Mid-year update 2006

UK
VFR
Flight Guide

UK

VFR
Flight Guide

FREE
Update
Service

To receive your free printed and email updates, please fill in your name and address on the form below:

(Please use block capitals)

Name _____

Address _____

_____

_____

Postcode _____

Email _____

Return this form to:

UK VFR Flight Guide
1a, Ringway Trading Estate,
Shadowmoss Road,
Manchester M22 5LH

(please send this page, photocopies cannot be accepted)

Are you flying with out-of-date charts?

Chart Subscription Service Order Information

Join the AFE subscription service, making life easy. Every time a new chart or UK VFR Flight Guide is published we will send it to you.

Telephone Orders:

Phone 0161 499 0023 with your credit card details, stating which charts are required on a regular basis and we will do the rest.

Single Orders (non subscription)

Please state edition required. This service is also available through our website. www.afeonline.com

Chart	Price
1:500,000	£13.99
1:250,000	£13.99
Ireland	£10.95
Low Countries	£12.95
Italy	£14.95
Germany	£11.95
France	£13.95
Spain	£12.95
Austria	£13.95
Switzerland	£13.95
Denmark	£19.95
Norway	£19.95
VFR Flight Guide:	
soft-bound	£21.95
spiral-bound	£21.95
loose-leaf	£24.95
UK En-route Guide	£15.95
UK AIM	£16.95
VFR Ireland	£16.95

Postage	
1-3 charts	£2.99
4+ charts	£4.99
VFR Flight Guide	£2.99
UK En-route Guide	£2.99
UK AIM	£2.99
VFR Ireland	£2.99

Chart	New Edition	Expected Date
1:500,000		
Southern England	33	Mar 2007
Northern England	30	May 2007
Scotland	25	Dec 2007
London Heli Routes	12	Available
1:250,000		
Central England	7	April 07
England South	11	Feb 2007
England East	7	Available
Borders	5	Available
West & South Wales	6	Aug 2007
Scotland East	4	Available
Scotland West	4	Available
Northern Ireland	5	Jun 2007
UK VFR Flight Guide	2008	Dec 2007
VFR Ireland	2008	Jan 2008
UK En-route Guide	2007	Summer 2007
UK AIM	2007	Summer 2007

Qty	Description	Single order (Tick box)	£
		☐	
		☐	
		☐	
		☐	
		☐	

Name:

AFE catalogue FREE tick box ☐   NIL

Address:

Sub Total

Postage

AFE   TOTAL

Post Code:

Tel:

Please debit my card:

Type: VISA / Mastercard / Switch Issue No.____

Tick box ☐ ☐ ☐ other ____

Card No. ____

Expiry date /

Signature ____

Airplan Flight Equipment Ltd
1a Ringway Trading Estate
Shadowmoss Road
Manchester M22 5LH

Tel: 0161 499 0023
Fax: 0161 499 0298

Tel: 0161 499 0023
www.afeonline.com

2007
UK VFR
Flight Guide

2007
UK VFR
Flight Guide

Published by

Camber Publishing Ltd

Distributed to the aviation trade by:

AFE Ltd (Manchester Office)
1a Ringway Trading Estate,
Shadowmoss Road,
Manchester M22 5LH
Tel: 0161 499 0023 **Fax:** 0161 499 0298

AFE Ltd (Oxford Office)
The Pilot shop
Oxford Airport
Oxford
OX5 1QX
Tel: 01865 841441 **Fax:** 01865 842495

Distributed to the book trade by:

Crécy Publishing Ltd
1a Ringway Trading Estate,
Shadowmoss Road,
Manchester M22 5LH

Tel: 0161 499 0024 **Fax:** 0161 499 0298

Spiral-bound   ISBN 1 874783 64 0

Loose-leaf   ISBN 1 874783 69 1

Softback   ISBN 1 874783 74 8

www.afeonline.com

2007 UK VFR Flight Guide

Compiled by Louise Southern

Designed by Robert Taylor
GDi studio

Contributors:

John Dale

Jeremy M Pratt

Mike Rudkin

Chris Walsh

Effective information date 23.11.06

Important

The UK VFR Flight Guide is a guide only and it is not intended to be taken as an authoritative document. In the interests of safety and good airmanship the AIP (including supplements, amendments and AIRACs), Pre-flight Information Bulletins, NOTAMS and AICs should be checked before flight as information can, and does, change frequently and often with little notice. Whilst every care has been taken in compiling this guide, relying where possible on official information sources, the publisher and editorial team will not be liable in any way for any errors or omissions whatsoever.

Regular amendments available at: **www.afeonline.com**

Contents

Flight Planning Airmet

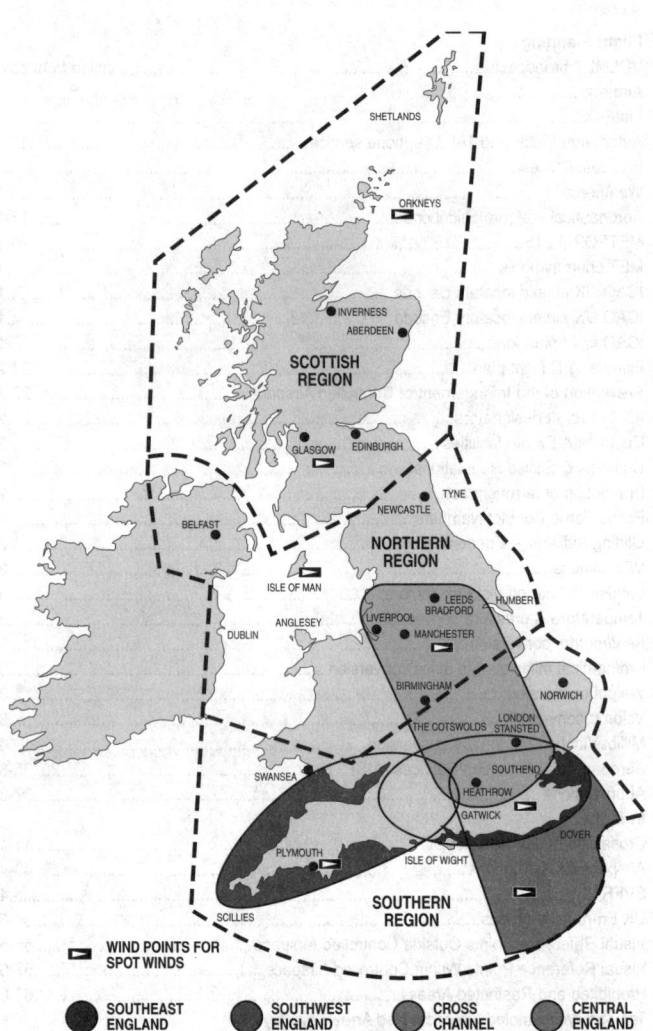

WIND POINTS FOR SPOT WINDS

- SOUTHEAST ENGLAND
- SOUTHWEST ENGLAND
- CROSS CHANNEL
- CENTRAL ENGLAND

AIRMET – Fax

09060 700 510	Airmet Index Page
09060 700 507	Regional Airmet South Text
09060 700 508	Regional Airmet North Text
09060 700 509	Regional Airmet Scottish Text
09060 700 511	Airmet UK Weather Text
09060 700 512	Airmet UK Upper Winds Text
09060 700 513	Airmet UK Update and Outlook
09060 700 514	Airmet South West England Text
09060 700 515	Airmet South East England Text
09060 700 516	Airmet Central England Text
09060 700 517	Airmet Cross Channel Text

Note: 090607 calls cost 75p/minute at all times

Weather helpdesk 0871 200 3985

MetFAX Helpline:
Tel: 08700 750075
Fax: 08700 750076

Fax Number	Product Description
09060 100 400	Main Index of all Fax services
09060 700 501	Aviation Index page
09060 700 502	Surface Analysis chart
	Surface T+24 Forecast chart
09060 700 503	F215 UK Low Level Weather chart
	F214 UK Spot Wind chart
09060 700 504	Surface T+48, 72, 96 & 120 Forecast chart
	3 day planning text (S England, S Wales)
09060 700 544	Surface T+48, 72, 96 & 120 Forecast chart
	3 Day planning text (N England, N Wales)
09060 700 505	Explanatory notes for F215
09060 700 506	4 Tephigrams temp/height chart

	Satellite Images
09060 700 538	Guide to satellite images
09060 700 537	Satellite Image (Visible & Infra-Red)
09060 700 539	Satellite Image (Infra-Red)

	European
09060 700 541	RAFC European FL100-450 Sig Wx.
	F614 European med-high Spot Winds
09060 700 542	F415 European Low Level Weather
	F414 European Low Level Spot Winds

	TAF and METAR Bulletins
09060 700 520	TAF & METAR Index Page
09060 700 521	METAR 1 – S England, South Wales, Channel Islands
09060 700 522	METAR 2 – SE England, Midlands, Wales
09060 700 523	METAR 3 – North England, Scotland, Ireland
09060 700 524	METAR 4 – SE England, Channel Islands, France
09060 700 525	METAR 5 – Europe
09060 700 530	TAF – 18hr Bulletin
09060 700 531	TAF 1 – S England, South Wales, Channel Islands
09060 700 532	TAF 2 – SE England, Midlands, East Anglia. Wales
09060 700 533	TAF 3 – North England, Scotland, Ireland
09060 700 534	TAF 4 – SE England, Channel Islands, France
09060 700 535	TAF 5 – Europe
09060 700 540	TAF & METAR Decode

METAR Bulletins compiled every 30 minutes

Note: 09060 calls cost 75p/minute at all times

The automated METAR and TAF service is accessed by telephoning: **09063 800 400**
This is a premium rated number.
Once connected press the star (*) key followed by the appropriate three digit code number.

Code	ICAO	Aerodrome	Hours	METAR	9hr TAF	24hr TAF
222	PD	Aberdeen	0500-2100	•	•	•
224	JA	Alderney	0700-1800	•	•	
228	AA	Belfast Aldergrove	H24	•	•	•
232	AC	Belfast City	0500-2100	•	•	
234	PL	Benbecula	0700-1500	•	•	
236	KB	Biggin Hill	0700-1900	•		
238	BB	Birmingham	H24	•	•	•
242	NH	Blackpool	0600-2000	•	•	
244	DM	Boscombe Down	H24	•		
246	HH	Bournemouth	0600-2000	•	•	•
252	GD	Bristol	H24	•	•	•
254	VN	Brize Norton	H24	•		
256	SC	Cambridge	0600-1800	•	•	
366	EC	Campbeltown	0600-2400	•		•
258	FF	Cardiff	H24	•	•	•
262	NC	Carlisle	0800-1600	•	•	
266	BE	Coventry	H24	•	•	•
268	TC	Cranfield	0700-1700	•	•	
272	DR	Culdrose	H24	•	•	
274	NX	Nottingham East Midlands	H24	•	•	•
276	PH	Edinburgh	H24	•	•	•
278	TE	Exeter	0600-2400	•	•	
282	LF	Farnborough	0600-1800	•	•	•
286	PF	Glasgow	H24	•	•	•
288	BJ	Gloucestershire	0800-1700	•	•	
292	JB	Guernsey	0300-2000	•	•	
296	NJ	Humberside	0500-2000	•	•	
298	PE	Inverness	0600-2000	•	•	
322	NS	Isle of Man	H24	•	•	
324	JJ	Jersey	0300-2000	•	•	
326	QK	Kinloss	H24	•	•	•
328	PA	Kirkwall	0500-1700	•	•	
334	NM	Leeds Bradford	H24	•	•	•
336	XE	Leeming	H24	•	•	
338	QL	Leuchars	H24	•	•	•
342	GP	Liverpool	H24	•	•	•
344	LC	London City	0600-1900	•	•	
346	KK	London Gatwick	H24	•	•	•
348	LL	London Heathrow	H24	•	•	•
352	SS	London Stansted	H24	•	•	•
354	AE	Londonderry	0500-1900	•	•	
356	QS	Lossiemouth	H24	•	•	•
358	GW	London Luton	H24	•	•	•
364	DL	Lyneham	H24	•	•	
368	CC	Manchester	H24	•	•	•
372	MH	Manston	0600-2100	•	•	
374	YM	Marham	H24	•	•	
376	NT	Newcastle	H24	•	•	•
377	WU	Northolt	0500-2300	•		
378	SH	Norwich	0500-0100	•	•	
382	VO	Odiham	H24	•	•	
386	HD	Plymouth	0600-1800	•	•	
388	PK	Prestwick	H24	•	•	•
392	DG	St Mawgan	H24	•	•	•
394	PM	Scatsa	0700-1700	•	•	
396	HE	Scillies St Mary's	0700-1600	•	•	
398	OS	Shawbury	H24	•	•	
410	SY	Sheffield City	0600-2000	•	•	
422	KA	Shoreham	0700-1700	•	•	
424	HI	Southampton	0500-1900	•	•	
426	MC	Southend	H24	•	•	
428	PO	Stornoway	0600-1500	•		•
432	PB	Sumburgh	0500-2100	•	•	

Flight Planning

Automated Metar and TAF telephone service

Code	ICAO	Aerodrome	Hours	METAR	9hr TAF	24hr TAF
436	NV	Durham Tees Valley	0600-2100	•	•	
438	PU	Tiree	0900-1300	•	•	
444	OV	Valley	H24	•	•	
446	XW	Waddington	H24	•		•
448	UW	Wattisham	H24	•	•	
452	PC	Wick	0600-200	•	•	
454	XT	Wittering	H24	•	•	
456	DY	Yeovilton	H24	•	•	
522	EHAM	Amsterdam		•	•	•
524	LFOB	Beauvais		•	•	
526	LFBR	Brest		•	•	
528	EBBR	Brussels		•	•	•
532	LFRK	Caen		•	•	
536	LFRC	Cherbourg		•	•	
538	EICK	Cork		•	•	
542	LFRG	Deauville		•	•	
544	LFRD	Dinard		•	•	
546	EIDW	Dublin		•	•	•
548	LFRM	Le Mans		•	•	
552	LFAT	Le Touquet		•	•	
554	LFQQ	Lille		•	•	•
556	ELLX	Luxembourg		•	•	
562	EBOS	Ostend		•	•	
564	LFPG	Paris Charles De Gaulle		•	•	•
566	LFPB	Paris Le Bourget		•	•	•
568	LFPO	Paris Orly		•	•	
572	LFRN	Rennes		•	•	
574	LFSR	Reims		•	•	
576	EHRD	Rotterdam		•	•	•
578	EINN	Shannon		•	•	•
582	LFPN	Toussus Le Noble		•	•	

Forecast Offices

The following offices are able to provide TAFs and METARs if you are unable to obtain them from another source, and can also provide clarification of a TAF or METAR you have already received.

Belfast/AldergroveAirport*	01849 423275
Birmingham Weather Centre	0845 3000300
Cardiff Weather Centre	02920 390492
Exeter Weather Centre	0870 900 0100
	01392 885680
Glasgow Weather Centre*	0141 221 6116
Isle of Man Airport	01624 821641
Jersey Airport	01534 492256
Jersey Airmet	01534 492256
	09006 650033
Leeds Weather Centre	01132 457687
Manchester Weather Centre*	0161 429 0927
Newcastle Weather Centre	0191 232 4245
Sella Ness	01806 242069

*These Forecast Offices can be consulted to clarify a forecast, for special forecasts and for route forecasts.

email: aviation@metoffice.com

www.metoffice.com

Weathercall is the UK's most used telephone based weather forecast.
Weathercall by telephone 6 hr town forecast updated hourly.
Weathercall by telephone 10 day forecast updated 3 time daily.
Weathercall by fax forecast updated daily at 7:00.

Weather call by phone

To use Weathercall, dial the number for your area and choose from the following list of options:

Press 1 for 10 day regional outlook forecast
Press 2 for the forecast for your town, covering the next 6 Hrs
Press 3 for a barometric pressure reading
Press 4 to leave your address to receive a Weathercall Card

Greater London	09014 722051
Kent, Surrey & Sussex	09014 722052
Dorset, Hampshire & Isle of Wight	09014 722053
Devon & Cornwall	09014 722054
Wiltshire, Gloucestershire, Avon & Somerset	09014 722055
Berkshire, Buckinghamshire & Oxfordshire	09014 722056
Bedfordshire, Hertfordshire & Essex	09014 722057
Norfolk, Suffolk & Cambridgeshire	09014 722058
Glamorgan & Monmouthshire	09014 722059
Shropshire, Herefordshire & Worcestershire	09014 722060
West Midlands, Staffordshire & Warwickshire	09014 722061
Nottinghamshire, Leicestershire, Northants & Derbyshire	09014 722062
Lincolnshire	09014 722063
Carmarthenshire, Credigion & Pembrokeshire	09014 722064
Anglesey, Gwynedd, Wrexham & Denbighshire	09014 722065
North West England	09014 722066
York, East Riding, South, West & North Yorkshire	09014 722067
Durham, Northumberland & Tyne & Wear	09014 722068
Cumbria, Lake District & Isle of Man	09014 722069
Dumfries & Galloway	09014 722070
Central Scotland & Strathclyde	09014 722071
Fife, Lothian & Borders	09014 722072
Tayside	09014 722073
Grampian & East Highlands	09014 722074
West Highlands & Islands	09014 722075
Caithness, Sutherland, Orkneys & Shetland	09014 722076
Northern Ireland	09014 722077

Weathercall by Fax

	10 day forecast 2-5 day regional forecast	5 day regional forecast
South East	09065 300128	09060 100411
South West	09065 300129	09060 100412
Wales	09065 300130	09060 100413
North West & North Wales	09065 300131	09060 100416
North East	09065 300132	09060 100417
Scotland	09065 300133	09060 100418
Northern Ireland	09065 300134	09060 100419
Midlands	09065 300135	09060 100414
National	09065 300136	09060 100410
East Anglia	09065 300137	09060 100415
Synoptic chart (today & tomorrow)	09065 300138	
Synoptic chart (following 4 days)	09065 300139	

Additional services by fax

Weather Radar Sequence	09060 100425
Surface analysis chart	09060 100444
User guide to surface charts	09060 100445
UK Plotted chart	09060 100447

Call charges (based upon calls from a BT Landline)
Weathercall by telephone (09014) 60p per minute
Weathercall 5 day forecast & fax services (09060) £1 per minute
Weathercall 10 day forecast by fax (09065) £1.50 per minute
www.metoffice.com – Aviation section

Sample METAR:

LOCATION	ISSUE DATE/TIME	OBSERVATION DATE/TIME	WIND	VISIBILITY	WEATHER	CLOUD	CLOUD	CLOUD	CLOUD	AIR TEMP /DEWPOINT	QNH	MILITARY WEATHER STATE CODE
EGQM	061159	061200Z	04028G39KT	3500	+RA	FEW005	SCT012	OVC020		07/05	Q0983	YLO

Sample TAF:

LOCATION	ISSUE DATE/TIME	FORECAST DATE/PERIOD	WIND	VISIBILITY	WEATHER	CLOUD	CLOUD	SUPPLEMENTARY INFORMATION
EGNT	060841Z	061019	04025G35KT	7000	RA	SCT008	BKN015	TEMPO 1019 05030G45KT 3000 BKN008

LOCATION INDICATOR
The ICAO Four Letter Code for the airfield

TIME
The first number group will be the issue time of the METAR/TAF as a six number group, the first two numbers being the date. The second six number group will be the date (first two numbers) followed by:
- METAR. The observation time in hours and minutes UTC, followed by Z (Zulu).
- TAF The period of forecast validity in UTC.

WIND
The surface wind direction is given in degrees true (three digits) rounded to the nearest 10°, followed by wind speed (two digits). Wind speed may be given in knots (KT), kilometres per hour (KMH) or metres per second (MPS).

G   Wind Gust
00000   Wind Calm
VRB   Variable Wind Direction
V   Variation in wind direction of 60° or more

VISIBILITY
The minimum horizontal visibility is given in metres.
9999   Visibility 10km or greater
0000   Visibility less than 50 m
- METAR only. Where there is a marked difference in visibility depending on direction, more than one visibility may be reported, followed by direction in which that visibility exists e.g. S = south, NE = north east etc.

RUNWAY VISUAL RANGE – METAR Only
R   RVR, followed by runway designator and the touchdown zone visibility in metres. If visibility is greater than the maximum RVR that can be assessed, or more than 1500 metres, it will be preceded by a P. M = RVR below the minimum that can be assessed.
At non-UK aerodromes the additional designator may be added after the RVR: U = Up; D = Down; N = No change. If there is a significant variability in RVR the letter V will be used in-between the minimum and maximum RVRs.

WEATHER

Weather Phenomena

Description	Precipitation	Visibility Factor	Other
MI Shallow	DZ Drizzle	BR Mist	PO Well developed dust/sand whirls
BC Patches			
PR Partial Covering	RA Rain	FG Fog	
DR Drifting	SN Snow	FU Smoke	SQ Squalls
BL Blowing	SG Snow Grains	VA Volcanic Ash	FC Funnel Cloud(s) (tornado or water-spout)
SH Shower(s)	IC Diamond Dust	DU Widespread Dust	SS Sandstorm
TS Thunderstorm	PE Ice-Pellets	SA Sand	DS Duststorm
FZ Super-Cooled	GR Hail	HZ Haze	
	GS Small Hail		

Intensity or Proximity Qualifier
- Light i.e. -SH
Moderate (no qualifier) i.e. SH
+Heavy i.e. +SH
VC In the vicinity (within 8 km of the airfield, but not actually at the airfield)
NSW (TAF only) = No Significant Weather

Flight Planning   Aeronautical Meteorological Codes

13

CLOUD

Cloud amount may be described as:

FEW (few)	1-2 OKTAS
SCT (Scattered)	3-4 OKTAS
BKN (Broken)	5-7 OKTAS
OVC (Overcast)	8 OKTAS
Note: 1 OKTA	1/8 cloud cover

Cloud base is given in hundreds of feet above aerodrome level (aal).f

Cloud type is not identified, except:

CB	Cumulo-nimbus
TCU	Towering Cumulus
SKC	Sky Clear
NSC	No Significant Cloud (TAF only)

If the sky is obscured the letters VV are inserted followed by the vertical visibility in hundreds of feet.

VV///   Sky obscured, vertical visibility cannot be assessed.

CAVOK (Pronounced KAV-O-KAY) will be used to replace the visibility, RVR, weather and cloud groups if the following conditions apply:

a Visibility: 10km or more

b Cloud: no cloud below 5000ft or below highest Minimum Sector Altitude, whichever is greater and no CB at any height

c No significant weather at or near the airfield

AIR TEMPERATURE/DEWPOINT

These are given in degrees Celsius

M   Minus

QNH

Rounded down to the next whole millibar and given as a four figure group in millibars/hectopascals, preceded by Q. If the value is less than 1000, the first number is 0.

SUPPLEMENTARY INFORMATION

METARs

RE   Recent weather

WS   Windshear

TREND. Certain major aerodromes will include a trend indicator for any forecast change in conditions during the two hours after the observation time.

BECMG Becoming. TEMPO = Temporary; may be followed by time (in hours and minutes UTC) preceded by FM (from), TL (until) or AT (at).

NOSIG No significant changes forecast during the trend period.

BECMG is an expected permanent change in conditions, expected to last less than one hour in each instance and not total more than half the forecast period.

TEMPO is a temporary fluctuation in conditions expected to last less than 1hour at a time and not occur in total during more than half the forecast period.

TAFs

Probability:

PROB 30	30% probability
PROB 40	40% probability

The abbreviations FM, TEMPO and BECMG are followed by time(s) (UTC) to the nearest hour.

AMENDMENTS

AMD is inserted after TAF and before the ICAO four letter code. AMD is used when the original TAF is withdrawn and replaced for some reason.

RETARD

(R) Used when the TAF is received late. Most often seen on METFAX.

MILITARY WEATHER STATE COLOUR CODES

– MINIMUM weather conditions

Colour	Visibility	Base of lowest cloud: 3/8 (scattered) or more
Blue	8km	2500ft AGL
White	5km	1500ft AGL
Green	3700m	700ft AGL
Yellow	1600m	300ft AGL
Amber	800m	200ft AGL
Red	Less than 800m	Below 200ft AGL or sky obscured
Black	Airfield not usable for reasons other than cloud base or visibility. Black will precede actual colour code	

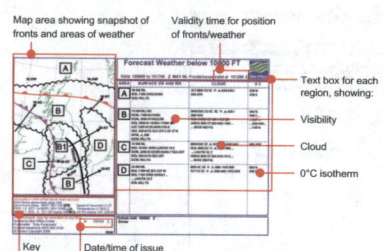

Map area showing snapshot of fronts and areas of weather

Validity time for position of fronts/weather

Text box for each region, showing:

Visibility

Cloud

0°C isotherm

Key

Date/time of issue

Map area

The map area will still appear on the sig Wx chart showing a snapshot of the fronts and areas of weather at a specific validity time (VT) shown at the top right of the chart.
Only sig wx areas, fronts and speed of movement will be shown on the map area. The 0 °C isotherm boxes have been moved to the text box allocated to a particular area.
The 'top' of the chart will now be 10,000 ft instead of 15,000ft.

Weather

The text boxes on the right will show the weather for each area of the map and have been designed to follow the TAF code appearing in the same order; visibility and weather followed by cloud. The METAR weather codes will also be used in this section to refer to specific forecast weather types (e.g. TS, +RA, FG etc.)

Cloud

Cloud amount will be: FEW, SCT, BKN or OVC, followed by the cloud type (e.g. ST, CU, CB, SC, AC). An additional two symbols may then appear to indicate whether MOD/SEV ICE or TURB is expected in this cloud. A key to the symbols is included in the lower left corner of the chart.
Cloud heights then appear in 100s of feet in the form 020/050 (in this case the cloud base is 2,000 ft and the top 5,000 ft AMSL). If a cloud top is expected to extend above 10,000 ft then XXX will appear. For example, BKN/OVC STSC 008/060 indicates 5 – 8 oktas of stratus and strato-cumulus base 800 ft top 6,000 ft AMSL with moderate turbulence and moderate icing expected within.

Key:		
MOD ICE		Moderate icing
SEV ICE		Severe icing
MOD TURB		Moderate turbulence
SEV TURB		Severe turbulence

Mountain wave

Wherever necessary, mountain wave forecasts will appear in the 'visibility and weather' box as MTW followed by a vertical speed VSP and height(s) above mean sea level.
e.g. 'MTW MAX VSP 700 FPM AT 080'. Mountain wave maximum vertical speed 700 ft per minute at 8,000 ft with moderate/severe turbulence expected

Issue/validity times

In order to meet customer requests, the chart times have been altered slightly to cover a nine-hour period instead of just six hours. Charts will be available at similar times to those currently in place. The table below summarises the times for the new charts:

Chart	Issue time	Valid for flights between	Validity time*	Outlook to	Prognosis
UK low-level	0330	0800 and 1700	1200	0000	1800
sig weather (F215)	0930	1400 and 2300	1800	0600	0000
	1530	2000 and 0500	0000	1200	0600
	2130	0200 and 1100	0600	1800	1200
European low-level	0330	0800 and 1700	1200	n/a	n/a
sig weather (F415)	0930	1400 and 2300	1800	n/a	n/a
	1530	2000 and 0500	0000	n/a	n/a
	2130	0100 and 1100	0600	n/a	n/a

*Validity time is the time at which the position of the fronts and areas of weather are valid.
All times will remain in UTC (denoted by 'Z' or 'Zulu' on the new briefing charts).

Prognosis

The prognosis chart (forecast for six hours on) will no longer appear on the chart, but will be shown below the main F215 chart on the Met Office web site. This prognosis chart shows only the expected positions of the principal synoptic features and mean sea level isobars at the end of the period. Weather zones are not given on the prognosis chart.

UK and European spot winds charts (F214 and 414)

In response to customer requests, the Met Office has also agreed to change the chart validity times of the F214 and F414 spot winds charts in order to bring them into line with the new F215 and F415 Sig Wx charts. As a result, the spot wind charts will have improved issue times and validity times as set out in the table below:

Chart	Issue time	Valid for flights between	Validity time*	Outlook to
UK spot winds (F214)	0000	0300 and 0900	0600	n/a
	0600	0900 and 1500	1200	n/a
	1200	1500 and 2100	1800	n/a
	1800	2100 and 0300	0000	n/a
European spot winds (F414)	0000	0300 and 0900	0600	n/a
	0600	0900 and 1500	1200	n/a
	1200	1500 and 2100	1800	n/a
	1800	2100 and 0300	0000	n/a

Amendment of charts

Only the current chart will be amended, therefore a chart will be subject to amendment as soon as it has been issued.

Example for F215 and F415

If we consider three chart issues of F215/F415, the 0200 – 1100 chart issued at 2100, the 0800 – 1700 chart issued at 0300 and the 1400 – 2300 issued at 0900. If the actual weather were to change from the forecast weather at say, 1000 with un-forecast thunderstorms which are now forecast to last all day, the 0800 – 1700 chart would be amended instantly since this is the current chart. The previous chart valid 0200 – 1100 would not be amended since it is no longer current (even though it's period is unfinished). If forecasters believe that the thunderstorms will also affect the period 1400 – 2300, then this chart would also be amended.
Users are advised to use the latest chart wherever possible since this should include the most up-to-date information and amendments as necessary.

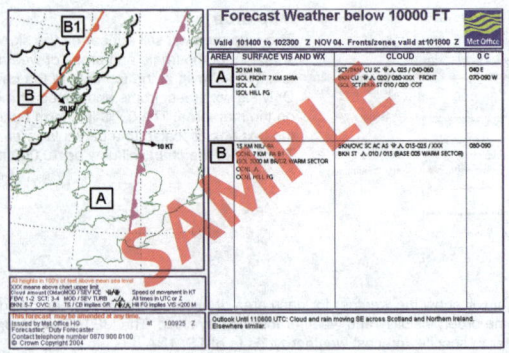

MET chart symbols

Pressure Systems, Fronts and Convergence Zones		Temperature and Tropopause		
▲▲	Cold front at surface	Tropopause 'High' centre and altitude (FL 400)		
⏺⏺	Warm front at surface	Tropopause 'Low' centre and altitude (FL 340)		
▲⏺▲	Occluded front at surface	0°C	130	Freezing level (in thousands of feet as a Flight Level)
▼⏺	Quasi-stationary front at surface	-62	400	Temperature and Flight Level of the tropopause
⌁	Convergence line	**Wind & Temperature at Altitude Charts Pressure**		
⦀⦀	Intertropical convergence zone	L	Centre of a low-pressure system	
L x 999	Centre of low pressure area (with indication of pressure at centre)	H	Centre of a high-pressure system	
H ◯ 1020	Centre of high pressure area (with indication of pressure at centre)	**Temperature**		
10	Speed of movement	0°C	In degrees Celsius	
→	Direction of movement	**Wind**		
SLW	Slow		Arrow shaft marks wind direction	
STNR	Stationary		Each long feather equals 10 knots	
Zone Boundaries			Each half feather equals 5 knots	
∿	Boudary of area of significant weasther		Each solid triangle equals 50 knots	
/// ///	Rain *	0	Calm	
,	Drizzle *	◤◤ FL 380	Flight level of jetstream	
✱	Snow *			
▽	Shower *	**Cloud Quantities**		
▲	Hail *	SKC	Sky Clear	
⏝	Light Icing *	FEW	Few (1 to 2 oktas)	
=	Widespread Mist *	SCT	Scattered (3 to 4 oktas)	
≡	Widespread Fog *	BKN	Broken (5 to 7 oktas)	
⇸	Freezing Fog *	OVC	Overcast (8 oktas)	
↦	Widespread Smoke *	LYR	Layers	
∿	Freezing Rain	**For Cumulonimbus only:**		
⏝	Moderate Icing	ISOL	Isolated	
⏝	Severe Icing	OCNL	(occasional) Well Separated	
⊙⏝	Freezing Precipitation	FRQ	(frequent) Hardly or not at all separated	
⋀	Moderate Turbulence	EMBD	Embedded in other cloud	
▲	Severe Turbulence	**Localisation**		
⌇	Severe Sand or Dust Haze	COT	Coast	
⌇	Widespread Sandstorm or Duststorm	LAN	Land	
∞	Widespread Haze	LOC	Locally	
CAT	Clear Air Turbulence	MAR	At Sea (maritime)	
⤬	Severe Line Squall	MON	Mountains	
⨝	Thunderstorm	SFC	Surface	
◍	Marked Mountain Waves	VAL	Valleys	
⎈	Tropical Cyclone			
* these symbols are not used at high altitude				

Code	Location	Code	Location	Code	Location	Code	Location
EGAA	Belfast Aldergrove	EGFA	West Wales	EGNF	Netherthorpe	EGSP	Peterborough
EGAB	Enniskillen	EGFC	Cardiff Heliport	EGNG	Bagby		Sibson
EGAC	Belfast City	EGFE	Haverfordwest	EGNH	Blackpool	EGSQ	Clacton
EGAD	Newtownards	EGFF	Cardiff	EGNI	Skegness	EGSR	Earls Colne
EGAE	Londonderry	EGFH	Swansea	EGNJ	Humberside	EGSS	London Stansted
EGAL	Langford Lodge	EGFP	Pembrey	EGNL	Barrow	EGST	Elmsett
EGBB	Birmingham	EGGD	Bristol	EGNM	Leeds Bradford	EGSU	Duxford
EGBC	Cheltenham	EGGP	Liverpool	EGNO	Warton	EGSV	Old Buckenham
	Racecourse	EGGW	London Luton	EGNR	Hawarden	EGSW	Newmarket
EGBD	Derby	EGHA	Compton Abbas	EGNS	Isle of Man		Racecourse
EGBE	Coventry	EGHB	Maypole	EGNT	Newcastle	EGSX	North Weald
EGBG	Leicester	EGHC	Lands End	EGNU	Full Sutton	EGSY	Sheffield City
EGBJ	Gloucestershire	EGHD	Plymouth City	EGNV	Durham Tees	EGTA	Aylesbury
EGBK	Northampton	EGHE	Scilly Isles		Valley	EGTB	Wycombe Air Park
EGBL	Long Marston	EGHF	Lee-on-Solent	EGNW	Wickenby	EGTC	Cranfield
EGBM	Tatenhill	EGHG	Yeovil	EGNX	Nottingham East	EGTD	Dunsfold
EGBN	Nottingham	EGHH	Bournemouth		Midlands	EGTE	Exeter
EGBO	Wolverhampton	EGHI	Southampton	EGNY	Beverley	EGTF	Fairoaks
EGBP	Kemble	EGHJ	Bembridge	EGOD	Llandbedr	EGTG	Bristol Filton
EGBS	Shobdon	EGHK	Penzance Heliport	EGOE	Ternhill	EGTH	Shuttleworth
EGBT	Turweston	EGHL	Lasham	EGOP	Pembrey	EGTK	Oxford
EGBV	Silverstone	EGHN	Sandown	EGOS	Shawbury	EGTO	Rochester
EGBW	Wellesbourne	EGHO	Thruxton	EGOV	Valley	EGTP	Perranporth
	Mountford	EGHP	Popham	EGOW	Woodvale	EGTR	Elstree
EGCB	Manchester	EGHR	Chichester	EGOY	West Freugh	EGTU	Dunkeswell
	Barton	EGHS	Henstridge	EGPA	Kirkwall	EGTW	Oaksey Park
EGCC	Manchester	EGHT	Tresco Heliport	EGPB	Sumburgh	EGUB	Benson
EGCD	Manchester	EGHU	Eaglescott	EGPC	Wick	EGUC	Aberporth
	Woodford	EGHY	Truro	EGPD	Aberdeen	EGUL	Lakenheath
EGCE	Wrexham	EGJA	Alderney	EGPE	Inverness	EGUN	Mildenhall
EGCF	Sandtoft	EGJB	Guernsey	EGPF	Glasgow	EGUO	Colerne
EGCG	Strubby Heliport	EGJJ	Jersey	EGPG	Cumbernauld	EGUU	Uxbridge
EGCH	Holyhead	EGKA	Shoreham	EGPH	Edinburgh	EGUW	Wattisham
EGCJ	Sherburn-in-Elmet	EGKB	Biggin Hill	EGPI	Islay	EGUY	Wyton
EGCK	Caernarfon	EGKD	Albourne	EGPJ	Fife	EGVA	Fairford
EGCL	Fenland	EGKE	Challock	EGPK	Glasgow	EGVH	Hereford
EGCN	Doncaster	EGKG	Goodwood		Prestwick	EGVN	Brize Norton
	Sheffield		Racecourse	EGPL	Benbecula	EGVO	Odiham
EGOP	Southport Sands	EGKH	Lashenden	EGPM	Scatsta	EGVP	Middle Wallop
EGCP	Thorne	EGKK	London Gatwick	EGPN	Dundee	EGWC	Cosford
EGCS	Sturgate	EGKL	Deanland	EGPO	Stornoway	EGWE	Henlow
EGCT	Tilstock	EGKR	Redhill	EGPR	Barra	EGWN	Halton
EGCV	Sleap	EGLA	Bodmin	EGPS	Peterhead	EGWU	Northolt
EGCW	Welshpool	EGLB	Brooklands		Heliport	EGXC	Coningsby
EGDC	Chivenor	EGLC	London City	EGPT	Perth	EGXD	Dishforth
EGDD	Bicester	EGLD	Denham	EGPU	Tiree	EGXE	Leeming
EGDG	St Mawgan	EGLF	Farnborough	EGPW	Unst	EGXF	Forrest Moor
EGDL	Lyneham	EGLG	Panshanger	EGQB	Ballykelly	EGXG	Church Fenton
EGDM	Boscombe Down	EGLI	Isleworth	EGQK	Kinloss	EGXH	Honington
EGDN	Netheravon	EGLJ	Chalgrove	EGQL	Leuchars	EGXJ	Cottesmore
EGDP	Portland	EGLK	Blackbushe	EGQM	Boulmer	EGXM	Benbecula
EGDR	Culdrose	EGLL	London Heathrow	EGQS	Lossiemouth	EGXP	Scampton
EGDX	St Athan	EGLM	White Whaltham	EGSA	Shipdham	EGXT	Wittering
EGDY	Yeovilton	EGLS	Old Sarum	EGSB	Bedford	EGXU	Linton-on-Ouse
EGEC	Campbeltown	EGLT	Ascot Racecourse	EGSC	Cambridge	EGXV	Leconfield
EGED	Eday	EGLW	London heliport	EGSD	Great Yarmouth	EGXW	Waddington
EGEF	Fair Isle	EGMA	Fowlmere	EGSF	Peterborough	EGXZ	Topcliffe
EGEG	Glasgow City	EGMC	Southend		Conington	EGYB	Brampton
	Heliport	EGMD	Lydd	EGSG	Stapleford	EGYC	Coltishall
EGEH	Whalsay	EGMF	Farthing Corner	EGSH	Norwich	EGYD	Cranwell
EGEN	North Ronaldsay	EGMH	Manston	EGSI	Marshland	EGYE	Barkston Heath
EGEO	Oban	EGMJ	Little Gransden	EGSJ	Seething	EGYM	Marham
EGEP	Papa Westray	EGML	Damyns Hall	EGSK	Hethel	EGYP	Mount Pleasant
EGER	Stronsay	EGNA	Hucknall	EGSL	Andrewsfield		
EGES	Sanday	EGNB	Brough	EGSM	Beccles		
EGET	Lerwick	EGNC	Carlisle	EGSN	Bourn		
EGEW	Westray	EGNE	Retford	EGSO	Crowfield		

Flight Planning

ICAO airfield locators Decode

Flight Planning — ICAO airfield locators Encode

Aberdeen	EGPD
Aberporth	EGUC
Albourne	EGKD
Alderney	EGJA
Andrewsfield	EGSL
Ascot Racecourse	EGLT
Aylesbury	EGTA
Bagby	EGNG
Ballykelly	EGQB
Barkston Heath	EGYE
Barra	EGPR
Barrow	EGNL
Beccles	EGSM
Bedford	EGSB
Belfast Aldergrove	EGAA
Belfast City	EGAC
Bembridge	EGHJ
Benbecula	EGPL
Benson	EGUB
Beverley	EGNY
Bicester	EGDD
Biggin Hill	EGKB
Birmingham	EGBB
Blackbushe	EGLK
Blackpool	EGNH
Bodmin	EGLA
Boscombe Down	EGDM
Boulmer	EGQM
Bourn	EGSN
Bournemouth	EGHH
Brampton	EGYB
Bristol	EGGD
Bristol Filton	EGTG
Brize Norton	EGVN
Brooklands	EGLB
Brough	EGNB
Caernarfon	EGCK
Cambridge	EGSC
Campbeltown	EGEC
Cardiff Heliport	EGFC
Cardiff	EGFF
Carlisle	EGNC
Chalgrove	EGLJ
Challock	EGKE
Cheltenham Racecourse	EGBC
Chichester	EGHR
Chivenor	EGDC
Church Fenton	EGXG
Clacton	EGSQ
Colerne	EGUO
Coltishall	EGYC
Compton Abbas	EGHA
Coningsby	EGXC
Cosford	EGWC
Cottesmore	EGXJ
Coventry	EGBE
Cranfield	EGTC
Cranwell	EGYD
Crowfield	EGSO
Culdrose	EGDR
Cumbernauld	EGPG
Damyns Hall	EGML
Deanland	EGKL
Denham	EGLD
Derby	EGBD
Dishforth	EGXD
Doncaster Sheffield	EGCN
Dundee	EGPN
Dunkeswell	EGTU
Durham Tees Valley	EGNV
Duxford	EGSU
Eaglescott	EGHU
Earls Colne	EGSR
Eday	EGED
Edinburgh	EGPH
Elmsett	EGST
Elstree	EGTR
Enniskillen	EGAB
Exeter	EGTE
Fair Isle	EGEF
Fairford	EGVA
Fairoaks	EGTF
Farnborough	EGLF
Farthing Corner	EGMF
Fenland	EGCL
Fife	EGPJ
Forest Moor	EGXF
Fowlmere	EGMA
Full Sutton	EGNU
Glasgow City Heliport	EGEG
Glasgow	EGPF
Gloucestershire	EGBJ
Goodwood Racecourse	EGKG
Great Yarmouth	EGSD
Guernsey	EGJB
Halton	EGWN
Haverfordwest	EGFE
Hawarden	EGNR
Henlow	EGWE
Henstridge	EGHS
Hereford	EGVH
Hethel	EGSK
Hollyhead	EGCH
Honington	EGXH
Hucknall	EGNA
Humberside	EGNJ
Inverness	EGPE
Islay	EGPI
Isle of Man	EGNS
Isle of Wight	EGHN
Isleworth	EGLI
Jersey	EGJJ
Kemble	EGBP
Kinloss	EGQK
Kirkwall	EGPA
Lakenheath	EGUL
Lands End	EGHC
Langford Lodge	EGAL
Lasham	EGHL
Lashenden	EGKH
Leconfield	EGXV
Leeds Bradford	EGNM
Leeming	EGXE
Lee-on-Solent	EGHF
Leicester	EGBG
Lerwick	EGET
Leuchars	EGQL
Linton-on-Ouse	EGXU
Little Gransden	EGMJ
Liverpool	EGGP
Llandbedr	EGOD
London City	EGLC
London Gatwick	EGKK
London Heathrow	EGLL
London Heliport	EGLW
London Luton	EGGW
London Stansted	EGSS
Londonderry	EGAE
Long Marston	EGBL
Lossiemouth	EGQS
Lydd	EGMD
Lyneham	EGDL
Manchester Barton	EGCB
Manchester Woodford	EGCD
Manchester	EGCC
Manston	EGMH
Marham	EGYM
Marshland	EGSI
Maypole	EGHB
Middle Wallop	EGVP
Mildenhall	EGUN
Mount Pleasant	EGYP
Netheravon	EGDN
Netherthorpe	EGNF
Newcastle	EGNT
Newmarket Racecourse	EGSW
Newtownards	EGAD
North Ronaldsay	EGEN
North Weald	EGSX
Northampton	EGBK
Northolt	EGWU
Norwich	EGSH
Nottingham	EGBN
Nottingham East Midlands	EGNX
Oaksey Park	EGTW
Oban	EGEO
Odiham	EGVO
Old Buckenham	EGSV
Old Sarum	EGLS
Oxford	EGTK
Panshanger	EGLG
Papa Westray	EGEP
Pembrey	EGOP
Penzance Heliport	EGHK
Perranporth	EGTP
Perth	EGPT
Peterborough Conington	EGSF
Peterborough Sibson	EGSP
Peterhead Heliport	EGPS
Plymouth	EGHD
Popham	EGHP
Portland	EGDP
Portsmouth	EGVF
Prestwick	EGPK
Redhill	EGKR
Retford	EGNE
Rochester	EGTO
Sanday	EGES
Sandtoft	EGCF
Scampton	EGXP
Scatsta	EGPM
Scilly Isles	EGHE
Seething	EGSJ
Shawbury	EGOS
Sheffield City	EGSY
Sherburn-in-Elmet	EGCJ
Shipdham	EGSA
Shobdon	EGBS
Shoreham	EGKA
Shuttleworth	EGTH
Silverstone	EGBV
Skegness	EGNI
Sleap	EGCV
Southampton	EGHI
Southend	EGMC
Southport Sands	EGCO
St Athan	EGDX
St Mawgan	EGDG
Stapleford	EGSG
Stornoway	EGPO
Stronsay	EGER
Strubby Heliport	EGCG
Sturgate	EGCS
Sumburgh	EGPB
Swansea	EGFH
Tatenhill	EGBM
Ternhill	EGOE
Thorne	EGCP
Thruxton	EGHO
Tilstock	EGCT
Tiree	EGPU
Topcliffe	EGXZ
Tresco Heliport	EGHT
Truro	EGHY
Turweston	EGBT
Unst	EGPW
Uxbridge	EGUU
Valley	EGOV
Waddington	EGXW
Warton	EGNO
Wattisham	EGUW
Wellesbourne Mountford	EGBW
Welshpool	EGCW
West Freugh	EGOY
Westray	EGEW
West Wales	EGFA
Whalsay	EGEH
White Whaltham	EGLM
Wick	EGPC
Wickenby	EGNW
Wittering	EGXT
Wolverhampton	EGBO
Woodvale	EGOW
Wrexham	EGCE
Wycombe Air Park	EGTB
Wyton	EGUY
Yeovil	EGHG
Yeovilton	EGDY

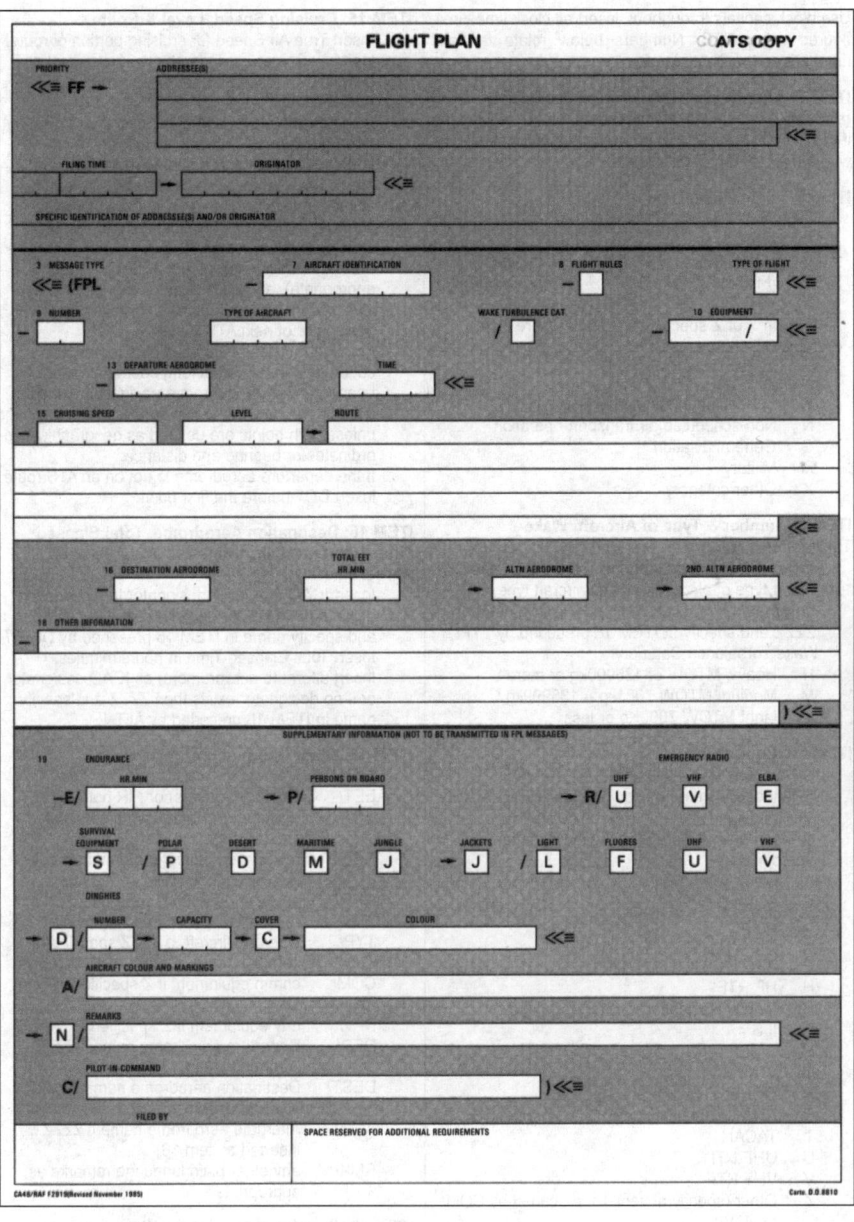

Flight Planning   ICAO flight plan form

Filing a VFR Flight Plan

Use block capitals throughout, insert all clock times in 4 figures using UTC. Numbers below relate to item numbers on the flight plan form.

ITEM 7: Aircraft Identification. The aircraft's registration (when it is being used as the RT callsign, or if the aircraft in non-radio) or the flight identification, with a maximum of 7 characters.

ITEM 8: Flight Rules/Type of Flight
Flight Rules
I   IFR
V   VFR
Y   IFR first
Z   VFR first
If using Y or Z specify in ITEM 15 where flight rules will change.

Type of Flight
S   Scheduled air service
N   Non-scheduled air transport operation
G   General aviation
M   Military
X   Other category

ITEM 9: Number & Type of Aircraft, Wake Turbulence Category.
Insert number of aircraft *only* if more than one. Insert type of aircraft as ICAO aircraft type designator. If no such designator exists insert ZZZZ and specify at ITEM 18 preceded by TYP/.
Wake Turbulence Category
H   Heavy, MTOW of 136000kg or more
M   Medium MTOW 7001kg – 135999kg
L   Light MTOW 7000Kg or less

ITEM 10: Equipment,
N No comm/nav equipment
S Standard comm/nav equipment (VHF RTF, ADF, VOR, ILS)
or insert one or more of the following letters as appropriate;
A   Loran A
C   Loran C
D   DME
E   DECCA
F   ADF
H   HF RTF
I   Inertial Navigation
L   ILS
M   OMEGA
O   VOR
P   DOPPLER
R   RNAV Route Equipment
T   TACAN
U   UHF RTF
V   VHF RTF
Z   Other (specify at item 18, preceded by COM/ or NAV/)
SSR Equipment; after the slash (/)
N   None
A   Transponder Mode A
C   Transponder Mode C

ITEM 13: Departure Aerodrome and **Time**.
Insert ICAO four letter aerodrome designator. If no ICAO designator exists enter ZZZZ and specify in ITEM 18, preceded by DEP/.
Insert estimated off-block time (UTC).

ITEM 15: Cruising Speed, Level & Route.
Insert True Air Speed for cruising portion of route. Use four figures preceded by K (Kilometres) or N (Knots). For Mach number three numbers preceded by M.
Insert cruising level as Flight Level (F followed by three numbers); or Altitude (A followed by three figures showing hundreds of feet); or Standard Metric Level (S followed by tens of metres); or altitude in tens of metres (M followed by four figures) or VFR for VFR flight with no specific cruising level.
For route, designator of first ATS route (if appropriate), and each point of change of speed, level, ATS route or flight rules, followed by designator of next ATS route.
For flight outside designated ATS routes, use coded designator, or lat/long coordinates, or bearing and distance from a navigation aid. DCT (Direct) can be used to join successive points unless both points are defined as geographical co-ordinates or bearing and distance.
If the departure aerodrome is not on an ATS route, insert DCT before the first point.

ITEM 16: Destination Aerodrome, Total Elapsed Time, Alternate Aerodrome and **2nd Alternate Aerodrome**.
Insert ICAO four letter designator for destination aerodrome, if no designator exists enter ZZZZ, and specify name in ITEM 18 preceded by DEST/.
Insert Total Elapsed Time in hours/minutes.
Insert alternate aerodrome(s) as ICAO designator, or if no designator exists then ZZZZ and specify name in ITEM 18 preceded by ALTN/.

ITEM 18: Other Information.
0 if None
EET/   signficant point(s) or FIR boundary designator(s) with estimated *elapsed* time(s).
REG/   registration if different to aircraft identification in ITEM 7
OPR/   name of operator if appropriate
STS/   reason for special handling by ATC
TYP/   types of aircraft, if ZZZZ specified at item 9
COM/   comm equipment if Z specified in item 10
NAV/   nav equipment if Z specified in item 10
DEP/   Departure aerodrome name if ZZZZ inserted at item 13
DEST/   Destination aerodrome name if ZZZZ inserted at item 16
ALTN/   Alternate aerodrome name if ZZZZ inserted at item 16
RMK/   any other plain language remarks as appropriate

ITEM 19: Supplementary Information.
Endurance:
E/ – fuel endurance in a four-figure group to express hours/minutes
Persons on Board:
P/ –
Emergency Radio:
R/   Radio
Cross out U if UHF 243MHz not available.
Cross out V if VHF 121.5MHz not available.
Cross out E if emergency locater beacon – aircraft (ELBA) not available.

20

Survival Equipment:

S/ Survival Equipment

Cross out all indicators if survival equipment not carried

Cross out P if polar survival equipment not carried

Cross out D if desert survival equipment not carried

Cross out M if maritime survival equipment not carried

Cross out J if jungle survival equipment not carried

Jackets:

J/ Jackets

Cross out all indicators if no life-jackets are carried

Cross out L if life-jackets are not equipped with lights

Cross out F if life-jackets are not equipped with flourescein

Cross out U or V to indicate radio capability of life-jackets.

Dingies:

Number Cross out indicators D and C if no dinghies are carried, or insert number

Capacity Insert total capacity, in persons, of dinghies carried

Cover Cross out C if dinghies are not covered

Colour Insert colour of dinghies carried

Aircraft Colour and Markings:

A/ Aircraft colour and markings – insert colour of aircraft and significant markings

Remarks:

N/ Remarks – Cross out indicator N if no remarks, or indicate other survival equipment/remarks.

Pilot in Command:

C/ Pilot – Insert name of pilot in command

Filing a flight plan

A VFR flight plan must be filed at least 60 minutes before clearance to start or taxi is requested. Normally the flight plan is filed at the departure airfield who will pass it on to the relevant Parent ATSU Flight Briefing Unit. If the departure airfield will not be able to file the flight plan, it should be telephoned or faxed directly to the appropriate Parent ATSU Flight Briefing Unit:

Flight Briefing Unit Telephone Number	Fax Number
LONDON/Heathrow EGLL	
0208 745 3111	0208 745 3491
0208 745 3163	0208 745 3492
Manchester EGCC	
0161 499 5502	0161 499 5504
0161 499 5500	0161 499 5501
Scottish ACC EGPX	
01292 692679	01292 671048

The ATSU or FBU must be advised as soon as possible of any cancellations, delays that will exceed 30 minutes, or changes to flight plan details.

If the flight lands at a place other than the flightplan destination, the destination must be informed within 30 minutes of the planned ETA there.

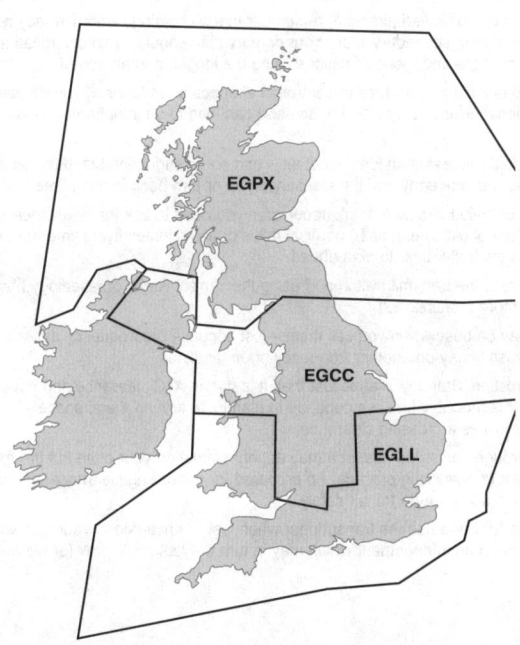

IMPORTANT NOTICE

Prevention of the Infringement of Controlled Airspace

THE NUMBER of reported infringements of controlled airspace is rising

2003: 181 reported infringements

2004: 202 reported infringements

2005: 373 reported infringements

2006: 334 reported infringements (January to August only)

Since 2005 NATS has reminded air traffic controllers to report all controlled airspace infringements however minor, this will explain some of the increase shown that year. However the number of risk bearing infringements has increased by the same amount and these would have been previously reported.

While infringements can occur in any controlled airspace, certain hotspot areas have become apparent, some of which are listed below

Luton/Stansted area

London City Airport

Western part of London Control Zone (White Waltham area)

Red Arrows Displays (Temporary Restricted Areas)

Particular care should be taken while operating in these areas

A UK based website devoted solely to Airspace Infringements is run by the General Aviation Safety Council (GASCo) on behalf of the Civil Aviation Authority. This site (The Fly on Track Website) contains lots of useful information which will aid pilots in avoiding infringements of controlled airspace; the following information is taken from the site.

The Web address for the Fly on Track Website, AIS (UK Aeronautical Information Service) and Nats (National Air Traffic Services) Website are listed below

Fly on Track	www.flyontrack.co.uk
AIS (UK Aeronautical Information Service)	www.ais.org.uk
NATS (National Air Traffic Services)	www.nats.co.uk

How NOT to Infringe

1 Contains good advice on VFR navigation, but it only works if you read and apply it! There are other relevant leaflets there too – for example: GPS use and Radio

2 If you plan a route through controlled airspace, remember that a crossing clearance may not always be possible and consider that route as your 'secondary' plan. Your primary plan should avoid controlled airspace – and don't forget to make your overall time and fuel calculations using the longer, primary route!

3 Where possible, avoid planning to fly close to controlled airspace boundaries. If you do need to do so, be very careful. A small navigational error or distraction of any sort can lead to an infringement – and it doesn't take much to ruin your day!

4 Pilot workload rises rapidly in less than ideal weather – and so do infringements. If the weather starts to deteriorate, consider your options early and if necessary divert or turn back in good time.

5 If you wish to transit controlled airspace, think about what you need to ask for in advance and call the appropriate Air Traffic Control (ATC) unit at 10 nautical miles or five minutes flying time from the airspace boundary. This gives the controller time to plan ahead.

6 Thinking before you press the transmit switch and using the correct Radio phraseology helps air traffic control to help you – and sounds more professional!

7 Be aware that ATC may be busy when you call them – just because the frequency doesn't sound busy doesn't mean that the controller isn't busy on another frequency or on landlines.

8 Remember – the instruction 'Standby' means just that; it is not an ATC clearance and not even a precursor to a clearance. The controller is probably busy so continue to plan to fly around the airspace. Only fly across the airspace if the controller issues a crossing clearance.

9 Your planned route through controlled airspace may appear simple on your chart but the traffic patterns within that airspace may make it unrealistic in practice. Be prepared for a crossing clearance that does not exactly match your planned route but will allow you to transit safely.

10 Don't be afraid to call ATC and use the transponder when lost or uncertain of your position – overcoming your embarrassment may prevent an infringement which may in turn prevent an Airprox (or worse).

DON'T INFRINGE AIR DISPLAY AIRSPACE

Every year the Temporary Restricted Airspace established around certain air shows in the UK attracts infringements. For example, between 2002 and 2005 Red Arrows Temporary Restricted Airspace was infringed on 14 occasions.

At best, infringements will lead to displays – including those by the Red Arrows – being disrupted and thousands of members of the paying public being denied the chance to see solo and team aerobatic performances. Some are cancelled as a result or called off half way through – for example the 2006 Kemble display.

All such incursions have flight safety implications and could lead to accidents and loss of life.

In many cases infringements occur because pilots simply haven't briefed themselves properly before taking off. All pilots should be aware of the briefing options available to ensure that they are not one of the infringements statistics. There are several ways to obtain pre-flight briefing information:

One of the easiest ways to check on temporary restricted airspace (such as Red Arrows displays) is by calling the dedicated free phone **AIS Information Line** on **0500 354 802**

Check **NOTAMs** on the **AIS Website** contact the **NOTAM Office** on **020 8745 3451** or **3450** (24-hour facility).

Alternatively, check **Pre-Flight Information Bulletins** (PIBs) on the AIS website. PIB Help is also available there. PIBs may also be accessed through the **Nats Website,** even if the AIS website is down.

Check Aeronautical Information Circulars (AICs), also on the **AIS Website**

Mauve AICs notify the establishment of Temporary Restricted Airspace around all of the Red Arrow's display sites and certain air shows.

Yellow AICs providing details of major displays or rallies may also be published.

A number of major events are notified by both Mauve and Yellow AICs.

Wherever and whenever you fly during the summer make sure you're properly briefed and that you don't end up as a Air Display infringement statistic.

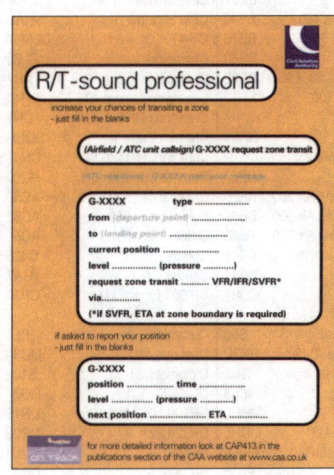

Name/Model	ICAO
2/180 Gyroplane	HG18
47G2/Bell	KH2
47G2A/Bell	KH2A
47G3B-KH4/Bell	KH4
A109/109A/II	A109
AB 47 G/G-2/2A/2A1/ 3B1/4/4A	A47G
AB 47 J/J-2A/3/3B-1	A47J
Aero145	O145
Aero Commander 685	AC85
Aero Commander 695	AC95
Aero-Jodel D-11A	AE11
Aeronca Champion	AR58
Aeronca Chief/Super Chief	AR11
Aeronca Sedan	AR15
Aero Star	TS60
Aero Star 600/700	PA60
Aircoupe A2	FO2
Aircruiser	VT11
Air Cruiser	AC72
Airtourer	VT10
ARV ARV-1	ARV1
Autogyro (Ultralight/Microlight)	GYRO
Balloons	BALL
Beagle Pup B121	BT12
Beech Bonanza 33	BE33
Beech Bonanza 35	BE35
Beech Bonanza 36	BE36
Beech Baron 55	BE55
Beech Baron 58	BE58
Beech Beech F90	BE9T
Beech Beech Jet 400	BE40
Beech Duchess 76	BE76
Beech Duke 60	BE60
Beech King Air C90, E90	BE9L
Beech King Air 100	BE10
Beech Starship, Model 2000	BEST
Beech Sundowner 23/ Musketeer 23	BE23
Beech Super King Air 200	BE20
Beech Super King Air 300	BE30
Beech Super King Air 350	B350
Beech Twin Beech 18	BE18
Bell 412	NB12
Bell B/A 206B-1	CCB4
Bell Jet Ranger/ Long Sea Ranger	B06
BN-2A/B Islander/Defender	BN2P
BN-2A Mk111 Trislander	TRIS
BO 105	NB05
BO 105A/C/D/S	MBH5
BO 105LS A-1, A-3	MDH5
BO 209, S Monsun	MB09
Brave	PA36
Buccaneer/LA-4/200EP/EPR	LA4
Buecker BUE 131 Jungmann BJ31	
CAP 10/10B	CP10
CAP 20/20L	CP20
CAP 21	CP21
CAP 230	CP23
Cessna 120	C120
Cessna 140	C140
Cessna 150	C150
Cessna 152	C152
Cessna 170	C170
Cessna 172/Skyhawk/ HawkXPII/Cutlass	C172
Cessna 172RG	C72R
Cessna 177RG	C77R
Cessna 185/Skywagon	C185
Cessna 190	C190
Cessna 195	C195
Cessna 310/T310	C310
Cessna 337	C337
Cessna Pressurised 337	P337
Cessna 340/340A	C340
Cessna 401/402/4026	C402
Cessna 411	C411
Cessna Caravan 1	C208
Cessna Cardinal 177	C177
Cessna Centurion/ Turbo Centurion 210	C210
Cessna Chancellor 414A	C414
Cessna Citation Jet 522	C525
Cessna Citation	C500
Cessna Citation II/S2	C550
Cessna Citation III/VI/VII	C650
Cessna Citation V	C560
Cessna Conquest/ Conquest II	C441
Cessna Crusader T303	C303
Cessna Golden Eagle 421	C421
Cessna Pressurised Centurion	P210
Cessna Skylane 182/RG, Turbo Skylane/RG	C182
Cessna Skymaster	C336
Cessna Stationair/Turbo Stationair/6	C206
Cessna Stationair/ Turbo Stationair 7/8	C207
Cessna Titan	C404
CFM Shadow	SHAD
CH-47	CEM47
Champion	CL60
Champion Citabria	AR7
Champion Lancer 402	CH40
Chipmunk DHC-1	DH1
Christen Eagle II	SOCH
Commander 112/114	CM11
Commander 200	M200
Commander 500	AC50
Commander 520	AC52
Commander 560	AC56
Corsair	C425
Cougar GA-7	GA7
CP 301 Emeraude	CP30
Decathlon	BL8
Diamond 1/1A	MU30
Diplomate ST 10	S10a
DO27	DO27
DR100,105,1050,1051	DR10
DR220,221	DR22
DR 250	DR250
DR 300	DR30
DR 360	DR36
DR 400	DR 40
Ecureuil AS350	S350
Ecureuil AS351	S351
Ecureuil AS355	S355
Europa	EUPA
Falco	F8L
Falcon 10	FA10
Falcon 20FJF/20C/ 20D/20E/20F	FA20
Falcon 20G/20GF, Mystere Falcon 200	FA21
Falcon 50	FA50
Falcon 900	FA90
G109/109B	G109
G115/115A	G115
Gardan GY100	GY10
Gazelle Sa341/342	GAZL
Glassair II/III	GLAS
Glider/Sailplane	GLID
Grumman Cheetah, Tiger, Traveler	AA5
Grumman Yankee AA-1B	AA1
Gulfstream I	G159
Gulfstream II/III/IV	GULF
HN-300C	BI30
Horizon GY 80	S80
HR 100	HR10
HR 200	HR20
HS125	HS25
Jet Commander	JCOM
Jet Commander 840/980/1000	AC6T
Jetstream 31/32	JSTA
Jodel D112/D120	D11
Jodel D140	D140
Kachina 2150A	MOR2
Kitfox	FOX
L-4-200 Buccaneer	LA4
LA-250	LA25
Lancair 235/320/360	LNC2
Lancair IV	LNC3
Learjet 23	LJ23
Learjet 24	LJ24
Learjet 25	LJ25
Learjet 28	LJ28
Learjet 31	LJ31
Learjet 35	LJ35
Learjet 55	LJ55
Learjet 60	LJ60
Luscombe 11	L11
Maule M-4	M4
Maule M-5	M5
Maule M-6	M6
Maule M-7	M7
Mooney 20, 21, 22, 201, 231	M20
Meta-Sokol L40	O40
MU2	MU2
P64-Oscar	OSCR
Pilatus PC-12	PC12
Piper Apache	PA23
Piper Aztec	PA27
Piper Cherokee/Archer II/ Dakota/Warrior	PA28
Piper Cherokee Arrow	P28R
Piper Cherokee 6/Lance/ Saratoga	PA32
Piper Cheyenne I/II	P31T
Piper Cheyenne III/IV	PA42
Piper Chieftain/Navajo	PA31
Piper Clipper	PA16
Piper Commanche	PA24
Piper Cub Special	PA11
Piper Cub Trainer	J2
Piper Cub Trainer 3	J3
Piper Family Cruiser	PA14
Piper Malibu	PA46
Piper Pacer	PA20
Piper Seminole	PA44
Piper Seneca	PA34
Piper Super Cruiser	PA12
Piper Super Cub	PA18
Piper Tri-Pacer/Colt	PA22
Piper Twin Commanche	PA30
Piper Vagabond	PA17
Piper Vagabond Trainer	PA15
R 1180T, 1180TD	R100
R 2160, 2160D, 2100, 2100A, 2112	R200
R 3000/3100/3120/3140	R300
Rallye	RALL
RF3	RF3
RF4	RF4
RF5	RF5
RF6	RF6
RF6B	SPF6B
RF7	SPF7
RF9	RF9
Robinson R22	R22
Robinson R44	R44
SF260	F260
SF260TP	F26T
Stagger Wing 17	BE17
Stampe	SV4
Stearman	B75
Steen Skybolt	BOLT
Super Acro Sport	ASPO
Swift	GC1
T67M Firefly 160	RF6
Tampico TB-09	TAMP
TBM 706	TBM7
Texan	T6
Tiger Moth 82A	DH82
Tobago TB-10	TOBA
Tomahawk	PA38
Trinidad TB-20/21	TRIN
Turbo Commander 690C	
Turbulent	D31
Twin Otter DHC-6	DH6
Vari-Eze	KREZ
Vari EZE/Long EZ	LGEZ
Yak 50	YK50
Yak 52	YK52
Zlin 42	Z42
Zlin 43	Z43
Z-50L	Z50

The following airports have been designated as Customs and Excise Airports by the DTLR:

Aberdeen/Dyce	
Belfast Aldergrove	2
Biggin Hill	1
Birmingham	
Blackpool	1
Bournemouth	
Bristol	
Cambridge	1
Cardiff	
Coventry	1
Durham Tees Valley	
Nottingham East Midlands	
Edinburgh	
Exeter	1
Glasgow	2
Humberside	1
Isle of Man	1
Leeds/Bradford	
Liverpool	
London City	1
London Gatwick	2
London Heathrow	2
London Luton	
London Stansted	
Lydd	1
Manchester	2
Manston	1
Newcastle	
Norwich	
Plymouth	2
Sheffield	1
Shoreham	1
Southampton	
Southend	
Sumburgh	1

1 Aerodromes are NOT Ports of Entry under the Immigration Act 1971
2 Aerodromes are Sanitary Airport under the International Sanitary Regulations

1 Aircrew

1.1 Arriving on Flights from other EU Countries

1.1.1 The duty/tax free allowances do not apply to intra EU crew. No declaration is required to be made. Also, there is no Customs restriction on crew members' exit route from the airport (although in practice at most larger airports their movements are constrained by security measures).

1.2 Arriving on Flights from Non-EU Countries

1.2.1 The Customs office at the airport of arrival will be able to advise on the arrangements in operation there for clearance of aircrew. Normally, this will involve the crew members in either:

a Making a declaration on Form C909; or

b making an oral declaration in the Red Channel or at the Red Point, if they are carrying goods in excess of the customs allowances for aircrew.

1.2.2 The terms of this paragraph apply not only to crew who have arrived on a direct flight from outside the EU, but also to crew whose aircraft has made a stopover at another EU airport.

1.3 Departing on Flights to Non-EU Destinations

1.3.1 It is not normally necessary for crews' effects to be made available for Customs, except when refund of VAT is being claimed under the Retail Export Scheme. VAT leaflet 704/1/93 explains the conditions under which aircrew are eligible for the Scheme, and the procedures to be followed.

2 Passengers

2.1 Arriving on Domestic Flights

2.1.1 The hold baggage of passengers who arrived in the United Kingdom from a non-EU Country and have transferred to a domestic flight will be subject to Customs control at the destination airport, if it has not been cleared at the airport of arrival in the United Kingdom. The Customs office at the destination airport should be contacted for details of the arrangements.

2.2 Arriving on Flights from other EU Countries

2.2.1 Passengers on direct flights from other EU Countries are not normally required to make any declaration and at most airports proceed through a separate EU exit.

2.2.2 The only exception is for passengers who commenced their journey outside the EU and have transferred to a flight to the United Kingdom after arriving in another EU Country. After reclaiming their hold baggage, such passengers must make an oral declaration in the Red Channel or at the Red Point, if they are carrying goods in excess of Customs allowances. Passengers with nothing to declare should proceed through the Green Channel.

2.3 Arriving on Flights from Non-EU Countries

2.3.1 After disembarkation, passengers completing their journey at a United Kingdom airport reclaim any hold baggage, and if they are carrying goods in excess of Customs allowances they must make an oral declaration in the Red Channel or at the Red Point. Passengers with nothing to declare should proceed through the Green Channel. These procedures apply not only to passengers who have arrived on a direct flight from outside the EU, but also to passengers whose aircraft has made a stopover at another EU airport.

2.3.2 Passengers who are transferring to a flight to another EU Country do not reclaim their hold baggage, but must declare any goods in their cabin baggage which are in excess of customs allowances.

2.3.3 Passengers who are transferring to a flight to a non-EU Country are not required to make any declaration to Customs.

2.3.4 The Customs office for the airport of arrival should be contacted for advice on the arrangements there for passengers transferring to a flight to another United Kingdom airport, as these may vary depending on local circumstances.

3 Further Information

3.1 Further information on the Customs requirements for international travellers, including details of Customs allowances is in HM Customs and Excise Notice 1.

It is a requirement of the Act that the commander of any aircraft flying between Great Britain and the Republic of Ireland, Northern Ireland, the Isle of Man or the Channel Islands or Inbound to Great Britain from those places must, on exit or entry to Great Britain, land at an airport designated in the act. The same requirement exists for flights entering or leaving Northern Ireland when flying to or from Great Britain, the Republic of Ireland, the Isle of Man or the Channel Islands.

To comply with the requirements of this legislation the captains of aircraft affected by the Act **must.**

1 Obtain clearance from the examining Police officer before take-off from and after landing at an airport designated in the act.

2 Must comply with the requirements of the examining officer in respect of any examination of the captain, passengers, or crew, if carried.

Designated Airports in Gt. Britain, Northern Ireland, Isle of Man, & Channel Islands
ABERDEEN
ALDERNEY
BELFAST ALDERGROVE
BELFAST CITY
BIGGIN HILL
BIRMINGHAM
BLACKPOOL
BOURNEMOUTH
BRISTOL
CAMBRIDGE
CARDIFF
CARLISLE
COVENTRY
DURHAM TEES VALLEY
EDINBURGH
EXETER
GLASGOW
GLOUCESTERSHIRE
GUERNSEY
HUMBERSIDE
ISLE OF MAN
JERSEY
LEEDS BRADFORD
LIVERPOOL
LONDON CITY
LONDON GATWICK
LONDON HEATHROW
LONDON LUTON
LONDON STANSTED
LONONDERRY
LYDD
MANCHESTER
MANSTON
NEWCASTLE
NORWICH
NOTTINGHAM EAST MIDLANDS
PLYMOUTH
PRESTWICK
SHEFFIELD CITY
SOUTHAMPTON
SOUTHEND

BRISTOL FILTON is not an airport designated under the act but the same facility will be available if application is made at least 24hrs prior to the flight. Such application should be made during normal office hours to. **Tel:** 01272 699094

Flights from Non Designated Airports
If a pilot wishes to make a direct flight from anon-designated airport he/she **must** seek prior permission from the Chief Constable in whose area then on-designated airport is located. Permission should be sought **as far in advance as possible.**

Requirements for Civil Helicopters
Pilots of civil helicopters flying into Northern Ireland are required to notify the Police Service of Northern Ireland (PSNI) control and Information centre. **Tel:** 01232 650222 Ex 22430, of the point and time for crossing the Northern Ireland coast, **this is in addition to the normal requirements of the Act.** Any amendment to the crossing point and/or time must be advised to **Belfast Aldergrove APP** who will notify the PSNI on the pilots behalf.

Avon and Somerset	0845 456 7000
Bedfordshire	01234 841212
Cambridgeshire	01480 456111
Cheshire	01244 350000
Cleveland	01642 326326
Cumbria	01768 891999
Derbyshire	0845 123 3333
Devon and Cornwall	0845 277 7444
Dorset	01305 251212
Durham	0191 386 4929
Dyfed-Powys	01267 232000
Essex	01245 491491
Gloucestershire	0845 090 1234
Greater Manchester	0161 872 5050
Gwent	01633 838111
Hampshire	0845 045 4545
Hertfordshire	01707 354000
Humberside	01482 326111
Kent	01622 690690
Lancashire	0845 125 3545
Leicestershire	0116 222 2222
Lincolnshire	01522 532222
London (Metropolitan)	0207 230 1212
London (City)	0207 601 2455
Merseyside	0151 709 6010
Norfolk	01953 424242
Northampton	01604 700700
Northumbria	01661 872555
North Wales	0845 607 1002
North Yorkshire	0845 606 0247
Nottinghamshire	0115 9670999
South Wales	01656 655555
South Yorkshire	0114 220 2020
Staffordshire	01785 257717
Suffolk	01473 613500
Surrey	0845 125 2222
Sussex	0845 607 0999
Thames Valley	0845 850 5505
Warwickshire	01926 415000
West Mercia	01905 723000
West Midlands	0845 113 5000
West Yorkshire	0845 606 0606
Wiltshire	01380 722341

Scotland

Central Scotland	01786 456000
Dumfries and Galloway	01387 252112
Fife	01592 418888
Grampian	0800 371553
Lothian and Borders	0131 311 3131
Northern	01463 715555
Strathclyde	0141 532 2000
Tayside	01382 223200

Northern Ireland

Police Service of Northern Ireland (PSNI)	02890 650222

Isle of Man & Channel Islands

Isle of Man	01624 631212
Jersey	01534 612612
Guernsey	01481 725111

(Who also have responsibility for Alderney)

As you may notice from this guide, the number of gliding airfields that will accept powered aircraft is increasing. There are a number of hazards and practices associated with such airfields which are unfamiliar to the powered pilot. The following points are designed as general guidance and pilots intending to visit a gliding airfield **are strongly advised to ensure they are properly briefed on the specific field they intend to visit.** All gliding airfields require telephone PPR so this is not another chore to remember. **There is nothing more likely to reverse the trend of gliding airfields accepting powered aircraft than demonstrations of poor airman ship or obstruction of their activities.** Having said the heavy bit, GO OUT AND ENJOY!

1 MAINTAIN A VERY GOOD LOOKOUT. Not only does steam give way to sail but remember, a glider cannot go around! Even the hottest competition model will continue to descend when committed to a landing. DO NOT OBSTRUCT THE LANDING AREA! Remember that Gliding fields are primarily for gliding, you are a guest and give preference at all times.

2 FLYING IN THE LOCAL AREA WHEN JOINING OR LEAVING THE CIRCUIT? Then there are two very relevant tips to remember. Firstly… **keep a very good lookout close to cloud base**… On thermic days this is where the Gliders will be, an unstable day with developing, or developed Cumulus will see many gliders turning beneath them, if you are descending through cloud it makes sense to do this further from your destination than you might normally do. Secondly… By the very nature of their activities glider pilots are more used to flying in close proximity to other aircraft than we powered pilots. Sometimes this can be very disconcerting! (It certainly has worried me when I've gone gliding)! But remember, as they do it a lot they are very aware of aircraft in their proximity, keep a very good lookout and may even have heard you coming! The best reaction is to assume you have not been seen and apply the Rules of the Air.

3 USE THE GLIDER COMMON FREQUENCIES. All gliding fields require PPR, when you get it make sure you know which of the common gliding frequencies are used by the local club and make circuit reports on it. You are very unlikely to get an answer but at least someone **MAY** know you are there. Remember, not all local Gliders will be listening out on radio, traffic awareness is not its primary function so **remain vigilant at all times.**

4 LOOK OUT FOR CABLES. Do not carry out overhead joins, as this is where the winch will deposit any departing gliders, sometimes up to 3000ft agl! You may see the cable drogue parachute but you will **not** see the cable. If you hit it in flight it will kill you, which would really spoil your visit! Remember also that tug aircraft will be towing cables, don't get too close and **always give them priority,** they have a job to do and this is only courteous airmanship.

5 LANDING (LOOK OUT FOR CABLES AGAIN)! After landing, roll beyond the launch point. This is because most gliders will be planning their landing to arrive at the launch point so that it is only a short push, (or tow), to regain the end of the launch queue. They'll then have plenty of room to land behind and to the right of you, (remember the Rules of the Air). It's quite obvious where the launch point is as the launch control caravan will be here and so will the launch queue of gliders. Give them a wide berth and do not land if a launch is in progress. After landing turn **left** and wait. Have a good look up final approach and on the base legs. Nothing coming? Then taxi back down the strip keeping close to the edge. If a tug or Glider should appear on final then stop and wait until it has landed. Continue to taxi back and **pass behind the launch queue. Don't taxi in front of the queue, you will be crossing the cables, the danger of this is quite obvious.** Park by the Launch control caravan but not between it and the winch as you will be obstructing the winch drivers view of the control caravan's visual signals, (a bit like an Aldis light).

6 BE AWARE OF YOUR PROPWASH. When manoeuvring or parking be very aware of your prop wash if you are using increased revs. The area around the launch point is generally very busy with people awaiting a launch, gliders being towed or manhandled, trailers, caravans, and vehicles. The possibilities for damage caused by loose stones or prop wash is self-evident.

7 DEPARTING. The same rules apply. Don't take off until the launch cable is on the ground following a launch remember the drogue chute on the cable will make this easy to accertain. Continue to be extremely vigilant until well clear of the site. At sites, which have Aerotow facilities, it is quite likely that there will be noise abatement routes or procedures. Find out if there are and follow them!

IF YOU ARE IN ANY DOUBT ABOUT LOCAL PROCEDURES THEN ASK ONE OF THE RESIDENT INSTRUCTORS. THERE WILL ALMOST CERTAINLY BE ONE NEAR THE LAUNCH CONTROL CARAVAN.

8 BAD GROUND. Many gliding fields are exactly that, a large field with useable and, sometimes, very unusable areas. Ensure you know where the area suitable for powered aircraft use is. Currock Hill is a case in point where a very large grass area has a relatively small area suitable for powered aircraft use.

Gliding fields invariably have some form of catering and facilities for an overnight stay at very reasonable cost. They are not as forbidding as they may seem to power pilots but when you do visit them show them you are a good airman. This article is by no means comprehensive and I find I learn something new at each site I visit. By showing the Gliding fraternity that we are considerate of their operations, the more likely it is that they will be willing to allow powered aircraft the use of their sites, which opens up a whole new range of airfields to visit.

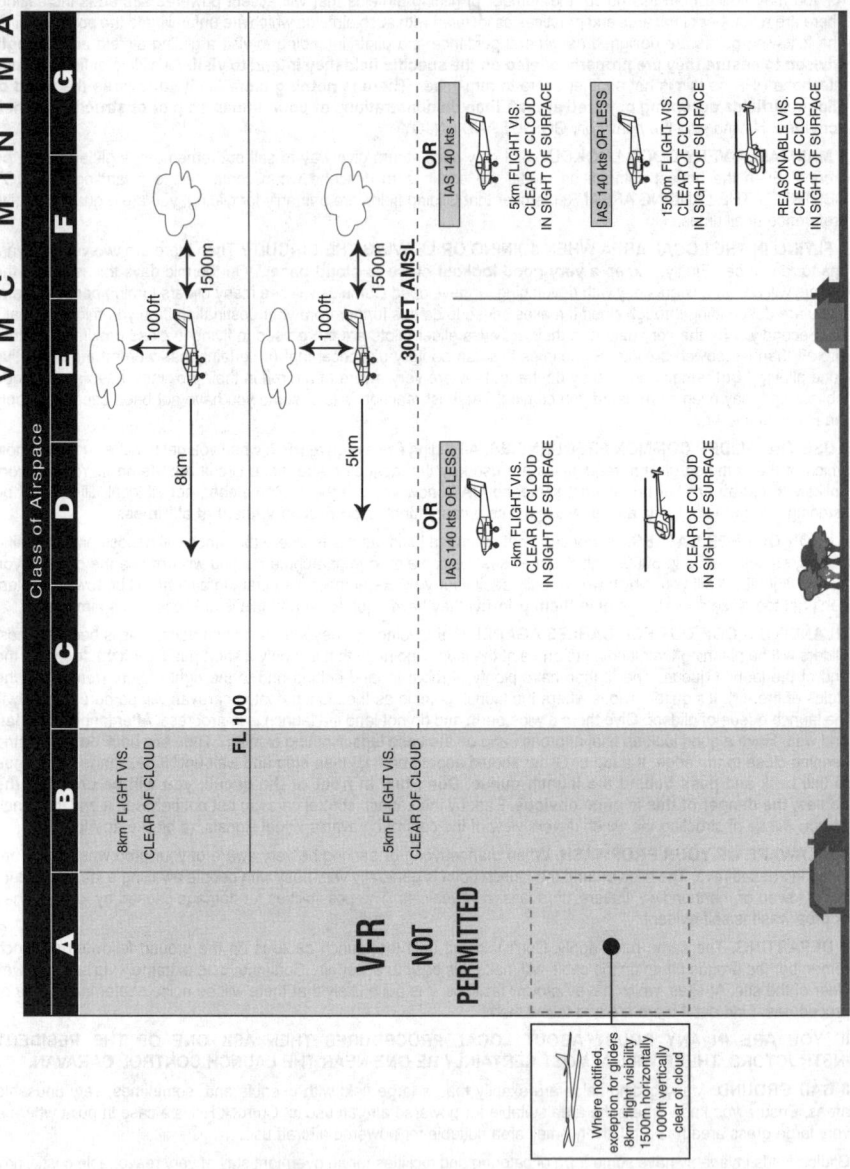

V M C   M I N I M A

Class of Airspace

A — VFR NOT PERMITTED

B — 8km FLIGHT VIS. CLEAR OF CLOUD

C — 5km FLIGHT VIS. CLEAR OF CLOUD

FL 100

FL 100 / **D** / **E** — 1000ft, 1500m, 8km

F / **G** — 1000ft, 1500m, 5km

3000FT AMSL

OR — IAS 140 kts OR LESS — 5km FLIGHT VIS. CLEAR OF CLOUD IN SIGHT OF SURFACE

CLEAR OF CLOUD IN SIGHT OF SURFACE

OR — IAS 140 kts + — 5km FLIGHT VIS. CLEAR OF CLOUD IN SIGHT OF SURFACE

IAS 140 kts OR LESS — 1500m FLIGHT VIS. CLEAR OF CLOUD IN SIGHT OF SURFACE

REASONABLE VIS. CLEAR OF CLOUD IN SIGHT OF SURFACE

Where notified, exception for gliders 8km flight visibility 1500m horizontally 1000ft vertically clear of cloud

Take-off Distance Factors				Landing Distance Factors		
VARIATION	**INCREASE IN TAKE-OFF DISTANCE (to 50')**	**FACTOR**		**VARIATION**	**INCREASE IN LANDING DISTANCE (from 50')**	**FACTOR**
10% increase in aircraft weight	20%	1.2		10% increase in aircraft weight	10%	1.1
Increase of 1000' in runway altitude	10%	1.1		Increase of 1000' in runway altitude	5%	1.05
Increase in temperature of 10°C	10%	1.1		Increase in temperature of 10°C	5%	1.05
Dry Grass				Dry Grass		
– Up to 20cm (8 in)	20%	1.2		– Up to 20cm (8 in)	15%	1.15
Wet Grass				Wet Grass		
– Up to 20cm (8 in)	30%	1.3		– Up to 20cm (8 in)	35%	1.35
				Very short grass may increase	<60%	<1.6
Wet Paved Surface	–	–		Wet Paved Surface	15%	1.15
2% uphill slope	10%	1.1		2% downhill slope	10%	1.1
Tailwind component of				Tailwind component of		
10% of lift off speed	20%	1.2		10% of landing speed	20%	1.2
Soft ground or snow *	at least 25%	at least 1.25		snow *	at least 25%	at least 1.25
Additional safety factor	–	**1.33**		**Additional safety factor**	–	**1.43**

The Take-off Run Available (TORA)
The TORA is the length of the runway available for the take-off ground run of the aircraft. This is usually the physical length of the runway.

The Emergency Distance (ED)
The ED is the length of the TORA plus the length of any stopway. A stopway is area at the end of the TORA prepared for an aircraft to stop on in the event of an abandoned take off. The ED is also known as the ACCELERATE – STOP DISTANCE AVAILABLE.

The Take-off Distance Available (TODA)
The TODA is the TORA plus the length of any clearway. A clearway is an area over which an aircraft may make its initial climb (to 50' in this instance). The TODA will not be more than 1.5 x TORA.

The Landing Distance Available (LDA)
The LDA is the length of the runway available for the ground run of an aircraft landing. In all cases the landing distance required should never be greater than the landing distance available.

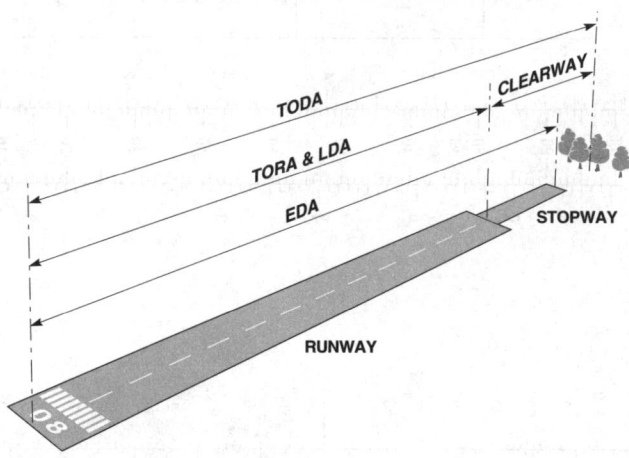

Flight Planning — Conversions

Temperature & Pressure

TEMPERATURE
°C 50 40 30 20 10 0 −10 −20 −30 −40 −50 −60
°F 120 110 100 90 80 70 60 50 40 30 20 10 0 −10 −20 −30 −40 −50 −60 −70

PRESSURE
Bars 7 6 5 4 3 2 1 0
lbs/sq" 100 90 80 70 60 50 40 30 20 10
Kg/cm² 7 6 5 4 3 2 1 0

Metric/Imperial Measurement

Metres	Feet	Feet	Metres
1	3.28	1	0.30
2	6.56	2	0.61
3	9.84	3	0.91
4	13.12	4	1.22
5	16.40	5	1.52
6	19.69	6	1.83
7	22.97	7	2.13
8	26.25	8	2.44
9	29.53	9	2.74
10	32.81	10	3.05
20	65.62	20	6.10
30	98.43	30	9.14
40	131.23	40	12.19
50	164.04	50	15.24
60	196.85	60	18.29
70	229.66	70	21.34
80	262.47	80	24.38
90	295.28	90	27.43
100	328.08	100	30.48
200	656.16	200	60.96
300	984.25	300	91.44
400	1,312.34	400	121.92
500	1,640.42	500	152.40
600	1,968.50	600	182.88
700	2,296.59	700	213.36
800	2,624.67	800	243.84
900	2,952.76	900	274.32
1000	3,280.84	1000	304.80
2000	6,561.70	2000	609.60
3000	9,842.50	3000	914.40
4000	13,123.40	4000	1,219.20
5000	16,404.20	5000	1,524.00
6000	19,685.00	6000	1,828.80
7000	22,965.90	7000	2,133.60
8000	26,246.70	8000	2,438.40
9000	29,527.60	9000	2,743.20
10000	32,808.40	10000	3,048.00

Km/Nautical Miles/Statute Miles

NM	Km	St	Km	NM	St
1	1.85	1.15	1	.54	.62
2	3.70	2.30	2	1.08	1.24
3	5.56	3.45	3	1.62	1.86
4	7.41	4.60	4	2.16	2.49
5	9.26	5.75	5	2.70	3.11
6	11.11	6.90	6	3.24	3.73
7	12.96	8.06	7	3.78	4.35
8	14.82	9.21	8	4.32	4.97
9	16.67	10.36	9	4.86	5.59
10	18.52	11.51	10	5.40	6.21
20	37.04	23.02	20	10.80	12.43
30	55.56	34.52	30	16.20	18.64
40	74.08	46.03	40	21.60	24.86
50	92.60	57.54	50	27.00	31.07
60	111.12	69.05	60	32.40	37.28
70	129.64	80.55	70	37.80	43.50
80	148.16	92.06	80	43.20	49.71
90	166.68	103.57	90	48.60	55.92
100	185.2	115.1	100	54.0	62.1
200	370.4	230.2	200	108.0	124.3
300	555.6	345.2	300	162.0	186.4
400	740.8	460.3	400	216.0	248.6
500	926.0	575.4	500	270.0	310.7
600	1111.2	690.5	600	324.0	372.8
700	1296.4	805.6	700	378.0	435.0
800	1481.6	920.6	800	432.0	497.1
900	1666.8	1035.7	900	486.0	559.2

Conversion Factors:

Centimetres to Inches x .3937
Inches to Centimetres x 2.54
Metres to Feet x 3.28084
Feet to Metres x 0.3048

Statute Miles to Nautical Miles x 0.868976
Statute Miles to Kilometres x 1.60934
Kilometres to Statute Miles x 0.62137
Kilometres to Nautical Miles x 0.539957
Nautical Miles to Statute Miles x 1.15078
Nautical Miles to Kilometres x 1.852

Volume (Fluid)

Litres	Imp. Gall	U.S. Gall
1	0.22	0.26
2	0.44	0.53
3	0.66	0.79
4	0.88	1.06
5	1.10	1.32
6	1.32	1.59
7	1.54	1.85
8	1.76	2.11
9	1.98	2.38
10	2.20	2.64
20	4.40	5.28
30	6.60	7.93
40	8.80	10.57
50	11.00	13.21
60	13.20	15.85
70	15.40	18.49
80	17.60	21.14
90	19.80	23.78
100	22.00	26.42
200	44.00	52.84
300	66.00	79.26
400	88.00	105.68
500	110.00	132.10
600	132.00	158.52
700	154.00	184.94
800	176.00	211.36
900	198.00	237.78
1000	220.00	264.20

U.S. Gall	Imp. Gall	Litres
1	0.83	3.79
2	1.67	7.57
3	2.50	11.36
4	3.33	15.14
5	4.16	18.93
6	5.00	22.71
7	5.83	26.50
8	6.66	30.28
9	7.49	34.07
10	8.33	37.85
20	16.65	75.71
30	24.98	113.56
40	33.31	151.41
50	41.63	189.27
60	49.96	227.12
70	58.29	264.97
80	66.61	302.82
90	74.94	340.68
100	83.27	378.54

Imp. Gall	U.S. Gall	Litres
1	1.20	4.55
2	2.40	9.09
3	3.60	13.64
4	4.80	18.18
5	6.00	22.73
6	7.21	27.28
7	8.41	31.82
8	9.61	36.37
9	10.81	40.91
10	12.01	45.46
20	24.02	90.92
30	36.03	136.38
40	48.04	181.84
50	60.05	227.30
60	72.06	272.76
70	84.07	318.22
80	96.08	363.68
90	108.09	409.14
100	120.09	454.60

Conversion Factors:

Imperial Gallons to Litres x 4.54596
Litres to Imperial Gallons x 0.219975
U.S. Gallons to Litres x 3.78541
Litres to U.S. Gallons x 0.264179
Imperial Gallons to U.S. Gallons x 1.20095
U.S. Gallons to Imperial Gallons x 0.832674

Weight lbs/Kg

lbs	Kg	Kg	lbs
1	.45	1	2.20
2	.91	2	4.41
3	1.38	3	6.61
4	1.81	4	8.82
5	2.27	5	11.02
6	2.72	6	13.23
7	3.18	7	15.43
8	3.63	8	17.64
9	4.08	9	19.84
10	4.54	10	22.05
20	9.07	20	44.09
30	13.61	30	66.14
40	18.14	40	88.18
50	22.68	50	110.23
60	27.22	60	132.28
70	31.75	70	154.32
80	36.29	80	176.37
90	40.82	90	198.42
100	45.4	100	220.5
200	90.7	200	440.9
300	136.1	300	661.4
400	181.4	400	881.8
500	226.8	500	1102.3
600	272.2	600	1322.8
700	317.5	700	1543.2
800	362.9	800	1763.7
900	408.2	900	1984.2
1000	453.6	1000	2204.6
2000	907.2	2000	4409.2
3000	1360.8	3000	6613.9
4000	1814.4	4000	8818.5
5000	2268.0	5000	11023.1
6000	2721.5	6000	13227.7
7000	3175.1	7000	15432.3
8000	3628.7	8000	17637.0
9000	4082.3	9000	19841.6
10000	4535.9	10000	22046.2

Km/Nautical Miles/Statute Miles

ST	NM	Km
1	.87	1.61
2	1.74	3.22
3	2.61	4.83
4	3.48	6.44
5	4.34	8.05
6	5.21	9.66
7	6.08	11.27
8	6.95	12.87
9	7.82	14.48
10	8.69	16.09
20	17.38	32.19
30	26.07	48.28
40	34.76	64.37
50	43.45	80.47
60	52.14	96.56
70	60.83	112.65
80	69.52	128.75
90	78.21	144.84
100	86.9	161.0
200	173.8	321.9
300	260.7	482.8
400	347.6	643.7
500	434.5	804.7
600	521.4	965.6
700	608.3	1126.5
800	695.2	1287.5
900	782.1	1448.4

Conversion Factors:

lbs to Kilograms x 0.45359
Kilograms to lbs x 2.20462

Flight Planning   Conversions

Flight Planning — Conversions

Millibars/Inches

Mbs	ins	Mbs	ins	Mbs	ins	Mbs	ins	Mbs	ins
950	28.054	970	28.644	990	29.235	1010	29.825	1030	30.416
951	28.083	971	28.674	991	29.264	1011	29.855	1031	30.445
952	28.113	972	28.703	992	29.294	1012	29.884	1032	30.475
953	28.142	973	28.733	993	29.323	1013	29.914	1033	30.504
954	28.172	974	28.762	994	29.353	1014	29.943	1034	30.534
955	28.201	975	28.792	995	29.382	1015	29.973	1035	30.564
956	28.231	976	28.821	996	29.412	1016	30.002	1036	30.593
957	28.260	977	28.851	997	29.441	1017	30.032	1037	30.623
958	28.290	978	28.880	998	29.471	1018	30.062	1038	30.652
959	28.319	979	28.910	999	29.500	1019	30.091	1039	30.682
960	28.349	980	28.939	1000	29.530	1020	30.121	1040	30.711
961	28.378	981	28.969	1001	29.560	1021	30.150	1041	30.741
962	28.408	982	28.998	1002	29.589	1022	30.180	1042	30.770
963	28.437	983	29.028	1003	29.619	1023	30.209	1043	30.800
964	28.467	984	29.058	1004	29.648	1024	30.239	1044	30.829
965	28.496	985	29.087	1005	29.678	1025	30.268	1045	30.859
966	28.526	986	29.117	1006	29.707	1026	30.298	1046	30.888
967	28.556	987	29.146	1007	29.737	1027	30.327	1047	30.918
968	28.585	988	29.176	1008	29.766	1028	30.357	1048	30.947
969	28.615	989	29.205	1009	29.796	1029	30.386	1049	30.977

Mbs	ins
1050	31.007

To convert Inches into millibars multiply by 33.86
To convert millibars into Inches multiply by 0.0295

AIS useful telephone numbers:
For clarification or up-dated information regarding:
Pre-flight information bulletins Tel: 0208 745 3464
Foreign Library Tel: 0208 745 3471/3464
UK AIP Tel: 0208 745 3456/3450

Pre-flight information bulletins can be accessed from the internet www.ais.org.uk
For information regarding Temporary Restricted Airspace
Red Arrows Displays
Emergency Restrictions of Flying
Royal Flights
Freephone telephone number is available Tel: 0500 354802

AOPA
Aircraft Owners & Pilots Association
Tel: 0207 834 5631
Fax: 0207 834 8623
Email: info@aopa.co.uk
Web: www.aopa.co.uk

ASG
Air Safety Group
Tel: 01483 764413
Email: secretary:airsafetygroup.org

BAEA
British Aerobatic Association
Tel: 01234 713245
Email: info@aerobatics.org.uk
Web: www.aerobatics.org.uk

BALPA
British Air Line Pilots Association
Tel: 0208 476 4000
Fax: 0208 476 4077
Email: balpa@balpa.org.uk
Web: www.balpa.org.uk

BBAC
British Balloon & Airship Club
Tel: 0117 9531231
Email: information@bbac.org
Web: www.bbac.org

BGA
British Gliding Association
Tel: 0116 253 1051
Fax: 0116 251 5939
Email: office@gliding.co.uk
Web: www.gliding.co.uk

BHAB
British Helicopter Advisory Board
Tel: 01276 856100
Fax: 01276 856126
Email: info@bhab.demon.org
Web: www.bhab.org

BHPA
British Hang Gliding & Paragliding Association
Tel: 0116 261 1322
Fax: 0116 261 1323
Email: office@bhpa.co.uk
Web: www.bhpa.co.uk

BMAA
British Microlight Aircraft Association
Tel: 01869 338888
Fax: 01869 337116
Email: general@bmaa.org
Web: www.bmaa.org

BPA
British Parachute Association
Tel: 0116 278 5271
Fax: 0116 247 7662
Email: skydive@bpa.org.uk
Web: www.bpa.org.uk

BWPA
British Women Pilots Association
Tel: 01342 892739
Email: enquires@bwpa.co.uk
Web: www.bwpa.co.uk

FFA
Flying Farmers Association
Tel: 01944 738281
Fax: 01944 738240
Email: chix@farmline.com
Web: www.ffa.org.uk

GAMTA
General Aviation Manufacturers & Traders Association
Tel: 01844 238020
Fax: 01844 238087
Email: info@bbga.aero
Web: www.bbga.aero

GAPAN
Guild of Air Pilots & Air Navigators
Tel: 0207 404 4032
Fax: 0207 404 4035
Email: gapan@gapan.org
Web: www.gapan.org

GASCO
General Aviation Safety Council
Tel/Fax: 01634 200203
Email: info@gasco.org.uk
Web: www.gasco.org.uk

JAA
Joint Aviation Authorities
Tel: +31 23 5679700
Fax: +31 23 5621714
Web: www.jaa.nl

LFA
Lawyers Flying Association
Tel: 0207 796 6516
Fax: 0207 796 6783
Email: tony@stapley.co.uk
Web: www.stapley.co.uk/lfa.htm

PFA
Popular Flying Association
Tel: 01280 846786
Fax: 01280 846780
Email: office@pfa.org.uk
Web: www.pfa.org.uk

Aeronautical Information Services (AIS)

Flight Planning

CAA Headquarters
CAA House
45-59 Kingsway
London
WC2B 6TE
Tel: 0207 379 7311 (Switchboard)

CAA Safety Regulation Group
Aviation House
South Area London Gatwick Airport
Gatwick
Tel: 01293 567171 (Switchboard)
Web: www.caa.co.uk

NATS
Fifth Floor
Brettenham House South
Lancaster Place
London
WC3E 7EN
Tel: 0207 309 8666
Web: www.nats.co.uk

AFE Manchester
1a Ringway Trading Estate
Shadowmoss Road
Manchester
M22 5LH
Tel: 0161 499 0023
Fax: 0161 499 0298
Email: enquiries@afeonline.com
Web: www.afeonline.com

AFE Oxford
The Pilot Shop
Oxford Airport
Oxford
OX5 1QX
Tel: 01865 841441
Fax: 01865 842495
Email: oxford@afeonline.com
Web: www.afeonline.com

Pre-flight abbreviations Coverage:

A1	*Route and general information.*
A2	*Selected international airfields within the London FIR.*
A3	*Other selected airfields.*
A4	*Selected airfields in the Scottish FIR.*
A5	*Other (smaller) airfields and obstacles.*
A6	*Permanent NOTAMs (usually cross-referring to AIP amendments).*
A8	*Royal Flights and navigation warnings.*
	For clarification or up-dated information regarding pre-flight information bulletins, call 0208 745 3464 / 3452
	For clarification or up-dated information regarding NOTAMs, call 0208 745 3450

°C	Degrees Compass
°M °m	Degrees Magnetic
°T	Degrees True
ACFT	Aircraft
AD	Aerodrome
A/G	Air/Ground Station
ABn	Aerodrome Beacon
ADF	Automatic Direction Finder
ADIZ	Air Defense Identification Zone (US)
ADR	Advisory Zone
AFIS	Aerodrome Flight Information Service
AGCS	Air Ground Comunication Service
AGL, agl	Above Ground Level
AI	Attitude Indicator
AIAA	Area of Intense Aerial Activity
AIC	Aeronautical Information Circular
AIP	Aeronautical Information Publication
airex	*Air Exercise (usually by military aircraft)*
AIS	Aeronautical Information Service
alt	*alternate or alternative*
alt, Alt	altitude
ALTN	Alternate Destination
AM	Amplitude Modulation
amdt	*amendment*
AME	Authorised Medical Examiner
amsl	Above Mean Sea Level
ANO	Air Navigation Order
AOPA	Aircraft Owners & Pilots Association
Ap	Approach lights
APAPI	Abbreviated Precision Approach Path Indicator
APP	Approach
aprx	*approximately*
ARA	Advisory Radio Area
ARP	*Aerodrome Reference Point*
ARP	Aerodrome Reference Point
arr	Arrangement
Arr	Arrival
ASR	Altimeter Setting Region
ATA	Actual Time of Arrival
ATC	Air Traffic Control
ATIS	Automatic Terminal Information Service
ATPL	Air Transport Pilot Licence (UK)
ATS	Air Traffic Services
ATSU	Air Traffic Service Unit
ATZ	Aerodrome Traffic Zone
authy	*authority*
AUW	All Up Weight
AVASIS	Abbreviated VASIS
avbl	*Available*
AVGAS	Aviation Gasoline

Awy, *awy(s)*	*airway(s)*
Az	Azimuth
BAA	Britsh Airports Authority
bdry	*boundary*
blks	*blocks (usually referring to sections of apron or manoeuvring area)*
Bn	Beacon
Brg, *brg*	Bearing
btn	*between*
C of A	Certificate of Airworthiness
C of E	Certificate of Experience
C of G	Centre of Gravity
C of T	Certificate of Test
C	Centre (runway designator)
c/l	*centre line*
C/S, *c/s*	Callsign
CAA	Civil Aviation Authority
CAAFU	Civil Aviation Authority Flying Unit
CAP	Civil Air Publication
CAS	Calibrated Airspeed
cas	*controlled air space*
CDI	Course Deviation Indicator
CFI	Chief Flying Instructor
CHAPI	Compact Helicopter Approach Path Indicator
chg	*change*
chk	*check*
CIV, civ	Civilian
CLNC, clnc	Clearance
clsd	*closed*
CMATZ	Combined Military Aerodrome Traffic Zones
com, COM	Communication
CSU	Constant Speed Unit
CTA	Control Area
CTR	Control Zone
DA	Decision Altitude
DAAIS	Danger Area Activity Information Service
DACS	Danger Area Crossing Service
Dept	Departure/Depart
DEST	Destination
DF	Direction Finding
DH	Decision Height
DI	Direction Indicator
Dist, *dist*	Distance
Dly, *dly*	Daily
DME	Distance Measuring Equipment
DR	Dead Reckoning
EAS	Equivalent Air Speed
EEC	European Economic Community
EGT	Exhaust Gas Temperature
Elev, *elev*	Elevation
eqpt	*equipment*
est	*established*
ETA	Estimated Time of Arrival
ETD	Estimated Time of Departure
ETE	Estimated Time En route
Ex, *exc*	Except
Ext	Extension
	extending/retracting
Extv	Extensive
FAA	Federal Aviation Authority
FAF	Final Approach Fix
FAP	Final Approach Point
FAT	Final Approach Track
FBO	Fixed Base Operator
Fcst	Forecast
FIR	Flight Information Region

Flight Planning · *Abbreviations*

FIS	Flight Information Service	LITAS	Low Intensity Two-colour Approach Slope System
FL	Flight Level	LLZ	Localizer – Instrument Landing System (ICAO)
FLT, *flt*	Flight		
FM	Frequency Modulation		
fm	*from*	LMT	Local Mean Time
FPL	Filed Flight Plan	LOC	Locater Beacon
FPM	Feet Per Minute	LOM	Locater Outer Marker
freq	*Frequency*	Long	Longitude
FT, ft	Feet	LORAN	Long Range Aid to Navigation
G/S	Ground Speed	Ltrs	Litres
GA	General Aviation	M, *m*	Metres
GEN	General	Mag, *mag*	Magnetic
Gn	Green	MAP	Missed Approach Point
GND	Ground Control	MATZ	Military Aerodrome Traffic Zone
GP	Glide Path	MAX, *max*	Maximum
GPS	Global Positioning System	Mb	Millibar
GPWS	Ground Proximity Warning System	MDA	Minimum Descent Altitude
Grad	Gradient	MDH	Minimum Descent Height
H24	Continuous Service (24 hours)	MEF	Maximum Elevation Figures
Hdg	Heading	MET, *met*	Meteorological, Meteorology
HEL	*helicopter*	METAR	Aviation routine weather report
HF	High Frequency	MF	Medium Frequency
Hgt, *hgt*	Height	MHz	Megahertz
HI	Heading Indicator	MIL, *mil*	Military
HIRTA	High Intensity Radio Transmission Area	Min	Minute(s)
HJ, *HJ*	Sunrise to Sunset	Min	Minimum
HN, *HN*	Sunset to Sunrise	*mkd*	*marked*
HO	Service available to meet Operation requirements	Mkr	Marker
		MM	Middle Marker
Hol(s)	Holiday(s)	MOD	Ministry of Defence
hPa	Hectopascal	Mod	Modified
Hrs	Hour(s)	MSA	Minimum Sector Altitude
HSI	Horizontal Situation Indicator	MSD	Minimum Separation Distance
HT	High Tension	MSL	Mean Sea Level
HX	No specific working hours	MTA	Military Training Area
IAF	Initial Approach Fix	MTOW	Maximum Take Off Weight
IAP	Instrument Approach Procedure	MTWA	Maximum Total Weight Authorised
IAS	Indicated Airspeed	*mvmt*	*movement*
IBn	Identification Beacon	NATS	National Air Traffic Service
ICAO	International Civil Aviation Organisation	Nav aid	Navigation Aid
Ident	Identification	Nav	Navigation
IFR	Instrument Flight Rules	NDB	Non-Directional Beacon
ILS	Instrument Landing System	NM, nm	Nautical Miles
IM	Inner Marker	*no*	*number*
IMC	Instrument Meteorological Conditions	NOTAM	Notice To Airmen
In(s)	Inch(es)	O/H, *O/H*	Overhead
Inbd	Inbound	O/R, *o/r*	On Request
Info	Information	OBI	Omni Bearing Indicator
Inop	Inoperative	OBS	Omni Bearing Selector
intxn	*intersection*	Obst, *obst*	Obstruction
IR	Instrument Rating	OCA	Obstacle Clearance Altitude
ISA	International Standard Atmosphere	OCH	Obstacle Clearance Height
Kg,kg	Kilograms	OCL	Obstacle Clearance Limit
kHz	Kilohertz	OCNL	Occasionally
Km	Kilometres	OM	Outer Marker
Kts	Knots	*opr*	*operating*
L	Left (runway designator)	OPS, *ops*	Operations
LARS	Lower Airspace Radar Service	OT	Other Times
Lat	Latitude	PAPI	Precision Approach Path Indicators
lbs	Pounds	PAR	Precision Approach Radar
Lctr	Locater Beacon	Pax	Passenger(s)
LCZ	Localizer – Instrument Landing System	*perm*	*permanently*
LDA	Landing Distance Available	PFA	Popular Flying Association
ldg	*landing*	PH, *ph*	Public Holidays
LFA	*Low Flying Area*	*PJE*	*Parachute Jumping Exercise*
LFZ	*Local Flying Zone*	PN	*Prior Notice*
lgts	*lights*	PNR	Prior Notice Required
LH	Left Hand	POB	Persons on Board
LHS	Left Hand Side	Posn	Position

(left margin, rotated) Abbreviations   Flight Planning

PPL	Private Pilot's Licence	temp	temporary
PPO	Prior Permission Only	tfc	traffic
PPR	Prior Permission Required	Thr	Threshold
proc	procedure	til	until
Prop	Propellor	tkof	take-off
Psi	Pounds per Square Inch	TL, trans lev	Transition Level
psn	position	TMA	See TCA
pt	point	TODA	Take Off Distance Available
pwr	power	TORA	Take Off Run Available
QDM	Magnetic Bearing TO Station	trk	track
QDR	Magnetic Bearing FROM Station	trng	training
QFE	Atmospheric Pressure at aerodrome elevation (or runway threshold)	TT	Total Time
		TTSN	Total Time Since New
QNH	Altimeter sub-scale setting to obtain ALTITUDE amsl	TVOR	Terminal VOR
		TWR	Tower
QTE	True Bearing FROM Station	Twy	Taxiway
QUJ	True Bearing TO Station	tx	transmission or transmit
R	Radial (° FROM a beacon/position)	Tx	Transmitter
R	Right (runway designator)	u/s	unserviceable
RAD	Radar	UFN	Until Further Notice
Rad	Radius	UHF	Ultra High Frequency
RAMP	Ramp Control	UIR	Upper Flight Information Region
RAS	Radar Advisory Service	Unltd, unl	Unlimited
RAS	Recitified Air Speed	Unsvc, u/s	Unserviceable
RASA	Radar Advisory Service Area	UTC	Co-ordinated Universal Time
RCC	Rescue Co-ordination Centre	Va	Design Manoeuvring Speed
rcl	runway centre line	VAR	Magnetic Variation
rcvd	received	VASI	Visual Approach Slope Indicator
ref	reference	VDF	VHF Direction Finder
RFF	Rescue and Fire Fighting (category)	Vfe	Maximum speed with flaps extended
Rgn	Region	VFR	Visual Flight Rules
RH	Right Hand	VHF	Very High Frequency
RHS	Right Hand Side	Vis	Visibility
RIS	Radar Information Service	Vle	Maximum speed with landing gear extended
RMI	Radio Magnetic Indicator		
RMKs rmks	Remarks	VLF	Very Low Frequency
RNAV	Area Navigation System	Vlo	Maximum speed with landing gear extended
RPS	Regional Pressure Setting	VMC	Visual Meteorological Conditions
RT, rtf	Radiotelephony	Vmca	Minimum control speed with critical
RVR	Runway Visual Range	Vne	Never Exceed Speed
Rwy	Runway	Vno	Maximum Normal Operating Speed
Rx	Receiver	VOLMET	Spoken Meteorological Information for aircraft in flight
SAR, SAR	Search and Rescue		
Sched, sched	Schedule	VOR	VHF Omni Range
sec	sector	VRP	Visual Reference Point
sfc, SFC	Surface	Vx	Speed for best angle of climb
shld	should	Vy	Speed for best rate of climb
SID	Standard Instrument Departure	W/P	Waypoint
SL	Sea Level	W/V	Wind Velocity
SMOH	Since Major Overhaul	wdn	withdrawn
SR	Sunrise	wef, wef	With Effect From
SRA	Surveillance Radar Approach	wfu, wfu	withdrawn from use
SS	Sunset	wi	within
SSA	Sector Safe Altitude	WIE	With Immediate Effect
SSR, ssr	Secondary Surveillance Radar	WIP	Work In Progress
STAR	Standard Instrument Arrival Route	Wx	Weather
stn, Stn	Station	XPDR	Transponder
STOL	Short Take Off and Landing	Z	Zulu (UTC)
svce	service		
SVFR	Special Visual Flight Rules		
TA, trans alt	Transition Altitude		
TACAN	Tactical Air Navigation Aid		
TAF	Terminal Area Forecast		
TAS	True Air Speed		
tbn	to be notified		
TBO	Time Between Overhauls		
TCA	Terminal Control Area		
TDZ	Touch Down Zone		
Temp	Temperature		

Abbreviations

Flight Planning

In-flight

Crosswind/Headwind calculator – use of the wind component graph

This graph can be used to find the head/tail wind component and the crosswind component, given a particular wind velocity and runway direction.

EXAMPLE:

Runway 27

Surface wind 240°/15 knots

The angle between the runway direction (270°) and wind direction(240°) is 30°. Now on the graph locate a point on the 30° line, where it crosses the 15 knot arc. From this point take a horizontal line to give the headwind component (13 knots) and a vertical line to give the crosswind component (8 knots).

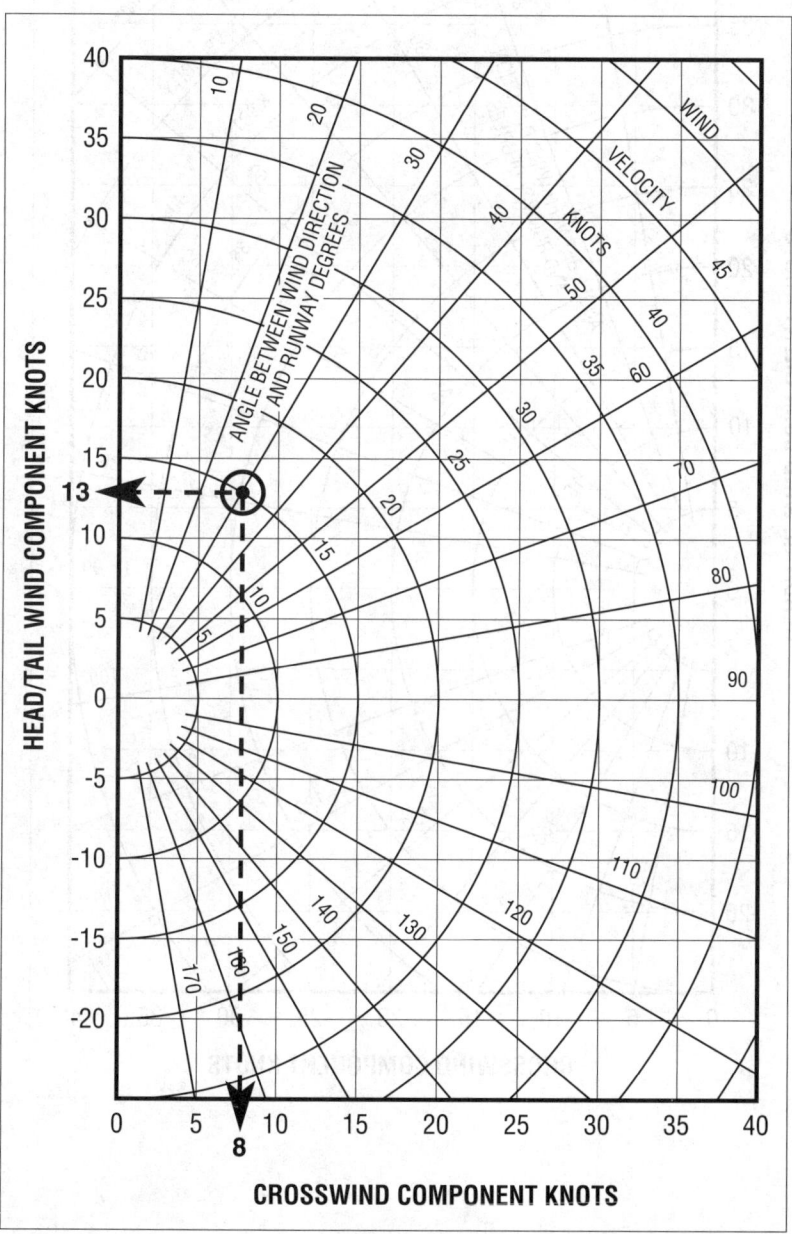

CROSSWIND COMPONENT KNOTS

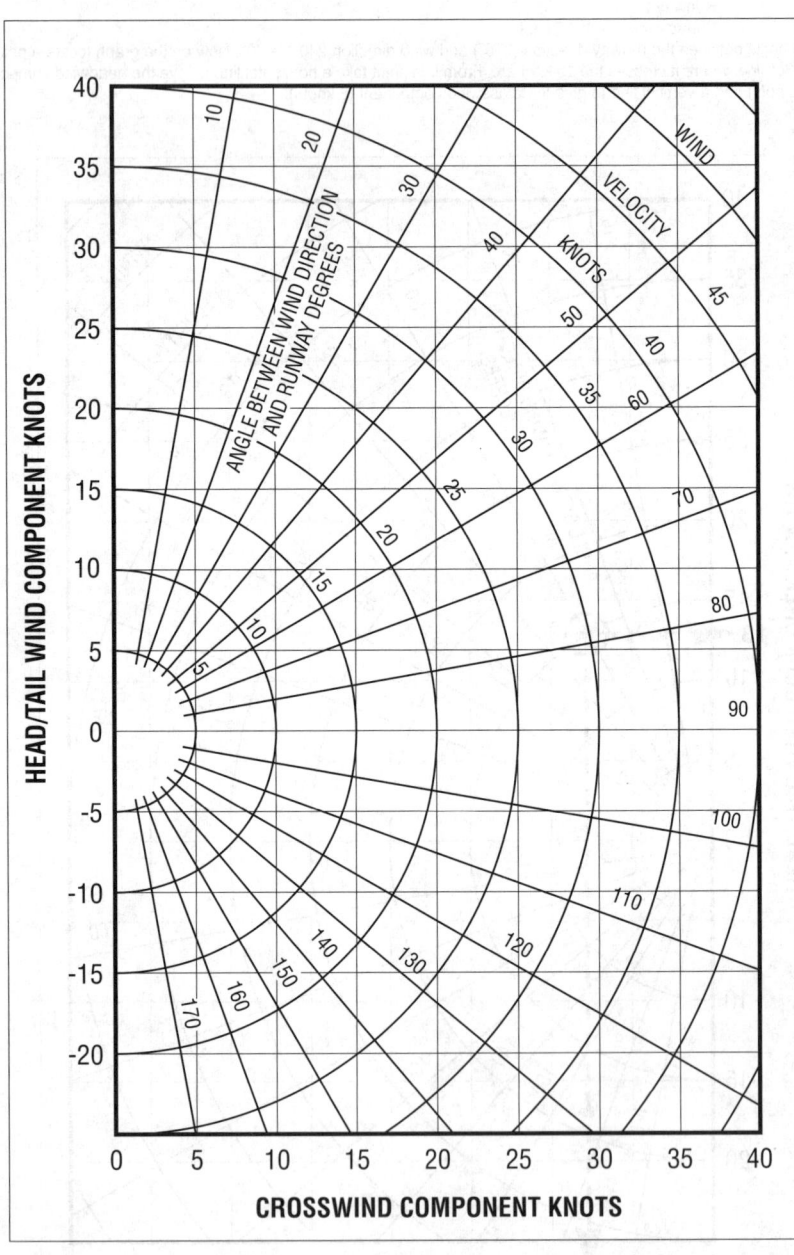

Class A Airspace

	IFR	VFR
Service	Air Traffic Control Service	
Separation	Separation provided between all IFR flights by ATC	
ATC Rules	Flight plan required (**See Note 1**) ATC clearance required Radio communication required ATC instructions are mandatory	VFR FLIGHT NOT PERMITTED
VMC Minima	Not applicable (**See Note 2**)	
Speed Limitations	As published in procedures or instructed by ATC	

Note 1: In certain circumstances, Flight Plan requirements may be satisfied by passing flight details on RTF (detailed at ENR 1.10).

Note 2: For the purposes of:

(**a**) Climbs and descents maintaining VMC;

(**b**) powered aircraft – Airways crossings (ENR 1.1.1.3, paragraph 5.1.6.1); and

(**c**) powered aircraft – other penetrations of Airways (ENR 1.1.1.3, paragraph 5.1.6.2).

In Class A Airspace, the VMC minima are to be:

At or above FL 100:	8km flight visibility 1500 m horizontal and 1000ft vertical distance from cloud
Below FL 100:	5km flight visibility 1500 m horizontal and 1000ft vertical distance from cloud

Class B Airspace

	IFR	VFR
Service	Air Traffic Control Service	
Separation	Separation provided between all flights by ATC	
ATC Rules	Flight plan required (See Note) ATC clearance required Radio Communications required ATC instructions are mandatory	
VMC Minima	Not applicable	**At or above FL100** 8km flight visibility Clear of cloud **Below FL100** 5km flight visibility Clear of cloud
Speed Limitations	As published in procedures or instructed by ATC	

Note: In certain circumstances, Flight Plan requirements may be satisfied by passing flight details on RTF (detailed at ENR 1.10).

Airspace classifications

In-flight

43

Class C – Controlled Airspace

	IFR	VFR
Service	Air Traffic Control Service	
Separation	Separation provided between all IFR flights	All VFR flights separated from all IFR flights by by ATC. Traffic information provided on other VFR flights to enable pilots to effect own traffic avoidance and integration
ATC Rules	Flight plan required (See Note) ATC clearance required Radio communication required ATC instructions are mandatory	
VMC Minima	Not applicable	**At or above FL100** 8km flight visibility 1500m horizontal and 1000ft vertical distance from cloud **Below FL100** 5km flight visibility 1500m horizontal and 1000ft vertical distance from cloud or **At or below 3000ft** **(a)** aircraft (except helicopters) 140ft IAS or less: 5km flight visibility and clear of cloud and in sight of the surface; **(b)** helicopters: clear of cloud and in sight of the surface
Speed Limitation	As published in procedures or instructed by ATC	**Below FL100** 250kt IAS or Lower when published in procedures or instructed by ATC

Note: In certain circumstances, Flight Plan requirements may be satisfied by passing flight details on RTF (detailed at ENR 1.10).

Class D Airspace

	IFR	VFR
Service	Air Traffic Control Service	
Separation	Separation provided between all IFR flights by ATC Traffic information provided on conflicting ATC VFR flights	ATC separation not provided Traffic information provided on IFR and other VFR flights to enable pilots to effect own traffic avoidance and integration.
ATC Rules	Flight plan required (See Note 1) ATC clearance required Radio communication required ATC instructions are mandatory	
VMC Minima	Not applicable	**At or above FL100** 8km flight visibility 1500m horizontal and 1000ft vertical distance from cloud **Below FL100** 5km flight visibility 1500m horizontal and 1000ft vertical distance from cloud **or** **At or below 3000ft** **(a)** aircraft (except helicopters) 140kt IAS or less 5km flight visibility and clear of cloud and in sight of the surface. **(b)** helicopters clear of cloud and in sight of the surface.
Speed Limitation	**Below FL100** 250kt IAS **or** Lower when published in procedures or instructed by ATC	

Note 1: In certain circumstances, Flight Plan requirements may be satisfied by passing flight details on RTF (detailed at ENR 1.10).

Class E Airspace

	IFR	VFR
Service	Air Traffic Control Service	Air Traffic Control Service to communicating flights
Separation	Separation provided between all IFR flights by ATC Traffic information provided on conflicting VFR flights	ATC separation not provided Traffic information provided on request, as far as practicable on IFR and other known VFR flights to enable pilots to effect own traffic avoidance and integration
ATC Rules	Flight plan required (See Note) ATC clearance required Radio Communications required ATC instructions are mandatory	None However pilots are encouraged to contact ATC and comply with instructions
VMC Minima	Not applicable	**At or above FL100** 8km flight visibility 1500m horizontal and 1000ft vertical distance from cloud **Below FL100** 5km flight visibility 1500m horizontal and 1000ft vertical distance from cloud **or** **At or below 3000ft** **(a)** Aircraft (except helicopters): 140kt IAS or less 5km visibility and clear of cloud and in sight of surface **(b)** helicopters: clear of cloud and in sight of surface
Speed Limitations	Below FL100 250kt IAS **or** lower when published in procedures or instructed by ATC	

Note: In certain circumstances, Flight Plan requirements may be satisfied by passing flight details on RTF (detailed at ENR 1.10).

Class F Airspace

	IFR	VFR
Service	Air Traffic Advisory Service to participating Flights	Air Traffic Services as appropriate
Separation	Separation provided between participating IFR flights by ATC	ATC separation not provided
ATC Rules	Participating flight Flight plan required (See Note) ATC clearance required Radio communication required ATC instructions are mandatory	None
VMC Minima	Not applicable	**At or above FL100** 8km flight visibility 1500m horizontal and 1000ft vertical distance from cloud **Below FL100** 5km flight visibility 1500m horizontal and 1000ft vertical distance from cloud **or** **At or below 3000ft** (a) aircraft (except helicopters) greater than 14kt IAS 5km flight visibility and clear of cloud and in sight of the surface (b) aircraft (except helicopters) 140kt IAS or less 1500m flight visibility clear of cloud and in sight of the surface (c) helicopters at a speed which, having regard to the visibility, is reasonable: clear of cloud and in sight of the surface
Speed Limitations	**Below FL100** 250kt IAS **or** lower when published in procedures or instructed by ATC	

Note: In certain circumstances, Flight Plan requirements may be satisfied by passing flight details on RTF (detailed at ENR 1.10).

Class G Airspace

	IFR	VFR
Service	Air Traffic Services as appropriate	
Separation	ATC separation not provided (See Note 1)	
ATC Rules	None (See Note 2)	
VMC Minima	Not applicable	**At or above FL100** 8km flight visibility 1500m horizontal and 1000ft vertical distance from cloud **Below FL100** 5km flight visibility 1500m horizontal and 1000ft vertical distance from cloud **or** **At or below 3000ft** **(a)** Aircraft (except helicopters) greater than 140kt IAS 5km flight visibility clear of cloud and in sight of the surface **(b)** Aircraft (except helicopters) 140kt IAS or less 1500m flight visibility clear of cloud and in sight of the surface **(c)** helicopters at a speed which, having regard to the visibility, is reasonable clear of cloud and in sight of the surface.
Speed Limitations	**Below FL100** 250kt IAS **or** lower when published in procedures or instructed by ATC	

Note 1: Where Air Traffic Control units provide ATS to traffic outside Controlled Airspace, separation may be provided between known flights.

Note 2: Aircraft receiving services from Air Traffic Control units are expected to comply with clearances and instructions unless the pilot advises otherwise.

Special VFR Flight: A flight made at any time in a Control Zone which is Class A airspace, or in any other control zone in Instrument Meteorological Conditions or at night, in respect of which the appropriate air traffic control unit has given permission for the flight to be made in accordance with special instructions given by that unit instead of in accordance with the Instrument Flight Rules and in the course of which the aircraft complies with any instructions given by that unit and remains clear of cloud and in sight of the surface.

1 Clearance for Special VFR flight in the UK is an authorisation by ATC for a pilot to fly within a Control Zone although he is unable to comply with IFR. In exceptional circumstances, requests for Special VFR flight may be granted for aircraft with an all-up-weight exceeding 5700kg and capable of flight under IFR. Special VFR clearance is only granted when traffic conditions permit it to take place without hindrance to the normal IFR flights, but for aircraft using certain notified lanes, routes and local flying areas see paragraph 2.2. Without prejudice to existing weather limitations on Special VFR flights at specific aerodromes (as detailed within the AD 2 Section) ATC will not issue a Special VFR clearance to any fixed-wing aircraft intending to depart from an aerodrome within a Control Zone, when the official meteorological report indicates that the visibility is 1800m or less and/or the cloud ceiling is less than 600ft.

2 Aircraft using the access lanes and local flying areas notified for Denham, White Waltham and Fairoaks in the London CTR and any temporary Special Access Lanes which may be notified from time to time will be considered as Special VFR flights and compliance with the procedures published for the relevant airspace will be accepted as compliance with ATC clearance. Separate requests should not be made nor will separate clearances be given. Separation between aircraft which are using such airspace cannot be given, and pilots are responsible for providing their own separation from other aircraft in the relevant airspace.

3 When operating on a Special VFR clearance, the pilot must comply with ATC instructions and remain at all times in flight conditions which enable him to determine his flight path and to keep clear of obstacles. Therefore, it is implicit in all Special VFR clearances that the aircraft remains clear of cloud and in sight of the surface. It may be necessary for ATC purposes to impose a height limitation on a Special VFR clearance which will require the pilot to fly either at or not above a specific level

4 A full flight plan, Form CA48/RAF2919, is not required for Special VFR flight but ATC must be given brief details of the call sign, aircraft type and pilots intentions. These details may be passed either by RTF or, at busy aerodromes, through the Flight Clearance Office. A full flight plan must be filed if the pilot wishes the destination aerodrome to be notified of the flight.

5 Requests for Special VFR clearance to enter a Control Zone, or to transit a Control Zone, may be made to the ATC authority whilst airborne. Aircraft departing from aerodromes adjacent to a Control Zone boundary and wishing to enter may obtain Special VFR clearance either prior to take-off by telephone or by RTF when airborne. In any case, all such requests must specify the ETA for the selected entry point and must be made 5-10 minutes beforehand.

6 ATC will provide standard separation between all Special VFR flights and between such flights and other aircraft under IFR. However, pilots with a Special VFR clearance should note that they cannot be given separation from aircraft flying in the lanes, routes and local flying areas detailed in paragraph 2.2; nor from aircraft flying in any temporary Special Access Lanes which may be notified from time to time.

7 A Special VFR clearance within a Control Zone does not absolve the pilot from the responsibility for avoiding an Aerodrome Traffic Zone unless prior permission to penetrate the ATZ has been obtained from the relevant ATC Unit.

8 Because Special VFR flights are made at the lower levels, it is important for pilots to realise that a Special VFR clearance does not absolve them from the need to comply with the relevant low flying restrictions of Rule 5 of the Rules of the Air Regulations 1996 (other than the 1500ft rule where the clearance permits flight below that height). In particular, it does not absolve pilots from the requirement that an aircraft, other than a helicopter, flying over congested areas must fly at such a height as would enable it to clear the area and alight without danger to persons or property on the ground in the event of an engine failure and that a helicopter, whether flying over a congested area or not, must fly at such a height as would enable it to alight without danger to persons or property on the ground in the event of an engine failure. In addition there are special rules applicable to flight by helicopters over London.

Special VFR flight

In-flight

Note: DMEs associated with a specific runway normally read distance from the threshold of the runway in use.

Station	Navaid	Ident	Freq	Range	Co-ordinates
Aberdeen	Lctr	ATF	348.00	25	N5704.65 W00206.34
	NDB	AQ	336.00	15	N5708.30 W00224.28
	VOR/DME	ADN	114.30		N5718.63 W00216.03
	DME 16	I-AX	109.90		N5712.07 W00212.04
	DME 34	I-ABD	109.90		N5712.07 W00212.04
Aberporth/West Wales	NDB	AP	370.50	15	N5206.99 W00433.58
Alderney	Lctr	ALD	383.00	30	N4942.53 W00211.98
Ballykelly	TACAN	BKL	109.10		N5503.65 W00700.80
Barkway	VOR/DME	BKY	116.25		N5159.38 E00003.71
Barra	NDB	BRR	316.00	15	N5701.55 W00726.95
Barrow	NDB	WL	385.00	15	N5407.61 W00315.78
	DME	WL	109.40		N5407.59 W00315.79
Belfast Aldergrove	VOR/DME	BEL	117.20		N5439.66 W00613.79
	Lctr	OY	332.00	15	N5441.56 W00605.12
	DME 25	I-AG	109.90		N5439.63 W00612.02
	DME 17	I-FT	110.90		N5439.31 W00613.74
Belfast City	Lctr	HB	420.00	15	N5436.93 W00552.86
	DME 22	I-BFH	108.10		N5437.17 W00552.50
	DME 04	HBD	108.10		N5437.17 W00552.50
Benbecula	VOR/DME	BEN	113.95		N5728.67 W00721.92
	DME	BCL	108.10	25	N5728.51 W00722.22
	NDB	BBA	401.00	40	N5728.57 W00722.15
Benson	TACAN	BSO	110.00		N5136.87 W00105.95
Berry Head	VOR/DME	BHD	112.05		N5023.91 W00329.61
Biggin Hill	DME 21	I-BGH	109.35		N5120.22 E00002.10
	VOR/DME	BIG	115.10		N5119.85 E00002.08
Birmingham	Lctr	BHX	406.00	25	N5227.27 W00145.14
	DME 15	I-BIR	110.10		N5227.27 W00145.14
	DME 33	I-BM	110.10		N5227.27 W00145.14
Blackbushe	NDB	BLK	328.00	15	N5119.40 W00050.69
	DME	BLC	116.20		N5119.40 W00050.69
Blackpool	Lctr	BPL	420.00	15	N5346.37 W00301.67
	DME 28	I-BPL	108.15		N5346.22 W00301.71
Boscombe Down	TACAN	BDN	108.20		N5108.93 W00145.15
Bourn	NDB	BOU	391.50	15	N5212.67 W00002.70
Bournemouth	Lctr	BIA	339.00	20	N5046.66 W00150.54
	Lczr 26	IBH	110.50		N5046.64 W00151.56
	DME 08	I-BMH	110.50		N5046.72 W00150.38
	DME 26	I-BH	110.50		N5046.72 W00150.38
Bovingdon	VOR/DME	BNN	113.75		N5143.56 W00032.98
Brecon	VOR/DME	BCN	117.45		N5143.53 W00315.78
Bristol	Lctr	BRI	414.00	40	N5122.89 W00243.05
	DME 09	I-BON	110.15		N5122.89 W00243.20
	DME 27	I-BTS	110.15		N5122.89 W00243.20
Bristol Filton	Lctr	OF	325.00	25	N5131.31 W00235.41
	DME 09	I-BRF	110.55		N5131.25 W00235.48
	DME 27	I-FB	110.55		N5131.25 W00235.48
Brize Norton	TACAN	BZN	111.90		N5144.89 W00136.21
	Lctr	BZ	386.00	20	N5144.95 W00136.10
Brookmans Park	VOR/DME	BPK	117.50		N5144.98 W00006.40
Brough	NDB	BV	372.00	15	N5343.52 W00034.89
Burnham	NDB	BUR	421.00	15	N5131.13 W00040.61
Caernarfon	NDB	CAE	320.00	15	N5306.00 W00420.40
Cambridge	Lctr	CAM	332.50	15	N5212.65 E00010.96
	DME 23	I-CMG	111.30		N5212.42 E00010.88
Campbeltown	NDB	CBL	380.00	15	N5526.14 W00541.28
Cardiff	Lctr	CDF	388.50	40	N5123.60 W00320.27
	DME 12	I-CDF	110.70		N5123.92 W00320.43
	DME 30	I-CWA	110.70		N5123.92 W00320.43
Carlisle	Lctr	CL	328.00	20	N5456.40 W00248.33
	DME	CO	110.70		N5456.40 W00248.31
Carnane	NDB	CAR	366.50	25	N5408.46 W00429.50
Chiltern	NDB	CHT	277.00	25	N5137.38 W00031.11
Clacton	VOR/DME	CLN	114.55		N5150.91 E00108.85
Compton	VOR/DME	CPT	114.35		N5129.50 W00113.18
Compton Abbas	NDB	COM	349.50	10	N5057.97 W00209.31

Station	Navaid	Ident	Freq	Range	Co-ordinates
Coningsby	TACAN	CGY	111.10		N5305.46 W00010.14
Cottesmore	TACAN	CTM	112.30		N5244.12 W00039.04
Coventry	Lctr	CT	363.50	20	N5224.66 W00124.35
	DME 23	I-CT	109.75		N5222.23 W00128.84
	DME 05	I-CTY	109.75		N5222.23 W00128.84
Cranfield	Lctr	CIT	850.00	15	N5207.81 W00033.41
	VOR	CFD	116.50		N5204.45 W00036.64
Cranwell	NDB	CWL	423.00	25	N5301.58 W00029.34
	TACAN	CWZ	117.40		N5301.72 W00029.13
Cumbernauld	NDB	CBN	374.00		N5558.53 W00358.48
	DME	CBN	117.55		N5558.53 W00358.47
Daventry	VOR/DME	DTY	116.40		N5210.81 W00106.83
Dean Cross	VOR/DME	DCS	115.20		N5443.31 W00320.43
Detling	VOR/DME	DET	117.30		N5118.23 E00035.83
Doncaster Sheffield	NDB	FNY	338.00		N5328.49 W00100.10
	DME	I-FNL	110.95		N5328.49 W00100.12
Dover	VOR/DME	DVR	114.95		N5109.75 E00121.55
Dundee	Lctr	DND	394.00	25	N5627.30 W00306.90
	DME 10	I-DDE	108.10		N5627.10 W00301.55
Durham Tees Valley	Lctr	TD	347.50	25	N5433.63 W00120.02
	DME 05	I-TSE	108.50		N5430.49 W00125.68
	DME 23	I-TD	108.50		N5430.49 W00125.68
Edinburgh	Lctr	EDN	341.00	35	N5558.70 W00317.12
	Lctr	UW	368.00	25	N5554.30 W00330.15
	DME 06	I-VG	108.90		N5557.10 W00322.37
	DME 24	I-TH	108.90		N5557.10 W00322.37
Enniskillen	NDB	EKN	375.50	15	N5423.65 W00738.60
	DME	ENN	116.75		N5423.92 W00739.22
Epsom	NDB	EPM	316.00	25	N5119.16 W00022.31
Exeter	Lctr	EX	337.00	25	N5045.13 W00317.70
	DME 08	I-ET	109.90		N5044.12 W00324.86
	DME 26	I-XR	109.90		N5044.12 W00324.86
Fairford	TACAN	FFA	113.40		N5140.81 W00147.86
	DME 09	I-FFD	111.10		N5140.90 W00147.86
	DME 27	I-FFA	111.10		N5140.90 W00147.86
Fairoaks	NDB	FOS	348.00	8	N5120.82 W00033.83
	DME	FRK	109.85		N5120.82 W00033.83
Farnborough	DME 24	I-FNB	111.50		N5116.59 W00046.68
	DME 06	I-FRG	111.55		N5116.59 W00046.68
Gamston	VOR/DME	GAM	112.80		N5316.88 W00056.83
Glasgow	VOR/DME	GOW	115.40		N5552.23 W00426.74
	DME 05	I-UU	110.10		N5552.18 W00426.04
	DME 23	I-OO	110.10		N5552.18 W00426.04
	Lctr	GLW	331.00	25	N5552.19 W00426.02
Gloucestershire	Lctr	GST	331.00	25	N5153.51 W00210.07
	DME	GOS	115.55		N5153.53 W00210.08
Goodwood	VOR/DME	GWC	114.75		N5051.31 W00045.40
Great Yarmouth	Lctr	ND	417.00	10	N5238.15 E00143.62
Guernsey	VOR/DME	GUR	109.40		N4926.23 W00236.22
	NDB	GUY	361.00	30	N4926.23 W00236.03
	DME 09	I-UY	108.10		N4926.00 W00236.00
	DME 27	I-GH	108.10		N4926.00 W00236.00
Haverfordwest	NDB	HAV	328.00	10	N5149.93 W00458.10
	DME	HDW	116.75		N5149.93 W00458.18
Hawarden	Lctr	HAW	340.00	25	N5310.75 W00258.77
	DME 05	I-HWD	110.35		N5310.73 W00258.73
	DME 23	I-HDN	110.35		N5310.73 W00258.73
Henton	NDB	HEN	433.50	30	N5145.58 W00047.41
Honiley	VOR/DME	HON	113.65		N5221.40 W00139.81
Humberside	Lctr	KIM	365.00	15	N5334.43 W00021.22
	DME 21	I-HS	108.75		N5334.43 W00021.20
Inverness	VOR/DME	INS	109.20		N5732.55 W00402.49
	DME 05	I-LN	108.50		N5732.51 W00402.77
	DME 23	I-DX	108.50		N5732.51 W00402.77
	NDB	IVR	328.00		N5732.51 W00402.76
Islay	NDB	LAY	395.00	20	N5540.97 W00614.96
	DME	ISY	109.95		N5540.97 W00614.96
Isle of Man	VOR/DME	IOM	112.20		N5404.01 W00445.81

Station	Navaid	Ident	Freq	Range	Co-ordinates
	Lctr	RWY	359.00	20	N5404.86 W00437.37
	DME 26	I-RY	111.15		N5404.86 W00437.37
	DME 08	I-RH	111.15		N5404.86 W00437.37
Jersey	Lctr	JW	329.00	25	N4912.35 W00213.20
	VOR/DME	JSY	112.20		N4913.26 W00202.76
	DME 09	I-JJ	110.90		N4912.50 W00212.12
	DME 27	I-DD	110.30		N4912.57 W00211.34
Kinloss	NDB	KS	370.00	20	N5739.03 W00335.23
	TACAN	KSS	109.80		N5739.56 W00332.11
Kirkwall	Lctr	KW	395.00	40	N5857.56 W00253.96
	VOR/DME	KWL	108.60		N5857.58 W00253.63
	DME 09	I-ORK	110.10		N5857.54 W00253.96
	DME 27	I-KIR	110.10		N5857.54 W00253.96
Lakenheath	TACAN	LKH	110.20		N5224.39 E00032.88
Lambourne	VOR/DME	LAM	115.60		N5138.76 E00009.10
Lands End	VOR/DME	LND	114.20		N5008.18 W00538.21
Lashenden	DME	HLS	115.95		N5109.28 E00038.88
	NDB	LSH	340.00	15	N5109.28 E00038.88
Leeds Bradford	Lctr	LBA	402.50	25	N5351.90 W00139.17
	DME 32	I-LF	110.90		N5351.78 W00139.57
	DME 14	I-LBF	110.90		N5351.78 W00139.57
Leeming	TACAN	LEE	112.60		N5417.83 W00132.21
Leicester	NDB	LE	383.50	10	N5236.38 W00102.10
Lerwick	NDB	TL	376.00	25	N6011.30 W00114.78
Leuchars	TACAN	LUK	110.50		N5622.37 W00251.82
Lichfield	NDB	LIC	545.00	50	N5244.80 W00143.16
Linton-On-Ouse	TACAN	LOO	109.00		N5403.03 W00114.94
Liverpool	Lctr	LPL	349.50	25	N5320.38 W00243.51
	DME 09	LVR	111.75		N5319.95 W00250.95
	DME 27	I-LQ	111.75		N5319.95 W00250.95
London	VOR/DME	LON	113.60		N5129.23 W00028.00
Londonderrry	Lctr	EGT	328.50	25	N5502.73 W00709.30
	DME 26	I-EGT	108.30		N5502.51 W00709.56
London City	NDB	LCY	322.00	10	N5130.27 E00004.05
	DME 10	LST	111.15		N5130.35 E00003.32
	DME 28	LSR	111.15		N5130.35 E00003.32
London Gatwick	NDB	GE	338.00	15	N5109.86 W00004.14
	Lctr	GY	365.00	15	N5107.83 W00018.95
	DME 08R	I-GG	110.90		N5109.16 W00011.53
	DME 26L	I-WW	110.90		N5109.16 W00011.53
London Heathrow	DME 09R	I-BB	109.50		N5127.83 W00027.51
	DME 09L	I-AA	110.30		N5128.73 W00027.55
	DME 27R	I-RR	110.30		N5128.73 W00027.55
	DME 27L	I-LL	109.50		N5127.83 W00027.51
London Luton	Lctr	LUT	345.00	20	N5153.68 W00015.15
	DME 08	I-LTN	109.15		N5152.39 W00022.10
	DME 26	I-LJ	109.15		N5152.39 W00022.10
London Stanstead	NDB	SSD	429.00	20	N5153.68 E00014.70
	DME 05	I-SED	110.50		N5153.16 E00014.02
	DME 23	I-SX	110.50		N5153.16 E00014.02
Lydd	DME	I-LDY	108.15		N5057.52 E00056.35
	Lctr	LAA	397.00		N5057.31 E00056.21
Lyneham	NDB	LA	282.00	40	N5130.49 W00200.36
	TACAN	LYE	109.80		N5130.61 W00159.54
Machrihanish	VOR/DME	MAC	116.00		N5525.80 W00539.02
Manchester	Lctr	MCH	428.00	15	N5321.20 W00216.38
	VOR/DME	MCT	113.55		N5321.42 W00215.73
	DME 06L	I-MM	109.50		N5321.19 W00216.38
	DME 24R	I-NN	109.50		N5321.19 W00216.38
	DME 06R	I-MC	111.55		N5320.35 W00217.57
Manchester Woodford	Lctr	WFD	380.00	15	N5320.26 W00209.50
	DME 25	I-WU	109.15		N5320.33 W00209.00
Manston	DME	I-MSN	111.75		N5120.48 E00120.78
	Lctr	MTN	347.00	20	N5120.27 E00120.46
Marham	TACAN	MAM	108.70		N5238.84 W00033.20
Mayfield	VOR/DME	MAY	117.90		N5101.03 E00006.96
Midhurst	VOR/DME	MID	114.00		N5103.23 W00037.50
Mildenhall	TACAN	MLD	115.90		N5221.80 E00029.30

Station	Navaid	Ident	Freq	Range	Co-ordinates
Newcastle	VOR/DME	NEW	114.25		N5502.31 W00141.90
	Lctr	NT	352.00	40	N5503.02 W00138.56
	DME 07	I-NC	111.50		N5502.22 W00141.35
	DME 25	I-NWC	111.50		N5502.22 W00141.35
New Galloway	NDB	NGY	399.00	35	N5510.65 W00410.11
Northampton	NDB	NN	378.50	15	N5217.95 W00047.86
Northolt	DME 25	I-NHT	108.55		N5132.98 W00025.96
Norwich	Lctr	NH	371.50	20	N5240.59 E00123.08
	Lctr	NWI	342.50	20	N5240.65 E00117.49
	DME 27	I-NH	110.90		N5240.65 E00116.99
Nottingham	NDB	NOT	430.00	10	N5255.30 W00104.77
Nottingham East Mids	Lctr	EME	353.50	20	N5249.96 W00111.67
	Lctr	EMW	393.00	10	N5249.72 W00127.27
	DME 09	I-EMW	109.35		N5249.97 W00119.67
	DME 27	I-EME	109.35		N5249.97 W00119.67
Ockham	VOR/DME	OCK	115.30		N5118.30 W00026.83
Odiham	TACAN	ODH	109.60		N5113.97 W00056.91
Ottringham	VOR/DME	OTR	113.90		N5341.90 W00006.21
Oxford	Lctr	OX	367.50	25	N5149.95 W00119.39
	DME	OX	117.70		N5149.95 W00119.37
Penzance	NDB	PH	333.00	15	N5007.70 W00531.70
Perth	VOR	PTH	110.40		N5626.55 W00322.11
Plymouth	Lctr	PY	396.50	20	N5025.46 W00406.74
	DME31	I-PLY	109.50		N5025.46 W00406.71
Pole Hill	VOR/DME	POL	112.10		N5344.63 W00206.20
Prestwick	NDB	PIK	355.00	30	N5530.37 W00434.64
	Lctr	PW	426.00	30	N5532.66 W00440.89
	DME 31	I-KK	110.30		N5530.47 W00435.65
	DME 13	I-PP	110.30		N5330.47 W00435.65
Redhill	NDB	RDL	343.00	10	N5112.97 W00008.33
Rochester	NDB	RCH	369.00	10	N5121.23 E00030.22
St Abbs	VOR/DME	SAB	112.50		N5554.45 W00212.38
St Athan	TACAN	SAT	114.80		N5124.38 W00326.09
St Mawgan	NDB	SM	356.50	20	N5026.89 W00459.67
	TACAN	SMG	112.60		N5026.07 W00501.82
Scampton	TACAN	WAD	117.10		N5309.92 W00031.62
Scatsta	Lctr	SS	315.50	25	N6027.61 W00112.92
Scilly Isles	Lctr	STM	321.00	15	N4954.85 W00617.47
Scotstownhead	NDB	SHD	383.00	80	N5733.55 W00149.03
Seaford	NDB	SFD	117.00		N5045.63 E00007.31
Shawbury	VOR/DME	SWB	116.80		N5247.88 W00239.75
Shefield City	NDB	SMF	333.00	15	N5323.56 W00122.99
	DME	SFH	111.36		N5323.58 W00122.99
Sherburn-In-Elmet	NDB	SBL	323.00	10	N5347.37 W00112.50
Shipdham	NDB	SDM	348.20	10	N5237.42 E00055.50
Shobdon	NDB	SH	426.00	20	N5214.68 W00252.55
Shoreham	Lctr	SHM	332.00	10	N5050.13 W00017.73
	DME	SRH	109.95		N5050.17 W00017.60
Sleap	NDB	SLP	382.00	10	N5250.02 W00246.07
Southampton	Lctr	EAS	391.50	15	N5057.30 W00121.36
	VOR/DME	SAM	113.35		N5057.31 W00120.70
	DME 20	I-SN	110.75		N5057.31 W00121.36
Southend	Lctr	SND	362.50	20	N5134.56 E00042.01
	DME 24	I-ND	111.35		N5134.22 E00041.86
Stornoway	Lctr	SAY	431.00	40	N5812.93 W00619.74
	DME 18	STW	110.90		N5812.91 W00619.75
	DME 36	SOY	110.90		N5812.91 W00619.75
	VOR/DME	STN	115.10		N5812.41 W00610.98
Strumble	VOR/DME	STU	113.10		N5159.68 W00502.40
Sumburgh	Lctr	SBH	351.00	25	N5952.94 W00117.69
	VOR/DME	SUM	117.35		N5952.72 W00117.19
	DME 09	SUB	108.50		N5952.93 W00117.72
	DME 27	I-SG	108.50		N5952.93 W00117.72
Swansea	Lctr	SWN	320.50	15	N5136.30 W00404.31
	DME	SWZ	110.30		N5136.36 W00404.24
Talla	VOR/DME	TLA	113.80		N5529.95 W00321.16
Tattenhill	NDB	TNL	327.00	10	N5248.88 W00146.00
Tiree	VOR/DME	TIR	117.70		N5629.59 W00652.53

Station	Navaid	Ident	Freq	Range	Co-ordinates
Trent	VOR/DME	TNT	115.70		N5303.23 W00140.20
Turnberry	VOR/DME	TRN	117.50		N5518.80 W00447.03
Valley	TACAN	VYL	108.40		N5315.45 W00432.65
Waddington	TACAN	WAD	117.10		N5309.92 W00031.61
Wallasey	VOR/DME	WAL	114.10		N5323.51 W00308.06
Warton	NDB	WTN	337.00	15	N5345.10 W00251.13
	TACAN	WTN	113.20		N5344.42 W00253.57
	DME 26	I-WQ	109.90		N5344.85 W00252.27
Wattisham	TACAN	WTZ	109.30		N5207.32 E00056.43
Welshpool	NDB	WPL	323.00	10	N5237.80 W00309.23
	DME	WPL	115.95		N5237.78 W00309.23
Westcott	NDB	WCO	335.00	30	N5151.18 W00057.75
Whitegate	NDB	WHI	368.50	25	N5311.10 W00237.38
Wick	Lctr	WIK	344.00	30	N5826.80 W00303.78
	VOR/DME	WCK	113.60		N5827.53 W00306.02
Wittering	TACAN	WIT	117.60		N5236.47 W00029.92
Wolverhampton	Lctr	WBA	356.00	25	N5230.95 W00215.71
	DME	WOL	108.60		N5230.95 W00215.71
Woodley	NDB	WOD	352.00	25	N5127.16 W00052.73
Yeovil	Lctr	YVL	343.00	20	N5056.48 W00239.87
	DME	YVL	109.05	25	N5056.45 W00239.20
Yeovilton	TACAN	VLN	111.00		N5100.38 W00238.32

En-route nav aids

In-flight

Airfield	VRP	Position
Benbecula	Lochmaddy Pier	N5735.77 W00709.40
Benbecula	Monarch Isle Lighthouse	N5731.57 W00741.67
Biggin Hill	Sevenoaks	N5116.60 E00010.90
Blackpool	Fleetwood Golf Course	N5355.13 W00302.72
Blackpool	Inskip Disused AD	N5349.63 W00250.05
Blackpool	Kirkham	N5346.95 W00252.28
Blackpool	Marshside	N5341.78 W00258.23
Blackpool	Poulton Railway Station	N5350.90 W00259.42
Boscombe Down	Alderbury	N5102.90 W00143.90
Bristol Filton	M5 Bridge over River Avon	N5129.33 W00241.58
Bristol Filton	Old Severn Bridge	N5136.67 W00238.62
Bristol Filton	Thornbury	N5136.67 W00231.10
Carlisle	Gretna	N5459.73 W00304.05
Carlisle	Halthwistle	N5458.13 W00227.73
Carlisle	Penrith	N5439.87 W00245.02
Carlisle	Wigton	N5449.48 W00309.67
Coventry	Bitteswell Disused AD	N5227.47 W00114.78
Coventry	Cement Works	N5216.35 W00123.07
Coventry	Draycott Water	N5219.57 W00119.58
Coventry	Nuneaton Disused AD	N5233.90 W00126.88
Cranfield	Olney Town	N5209.20 W00042.10
Cranfield	Stewartby Brickworks	N5204.40 W00031.05
Cranfield	Woburn Town	N5159.40 W00037.15
Dundee	Broughty Castle	N5627.75 W00252.18
Exeter	Axminster	N5046.90 W00259.90
Exeter	Crediton	N5047.43 W00339.08
Exeter	Cullompton	N5051.47 W00323.63
Exeter	Exmouth	N5037.48 W00324.13
Exeter	Topsham	N5041.38 W00328.82
Farnborough	Alton	N5109.12 W00057.97
Farnborough	Bagshot	N5120.95 W00041.95
Farnborough	Farnborough Railway Station	N5117.79 W00045.30
Farnborough	Guilford	N5114.37 W00035.10
Farnborough	Hook	N5116.77 W00057.72
Humberside	Brigg	N5333.20 W00029.20
Humberside	Castor	N5329.77 W00019.10
Humberside	Elsham Wolds	N5336.52 W00025.68
Humberside	Immingham Docks	N5337.70 W00011.60
Humberside	Laceby Crossroads	N5332.12 W00010.82
Humberside	North Tower Humber Bridge	N5342.85 W00027.03
Inverness	Dingwall	N5735.97 W00425.88
Inverness	Dores	N5722.92 W00419.92
Inverness	Invergordon	N5741.53 W00410.05
Inverness	Lochindrob	N5724.17 W00342.95
Inverness	Tomatin	N5720.02 W00359.50
Islay	Mull of Oa	N5535.50 W00620.30
Islay	North Coast	N5556.00 W00609.90
Islay	Port Ellen	N5538.00 W00611.40

Airfield	VRP	Position
Islay	Rhinns Point	N5540.40 W00629.10
Kirkwall	Foot	N5901.72 W00248.38
Kirkwall	Lamb Holm Island	N5853.23 W00253.60
Kirkwall	Stromberry	N5901.82 W00256.02
Londonderry	Buncrana	N5508.00 W00727.40
Londonderry	Coleraine	N5507.90 W00640.30
Londonderry	Dungiven	N5455.70 W00655.50
Londonderry	Moville	N5511.40 W00702.40
Londonderry	New Buildings	N5457.50 W00721.50
Middle Wallop	Andover	N5112.54 W00131.65
Middle Wallop	Grateley	N5110.24 W00136.57
Middle Wallop	Harewood	N5110.64 W00127.64
Middle Wallop	Stockbridge	N5106.81 W00129.22
Old Sarum	Alderbury	N5102.90 W00143.90
Plymouth	Avon Estuary	N5017.00 W00353.00
Plymouth	Ivy Bridge	N5023.08 W00355.10
Plymouth	Saltash Roundabout	N5025.13 W00414.08
Plymouth	Yelverton Roundabout	N5029.52 W00405.22
Scatsta	Brae	N6023.82 W00121.23
Scatsta	Fugla	N6026.95 W00119.43
Scatsta	Hillswick	N6028.55 W00129.32
Scatsta	Voe	N6021.00 W00115.97
Scilly Isles	Pendeen Lighthouse	N5009.88 W00540.30
Scilly Isles	St Martins Head	N4958.05 W00615.95
Shoreham	Brighton Marina	N5048.65 W00006.05
Shoreham	Lewes Int A27/A26 Jct	N5051.87 E00001.45
Shoreham	Littlehampton	N5048.77 W00032.78
Shoreham	Washington Int A24/A283	N5044.57 W00024.47
Southend	Billericay	N5138.00 E00025.00
Southend	Maldon	N5143.70 E00041.00
Southend	Sheerness	N5126.50 E00044.90
Southend	South Woodham Ferrers	N5139.00 E00037.00
Southend	St Marys Marsh	N5128.50 E00036.00
Warton	Blackburn	N5344.85 W00228.78
Warton	Formby Point	N5333.12 W00306.32
Warton	Garstang	N5354.38 W00246.55
Warton	M6/M58 Jct	N5332.07 W00241.87
Wick	Castletown Disused AD	N5835.07 W00321.01
Wick	Duncansby Head Lighthouse	N5838.60 W00301.50
Wick	Keiss Village	N5832.00 W00307.40
Wick	Loch Watten	N5829.00 W00320.10
Wick	Lybster Village	N5818.00 W00317.10
Wick	Thrumster Masts	N5823.58 W00307.43

Airfield	VRP	Position
Aberdeen	Banchory	N5703.00 W00230.10
Aberdeen	Core Hill TV Mast	N5723.20 W00224.00
Aberdeen	Insch	N5720.57 W00236.85
Aberdeen	Peterhead	N5730.42 W00146.60
Aberdeen	Stonehaven	N5657.75 W00212.60
Aberdeen	Turiff	N5732.32 W00227.60
Belfast Aldergrove	Ballymena	N5451.80 W00616.40
Belfast Aldergrove	Cluntoe Disused AD	N5437.23 W00632.03
Belfast Aldergrove	Divis	N5436.45 W00600.57
Belfast Aldergrove	Glengormley M2 J4	N5440.83 W00558.90
Belfast Aldergrove	Larne	N5451.20 W00549.52
Belfast Aldergrove	Portadown	N5425.50 W00626.85
Belfast Aldergrove	Toome Disused AD	N5445.47 W00629.67
Belfast City	Comber	N5433.05 W00544.75
Belfast City	Groomsport	N5440.50 W00537.08
Belfast City	Saintfield	N5427.62 W00549.97
Belfast City	Whitehead	N5445.17 W00542.57
Bournemouth	Hengistbury Head	N5042.72 W00144.93
Bournemouth	Sandbanks	N5041.00 W00156.83
Bournemouth	Stoney Cross Disused AD	N5054.70 W00139.42
Bournemouth	Tarrant Rushton Disused AD	N5051.00 W00204.70
Bristol	Barrow Tanks Reservoirs	N5124.58 W00239.77
Bristol	Bath	N5122.70 W00221.42
Bristol	Cheddar Reservoir	N5116.78 W00248.08
Bristol	Chew Valley	N5119.50 W00235.70
Bristol	Churchill	N5120.00 W00247.60
Bristol	Clevedon	N5126.35 W00251.08
Bristol	East Nailsea	N5125.80 W00244.10
Bristol	Hicks Gate Roundabout	N5125.52 W00231.00
Bristol	Portishead	N5129.70 W00246.42
Bristol	Radstock	N5117.53 W00226.92
Bristol	Weston Super Mare	N5120.70 W00258.33
Brize Norton	Bampton	N5143.50 W00132.80
Brize Norton	Burford	N5148.40 W00138.20
Brize Norton	Charlbury	N5152.30 W00128.90
Brize Norton	Faringdon	N5139.30 W00135.20
Brize Norton	Farmoor Reservoir	N5145.20 W00121.40
Brize Norton	Lechlade	N5141.60 W00141.40
Brize Norton	North Leach Roundabout	N5150.25 W00150.15
Cardiff	Cardiff Docks	N5127.40 W00309.10
Cardiff	Flat Holm Lighthouse	N5122.55 W00307.13
Cardiff	Lavernock Point	N5124.38 W00310.23
Cardiff	M4 J36	N5131.93 W00334.40
Cardiff	Minehead	N5112.35 W00328.50
Cardiff	Nash Point Lighthouse	N5124.08 W00333.33
Cardiff	Nash South	N5122.88 W00333.45
Cardiff	St Hilary TV Mast	N5127.45 W00324.18
Cardiff	Wenvoe TV Mast	N5127.57 W00316.90

Airfield	VRP	Position
Channel Islands	Alderney NDB	N4942.53 W00211.98
Channel Islands	Carteret Lighthouse	N4922.00 W00148.00
Channel Islands	Casquets Lighthouse	N4943.00 W00222.00
Channel Islands	Corbiere Lighthouse	N4911.00 W00215.00
Channel Islands	East of Iles Chausey	N4853.00 W00139.00
Channel Islands	Granville	N4850.00 W00139.00
Channel Islands	Ile de Brehat	N4851.00 W00300.00
Channel Islands	Minquiers	N4857.00 W00208.00
Channel Islands	North East Point	N49.30.42 W00230.52
Channel Islands	South East Corner	N4910.00 W00202.00
Channel Islands	St Germain	N4914.00 W00138.00
Channel Islands	West of Minquiers	N4857.00 W00218.00
Durham Tees Valley	A1(M)/A66(M) Jct	N5430.00 W00137.60
Durham Tees Valley	Hartlepool	N5441.00 W00112.83
Durham Tees Valley	Northallerton	N5420.33 W00125.92
Durham Tees Valley	Redcar Racecourse	N5436.43 W00103.85
Durham Tees Valley	Sedgefield Racecourse	N5438.75 W00128.10
Durham Tees Valley	Stokesley	N5428.18 W00111.68
Edinburgh	Arthurs Seat	N5556.63 W00309.70
Edinburgh	Bathgate	N5554.17 W00338.42
Edinburgh	Cobbinshaw Reservoir	N5548.47 W00334.00
Edinburgh	Dalkeith	N5553.60 W00304.10
Edinburgh	Forth Rd Bridge North Tower	N5600.37 W00324.23
Edinburgh	Hillend Ski Slope	N5553.30 W00312.50
Edinburgh	Kelty	N5608.08 W00323.25
Edinburgh	Kirkcaldy Harbour	N5606.83 W00309.00
Edinburgh	Kirkliston	N5557.33 W00324.18
Edinburgh	Kirknewton	N5553.25 W00325.08
Edinburgh	M9 J2	N5558.90 W00330.72
Edinburgh	Musselburgh	N5556.83 W00302.42
Edinburgh	Penicuik	N5549.92 W00313.42
Edinburgh	Polmont	N5559.33 W00341.00
Edinburgh	West Linton	N5545.17 W00321.45
Glasgow	Alexandria	N5559.33 W00434.58
Glasgow	Ardmore Point	N5558.28 W00441.95
Glasgow	Baillieston	N5551.17 W00405.37
Glasgow	Barrhead	N5548.00 W00423.50
Glasgow	Bishopton	N5554.13 W00430.10
Glasgow	Dumbarton	N5556.67 W00434.10
Glasgow	East Kilbride	N5545.83 W00410.33
Glasgow	Erskine Bridge	N5555.22 W00427.77
Glasgow	Greenock	N5556.83 W00445.08
Glasgow	Inverkip Power Station	N5553.90 W00453.20
Glasgow	Kilmacolm	N5553.67 W00437.65
Glasgow	Kilmarnock	N5536.75 W00429.90
Glasgow	Kingston Bridge	N5551.37 W00416.18
Isle of Man	Laxey	N5413.75 W00424.10
Isle of Man	Peel	N5413.33 W00441.50

Airfield	VRP	Position
Leeds Bradford	Dewsbury	N5341.50 W00138.10
Leeds Bradford	Eccup Reservoir	N5352.27 W00132.60
Leeds Bradford	Harrogate	N5359.50 W00131.60
Leeds Bradford	Keighley	N5352.00 W00154.60
Liverpool	Aintree Racecourse	N5328.60 W00256.58
Liverpool	Burtonwood	N5325.00 W00238.28
Liverpool	Chester	N5311.70 W00250.68
Liverpool	Kirkby	N5328.80 W00252.90
Liverpool	Neston	N5317.50 W00303.60
Liverpool	Oulton Park	N5310.57 W00236.80
Liverpool	Seaforth	N5327.68 W00302.08
Liverpool	Stretton Disused AD	N5320.77 W00231.58
London Gatwick	Billinghurst	N5100.90 W00027.00
London Gatwick	Dorking	N5113.62 W00020.10
London Gatwick	Guildford	N5114.37 W00035.10
London Gatwick	Handcross	N5103.17 W00012.13
London Gatwick	Haywards Heath	N5100.45 W00005.77
London Gatwick	Tunbridge Wells	N5108.00 E00015.90
London Luton	Hemel	N5145.37 W00024.97
London Luton	Hyde	N5150.65 W00021.97
London Luton	Pirton	N5158.30 W00019.90
London Stansted	Audley End Railway Station	N5200.25 E00012.42
London Stansted	Braintree	N5152.70 E00033.23
London Stansted	Chelmsford	N5144.00 E00028.40
London Stansted	Diamond Hangar	N5152.67 E00014.15
London Stansted	Epping	N5142.00 E00006.67
London Stansted	Great Dunmow	N5152.30 E00021.75
London Stansted	Haverhill	N5204.95 E00026.07
London Stansted	North End Hangar 4	N5153.32 E00013.53
London Stansted	Nuthampstead AD	N5159.40 E00003.72
London Stansted	Puckeridge A10/A120 Jct	N5153.10 E00000.27
London Stansted	Ware	N5148.70 W00001.60
Lyneham	Avebury	N5125.68 W00151.28
Lyneham	Blakehill Farm	N5137.00 W00153.10
Lyneham	Calne	N5126.20 W00200.30
Lyneham	Chippenham	N5127.60 W00207.40
Lyneham	Clyffe Pypard	N5129.40 W00153.70
Lyneham	Devizes	N5120.80 W00159.30
Lyneham	M4 J15	N5131.60 W00143.48
Lyneham	M4 J16	N5132.70 W00151.25
Lyneham	M4 J17	N5130.88 W0020730
Lyneham	Malmesbury	N5135.10 W00206.20
Lyneham	Marlborough	N5125.20 W00143.70
Lyneham	Melksham	N5122.50 W00208.30
Lyneham	South Marston	N5135.40 W00144.10
Lyneham	Wroughton	N5130.55 W00147.98
Manchester	Alderley Edge Hill	N5317.72 W00212.73
Manchester	Barton AD	N5328.27 W00223.42

Airfield	VRP	Position
Manchester	Buxton	N5315.35 W00154.77
Manchester	Congleton	N5309.90 W00210.85
Manchester	Hill Top	N5320.50 W00210.45
Manchester	Jodrell Bank	N5314.18 W00218.55
Manchester	Rostherne	N5321.23 W00223.12
Manchester	Sale Water Park	N5326.00 W00218.17
Manchester	Stretton Disused AD	N5320.77 W00231.58
Manchester	Swinton Intercharge	N5331.40 W00221.60
Manchester	Thelwall Viaduct	N5323.43 W00230.35
Newcastle	Blaydon	N5458.10 W00141.62
Newcastle	Blyth Power Station	N5508.50 W00131.50
Newcastle	Bolam Lake	N5507.88 W00152.47
Newcastle	Durham	N5446.43 W00134.60
Newcastle	Hexham	N5458.25 W00206.17
Newcastle	Morpeth Railway Station	N5509.75 W00140.97
Newcastle	Ouston Disused AD	N5501.50 W00152.52
Newcastle	Stagshaw Masts	N5502.00 W00201.42
Newcastle	Tyne Bridges	N5458.05 W00136.42
Nottingham East Midlands	Bottesford	N5257.88 W00046.90
Nottingham East Midlands	Church Boughton	N5253.17 W00141.90
Nottingham East Midlands	M1 J22	N5241.73 W00117.55
Nottingham East Midlands	M42 J11	N5241.33 W00132.88
Nottingham East Midlands	Melton Mowbray	N5244.37 W00053.57
Nottingham East Midlands	Trowell	N5257.70 W00116.05
Prestwick	Culzean Bay/Castle	N5522.17 W00446.08
Prestwick	Cumnock	N5527.33 W00415.45
Prestwick	Doonfoot	N5526.25 W00439.03
Prestwick	Heads of Ayr	N5525.97 W00442.78
Prestwick	Irvine Harbour	N5536.50 W00440.90
Prestwick	Kilmarnock	N5536.75 W00429.90
Prestwick	Pladda	N5525.58 W00507.07
Prestwick	West Kilbride	N5541.13 W00452.08
Sheffield City	Barnsley Railway Station	N5333.27 W00128.65
Sheffield City	Chesterfield Railway Station	N5314.25 W00125.22
Sheffield City	Old Coates Crossroads	N5323.52 W00107.12
Sheffield City	Redmires Reservoir	N5321.92 W00136.42
Southampton	Bishops Waltham	N5057.28 W00112.58
Southampton	Calshot	N5049.07 W00119.75
Southampton	Romsey	N5059.45 W00129.75
Southampton	Totton	N5055.20 W00129.33
Sumburgh	Bodam	N5955.10 W00116.10
Sumburgh	Mousa	N6000.00 W00109.60

PROHIBITED   Area (prefix P). Airspace within which the flight of ACFT is prohibited.
RESTRICTED   Area (prefix R). Airspace within the flight of ACFT is restricted in accordance with certain specified condition.

All prohibited and restricted areas extend upwards from the surface, unless otherwise noted.
# indicates an area where pilots are warned that entry (even if in advertent) might make the ACFT liable to counter measures.
The phrase 'subject to appropriate permission' should be taken to mean that prior written permission must be obtained from the authority listed in the RAC section of the AIP, and the flight must be carried out subject to any conditions contained within such permission.

**ALWAYS CHECK PROHIBITED/RESTRICTED AREA INFORMATION BY THE LATEST AIP & NOTAM INFORMATION,
IF IN DOUBT – STAY OUT!**

Identification/ Name	Upper Vertical Limit (AMSL)	Type of restriction	Remarks
R002 Devonport	2000	Restricted	Flight permitted if taking off or landing at HMS Drake Helicopter Landing Site subject to appropriate permission. Helicopters are permitted to take-off or land at a ship in the Devonport Dockyard subject to appropriate permission.
P047 Winfrith	1000	Prohibited	
R063 Dungeness	2000	Restricted	Flight permitted if taking off or landing at the helicopter area at Dungeness, subject to appropriate permission.
			Flight permitted if taking off or landing at London Ashford Airport (Lydd) in accordance with normal practice, remaining at least 1.5nm from Dungeness.
R095 Sark	2374	Restricted	Flight not permitted without permission from States Board of Administration, Guernsey.
			Sark is within UK territorial waters although within Brest FIR.
R101 Aldermaston	2400	Restricted	Flight permitted if taking off or landing at the helicopter landing area at Aldermaston, subject to appropriate permission.
R104 Burghfield	2400	Restricted	Flight permitted if taking off or landing at the helicopter landing area at Burghfield, subject to appropriate permission.
R105 Highgrove House	2000	Restricted	Applies only to helicopters and microlight ACFT.
P106 Harwell	2500	Prohibited	Flight permitted if taking off or landing at the helicopter landing area at Harwell, subject to appropriate permission.
R107 Belmarsh	2000	Restricted	Applies only to helicopters. Flight by helicopter permitted if carrying out an IFR approach from the E to London City AD.
			Flight permitted by any helicopter operated by or on behalf of a Police Force for any area within the UK.
R153 Hinkley Point	2000	Restricted	Flight permitted if taking off or landing at the helicopter area at Hinkley Point, subject to appropriate permission.
			Flight permitted by a helicopter flying within Bridgewater Bay Danger Area with permission from person in charge of the area, remaining at least 1nm from Hinkley Point.
R154 Oldbury	2000	Restricted	Flight permitted if taking off or landing at the helicopter area at Oldbury, subject to appropriate permission.
R155 Berkeley	2000	Restricted	Flight permitted if taking off or landing at the helicopter area at Berkeley, subject to appropriate permission.
R156 Bradwell	2000	Restricted	Flight permitted if taking off or landing at the helicopter area at Bradwell, subject to appropriate permission. Flight at a height >1500ft amsl whilst conducting Instrument APP procedure at Southend Airport.
R157 Hyde Park	1400	Restricted	Flight permitted by any aircraft flying in accordance with a special notification flight or any helicopter flying on route H4 with clearances issued by the appropriate ATC unit.
R158 City of London	1400	Restricted	Flight permitted by any aircraft flying in accordance with a special notification flight or any helicopter flying on route H4 with clearances issued by the appropriate ATC unit.
R159 Isle of Dogs	1400	Restricted	Flight permitted by any aircraft flying in accordance with a special notification flight or any helicopter flying on route H4 with clearances issued by the appropriate ATC unit.
R160 The Specified Area	Unlimited	Restricted	Except with PPR from CAA helicopters shall not fly over this area of Central London below such height deemed safe in the event of egine failure.
R204 Long Lartin	2200	Restricted	Applies only to helicopters other than Police Force Operations.
R212 Whitemoor	2000	Restricted	Applies only to helicopters other than Police Force Operations.
R214 Woodhill	2400	Restricted	Applies only to helicopters other than Police Force Operations.
R217 Sizewell	2000	Restricted	Flight permitted if taking off or landing at the helicopter area at Sizewell, subject to appropriate permission.
R218 Trawsfynydd	2700	Restricted	Flight permitted if taking off or landing at the helicopter area at Trawsfynydd, subject to appropriate permission.
R311 Capenhurst	2200	Restricted	

Identification/ Name	Upper Vertical Limit (AMSL)	Type of restriction	Remarks
R312 Springfields	2100	Restricted	Flight permitted at not less than 1670ft amsl for the purpose of landing at Blackpool AD. Flight permitted S of a line N5346.44 W00244.54 to N5345.13 W00250.44 for the purpose of landing or taking off at Warton AD. Flight permitted if taking off or landing at the helicopter landing area at Springfields, subject to appropriate permission.
R313 Scampton	9500	Restricted	Active Mon-Fri 0830-1700 (Winter), 0730-1600 (Summer) and as notified by NOTAM when Red Arrows are training. Pre-flight information Tel: 01522 733055 Tel: 01522 727451/727452. Waddington RAD 127.35
R315 Full Sutton	2000	Restricted	Applies only to helicopters other than Police Force Operations.
R319 Manchester	1700	Restricted	Applies only to helicopters other than Police Force Operations
R321 Wakefield	1600	Restricted	Applies only to helicopters other than Police Force Operations
R322 Wylfa	2100	Restricted	Flight permitted <2000ft agl, whilst operating in accordance with RAF Valley. Flight permitted if taking off or landing at the helicopter area at Valley, subject to the appropriate permission.
R413 Sellafield	2200	Restricted	Flight permitted if taking off or landing at the helicopter landing area at Sellafield, subject to appropriate permission.
P414 Lisburn #	2000	Prohibited	
P417 Omagh #	2500	Prohibited	
R421 Belfast #	2000	Restricted	Flight permitted for the purpose of landing or taking off at Belfast City AD if the ACFT is under the control of Belfast/City ATC.
P422 Londonderry #	2500	Prohibited	
P424 Armagh #	2500	Prohibited	
P425 Ballykinler #	2000	Prohibited	
R431 Maghaberry #	2000	Restricted	Flight permitted for the purpose of landing or taking off at Belfast Aldergrove if the ACFT is under the control of Belfast Aldergrove ATC.
R432 Frankland/Durham	2200	Restricted	Applies only to helicopters other than Police Force Operations
P434 Dungannon #	2500	Prohibited	
P436 South Armagh #	2500	Prohibited	
P438 Enniskillen Town #	2000	Prohibited	
R444 Heysham	2000	Restricted	Flight permitted if taking off or landing at the helicopter area at Heysham, subject to appropriate permission. Microlight access to Middleton Sands obtained via BMAA office.
R445 Barrow in Furness	2000	Restricted	Flight permitted if taking off or landing at the helicopter area at Barrow in Furness, subject to appropriate permission.
R446 Hartlepool	2000	Restricted	Flight permitted if taking off or landing at the helicopter area at Hartlepool, subject to appropriate permission. Flight <1800ft amsl whilst conducting an Instrument APP to Durham Tees Valley AD.
R501 Chapelcross	2400	Restricted	Flight permitted if taking off or landing at the helicopter landing area at Chapelcross. Subject to appropriate permission.
P502 Magilligan Camp #	2000	Prohibited	
R503 Ballykelly #	2000	Restricted	Flight permitted if making an instrument APP to Rwy26/08 at Londonderry AD: or after Dept Rwy26/08 whilst maintaining Rwy heading provided that the ACFT is under control of Londonderry ATC.
R504 Shotts	2800	Restricted	Flight permitted by any helicopter operated by or on behalf of a Police Force for any area of the UK
R515 Hunterston	2000	Restricted	Flights permitted for purpose of landing or take off at the Helicopter area at Hunterston. Subject to appropriate permission.
R516 Torness	2100	Restricted	Flights permitted for purpose of landing or take off at the Helicopter area at Torness. Subject to appropriate permission.
R603 Rosyth	2000	Restricted	Flight permitted within 'Kelty Lane' if APP to land at, or Dept from, Edinburgh AD
R610A The Highlands	5000	Restricted	Flight permitted outside the Hrs of the Highlands Restricted Area (HRA) and during Scottish public holidays. Areas generally active Mon-Thu 1500-2300 (Winter) 1400-2200 (Summer) When HRA is active, crossing permission may be possible from Tain Range 122.75. Entry may also be possible subject to authorisation if requested from the Military Tactical Booking Cell Tel: 0800 515544 before the proposed flight.
R610B The Highlands	5000	Restricted	Lower limit 750ft AMSL. See notes for R610A.
R610C The Highlands	2000	Restricted	See notes for R610A.
R610D The Highlands	2000	Restricted	See notes for R610A.
P611 Coulport/Faslane	2200	Prohibited	
R612 Arbroath	6000	Restricted	Activity info available from Leuchars Tel: 01334 838722
P813 Dounreay	2100	Prohibited	

Temporary Restricted Airspace, Red Arrows Displays, Emergency Restrictions of Flying and Royal Flights

The latest information regarding Temporary Restricted Airspace, Red Arrows displays, Emergency Restrictions of Flying and Royal flights is all available by dialling a specially provided Freephone number. The number is:

0500 354802

Danger Areas

DANGER Area (D) Airspace within which activities dangerous to the flight of ACFT may exist or take place.
DACS Danger Area Crossing Service
DAAIS Danger Area Activity Information Service
The first frequency given is the primary frequency to be contacted during the Hrs of operation. Where a second frequency is given , this should be called if contact cannot be established on the first frequency. The second frequency is sometimes a FIR controller frequency. These frequencies often are very busy, or even not manned, so you cannot always rely on establishing contact and obtaining a DACS/DAAIS on such a frequency.
All danger areas extend upwards from the surface, unless otherwise noted.
= Hrs of activity are one hour earlier during the summer period.

ALWAYS CHECK DANGER AREA INFORMATION BY THE LATEST AIP, PRE-FLIGHTINFORMATION BULLETIN & NOTAM INFORMATION. AND IF IN DOUBT – STAY OUT!
*Subject to co-ordination procedures above 22000

Identification/ Name	Upper Limit (AMSL)	Hours of Activity (UTC)	Remarks
D001 Trevose Head	1000	Mon-Thu 0800-2359 Fri 0800-1800 #	DACS: St Mawgan APP 128.725
			DAAIS: London Info 124.750
D003 Plymouth	Up to 55000 SFC*	Mon-Thu 0800-2359 Fri 0800-1600 # & as notified	DACS: Plymouth Mil 121.250 London Info 124.750 Pre-flight Info Tel: 01752 557550
D004 Plymouth	Up to 55000 SFC*	Mon-Thu 0800-2359 Fri 0800-1600 # & as notified	DACS: Plymouth Mil 121.250 London Info 124.750 Pre-flight Info Tel: 01752 557550
D006 Falmouth Bay	1500	Mon-Thu 0800-2359 Fri 0800-1600 # & as notified	DACS: Culdrose APP 134.050 DAAIS: London Info 124.750 Pre-flight Info Tel: 01326 552201
D006A Falmouth Bay	Up to 22000	Mon-Thu 0800-2359 Fri 0800-1600 # & as notified	DACS: Plymouth Mil 121.250 London Info 124.750 Pre-flight Info Tel: 01326 552201
D007 Fowey Inner	2000	Mon-Thu 0800-2359 Fri 0800-1600 # & as notified	DACS: Plymouth Mil 121.250 London Info 124.750 Pre-flight Info Tel: 01637 872201 Ex 2045/2046
D007A Fowey	Up to 22000	Mon-Thu 0800-2359 Fri 0800-1600 # & as notified	DACS: Plymouth Mil 121.250 London Info 124.750 Pre-flight Info Tel: 01752 557550
D007B Fowey	Up to 22000	Mon-Thu 0800-2359 Fri 0800-1600 # & as notified	As for D007A
D008 Plymouth	Up to 55000	Mon-Thu 0800-2359 Fri 0800-1600 # & as notified	As for D007A
D008A Plymouth	Up to 22000	Mon-Thu 0800-2359 Fri 0800-1600 # & as notified	As for D007A
D008B Plymouth	Up to 55000 SFC*	Mon-Thu 0800-2359 Fri 0800-1600 # & as notified	As for D007A
D009 Wembury	Up to 22000	Mon-Thu 0800-2359 Fri 0800-1600 # & as notified	As for D007A
D009A Wembury	Up to 55000	Mon-Thu 0800-2359 Fri 0800-1600 # & as notified	As for D007A
D011 Dartmoor	10000 OCNL Notification to 24100	Mon-Fri 0800-2359 # & as notified	Nil
D012 Lyme Bay	Up to 18000 OCNL Notification to 25000	Mon-Thu 0800-2359 # Fri 0800-1600 # & as notified	DACS: Plymouth Mil 124.150 or London Info 124.750 Pre-flight Info Tel: 01752 557550
D013 Lyme Bay	Up to 60000	Mon-Thu 0800-2359 # Fri 0800-1600 # & as notified	As D012

Identification/ Name	Upper Limit (AMSL)	Hours of Activity (UTC)	Remarks
D014 Portland	5000 OCNL Notification to 15000	Mon-Thu 0800-2359 Fri 0800-1600 # & as notified	DACS: Plymouth Mil 124.150 or London Info 124.750 Tel: 01752 557550
D015 Bovington	3600	When notified	DAAIS: Bournemouth TWR 125.600
D017 Portland	22000 OCNL Notification to 55000	Mon-Thu 0800-2359 # Fri 0800-1600 # & as notified	DACS: Plymouth Mil 124.15 or London Info 124.750 Pre-flight Info Tel: 01752 557550
D021 Portland	Up to 15000	Mon-Thu 0800-2359 # Fri 0800-1600 # & as notified	As D017
D023 Portland	22000 OCNL Notification to 55000	Mon-Thu 0800-2359 # Fri 0800-1600 # & as notified	As D017
D026 Lulworth	15000	Mon-Fri 0800-2359# & as notified	DAAIS: London Info 124.750 Pre-flight Info Tel: 01752 557550
D031 Portland	As notified up to 15000	Mon-Thu 0800-2359 # Fri 0800-1600 # & as notified	DACS: Plymouth Mil 124.150 London Info 124.750 Pre-flight Info Tel: 01752 557550
D036 Portsmouth	19000 OCNL Notification to 55000	Mon-Thu 0800-1700 # Fri 0800-1400 # & as notified	DACS: Plymouth Mil 124.150 DAAIS: London Info 124.750 Pre-flight Info Tel: 01752 557751
D037 Portsmouth	55000	Mon-Fri 1000-1800 # & as notified	DAAIS: London Info 124.750 or 124.600
D038 Portsmouth	55000	Mon-Fri 0800-1800 # & as notified	As D037
D039 Portsmouth	55000	Mon-Fri 0800-1800 # & as notified	As D037
D040 Portsmouth	22000 OCNL Notification to 55000	Mon-Fri 0800-1800 # & as notified	As D037
D044 Lydd Ranges	4000	H24	DAAIS: Lydd Info 120.700 London Info 124.600
D061 Woodbury Common	1500	When notified	DAAIS: Exeter APP 128.975 when open
D064A South West MDA	FL 660 10000 ONCL Notification from ALT 5000 to FL 660	When Notified	Air combat and training exercises of ACFT engaged in high energy manoeuvres Pre flight notification Tel: RAF Boulmer 01665 572312
D064B South West MDA	FL 660 10000 ONCL Notification from AIT 5000 to FL 660	When notified	As D064A
D064C South West MDA	FL 660 10000 ONCL Notification from ALT 5000 to FL 660	When notified	As D064A
D110 Braunton Burrows	2000	When notified	DAAIS: London Info 124.750
D113A Castlemartin	15200 ONCL Notification to 40000	Mon-Fri 0830-2359 # & as notified	DAAIS: London Info 124.750
D113B Castlemartin	1500 ONCL Notification up to 45000	Mon-Fri 0830-2359 # & as notified	DAAIS: london 124750
D115A Manorbier	23000 ONCL Notification to 27000	Mon-Fri 0830-1700 # & as notified	DAAIS: London Info 124.750

Identification/ Name	Upper Limit (AMSL)	Hours of Activity (UTC)	Remarks
D115B Manorbier	40000 OCNL Notification to 50000	Mon-Fri 0830-1700 # & as notified	DAAIS: London Info 124.750
D117 Pendine	23000 ONCL Notification to 27000	Mon-Fri 0800-1800 # & as notified No firing during public holidays	DAAIS: Pembrey Range 122.750 London Info 124.750
D118 Pembrey	23000	Mon-Thu 0900-1700 # Fri 0900-1400 # & as notified	DAAIS: Pembrey Range 122.750
	5000	SR-SS outside main activity ops Hrs	DAAIS: not available
D119 Bridgewater Bay	5000	When notified	DAAIS: Yeovilton APP 127.350 London Info 124.750
D121 St. Thomas Head	600	H24	DAAIS: Bristol APP 125.650 London Info 124.750
D123 Imber	Up to 50000	H24	DACS: Salisbury Ops 122.750 DAAIS: ATIS 122.75 0 Pre-flight Info Tel: 01980 674730 or Tel: 01980 674710 DAAIS: Tel: 01980 674739
D124 Lavington	As notified up to unlimited	When notified	As D123
D125 Larkhill	Up to 50000	H24	As D123
D126 Bulford	1400 OCNL Notification to 2500	H24	As D123
D127 Porton	12000 8000 OCNL Notification to 12000	0600-1800 daily 1800-0600 daily	DAAIS: Boscombe Down Zone 126.700 London Info 124.750
D128 Everleigh	1400 OCNL Notification to 50000	H24	As D123
D129 Weston-on-Green	FL120	H24	DAAIS: Brize RAD 124.275
D130 Longmoor	1800 2300	H24 Mon-Fri	Farnborough APP 125.250 London Info 124.600 Pre flight Info Tel: 0208 7453451
D131 Hankley Common	1400	When notified	DAAIS: Farnborough APP 125.250 London Info 124.600
D132 Ash Ranges	As notified up to 2500	When notified	DAAIS: Farnborough APP 125.250 London Info 124.600
D133 Pirbright	1200 OCNL Notification to 2400	0800-2359# & as notified	DAAIS: Farnborough APP 125.250 London Info 124.600
D133A Pirbright	1200	0800-2359 # & as notified	As D133
D136 Shoeburyness	10000	When notified Mon-Fri 0800-1800 #	DAAIS: Southend APP 130.775 London Info 124.600
D138 Shoeburyness	Up to 35000 OCNL Notification to 60000	Mon-Fri 0600-1800 # & when notified	As D136
D138A Shoeburyness	Up to 35000 OCNL Notification to 60000	Mon-Fri 0600-1800 # & when notified	As D136
D138B Shoeburyness	5000	When notified as D138	As D136
D139 Fingringhoe	1500 OCNL Notification to 2000	H24	Nil
D141 Hythe Ranges	3200	H24	DAAIS: Lydd Info 120.700 London Info 124.600
D145 Hullavington	2000	When notified	DAAIS: Lyneham Zone 123.400
D146 Yantlet	3000	When notified 0800-1700 #	DAAIS: Southend APP 130.775
D147 Pontrilas	10000	H24	Nil
D201 Aberporth	Unlimited	Mon-Fri 0800-2300 # & as notified	DACS: Aberporth Info 119.650 Swanwick Mil 135.150
D201A Aberporth	Unlimited	Mon-Fri 0800-2300 # & as notified	As D201

Identification/ Name	Upper Limit (AMSL)	Hours of Activity (UTC)	Remarks
D201B Aberporth	Unlimited	When notified	As D201
D201C Aberporth	Unlimited FL 55	Mon-Fri 0800-2300 # & as notified	As D201
D201D Aberporth	Unlimited FL 55	Mon-Fri 0800-2300 # & as notified	As D201
D202 Llanbedr	6000	Mon-Fri 0800-2300 # & as notified	DACS: Llanbedr RAD 122.500
D203 Sennybridge	23000 OCNL Notification to 50000	Mon-Fri 0800-1800 #	Nil
	18000 ONCL Notification to 50000	Mon-Fri 1800-0800 #	Nil
		When notified	Nil
D206 Cardington	6000	Mon 0400 to Fri 2259 & as notified	Nil
D207 Holbeach	23000	Mon-Thu 0900-1700 Fri 0900-1200 # Sept – April inc Tue & Thur 1700-2200 # & as notified	DAAIS: London Info 124.600 DAAIS: Not available
	5000	SR-SS outside main activity Ops Hrs	Nil
D208 Stanford	2500 OCNL Notification to 7500	H24	DAAIS: Lakenheath Zone 128.900
D211 Swynnerton	As notified up to 2400	When notified	Nil
D213 Kineton	2400	When notified	DAAIS: Coventry APP 119.250 Coventry ATIS 126.050
D215 North Luffenham	2400	When notified	DAAIS: Cottesmore APP 130.200
D216 Credenhill	2300 OCNL Notification to 10000	H24	Nil
		When notified	Nil
D304 Upper Hulme	3500	When notified 0800-1800 # occassionaly up to 2100 Oct-Mar inc	DAAIS: Manchester APP 135.000
D305 Beckingham	1500	When notified	Nil
D306 Cowden	5000	SR-SS	Nil
D307 Donna Nook	20000 OCNL Notification to 23000	Mon-Thu 0900-1630 Fri 0900-1500 # Sep-Apr inc Tue & Thu 1630-2200 # & as notified	DAAIS: Donna Nook Range Control 122.750
	5000	SR-SS outside main activity Ops Hrs	DAAIS: Not available
D308 Wainfleet	23000	Mon & Wed 1400-2200 # Tue & Thurs 0900-1700 # Fri 0900-1500 # & as notified Mon-Fri only	DAAIS: Wainfleet Range Control 122.750
	5000	SR-SS outside main activity Ops Hrs	DAAIS: Not available
D314 Harpur Hill	2900	Mon-Fri 0800-1900 #	DAAIS: Manchester APP 135.000
D323A Southern MDA	As notified up to FL 660 As notified up from FL 50	When notified	Pre-flight RAF Boulmer Tel: 01665 572312 Airspace Booking Tel: 01489 612495
D323B Southern MDA	As notified up to FL 660 As notified up from FL 50	When notified	As D323A
D323C Southern MDA	As notified up to FL 660 As notified up from FL 50	Mon-Fri 0800-1800 # & as notified	As D323A
D323D Southern MDA	As notified up to FL 660 As notified up from FL 250	When notified	As D323A
D323E Southern MDA	As notified up to FL 660 As notified up from FL 250	When notified	As D323A
D323F Southern MDA	As notified Up to FL 660 As notified up From FL 250	When notified	As D323A

Identification/ Name	Upper Limit (AMSL)	Hours of Activity (UTC)	Remarks
D401 Ballykinler	3200	0800-2359 # daily	Nil
D402A Luce Bay (N)	3000 OCNL Notification to 23000	When notified	DACS/DAAIS: Range Control 130.050 Scottish Mil via Scottish Info 119.875
D402B Luce Bay (N)	3000 OCNL Notification to 23000	When notified	As D402A
D402C Luce Bay (N)	4000	Mon-Fri 0730-1530 #	As D402A
D403 Luce Bay	Up to 35000 & as notified	Mon-Thu 0900-2230 # Fri 0900-1630 #	As D402A
D403A Luce Bay	3000	Mon-Thu 0900-1800 Fri 0900-1630	As D402A
D405 Kirkcudbright	15000 OCNL Notification to 50000	Mon-Fri 0800-2359 # & when notified	Kirkcudbright Range 122.100 (0800-1630 (L)
D405A Kirkcudbright	1000	Mon-Fri 0800-2359 #	As for D405
D406 Eskmeals	Up to 50000 OCNL Notification to 80000	Sep-Mar: Mon-Fri 0800-1700 Apr-Aug: Mon-Fri 0700-1900 # & as notified	DAAIS: London Info 125.475
D406B Eskmeals	As notified up to 50000 OCNL Notification to 80000	When notified	DAAIS: London Info 125.475
D406C Eskmeals	As notified up to 50000	When notified	DACS: Eskmeals Range 122.750
D407 Warcop	10000 OCNL Notification to 13500	Mon-Sat 0730-0200 Sun 0730-1300 #	Nil
D408 Feldom	2500 OCNL Notification to 5600	Tue-Sun 0830-1630 # & as notified	DAAIS: Leeming APP 127.750 London Info 125.475
D409 Catterick	3400	When notified	DAAIS: Leeming APP 127.750 London Info 125.475
D410 Strensall	1000	When notified 0800-1800 #	Nil
D411 Portpatrick	1000	Mon-Fri 0800-1630 # & as notified	DACS: West Freugh APP 130.050 DAAIS: Scottish Info 119.875
D412 Staxton	10000	When notified	DAAIS: London Info 125.475 Airspace Booking Tel: 01489 612495
D441 Ellington Banks	2400	When notified Mon-Sat 0900-1700	DAAIS: Linton APP 118.550
D442 Bellerby	3000	H24	Nil
D505 Magilligan	2000 OCNL Notification to 6500	0800-2359 # daily	Nil
D508 Ridsdale	4100	Mon-Fri 0800-1700 # & as notified	DACS: Newcastle APP 124.375 Pre-flight Info Newcastle ATC Tel: 0870 122 1448 Ex 3251
D509 Campbeltown	As notified up to 55000	When notified	DAAIS: Scottish Info 119.875
D510 Spadeadam	5500 ONCL Notification to 18000	Mon-Thurs 0900-1700 # Fri 0900-1600 # & as notified	DAAIS: Newcastle APP 124.375 Carlisle TWR 123.600 DACS: Spadeadam 128.725
D510A Spadeadam	5500 ONCL Notification to 15000	Mon-Thurs 0900-1700 # Fri 0900-1600 # & as notified	As D510
D512 Otterburn	18000 OCNL Notification to 25000	H24	DAAIS: Scottish Info 119.875
D512A Otterburn	22000	When notified	As D512
D513 Druridge Bay	10000	When notified	DAAIS: Scottish Info 119.875 Tel: 01489 612495
D513A Druridge Bay	As notified up to 23000	When notified	As D513
D513B Drurudge Bay	As notified up to 23000	When notified	As D512

Danger Areas

In-flight

Identification/ Name	Upper Limit (AMSL)	Hours of Activity (UTC)	Remarks
D601 Garelochhead	4000	0800-2359 # daily & as notified	Nil
D602 Cultybraggan	2500	When notified	Nil
D604 Barry Buddon	1500 OCNL Notification to Max ALT 9000	H24	DAAIS: Leuchars APP 126.500
D609 St. Andrews	1000 OCNL Notification to 5000	H24	DAAIS: Scottish Info 119.875
D613A Central MDA	As notified up to FL 660 As notified up from FL 100	When notified	Pre-flight RAF Boulmer Tel: 01665 572312 Airspace Booking Tel: 01489 612495
D613B Central MDA	As notified up to FL 660 As notified up from FL 100	When notified	As D613A
D613C Central MDA	As notified up to FL 660 As notified up from FL 100	When notified	As D613A
D701 Hebrides	Up to 30000	Mon-Fri 1000-1800 # & as notified.	DAAIS: Scottish Info 127.275. When D701A is activated, D701 becomes an integral part of it & is activated to the same altitude.
D701A Hebrides	As notified up to unlimited	When notified	DAAIS: Scottish Info 127.275
D701B Hebrides	As notified up to unlimited	When notified	DAAIS: Scottish Info 127.275 Above FL 55 Stationary Temporary Airspace Reservation will be iniated by RSO Hebrides via Shanwick Oceanic.
D701C Hebrides	10000 OCNL Notification to 15000	When notified	DAAIS: Scottish Info 127.275
D701D Hebrides	As notified up To unlimited	When notified	DAAIS: Scottish Info 127.275 Above FL 55 Stationary Temporary Airspace Reservation will be iniated by RSO Hebrides via Shanwick Oceanic.
D701E Hebrides	10000	When notified Mon-Fri 1630-SS Sat 1300-SS #	DAAIS: Scottish Info 127.275 Activated after normal civilian ACFT movements at Benbecula have ceased.
D702 Fort George	2100	0800-1600 # daily & as notified	DAAIS: Inverness TWR 122.600 Scottish Info 129.225
D703 Tain	15000 ONCL Notification to 22000 5000	Mon-Thu 0900-2200 Fri 0900-1400 SR-SS outside main Ops Hrs	ACFT visiting Dornoch or Fearn AD during range opening Hrs Contact Tain Range 122.750 DAAIS: not available
D710 Raasay	1500	When notified Mon-Sat SR-SS	DAAIS: Scottish Info 127.275
D712A Northern MDA	As notified up to FL 660 As notified up from FL 250	When notified	Pre-flight RAF Boulmer Tel: 01665 572312 Airspace Booking Tel: 01489 612495
D712B Northern MDA	As notified up to FL 660 As notified up from FL 250	When notified	As D712A
D712C Northern MDA	As notified up to FL 660 As notified up from FL 250	When notified	As D712A
D712D Northern MDA	As notified up to FL 660 As notified up from FL 250	When notified	As D712A
D801 Cape Wrath (NW)	As notified up to 55000	When notified	DAAIS: Scottish Info 129.225

Identification/ Name	Upper Limit (AMSL)	Hours of Activity (UTC)	Remarks
D802 Cape Wrath (SE)	As notified up to 55000	When notified	As D801
D803 Garvie Island	As notified up to 40000	When notified Mon-Fri 0800-1800 #	DAAIS: Scottish Info 129.225
D807 Moray Firth	1500	Mon-Fri 0700-2359 # & as notified	DAAIS: Lossiemouth Dept 119.350
D809 (N) Moray Firth (North)	As notified up to 55000	When notified	DAAIS: Scottish Info 129.225
D809 (C) Moray Firth (Central)	As notified up to 55000	When notified	As D809 (N)
D809 (S) Moray Firth (South)	As notified up to 55000	When notified	As D809 (N)

Culdrose
Vertical limits:	Surface to 5800ft
Activity:	Considerable helicopter & fixed-wing activity. Night operations may take place with ACFT using reduced navigation/anti-collision lights.
Active Times:	Peak activity Mon-Thur 0730-1600 Fri 0730-1530 (Summer) + 1Hr (Winter)
Contact Frequencies:	Culdrose LARS 134.050

Kinloss/Lossiemouth
Vertical limits:	Surface to FL150
Activity:	Intensive military activity
Active Times:	Peak activity Mon-Thur 0700-2259 Fri 0700-1700 (Summer) + 1Hr (Winter)
Contact Frequencies:	Lossiemouth LARS 119.350

Lincolnshire
Vertical limits:	2500ft ALT to FL180
Activity:	Considerable military flight training
Active Times:	Peak activity Mon-Fri 0600-1500 (Summer) + 1Hr (Winter)
Contact Frequencies:	Waddington LARS 127.350
	Cottesmore LARS 130.200
	Coningsby LARS 120.800

Oxford
Vertical limits:	Surface to 5000ft ALT
Activity:	Intensive military and civilian activity from the many aerodromes in this area, heavy jet, training, instrument etc.
Active Times:	Permanently active
Contact Frequencies:	Brize Radar LARS 124.275

Spadeadam
Vertical limits:	Surface to 4500ft
Activity:	Military activity associated with electronic warfare training range D510
Active Times:	Peak activity Mon-Thur 0800-1600 Fri 0500-1500 (Summer) + 1Hr (Winter) and as notified
Contact Frequencies:	DACS: Spadeadam APP 122.100 Hrs as above
	DAAIS: Newcastle LARS 124.375 H24
	Carlisle APP 123.600

Shawbury
Vertical limits:	Surface to FL70
Activity:	Intensive instrument training, general handling and training by military helicopters and fixed-wing ACFT. Night operations may take place with ACFT using reduced navigation/anti-collision lights.
Active Times:	Permanently active Mon-Thu 0600-1230 Fri 0600-1600 (Summer) + Hr (Winter)
Contact Frequencies:	Shawbury LARS 120.775

Vale of York
Vertical limits:	Surface to FL200
Activity:	Considerable military flight training
Active Times:	Peak activity Mon-Thur 0600-2259 Fri 0600-1500 (Summer) + 1Hr (Winter)
Contact Frequencies:	Leeming LARS 127.750
	Linton LARS 129.150

Valley
Vertical limits:	2000ft to 6000ft
Activity:	Considerable flight training
Active Times:	Peak activity Mon-Thur 0700-1700 Fri 0700-1600 (Summer) + 1Hr (Winter)
Contact Frequencies:	Valley LARS 125.225
	London Flight Info. 124.750

Wash
Vertical limits:	Surface to FL50
Activity:	Holding patterns associated with Danger Areas D207 & D308
Active Times:	Permanently active Mon-Fri
Contact Frequencies:	Waddington LARS 127.350 H24
	Coningsby LARS 120.800
	Marham LARS124.150

Yeovilton
Vertical limits	Surface to 6000ft ALT
Activity	Intense helicopter instrument flying training. Night operations may take place with ACFT using reduced navigation/anti-collision lights.
Active Times	Mon-Thu 0730-1600 Fri 0730-1500 (Summer) + 1Hr (Winter)
Contact Frequencies	Yeovilton LARS 127.350
	Plymouth Military Radar 124.150

Vertical limits:	FL50 to FL245, but excluding controlled airspace.
Activity:	Considerable test flight activity. Such flights often have limited manoeuvrability and may not be able to comply with the rules of the air.
Hours of operation:	Mon-Thu 0830-1700 Fri 0830-1600 (Summer)
	Mon-Thu 0930-1830 Fri 0930-1030(Winter)
Contact Frequencies:	Boscombe Down 126.700
	Boscombe LARS 126.700
	Bournemouth APP 119.475
	Bristol LARS 125.650
	Bristol Filton LARS 122.725
	Brize LARS 124.275
	Cardiff LARS 126.625
	Exeter LARS 128.975
	Farnborough LARS 125.25
	London Radar 135.180
	Lyneham Zone 123.400
	Middle Wallop APP 118.275
	Plymouth LARS 121.25 & 124.15
	Southampton APP 128.850
	Yeovilton LARS 127.350

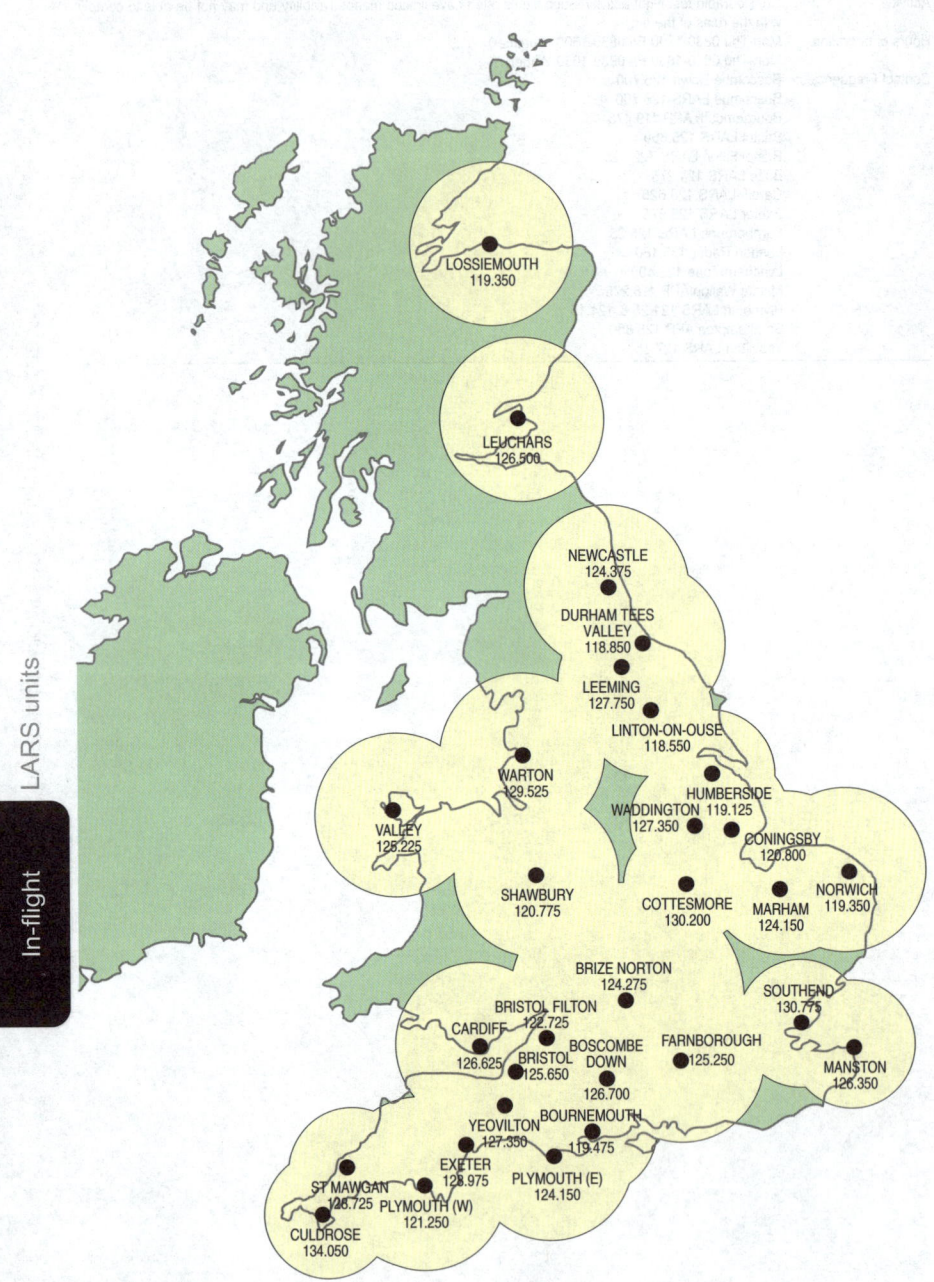

LOSSIEMOUTH
119.350

LEUCHARS
126.500

NEWCASTLE
124.375

DURHAM TEES
VALLEY
118.850

LEEMING
127.750

LINTON-ON-OUSE
118.550

WARTON
129.525

HUMBERSIDE
WADDINGTON 119.125
127.350

VALLEY
125.225

CONINGSBY
120.800

NORWICH
119.350

SHAWBURY
120.775

COTTESMORE
130.200

MARHAM
124.150

BRIZE NORTON
124.275

SOUTHEND
130.775

BRISTOL FILTON
122.725

CARDIFF

BOSCOMBE
DOWN

FARNBOROUGH
125.250

BRISTOL
126.625   125.650

126.700

MANSTON
126.350

YEOVILTON
127.350

BOURNEMOUTH
119.475

ST MAWGAN
126.725 PLYMOUTH (W)

EXETER
128.975

PLYMOUTH (E)
124.150

121.250

CULDROSE
134.050

Lower Airspace Radar Service (LARS) Units

Even outside the published hours, pilots should attempt to contact the LARS unit in case it is open beyond normal hours. Some LARS units (mostly military ones) may close for up to a week during holiday periods - see Pre-flight Information Bulletins.

LARS	Contact Frequency	ATC Hours
Boscombe Down	Boscombe Zone 126.700	H24 not available weekends & PH
Bournemouth	Bournemouth 119.475	0630-2130
Bristol	Bristol APP 125.650	H24
Bristol Filton	Filton APP 122.725	Mon-Fri 0700-1700 (Summer) + 1Hr (Winter) Service north of River Avon
Brize Norton	Brize 124.275	H24
Cardiff	Cardiff APP 126.625	0445-2200 (Summer) + 1Hr (Winter)
Coningsby	Coningsby 120.800	Mon-Fri 0800-1700
Cottesmore	Cottesmore 130.200	Mon-Fri 0800-1700
Culdrose	Culdrose 134.050	Mon-Thu 0830-1700 or SS Fri 0830-1400 or SS
Durham Tees Valley	Teeside APP 118.850	H24
Exeter	Exeter APP 128.975	Mon 0600-2359 Tue-Fri 0001-0100 0600-2359 Sat 0001-0100 0530-2000 Sun 0700-2359 (Summer) Mon 0001-0100 0700-2359 Tue-Fri 0001-0200 0700-2359 Sat 0001-0200 0800-1700 Sun 0830-2359 (Winter)
Farnborough	Farnborough 125.250	0700-1900 (Summer) + 1Hr (Winter)
Humberside	Humberside APP 119.125	Sun-Fri 0530-1915 Sat 0530-1900 (Summer) + 1Hr (Winter)
Leeming	Leeming 127.750	Mon-Thu 0800-2359 Fri 0800-1800 Sat, Sun & PH 0800-1800
Leuchars	Leuchars 126.500	H24
Linton-On-Ouse	Linton 118.550	Mon-Thu 0730-1715 Fri 0730-1700
Lossiemouth	Lossiemouth 119.350	Mon-Fri during Inverness AD Op Hrs
Manston	Manston 126.350	0900-1700
Marham	Marham 124.150	Mon-Thu 0800-2359 Fri 0800-1800
Newcastle	Newcastle APP 124.375	H24
Norwich	Norwich APP 119.350	0900-1700
Plymouth*	Plymouth MIL 121.250	Mon-Fri 0630-2230
	Plymouth MIL 124.150	Mon-Fri 0630-2230
St Mawgan	St Mawgan 128.725	Mon-Thu 0650-2359 Fri-Sun 0650-2200
Shawbury	Shawbury 120.775	Mon-Thu 0830-1730 Fri 0830-1700
Southend	Southend 130.775	0900-1800
Valley	Valley 125.225	Mon-Thu 0800-1800 Fri 0800-1700
Waddington	Waddington 127.350	H24
Warton	Warton 129.525	Mon-Thu 0630-1900 Fri 0630-1600 (Summer) + 1Hr (Winter)
Yeovilton	Yeovilton 127.350	Mon-Thu 0830-1700 Fri 0830-1400

*ACFT operating E of western edge of Awy A25 call Plymouth Military 124.150
ACFT operating W of western edge of Awy A25 call Plymouth Military 121.250

Military Aerodrome Traffic Zone (MATZ) Units

If planning to enter or pass close to a MATZ, pilots are strongly advised to call on the appropriate frequency, even outside the notified hours of operation. Some MATZ may close for up to a week during holiday periods – see Pre-flight Information Bulletins.

ATZ	Contact Frequency	ATC Hours
Barkston Heath	Cranwell 119.375	Mon-Thu 0830-1730 Fri 0830-1700
Benson	Benson 120.900	H24
Boscombe Down	Boscombe Zone 126.700	H24
Church Fenton	Fenton 126.500	H24
Coningsby	Coningsby 120.800	H24
Cottesmore	Cottesmore 130.200	H24
Cranwell	Cranwell 119.375	H24
Culdrose	Culdrose 134.050	H24
Dishforth	Leeming 127.750	H24
Fairford	Brize Radar 119.000	H24
Honington	Lakenheath 128.900	H24
Kinloss	Lossiemouth 119.350	H24
Lakenheath	Lakenheath 128.900	H24
Leeming	Leeming 127.750	H24
Leuchars	Leuchars 126.500	H24
Linton-On-Ouse	Linton 118.550	Mon-Thu H24 Fri-Sun 0700-2359 Summer 1Hr earlier
Lossiemouth	Lossiemouth 119.350	H24
Marham	Marham 124.150	H24
Merryfield	Yeovilton 127.350	Mon-Fri 0700-1700 Summer 1Hr earlier
Middle Wallop	Boscombe Zone 126.700	H24
Mildenhall	Lakenheath 128.900	H24
Mona	Valley 125.225	H24
Odiham	Odiham 131.300	H24
Predannack	Culdrose 134.050	H24
St Mawgan	St Mawgan 128.725	H24
Scampton	Waddington 127.350	H24
Sculthorpe	Marham 124.150	H24
Shawbury	Shawbury 120.775	H24
Ternhill	Shawbury 120.775	H24
Topcliffe	Leeming 127.750	H24
Valley	Valley 125.225	H24
Waddington	Waddington 127.350	H24
Warton	Warton 129.525	H24
Wattisham	Wattisham 125.800	H24
Wittering	Cottesmore 130.200	H24
Yeovilton	Yeovilton 127.350	H24

MATZ Units

In-flight

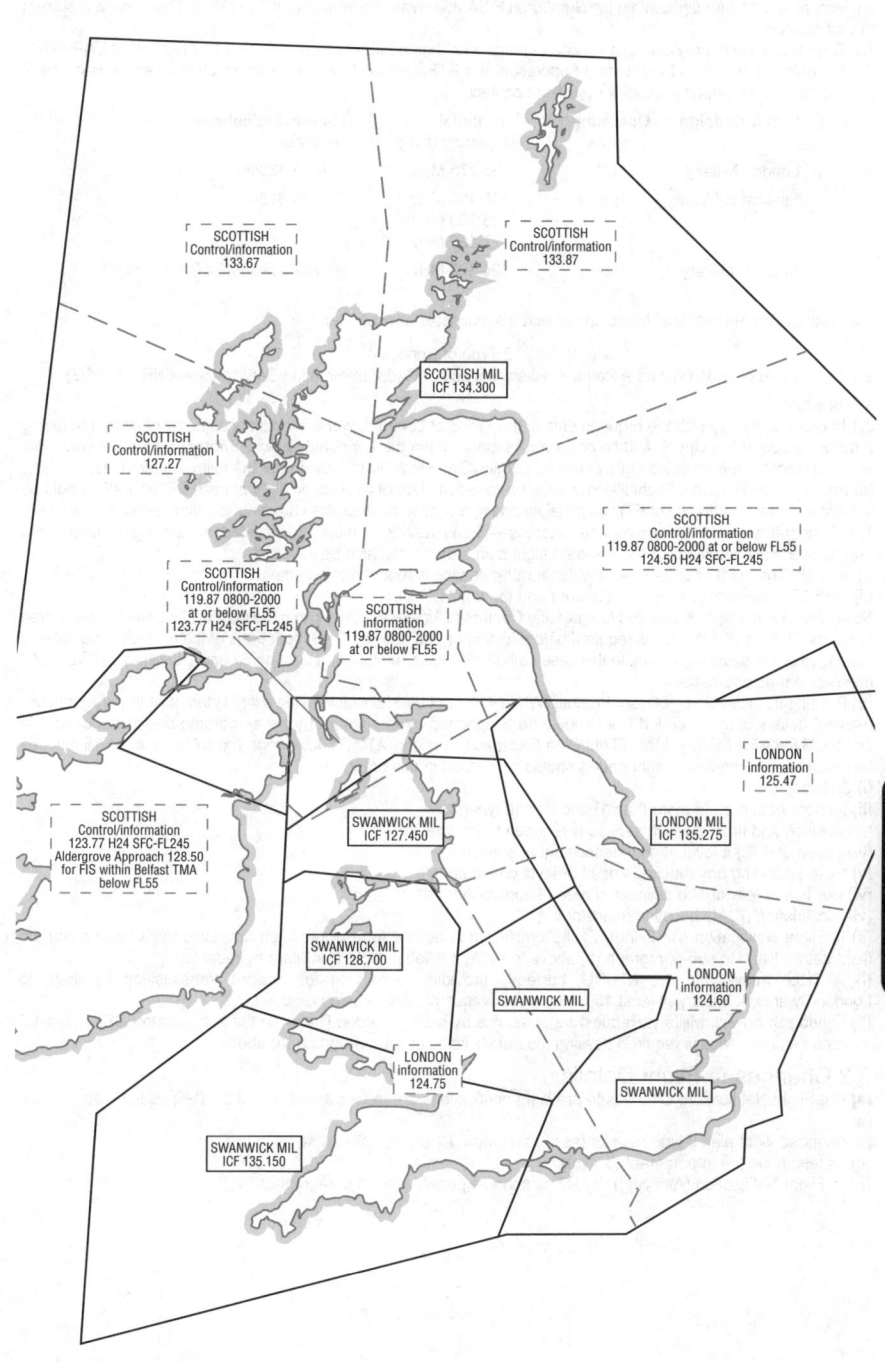

1 Availability of Service

1.1 This service is available to all aircraft flying outside Controlled airspace in the UK FIR except for flight along advisory routes and for flight within the Sumburgh FISA. It is available from FL 100 to FL 240. This service is subject to Unit capacity.

1.2 The military Units providing this service together with their boundaries are depicted on the chart at ENR 6-1-6-4. The table below shows their hours of operation, the RTF operating frequency on which this service is normally provided and a telephone number for pre-flight contact.

Unit & Callsign	Operating Hours	Initial frequency (ICF)	Contact telephone number
London Military	H24	135.275 MHz	01895 426464
Swanwick Military	H24	135.150 MHz 128.700 MHz 127.450 MHz	01489 612417
Scottish Military	H24	134.300 MHz	01292 479800 Ex 6020 or 6002

1.3 Participating aircraft must be equipped with a serviceable transponder.

2 Type of Service

2.1 The service provided will be a Radar Advisory Service or Radar Information Service (See ENR 1.6.1.1/2).

3 Procedures

3.1 In order to comply with the requirements of the FPPS at London/Swanwick Military captains of aircraft requiring a radar service in the Upper, Middle or Lower Airspace within the London/Swanwick Military area of responsibility are to pre-notify their intended flight details to London/Swanwick Military by one of the following methods:

(a) Pre-flight Notification – Flight Plans. As the preferred method of notification flight plans (F2919/CA48) should be submitted as far in advance of ETD as possible and in any case not less than 30 minutes before service is required. The London/Swanwick Military signals address – EGWDZQZX – must be included on the flight plan. When appropriate these additions to the standard flight plan format must also be included:

(i) Item 18. The point and the time at which a radar service is required to commence;

(ii) Item 15. The point of entry into the area and the point of exit.

Note: Item 15. If a flight is planned to enter any Controlled Airspace (CAS) within the London/Swanwick Military area of responsibility and a service is required before joining or after leaving CAS, both parts of the route may be entered in Item 15 of the same flight plan. In this case both IFPS – EGZYIFPS – and London/Swanwick Military EGWDZQZX must appear as addressees.

(b) Pre-Flight Notification – Military Prenote. When it has not been possible to file a flight plan, as sub-paragraph (a), relevant details of the intended flight should be telephoned by the pilot or by his aerodrome operations or ATC to London/Swanwick Military, Main Flight Plan Reception Section, (ATOTN Telephone Ext 6710) at least 15 minutes before service is required. Flight details should be passed in this order:

(i) Callsign;

(ii) number of aircraft (if more than 1) and aircraft type(s);

(iii) position and time at which service is required to commence;

(iv) speed and flight level at commencement of service;

(v) route (including any required speed or level changes);

(vi) position of leaving the delineated area (if applicable); and

(vii) destination (ICAO Location Indicator).

(c) In-Flight Notification (Air Filing). Exceptionally, when neither form of pre-flight notification has been made the flight details listed in sub-paragraph (b) above, may be notified in flight (Air Filed) by radio to:

(i) ATCRU. Airfile with the ATCRU, currently providing a service for onward transmission by them to London/Swanwick Military at least 15 minutes in advance of service being required;

(ii) London/Swanwick Military. Request radar service by calling London Radar on the appropriate (ICF), at least 5 minutes before service is required passing the details listed in sub-paragraph (b) above.

3.2 Changes to Flight Details

(a) Pre-Flight Notification. Changes to pre-flight notifications are to be passed to LATCC (Mil) as soon as possible by:

(i) Amended flight plan if time permits (as in paragraph 3.1 (a) (ii)); otherwise

(ii) by telephone (as in paragraph 3.1 (b)).

(b) In-Flight Notification (Air Filing). By RT as soon as possible (as in paragraph 3.1 (c))

SAFETYCOM was introduced in the UK in November 2004. It is a common frequency for use by aircraft operating in the vicinity of an aerodrome or landing site within the UK that does not have an assigned frequency.

SAFETYCOM Frequency – 135.475 MHz

SAFETYCOM is NOT an air traffic service. It is available to assist pilots to avoid potential collisions between arriving and departing aircraft and should be only used to broadcast the pilot's intentions.

Transmissions made on SAFETYCOM are to be made only when the aircraft is below 2000ft, above an aerodrome or location elevation or below 1000ft above circuit height (if applicable). SAFETYCOM transmissions can only be made within 10nm of the aerodrome or landing location.

The SAFETYCOM frequency must only be used to transmit information regarding the pilot's intentions, there will be NO response from the ground, except when the pilot of an aircraft on the ground needs to transmit his intentions.

The SAFETYCOM frequency must NOT be used as a 'chat' frequency at any time.

Pilots are advised to brief themselves on the format of calls using CAP413.

The use of SAFETYCOM is not mandatory.

SAFETYCOM is not recommended for use at aerodromes that have assigned frequencies for communications. Pilots remain responsible for obtaining any clearance that is necessary to enter controlled airspace.

Sunrise and sunset tables

DATE	EGAA Belfast Aldergrove SR/SS	EGBB Birmingham SR/SS	EGFF Cardiff SR/SS	EGPH Edinburgh SR/SS	EGLL London Heathrow SR/SS	EGCC Manchester SR/SS
Jan 1	0848/1609	0818/1604	0819/1616	0845/1550	0807/1602	0825/1601
Jan 15	0840/1630	0811/1623	0812/1634	0835/1612	0800/1621	0817/1621
Feb 5	0808/1711	0743/1700	0746/1710	0801/1655	0733/1657	0748/1700
Feb 19	0739/1740	0716/1727	0720/1736	0730/1726	0708/1723	0720/1727
Mar 5	0706/1808	0645/1753	0651/1800	0656/1755	0638/1747	0648/1754
Mar 19	0631/1836	0613/1818	0619/1824	0619/1824	0607/1812	0615/1820
Apr 1	0558/1901	0542/1841	0550/1846	0545/1851	0537/1833	0544/1844
Apr 15	0523/1928	0510/1905	0519/1909	0509/1919	0506/1857	0511/1909
May 6	0436/2008	0427/1941	0437/1944	0419/2002	0424/1931	0426/1947
May 20	0411/2033	0404/2003	0415/2005	0453/2028	0402/1953	0402/2020
June 3	0354/2053	0349/2021	0401/2022	0334/2050	0348/2010	0346/2029
June 17	0347/2105	0344/2033	0356/2032	0327/2102	0343/2020	0340/2040
July 1	0352/2105	0349/2033	0401/2033	0332/2102	0348/2021	0345/2040
July 15	0407/2054	0402/2023	0414/2024	0348/2050	0401/2012	0359/2030
Aug 5	0441/2019	0433/1952	0443/1955	0424/2013	0430/1943	0431/1958
Aug 19	0507/1949	0456/1925	0505/1928	0452/1941	0452/1916	0455/1929
Sept 2	0533/1915	0519/1854	0527/1858	0519/1906	0514/1846	0519/1857
Sept 16	0559/1840	0542/1821	0549/1826	0546/1829	0536/1814	0544/1823
Oct 7	0638/1747	0618/1731	0623/1739	0627/1734	0610/1726	0621/1732
Oct 21	0705/1713	0642/1700	0647/1708	0656/1659	0634/1656	0646/1700
Nov 4	0733/1643	0708/1632	0711/1642	0726/1627	0659/1629	0713/1632
Nov 18	0801/1619	0733/1610	0735/1621	0755/1601	0723/1608	0739/1609
Dec 2	0825/1603	0756/1557	0757/1608	0821/1544	0745/1555	0802/1554
Dec 16	0843/1558	0812/1553	0813/1605	0839/1539	0800/1552	0819/1550

Safetycom – Sunrise and sunset tables

In-flight

ENGLAND

Bedfordshire
Cranfield
Dunstable Downs
Henlow
Little Staughton
London Luton
Long Acres Farm
Sackville Farm
Shuttleworth
Berkshire
Brimpton
Newbury Racecourse
White Waltham
Bristol
Bristol
Bristol Filton
Buckinghamshire
Aylesbury
Denham
Finmere
Halton
Thornborough Grounds
Turweston
Wycombe Air Park
Cambridgeshire
Bourn
Cambridge
Chatteris
Duxford
Jubilee Farm
Kimbolton
Kingfisher Bridge
Lark Engine Farmhouse
Little Gransden
Marshland
Peterborough Conington
Peterborough Sibson
Sutton Meadows
Wallis International
Wyton
Cheshire
Arclid
Ashcroft
Lymm Dam
Stretton
Cornwall
Bodmin
Culdrose
Davidstow Moor
Lands End
Lower Botrea
Perranporth
Predannack
Roserrow
St Mawgan
Truro
Woodlands
Cumbria
Barrow
Cark
Carlisle
Kirkbride
Derbyshire
Camphill
Coal Aston
Derby
Grangewood
Devon
Belle Vue
Chivenor

Dunkeswell
Eaglescott
Eggesford
Exeter
Farway Common
Gorrell Farm
Halwell
Lundy Island
Plymouth City
Salcolmbe
Sheepwash
Stoodleigh Barton
Dorset
Bournemouth
Compton Abbas
Newton Peveril
Stalbridge
Durham
Durham Tees Valley
Fishburn
Peterlee
East Yorkshire
Beverley
Breighton
Eddsfield
Full Sutton
Garton Field
Hollym
Melbourne
Pocklington
South Cave
East Sussex
Deanland
Old Hay
Swanborough Farm
Essex
Andrewsfield
Audley End
Boones Farm
Clacton
Damyns Hall
Earls Colne
Great Oakley
Hunsdon
Laindon
London Stansted
North Weald
Rayne Hall Farm
Southend
Stapleford
Thurrock
West Hordon
Gloucestershire
Badminton
Bowldown
Gloucestershire
Kemble
Nympsfield
Orange Grove
Upper Harford
Greater London
Biggin Hill
Gerpins Farm
London City
Northolt
Greater Manchester
Manchester
Manchester Barton
Manchester Woodford
Hampshire
Bourne Park
Chilbolton

Colemore Common
Farnborough
Hook
Lasham
Middle Wallop
Odiham
Popham
Southampton
Thruxton
Herefordshire
Allensmore
Berrow
Cottered
Eastbach
Ledbury
Shobdon
Woonton
Hertfordshire
Elstree
Fowlmere
Graveley
Newnham
Nuthampstead
Panshanger
Plaistows
Rush Green
Top Farm
Isle of Man
Andreas
Ronaldsway
Isle of Wight
Bembridge
Binstead
Isle of Wight
Isle of Scilly
Scilly Isles
Kent
Challock
Clipgate
Farthing Corner
Folkestone
Laddingford
Lashenden
Lydd
Manston
Maypole
Payden Street
Pent Farm
Rochester
Stoke
Lancashire
Blackpool
St Michaels
Tarn Farm
Temple Breuer
Warton
Leicestershire
Battleflat Farm
Bruntingthorpe
Husbands Bosworth
Leicester
Measham Cottage Farm
Nottingham East Midlands
Saltby
Wharf Farm
Lincolnshire
Ashley's Field
Barkston Heath
Bucknall
Coningsby
Cranwell
Crowland

Fenland
Haxey
Hougham
Humberside
Louth Hall Farm
Louth Stewton
New York
North Coates
North Moor
Sandtoft
Scampton
Skegness
Strubby
Sturgate
Temple Bruer
Waddington
Wickenby
Wittering
Merseyside
Haydock Park
Ince
Liverpool
Woodvale
Middlesex
London Heathrow
Norfolk
Boughton North
Coltishall
Cromer
East Winch
Felthorpe
Great Massingham
Gunton Park
Kings Lynn
Langham
Little Snoring
Long Stratton
Ludham
Marham
Norwich
Old Buckenham
Seething
Shipdham
Tibenham
Tibenham Priory Farm
Weybourne
North Yorkshire
Bagby
Burn
Church Fenton
Dishforth
Elvington
Felixkirk
Kirkbymoorside
Leeming
Linton on Ouse
Sherburn in Elmet
Sutton Bank
Topcliffe
Whitby
Wombleton
Yearby
York Rufforth
Northamptonshire
Bakersfield
Deenethorpe
Easton Maudit
Hinton in the Hedges
Newark
Northampton
Pitsford
Rothwell

Spanhoe
Tower Farm
Northumberland
Eshott
Milfield
Nottinghamshire
Caunton
Grassthorpe Grange
Hucknall
Lambley
Langar
Nottingham
Retford/Gamston
Syerston
Oxfordshire
Benson
Bicester
Brize Norton
Chalgrove
Chiltern Park
Drayton St Leonard
Enstone
Oaklands
Oxford
Sandhill Farm
Shennington
Weston on the Green
Rutland
Cottesmore
Shacklewell
Wing Bottom
Shropshire
Knockin
Milson
Nesscliffe Camp
Peplow
Rednall
Seighford
Shawbury
Sherlowe
Sleap
Ternhill
Tilstock
Somerset
Clutton Hill Farm
Henstridge
Merryfield
Shepton Mallet
Weston Zoyland
Yeovil
Yeovilton
South Yorkshire
Doncaster Sheffield
Finningley Village
Netherthorpe
Sheffield City
Thorne
Staffordshire
Abbots Bromley
Otherton
Roddige
Sittles Farm
Tatenhill
Suffolk
Beccles
Crowfield
Cuckoo Tye Farm
Debach
Elmsett
Ipswich Monewden
Lakenheath
Mildenhall

Nayland
Newmarket Heath
Rougham
Waits Farm
Wattisham
Surrey
Blackbushe
Fairoaks
Redhill
Vallance by Ways
Gatwick
Tyne & Wear
Currock Hill
Newcastle
Warwickshire
Baxterley
Bidford
Bromsgrove
Green Farm
Home Farm
Little Chase Farm
Long Marston
Shotteswell
Stoke Golding
Swinford
Wellesbourne Mountford
West Midlands
Birmingham
Cosford
Coventry
Wolverhampton Business
West Sussex
Chichester
Chilsfold Farm
Jackrells Farm
London Gatwick
Shoreham
Truleigh Farm
West Yorkshire
Fadmoor
Garforth
Huddersfield Crossland
Moor
Leeds Bradford
Oxenhope
Walton Wood
Wiltshire
Boscombe Down
Clench Common
Colerne
Craysmarsh Farm
Draycott Farm
Fairford
Garston Farm
Lydeway Field
Lyneham
Manor Farm
Netheravon
Oaksey Park
Old Sarum
Redlands
Upavon
Wadswick Strip
Wing Farm
Worcestershire
Defford
Hanley William
Pound Green

WALES

Cardiff
Cardiff

Carmarthenshire
Pembrey
Denbighshire
Greenlands
Rhedyn Coch
Flintshire
Hawarden
Gwynedd
Caernarfon
Talybont
Isle of Anglesey
Mona
Valley
Pembrokeshire
Haverfordwest
Rosemarket
Upfield Farm
Powys
Breidden
Hardwicke
Lane Farm
Welshpool
Rhondda Cynon Taff
Rhigos
Swansea
Swansea
West Wales
Vale of Glamorgan
St Athan
Wrexham
Chirk
SCOTLAND
Aberdeenshire
Aberdeen
Hatton
Insch
Whiterashes
Angus
Aboyne
Argyll & Bute
Bute
Campbeltown
Colonsay
Coll
Gigha Island
Glenforsa
Islay
Oban
Tiree
Borders
Ayton Castle
Charterhall
Midlem
City of Edinburgh
Edinburgh
City of Glasgow
Glasgow
Dumfries & Galloway
Castle Kennedy
Wigtown
Dundee City
Dundee
East Lothian
East Fortune
Fife
Crail
Fife
Kingsmuir
Leuchars
Highland
Castletown
Dornoch

Fearn
Feshiebridge
Inverness
Isle of Skye
Knockbain Farm
Plockton
Strathaven
Wick
Moray
Kinloss
Lossiemouth
North Lanarkshire
Cumbernauld
Orkney Islands
Eday
Flotta
Kirkwall
Lamb Holm
North Ronaldsay
Papa Westray
Sanday
Stronsay
Westray
Perth & Kinross
Crieff
Errol
Perth
Portmoak
Shetland Islands
Fetlar
Foula
Lerwick
Out Skerries
Papa Stour
Scatsta
Sumburgh
Unst
Whalsay
South Ayrshire
Prestwick
Western Isles
Sollas
Stronsay

CHANNEL ISLANDS

Alderney
Guernsey
Jersey
IRELAND
Northern Ireland
Ballykelly
Belfast Aldergrove
Belfast City
Bellarena
City of Derry
Donaghcloney
Donemana
Dunnyvadden
Enniskillen
Movenis
Newtownards

Airfields in BLOCK CAPITALS are in the main listing with an airfield diagram. Airfields in Lower Case are in the Private Airfields text listing.

ABBOTS BROMLEY
ABERDEEN
Aboyne
ALDERNEY
Allensmore
ANDREAS
ANDREWSFIELD
ARCLID
ASHCROFT
ASHLEY'S FIELD
AUDLEY END
AYLESBURY
AYTON CASTLE
BADMINTON
BAGBY
BAKERSFIELD
Ballykelly
BARKSTON HEATH
BARRA
BARROW
BATTLEFLAT FARM
BAXTERLEY
BECCLES
BELFAST ALDERGROVE
BELFAST CITY
BELLARENA
BELLE VUE
BEMBRIDGE
BENBECULA
BENSON
BERROW
BEVERLEY
BICESTER
BIDFORD
BIGGIN HILL
Binstead
BIRMINGHAM
BLACKBUSHE
BLACKPOOL
BODMIN
BOONES FARM
BOSCOMBE DOWN
BOUGHTON
BOURN
BOURNE PARK
BOURNEMOUTH
BOWLDOWN
BREIGHTON
Briedden
BRIMPTON
BRISTOL
BRISTOL FILTON
BRIZE NORTON
Bromsgrove
BRUNTINGTHORPE
BUCKNALL
BURN
BUTE
CAERNARFON
CALAIS-DUNKIRK
CAMBRIDGE
CAMPBELTOWN
Camphill
CARDIFF
CARK

CARLISLE
CASTLE KENNEDY
Caunton
CHALGROVE
Challock
CHARTERHALL
CHATTERIS
CHICHESTER
CHILBOLTON
CHILSFOLD FARM
CHILTERN PARK
CHIRK
CHIVENIR
CHURCH FENTON
CLACTON
CLENCH COMMON
CLIPGATE
CLUTTON HILL FARM
COAL ASTON
COLEMORE COMMON
COLERNE
Coll
COLONSAY
COMPTON ABBAS
CONINGSBY
COSFORD
COTTERED
COTTESMORE
COVENTRY
CRAIL
CRANFIELD
CRANWELL
CROMER
CROWFIELD
CROWLAND
Craysmarsh Farm
CUCKOO TYE FARM
CULDROSE
CUMBERNAULD
CURROCK HILL
DAMYNS HALL
DAVIDSTOW MOOR
DEANLAND
DEBACH
DEENTHORPE
DEFFORD
DENHAM
DERBY
DINARD
DISHFORTH
DONAGHCLONEY
DONCASTER SHEFFIELD
Donemana
DORNOCH
Downland
DRAYCOTT FARM
DRAYTON ST LEONARD
DUBLIN
DUNDEE
DUNKESWELL
DUNNVADDEN
Dunstable Downs
DURHAM TEES VALLEY
DUXFORD
EAGLESCOTT
EALRS COLNE
EAST FORTUNE
East Lochlane Farm
East Winch
EASTBACH

EASTON MAUDIT
EDAY
EDDSFIELD
EDINBURGH
EGGESFORD
ELMSETT
ELSTREE
ELVINGTON
ENNISKILLEN
ENSTONE
Errol
ESHOTT
EXETER
FADMOOR
FAIR ISLE
Fairford
Fanners Farm
FARIOAKS
FARNBOROUGH
FARTHING CORNER
FARWAY COMMON
Fearn
Felixkirk
FELTHORPE
FENLAND
FESHIEBRIDGE
FETLAR
FIFE
FINMERE
FINNINGLEY VILLAGE
FISHBURN
Flotta
Folkestone
FOULA
FOWLMERE
FULL SUTTON
GARFORTH
GARSTON FARM
GARTON FIELD
GERPINS FARM
GIGHA ISLAND
GLASGOW
GLENFORSA
GLOUCESTERSHIRE
GORREL FARM
GRANGEWOOD
Grassthorpe Grange
GRAVELEY
GREAT MASSINGHAM
GREAT OAKLEY
Green Farm
GREENLANDS
GUERNSEY
Gunton Park
HALTON
Halwell
HANLEY WILLIAM
HARDWICKE
Hatton
HAVERFORDWEST
HAWARDEN
HAXEY
HAYDOCK PARK
Haywood
HENLOW
HENSTRIDGE
HINTON IN THE HEDGES
HOLLYM
Home Farm
Hook

HOUGHAM
HUCKNALL
HUDDERSFIELD
HUMBERSIDE
HUNSDON
HUSBANDS BOSWORTH
INCE
INSCH
INVERNESS
IPSWICH MONEWDEN
ISLAY
ISLE OF MAN
ISLE OF SKYE
ISLE OF WIGHT
JACKRELLS FARM
JERSEY
Jubilee Farm
KEMBLE
Kimbolton
Kingfisher Bridge
Kings Lynn
KINGSMUIR
KINLOSS
KIRKBRIDE
KIRKBYMOORSIDE
Kirkcudbright
KIRKWALL
Knockbain Farm
KNOCKIN
LA ROCHELLE
LADDINGFORD
Laindon
LAKENHEATH
LAMB HOLM
LAMBLEY
LANDS END
Lane Farm
LANGAR
Langham
Lark Engine Farmhouse
LASHAM
LASHENDEN
LE TOUQUET
LEDBURY
LEEDS BRADFORD
LEEMING
LEICESTER
LERWICK
LEUCHARS
LINTON ON OUSE
Little Chase Farm
LITTLE GRANSDEN
LITTLE SNORING
LITTLE STAUGHTON
LIVERPOOL
LONDON CITY
LONDON GATWICK
LONDON HEATHROW
LONDON LUTON
LONDON STANSTED
LONDONDERRY
LONG ACRES FARM
LONG MARSTON
LONG STRATTON
LOSSIEMOUTH
LOUTH
LOUTH HALL FARM
Lower Botrea
LUDHAM
LUNDY ISLAND

LYDD
LYDEWAY FIELD
LYMM DAM
LYNEHAM
MANCHESTER
MANCHESTER BARTON
MANCHESTER WOODFORD
MANOR FARM
MANSTON
MARHAM
MARSHLAND
MAYPOLE
MEASHAM COTTAGE FARM
Melbourne
MERRYFIELD
MIDDLE WALLOP
MIDLEM
MILDENHALL
MILFIELD
MILSON
MITCHELS FARM
MONA
MOVENIS
NAYLAND
Nescliffe Camp
NETHERAVON
NETHERTHORPE
NEW YORK
Newark
NEWBURY RACE COURSE
NEWCASTLE
NEWMARKET HEATH
NEWNHAM
NEWTON PEVERIL
NEWTOWNARDS
NORTH COATES
NORTH MOOR
NORTH RONALDSAY
NORTH WEALD
NORTHAMPTON
NORTHOLT
NORWICH
NOTTINGHAM
NOTTINGHAM EAST MIDLANDS
NUTHAMPTSTEAD
Nympsfield
OAKLANDS
OAKSEY PARK
OBAN
ODIHAM
OLD BUCKENHAM
Old Hay
OLD SARUM
ORANGE GROVE
OSTEND
OTHERTON
OUT SKERRIES
OXENHOPE
OXFORD
PANSHANGER
PAPA STOUR
PAPA WESTRAY
Payden Street
PEMBREY
Pent Farm
PEPLOW
PERRANPORTH
PERTH
PETERBOROUGH CONINGTON
PETERBOROUGH SIBSON

PETERLEE
PITTSFORD
PLAISTOWS
PLOCKTON
PLYMOUTH CITY
POKLINGTON
POPHAM
Portmoak
POUND GREEN
PREDANNACK
PRESTWICK
RAYNE HALL FARM
REDHILL
REDLANDS
REDNAL
RETFORD
RHEDYN COCH
Rhigos
ROCHESTER
RODDIGE
Rosemarket
ROSERROW
ROSSALL FIELD
ROTHWELL
ROUGHAM
RUSH GREEN
ST ATHAN
ST MAWGAN
ST MICHAELS
SACKVILLE FARM
SALCOMBE
SALTBY
SANDAY
SANDHILL FARM
SANDTOFT
SCAMPTON
SCATSTA
SCILLY ISLES
SEETHING
Seighford
Sennybridge
Shacklewell
SHAWBURY
Sheepwash
SHEEPWASH
SHEFFIELD CITY
SHENNINGTON
SHERBURN IN ELMET
SHERLOWE
SHIPDHAM
SHOBDON
SHOREHAM
SHOTTESWELL
SHUTTLEWORTH
SITTLES FARM
SKEGNESS
SLEAP
Sollas
SOUTH CAVE
SOUTHAMPTON
SOUTHEND
SPANHOE
STAPLEFORD
STOKE
STOKE GOLDING
Stoodleigh Barton
STORNOWAY
STRATHALLAN
Strathaven
Stretton

Airfield directory listing

In-flight

STRONSAY
STRUBBY
STURGATE
SUMBURGH
Sutton Bank
SUTTON MEADOWS
SWANBOROUGH FARM
SWANSEA
SWINFORD
SYERSTON
TALYBONT
TATENHILL
TEMPLE BRUER
TERNHILL
Thornborough Grounds
THORNE
Thorpe le Soken
THRUXTON
THURROCK
Tibenham
TIBENHAM
TILSTOCK
TIREE
TOP FARM
TOPCLIFFE
Tower Farm
Truleigh Farm
TRURO
TURWESTON
UNST
UPAVON
UPFIELD FARM
UPPER HARFORD
Vallance by ways Gatwick
VALLEY
WADDINGTON
Wadswick Strip
WALLIS INTERNATIONAL
WALTON WOOD
WARTON
WATTISHAM
WELLESBOURNE MOUNTFORD
WELSHPOOL
WESTON ZOYLAND
West Hordon
WEST WALES
Weston on the Green
WESTRAY
WEYBOURNE
WHALSAY
WHARF FARM
Whitby
WHITE WALTHAM
WHITERASHES
WICK
WICKENBY
Wigtown
WING FARM
WITTERING
WOLVERHAMPTON
WOMBLETON
Woodlands
WOODVALE
Woonton
WYCOMBE
WYTON
YEARBY
YEOVIL
YEOVILTON
YORK

For	See
Aberporth	West Wales
Aldergrove	Belfast
	Aldergrove
Aviemore	Feshiebridge
Baldock	Newnham
Banbury	Shotteswell
Barham	Clipgate
Barton	Manchester
	Barton
Bedford	Castle Mill
Bembridge	Isle of Wight
Bigglewade	Shuttleworth
Bolt Head	Salcolmbe
Booker	Wycombe Air Park
Bradford	Leeds Bradford
Braintree	Rayne Hall Farm
Broadford	Isle of Skye
Buntingford	Cottered
Castle Donington	Nottingham East Midlands
Cherry Tree Farm	Monewden
Chester	Hawarden
Church Farm	Shotteswell
City of Derry	Londonderry
Cleobury Mortimer	Milson
Conington	Peterborough
	Conington
Croft Farm	Defford
Crosland Moor	Huddersfield
Dalcross	Inverness
Doncaster	Thorne
Dyce	Aberdeen
East Midlands	Nottingham East Midlands
Edgehill	Shenington
Eglington	Londonderry
Emlyn's Field	Greenlands
Emlyn's Other Field	Rhedyn Coch
Filton	Bristol Filton
Finningley	Doncaster Sheffield
Gamston	Retford
Gatwick	London Gatwick
Glenrothes	Fife
Goodwood	Chichester
Grange over Sands	Cark
Great Yarmouth	North Deenes
Halfpenny Green	Wolverhampton Business Airport
Headcorn	Lashenden
Heathrow	London Heathrow
Hurn	Bournemouth
Jericho Farm	Lambley
Kidlington	Oxford
Laurelhill	Donaghcloney
Lewes	Deanland
Lichfield	Sittles Farm
Lincoln	Wickenby
Linley Hill	Beverley
Liverpool	Liverpool John Lennon
Luton	London Luton
Machrinhanish	Campbeltown
Machrins	Colonsay

For	See
Marshland	Wisbech
Monewden	Ipswich Monewden
Moors National Park	Fadmoor
Mount Airey	South Cave
Muckleburgh	Weybourne
Mull	Glenforsa
Newquay	St Mawgan
Newton le Willows	Haydock Park
Ninescores Farm	Finingley Village
North Connel	Oban
North Reston	Louth Hall Farm
Northreeps	Cromer
Old Warden	Shuttleworth
Oswestry	Knockin
Peterhead	Longside
Pickering	Wombleton
Priory Farm	Tibenham
Riseley	Sackville Farm
Robin Hood Int	Doncaster Sheffield
Ronaldsway	Isle of Man
Royston	Nuthampstead
Rufforth	York
Rugby	Husbands Bosworth
Sandown	Isle of Wight
Sandy	Long Acres Farm
Scone	Perth
Scunthorpe	North Moor
Sibson	Peterborough Sibson
Sorbie	Kingsmuir
Spalding	Crowland
Spence	Eastbach
St Angelo	Enniskillen
St Just	Lands End
St Marys	Scilly Isles
Stansted	London Stansted
Staverton	Gloucestershire
Stewton	Louth
Stoneacre Farm	Farthing Corner
Stonefield Park	Chilbolton
Sywell	Northampton
Tarn Farm	Rossall Field
Teeside	Durham Tees Valley
Thame	Aylesbury
Thirsk	Bagby
Thorne	Doncaster
Tingwall	Lerwick
Tollerton	Nottingham
York	Elvington
Velcourt	Ledbury
Walney Island	Barrow
Wasing Lower Farm	Brimpton
Westland	Yeovil
Withybush	Haverfordwest
Woodford	Manchester Woodford
Yeatsall Farm	Abbots Bromley

Key to airfield directory maps

800m x 46m	Hard Rwy, with the Rwy length and width in metres
800m x 18m	Soft Rwy, with the Rwy length and width in metres
60	The Runway QDM (the magnetic direction of the runway in tens of degrees)
	Displaced threshold
	Hard Twy, Apron or manoeuvring area
	Grass Twy, Apron or manoeuvring area
	Dissused Rwy
	Dissused Twy, Apron or manoeuvring area
H1 H	Holding point
01 LP	Launch Point
H	Helipad
A A H	Helicopter holding point
T	Signal square
	Windsock
C	Control, the point for pilots to report
	Parachuting area
	Buildings or built-up area (non aviation)
	Buildings (aviation)
	Track
A47	Road
M6	Dual carriageway or Motorway
	Railway
	Disused Railway
	Overhead powerlines
	Cuttings and embankments
	Trees or bushes
	Hedge
	Footpath or Bridleway
	Fence
	Stone wall
	Ditch or dyke
	Grass boundary
	Waterway
	Coastline
	High ground
	Marsh
	Do NOT overfly
	Quarry

N	This way up
	Golf course
	Camp site
	Faiground
	Church
	Steeple
	Lamp post
	Balloons
	Lighthouse/ship
	Windmill
	Wind turbine
	Pylon
343 (321)	Masts/Obstructions
•785	Spot height
	Undulations
	Uneven section
	Downslope/Upslope
	Steep rise
	Arrester gear
ILS/DME I-AX 109.90	ILS, ILS/DME, LLZ or LLZ/DME, next to the Thr of thr Rwy it serves
	NDB
	Co-located NDB/DME
	VDF
	VDF/DME
	DME
	VOR
	Co-locatedVOR/DME
	TACAN
H	Heliport
⊗	Disused A/D
G	Gliding
M	Microlights
	Hang Gliding
	Bird Sanctuary
VRP INSCH	Visual Reporting Point (VRP)
	Hospital

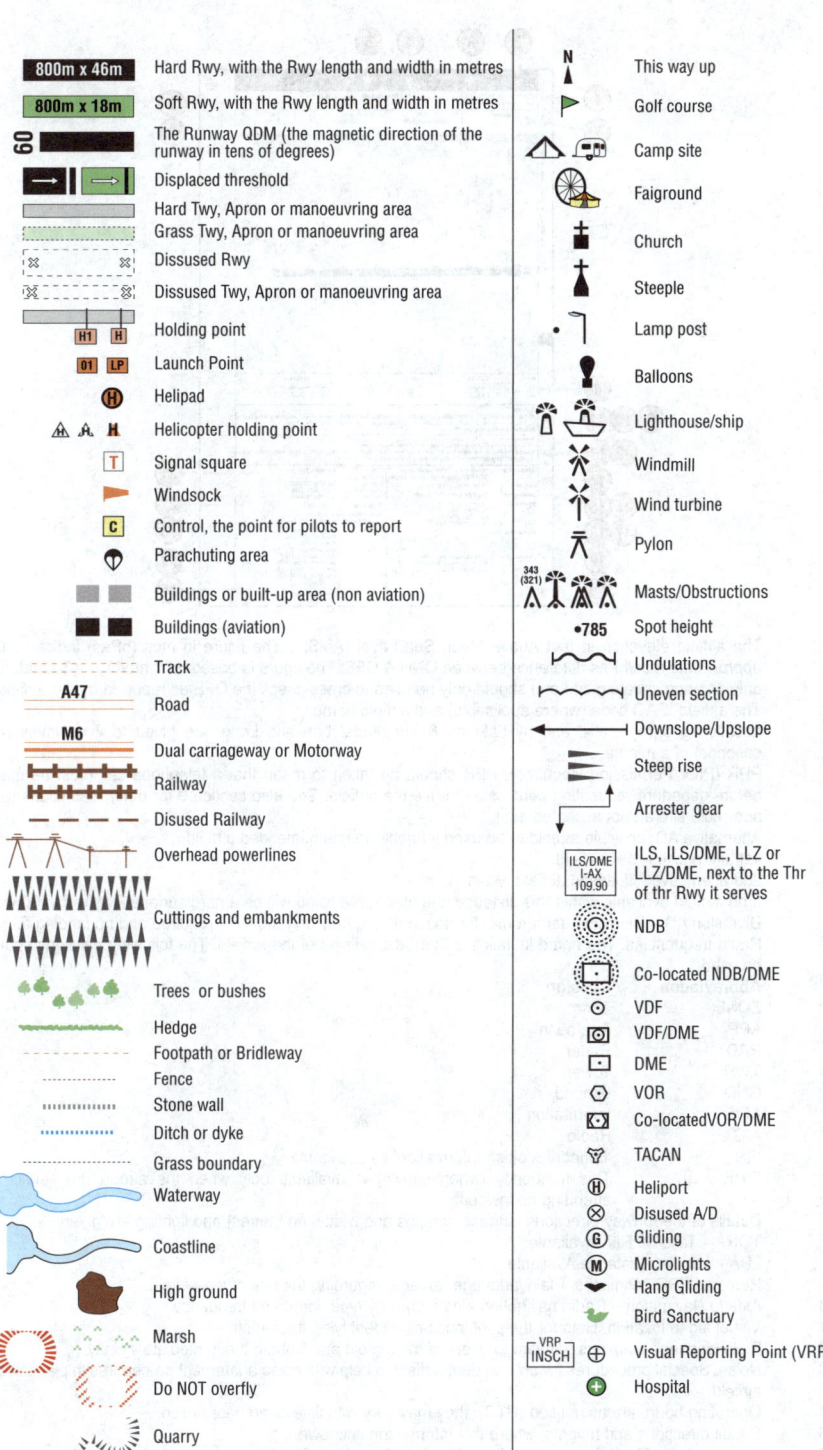

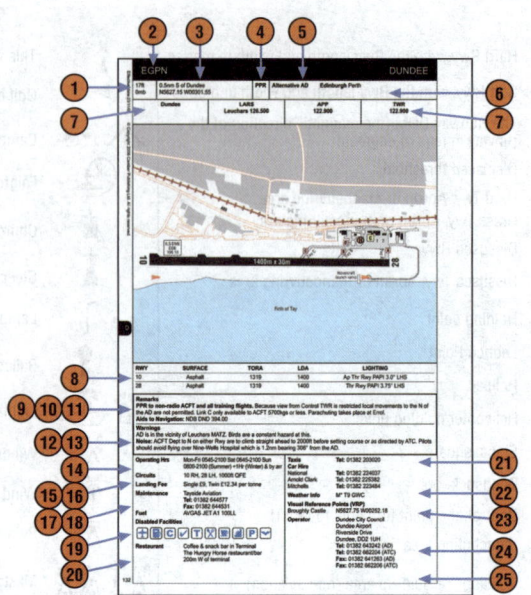

1	The airfield elevation in feet Above Mean Sea Level (AMSL). The figure in mbs (hPas) indicates the *approximate* mbs/hPas difference between QNH & QFE. The figure is based on 1 mb/hPa = 30 feet. It is only an approximate guide and should only be used to cross-check the QFE as reported by the airfield.
2	The airfield ICAO code (where applicable) and airfield name.
3	Location geographically, and by Latitude & Longitude. Lat. and Long. are given to 2 decimals (*not* seconds) of a minute.
4	PPR (Prior Permission Required). PPR should be taken to mean that a telephone call must be made before departure requesting permission to use the airfield. See also section 9 for other restrictions (e.g. non-radio aircraft not accepted etc.).
5	Alternative AD. possible airfield to be used if unable to reach intended airfield.

1st alternative – IFR airfield

2nd alternative – licensed airfield within 30nm

If no airfield available within this distance, the alternative listed will be a hard surface Rwy within 30nm.

6	Diversion AD – Diversion aerodrome, for use in emergency only, no PPR required and no landing fees
7	Radio frequencies. The name in italics is the radio callsign of the airfield. The following callsigns should be used:

Abbreviation	Callsign
ZONE	Zone
APP	Approach
RAD	Radar
TWR	Tower
GND	Ground
AFIS	Information
A/G	Radio
FIS	'London/Scottish Information' as applicable
FIRE	This frequency (when shown) is available only when the airport fire service is attending an incident.

8	Details of the runway directions, surface, lengths and widths (in metres) and lighting are given.
	TORA = Take-off Run Available
	LDA = Landing Distance Available.
9	Remarks/PPR conditions. Plain language remarks regarding the use of the airfield.
10	Aids to Navigation – Radio navigation aids shown by type, ident and frequency.
11	Visual aid to location. Help for the pilot in locating/identifying the airfield
12	Plain language warnings relevant to users of the airfield and flight in the immediate vicinity.
13	Noise. Special procedures for arr and dept airfield to help with noise abatement procedures in place at the airfield.
14	Operating hours are as notified (UTC), they may vary with little or no prior notice.
15	Circuit directions and heights, where this information is known
16	Landing fees. This information is based on supplied data. Special rates or supplements may apply at certain times, airfield pages are not amended for a change of landing fee information only.

17	Maintenance availability where known
18	Fuel availability. Please note that at many airfields fuel is not available at all times when the airfield is open.
19	Disabled Facilities

⊞ Access to airside

⬛ Help for refueling

C Access or help to pay landing fee and sign in/out and flight breifing where applicable

☎ Assistance is available with prior notice only

✔ Assistance is available without prior notice

✘ No wheelchair access available on this airfield

T Wheelchair access toilet close by

✕ Access to airfield café

☕ Access for hot drinks only

⬛ Access to pilot shop

P Disabled parking reserved close to facilities

◡ Flight training for the disabled available

20	Restaurants. Basic detail where known. Inclusion of a company name or telephone number does not imply recommendation or endorsement by the airfield operator or the publisher.
21	Taxis/Car Hire. Basic detail where known. Inclusion of a company name or telephone number does not imply recommendation or endorsement by the airfield operator or the publisher.
22	Weather Information. Weather reports & forecasts available for the airfield and where they can be obtained:

M	METAR (usually only available during the normal opening hours of the airfield).
M*	METAR not distributed. It will probably be necessary to contact the airfield direct for this report.
T9	9 hour TAF
T24	24 hour TAF
T	TAF of other duration (mostly military airfields).
Fax	METAR & TAF available via MetFAX service (see Met section of Flight Planning for full details).
123	Three figure airfield code for use with automated METAR & TAF telephone service. (see Met section of Flight Planning for full details).
A	ATIS (see radio box for frequency).
VS	METAR included on VOLMET South broadcast.
VN	METAR included on VOLMET North broadcast.
VM	METAR included on VOLMET Main broadcast.
VSc	METAR included on VOLMET Scottish broadcast.
AirS	Airfield is within AIRMET Southern coverage *.
AirN	Airfield is within AIRMET Northern coverage *.
AirSc	Airfield is within AIRMET Scottish coverage *.
AirSE	Airfield is within AIRMET Southeast England coverage *.
AirCen	Airfield is within AIRMET Central England coverage *.
AirSW	Airfield is within AIRMET Southwest England coverage *.

* Used only if TAFs are not available. Where coverage overlaps the most localised forecast is given.

Forecast office. Where no forecast office is designated, that designated to other airfields in the area is given. Forecast office telephone numbers are given in the MET section of the Flight Planning pages. For military and government airfields the stated Forecast Office may be able to provide METARs and TAFs.

BEL	Belfast/Aldergrove Airport
MOEx	Exeter Weather Centre
GWC	Glasgow Weather Centre
IOM	Isle of Man Airport
JER	Jersey Airport
MWC	Manchester Weather Centre

23	Visual Reference Points (VRP's)
24	The postal address, telephone and fax numbers of the airfield operator
25	Other information, such as controlled airspace regulations, special procedures, may also be listed after the main airfield page.

400ft 13mb	4nm N of Rugeley N5249.50 W00154.00	PPR	Alternative AD	Nottingham East Midlands Tatenhill

Non-Radio	APP East Mids 134.175	A/G Tatenhill 124.075	Safetycom 135.475

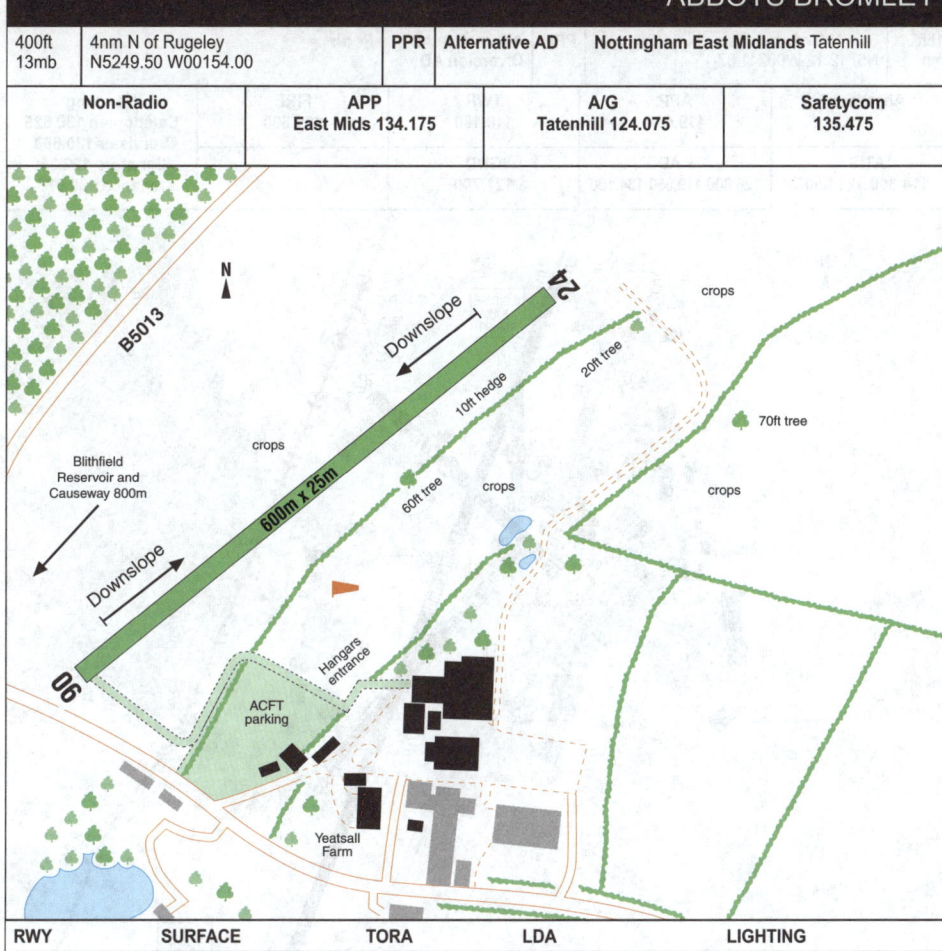

A

RWY	SURFACE	TORA	LDA	LIGHTING
06/24	Grass	600x25	U/L	Nil

Remarks
PPR by telephone essential. AD situated close to ene of causeway carrying B5013 across Blithfield Reservoir. AD based ACFT are mainly active at weekends. AD close to Tatenhill ATZ visitors advised to call Tatenhill.

Warnings
Cross Hayes gliding site with winch launching 2nm SE of AD. Keep good lookout for Gliders. Tatenhill ATZ 4nm to E. During the week low flying military ACFT may be encountered, keep a good lookout.
Noise: Avoid over flight of Abbots Bromley village close to E of AD

Operating Hrs	SR-SS daily	**Operator**	Mr Richard Hall Yeatsall Farm Abbots Bromley Staffs WS15 3DY **Tel:** 01283 840343
Circuits	24 RH, 06 LH, 800ft QFE		
Landing Fee	Nil		
Maintenance	Nil		
Fuel	Nil		
Disabled Facilities Nil			

Restaurant/Accomodation
B&B available at Marsh Farm in Abbots Bromley
Marsh Farm   **Tel:** 01283 840323

Taxis
Rugeley   **Tel:** 01889 586061
Car Hire   Nil

Weather Info   AirCen MWC

215ft 7mb	5nm NW of Aberdeen N5712.12 W00211.87	PPR	Alternative AD Diversion AD	Perth

Aberdeen	APP 119.050	TWR 118.100	FIRE 121.600	Handling Caledonian 130.625 Servisair 130.600 Signature 122.350 Aviance 130.075
ATIS 114.300 121.850	RAD 128.300 119.050 134.100	GND 121.700		

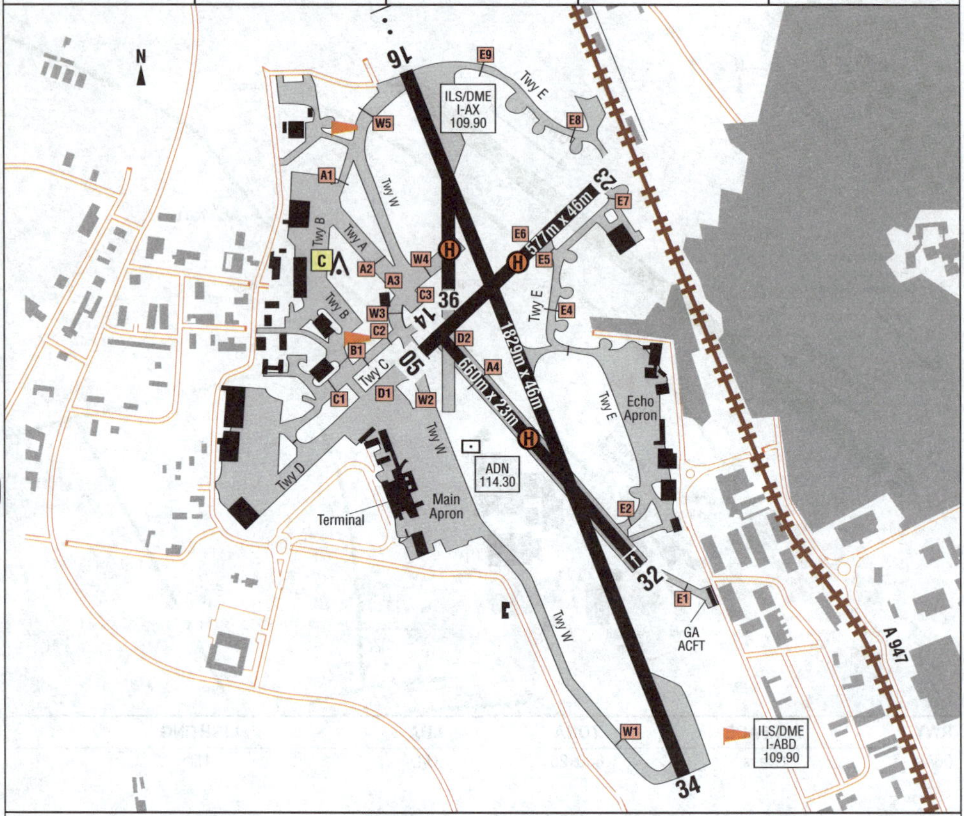

RWY	SURFACE	TORA	LDA	LIGHTING
16/34	Asphalt	1829	1829	App Thr Rwy PAPI 3° LHS
36	Asphalt	Helistrip	260x23	Nil
05/23	Asphalt	Helistrip	577x46	23-Thr Rwy CHAPI 6°
14/32	Asphalt	Helistrip	660x23	Nil

Remarks

PPR to non-radio ACFT. Helicopter operations outside published Hrs. ACFT to join final not less than 1000ft QFE. All telephone calls are recorded.

Handling: All Arr light ACFT will be directed to Signature at the Flying Club unless another handling agent has been specified.

Aids to Navigation: VOR/DME ADN 114.30. NDB ATF 348.00. NDB AQ 336.00.

Warnings

TV masts 1290ft amsl 12.5nm NW 648ft amsl 146°/2.9nm. Intense helicopter activity adjacent to full length of E apron Light ACFT beware of large helicopter down wash/vortices. Rwy16 PAPIs should not be used until on extended centre line. Moderate/severe turbulence and windshear may be experienced on APP to all Rwys when the 1000ft wind exceeds 15kt indirection 200-320°. Model ACFT flying up to 13kg not above 400ft agl at Haremoss 1.5 NW of Portlethen.

Operating Hrs	0510-2130 (PPR 2130-0510) (Summer) +1Hr (Winter)	Handling	Tel: 01244 770222 (Caledonian) Tel: 01244 723357 (Servisair) Tel: 01244 723636 (Signature) Tel: 01224 795802 (Aviance)
Landing Fee	On application		
Maintenance	By arr		
Fuel	Tel: 0860 310313 AVTUR JET A1	Disabled Facilities	

Restaurants	Buffet & bar at AD	Operator	Aberdeen Airport Ltd

Restaurants	Buffet & bar at AD	
Car Hire		
Avis	**Tel:** 01224 722282	
Europcar	**Tel:** 01224 770770	
Enterprise	**Tel:** 01224 348484	
Hertz	**Tel:** 01224 722373	
Budget	**Tel:** 01224 771777	
Taxis	Available at terminal	
Weather Info	M T9 T18 Fax 222 A Vsc GWC	

Operator

Aberdeen Airport Ltd
Aberdeen Airport
Dyce, Grampian
Scotland, AB21 7DU
Tel: 0870 040 0006 (AD)
Tel: 01224 723714 (NATS)
Fax: 01224 727176 (ATC)
Fax: 01224 725721 (AD)
www.aberdeenairport.com

CTA/CTR-CLASS D AIRSPACE
Normal CTA/CTR-Class D Airspace rules apply
Transition Altitude 6000ft

Entry/Exit Lanes
To facilitate the operation of ACFT to and from Aberdeen, the following entry/exit lanes have been established. They are all 3nm wide:
1 Peterhead lane
2 Stonehaven lane
3 Inverurie lane– for ACFT taking off from Rwy16 or landing on Rwy34 follow A96 until Kintore.
Use of lanes is subject to ATC clearance. ACFT in lanes must remain clear of cloud, in sight of the surface, fly not above 2000ft QNH with a min visibility of 3 km. ACFT using the lane shall keep the centre line on the left. Pilots must maintain adequate clearance from the GND or other obstacles

A

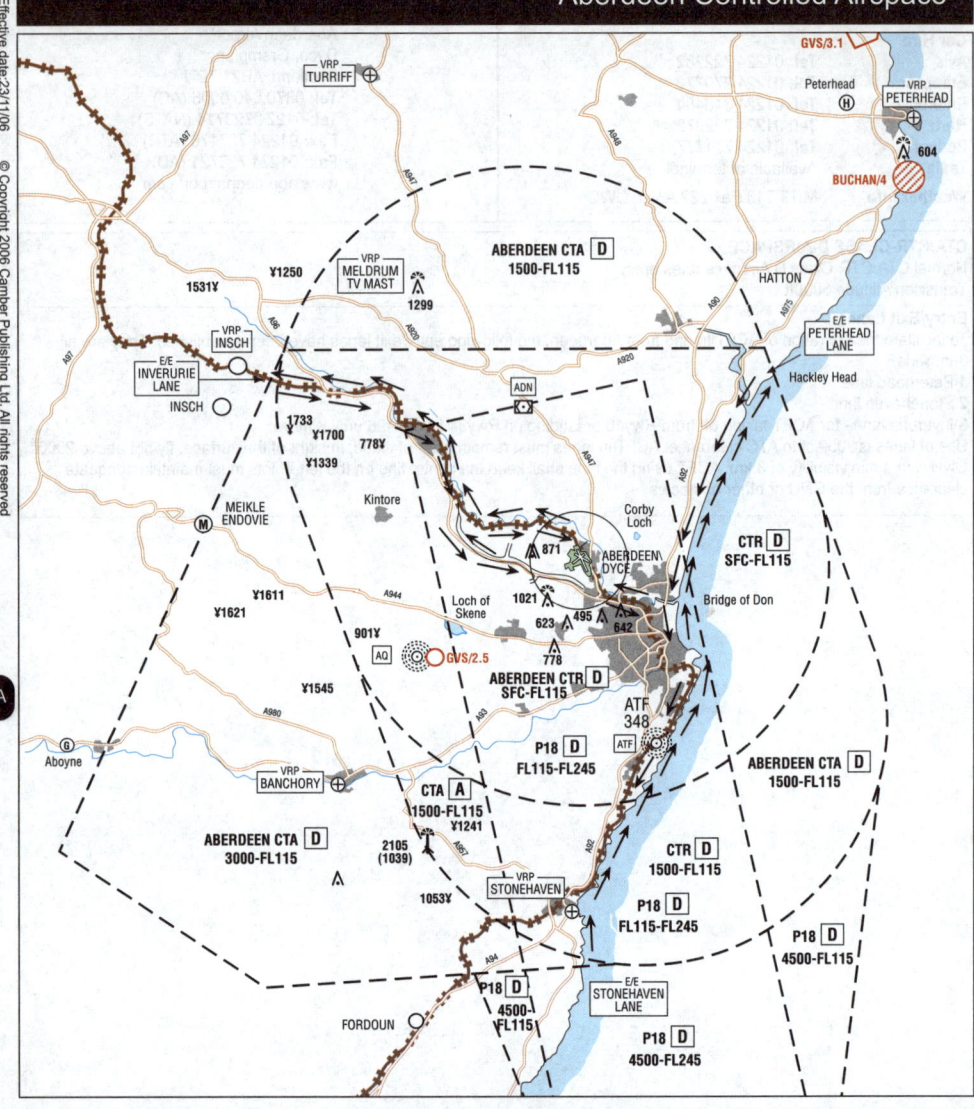

Visual Reference Points (VRP)

VRP	VOR/NDB	VOR/DME
Banchory	ADN 211°/ATF 268°	ADN 211°/17nm
N5703.00 W00230.10		
Core Hill TV Mast	ADN 321°/AQ 005°	ADN 321°/6nm
N5723.20 W00224.00		
Insch	ADN 284°/AQ 336°	ADN 284°/11nm
N5720.57 W00236.85		
Peterhead	ADN 058°/SHD 162°	ADN 058°/20nm
N5730.42 W00146.60		
Stonehaven	ADN 179°/ATF 211°	ADN 179°/21nm
N5657.75 W00212.60		
Turiff	ADN 340°/SHD 272°	AND 340°/15nm
N5732.32 W00227.60		

290ft 10mb	1nm SW of St Annes N4942.37 W00212.88	**Alternative AD Diversion AD**	**Jersey** Guernsey

Alderney	**APP** Guernsey 128.650	**TWR** Alderney 125.350	**GND** 130.500	**FIRE** 121.600

RWY	SURFACE	TORA	LDA	LIGHTING
03/21	Grass	497	497	Nil
14/32	Grass	732	732	Thr Rwy APAPI 3.5° LHS
08/26	Asphalt	880	880	App Thr Rwy APAPI 3° LHS

Rwy08/26 18m asphalt with 2.5m grass either side

Remarks

Not available to non-radio ACFT. PPR for parking on hard apron. Hi-Vis. Channel Islands CTR regulations apply. ACFT must be able to maintain R/T communication with Jersey Zone, Guernsey APP & Alderney TWR. Instrument training must be booked in advance with Guernsey APP. Duty free shop
Aids to Navigation: NDB ALD 383.00

Warnings

Exercise caution because of turbulence caused by nearby cliffs. Rwy surfaces undulating. Rwy03/21 & Rwy14/32 are marked by inset concrete blocks. Low boundary fence with orange/white markers short of Rwy03 & 32 Thr. ACFT using Rwy08/26 may see a white RVR light at upwind ends when Rwy lights are on. AD boundary fence 0.9m high lies within the Rwy14/32 and Rwy03/21 Rwy strips. Third party insurance is required in the sum of £500,000. Animals grazing infields on final APP. Due to coastal location, birds are a hazard throughout most of the year, particularly in the migration season.
Noise: Avoid over flying St Annes below 700ft aal.

Operating Hrs	Mon-Thu 0640-1730 Fri-Sun 0640-1830 (Summer) Mon-Sat 0740-1830 Sun 0855-1830 (Winter)
Circuits	26, 32 LH, 08, 14 RH, 700ft QFE No circuits 03/21

Landing Fee
£9.10 per 1000kgs or part there of (flights over 55nm)
£7.35 per 1000kgs or part thereof (flights under 55nm)
£5.30 per 1000kgs or part there of (local flights)
Fuel uplift or overnight stay discounts – Single £6 Twin £12

Maintenance	Nil
Fuel	AVGAS 100LL 0700-1730 (Daily) Sun 0900-1830 (Winter)

Disabled Facilities Nil

Restaurants	Light refreshments available at AD	Operator	States of Guernsey
Taxis			States of Guernsey Airport
Alderney Taxis	**Tel:** 01481 822611/822992		Guernsey, Channel Islands
Cycle Hire			**Tel:** 01481 822851 (Alderney ATC)
J B Cycle Hire	**Tel:** 01481 822294/822762		**Tel:** 01481 237766 Ex 2130
Weather Info	M T9 Fax 224 JER		(Guernsey APP)
	Tel: 01481 238957 (METAR & TAF)		**Tel:** 01481 237766 (Guernsey ATC)
			Tel: 01481 822851
			(PPR Hard apron only)
			Fax: 01481 822352 (Alderney ATC)

CTR Class D Airspace

Normal CTA/CTR Class D Airspace rules apply

Alderney Control Zone Radius 5nm SFC/2000ft aal

1 Unless otherwise authorised by Guernsey ATC, an ACFT shall not fly at less than 2000ft above AD elevation and within 5nm of the AD.

2 If at any time the ACFT is less than 2000ft within 5nm of the AD, then a continuous watch is to be made with **Guernsey ATC**

3 Carriage of SSR transponders is mandatory within the Channel Isles CTR.

4 If R/T failure occurs track 070° out of the zone from Alderney from overhead the AD at 2000ft.

Channel Island Visual Reference Points (VRP)

VRP	VOR/DME	VOR/DME	VOR/DME
Carteret Lighthouse	JSY 051°/13nm	GUR 101°/32nm	
N4922.00 W00148.00			
Casquets Lighthouse	JSY 340°/32nm	GUR 032°/19nm	
N4943.00 W00222.00			
Corbiere Lighthouse	JSY 257°/8nm	GUR 141°/21nm	DIN 353°/36nm
N4911.00 W00215.00			
Heauville	JSY 026°/24nm	GUR 078°/33nm	
N4934.60 W00148.06			
NE Point of Guernsey	JSY 317°/25nm	GUR 045°/6nm	
N4930.42 W00230.52			
NW corner of Jersey	JSY 289°/8nm	GUR 131°/18nm	
N4915.30 W00214.50			
Point de Rozel	JSY 029°/18nm	GUR 088°/30nm	
N4928.60 W00150.60			
St. Germain	JSY 091°/16nm	GUR 111°/40nm	DIN 028°/43nm
N4914.00 W00138.00			
SE Corner of Jersey	JSY 176°/3nm	GUR 130°/28nm	DIN 007°/35nm
N4910.00 W00202.00			
W of Cap de la Hague	JSY 008°/30nm	GUR 058°/29nm	
N4943.00 W00200.00			

See Channel Island transit Corridor chart – Jersey

ANDREAS

110ft 3mb	3nm NW of Ramsey N5422.03 W00426.45		PPR	Alternative AD	Ronaldsway
Andreas Base		**ATIS** Ronaldsway 123.875		**APP** Ronaldsway 120.850	**A/G** 130.100

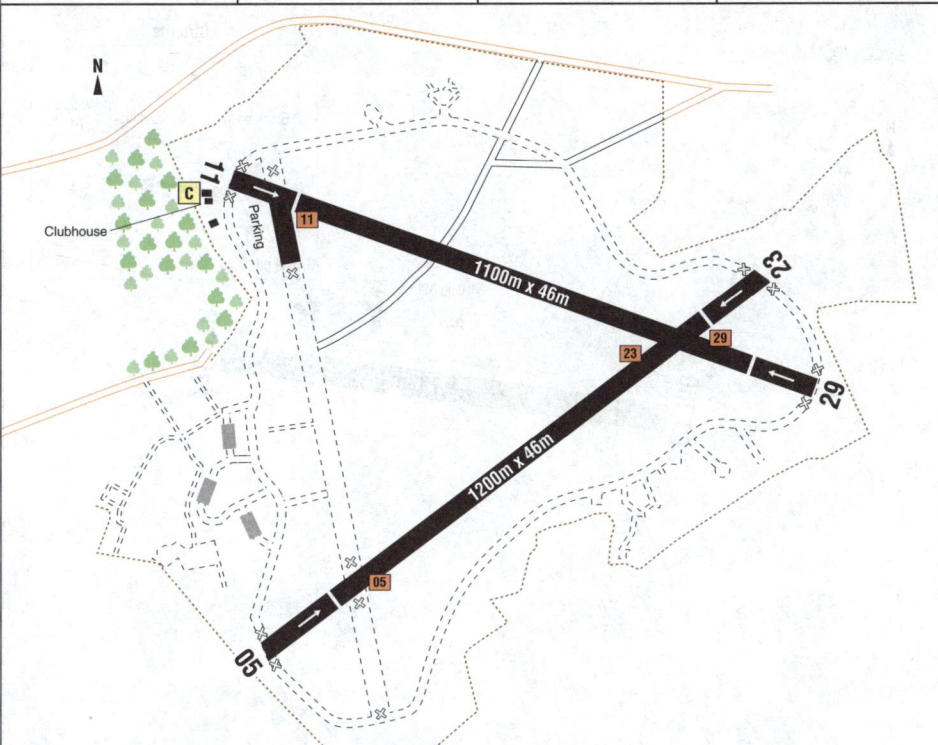

RWY	SURFACE	TORA	LDA	LIGHTING
11/29	Asphalt	900x46	U/L	Nil
05/23	Asphalt	1000x46	U/L	Nil

Remarks
PPR by telephone. Visiting ACFT welcome at pilots own risk. Gliding operations are by winch and Aerotow. When gliding in progress Andreas Base active. AD uses WW2 site, marked areas are useable, Rwy surfaces may have loose stones. AD is not notified as a point of entry for I.O.M. under the prevention of Terrorism legislation.

Warnings
Power and Gliding ops may be on different Rwys. Non-radio traffic occasionally operates from Andreas. Vehicle access to AD strictly controlled due to Rwy acess. See website for details.
Caution: Winch cables on active Rwys, right side of Rwy, full length.
Noise: Avoid over flying all local houses.

Operating Hrs	SR-SS	**Operator**	Andreas Gliding Club
Circuits	1000ft QFE details with PPR No overhead joins		Andreas Airfield Braust Farm Lezayre
Landing Fee	Nil		Isle of Man
Maintenance	Nil		**Tel:** 01624 817659 (Bob Fennell)
Fuel	Nil		**Tel:** 01624 861863 (Tom Wiseman)
Disabled Facilities	Nil		bob@manxgliding.flyer.co.uk
Restaurant	Nil		www.manxgliding.org
Taxi/Car Hire	Nil		
Weather Info	MOEx		

EGSL

ANDREWSFIELD

286ft 10mb	4nm WNW of Braintree N5153.70 E00026.95	PPR	Alternative AD Diversion AD	Southend Earls Colne

Andrewsfield	APP Essex RAD 120.625	A/G 130.550

Circuits

Black barn · Salings · Water Twr · Gravel pits · A120

Visiting ACFT · C

799m x 18m x 18m

09L 09R · 27L 27R

N

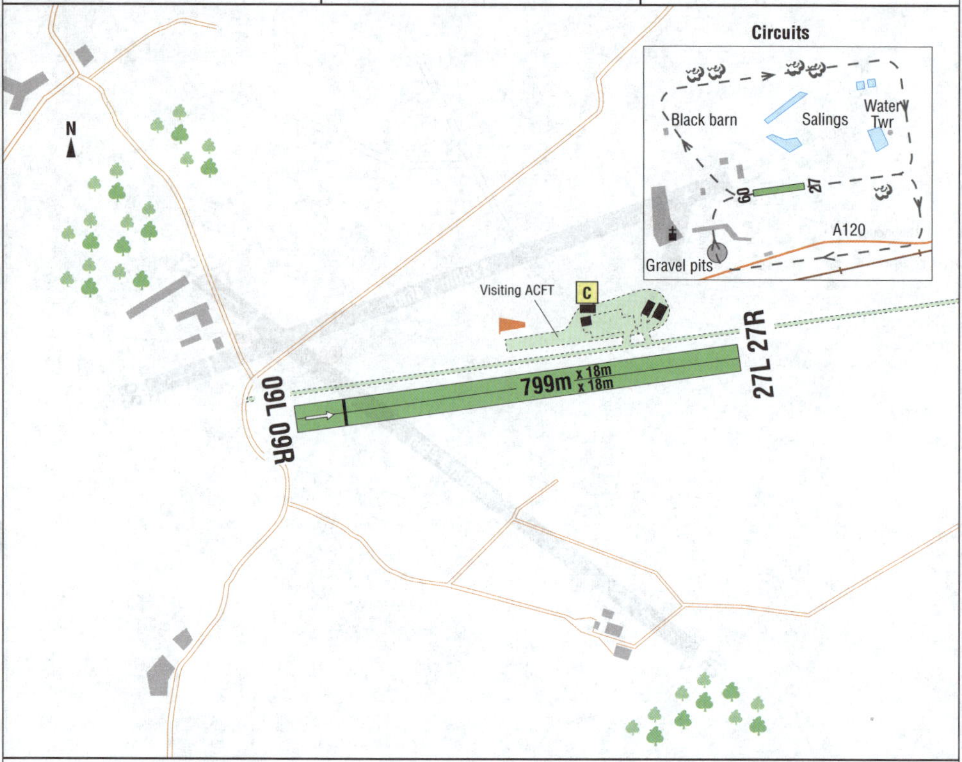

RWY	SURFACE	TORA	LDA	LIGHTING
09L/R	Grass	799	720	Thr Rwy
27L/R	Grass	799	799	Thr Rwy APAPI 3° LHS

Operating as two parallel Rwys

Remarks
PPR by telephone only. Not available for public transport flights. Use at night by ACFT requiring a licensed AD is confined to operations by Andrewsfield Aviation Ltd using Rwy27. Rwy09 not available for landings by night by ACFT required to use a licensed AD.

Warnings
Located on E edge of Stansted CTR and under the Stansted CTA (base 2000ft AMSL).

Operating Hrs	0900-1800 (Summer) 0830-1800 (Winter) & by arr	**Car Hire** The Oak Garage	**Tel:** 01371 820227
Circuits	RH 700ft QFE	**Weather Info**	AirCen MOEx
Landing Fee	Single £8 Helicopters £12	**Operator**	Andrewsfield Aviation Ltd Sailing Airfield, Stebbing Great Dunmow, Essex, CM6 3TH **Tel:** 01371 856744 **Fax:** 01371 856500 aviation@andrewsfield.freeserve.co.uk
Maintenance MK Aero support **Fuel**	**Tel:** 01371 856796 AVGAS 100LL		

Disabled Facilities

Restaurants Hot & cold food available

Taxis
Style Travel   **Tel:** 01371 853016

262ft 9mb	2nm E of Sandbach N5308.50 W00219.00	**PPR**	**Alternative AD**	**Liverpool** Manchester Barton

Non-Radio	**ATIS** Manchester 128.175 (Arr)	**Safetycom** 135.475

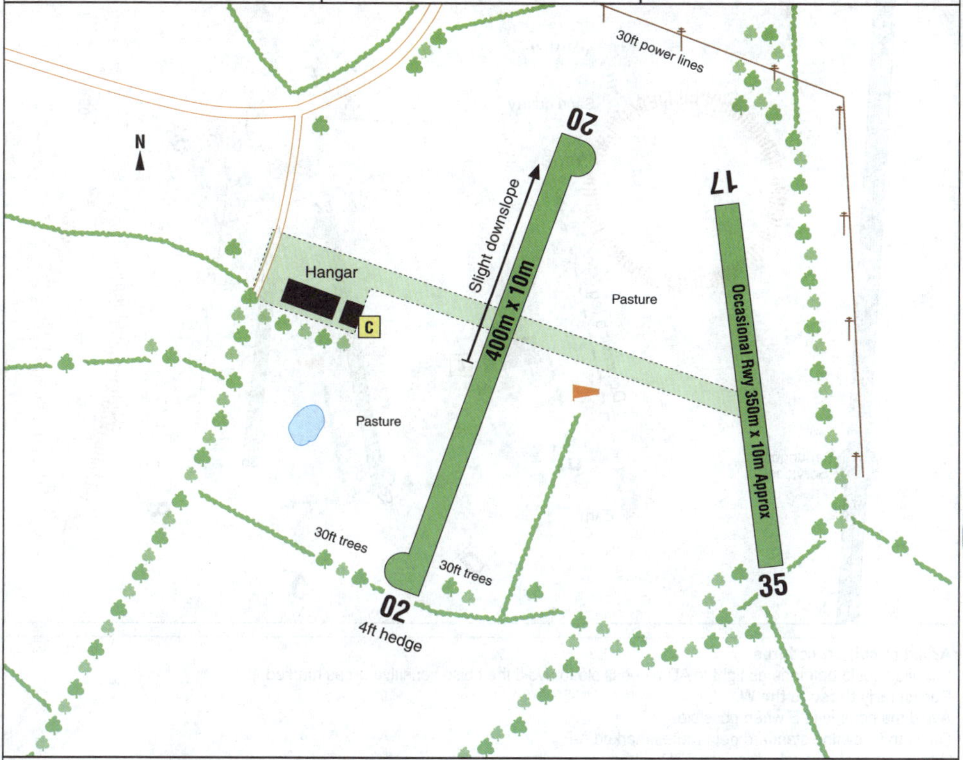

(Airfield diagram)

Labels on diagram: 30ft power lines · 20 · 17 · Hangar · C · Slight downslope · 400m x 10m · Pasture · Occasional Rwy 350m x 10m Approx · N · Pasture · 30ft trees · 30ft trees · 02 · 4ft hedge · 35

RWY	SURFACE	TORA	LDA	LIGHTING
02/20	Grass	400x10m	U/L	Nil

Rwy20 surface undulates
Rwy17/35 (350x10m) avail certain times due to crop rotation
Twy w of windsock can be used in strong crosswinds

Remarks
PPR by telephone essential. Visiting ACFT welcome at pilots own risk. AD used as microlight training site.

Warnings
4ft hedge Rwy02 Thr. 30ft trees abeam Rwy02 Thr 30ft power lines cross final APP Rwy20 approx 175m from Thr. Manchester CTR boundary is 2.5nm to N.
Noise: See overleaf for specific noise info

Operating Hrs	SR-SS	**Operator**	Arclid Resident Flyers
Circuits	02 LH, 20 RH 500ft QFE		C/O John Bradbury (CFI)
Landing Fee	£2		Cheshire Microlight Centre
Maintenance	By prior arr		4 Adlington Drive
Fuel	By prior arr		Sandbach
Disbabled Facilities			Cheshire,CW11 1DX

Restaurants	Nil
Taxis/Car Hire	Nil
Weather Info	AirCen MWC

Tel: 01270 764713 (Home/Office)
Tel: 07831 274201 (Airfield/Mobile)
enquire@cheshiremicrolights.co.uk
www.cheshiremicrolights.co.uk

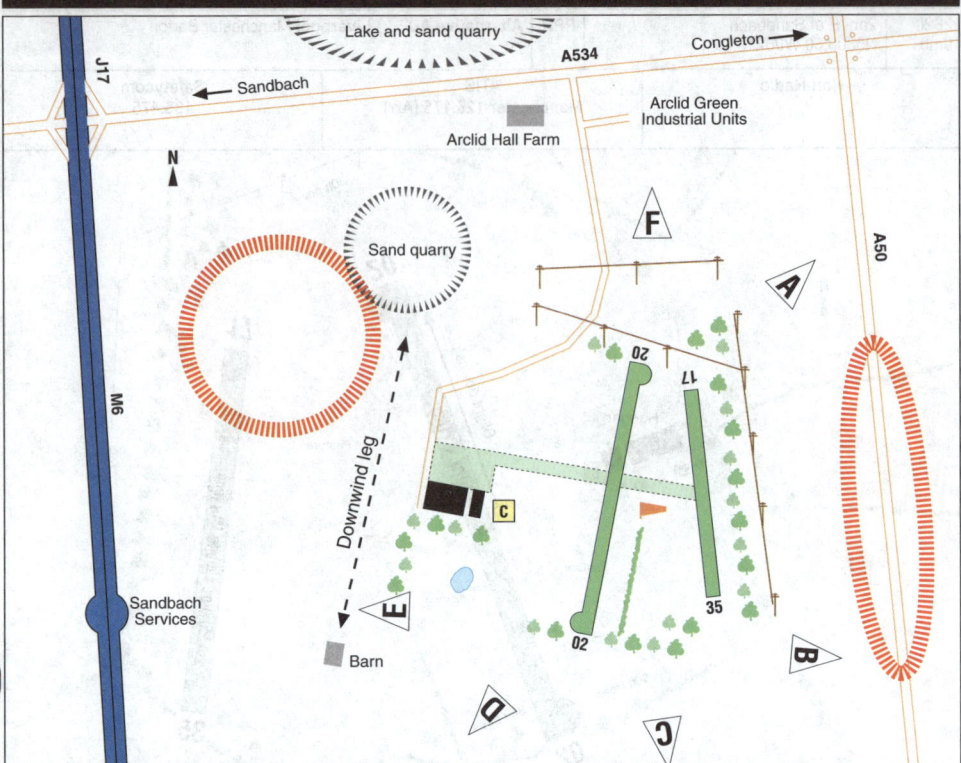

Arclid circuit procedures

Circuits should be made as tight to AD as possible to avoid the noise sensitive areas marked.

Particularly those to the W.

Avoid the houses to E when possible.

Depts to follow the standard dept routes marked A-F.

When you book out, take the next SDR in turn.

150ft 5mb	3.2nm SW of Winsford N5309.85 W00234.29	PPR	Alternative AD Diversion AD	Liverpool Hawarden

Ashcroft	ATIS Manchester 128.175 (Arr) Liverpool 124.325	APP Liverpool 119.850	A/G 122.525 Not always manned

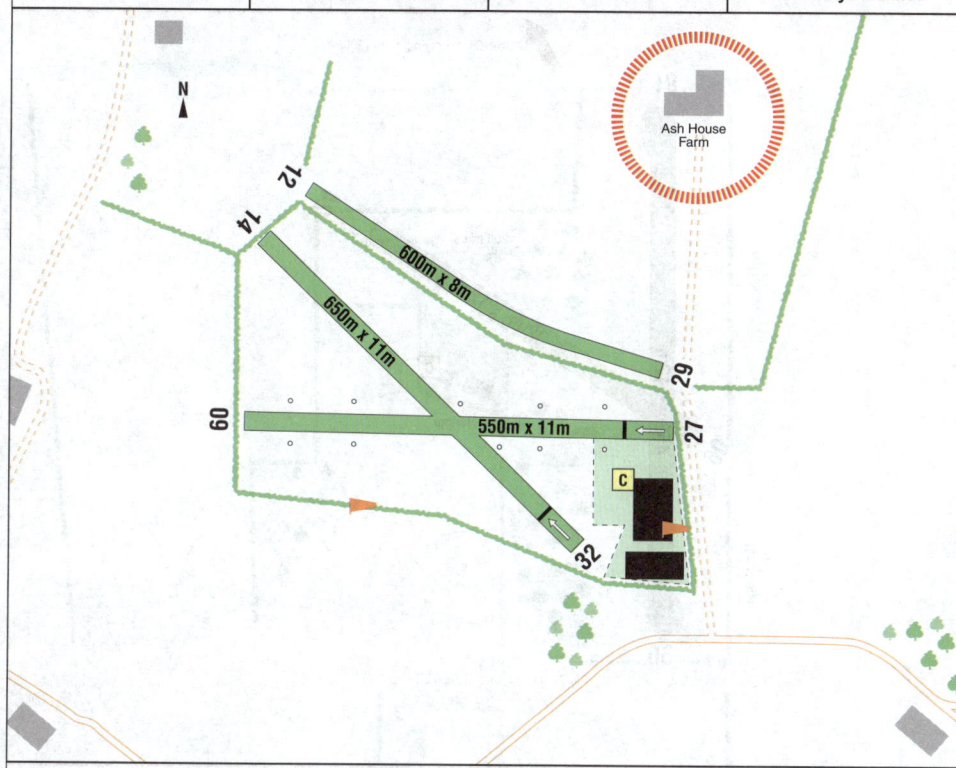

RWY	SURFACE	TORA	LDA	LIGHTING
09/27	Grass	550x11	U/L	Ltd
14/32	Grass	650x11	U/L	Nil
12/29	Grass	600x8	U/L	Nil

Displaced Thr Rwy27 & Rwy32 50m

Remarks
Strict PPR. Previous farm strip experience essential. Pilots use the strip entirely at their own risk and discretion. Use mown strips only, there may be long grass either side of the Rwys.

Warnings
Rwy12/29 curved, restricted use available to authorised pilots only. Rwy14/32 waterlogged after heavy rain. Raised white Rwy markers along either side of Rwy09/27. Severe downdrafts when landing on Rwy27 with SW winds >10kts.
Noise: Essential no flying on N side of AD, avoid all local farmhouses.

Operating Hrs	SR-SS	**Taxis**	
Circuits	South 800ft QFE	Winsford Taxis	**Tel:** 01606 550055
Landing Fee	Microlights £5	Tonys Taxis	**Tel:** 01606 559348
	Parking £5 per day	**Weather Info**	AirCen MWC
	ACFT < 200hp £8	**Operator**	Steve Billington
	ACFT > 200hp £15		Ashcroft Farm, Darnhall
Maintenance	Nil		Winsford, Cheshire, CW7 4DQ
Fuel	Nil		**Tel:** 01270 528697
Disabled Facilities	Nil		ashcroftair@btinternet.com
Restaurants	Boot & Slipper 2nm from AD		www.ashcroftair.co.uk
	Tel: 01270 528238		

ASHLEY'S FIELD

8ft 0mb	4.5nm NNW of Skegness N5313.00 E00016.25	PPR	Alternative AD	Doncaster Wickenby

Non Radio	LARS Waddington 127.350 Coningsby 120.800	Safetycom 135.475

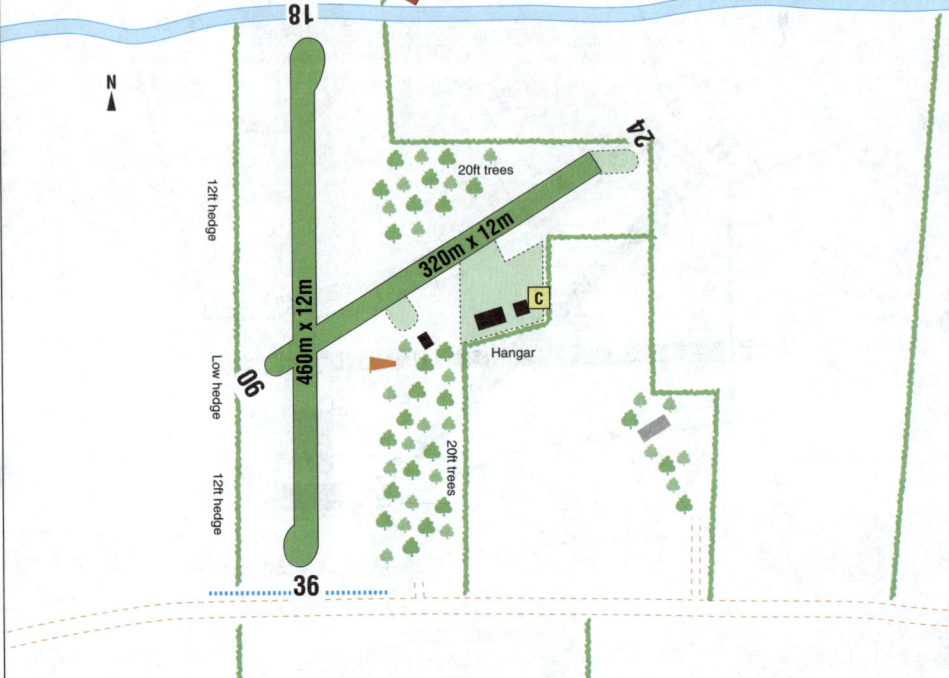

Do NOT overfly pig farm (200m)

18

N

24

12ft hedge

20ft trees

320m x 12m

C

460m x 12m

06

Low hedge

Hangar

12ft hedge

20ft trees

36

A

RWY	SURFACE	TORA	LDA	LIGHTING
18/36	Grass	460x12	U/L	Nil
06/24	Grass	320x12	U/L	Nil

Remarks

PPR by telephone essential. All visitors must be met by prior arrangement AD is very isolated, no public transport is available. Rwys regularly cut and in excellent condition.

Warnings

Rwy36 has slight downslope at N end. Low hedges at Rwy06/24 Thr. Rwy36 APP is over a public road.
Caution: Vehicles on Airfield.
Noise: Avoid over flying pig farm to NNE of AD.

Operating Hrs	SR-SS	**Operator**	John Rogers
Circuits	18 & 06 RH, 24 &36 LH.		The Captain's Table
Landing Fee	Available with PPR		Witham Bank
Maintenance	Nil		Chapel Hill
Fuel	Nil		Lincolnshire
Disabled Facilities	Nil		LN4 4QA
Restaurant	Nil		**Tel:** 01526 343757
Taxi/Car Hire	Available with PPR		
Weather Info	AirCen MWC		

283ft 11mb	1nm SW of Saffron Walden N5200.52 E00013.57	PPR	**Alternative AD** **Diversion AD**	**Cambridge** Duxford

Non-radio	**APP** **Essex RAD 120.625**	**Safetycom** **135.475**

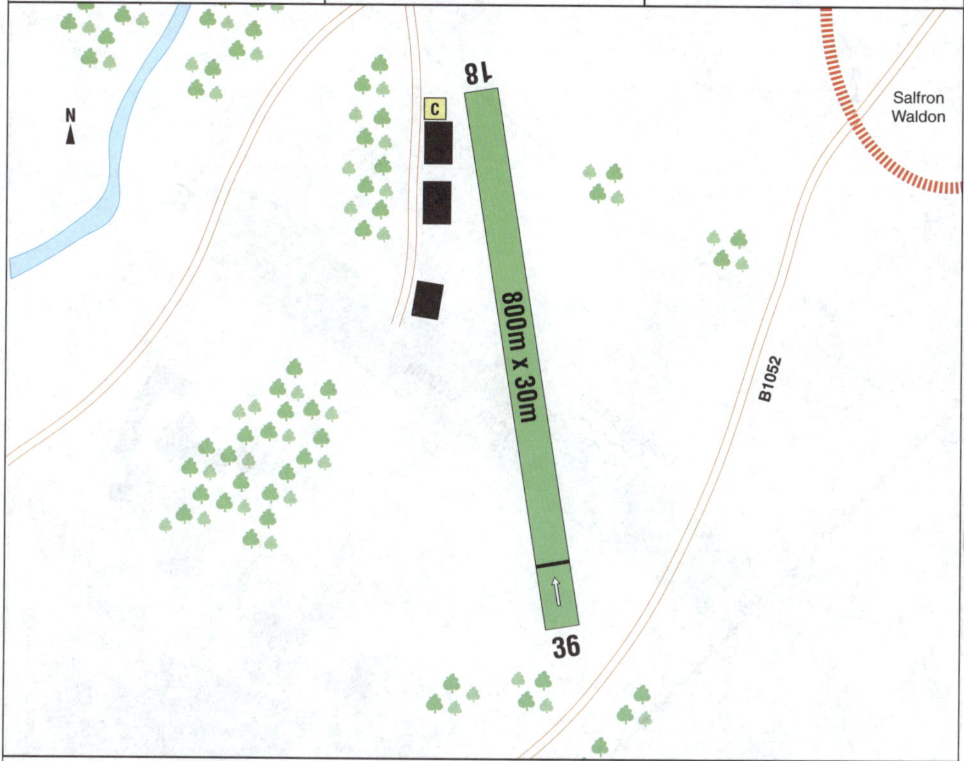
N
18
C
800m x 30m
36
B1052
Salfron
Waldon

RWY	SURFACE	TORA	LDA	LIGHTING
18/36	Grass	800x30	U/L	Nil

Rwy18 slight upslope
Rwy36 APP tall trees reduce LDA to 700m

Remarks
AD situated on the edge of Stansted CTA. Inbound ACFT to contact Essex RAD. Visiting pilots must report to the control point at the green hangar to sign movements book.

Warnings
Caution is necessary on APP Rwy36 due to a line of trees across the extended centre line 50m before the AD boundary.
Noise: Avoid over flying Saffron Walden 1nm NE of AD.

Operating Hrs By arr SR-SS
Circuits 18 RH, 36 LH
Landing Fee Single £5 Twin £10 (private)
Single/Twin £10 (commercial)
Maintenance Nil
Fuel Nil
Disabled Facilities

Taxis
Adtax **Tel:** 01799 521164

Car Hire
Practical Car Hire **Tel:** 01799 541456
Weather Info AirCen MOEx
Operator Audley End Development Co Ltd
Bruncketts Wendens Ambo
Saffron Walden, Essex, CB11 4JL
Tel: 01799 541354/541956
Fax: 01799 542134
aee@tdirect.net

Effective date:23/11/06

A

EGTA

AYLESBURY

289ft 9mb	3nm NE of Thame N5146.52 W000546.40	PPR	Alternative AD	Cranfield Wycombe

Non-radio	APP Luton 129.550	Safetycom 135.475

A

RWY	SURFACE	TORA	LDA	LIGHTING
06/24	Grass	1000x100	U/L	Nil

Remarks
PPR by telephone essential at all times. Gliding site but light ACFT & microlights welcome at own risk. Please park adjacent to glider launch point at Thr of Rwy in use.

Warnings
No overhead joins due launch cables. AD may suffer from water logging after periods of heavy rain. The gliding club advise that although they are always happy to see powered visitors they have no facilities – not even a loo!
Noise: Avoid over flying village of Haddenham 1.5nm SE of AD

Operating Hrs	Weekends only Sat-Sun (Summer) Sun only (Winter)	**Operator**	Upward Bound Trust Gliding Club Mr M Clark 27 Crotch Crescent New Marston, Oxon, OX3 0JL **Tel:** 01865 865165 (Day) **Tel:** 01865 721090 (Evenings) www.ubt.org.uk
Circuits	All circuits on N side 1000ft QFE No overhead joins Keep good lookout for gliders		
Landing Fee	Donations gratefully received		
Maintenance	Nil		
Fuel	Nil		
Disabled Facilities	Nil		
Restaurants	Nil		
Taxis/Car Hire	Nil		
Weather Info	AirCen MOEx		

220ft 7mb	2nm SW Eyemouth N5551.00 W00206.50	PPR	Alternative AD	Edinburgh Charterhall

Non-Radio	FIR Scottish 119.875	Safetycom 135.475

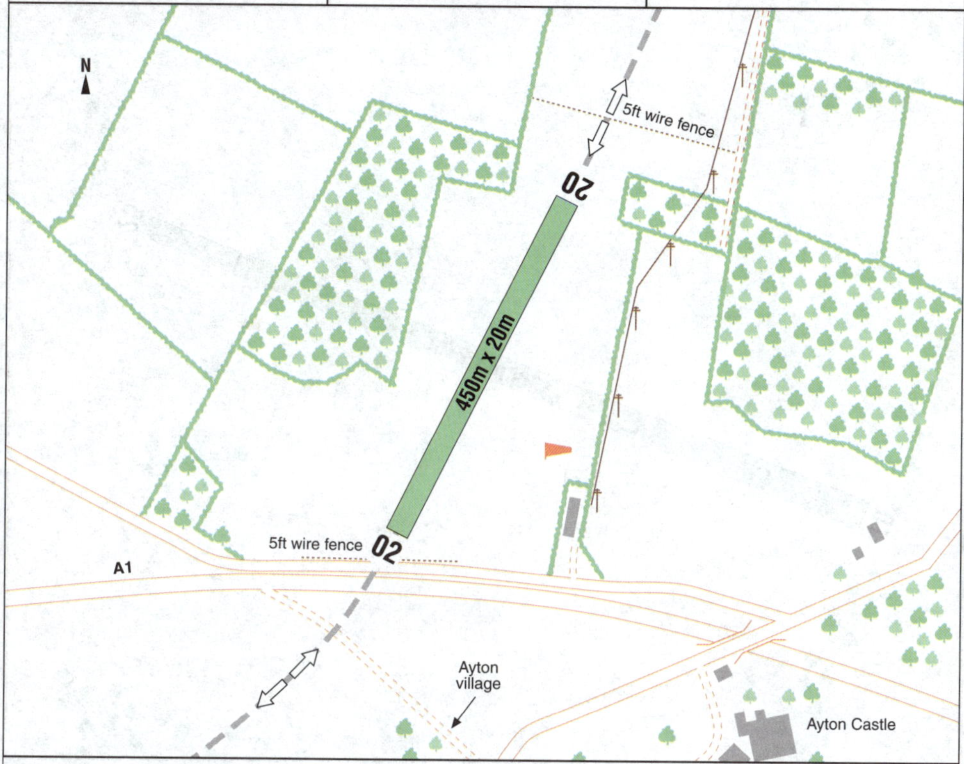

N

5ft wire fence

20

450m x 20m

5ft wire fence

02

A1

Ayton village

Ayton Castle

A

RWY	SURFACE	TORA	LDA	LIGHTING
02/20	Grass	450x20	U/L	Nil

Remarks

PPR by telephone. Visiting ACFT welcome at pilots own risk. Sheep graze AD.

Warnings

Low-level military ACFT may be encountered, particularly weekdays. Electricity cables run parallel to Rwy 100m to E. Low wire fences close to Rwy Thr. Adjacent woods may cause turbulence.
Noise: Avoid over flying local habitation, particularly Ayton village. Execute curved APP/Dept.

Operating Hours	SR-SS
Circuits	LH 1000ft QFE
Landing Fee	Nil
	Donation to grass cutting always welcome
Maintenance	Nil
Fuel	Nil

Disabled Facilities

Restaurants/Accomodation
Churches Hotel   **Tel:** 01890 750401 (Eyemouth)
The Craw Inn   **Tel:** 01890 761253 (Auchencrow)

Taxis
Eyemouth Taxis   **Tel:** 01890 781533

Car Hire
Blackburn & Price   **Tel:** 01289 307436 (Berwick-on-Tweed)
Weather Info   AirSC GWC
Operator   Mr D Liddell-Grainger
Ayton Castle
Berwickshire, TD14 5RD
Tel: 01890 781212 (Castle)
Fax: 01890 781550

495ft 17mb	3.5nm ENE of Chipping Sodbury N5132.98 W00217.92	PPR	Alternative AD	Bristol Filton Kemble

Badminton	APP Lyneham 123.400 Bristol Filton 122.725	A/G 123.175

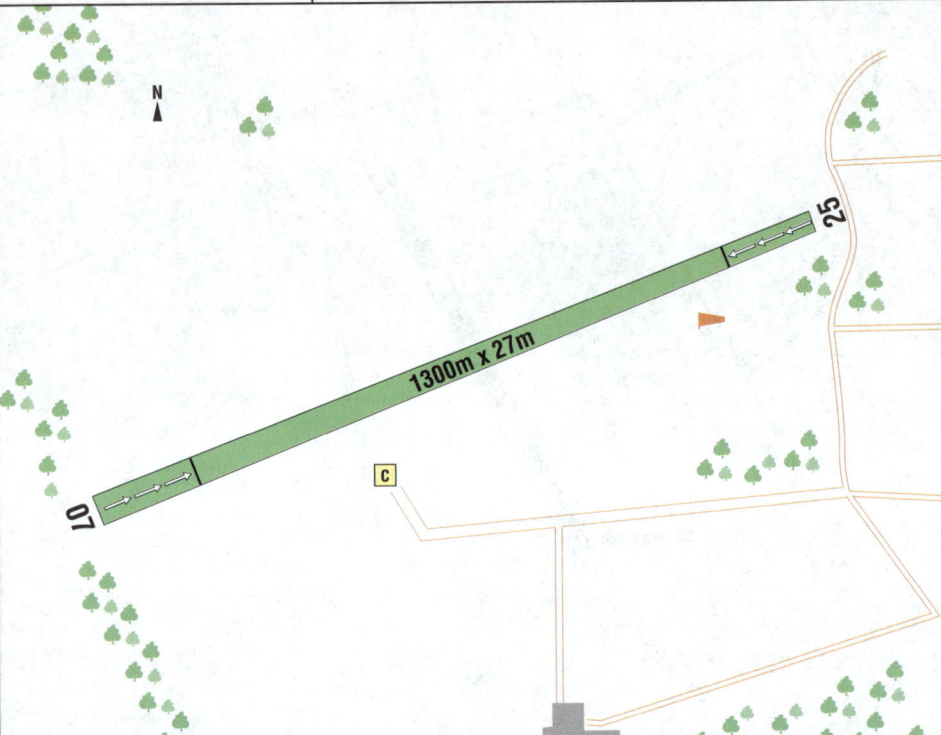

RWY	SURFACE	TORA	LDA	LIGHTING
07	Grass	1250x27	U/L	Nil
25	Grass	1250x27	U/L	Nil

Displaced Thr Rwy07 50m
Displaced Thr Rwy25 50m

Remarks
PPR by telephone only. Rwy25 APP should be high enough to cross the public road safely.

Warnings
Care must be taken during August and March when Rwy may be fenced against stock. Horse trials in May.
Noise: Avoid over flying the villages of Badminton and Little Badminton.

Operating Hrs	By arr	**Operator**	Mr H Richardson
Circuits	07 LH, 25 RH		Badminton Airfield
Landing Fee	On Application		Badminton, Glos, GL9 1DD
Maintenance	Nil		**Tel: 01454 218888** (Hangar)
Fuel	100LL		**Tel: 01454 218220**
Disabled Facilities	Nil		**Tel: 01249 721076**
Restaurants	Nil		**Fax: 01454 218159**
Taxis/Car Hire	Nil		
Weather Info	AirSW MOEx		

160ft 5mb	2nm SE of Thirsk N5412.62 W00117.55	PPR	Alternative AD Diversion AD	Durham Tees Valley Wombleton

Bagby	APP Topcliffe 125.000	A/G 123.250 Not always manned

RWY	SURFACE	TORA	LDA	LIGHTING
06/24	Grass	710x20	U/L	Rwy Single PAPI 4°
15/33	Grass	450x20	U/L	Nil

Rwy06 Upslope 2.5%, Rwy33 Upslope 1.5%
Rwy06/24 Electric Rwy lighting available

Remarks
PPR essential during winter months. Light ACFT including twins are welcome. During Topcliffe Hrs of operation special dept procedures apply, details available on arrival. Microlight training takes place on AD. ACFT parking, A – short term, B – long term.

Warnings
Non radio ACFT telephone briefing recommended weekdays.
Noise: Do not over fly the villages of Bagby and Thirkleby. Compulsory routing via sewage works on Rwy15/33.

Operating Hrs	0830-SS (L) & by arr (Home ACFT) Closed Tues 1700-1930 Services available 0930-1900 (L) (Visiting ACFT) PPR outside these times	**Taxis** Jeb Chapmans **Car Hire**	**Tel:** 07973 443169 **Tel:** 07960 568299
Circuits	06, 15 RH, 33, 24 LH 800ft	Moss Motors	**Tel:** 01845 522042
Landing Fee	All landings free with fuel uplift	**Weather Info**	AirN MWC
Maintenance	M3 G Fox Engineering **Tel:** 01845 597707	**Operator**	Mr J M Dundon Bagby Airfield Bagby, Thirsk, YO7 2PH **Tel:** 01845 597385 (AD) **Tel/Fax:** 01845 597747 (Office) **Tel:** 07774 680186 bagbyair@aol.com www.egng.co.uk
Fuel	AVGAS 100LL JET A1		
Disabled Facilities Nil			
Accomodation	Hotels in Thirsk		
Restaurants	Bar meals & club facilities at AD 1200-1300 weekdays 1100-1400 weekends		

103

340ft 11mb	2nm NE of Corby N5230.10 W00038.15	PPR	Alternative AD	Cranfield Peterborough Conington

Non-Radio	LARS Cottesmore 130.200	Safetycom 135.475

B

Weldon village 1nm
DO NOT overfly

N

Laundimer Farm

Hangar

50ft tree

25

8ft hedge

crops

490m x 15m

Swimming lake

crops

07

crops

40ft tree

40ft tree

Laundimer Woods

RWY	SURFACE	TORA	LDA	LIGHTING
07/25	Grass	490x15	U/L	Nil

Remarks
PPR by telephone. Visiting ACFT, including Microlights welcome at pilots own risk. Rwy25 boggy during Winter months. Cottesmore active Mon-Fri only.
Visual aids to location: AD located at top of hill adjacent to extensive Woods, (S of strip). Rockingham Motor Racing circuit 1.5nm to NW.

Warnings
8ft hedge at Rwy25 Thr. 50ft tree to N Rwy25 APP on very short final. 40ft tree to S Rwy07 Thr. Crops grown up to edges of strip. Deenethorpe AD 1nm NE. Lyveden Gliding site 1.5nm SE, beware of cables up to 2000ft agl. Wittering MATZ 3.5nm NNE, Harrier ACFT may be encountered mainly during weekdays, keep a good lookout.
Noise: Avoid over flying local habitation, particularly Weldon village to NW.

Operating Hrs	SR-SS daily	Operator	Mr T D Baker
Circuits	25 LH, 07 RH		Laundimer House
Landing Fee	Nil		Bears Lane, Weldon,
Maintenance	Nil		Northants, NN17 3LH
Fuel	MOGAS by arr		**Tel/Fax:** 01536 206770
Disabled Facilities	Nil		bearsbaker@aol.com (AD)
Restaurants/ Accomodation	B&B available from Laundimer house		Pauline@laundimerhouse.co.uk (B&B)
Taxis/Car Hire	Nil		
Weather Info	AirCen MWC		

| 367ft | 3nm NE of Grantham | PPR | Alternative AD | Cranwell Langar |
| 12mb | N5257.74 W00033.70 | MIL | Diversion AD | |

| Barkston | | APP | | TWR |
| | | Cranwell 119.375 | | 120.425 |

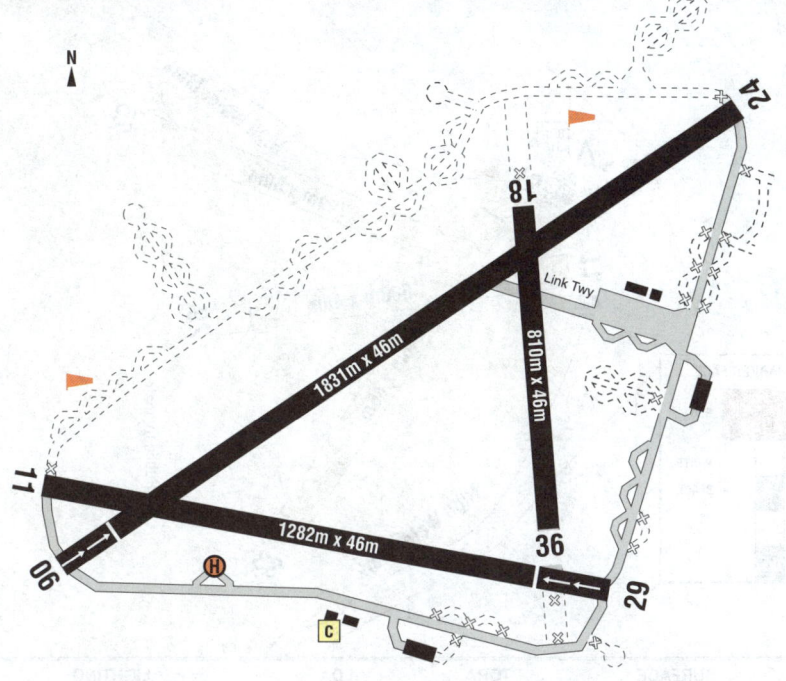

RWY	SURFACE	TORA	LDA	LIGHTING
06	Concrete	1831	1677	Thr Rwy PAPI 3° LH
24	Concrete	1831	1829	Ap Thr Rwy PAPI 3° LH
11	Asphalt	1282	1280	Thr Rwy PAPI 3° LH
29	Asphalt	1282	1125	Thr Rwy PAPI 3° LH
18/36	Asphalt	810	796	Nil

Remarks

PPR by telephone essential. AD not available for use outside published Hrs. RAF AD. Extensive military training on AD. Model ACFT club and RAF Cranwell Motor Club use AD at weekends.

Warnings

AD regularly active outside normal operational Hrs. Considerable aerobatic activity may be encountered in the ATZ and local area at any time. Due to the close proximity of neighbouring AD and over lapping RAD patterns, all ACFT on instrument APP may be subject to a RIS, FIS or procedural service.
Noise: Avoid over flying Belton, Bottesford and Ancaster villages.

Operating Hrs	Mon-Thu 0830-1730 Fri 0830-1700 (L)
Circuits	11, 18 LH, 36, 06, 24, 29, LH 1000ft QFE
Landing Fee	Available with PPR
Maintenance	Nil for visiting ACFT
Fuel	Not available to visiting ACFT
Disabled Facilities	

Restaurants	Nil
Taxis/Car Hire	Nil
Weather Info	AirCen MWC
	ATIS **Tel:** 01400 265023

Visual Reporting Points (VRP)

Point Oscar	Roundabout on A15/A52 W of Theekingham, S of Osbournby.
Point Alpha	E of Bottesford on E edge of A1 southbound road
Operator	Defence Elementary Flying Training School RAF Barkston Heath Grantham, Lincs NG32 2DQ **Tel:** 01400 265200 (PPR)

B

5ft 0mb	Foreshore of Traigh Mhor N5701.37 W00726.58	PPR	Alternative AD Diversion AD	Benbecula Tiree

Barra	FIS Scottish 127.275	AFIS Tiree 122.700 Barra 118.075	APP Benbecula 119.200

APP MARKER FACE
- RED
- WHITE
- BLACK

Runway labels on chart: BRR 316, 35ft agl, Terminal, High Water Mark, Public footpath, 25, 29, 33, 15, 11-07, 799m x 60m, 680m x 46m, 846m x 46m

RWY	SURFACE	TORA	LDA	LIGHTING
07/25	Sand	799	799	Nil
11	Sand	667	617	Nil
29	Sand	667	597	Nil
15	Sand	846	796	Nil
33	Sand	846	776	Nil

Remarks

PPR is essential to obtain information on surface conditions, in addition to other information. The obstacle clearance surfaces of Rwy07/25 are infringed at both ends. A weather minima of 3km visibility and cloud base of 1000ft aal must be strictly adhered to.

Warnings

Landing and take-off areas may be considerably ridged by hard sand and contain pools of standing water which are hazards to ACFT. The bearing strength, braking action and contamination of the beach is unknown, variable and unpredictable. Some down draughts may be experienced at the W end of Rwy07/25 in strong wind from the W through S. Rwy07/25 will be marked by black/white boxes on the landward side of Thr on request. The E end of Rwy07/25 is generally unfit for use due to water logging & sand ridging.

Operating Hrs	Mon-Fri 0945-1215 & 1400-1630 Sat 1215-1330 & 1400-1630 (1 Apr-27 Oct) Sun Closed All times subject to tidal variation	**Taxis** Barra Taxi J Campbell D Sinclair	**Tel:** 01871 810999 **Tel:** 01871 810216 **Tel:** 01871 890253
Circuits	Variable	**Car Hire** Macmillan Self Dri.	**Tel:** 01871 890366
Landing Fee	£13.84 up to 3000kgs Booked in advance VFR cash/cheque on the day	Barra Car Hire H MacNeil	**Tel:** 01871 810243 **Tel:** 01871 810262
		Bus	Post bus drops passengers at Castlebay
Maintenance	Nil	**Weather Info**	AirSc GWC
Fuel	Nil	**Operator**	HIAL Barra Aerodrome Eoligarry Isle of Barra, HS9 5YD **Tel:** 01871 890212 (PPR) **Fax:** 01871 890220 www.highlands-and-islands-airports.com
Disabled Facilities	Nil		
Restaurants Heathbank Hotel (4 miles) May to Sept only Craigard/Castlebay Hotels (12 miles) open all year			

B

44ft 2mb	1.5nm NW of Barrow in Furness N5407.87 W00315.81	PPR	**Alternative AD** **Diversion AD**	**Blackpool** Cark

	Walney	**AFIS** **123.200**	

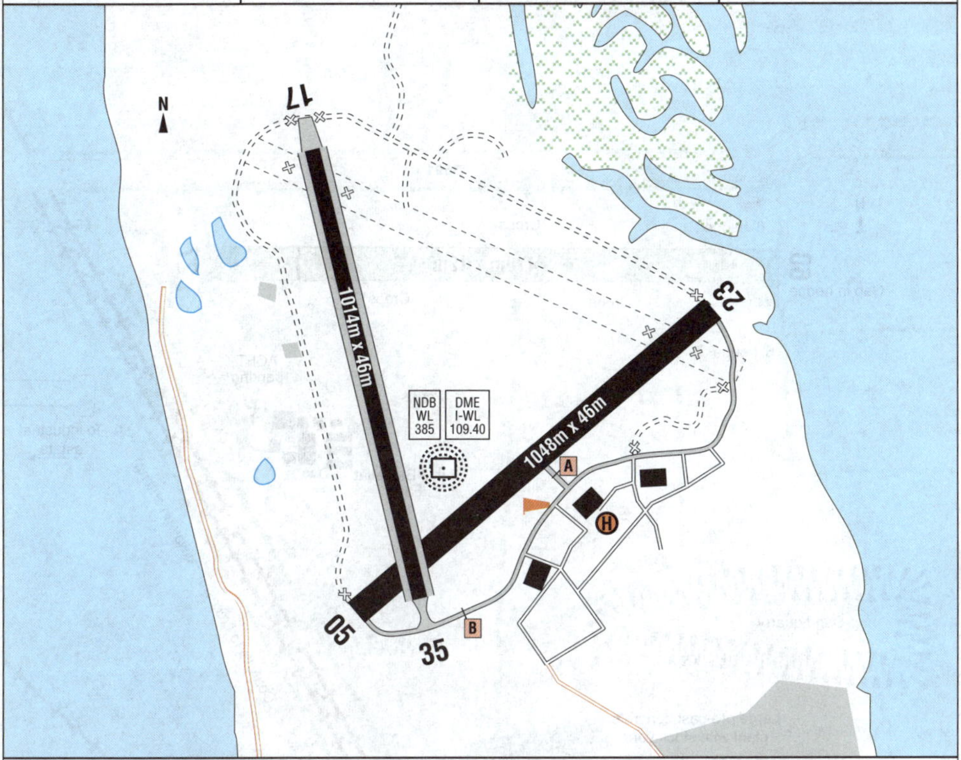

N
17
23
05
35
1014m x 46m
1048m x 46m
NDB
WL
385
DME
I-WL
109.40
A
B
H

RWY	SURFACE	TORA	LDA	LIGHTING
05	Asphalt	1014x46	U/L	Thr Rwy APAPI 4° LHS
23	Asphalt	1014x46	U/L	Thr Rwy APAPI 3.5° LHS
17	Asphalt	1011	1011	Thr Rwy APAPI 4° RHS
35	Asphalt	1011	1011	Thr Rwy APAPI 3° LHS

Remarks

PPR strictly by telephone. Non-radio ACFT not accepted. AD closed to all traffic except home based ACFT and gliders at weekends, PH and other notified periods. Landings absolutely prohibited when AD is closed.

Warnings

Glider launching takes place on the AD. Rwy17/35 has centre strip 23m wide, Rwy edge lights still 46m wide. Restricted area R445 2nm SE of AD

Operating Hrs Mon Thu 0700-1530 Fri 0700-1200 (Summer) +1Hr (Winter)

Circuits Variable

Landing Fee £5.00 per half tonne

Maintenance Nil

Fuel Jet A1

Disabled Facilities

Restaurants Nil
Ferry Hotel restaurant 20 mins walk

Taxis
Acacia Cars **Tel:** 01229 830055
D&S Contracts **Tel:** 01229 822020

Car Hire
Avis **Tel:** 01229 829555
Hertz **Tel:** 01229 836666

Weather Info M* AirN MWC

Operator Bae Systems (Marine) Ltd
Barrow/Walney Island Aerodrome
Cumbria, LA14 3YJ
Tel: 01229 470087/471407 (Flt Ops)
Tel: 01229 470619 (ATC)
Fax: 01229 470619

Effective date:23/11/06

525ft 17mb	2nm S of Coalville N5241.83 W00121.02	PPR	Alternative AD	Nottingham East Midlands Leicester

Non Radio	ATIS East Mids 128.225	APP East Mids 134.175	Safetycom 135.475

B

N

6' hedge

Gap in hedge

60

Crops

470m x 12m

27

Crops

Crops

6' hedge

Ponds

ACFT parking

Twy

B591

Little Battleflat Farm

To industrial estate

Coalville to Leicester railway (in cutting)

Sand quarry

Large pre-cast concrete plant with stock yard

RWY	SURFACE	TORA	LDA	LIGHTING
09/27	Grass	470x12	U/L	Nil

Displaced Thr Rwy27

Remarks
Good flat strip with clear APP Rwy09. Obstructions on Rwy27 APP see warnings.
Visual aid to location: White farm buildings S of Rwy27 Thr and Coalville-Leicester railway which crosses Rwy27 APP. Also sand quarry and large concrete works with stock yard SSW of AD.

Warnings
30ft tree bordering farm track which crosses Rwy27 Thr. B591 borders the strip to N, crops are grown to the Rwy edges. AD is beneath the East Mids CTZ, (Class D 2500ft base).
Noise: Avoid over flying local habitation. Please fly over local industrial estate to minimise disturbance.

Operating Hrs	SR-SS	**Operator**	Mrs J Lees Little Battleflat Farm Ellistown, Leicester, LE67 1FB **Tel:** 01530 832567
Circuits	1000ft QFE		
Landing Fee	Nil		
Maintenance	Nil		
Fuel	Nil		
Disabled Facilities	Nil		
Restaurant	Nil		
Taxi/Car Hire	Nil		
Weather Info	AirCen MWC		

420ft 14mb	4.5nm SE of Tamworth N5234.00 W00136.60	PPR	Alternative AD	Birmingham Tatenhill

Baxterley	APP Brimingham 118.050	A/G 120.300 only monitored during events

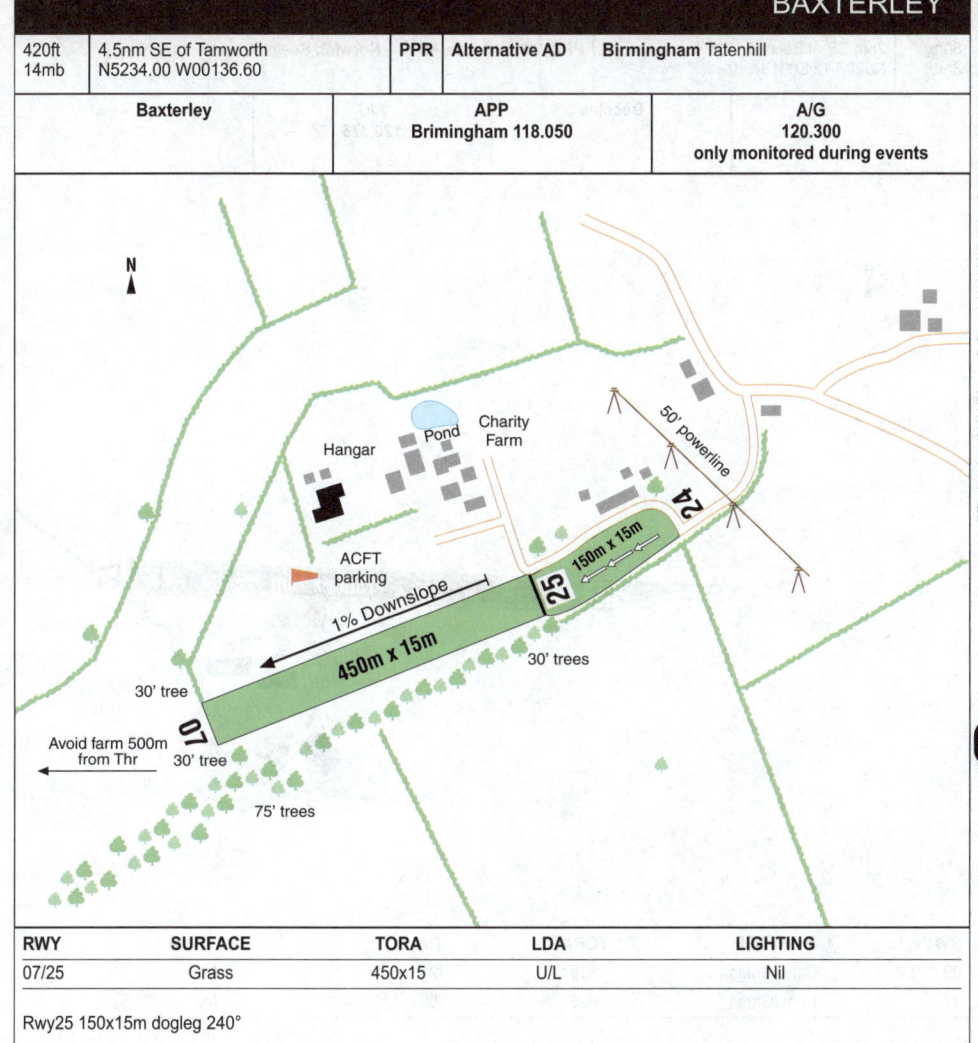

RWY	SURFACE	TORA	LDA	LIGHTING
07/25	Grass	450x15	U/L	Nil

Rwy25 150x15m dogleg 240°

Remarks
PPR by telephone. Situated close to NE corner of Birmingham CTR (base 2000ft), visitors advised to contact Birmingham APP. Organised Fly-ins and events during summer months. Check aviation press for details. BAX displayed on hangar roof.

Warnings
50ft agl power lines 70m from Rwy25 Thr (measured from beginning of dogleg extension). Mature trees to S of Rwy that may cause turbulence, they decrease in size from Rwy07 Thr towards Rwy25. 1% down slope Rwy25.Occasional model ACFT activity. **Noise:** Avoid over flying local habitation, particularly farm 500m out Rwy07 APP.

Operating Hrs	SR-SS		Operator	Ken Broomfield
Circuits	S 1000ft QFE			Charity Farm
Landing Fee	Nil			Baxterley, Warks
Maintenance	Nil			**Tel:** 01827 874572
Fuel	AVGAS available by prior arr			**Fax:** 01827 874898
Disabled Facilities	Nil			(Operates as voice info line
Restaurant	Refreshments available with 24Hrs notice			on fly-in days)
Taxi/Car Hire	Available on request			
Weather Info	AirCen MWC			

80ft 3mb	2nm SE of Beccles N5226.12 E00137.10	PPR	Alternative AD	Norwich Seething	
	Beccles			A/G 120.375	

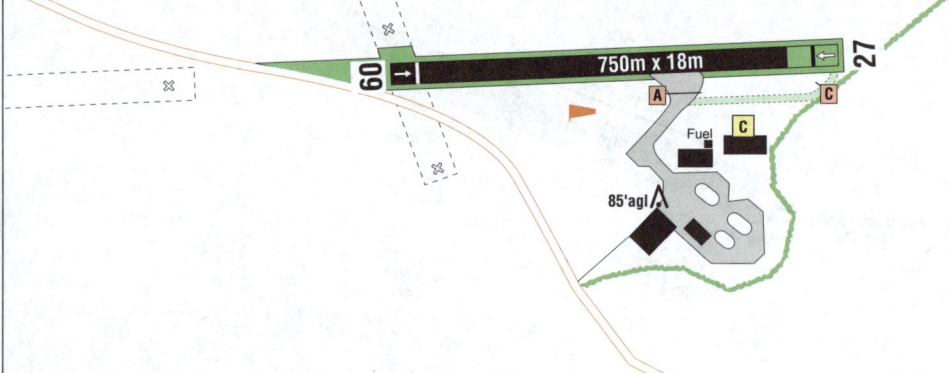

RWY	SURFACE	TORA	LDA	LIGHTING
09	Conc/Grass	568	624	Nil
27	Conc/Grass	656	568	Nil

Rwy27 first 250m Grass

Remarks
AD on part of old WWII AD. All other hard surfaces not available to ACFT.

Warnings
85ft agl mast on hangar roof. Helicopters should conform to circuit pattern. Windshear may be experienced on final APP Rwy27 in SW winds.

Noise: Avoid over flying local villages.

Operating Hrs	0900-1800 (Summer) 0900-SS (Winter)	**Operator**	Mr R D Forster
Circuits	09 RH, 27 LH 1000ft agl		Rain Air Ltd
Landing Fee	Single £8 Twin £10		Beccles Airfield
Maintenance			Beccles, LN34 7TE
Rainair	**Tel:** 07767 827172		**Tel:** 07767 827172
Fuel	AVGAS 100LL		**Fax:** 01502 475157
	available during full opening Hrs		info@rainair.co.uk
Disabled Facilities	Nil		www.rainair.co.uk
Restaurant	Tea Coffee & light snacks available		
Taxi/Car Hire			
Gold Taxi	**Tel:** 01502 711611		
Weather Info	AirS MOEx		

268ft 9mb	11.5nm NW of Belfast N5439.45 W00612.95	PPR	Alternative AD	Belfast City Newtownards

Aldergrove	ATIS 128.200	APP 128.500	RAD 120.900
DIR 129.000	TWR 118.300	GND 121.750	FIRE 121.600

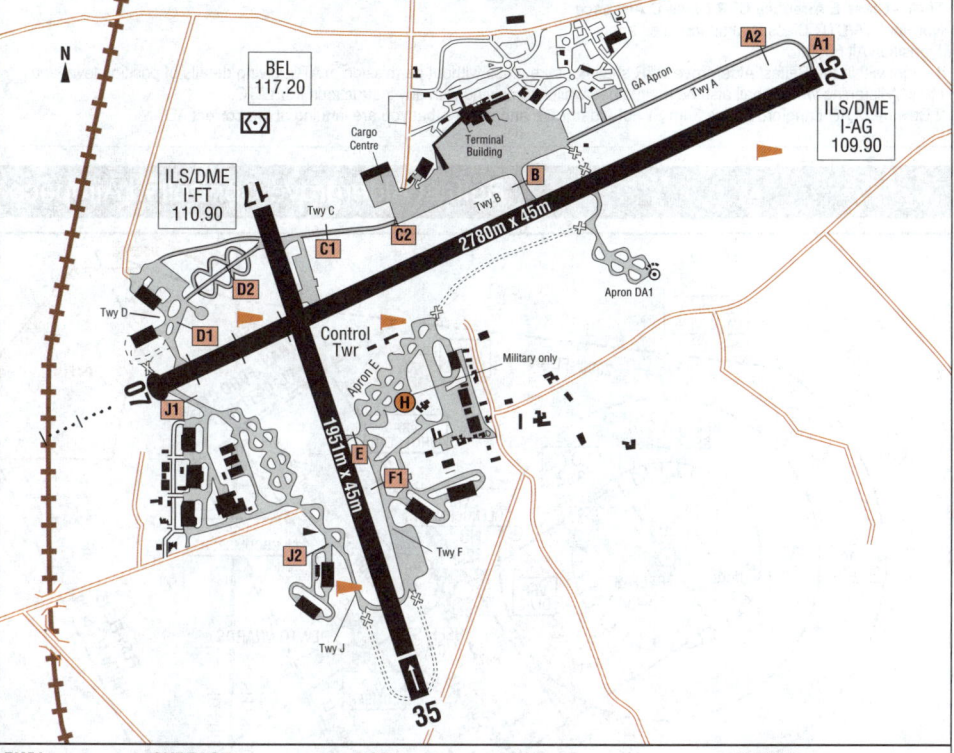

RWY	SURFACE	TORA	LDA	LIGHTING
07/25	Asphalt	2780	2780	Ap Thr Rwy PAPI 3° LHS
17	Asphalt	1791	1791	Ap Thr Rwy PAPI 3° LHS
35	Asphalt	1891	1799	Ap Thr Rwy PAPI 3° LHS

Remarks

PPR to non-radio ACFT. Pilots must present ACFT and contents to police on Arr from and prior to Dept for international flights. Twy J U/L for civil use only. ACFT below 2000kg AUW will park, normally self-manoeuvring on the GA apron, or as directed. For training contact the AD Duty Officer. Illuminated wind direction indicators at Thr Rwy17, 25 & 35. Certain customs facilities available. Handling available from Executive Jet Centre or Woodgate Executive Air Charter.
Aids to Navigation: NDB OY 332.00

Warnings

Severe bird hazard during autumn and winter months; pilots will be advised by ATC. Helicopters frequently operate at low level S of Rwy25, but will remain at least 250m from that Rwy until further cleared by ATC. Beware of AD Langford Lodge 3nm SW of Aldergrove and ensure that you are landing at the correct AD. Langford Lodge U/L AD with crossed Rwy07/25 & Rwy03/21 situated 3nm SW of Aldergrove. Model ACFT flying takes place at Langford Lodge, not above 400ft or 200ft when Rwy07 in use. Model ACFT flying at Nutts Corner, disused AD 3nm SE of Aldergrove

Operating Hrs	H24	**Disabled Facilities** Available	
Circuits	LH except Rwy25	**Handling**	**Tel:** 02894 422646 (Executive Jet Centre)
Landing Fee	Under 2mt or flights within 185km £14.99 Parking £11.99 (per 24Hrs)		**Tel:** 02894 422478 (Woodgate Air Charter)
Maintenance	Woodgate Air Maintenance **Tel:** 02894 422017		**Fax:** 02894 422640 (Executive Jet Centre) **Fax:** 02894 452649 (Woodgate Air Charter)
Fuel	JET A1 AVGAS 100LL, 0900-1700 (L) Out of Hrs by prior arr with **Tel:** 02894 422478 (Executive Air Service)	**Restaurant**	Buffet & bars available at terminal

B

Taxis	Available at Terminal Buses every 30 mins	Operator	Belfast International Airport Belfast, BT29 4AB
Car Hire			**Tel:** 02894 484281 (ATC/Flight Planning)
Avis	**Tel:** 02894 422333		**Tel:** 02894 484313 (Duty Ops/Manager)
Europcar	**Tel:** 02894 423444		**Fax:** 02894 423883 (AD)
Hertz	**Tel:** 02894 422533		
Weather Info	M T9 T18 Fax 228 A VSc BEL		

TMA – Class E Airspace CTR Class D Airspace
Normal CTA/CTR Class D Airspace rules apply
Transition Alt 6000ft
1 Flight within the Belfast Aldergrove CTR shall not take place without permission of ATC, giving details of position level and track. A listening watch shall also be maintained whilst complying with any instructions from ATC.
2 Beware of AD Langford Lodge 3nm SW of Aldergrove and ensure that you are landing at the correct AD.

Belfast Aldergrove Controlled Airspace

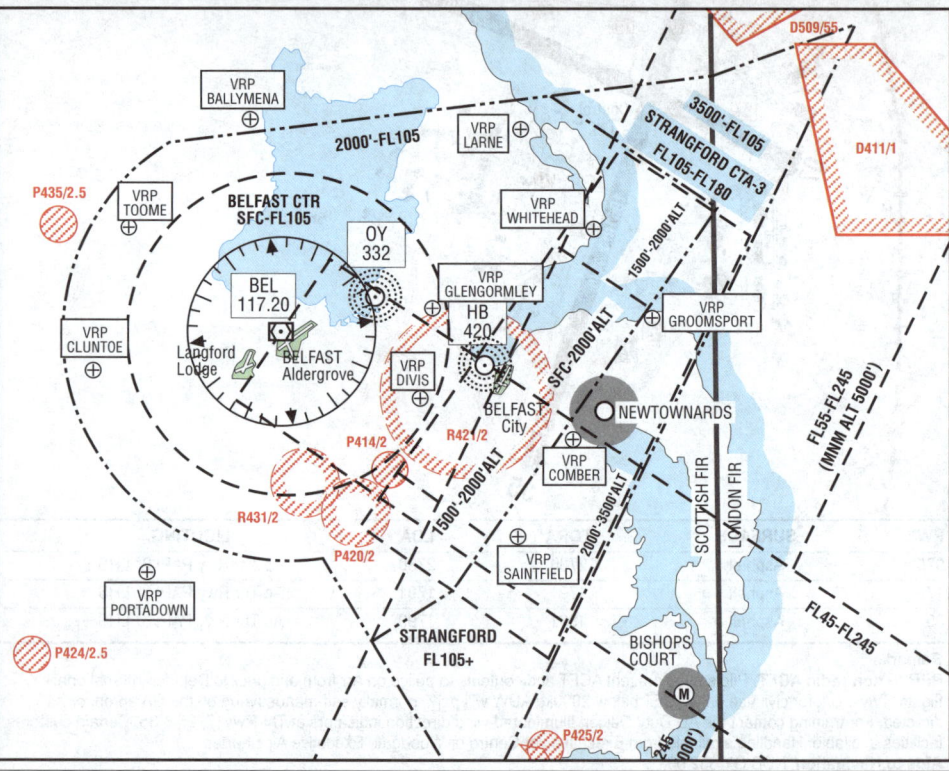

B

Visual Reference Points (VRP)

VRP	VOR/VOR	VOR/NDB	VOR/DME
Ballymena N5451.80 W00616.40	BEL 359°/MAC 218°	BEL 359°/HB 323°	BEL 359°/12nm
Cluntoe (Disused AD) N5437.23 W00632.03	BEL 263°/MAC 218°	MAC 218°/OY 260°	BEL 263°/11nm
Divis N5436.45 W00600.57	BEL 118°/DUB 014°	BEL 118°/HB 269°	BEL 118°/8nm
Glengormley (M2 J4) N5440.83 W00558.90	BEL 088°/TRN 232°	BEL 088°/HB 324°	BEL 088°/9nm
Larne N5451.20 W00549.52	BEL 056°/MAC 196°	MAC 197°/OY 048°	BEL 056°/18nm
Portadown N5425.50 W00626.85	BEL 214°/DUB 001°	DUB 001°/OY 224°	BEL 214°/16nm
Toome (Disused AD) N5445.47 W00629.67	BEL 308°/MAC 222°	MAC 222°/OY 291°	BEL 308°/11nm

EGAC

BELFAST CITY

15ft 1mb	E side of Belfast Docks N5437.08 W00552.35		**Alternative AD** **Diversion AD**	**Belfast Aldergrove** Newtownards	
	Belfast		**ATIS** 136.625		**APP** 130.850
	RAD 134.800		**TWR** 122.825		**Handling** 129.750

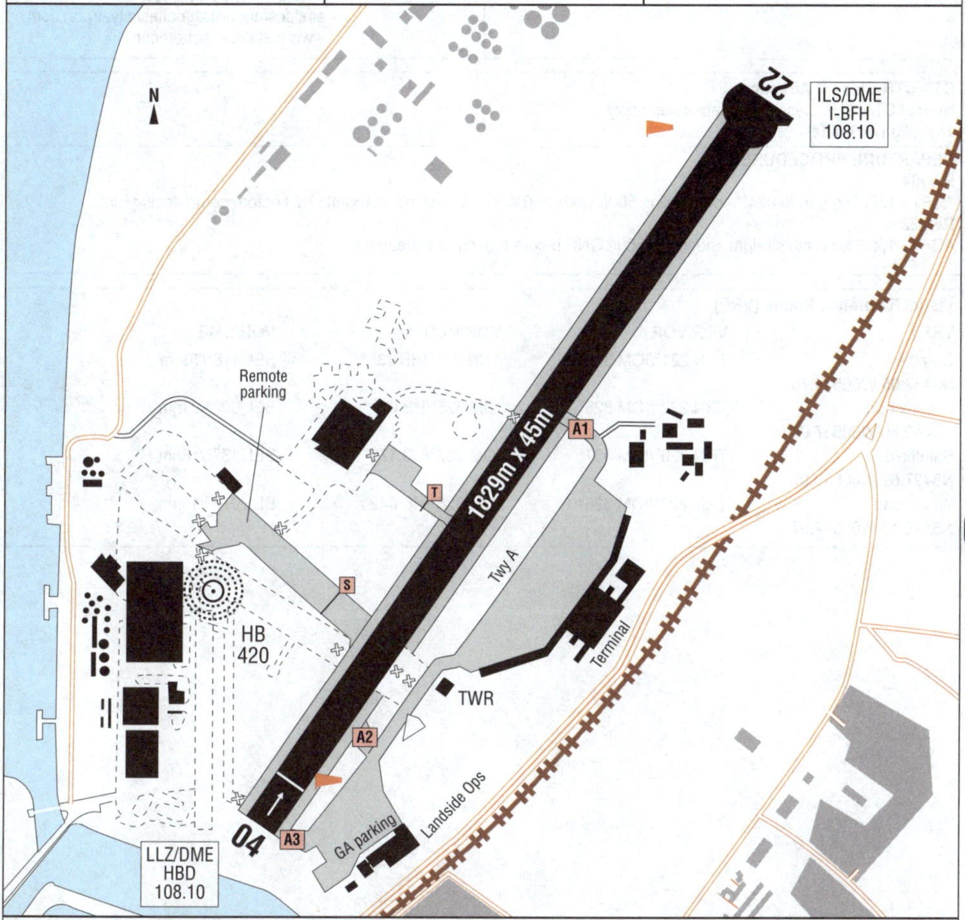

N

Remote parking

22

ILS/DME
I-BFH
108.10

1829m x 45m

A1

T

Twy A

S

HB
420

Terminal

TWR

A2

04

A3

GA parking

Landside Ops

LLZ/DME
HBD
108.10

B

RWY	SURFACE	TORA	LDA	LIGHTING
04	Asphalt	1829	1737	Ap Thr Rwy PAPI 3° LHS
22	Asphalt	1767	1767	Ap Thr Rwy PAPI 3° LHS

Remarks

ACFT Dept under IFR and VFR must comply with published noise abatement procedures if weather conditions permit.

Warnings

AD located within restricted area R421. Many obstacles on Rwy04 APP. Windshear on APP Rwy22 and Rwy04 Dept with wind 100°-160° >15kts.

Operating Hrs	Mon-Sat 0530-2030 Sun 0715-2030 (Summer) +1Hr (Winter) & by arr		**Disabled Facilities**	
Circuits	04 LH, 22 RH, 1500ft QNH			
Landing Fee	On Application Ground Handling available published Hrs		**Handling**	**Tel:** 02890 935027 **Fax:** 02890 935160
Maintenance **Fuel**	Nil JET A1 Available published Hrs		**Restaurants**	Buffet & bar at Terminal

Taxis	Airport Taxi Rank	Operator	Belfast City Airport Ltd
Car Hire			Sydenham by-Pass, Belfast, BT3 9JH
Avis	**Tel:** 02890 420404		**Tel:** 02890 454871 (ATC)
National	**Tel:** 02890 739400		**Tel:** 02890 939093 (AD)
Europcar	**Tel:** 02890 450904		**Tel:** 02890 935027
Hertz	**Tel:** 02890 732451		(Airside Standards Dept)
Weather Info	M T9 Fax 232 BEL		**Fax:** 02890 935123 (ATC)
	ATIS **Tel:** 02890 935124		**Fax:** 02890 939094 (Admin)
			Fax: 02890 90739582
			(Airside Standards Dept)
			airsidestandards@belfastcityairport.com
			www.belfastcityairport.com

CTA/CTR-Class D Airspace
Normal CTA/CTR Class D Airspace rules apply
Transition Alt 6000ft

DEPARTURE PROCEDURES
Rwy04
ACFT <13000kg turn to 034°M on passing 500ft QNH or 0.4nm DME, climb to 1500ft QNH before commencing turn.
Rwy22
ACFT <13000kg climb straight ahead to 1500ft QNH before turning onto heading.

Visual Reference Points (VRP)

VRP	VOR/VOR	VOR/NDB	VOR/DME
Comber	TRN 221°/IOM 315°	TRN 221°/HB 135°	BEL 118°/18nm
N5433.05 W00544.75			
Groomsport	TRN 222°/IOM 325°	IOM 325°/HB 074°	BEL 093°/21nm
N5440.50 W00537.08			
Saintfield	TRN 220°/IOM 307°	IOM 307°/HB 175°	BEL 137°/18nm
N5427.62 W00549.97			
Whitehead	TRN 228°/IOM 326°	IOM 326°/HB 042°	BEL 078°/19nm
N5445.17 W00542.57			

B

15ft 0mb	4nm N of Limavady (Disused AD) N5508.30 W00658.00	PPR	Alternative AD	Londonderry
Bellarena Base		**A/G 130.100**		**Used during glider ops If no response make blind calls**

13

N

11

500m x 30m

500m x 30m

29 31

4ft wire fence

Hangar

Gliding Club

Glider trailers

Private House

B

RWY	SURFACE	TORA	LDA	LIGHTING
13/31	Grass	500x30	U/L	Nil
11/29	Grass	500x30	U/L	Nil

Remarks

PPR by telephone essential. Primarily a gliding site but occasional visits by light ACFT welcome at own risk. Rwys are not marked but are the best runs on a large field of coastal turf. Although we quote Rwy widths the large run-off area make these figures academic.

Warnings

AD is surrounded to the land ward by a wire fence 4ft high. Glider launching by aerotow please keep a good lookout for tugs & gliders. High GND 1263ft amsl 1.8nm to E & SE.

Operating Hrs	0930 (L) to 30mins after SS Sat/Sun & PH 7 day Ops through Easter week & 1week in July	Taxis	Tel: 02897 7750561 Tel: 02897 7750489
Circuits	LH 1000ft QFE	Car Hire	Tel: 02870 343654
Landing Fee	Nil	Weather Info	AirN BEL
Maintenance	Nil	Operator	Ulster Gliding Club
Fuel	Nil		Bellarena Airfield Co Londonderry Northern Ireland
Disabled Facilities			Tel: 02877 750301 (Clubhouse manned at weekends)

Restaurants/ Accommodation	There are a number of restaurants in Limavady & local hotels & B&B

675ft 22mb	2.5nm NE of Torrington N5058.57 W00405.73		**PPR**	**Alternative AD Diversion AD**	**Exeter** Eaglescott
	Belle Vue			**A/G 123.575**	

1193'

Huntshaw Cross

625m x 20m

26

08

Deep Moor Scrap yard

Land fill site

RWY	SURFACE	TORA	LDA	LIGHTING
08/26	Grass	625x20	U/L	Nil

Displaced Thr Rwy26 100m

Remarks
PPR by telephone. Microlight activity. Visiting ACFT welcome at pilots own risk. Microlights with cruise speed above 45kts permitted. Taxi on the Rwy unless otherwise directed. Eaglescott AD, gliding parachuting, microlights and fixed wing activity 5nm SE avoid ATZ unless transit authorised. Camping and caravaning available. Model ACFT flying takes place occasionally S of AD.

Warnings
Devon Air Ambulance based on AD, H24 operations. Radio mast with guy lines 537agl (1193ft amsl) 300m N of AD. Beware of grazing sheep. Rwy08 APP should be sufficiently high to give good clearance of public road close to Thr. Electric fences sometimes adjacent to Rwy on S side.
Noise: Avoid over flying all settlements and farms within 3nm, particularly scrap yard 0.75nm SW of Rwy08 Thr. Dept climb out on Rwy heading until 2nm to clear area.

Operating Hrs	Mon-Sat 0800-2100 or SS Sun/PH 0900-1800 landing only until 2100	**Taxis/Car Hire**	Details available from operator
		Weather Info	AirSW MOEx
Circuits	LH 1000ft QFE	**Operator**	Mr D R Easterbrook Belle Vue Aerodrome
Landing Fee	£5 Overnight parking £3 per night		Yarnscombe, Barnstaple North Devon, EX313ND **Tel/Fax:** 01805 623113
Maintenance	Nil		**Tel:** 07971 278984
Fuel	MOGAS available 1nm distance		**Tel:** 01237 477248
Disabled Facilities	Nil		(Tony Hodder – Wingnuts Flying Club)
Restaurants	Self service refreshments at AD B&B within 1km details available from operator		

53ft 2mb	2.3nm NE of Sandown (Isle of Wight) N5040.68 W00106.57		**Alternative AD** **Diversion AD**	**Southampton** Isle of Wight
	Bembridge		**A/G** **123.250**	

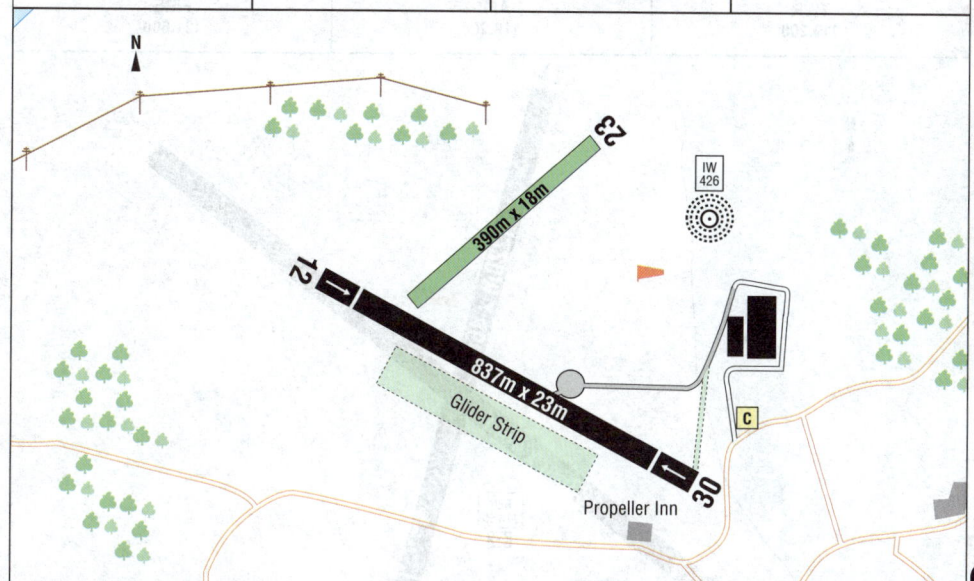

RWY	SURFACE	TORA	LDA	LIGHTING
12	Concrete	837	775	Thr Rwy APAPI 4° LHS
30	Concrete	837	751 (Day) 699 (Night)	Thr Rwy APAPI 4° LHS
23	Grass	390x10m	U/L	Nil

Rwy23 Landing Only

Remarks
Non-radio ACFT not accepted. When gliders are operating, join by over-flying the AD at 1500 ft QFE on the Rwy QDM. When overhead the upwind end of the Rwy turn left/right (depending on circuit direction) to level at circuit height (1000ft QFE) on crosswind leg prior to turning downwind. AD licensed Mon-Fri and U/L Sat-Sun. Certain customs facilities available.

Warnings
Rwy23 only to be used for landing due to high GND to SW. Trees and rising GND within the APP area to Rwy30. Severe turbulence can be experienced on APP in winds above 25kts, from 90° through S to 90°. Vehicles pass under Rwy30 APP. Manufacturers' demonstration flights may take place without notice at any time including weekends, during daylight Hrs, within 1.5nm of the AD boundary and up to 3000ft agl. Visiting ACFT must be prepared to remain clear until advised. Glider activity at times mainly weekends. Tailwinds can be experienced at both ends of Rwy.
Caution: When taxing due to width of Twy.
Noise: Avoid over flying Bembridge village and bird sanctuary 0.5nm N of AD.

Operating Hrs	U/L 0900-1800 (Summer) Mon-Fri 0900-1800 Fri-Sun 0900-1630 (Winter). Licenced Call Mon-Thu 0900-1615 Fri 0900-1215, Cat I Mon-Thu 1615-1800 Fri 1215-1800 Sat-Sun 0900-1800 (Summer), Cat I Mon-Thu 1615-1800 Fri 1215-1630 Sat-Sun 0900-1630 (Winter)	**Restaurants** Propeller Inn	**Tel:** 01983 873611 (bar snacks) at AD
		Taxis Bembridge Harbour	**Tel:** 01983 874132
		Car Hire South Wight Rentals	**Tel:** 01983 864263
Circuits	12 LH, 30 RH, 1000ft QFE Gliders will be flying opposite circuit	**Weather Info**	AirS MOEx
Landing Fee	< 750kg £5, 751-1500kg £10.75 >150001 kg £5 per 500kg Overnight parking £5 Touch & Go 50% of landing or £20 per Hr	**Operator**	B-N Group Ltd The Airport, Bembridge Isle of Wight, PO35 5PR **Tel:** 01983 871538/873331 (ATC) **Tel/Fax:** 01983 871566 ats@eghj.com www.ehgj.com
Maintenance	Nil		
Fuel	AVGAS 100LL JET A1 by prior arr during operational Hrs		
Disabled Facilities	Nil		

19ft 1mb	W side of Isle of Benbecula N5728.87 W00721.77	PPR	Alternative AD Diversion AD	Tiree Barra

Benbecula		ATIS 113.950		APP 119.200
TWR 119.200		**AFIS 119.200**		**FIRE 121.600**

RWY	SURFACE	TORA	LDA	LIGHTING
06	Bitumen	1836	1717	Ap Thr Rwy PAPI 3°LHS
24	Bitumen	1688	1688	Ap Thr Rwy PAPI 3°LHS
17/35	Asphalt	1220	1220	Nil

Starter extension Rwy35 100m (available on request, day only)

Remarks

PPR 3Hrs notice required. Built in tie-downs on N section of main apron. Low intensity battery edge lights available Rwy17/35 for air ambulance or SAR ACFT only. Rwy17/35 not available to ACFT >5700kg unless Rwy06/24 is not available & surface wind conditions dictate. Prefered Rwy for landing Rwy24 Dept Rwy06. AFIS may be provided outside APP/TWR Hrs of service by arr for Air Ambulance or SAR flights. Training flights are subject to prior approval from ATC.

Warnings

Twys closed except between Thr Rwy06 and apron. Rwy06 end lights visible for last 50m of landing run only. Rwy17/35 is subject to standing water. Grass areas soft and unsafe. Only marked Twy to be used. Intense military activity takes place in the vicinity. ATC will advise when Danger Area D701 A-E is active.

		Taxi	
Operating Hrs	Mon & Fri 0730-1645 Tue-Thu 0730-1515	Buchanan's	**Tel:** 01870 602277
	Sat 0730-0930 1345-1545 Sun 1000-1130 (Summer) +1Hr	MacVicar's	**Tel:** 01870 602307
	(Winter) & by arr	Maclennan's	**Tel:** 01870 602191
Circuits	Nil	**Car Hire**	
Landing Fee	£13 ACFT under 3MT	Maclennan's	**Tel:** 01870 602191
	VFR cash/cheque on day	**Weather Info**	M T9 Fax 234 GWC
			Tel: 01870 604818
Maintenance	Nil		
Fuel	JET A1	**Visual Reference Points (VRP)**	
	Mon-Fri 0900-1600 (L) & by arr	Lochmaddy Pier	N5735.76 W00709.40
Loganair Fuels	**Tel:** 01870 603147/0141 842 7455	Monach Islands Lighthouse	N5731.57 W00741.67
	Fax: 01870 602714	**Operator**	HIAL Benbecula Aerodrome
Disabled Facilities Nil			Balvanich, Isle of Benbecula
			Western Isles HS7 5LW
Restaurants/Accommodation			**Tel:** 01870 602051
Light refreshments available at AD Cafe/Bar			**Fax:** 01870 604826
Accommodation in local Hotels			www.highlands-and-islands-airports.uk.com

226ft 7mb	11nm SE of Oxford N5136.98 W00105.75		PPR MIL	Alternative AD Diversion AD	Oxford Wycombe

Benson	Zone 120.900	APP 136.450	TWR 127.150

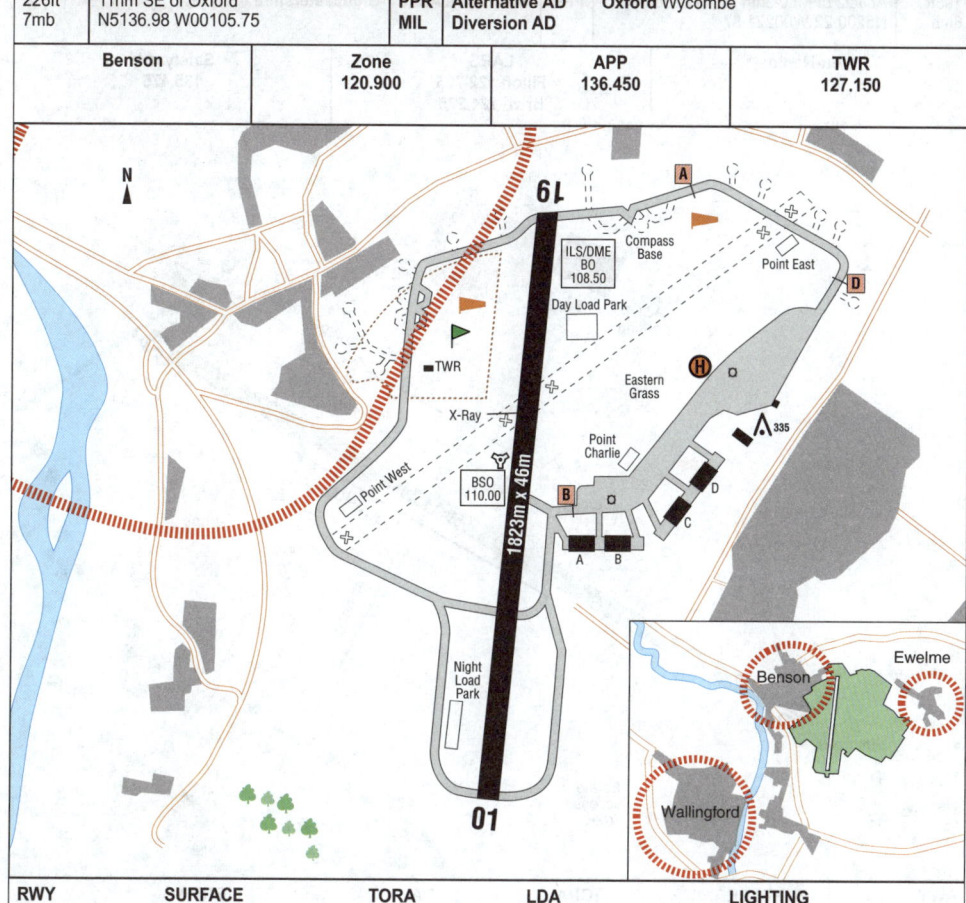

RWY	SURFACE	TORA	LDA	LIGHTING
01/19	Asph/Conc	1823	1823	Ap Thr Rwy PAPI 3°

Remarks

Strict PPR 24Hrs notice required for private ACFT. VFR Arr below 3000ft are to contact Benson Zone at least 5nm before MATZ boundary or to be under control of Brize RAD. After landings & before take-off pilots must report personally to operations. ACFT to use Twys E side Rwy01/19 only. The E parallel and Twys to W of Rwy01/19 are for use by station based ACFT only. No visitors outside Hrs. GND handling facilities available Mon-Fri 0900-1730 for visiting ACFT. Visitors restricted to landings and take-offs only.

Visual aid to location: Ibn BO Red

Warnings

Serious risk of bird strikes. Regular glider, helicopter & light ACFT activity in the MATZ. Caution on 90° bend en-route to Rwy24 from the apron, braking action poor when wet with adverse camber. High traffic density due to Oxford AIAA. Do not climb above 4000ft QNH until clear of N boundary Awy G1 S of Benson, base 4500ft. London QNH. Intensive MATZ crossing traffic. Public road crosses the undershoot of Rwy19 150m from Thr. Caution, fixed wing and rotary activity takes place outside published Hrs.

Noise: Avoid over flying the villages of Benson, Ewelme and Wallingford.

Operating Hrs	Hrs of operation	**Operator**	RAF Benson
Circuits	01 RH, 19 LH		Oxon
Landing Fee	Charges in accordance with MOD policy Contact Station Ops for details		OX10 6AA **Tel:** 01491 827015 **Tel:** 01491 827016
Maintenance	Nil		**Fax:** 01491 838747 (Ops)
Fuel	AVGAS JET A1 100LL FSII by arr		
Disabled Facilities	Nil		
Restaurants	Nil		
Taxis/Car Hire	Nil		
Weather Info	AirSE MOEx		

B

| 195ft
6mb | At Jct2 of M50 3nm SE of Ledbury
N5200.22 W00221.87 | **PPR** | **Alternative AD** | **Gloucestershire** Kemble |

| **Non-Radio** | **LARS**
Filton 122.725
Brize 124.275 | **Safetycom**
135.475 |

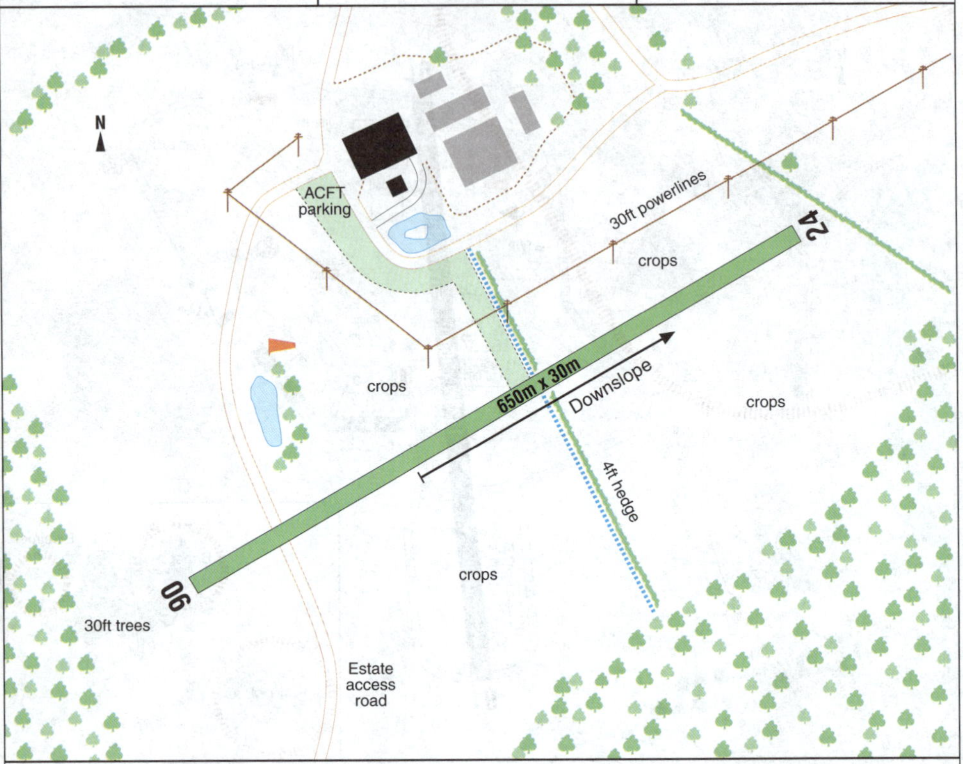

B

Chart labels:
N

ACFT parking

30ft powerlines

crops

24

650m x 30m

Downslope

crops

4ft hedge

crops

06

30ft trees

crops

Estate access road

RWY	SURFACE	TORA	LDA	LIGHTING
24/06	Grass	650x30	U/L	Nil

Remarks
PPR by telephone. Visiting ACFT welcome at pilots own risk. AD is part of a working farm. Crops may be grown up to Rwy edge.

Warnings
Rwy06 downslope particularly after Rwy midpoint. Vehicles regularly use estate access road which crosses Rwy close to Rwy06 Thr. Road surface is concrete.
Caution: Twy has a ditch on E side. Powerlines on AD diagram. Mast 0.5nm SW of AD 630ft amsl. Great Malvern HIRTA is 5nm NNE up to 4000ft amsl.
Noise: Do not over fly Bromesberrow Heath 1nm SW of AD.

Operating Hrs	SR-SS	**Operator**	Dr The Hon G Greenall Bromesberrow Place Ledbury Herefordshire HR8 1RZ **Tel:** 01531 650102 **Fax:** 01531 650056 gilgreenall@bromesberrow.com
Circuits	Variable at 1000ft QFE		
Landing Fee	Advised with PPR		
Maintenance	Nil		
Fuel	AVGAS 100LL		

Disabled Facilities

Taxi/Car Hire	Nil
Weather Info	AirSW MOEx

5ft 0mb	4nm NE of Beverley N5353.92 W00021.72	PPR	Alternative AD Diversion AD	Humberside Full Sutton
	Beverley		**A/G 123.050**	

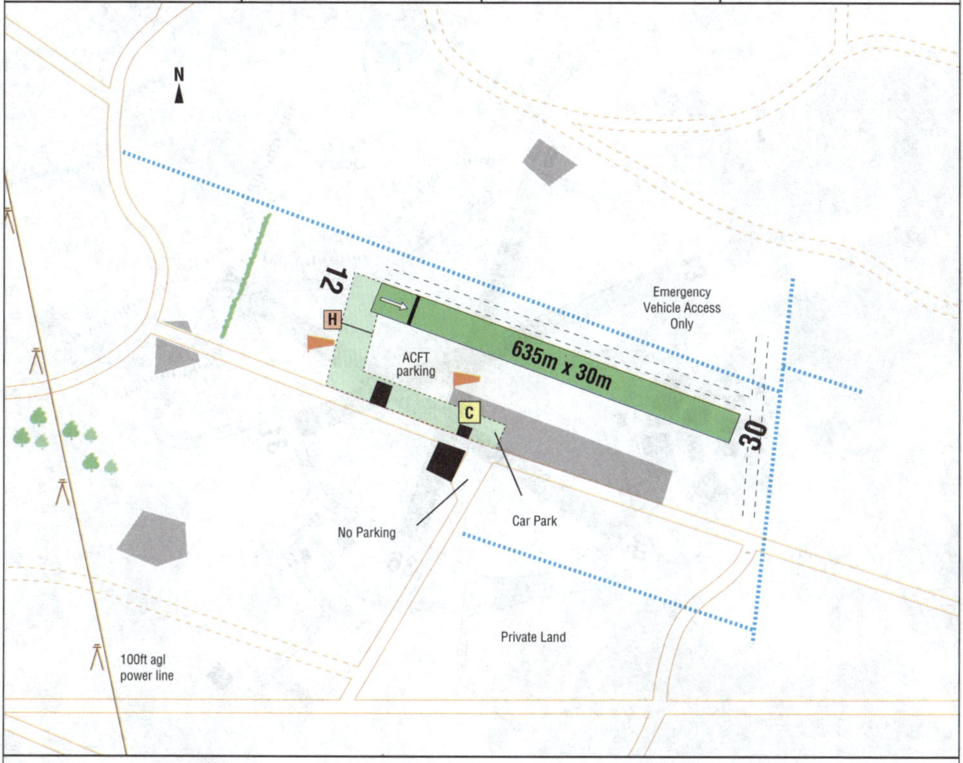

Airfield diagram: Rwy 12/30, 635m x 30m grass. H (helicopter), C (car park), ACFT parking, No Parking, Car Park, Private Land, Emergency Vehicle Access Only, 100ft agl power line.

B

RWY	SURFACE	TORA	LDA	LIGHTING
12	Grass	635	635	Nil
30	Grass	635	635	Nil

Remarks
PPR. Non-radio ACFT not accepted. Licensed AD not available for public transport flights required to use a licensed AD. Due to the proximity of electric transmission line no right base join for Rwy12. No right turns due to possible conflict with SAR helicopter activity

Warnings
Power line 100ft aal crosses extended Rwy centre line 1200m 300° from ARP. Pilots using Rwy12 must have visual contact with the power line before starting final APP. A dyke 30m before Rwy30 Thr marked with red and white warning markings. A second dyke runs parallel to Rwy30, 23m from the right-hand edge.
Noise: Avoid over flying Leven village 1.5nm E of AD. Dept from Rwy12 turn left before reaching Leven village.

Operating Hrs	0900-1800 (Summer) 0900-SS (Winter) Closed Monday	**Taxis** Alpha	**Tel:** 01482 881461
Circuits	ACFT to join overhead at 1500 ft QFE All circuits N. Avoid Leconfield ATZ 12 LH, 30 RH, 1000 ft QFE	Bradcabs **Car Hire** Andrews	**Tel:** 01482 868396 **Tel:** 01482 867360
Landing Fee	Single £7 Twin £15 (< 2 Tonne)	Beverly Ford	**Tel:** 01482 866900
Maintenance	Nil	**Weather Info**	AirN MWC
Fuel	AVGAS 100LL	**Operator**	Hull Aero Club Linley Hill Airfield Leven Humberside, HU17 5LT **Tel/Fax:** 01964 544994
Disabled Facilities			
Restaurants	Tea, coffee & sweets available in club house		

EGDD

BICESTER

267ft 9mb	0.25nm NNE of Bicester N5154.91 W00108.11	PPR	Alternative AD	Oxford Turweston

Bicester Radio	LARS Brize 124.275	A/G 129.975

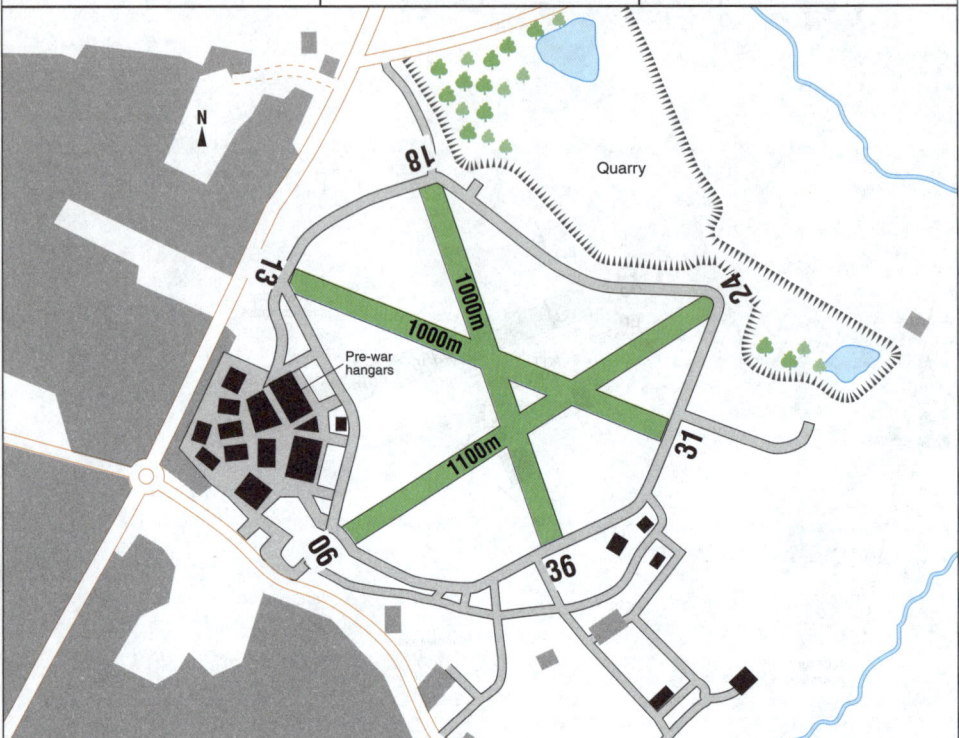

RWY	SURFACE	TORA	LDA	LIGHTING
06/24	Grass	1100	U/L	Nil
13/31	Grass	1000	U/L	Nil
18/36	Grass	1000	U/L	Nil

Remarks

PPR by telephone. Gliding takes place 7 days a week including winch launch and aerotow. AD pre-war RAF grass field. Light ACFT welcome when on gliding business. Visiting pilots keep a good lookout for Gliders at all times. AD surface is short cut grass. Although the above runs are quoted and shown on diagram. Grass area inside peri-track usable with care as GND rough due to collapsed drains. An excellent website is available which provides local info.
Visual aid to location: 'C' type hangars in technical area in SW corner of AD.

Warnings

Rwy in use recognised by launch point. Gliders and powered ACFT operate on both sides of circuit. Once established in the circuit ACFT must remain on same side and land on that side of launch point. ACFT must not cross over to another Rwy. No overhead joins at any time due cables. D129, Weston on the Green, is close to SW of AD. Visiting pilots must ensure they do not penetrate the area.

Operating Hrs	SR-SS	**Taxis/Car Hire**	Nil
Circuits	Telephone briefing essential with PPR on day of intended arrival.	**Weather Info**	AirCen MOEx
		Operator	Windrushers Gliding Club
Landing Fee	Nil		Bicester Airfield
Maintenance	Nil		Skimmingdish Lane
Fuel	AVGAS 100LL		Bicester
Disabled Facilities	Nil		Oxfordshire
			OX26 5HA
			Tel: 01869 243030
			Tel: 07986 049036
Restaurants	Food & drink available weekend		fly@windrushers.org.uk
			www.windrushers.org.uk

122

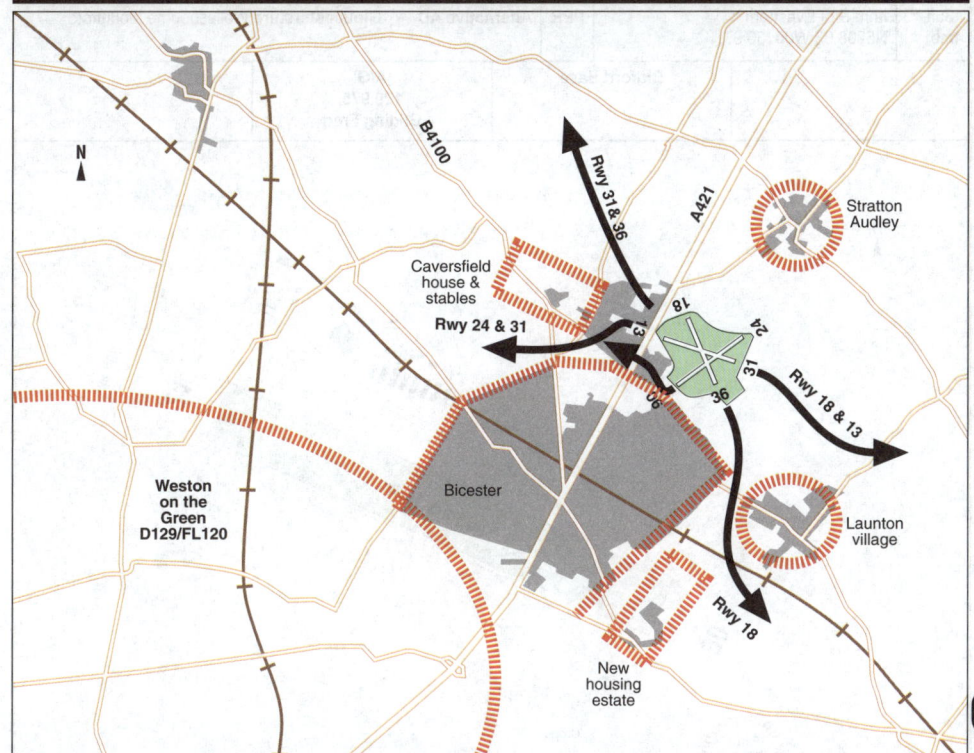

Prior to dept all non Bicester based ACFT must book out using the powered ACFT book, immediately prior to start up. A verbal dept briefing **must** be obtained from duty instructor.

All pilots must be aware of the possibility of noise complaints at ALL times. Avoid Bicester Town and all villages and farms wherever possible by following the designated routes.

Rwy24
Aim to pass L of main hangar, turn R onto 300°, keeping Bicester town on your L.

Rwy31
Turn 45° R or L after take-off to avoid Caversfield House and stables.

Low powered ACFT are advised to climb straight ahead, then turn R onto 360°.

Rwy18
Fly 130° after take off to avoid Launton village or fly 200° to pass between Launton and Bicester (following the ring road).

Rwy36 & 06
Avoid the village of Stratton Audley

NOTE: Engine failure options are severely limited from Rwy18, 36 & 06

135ft 4mb	4nm E of Evesham N5208.03 W00150.97	PPR	Alternative AD	Gloucestershire Wellesbourne Mountford

	Bidford Base	A/G 129.975 Gliding Freq	

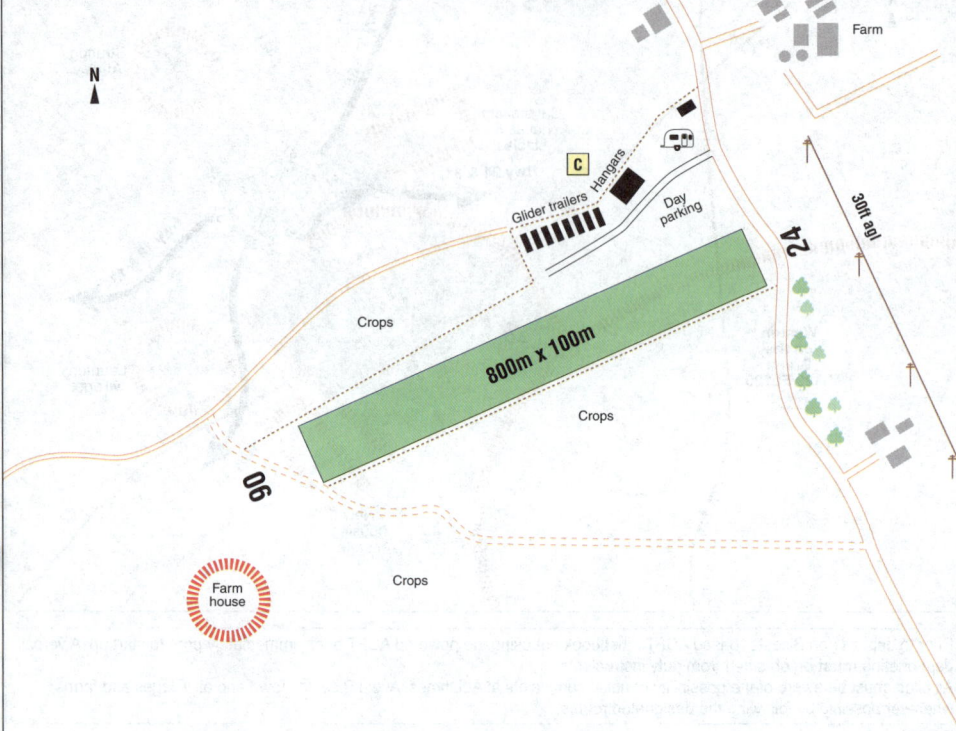

RWY	SURFACE	TORA	LDA	LIGHTING
06/24	Grass	800x100	U/L	Nil

Remarks

PPR essential by telephone for daily gliding & noise briefing. Gliding site aerotow only. Powered visitors should keep a good look out for gliders ensuring their operations are not obstructed.

Warnings

Power lines 300m from Rwy24 Thr. AD situated within Restricted area R204, applicable to helicopters only. Crops grown up to S of AD. **Noise:** Avoid over flying local villages.

Operating Hrs	0800-SS (L)	**Operator**	Bidford Gliding Centre Bidford Airfield Bidford-on-Avon Warks, B504PD **Tel:** 01789 772606 (AD) office@bidfordgliding.co.uk www.bidfordgliding.co.uk
Circuits	S 1000ft QFE		
Landing Fee	£5 Free with fuel uplift		
Maintenance	Bidford Gliding Centre (Gliders & powered ACFT) **Tel/Fax:** 01789 490174		
Fuel	AVGAS 100LL		
Disabled Facilities	Nil		
Restaurants/ Accomodation	Cafe & camping on site		
Taxis	**Tel:** 01789 262600		
Car Hire	**Tel:** 01905 792307		
Weather Info	AirCen MOEx		

598ft 20mb	12nm SSE of London N5119.85 E00001.95		Alternative AD	**Southend** Redhill

Biggin	**ATIS** 121.875 (Arr)	**APP** 129.400
RAD **Thames 132.700**	**TWR** **134.800**	**FIRE** 121.600

RWY	SURFACE	TORA	LDA	LIGHTING
03	Concrete	1778	1558	Thr Rwy APAPI 4° LHS
21	Concrete	1670	1670	Ap Thr Rwy PAPI 4° LHS
11/29	Asphalt	792	792	Nil

Remarks
PPR Helicopters. AD not available to non-radio ACFT or microlights. Hi Vis. When taking off, going around or making touch and goes remain at, or below, 500ft QFE until the upwind end of the Rwy. Joining the circuit at 1000ft QFE across the upwind end of the Rwy in use. Inbound IFR flights requiring RAD service, contact Thames RAD. AD rules and conditions of use are available from the operator.

Warnings
Windshear and turbulence on short final Rwy03 with NE winds. Aerobatic manoeuvres and low fly pasts are prohibited unless participating in an organised flying display.
Caution: Reduced wing tip clearance between taxing and parked ACFT on apron adjacent to TWR. Marshalling guidance provided.
Noise: All types of ACFT and helicopters must avoid noise sensitive areas surrounding AD, helicopters must conform to normal fixed wing Dept and circuit procedures unless otherwise instructed by ATC. Routes published by AD authority.

Operating Hrs	Mon-Fri 0630-2000 Sat-Sun & PH 0800-1900 (Summer) +1Hr (Winter)	**Landing Fee**	Up to 0.8 tonnes £17.99 0.8-1.7 tonnes £21.15
Circuits	03, 11 LH, 21, 29 RH 1000ft QFE		

Maintenance		Weather Info	M T9 Fax 236 A MOEx
Shipping & Airlines Ltd **Tel:** 01959 573404		**Operator**	Regional Airports Ltd
Falcon Flying Services **Tel:** 01959 575923			Biggin Hill Airport
Fuel	AVGAS JET A1 100LL		Kent, TN16 3BN
Disabled Facilities Nil			**Tel:** 01959 574677 (ATC)
			Tel: 01959 57111 (Admin)
Restaurants	Restaurant/refreshments available at AD		**Tel:** 01959 574737 (Fuel)
Taxis			**Tel:** 01959 574679 (Handling)
Luxury Cars	**Tel:** 01959 578550/567		**Fax:** 01959 576404 (Ops)
Car Hire			enquiries@bigginhillairport.com
Budget Rent-a-Car	**Tel:** 0208 4647736		www.bigginhillairport.com

B

Biggin Hill Noise Procedures

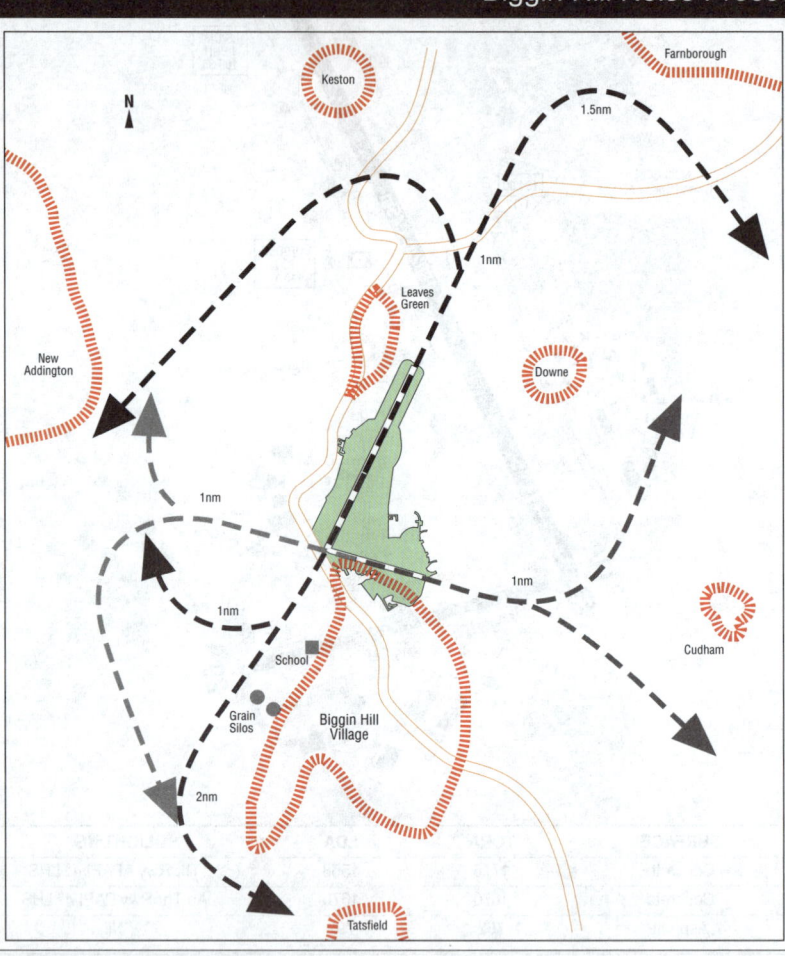

Visual Reference Points (VRP)
Sevenoaks   N5116.60 E00010.90

VFR DEPT ROUTES
Transition Alt 6000ft. Light twins and singles only

Rwy21
Dept E, S or NE avoid built up areas. Keep school and silos on LH. Straight ahead for 2nm then L turn. Dept to W or N straight ahead for 1nm then turn R. Keep school on LH

Rwy03
Dept to E or S, NE; straight ahead for 1.5nm then R turn. Caution; ACFT joining dead side Rwy03/21 at Alt 1600ft. Avoid Farnborough and Downe. Dept to N and W; straight ahead for 1nm then L turn. Avoid built up areas

Rwy29
Dept to S, E, straight ahead for 1nm then L turn. Keep silos on LH. Caution; ACFT joining dead side Rwy11/29 at Alt 1600ft. Dept to N, NE; straight ahead for 1nm R turn. Avoid Leaves Green. Dept to W; straight ahead for 1nm then turn on track.

Rwy11
All directions; straight ahead for 1nm then L or R on track. Avoid Cudham, Downe, Biggin Hill. Caution; if turning W or S due to ACFT joining dead side Rwy11/29 at Alt 1600ft.

327ft 11mb	5.5nm ESE of Birmingham N5227.23 W00144.88	**PPR**	**Alternative AD**	**Coventry** Wellesbourne Mountford

Birmingham		**ATIS** 136.025	**APP** 118.050	**DEL** 121.975
RAD 118.050 131.325		**TWR** 118.300	**GND** 121.800	**FIRE** 121.600

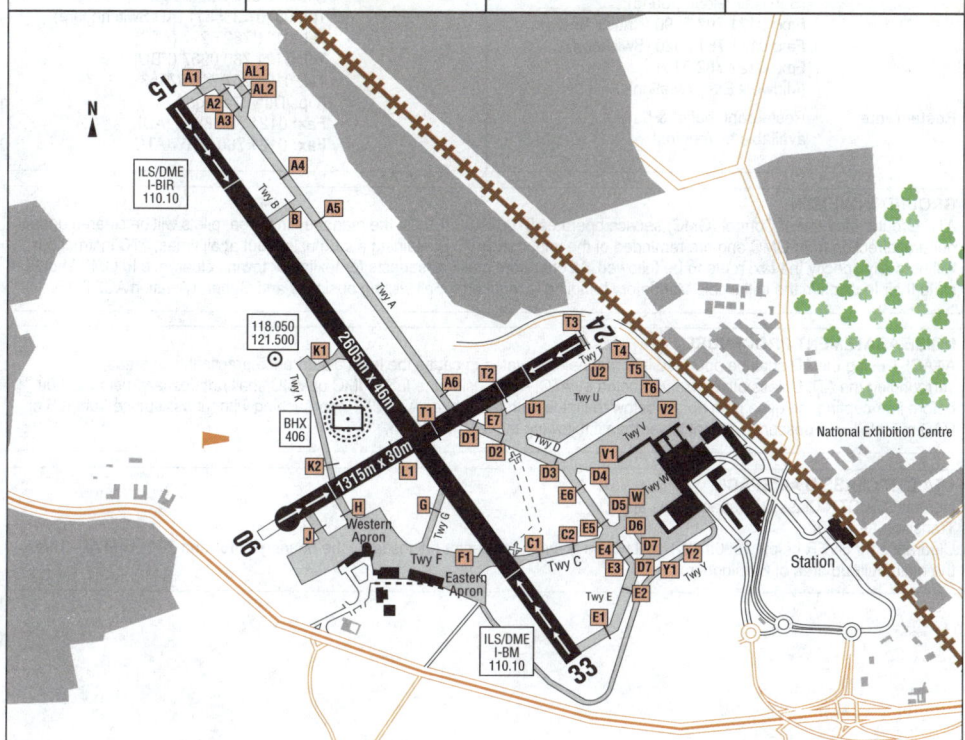

RWY	SURFACE	TORA	LDA	LIGHTING
06	Asphalt	1260	1025	APAPI 3.5° LHS
24	Asphalt	1315	1188	PAPI 3.5° LHS
15	Asphalt	2575	2279	Ap Thr Rwy PAPI 3° LHS
33	Asphalt	2600	2304	Ap Thr Rwy PAPI 3° LHS

Rwy06/24 daylight use only

Remarks
PPR to non-radio ACFT. Hi-Vis. Use of AD for training purposes is subject to the approval of Airport Managing Director & ATC. Training ACFT must climb straight ahead to1000ft aal before turning, unless otherwise instructed by ATC. Training flights including ILS go-arounds by ACFT not based at Birmingham, likely to cause nuisance to surrounding area, are prohibited between 1800-0800 (L). ACFT must not join the final APP track to any Rwy below 1500ft aal, unless they are propeller driven ACFT whose MTWA does not exceed 5700kg in which case the minimum height is 1000ft aal. Mandatory handling for GA ACFT. Marshalling is mandatory for all ACFT parking on W apron. Twy T & U are not available at night. Use minimum power manoeuvring on Twy T & U. Use of Twy C prohibited when Rwy33 in use.
Helicopter Operations: Helicopters to land as instructed by ATC.
Visual aids to location: IBn BM Green.

Warnings
Twy D to rear of stands 44-51 restricted to ACFT with max wing span of 38.5m.

Operating Hrs	H24	**Maintenance**	Available plus hangarage
Circuits	Variable circuits 1000ft QFE for light ACFT	**Fuel**	Arrange through handling agents AVTUR JET A1
Landing Fee	Up to 1MT £14.80 Up to 1.5MT £22.21 Up to 2MT £29.61 Up to 3MT £39.52 & parking	**Disabled Facilities**	Available

B

Handling	Tel: 0121 782 1999 (Signature)	Taxis	Available at Terminal
	Tel: 0121 767 7715 (Aviance)	Car Hire	
	Tel: 0121 767 772 (Servisair Globeground)	Avis	Tel: 0121 782 6183
	Tel: 0121 767 7518 (British Airways)	Hertz	Tel: 0121 782 5158
	Tel: 0121 781 0005 (Swissport)	Europcar	Tel: 0121 782 6507
	Tel: 0121 782 5100	Weather Info	M T9 T18 Fax 238 A VS MWC
	(Midwest Exec Aviation)		ATIS Tel: 0121 780 0910
	Fax: 0121 7821899 (Signature)	Operator	Birmingham International Airport Ltd
	Fax: 0121 782 7766		Birmingham, B26 3QJ
	(Servisair Globeground)		Tel: 08707 335511 (AD Switchboard)
	Fax: 0121 767 7590 (British Airways)		Tel: 0121 782 6227 (ATC)
	Fax: 0121 781 0020 (Swissport)		Tel: 0121 780 0907 (FBU)
	Fax: 0121 782 5101		Tel: 0121 767 7139/7153
	(Midwest Exec Aviation)		(Ops/Duty Manager)
Restaurants	Restaurant, buffet & bar		Fax: 0121 782 8802 (AD)
	available at Terminal		Fax: 0121 780 0917 (ATC)

GROUND MOVEMENT

ATC Ground Movement Control (GMC) service operates 0700-2100 (L). On the manoeuvring area, pilots will be cleared under general direction from GMC and are reminded of the importance of maintaining a careful lookout at all times. ATC instructions will normally specify the taxi route to be followed. All operators making requests for taxiing or towing clearance to GMC should state their location in the initial call. Mandatory handling is required for all visiting business and General Aviation ACFT.

NOISE ABATEMENT PROCEDURE

All ACFT using the AD shall be operated in a manner calculated to cause the least disturbance practicable in areas surrounding the AD. Unless otherwise instructed by ATC, ACFT using the ILS in IMC or VMC shall not descend below 2000ft before intercepting the glide path nor fly below the glide path there after. An ACFT approaching without assistance from ILS or RAD must follow a descent path not lower than if following the ILS glide path.

CTA/CTR CLASS D AIRSPACE

Normal CTA/CTR Class D Airspace rules apply.
Transition Alt 4000ft
Clearance for SVFR below 1500ft QNH will not be given in the sector enclosed by the bearings 245° and 360° from AD. This is the main built-up area of Birmingham.

EGLK

BLACKBUSHE

325ft 11mb	8.5nm SE by S of Reading N5119.43 W00050.85	**PPR**	**Alternative AD Diversion AD**	Farnborough Fairoaks

Blackbushe	**APP** Farnborough 125.250	**AFIS** 122.300	**A/G** 122.300

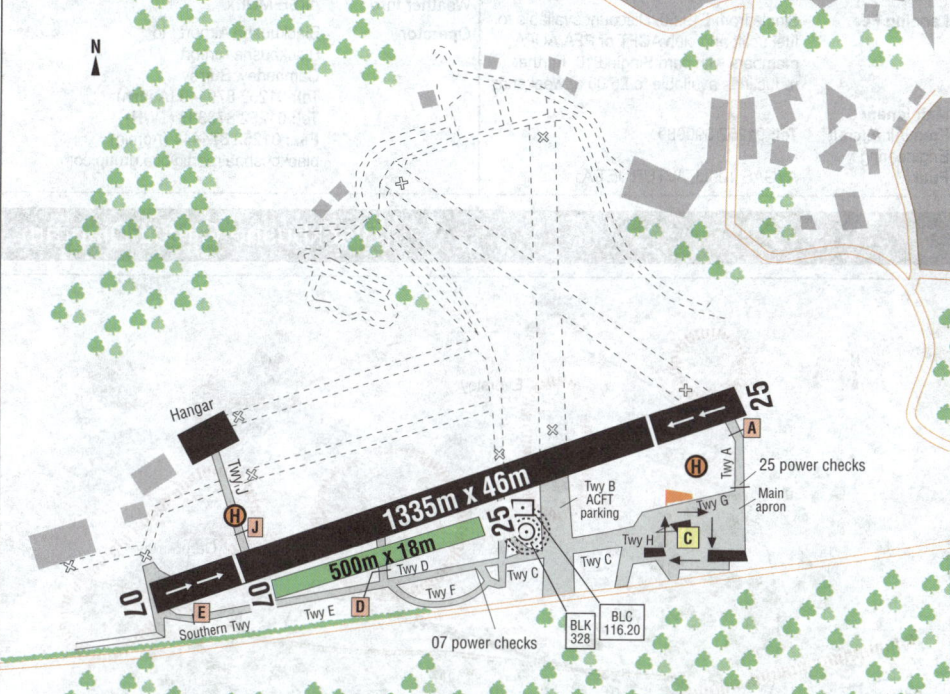

RWY	SURFACE	TORA	LDA	LIGHTING
07	Asphalt	1237	1102	Thr Rwy PAPI 3.1° LHS
25	Asphalt	1237	1059	Thr Rwy PAPI 3.1° LHS
07/25	Grass		Helicopters Only	CHAPI 5°

Helipad On Twy J

Remarks

PPR by telephone. Some PHs AD is not available for ACFT required to use a licensed AD. APP Blackbushe remaining N of the M3 to avoid ACFT using Farnborough. Pilots are responsible for their passengers whilst on the airside of AD. Due to planning restrictions the following ACFT may not land at this AD: Cessna Skymaster (C336/337/L); Dornier 28D Sky Servant(D08D/L); Gates Learjet 23, 24, 25, 28, 29 (LR23, 24, 25, 28/L, 29/M); Piaggio P166 (P166/L).
Visual Aids to location: Abn White flashing.

Warnings

AD is frequently used outside the published Hrs of operation by fixed and rotary wing ACFT. Pilots operating at any time in the vicinity of the AD should therefore call Blackbushe AFIS/AG to check if the AD is active. Pilots are further cautioned that no reply does not necessarily imply no traffic in the ATZ, and a very careful lookout should be maintained. Avoidance of the ATZ if at all possible is preferable. Helicopter specific lighting aids have been installed on Twy J, these consist of illuminated Tee and CHAPI 5.0°. Fixed-wing pilots should ignore indications from this lighting. An additional AD beacon situated on the roof of a hangar (287° 0.3nm from the ARP) may be illuminated, but only outside notified AD Hrs. A section of disused Rwy01/19, to the S of Rwy07/25, is marked as ACFT parking area. The grassed surface S of Rwy07/25 grass between Twys C & D is unsuitable for use by certain types of helicopter due to its poor grading. Pilots are cautioned to positively ascertain that the grading of this area is suitable for their operational requirements. Visual glide slope guidance signals for both Rwy07& 25 are visible to the S of the extended Rwy centre lines where normal obstacle clearance is not guaranteed. They should not be used until aligned with the Rwy. A public footpath crosses the centre of the AD from SE to NW. Fuel normally available on PH. Caution large concentrations of birds on and in the vicinity of AD.
Noise: Avoid over flying Yateley to NE and Hartley-Wintney W of AD

Operating Hrs	0700-1700 (Summer) +1Hr (Winter) & by arr
Circuits	All circuits S of AD Single engined ACFT 800ft QFE Twin engined & executive ACFT 1200ft QFE Night circuit height for all ACFT 1000ft QFE
Landing Fee	Single from £19.50. Discount available for fuel uplift and club ACFT or PFA/AOPA members with card Single £10. Further reductions available to £5.00 at weekends
Maintenance PremiAir Aircraft Engineering	Tel: 01252 890089
Fuel	AVGAS 100LL AVTUR JET A1

Disabled Facilities	Nil
Restaurants	Club facilities – Biggles Bistro
Taxis A2B Taxis	Tel: 01276 64488/64499
Car Hire Avis Europcar	Tel: 01344 417417 Tel: 01276 451570
Weather Info	AirSE MOEx
Operator	Blackbushe Airport Ltd Blackbushe Airport Camberley, Surrey Tel: 01252 879449 (Admin) Tel: 01252 873338 (TWR) Fax: 01252 874444 (Admin) blackbusheairport@bca.group.com

Blackbushe Circuit Diagram

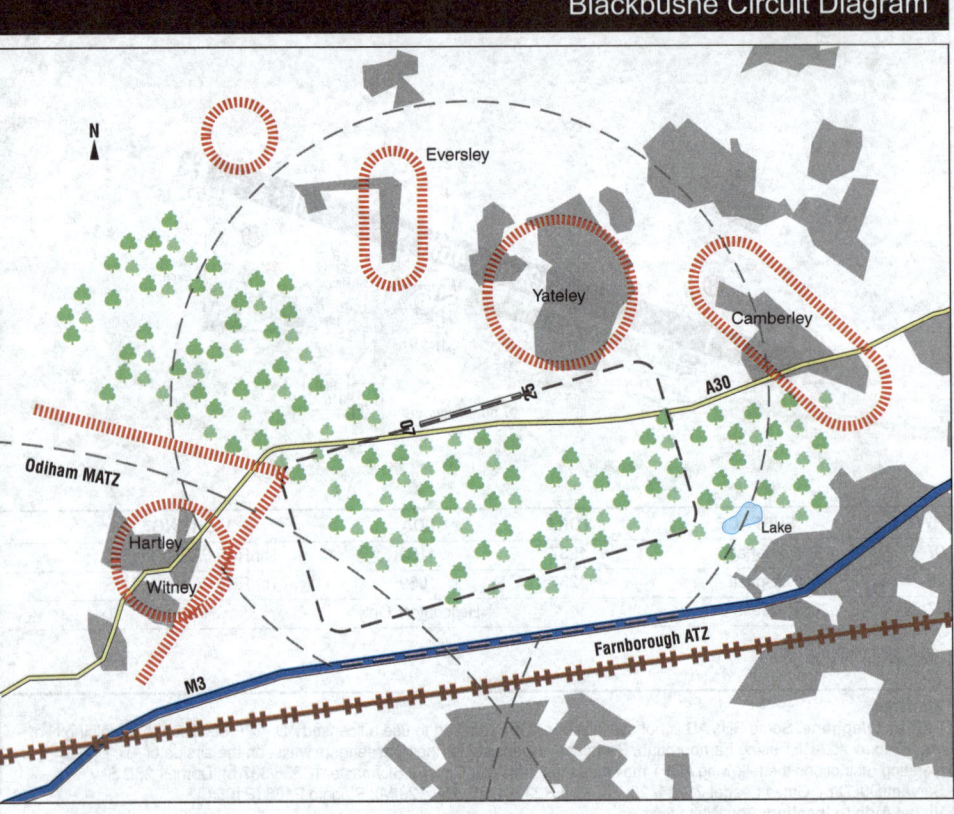

EGNH   BLACKPOOL

34ft 1mb	2.6nm SSE of Blackpool N5346.30 W00301.72	PPR	Alternative AD	Warton Woodvale

Blackpool	ATIS 121.750	APP Warton 129.525	APP 119.950
RAD 135.950	TWR 118.400	FIRE 121.600	

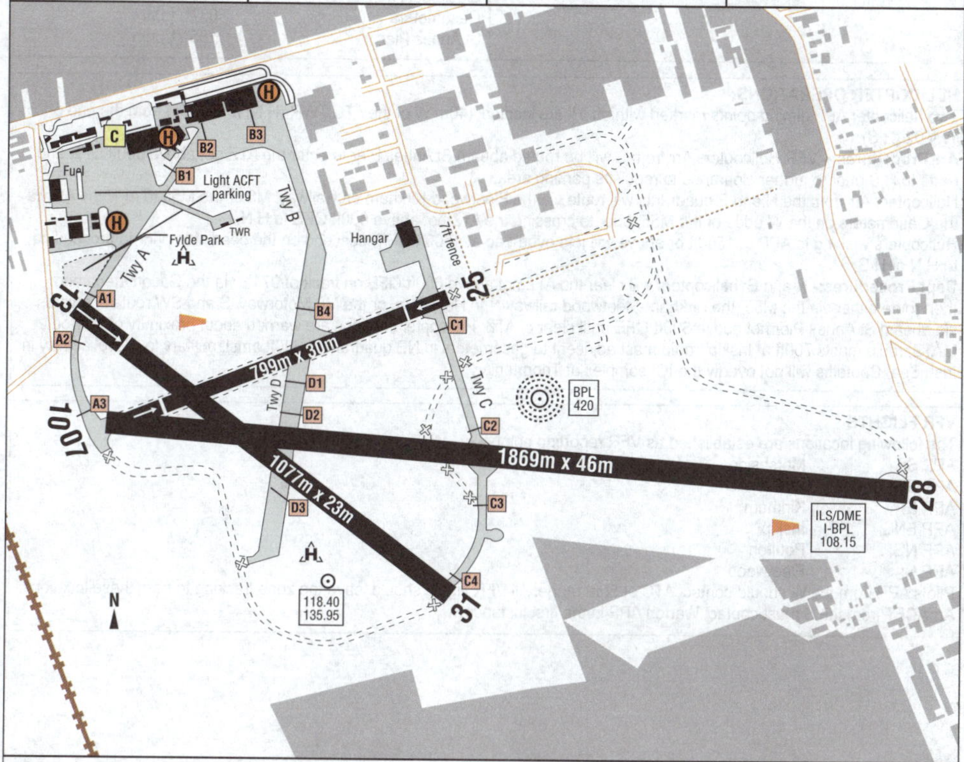

Effective date:23/11/06

B

RWY	SURFACE	TORA	LDA	LIGHTING
07	Asphalt	700	610	Nil
25	Asphalt	799	700	Nil
10/28	Asphalt	1869	1869	Ap Thr Rwy PAPI 3°
13	Asphalt	1077	927	Nil
31	Asphalt	1077	1077	Nil

Remarks

PPR to non-radio ACFT. Hi-Vis. All inbound ACFT to make initial call to APP. Landing and taxiing on grass areas by fixed-wing ACFT is prohibited. The portion of Twy which passes between the hangars and the ACFT parking area is only suitable for ACFT with wingspan of up to 19m. Grass parking known as Fylde Park is provided to N of Rwy13 under shoot. ACFT using Blackpool AD do so in accordance with Blackpool AD terms and conditions (available on application). All Depts must book out with ATC via telephone.

Warnings

Operating Hrs	0600-2000 (Summer) 0700-2100 (Winter) & by arr
Circuits	25, 28, 31 RH 07, 10, 13 LH
Landing Fee	0-500kgs £7.50 501-1000kgs £15.00 1001-1500kgs £22.50 PFA discount £2.00 on the above rates with membership card
Maintenance	Westair **Tel:** 01253 404925
Fuel	AVGAS JET A1 100LL

Handling
Hanger 3   **Tel:** 01253 407070
                Fax: 01253 405100

Disabled Facilities

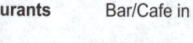

Restaurants   Bar/Cafe in terminal
Taxis
Black Taxi   Freephone in terminal
Car Hire
Hertz   **Tel:** 01253 344010
Weather Info   M T9 Fax 242 A VN MWC

131

Operator	Blackpool Airport Ltd Blackpool Airport, Blackpool Lancashire, FY4 2QY **Tel:** 01253 343434 **Fax:** 01253 405009 **Tel:** 01253 472527 (ATC) **Fax:** 01253 402004 (ATC)

Visual Reference Points (VRP)

Fleetwood Golf Course	N5355.13 W00302.72
Inskip Disused AD	N5349.63 W00250.05
Kirkham	N5346.95 W00252.28
Marshide	N5341.78 W00258.23
Poulton Railway Station	N5350.90 W00259.42

Pilots may also be requested to route via the following positions

Blackpool (Tall) TWR	338°/2.6nm
Gasometers	037°/1.8nm
St Annes Pier	185°/1.5nm

HELICOPTER OPERATIONS
Two helicopter APP aiming points marked with an 'H' are located 140m W of the ATC TWR (H N) and 100m from the end of Twy 02 (H S).

Arr Procedures – VFR Helicopters Arr from S will be routed abeam St Annes Pier to enter the ATZ not above 600ft QFE and route to H S prior to further clearance to requisite parking area.

Helicopters Arr from the N and E quadrants will route via the Fleetwood-Kirkham on Railway. M6 or the M55 to APP the AD via the Gasometers on the W edge of the M55, prior to crossing the ATZ not above 600ft QFE to H N.

Helicopters wishing to APP at 1500ft or above will join overhead at 1500ft QFE, descend on the dead side prior to proceeding to H N or H S.

Dept Procedures:- N and E: helicopters will clear the ATZ not above 600ft QFE on track of 071°, via the Gasometers, and then route either via the M55, the Kirkham-Fleetwood railway N to Heysham, or the M6 Motorway. S and SW route seawards via abeam St Annes Pier not above 600ft QFE until clear of ATZ. Helicopter captains are warned about proximity of Warton MATZ, radio masts 700ft at Inskip, radio mast adjacent to gasometers in NE quadrant at 300ft amsl, military low level activity in Irish Sea. Captains will not overfly the ICI complex at Thornton.

VFR FLIGHTS
The following locations are established as VFR reporting points:

APP S:	Marshside
APP SE:	Warton AD
APP E:	Kirkham
APP ENE:	Inskip
APP NE:	Poulton
APP N:	Fleetwood

Pilots APP from the W should contact ATC at 5nm range. All VFR flights should leave the zone tracking to/from these locations. Arr ACFT from the S must contact Warton APP in the first instance.

650ft 21mb	3.5nm NE of Bodmin N5029.98 W00439.95	PPR	Alternative AD Diversion AD	St Mawgan Perranporth

Bodmin	APP St Mawgan 128.725	A/G 122.700

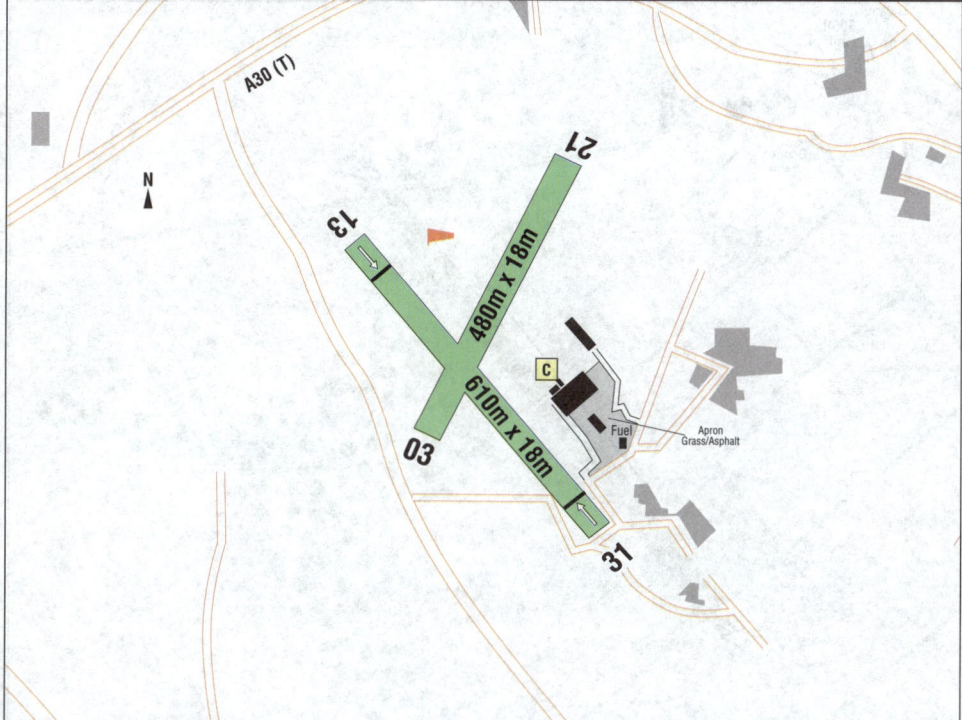

RWY	SURFACE	TORA	LDA	LIGHTING
03/21	Grass	480	480	Nil
13	Grass	598	598	Nil
31	Grass	610	540	Nil

Remarks
PPR. AD not available for night flying. AD limited to ACFT take off weight <2490kg. AD closed 2200-0700 (L). Customs available by arr.

Warnings
Windshear may be encountered in strong winds. Due to the convex nature of the AD the Rwy stop-ends are not visible from the take-off position.
Caution: When taxiing to the apron or fuel bay. Rifle range 1.4nm to E safety height 1000ft

Operating Hrs	0830-1930 (Summer) 0830-1730 or SS (Winter) & by arr	**Weather Info**	AirSW MOEx
Circuits	03, 31 LH, 21, 13 RH 800 ft QFE	**Operator**	Cornwall Flying Club Ltd Bodmin Airfield, Cardinham, Bodmin, Cornwall, PL30 4BU **Tel:** 01208 821419 **Tel:** 01208 821463 **Fax:** 01208 821711
Landing Fee	Single £8		
Maintenance	Hangarage available		
Fuel	AVGAS 100LL		
Disabled Facilities	Nil		
Restaurants	Restaurant open 5 days a week 1030-1500 (L) also pilot shop		
Taxis Bodmin Taxi Serv	**Tel:** 01208 72345		
Car Hire Ford Rental	**Tel:** 01208 893006		

B

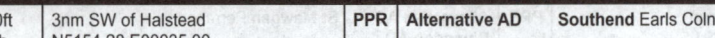

BOONES FARM

270ft 9mb	3nm SW of Halstead N5154.28 E00035.00	PPR	Alternative AD	Southend Earls Colne

Non-Radio	ATIS Stansted 127.175	APP Essex RAD 120.625	Safetycom 135.475

(Airfield diagram: Runway 04/22 grass strip 738m x 46m, "Slight dip" in centre. Hangars and Boones Farm to the NW. 305ft agl mast NW. Crops and trees to the E/SE. 30ft powerlines crossing NE. 45ft tree, 30ft tree, 3ft hedge near Rwy22 threshold. 3ft hedge at Rwy04 threshold. North arrow pointing up.)

RWY	SURFACE	TORA	LDA	LIGHTING
04/22	Grass	738x46	U/L	Nil

Slight dip in centre of Rwy

Remarks
PPR. Visiting ACFT welcome at pilots own risk. AD close to London Stansted CTA/CTR and Earls Colne ATZ visiting pilots are advised to exercise caution with flight planning. Avoid inadvertent penetration of controlled airspace. Essex RAD is NOT a LARS unit. ACFT operating in vicinity of CTA/CTR are advised to select 7000 with mode C on transponder, (If fitted), and monitor the Essex RAD freq

Warnings
Occasional Deer may cross strip. Radio mast 305ft agl to NW of AD. Low hedge at both Thr, 2 trees to N of Rwy22 Thr. Trees close to S of Rwy may cause turbulence. 30ft power line crosses Rwy22 APP 450m from Thr.
Noise: Avoid over flying village of High Garret NW or AD or local habitation.

Operating Hrs	SR-SS	**Weather Info**	AirCen MOEx
Circuits	1000ft QFE to SE only	**Operator**	Mr John M Wicks
Landing Fee	Nil		Boones Farm
Maintenance	Nil		Hallstead Road
Fuel	Nil		High Garret
			Braintree
Disabled Facilities			Essex CM7 5PB
			Tel: 01376 348882
			wixies@aol.com

Restaurants
Hare & Hounds   **Tel:** 01376 330330

Taxis/Car Hire   **Tel:** 01376 330330

407ft 13mb	1.5nm SE of Amesbury N5109.13 W00144.84	PPR MIL	Alternative AD Diversion AD	Bournemouth Thruxton

Boscombe	Zone 126.700	APP 130.000	TWR 130.750	GND 130.750

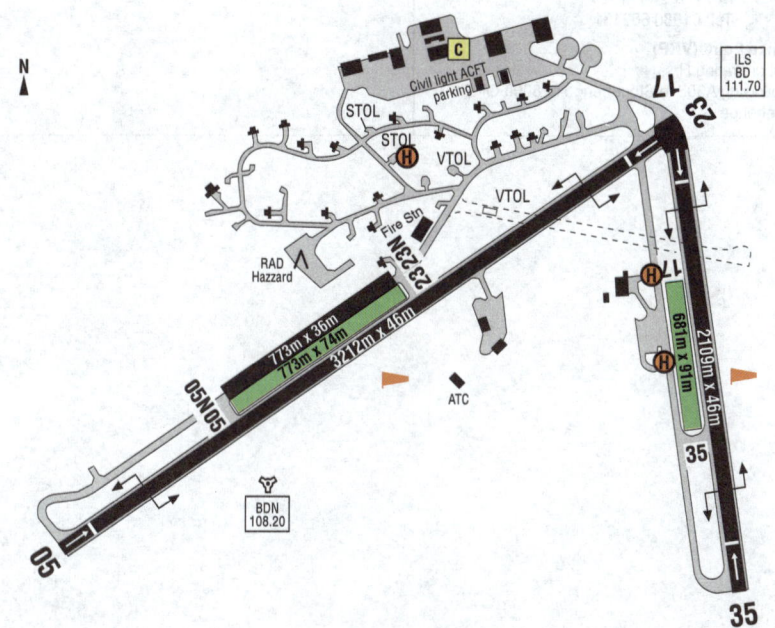

RWY	SURFACE	TORA	LDA	LIGHTING
05	Asphalt	3212	3209	Ap Thr Rwy PAPI 3°
23	Asphalt	3212	3109	Ap Thr Rwy PAPI 3°
17/35	Asphalt	1913	1913	Ap Thr Rwy PAPI 3°
17/35	Grass	681	681	Nil
23/05N	Asphalt	773	773	Nil
23/05	Grass	773	773	Nil

Remarks

Strict PPR from Main Flying Ops. PPR to civil ACFT is limited Mon-Thur 0900-1700 Fri 0900-1600. No training flights. Pilots operating over Salisbury Plain must, before recovery to Boscombe Down, establish RT contact for RAD Sequencing and avoidance of circuit traffic. Visiting ACFT to call at min 20nm. All procedures within 10nm and below 3000ft are flown on Boscombe QFE. After landing visiting ACFT must obtain ATC permission before vacating Rwy. Outside published Hrs VHF only ACFT inbound call Boscombe Zone 20nm from AD. If no reply contact Boscombe TWR for info on ACFT ops. No response on either freq means ATC closed. The ATZ will remain active with Bustard Flying Club ACFT.

Warnings

Intensive test flying at this AD. Beware of close proximity 'Salisbury Plain' Danger Areas D123, D124, D125, D126 – DACS Salisbury Ops and also of D127 Porton Down. After dark up to 2359 Hrs Mon-Fri MATZ may contain unlit ACFT, AD and obstruction lights may be extinguished during flying. Light ACFT & heli flying in daylight outside AD Hrs. Radiation hazard (525ft radius up to 500ft agl extends to within 500ft of Rwy05/23). Possible inadvertent actuation of electrically initiated explosive devices. RAF barriers installed for all Rwys. Arrester gears are fitted 435m from 05 Thr, 372m from 23 Thr, 273m from 17 Thr, 427m from 35 Thr. Rwy05/23 overrun cable normally up. Rwy17/35 both cables normally down. No gliding permitted. No deadside on AD below 1200ft QFE. Helicopters operate southside normally up to 500ft QFE. Light ACFT operate to parallel section of N Twy from non-standard 800ft N circuit

Noise: Avoid over flying Cholderton Rare Breeds Farm, Arundel Farm and all nearby villages

Operating Hrs		Circuits	Variable
Military	Mon-Thu 0830-1730 Fri 0830-1630 (L)	**Landing Fee**	Charges in accordance with MOD policy
Civil	Mon-Thu 0900-1700 Fri 0900-1600 (L)		Contact Station Ops for details

| Maintenance | Nil |
| Fuel | AVGAS 100LL JET A1 with FSII |

Disabled Facilities

Restaurants	Nil
Taxis/Car Hire	Available by private arr
Weather Info	M T Fax 244 MOEx **Tel**: 01980 662131

Visual Reference Point (VRP)
Outside normal operating Hrs.
Join from W, following A303 to Stonehenge at 800ft QFE.
Report at Stonehenge

| Operator | MOD Boscombe Down Salisbury Wiltshire SP4 0JF **Tel:** 01980 663051/2 (Ops) **Tel:** 01980 663246/2114 (ATC) **Fax:** 01980 663225 |

B

70ft 2mb	4nm SSW of RAF Marham N5235.52 E00030.95	PPR	Alternative AD	Norwich Old Buckenham

Non-Radio	APP Marham 124.150	Safetycom 135.475

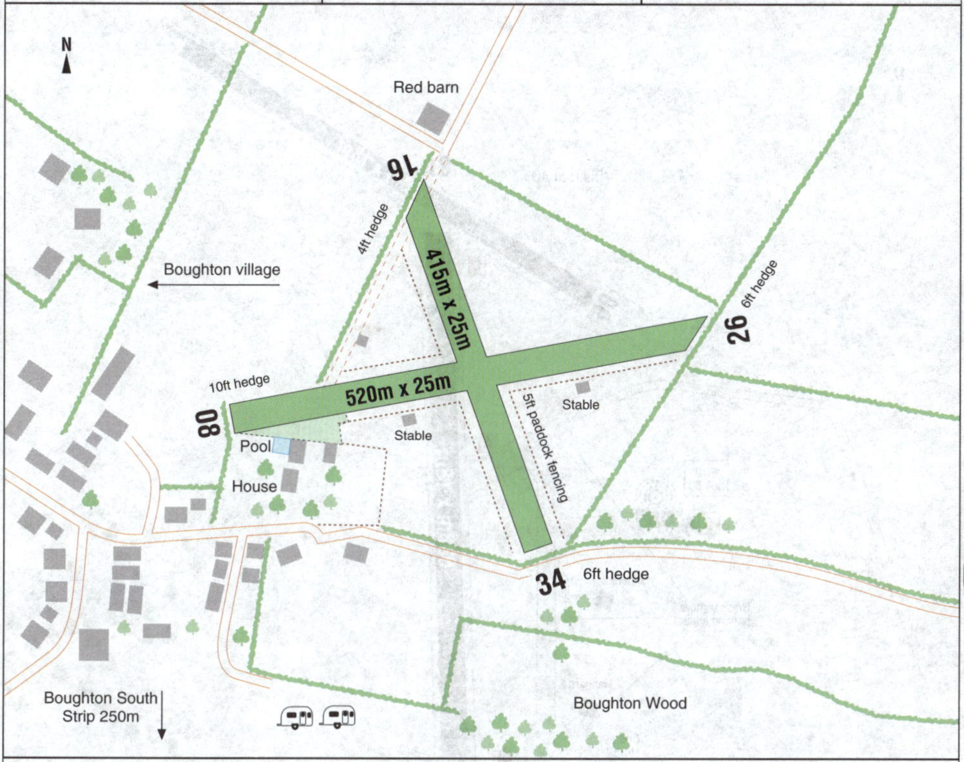

N

Red barn

16

Boughton village

4ft hedge

415m x 25m

6ft hedge

26

10ft hedge

520m x 25m

5ft paddock fencing

Stable

08

Pool

Stable

House

34   6ft hedge

Boughton South Strip 250m

Boughton Wood

B

RWY	SURFACE	TORA	LDA	LIGHTING
08/26	Grass	520x25	U/L	Nil
16/34	Grass	415x25	U/L	Nil

Remarks
PPR by telephone. Visiting pilots welcome at own risk. Free lift to Oxborough Hall for National Trust members.

Warnings
AD situated within Marham MATZ. Arr/Dept ACFT contact Marham APP. Rwys are bordered by 5ft paddock fence. A 6ft hedge runs across Rwy26 Thr. Caution: There is another Boughton AD (single Rwy) to S.
Noise: Avoid over flying the village of Boughton.

Operating Hrs	SR-SS + 30 mins	**Weather Info**	AirS MOEx
Circuits	See remarks	**Operator**	Mr P Coulten
Landing Fee	Nil		Oxborough Road, Boughton
Maintenance	Nil		Kings Lynn, Norfolk
Fuel	Nil		**Tel/Fax:** 01366 500315 (Home)
			Tel: 07771 552870
Disabled Facilities			paulcoulten@btinternet.com

Restaurants   Tea & coffee available at the farmhouse
Taxis
Barry's Cars   **Tel:** 01366 385888
Car Hire
Bees Motors   **Tel:** 01366 384109

137

226ft 7mb	7nm W of Cambridge N5212.63 W00002.55	PPR	Alternative AD Diversion AD	Cambridge Little Gransden

	Bourn	A/G 124.350

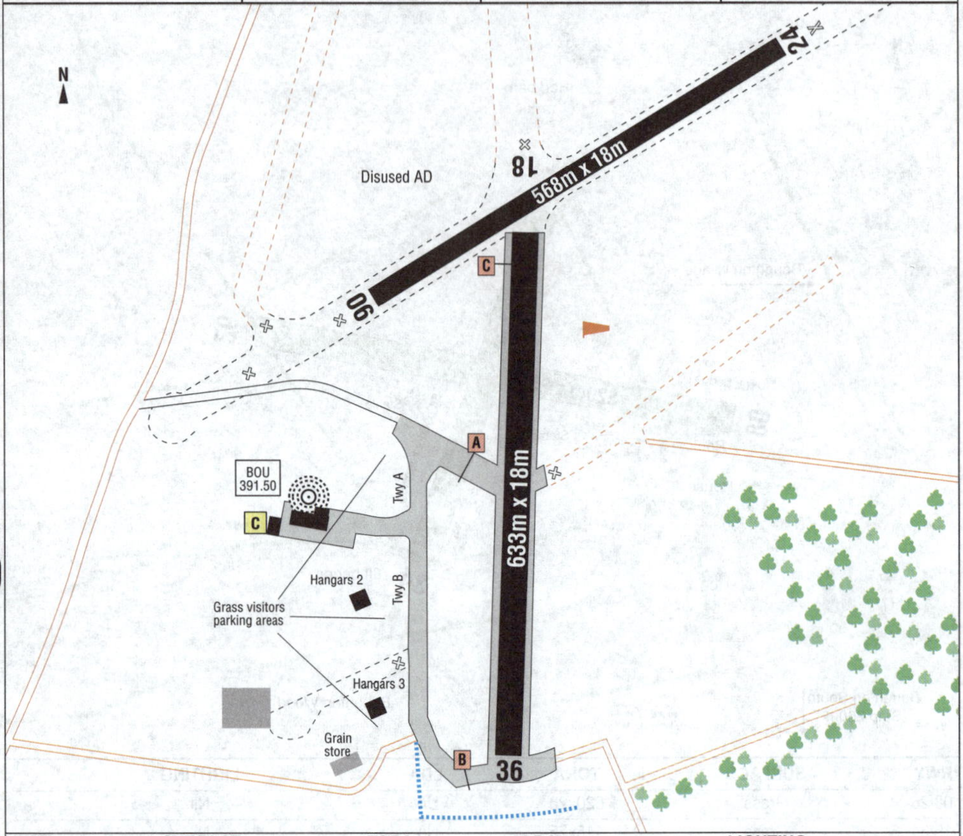

B

Disused AD

568m x 18m
06 / 18 / 24
633m x 18m
36

BOU 391.50

Twy A
Twy B
Hangars 2
Grass visitors parking areas
Hangars 3
Grain store

Hold A
Hold B
Hold C

RWY	SURFACE	TORA	LDA	LIGHTING
18/36	Bitumen	633	633	Nil
06/24	Bitumen	568	568	Nil

Remarks
PPR by telephone. The licensed area is situated on WWII AD on which non-aviation activities also take place. Not available for use by public transport passenger flights required to use a licensed AD or at night. Power checks for Rwy36 to be completed at Hold A.

Warnings
There are a number of other licensed AD in the vicinity and intensive gliding with winch launching cables to 3000ft agl takes place at Gransden Lodge 3nm SW Bourn. No engine run ups at Hold B.
Noise: Avoid over flying all local villages.

Operating Hrs	0900-1700 (Summer) 0930-1700 or SS (Winter) & by arr Closed on all Bank Holiday Mondays	**Taxis/Car Hire**	Arrangement on arrival
		Weather Info	AirCen MOEx
Circuits	36, 24 RH, 18, 06 LH 1000ft QFE	**Operator**	Rural Flying Corps Bourn Aerodrome Bourn, Cambs, CB37TQ **Tel/Fax**: 01954 719602 info@rfcbourn.flyer.co.uk www.rfcbourn.flyer.co.uk
Landing Fee	Single £5 Twin £10 Microlight £1 Classic & interesting ACFT free at discretion of duty instructor		
Maintenance	Nil		
Fuel	Nil		

Disabled Facilities

 C  P

Restaurants   Tea & coffee only available at AD

BOURNE PARK

550ft 18mb	3.5nm NNE of Andover N5115.96 W00127.43	**PPR**	**Alternative AD**	**Southampton** Thruxton

Non-Radio	**LARS** Boscombe 126.700	**RAD** Middle Wallop 123.300	**Safetycom** 135.475

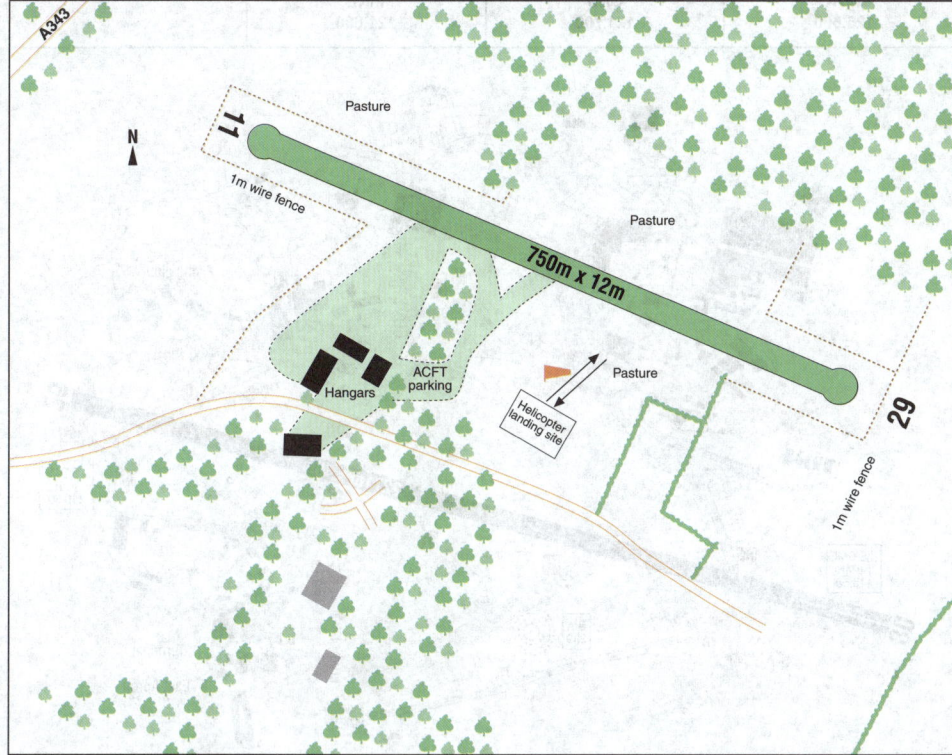

RWY	SURFACE	TORA	LDA	LIGHTING
29/11	Grass	750x12	U/L	Nil

Remarks
PPR by telephone essential. Pilots welcome at own risk. AD home to Aerofab restorations. Boscombe & Middle Wallop MATZ's are close to S/SW.

Warning
Rwy11 has slight upslope. AD close to Boscombe & Middle Wallop areas of aerial activity and military aircraft, particularly helicopters may be encountered down to low level. Windshear may be encountered on Rwy11 APP when there are moderate/strong winds from E.
Noise: Avoid over flying of all local houses and villages.

Operating Hrs	SR-SS	**Operator**	John King
Circuits	LH 1000ft QFE		Aerofab Restorations
Landing Fee	A packet of biscuits		Bourne Park Estates
Maintenance	M3 Aerofab Restorations (fixed wing) E4 M5 Falcon Aviation (Gazelle helicopters)		Andover Hants SP11 0DG
Fuel	Nil		**Tel:** 01264 736635
Disabled Facilities	Nil		
Restaurants	Nil		
Taxis/Car Hire	Nil		
Weather Info	AirSW MOEx		

38ft 1mb	3.5nm NNE of Bournemouth N5046.80 W00150.55	PPR	Alternative AD Diversion AD	Southampton Compton Abbas

Bournemouth	ATIS 121.950	APP 119.475	RAD 119.475 118.650

TWR 125.600	GND 121.700	FIRE 121.600	

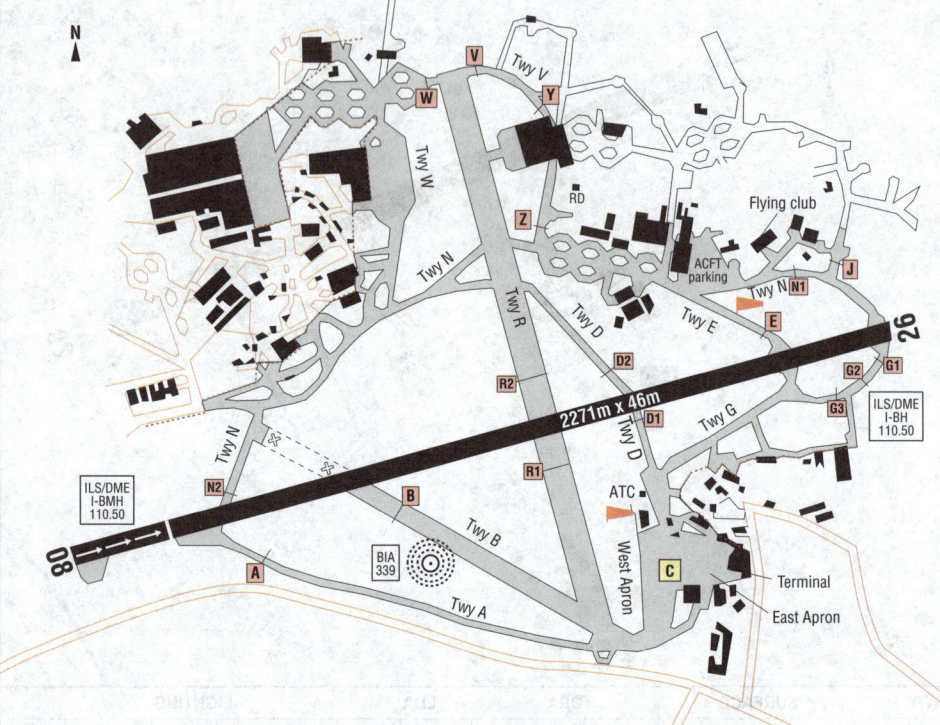

RWY	SURFACE	TORA	LDA	LIGHTING
08	Asphalt	2271	1838	Ap Thr Rwy PAPI 3° LHS
26	Asphalt	2026	1970	Ap Thr Rwy PAPI 3° RHS

Rwy26 2211m available on request

Remarks

PPR to non-radio and light ACFT. Hi-Vis. Escorts may accompany no more than 3 persons who do not have Hi-Vis clothing. It is prohibited to taxi any ACFT on U/L part of AD where vehicles operate on the road system. In these areas towing only approved subject to look-outs., asphalt or grass areas S of Twy G. Long or short stay. ACFT to be parked at least 25m from Twy edge. Pilots to state parked position on initial contact with ATC. Booking out via RTF not permitted. Flight plans to be filed at Flight Clearance Office at Bournemouth Handling in person. Prop swinging may only be carried out as a 2-person operation, this is to include PIC and person familiar with prop swinging procedures. All ACFT MTWA 3 tonnes or greater intending to park on the E or W apron require marshaller guidance before leaving the apron taxi-lane for stand positioning. All GND running of engines must have the approval of AD Authority and be booked through ATC. All ACFT that use E or W aprons and/or the terminal facilities are required to be handled by an approved handling agent. All visiting ACFT <3 tonnes must contact Bournemouth Handling to obtain a PPR number. ACFT not complying to this will not be able to land.

Warnings

With the exception of Twy B & R all Twys are only 15m wide and so are not suitable for use by ACFT with a wheel base that exceeds 18m or a wheel span greater than 9m. Use of spur Twy that abut V and G is limited to ACFT with a wingspan not exceeding 15m or wheel base not exceeding 4.5m. The SE Twy is routed through the apron area. The entire area bounded by the S and by a single yellow painted line near the Control tower to the N is designated as apron area for air traffic control purposes. Pilots are to exercise caution in this area, and when using the NE Twy, due to movements of pedestrians and vehicles. Twy V & W are unlit and unsuitable for use during dark. Pilots wishing to use Twy V & W during dark should request a follow me vehicle at the earliest opportunity.

Operating Hrs	0530-2030 (Summer) 0630-2130 (Winter) & by arr	Circuits	Only available to AD based ACFT ACFT less than 5700kgs 1000ft All other ACFT/jet ACFT 1500Ft After 2030 (L) all ACFT 1500ft QFE

Landing Fee	On application (payable at terminal info desk)
Maintenance	Available Full up to 5700kg MAUW
Fuel	AVGAS 100LL Jet A1 Refuelling facilities available daily 0700-2130 with:
Shell	**Tel:** 01202 575037 by prior arr only outside these times with:
Esso	**Tel:** 01202 594000
Disabled Facilities	Available
Handling	**Tel:** 01202 364252 (Servisair – Charter/Scheduled/Executive) **Tel:** 01202 364373 (Execair – Executive) **Tel:** 01202 364317 (Bournemouth Handling) **Fax:** 01202 364253 (Servisair – Charter/Scheduled/Executive) **Fax:** 01202 364374 (Execair –Executive)

Restaurants	Cafeteria in terminal Flybites on NW sector of AD
Taxis	At terminal or
Country Cabs	**Tel:** 01202 536276
United	**Tel:** 0800 304555
Car Hire	
Avis	**Tel:** 01202 293218
Hertz	**Tel:** 01202 291231
Weather Info	M T9 Fax 246 A VS MOEx
Operator	Bournemouth Airport Plc Christchurch Dorset BH23 6SE **Tel:** 01202 364150 (ATC) **Tel:** 01202 364170 (AD Duty Manager) **Fax:** 01202 364159 (ATC) www.flybournemouth.com

Bournemouth Controlled Airspace

Visual Reference Points (VRP)

VRP	VOR/NDB	VOR/DME
Hengistbury Head N5042.72 W00144.93	SAM 229°/BIA 141°	SAM 229°/21nm
Sand Banks N5041.00 W00156.83	Not suitable VOR/NDB	SAM 237°/28nm
Stoney Cross (Disused AD) N5054.70 W00139.42	SAM 260°/BIA 045°	SAM 260°/12nm
Tarrant Rushton (Disused AD) N5051.00 W00204.70	SAM 260°/BIA 299°	SAM 260°/29nm

CTR–Class D Airspace
Normal CTA/CTR Class D Airspace rules apply. Transition Alt 4000ft

141

500ft 16mb	3.5nm WSW of Tetbury N5137.72 W00014.75		PPR	Alternative AD	Gloucestershire Kemble

Non-Radio	LARS Filton 122.725	LARS Brize 124.275	Safetycom 135.475

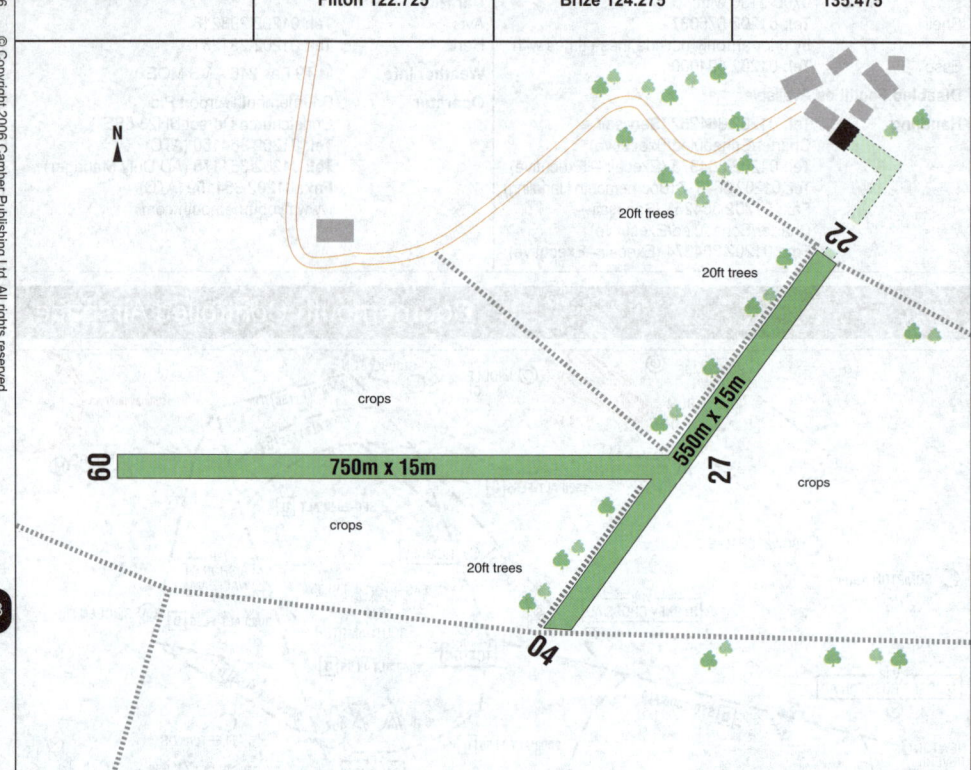

RWY	SURFACE	TORA	LDA	LIGHTING
09/27	Grass	750x15	U/L	Nil
04/22	Grass	550x15	U/L	Nil

Remarks
PPR by telephone. Very well maintained strip. Crops may be grown close to both sides Rwy09/27 & E of Rwy04/22. Agricultural events may take place on the owners property.

Warnings
Stone walls border some Rwy edges and Thrs, see diagram. A stone wall encroaches Rwy22 Thr. Wire fences may be along grass Twy leading to hangar. Individual trees border Rwy04/22 on W side and may generate turbulence under certain wind conditions. R105/2.0 to E of AD, relevant to helicopters only.
Noise: Avoid over flying all local habitation.

		Operator	Mr Greville Vernon
Operating Hours	SR-SS		Bowldown Farms Ltd
Circuits	Advised with PPR		Bowldown
Landing Fee	Nil		Weston Birt
Maintenance	Nil		Tetbury
Fuel	Nil		Gloucestershire
Disabled Facilities	Nil		GL8 8UD
Taxi/Car Hire	Nil		**Tel:** 01666 890224
Weather Info	AirSW MOEx		**Tel:** 07764 348651

20ft 1mb	5nm ENE of Selby N5348.12 W00054.85		**PPR**	**Alternative AD** **Diversion AD**	**Humberside** Sherburn in Elmet
		Breighton		**A/G** **129.800**	

N

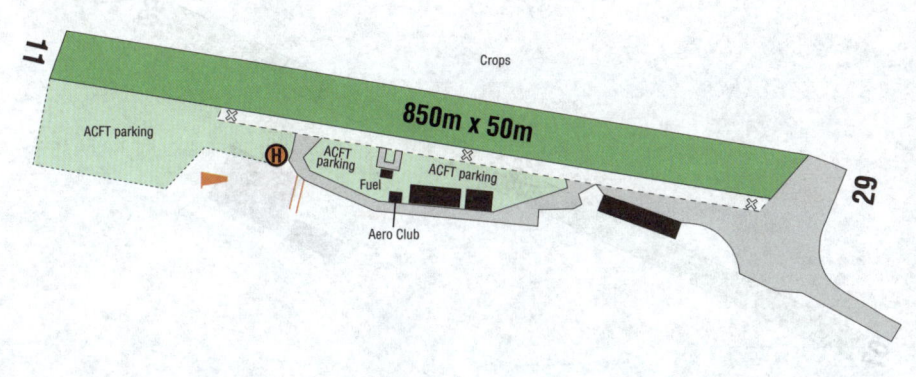

11

29

Crops

850m x 50m

ACFT parking

ACFT parking

ACFT parking

Fuel

Aero Club

B

RWY	SURFACE	TORA	LDA	LIGHTING
11/29	Grass	850x50m	U/L	Nil

Remarks

PPR. Visiting ACFT, including non radio, welcome on prior permission and at pilot's own risk. Situated at SW corner of disused military AD. Home of vintage and classic ACFT. Live side join required due to frequent aerobatic activity on N side of Rwy centre line. Vintage & Classic ACFT especially welcome.

Warning

Special rules apply on display days.
Noise: Avoid over flying the villages of Breighton and Bubwith.

Operating Hrs	Mon-Fri 0730-SS Sat-Sun 0900-SS (Summer) +1Hr (Winter)		**Taxis** **Car Hire**	On request through AD
Circuits	29 LH, 11 RH, 700ft QFE all circuits S No overhead joins.		National **Weather Info**	**Tel:** 01904 612141 AirN MWC
Landing Fee	Nil		**Operator**	Real Aeroplane Company Ltd
Maintenance	Real Aeroplane Co **Tel:** 01757 289065			The Aerodrome Breighton Selby Yorks YO8 7DH
Fuel	AVGAS JET A1 100LL Limited over night hangarage available			**Tel:** 01757 289065 realaero@aol.com www.realaero.com

Disabled Facilities

Restaurants   Refreshments & food at weekends

210ft 7mb	5.5nm ESE of Newbury N5123.03 W00110.35	PPR	Alternative AD Diversion AD	Farnborough Blackbushe
	Brimpton		A/G 135.125 Not always manned	

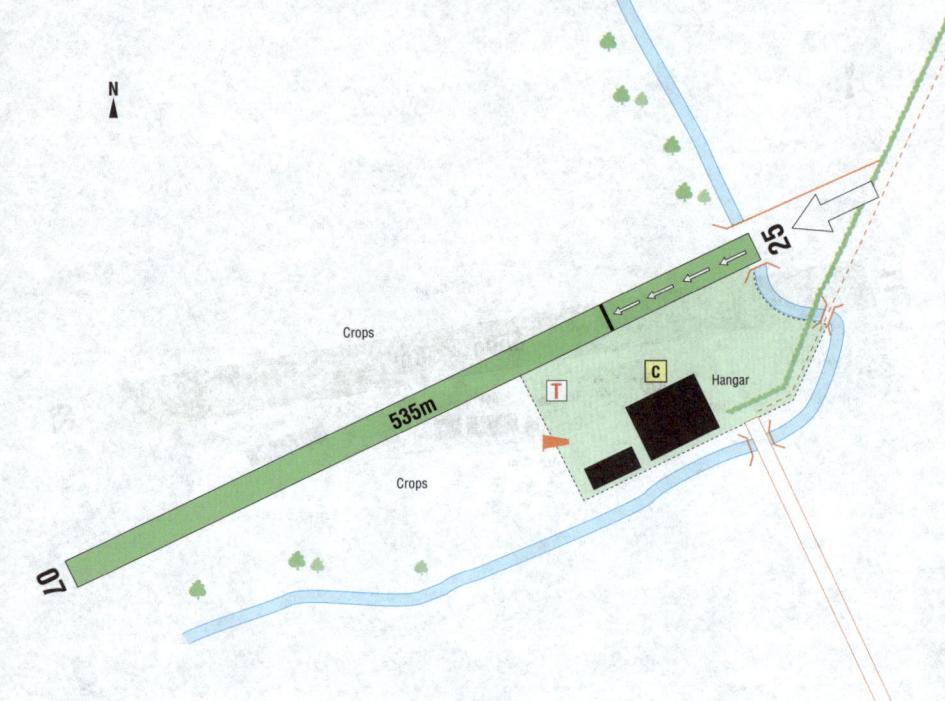

RWY	SURFACE	TORA	LDA	LIGHTING
07	Grass	535	U/L	Nil
25	Grass	635	U/L	Nil

Displaced Thr Rwy25 100m

Remarks
PPR strictly by telephone.

Warnings
AD situated just within NW edge of Atomic Weapons Establishment Restricted Area R101/2.4 and operates under special exemption. All APP to AD must be from N. Flying S of AD below 2400ft AGL prohibited unless landing or taking-off.
Noise: Avoid over flying the villages of Brimpton, Aldermaston, Woolhampton and local habitation.

Operating Hrs	0830-dusk (L)	**Car Hire**	
Circuits	07 LH, 25 RH 800ft QFE No overhead joins	National	**Tel:** 01635 582525
		Weather Info	AirSW MOEx
Landing Fee	Single £5 Twin £10	**Operator**	Alan House Sylmar Aviation Manor View Hopgoods Green Bucklebury RG7 6TA **Tel:** 01635 866088 **Tel:** 07836 775557 **Tel:** 0118 971 3822 (Clubhouse)
Maintenance	Limited		
Fuel	Nil		
Disabled Facilities			

Restaurants — Light snacks available in clubhouse

Taxis
JDM Taxis **Tel:** 01635 826763
CDC Taxis **Tel:** 01635 866730

144

EGGD

BRISTOL

622ft	7nm SW of Bristol	PPR	Alternative AD	Bristol Filton Kemble
21mb	N5122.95 W00243.13		Diversion AD	

Bristol		ATIS 126.025		APP 125.650		RAD 136.075
TWR 133.850		GND 121.925		FIRE 121.600		

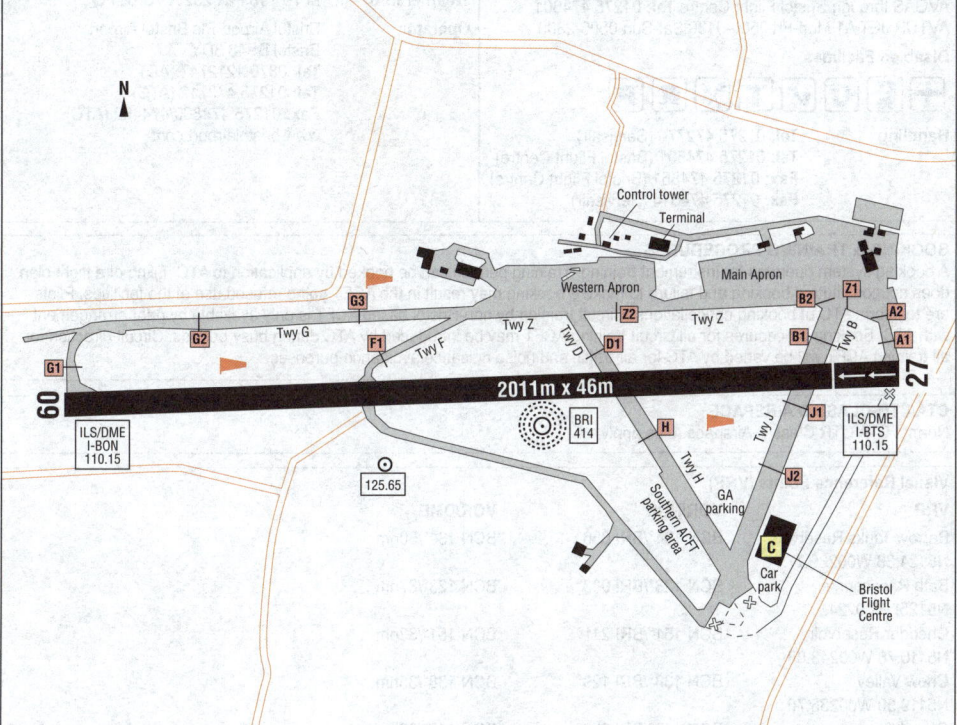

RWY	SURFACE	TORA	LDA	LIGHTING
09	Asphalt	2011	1938	Ap Thr Rwy PAPI 3° LHS
27	Asphalt	2011	1876	Ap Thr Rwy PAPI 3° LHS

Remarks

Non-radio ACFT not accepted. Hi-Vis. Training is not permitted 2200-0700 (L). See 'Booking & Training Procedures'. Propeller driven ACFT of more than 5700kg MTWA must not join final APP track to any Rwy at a height of less than 1000ft QFE. Parking & start up procedure for all ACFT on main aprons is under guidance of apron marshaller following clearance from ATC. Grass areas unsuitable for parking ACFT. Light ACFT Ops:Rwy27 – Pilots to arrange flight to minimise noise nuisance. ACFT landing Rwy27 follow descent profile not below that indicated by PAPI's. Rwy09 – Practice EFATO manoeuvres not permitted. Pilots should avoid over flying Felton Village whenever possible, when Dept Rwy09 and requiring to turn left, ACFT shall climb ahead to 1nm DME before commencing turn. GND running of engines subject to ATC approval at night. Helicopter Operation: Do not over fly noise sensitive area to N of AD boundary below 500ft QFE. Helicopters wishing to Dept/Arr via E/NE AD boundary use Rwy then turn N following A38. Helicopters Dept/Arr from W do so along line of Twy G. W Dept should not turn N until crossing AD boundary. W Arr avoid Felton Village. Helicopters avoid all noise sensitive areas & not permitted to overfly apron. Designated helicopter training area S of AD. Parallel Arr/Dept not permitted to/from Twy G except when traffic using Rwy is VFR. Due to restricted GA parking, operators of inbound GA flights must pre notify handling agents with ETA and duration of stay

Warnings

GND signals not displayed, except light signals. Hot air balloon activity in VMC & daylight Hrs from site 4.5nm NE of AD & downwind of site. Balloons may pass below CTA or if radio equipped, within the CTR/CTA. Pilots will be notified by ATC of known balloon activity which may affect their flights. Glider and hang glider activity takes place along the Mendip Hills, to the south of the AD. ATC will only be notified of such activity when gliders and hang gliders are operating within designated areas within the CTR/CTA and so pilots may not always receive warning of the activity. Bird scaring is carried out on a regular basis but birds may not always be detected on the extreme W end of the AD and on the APP and Dept tracks of all Rwys. Pilots must conform to the noise abatement techniques laid down for the type of ACFT and operate so as to cause the least disturbance practicable in areas surrounding the AD. Pilots may experience wind shear/turbulence especially if the wind is strong, SE Rwy09, W Rwy27.

Operating Hrs	H24
Circuits	Variable 1000ft QFE for non-jet ACFT Rwy09 RH only but ATC may vary Rwy27 LH. Helicopters 700ft QFE
Landing Fee	On Application to BFC Night surcharges 2300-0700 (L)
Maintenance	Bristol Flight Centre Tel: 01275 474501
Fuel	AVGAS 0800-2000 (L)

Surcharge applies outside these Hrs
AVGAS through Bristol Flight Centre Tel: 01275 474601
AVTUR JET A1 Mon-Fri 0500-0130 Sat-Sun 0500-2300

Disabled Facilities

Handling	Tel: 01275 472776 (Servisair)
	Tel: 01275 474501 (Bristol Flight Centre)
	Fax: 01275 474851 (Bristol Flight Centre)
	Fax: 01275 474514 (Servisair)

Restaurants
Restaurant refreshments & club facilities available
Duty-Free Shop & 24Hr (airside) bar

Taxis	
Bristol Int Cars	Tel: 01275 474888
CarHire	
Avis	Tel: 01275 473536
Europcar	Tel: 01275 474623
Hertz	Tel: 01275 472807
Weather Info	M T9 T18 Fax 252 A VS BCFO
Operator	Bristol Airport Plc Bristol Airport Bristol BS48 3DY Tel: 0870 1212747 (AD) Tel: 01275 473712 (ATC) Fax: 01275 474800/474482 (ATC) www.bristolairport.com

---

BOOKING & TRAINING PROCEDURES
A booking system operates for instrument training. Training periods can be booked by application to ATC. Filing of a flight plan does not constitute a booking and failure to make a booking may result in the ACFT being refused use of the facilities. Pilots are to inform ATC of booking cancellations. Circuit training by non-Bristol based ACFT is only available by prior arrangement with ATC. Booking procedures for all circuit training ACFT may be introduced by ATC during busy periods. Circuit direction for all training ACFT will be varied by ATC for air traffic and noise nuisance avoidance purposes.

CTA/CTR-CLASS D AIRSPACE
Normal CTA/CTR Class D Airspace rules apply.

Visual Reference Points (VRP)

VRP	VOR/NDB	VOR/DME
Barrow Tanks Reservoir N5124.38 W00239.77	BCN 134°/BRI 056°	BCN 134°/30nm
Bath Racecourse N5125. W00224.	BCN 123°/BRI 083°	BCN 123°/37nm
Cheddar Reservoir N5116.78 W00248.08	BCN 151°/BRI 211°	BCN 151°/32nm
Chew Valley N5119.50 W00235.70	BCN 138°/BRI 129°	BCN 138°/35nm
Churchill N5120.00 W00247.60	BCN 147°/BRI 229°	BCN 147°/29nm
Clevedon N5126.35 W00251.08	BCN 142°/LA 267°	BCN 142°/23nm
East Nailsea N5125.80 W00244.10	BCN 136°/BRI 352°	BCN 136°/27nm
Frome N5113. W00219.	BCN 133°/LA 219°	BCN 133°/27nm
Hicks Gate Roundabout N5125.52 W00231.00	BCN 127°/BRI 074°	BCN 127°/33nm
M4 J18 N5125. W00231.	BCN 115°/BRI 066°	BCN 115°/37nm
M5 Sedgemoor Services N5116. W00255.	BCN 158°/BRI 232°	BCN 158°/37nm
M5 Avon Bridge N5129. W00241.	BCN 127°/BRI 012°	BCN 127°/26nm
Old Severn Bridge (M48) N5136. W00238.	BCN 110°/BRI 015°	BCN 110/24nm
Radstock N5117.53 W00226.92	BCN 134°/LA 236°	BCN 134°/40nm
Wells Mast N5114. W00237	BCN 144°/BRI 161°	BCN 144°/38nm
Weston Aerodrome N5120. W00256.	BCN 156°/BRI 256°	BCN 156°/26nm

NB: ACFT entering the Bristol CTR/CTA via M5 Avon Bridge, Hicks Gate, Radstock or Cheddar VRP's may be required to hold at East Nailsea, Barrow Tanks Reservoirs, Churchill or Chew Valley VRPs as appropriate. The Wells Mast is referred to as the Mendip Mast at AIP ENR 5.4.1. Pilots are advised to use caution when routing via this VRP due to the nature of this lighted Air Navigation obstacle at height 1009ft agl, 2003ft amsl

B

Effective date:23/11/06

386
CARDIFF CTA D
L9 A FL245 FL75
FL75 5500
M4 J24
M4
348
VRP M4 J24
336
Y9 A FL245 FL105
FL105
480
428
cables
400
400
UPFIELD Fm
COTSWOLD CTA A
FL105 FL245
Cardiff CTA D
4000 FL105
cables
329

OLD SEVERN BRIDGE
430
521
cables
R154 2000 SFC
VRP THORNBURY
COTSWOLD CTA A
FL245 FL105
R105 2000 SFC
CHARLTON PARK
VRP MALMSBURY
D145 2000 SFC
LYNEHAM CTA D
FL105
L9 A FL245 FL65
HULLAVINGTON
3500
VRP M4 J17
BRISTOL CTA D
FL65 FL105

493
BRISTOL CTA D
4000 FL105
420
368
394
M5 AVON BRIDGE
BADMINTON
racing circuit
BRISTOL CTA D
4500 FL105
VRP M4 J18
GARSTON Fm

BRISTOL Filton
CARDIFF CTA D
FL105 3000
VRP CLEVEDON
BALLOONS
EAST NAILSEA
377
328
590 AMSL CAPTIVE BALLOON
402
HICKS GATE R ABOUT
886
BATH RACECOURSE
COLERNE
CHIPPENHAM

CARDIFF CTA D
2000 FL105 1500
BRISTOL CTA D
2000 FL105 1500
D121 600 SFC
BRISTOL CTA D
1500 FL105
PEWISH
BRI BRISTOL
BARROW TANKS RESERVOIR
BRISTOL CTR D
SFC FL105
BRISTOL CTA D
1500 FL105
COTSWOLD CTA D
FL245 FL105
WINSLEY
LYNEHAM CTR D
3500 SFC
MELKSHAM

WESTON AERODROME
WESTON
CHURCHILL
1158
CLUTTON HILL
571
VRP CHEW VALLEY
BRISTOL CTA D
2000 FL105
BRISTOL CTA D
3500 FL105

KEEVIL

CARDIFF CTA D
FL105 3000
M5 SEDGEMOOR SERVICES
CHEDDER RESERVOIR
BRISTOL CTA D
3000 FL105
HALESLAND
1000
2003
FRANKLYNS FIELD
VRP RADSTOCK
500

N862 A FL245 FL105
WELLS MAST
VRP FROME
WING Fm

R153 2000 SFC
YEOVILTON NORTH AIAA
6000 SFC
D123 150000 SFC

A39
A361
A359
A360

B

226ft 8mb	4nm N of Bristol N5131.17 W00235.45	PPR	Alternative AD	Bristol Kemble

Bristol Filton	APP 122.725	RAD 122.725	TWR 132.350	FIRE 121.600

N

ILS/DME I-BRF 110.55

122.725

OF 325

G

D   **C**

Twy C

Apron 2

Apron 3

Apron 4

Twy B

C

B

Twy A

A

ILS/DME I-FB 110.55

Apron 1

E

F

H

60 →   **2467m x 91m**   ← **27**

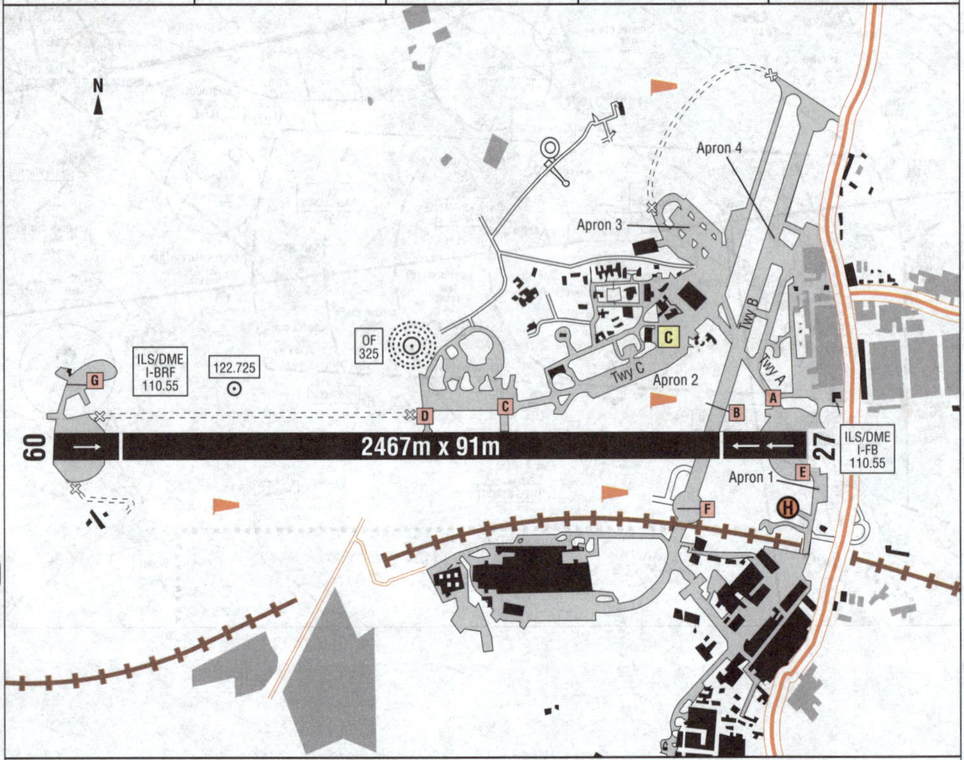

RWY	SURFACE	TORA	LDA	LIGHTING
09	Concrete	2300	2125	Ap Thr Rwy PAPI 3° LHS RHS
27	Concrete	2300	2060	Ap Thr Rwy PAPI 3° LHS RHS

Remarks

PPR by telephone. ACFT on APP Rwy27 are to cross A38 not below 100ft agl. Instrument training not available to ACFT without a serviceable transponder. All ACFT to contact APP not RAD at weekends.

Warnings

Not all Twys are available for use. Deviation from the marked manoeuvring area can be hazardous. Rwy09/27 subject to slow clearance of standing water after heavy rain. Pilots must request start clearance and have a marshaller in attendance. Pilots must ensure that at all times ACFT are operated to cause the least disturbance practicable in areas surrounding the AD. **Noise**: Subject to ATC operations at the time, Dept ACFT will be offered Rwy27, Arr Rwy09 whenever possible, together with the surface wind and Rwy status. NB weekend contact RAD. Pilots are to avoid flying over built up areas.

Operating Hrs	Mon 0600-1930 Tue-Fri 0545-1930 Sat-Sun 0800-1600 (Summer) +1Hr (Winter)	**Car Hire**	
		Flight Operations	**Tel:** 0117 9699094
Circuits	Jet/Turbo Prop ACFT, 2000ft QFE Other ACFT, 27 LH, 09 RH, 500ft QFE	**Weather Info**	M T9 Fax MOEx
		Visual Reference Points (VRP)	
Landing Fee	£17.00 per metric tonne or part thereof	Old Severn Bridge	N5136.67 W00238.62
Maintenance	Hangarage on request	M5 bridge over	
Fuel	AVGAS 100LL (subject to avail) JET A1	River Avon	N5129.33 W00241.58
Disabled Facilities		Thornbury	N5136.67 W00231.10

Operator

BAe Property Services
PO Box 77
Bristol, BS99 7AR
Tel: 0117 9699094
Fax: 0117 9362474
bristolfilton.flightops@baesystems.com
www.bristolfilton.co.uk

Restaurants   Refreshments at BAe Flight Operations

Taxis
Eurotaxis   **Tel:** 01454 320101
Spirit Taxis   **Tel:** 0117 3731111

EGVN   BRIZE NORTON

288ft 10mb	4nm WSW of Witney N5145.00 W00135.02	PPR MIL	Alternative AD Diversion AD	Oxford Kemble

Brize	LARS 124.275	Zone 119.000	RAD 124.275	DIR 133.755
APP 127.250	TWR 123.725	GND 121.725	OPS 130.075	

N

Wash Bay

E1 E2

Terminal & Ops

D1

Twy E

E3

E3

26

F2

Twy F

F1

F2

BZN
111.90

D

D

Twy D

G2

ILS/DME
BZB
111.90

BZ
386

K

3050m x 56m

C

119.000
124.275

Twr

C

C

Twy C

Twy G

08

A

B2

G1

Twy B

Twy G

B

Twy A

B

ILS/DME
BZA
111.90

B

RWY	SURFACE	TORA	LDA	LIGHTING
08/26	Asphalt	3050	3050	Ap Thr Rwy PAPI 3°

Remarks

PPR 24Hrs notice required. Located within the Brize Norton CTR. No visiting ACFT between 1700-0800 (L). No 180° turns on Rwy. Light ACFT can expect to see vehicular traffic crossing at the upwind end of the Rwy.

Free fall parachuting takes place up to FL150 SR-SS. ACFT with wing span >60m are not permitted to use Twy B.
Noise: Rwy26 Visual circuits should avoid Cotswold Wildlife Park, Shilton, Witney. Rwy08 visual circuits avoiding Witney. Light ACFT will normally be required to enter or leave the Brize Norton CTR via Burford or Faringdon VRP's. Arr ACFT are to proceed at 1000ft QFE directly from the VRP's to base leg, or as directed by ATC.

Operating Hrs	H24	**Taxis/Car Hire**	Nil
Circuits	Light ACFT Variable 1000ft QFE Other ACFT 1500ft	**Weather Info**	M T Fax 254 MOEx
		Operator	RAF Brize Norton
Landing Fee	Charges in accordance with RAF policy Contact Station Ops for details		Oxon OX8 3LX **Tel:** 01993 842551 Ex 7551 (Ops)
			Tel: 01993 842551 Ex 7433 (PPR)
Maintenance	Nil		**Tel:** 01993 845886 (Brize Norton FC)
Fuel	JET A1 FS11 AVGAS		

Disabled Facilities

Restaurants   Nil

CTA/CTR-Class D Airspace
Normal CTA/CTR Class D Airspace rules apply
To assist Brize RAD in ensuring access to its airspace pilots should make an R/T call when 15nm or 5 minutes flying time from the zone boundary, whichever is the earlier.

149

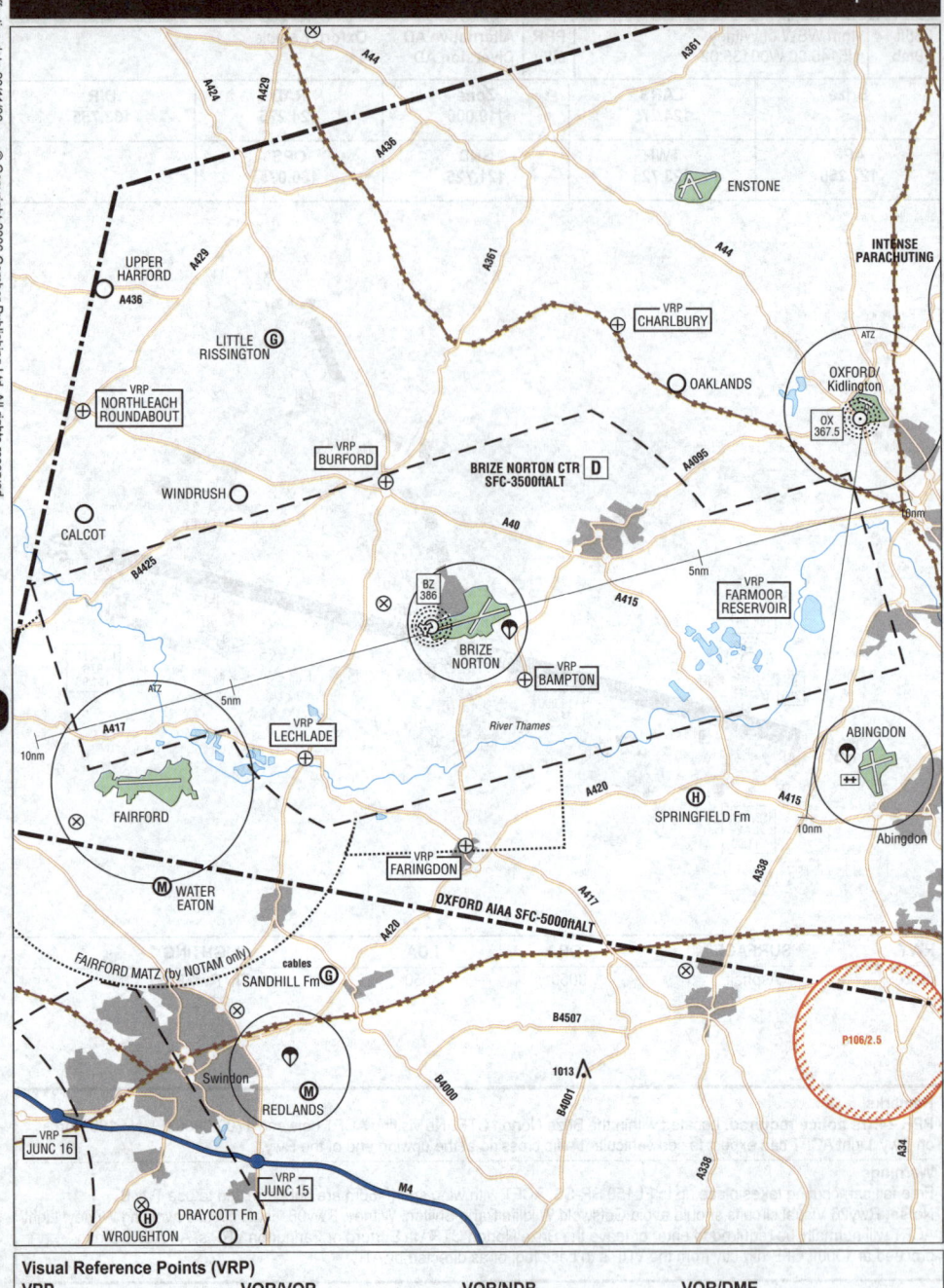

Visual Reference Points (VRP)

VRP	VOR/VOR	VOR/NDB	VOR/DME
Bampton N5143.30 W00132.48	CPT 322°/DTY 213°	CPT 322°/BZ 127°	CPT 322°/19nm
Burford N5148.24 W00132.12	CPT 324°/DTY 223°	CPT 324°/BZ 342°	CPT 324°/24nm
Charlbury N5152.18 W00128.54	CPT 340°/DTY 219°	CPT 340°/BZ 034°	CPT 340°/25nm
Faringdon N5139.18 W00135.12	CPT 309°/DTY 212°	CPT 309°/BZ 177°	CPT 309°/17nm
Farmoor Reservoir N5145.12 W00121.24	CPT 345°/DTY 202°	CPT 345°/BZ 091°	CPT 345°/17nm
Lechlade N5141.36 W00141.25	CPT 308°/DTY 219°	CPT 308°/BZ 227°	CPT 308°/21nm
Northleach Roundabout N5150.15 W00150.09	CPT 320°/DTY 235°	CPT 320°/BZ 304°	CPT 320°/31nm

BRUNTINGTHORPE

467ft 16mb	6nm S of Leicester N5229.22 W00107.84	PPR	Alternative AD Diversion AD	Coventry Leicester

	Bruntingthorpe	A/G 122.825 (By arr)	

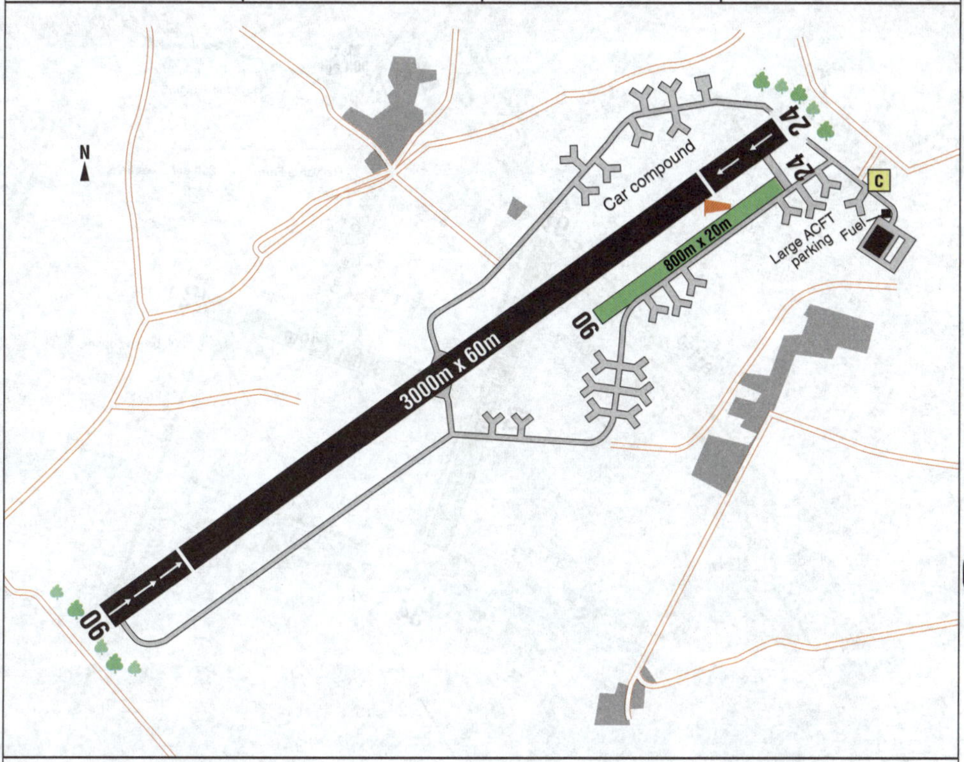

B

RWY	SURFACE	TORA	LDA	LIGHTING
06/24	Asphalt	2630x60	U/L	Nil
06/24	Grass	800x60	U/L	Nil

Remarks
PPR by telephone. AD used intensively by the motor industry for vehicle proving. Extensive long term parking/storing facilities available for large ACFT. ACFT museum unique collection of Cold War jets open Sun 1000-1600.

Warnings
Earth banks with trees up to 40' close to both Thrs. Grass Rwy has been reduced to 800m due to new track at Rwy24 Thr.
Noise: Do not over fly local villages.

Operating Hrs	Available on request	**Operator**	C Walton Ltd
Circuits	Avoid over flying habitation		Bruntingthorpe Aerodrome
Landing Fee	On application		Lutterworth, Leics, LE17 5QN
Maintenance	Nil		**Tel:** 01162 478030
Fuel	Nil		**Tel:** 01162 799315 (Security)
			Fax: 01162 478031
Disabled Facilities			www.bruntingthorpe.com

 ✈ ☎ ✕ T P

Restaurants	Pubs 10min walk in Bruntingthorpe village
Taxis/Car Hire	By arrangement on arrival
Weather Info	AirCen MCW

50ft 1mb	5nm WSW of Horncastle N5311.97 W00015.17	PPR	Alternative AD	Nottingham East Midlands Wickenby

Non-Radio	LARS Coningsby 120.800	LARS Waddington 127.350	Safetycom 135.475

RWY	SURFACE	TORA	LDA	LIGHTING
07/25	Grass	300x20	U/L	Nil
16/34	Grass	300x20	U/L	Nil

Remarks

PPR by telephone. Suitable for Microlights or STOL ACFT. AD is bordered by drainage dyke to S and road to N. Visitors ensure they have identified current Rwys.

Visual Aid to Location: Church in Bucknall Village and Sewage Farm close NE of strip.

Warnings

Road and low hedge cross Rwy16 Thr. 30ft trees cross Rwy34 APP just short of Rwy Thr. A public bridleway crossed Rwy25 Thr. There is a low hedge, with a gap for taxiing which divides Rwy07/25 from 16/34. AD is close to N boundary of Coningsby MATZ.

Noise: Avoid over flight of Bucknall village to NE.

Operating Hrs	SR-SS	**Operator**	Allan Todd & Tony Brumpton
Circuits	07, 25 to S, 16, 34 to E Always away from village		Hallyards Farm, Bucknall Lincoln, LN10 5DT **Tel:** 01526 388249 (Allan Todd) **Tel:** 07970 496811 allan@todd.flyer.co.uk
Landing Fee	Nil		
Maintenance	Nil		
Fuel	MOGAS available by arrangement		
Disabled Facilities	Nil		
Restaurants	Nil		
Taxis/Car Hire	Nil		
Weather Info	AirN MWC		

20ft 0mb	2nm S of Selby N5344.73 W00104.97	PPR	Alternative AD	Leeds Bradford Sherburn in Elmet

Burn Base	APP Fenton 126.500	A/G 130.100 (Not always manned)

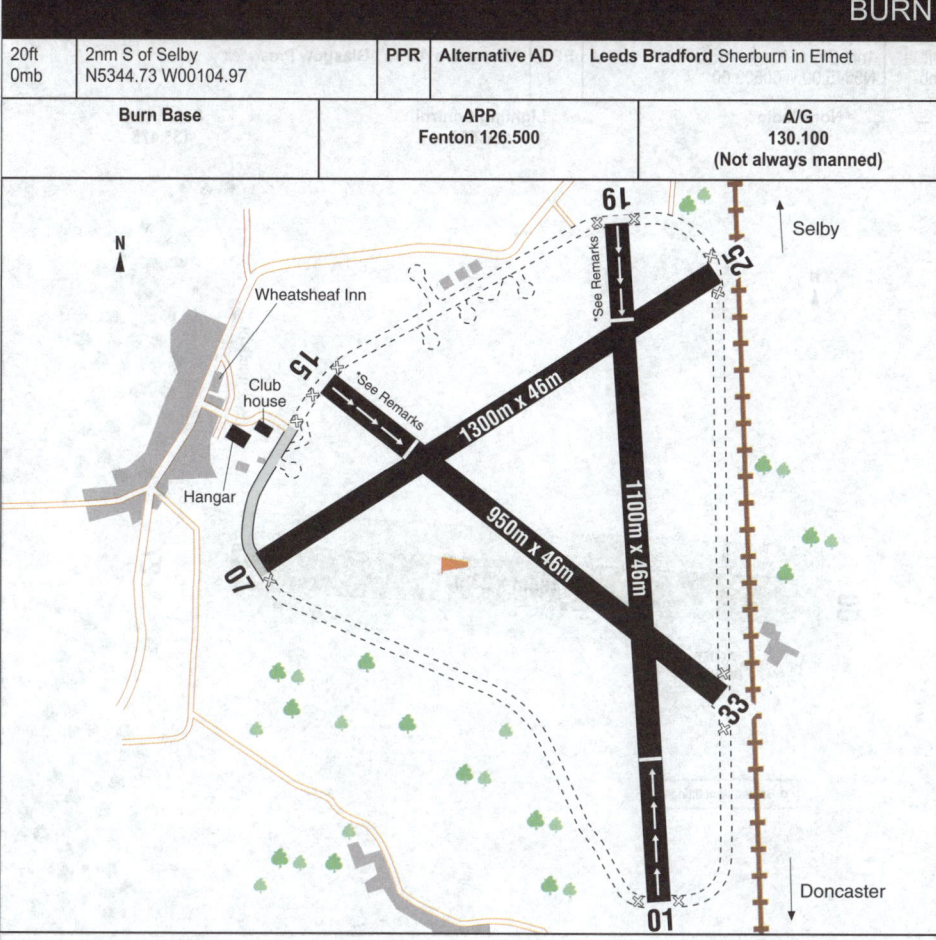

RWY	SURFACE	TORA	LDA	LIGHTING
07/25	Asphalt	1300x46	U/L	Nil
01/19	Asphalt	1100x46	U/L	Nil
15/33	Asphalt	950x46	U/L	Nil

Rwys in moderate condition

Remarks
PPR by telephone. AD a gliding site, powered ACFT welcome at pilots own risk. Pilots with Silver 'C' gliding qualification are always welcome. All visiting pilots must obtain a full briefing to ensure safe integration when gliding is in progress. Rwy01/19 & Rwy33/15 have displaced Thr to avoid rough portions of Asphalt; these areas must NOT be used.

Warnings
Gliding by winch launch and aerotow to 2000ft agl. DO NOT join overhead when gliding is in progress. Powered ACFT and Gliders may operate from different Rwys. When gliding club is closed all gates are locked. Access arranged with PPR gliding not in progress. Farming activity, horse riders, and walkers near Rwys. Twy are not suitable for ACFT use except between Rwy07 Thr and Clubhouse/Hangar.

Operating Hrs	SR-SS	**Taxis**	
Circuits	Visitors normally LH 1000ft QFE. Orbit AD at 1000ft QFE to indicate intention to land. DO NOT join overhead. Club tugs & Gliders Variable	Selby Taxis	**Tel:** 01757 212285
		Station Taxis	**Tel:** 01757 702567
		Den's Cabs	**Tel:** 01757 291541
		Car Hire	Nil
Landing Fee	£10 includes temporary membership BGA members free	**Weather Info**	AirN MWC
		Operator	Burn Gliding Club Ltd
Maintenance	Nil		Park Lane
Fuel	AVGAS 100LL		Burn, Selby
Disabled Facilities			North Yorkshire, YO8 8LW
			Tel: 01757 270296 (Clubhouse)
			Tel: 07712 467401 (Launch Point)
			Tel: 01757 210896/ 270422 (PPR/Briefing)
			Tel: 01405 860144 (PPR/Briefing)
Restaurants	Good local Pubs		

153

50ft 1mb	1nm SW of Kingarth N5545.00 W00503.00	**PPR**	**Alternative AD**	**Glasgow** Prestwick

Non-Radio	**Lighting Control** **130.650**	**Safetycom** **135.475**

RWY	SURFACE	TORA	LDA	LIGHTING
09	Grass	500x23	U/L	Rwy Thr APAPI 4.5° LHS
27	Grass	500x23	U/L	Rwy Thr APAPI 5.0° LHS

Remarks
PPR by telephone. Available to visiting ACFT at Pilots own risk during daylight Hrs only. AD lighting not available for visitors but provided for Loganair Air Ambulance operations only.

Warnings
Rwy27 APP is through a gap cut in an extensive stand of trees. High GND to SE to 516ft amsl. Strip slopes down from Rwy27 to Rwy09 with 1 degree gradient. Caution AD light fittings raised above Rwy surface. Sector Safety Altitude for AD of 3600ft (NE sector). 2600ft (SE sector). 3900ft (SW sector) 3500ft (NW sector). **Remember- these figures are for the guidance of Air Ambulance experienced pilots. Visitors should exercise extreme caution.** There is Class E airspace, Scottish TMA with base 3000ft QNH to E of AD.

Operating Hrs	SR-SS	**Weather Info**	AirSC GWC
Circuits	Circuits to N	**Operator**	Mr N Mellish
Landing Fee	Nil		Mount Stuart Trust
Maintenance	Nil		Estate Office
Fuel	Nil		Mount Stuart
Disabled Facilities			Rothesay
☒			Isle of Bute, PA20 9LR
			Tel: 01700 502627
			(Mon-Fri 0900-1700 (L))
			Fax: 01700 505313
Restaurant	Within walking distance of Kingarth village		nick.mellish@bute.estate.com
Taxi/Car Hire	Nil		

14ft 0mb	3.5nm SW of Caernarfon N5306.25 W00420.42	PPR	Alternative AD Diversion AD	Liverpool Mona

Caernarfon	LARS Valley 125.225	A/G 122.250

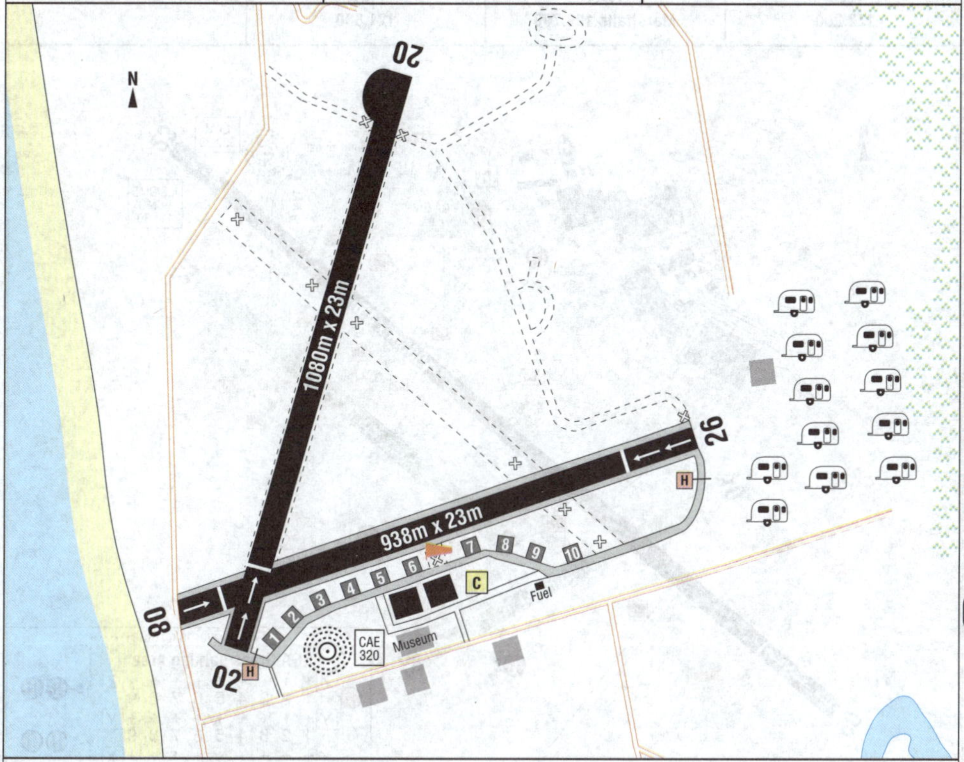

(Airport diagram: runways 02/20 1080m x 23m, 08/26 938m x 23m; Museum, CAE 320, Fuel, caravan sites, taxiways. North arrow.)

RWY	SURFACE	TORA	LDA	LIGHTING
08	Asphalt	880	880	Nil
26	Asphalt	880	759	Nil
02	Asphalt	1080	1003	Nil
20	Asphalt	1044	1044	Nil

Remarks
PPR. Hi-Vis. Arr ACFT contact Valley. Join the circuit at 1300ft QFE. No taxiing on grass surfaces. Dept ACFT, unless otherwise instructed should call Valley immediately after take-off. Certain customs facilities available. Aviation museum on AD.

Warnings
AD in vicinity of Valley CMATZ. Extensive high GND to S and E of AD. TV mast 1983ft AMSL 5nm S of AD. Transient obstacles, vehicles (16ft) on road across Rwy02 APP centre line. Microlight and gliding activity on AD.
Noise: Avoid over flight of any caravan site within ATZ (Apart from final Rwy26).

Operating Hrs	0800-1800 (Summer) 0900-1630 (Winter)	**Restaurants**	Dakota Cafe **Tel:** 01286 830800
Circuits	02, 26 RH, 08, 20 LH, 800ft QFE	**Taxis/Car Hire**	AD will assist
Landing Fee	Single £12, Twin £20 Microlight £7.50	**Weather Info**	AirN MWC
Maintenance	Apache Aviation **Tel:** 01286 832407	**Operator**	Air Caernarfon Ltd
Fuel	AVGAS 100LL JET A1 with oils W100 & W80		Dinas Dinlle Gwynedd LL54 5TP **Tel:** 01286 830800 **Fax:** 01286 830280 info@qdm-aviation.com www.air-world.co.uk

Disabled Facilities

EGSC

CAMBRIDGE

47ft 2mb	1.5nm E of Cambridge N5212.30 E00010.50	PPR	Alternative AD Diversion AD	Cranfield Bourn

Cambridge	ATIS 134.600	APP 123.600	RAD 124.975

TWR 122.200	OPS Marshalls 129.700	FIRE 121.600	

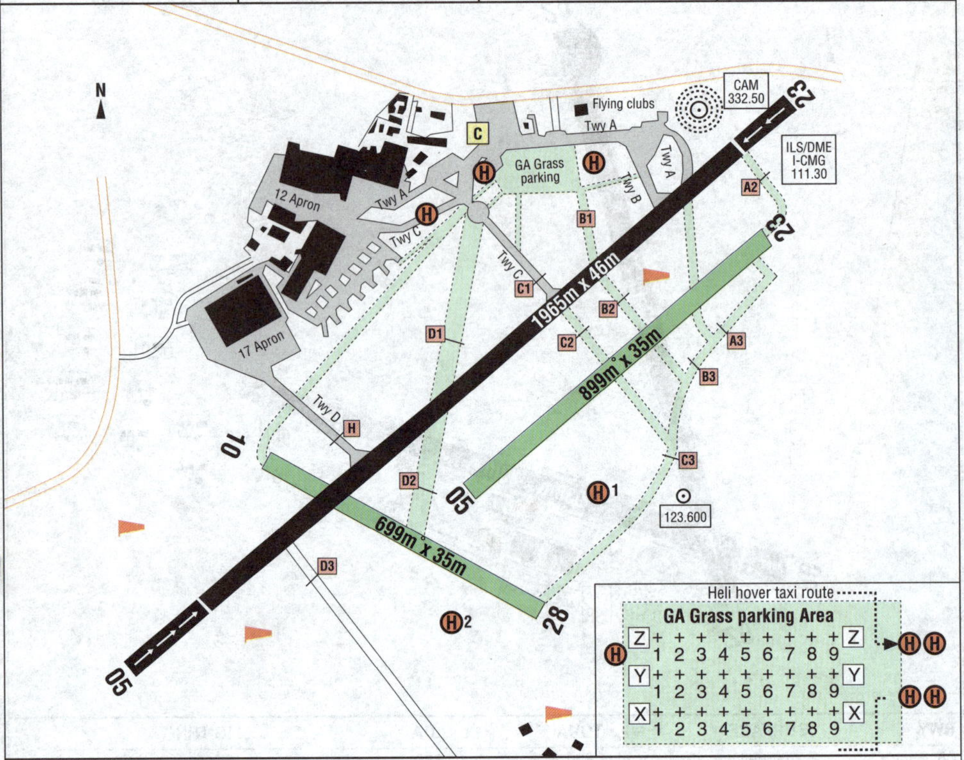

C

Map labels:
- N
- CAM 332.50
- ILS/DME I-CMG 111.30
- Flying clubs
- Twy A
- 12 Apron
- GA Grass parking
- Twy A
- Twy B
- Twy C
- 17 Apron
- Twy D
- 1965m x 46m
- 899m x 35m
- 699m x 35m
- 10
- 05
- 28
- 23
- 123.600
- A2, A3, B1, B2, B3, C1, C2, C3, D1, D2, D3

Heli hover taxi route

GA Grass parking Area

Z	+	+	+	+	+	+	+	+	Z
	1	2	3	4	5	6	7	8	9
Y	+	+	+	+	+	+	+	+	Y
	1	2	3	4	5	6	7	8	9
X	+	+	+	+	+	+	+	+	X
	1	2	3	4	5	6	7	8	9

RWY	SURFACE	TORA	LDA	LIGHTING
05	Asphalt	1851	1635	Ap Thr Rwy PAPI 3° LHS
23	Asphalt	1892	1747	Ap Thr Rwy PAPI 3° LHS
05/23	Grass	899	899	Nil
10/28	Grass	699	699	Nil

Remarks

Not available to non-radio ACFT or Microlights. Hi vis. Preferred Arr Rwy23, Dept Rwy05. ACFT APP Asph Rwy05/23 not below PAPI glide slope from 1000ft. Parallel Rwy ops may be in progress. Rwy05/23 grass go-a rounds remain S of Rwy05/23 grass centre line. ACFT taxiing on grass to keep to Twys. Long grass is unsuitable for manoeuvring. Holding position signs and yellow Twy markings are provided between Twy A, B, C, D and the main Rwy. Holding points for grass Rwy are marked with rectangular day glo markers marked with the Rwy designator. A security charge may be levied for secure parking. Handling available

Helicopter Hover Taxi Route: Helis are to hover into W H via SE corner, E & N side of GA grass parking area. Exit in reverse direction.

Visual aid to location: IBN flashing green Cl.

Warnings

Turbulence and wind shear may be experienced shortly after Dept Rwy28 when there is a strong N wind.

Noise: Avoid over-flying Cambridge below 2000ft. Helicopters should APP vis Heli VRP to N E &S of AD, avoiding over flying Cambridge city and surrounding villages.

Operating Hrs	Mon-Fri 0630-1900 Sat-Sun 0700-1800 (Summer) +1Hr (Winter) & by arr	Maintenance Fuel	Available by arr JET A1 AVGAS 100LL
Circuits	23, 28 LH, 05, 10 RH 1500ft Twins, Fixed wing 1000ft, 700ft Helicopters (QFE)	Disabled Facilities	
Landing Fee	£19.00 up to 1.5MT pay on day		

Handling	Tel: 01223 373214/3285	Operator	Marshall Aerospace
	(Cambridge Airport Handling)		The Airport
Restaurants	Restaurant Mon-Fri 0730-1400		Cambridge, CB5 8RX
	Coffee Shop Mon-Fri 0800-1630		**Tel:** 01223 373213 (ATC)
			Tel: 01223 373214 (Ops)
Taxis			**Fax:** 01223 373833 (ATC)
Cabco A1	**Tel:** 01223 711111		
Car Hire			
Hertz	**Tel:** 01223 416634		
Avis	**Tel:** 01223 212551		
Weather Info	M T9 Fax 256 MOEx		

Helicopter VRP

November
N5214.38 E00011.25 Reservoir/lake 0.25nm
NE Horningsea

Echo
N5212.47 E00014.54 Plantation S of A14

Sierra
N5209.51 E00010.27 Golf Course

MINIMUM NOISE PROCEDURE
Rwy05 RTO climb ahead thru 500ft QFE before turning
Rwy05 LTO climb ahead thru 2000ft QFE before turning
Rwy23 LTO climb ahead thru 500ft QFE before turning
Rwy23 RTO climb ahead thru 2000ft QFE before turning

Effective date:23/11/06

C

42ft 2mb	3nm WNW of Campbletown N5526.23 W00541.18	PPR	Alternative AD Diversion AD	Prestwick
	Campbeltown		AFIS 125.900	

3049m x 46m

Northern Twy

Southern Parallel Twy

Light ACFT Apron

CBL 380

S MID

N

C

Terminal

Fuel Apron

Fuel

MAC 116.00

11

29

RWY	SURFACE	TORA	LDA	LIGHTING
11	Conc/Asph	2869	2727	Ap Thr Rwy PAPI 3°
29	Conc/Asph	2899	2497	Ap Thr Rwy PAPI 3°

Rwy29 first 402m sterile for landing
Rwy11 first 322m sterile for landing

Remarks
Non-radio ACFT not accepted. Circling is not permitted S of AD. No GND signals. Fuel and long stay on the apron.

Warnings
Serious risk of bird strikes. High GND 1159ft amsl 135°/4nm & 1465ft amsl 230°/5nm. Markings for military emergency Rwy visible S of parallel Twy, outside licensed AD. Pilots ignore theses markings, use Rwy29/11 for take-off & landing.

Operating Hrs	0930-1730 (L) Mon-Fri	**Taxis**	
Circuits	11 LH, 29 RH, 1500ft QFE	McKerrals	**Tel:** 01586 553131
	No circuits to S of AD	**Car Hire**	
Landing Fee	£12 up to 3MT	Campbeltown	**Tel:** 01586 552772
	VFR cash or Cheque on day	**Weather Info**	M T Fax 366 GWC
Maintenance	Nil	**Operator**	HIAL Campbeltown
Fuel	AVGAS 100LL		Argyll PA28 6NU
	Tel: 01586 553797		**Tel:** 01586 553797 (ATC)
	Fax: 01586 552620		**Fax:** 01586 552620
			www.highlands-and-islands-airports.uk.com

Disabled Facilities

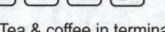

Restaurant   Tea & coffee in terminal

EGFF

CARDIFF

220ft 8mb	8.5nm SW of Cardiff N5123.80 W00320.60		PPR	Alternative AD	Bristol Swansea

Cardiff	ATIS 132.475	LARS 126.625	APP 126.625
RAD 125.850	TWR 125.000	Signature 122.350	

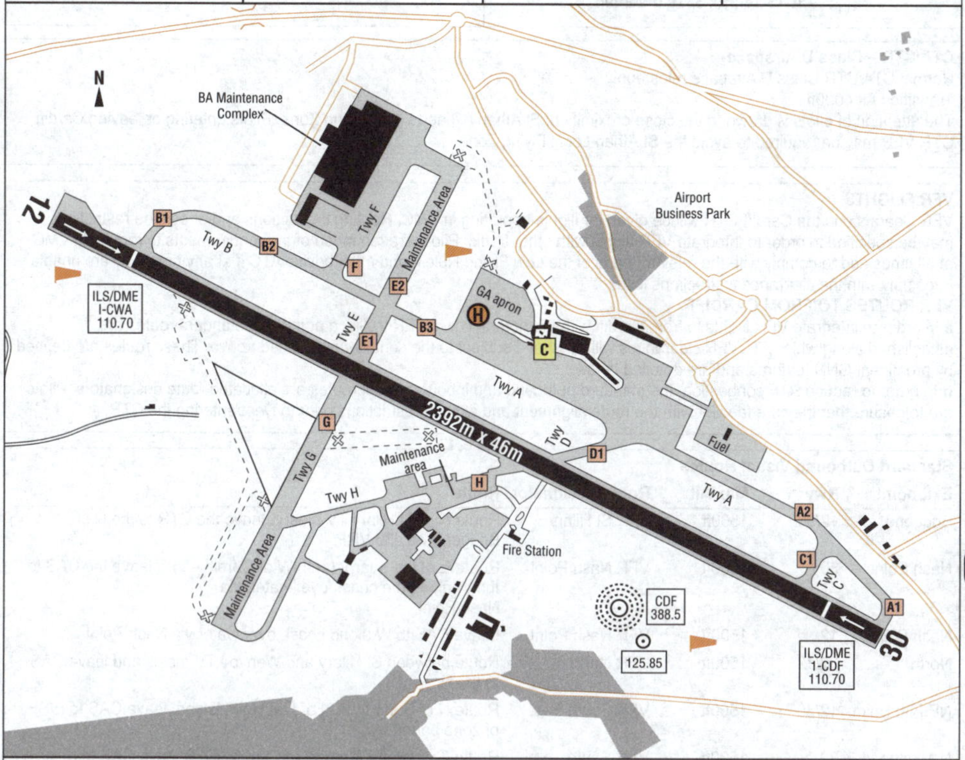

C

BA Maintenance Complex

N

Airport Business Park

Twy F

Maintenance Area

12

B1

Twy B

B2

F

E2

E1

B3

GA apron

H

C

Twy A

ILS/DME I-CWA 110.70

Twy E

Twy A

G

2392m x 46m

Twy D

D1

Fuel

Maintenance area

Twy G

H

Twy H

Fire Station

A2

Maintenance Area

CDF 388.5

C1

Twy C

125.85

ILS/DME I-CDF 110.70

A1

30

RWY	SURFACE	TORA	LDA	LIGHTING
12	Asphalt	2352	2133	Ap Thr Rwy PAPI 3° LHS
30	Asphalt	2354	2201	Ap Thr Rwy PAPI 3° LHS

Remarks

PPR essential. All training in Cardiff CTR/CTA is PPR from Cardiff APP. A helicopter set-down point, marked with an 'H', is situated on the parallel Twy to the W of stand 2. ACFT will be allowed to ground taxi or hover taxi to the helicopter alighting pad located to the W of the W pier, as instructed by ATC. Flight clearance is located on the first floor of the Control TWR building. Access from airside is via the domestic pier. Asymmetric training must be approved by ATC and ACFT wishing to instrument train in Cardiff Zone must have a functioning transponder with Mode C. Landing fees can be paid at the Bureau De Change between 0800-1700 Monday to Friday, otherwise at the Information Desk in the terminal, also at Cardiff-Wales Flying Club on the S side of AD. Handling is mandatory for all ACFT other than Cardiff based flying club.

Warnings

Possible turbulence on short finals when landing on Rwy30 in strong W to S winds. Due to proximity of RAF St Athan (3nm W) overhead joining will not normally be approved. When inbound to Rwy12 or outbound from Rwy30 at Cardiff be aware of the close proximity of RAF St Athan and the St Athan Local Flying Zone to the Cardiff Arr/Dept tracks. VFR flights to/from Cardiff AD may be required to enter/leave the CTR at VRPs which avoid the St Athan Local Flying Zone.
Noise: ACFT must be operated to cause the least disturbance practicable to areas surrounding the AD. Single engine ACFT should avoid over flying the chemical complex at Barry.

Operating Hrs	H24
Circuits	30 RH, 12 LH or as instructed by ATC
Landing Fee	On application

Maintenance
LAM   **Tel: 01446 710106**
Fuel   **AVGAS 100LL JET A1**
JET A1 by arr with Air BP (H24)
AVGAS (H24)
Tel: 01446 710000 (H24)

Disabled Facilities

Handling	**Tel: 01446 712637 (Signature)**
Restaurants	G/A CTR on S side
	Licensed Buffet and Cafeteria in Terminal

Taxis		Operator	Cardiff International Airport Ltd
Cardiff Airport Taxis **Tel:** 01446710693			Vale of Glamorgan, CF26 3BD
	Frequent buses to/from Cardiff & Barry		**Tel:** 01446 712562 (ATC)
Car Hire			**Tel:** 01446 711111 (AD Auth)
Avis	**Tel:** 01446 719569		**Fax:** 01446 711838 (ATC)
Europcar	**Tel:** 01446 711924		**Fax:** 01446 711675 (AD Auth)
Hertz	**Tel:** 01446 711722		
Weather Info	M T9 T18 Fax 258 A VS MOEx		
	ATIS **Tel:** 01446 729319		
	ATIS **Tel:** Ex 3319 (Internal)		

CTA/CTR – Class D Airspace
Normal CTA/CTR Class D Airspace rules apply
Transition Alt 4000ft
The attention of pilots is drawn to the close proximity of St Athan AD and Local Flying Zone. Pilots entering or leaving Cardiff CTR VFR may be required to avoid the St Athan Local Flying Zone.

VFR FLIGHTS
VFR clearance in the Cardiff CTR will be given for flights operating in VMC. Routing instructions and/or altitude restrictions may be specified in order to integrate VFR flights with other traffic. Pilots are reminded of the requirements to remain in VMC at all times and to comply with the relevant parts of the Low Flying Rules, and must advise ATC if at any time they are unable to comply with the clearance instructions issued.
VFR ROUTES TO/FROM CARDIFF
a In order to integrate VFR flights to/from Cardiff with the normal flow of IFR traffic, a number of standard routes are established along which ATCVFR clearances will be issued subject to the conditions specified above. These routes are defined by prominent GND features and are detailed below.
b In order to reduce RTF congestion, the standard outbound and inbound visual routes are allocated route designators. Pilots are to ensure that they are familiar with the route alignment and altitude restrictions prior to Dept/entering the CTR.

Standard Outbound Visual Routes
Exit point	Rwy	Max Alt	Route Designator	Route
Bridgend	12/30	1500ft	VFR St Hilary	Route N of St Hilary TV mast & leave the CTR to the N of Bridgend via J36 VRP.
Nash Point	30	1500ft	VFR Nash Point	Route E of the quarry (1nm W of Cardiff AD) & leave the CAS to the W along the coast, over water, via Nash Point.
Nash Point	12	1500ft	VFR Nash Point	Leave CAS to W along coast, over water via Nash Point
North	30/12	1500ft	VFR North	Route between St Hilary and Wenvoe TV masts and leave CAS to the N.
NE Flat Holm	12/30	1500ft	VFR South East	Route N of Barry then N of Flat Holm Island, leave CAS to E/SE of zone boundary.
N Minehead	30	1500ft	VFR South	Route E of quarry (1nm W of Cardiff AD) & leave CAS to S towards Minehead VRP
N Minehead	12	1500ft	VFR South	Route S & leave CAS to S towards Minehead VRP.

Standard Inbound Visual Routes
Entry point	Rwy	Max Alt	Route Designator	Route
Bridgend	30/12	1500ft	VFR St Hilary	Enter CAS via Bridgend, route N of St Hilary TV mast, then as directed by ATC.
North	30/12	1500ft	VFR North	Enter CAS from N between St Hilary and Wenvoe TV masts, then as directed by ATC.
Wenvoe	30/12	1500ft	VFR Wenvoe	Enter CAS via Wenvoe TV mast, then as directed by ATC.
Cardiff Docks	30/12	1500ft	VFR Cardiff Docks	Enter CAS via Cardiff Docks, then as directed by ATC.
NE of Flat	30/12	1500ft	VFR Flat Holm	Enter CAS via Weston Super Mare, route N of Flat Holm Lighthouse towards Lavernack Point, then as directed by ATC.
N Minehead	30	1500ft	VFR South	Enter CAS form S, then as directed by ATC.
N Minehead	12	1500ft	VFR South	Enter CAS from S, remaining E of the quarry (1nm W of Cardiff AD), then as directed by ATC.
Nash Point	30	1500ft	VFR Nash Point	Enter CAS via Nash Point, route along the coast, over water, then as directed by ATC.
Nash Point	12	1500ft	VFR Nash Point	Enter CAS via Nash Point, route along coast, over water, E of quarry (1nm W of Cardiff AD), then as directed by ATC.

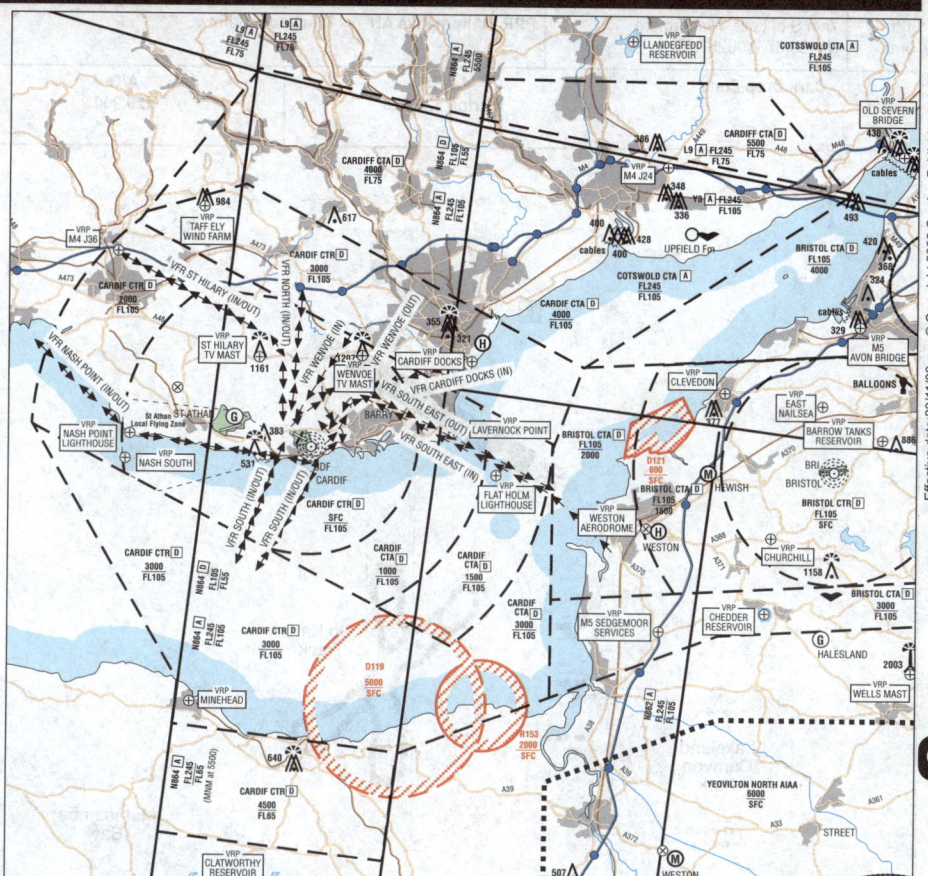

C

Visual Reference Points (VRP)

VRP	NDB/DME	VOR/DME
Cardiff Docks N5127.40 W00309.10	CDF 064°/*I-CWA (I-CDF) 7nm	BCN 171°/17nm
Clatworthy Reservoir N5104. W00322.	CDF 187°/*I-CWA (I-CDF) 19nm	BCN 189°/39nm
Flat Holm Lighthouse N5122.55 W00307.13	CDF 100°/*I-CWA (I-CDF) 8nm	BCN 169°/22nm
Lavernock Point N512423.38 W00310.23	CDF 086°/*I-CWA (I-CDF) 6nm	BCN 173°/20nm
Llandegfedd Reservoir N5121. W00258.00	CDF 041°/*I-CWA (I-CDF) 22nm	BCN 104°/11nm
M4 J24 N5136. W00255.00	CDF 055°/*I-CWA (I-CDF) 20nm	BCN 124°/15nm
M4 J36 N5131.93 W00334.40	CDF 317°/*I-CWA (I-CDF) 12nm	BCN 229°/16nm
Minehead N5112.35 W00328.50	CDF 207°/*I-CWA (I-CDF) 8nm	BCN 198°/32nm
Nash Point Lighthouse N5124.08 W00333.33	CDF 277°/*I-CWA (I-CDF) 8nm	BCN 213°/22nm
Nash South (on St Athan C/L 1nm S of Nash Point) N5122.88 W00333.45	CDF 269°/*I-CWA (I-CDF) 8nm	BCN 212°/23nm
Old Severn Bridge (M48) N5136. W00238.	CDF 067°/*I-CWA (I-CDF) 29nm	BCN 110°/24nm
St Hilary TV Mast ** N5127.45 W00324.18	CDF 330°/*I-CWA (I-CDF) 4nm	BCN 201°/17nm
Taff Ely Wind Farm N5134. W00328.	CDF 338°/*I-CWA (I-CDF) 117nm	BCN 223°/12nm
Wenvoe TV Mast ** N5127.60 W00316.95	CDF 031°/*I-CWA (I-CDF) 5nm	BCN 186°/16nm

Note: * DME frequency-paired with ILS gives zero range indication from the Thr of the Rwy with which it is associated
** Caution to be exercised when routing via St Hilary TV mast 1164ft amsl/745ft agl
*** Caution to be exercised when routing via Wenvoe TV mast 1212ft amsl/787ft agl

17ft 0mb	7nm S of Lake Windermere N5409.87 W00257.53	**PPR**	**Alternative AD**	**Blackpool** Barrow
Cark Drop Zone			**LARS** Warton 129.525	**A/G** 129.900

RWY	SURFACE	TORA	LDA	LIGHTING
06/24	Asphalt	400x15	U/L	Nil

Rwy06/24 200m over run
Rwy surfaces rough

Remarks
PPR by telephone. Primarily a parachute centre but light ACFT welcome at own risk. Parachutists exit free-fall up to FL140. Parachutes open from 2200ft down. Radio usually manned only at weekends. If no reply please make blind calls.

Warnings
The 2 other Rwys are fenced off and unusable. Portions of WW II Rwy06/24 are overgrown and unusable but serviceable portion is clearly visible. Windsock at weekends only. Occasionally live stock on AD. Power lines 550m from Rwy06 Thr.
Noise: Avoid over flying local habitation.

Operating Hrs	SR-SS	**Operator**	North West Parachute Centre
Circuits	No overhead joins Circuits over the sea at 1000ft QFE		Cark Airfield Moore Lane Flookburgh
Landing Fee	Single £10, Twin £20, Microlight £5		Grange-over-Sands Cumbria
Maintenance	Nil		**Tel:** 01539 558672
Fuel	Nil		(PPR AD weekends)
Disabled Facilities	Nil		
Restaurants	Snacks at weekends		
Taxis	**Tel:** 01539 533792		
Car Hire	Nil		
Weather Info	AirN MWC		

162

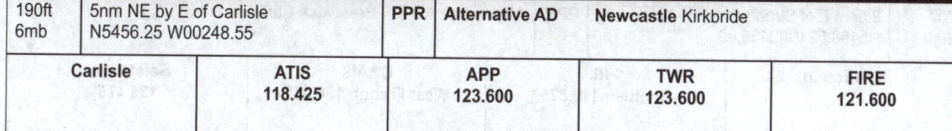

EGNC   CARLISLE

190ft 6mb	5nm NE by E of Carlisle N5456.25 W00248.55	PPR	Alternative AD	Newcastle Kirkbride

Carlisle	ATIS 118.425	APP 123.600	TWR 123.600	FIRE 121.600

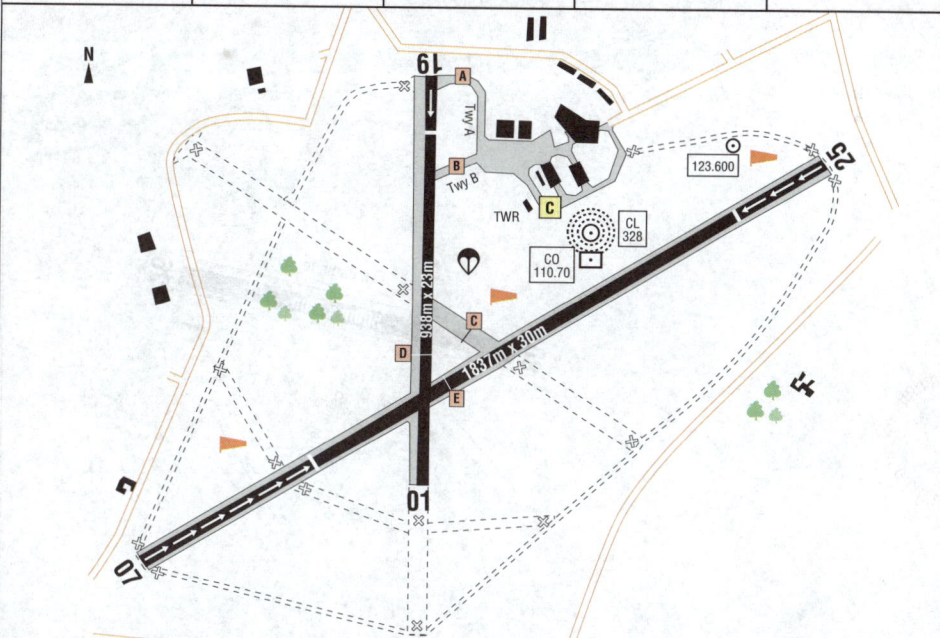

RWY	SURFACE	TORA	LDA	LIGHTING
01	Asphalt	803	803	Nil
19	Asphalt	938	809	Nil
07	Asphalt	1659	1321	Thr Rwy PAPI 3.5° LHS
25	Asphalt	1714	1469	Ap Thr Rwy PAPI 3.5° LHS

Displaced Thr Rwy25 245m, Displaced Thr Rwy19 129m, Displaced Thr Rwy07 458m

Remarks
PPR. AD is not available to non-radio ACFT. Hi-vis. All ACFT using AD must comply with the AD terms & conditions available via AD Ops. AD used out of Hrs. Certain customs facilities available. Aviation museum on AD.

Warnings
Danger Area D510 5nm NE of AD. DAAIS available from Carlisle APP. The ends of TORA/ED/LDA on Rwy07/25 are shown by red edge lights only. The red lights across the Rwys mark the end of useable pavement. Rwy07/25 lighting is at full width 46m. The only useable Twys are from the apron to the Rwy19 Thr and the disused Rwy13/31 that links Rwy01/19 with Rwy07/25. Free fall parachuting on AD. During adverse weather conditions NDB CL is subject to failure, use with caution.

Operating Hrs	0800-1730 (Summer) +1Hr (Winter) & by arr	**Car Hire**	
Circuits	Variable	National	**Tel:** 01228 542707
Landing Fee	On application	Avis	**Tel:** 01228 590580
Maintenance	Northumberland Aircraft Maintenance **Tel:** 01670 731189 (M3) **Tel:** 07962 167468	Enterprise	**Tel:** 01228 599877
		Weather Info	M T9 Fax 262 MWC ATIS **Tel:** 01228 574123
Fuel	AVGAS 100LL AVTUR JET A1 by prior arr Oil W80 S80 W100 S100 Multi	**Visual Reference Points (VRP)**	
Disabled Facilities		Gretna	N5459.73 W00304.05
		Haltwistle	N5458.13 W00227.73
		Penrith	N5439.87 W00245.02
		Wigton	N5449.48 W00309.67

Restaurants
Airport Café/Bar   **Tel:** 01228 573443

Taxis
Radio Taxis   **Tel:** 01228 527575
Airbus 2000   **Tel:** 01697 73735
Executive Cars   **Tel:** 01228 404305

Operator   Stobart Air Ltd
Carlisle Airport
Carlisle, CA6 4NW
Tel: 01228 573641 (Admin/Ops)
Fax: 01228 573310
enquiries@carlisleairport.co.uk
www.carlisleairport.co.uk

C

CASTLE KENNEDY

70ft 2mb	2.5nm E of Stranraer N5453.52 W00456.09	PPR	Alternative AD	Prestwick Carlisle

	FIR	DAAIS	Safetycom
Non-Radio	**Scottish 119.875**	**West Freugh 130.050**	**135.475**

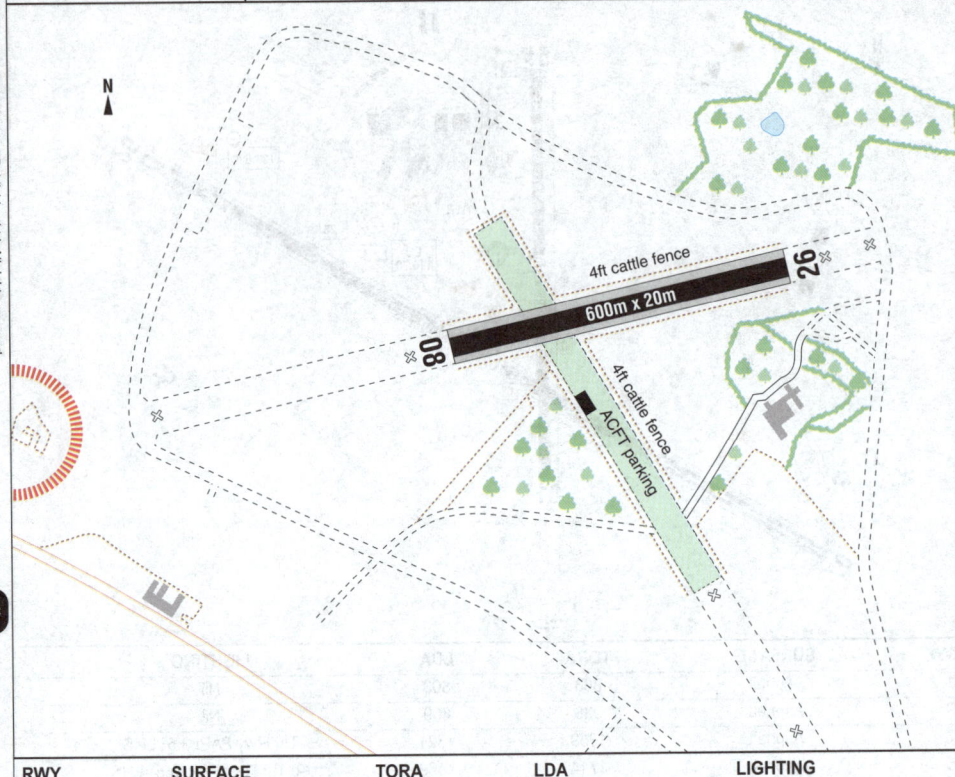

N

4ft cattle fence

26

600m x 20m

08

4ft cattle fence

ACFT parking

C

RWY	SURFACE	TORA	LDA	LIGHTING
08/26	Asphalt	600x20	U/L	Nil

Remarks
Strictly PPR due to activities on AD. Contact via website or telephone. Visiting ACFT welcome at their own risk and at pilots discretion. WW2 AD, useable areas marked with white brackets painted on Rwy. Website provides news and info on events. Aerial photo also available.

Warnings
AD situated on the edge of D402A . Pilots to contact West Freugh Ops, and check NOTAM's to ascertain danger area activity. West Freugh is under care & maintenance, A/G is manned, provides range activity info. Military ACFT may still use West Freugh. Wind shear may be encountered due trees to N & S of Rwy. Model ACT use area N of Rwy intersection, they are forbidden from operating within 60m if Rwy08/26
Noise: Rwy26 left turn ASAP after take off, track 240° to avoid house at W end of Rwy. Avoid over flying all local properties.

Operating Hrs	SR-SS	**Taxis**	
Circuits	08 RH, 26 LH. Join over head 1200ft QFE, descend downwind leg	McLeans	**Tel:** 01776 702222
		Car Hire	Nil
Landing Fee	Micro/Ultralight £5, Single £10, Twin £20 All money towards developments	**Weather Info**	AirSc GWC
		Operator	Stair Estates, Estate Office Rephad, Stranraer Wigtownshire DG9 8BX
Maintenance	Nil		**Tel:** 01776 702024 (AD)
Fuel	Nil		**Tel:** 07774 116424 (AD mobile)
Disabled Facilities			**Tel:** 01776 888741 (West Freugh Ops)
☒			**Fax:** 01776 706248 (AD)
			enquires@castlekennedyairfield.co.uk
Restaurants			www.castlekennedyairfield.co.uk
The Plantings Inn	**Tel:** 01581 400633 (also B&B 400m)		

EGLJ

CHALGROVE

230ft 7mb	8nm SE of Oxford N5140.53 W00104.38		**Alternative AD Diversion AD**	**Oxford** Wycombe

Chalgrove	Zone **Benson 120.900**	A/G **125.400**

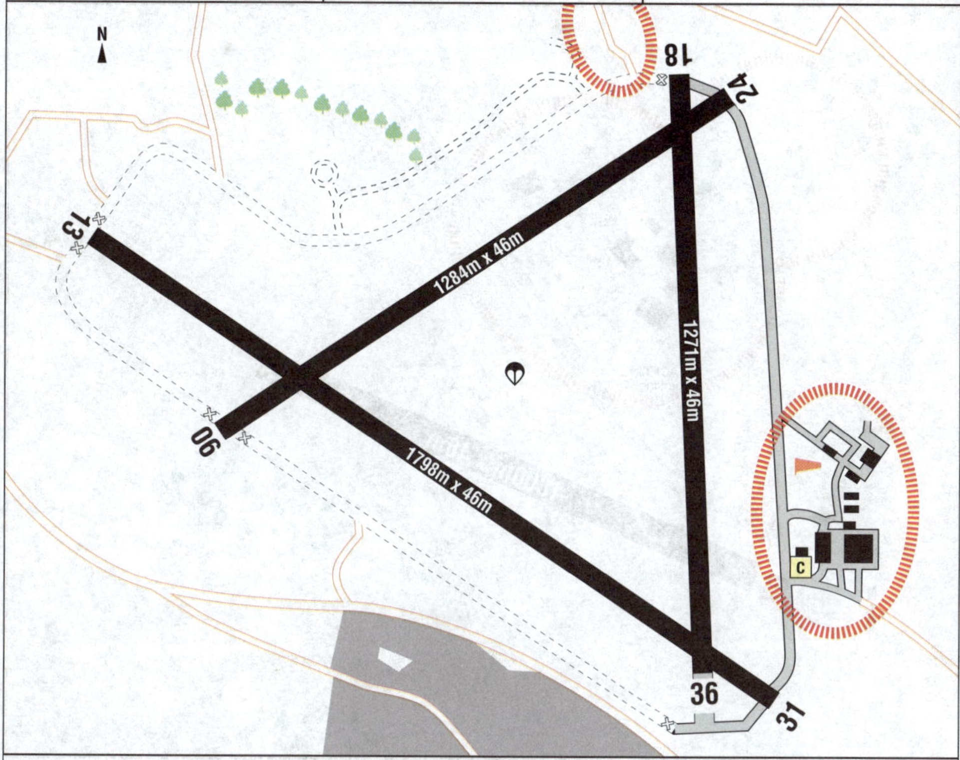

N

Runways depicted: 18, 24, 13, 06, 36, 31

- 1284m x 46m
- 1271m x 46m
- 1798m x 46m

C

RWY	SURFACE	TORA	LDA	LIGHTING
06/24	Asphalt	1289	1289	Rwy
13/31	Asphalt	1801	1801	Thr Rwy
18	Asphalt	1270	1270	Ap Rwy
36	Asphalt	1270	1224	Rwy

Rwy18 no departures

Remarks
Strictly PPR by telephone. For ACFT visiting company only, no public transport/corporate movements will be approved. AD licensed for daytime use only, however company operations may take place at night. Visiting ACFT operations will be prohibited during testing.

Warnings
AD situated within the Benson MATZ, Arr/Dept ACFT contact Benson APP. Over flight of hangar and associated buildings prohibited below1000ft QFE. Take-off, landing, and taxiing on grass areas prohibited due to obstructions. GND level tests from a Meteor ACFT on Rwy13/31 at speeds between 60-130kts. In flight tests from a Meteor ACFT above Rwy06/24 at heights between 250-1000ft QFE at speeds up to 450kts. Ejector seat testing may take place at any time during daylight Hrs from the centre of the AD up to 600ft agl. Parachute drop tests from 5500ft QFE overhead AD from helicopters
Noise: Avoid over flying Chalgrove village

Operating Hrs	Mon-Thu 0730-1530 Fri 0730-1130 (Summer) +1Hr (Winter) AD closed at weekends & PH	**Restaurants**	Nil
		Taxis	Operator can advise
		Car Hire	Nil
Circuits	N 1000ft QFE	**Weather Info**	AirSE MOEx
Landing Fee	Advised with PPR	**Operator**	Martin-Baker Aircraft Co Ltd
Maintenace	Nil		Chalgrove Airfield, Chalgrove
Fuel	JET A1		Oxford, OX44 7RJ
Disabled Facilities			**Tel:** 01865 892200
			Fax: 01865 892214

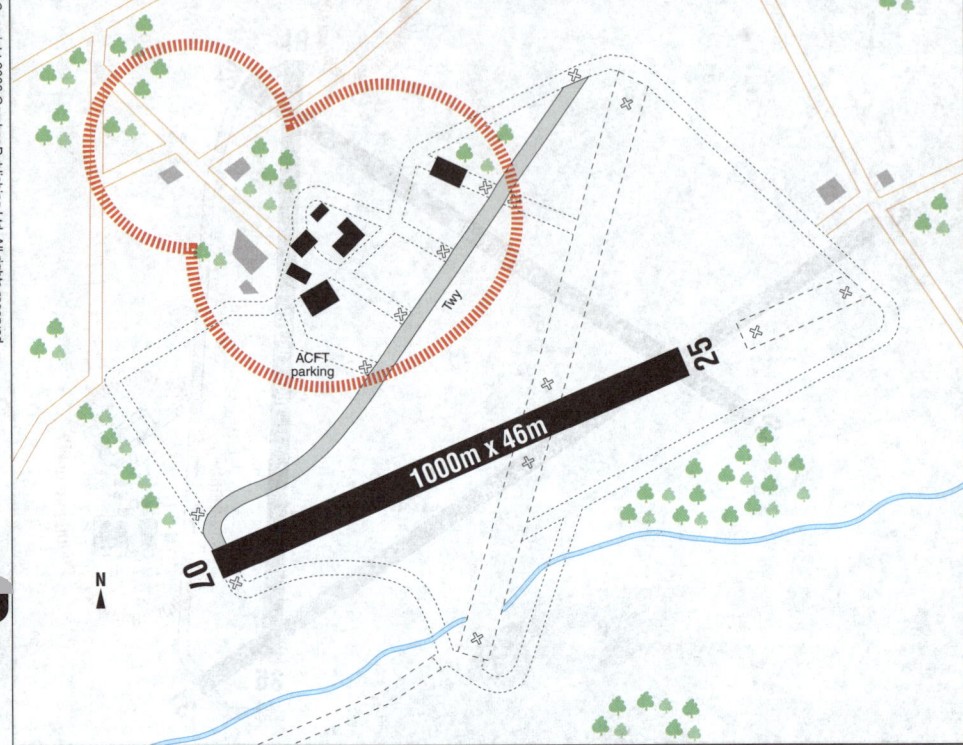

CHARTERHALL

350ft 12mb	4.5nm SSW of Duns N5542.45 W00222.64	PPR	Alternative AD Diversion AD	Edinburgh Eshott

Non Radio	FIS Scottish 119.875	Safetycom 135.475

C

N

Twy

ACFT parking

07

1000m x 46m

25

RWY	SURFACE	TORA	LDA	LIGHTING
07/25	Asphalt	1000x46	U/L	Nil

Remarks
PPR essential. Light ACFT accepted at the pilot's own risk. Microlight activity on AD.

Warnings
Rwy and AD surface rough. AD used for farming beware of animals on the Rwy. A fence crosses E end of Rwy. MOD training takes place on AD

Operating Hrs	SR-SS
Circuits	07 RH, 25 LH, 1000ft QFE
Landing Fee	£20
Maintenance	Nil
Fuel	Nil
Disabled Facilities	Nil
Taxis Robertson	**Tel:** 01361 882340
Car Hire	Nil
Weather Info	AirSc MWC

Operator	Mr A R Trotter Charterhall, Duns Berwickshire **Tel:** 01890 840301 **Fax:** 01890 840651 info@charterhall.net www.charterhall.net

5ft 0mb	2nm N of Chatteris N5229.12 E00005.43		PPR	Alternative AD	Cambridge Peterborough Conington
	Chatteris			A/G 129.900	Only manned during parachuting

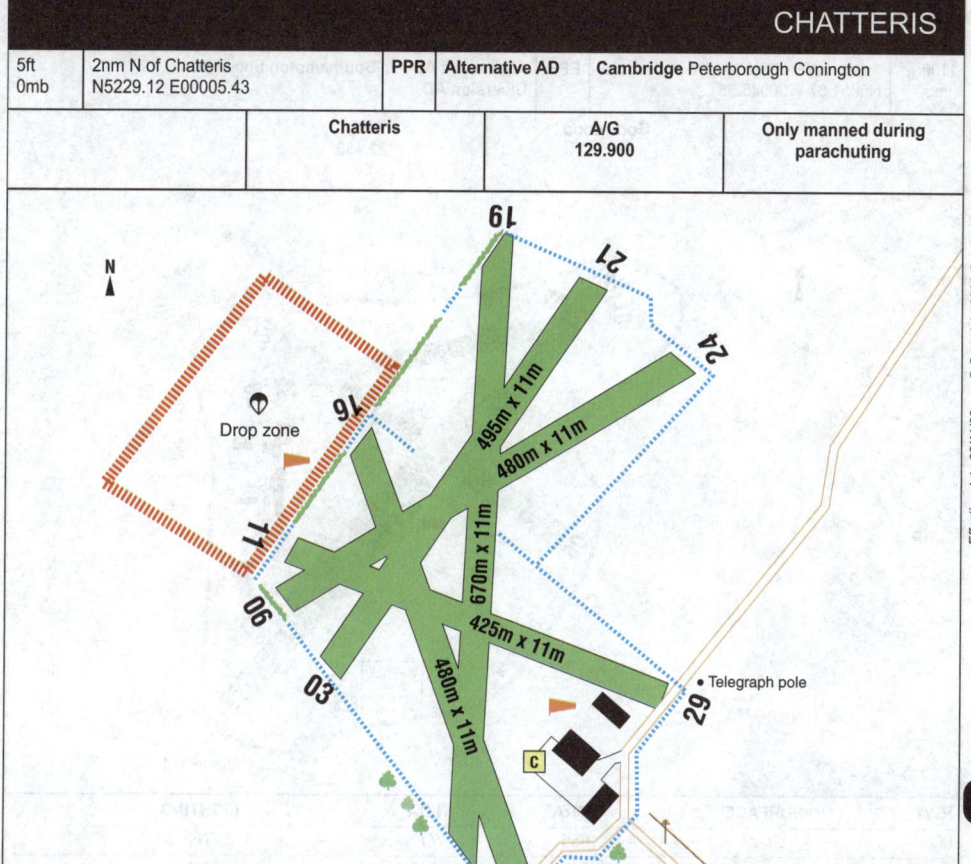

RWY	SURFACE	TORA	LDA	LIGHTING
01/19	Grass	670x11	U/L	Nil
06/24	Grass	480x11	U/L	Nil
03/21	Grass	495x11	U/L	Nil
16/34	Grass	480x11	U/L	Nil
11/29	Grass	425x11	U/L	Nil

Rwy34 & 29 microlight use only

Remarks
PPR strictly by telephone due to parachuting ops. Parachutists free-fall from FL150. Microlights also operate.

Warnings
Do not over fly the drop zone at any time. Telegraph pole on short final Rwy29. Public road crosses the undershoot Rwy29, please be aware of vehicles & pedestrians. AD is in an area of intense military low flying, keep a good lookout at all times.
Noise: Avoid over flying local habitation.

Operating Hrs	SR-SS	**Weather Info**	AirS MOEx
Circuits	19, 21, 24 LH, 01, 03, 06 RH, 700ft QFE No dead side	**Operator**	Chatteris Leisure Ltd Chatteris Airfield, Stonea March, Cambs, PE15 0EA **Tel:** 01473 829982 (PPR Weekends) **Tel:** 01354 740810 (PPR AD) **Fax:** 01354 740406 chatpara@aol.com
Landing Fee	Light ACFT £5, Microlight £3 except where reciprocal arr exists		
Maintenance	Nil Hangarage overnight by prior arr		
Fuel	AVGAS 100LL JET A1 by arr only		
Disabled Facilities	Nil		
Restaurants	Cafe at AD Thu-Sun 0800-2000 (L)		
Taxis	Tel: 01354 658083		
Car Hire	Tel: 01354 652361		

110ft 3mb	1.5nm NNE of Chichester N5051.57 W00045.55	PPR	Alternative AD Diversion AD	Southampton Shoreham

	Goodwood	AFIS 122.450	

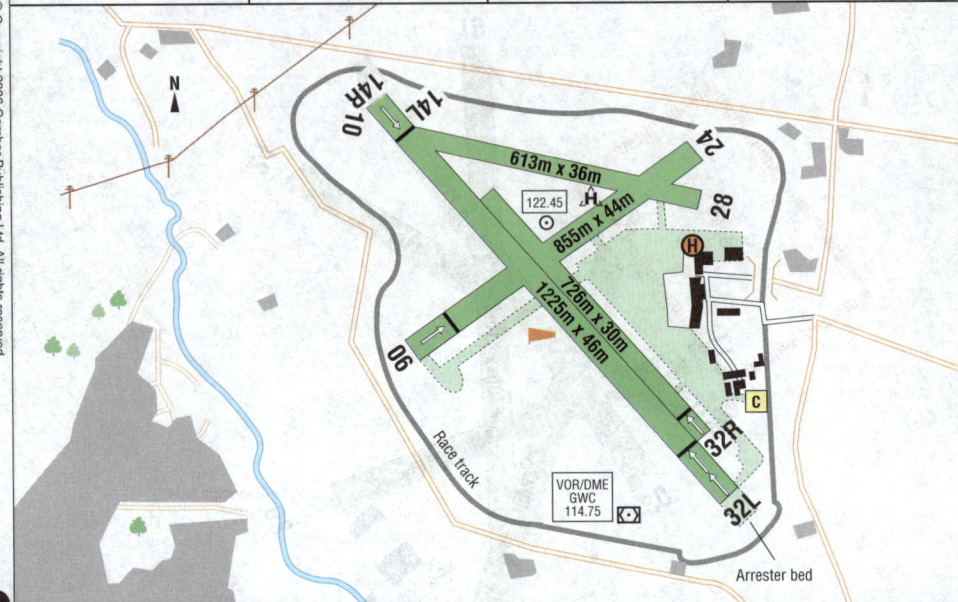

RWY	SURFACE	TORA	LDA	LIGHTING
06	Grass	855	710	Nil
24	Grass	845	845	Nil
32l	Grass	1129	1049	Thr Rwy
32r	Grass	726	726	Nil
14r	Grass	1170	1087	Thr Rwy APAPI 3° LHS
14l	Grass	726	726	Nil
10/28	Grass	613	613	Nil

Remarks
PPR by telephone recommended. Rwy14R has U/L starter extension for CEGA ACFT only. Helis must not taxi across road between fire station & TWR. Helis taxiing from parking area must taxi W of TWR. White Frangible Rwy edge markers on all Rwys.

Warning
When Rwy06/24 & 10/28 in use fixed-wing circuits, opposite direction heli circuits flown from Rwy32L Thr. Arrester bed shingle at end Rwy14R. When Relief Rwy14L/32R in use (Nov-Mar) Thr will be marked with black & white prismatic markers. Motor racing track on perimeter in constant use daylight Hrs not to be used for taxiing ACFT any time. Helis not permitted join circuit below 700ft QFE unless weather dictates lower height.
Noise: Helis avoid routing over Chichester, Westerton & Summersdale

Operating Hrs	0800-1700 (Summer) Nov Feb & Mar 0900-1700 Dec-Jan 0900-1600 & by arr	**Taxi** Dunnaways	**Tel:** 01243 782403
		Car Hire	
Circuit	06, 14, 10 LH, 24, 28, 32 RH ACFT 1200ft QFE, Heli 900ft QFE or as directed by AFIS Sun – no heli circuits – no FW circuits after 1400(L)	National Wessex Car Rental	**Tel:** 01243 202426 **Tel:** 01243 779977
		Weather Info	AirSE MOEx
Landing Fee	PA28 £14.95	**Operator**	Goodwood Road Racing Co Ltd Chichester (Goodwood) Aerodrome Chichester West Sussex, PO18 0PH **Tel:** 01243 755060 (Admin) **Tel:** 01243 755061 (ATC) **Fax:** 01243 755062 (ATC) control@goodwood.co.uk www.goodwood.co.uk
Maintenance	Goodwood ACFT Maintenance **Tel:** 01243 755064		
Fuel	AVGAS 100LL JET A1		
Disabled Facilities			

Restaurants	On AD by motor circuit pits and in Goodwood Flying Club

Helicopter Circuits

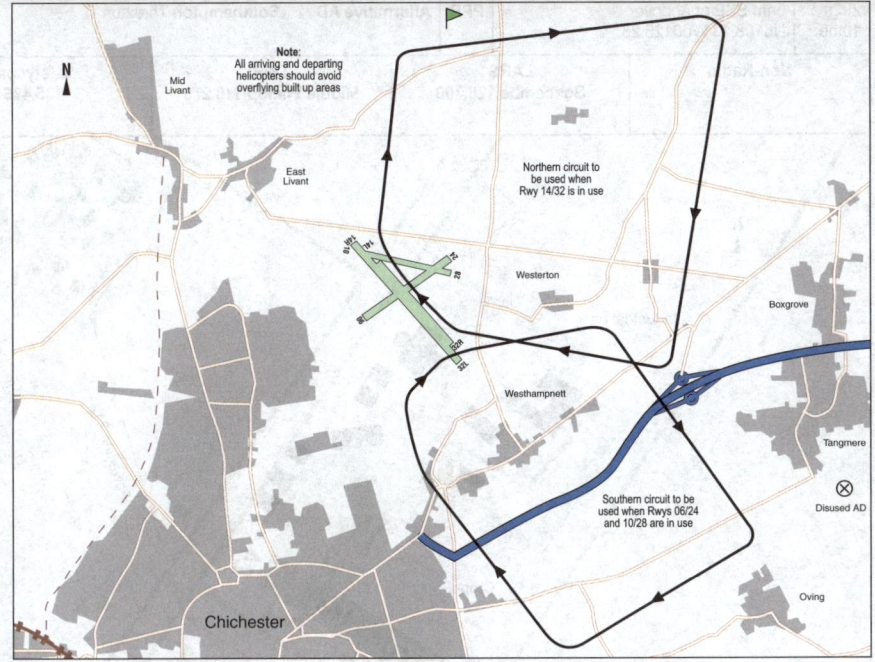

Fixed Wing Circuits

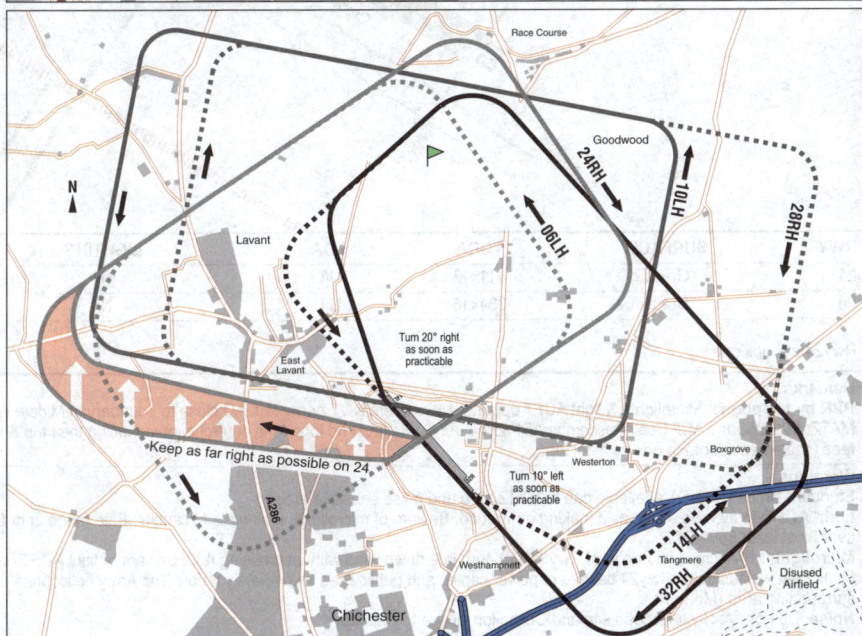

C

Circuit Height 1200ft QFE

Rwy06 Arr No low APP over built up areas in the undershoot

Rwy24 Dept ASAP after takeoff, turn R to avoid built up areas, maintain HDG until circuit height. No practice EFATO until W A286

Rwy14L/R Arr No low APP over East Lavant, light ACFT land beyond the intersection Rwy10/14

Rwy14L/R Dept ASAP after takeoff turn L 10° to avoid over flight of school and houses on Dept path. No practice EFATO until well clear of houses and school

Rwy32L/R Arr Follow defined circuit path turning base leg S of dual carriageway

Rwy32L/R Dept ASAP after takeoff turn R 20° to avoid East Lavant, maintain HDG until beyond village. No practice EFATO until well clear of East Lavant village

Rwy10 Arr Follow defined circuit, avoiding Lavant village on base leg

Rwy28 Dept Maintain Rwy HDG until clear of Lavant Village

292ft 10mb	5nm SSE of Andover N5108.13 W00125.28	PPR	Alternative AD	Southampton Thruxton

Non-Radio	LARS Boscombe 126.700	TWR Middle Wallop 118.275	Safetycom 135.475

RWY	SURFACE	TORA	LDA	LIGHTING
24	Grass	411x18	U/L	Nil
06	Grass	384x18	U/L	Nil

Rwy24 2% upslope

Remarks
PPR by telephone. Microlights & light ACFT operate. Helicopters NOT permitted. AD close to boundary of Middle Wallop MATZ. In/Outbound ACFT call Boscombe APP/Zone. All flights must be logged in control caravan facing the strip & landing fees (sealed envelope) in box by flight log.

Warnings
Standard circuit join NOT available due to MATZ stub and noise sensitive areas.
Light ACFT: to fly wide circuit as if making go-around. Beware of microlights making tight circuits. Rifle range 2nm E of AD, over fly at least 500ft QFE.
Microlights: Fly across mid-point of Rwy (150°), turn late down wind without crossing A30. Beware of light ACFT on longer finals from wide circuits. Rwy24 beware of power cables and public road immediately before Thr. Army helicopters operate in surrounding area (Mon-Fri).
Noise: Do not over fly telescope site and Chilbolton village to N of AD.

Operating Hrs	0800-2100 (L) No night flying No flying training	**Restaurants** Les Copains D'abord **Tel:** 01264 810738
Circuits	24 LH, 06 RH, All circuits S 600ft QFE	Abbots Mitre **Tel:** 01264 860348 (pub)
		Taxis/Car Hire Nil
Landing Fee	£3	**Weather Info** AirSW MOEx
Maintenance	M3 Hants Light Plane Services **Tel:** 01264 860056	**Operator** Stonefield Park & Chilbolton Flying Club 5 Augustus Gardens
Fuel	Nil	Camberley Surrey GU15 1 HL
Disabled Facilities	☒	**Tel:** 01276 691563 (Colin Marsh PPR) ppr@chilbolton.flyer.co.uk

140ft 4mb	5nm S of Dunsfold AD N5104.31 W00036.27	**PPR**	**Alternative AD**	**Shoreham** Goodwood

Non-Radio	**LARS** Farnborough 125.250	**Safetycom** 135.475

30ft power cables

ACFT parking

600m x 7m

08

26

Run up area

30ft power cables

RWY	SURFACE	TORA	LDA	LIGHTING
08	Grass	470x7	U/L	Nil
26	Grass	470x7	U/L	Nil

Rwy26 2% upslope

Remarks
PPR by telephone essential. Sheep may be grazing and electric wire fence established across strip. Windsock displayed. LDA provided by operator Rwy 08-600m Rwy26-470m

Warnings
Domestic power cables run close to AD on SW corner. AD may be waterlogged after prolonged wet weather. Gatwick CTA close to E.
Noise: Avoid all local villages, houses and Farms. Also fields containing livestock.

Operating Hrs	SR-SS	**Operator**	Mr I Charlton
Circuits	N over woods 1000ft QFE. Keep tight to AD		Chilsfold Farm Northchapel Petworth West Sussex GU28 9JZ **Tel:** 01428 707655
Landing Fee	Notified with PPR		
Maintenance	Nil		
Fuel	Nil		
Disabled Facilities	Nil		
Restaurants	Nil		
Taxis/Car Hire	Nil		
Weather Info	AirSE MOEx		

180ft 6mb	7nm W of Henley-on-Thames N5133.36 W00106.59	PPR	Alternative AD	Oxford Wycombe

Chiltern Park	Zone Benson 120.900	A/G 134.025

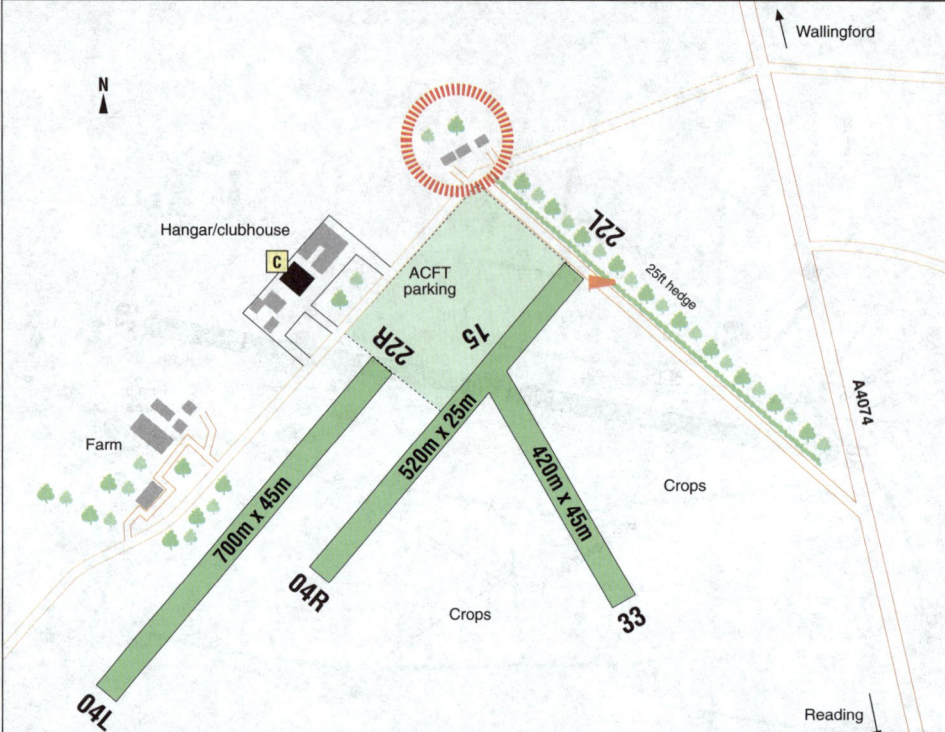

RWY	SURFACE	TORA	LDA	LIGHTING
04L/22R	Grass	700x45	U/L	Nil
04R/22L	Grass	520x25	U/L	Nil
15/33	Grass	420x45	U/L	Nil

Remarks
PPR by telephone. Primarily a Microlight AD but suitable light ACFT, helicopters and gliders welcome at pilots own risk. Join on permanent deadside to E of AD at 1000ft, descend to circuit height.

Warnings
AD located within the Benson MATZ, inbound ACFT call Benson APP. Benson has intensive helicopter activity during weekdays but may operate at weekends for exercises.
Noise: Avoid all local habitation, Arr/Dept via SSW.

Operating Hrs	Mon-Sat SR-SS Sun 1100-SS	**Operator**	Dennis Pearson
Circuits	All circuits to W 500ft		Chiltern Aero Club
Landing Fee	Fixed wing £5		Chiltern Park Aerodrome
	Helicopters £10		Ipsden, Wallingford
	Gliders £10		Oxon, OX10 6AS
	Free ACFT >50yrs old		**Tel:** 01491 875200
			Tel: 07739 802010
Maintenance	Nil		www.chiltern.aero
Fuel	Nil		
Disabled Facilities	Nil		
Restaurants	Local Pub 2.5 miles from AD		
Taxis	**Tel:** 01491 837022		
Car Hire	Nil		
Weather Info	AirSE MOEx		

448ft 14mb	1nm E of Chirk N5257.00 W00303.00	**PPR**	**Alternative AD**	**Hawarden** Sleap

Non-radio	**LARS** **Shawbury 120.775**	**Safetycom** **135.475**

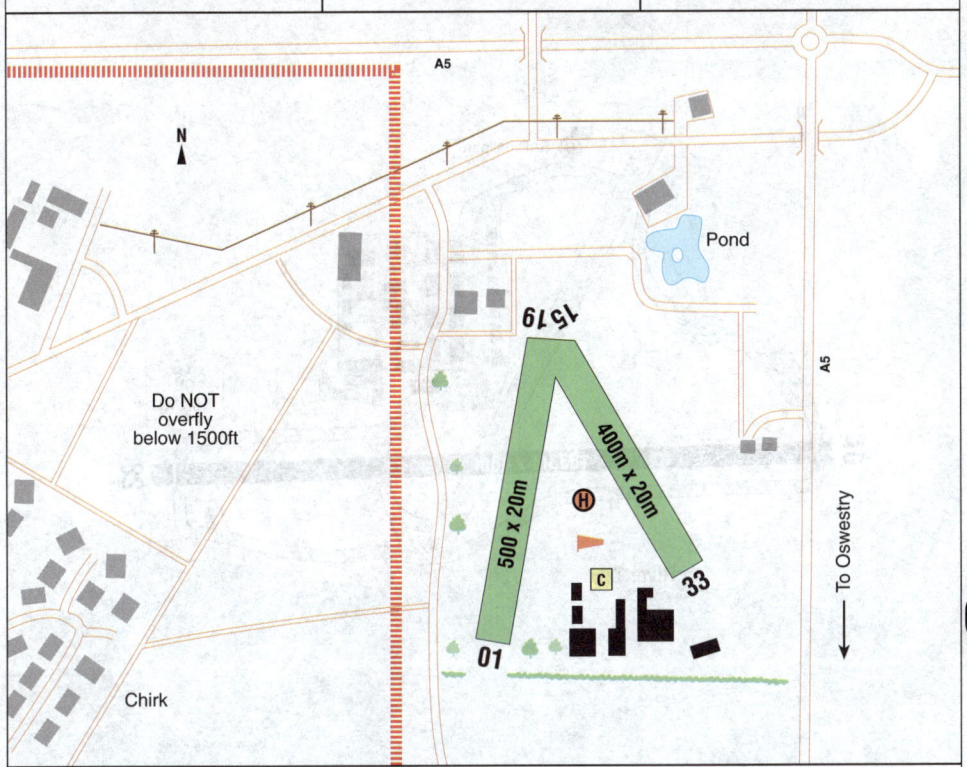

RWY	SURFACE	TORA	LDA	LIGHTING
01/19	Grass	500x20	U/L	Nil
15/33	Grass	400x20	U/L	Nil

Remarks
PPR essential. Primary a microlight AD but STOL ACFT welcome at pilots own risk. Rwys have no designator markings or edge marks.
Visual aid to location: AD is easily identifiable by white concrete 'H' in the centre of AD.

Warnings
Rwy01 has slight down slope. Sheep may be grazing if microlights are not active.
Noise: Area to W of AD is particularly noise sensitive and should not be over flown below 1500ft.

Operating Hrs	PPR AD Closed Apr-Nov Sat 1200 – Mon 0900	**Operator**	Mr R Everitt (Operator) **Tel:** 01691 774137 **Tel:** 07974 952118 Mr J Pierce (Owner) **Tel:** 01691 772659
Circuits	15, 19 LH, 01, 33 RH, 600ft QFE		
Landing Fee	Nil		
Maintenance	BMAA & PFA types		
Fuel	Nil		
Disabled Facilities	Nil		
Restaurants	Cafe on AD Mon-Fri		
Taxis/Car Hire	Nil		
Weather Info	AirCen MWC		

Effective date:23/11/06

EGDC

CHIVENOR

27ft 1mb	4nm WNW Barnstaple N5105.23 W00409.02	PPR MIL	Alternative AD	Cardiff Eaglescott
Chivenor		**A/G 130.200**		**When gliders operate C/S Alpha Charlie Base**

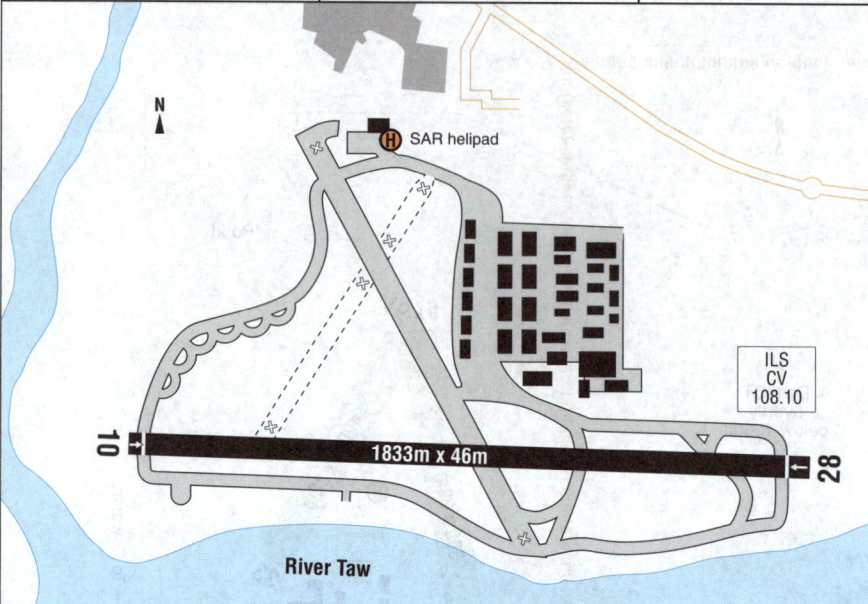

N

H SAR helipad

ILS CV 108.10

10

1833m x 46m

28

River Taw

RWY	SURFACE	TORA	LDA	LIGHTING
10/28	Asph/Conc	1833	U/L	Ap Rwy

Remarks

PPR with 24Hrs notice required. Applications should be made during office hours. Helicopters only not available to fixed wing ACFT. Military SAR helicopter activity H24. Powered gliders operate WE, PH and some evenings.

Warnings

AD Disused. Rwy and AD lighting maintained for SAR helicopter use and obstacles are frequently placed on Rwy and Twys.

Operating Hrs	SAR Helis H24 Visiting ACFT 0800-2200 (L)	Operator	Air Operations A Flight 22 Sqd RMB Chivenor Barnstable Devon EX31 4AZ **Tel:** 01271 857220 (PPR)
Circuits	To S 1000ft QFE		
Landing Fee	Charges in accordance with MOD policy Contact Station Ops for details		
Maintenance	Nil		
Fuel	Not available for visitors		
Disabled Facilities	Nil		
Restaurants	Nil		
Taxis/Car Hire	Nil		
Weather Info	AirSW MOEx		

29ft 1mb	4nm SE of Tadcaster N5350.06 W00111.73	PPR MIL	Alternative AD Diversion AD	Leeds Bradford Sherburn in Elmet

Fenton	LARS Linton 118.550	APP 126.500

PAR 123.300	TWR 122.100	GND 121.950

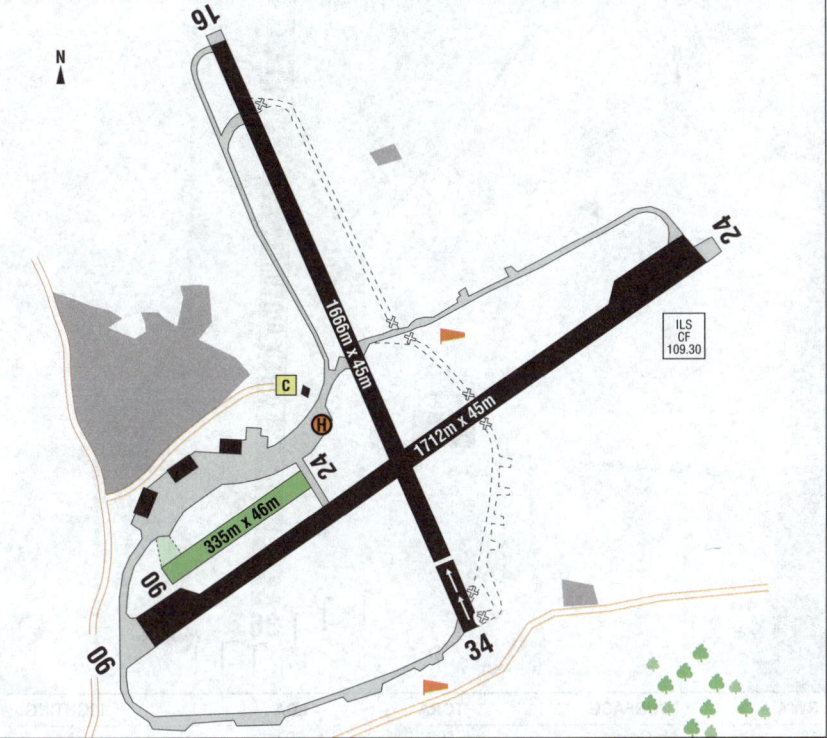

RWY	SURFACE	TORA	LDA	LIGHTING
06	Asph/Conc	1711	1711	Ap Thr Rwy PAPI 3°
24	Asph/Conc	1712	1877	Ap Thr Rwy PAPI 3°
16	Asphalt	1666	1666	Thr Rwy PAPI 3°
34	Asphalt	1666	1467	Thr Rwy PAPI 3°
06/24	Grass	335x46	U/L	Nil

Displaced Thr Rwy06/34

Remarks
PPR by telephone 24Hrs notice required. Satellite AD to Linton-on-Ouse. Intensive flying at this AD due to the flying training school.
Visual aids to location: Ibn CF Red.

Warnings
Public road (controlled by traffic lights) crosses final APP Rwy06 225m from Thr. Civil AD – Sherburn-in-Elmet –3nm to SW.

Operating Hrs	Mon-Thu 0700-1615 Fri-Sun 0700-1600 (Summer) +1Hr (Winter)	**Restaurants**	Nil
Circuits	24, 34 RH, 06, 16 LH 1000ft QFE, 800ft Light ACFT	**Taxis** Windmill	**Tel:** 01937 232979
		Car Hire	
Landing Fee	Charges in accordance with MOD policy Contact Station Ops for details	National (Leeds)	**Tel:** 01132 777957
		Weather Info	AirN MWC
Maintenance	Nil	**Operator**	RAF Church Fenton
Fuel	JET A1 AVGAS 100LL (Ltd quantities) by arr 24Hrs notice required		Tadcaster North Yorkshire, LS24 9SE **Tel:** 01347 848261 Ex 7491/2 (PPR Linton-on-Ouse)
Disabled Facilities			

37ft 1mb	2nm W of Clacton (1nm W of Clacton pier) N5147.10 E00107.80	PPR	Alternative AD Diversion AD	Southend Elmsett

Clacton	LARS Southend 130.775	A/G 118.150

C

610m x 18m

18

36

N

Fuel

Visitor parking

A

B

C

RWY	SURFACE	TORA	LDA	LIGHTING
18	Grass	596	502	Nil
36	Grass	600	542	Nil

Remarks

PPR by telephone essential. Visiting ACFT welcome at pilot's own risk. Telephone briefing necessary prior to visit. No overhead join.

Aids to Navigation: VOR/DME CLN 114.55

Warnings

There is a line of lamp posts 16ft agl on the public Rd crossing APP Rwy36 just before the AD boundary. A public footpath crosses the AD.

Operating Hrs	0900-1730 or SS (Summer) 1000-1600 or SS (Winter)	**Taxis** George Won	
		AJ	**Tel:** 01255 220050/270630 **Tel:** 01255 474444
Circuits	18 RH, 36 LH, 1000ft QFE	**Car Hire**	Nil
Landing Fee	Single £7.50	**Weather Info**	AirS MOEx
Maintenance		**Operator**	Clacton Aero Club
CAS Engineering	**Tel:** 01255 424671		Clacton Aerodrome
Fuel	Nil		West Road
Disabled Facilities	Nil		Clacton-On-Sea
Restaurants	Refreshments available at AD		Essex, CO15 1AG **Tel:** 01255 424671 **Fax:** 01255 475364

623ft 20mb	2nm S of Marlborough N5123.37 W00143.94	PPR	Alternative AD	Oxford Thruxton

Clench Common	Zone Lyneham 123.400	A/G 129.825

Wernham Farm

Disused Railway

N

16

396m x

4ft fence

443m x

08

28m

28m

26

34

Clench Common

Cutleys Farm

RWY	SURFACE	TORA	LDA	LIGHTING
08/26	Grass	443x28	U/L	Nil
16/34	Grass	396x28	U/L	Nil

Rwy34 upslope on first third

Remarks
PPR by telephone Primarily a microlight school but STOL ACFT welcome at own risk. AD is close to the S boundary of the Lyneham CTR.

Warnings
4ft high fence close to Rwy16 Thr.
Noise: Avoid over flying Clench Common village and Wernham Farm

Operating Hrs	Mon-Sat 0800-2000 Sun 1000-1900 or SS (L) whichever earliest	**Operator**	Graham Slater, GS Aviation Clench Common Airfield Marlborough Wiltshire, SN8 4NZ **Tel:** 01672 515535 **Tel:** 07831 350928 **Fax:** 01672 511574 info@gsaviation.co.uk
Circuits	08, 34 RH, 16, 26 LH Join overhead at 1500ft QFE then descend to 500ft QFE on dead side		
Landing Fee	£3		
Maintenance Fuel	Workshop facilities for microlights MOGAS (local garage by arr)		
Disabled Facilities			

Restaurants	Hot drinks available
Taxis/Car Hire	**Tel:** 01672 511088
Weather Info	AirSW MOEx

177

406ft 13mb	6nm SSE of Canterbury N5111.11 E00109.30	PPR	Alternative AD	Manston Rochester
Non-Radio		**LARS** **Manston 126.350**		**Safetycom** **135.475**

N

20

490m x 30m

ACFT parking

C

02

7ft hedge

RWY	SURFACE	TORA	LDA	LIGHTING
02/20	Grass	490x30m	U/L	Nil

Rwy02 slight downslope

Remarks
PPR by telephone essential. Visiting ACFT welcome at pilots own risk. Visitors are requested to complete AD log before dept. Short field experience is helpful.
Visual aid to location: Golf course 0.5nm ENE.

Warnings
Trees border strip to E and N, may generate turbulence. Low hedge by Rwy02 Thr. Trees on short final Rwy20.
Noise: No over flight of local villages. No local flying.

Operating Hrs	SR-SS	**Operator**	Mr R G Akehurst
Circuits	20 RH, 02 LH, 1000ft QFE		Clipgate Farm
Landing Fee	Nil		Lodge Lees
			Barham
Maintenance	Nil		Canterbury
Fuel	Nil		Kent, CT4 6NS
Disabled Facilities			**Tel:** 01227 831327
			Fax: 01227 832906
			Tel: 07973 176879
			bob@clipgate.co.uk
			www.clipgate.co.uk

C ✔ ☕ **P**

Restaurants	
Accomodation	Caravans and camping on site
Taxis	Nil
Car Hire	Nil
Weather Info	AirSE MOEx

CLUTTON HILL FARM

600ft 20mb	5nm WSW of Bath N5120.57 W00231.22	PPR	Alternative AD	Bristol Filton Kemble

Non-radio	ATIS Bristol 126.025	APP Bristol 125.650	Safetycom 135.475

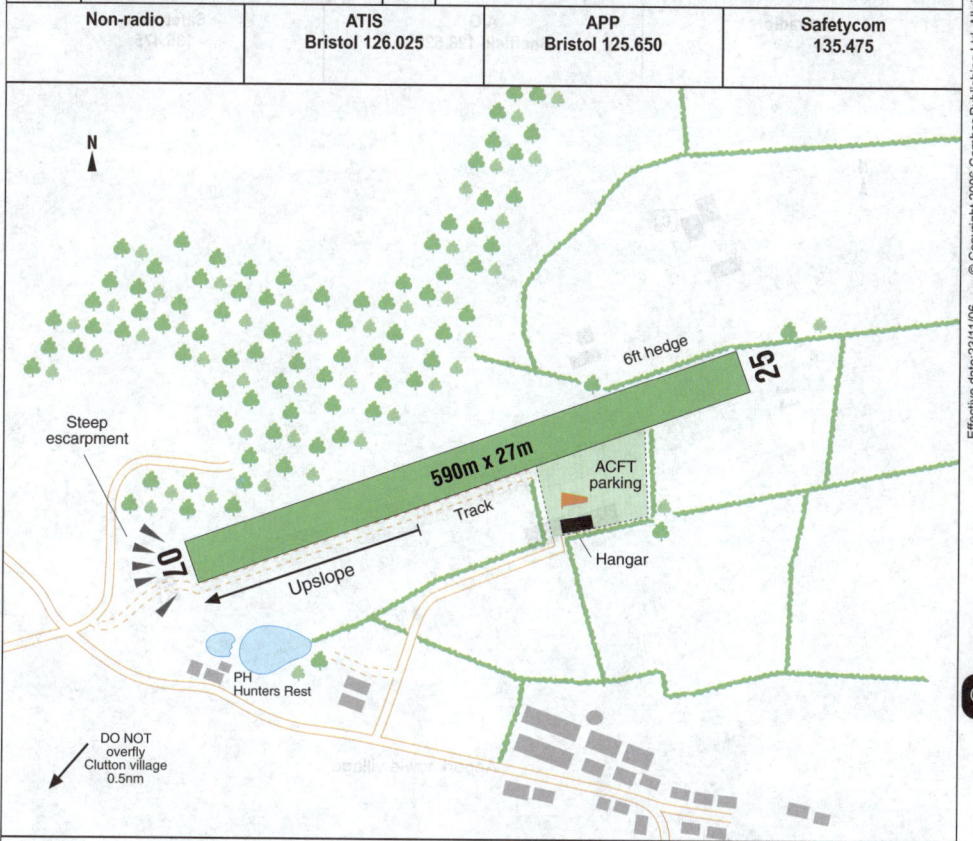

RWY	SURFACE	TORA	LDA	LIGHTING
07/25	Grass	590x27	U/L	Nil

Remarks
PPR by telephone. Microlights not accepted. Visiting ACFT are welcome at pilots own risk. The Bristol CTA (Base 1500ft) lies over the AD. Arr/Dept ACFT must call Bristol APP. Useful Weather Info can be obtained from Bristol ATIS

Warnings
Marked upslope at W end of Rwy & steep escarpment up to Rwy07 Thr. The combination of this may be a marked roll-over effect for Rwy25 Dept. Trees close to N side of Rwy25 Thr, they may generate turbulence & obscure view of Rwy when downwind Rwy07.
Noise: AD is in a very noise sensitive area, extreme care should be taken to avoid over flight of local villages, particularly Clutton to the SW.

Operating Hrs	SR-SS		Operator	Clutton Hill Agricultural Services Ltd
Circuits	08 LH, 26 RH, 600ft QFE			Clutton Hill Farm
Landing Fee	£5			Clutton, Bristol, Somerset
Maintenance	Nil			**Tel:** 01761 452458
Fuel	Nil			**Tel:** 07751 673369
Disabled Facilities	Nil			
Restaurants				
Hunters Rest	**Tel:** 01761 452303			
Taxis	**Tel:** 01761 417166			
Car Hire	Nil			
Weather Info	AirSW MOEx			

720ft	5nm S of Sheffield	PPR	Alternative AD	Nottingham East Midlands Retford
24mb	N5318.28 W00125.83			

Non radio	A/G Sheffield 128.525	Safetycom 135.475

N ↑

C

732m x 20m

11

29

Apperknowle village
↓

RWY	SURFACE	TORA	LDA	LIGHTING
11/29	Grass	732x20	U/L	Nil

Rwy11 1.6% upslope

Remarks
PPR strictly by telephone.

Warnings
Sheffield city ATZ to NE of AD.

Operating Hrs	SR-SS		Operator	Mr W H Valle
Circuits	Nil			Bentley Farm
Landing Fee	On application			Summerley, Apperknowle
Maintenance	Nil			Sheffield
Fuel	Nil			**Tel: 01246 412305 (AD)**
Disabled Facilities	Nil			
Restaurants	Nil			
Taxis/Car Hire	Nil			
Weather Info	AirCen MWC			

COLEMORE COMMON

Effective date:23/11/06

610ft 20mb	4nm SSE of Alton N5103.76 W00100.58	PPR	Alternative AD	Southampton Goodwood
Colemore Common		**LARS** Farnborough 125.250		**A/G** Microlight freq 129.825

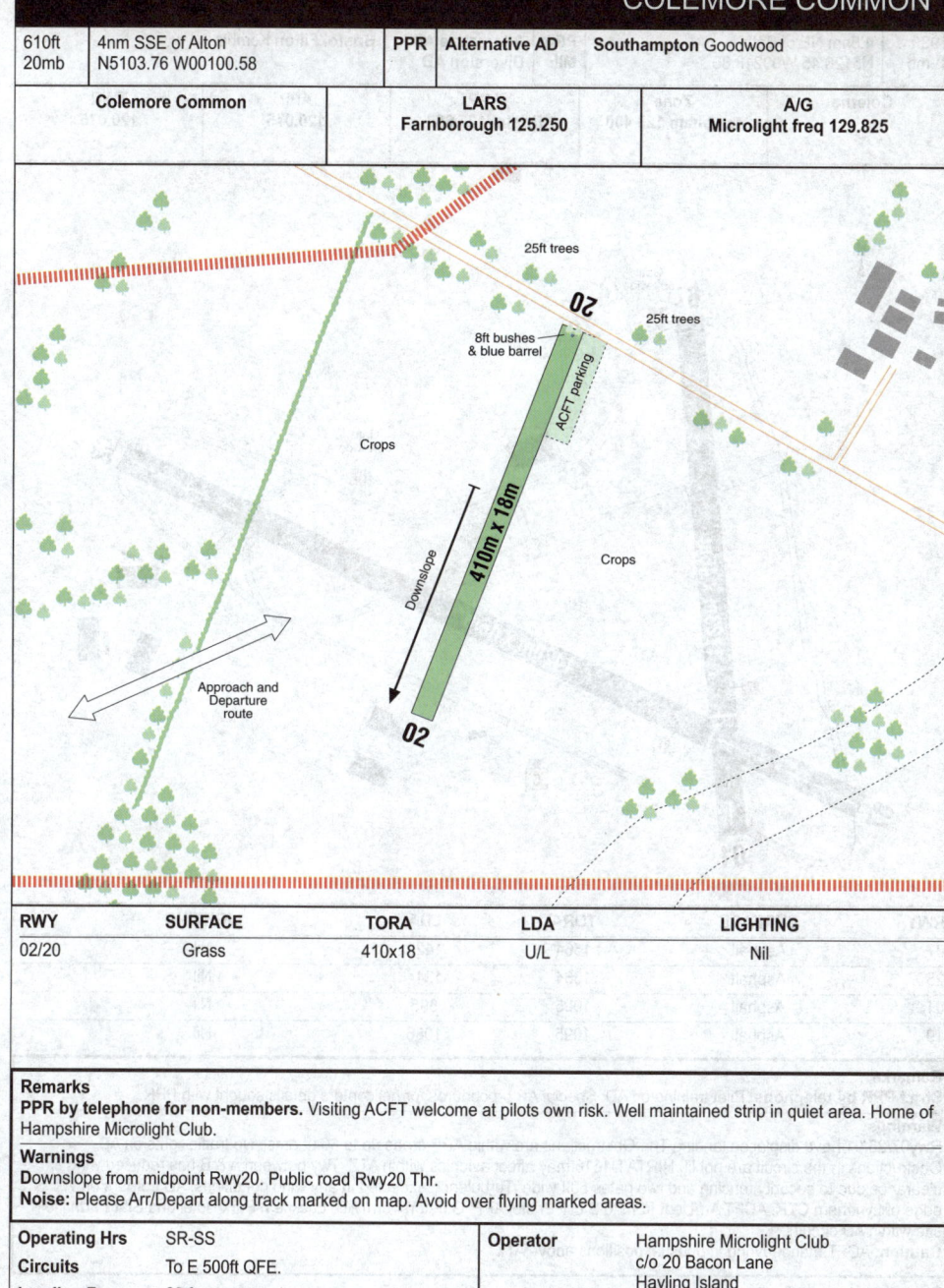

25ft trees
25ft trees
8ft bushes & blue barrel
ACFT parking
Crops
Crops
Downslope
410m x 18m
20
02
Approach and Departure route

C

RWY	SURFACE	TORA	LDA	LIGHTING
02/20	Grass	410x18	U/L	Nil

Remarks
PPR by telephone for non-members. Visiting ACFT welcome at pilots own risk. Well maintained strip in quiet area. Home of Hampshire Microlight Club.

Warnings
Downslope from midpoint Rwy20. Public road Rwy20 Thr.
Noise: Please Arr/Depart along track marked on map. Avoid over flying marked areas.

Operating Hrs	SR-SS	**Operator**	Hampshire Microlight Club c/o 20 Bacon Lane Hayling Island Hampshire PO11 0DN **Tel:** 023 9246 8806 (PPR) **Tel:** 078 3475 2083 (PPR) daryl@darylcornelius.com www.hmfclub.com
Circuits	To E 500ft QFE.		
Landing Fee	£3 for non members Leave money in blue barrel Rwy20 Thr		
Maintenance	Nil		
Fuel	Nil		
Disabled Facilities	Nil		
Restaurant	Nil		
Taxi/Car Hire	Nil		
Weather Info	MOEx		

| 593ft | 4.5nm NE of Bath | PPR | Alternative AD | Bristol Filton Kemble |
| 19mb | N5126.45 W00216.80 | MIL | Diversion AD | |

Colerne	Zone	APP	APP	TWR
	Lyneham 123.400	Bristol 125.650	120.075	120.075

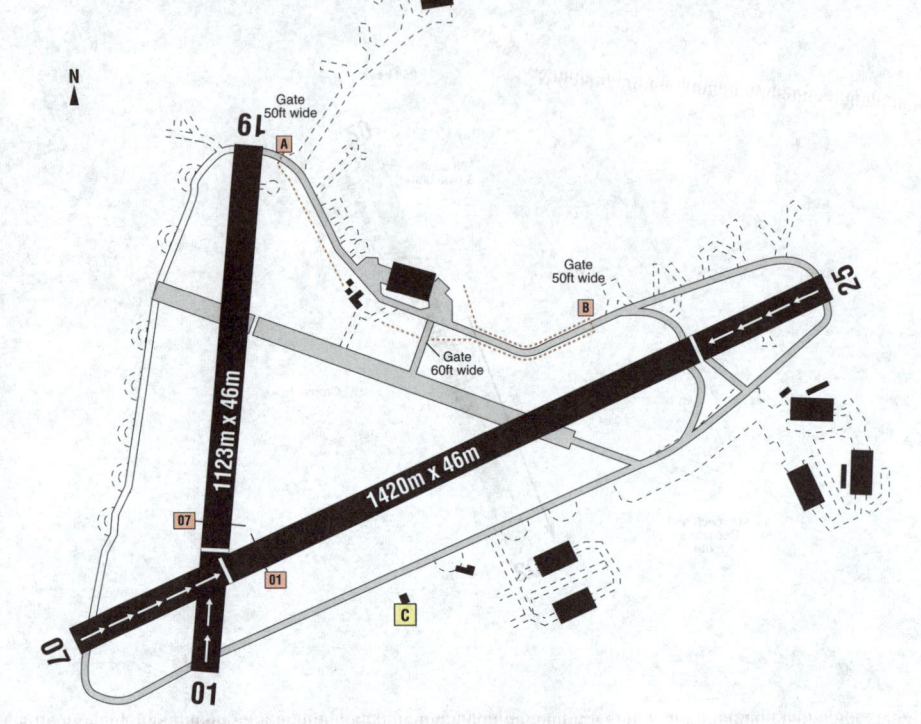

RWY	SURFACE	TORA	LDA	LIGHTING
07	Asphalt	1664	1422	Nil
25	Asphalt	1664	1344	Nil
01	Asphalt	1095	895	Nil
19	Asphalt	1095	1086	Nil

Remarks
Strict PPR by telephone. Pilot training on AD. Special Arr procedures for helicopters details sought with PPR.

Warnings
Rwy07/25/01 have displaced landing Thr. Obstructions are within APP areas up to 604ft amsl. No traffic lights on AD. Obstructions in the circuit are not lit. HIRTA D1616 may affect avionics within ATZ. Twy between A & B has reduced wing tip clearance due to security fencing and two gates 50ft wide. Turbulence expected in any wind conditions. AD borders on W edge of Lyneham CTR. ACFT Arr/Dept from/to S call Bristol APP. Garston Farm AD, Lucknam Park Hotel and Star Farm Heli site within AD circuit.
Caution: ACFT manoeuvring in unusual positions above ATZ.

Operating Hrs	As required by RAF operations	**Taxi**	
Circuits	As instructed by ATC at 800ft QFE	Grahams	**Tel:** 0785 0874141
Landing Fee	Charges in accordance with MOD policy	**Car Hire**	Nil
	Contact Station Ops for details	**Weather Info**	AirSW MOEx
		Operator	BUAS Colerne
Maintenance	Nil		Azimghur Barracks
Fuel	AVGAS 100LL		Colerne Airfield
	strictly by prior arrangement		Wiltshire
			SN14 8QY
Disabled Facilities	Nil		**Tel:** 01225 745338
Restaurants	Nil		

COLONSAY

Effective date:23/11/06

24ft 1mb	W side of Colonsay Island N5603.45 W00615.62	PPR	Alternative AD	Islay Tiree

Non Radio	FIS Scottish 127.275	AFIS Tiree 122.700	Safetycom 135.475

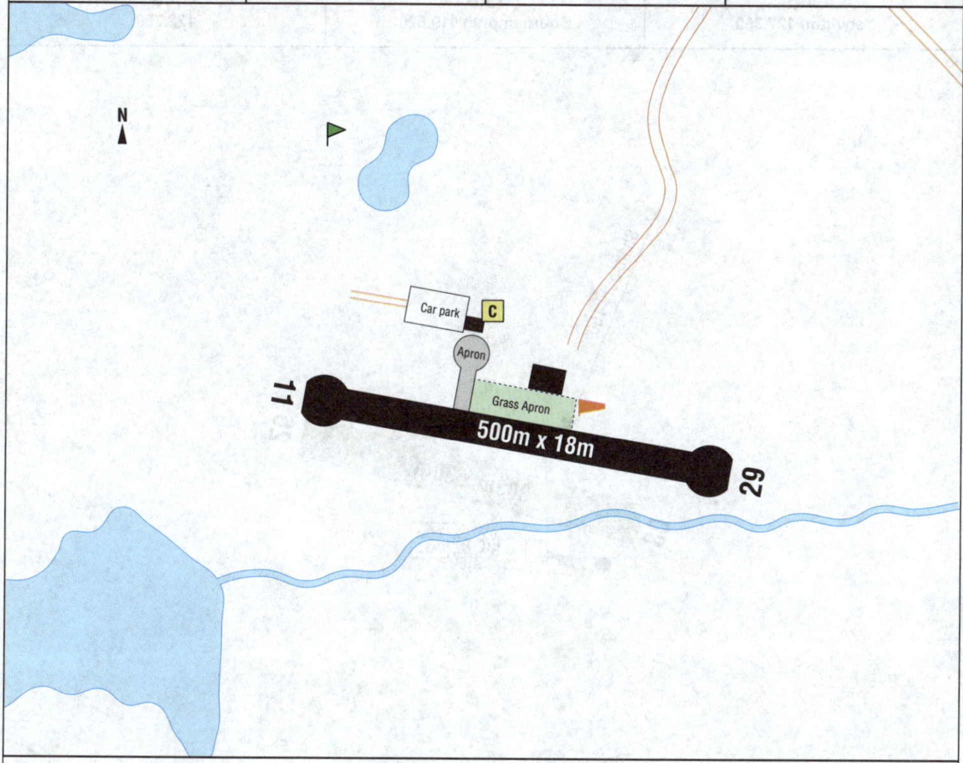

Car park

C

Apron

Grass Apron

11

29

500m x 18m

N

C

RWY	SURFACE	TORA	LDA	LIGHTING
11/29	Tarmac	500x18	U/L	Nil

Remarks
PPR by letter, fax or email (24hrs notice required). Visiting light ACFT at pilot's own risk. Applications for PPR must include acceptance of own risk. All circuits to the S to minimise domestic and wildlife disturbance.

Warnings
Noise: Avoid over-flying bird sanctuaries which extend along the coast to N of AD

Operating Hrs	SR-SS	Operator	Argyll & Bute Council c/o Colonsay Estate Colonsay Estate Office Isle of Colonsay Argyll, PA61 7YU **Tel:** 01951 200211 **Fax:** 01951 200369 alexhoward@dial.pipex.com
Circuits	All circuits to S		
Landing Fee	<500kg £9.10 >501kg £12.20		
Maintenance	Nil		
Fuel	Nil		
Disabled Facilities			

  T P

Taxis/Hire Car	Transport on request
Weather Info	AirSc GWC

811ft 27mb	2.7nm S of Shaftesbury N5058.03 W00209.22	PPR	Alternative AD Diversion AD	Bournemouth Old Sarum
Compton		**LARS** Bournemouth 119.475		**LARS** Boscombe Down 126.700
LARS Yeovilton 127.350		**RAD** Bournemouth 119.620		**A/G** 122.700

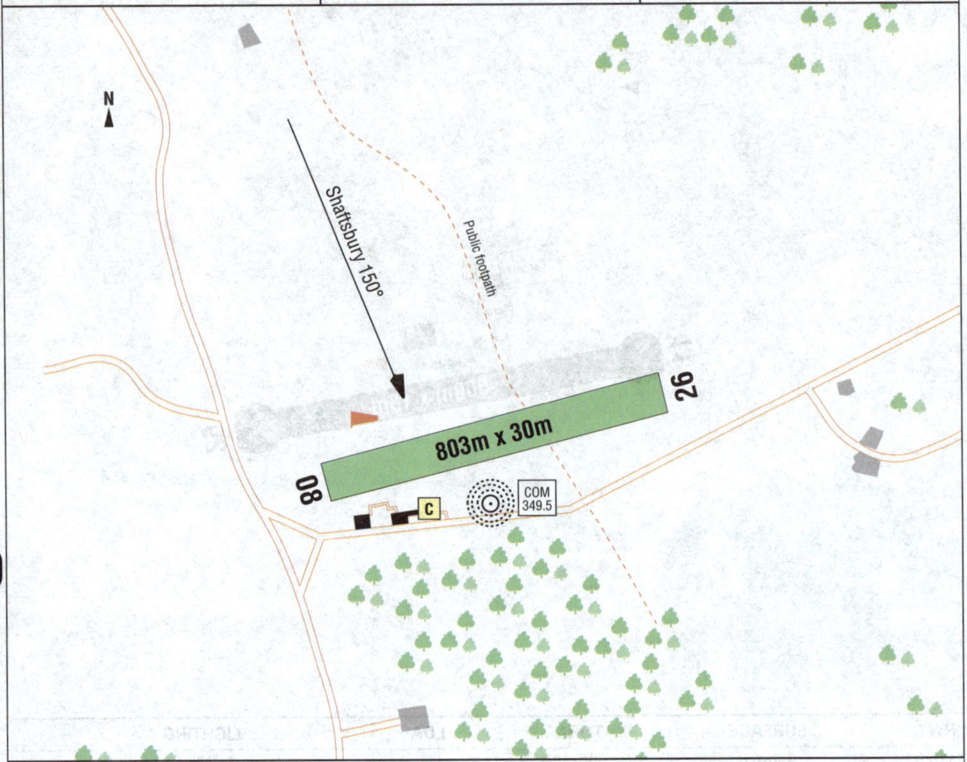

N

Shaftsbury 150°

Public footpath

803m x 30m

26

08

COM 349.5

C

RWY	SURFACE	TORA	LDA	LIGHTING
08/26	Grass	799	803	Nil

Remarks
AD is not available at night by flights required to use a licensed AD. ACFT to clear left after landing on Rwy26 and right after landing on Rwy08. Over flights not below 3000ft altitude. RAD available Bournemouth (7 days), weekdays only from Boscombe Down LARS or Yeovilton LARS. ACFT Arr from E via 'SAM' can track SAM 281° outbound to Shaftesbury (SAM DME 32.5nm) then track 150° to Compton Abbas. Falconry Centre and Movie Aviation Museum in AD, open daily.
Visual aid to location: White strobe flashes during AD operating Hrs.

Warnings
Mast 55ft agl S of AD boundary. Check for aerobatics and formation flying taking place within ATZ. Due to prop wash, all ACFT to park E of flashing beacon. GND to the N of the Rwy has a steep slope gradient. Turbulence & wind shear will be experienced with southerly winds above 10kts.Particularly affected are Rwy08 Arr in SE winds & climb out Rwy26 with S or SW winds.
Noise: Avoid over-flying villages around the AD. Rwy26 Dept turn right to over fly Melbury Hill as soon after crossing AD boundary as safety permits. Noise abatement procedures must be obtained prior to Dept

Operating Hrs	0900-2000 (Summer) 0900-1700 (Winter)	**Restaurant**	Licensed restaurant & bar at AD 0930-1800 (Summer) 0930-1700 (Winter) Available for corporate entertainment
Circuits	08 LH, 26 RH, 800ft QFE Microlights 500ft QFE inside Fixed wing circuit		
		Taxis	
		Hiltop	**Tel:** 01747 855555
Landing Fee	£8.50 all types	**Car Hire**	Operator can arr on request
Maintenance	Airtime **Tel:** 01747 812791 Hangarage available	**Weather Info**	AirSW MOEx
		Operator	Compton Abbas Airfield Ltd Ashmore, Dorset, SP5 5AP **Tel:** 01747 811767 **Fax** 01747 811161 fly@abbasair.com www.abbasair.com
Fuel	AVGAS 100LL		
Disabled Facilities			

EGXC

CONINGSBY

25ft 1mb	8nm NW of Boston N5305.58 W00009.95	PPR MIL	Alternative AD Diversion AD	Nottingham East Midlands Wickenby

Coningsby	LARS Waddington 127.350	APP 120.800	TWR 124.675	GND 122.100 (on request)

Effective date:23/11/06

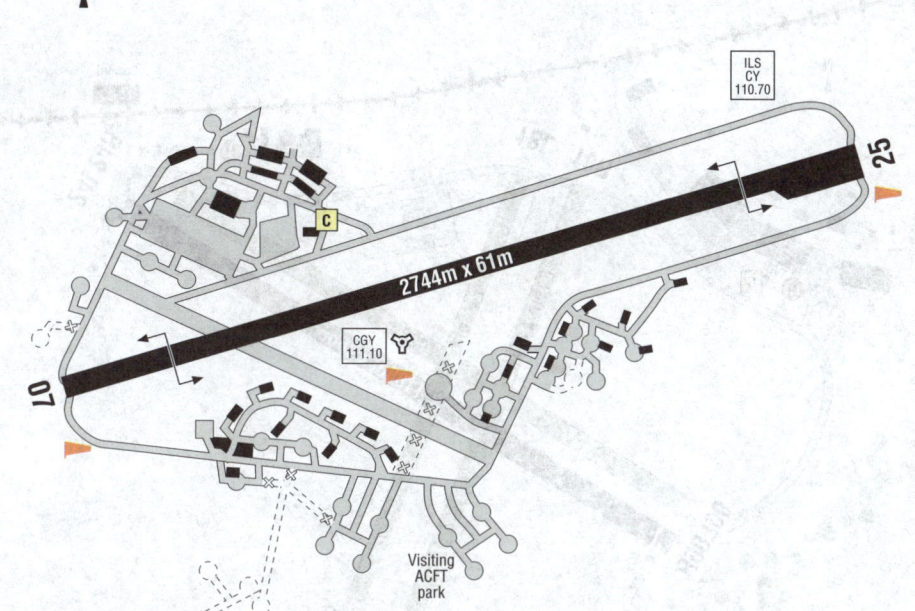

Visiting ACFT park

RWY	SURFACE	TORA	LDA	LIGHTING
07	Asph/Conc	2744	2744	Ap Thr Rwy PAPI 3°
25	Asph/Conc	2744	2744	Ap Thr Rwy PAPI 3°

Arrestor gear cables 396m from both Thrs. Rwy25 APP down, overrun up
Rwy07 both up. Arrestor cables up outside operating hrs

Remarks
PPR strictly by telephone. RAF AD within active MATZ. Based jet ACFT carry out high energy manoeuvres within the vicinity of the AD. Civil visiting ACFT accepted only by telephone permission, may be subject to refusal or specified arrival conditions. Traffic is particularly severely restricted when Rwy07 in use. Frequent weekend movements, contact Waddington LARS for AD status.
Visual Aid to location: I Bn CY Red

Warnings
Vintage ACFT of the Battle of Britain Memorial Flight (BBMF) fly circuits to N of main Rwy and grass strip between 500 – 1000ft QFE. The grass strip is not available to visiting ACFT. Harrier ACFT conduct VSTOL manoeuvres at various locations on AD.
Caution: Arrester cables. Be sure you have identified their position and land beyond. Danger of severe turbulence
Noise: Do not over fly Engine de-tuner in SW dispersal when notified as active, avoid by 1000ft agl by 0.6nm radius. Light ACFT and helicopters may turn on route above 1000ft agl.

Operating Hrs	0800-1700 Mon-Fri (L). ATZ operational H24	Restaurants	Nil
Circuits	25 LH, 07 RH, 1000ft QFE	Taxis/Car Hire	Nil
Landing Fee	Charges in accordance with MOD policy Contact Station Ops for details	Weather Info	AirS MOEx
		Operators	RAF Coningsby
Maintenance	Not normally available to Civil visitors		Lincoln
Fuel	AVGAS 100LL JET A1 strictly by prior arr		LN4 4SY Tel: 01526 342581 (Ops) Tel: 01526 347716/347959 (Ops) Tel: 01526 347443 (ATC)

Disabled Facilities

| 272ft | 7nm NW of Wolverhampton | PPR | Alternative AD | Birmingham Wolverhampton |
| 9mb | N5238.40 W00218.33 | MIL | Diversion AD | |

| Cosford | LARS | APP |
| | Shawbury 120.775 | 135.875 |

| GND | TWR | A/G |
| 128.650 | 128.650 | BFC Base 135.875 |

C

[Airport diagram showing runways:
18L 18R, 24L 24R, Cosford, Air Ambulance (H), TWR (H), C, 849m x 46m, 849m x 46m, 1028m x 46m, 1186m x 46m, 06L 06R, 36L 36R]

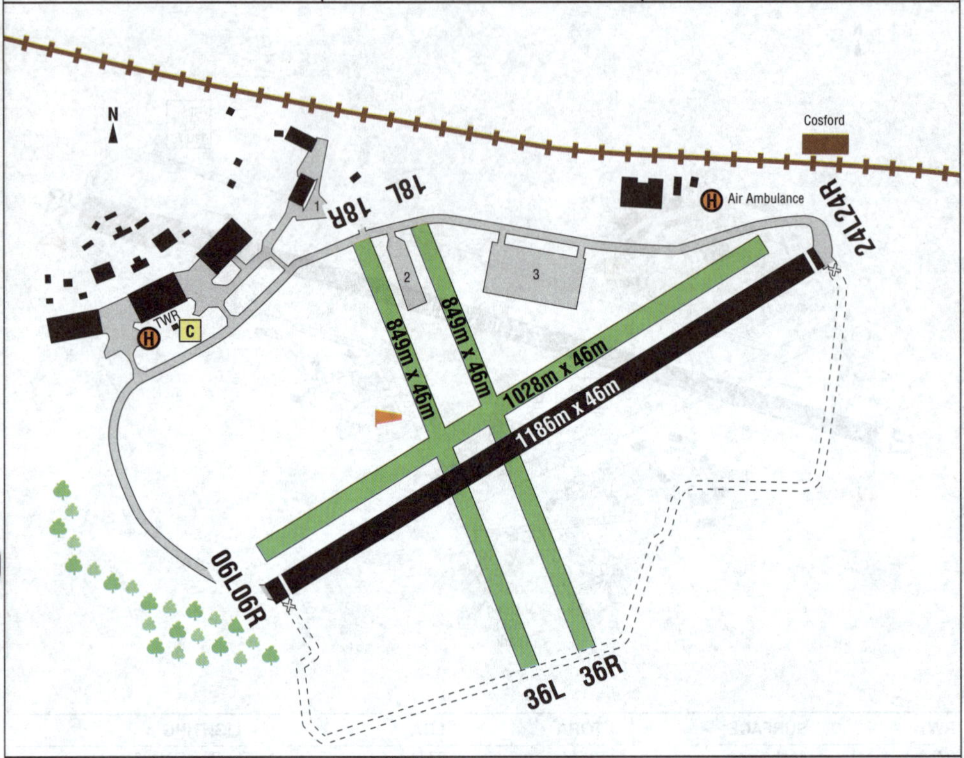

RWY	SURFACE	TORA	LDA	LIGHTING
06/24	Asphalt	1185	1141	Nil
24R/06L	Grass	1028	1028	Nil
18L/36R	Grass	849	849	Nil
18R/36L	Grass	849	849	Nil

Remarks
PPR. Ab initio pilot training takes place here. No civil ACFT accepted Sat/Sun. AD may close at indeterminate times if not required by station based training ACFT. ATZ remains active H24. Visiting civil ACFT will not be accepted if visibility is <5km. Air ambulance operations daily until 2000 (L). Cosford Flying Club operations until dusk

Warnings
Glider and powered glider activity outside published Hrs and at weekends. Railway embankment 20ft aal 274m before Rwy24 Thr. Ravine 91m before Rwy06 Thr. Air Ambulance activity H24. Grass Rwys used by light ACFT and gliders and are not available for use by civilian ACFT.
Caution: full obstacle clearance criteria not met on APP. Up to 12 light ACFT operating at any one time.
Noise: ACFT to avoid Albrighton village 1nm SE.

Operating Hrs	Mon-Fri 0900-1700 (L) or as requested by OC flying	Restaurants	In Aerospace Museum
		Taxis/Car Hire	Nil
Circuits	All to S	Weather Info	AirCen MWC
Landing Fee	Charges in accordance with MOD policy Contact Station Ops for details	Operator	RAF Cosford Wolverhampton West Midlands, WV7 3EX
Maintenance	Nil		**Tel:** 01902 377567
Fuel	Nil		**Tel:** 01902 337030
Disabled Facilities			**Tel:** 01902 377582

COTTERED

390ft 13mb	5nm SE of Baldock N5157.50 W00006.00	**PPR**	**Alternative AD**	**Cambridge** Duxford

Non-Radio	ATIS Luton 120.575	APP Luton 129.550	Safetycom 135.475

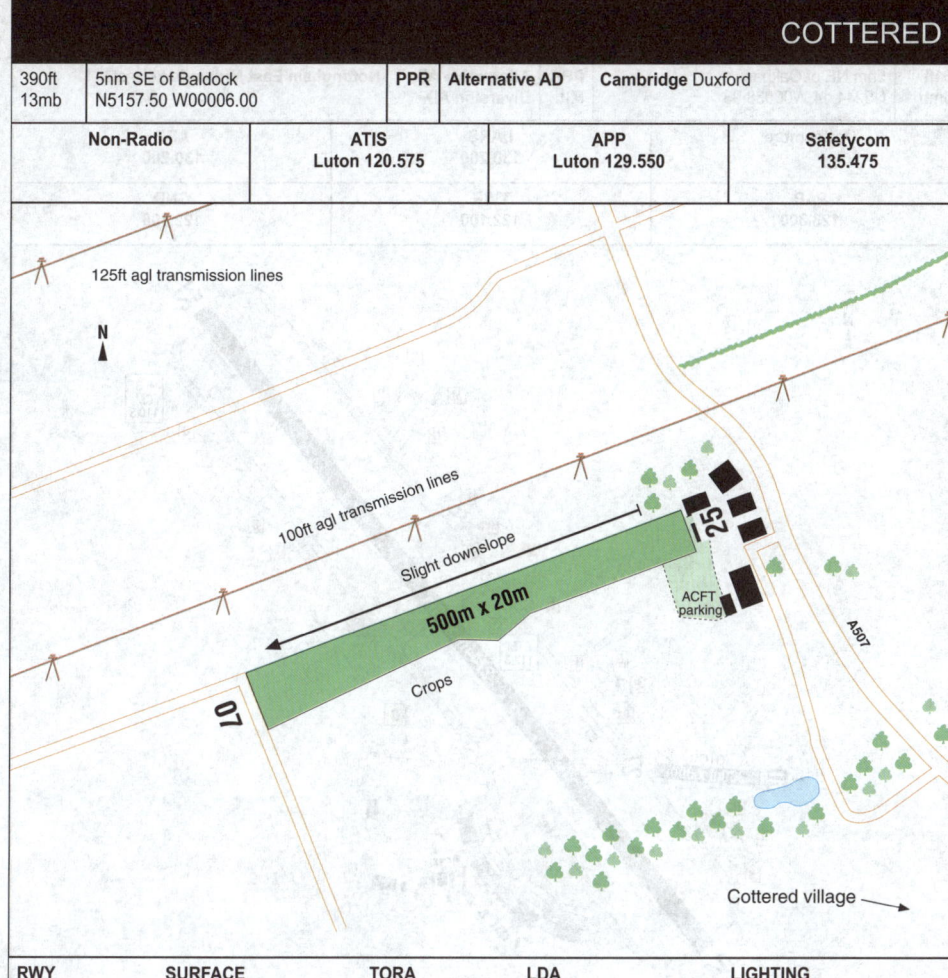

(map labels:) 125ft agl transmission lines · N · 100ft agl transmission lines · Slight downslope · 500m x 20m · 07 · 25 · ACFT parking · Crops · A507 · Cottered village →

RWY	SURFACE	TORA	LDA	LIGHTING
07/25	Grass	500x20	U/L	Nil

Rwy25 slight downslope

Remarks
PPR by telephone. Visiting ACFT operate at own risk. Strip width is given as 20m there is a wider section at the midpoint and to the S Rwy07 Thr.

Warnings
AD is situated below Luton CTA (base 2500ft QNH). Trees and farm buildings close to Rwy25 Thr. Farm track runs down N side of strip and branches across Rwy07 Thr. 100ft agl transmission line parallel to AD 80m to N side with a second line 1000 metres further to the N. Crops are grown close to the strip edge.
Noise: Do not over fly Cottered village SE of AD

Operating Hrs	SR-SS		**Operator**	Kingsley Brothers Childs Farm Cottered, Buntingford, Herts **Tel:** 01763 281256 **Fax:** 01763 281652
Circuits	1000ft QFE			
Landing Fee	£6			
Maintenance	Nil			
Fuel	Nil			
Disabled Facilities	✔ P			
Restaurants	Bull Pub Cottered Village			
Taxis/Car Hire	Nil			
Weather Info	AirSE MOEx			

461ft 15mb	5nm NE of Oakham N5244.14 W00038.93	PPR MIL	Alternative AD Diversion AD	Nottingham East Midlands Leicester

Cottesmore	LARS 130.200	APP 130.200
PAR 123.300	TWR 122.100	GND 122.100

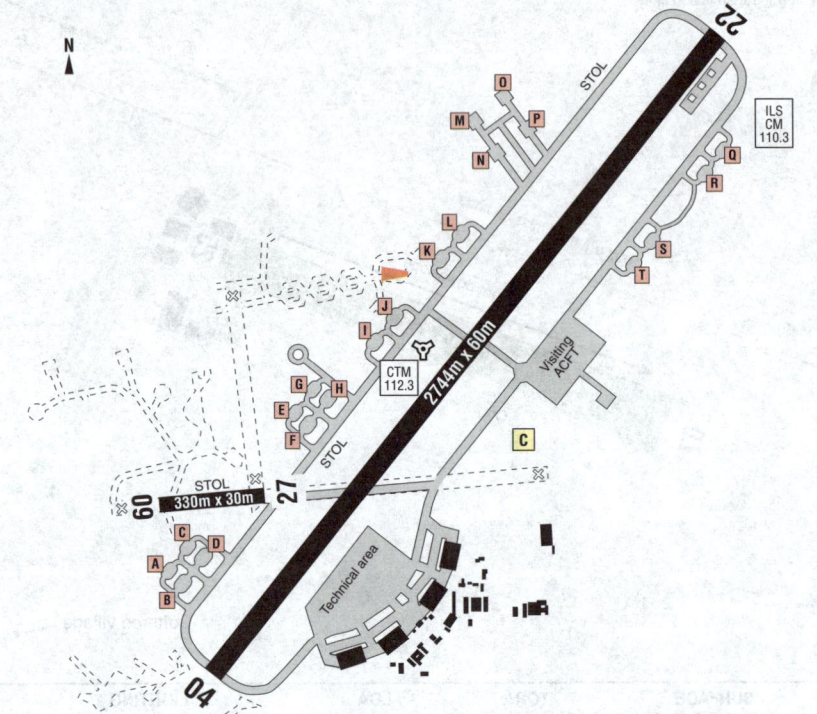

RWY	SURFACE	TORA	LDA	LIGHTING
22/04	Asph/Conc	2744	2744	Ap Thr Rwy PAPI 2.5°
09/27	Asphalt	329x46	U/L	Nil

Remarks
24Hrs PPR by telephone essential. RAF AD with intensive fast jet operations. AD situated within CMATZ with RAF Wittering, Cottesmore is controlling authority. Inbound ACFT/Helicopters contact Cottesmore not less than 15nm before the MATZ boundary.

Warnings
N Twys have non-standard markings for use as STOL strips by based ACFT only. Based ACFT will carry out variable circuits. There is a significant bird hazard on AD. Visiting ACFT may be required to operate under RAD control to comply with local noise restrictions/ be sequenced in traffic. Visiting ACFT prohibited before 0830 (L). Due to restricted wing tip clearance visiting ACFT with wingspan exceeding 16m will not be permitted to use S Twy between Rwy04 Thr and the technical area.
Noise: Visiting ACFT to climb to 1000ft QFE or higher to leave the local area. Over flight of local villages within 10nm of Cottesmore is to be avoided.

Operating Hrs	Mon-Fri 0700-1600 (Summer) +1Hr (Winter). Visiting ACFT prohibited before 0830 (L). ATZ active H24	Restaurants	Nil
		Taxis/Car Hire	Nil
Circuits	Variable but visiting ACFT should expect 22 RH, 04 LH, 1200ft QFE	Weather Info	M T Fax MOEx ATIS **Tel:** 01572 812241 Ex 7602 Met Office **Tel:** 01572 812241 Ex 7337
Landing Fee	Charges in accordance with MOD policy Contact Station Ops for details	Operator	RAF Cottesmore Oakham Leicestershire LE15 7BL **Tel:** 01572 812241 Ex 7330/7270
Maintenance	Nil for civil visitors		
Fuel	JET A1 by prior arr		
Disabled Facilities			

267ft	3nm SSE of Coventry		PPR	Alternative AD	Birmingham Wellesbourne Mountford
9mb	N5222.18 W00128.78			Diversion AD	

Coventry		ATIS	126.050	APP	119.250	RAD	122.000
TWR	119.250 124.800	GND	121.700	FIRE	121.600		

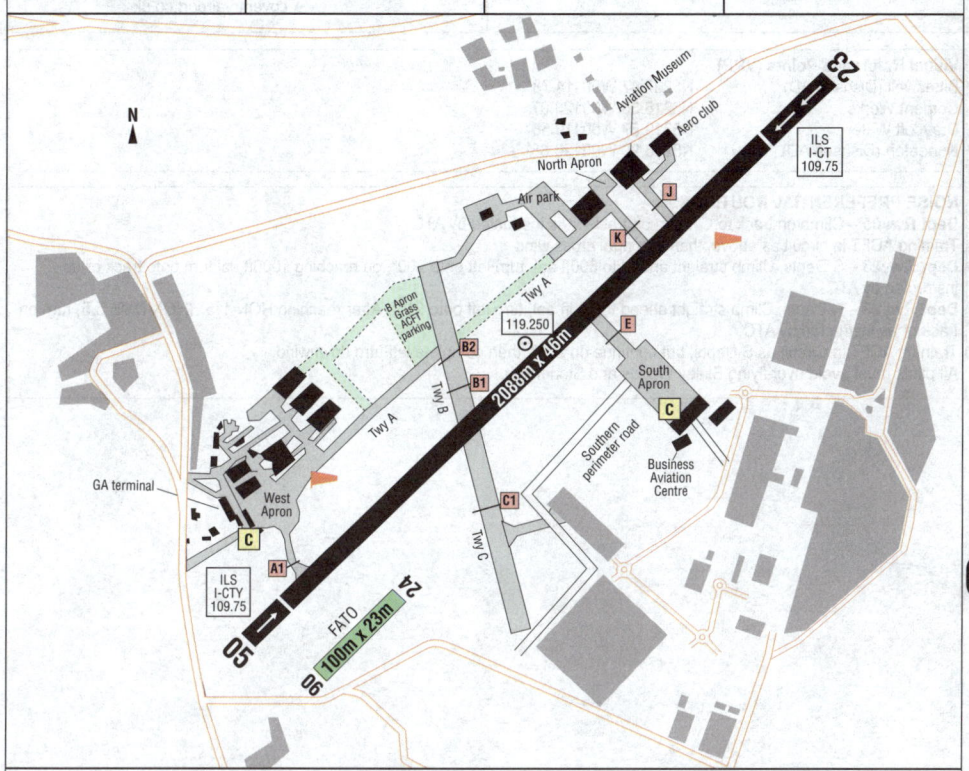

RWY	SURFACE	TORA	LDA	LIGHTING
05	Asphalt	1615	1795	Ap Thr Rwy PAPI 3° LHS
23	Asphalt	1825	1615	Ap Thr Rwy PAPI 3° LHS
FATO				
06/24	Grass	100x23	U/L	Nil

Remarks

PPR essential ACFT <500kgs not permitted. Circuit and instrument training can be pre-booked with ATC. Non-radio ACFT join overhead at 1500ft QNH. Helicopter training flights operating at 700ft QFE and below might not comply with normal R/T procedure. Helicopter circuits will normally operate from a grass area (as directed by ATC) circuit height 700ft QFE (except at night when main Rwy is used). Pilots required to book-out by telephone. An ATC GMC service in use during busy periods when notified by NOTAM. GMC is for booking out. A careful lookout should be maintained at all times. ATC instructions will specify the taxi route to be followed. Light ACFT are to self manoeuvre for parking only if instructed by ATC.

Aids to Navigation: NDB CT 363.50

Warnings

Turbulence on short finals Rwy23 in SW winds. Helicopter Ops N Rwy23 APP 3.5nm from touchdown. Adhere to standard RTF procedures. ACFT with a wingspan in excess of 18m may require marshalling when taxiing. Regular bird scaring. Due to close proximity of Birmingham AD, pilots must ensure their flight remains clear of Birmingham CTR/CTZ, unless ATC clearance is issued.

Operating Hrs	H24	**Maintenance**	
Circuits	05 RH, 23 LH	Atlantic Aero Eng	**Tel:** 02476 762225
	Circuits to SE 1000ft QFE	Fuel	AVGAS JET A1 100LL
			Oils W80 W20/50S100
Landing Fee	£0.16 per kg AUW	**Disabled Facilities**	Available
	Circuit & Instrument training	**Restaurants**	Refreshments available in Business
	50% discount for PPR/Training		Aviation Centre & GA Terminal

Taxis		Operator	West Midlands International Airport Ltd
PABT	**Tel:** 02476 304777		Phoenix House
Car Hire			Siskin Parkway West
Avis	**Tel:** 02476 225500		Coventry Airport South
National	**Tel:** 02476 677042		Coventry, CV8 3AZ
Hertz	**Tel:** 02476 251741		**Tel:** 02476 308600 (Admin)
Weather Info	M T9 Fax 266 MWC		**Tel:** 02476 308638 (ATC)
	ATIS **Tel:** 024 7633 2668		**Fax:** 02476 882669 (ATC)
			charrison@coventryairport.co.uk
			www.coventryairport.co.uk

Visual Reference Points (VRP)

Bitteswell (Disused AD)	N5227.47 W00114.78
Cement Works	N5216.35 W00123.07
Draycott Water	N5219.57 W00119.58
Nuneaton (Disused AD)	N5233.90 W00126.88

NOISE PREFERENTIAL ROUTINGS:

Dept Rwy05 – Climb on track to CT, turn on track or as instructed by ATC.
Training ACFT in circuit as above, then turn right cross wind
Dept Rwy23 – S Depts: Climb straight ahead to 500ft aal, turn left onto 200°, on reaching 1000ft aal turn onto track or as instructed by ATC.
Dept Rwy23 – N Depts: Climb straight ahead to 500ft aal, turn left onto 215°. After reaching HON 115° (HON DME 5.5) turn on track or as instructed by ATC.
Training ACFT in Circuit as S Depts, but continue on 200°, then complete left turn downwind.
All pilots must avoid over flying Binley Woods and Stoneleigh.

C

71ft 2mb	10nm S of St Andrews N5616.08 W00236.33	PPR	Alternative AD	Dundee Fife

Non-Radio	LARS Leuchars 126.500	Safetycom 135.475

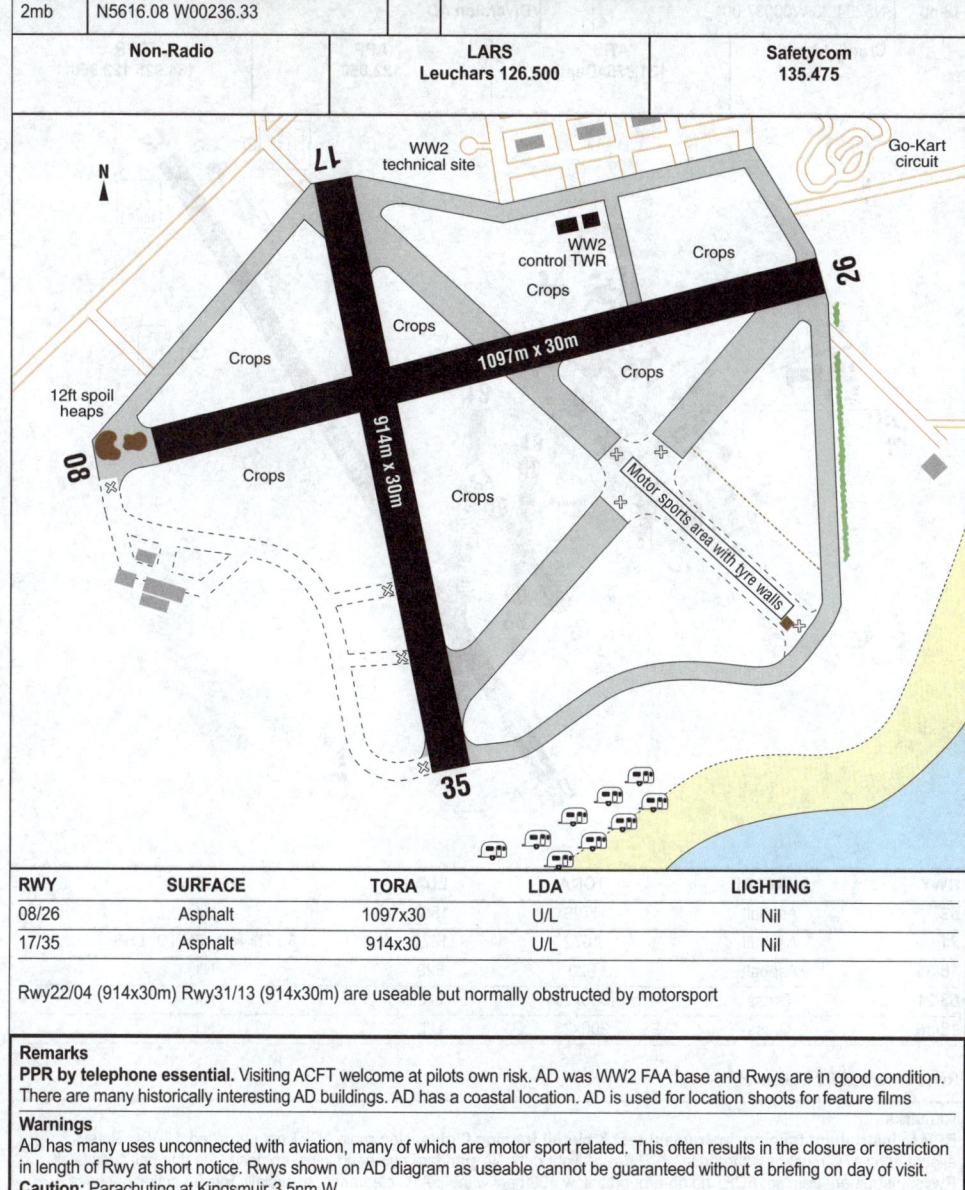

RWY	SURFACE	TORA	LDA	LIGHTING
08/26	Asphalt	1097x30	U/L	Nil
17/35	Asphalt	914x30	U/L	Nil

Rwy22/04 (914x30m) Rwy31/13 (914x30m) are useable but normally obstructed by motorsport

Remarks
PPR by telephone essential. Visiting ACFT welcome at pilots own risk. AD was WW2 FAA base and Rwys are in good condition. There are many historically interesting AD buildings. AD has a coastal location. AD is used for location shoots for feature films

Warnings
AD has many uses unconnected with aviation, many of which are motor sport related. This often results in the closure or restriction in length of Rwy at short notice. Rwys shown on AD diagram as useable cannot be guaranteed without a briefing on day of visit.
Caution: Parachuting at Kingsmuir 3.5nm W

Operating Hrs	SR-SS		Operator	William Robertson
Circuits	LH 1000ft QFE			Balcomie Road
Landing Fee	£15			Crail, Fife, KY10 3XL
Maintenance	Nil			**Tel:** 01333 451839
Fuel	Nil			**Fax:** 01333 451842
Disabled Facilities				m3@sol.co.uk
				www.crailthrash.co.uk
Restaurants	Nil			
Taxis/Car Hire	Nil			
Weather Info	AirSC GWC			

191

EGTC

CRANFIELD

358ft 12mb	7nm SW of Bedford N5204.33 W00037.00	PPR	Alternative AD Diversion AD	Cambridge Northampton

Cranfield	ATIS 121.875 (Dept)	APP 122.850	TWR 134.925 122.850

(airport diagram)

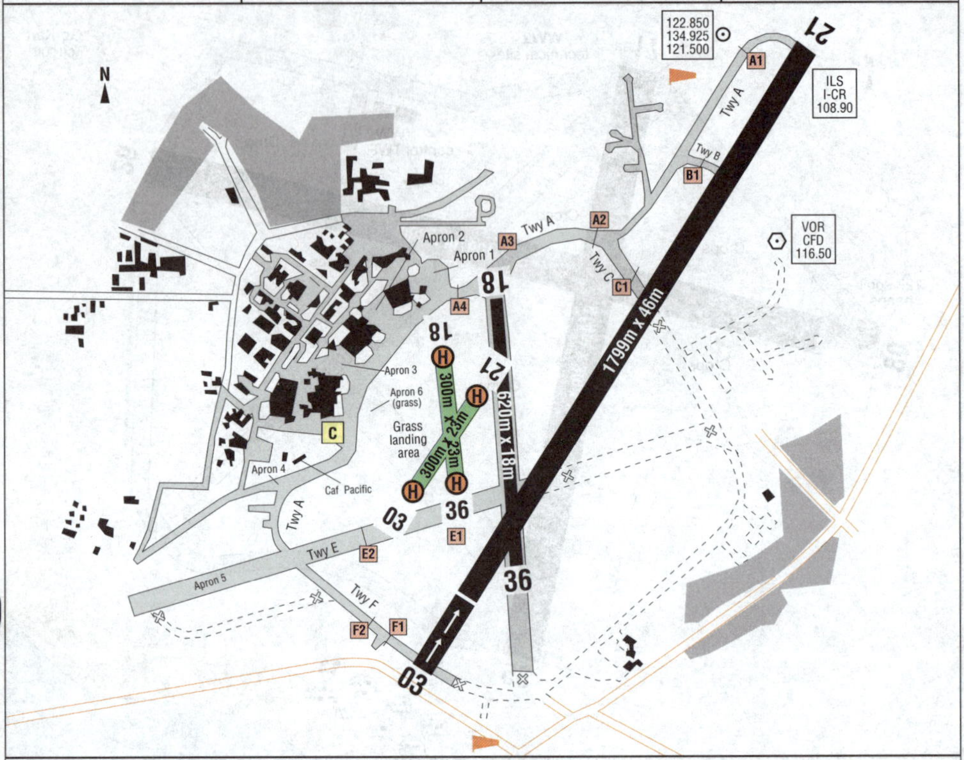

RWY	SURFACE	TORA	LDA	LIGHTING
03	Asphalt	1799	1594	Nil
21	Asphalt	1672	1672	Ap Thr Rwy PAPI 3° LHS
18/36	Asphalt	620	620	Nil
03/21	Grass	300x23	U/L	Nil
18/36	Grass	300x23	U/L	Nil

Rwy21 licensed for night use

Remarks

PPR to instrument training, instrument test & circuit training flights. Non-radio ACFT not permitted. Hi-Vis. Slots allocated by ATC must be adhered to. PPR day of flight only. No standard overhead joins, no dead side due heli circuits all Rwys. Instrument training: ACFT no go-around below 400ft agl without ATC clearance, especially Rwy03 active opposite direction. VFR traffic join via VRP. Rwy18 light ACFT day only. All helis must request start-up clearance. 12 Hrs notice Customs, details to ATC only.

Aids to Navigation: NDB CIT 850.00

Warnings

Intensive flight training AD. S 300m of Rwy18/36 unfit-use. Helicopter operations on grass area NW of main Rwy intersection. All fixed wing ACFT entering/exiting the grass via N Twy to use concrete entry/exit points. Windshear may be experienced Dept Rwy36, Arr Rwy18.
Caution: Twy E congested with parked ACFT, min wing tip clearance may not be available
Noise: Avoid over flying all buildings and structures 1500m W of disused Rwy below 500ft QFE.

Operating Hrs	Landing Fee	On application
Mon-Fri 0730-1800 Sat-Sun & PH 0800-1700 (Summer) Mon-Fri 0830-1900 Sat-Sun & PH 0900-1800 (Winter) Extensions by arr Tel: 01234 754784	Maintenance Fuel	Various AVGAS 100LL JET A1

Circuits Fixed wing day 800ft QFE
Night 1200ft QFE

Disabled Facilities

Handling	Tel: 01234 752220/754789
	Fax: 01234 752221/754785
Restaurants	Café Pacific Restaurant/Bar
Mon-Fri 0800-1700 Sat 0900-1600 Sun 1000-1400
	Tel: 01234 754611
Taxis	Tel: 01234 750005
Car Hire	
Budget	Tel: 01908 373111
Hertz	Tel: 01908 374492
Weather Info	M T9 Fax 268 A MOEx

Visual Reference Points (VRP)

Olney Town	N5209.20 W00042.10
(Rwy04, 18 & 36 only)	
Stewartby Brickworks	N5204.40 W00031.05
Woburn Town	N5159.40 W00037.15

Operator

Cranfield University
Cranfield
Beds, MK43 0AL
Tel: 01234 754784 (Admin)
Tel: 01234 754761 (ATC)
Fax: 01234 754785 (ATC)
Fax: 01234 751805 (Admin)
airport@cranfield.ac.uk
www.cranfieldairport.co.uk

Effective date:23/11/06

C

218ft	9nm NE of Grantham	**PPR**	**Alternative AD**	**Nottingham East Midlands** Syerston
7mb	N5301.82 W00028.99	**MIL**	**Diversion AD**	

Cranwell		**ATIS** 135.675		**APP** 119.375
PAR 123.300		**TWR** 125.050		**A/G** 119.375

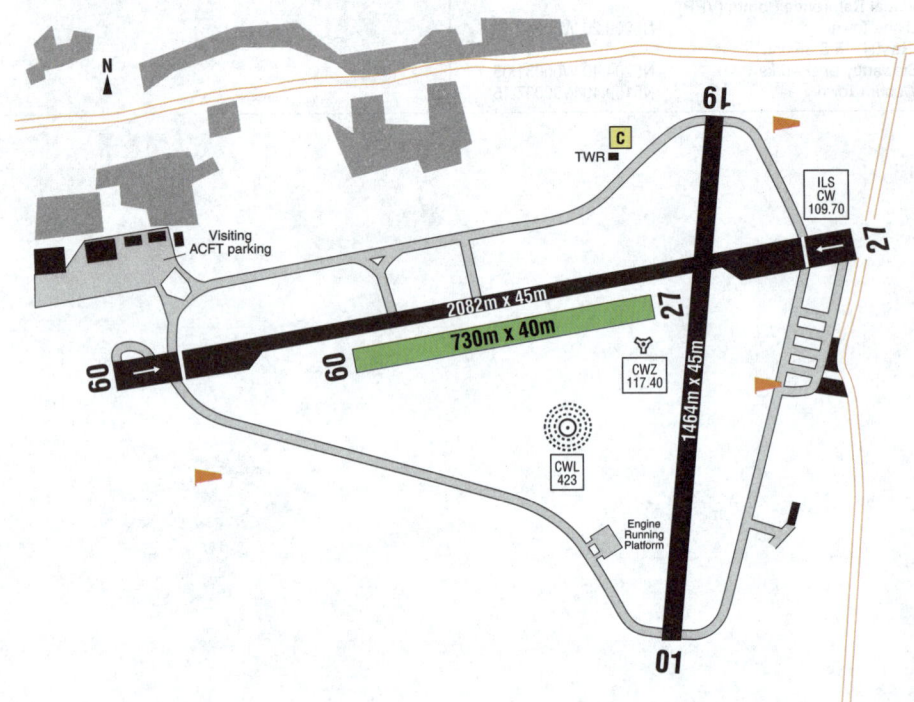

RWY	SURFACE	TORA	LDA	LIGHTING
09	Asph/Conc	2082	1918	Ap Thr Rwy PAPI 3°
27	Asph/Conc	2082	1989	Ap Thr Rwy PAPI 3°
01/19	Asph/Conc	1464	1464	Thr Rwy PAPI 3°
09/27	Grass	730	730	Nil

Remarks
Grass AD N of main AD is for glider ops only. ACFT inbound to either Cranwell or Barkston Heath are to call Cranwell APP at least 5nm before the boundary of the Cranwell/Barkston Heath CMATZ. ACFT must adhere to slot times. Light ACFT may operate outside normal operating times using A/G. Visiting ACFT note there is a grass strip S of and parallel to Rwy09/27 active with ACFT not using RTF.
Visual aid to location: Abn White; Ibn CW Red.

Warnings
Public roads cross APP to all Rwys. Motorised glider towing up to 3000ft and winch launching up to 2000ft takes place on the grass AD to N of main AD during daylight Hrs evenings & weekends. ATZ active H24.
Noise: On Dept climb straight ahead to 1000ft QFE before turning, avoiding all local villages.

Operating Hrs	As required 3FTS operations (ATZ H24)	**Restaurants**	Nil
Circuits	27 LH, 09 RH, 01 & 19 variable CCT 1000ft QFE, Light ACT 800ft AFE	**Taxis/Car Hire**	Nil
		Weather Info	AirCen MWC
Landing Fee	Charges in accordance with MOD policy Contact Station Ops for details	**Operator**	RAF Cranwell Sleaford Lincs NG34 8HB
Maintenance	Nil		**Tel:** 01400 261201 Ex 7377
Fuel	AVGAS 100LL AVTUR FS11 By arr min notice of 24Hrs & max uplift of 500Imp Galls		**Tel:** 01400 261201 Ex 7182 (Ops)
Disabled Facilities			

CROMER

188ft 6mb	2nm SE of Cromer N5254.09 E00119.73		**PPR**	**Alternative AD Diversion AD**	**Norwich** Old Buckenham

Cromer	**ATIS** Norwich 128.625	**LARS** Norwich 119.350	**A/G** 129.825

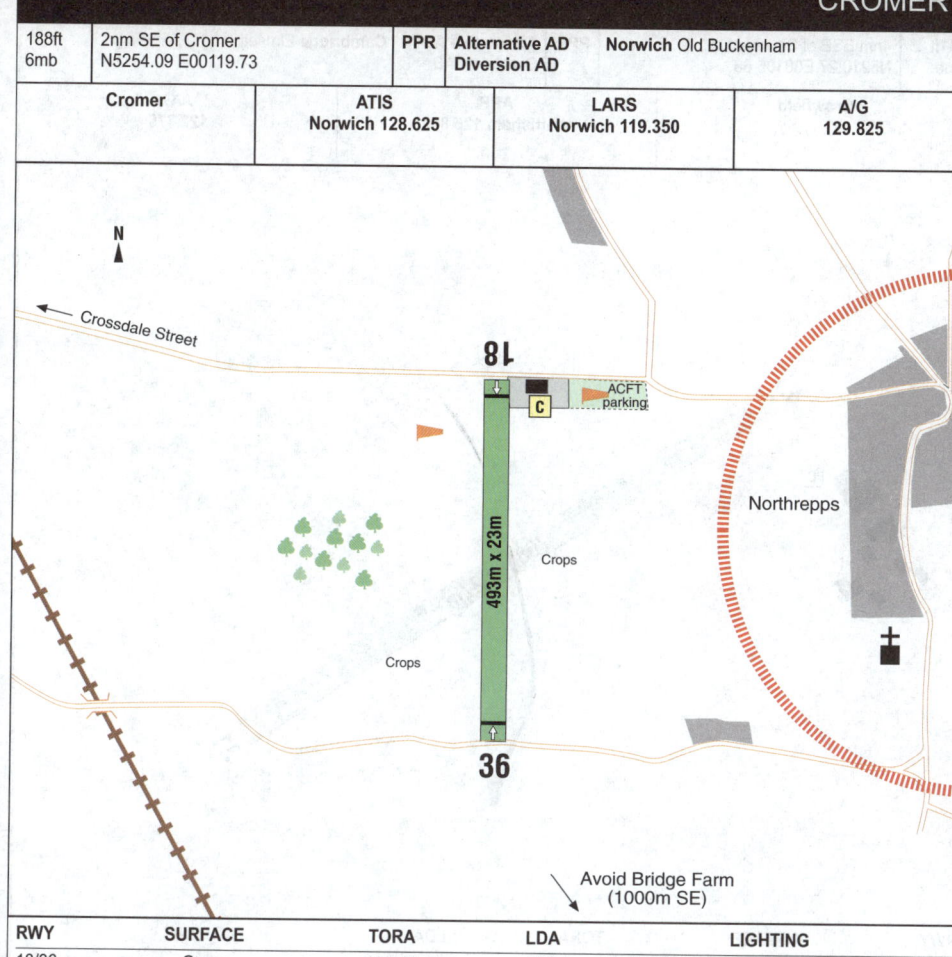

Crossdale Street

18

C ACFT parking

493m x 23m

Crops

Crops

36

Northrepps

Avoid Bridge Farm (1000m SE)

C

RWY	**SURFACE**	**TORA**	**LDA**	**LIGHTING**
18/36	Grass	493x23	U/L	Nil

Rwy36 1.8% upslope

Remarks
PPR essential for briefing. Light ACFT & helicopters welcome at pilots own risk. Extensive microlight and paramotor activity at AD. Military and civil helicopter training may take place at short notice. Any training is by strict arrangement only. Intensive military & civil low flying in the area including off-shore civil helicopters, Model ACFT flying may take place weekdays. All visiting ACFT must book each flight in and out. New extended parking/heli area to E of existing parking area.

Warnings
Dept are normally restricted to Rwy18 which has a 1.8% downslope and public road close to Thr. Public footpath close to Thr Rwy36. SAR helicopters may operate from AD. Heavy SAR helicopters landing area on Rwy, users must be prepared for AD to be unavailable to fixed wing ACFT at short notice. Civil and military helicopter under slung load training may take place on weekdays. **Noise:** Avoid over flying Northrepps, Crossdale Street & Bridge Farm below 500ft QFE.

Operating Hrs	SR-SS		**Taxis**	
Circuits	36 RH, 18 LH, 600 QFE		A1 Cabs	**Tel:** 01263 513371
Landing Fee	Private £5 Microlights £4		ACE	**Tel:** 01263 511749
	Commercial on application		**Car Hire**	Available in Cromer
	Camping £2 per night		**Bike Hire**	Available in Cromer
	Long term parking by arr		**Weather Info**	AirS MOEx
Maintenance	Nil		**Operator**	Chris Gurney
Fuel	AVGAS 100LL by arr			Heath Cottage
	MOGAS			Northrepps, Cromer
Disabled Facilities	Nil			Norfolk, NR27 9LB
				Tel: 01263 513015
Restaurants	Light refreshments available on AD			**Tel:** 07886 264992
Cromer Tourist Info	**Tel:** 01263 512497			**Fax:** 01263515516
Accomodation	Camping and B&B available on AD			northrepps@hotmail.com
				www.chris.gurney.co.uk

195

201ft 7mb	4nm ESE of Stowmarket N5210.27 E00106.66	PPR	**Alternative AD** **Diversion AD**	**Cambridge** Elmsett

Crowfield	**APP** **Wattisham 125.800**	**A/G** **122.775**

768m x 27m

13

31

N

C

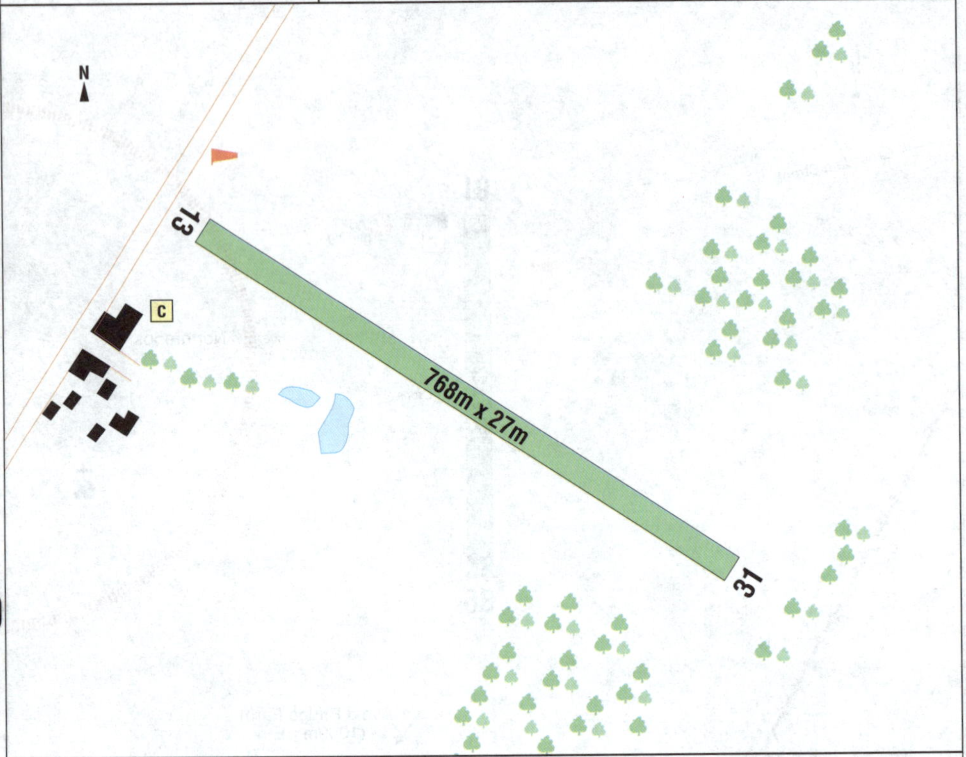

RWY	SURFACE	TORA	LDA	LIGHTING
31	Grass	768x27	U/L	Nil
13	Grass	768x27	U/L	Nil

Remarks
PPR by telephone only. No multi engined ACFT. No singles more than 148kw/1200kgs AUW. No Gliders, Microlights or Helicopters. Total daily movements restricted. Arr must contact Wattisham APP when at least 15nm from Wattisham. Dept unless otherwise instructed ACFT must fly not above 800ft QFE while under Wattisham MATZ. Contact Wattisham before takeoff if possible or ASAP after take-off.

Warnings
Noise: Please operate with consideration, this AD is in a noise sensitive area, avoid all local villages.

Operating Hrs	0800-1900 (Summer) 0900-1800 or SS (Winter)	**Car Hire**	By arr
		Weather Info	AirS MOEx
Circuits	31 variable, 13 LH, 800ft QFE	**Operator**	Mr A C Williamson
Landing Fee	£5		Crowfield Aerodrome
Maintenance	Nil		Coddenham Green, Ipswich
Fuel	AVGAS 100LL Oils W100 W80 100 80		Suffolk, IP6 9UN **Tel:** 01449 711017 **Fax:** 01449 711054

Disabled Facilities

Restaurants	Coffee & tea available
Taxis Stowmarket	By arr or **Tel:** 01449 677777

10ft	4nm S of Spalding (On Crowland Rd)	PPR	Alternative AD	Cambridge Fenland
0mb	N5242.53 W00008.57			

Crowland	LARS Cottesmore 130.200	A/G 129.975

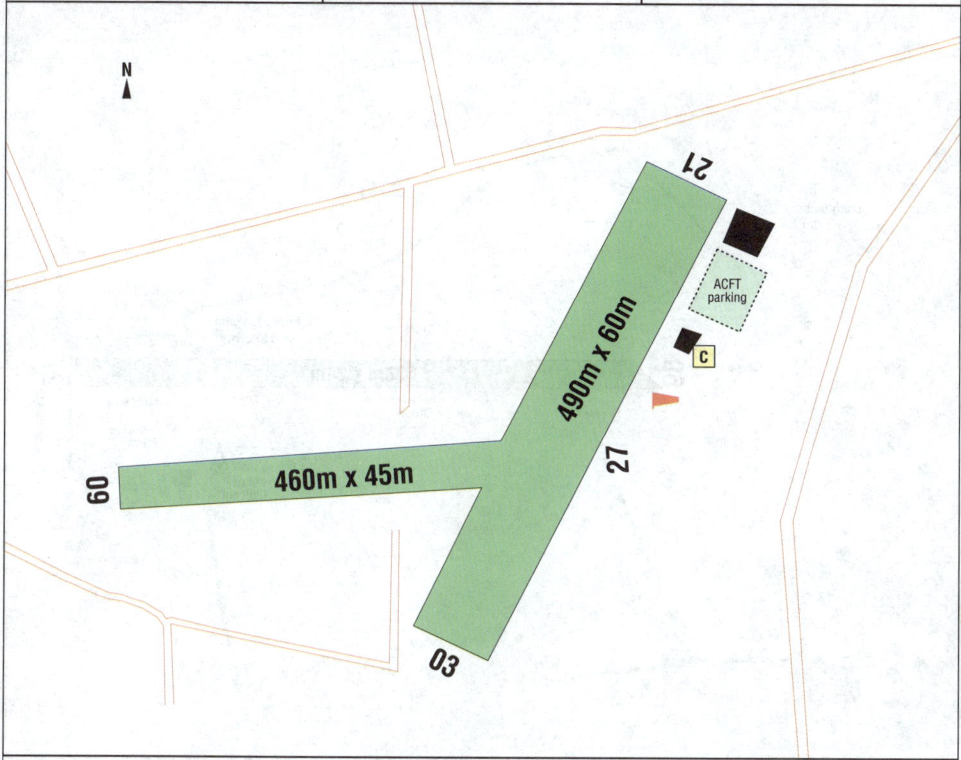

N

21

ACFT parking

C

490m x 60m

27

60

460m x 45m

03

C

RWY	SURFACE	TORA	LDA	LIGHTING
03/21	Grass	490x60	U/L	Nil
09/27	Grass	460x45	U/L	Nil

Remarks
PPR by telephone. Visitors welcome at pilot's own risk. Good APP. Frequent aero-tow glider flying. RAF Wittering MATZ panhandle begins 5nm WSW of Crowland.

Warnings
Intensive military low-flying activity Mon-Fri in the vicinity. Mast 200 ft agl situated S of Crowland. AD surface rough in places.

Operating Hrs	SR-SS	**Operator**	Peterborough & Spalding Gliding Club
Circuits	Variable 800-1000 QFE		Postland, Crowland
Landing Fee	Nil		Lincs, PE6 0JW
Maintenance	Nil		**Tel:** 07913 945634
Fuel	Nil		www.psgc.co.uk

Disabled Facilities

Restaurants	Light refreshments when gliding in progress
Taxis/Car Hire	**Tel:** 01775 711122
Weather Info	AirS MOEx

CUCKOO TYE FARM

240ft 8mb	2nm N of Sudbury N5204.50 E00045.50	PPR	Alternative AD	Southend Elmsett

Non-Radio	APP Wattisham 125.800	Safetycom 135.475

N

Long Melford 1000m

A134

Crops

Crops

Crops

Parked ACFT

Public footpath crosses Rwy

60 ———— 660m x 24m ———— 27

Crops

Cuckoo Tye Farm

Mast 120ft agl

Low hedge

C

RWY	SURFACE	TORA	LDA	LIGHTING
09/27	Grass	660x24	U/L	Nil

Remarks
PPR by telephone. Visiting ACFT welcome at pilots own risk. AD close to SW panhandle of Wattisham MATZ, Wattisham is busy with military helicopter traffic during weekdays. Operator advises that inbound and outbound ACFT call Wattisham APP. **Visual aid to location:** A Cessna 172 is parked close to Rwy09 Thr.

Warnings
A public footpath crosses Rwy but is rarely used. A134 crosses Rwy27 APP on short final. Crops are grown close to Rwy edges. Horse riders use the unclassified roads close to AD, care should be taken not to over fly them. Radio mast on the workshop S of AD. **Noise:** Avoid local houses, particularly Long Melford.

Operating Hrs	SR-SS	**Operator**	Mr P J Miller
Circuits	LH 1000ft QFE		Cuckoo Tye Farm
Landing Fee	Nil		Acton, Sudbury
Maintenance	Nil		Suffolk, CO10 0AE
Fuel	Nil		**Tel:** 01787 377233
Disabled Facilities	Nil		**Tel/Fax:** 01787 881706
Restaurants	Nil		peter@cuckootye.co.uk
Taxi **SCC**	**Tel:** 01787 373222		
Car Hire	Nil		
Weather Info	AirCen MOEx		

EGDR

267ft 9mb	1nm SE of Helston N5005.17 W00515.34	PPR MIL	Alternative AD Diversion AD	St Mawgan Lands End

Culdrose	LARS 134.050	APP 134.050
PAR 123.300 122.100	SRE 134.050 122.100	TWR 122.100 123.300

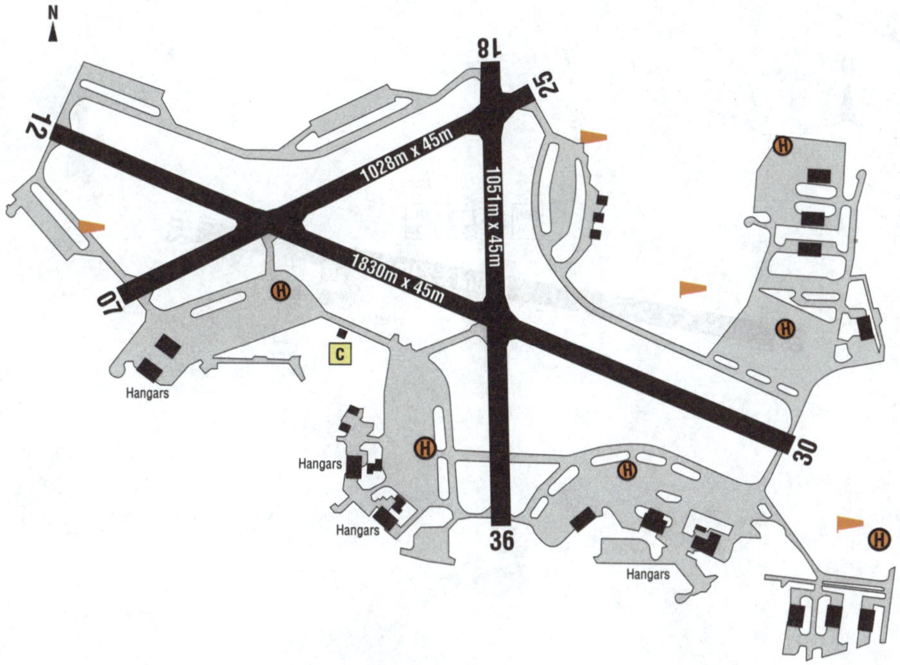

N

18 / 25 / 12 / 07 / 30 / 36

1028m x 45m
1051m x 45m
1830m x 45m

Hangars
Hangars
Hangars
Hangars

C

RWY	SURFACE	TORA	LDA	LIGHTING
07/25	Asphalt	1028	1028	Ap Rwy PAPI 3°
12/30	Asphalt	1830	1830	Ap Rwy PAPI 3°
18/36	Asphalt	1051	1051	Ap Rwy PAPI 3°

Remarks
PPR 24Hrs required. Inbound ACFT to contact Culdrose APP at 20nm. RAD let down mandatory.
Visual aid to location: Ibn CU Red.

Warnings
High intensity helicopter operations in the area and at Preddannack. Glider launching at weekends and evenings. More than one Rwy may be used simultaneously. No visual signals.
Noise: Avoid over flying Helston

Operating Hrs	Mon-Thu 0730-1600 or SS Fri 0730-1300 or SS (Summer) +1Hr (Winter)	**Restaurants**	Nil
Circuits	Helicopter circuits LH & RH No dead side	**Taxis/Car Hire**	Nil
		Weather Info	M T Fax 272 MOEx
Landing Fee	Charges in accordance with MOD policy Contact Station Ops for details	**Operator**	RNAS Culdrose Helston Cornwall
Maintenance	Nil		TR12 7RH
Fuel	AVGAS 100LL JET A1 By arr		**Tel:** 01326 574121 Ex 2415 (ATC) **Tel:** 01326 574121 Ex 2620 (PPR/Ops)

Disabled Facilities

350ft 13mb	16nm NE of Glasgow N5558.48 W00358.53	PPR	Alternative AD Diversion AD	Glasgow Fife
	Cumbernauld		A/G 120.600	

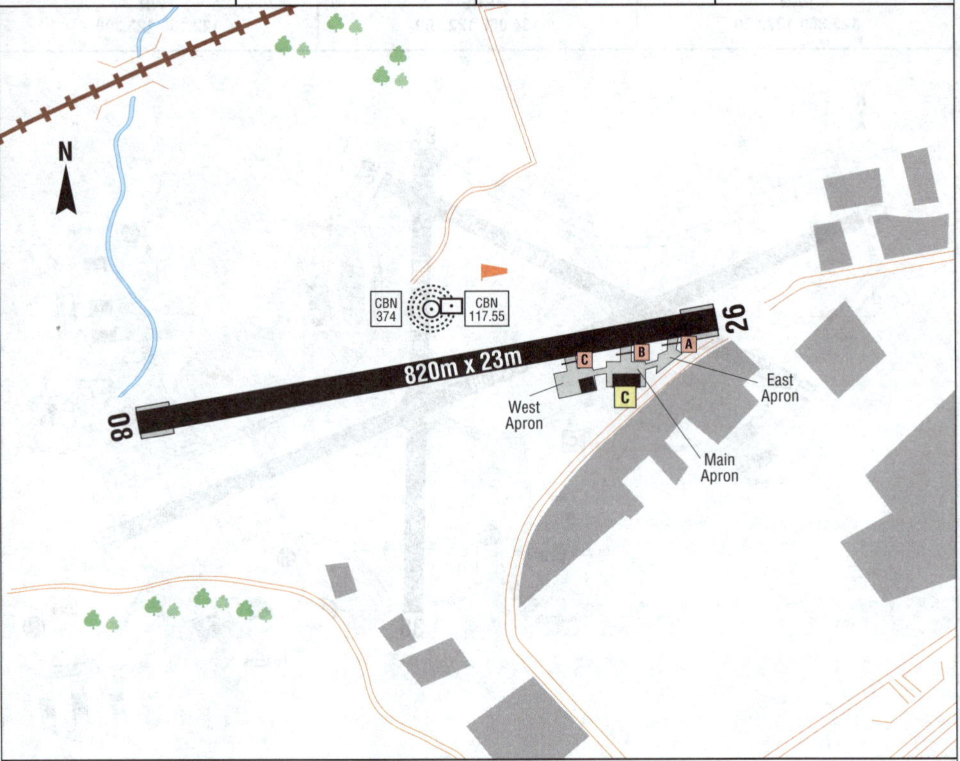

N

CBN 374   CBN 117.55

820m x 23m

80

26

West Apron

C   B   A

C

Main Apron

East Apron

RWY	SURFACE	TORA	LDA	LIGHTING
08	Asphalt	820	820	Thr Rwy APAPI 4° LHS
26	Asphalt	820	820	Thr Rwy APAPI 3.5° LHS

Remarks
Certain customs facilities available. In IFR, suitably equipped ACFT may let down at Edinburgh and proceed to Cumbernauld VMC.
Visual aids to location: White strobe on roof of Control TWR, available on request. If no reply on A/G observe signal square, proceed with overhead join and make A/G standard calls.

Warnings
AD is situated under Scottish TMA. Traffic in transit should anticipate local circuit activity at this AD. Microlight flying takes place at AD.
Noise: Avoid over flying Dullatur village 0.75mile W of Rwy08 Thr. Also Banton and High Banton N of AD.

Operating Hrs	0700-2000 (Summer) 0900-1700 (Winter) & by arr	**Restaurant**	Nil
		Taxis	
Circuits	26 RH, 08 LH, 1000ft QFE Join overhead 2000ft QFE descend on dead side to join circuit	Central	**Tel:** 01236 722772
		Car Hire	
		Robinsons	**Tel:** 01236 729232
Landing Fee	Visitors: Single £17.50 Twin 43.80 (up to 3000Kg). Local Club: Single £10.60	**Weather Info**	AirSc GWC
		Operator	Cumbernauld Airport Ltd
Maintenance	Cormack Aircraft Services Ltd **Tel:** 01236 457777 info@cormackaircraft.com		Duncan Macintosh Road Ward Park, North Cumbernauld G68 0HH
Fuel	AVGAS JET A1 100LL available operating Hrs VISA/Mastercard accepted		**Tel:** 01236 722100 **Tel:** 01236 722822 (ATC) **Fax:** 01236 781646

Disabled Facilities

800ft 26mb	8nm SW of Newcastle Airport N5456.03 W00150.73	PPR	Alternative AD	Newcastle Eshott

Currock Base	APP Newcastle 124.375	A/G 130.125

RWY	SURFACE	TORA	LDA	LIGHTING
06/24	Grass	600x50	U/L	Nil

Remarks
PPR and briefing by telephone. Primarily a gliding site but light ACFT welcome at pilot's own risk. The whole of the field (90 acres) is used for gliding but only the strip shown is recommended for visitors. AD is situated within Newcastle CTR, clearance to enter must be obtained from Newcastle APP.

Warnings
When Rwy24 in use do not land short of the windsock due to steep upslope to Thr and possible wind shadow effect. Slight upslope to Rwy24. Gliders launch with winch and aero tow. Launch positions may not be co-located.

		Operator	Northumbria Gliding Club Ltd
Operating Hrs	Sat-Sun & Wed 0900-SS (L) & by arr		Currock Hill, Chopwell
Circuits	Powered ACFT to S 800ft QFE gliders variable		Newcastle, NE17 7AX **Tel:** 01207 561286
Landing Fee	Private £5 Commercial £10		info@northumbria.flyer.co.uk www.northumbria-gliding-club.co.uk
Maintenance	Nil		
Fuel	AVGAS 100LL by prior arr		
Disabled Facilities	Nil		

Restaurants
Tea, coffee & snacks available when gliding in progress
Four Seasons **Tel:** 01207 561208 (10 min walk)

Taxis	**Tel:** 0191 4131143
Car Hire	Nil

Weather Info AirN MWC

C

201

DAMYNS HALL

56ft 2mb	2nm S of Upminster N5131.77 W00014.73	PPR	Alternative AD	Southend	Stapleford

Hornchurch Radio	APP London City 132.700	A/G 119.550

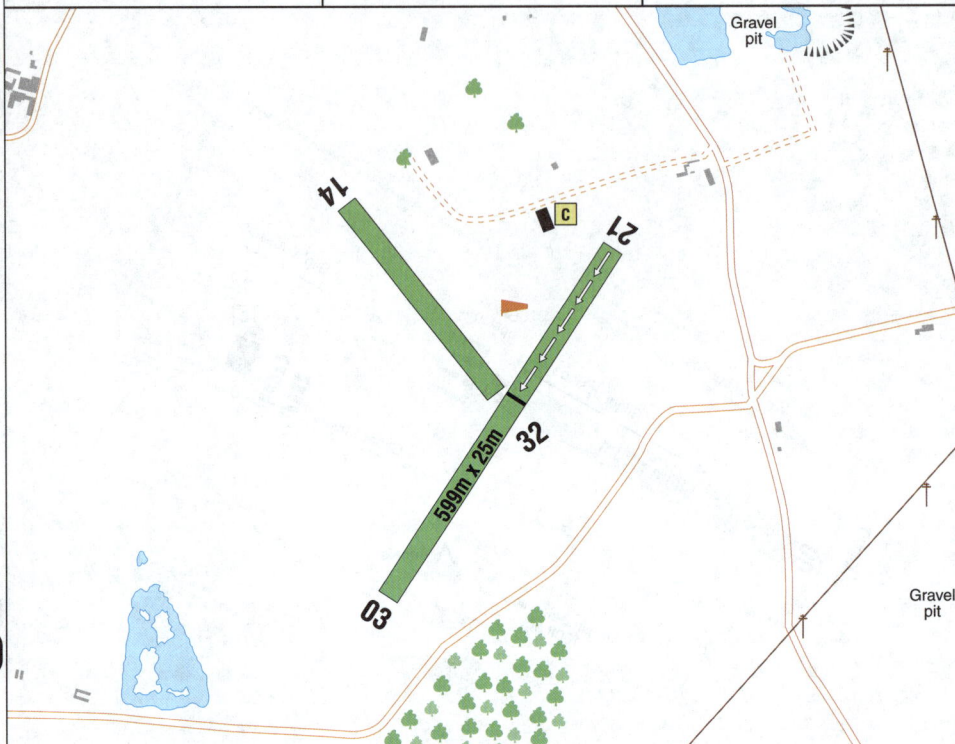

RWY	SURFACE	TORA	LDA	LIGHTING
03	Grass	341	595	Nil
21	Grass	595	341	Nil

Remarks
Strict PPR by telephone. Visitors welcome at own risk. Helicopter joining procedures available with PPR. Hangar space available on request.

Warnings
Uphill slope Rwy03, prefered landing in light winds. AD close to London City CTA Class D Airspace – 1nm W of AD. London City CTR Class D Airspace 2.3nm W of AD. ACFT must contact London City APP before entering the ATZ. Gerpins Farm Airfield 0.6nm W of AD. Thurrock 4.6nm E of AD. Keep good look out for ACFT using these AD.
Noise: Avoid over flying the following villages surrounding the AD. Rainham SW of AD. South Ockendon SE of AD. Hornchurch NW of AD. Aveley S of AD. Upminster N of AD.

Operating Hrs	Thu-Sun 1000-1700 (Summer) Fir-Sun 1000-1600 (Winter)	**Operator**	Damyns Hall Aerodrome Aveley Road Hornchurch Essex RM14 2TN **Tel:** 02476 511615 **Fax:** 02476 511549
Circuits	21 LH, 03 RH 1000ft QFE		
Landing Fee	Available with PPR		
Maintenance	Nil		
Fuel	AVGAS JET A1		
Restaurants	Nil		
Taxi/Car Hire	Nil		
Weather Info	AirSE MOEx		

969ft 33mb	3nm ENE of Camelford N5038.25 W00437.13		PPR	Alternative AD Diversion AD	Plymouth Bodmin

Non radio	LARS St Mawgan 128.725	A/G 129.825 (Microlight freq)	Safetycom 135.475

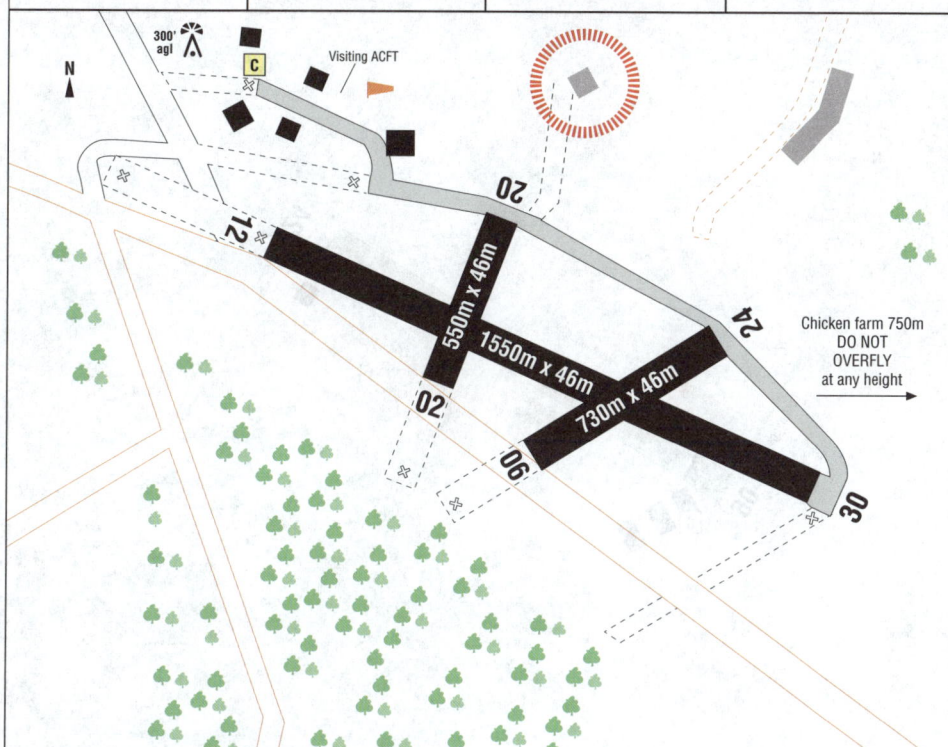

Chicken farm 750m
DO NOT
OVERFLY
at any height →

RWY	SURFACE	TORA	LDA	LIGHTING
12/30	Concrete	1550x46	U/L	Nil
06/24	Concrete	730x46	U/L	Nil
02/20	Concrete	550x46	U/L	Nil

Remarks
PPR by telephone. Situated on unfenced moorland. Windsock displayed when flying in progress. Beware of livestock and people on Rwys. Gliding at weekends. Microlight activity at any time

Warnings
A road running SE/NW bisects the AD. Only Rwy to NE of road are useable. Radio TWR 236ft aal in NW corner of AD, 200m from signals square.
Noise: Avoid over flying villages NW of AD. No flying within 1/2nm radius of farm 1.5miles E of AD at N5038.45 W00434.30

Operating Hrs	0800-1700 (Summer) +1Hr (Winter)	Operator	Moorland Flying Club
Circuits	All S		Davidstow Airfield
Landing Fee	No charge for flyers spending money in the local area		Camelford, PL32 9YF **Tel:** 01840 261517 letsflywithsteve@aol.com
Maintenance	For microlights		
Fuel	Nil		
Disabled Facilities	Nil		
Restaurants	Available in Camelford 1m NW		
Taxis	**Tel:** 01840 213867		
Car Hire	Nil		
Weather Info	AirSW MOEx		

60ft 2mb	5nm E of Lewes N5052.73 E00009.38	PPR	Alternative AD	Shoreham Lashenden

	Deanland	A/G 129.725 (not always manned)	

RWY	SURFACE	TORA	LDA	LIGHTING
06	Grass	500x27	U/L	Rwy
24	Grass	500x27	U/L	Rwy

Remarks

PPR by telephone. No microlights of any type. Available for single-engined ACFT only. Considerate pilots welcome at own risk but ACFT performance must be compatible with the length of the strip and pilot must have short field experience. Please enter flight details in movements book at the 'Control Point'. ACFT insurance must cover operational risks at strips. No local or training flights. **Arr:** large circuits with a minimum of 1.5nm final maintaining the Rwy centre line. **Under no circumstances cut the corners. Dept:** Climb accurately maintaining Rwy centre line for 1.5nm before turning on track. **Under no circumstances make early turns.**

Warnings

After prolonged or heavy rainfall the Rwy will become water logged, please check by phone. Make blind calls if radio unmanned. Model ACFT flying takes place on AD. Police helicopter operations may occur at any time
Caution: Private strip 1nm from end of Rwy24 to SW.
Noise: Do not over fly any local houses, the caravan park and village of Ripe

Operating Hrs	SR-SS		Weather Info	AirSE MOEx
Circuits	O6 LH, 24 RH, 1000ft QFE		Operator	Messrs Brook & Price Deanland Airfield c/o DJ Brook, BCL House Gatwick Road, Crawley Sussex RH10 9AX **Tel:** 01323 811410 (AD) **Tel:** 07785 316368 **Tel:** 01323 811858 **Tel:** 01903 774379 **Fax:** 01293 429836 david@gatwick-group.co.uk www.deanland-airfield.co.uk
Landing Fee	Private minimum charge £3 Over night park £3, Commercial by arr.			
Maintenance David Hockings	**Tel:** 07710 329369			
Fuel	Nil			
Disabled Facilities	Nil			
Restaurant	Nil			
Taxis Becks	**Tel:** 01273 483838			
Car Hire	Nil			

DEBACH

180ft 6mb	3nm NW of Woodbridge N5208.11 E00116.16	PPR	Alternative AD	Norwich Crowfield

Non-Radio	APP Wattisham 125.800	Safetycom 135.475

Restored WW2 control tower

30ft powerlines

crops

24

Access to restored control tower

crops

500m x 25m

crops

06

ACFT parking

crops

RWY	SURFACE	TORA	LDA	LIGHTING
24/06	Grass	500x25	U/L	Nil

Remarks

Strictly PPR by telephone. Visiting ACFT are limited, permission may be denied. Visiting ACFT should park at either end of strip on hard surface. Other parts of AD are not suitable for ACFT use. AD located on SW portion of the last 8th AF base to be operational during WW2. Home of the 493rd BG, Helton's Hellcats, (B17's). WW2 Watch Office and other buildings have been restored to original condition. There is an annual open day, (Sun 10th June 2007 with a dance on Sat 9th. Camping available on W/E of open day). Access is not normally available on other days.

Warnings

30ft power lines run close to Rwy24 final but do not cross APP. Crops grown up to Rwy edges. Model ACFT use AD at weekends & PH. The 'two tone' cut on the strip at the W end is the model ACFT operating area. Monewden AD 1nm to N. National grid transmission lines cross extreme SE corner of WW2 airfield but should not affect normal circuit.
Noise: Please avoid flying over all local houses.

Operating Hrs	SR-SS	**Weather Info**	AirS MOEx
Circuits	LH 1000ft QFE	**Operator**	Richard Taylor
Landing Fee	Nil		Grove Farm
Maintenance	Nil		Clopton
Fuel	Nil, available from Crowfield		Suffolk
Disabled Facilities	Nil		**Tel:** 01473 737236
Restaurants	Nil		**Tel:** 07850 078432
Taxis	Nil		www.493bgdebach.co.uk
Car Hire	Nil		

205

328ft 11mb	4nm E of Corby N5230.37 W00035.35	PPR	Alternative AD	Cambridge Peterborough Conington

Non-Radio	LARS Cottesmore 130.200	Safetycom 135.475

RWY	SURFACE	TORA	LDA	LIGHTING
04/22	Asphalt	1200x30	U/L	Nil

Remarks
PPR by telephone. ACFT Arr & Dept are advised to contact Cottesmore app.

Warnings
Rwy04 Thr inset by 400m Rwy22 Thr by 237m. Microlights operate outside AD Hrs. Beware close proximity of Lyveden gliding site.
Noise: ACFT should avoid over flying Deene Park (1.5nm W of AD) below 2000ft and Deenthorpe village.

Operating Hrs	Sat-Sun & PH 0800-1630 (Summer) Sat-Sun & PH 0900-SS (Winter) Other Hrs strictly PPR	**Operator**	Mr A P I Campbell Estates Office Deene Park, Corby Northants, NN17 3EW **Tel:** 01780 450361 **Fax:** 01780 450282
Circuits	04 RH, 22 LH, 800ft Join overhead at 2000ft.		
Landing Fee	Single £5 Twin £10 penalty for no PPR		
Maintenance	Nil		
Fuel	Nil		
Disabled Facilities	Nil		
Restaurants	Nil		
Taxis/Car Hire	Nil		
Weather Info	AirCen MWC		

70ft 2mb	0.5nm SE of Defford Disused AD N5205.13 W00208.15	PPR	Alternative AD	Gloucestershire Wellesbourne Mountford

Defford	A/G 119.100	Please make routine circuit calls

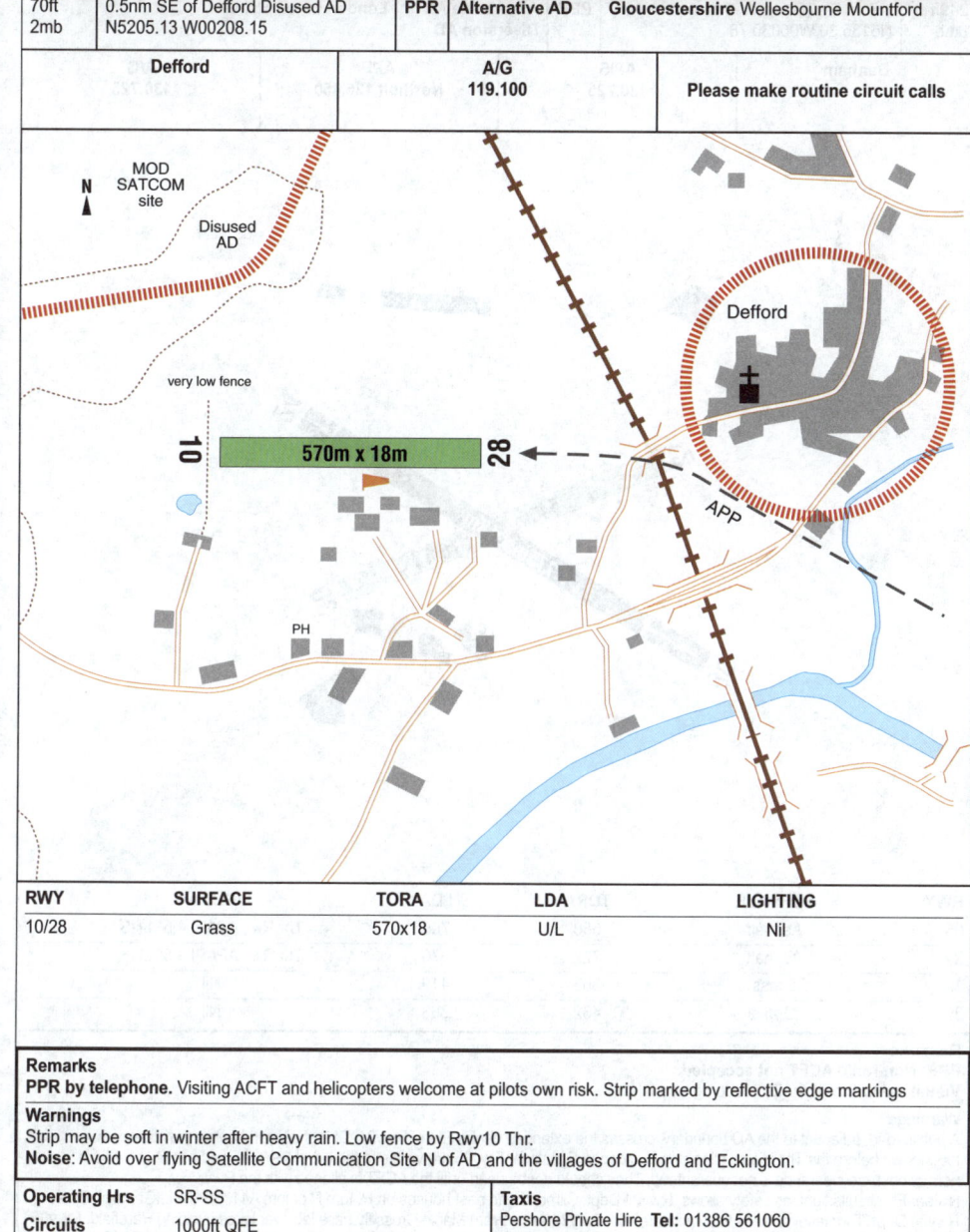

RWY	SURFACE	TORA	LDA	LIGHTING
10/28	Grass	570x18	U/L	Nil

Remarks
PPR by telephone. Visiting ACFT and helicopters welcome at pilots own risk. Strip marked by reflective edge markings

Warnings
Strip may be soft in winter after heavy rain. Low fence by Rwy10 Thr.
Noise: Avoid over flying Satellite Communication Site N of AD and the villages of Defford and Eckington.

Operating Hrs	SR-SS
Circuits	1000ft QFE
Landing Fee	Nil but donations to Mission Aviation Fellowship gratefully received
Maintenance	Nil
Fuel	Nil

Disabled Facilities

Restaurants Pub 400m from AD
Farm shop and tearoom on AD

Taxis
Pershore Private Hire **Tel:** 01386 561060
Eckington Taxis **Tel:** 01386 750407
Car Hire
PJ Nichols **Tel:** 01386 555555
Bredon Motors **Tel:** 0800 614809

Weather Info Air Cen MOEx

Operator Mr C H Porter
The Croft Farm
Defford, Worcs, WR8 9BN
Tel: 07767 606172
Tel: 07767 796355
clive.porter@croftfarm.fsnet.co.uk
www.defford-croftfarm.co.ul

207

| 249ft | 1.5nm E of Gerrards Cross | PPR | Alternative AD | London Luton Elstree |
| 8mb | N5135.30 W00030.78 | | Diversion AD | |

Denham	AFIS 130.725	APP Northolt 126.450	A/G 130.725

RWY	SURFACE	TORA	LDA	LIGHTING
06	Asphalt	686	706	Thr Rwy APAPI 4.5° LHS
24	Asphalt	728	670	Thr Rwy APAPI 4.5° LHS
12	Grass	363	419	Nil
30	Grass	432	363	Nil

Remarks
PPR. Non-radio ACFT not accepted.
Visual aid to location: ID beacon green DN.

Warnings
A public road, adjacent to the AD boundary, crosses the extended centre line of Rwy24. Do not descend below the glide-path, or touchdown before the Thr. Visual glide slope guidance signals for Rwy06 are visible to the left of the extended centre line where normal obstacle clearance is not guaranteed. They should not be used until the ACFT is aligned with the Rwy.
Noise: Fly circuits tight, as safety allows. Rwy24 Dept. Climb ahead past houses on R, turn R before A413, to avoid Gerrards Cross. Rwy06 Dept. Turn leftover lakes to avoid Harefield. **Rwy24 Arr** – From Maple Cross fly base leg over lakes avoiding Harefield. **Rwy06 Arr** – From Chalfont St Giles fly base leg E of A413 avoiding Gerrards Cross. In circuit stay S Hog trough Wood avoid Chalfont St Peter. Additional restrictions for twins & helicopters at weekends. ACFT flying N of London should fly as high as permitted.

Operating Hrs	Licensed Hrs 0800-1630 or SS (Summer) 0900-1730 or SS (Winter). AD available 0900-1900 (Summer) 0800-1800 (Winter) & by arr	**Taxis** Cabline **Car Hire** National Lordship Motors	**Tel:** 01895 270001 **Tel:** 01753 534442 **Tel:** 01753 883120
Circuits	06 LH, 24 RH, 12 30 variable Max 750ft QFE (1000ft QNH) No overhead joins	**Weather Info** **Operator**	AirSE MOEx Bickerton's Aerodromes Ltd Denham Aerodrome
Landing Fee	Up to 1 tonne £10.00 inc VAT		Uxbridge, Middlesex, UB9 5DE
Maintenance	Ltd		**Tel:** 01895 832060 (Admin 0900-1300)
Fuel	AVGAS 100LL JET A1 by arr		**Tel:** 01895 832161 (ATS)
Disabled Facilities	Available		**Fax:** 01895 833486
Restaurant	Restaurant & club facilities available		

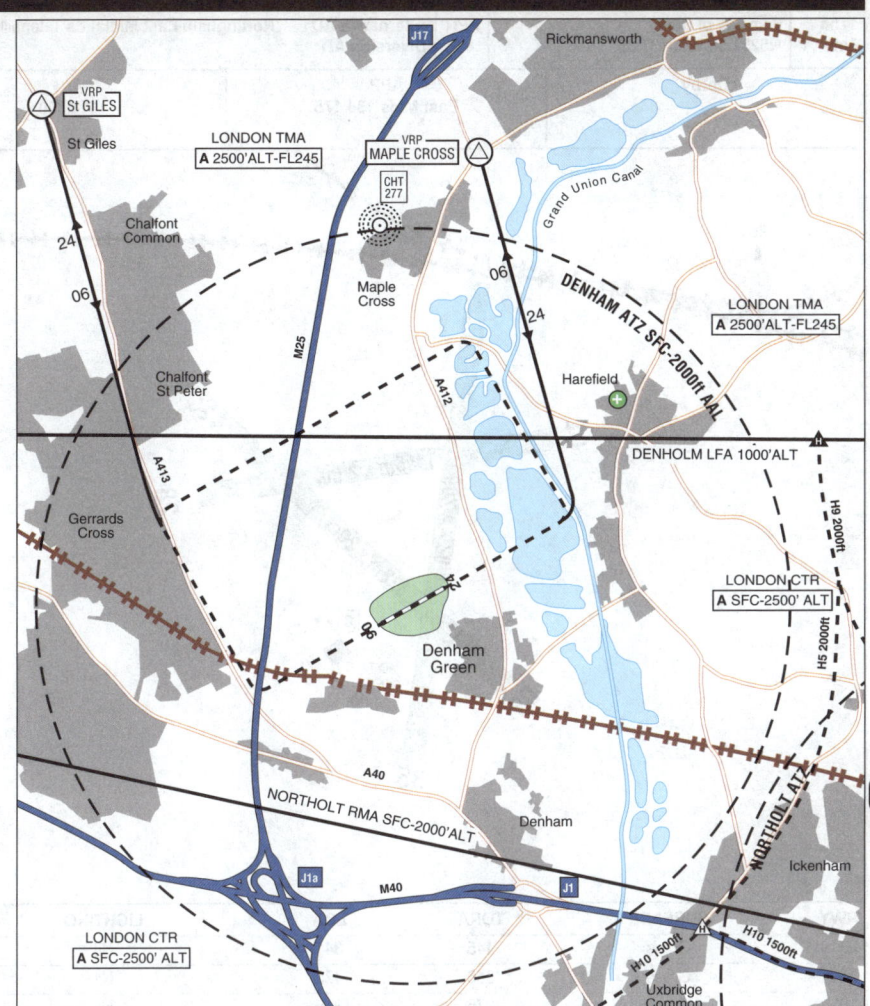

D

Visual Reference Point (VRP)

	VOR/DME	VOR/DME	NDB
Maple Cross N5137.77 W00030.25	BNN 166°/6nm	BPK 247°/17nm	CHT 058°
Chalfont St Giles N5138.02 W00034.02	BNN 190°/6nm	BPK 250°/19nm	CHT 293°

Flight without compliance to IFR within the Denham ATZ is permitted subject to the following conditions:
1 ACFT must remain clear of cloud and in sight of the surface.
2 Fly NOT above 1000ft QNH within London CTR
3 Minimum flight visibility 3km
DO NOT proceed S of A40. Pilots flying in the ATZ are responsible for providing their own separation from other ACFT flying in the relevant airspace. Safety must take precedence.

Joining Procedures – THERE ARE NO OVERHEAD JOINS
Rwy06 Join via Chalfont St Giles (N5138.02 W00034.02) directly to base leg to the E of the A413 to avoid Gerrards Cross.
Rwy24 Join via Maple Cross (N5137.77 W00030.25) directly to base leg over the lakes to avoid Harefield. Joining traffic MUST establish radio contact with Denham at 10nm range & then report at St Giles or Maple Cross as appropriate to Rwy in use.

Circuit Traffic
Circuit traffic should stay S of Hog Trough Wood to avoid a noise sensitive area in Chalfont St Peter. Additional restrictions apply to twin engined ACFT & helicopters.

Dept Procedures
Rwy06 Turn left over the lakes to avoid Harefield.
Rwy24 After take-off continue straight ahead until past the houses on the right, then turn right before the A413 to avoid over flying Gerrards Cross.

Effective date:23/11/06

175ft	6nm SW of Derby	PPR	Alternative AD	Nottingham East Midlands Tatenhill
6mb	N5251.58 W00137.05		Diversion AD	

Derby	APP East Mids 134.175	A/G 118.350

RWY	SURFACE	TORA	LDA	LIGHTING
23	Grass	445	341	Nil
05	Grass	356	430	Nil
10	Grass	276	315	Nil
28	Grass	300	291	Nil
17	Grass	513	No Landing	Nil
35	Grass	No Take-Off	528	Nil

Remarks

PPR. Non-radio ACFT not accepted. Overhead joins are not permitted. Not available at night or to Public Transport flights required to use a licensed AD. Special Arr & Dept procedures apply, which can be obtained when telephoning for PPR. Displaced Thr are marked by black and white wing bars. Derby is under the East Midlands CTA (base 1500ftAMSL over the AD). Rwy10/28 is only to be used for instruction when a QFI acts as pilot in command.

Warnings

Power line 100ft aal crosses Rwy23 APP 1200m from touchdown. Trees on the APP Rwy23 may cause turbulence and block the view of APP ACFT to ACFT on the GND. There are no QDM marks on the Rwys. Due to short LDA's on Rwy28/10 and Rwy23/05 an early go around decision is vital. DO NOT attempt to land long.
Noise: Avoid over flying local villages.

Operating Hrs	Mon-Sat 0900-1800 Sun & PH 0930-1800 (Summer) Mon-Sat 0900-SS Sun & PH 0930-SS (Winter)	**Disabled Facilities** Nil	
		Restaurants	Tea & Coffee in club house
		Taxis	
Circuits	05 LH, 23 RH, 1000ft QFE	Stretton	**Tel:** 01283 511876
Landing Fee	Single £6, Twin/Heli £10	A1	**Tel:** 01283 838383
		Car Hire	
Maintenance	Airspeed Aviation Ltd **Tel:** 01283 733803	Hertz	**Tel:** 01332 205215
		National	**Tel:** 01332 382251
Fuel	AVGAS 100LL	**Weather Info**	AirCen MWC

Operator　　Derby Aero Club
Derby Aerodrome
Hilton Road, Egginton
Derby, DE65 6GU
Tel: 01283 733803
Fax: 01283 734829
www.derbyaeroclub.com

Derby Circuit Procedures

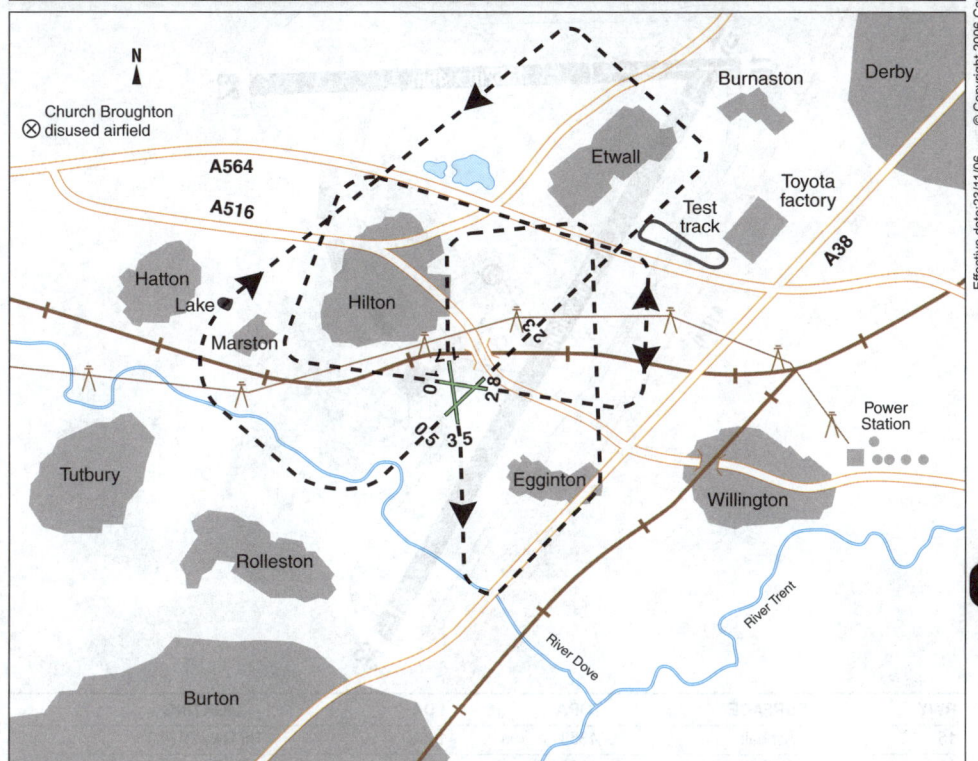

Rwy23
Turn crosswind S of river Dove but before Rolleston. Turn downwind at small lake between Hatton & Marston
Turn base leg between Burnaston & Etwall. Final APP will over fly Toyota test track

Rwy05
Turn crosswind abeam Toyota factory pass between Burnaston & Etwall. Turn downwind to remain W of Hilton. Turn base leg by initially turning at small lake to remain clear of Hatton & Marston, then follow course of river Dove to final remaining clear of Rolleston

Rwy28
Turn crosswind before Marston but remain W of Hilton. Turn downwind following course of A564. Turn base leg at Toyota test track. Continue to final

Rwy10
Turn crosswind abeam Toyota test track. Turn downwind following course of A564. Turn base leg W of Hilton & E of Marston
Continue to final

Rwy17 (Dept Only)
Turn crosswind at river Dove, intercept A38 to avoid Egginton. Turn downwind to Toyota test track. Continue onto base leg

Rwy35 (Arr Only)
Turn crosswind to avoid Etwall. Turn downwind at Toyota test track. Then leave the circuit

D

117ft 4mb	3.5nm E of Ripon N5408.23 W00125.22	PPR MIL	Alternative AD Diversion AD	Durham Tees Valley Sherburn in Elmet	

Dishforth	LARS Leeming 127.750	APP Topcliffe 125.000	TWR Dishforth 122.100	A/G 130.100 Glider Ops

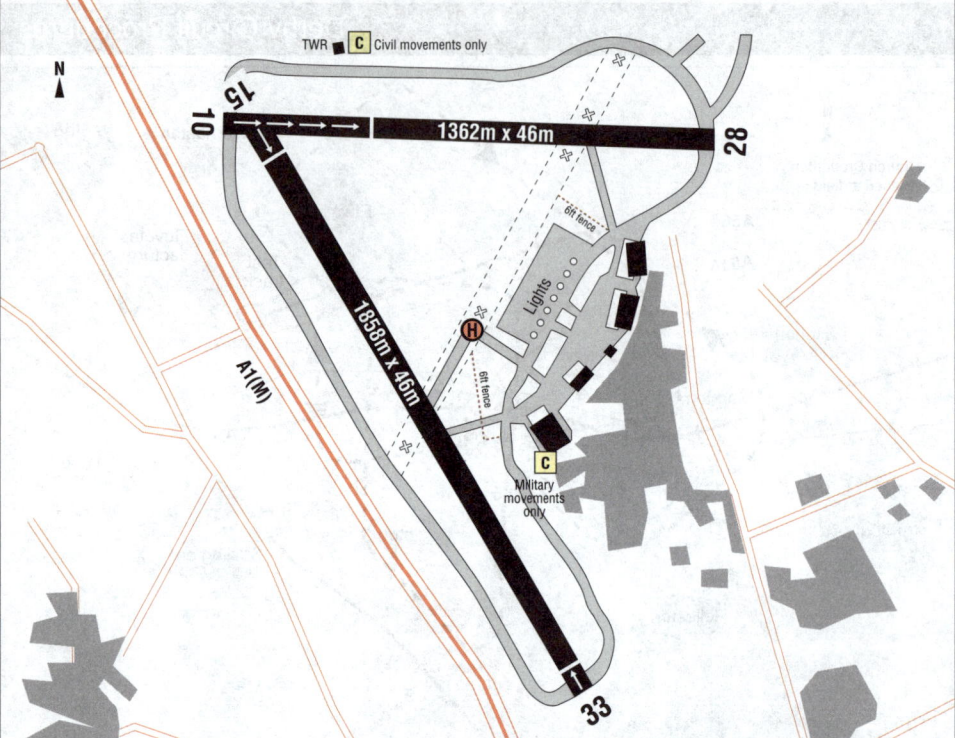

RWY	SURFACE	TORA	LDA	LIGHTING
15	Asphalt	1858	1636	Thr Rwy PAPI 3°
33	Asphalt	1858	1782	Ap Thr Rwy PAPI 3°
10	Asphalt	1362	936	Nil
28	Asphalt	1362	1362	Nil

Remarks

First 96m of Rwy33 and the first 426m of Rwy10 are sterile. Pilots should contact Leeming LARS before entering the area.

Warnings

Rwy10/28 not available for fixed wing ACFT. High intensity military flying during operational Hrs. Glider flying outside AD Hrs, evenings and weekends. Army helicopter operations may take place at any time.

Noise: Avoid over flying Boroughbridge, Kirby Hill & Dishforth.

Operating Hrs	Mon-Fri 0830-1700 & as required	**Operator**	British Army Dishforth, Thirsk, North Yorkshire **Tel:** 01423 321633 (PPR Dishforth TWR) **Tel:** 01423 321561 (Army Ops) **Fax:** 01423 321664
Circuits	10, 15 RH, 28, 33 LH, 1000ft QFE		
Landing Fee	Charges in accordance with MOD policy Contact Station Ops for details		
Maintenance	Nil		
Fuel	JET A1 (not normally available to civil visitors)		
Disabled Facilities	Nil		
Restaurants	Nil		
Taxis/Car Hire	Nil		
Weather Info	AirN MWC		

D

180ft 6mb	0.5nm S of Donaghcloney N5424.19 W00615.61	**PPR**	**Alternative AD**	**Belfast Aldergrove** Newtownards

Non-Radio	**FIS** Scottish 119.875	**APP** Aldergrove 128.500*	*If operating below or in proximity to the Belfast TMA	**Safetycom** 135.475

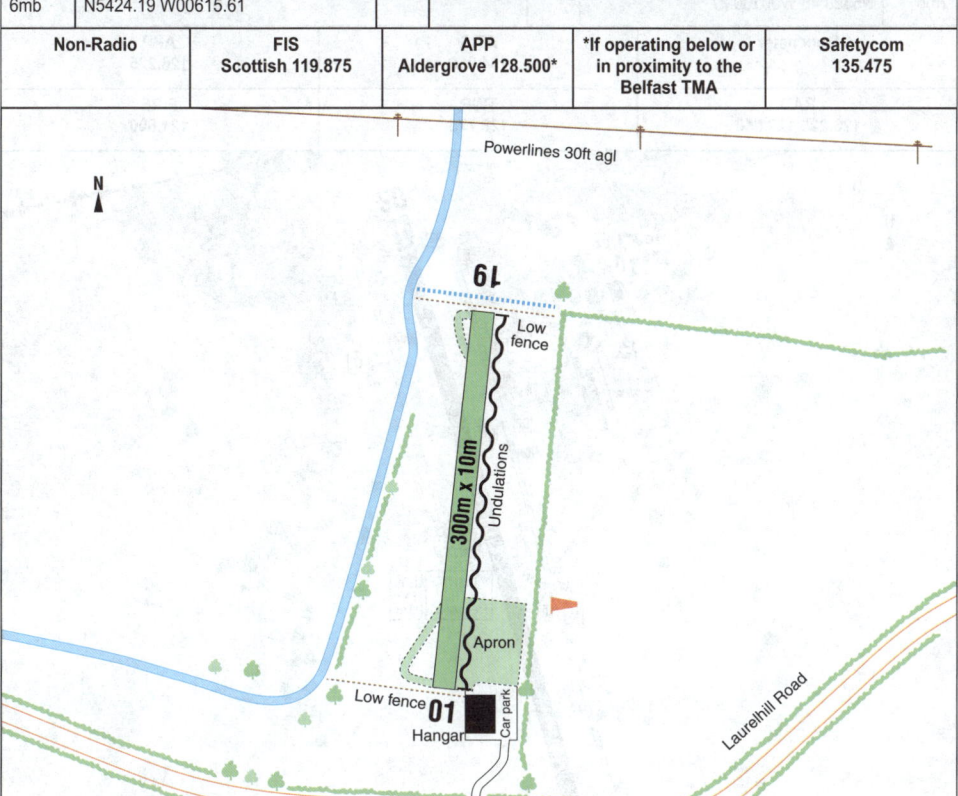

Powerlines 30ft agl

N

19

Low fence

300m x 10m

Undulations

Apron

Low fence **01**

Hangar

Car park

Laurelhill Road

RWY	SURFACE	TORA	LDA	LIGHTING
01	Grass	300x10	U/L	Nil
19	Grass	300x10	U/L	Nil

Rwy has significant undulations over full length

Remarks
PPR by telephone. Visiting ACFT/Microlights welcome at pilots own risk. AD is not notified as a designated point of entry/exit for Northern Ireland under the prevention of Terrorism act but this can be arranged via The Police Service of Northern Ireland. Hangarage is limited, visiting Microlights can be accommodated with prior arrangement.

Warnings
First time visiting pilots should obtain a telephone briefing. Rwy has significant undulations over full length. Low fences adjacent to both Rwy Thr. Powerlines 30ft agl, cross Rwy19 APP on short final. AD situated just to S of Belfast TMA, base altitude 2000ft QNH.
Noise: Avoid over flying houses to E of AD.

Operating Hrs	SR-SS	**Operator**	Fred Cameron
Circuits	19 RH 01 LH		**Tel:** 07880 504626
Landing Fee	Nil		**Tel:** 02890 650222 (PSNI)
Maintenance	Microlights only **Tel:** 02897 532558		**Fax:** 02840 621915 fly@euroflight.co.uk
Fuel	MOGAS avail by prior arr		
Disabled Facilities	Nil		
Restaurants	Nil		
Taxis	**Tel:** 02840 624794		
Car Hire	Nil		
Weather Info	AirN BEL		

EGCN   DONCASTER SHEFFIELD

Effective date:23/11/06

| 55ft
2mb | 3nm SE of Doncaster
N5328.48 W00100.27 | PPR | Alternative AD | Gamston Sandtoft |

Doncaster	ATIS 134.950	APP 126.225

RAD 126.225 129.050	TWR 128.775	FIRE 121.600

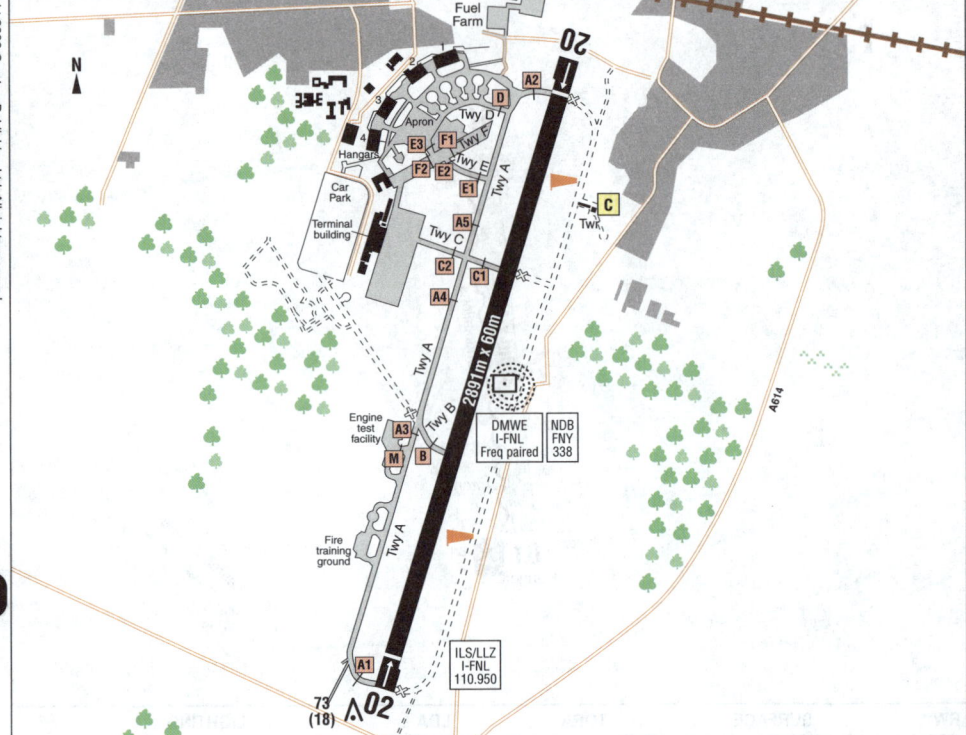

RWY	SURFACE	TORA	LDA	LIGHTING
02	Asphalt	2893	2741	Ap Thr Rwy PAPI 3.1°
20	Asphalt	2756	2604	Ap Thr Rwy PAPI 3°

Remarks
PPR Non-radio. Hi-Viz & photo ID. Pilots are requested to book-in via Signature Flight Support before starting their journey. Visual circuit training not permitted on Sun & PH.

Warnings
Bird concentrations on all areas under agricultural use on Rwy02/20 APP.

Operating Hrs	H24	**Weather Info**	M T9 MWC ATIS **Tel:** 0870 8332210 (External) ATIS **Tel:** Ex 4854 (Internal)
Circuits	02 RH 1000ft QFE 20 LH 1000ft QFE No overhead joins	**Operator**	Robin Hood Airport Doncaster Sheffield Heyford Lane Doncaster Sheffield DN9 3RH
Landing Fee	Available on request		**Tel:** 01302 801010
Maintenance	Limited		**Tel:** 01302 625022 (Apron Ops) **Tel:** 01302 624871(ATC)
Fuel	AVTUR JET A1		**Fax:** 01302 801011
Disabled Facilities	Available		**Fax:** 01302 625023 (Apron Ops)
Handling	**Tel:** 01302 624844 (Signature Flight Support) **Fax:** 01302 624846 (Signature Flight Support) **Tel:** 01302 623070 (Cargo) **Fax:** 01302 623073 (Cargo)		**Fax:** 01302 624862 (ATC)
Restaurants	Available in terminal		
Taxi/Car Hire	Available in terminal		

214

DORNOCH

3ft 0mb	1nm S of Dornoch N5752.14 W00401.32	PPR	Alternative AD Diversion AD	Inverness Wick

Non radio	LARS Lossiemouth 118.900	DAAIS Tain Range 122.750	Safetycom 135.475

775m x 23m

10 ... 28

RWY	SURFACE	TORA	LDA	LIGHTING
10/28	Grass	775x23	U/L	Nil

Remarks
PPR prospective visitors must telephone Council Offices, Dornoch during office Hrs. An entry/exit lane is established from the Danger Area boundary S to the AD via Embo from the surface to 1000ft amsl. Clearance to enter the Danger Area is required prior to Arr & Dept. Telephone available at AD.

Warnings
AD situated near W edge of Danger Area D703. DAAIS Tain Range. Landing strip is marked by 3ft high posts 90m either side of Rwy centreline and across ends.

Operating Hrs	SR-SS	**Operator**	The Highland Council Area Manager TEC Services, Victoria Road Brora, Sutherland, KW9 6QN **Tel:** 01862 812000 **Tel:** 01408 623400 **Tel:** 01862 810491 (Council Offices) **Fax:** 01408 621118
Circuits	Nil		
Landing Fee	On application		
Maintenance	Nil		
Fuel	Nil		
Disabled Facilities	Nil		

Restaurants
Royal Golf Hotel **Tel:** 01862 810283
Matlin House **Tel:** 01862 810335

Taxis/Car Hire
Hugh MacKay **Tel:** 01862 810612

Weather Info AirSc GWC

215

525ft 17mb	5nm S of Swindon N5129.75 W00144.62	PPR	Alternative AD	Oxford Kemble

Non-Radio	Zone Lyneham 123.400	Safetycom 135.475

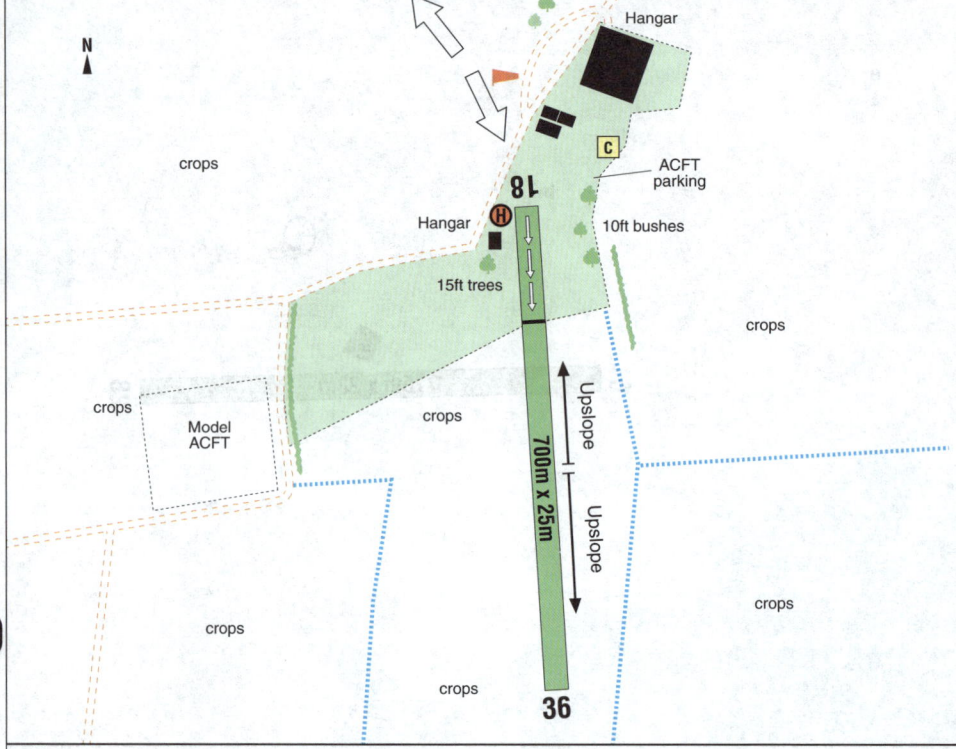

RWY	SURFACE	TORA	LDA	LIGHTING
18/36	Grass	700x30	U/L	Nil

Starter extension Rwy18 100m
Rwy18 has dip in centre

Remarks
PPR by telephone. Visiting ACFT welcome at pilots own risk. AD situated within Lyneham CTR.

Warnings
Crops are grown up to Rwy edges. Hangar close to Rwy18 Thr. Model helicopter flying takes place in area to W of Rwy18/36.
Noise: Make a curved APP Rwy18, climb out Rwy36 to avoid over flying of Farm buildings. Also note the position for power checks to be carried out.

Operating Hrs	SR-SS	**Operator**	Draycott Flight Centre Chiseldon Swindon Wilts, SN4 0HX **Tel:** 01793 741527
Circuits	RH 18, LH 36, 600ft Lyneham QFE No Circuit training		
Landing Fee	Nil		
Maintenance	Nil		
Fuel	100LL JET A1 Fuel accounts available		
Hangarage	Available		
Disabled Facilities	Nil		
Restaurants	Ops Room 'Summer House'		
Taxis/Car Hire	Nil		
Weather Info	Air SW MOEx Lyneham ATIS **Tel:** 01249 890381 Ex 7308		

150ft 5mb	7nm SE of Oxford N5139.85 W00107.56	PPR	Alternative AD	Oxford Chalgrove

Non Radio	Zone Benson 120.900	Safetycom 135.475

390m x 14m

RWY	SURFACE	TORA	LDA	LIGHTING
06/24	Grass	390x14	U/L	Nil

Remarks

PPR by telephone. Microlight AD but STOL ACFT and experienced pilots welcome at pilots own risk. AD located in Benson MATZ. The circuit passes over Drayton St Leonard at 1200ft QNH.

Warnings

Electric fences surround AD sides and Thr. When cattle are not grazing in the adjacent field Thr fences can be removed to provide extensions on Rwy24 & 06 for take-off only. AD is prone to flooding after heavy precipitation. Caution, parachuting takes place at Chalgrove, 2nm ENE.

Local procedures/Noise: Inbound ACFT should contact Benson APP before entering the MATZ or telephone Benson ATC. Dept telephone Benson before take-off.

Noise: To avoid local sensitive areas avoid conflict with Benson circuit Arr are to follow these procedures. Do not carry out overhead joins or circuits. If safety allows carry out a direct APP from a long final. APP Rwy24 offset to N to avoid Newington, The farm to the W, & the farm on the hill. APP Rwy06 should be slightly right of centreline to avoid Drayton St Leonard. Dept Rwy06 ASAP after take-off turn left onto N. Rwy24 ASAP after take-off turn left onto 220° to avoid Drayton St Leonard.

Operating Hrs	SR-SS
Circuits	See Local procedures/Noise
Landing Fee	Nil
Maintenance	Nil Limited outside parking available by arr
Fuel	Nil
Disabled Facilities	Nil
Restaurants	Nil
Taxis/Car Hire	Nil
Weather Info	AirSE MOEx

Operator

Mr George Farrant
Manor Farm
Drayton St Leonards, Wallingford
Oxon, OX10 7BE
Tel: 01865 890223
Fax: 01865 400064
Tel: 01491 837766 Ex 7555/7487
(Benson ATC)

217

17ft 0mb	0.5nm S of Dundee N5627.15 W00301.55	PPR	Alternative AD	Edinburgh Perth

Dundee	LARS Leuchars 126.500	APP 122.900	TWR 122.900

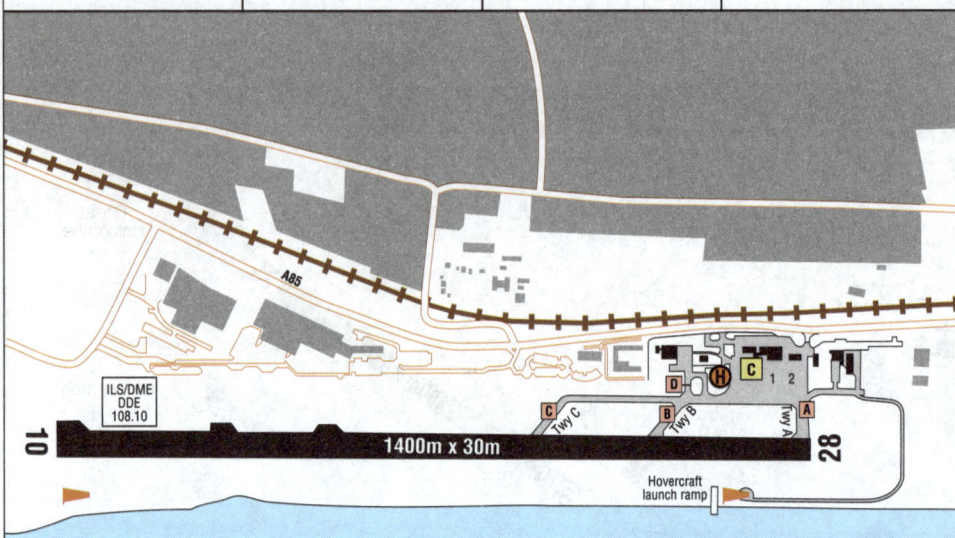

RWY	SURFACE	TORA	LDA	LIGHTING
10	Asphalt	1319	1400	Ap Thr Rwy PAPI 3.0° LHS
28	Asphalt	1319	1400	Thr Rwy PAPI 3.75° LHS

Remarks

PPR to non-radio ACFT and all training flights. Because view from Control TWR is restricted local movements to the N of the AD are not permitted. Link C only available to ACFT 5700kgs or less. Parachuting takes place at Errol.
Aids to Navigation: NDB DND 394.00

Warnings

AD is in the vicinity of Leuchars MATZ. Birds are a constant hazard at this.
Noise: ACFT Dept to N on either Rwy are to climb straight ahead to 2000ft before setting course or as directed by ATC. Pilots should avoid flying over Nine-Wells Hospital which is 1.2nm bearing 306° from the AD.

Operating Hrs	Mon-Fri 0545-2100 Sat 0645-2100 Sun 0800-2100 (Summer) +1Hr (Winter) & by arr	**Taxis**	Tel: 01382 203020
		Car Hire	
Circuits	10 RH, 28 LH, 1000ft QFE	National	**Tel:** 01382 224037
Landing Fee	Single £9, Twin £12.34 per tonne	Arnold Clark	Tel: 01382 225382
		Mitchells	**Tel:** 01382 223484
Maintenance	Tayside Aviation **Tel:** 01382 644577 **Fax:** 01382 644531	**Weather Info**	M* T9 GWC
		Visual Reference Points (VRP)	
Fuel	AVGAS JET A1 100LL	Broughty Castle	N5627.75 W00252.18
Disabled Facilities		**Operator**	Dundee City Council Dundee Airport Riverside Drive Dundee, DD2 1UH **Tel:** 01382 643242 (AD) **Tel:** 01382 662204 (ATC) **Fax:** 01382 641263 (AD) **Fax:** 01382 662206 (ATC)

Restaurant	Coffee & snack bar in Terminal The Hungry Horse restaurant/bar 200m W of terminal

839ft 28mb	14nm NE of Exeter N5051 60 W00314.08	PPR	Alternative AD	Exeter Eaglescott

	Dunkeswell	A/G 123.475

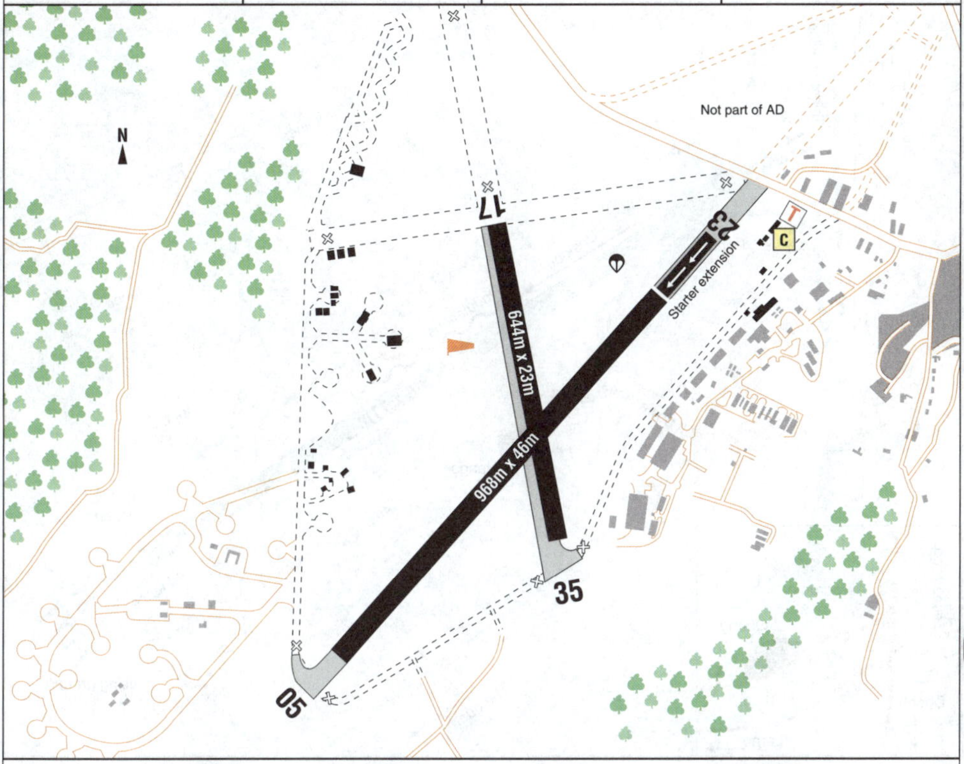

Not part of AD

Starter extension

968m x 46m

644m x 23m

RWY	SURFACE	TORA	LDA	LIGHTING
05/23	Asphalt	968	968	Rwy
17/35	Asphalt	644	644	Nil

Starter extension Rwy23 150m available on request

Remarks

Warnings

Gliders WSW of AD. Free-fall parachuting from up to FL150 on AD. Sheep grazing adjacent to Rwy. Pilots should positively identify Rwy23 displaced Thr before committing ACFT to finals. Only use established Twys or Rwys for taxi, peri-track is unsuitable. Large paved area to NE not part of AD.

Noise: Avoid over flying Dunkeswell below 500ft QFE.

Operating Hrs	0830-1830 (L) & by arr	**Weather Info**	T9 MOEx
Circuits	05, 35 RH, 17, 23 LH	**Operator**	Air Westward Ltd Dunkeswell Honiton Devon EX14 4LG **Tel:** 01404 891643 (AD info) **Fax:** 01404 891465 www.dsft.co.uk
Landing Fee	Single £9, Twin £4.50 per half metric tonne		
Maintenance	Flymoore Aircraft Engineering **Tel:** 01404 891504 Also limited hangerage available		
Fuel	AVGAS JET A1 100LL		

Disabled Facilities

Restaurants   Fully licenced bar & Restaurant open 24/7

Taxis/Car Hire

Honiton Garage   **Tel:** 01404 42036

219

490ft 16mb	2nm ESE of Ballymena N5450.87 W00612.38	PPR	Alternative AD	Belfast Aldergrove Newtownards

Dunnyvadden	ATIS Aldergrove 128.200	APP Aldergrove 128.500	A/G 122.300

Broughshane

Telephone lines

N

13

Pond

Pond

Upslope

Undulations

Power lines

4ft fence

4ft fence

540m x 11m

30ft power lines

Hangar

4ft fence

Pond

4ft fence

31

House

Rising ground

The quarry

Ballymena /

Aerodrome

Quarry

Doagh

A36

Larne

RWY	SURFACE	TORA	LDA	LIGHTING
13/31	Grass	540x11	U/L	Nil

Rwy13 upslope

Remarks
PPR strictly by telephone. Visitors welcome at own risk. Telephone briefing for visitors is mandatory. Pilots/ACFT must be experienced/suitable for operating from a short strip. Microlight activity at AD. Quarry 1 nm SE of AD on final for Rwy31 is a good locator Also wind farm 4.5nm SE on Elliot's Hill (1158ft amsl). AD is not notified as a designated point of entry/exit for Northern Ireland under the Prevention of Terrorism Act but this can be arranged by The Police Service of Northern Ireland.

Warnings
Parts of AD are prone to water logging after heavy rain – enquire when telephoning for PPR. Crosswind and terrain/tree induced turbulence/rotor are often a problem. Beware of trees on both APP Rwy31 has a 4ft fence at Thr. Rwy13 has telephone wires across APP. Farm road crosses strip at midpoint – beware loose stones. Keep a good lookout for slow moving farm vehicles especially where they might be partially obscured by the trees.

Operating Hrs	SR-SS		Weather Info	AIR BEL
Circuits	Standard overhead join LH 1000ft QFE		Operator	Christine Goodwin Dunnyvadden Aerodrome Craigadoo Rd, Ballymena Co Antrim, BT42 4RS **Tel:** 028 2565 0002 **Tel:** 028 9065 0222 (PSNI) radiochristine@hotmail.com
Landing Fee	Nil			
Maintenance	Nil possible hangarage by prior arr			
Fuel	MOGAS limited supplies by prior arr			

Disabled Facilities

Restaurants Nil

Taxis Operator can provide info

Car Hire Nil

220

D

120ft	4.7nm SE of Darlington		
4mb	N5430.55 W00125.77	**Alternative AD**	**Newcastle** Fishburn

Durham	**ATIS** **136.200**	**LARS** **118.850**	**APP** **118.850**
RAD **118.850**	**TWR** **119.800**	**FIRE** **121.600**	

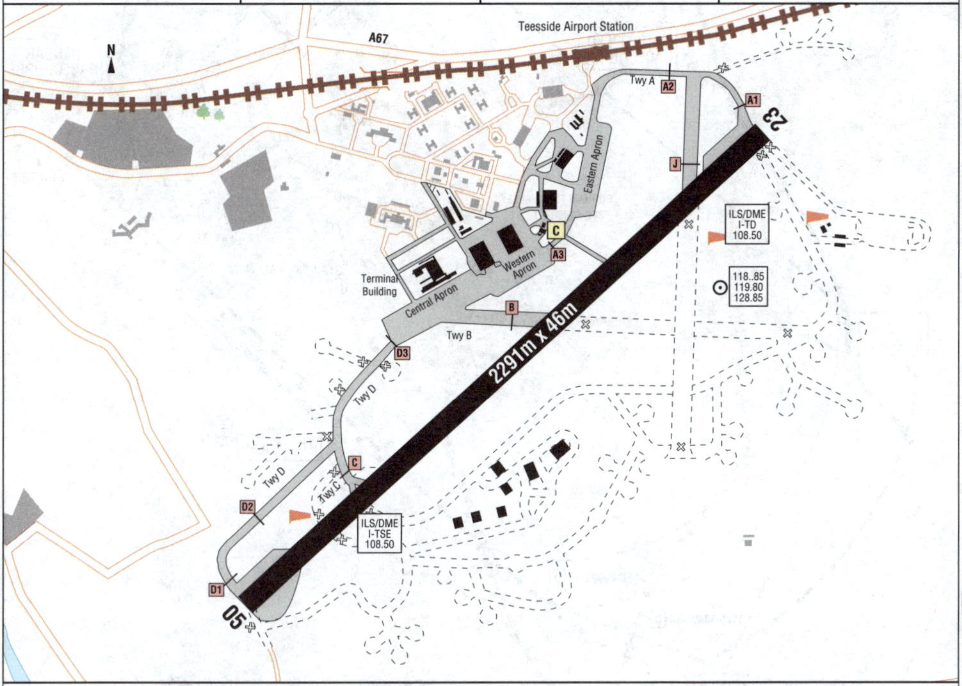

Teesside Airport Station

A67

Twy A — A2

A1

23

ILS/DME I-TD 108.50

118..85 119.80 128.85

Eastern Apron

J

C

Western Apron

A3

Terminal Building

Central Apron

B

Twy B

D3

Twy D

2291m x 46m

Twy D

C

Twy D

D2

Twy D

ILS/DME I-TSE 108.50

D1

05

D

RWY	SURFACE	TORA	LDA	LIGHTING
05	Asphalt	2291	2291	Ap Thr Rwy PAPI 3° LHS
23	Asphalt	2291	2291	Ap Thr Rwy PAPI 3° RHS

Remarks
Not available to non-radio ACFT. HI-Vis. Aerobatics and other unusual flight manoeuvres prohibited within ATZ except with prior written permission from AD MD. Training flights require arr with DO. Heli training is PPR from ATC. Unless otherwise instructed by ATC, ACFT using ILS in IMC or VMC shall not descend below 1800ft aal before intercepting the glide path, nor thereafter fly below it. ACFT APP without assistance from RAD or ILS must not fly lower than the ILS glide path or RAD APP procedure. Booking-out details will not be accepted on RT. ACFT exceeding 2 Tonnes subject to mandatory handling.
Aids to Navigation: NDB TD 347.50

Warning
Both ends of Rwy05/23 width is twice that of the associated edge lights take care to line up correctly, especially at night or in poor visibility. Deer hazard, report sightings to ATC.
Noise: Avoid over flying local villages, Middleton St George, Yarm, Middleton Oncrow and Eaglescliffe.

Operating Hrs	0500-2100 (Summer) +1Hr (Winter) & by arr	**Restaurant** St George Hotel	Restaurant & buffet at Terminal **Tel:** 01325 332631 (on AD)
Circuits	Variable Light ACFT 1000ft QFE Large ACFT minimum 1500ft QFE	**Taxis** **Buses**	Available at terminal available at Terminal to: Darlington, Stockton, Middlesborough & Redcar
Landing Fee	£15.39 per metric tonne. Singles up to 2MT 25% discount if paid at the time	**Car Hire**	
Maintenance	Nil	Avis Hertz	**Tel:** 01325 332091 **Tel:** 01325 332600
Fuel	AVGAS JET A1 100LL	Europcar	**Tel:** 01325 333329
Disabled Facilities		**Weather Info**	M T9 Fax 436 VN MWC

Handling	**Tel:** 01325 333125 (Servisair) **Tel:** 01325 332342 (Aviance) **Tel:** 01325 337733 (Midwest Exec (GA))	**Operator**	Durham Tees Valley Int Airport Ltd Darlington, Co Durham, DL2 1LU **Tel:** 01325 332811 **Fax:** 01325 332810

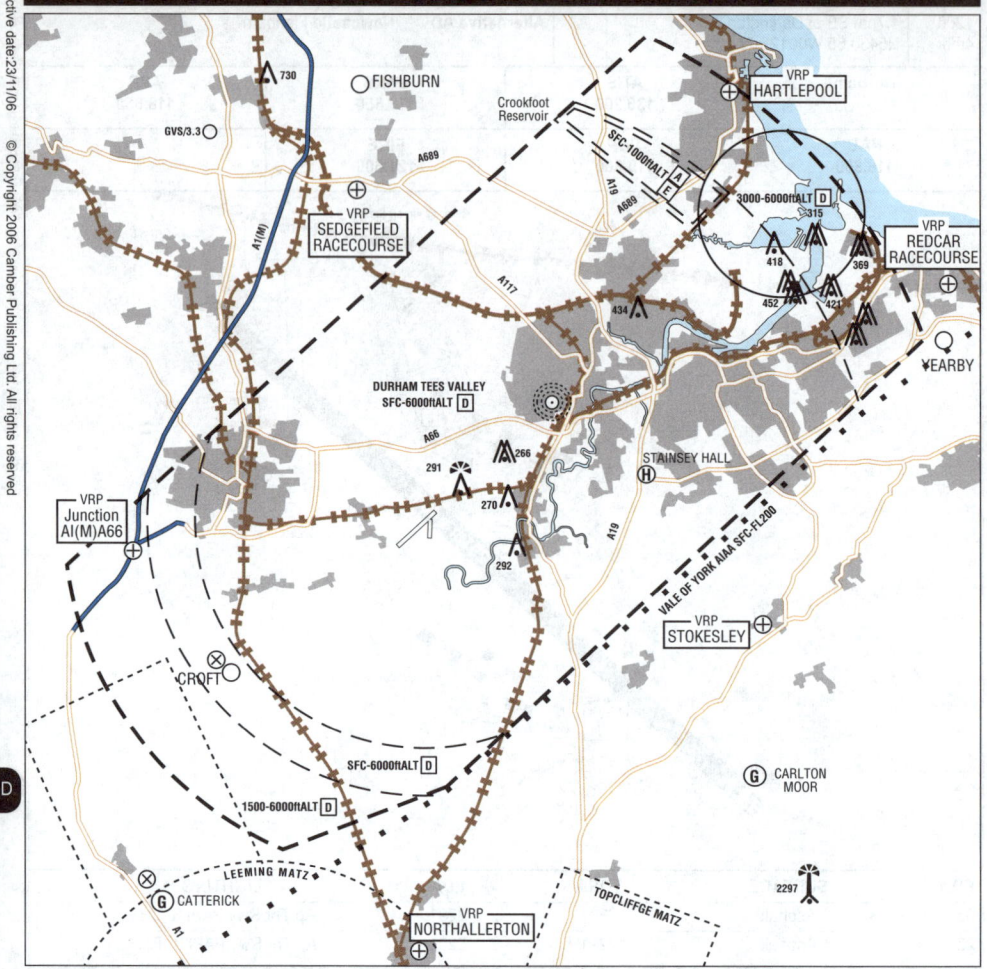

Visual Reference Points (VRP)

VRP	VOR/NDB	VOR/DME
Hartlepool N5441.00 W00112.83	NEW 144°/TD 033°	NEW 144°/27nm
Motorway Jct A1(M) & A66(M) N5430.00 W00137.60	NEW 179°/TD 255°	NEW 179°/32nm
Northallerton N5420.33 W00125.92		NEW 170°/43nm
Redcar Racecourse N5436.43 W00103.85	NEW 142°/TD 077°	NEW 142°/34nm
Sedgefield Racecourse N5438.75 W00128.10		NEW 164°/25nm
Stokesley N5428.18 W00111.68		NEW 156°/38nm

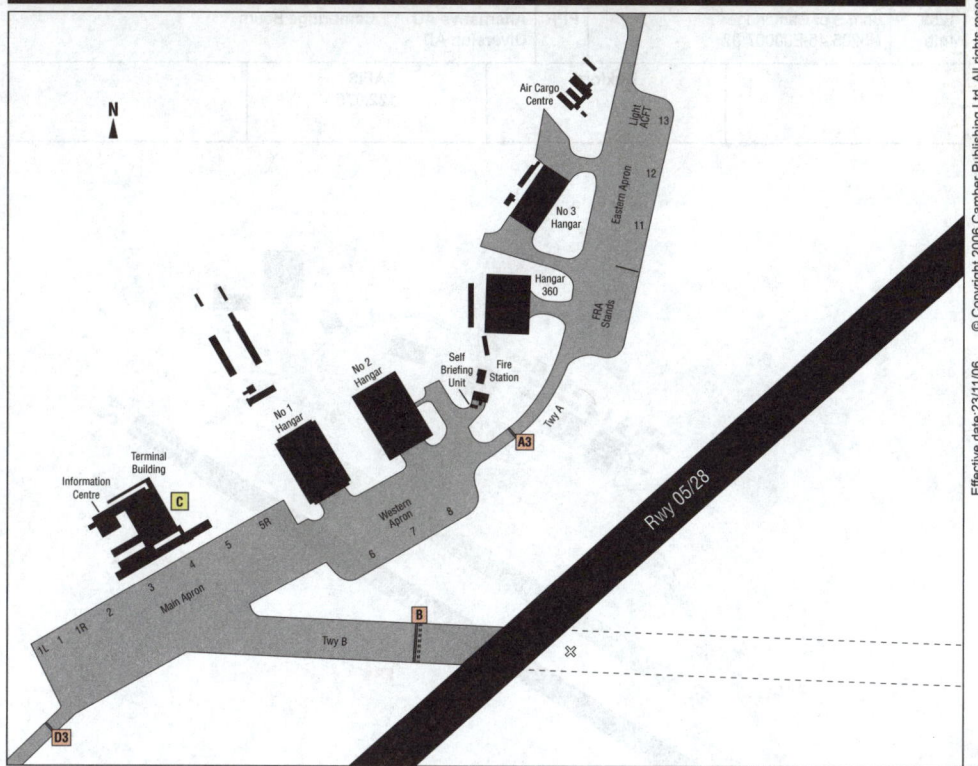

N

Air Cargo Centre

Light ACFT

13

Eastern Apron

12

No 3 Hangar

11

Hangar 360

FRA Stands

No 2 Hangar

Self Briefing Unit

Fire Station

Twy A

No 1 Hangar

A3

Terminal Building

Information Centre

C

Western Apron

5R

9

5

4

7

8

3

6

Main Apron

2

1L

1

1R

Rwy 05/28

B

Twy B

D3

D

125ft 4mb	8nm S of Cambridge N5205.45 E00007.92		PPR	Alternative AD Diversion AD	Cambridge Bourn
		Duxford		AFIS 122.075	

D

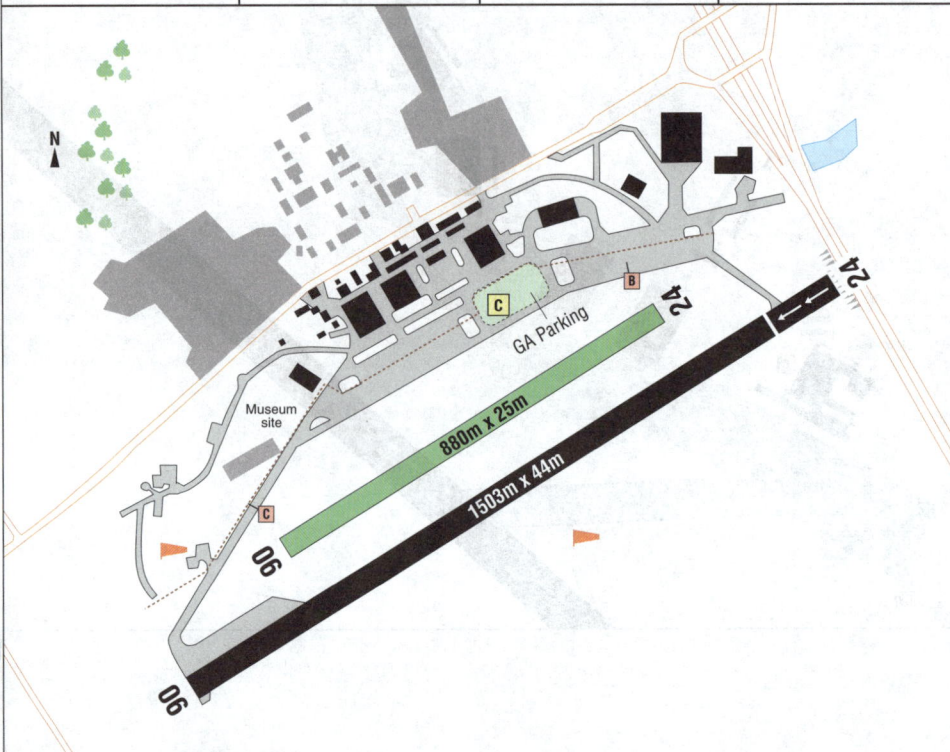

RWY	SURFACE	TORA	LDA	LIGHTING
06	Asphalt	1222	1222	Nil
24	Asphalt	1319	1219	Nil
06/24	Grass	880	880	Nil

Displaced Thr Rwy24 150m

Remarks
Strictly PPR by telephone. It is essential to obtain a briefing whether in or out bound. Powered ACFT circuits (from grass or paved Rwys) are normally to the S. The first 50m of Rwy24 (asphalt) is sterile and marked with yellow chevrons. Certain customs facilities available.

Warnings
AD may be closed due to adverse weather conditions. Wethersfield glider site to be avoided (Op Height 2000ft agl). Linton Zoo has birds of prey flying up to 2500ft.
Noise: Avoid over-flying the nearby villages of Duxford, Thriplow, Whittlesford and Fowlmere and adjacent bird sanctuary. Do not over fly Gas Venting Station to SE below 3200ft

Operating Hrs	0900-1700 or SS whichever earlier (Summer) +1Hr (Winter)	**Taxis** Academy Sawston	**Tel:** 01223 833030
Circuits	Variable 1000ft QFE No overhead/dead side joins	Mastercab **Car Hire**	**Tel:** 01223 566654
Landing Fee	On application	Willhire Veh Rental	**Tel:** 01223 414600
Maintenance	Aircraft Restoration Co **Tel:** 01223 835313	**Weather Info**	AirCen MOEx
Fuel	JET A1 AVGAS 100LL 1000-1600 (L) & by arr	**Operator**	Imperial War Museum Cambridgeshire County Council Duxford Airfield, Cambs, CB2 4QR **Tel:** 01223 833376 (ATC) **Tel:** 01223 835000 Ex 236 (Switchboard) **Fax:** 01223 830410 (ATC) airtraffic@iwm.org.uk www.iwm.org.uk
Disabled Facilities	Available		
Restaurant	Restaurant at AD		

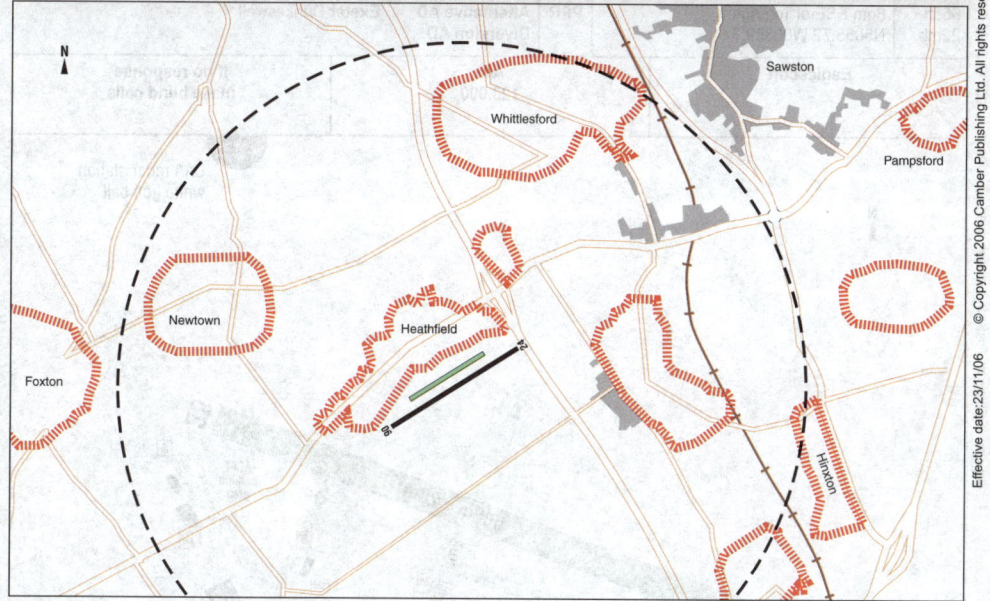

Arrival routes

Rwy06 Dept – continue straight ahead 2nm (BP roundabout) before turning on course

Rwy24 Dept – LH circuit, Continue on Rwy, Do not turn right until passing Royston or 2000ft QNH

Rwy24 Arr – LH circuit, join downwind, position for 2nm final (BP roundabout)

Rwy06 Arr – RH circuit, join downwind

Inbound routes to avoid Stansted Controlled Airspace

Inbound from S to pass W of Stansted – Route LAM VOR – BPK VOR – BKY VOR – Duxford AD

Inbound from S to pass E of Stanstead – Route Chelmsford VRP – Braintree VRP – Haverhill VRP – Duxford AD

Inbound from E – Route CLN VOR – Haverhill VRP – Duxford AD

Inbound from N to Rwy06 – Route via Sawston to join downwind

Inbound from N to Rwy24 – Route via Royston to join downwind

D

655ft 22mb	6nm ESE of Torrington N5055.72 W00359.37	PPR	Alternative AD Diversion AD	Exeter Dunkeswell
Eaglescott		**A/G 123.000**		**If no response make blind calls**

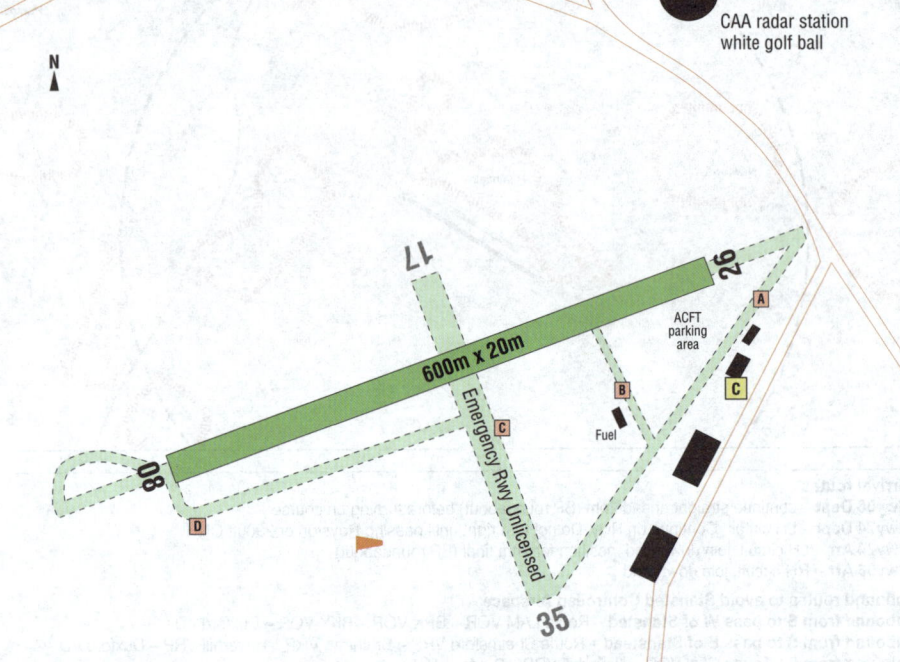

CAA radar station
white golf ball

N

600m x 20m

17

26

80

35

Emergency Rwy Unlicensed

ACFT parking area

A

B

C

C

D

Fuel

E

RWY	SURFACE	TORA	LDA	LIGHTING
08/26	Grass	600	600	Nil

Total usable run 900m
Starter extension Rwy08 120m
Starter extension Rwy26 180m
Emergency crosswind strip doubling as a Twy
Rwy35/17 (320m) is also available for light acft but is U/L

Remarks
PPR by telephone. AD licensed Sat-Sun & by arr. Not available at night for flights required to use a licensed AD or for public transport passenger flights required to use a licensed AD. Non-radio ACFT must contact AD prior to visit. If no response from A/G proceed with standard overhead join at 2000ft.

Warnings
Gliding by aerotow takes place at the AD using the area to the right of the Rwy in use. Microlight and model ACFT (SW corner) flying takes place at AD.

Operating Hrs	0700-2000 (Summer) 0800-SS (Winter)	Restaurants	Golf Club restaurant village cafe/restaurant in Atherington
Circuit	All arriving ACFT LH all Rwys 800ft Based gliders & Microlights RH	**Taxis** Barum Cabs	**Tel: 01271 24444**
		Car Hire	**Tel: 01271 42746**
Landing Fee	Single £5, Heli £7.50 Twins £10		
Maintenance	Nil	**Weather Info**	AirSW MOEx
Fuel	AVGAS JET A1 MOGAS 100LL	**Operator**	Devon Airsports Ltd
Hangarage	Available		Eaglescott Airfield Burrington, Umberleigh Devon, EX379LH **Tel:** 01769 520404 www.eaglescott-airfield.com

Disabled Facilities

  ✔

226

227ft 8mb	3nm SE of Halstead N5154.87 E00040.95	**PPR**	**Alternative AD**	**Cambridge** Andrewsfield

Earls Colne	**LARS** Southend 130.775	**A/G** 122.425

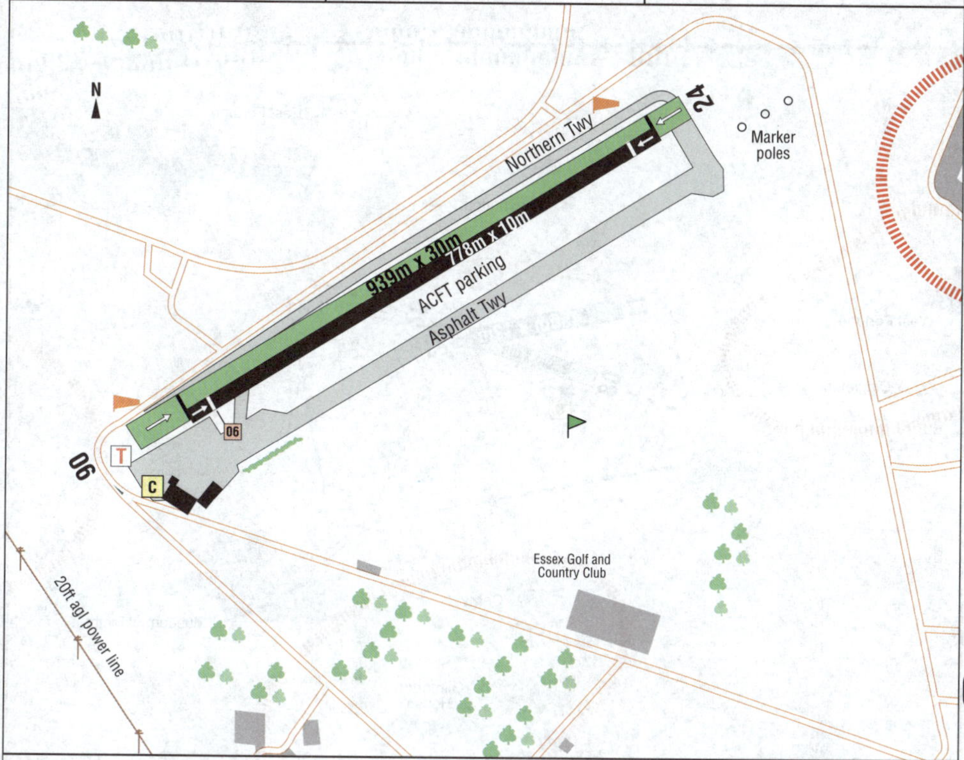

(Aerodrome chart: runway 06/24 aligned NE–SW, shown as "939m x 30m" grass and "778m x 10m" asphalt, with Northern Twy, ACFT parking, Asphalt Twy, Marker poles, Essex Golf and Country Club, 20ft agl power line, threshold markers 06 and 24)

RWY	SURFACE	TORA	LDA	LIGHTING
06	Grass/Asph	877	778	Thr Rwy By Arr
24	Grass/Asph	840	778	Thr Rwy By Arr

Displaced Thr Rwy06 99m
Displaced Thr Rwy24 62m

Remarks
PPR essential for helicopters. Not available at night for flights required to use a licensed AD. Pilots are advised that both Rwy are not available simultaneously, and should ensure they are aligned with the correct Rwy.

Warnings
Power lines cross Rwy06 APP. Pilots should not land before displaced Thr. Customs facilities available 4hr PNR
Noise: Rwy24 Dept climb ahead to 900ft QNH. Rwy06 Dept keep left of marker poles turning to the right after wooded area and mobile phone mast. Pilots are to obtain noise abatement brief prior to Dept. Avoid over flying Earls Colne village.

Operating Hrs	0900-1800 (Summer) 0900-SS (Winter)	**Taxis/Car Hire**	By arr
Circuits	24 LH, 06 RH 1000ft QFE	**Weather Info**	AirCen MOEx
Landing Fee	Single £12, Twin £17, Heli £25	**Operator**	Bulldog Aviation Ltd
Maintenance	Available		Earls Colne Airfield
Fuel	AVGAS 100LL		Colchester, Essex, CO6 2NS

Tel/Fax: 01787 223943 (AD Ops)
Tel: 01787 223676 (Flying School)
www.anglianflightcentres.co.uk

Disabled Facilities

Restaurant
Restaurant accomodation & leisure complex 2mins walk from AD swimming pool gymnasium 18 hole golf course & driving range (booking advised)   **Tel:** 01787 224466
Drapers Hotel   **Tel:** 01787 223666

115ft 4mb	2.5nm S of North Berwick N5600.07 W00243.99	PPR	Alternative AD	Edinburgh Fife
	East Fortune Micro		A/G 118.750	

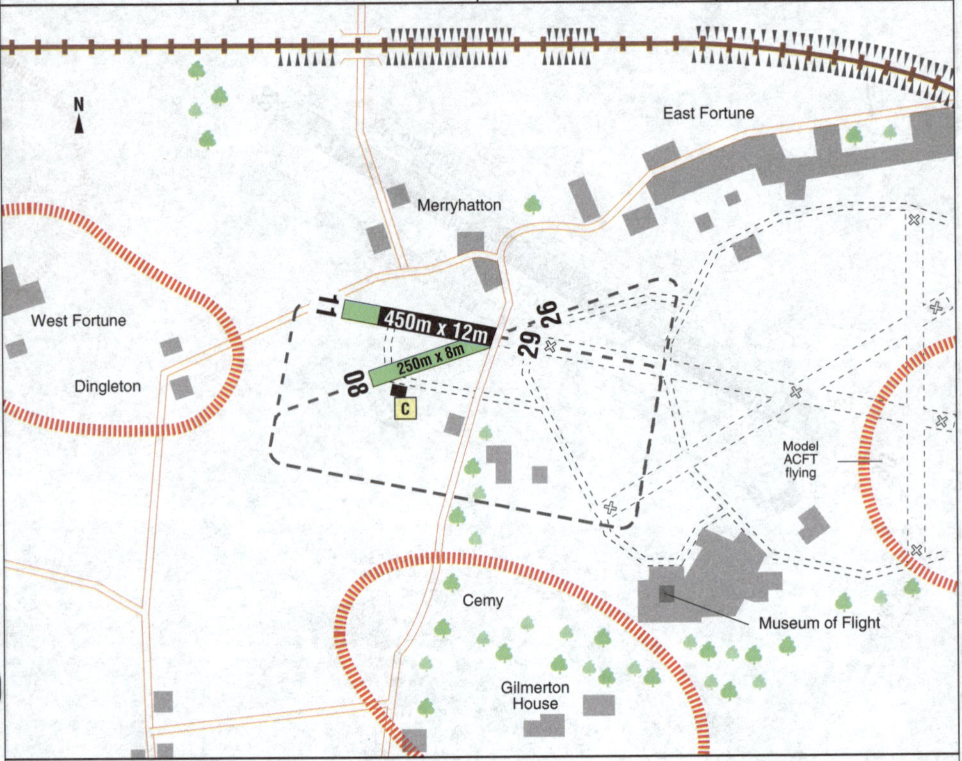

East Fortune

Merryhatton

West Fortune

Dingleton

11 **450m x 12m**

08 **250m x 8m**

29 **26**

C

Model ACFT flying

Cemy

Museum of Flight

Gilmerton House

RWY	SURFACE	TORA	LDA	LIGHTING
11/29	Grass/Conc	450x12	U/L	Nil
08/26	Grass/Conc	250x8	U/L	Nil

Remarks
PPR by telephone. Primarily a microlight AD, light ACFT welcome. During Sunday Market PPR may be refused to visitors. The useable portion of WWII AD is clearly marked out in NW corner. Do not use other parts of AD which are the property of other landowners. AD is home of Museum of Flight which is a short walk down the perimeter track.

Warnings
Public road crosses WWII Rwy close to Rwy29 Thr. There is considerable military low flying in the vicinity. Model ACFT flying takes place on E portion of AD.
Noise: Please follow circuit pattern marked on AD chart. Do not over fly Sunday market on E portion of AD

Operating Hrs	SR-SS	Taxis/Car Hire	
Circuits	Join overhead 1500ft QFE S 500ft QFE. Please follow tight circuit procedure on diagram	Jim's Taxi Johnny's Cab	**Tel:** 01620 894900 **Tel:** 01620 826222
		Weather Info	AirSC GWC
Landing Fee	Nil donations gratefully received	Operator	Mr G Douglas East of Scotland Microlights East Fortune **Tel:** 01620 880332 (AD) **Tel:** 01875 820102 (Mr Douglas) gordon@eosm.co.uk www.eosm.co.uk
Maintenance	Nil		
Fuel	MOGAS available in emergency		

Disabled Facilities

Restaurants
Tea, coffee & biscuits available most days
Restaurant in museum complex and local garden centre

EASTBACH

Effective date:23/11/06

600ft 20mb	6nm S of Ross on Wye N5150.13 W00235.98		PPR	Alternative AD	Gloucestershire Shobdon
Non-Radio		**APP** Gloucester 128.550		**LARS** Brize 124.275	**Safetycom** 135.475

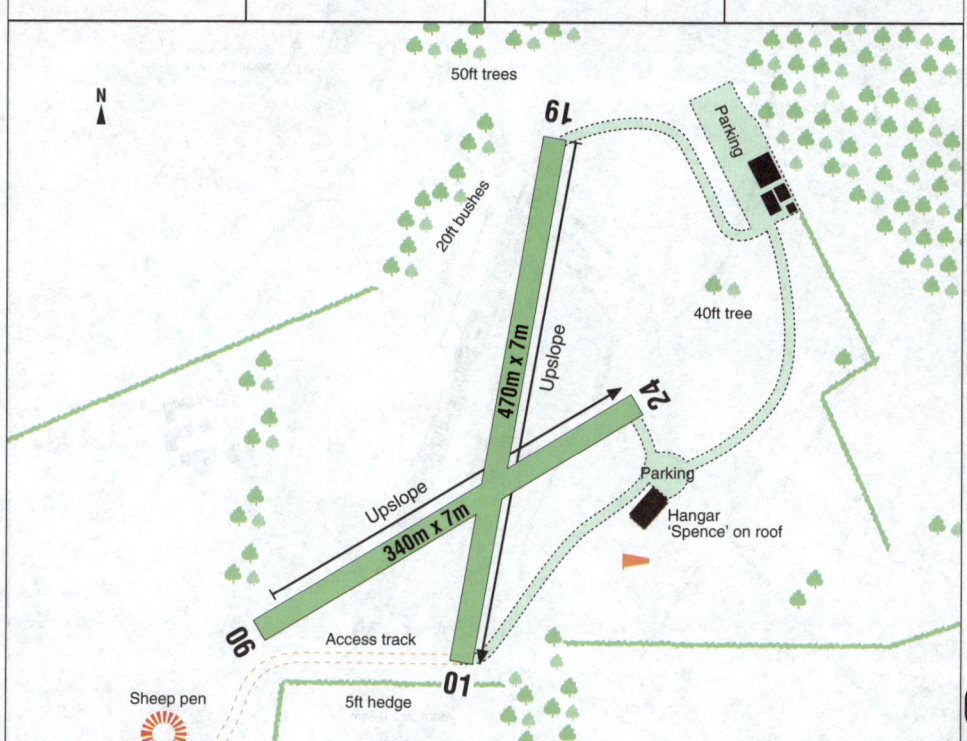

RWY	SURFACE	TORA	LDA	LIGHTING
01/19	Grass	470x7	U/L	Nil
06/24	Grass	340x7	U/L	Nil

Remarks
PPR by telephone. Visiting STOL ACFT welcome at pilot's own risk. AD situated on a hilltop. There is an upslope on Rwy 06 & 19. Visiting ACFT should land only on Rwy06 or 19, and Dept only on Rwy01 or 24. Very well maintained site with deep wooded escarpments to the NE & E.

Warnings
Because of the close proximity of woodland and escarpments pilots should be aware of rollover and turbulence even in light wind conditions. There is a copse of 50ft trees just right of short final Rwy19. Please use mown Twy. Windsock displayed on bank behind hangar in SE corner of AD. Access track crosses Rwy01 Thr.
Noise: Avoid over flying large house to the S of AD.

Operating Hrs	SR-SS	**Operator**	Spence Airfield Associates Ltd
Circuits	LH 1000ft QFE		Holtar Bungalow
Landing Fee	Nil		4 Albert Road
Maintenance	Nil		Coleford
Fuel	MOGAS by arr		Gloucester
			GL16 8DZ
Disabled Facilities	Nil		**Tel:** 01594 562653 (Graham Vaughan)
Restaurants	Nil		**Tel:** 07768 746055 (Mark Taylor)
Taxis/Car Hire	Nil		steveatholtar@tiscali.co.uk
Weather Info	AirCen MOEx		www.spenceairfield.co.uk

300ft 10mb	7nm ESE of Northampton N5212.80 W00042.10	PPR	Alternative AD	Cranfield Northampton

Non-Radio	ATIS Cranfield 121.875 (Dept)	Safetycom 135.475

Easton Maudit village DO NOT overfly

N

4ft hedge

16

30ft tree

30ft tree

Downslope

crops

604m x 23m

crops

125ft agl National Grid power lines

4ft hedge

34

20ft tree

Avoid farm 0·5nm

E

RWY	SURFACE	TORA	LDA	LIGHTING
16/34	Grass	604x23	U/L	Nil

Rwy16 recommended in light winds due to down slope at N end

Remarks
PPR by telephone. Authorised visitors welcome at pilot's own risk. Fuel available from Northampton Sywell 7nm NNW.

Warnings
Power lines run close to W of AD but do not obstruct APP/Dept. Low hedges at both Thrs. Crops grown close to Rwy edge.
Noise: Do not over fly Easton Maudit village and Farmhouse 0.5nm S of AD

		Operator	Tim Allebone
Operating Hrs	SR-SS		The Limes
Circuit	1000ft QFE		Easton Maudit
Landing Fee	Nil		Northants NN29 7NR
Maintenance	Nil		**Tel:** 01933 663225
Fuel	Nil		**Tel:** 07973 147143
Disabled Facilities			tim.allebone@virgin.net

Restaurant	Nil
Taxis/Car Hire	Nil
Weather Info	AirCen MOEx

230

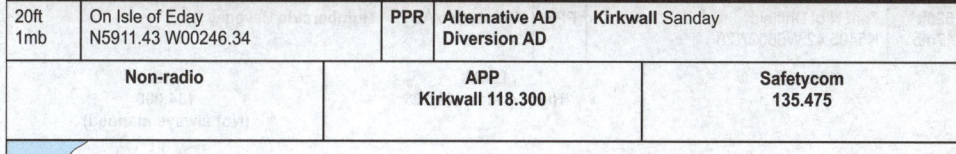

20ft 1mb	On Isle of Eday N5911.43 W00246.34	PPR	Alternative AD Diversion AD	Kirkwall Sanday

Non-radio	**APP** **Kirkwall 118.300**	**Safetycom** **135.475**

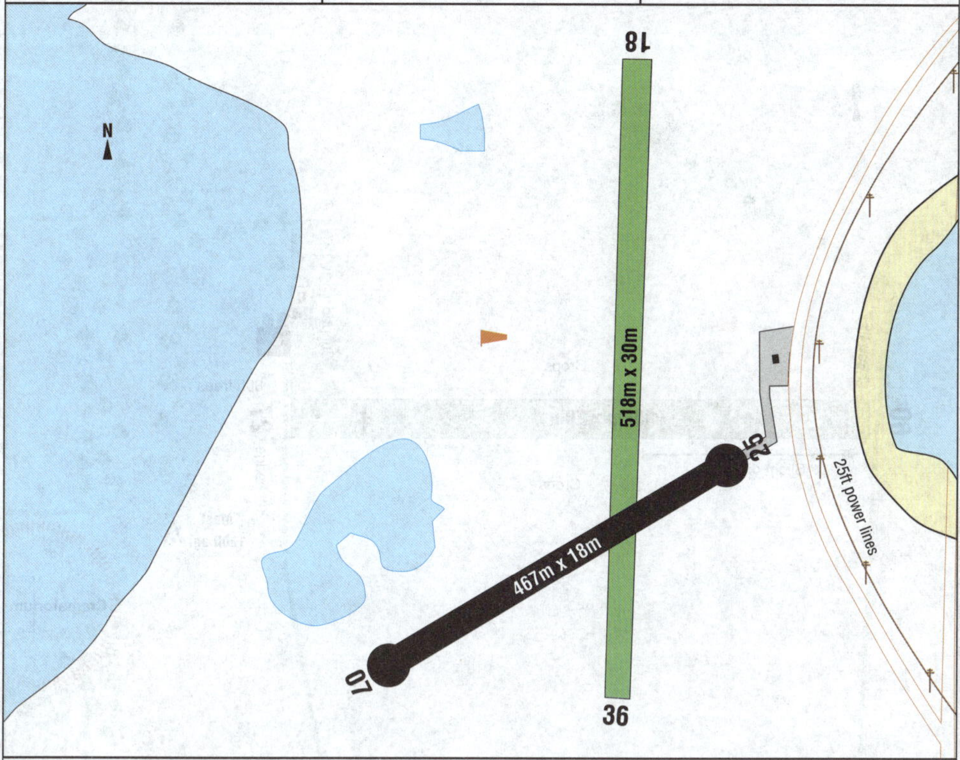

RWY	SURFACE	TORA	LDA	LIGHTING
18/36	Grass	518	518	Nil
07	Graded Hardcore	462	462	Nil
25	Graded Hardcore	467	462	Nil

Remarks
Licensed for day use only. RT contact with Kirkwall is recommended.
Visual aid to location: Flashing beacon on terminal building available on request.

Warnings
Rwy07/25 may become soft and waterlogged after periods of continuous rainfall, particularly at W end.

Operating Hrs	By arr	**Operator**	Orkney Islands Council Council Offices Kirkwall, Orkney, Scotland **Tel:** 01856 873535 **Fax:** 01856 876094
Circuits	Nil		
Landing Fee	Nil If fire cover provided then £18.91		
Maintenance	Nil		
Fuel	Nil		
Disabled Facilities	Nil		
Restaurants Blett Boathouse	**Tel:** 01857 622248		
Taxis Mr A Stewart	**Tel:** 01857 622206		
Car Hire	Nil		
Weather Info	AirSc GWC		

E

525ft 17mb	7nm N of Driffield N5406.42 W00027.26	PPR	Alternative AD	Humberside Beverley

Eddsfield	LARS Humberside 119.125	A/G 134.000 (Not always manned)

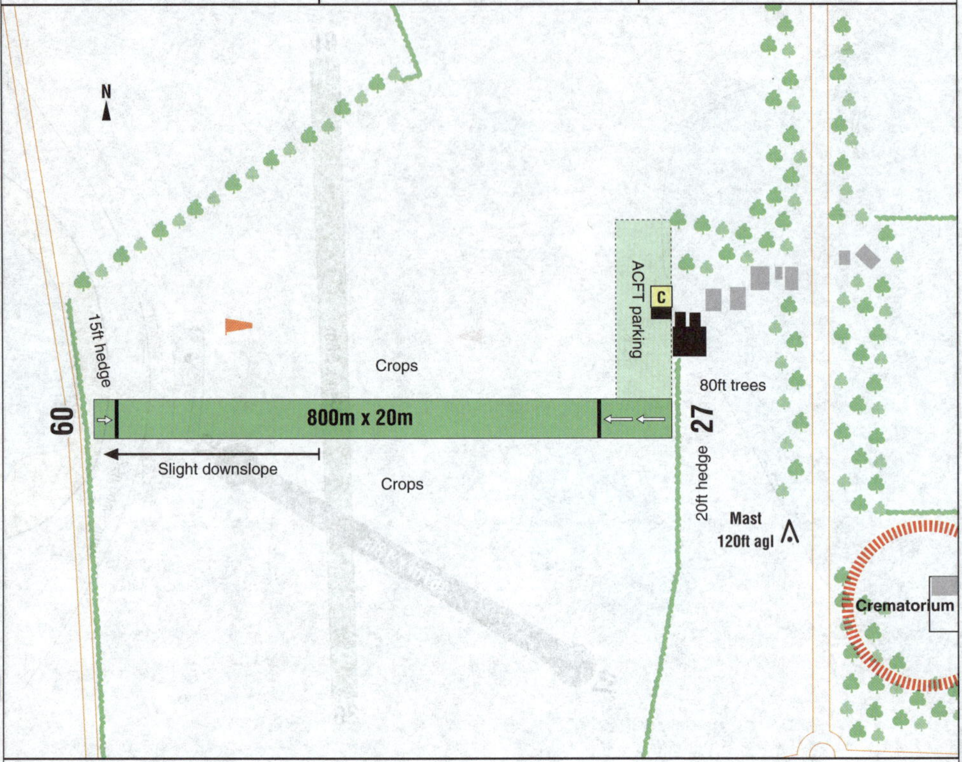

N

ACFT parking

C

15ft hedge

09

800m x 20m

Slight downslope

Crops

Crops

27

80ft trees

20ft hedge

Mast 120ft agl

Crematorium

E

RWY	SURFACE	TORA	LDA	LIGHTING
09	Grass	700x20	U/L	Nil
27	Grass	775x20	U/L	Nil

Remarks
PPR by telephone. Visiting ACFT welcome at pilot's own risk. Well equipped caravan clubhouse. Rwys well prepared with white designators.

Warnings
2 telecommunication masts close to S Rwy27 APP one on very short final is 120ft. The second approx 900m out is 150ft agl. Mature trees on short final for Rwy27 up to 80ft agl may cause rotor or roll-over, Rwy27 landing Thr is displaced to take them into account.
Noise: Do not over fly crematorium which is a new building S of Rwy27 APP on short final. Do not over fly Octon/Thwing village.

Operating Hrs	0900-SS	
Circuits	09 LH, 27 RH, 1000ft QFE	
Landing Fee	£3	
Maintenance	Nil	
Fuel	AVGAS JET A1 100LL	

Operator

Mr Ed Peacock
Octon Lodge
Langtoft, Driffield
East Yorkshire, YO25 3BJ
Tel: 01377 267368
Tel: 07792 398320
airfield@eastyorkshire.co.uk
www.eastyorkshire.co.uk/eddsfield

Disabled Facilities

Restaurants	The Old Mill 0.5nm from AD
Taxis/Car Hire	Nil
Weather Info	AirN MWC Live airfield weather on website

232

135ft 5mb	5nm W of Edinburgh N5557.00 W00322.35	PPR	Alternative AD Diversion AD	Glasgow Fife

Edinburgh	ATIS 131.350	APP 121.200	CTR 130.400 Gliders Transiting
RAD 128.975 121.200	**TWR** 118.700	**GND** 121.750	**FIRE** 121.600

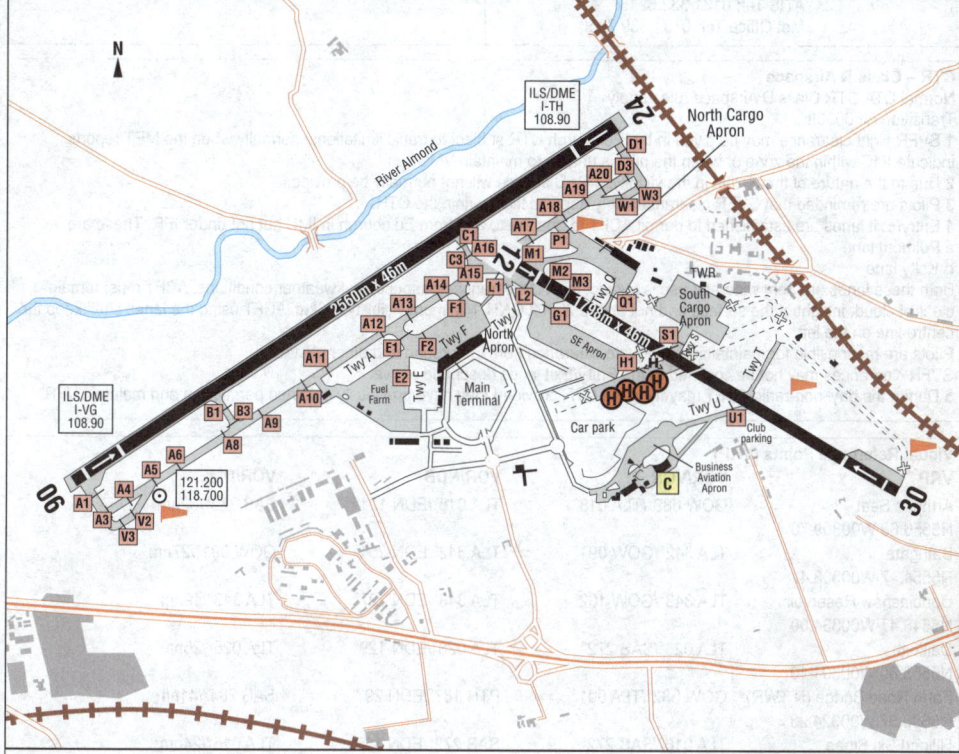

RWY	SURFACE	TORA	LDA	LIGHTING
06/24	Asphalt	2560	2347	Ap Thr Rwy PAPI 3° LHS
12	Asphalt	1798	1798	Ap Thr Rwy PAPI 3° LHS
30	Asphalt	1798	1746	Ap Thr Rwy PAPI 3.5° LHS

Rwy06/24 PPR 0800-1000 for training flights. Rwy12/30 sometimes unavailable for ACFT ops

Remarks

PPR to non-radio ACFT. All GA must make prior Arr with a handling agent for GND handling of all flights. All movements on GA apron must be marshalled. Due to Ltd parking space ALL ACFT are PPR with thier handling agent. Approved handling agents: Execair, Comet Handling or Servisair. All other GA ACFT may be required to go directly to GA terminal for off-loading/loading of passengers. Permission may be given for parking on the main apron for off-loading passengers interlining etc. But ACFT must move to GA apron ASAP. Transport to & from the main terminal is via your handing agent. All telephone calls are recorded.
Aids to Navigation: NDB EDN 341.00. NDB UW 386.00

Warnings

There is a large bird population around the AD and hence increased bird activity in the lower airspace, together with visible evidence of deterrent activity in the form of shell crackers being fired. All ACFT must be operated in a manner calculated to cause the least disturbance practicable in areas surrounding the AD. For visual APP Rwy06/24: Propeller driven ACFT whose MTWA does not exceed 5700kg will not join final below 1000ft QFE.

Operating Hrs	H24	**Disabled Facilites**	Available
Circuits	As directed by ATC	**Handling**	**Tel:** 0131 317 7447 (Signature)
Landing Fee	BAA Rates		**Tel:** 0131 339 4615 (Midwest Exec)
Maintenance	Aeroscot Engineering **Tel:** 0131 344 3349		**Tel:** 0131 399 1010 (Greer Aviation) **Fax:** 0131 317 7484 (Signature)
Fuel	AVGAS JET A1 100LL Signature or Greer Aviation		**Fax:** 0131 339 4625 (Midwest Exec) **Fax:** 0131 339 1020 (Greer Aviation)

Restaurant	Restaurants/buffet/bars available at Terminal	Operator	Edinburgh Airport Ltd

Restaurant	Restaurants/buffet/bars available at Terminal	**Operator**	Edinburgh Airport Ltd Edinburgh Airport Lothian EH12 9DN **Tel:** 0131 344 3139 (OPS) **Tel:** 0131 333 6239 (ATC) **Fax:** 0131 317 7638 (ATC) **Fax:** 0131 333 5055 (EAL)
Taxis	Available at Terminal		
Car Hire			
Avis	**Tel:** 0131 333 1866		
Europcar	**Tel:** 0131 333 2588		
Hertz	**Tel:** 0131 333 1019		
Alamo	**Tel:** 0131333 5100		
Weather Info	M T9 T18 Fax 276 A VSc GWC ATIS **Tel:** 0131 333 6216 Met Office **Tel:** 0131 339 7950		

CTR – Class D Airspace

Normal CTA/CTR Class D Airspace rules apply

Transition Alt 6000ft

1 SVFR flight clearance may be given in the Edinburgh CTR subject to traffic limitations; normally when the MET reports indicate IMC within the zone or when the pilot is unable to maintain VMC.

2 Due to the nature of the terrain in the vicinity, a RAD service will not normally be provided.

3 Pilots are reminded that SVFR clearances only apply to flight within the CTR.

4 Entry/Exit lanes are established to permit ACFT to operate to and from Edinburgh in IMC but not under IFR. These are:

a Polmont lane

b Kelty lane

Both these lanes are 3nm wide and use is subject to ATC clearance, irrespective of weather conditions. ACFT must remain clear of cloud, insight of the surface and not above 2000ft QNH. Minimum visibility is 3km. ACFT using the lanes shall keep the centre-line on the left.

Pilots are responsible for maintaining adequate clearance from the ground and other obstacles.

SVFR clearances may not be confined to the Entry/Exit lanes described above.

5 During the day, non-radio ACFT may fly in the CTR provided they have previously obtained permission and maintain VFR.

Visual Reference Points (VRP)

VRP	VOR/VOR	VOR/NDB	VOR/DME
Arthur's Seat N5556.63 W00309.70	GOW 089°/TLA 018°	TLA 018°/EDN 121°	SAB 278°/32nm
Bathgate N5554.17 W00338.42	TLA 342°/GOW 091°	TLA 342°/EDN 254°	GOW 091°/27nm
Cobbinshaw Reservoir N5548.47 W00334.00	TLA 343°/GOW 102°	TLA 343°/EDN 227°	TLA 343°/19nm
Dalkeith N5553.60 W00304.10	TLA 026°/SAB 272°	TLA 026°/EDN 129°	TLA 026°/26nm
Forth Road Bridge (N TWR) N5600.37 W00324.23	GOW 082°/TLA 001°	PTH 187°/EDN 297°	SAB 284°/41nm
Hillend Ski Slope N5553.30 W00312.50	TLA 016°/SAB 272°	SAB 272°/EDN 159°	TLA 016°/24nm
Kelty N5608.08 W00323.25	TLA 002°/SAB 293°	SAB 293°/EDN 344°	GOW 068°/39nm
Kirkcaldy Harbour N5606.83 W00309.00	TLA 015°/SAB 295°	SAB 295°/EDN 034°	GOW 076°/46nm
Kirkliston N5557.33 W00324.18	TLA 001°/GOW 086°	GOW 086°/EDN 255°	GOW 086°/36nm
Kirknewton N5553.25 W00325.08	GOW 093°/TLA 359°	GOW 093°/EDN 224°	GOW 093°/35nm
Musselburgh N5556.83 W00302.42	TLA 025°/SAB 279°	TLA 025°/EDN 107°	TLA 025°/29nm
Penicuik N5549.92 W00313.42	GOW 098°/TLA 016°	GOW 098°/EDN 171°	GOW 098°/41nm
Philipstoun (M9 J2) N5558.90 W00330.72	GOW 083°/TLA 354°	GOW 083°/UW 276°	GOW 083°/32nm
Polmont N5559.33 W00341.00	TLA 343°/SAB 280°	TLA 343°/EDN 277°	GOW 079°/27nm
West Linton N5545.17 W00321.45	TLA 004°/SAB 260°	SAB 260°/EDN 195°	TLA 004°/15nm

Effective date:23/11/06

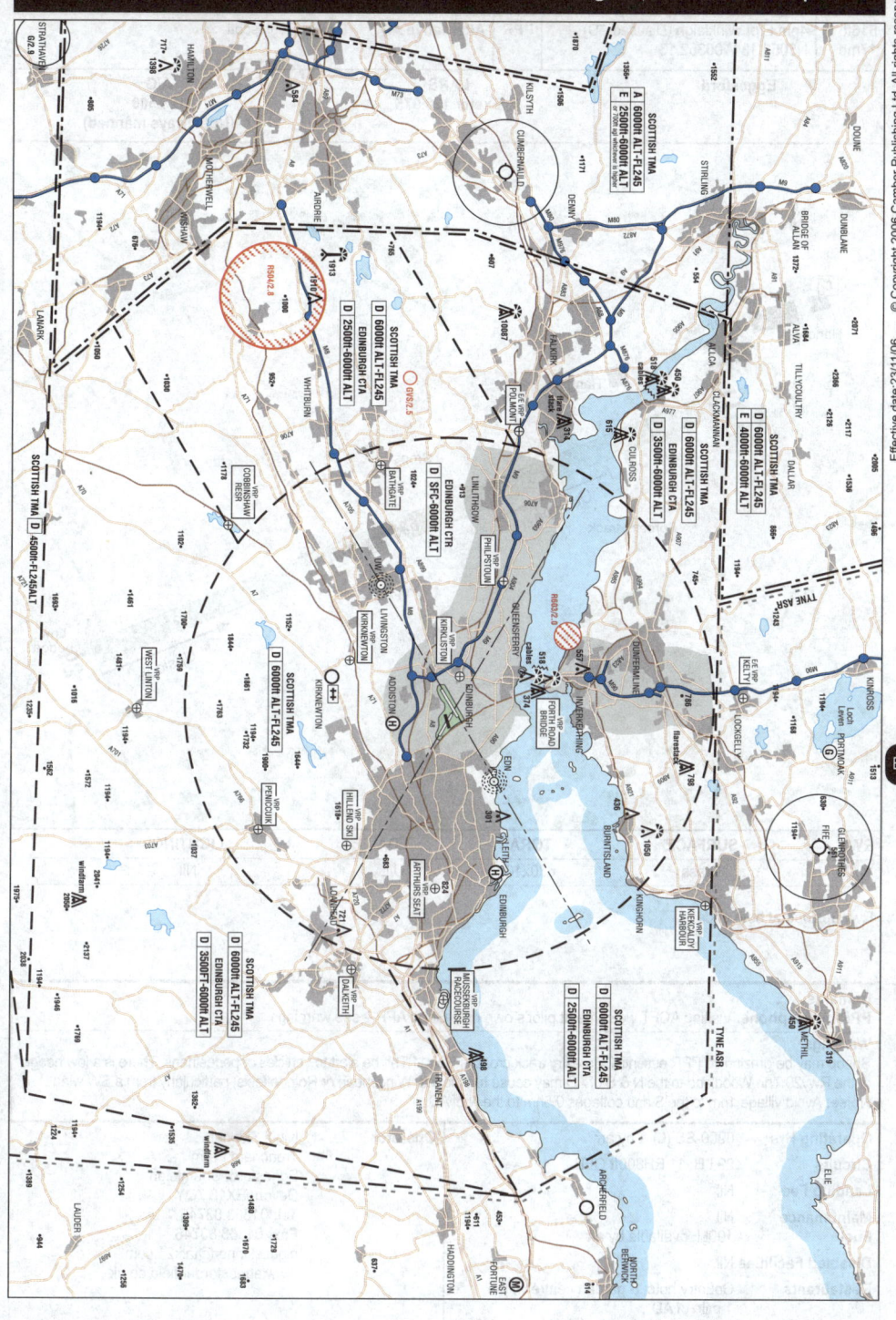

516ft 17mb	4nm E of Winkleigh (Disused AD) N5052.13 W00352.13	PPR	Alternative AD	Exeter Eaglescott

Eggesford	LARS Exeter 128.975	A/G 123.500 (Not always manned)

N

Trenchard Farm

C

Hangars

Fuel

ACFT parking

11

Hangar

Upslope

Forestry track

Crops

630m x 10m

Crops

Low hedge

Upslope

29

E

RWY	SURFACE	TORA	LDA	LIGHTING
11/29	Grass	630x10	U/L	Nil

Rwy upslope at both ends

Remarks

PPR by telephone. Visiting ACFT welcome at pilot's own risk. Good APP – see warnings

Warnings

Sheep may be grazing so PPR essential. Forestry track crosses Rwy11 Thr, be alert to vehicles or pedestrians. There is a low hedge at the Rwy29 Thr. Woodland to the N & S of AD may cause turbulence, Windshear, or Rotor effects, particularly from a SW wind.

Noise: Avoid village 1nm to the S and cottages 0.5nm to the N of AD.

Operating Hrs	0900-SS (L) & by arr	**Operator**	Nigel Skinner Trenchard Farm Eggesford, Chumleigh Devon, EX18 7QY **Tel:** 01363 83746 **Fax:** 01363 83746 nigel.skinner@talk21.com www.eggesfordairfield.co.uk
Circuits	29 LH, 11 RH800ft QFE		
Landing Fee	Nil		
Maintenance	Nil		
Fuel	100LL available by arr		
Disabled Facilities	Nil		
Restaurants	Country hotel & garden centre within 1 mile of AD		
Taxis	**Tel:** 01769 573636		
Car Hire	Nil		
Weather Info	AirSW MOEx		

246ft	3nm S of RAF Wattisham	PPR	Alternative AD	Southend Earls Colne
7mb	N5204.53 E00058.67		Diversion AD	

Elmsett	APP Wattisham 125.800	A/G 130.900

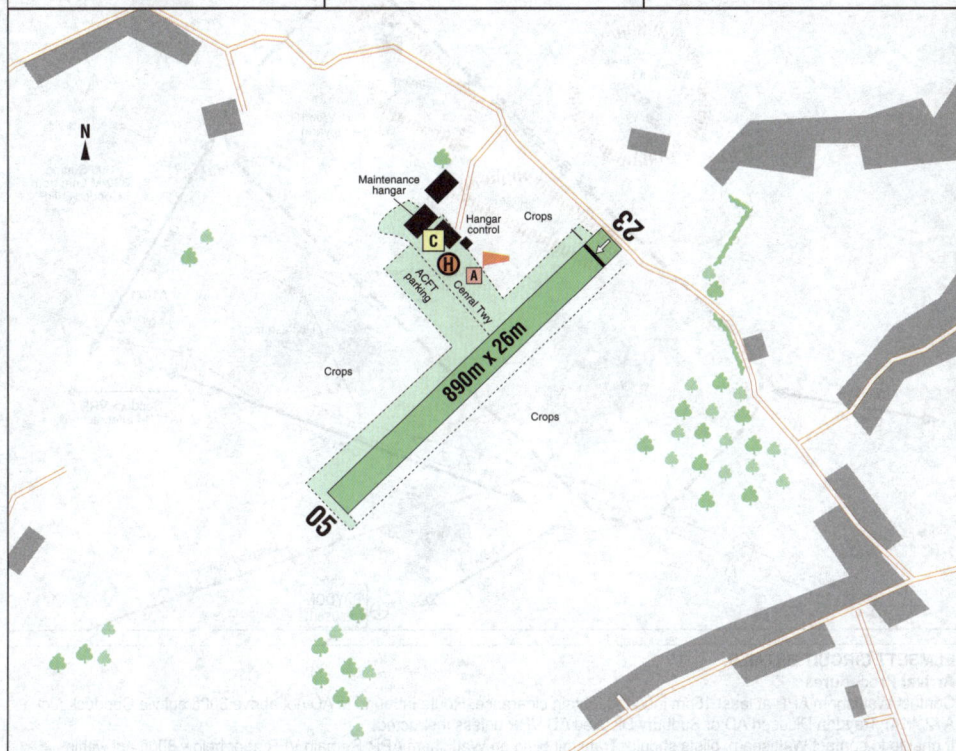

RWY	SURFACE	TORA	LDA	LIGHTING
05	Grass	890x26	U/L	Thr Rwy APAPI 3.75° LHS
23	Grass	890x26	U/L	Thr Rwy APAPI 4.0° LHS

Rwy05 1.8% upslope

Remarks

Strictly PPR by telephone. Arr Procedures: Contact Wattisham APP at least 15nm from Wattisham & obtain clearance. If unable to establish radio contact, route not above 800ft agl via VRP's at Raydon Disused AD or Copdock Jct A12/A14. Yak 50/52 ACFT must use Rwy23. Keep to circuit pattern to minimise noise. If no contact on ground, try ASAP after Dept. If no contact remain not above 800ft agl and Dept from circuit via Raydon or Copdock VRP's.

Warnings

Rwy lighting stands proud of surface exercise caution vacating Rwy. Crops up to edge of Rwy S side. Public right of way crosses APP Rwy23 70m from Thr. Taxiing beyond hold A not permitted when ACFT are taking-off or landing. Power checks Holding Point A only.

Noise: Keep well clear of all towns and villages marked. Avoid over flying villages within 5nm of AD, leave local area ASAP. Do not fly inside circuit pattern shown, especially on Dept.

Operating Hrs	Mon-Fri 0900-1700 (L)	Operator	Mr T D Gray
Circuits	05 RH, 23 LH, 800ft QFE		Poplar Aviation Ltd
Landing Fee	On application		Poplar Hall Farm, Elmsett
Maintenance	Aero Anglia		Ipswich, Suffolk, IP7 6LN
Fuel	AVGAS 100LL		**Tel:** 01473 824116
Disabled Facilities	Nil		**Fax:** 01473 822896
Restaurant	Hot drinks available		duncan@poplarhall.co.uk
Taxis/Car Hire	By arr		www.poplaraviation.co.uk
Weather Info	AirS MOEx		

E

ELMSETT CIRCUIT DETAILS:

Arrival Procedures:

Contact Wattisham APP at least 15nm inbound, obtain clearance. Route inbound to AD not above 800ft agl via Copdock (Jct A12/A14), Raydon Disused AD or Sudbury Disused AD VRP unless instructed.

If unable to contact Wattisham, pilots should: Transmit blind on Wattisham APP. Remain VFR at or below 800ft agl within Wattisham MATZ/Elmsett ATZ.

From Copdock VRP track 330°T to join left base Rwy23 or track 245°T to join at Raydon Disused AD for Rwy05

From Raydon Disused AD VRP track 300°T to join right base to join right base for Rwy05 or downwind Rwy23.

From Sudbury Disused AD VRP track 100°T to join finals Rwy05 or join circuit Rwy23.

DEPARTURE PROCEDURES:

Contact Wattisham APP before dept to obtain clearance.

If unable to contact Wattisham, pilots should: Transmit blind on Wattisham APP. Dept VFR in noise abatement circuit not above 800ft agl routing outbound via Copdock (Jct A12/A14), Raydon Disused AD VRP or Sudbury Disused AD VRP.

Rwy05: Copdock dept – Maintain Rwy track 050°T, climb to circuit height ASAP. Turn crosswind before Middle Wood, fly parallel to power lines, track 140°T till overhead electricity sub-station, track 150°T to VRP.

Rwy05: Raydon Dept – Maintain Rwy track 050°T, climb to circuit height ASAP. Turn crosswind before Middle Wood, fly parallel to power lines, track 140°T aiming for electricity sub-station. Turn downwind when between Wolves Wood and Hintlesham Wood, track 230°T. When S of Hadleigh track 140°T to VRP.

Rwy05: Sudbury dept – Maintain Rwy track 050°T, climb to circuit height ASAP. Turn crosswind before Middle Wood, fly parallel to power lines, track 140°T aiming for electricity sub-station. Turn downwind when between Wolves Wood and Hintlesham Wood, track 230°T. Turn right base S of Hadleigh, track 320°T keeping clear of town. When clear to SW track 280°T to VRP.

Rwy23: Copdock dept – Dept as for Raydon, track 065°T to VRP.

Rwy23: Raydon dept – Maintain Rwy track 230°T, climb to circuit height ASAP. Turn crosswind when SW of Hadleigh, track 140T keeping clear of twon. When S of Hadleigh track 120°T to VRP.

Rwy23: Sudbury dept – Maintain Rwy track 050°T, climb to circuit height ASAP. When W of Hadleigh track 280°T to VRP.

332ft 11mb	2.6nm E of Watford N5139.35 W00019.55	PPR	Alternative AD Diversion AD	London Luton Denham

Elstree	A/G 122.400	AFIS 122.400

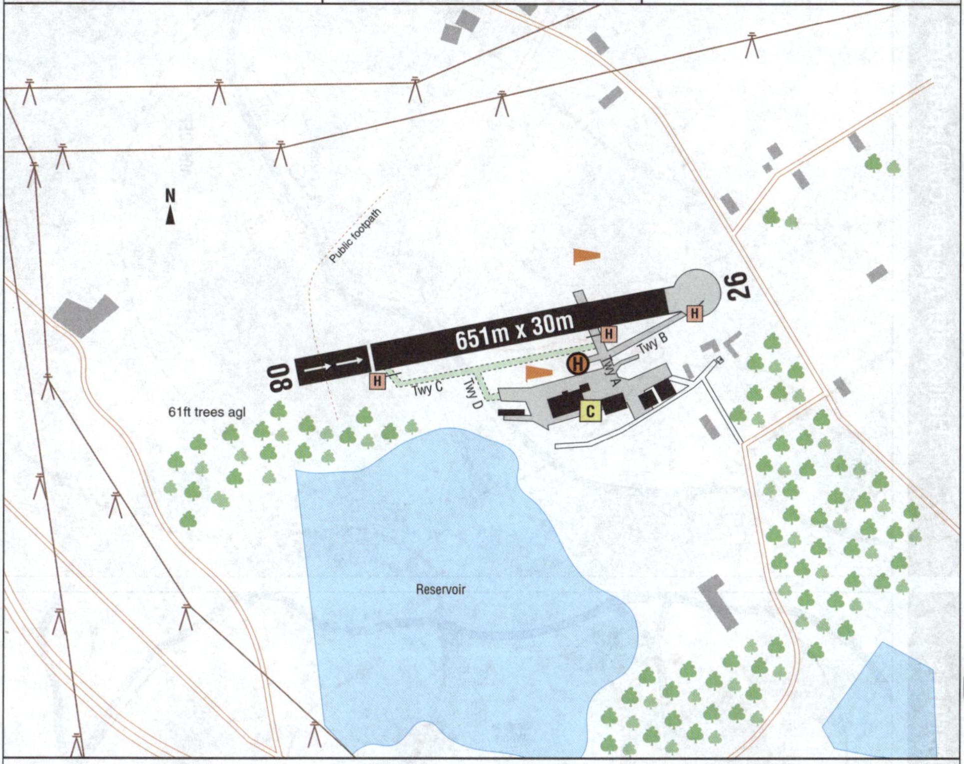

651m x 30m

Twy B

Twy C

Twy D

26

08

Public footpath

N

61ft trees agl

Reservoir

C

RWY	SURFACE	TORA	LDA	LIGHTING
08	Asphalt	651	651	Rwy
26	Asphalt	651	651	Thr Rwy LITAS 4.5° LHS

Pavement at W end provides 174x18 U/L stop way

Remarks
Strictly PPR by telephone. Not available to non-radio ACFT. Licensed night use Rwy26 only. ACFT must not join overhead. APP must be straight in from 4nm, reporting at the VRP's. Terms & conditions use available on request from AD operator. Specific Dept Routes.
Visual aids to location: Ibn Green EL, Abn White flashing.

Warnings
Distance between Twy centre line & parked ACFT 10.5m, but 8.5m on aprons. Taxi with extreme caution.
Noise: Obtain Noise Abatement dept instructions from Watch Office.

Operating Hrs	As required
Circuits	Reserved for flying training by Cabair and Firecrest
Landing Fee	On application

Maintenance
Cabair	**Tel:** 0208 953 3586
Metair	**Tel:** 0208 2073702
Fuel	JET A1 AVGAS 100LL

Disabled Facilites

Restaurants	Licensed restaurant at AD

Taxis
Allied	
Car Hire	**Tel:** 01923 232505
National	Available on request
	Tel: 01923 233340

Weather Info	AirSE MOEx
Operator	Montclare Shipping Co Ltd Elstree Aerodrome Borehamwood Hertfordshire, WD6 3AR **Tel:** 0208 953 7480 (ATC) **Fax:** 0208 207 3691 www.egtr.net

E

Helicopter Approach/Departures

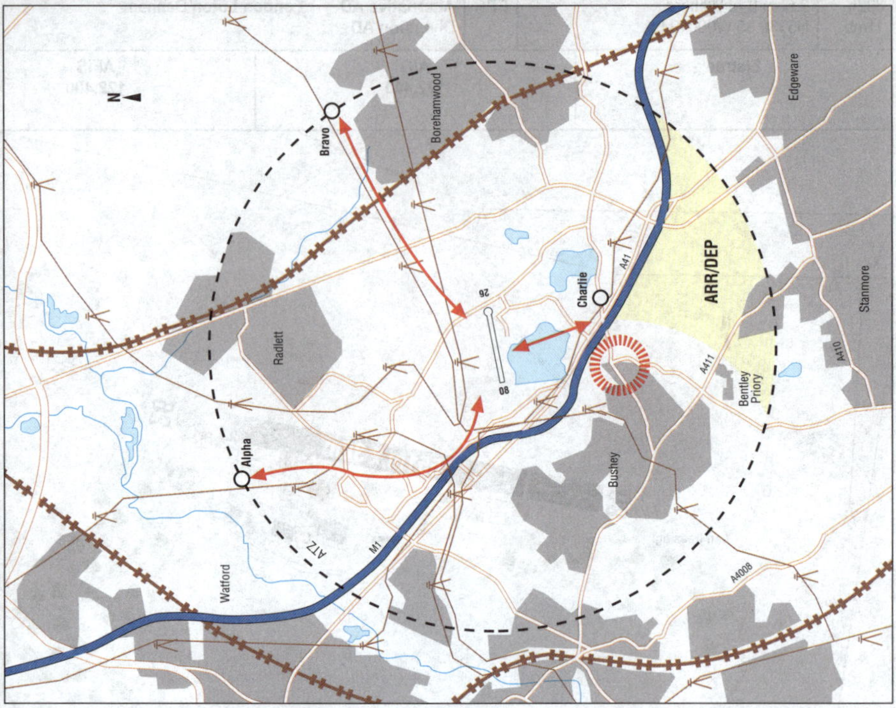

Fixed Wing Approach/Departures

E

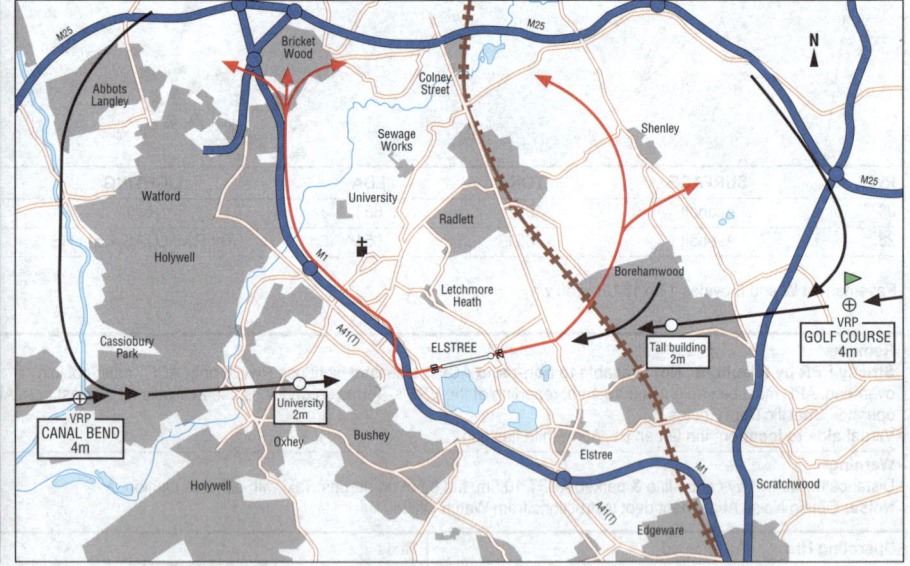

Visual Reporting Points (VRP)
Rwy08 Canal Bend
N5139.03 W00025.62 (4nm) University (2nm)
Rwy26 Golf Course
N5140.00 W00012.93 (4nm) Tall Building (2nm)

47ft 1mb	4nm SE of York N5355.28 W00059.55	PPR	Alternative AD	Leeds Bradford Sherburn in Elmet

York Radio		APP Fenton 126.500	A/G 119.625

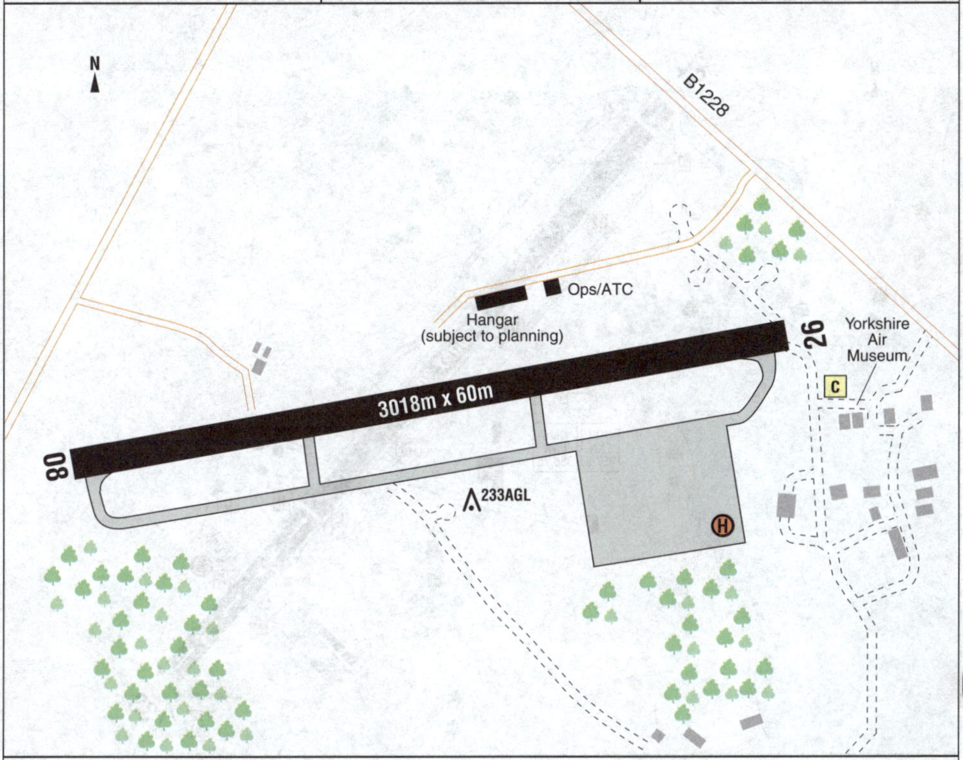

Airfield diagram showing Runway 08/26, 3018m x 60m, Hangar (subject to planning), Ops/ATC, Yorkshire Air Museum, 233AGL mast, and B1228 road.

RWY	SURFACE	TORA	LDA	LIGHTING
08/26	Asph/Conc	3018x60	U/L	Nil

Remarks
PPR strictly by telephone. Visitors welcome at pilots own risk. ACFT parking is by direction from the follow-me truck or by radio. Adjacent Yorkshire Air Museum has no authority to approve or deny ACFT movements. AD is used for events other than aviation activity. The museum has many interesting exhibits including an intact HP Halifax bomber from WW2. New hangar to be built on AD subject to planning permission.

Warnings
AD located under Church Fenton MATZ. 233ft agl radio mast S of Rwy mid point.
Noise: Avoid over flying all local habitation

		Taxis	
Operating Hrs	SR-SS	Crest Taxi	**Tel:** 01904 608322
Circuits	26 LH, 08 RH, 1000ft QFE	**Car Hire**	Nil
Landing Fee	On Application	**Weather Info**	AirN MWC
Maintenance	Nil	**Operator**	Elvington Park Ltd
Fuel	AVGAS JET A1 100LL		Halifax Way
Disabled Facilities			Pocklington Ind Estate

Pocklington, YO42 1NP
Tel: 01759 305851
aviation@elvington.biz
www.elvington.biz

Restaurants Café in Yorkshire Air Museum

155ft 5mb	4.5nm N of Enniskillen N5423.93 W00739.12	PPR	Alternative AD Diversion AD	Belfast Aldergrove Sligo

	Enniskillen	A/G 123.200

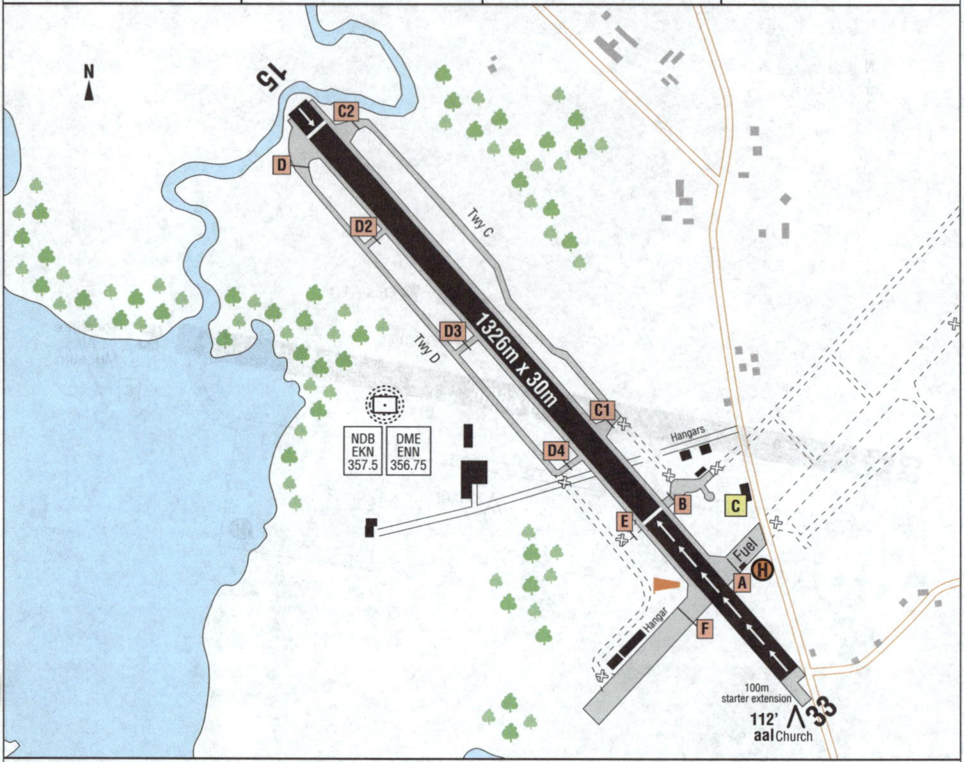

RWY	SURFACE	TORA	LDA	LIGHTING
15	Asphalt	1236	1286	Rwy PAPI 3.5° LHS
33	Asphalt	1337	1004	Rwy PAPI 4.5° LHS

Displaced Thr Rwy15 100m
Displaced Thr Rwy33 330m

Remarks
Not available to ACFT unable to communicate by radio unless the pilot has obtained a specific prior permission.
Rwy33 PAPIS not to be used for APP slope guidance unless aligned with Rwy.

Warnings
Twys C & D available to ACF with wingspan <12m. No turns below 300ft QFE. Low level circuits only permitted for practice bad weather flying.

Operating Hrs	Tue-Sun 0900-1700 (L) & by arr	**Operator** Enniskillen Airport Ltd
Circuits	15 RH, 33 LH 1000ft QFE Microlights & Helicopters 800ft QFE	Trory Enniskillen
Landing Fee	On application	Co Fermanagh Northern Ireland
Maintenance	Nil	BT94 2FP
Fuel	JET A1 AVGAS 100LL	**Tel:** 0286 6329000
Hangarage	Limited	**Fax:** 0286 6329100
Disabled Facilities		info@enniskillen-airport.co.uk www.enniskillen-airport.co.uk

Restaurants	Café St Angelo on AD
Taxis/Car Hire	Available on request
Weather Info	AirN BEL

550ft 18mb	4.5nm E of Chipping Norton N5155.69 W00125.71	PPR	Alternative AD Diversion AD	Oxford Turweston

	Enstone		A/G 129.875	

E

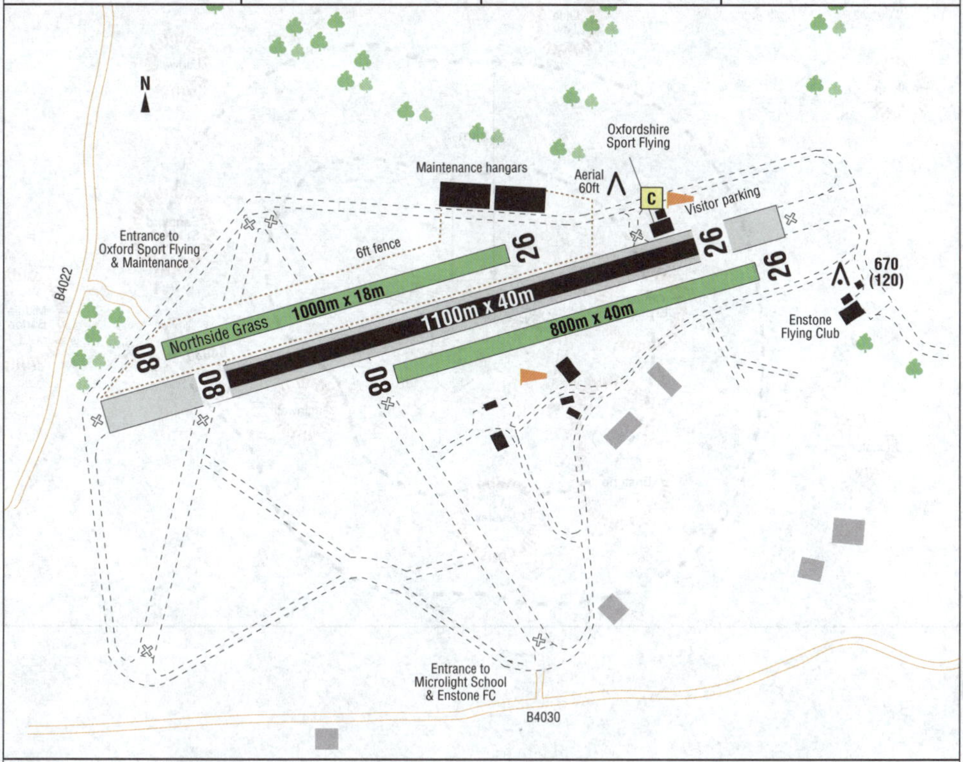

RWY	SURFACE	TORA	LDA	LIGHTING
08/26	Asphalt	1100x40	U/L	Nil
08/26	Grass	800x40	U/L	Nil

Remarks
PPR by telephone or radio. No Dept before 0800 or after 1930 or SS whichever is earlier. Gliding no longer takes place on AD, Grass Rwy S of main Rwy available to ACFT. N side grass strip operated by maintenance organisation. Use at own risk

Warnings
Rwys15/33 and 02/20 are not usable. Motor Gliders, Light ACFT and Microlights operate from this AD. Radio mast 120ft aal (670ft amsl) in SE corner of the AD.
Noise: Avoid over flying the noise sensitive villages of Great Tew, Little Tew, Ledwell, Sandford St Martin, Enstone and Church Enstone and Heythrop College.

Operating Hrs	0800-SS (L) Last dept 1930 (L)	**Accommodation** Swan Lodge	**Tel:** 01608 678736
Circuits	08 LH, 26 RH Motor gliders 600ft QFE Microlights 600ft QFE ACFT 800ft QFE	Pretty Bush Cotswold View **Taxis** Aston Cars	**Tel:** 01608 738262 **Tel:** 01608 810314 **Tel:** 01869 340460
Landing Fee	Single £7.50 Microlights £5.00 Twin £15	**Car Hire** Europcar **Weather Info**	**Tel:** 01295 51787 AirCen MOEx
Maintenance **Fuel**	Available **Tel:** 01608 683625 AVGAS 100LL	**Operator**	Oxfordshire Sport Flying Club Ltd Enstone Aerodrome, Church Enstone Oxon OX7 4NP

Disabled Facilities

Restaurants
Snacks on AD inc home made cakes @ OSF
Little Chef on A44 & the Crown Inn Church Enstone

Tel: 01608 677208
(Oxfordshire Sport Flying)
Tel: 01608 678204 (Enstone Flying Club)
Tel: 01608 678741 (Microlights)
Fax: 01608 677808
(Oxfordshire Sport Flying)
osf@enstoneaerodrome.co.uk
www.enstone-aerodrome.co.uk

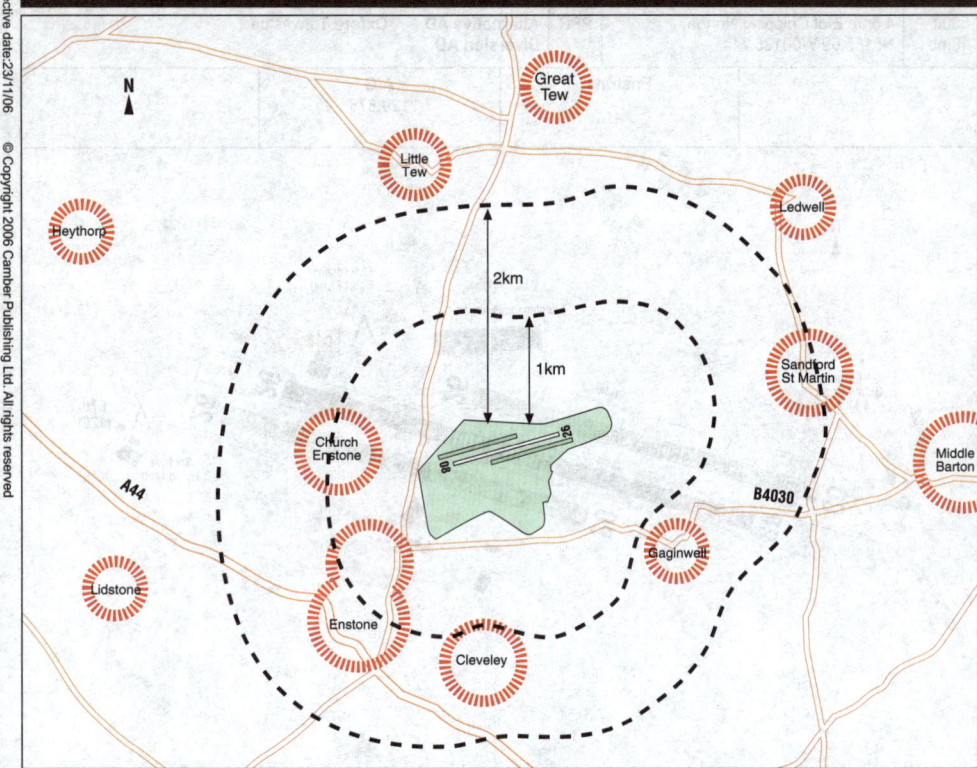

E

197ft 7mb	7nm N of Morpeth N5516.84 W00142.82	PPR	Alternative AD	Newcastle Peterlee

Eshott	APP Newcastle 124.375	A/G 122.850

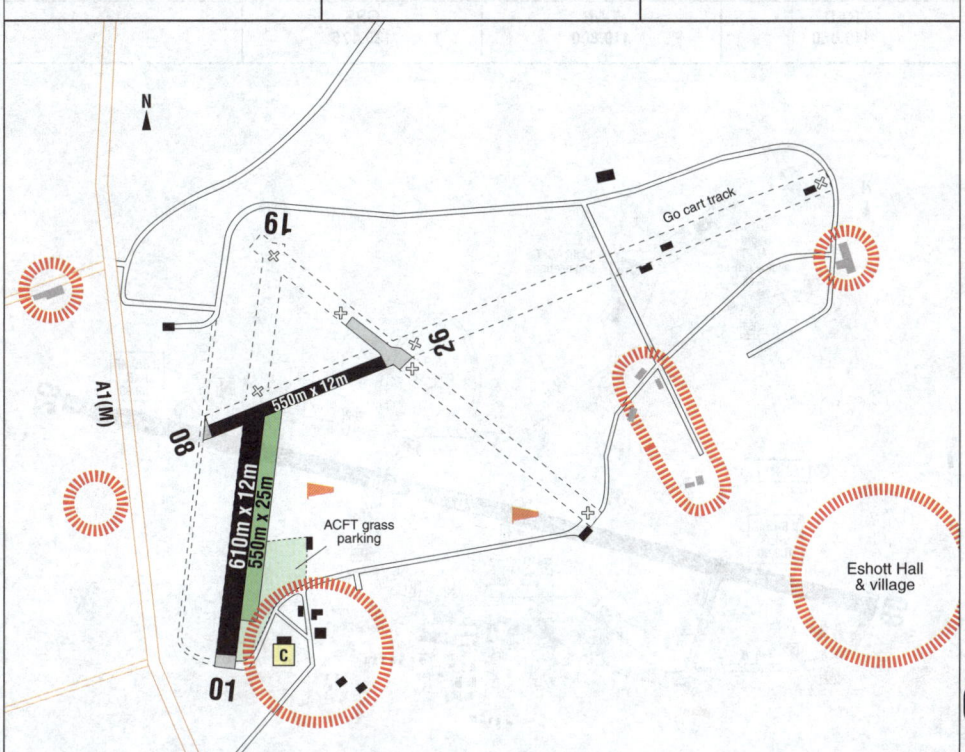

RWY	SURFACE	TORA	LDA	LIGHTING
01/19	Asphalt	610x45	U/L	Nil
01/19	Grass	550x25	U/L	Nil
08/26	Asphalt	490x20	U/L	Nil

Remarks
PPR only, essential for joining instructions. Please pay landing fee.

Warnings
Rwy08/26 has been resurfaced with Asphalt to a width of 12m. Asphalt E of the disused Rwy14/32 intersection is a go-kart racing track and not useable by ACFT. Intense microlight activity keep a good lookout, contact Newcastle APP for information.
Noise: Avoid over flying Felton village to N and farm buildings and houses in the immediate area

Operating Hrs	0900-1900 (L) No operations outside these Hrs	Operator	Eshott Airfield Ltd Bockenfield Felton Northumberland, NE65 9QJ **Tel:** 01670 787881 (Operator) **Tel:** 01670 787881 (AD) **Tel:** 07798 771415 www.eshottairfield.co.uk
Landing Fee	Microlight £0, Overnight parking £5 ACFT £5, Overnight parking £8		
Circuits	01, 08 RH, 19, 26 LH		
Maintenance	By arr		
Fuel	AVGAS		
Disabled Facilities	Nil		
Restaurants	Cafe on AD at weekends		
Taxis/Car Hire	AD operator will advise		
Weather Info	AirN MWC		

102ft 3mb	4nm NE of Exeter N5044.07 W00324.83		Alternative AD	Plymouth Dunkeswell

Exeter	ATIS 119.325	LARS 128.975	APP 128.975

RAD 119.050	TWR 119.800	OPS 130.175	

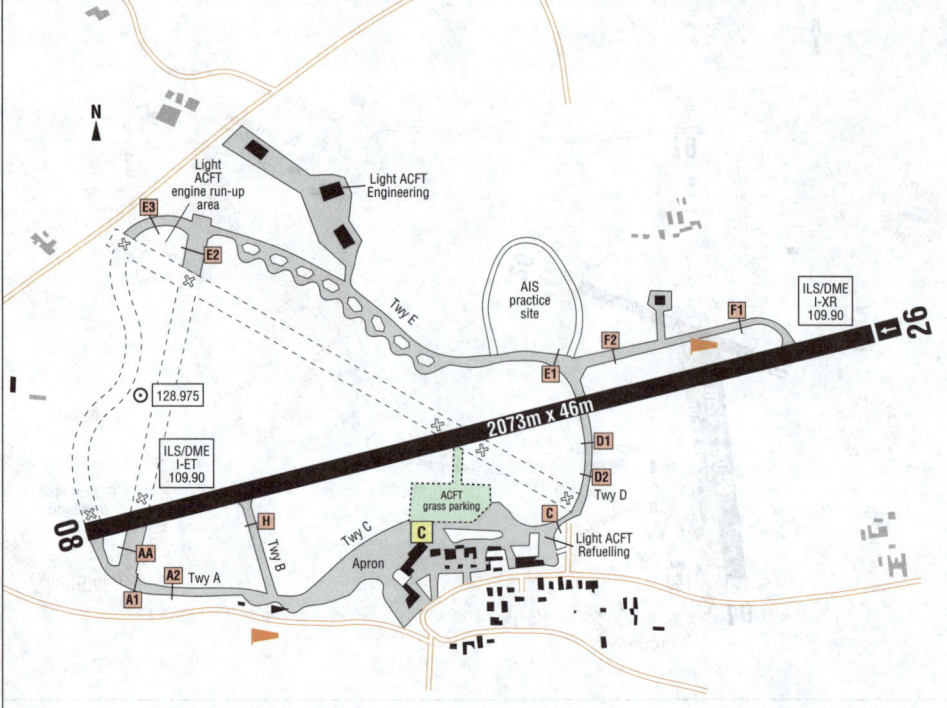

RWY	SURFACE	TORA	LDA	LIGHTING
08	Asphalt	2047	2037	Ap Thr Rwy PAPI 3° LHS
26	Asphalt	2073	2037	Ap Thr Rwy PAPI 3.5° LHS

Displaced Thr Rwy08 10m
Displaced Thr Rwy26 36m

Remarks

PPR to all ACFT >9m long via AD Ops. Non-radio ACFT not accepted. Hi-vis. Light ACFT pilots beware of elevated Rwy lights and PAPI 08/26. Twys except bravo are only 15m wide and thus not suitable for use by ACFT whose wheel base >18m and wheel span >9m. Twy E has green reflective centre line studs and blue edge studs from E1 to a line of amber studs across Twy. This Twy is limited to ACFT with wheel base <7.5m, wingspan <30m. The remainder of Twy is not suitable for ACFT with wheel base >7.5m and wingspan >15m. Twy F is not licensed, only 8m strip on Twy is useable by ACFT. Twy is only suitable for ACFT with <7.5m wheel base and <15m wingspan. Twy F is unlit, available in day light Hrs only. ACFT requiring apron parking must book with AD Ops prior to Arr. Pedestrians access on S of AD from/to grass or non-parking apron must be via airside barrier adjacent to fire section.
Fuelling: AVGAS pumps only. Max of 3 ACFT at fuelling apron at any one time. ACFT must call ATC prior to leaving fuelling apron.
Aids to Navigation: NDB EX 337.00

Warnings

ACFT APP without assistance from RAD shall follow a descent path no lower than the normal APP path indicated by the PAPIs. Restrictions on use for single engine ECFT – Rwy08 new displaced Thr not marked. Rwy08 not available for single engine ACFT precision APP and night use. Rwy26 900m available for single engine ACFT dept.
Noise: Pilots must ensure at all times that ACFT are operated to cause the least disturbance practicable in areas surrounding the AD, particularly the City of Exeter and Clyst Honiton village.

Operating Hrs	**Landing Fee**	On application from ATC or via website
Mon-Fri 0700-1900 Sat 0700-1800 Sun 0800-1900 (Summer) Mon 0001-0100 0700-2359 Tue-Fri 0001-0200 0700-2359 (PPR before 0800, after 1900) Sat 0001-0200 0800-1700 Sun 0830-2359 (PPR before 0900, after 1700) (Winter)	**Maintenance**	Iscavia Eng
		Tel: 01392 362415 (Iscavia Eng)
	Fuel	AVGAS JET A1 100LL

Disabled Facilities

Restaurant	Bar/Buffet facilities available
Taxis	
Corporate Cars	**Tel:** 01392 360214
Car Hire	
Avis	**Tel:** 01392 59713
Weather Info	M T9 Fax 278 MOEx
	Tel: 01392 3549150

Visual Reference Points (VRP)

Axminster	N5046.90 W00259.90
Crediton	N5047.43 W00339.08
Cullompton	N5051.47 W00323.63
Exmouth	N5037.48 W00324.13
Topsham	N5041.38 W00328.82

Operator	Exeter International Airport
	Exeter, Devon, EX5 2BD
	Tel: 01392 354915 (ATC)
	Tel: 01392 447433 (Ops)
	Fax: 01392 447422 (Ops)
	Fax: 01392 354967 (ATC)
	www.exeter-airport.co.uk

Effective date:23/11/06

E

780ft 26mb	4.5nm N of Wombleton N5418.52 W00058.43	PPR	Alternative AD	Durham Tees Valley Full Sutton
Fadmoor		**LARS** Linton 129.150		**A/G** 123.225 not manned

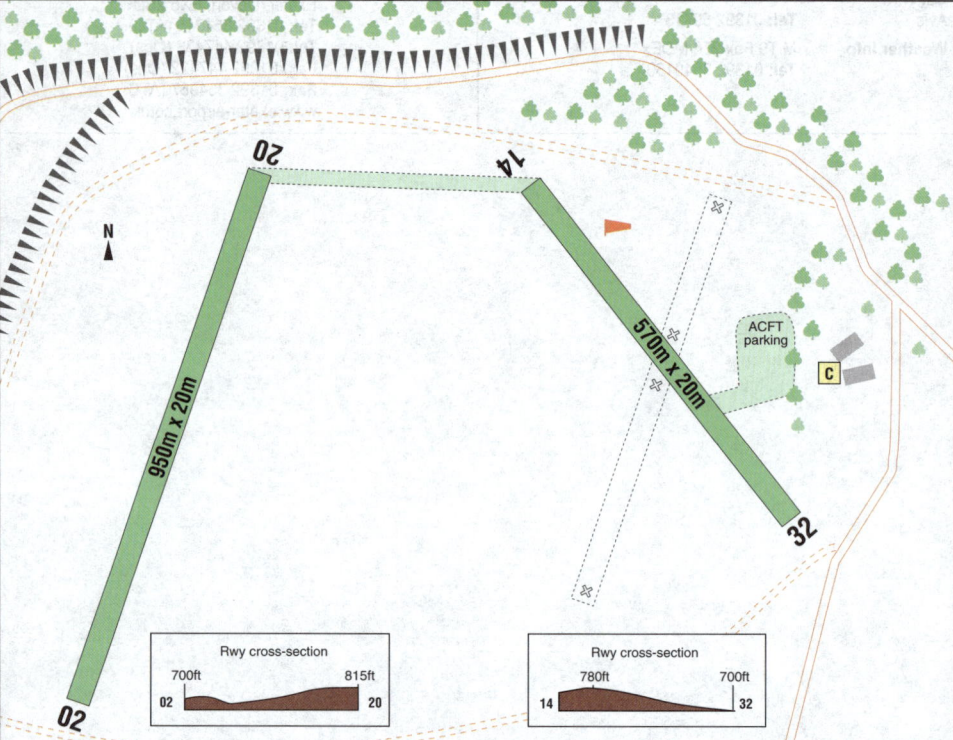

RWY	SURFACE	TORA	LDA	LIGHTING
02/20	Grass	950	U/L	Rwy
14/32	Grass	570	U/L	Rwy

Rwy02 or 32 preferred for landing

Remarks
PPR visiting ACFT accepted on agricultural business to purchase farm pork. AD subject to planning regulations. Pilots should have experience in grass field landings. AD situated on crown of hill, on edge of escarpment, at S edge of moorland. GND slopes away from all Thr. Self contained holiday flat available for rent from operator on AD phone number.

Warnings
Beware of low flying military ACFT above and below AD level.

Operating Hrs	Mon-Sat SR-SS Closed Sundays	**Operator**	P H Johnson Fadmoor Kirkbymoorside Yorkshire, YO62 7JH **Tel:** 01751 431171 (AD) **Tel:** 07989 383562 **Fax:** 01751 432727
Circuits	Nil		
Landing Fee	On application		
Maintenance	Nil Ltd hangerage		
Fuel	AVGAS 100LL		
Disabled Facilities	Nil		
Restaurants Plough Royal Oak	**Tel:** 01751 431515 (1 mile) **Tel:** 01751431414 (1 mile)		
Taxis/Car Hire	On request		
Weather Info	AirN MWC		

F

223ft 7mb	On Fair Isle N5932.15 W00137.68		PPR	Alternative AD Diversion AD	Sumburgh Sanday
Fair Isle			**APP** **Sumburgh 131.300**		**A/G** **118.025**

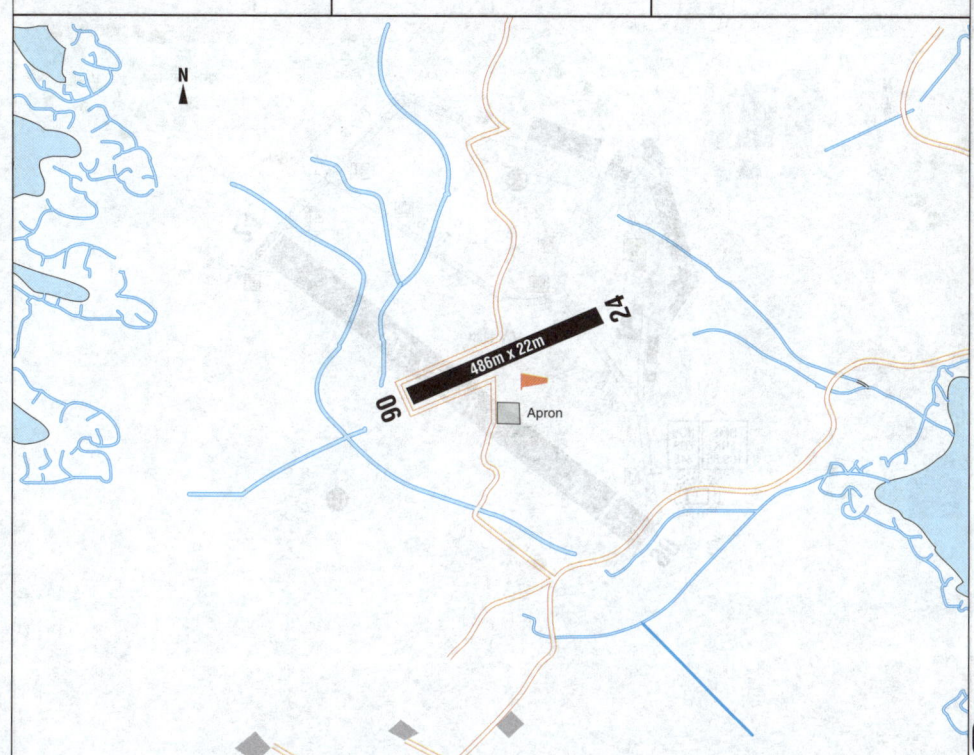

RWY	SURFACE	TORA	LDA	LIGHTING
06/24	Gravel	486	486	Nil

Remarks

PPR. GND falls away very steeply approx 30m beyond each Rwy end. Care should betaken to anticipate sudden wind changes which might result in a touch down short of Thr. Rwy surface prone to moss growth almost exclusively on E end and may be slippery, particularly when wet. Accommodation available at Fair Isle Observatory Lodge, E of AD. A/G is SR-SS only subject to PPR and as required for emergency use.

Warnings

Turbulence can be expected with a W wind. Avoid low flying over islands or cliffs. Rwy is banked above surrounding land. Weather conditions can change rapidly. Pilots can arrive, having had a favourable met. report, to find the Isle shrouded in fog/low cloud. Bird hazard, May-Aug particularly on Rwy06 APP.

Operating Hrs	SR-SS	**Taxis/Car Hire** J Stout	**Tel:** 01595 760222
Circuits	06 RH, 24 LH	**Weather Info**	AirSc GWC
Landing Fee	Single £10 Twin £15	**Operator**	The National Trust for Scotland
Maintenance	Nil		Fairlsle
Fuel	Nil		Shetland, ZE2 9JU
Disabled Facilities			**Tel:** 01595 760224 (Mr D Wheeler) **Fax:** 01595 760210 dave.wheeler@fairisle.org.uk www.fairisle.org.uk/egrf
Restaurants	Food & accomodation available at the Fair Isle Observatory Lodge **Tel:** 01595 760258		

80ft 3mb	2nm N of Woking N5120.88 W00033.53	PPR	Alternative AD Diversion AD	Farnborough White Waltham

Fairoaks	LARS Farnborough 125.250	AFIS 123.425	A/G 123.425

813m x 27m

108ft

DME FRK 109.85 | NDB FOS 348

Twy C · Twy B · Twy A

C1 · B2 · B1 · B3 · A3 · A2 · A1 · 24 · 06 · H · C · T

RWY	SURFACE	TORA	LDA	LIGHTING
06	Asphalt	813	760	Thr Rwy APAPI 3.5°
24	Asphalt	813	800	Thr Rwy APAPI 4.0°

Remarks

Not available to non-radio ACFT. Weight shift microlights not accepted. Airside passengers are pilots responsibility. New visitors should obtain a telephone briefing.
Visual aid to location: Abn flashing white.

Warnings

AD located inside S boundary of London Control Zone – special procedures apply. Due to a hump on Rwy Rwy24 red end lights are visible only for the last 150m of LDA. The last 3 Rwy edge lights are cautionary yellow. Exercise caution when taxiing through the apron/parking areas due to reduced wing tip clearances. Pilots of ACFT whose wingspan >15m should satisfy themselves that they have adequate clearance. Twy to SE of Rwy24 Thr is not available to ACFT required to use a licensed AD. Other ACFT should only use this Twy with the permission of AD management. Grass areas are subject to water logging. Public footpath crosses AD close to Rwy24 Thr. Helicopter training takes place on AD. AD is frequently used outside published Hrs, pilots in the vicinity should call Fairoaks to determine if it is active.
Noise: Inbound, do not over fly Knaphill below 1500ft QNH & avoid properties to NE of AD below 1000ft QFE.

Operating Hrs	Mon-Fri 0700-1900 (Mar-Aug) 0700-1800 (Sep) 0700-1700 (Oct) Sat 0700-1700 Sun & PH 0800-1700 (Summer) Mon-Sat 0800-1800 Sun & PH 0900-1800 (Winter)
Circuits	Variable
Landing Fee	On application

Maintenance
Mann Aviation **Tel:** 01276 857441
Fuel AVGAS JET A1 100LL
All aviation oils

Restaurants
Hangar Café **Tel:** 01276 855446
Taxis
Five Star **Tel:** 01483 755555
Boomerang **Tel:** 01483 714062
Car Hire
UK Airport Cars **Tel:** 0208 8180102
Weather Info M* AirSE MOEx

Disabled Facilities

Operator	Fairoaks Airports Ltd
	Fairoaks Airport
	Chobham, Woking
	Surrey, GU24 8HX
	Tel: 01276 857700 (Admin)
	Tel: 01276 857300 (ATC)
	Fax: 01276 856898
	Telex: 859033 FKSATC
	www.alanmann.co.uk

Fairoaks ATZ and Local Flying Area

Within the Local Flying Area (2nm radius centred on AD) flights may take place without compliance with IFR requirements subject to the following conditions.

1 ACFT to remain below cloud and in sight of the GND.

2 Maximum altitudes 800ft (QNH) when London Heathrow Rwy23 is in use. Otherwise maximum altitude is 1500ft (QNH).

3 Minimum visibility is 3km.

4 ACFT must not enter the Fairoaks ATZ without permission, even if operating on an SVFR clearance in the London CTR.

5 Inbound traffic APP from the S must remain W of the M25 whilst within the Fairoaks Local Flying Area.

6 Pilots of ACFT flying in the Local Flying Area are responsible for providing their own separation from other ACFT operating in the same airspace.

F

EGLF

FARNBOROUGH

238ft 8mb	1nm NNW of Aldershot N5116.55 W00046.58	PPR	Alternative AD Diversion AD	Southampton Blackbushe

Farnborough	ATIS 128.400	LARS 125.250	APP 134.350
RAD 125.250	TWR 122.500	FIRE 121.600	OPS 130.375 TAG Aviation

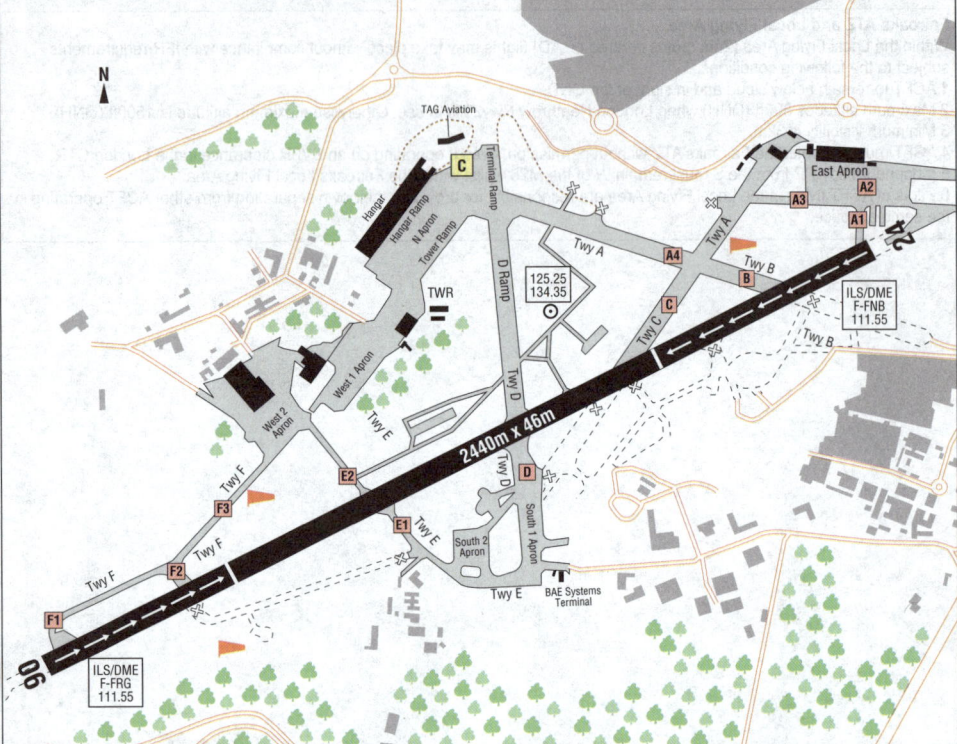

RWY	SURFACE	TORA	LDA	LIGHTING
06	Con/Asph	2000	1800	Ap Thr Rwy PAPI 3.5°
24	Con/Asph	2063	1800	Ap Thr Rwy PAPI 3.5°

Starter extension Rwy06 170m mandatory for all depts. Rwy06/24 friction surface no tight turns on asphalt section

Remarks

PPR. Pilots must book out by phone. All visiting ACFT must arrange handling and parking with TAG Aviation. Training available for home based ACFT only.

Visual aid to location: Flashing Green FH.

Warnings

Minimum obstacle clearance Rwy06/24 is not provided by PAR or PAPIs at less than 1nm from Thr. Danger Areas D132, D133A and D133 are within 3nm E of AD boundary. Traffic carrying out instrument APP Rwy28 at Odiham will pass approximately 1.5nm S of Farnborough AD at 1900ft QNH or lower. ATC brief available. Twy C and L the outer edges marked with yellow chevrons are not suitable for ACFT use. Single engine jet ACFT may not Dept Rwy06. AD will close prior to 2200 Mon-Fri when no operations expected.

Noise: All Dept are to use maximum climb until ACFT reaches initial clearance level.

		Maintenance	Farnborough Aviation Services Tel: 01252 524440
Operating Hrs	Mon-Fri 0600-2100 Sat-Sun & PH 0700-1900 (Summer) +1Hr (Winter)		
Circuits		Fuel	AVGAS 100LL JET A1 by arr with TAG Aviation
ACFT >2730Kg not below 1700ft QNH before turning base leg ACFT <2730Kg not below 1200ft QNH before turning base leg Avoid congested area 2nm W of AD unless ATC authorise		Disabled Facilities	Available
		Restaurants	Many pubs within walking distance
		Taxis/Car Hire	Can be arranged on Arr at AD
Landing Fee	Minimum charge including Nav & handling £50	Weather Info	M T9 Fax 282 MOEx METAR/TAF Tel: 09063 800400 Ex 282

Visual Reference Points (VRP)		Operator	TAG Aviation
Alton	N5109.12 W00057.97		Farnborough Airport
Bagshot	N5120.95 W00041.95		Hampshire, GU14 6XA
Guildford	N5114.37 W00035.10		**Tel:** 01252 526015 (ATC RAD)
Hook	N5116.77 W00057.72		**Tel:** 01252 526017 (ATC VIS)
Nokia Factory	N5117.55 W00047.88		**Tel:** 01252 524440 (TAG Aviation PPR)
			Fax: 01252 518771 (TAG Aviation)

Farnborough Helicopter VFR Arrival Routes

Effective date:23/11/06

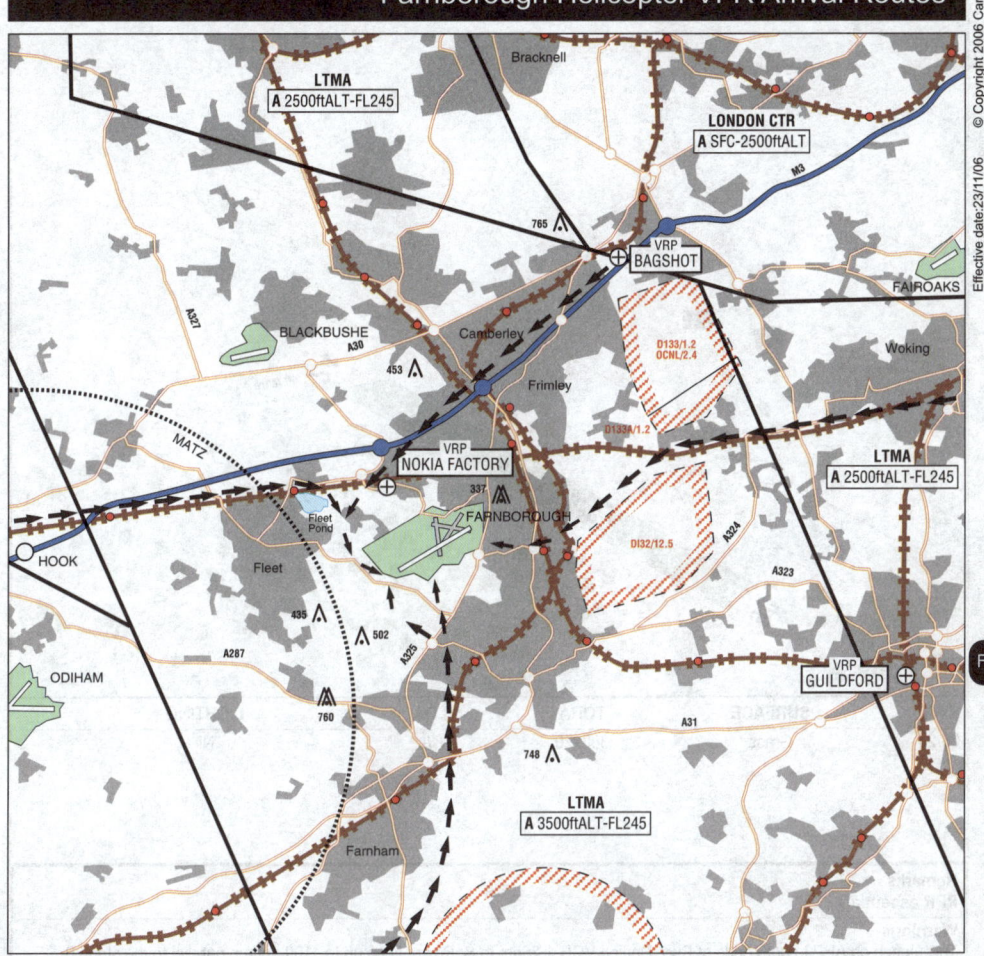

F

253

420ft 14mb	4nm S of Gillingham N5119.83 E00036.07	PPR	Alternative AD	Southend Rochester

Non-radio	APP Rochester 122.250	Safetycom 135.475

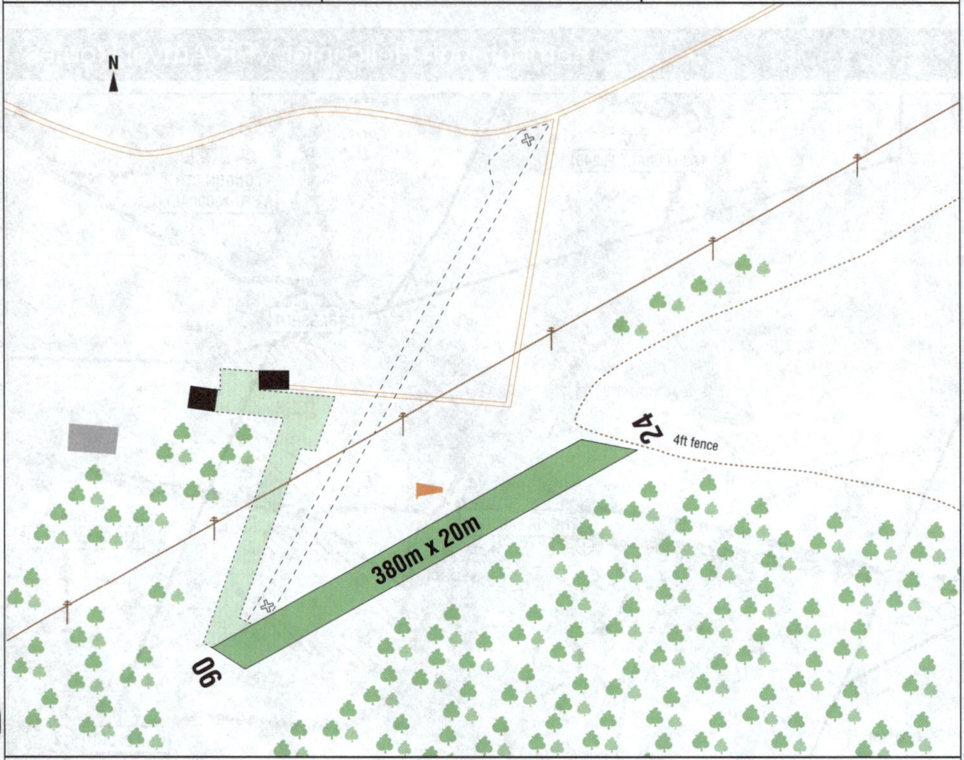

N

4ft fence

24

380m x 20m

06

RWY	SURFACE	TORA	LDA	LIGHTING
06/24	Grass	380x20	U/L	Nil

Remarks
PPR essential.

Warnings
Turbulence on APP to both ends of Rwy. Detling VOR 1.25nm to S. Power lines up to 110ft agl run parallel to the strip 80-100m NW of strip. GND in the immediate undershoot area of Rwy06 falls away steeply.

Noise: Avoid over flying farmhouse 400 yards to E of Rwy. Final APP Rwy24 to be made between farmhouse and Thr.

Operating Hrs	PPR	**Operator**	SBC
Circuits	24 LH, 06 RH		Stoneacre Farm
Landing Fee	£2 (£50 without PPR)		Matts Hill Road, Hartlip
Maintenance	Nil		Sittingbourne, Kent ME97XA
Fuel	Nil		**Tel:** 01634 264011

Disabled Facilities

Restaurants	Nil
Taxis/Car Hire	Nil
Weather Info	AirSE MOEx

771ft 25mb	4nm NE of Sidmouth N5044.15 W00311.46	PPR	Alternative AD Diversion AD	Exeter Dunkeswell

Farway Radio	LARS Exeter 128.975	A/G 119.425

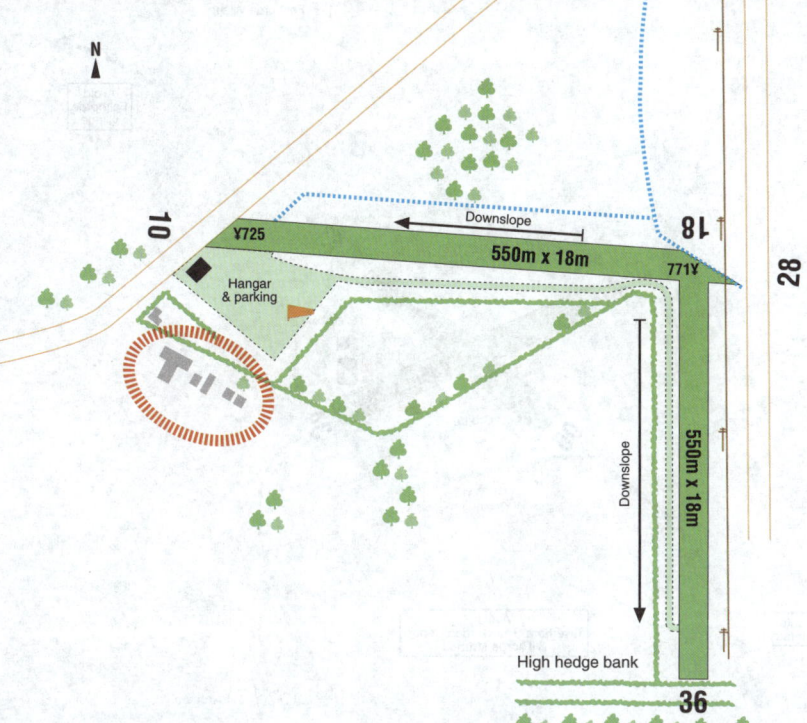

RWY	SURFACE	TORA	LDA	LIGHTING
10/28	Grass	550x18	U/L	Nil
18/36	Grass	550x18	U/L	Nil

Remarks

PPR. Contact Exeter LARS on arr & dept. There is an annual fly-in associated with Devon PFA Strut which is well worth a visit. See aviation press for details and Devon PFA Strut website.

Warnings

Sheep may be grazing. There are numerous hazards (mostly minor) relating to most Rwys which should be considered. Please study the AD diagram closely.
Noise: Avoid local habitation, particularly area SW of AD

Operating Hrs	SR-SS	**Operator**	Terry Case
Circuits	800ft QFE		Moorlands Farm
Landing Fee	Nil		Sidbury, Sidmouth
Maintenance	Nil		Devon, EX10 0QW
Fuel	Nil		**Tel/Fax:** 01395 597535
Disabled Facilities			**Tel:** 07779 538991
			Tel: 07772 532901
			twnc@onetel.net
			www.farwaycommon.com

Restaurants/Accommodation	Numerous local hotels & B&B
Taxis/Car Hire	Locally by arr
Weather Info	AirSW MOEx

F

120ft 4mb	4nm NW of Norwich Airport N5242.35 E00111.57	PPR	Alternative AD	Norwich Old Buckenham

Felthorpe	APP Norwich 119.350	A/G 123.500 (Not always manned)

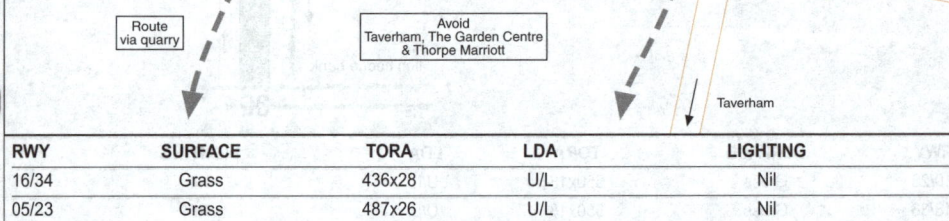

RWY	SURFACE	TORA	LDA	LIGHTING
16/34	Grass	436x28	U/L	Nil
05/23	Grass	487x26	U/L	Nil

Remarks
PPR by telephone. Visiting ACFT welcome at pilots own risk. Windsock and landing T displayed. Due to close proximity of Norwich AD all ACFT call Norwich APP. New 1.5m high fence across Rwy16 Thr. Club house open weekends.

Warnings
Trees at boundary may cause turbulence, even in light wind and also obscure view of ACFT in circuit when Dept. Space between Rwys cultivated, agricultural workers & machinery may be present. Busy public Rd on 2 sides of AD. New 1.5m high fence accross Rwy16 Thr.
Noise: Avoid over flying Felthorpe village to NE & Taverham to SSE, also Taverham nursery between AD & village.

Operating Hrs	SR-SS	**Weather Info**	AirS MOEx
Circuits	05 16 RH, 23 34 LH, 500ft QFE Over head joins 1000ft QFE	**Operator**	Felthorpe Flying Group Ltd Kevin Day, The Field Cottage King Street, Neathshield Norfolk NR12 8BW **Tel:** 01603 867691 (AD) **Tel:** 01692 630942 (Secretary) **Tel:** 07900 162459 (Secretary) **Tel:** 01483 746500 (Secretary Office)
Landing Fee	Nil		
Maintenance	Nil		
Fuel	Nil		

Disabled Facilities

Restaurant	Norwich approx 15mins drive

Taxis

Olivers Travels	**Tel:** 01603 261010
HP Private Hire	**Tel:** 01603 897261

Car Hire

National	**Tel:** 01603 631912

F

6ft 0mb	6nm SE of Spalding N5244.37 W00001.80	PPR	Alternative AD Diversion AD	Cambridge Peterborough Conington

Fenland	A/G 122.925	AFIS 122.925 (weekends & by arr)

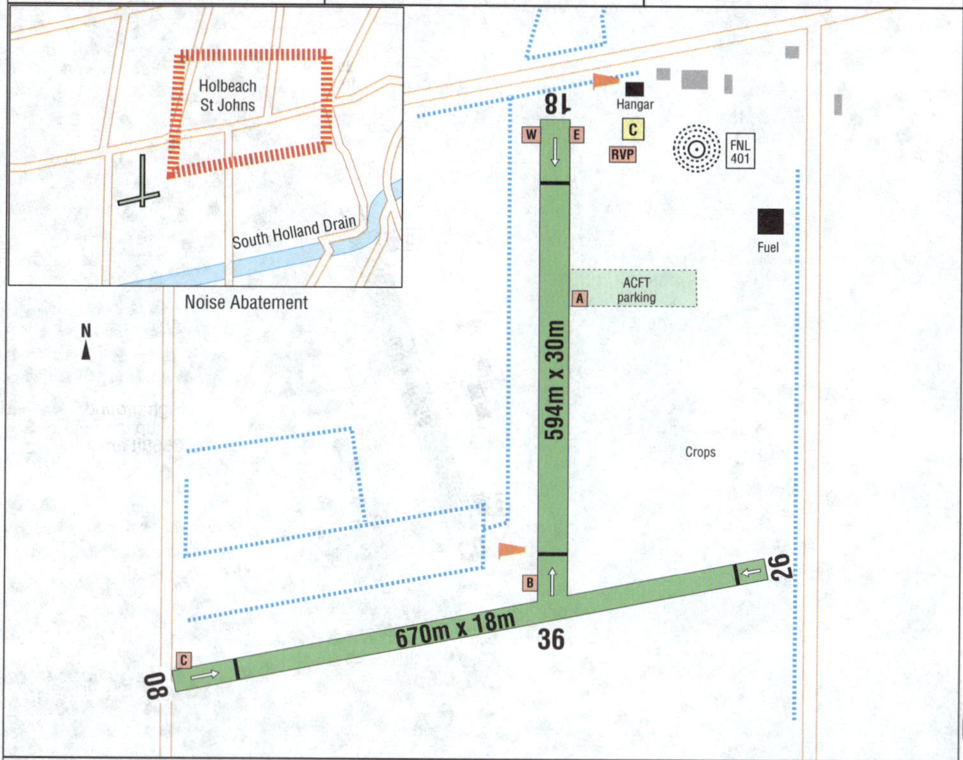

Holbeach
St Johns

South Holland Drain

Noise Abatement

N

18

Hangar

C

W   E

RVP

FNL
401

Fuel

A

ACFT
parking

Crops

B

670m x 18m

594m x 30m

36

26

08

C

RWY	SURFACE	TORA	LDA	LIGHTING
18	Grass	594	512	Thr Rwy LITAS 4.25°
36	Grass	594	591	Nil
08/26	Grass	670x18	U/L	Nil

Rwy18 lighting PPR

Remarks
PPR. AD not available for use by public transport passenger flights required to use a licensed AD. Certain customs facilities available.
Visual aid to location: Ibn FE Green

Warnings
AD is in a low flying military training area. All ACFT movements confined to marked grass strips and Rwy. Caution – Rwy08/26 may appear longer from the air than the actual usable length indicated on charts. Beware of drainage channels close to AD.
Noise: Rwy18 LH in use downwind is wide of the village to E of AD Do not fly between the village and AD, keep well wide to E.

Operating Hrs	Closed Monday Tue-Sun & PH 0900-SS (L) & by arr	
Circuits	08, 18 RH, 36, 26 LH, 1000ft QFE	
Landing Fee	Single £7.50 Twin £12.50 Micro £4	
Maintenance	Fenland AeroServices Ltd (Tue-Sun)	
Fuel	AVGAS JET A1 100LL available during operating Hrs	

Disabled Facilities

Restaurant
Fully licensed restaurant open Tue-Sun

Taxis	Phoenix Taxi Ser. **Tel:** 01406 22807
Car Hire	4 Star **Tel:** 01406 370882
Weather Info	AirS MOEx
Operator	Fenland Aero Club Ltd Fenland Aerodrome Jekylls Bank Holbeach St Johns Lincolnshire, PE128RQ **Tel:** 01406 540330 (Clubhouse/ATC) **Tel:** 01945 540461 (Flying School) www.fenlandairfield.co.uk

F

860ft 28mb	1.5nm SE of Loch Insh N5706.00 W00353.08	PPR	Alternative AD	Inverness Perth

	Feshiebridge	A/G 130.100 (Glider freq)	

River Feshie

N

80' Tree

21

900m x 8m

03

High ground up to 3668ft amsl

F

RWY	SURFACE	TORA	LDA	LIGHTING
03/21	Grass	900x8	U/L	Nil

Rwy21 slight upslope in last 25%

Remarks
PPR by telephone. Primarily a gliding field with both winch and aerotow. Powered ACFT welcome. AD situated in stunning countryside but due consideration should be given for mountain weather and turbulence. Parking by the control caravan parked at appropriate landing Thr. Pilots are welcome to camp on AD.

Warnings
Caution turning off strip: Rwy smooth but lower than surrounding land with varying 'kerb effect' up to approx. 15cm (6"). There is an 80ft tree on centre line approx. 250m Rwy21 Thr, also low fence crosses 25m away from Rwy21 APP Thr. Give priority to gliders, they may block the Rwy for short periods during launch and retrieval. Information is passed by control on glider common freq. Make normal circuit calls on this freq. High GND up to 3668ft immediately to E and heavily wooded areas close to E & SE.

Operating Hrs	SR-SS	**Taxis**	**Tel:** 01479 810118
Circuits	21 RH, 03 LH	**Car Hire**	
	Gliders use L & R circuit on both Rwys	Budget	**Tel:** 01463 713333
Landing Fee	£10 inc day membership to club	**Weather Info**	AirSc GWC
Maintenance	Nil	**Operator**	Cairngorm Gliding Club
Fuel	Nil		Miss J Williamson
Disabled Facilities	Nil		Balnespick, Kincraig
			Kingussie, Inverness
Restaurant	Tea & coffee available at control TWR		**Tel:** 01540 651246 (Landowner)
	Aviemore Tourist Board		**Tel:** 01540 651317 (AD)
	Tel: 01479 810363		**Tel:** 07770 454593
	(for restaurants/accommodation etc)		

FETLAR

270ft 9mb	1nm NW of Houbie Isle of Fetlar N6036.23 W00052.33	PPR	Alternative AD	Scatsta Unst

Non-radio	APP Sumburgh 131.300	Safetycom 135.475

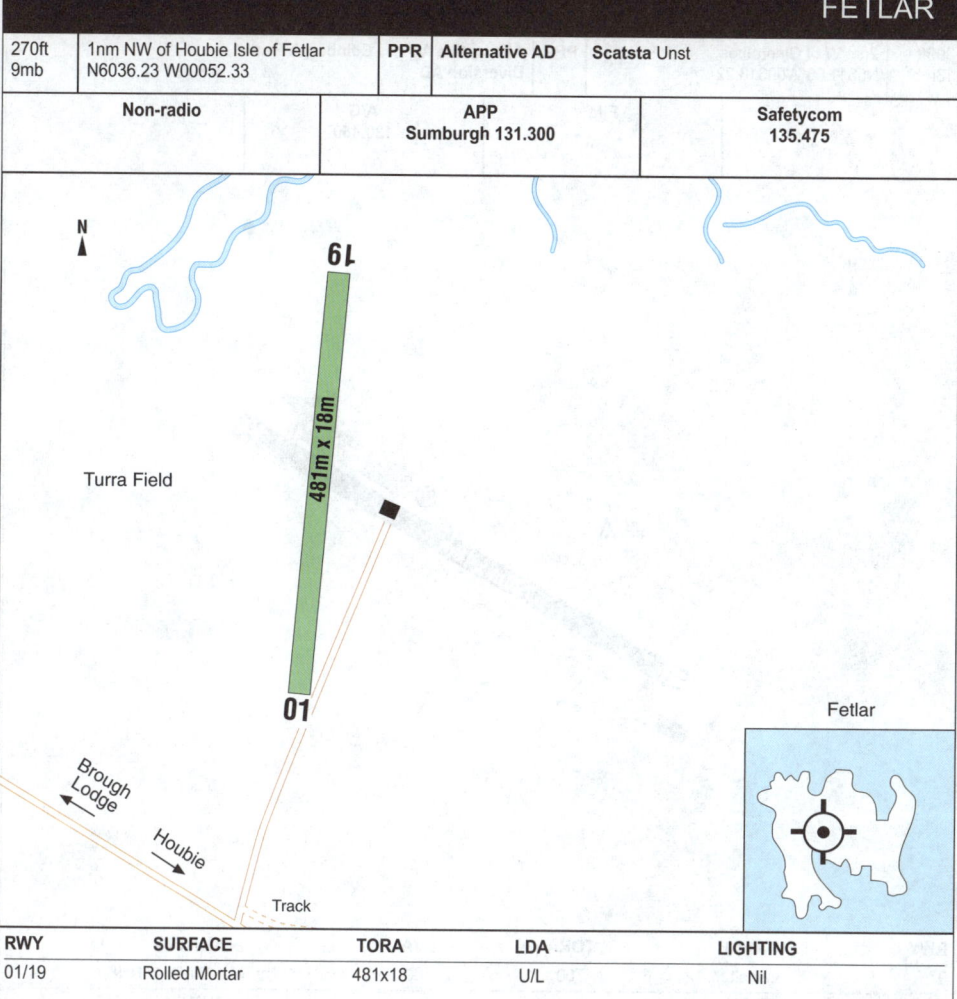

F

RWY	SURFACE	TORA	LDA	LIGHTING
01/19	Rolled Mortar	481x18	U/L	Nil

Remarks

PPR by telephone. AD is available for visiting ACFT. We strongly advise that visitors also contact Loganair to establish the operating times of their services. As there is extremely limited off Rwy parking, your ACFT could obstruct the Rwy for essential services (see warnings). A windsock is provided with PPR. There is no fire cover on AD.

Warnings

Although the Rwy has no gradient the surface is rough and could cause prop-strike to nose wheel ACFT with little prop clearance. Parking off-Rwy should only be attempted with extreme care, after first investigating on foot. The highest point on the Island (Vord Hill 522ft amsl) is 1.5nm out close to left of Rwy19 APP. The AD is on common land and sheep may stray onto the Rwy at any at any time. Moss growth may affect braking action.

Operating Hrs	SR-SS	**Taxis/Car Hire**	Nil
Circuits	1000ft QFE		Mr Leaper can provide transport by arr
Landing Fee	Nil	**Weather Info**	AirSC GWC
Maintenance	Nil	**Operator**	Fetlar Development Group
Fuel	Nil		Fetlar Aerodrome
Disabled Facilities Nil			Shetland, ZE2 9DJ
Restaurants/Accomodation			**Tel:** 01957 733267 (Mr R Leaper)
B&B	**Tel:** 01957 733227 (Mrs L Boxall)		**Tel:** 01595 840246 (Loganair)
	Tel: 01957 733242 (P Kelly)		

399ft 13mb	2nm W of Glenrothes N5611.00 W00313.22	PPR	Alternative AD Diversion AD	Edinburgh Perth

	Fife		A/G 130.450	

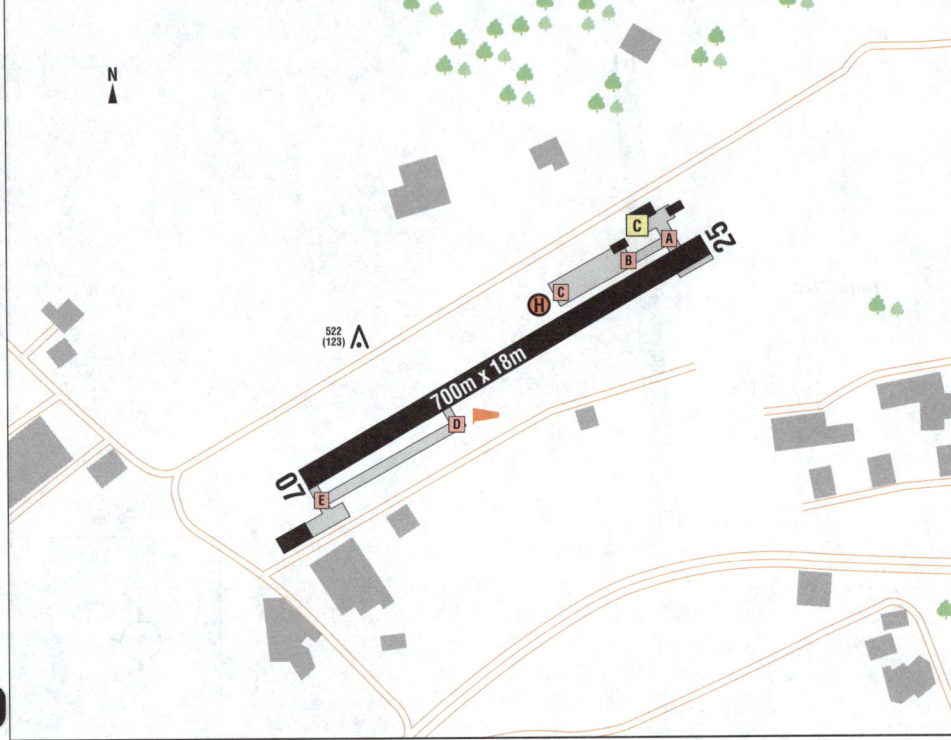

RWY	SURFACE	TORA	LDA	LIGHTING
07	Asphalt	700	700	Thr Rwy APAPI 4° RHS
25	Asphalt	700	700	Thr Rwy APAPI 4.25° LHS

Remarks
PPR. Pilots should avoid flying over the town of Glenrothes and are advised when taking off from Rwy07 to turn right on reaching 300ft aal.

Warnings
Caution: Road close to Rwy07 Thr
Noise: Avoid over flying Kinglasie SW of AD. When turning finals for Rwy25 at 300ft avoid all houses.

Operating Hrs	Mon-Sat 0700-2100 Sun 0830-2030 (L)	Weather Info	AirSC GWC
Circuits	25 LH, 07 RH	Operator	Tayside Aviation Ltd
Landing fees	Single £8 Twin £16 Commercial Twin £32 Light Commercial Twin £16 £5 voucher issued per landing, redeemable in Tipsy Nipper on day of landing Hangarage available on request		Fife (Glenrothes) Airport Fife, KY6 2SL **Tel:** 01592 753792 **Fax:** 01592 612812 enquiries@taysideaviation.co.uk www.taysideaviation.co.uk
Maintenance	Nil		
Fuel	AVGAS 100LL		
Disabled Facilities	Available		
Restaurant	Tipsy Nipper fully licensed restaurant refreshments & club facilities		
Taxis/Car Hire	By arrangement on arrival		

F

405ft 14mb	2.5nm WSW of Buckingham N5159.13 W00103.36	PPR	Alternative AD Diversion AD	Cranfield Turweston

	Non Radio		Safetycom 135.475	

RWY	SURFACE	TORA	LDA	LIGHTING
10/28	Asphalt	701x46	U/L	Nil
10/28	Grass	600x30	U/L	Nil

Remarks
PPR by telephone. Visiting light ACFT welcome at pilot's own risk.

Warnings
Power cables to S and W of Rwy. Barbed wire and netting fence along S of Rwy. Surface best at E end of Rwy. One low level circuit should be made prior to landing in order to permit lorries and model ACFT to clear the Rwy. Do not over-fly the market which is held adjacent to the AD on Sundays.
Noise: Do not over fly villages of Tingewick and Finmere.

Operating Hrs	Available on request	**Weather Info**	AirCen MOEx
Circuits	28 LH, 10 RH	**Operator**	Colin Thomas
Landing Fee	Nil		
Maintenance	Nil		
Fuel	Nil		
Disabled Facilities	Nil		

Restaurants
Royal Oak **Tel:** 01280 848373 (Tingewick)

Taxis
A.K.Cars **Tel:** 01280 817338
Buckingham Taxis **Tel:** 01280 812038
Car Hire
Bucks Self Drive **Tel:** 01280 822493

5ft 0mb	3nm NE of Doncaster Sheffield AD N5330.71 W00056.27	PPR	Alternative AD	Humberside Sandtoft

Non-Radio	LARS Humberside 119.125	APP Doncaster Sheffield 126.225	TWR Doncaster Sheffield 128.775	Safetycom 135.475

F

Wroot

N

20

1200m x 30m

02

Hangar

ACFT parking

Ninescores Farm

RWY	SURFACE	TORA	LDA	LIGHTING
02/20	Grass	1200x30	U/L	Available on request

Remarks
PPR by telephone. No Microlights. Visiting ACFT welcome at pilots own risk. Rwy is flat and well maintained with no APP hazards. Windsock displayed.

Warnings
Drainage ditch close to Rwy20 Thr. Sandtoft ATZ NE of AD. Occasional military low flying activity takes place in the vicinity of the AD (mainly weekdays).
Noise: Avoid over flight of village of W root NE of AD.

Operating Hrs	SR-SS		**Operator**	Philip Hopkins & Sons
Circuits	LH 1000ft QFE			Ninescores Farm
Landing Fee	Nil			Finningley, Yorkshire, DN9 3DY
Maintenance	Nil			**Tel:** 01302 770274
Fuel	Nil			**Tel:** 07836 659322
Disabled Facilities	Nil			**Fax:** 01302 772800
Restaurants	Bawtry or Epworth			
Taxi				
Axholme Hire	**Tel:** 01427 871486			
Taxi & Mini Cab Co	**Tel:** 01427 533335			
Car Hire	Nil			
Weather Info	AirN MWC			

FISHBURN

377ft 12mb	2.5nm NNW of Sedgefield N5441.30 W00127.85	PPR	Alternative AD	Durham Tees Valley Peterlee

Fishburn	APP Durham 118.850	A/G 118.275

N

Crops

800m x 30m

26

08

Crops

Fishburn

F

RWY	SURFACE	TORA	LDA	LIGHTING
08/26	Grass	600x30	U/L	Nil

Rwy26 1.6% upslope

Remarks
PPR by telephone. Situated N of the Teesside CTR. Helicopters accepted.

Warnings
Join circuit from N only. Crops grown right up to Rwy edge.
Noise: Avoid over flying local habitation.

Operating Hrs	Mon-Sat 0800-2030 Sun 0930-2030 (L) (Last take-off 2000)
Circuits	08 LH, 26 RH, 800ft QFE
Landing Fee	Single £3 Twin £5 Cheques £1 surcharge
Maintenance	In emergency
Fuel	AVGAS 100LL Cheques £1 surcharge

Disabled Facilities

Restaurants
Snacks & hot drinks available in clubhouse

Taxis	
Ron's	**Tel:** 01740 621862
Turners	**Tel:** 01740 620338
Car Hire	
Turners	**Tel:** 01742 620338
Weather Info	AirN MWC
Operator	Beryl Morgan Airfield Cottage West House Farm Bishop Middleham Durham, DL17 9DY **Tel/Fax:** 0191 3770137 (Airfield) **Tel:** 0191 3778430 (Home) **Tel:** 07785 786716

150ft 5mb	Nr Hametown Isle of Foula N6007.33 W00203.12	PPR	Alternative AD	Lerwick Scatsta

Non-radio	APP Sumburgh 131.300	Safetycom 135.475

18

454m x 15m

Downslope

36

Hametoun

N

RWY	SURFACE	TORA	LDA	LIGHTING
18/36	Gravel	454x18	U/L	Nil

45m over run at S end

Remarks
PPR contact Airstrip Trust. Visiting ACFT accepted. All visitors must contact Directflight to check details of their services.There is no off-Rwy parking so visiting ACFT will constitute an obstruction to vital local services.

Warnings
AD is extremely hump backed giving rise to possible optical illusion on APP and roll-out. The paved surface is rough and could cause prop-strike to nose wheel ACFT with little prop clearance. The AD is prone to severe turbulence, particularly in cross winds. There are soft sections of the paved surface at the Rwy midpoint on either side of the centre line, ACFT should avoid turning here to prevent surface damage. High GND 0.5nm W of AD (814ft amsl) & 1.5nm NW (1373ft amsl). AD is on common land and sheep may stray onto strip at any time. High risk of bird strike in summer. Moss may effect braking. No windsock.
Important: ACFT parked on strip restrict scheduled & ambulance services –consult with Directflight.

		Operator	Mrs Isobel Holbourn
Operating Hrs	SR-SS		Foula Airstrip Trust
Circuits	1000ft QFE		**Tel:** 01595 753233 (Airstrip Trust)
Landing Fee	£30 per landing		**Tel:** 01957 753235 (Fire Service)
Maintenance	Nil		**Tel:** 01595 840246 (Directflight)
Fuel	Nil		
Disabled Facilities			
Restaurants	Nil		
Taxis/Car Hire	Nil		
Weather Info	AirSC GWC		

EGMA

17ft 4mb	7.5nm SSW of Cambridge N5204.65 E00003.70	PPR	Alternative AD Diversion AD	Cambridge Duxford

Fowlmere	APP Essex RAD 120.625	AFIS Duxford 122.075	A/G 135.700

704m x 30m

25

07

B

C

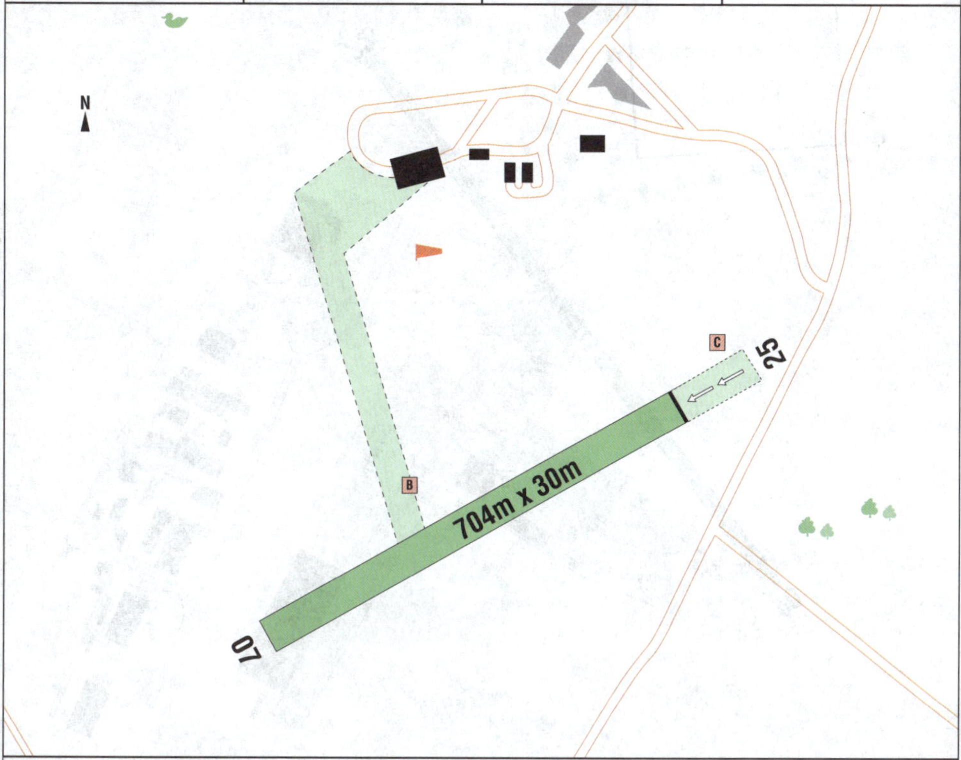

RWY	SURFACE	TORA	LDA	LIGHTING
07/25	Grass	704x30	U/L	Nil

Rwy25 150m of unmarked Rwy is available at E end for take-offs
Rwy07 150m of unmarked Rwy is available for landings & take-offs

Remarks
PPR strictly by telephone for briefing. Fowlmere is close to Duxford AD, 2.5nm WSW. Contact Duxford info prior to joining for Wy25 or dept Rwy07. Join via Royston Rwy25: follow railway NE between Melbourn & Meldrith keep N of bird sanctuary, turn right base between Fowlmere & Thirplow. Rwy07: Royston direct to long final.

Warnings
Back tracking is necessary for entry/exit on Rwy07/25. Pilots should not take-off or land while this is in progress. ACFT holding at the marked holding points will be clear of the Rwy and strips.
Noise: Strict compliance with noise abatement. Avoid making a low APP Rwy25 due public Rd, flying over Fowlmere village & built up areas in the vicinity. Bird reserve 700m NW of AD.

Operating Hrs	Tue-Fri & PH 0800-1200, Sat-Sun 0800-1200 (Summer) +1Hr (Winter)	**Taxis** Meltax	**Tel:** 01763 244444
Circuits	07 LH, 25 RH, 800ft QFE No overhead joins	**Car Hire** Kirkham Cars Ford	**Tel:** 01763 261116 **Tel:** 01763 242084
Landing Fee	Single £10 Twin £15	**Weather Info**	AirS MOEx
Maintenance	Modern Air	**Operator**	Modern Air (UK) Ltd
Fuel	AVGAS 100LL by arr		Fowlmere Aerodrome Royston, Herts, SG8 7SJ **Tel:** 01763 208281 (AD) **Tel:** 01223 833376 (Duxford ATC) **Fax:** 01763 208861

Disabled Facilities

Restaurants
Sheen Mill   **Tel:** 01763 261393 (Melbourne)
The Chequers **Tel:** 01763 208369 (Fowlmere)

86ft 3mb	7nm E of York N5358.83 W00051.88	PPR	Alternative AD Diversion AD	Humberside Sherburn in Elmet

	Full Sutton		A/G 132.325	

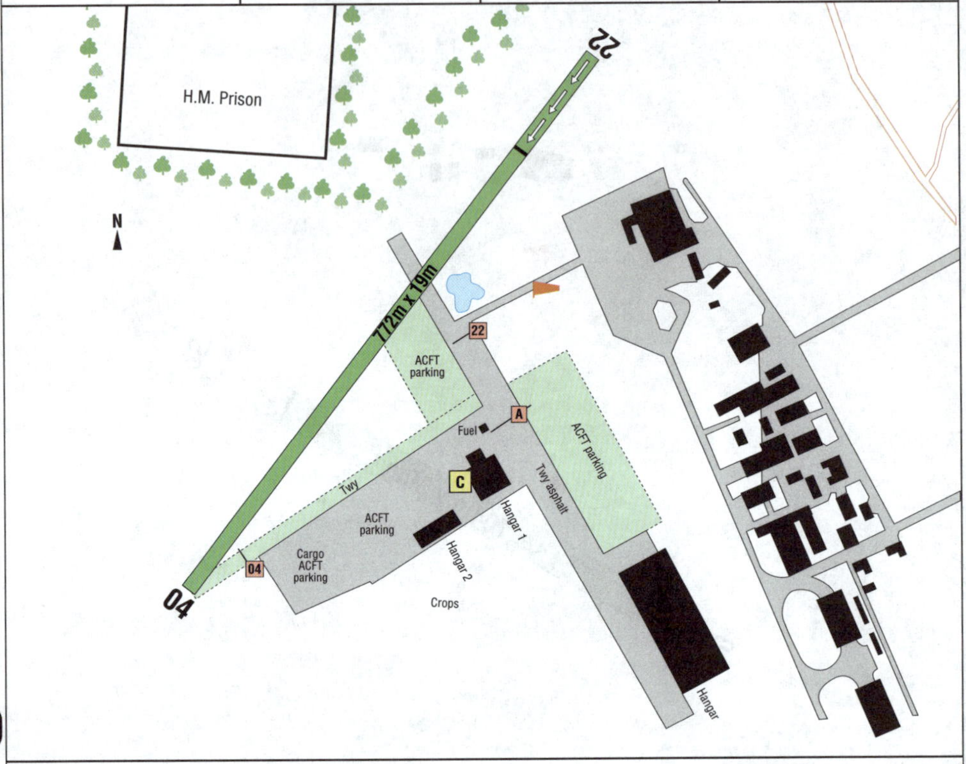

H.M. Prison

N

772m x 19m

22

ACFT parking

Fuel

A

C

ACFT parking

Twy

ACFT parking

Twy asphalt

Hangar 1

Cargo ACFT parking

Hangar 2

Crops

04

Hangar

F

RWY	SURFACE	TORA	LDA	LIGHTING
04	Grass	772	772	Nil
22	Grass	772	715	Nil

Displaced Thr Rwy22 79m

Remarks
PPR. Non–radio ACFT not accepted. Radio use is mandatory. AD not available to Public Transport flights which require a licensed AD.
Visual aid to location: 4 large grain silos E of AD.

Warnings
AD is within Restricted Area R315 (applies to helicopters only). Do not land short of displaced Thr. Intensive gliding at Pocklington, 4nm SE of AD. High GND up to 807ft amsl 4nm E of AD.When wind >240° windshear my be experienced Rwy22 Thr.
Noise: Do not over fly the prison on N side of AD under any circumstances. Dept Rwy22, fly over pig farm on climb out.

Operating Hrs Tue-Fri 0800-1800 Sat-Sun 0900-SS (Summer) Tue-Fri 0900-1700 Sat-Sun 0900-SS (Winter)	**Taxis** Hessles's Cabs	**Tel:** 01759 303176
Circuits 04 LH, 22 RH, 800ft QFE	**Car Hire** Avis National	**Tel:** 01904 610460 **Tel:** 01904 612141
Landing Fee Single £5, Twin £10	**Weather Info**	AirN MWC
Maintenance RH Aviation **Tel:** 01759 372849 **Fuel** AVGAS 100LL available by arr	**Operator**	Full Sutton Flying Centre Ltd Full Sutton Airfield Stamford Bridge York, YO4 1HS **Tel:** 01759 372717 **Tel:** 01759 373277 (Club) **Fax:** 01759 372991

Disabled Facilities

Restaurants Tea & coffee in clubhouse

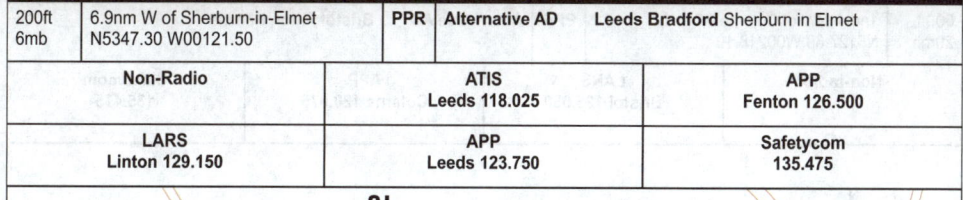

200ft 6mb	6.9nm W of Sherburn-in-Elmet N5347.30 W00121.50	PPR	**Alternative AD**	**Leeds Bradford** Sherburn in Elmet

Non-Radio	**ATIS** Leeds 118.025	**APP** Fenton 126.500
LARS Linton 129.150	**APP** Leeds 123.750	**Safetycom** 135.475

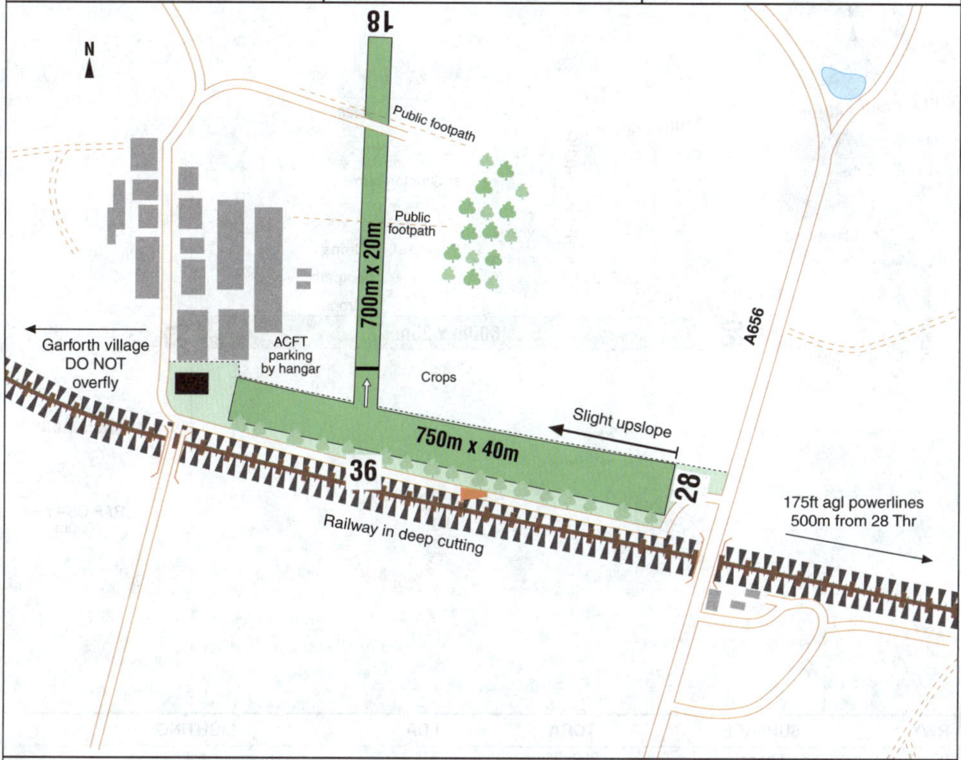

N

Public footpath

Public footpath

Garforth village DO NOT overfly

ACFT parking by hangar

Crops

700m x 20m

750m x 40m

Slight upslope

36

18

28

A656

Railway in deep cutting

175ft agl powerlines 500m from 28 Thr

G

RWY	SURFACE	TORA	TODA	LIGHTING
28	Grass	750x40	U/L	Nil
18/36	Grass	700x20	U/L	Nil

Rwy36 banked on either side for first 350m
Displaced Thr Rwy36 200m

Remarks
PPR by telephone. Microlights not accepted. Visitors welcome at pilots own risk. Rwy S edge is slightly curved. Operator advises pilots keep to line of A1 to remain clear of Church Fenton MATZ then follow railway line in on Rwy28 APP.
Visual aid to location: Railway cutting and industrial buildings to the W.

Warnings
AD situated between Church Fenton MATZ (usually closed weekends), and Leeds CTR/CTA (H24).
Caution: National Grid pylons & transmission lines 175ft agl cross Rwy28 APP 500m from Thr. A656 crosses short final Rwy28. 2 public footpaths cross Rwy18/36.
Noise: Do not over fly Garforth village close to W.

Operating Hrs	SR-SS	**Taxi**	
Circuits	28 36 RH, 18 LH	Garforth Cars	**Tel:** 0113 2872866
Landing Fee	Advised with PPR	D+D Services	**Tel:** 0113 2860114
Maintenance	Nil	**Car Hire**	
Fuel	AVGAS 100LL	Central Self Drive	**Tel:** 01977 603280
		L C H Leeds	**Tel:** 01132 468989 (Free delivery to AD)
Disabled Facilities		**Weather Info**	AirN MWC
		Operator	Chris Makin Sturton Grange, Garforth, Leeds LS25 2HB
Restaurants	The Swan, Aberford (3nm from AD) The Hilton Hotel, Garforth		**Tel:** 0113 2862631 **Fax:** 0113 2873747

600ft 20mb	1nm NNW of Colerne AD N5127.60 W00218.10	PPR	Alternative AD	Bristol Filton Kemble

Non-radio	LARS Bristol 125.650	APP Colerne 120.075	Safetycom 135.475

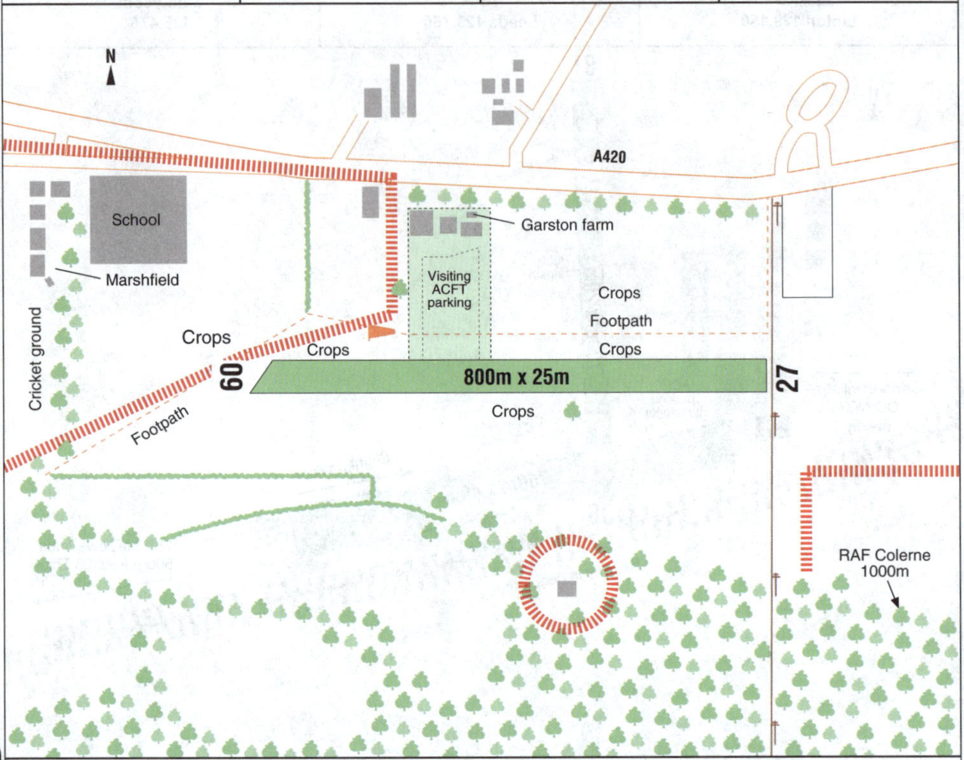

N

A420

School

Marshfield

Garston farm

Visiting ACFT parking

Crops

Footpath

Cricket ground

Crops

Crops

Crops

60

800m x 25m

27

Crops

Crops

Footpath

RAF Colerne 1000m

G

RWY	SURFACE	TORA	LDA	LIGHTING
09/27	Grass	850x25	U/L	Nil

Remarks
PPR by telephone. Visitors welcome at pilots own risk. Well maintained flat strip. NS Twy should never be used for arr or dept.

Warnings
AD situated within the Colerne ATZ. Arr ACFT must contact Colerne APP. Dept must call before take-off if no reply after 3 calls proceed with caution. Wires APP Rwy27 Thr from N & S but are underground 50m either side of the Thr. Wooded area to S of Rwy may cause turbulence at low levels. NO right turns Rwy27 Dept (due school). Right of way crosses Rwy09 Thr and Twy.
Noise: Do not over fly the school or Marshfield below 1500ft agl W of AD. Make glide app if possible and offset
Rwy09 APP by 30° to S to avoid Marshfield.
Rwy27 Dept turn left 30° ASAP to avoid village.
Rwy09 Depts climb ahead through 1400ft QNH before north to vacate Colerne ATZ.

Operating Hrs	SR-SS	**Weather Info**	AirSW MOEx
Circuits	N 1000ft QFE Downwind Rwy09 extended to avoid village	**Operator**	Mr M Ball Garston Farm, Marshfield Chippenham, Wilts, SN14 8LH
Landing Fee	Advised with PPR		**Tel:** 07901 755312
Maintenance	Nil		**Tel:** 01225 891284
Fuel	Nil		www.garstonfarm.flyer.co.uk

Disabled Facilities

Restaurants	3 pubs in village
Taxis	**Tel:** 01225 892005 **Tel:** 07968 899321
Car Hire	Nil

39ft 1mb	6.5nm NW of Withernsea N5347.40 W00005.16	PPR	Alternative AD	Humberside Beverley

Garton	LARS Humberside 119.125	A/G 122.075 Available on request

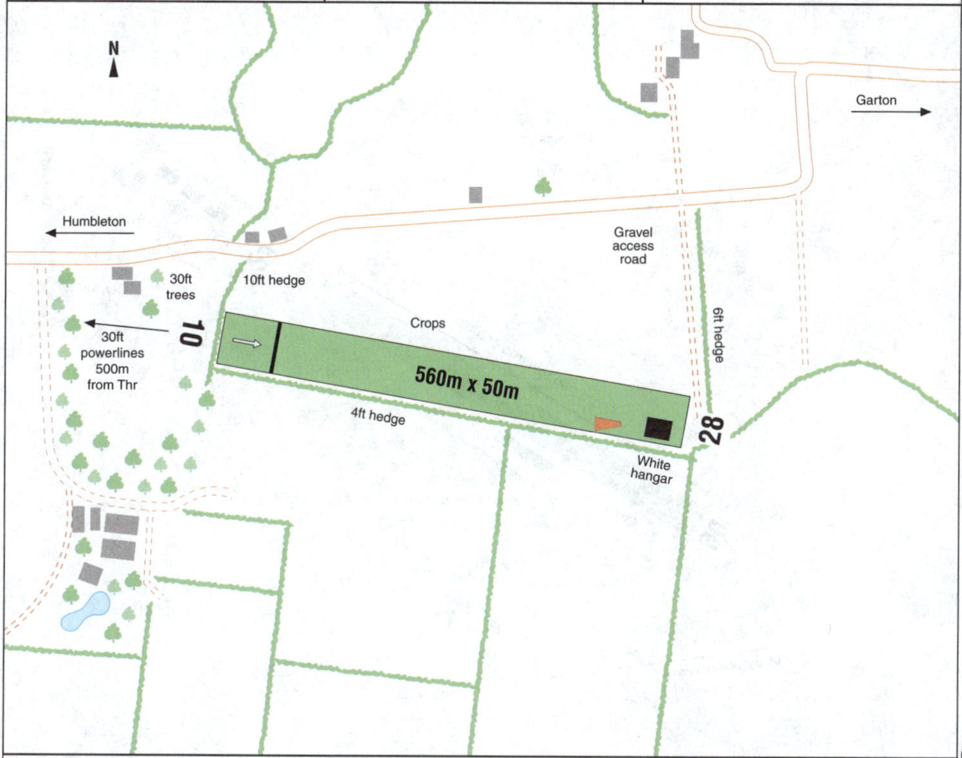

N↑

Garton →

← Humbleton

30ft trees

10ft hedge

Crops

Gravel access road

6ft hedge

10

30ft powerlines 500m from Thr

560m x 50m

4ft hedge

28

White hangar

RWY	SURFACE	TORA	LDA	LIGHTING
10	Grass	470x50	U/L	Nil
28	Grass	560x50	U/L	Nil

Remarks
PPR by telephone essential when a briefing will be provided. Visiting ACFT welcome at pilots own risk.
Visual aid to location: White hangar at E end of strip.

Warnings
D306 Cowden 2nm N. Closed for ACFT activity has 2nm exclusion zone due to unexploded ordnance. Crops to N edge of Rwy and low hedge runs along Rwy S edge
Caution: 10ft hedge and trees on W AD boundary. 30ft agl power lines cross Rwy10 APP 500m from Thr.
Noise: Avoid over flying local farms & houses.

Operating Hrs	SR-SS
Circuits	10 RH, 28 LH, 1000ft QFE
Landing Fee	Nil
Maintenance	Nil
Fuel	Nil

Disabled Facilities

Restaurant	Nil
Taxi/Car Hire	Nil
Weather Info	AirN MWC

Operator	Mr G Bantin c/o B&K Universal Ltd Grimston, Aldborough Hull, Yorkshire, HU11 4QE **Tel:** 01964 527555 **Fax:** 01964 527006 info@bku.com

G

GERPINS FARM

90ft 3mb	1nm S of Upminster N5131.80 E00014.78	PPR	Alternative AD	Southend Stapleford

Non-Radio	APP Thames 132.700	Safetycom 135.475

N

40ft trees

Dungraftin

T-type hangars
ACFT road crossing (residents)

Gerpins Farm

Crops

Slight rise towards centre

400m x 20m

ACFT parking

06

Crops

Xmas trees up to 12ft

40ft agl powerlines

9

RWY	SURFACE	TORA	LDA	LIGHTING
06/24	Surface	400x20	U/L	Nil

Remarks
PPR by telephone. Visiting ACFT welcome at pilots own risk. AD situated on reclaimed land and old gravel workings close to M25. Residents hangars and operators house across the lane from AD.

Warnings
AD close to edge of London City CTR (class D). Controlling authority is Thames RAD. Also under the London TMA (class A). Base 2500ft QNH. Long grass grown for Hay may be present up to Rwy edge. AD slightly convex in configuration.
Caution: AD is NOT Damyns Hall which is approx 700m to the ENE.
Noise: Avoid farm and buildings to NE of Rwy06 Thr.

Operating Hrs	SR-SS	**Operator**	Mr Derek Izod
Circuits	06 LH, 24 RH		Dungraftin
Landing Fee	Nil		Gerpins Lane
Maintenance	Nil		Upminster, RM14 2XR
Fuel	Nil		**Tel:** 01708 250315
Disabled Facilities Nil			izodair@supanet.com
Restaurants	Huntsman & Hounds or The Optimist within 20 mins walk		
Taxis Windmill	**Tel:** 01708 455444		
Car Hire	Nil		
Weather Info	AirSE MOEx		

46ft 2mb	1.5nm S of Village N5539.20 W00545.47	**PPR**	**Alternative AD** **Diversion AD**	**Prestwick** Campbeltown

Non-radio	**FIS** **Scottish 127.275**	**Safetycom** **135.475**

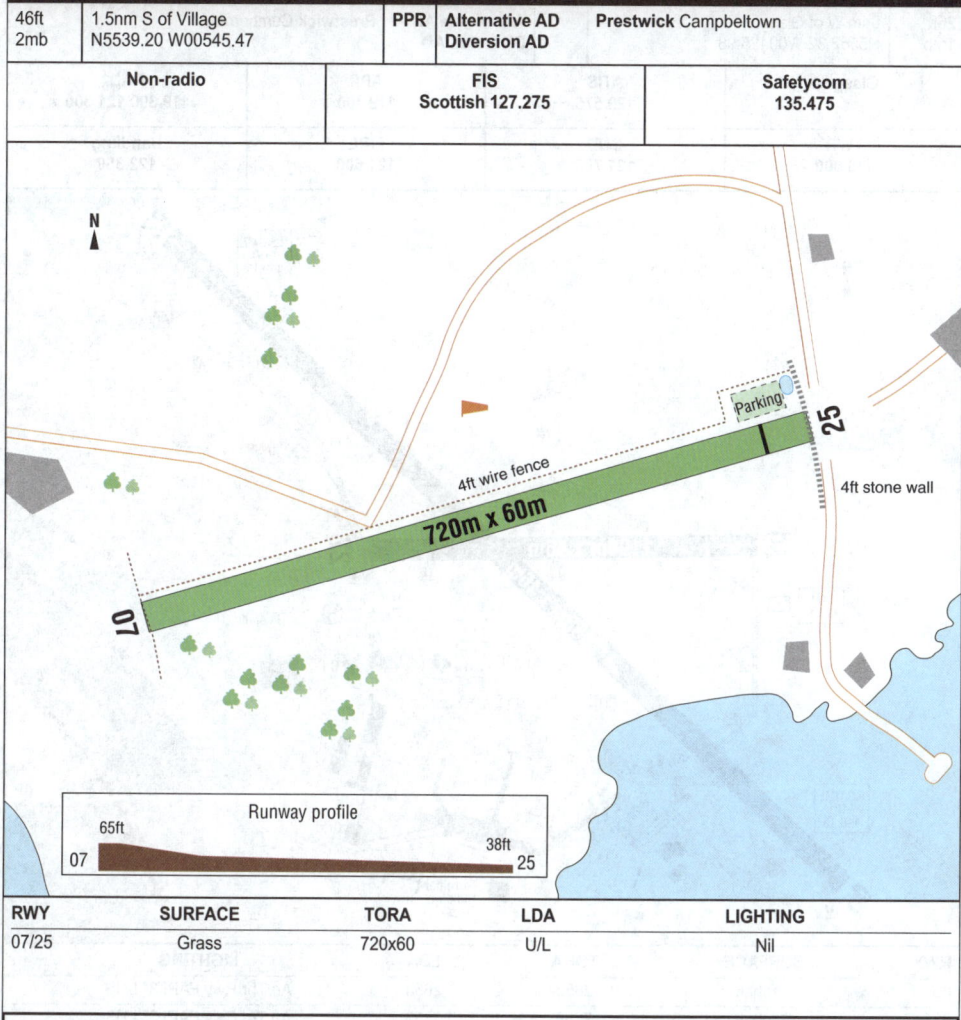

Runway profile

RWY	SURFACE	TORA	LDA	LIGHTING
07/25	Grass	720x60	U/L	Nil

Remarks
PPR by telephone. Visiting ACFT welcome. Tie-downs available N side of Rwy25 Thr. Guests of the Gigha Hotel (1.5m N) can be provided with transport to and from the hotel.

Warnings
Rwy has marked step down at Rwy07 Thr. See profile diagram. Shallow dyke on N side of apron. Access Twy is clearly visible as the grass is cut. Use mown entrance to apron only. The un-mown areas are bad ground containing rocks.
Noise: Avoid over flying the village on Sundays between 1200-1300 (L).

Operating Hrs	SR-SS	**Operator**	Holt Leisure Parks Ltd Achamore House Isle of Gigha Argyll, PA41 7AD **Tel:** 01583 505254 **Fax:** 01583 505244 www.isle-of-gigha.co.uk
Circuits	Nil		
Landing Fee	Single £15 Twin £25 £5 discount if staying overnight at Gigha Hotel		
Maintenance	Nil		
Fuel	MOGAS by arr		
Disabled Facilities	Nil		
Restaurants Gigha Hotel	**Tel:** 01583 505254 (Same as PPR)		
Taxis/Bike Hire Gigha Hotel A & V Oliver	**Tel:** 01583 505254 **Tel:** 01583 505251		
Weather Info	AirSc GWC		

271

26ft 1mb	6nm W of Glasgow N5552.32 W00425.98		Alternative AD Diversion AD	Prestwick Cumbernauld
Glasgow	**ATIS** 129.575		**APP** 119.100	**RAD** 119.300 121.300
TWR 118.800	**GND** 121.700		**FIRE** 121.600	**Handling** 122.350

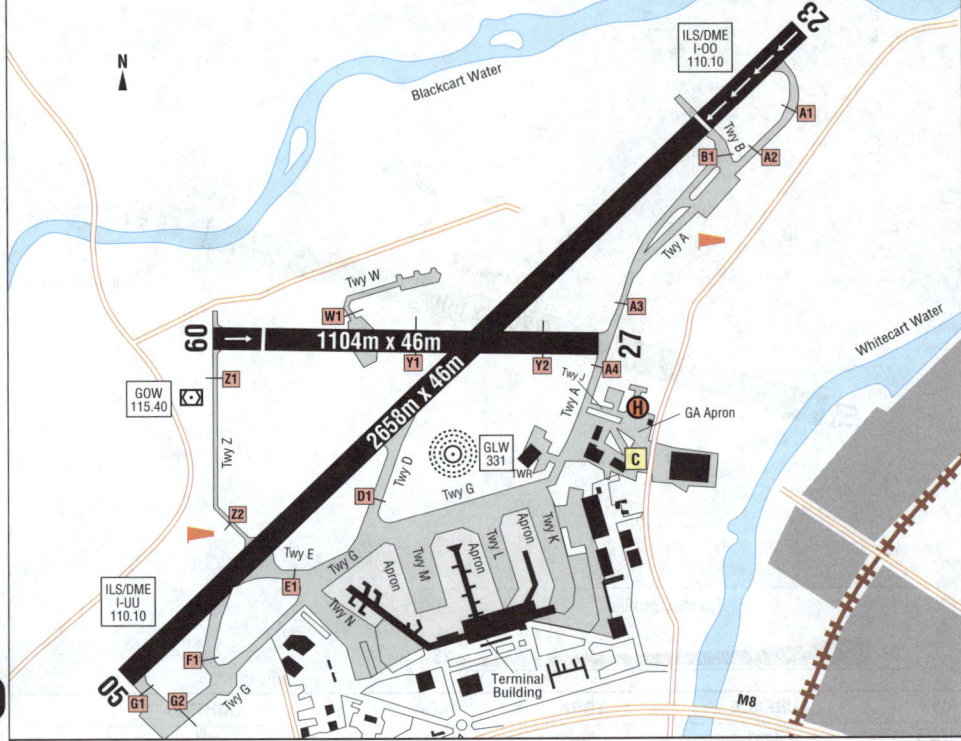

RWY	SURFACE	TORA	LDA	LIGHTING
05	Asphalt	2658	2658	Ap Thr Rwy PAPI 3° LHS
23	Asphalt	2658	2353	Ap Thr Rwy PAPI 3° LHS
09	Asphalt	1104	1042	Thr Rwy PAPI 3° LHS
27	Asphalt	1104	1104	Thr Rwy PAPI 3° LHS

Remarks
Use governed by Scottish CTR regulations. Filing a flight plan does not constitute permission to use Glasgow AD. All pleasure, training & non-business GA traffic subject to prior notification to ATC. Operators must make prior arr with handling agent for GND handling all flights. Use of AD for training purposes is subject to Operations Directors permission, Glasgow AD Ltd ATC. Visiting GA ACFT including international Arr will be parked on GA Park Stand 35. Pilots of international Arr and Dept GA ACFT are responsible for presenting their passengers to Customs and Immigration. Transport to and from the Customs Office will be provided by a Handling Agent.

Warnings
No GND signals except light signals. Large Whooper swans up to 12kgs are present around the AD from Sept-April. Flocks of up to 100 birds may fly at heights up to 500ft. The main flying activity of the swans is usually confined to short periods around dawn and dusk and ATC will endeavour to advise their presence when airborne. Hang Gliding takes place within the Glasgow CTR up to 2500ft amsl (occasionally 3000ft with ATC permission) and sites are considered active during all daylight Hrs. Pilots inbound to or outbound from the AD must operate ACFT so as to cause the least disturbance practicable to the areas in and around the AD.

Operating Hrs	H24 All flights subject to approval	**Disabled Facilities** Available	
		Handling	**Tel:** 0141 887 8348 (Signature)
Circuits	Nil	**Restaurant**	Restaurant buffet & bars in Terminal
Landing Fee	BAA rates	**Taxis**	Available at Terminal
Maintenance	Avail	**Car Hire**	
Fuel	AVGAS JET A1 100LL arr by mandatory handling agent	Avis	**Tel:** 0141 887 2261
		Hertz	**Tel:** 0141 887 2541

G

Weather Info	M T9 T18 Fax 286 A VSc GWC ATIS **Tel:** 0141 877 7449	**Operator**	Glasgow Airport Ltd Paisley, Strathclyde, PA3 2ST **Tel:** 0141 887 1111 (AD) **Tel:** 0141 840 8000 (NATS) **Tel:** 0141 840 8029 (ATC) **Tel:** 0141887 9319 (AIS) **Fax:** 0141 848 4354 (AD)

HELICOPTER OPERATIONS
Helicopters are not to move out of the alighting and parking area with out obtaining taxi instructions from ATC. Glasgow-based helicopters will park on the old Loganair Twy. Visiting helicopters will normally be allocated a stand on the W apron (Stands 31-34). Helicopters, inbound and outbound, are to avoid over flying AD buildings whenever possible. Inbound helis (other than large) will be routed to the helicopter app point – Rwy27 Thr. CASEVAC helicopters will be directed by ATC to alight on the main apron Twy, then to GND taxi to an ACFT stand.

USE OF RWYS
Rwy09/27 may be used at night by ACFT up to ATP size but only when the cross wind component on Rwy05/23 is greater than that specified in the ACFT's operations data manual. A Rwy lighting system including PAPI set at 5.25° can be made available at thirty minutes notice. Rwy09/27 is not available when low visibility procedures are in force.

GND MOVEMENT CONTROL
GMC is responsible for:
The surface movement of all ACFT on the Manoeuvring area excluding the Rwy in use.
Passing Air Traffic Control clearances to ACFT.
Passing parking instructions to all ACFT. All ACFT making requests for taxiing or towing clearance on the GND freq should state their location in the initial call.

CTR-CLASS D AIRSPACE
Normal CTA/CTR Class D Airspace rules apply
Transition Alt 6000ft
1 These rules do not apply to non-radio ACFT by day provided they have obtained permission and maintain 5km visibility 1500m horizontally and 1000ft vertically away from cloud.
2 SVFR clearances may be given that are not confined to Entry/Exit lanes.
3 When operating on a SVFR clearance, pilots must remain clear of cloud insight of the surface and remain in flight conditions that will ensure theycan determine their flight path and remain clear of obstacles.
4 Due to the nature of the terrain, a RAD service will not normally be provided to ACFT on a SVFR clearance.
5 SVFR clearance only applies to the CTR.
6 Entry/Exit lanes are established to permit ACFT to operate to and from Glasgow in IMC, but not under IFR these are a) Clyde lane b) Alexandria lane c) Barrhead E Kilbride Lane. All these lanes are 3nms wide and use of the lanes is subject to ATC clearance and radio contact with Glasgow App. ACFT must remain clear of cloud and in sight of the surface not above 2000ft. Minimum visibility is 3km.ACFT must keep the lane centre-line on the left, unless other wise instructed.

G

Visual Reference Points (VRP)

VRP	VOR/VOR	VOR/NDB	VOR/DME
Alexandria N5559.33 W00434.58	GOW 333°/TRN 015°	TRN 015°/GLW 331°	GOW 333°/8nm/TRN 015°/41nm
Ardmore Point N5558.28 W00441.95	GOW 311°/TRN 009°	TRN 009°/GLW 309°	GOW 311°/10nm
Baillieston N5551.17 W00405.37	TLA 316°/GOW 100°	TLA 316°/GLW 100°	GOW 100°/12nm
Barrhead N5548.00 W00423.50	TRN 030°/TLA 302°	TRN 030°/GLW 166°	GOW 162°/5nm/TRN 030°/32nm
Bishopton N5554.13 W00430.10	GOW 321°/TUR 020°	TRN 020°/GLW 315°	GOW 321°/3nm
Dumbarton N5556.67 W00434.10	GOW 322°/TRN 016°	TRN 016°/GLW 320°	GOW 322°/6nm/TRN 016°/39nm
East Kilbride N5545.83 W00410.33	TRN 043°/TLA 305°	TRN 043°/GLW 131°	GOW 130°/11nm
Erskine Bridge N5555.22 W00427.77	GOW 354°/TRN 022°	TRN 022°/GLW 347°	GOW 354°/3nm
Greenock N5556.83 W00445.08	GOW 299°/TRN 007°	TRN 007°/GLW 299°	GOW 299°/11nm
Inverkip Power Stn N5553.90 W00453.20	GOW 282°/TRN 360°	TRN 360°/GLW 282°	GOW 282°/15nm
Kilmacolm N5553.67 W00437.65	TRN 014°/GOW 288°	TRN 014°/GLW 288°	GOW 288°/6nm/TRN 014°/35nm
Kilmarnock N5536.75 W00429.90	GOW 192°/TRN 034°	GOW 192°/NGY 342°	GOW 192°/16nm
Kingston Bridge N5551.37 W00416.18	GOW 103°/TRN 033°	TRN 033°/GLW 103°	GOW 103°/6nm/TRN 033°/37nm

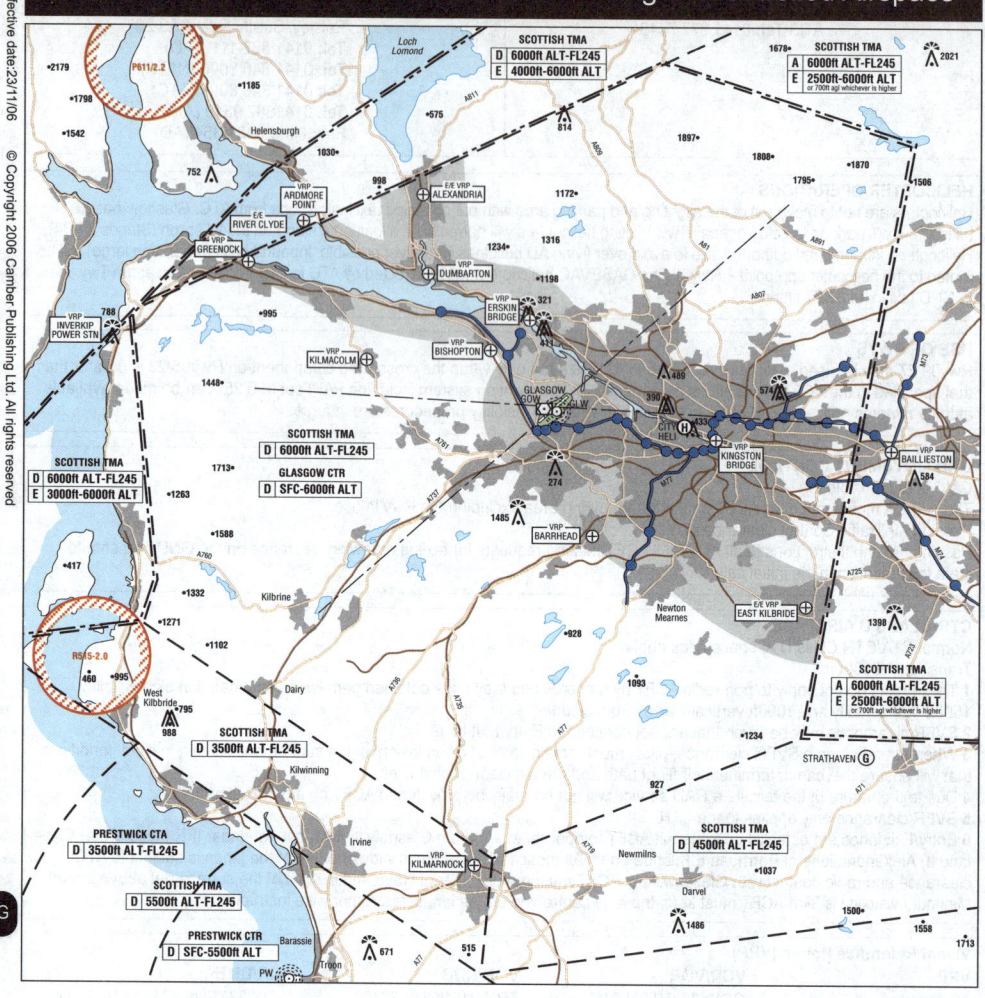

GLENFORSA

15ft 0mb	1nm E of Salen on Isle of Mull N5631.04 W00554.85	PPR	Alternative AD Diversion AD	Glasgow Tiree

Non-radio	FIS Scottish 127.275	Safetycom 135.475

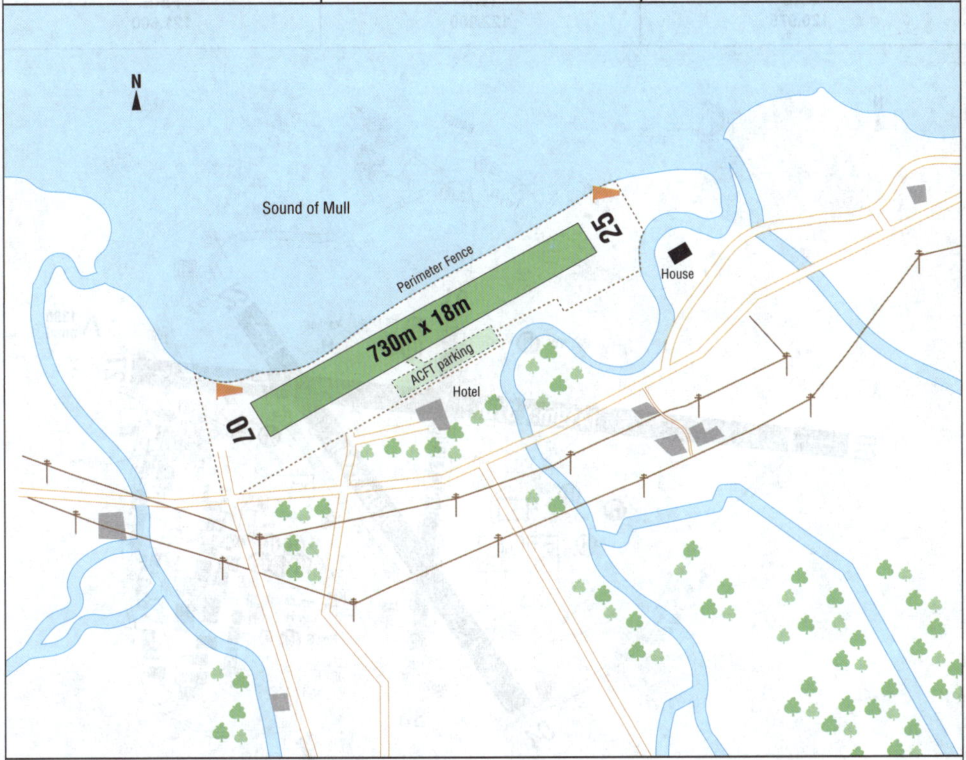

Sound of Mull

N

Perimeter Fence

730m x 18m

25

07

House

ACFT parking

Hotel

G

RWY	SURFACE	TORA	LDA	LIGHTING
07/25	Grass	730x18	U/L	Nil

Remarks
PPR essential 24Hrs notice. For advisory WX actuals and info on state of strip call AD. On rare occasions pilots are not met at the AD; please leave flight details at the adjacent cabin.

Warnings
Rwy07 requires a curved APP to keep clear of high GND to W. There is also high GND to the SE close to the AD. Sheep graze from Oct-Apr on the strip, removed at weekends. Keep a lookout for microlight activity at any time. Due to prolonged wet weather, permission to use AD may be suspended especially during the winter months.
Noise: Avoid over flying Glenforsa Hotel and village of Salen, also large new structure S of Rwy25 Thr

Operating Hrs	By arr	**Taxis**	
Circuits	Over sea 800ft QFE	R Atkinson	Tel: 01680 300441
Landing Fee	Private Single £12.20, Twin £18	**Car Hire**	
	Microlight £9.10	Mull Car Hire	Tel: 01680 300402
	Commercial £7.60 per half tonne		Tel: 07799 744908
Maintenance	Nil	**Weather Info**	AirSc GWC
Fuel	Oban from Paul Keegan	**Operator**	Argyll and Bute Council
	Tel: 01631 710384		Mr D S Howitt
	Tel: 07770 620988		Aerodrome Bungalow, Glenforsa
			Isle of Mull, Argyll, PA72 6JN
Disabled Facilities			Tel: 01680 300402 (D S Howitt)
			Tel: 07799 744908 (D S Howitt)

Restaurants
Glenforsa Hotel **Tel:** 01680 300377
Salen Hotel **Tel:** 01680 300324

EGBJ

GLOUCESTERSHIRE

101ft 3mb	3.5nm W of Cheltenham N5153.65 W00210.03		**Alternative AD**	**Bristol Filton** Kemble	
Gloucester		**ATIS** 127.475		**APP** 128.550	
RAD 120.975		**TWR** 122.900		**FIRE** 121.600	

RWY	SURFACE	TORA	LDA	LIGHTING
04	Asphalt	988	988	APAPI 4.5° LHS
22	Asphalt	988	900	APAPI 3.5° LHS
09	Asphalt	1271	1153	Thr Rwy PAPI 3° LHS
27	Asphalt	1317	997	Ap Thr Rwy PAPI 3.5° LHS
18/36	Asphalt	800	800	Nil
04/22	Grass	–	U/L	Nil

Remarks
PPR at all times for instrument training. Non-radio ACFT not accepted. Hi-vis. Permission to use AD outside scheduled Hrs to be obtained from ATC. APP will only provide FIS to ACFT within 10nm of AD, if traffic conditions permit. VFR ACFT outside this radius are requested not to call Gloucester. All pilots must book out at the Flight Briefing Unit via telephone.
Visual aid to location: Ibn Green Go.

Warnings
Twy C between Rwy09 & 04 Thr is edge-marked white reflective discs. Entry/exit curves to Rwys are marked by green reflective studs. Due to extensive standing water Rwy04/22 may not be usable after periods of heavy/prolonged rain. Use extreme caution when using Twy in maintenance area due vehicles & pedestrians. Caution: Bird hazzard, flocks of gulls may be encountered over AD at dawn /dusk.
Noise: Dept Rwy18 turn left 20°after passing upwind end of Rwy. Dept Rwy27 turn right 10° on crossing upwind end of Rwy to avoid housing estate, a left turn can be made after passing 700ft QFE. Dept Rwy22 no left turns until after passing Chosen Hill. Avoid over flying all adjacent villages to AD.

Operating Hrs	Mon-Fri 0730-1830 Sat-Sun 0800-1830 (Summer) Mon-Fri 0830-1930 Sat-Sun 0900-1800 (Winter) & by arr	Circuits	04, 09, 18 LH, 22, 27, 36 RH Fixed wing >1000ft QFE Heli 750ft QFE max
		Landing Fee	£10 <750kg, £17.63 751-1500kg, £11.75 with 50L fuel <1500kg

| Maintenance | Available + hangarage |
| Fuel | AVGAS JET A1 100LL |

Disabled Facilities

Handling	Tel: 01452 856333
	ops@jet1.co.uk
Restaurants	Cafe & Club facilities at AD
Taxis/Car Hire	Available from Ops
National	**Tel:** 01452421133
Weather Info	M T9 Fax 288 A MOEx

Operator

Gloucestershire Airport Ltd
Gloucestershire Aerodrome
Cheltenham, Glos, GL516SR
Tel: 01452 857700 Ex 223 (ATC/Briefing)
Tel: 01452 857700 Ex 227 (Admin)
Fax: 01452 715174
briefing@gloucestershireairport.co.uk
(ATC)
www.gloucestershireairport.co.uk

Effective date:23/11/06

G

520ft 17mb	14nm SW of Barnstaple N5056.70 W00423.20	**PPR**	**Alternative AD**	**Exeter** Eaglescott

Non Radio	**LARS** Exeter 128.975	**Safetycom** 135.975

N

18

8ft hedge

Gorrel Farm

Twy

Upslope with undulations

420m x 20m

Pasture

Pasture

36

RWY	SURFACE	TORA	LDA	LIGHTING
18/36	Grass	420x20	U/L	Nil

Remarks

PPR by telephone essential. Experienced strip flyers welcome at own risk. AD is located on a working farm and sheep may graze the Rwy at any time.

Warnings

Rwy is undulating and has a marked Upslope from S to N. ACFT land uphill Rwy36, take-off Rwy18. S end may become waterlogged after prolonged rain. High GND up to 771ft amsl surrounds the AD.

Noise: Avoid over flying of local farms and fields containing livestock.

Operating Hrs	SR-SS daily	**Operator**	Mr Frank Cox
Circuits	LH 1500ft QNH		Gorrel Farm
Landing Fee	Nil		Woolfardisworthy
Maintenance	Nil		Bideford
Fuel	Nil		Devon
			EX39 5QZ
			Tel/Fax: 01237 431503

Disabled Facilities

Taxi/Car Hire	Sams **Tel:** 01237 471800
Weather Info	AIRSW MOEx

330ft 11mb	5nm SSE of Burton Upon Trent N5244.00 W00135.00	PPR	Alternative AD	Nottingham East Midlands Tatenhill

Non-Radio	ATIS East Mids 128.225	APP East Mids 134.175	Safetycom 135.475

N

12

Slight upslope

30ft powerlines

1m wire fence

489m x 13m

Silage field

30

1m wire fence

Bridle track

Hangar

30ft powerlines

RWY	SURFACE	TORA	LDA	LIGHTING
12/30	Grass	489x13	U/L	Nil

Remarks
PPR by telephone. Visiting ACFT welcome at pilots own risk. Ltd parking available. AD not usable Nov-Mar. Windsock displayed with PPR.

Warnings
AD beneath East Midlands CTA, (base 2500ft QNH, Class D). Fence 1m high runs along N side of Rwy and across Rwy30 Thr. Rwy surface good but may become waterlogged after prolonged wet weather. 30ft powerlines approach Rwy on S side but go underground to cross Rwy. There is a bridle track close to the Rwy30 Thr, caution horses and riders.
Noise: Avoid over flying all local villages and houses.

Operating Hrs	SR-SS		Operator	Mr G T Leedham
Circuits	S 1000ft QFE			The Pines
Landing Fee	Nil			Grangewood
Fuel	Nil			Netherseal
Disabled Facilities	Nil			Derbyshire
Restaurants	Nil			DE12 8BE
Taxis/Car Hire	Nil			**Tel:** 01283 760309
Weather Info	AirCen MWC			**Tel:** 07790 223005

G

GRAVELEY

300ft 10mb	3nm SE of Hitchin N5156.45 W00012.10		**PPR**	**Alternative AD**	**Luton** Cranfield

Non-Radio	**ATIS** Luton 120.575	**APP** Luton 129.550	**Safetycom** 135.475

RWY	SURFACE	TORA	LDA	LIGHTING
01/19	Grass	500x15m	U/L	Nil

Remarks

PPR by telephone. Primarily a microlight site, light ACFT welcome at pilots own risk. There is a 'pick your own' fruit farm adjacent to AD which is owned by the airfield operator. (Usually available Jun-Sept).

Warnings

AD situated within Luton CTR. Clearance to enter CTR must be obtained from Luton APP. Non-Radio ACFT both inbound and outbound should telephone Luton ATC before take-off.

Noise: Avoid low over flying of the houses to NW of AD and Graveley village to the S & SW. This is a very noise sensitive area.

Operating Hrs	SR-SS	**Operator**	Mr T Franklin
Circuits	Join from N or E into overhead Circuit to E 500ft QFE		Graveley Hall Farm Hitchin Herts, SG4 7LY
Landing Fee	Nil		**Tel:** 01438 317112
Maintenance	Nil		**Tel:** 01582 395029 (Luton ATC)
Fuel	Nil		
Disabled Facilities	Nil		
Restaurants	Tea shop at farm during fruit picking season		
Taxis	**Tel:** 01438 317777		
Car Hire	Nil		
Weather Info	AirS MOEx		

GREAT MASSINGHAM

295ft 10mb	10nm E of Kings Lynn N5246.73 E00040.35	**PPR**	**Alternative AD**	**Norwich** Old Buckenham

Non radio	**LARS** Marham 124.150	**Safetycom** 135.475

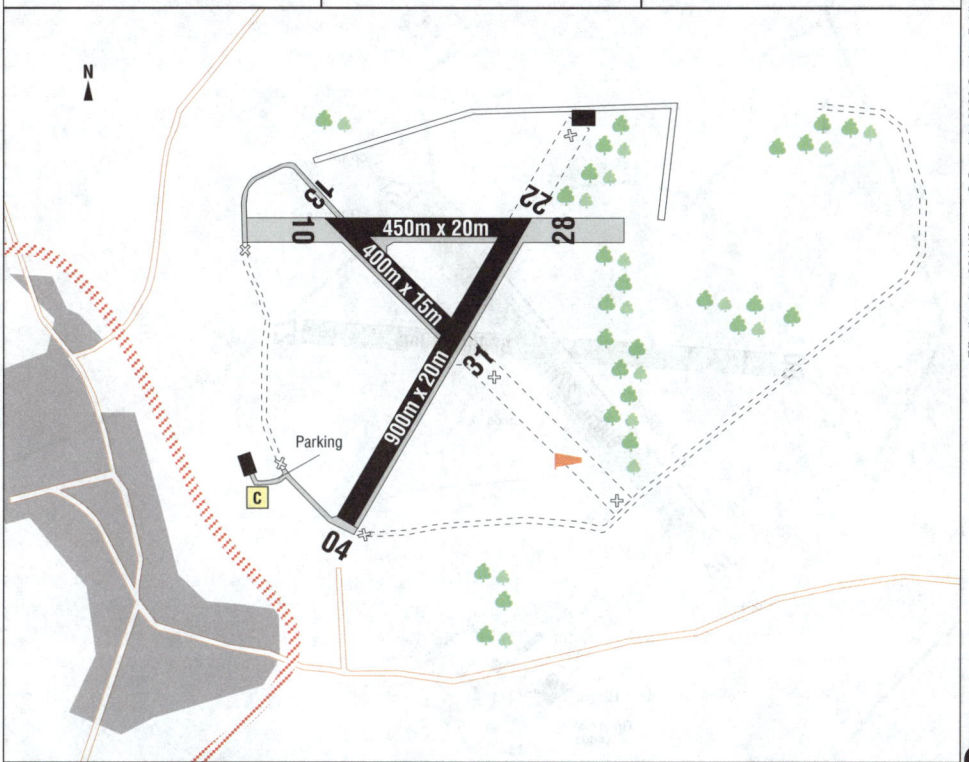

RWY	SURFACE	TORA	LDA	LIGHTING
04/22	Concrete	900x20	U/L	Nil
10/28	Concrete	450x20	U/L	Nil
13/31	Concrete	400x15	U/L	Nil

Remarks
PPR by telephone, non-radio ACFT not accepted. AD is unmanned. WW II AD. Radio contact with Marham essential (when open) due to proximity to Marham MATZ. No signals square. AD used by microlights, who may use short Rwy because of wind direction. ACFT parking next to hangar at SW corner of AD. Visiting pilots requested to complete movements book in control hut adjacent to hangar. No training flights permitted.

Warning
Agricultural operations may temporarily block Rwys.
Caution: pedestrians – perimeter track is a public footpath. ACFT using Rwy04/22 keep a good look out for microlights.
Noise: Avoid over flying Gt Massingham and other local villages. Dept Rwy22 turn left 20° to avoid houses.

Operating Hrs	SR-SS	**Operator**	Mr O C Brun
Circuits	04 RH, 22 LH		Leicester House
Landing Fee	Single £8, Twin £12		Great Massingham
	Overnight parking £4		Kings Lynn, Norfolk
Maintenance	Nil		PE32 2HB
Fuel	Nil		**Tel:** 01485 520257
Disabled Facilities	Nil		**Fax:** 01485 520234
Restaurants	Nil		
Taxis Silverlink	**Tel:** 01485 520938		
Car Hire	Nil		
Weather Info	AirS MOEx		

GREAT OAKLEY

60ft 2mb	3.5nm SW of Harwich N5154.00 E00110.30	PPR	Alternative AD	Southend Clacton

Non-Radio	LARS Southend 130.775	A/G 123.200

N

crops
15ft tree
crops
22
60
800m x 40m
27
Slight upslope
600m x 22m
crops
crops
04
crops
crops
ACFT parking
Hangar
Great Oakley Lodge

RWY	SURFACE	TORA	LDA	LIGHTING
04/22	Grass	600x22	U/L	Nil
09/27	Grass	850x40	U/L	Nil

Displaced Thr Rwy09 70m.
Displaced Thr Rwy27 70m

Remarks
PPR by telephone. Visiting ACFT welcome at pilots own risk. Course fishing available in 2 lakes, day tickets available. New clubhouse open.
Visual aid to location: Group of 3 small lakes SSE of AD.

Warnings
Crops grown up to strip edge. Tractor path crosses Rwy04 Thr. 15ft tree to S of Rwy22 Thr. Powerline 30ft agl crosses Rwy22 APP 350m from Rwy Thr.
Noise: Avoid over flight of local habitation, particularly Great Oakley village SSE of AD.

Operating Hrs	0830-2100 (L)	**Taxi** Harwich Taxis	**Tel**: 01255 551111
Circuits	22 27 RH, 04 09 LH, 1000ft QFE	**Car Hire**	Nil
Landing Fee	£5	**Weather Info**	AirS MOEx
Maintenance	Nil	**Operator**	Mr Tim Spurge
Fuel	Hangarage available on monthly basis AVGAS 100LL		Great Oakley Lodge Harwich, Essex, CO12 5AE **Tel**: 01255 880045 **Fax**: 01255 880244 **Tel**: 07770 880145 tim.spurge@btconnect.com www.greatoakleyairfield.co.uk
Disabled Facilities			

Restaurant	Tea & Coffee available on request Cold drinks in the clubhouse

588ft 19mb	4nm WSW of Holywell N5317.40 W00319.50	PPR	Alternative AD	Hawarden Caernarfon

Greenlands	A/G 129.825 (Microlight freq)	A/G 129.975 (Glider freq)	A/G Bryngwyn 118.325

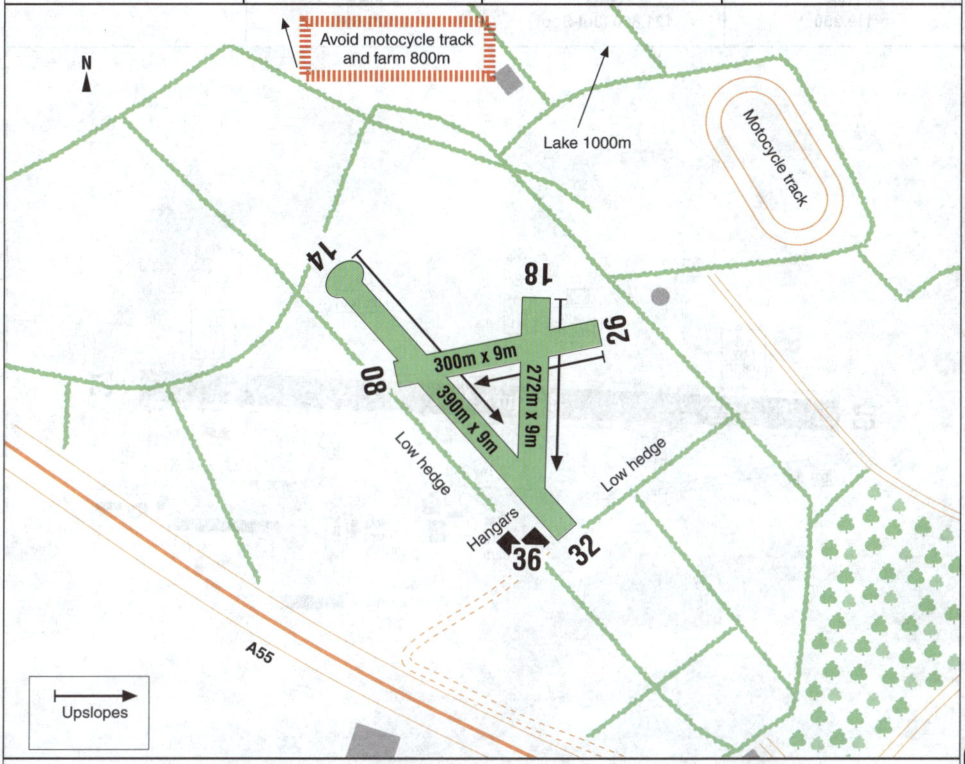
Avoid motocycle track and farm 800m
N
Lake 1000m
Motocycle track
14
18
26
08
300m x 9m
390m x 9m
272m x 9m
Low hedge
Low hedge
Hangars
36
32
A55
Upslopes

RWY	SURFACE	TORA	LDA	LIGHTING
14/32	Grass	390x9	U/L	Nil
08/26	Grass	300x9	U/L	Nil
18/36	Grass	272x9	U/L	Nil

Rwy14/26/18 upslope, Rwy14 Thr marked with red square

Remarks

PPR by telephone. Microlights operate from AD. Visiting ACFT welcome at pilots own risk. Windsock occasionally displayed on S AD boundary.

Visual aid to location: small lake to N and A55 dual carriageway to S.

Warnings

AD is convex, this may cause turbulence/roll-over on APP. Rwys become waterlogged during winter months and after heavy rain. Vintage military ACFT operate from strip to S of A55. Visitors are requested to call Bryngwyn to ascertain if strip is active.

Noise: Avoid over flying local habitation, particularly the Farmhouse & Motorcycle track 800m N of AD.

Operating Hrs	SR-SS
Circuits	Overhead join N 500ft QFE
Landing Fee	Nil
Maintenance	Nil
Fuel	MOGAS provided in cans by prior arr

Disabled Facilities

Restaurant/Accommodation

Travellers Inn **Tel:** 01352 720251 (200m from AD)

White House Hotel **Tel:** 01745 582155

Taxi/Car Hire	Nil
Weather Info	AirN MWC
Operator	Mr Richard Emlyn Jones Rhedyn Coch, Rhuallt St Asaph Denbighshire, LL17 0TT **Tel:** 01745 584051 **Tel:** 07880 733274

Effective date:23/11/06

G

336ft 11mb	2.5nm WSW of St Peter Port N4926.10 W00236.12	PPR	Alternative AD Diversion AD	Jersey Alderney

Guernsey	ATIS 109.40 (GUR VOR)	APP 128.650	RAD 118.900 124.500
TWR 119.950	GND 121.800 (Jul-Sep)	FIRE 121.600	

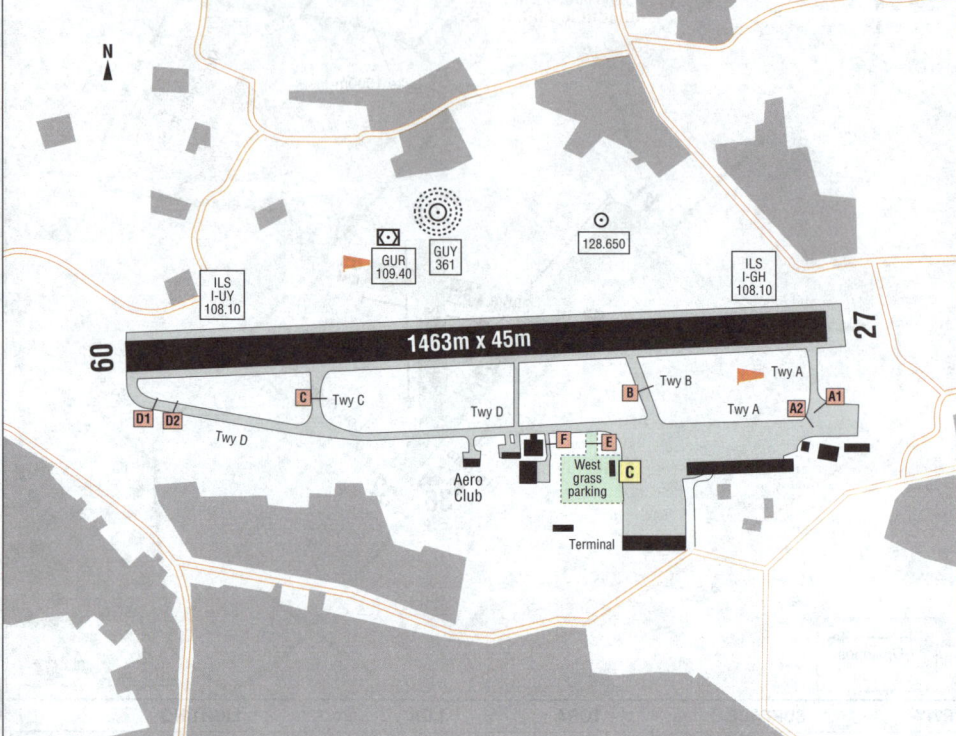

RWY	SURFACE	TORA	LDA	LIGHTING
09	Asphalt	1453	1453	Ap Thr Rwy PAPI 3° LHS
27	Asphalt	1463	1453	Ap Thr Rwy PAPI 3° LHS

Remarks

PPR. Hi-Vis. On Arr all GA pilots must report to the FBU for Special Branch and Customs Clearance. Use governed by regulations applicable to Channel Islands CTR. IMC flight to Guernsey by ACFT not equipped with VOR is by prior permission only. Model ACFT flying at Chouet Headland takes place up to 400ft amsl on any day of the year during daylight hours. All training must be booked in advance with ATC. Light ACFT grass parking to W of control TWR. Parking on hard apron PPR except schedule ACFT. Access to the terminal is via the public Rd or by arrangement with AD security. There is no access to the terminal from airside, access only via handling agents. All commercial flights and ACFT with MTOW >4 tonnes must use designated handling agent.

Warnings

Flight is not permitted at height less than 2000ft agl within 3nm of N4952.83 W00221.67 on Sark except with permission of States Guernsey Public Services Department. All ACFT are to avoid over flying the Princess Elizabeth hospital (2nm ENE of AD) at less than 1000ft agl. Light ACFT grass parking areas on W side of control TWR. All chocks and picketing blocks should be removed to edge of parking area after use. Down draught or turbulence may be experienced on APP to either Rwy in strong winds from any direction due to local terrains cliffs and valleys. Landing Rwy27 in strong SE-SW winds, buildings induce turbulence & windshear. All air crew & passengers must carry a means of identification to gain access airside. Due to coastal location birds are a hazard most of year, particularly during migration season. Firing at Fort le Marchant small arms range N4930.20 W00231.07, takes place seaward within 347-069°, radius 3000m. ACFT proceeding to and from stands 1, 2, A, B and the E apron must not cross Rwy27 holding point without clearance.

Noise: Rwy09/27 climb straight ahead thru 1500ft agl before turning on course. If on SVFR/VFR clearance not above 1000ft proceed to coast before turning on course. Rwy09/27 Arr join final APP not less than 500ft, maintain until intercepting glide path PAPI on directions.

Operating Hrs	0530-2000 (Summer) +1Hr (Winter) & by arr	**Weather Info**	M T9 Fax 292 A JER ATIS **Tel:** 01481 238957
Circuits	700ft QFE	**Operator**	States of Guernsey Airport Guernsey Channel Islands **Tel:** 01481 237766 **Tel:** 01481 237766 Ex 2130 (APC) **Tel:** 01481 237766 Ex 2131 (TWR) **Tel:** 01481 235791 (Fuel) **Fax:** 01481 239595 **Fax:** 01481 239440 (FBU) www.guernsey-airport.gov.gg
Landing Fee	Available on request		

Maintenance
ACFT Servicing **Tel:** 01481 265750 (Guernsey)
Fuel AVGAS JET A1 100LL
Purchasing fuel may result in reduced landing fees

Disabled Facilites

Restaurant	Buffet at Terminal
Taxis	
Taxi Rank	**Tel:** 01481 235283
Car Hire	
Harlequin	**Tel:** 01481 239511
Value Rent A Car	**Tel:** 01481 236344
Cycle Hire	
Rent-a-bike	**Tel:** 01481 249311
W Coast	**Tel:** 01481-253654

GUERNSEY CONTROL ZONE

Unless other wise authorised, a pilot who intends to fly in the Guernsey CTR must:
1 Contact Jersey Zone for entry into the Channel Islands Control Zone, giving details of the ACFT position, level and track.
2 Maintain a listening watch on the appropriate freq.
3 Comply with any instructions from ATC.
4 An ACFT shall not fly below 2000ft within 5nm of the AD, unless permission has been obtained.
5 SSR transponder equipment is mandatory within the Channel Islands Control Zone (Mode A).
6 In the event of radio failure the pilot should leave the Control Zone by maintaining track 225°T from overhead Guernsey Airport at 2000ft.
7 A VFR lane is established between GUR & ALD for traffic routing between the AD. The lane is 5nm either side of a line joining the AD, with a maximum alt of 2000ft, subject to ATC clearance.

Channel Island Visual Reference Points (VRP)

VRP	VOR/DME	VOR/DME	VOR/DME
Carteret Lighthouse N4922.00 W00148.00	JSY 051°/13nm	GUR 101°/32nm	
Casquets Lighthouse N4943.00 W00222.00	JSY 340°/32nm	GUR 032°/19nm	
Corbiere Lighthouse N4911.00 W00215.00	JSY 257°/8nm	GUR 141°/21nm	DIN 353°/36nm
Heauville N4934.60 W00148.06	JSY 026°/24nm	GUR 078°/33nm	
NE Point of Guernsey N4930.42 W00230.52	JSY 317°/25nm	GUR 045°/6nm	
NW corner of Jersey N4915.30 W00214.50	JSY 289°/8nm	GUR 131°/18nm	
Point de Rozel N4928.60 W00150.60	JSY 029°/18nm	GUR 088°/30nm	
St. Germain N4914.00 W00138.00	JSY 091°/16nm	GUR 111°/40nm	DIN 028°/43nm
SE Corner of Jersey N4910.00 W00202.00	JSY 176°/3nm	GUR 130°/28nm	DIN 007°/35nm
W of Cap de la Hague N4943.00 W00200.00	JSY 008°/30nm	GUR 058°/29nm	

See Channel Islands Transit Corridor – Jersey

G

370ft 12mb	3.5nm SE of Aylesbury N5147.55 W00044.27		PPR MIL	Alternative AD Diversion AD	Cranfield Wycombe
	Halton			A/G 130.425	

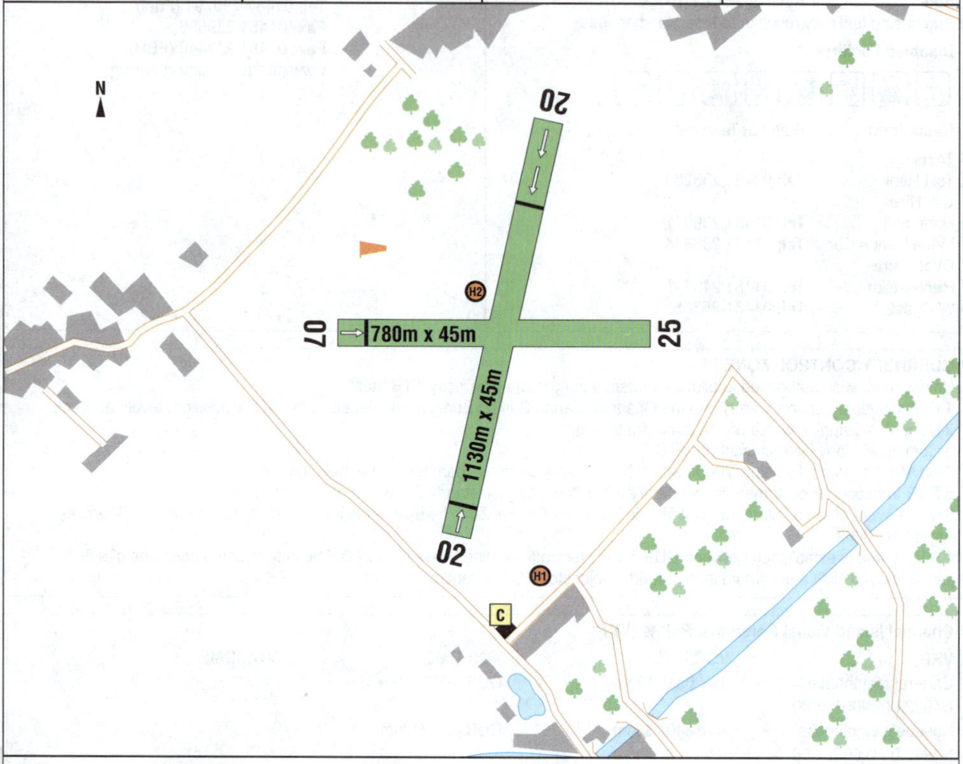

780m x 45m
1130m x 45m

N

07
25
20
02

H2
H1
C

RWY	SURFACE	TORA	LDA	LIGHTING
02	Grass	1130	1100	Nil
20	Grass	1130	840	Nil
07	Grass	780	780	Nil
25	Grass	780	780	Nil

Rwys have white sideline markers

Remarks
PPR 24Hrs notice required via RAF. Pilots of visiting ACFT are to obtain Arr procedure briefing by telephone before Dept. Inbound ACFT will be requested to route via VRPs.

Warnings
Intensive light ACFT and glider, tug, motor and winch. Cables up to 2000ft QFE. Mirror circuits with no dead side. Powered ACFT to NW and gliders to SE. Extensive soaring over ridge 5nm SE.
Noise: Dept routes for all Rwys.

Operating Hrs	Mon-Fri 0800-2000 Sat-Sun & PH 0900-2000 (L)	**Taxis/Car Hire**	Nil
		Weather Info	AirCen MOEx
Circuits	20, 26 RH, 02, 08 LH, 1000ft QFE	**Visual Reference Points (VRP)**	
Landing Fee	Charges in accordance with MOD policy Contact Station Ops for details	Lakes	2nm NE Rwy20/26
		Terrick	2nm SW min height 1500ft QFE
Maintenance	Nil	**Operator**	RAF Halton
Fuel	Nil		Aylesbury
Disabled Facilities			Bucks, HP22 5PG
			Tel: 01296 656367
			(PPR 0800-1700 Mon-Fri)

Restaurants Nil

H

645ft 21mb	12nm NW of Worcester N5217.98.W00228.22		PPR	Alternative AD	Birmingham Shobdon

Non Radio	APP Birmingham 118.050	LARS Brize 124.275	Safetycom 135.475

N

23

600m x 30m

C 05

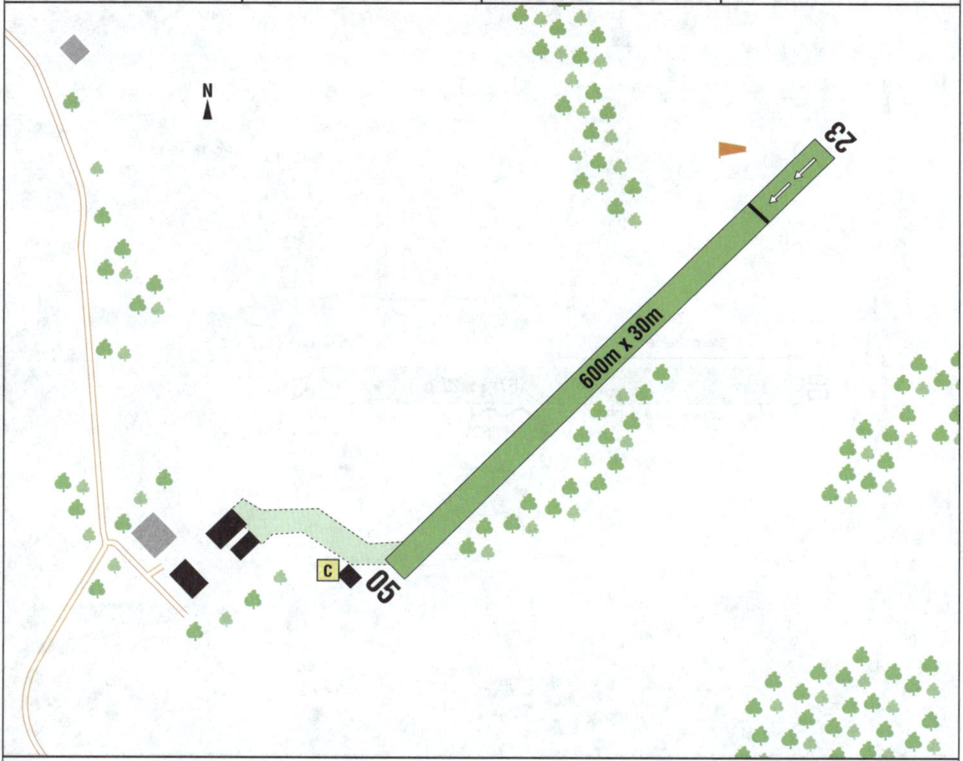

RWY	SURFACE	TORA	LDA	LIGHTING
05/23	Grass	600x30	U/L	Nil

Displaced Thr Rwy23 100m due to 18% upslope
Displaced end marked by 2 white chevrons

Remarks
PPR by telephone. AD on top plateau with steep upslope E end Rwy. Surface slightly undulating. Considerate visitors welcome at own risk.

Warnings
Strong S winds can cause turbulence Rwy23 APP due to local geography.
Noise: Please be considerate of local habitants, avoid over flying all local houses & maintain Rwy centreline on APP/dept.

Operating Hrs	0900-SS	**Weather Info**	AirN MWC
Circuits	LH 800ft QFE but can vary	**Operator**	Geoff & Angela Bunyan
Landing Fee	£5		Hanley House Farm
Maintenance	Nil		Hanley William
Fuel	Nil		Tenbury Wells
Disabled Facilities			Worcs, WR15 8QT
			Tel/Fax: 01886 853410
			www.hwas.orangehome.co.uk

Restaurants Light refreshments on site
The Fox Inn **Tel:** 01886 853189
Tally Ho Inn **Tel:** 01886 853241
The Baiting House **Tel:** 01886 853201
Upper Sapey Golf Club **Tel:** 01886 853506

Taxis/Car Hire
Swan Cabs **Tel:** 01584 810310

H

450ft 15mb	3nm ENE of Hay on Wye N5205.22 W00303.95	PPR	Alternative AD	Gloucestershire Shobdon

Non Radio	FIS London 124.750	Safetycom 135.475

B4348

5ft hedges

Grazing

Steep Upslope

6ft hedge

10ft hedge

09 ▬▬▬▬▬ **457m x 27m** ▬▬▬▬▬ 27

Wire fence removed with PPR

Undulations

ACFT parking

Grazing

5ft hedges

N

RWY	SURFACE	TORA	LDA	LIGHTING
09/27	Grass	457x27	U/L	Nil

Steep upslope from hedge to Rwy09 Thr

Remarks
PPR by telephone. Visitors welcome at pilots own risk. Sheep regularly graze and wire fence is sometimes erected across strip making PPR essential.
Visual aid to location: Large Orange windsock close to hangars and caravan.

Warnings
Not recommended for novice pilots. Rwy passes through gap in 5ft hedge at Rwy midpoint. Portion of Rwy between hedge gap & Rwy09 Thr rises 100ft: Land Rwy27 & dept Rwy09 unless very experienced with AD. See notes above reference the essential nature of PPR. AD is located within the Wye valley on the S on rising GND. Highest point is 4nm S 2306ft amsl. High GND up to 1044ft amsl 1.5nm to E. 6ft hedge close to Rwy27 Thr. 10ft hedge on short finals Rwy09.

Operating Hrs	SR-SS	**Operator**	Graham & Judy Pritchard
Circuits	N 1000ft QFE		New House Farm
Landing Fee	Nil		Hay on Wye
Maintenance	Nil		Herefordshire
Fuel	MOGAS available by prior arr		**Tel/Fax:** 01497 831259
Disabled Facilities			Tel: 07774 001446
			flyers@dsl.pipex.com
Restaurants	Nil		
Taxis/Car Hire	Nil		
Weather Info	AirN MWC		

H

159ft 5mb	2nm N of Haverfordwest N5149.98 W00457.67	PPR	Alternative AD	Swansea West Wales

Haverfordwest	A/G 122.200

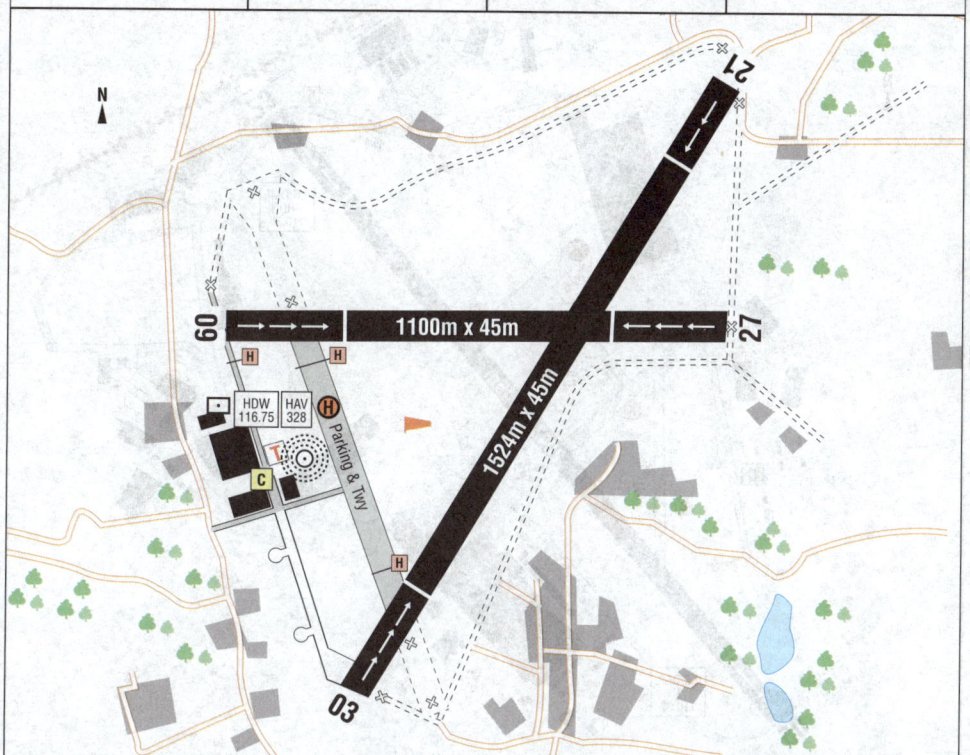

RWY	SURFACE	TORA	LDA	LIGHTING
03	Asphalt	1269	1202	Thr Rwy APAPI 3.5° LHS
21	Asphalt	1262	1269	Thr Rwy APAPI 3.5° LHS
09	Asphalt	1040	800	Nil
27	Asphalt	1010	800	Nil

Displaced Thr Rwy03 227m, Displaced Thr Rwy21 255m. Displaced Thr Rwy09 240m, Displaced Thr Rwy27 210m

Remarks
PPR essential. AD U/L Weekends. Flying training takes place at weekend by Haverfordwest Flying Training Centre. Microlight flying takes place on AD.
Visual aid to location: Ibn HW Green.

Warnings
A 3rd disused Rwy not available except as Twy between Rwy03 & 09 Thrs and as ACFT parking area. Rwy03/21 & 09/27 intersection liable to flooding during/after heavy rain.
Noise: Avoid local riding stables and residences N Rwy09/27, maintain circuit position on down wind leg.

Operating Hrs	Mon-Fri 0815-1530 (Summer) Mon-Fri 0915-1630 (Winter) except PH & by arr	Car Hire Days Drive	Tel: 01437 760860

Operating Hrs Mon-Fri 0815-1530 (Summer)
Mon-Fri 0915-1630 (Winter)
except PH & by arr
Circuits Fixed Wing LH Microlights RH
Landing Fee Single £10
Maintenance
Prestige **Tel:** 01437 766126
Fuel AVGAS JET A1 100LL & Oil
During AD opening hrs only
Disabled Facilities Nil
Restaurants Propellers Cafe
Taxis
Rocky's Taxis **Tel:** 01437 764822
Tel: 0800 074 8838

Car Hire
Days Drive **Tel:** 01437 760860
Weather Info AirS MOEx
Operator Pembrokeshire County Council
Fishguard Road
Haverfordwest
Dyfed SA62 4BN
Tel: 01437 764551 (Licensee)
Tel: 01437 765283 (PPR)
Tel: 01437 760822 (Club/AOC Ops)
Fax: 01437 769246(ATC)
hwestairport@haverfordwestairport.fsnet.co.uk
www.pembrokeshire.gov.ukk

Effective date:23/11/06

H

EGNR

HAWARDEN

45ft	3.5nm WSW of Chester	PPR	Alternative AD	Liverpool Sleap
1mb	N5310.68 W00258.67		Diversion AD	

Hawarden	APP 123.350	RAD 130.250	TWR 124.950

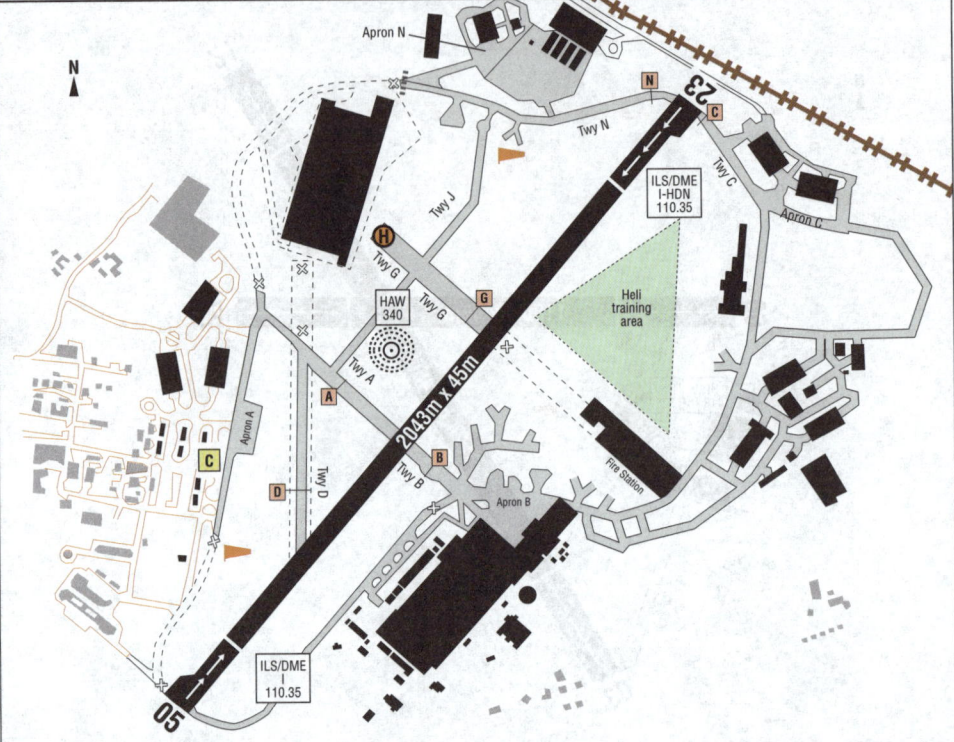

RWY	SURFACE	TORA	LDA	LIGHTING
05	Asph/Conc	1962	1663	Ap Thr Rwy PAPI 3.5° RHS
23	Asph/Conc	2043	1743	Ap Thr Rwy PAPI 3°LHS

Remarks
PPR (24 Hrs). Non-radio ACFT not accepted. Hi-Vis.

Warnings
Test flying takes place (including outside promulgated Hrs of ATC). Pilots are reminded of the proximity of Restricted Area R311 5nm N of AD. Compass deviation likely on new portion Rwy05/23 due to steel reinforcement. SFC winds over 15kts from E or W may cause turbulence from buildings. Apron N restricted to ACFT <17m wingspan. Apron N and parts of Twy N are not visible from ATC. Glider activity at Sealand 3nm NNW weekends up to 3000ft agl.

Noise: All ACFT are to climb ahead to 1.5nm before turning onto course or downwind into the circuit. Avoid over flight of local habitation below 1500ft.

Operating Hrs	Mon 0500-1800 Tue-Fri 0630-1800 Sat-Sun 0830-1500 (Summer) +1Hr (Winter)	**Taxis** Airport Service	**Tel:** 01244 346550
Circuits	05 RH, 23 LH, 1000ft QFE	Abbey Taxis	**Tel:** 01244 311804
Landing Fee	<1500kgs £17.48, 1500-2000kgs £28.40 2000-3000kgs £42.03 ACFT >3000kgs requires Handling Agent Weekend excess applied	Dee Cars **Car Hire** Avis Rent-a-Car National	**Tel:** 01244 671671 **Tel:** 01244 311463 **Tel:** 01244 390008
Maintenance	Hawarden Air Services **Tel:** 01244 538568	**Weather Info** **Operator**	M T9 MWC Airbus UK Ltd
Fuel	AVGAS JET A1 100LL By prior arr only 48Hrs notice required at weekends		Chester Hawarden Airport Broughton, Chester North Wales, CH4 0DR **Tel:** 01244 522012 (ATC)
Disabled Facilities	Nil		**Tel:** 01244 522013 (PPR)
Handling	**Tel:** 01244 536853 (Chester Handling)		**Fax:** 01244 523035
Restaurants	Nil		

H

11ft 0mb	12.5nm E of Doncaster N5329.42 W00049.79	PPR	Alternative AD	Humberside Sandtoft

Non Radio	LARS Waddington 127.350	APP Doncaster 126.225	TWR Doncaster 128.775	Safetycom 135.475

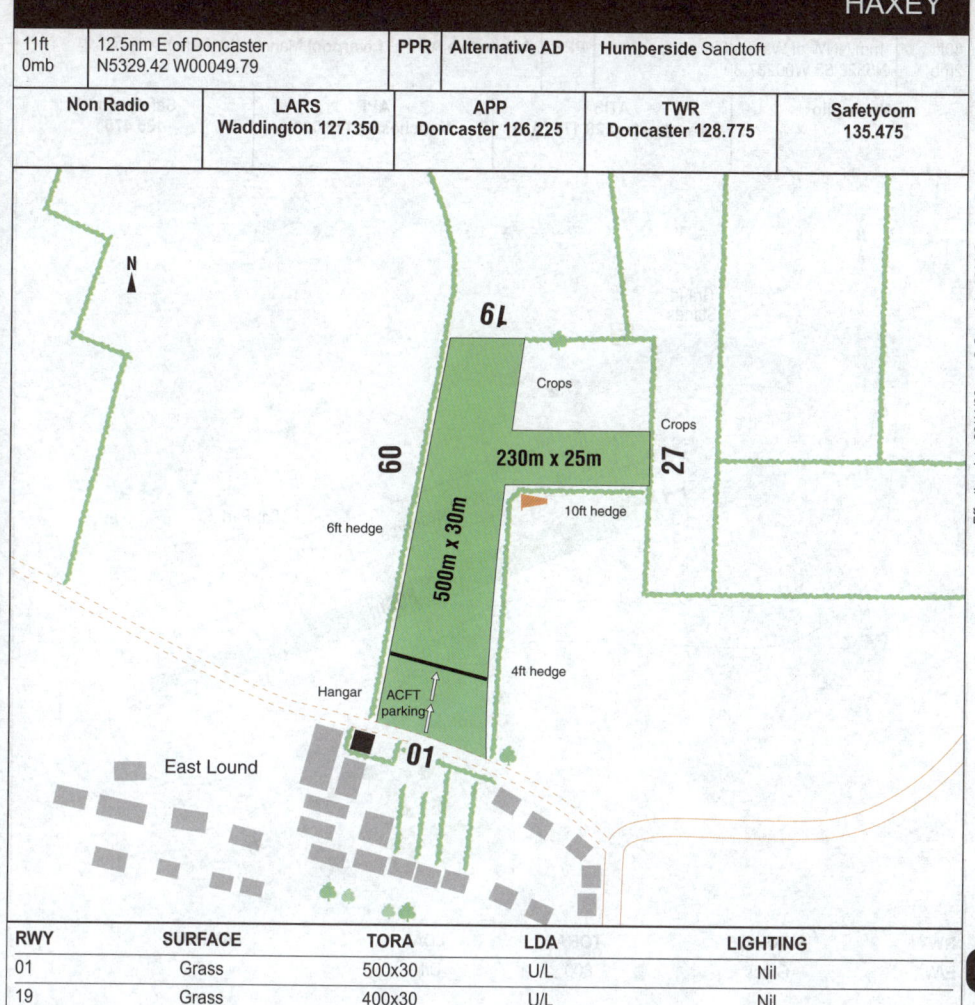

RWY	SURFACE	TORA	LDA	LIGHTING
01	Grass	500x30	U/L	Nil
19	Grass	400x30	U/L	Nil
27/09	Grass	230x25	U/L	Nil

Displaced Thr Rwy01, Rwy09 not available for take-off or landing

Remarks
PPR essential by telephone. All ACFT to contact Doncaster Sheffield ATC en-route and before dept.

Warnings
AD slightly undulating. Avoid obstructing farm track which crosses extreme S edge of AD.
Noise: Avoid over flying local villages and houses on short final on APP Rwy01 or Dept Rwy19

Operating Hrs	SR-SS	**Operator**	Mr J D Bingham
Circuits	Overhead join 01 LH, 19 27 RH		Haxey Airfield East Lound Doncaster DN9 2LR
Landing Fee	On application		**Tel:** 01427 752291
Maintenance	Nil		**Tel:** 01427 754077
Fuel	Can be arranged		**Tel:** 07702 039625
Disabled Facilities	Nil		**Tel:** 07926 809527
Restaurant	Various good pubs		fly.gassf@btinternet.com
Taxi/Car Hire			
Epworth Taxi	**Tel:** 01427 874569		
Weather Info	AirN MCW		

H

291

HAYDOCK PARK

80ft 2mb	4nm NNW of Warrington N5328.53 W00237.30	PPR	Alternative AD	Liverpool Manchester Barton

Non-radio	ATIS Manchester 128.175 (Arr)	APP Manchester 135.000	Safetycom 135.475

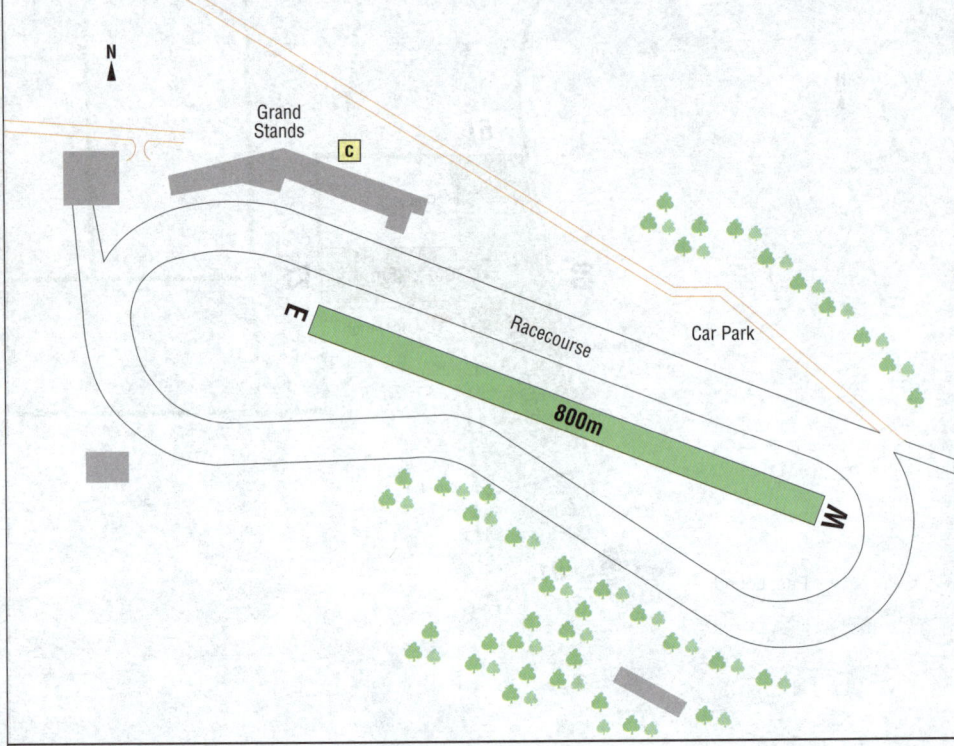

RWY	SURFACE	TORA	LDA	LIGHTING
E/W	Grass	800	U/L	Nil

Remarks
PPR essential. AD situated in Low Level Route within Manchester CTR. Primarily used on race days when all landings must be made 30mins before the first race. Light ACFT may be accepted on non race days at pilot's own risk. Windsock displayed on race days and when given sufficient prior notice. Limited helicopter servicing on race days.

Warnings
Care should be taken over rough GND, particularly at each end of Rwy. Parasending on race days.

Operating Hrs	Available on request	**Operator**	The Haydock Park Racecourse Ltd Newton-Le-Willows Merseyside, WA12 0HQ **Tel:** 01942 725963 Ex 208 (0900-1700 Mon-Fri) **Fax:** 01942 270879
Circuits	Nil		
Landing Fee	Light ACFT £25 Nil on race days		
Maintenance Ground Zero	Limited helicopter facilities race days **Tel:** 0161 7996967		
Fuel	Helicopter fuel available on race days		
Disabled Facilities	Nil		
Restaurants	Nil		
Taxis/Car Hire	Nil		
Weather Info	AirCen MWC		

H

170ft 5mb	4nm N of Hitchin N5201.17 W00018.10	PPR MIL	Alternative AD Diversion AD	Cranfield Little Gransden

Henlow	APP Luton 129.550	A/G 121.100	If no contact transmit normal calls blind & proceed with caution

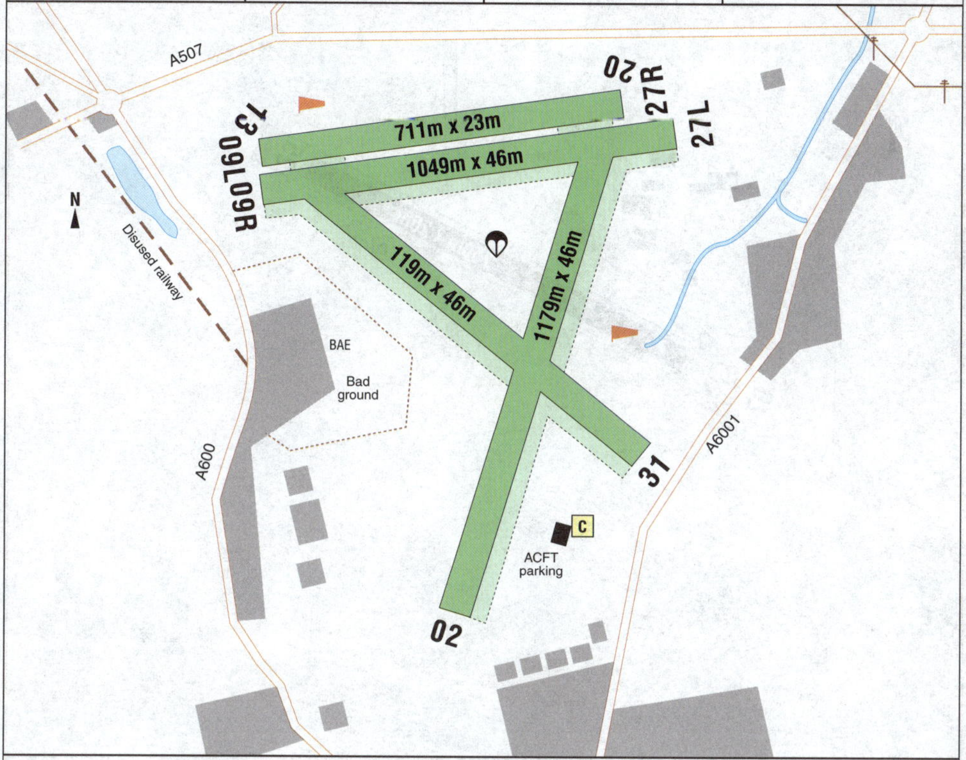

[Aerodrome chart showing runways 02/20, 09L/27R, 09R/27L, 13/31 with dimensions: 711m x 23m, 1049m x 46m, 119m x 46m, 1179m x 46m. Features: A507, Disused railway, A600, BAE Bad ground, A6001, ACFT parking, N arrow]

RWY	SURFACE	TORA	LDA	LIGHTING
02/20	Grass	1179	1052	Nil
09L/27R	Grass	711	711	Nil
09R/27L	Grass	1049	949	Nil
13/31	Grass	1119	1016	Nil

Rwys have white edge markings

Remarks
PPR 48Hrs notice by telephone. Civil flying training organisation operating on an RAF AD. Visitors PPR OC flying, or station duty officer 48Hrs beforehand and must obtain Arr briefing from flying club. Arr Standard OH join. During gliding operations route via local VRPs.

Warnings
Considerable ATC flying, some model ACFT flying & free-fall parachuting. Grass area consolidated with metal tracking that protrudes in places, remain within Rwys & Twys. Do not over fly the BAE complex.
Noise: Dept Normal procedure except Rwy02 No left turns before 700ft QFE. Rwy31 at 300ft QFE, turn left, track 295° until clear of ATZ.

Operating Hrs	0830-SS (L)	**Taxis/Car Hire**	By arr
Circuits	LH except 13 RH 27R (variable) 1000ft QFE	**Weather Info**	AirCen MOEx
Landing Fee	Charges in accordance with MOD policy	**Operator**	RAF Henlow Beds **Tel:** 01462 851515 Ex 6150 (PPR) **Tel:** 01462 851936
Maintenance	Nil		
Fuel	AVGAS 100LL		

Disabled Facilities

Restaurant Cafe & pub food in Henlow village

Visual Reference Points (VRP)
Blue Lagoon (Brick pit with blue water) 140°/2.25nm
Chick Sands (Aerial farm NW Shefford) 300°/2.5nm
Water TWR (Light concrete structure) 060°/3.5nm

H

| 184ft | 5nm SSE of Wincanton | **PPR** | **Alternative AD** | **Bournemouth** Compton Abbas |
| 6mb | N5059.30 W00221.52 | | **Diversion AD** | |

Henstridge	**LARS** Yeovilton 127.350	**A/G** 130.250

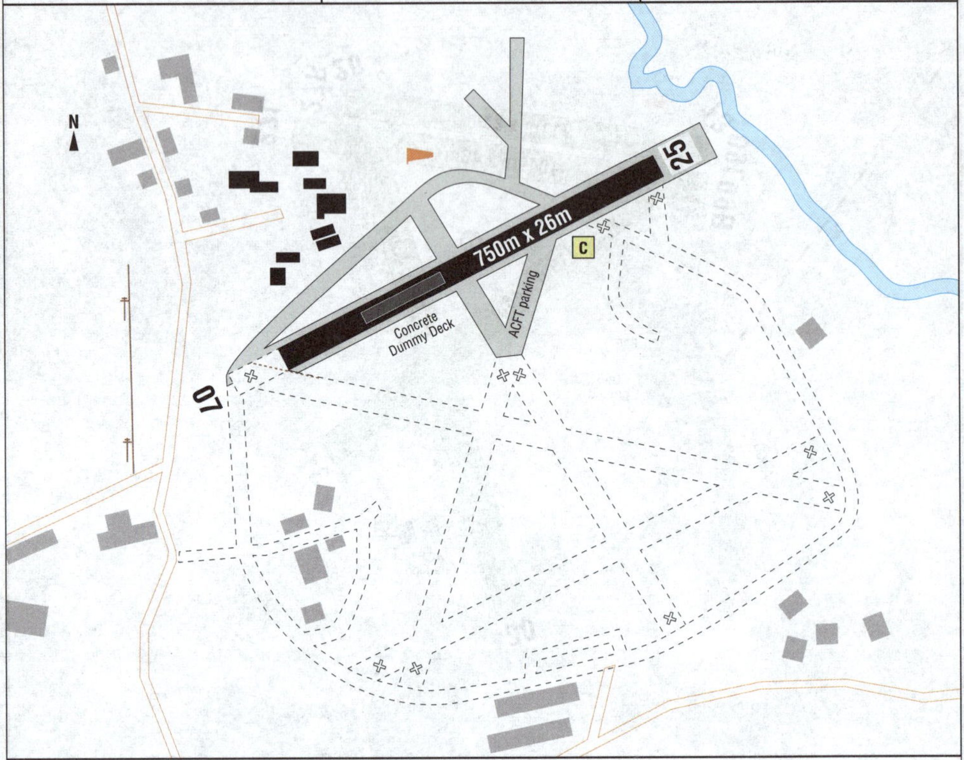

RWY	SURFACE	TORA	LDA	LIGHTING
07/25	Asph/Conc	750x26	U/L	Nil

Remarks
PPR non radio ACFT. Visiting ACFT welcome. Situated close to Yeovilton MATZ, call Yeovilton LARS. All other Rwys are not useable.
Visual aid to location: Rwy07/25 identified by the Concrete 'dummy deck' in the middle

Warnings
Keep a good lookout for high speed military ACFT and high intensity helicopter operations associated with Yeovilton.
Caution: Power cables 20ftagl cross Rwy07 final APP 230m from Thr. Fence 50m from Rwy07 Thr.
Noise: Avoid over flying near by villages and dwellings. Visit website for more noise abatement instructions.

Operating Hrs	0900-1800 or SS whichever earlier	**Operator**
Circuits	RH 800ft QFE	
Landing Fee	£8 Microlight & Gyro £4	
Maintenance	Nil	
Fuel	AVGAS JET A1 100LL	

Operator

EGHS Ltd
Henstridge Airfield
Somerset, BA8 0TN
Tel: 01963 364231
Fax: 01963 364351
www.henstridgeairfield.com

Disabled Facilities

Restaurant	Cafeteria Sat-Sun 0900-1430 Snacks Mon-Fri
Taxis	
Bill	**Tel:** 01963 362754
Car Hire	Nil
Weather Info	AirSW MOEx

H

505ft 17mb	2nm W of Brackley N5201.75 W00112.48		PPR	Alternative AD Diversion AD	Oxford Turweston
	Hinton			**A/G 119.450**	

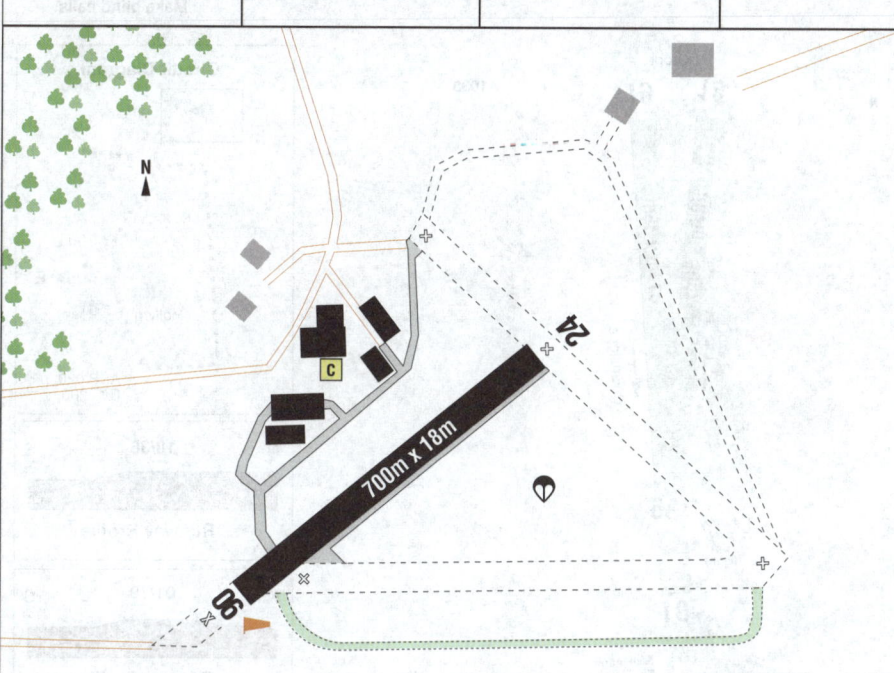

RWY	SURFACE	TORA	LDA	LIGHTING
06/24	Asphalt	700x18	U/L	Nil

Remarks
PPR by telephone. Visitors welcome. Gliding and parachuting daily throughout the year. All ACFT must call at least 5nm away.

Warnings
Rwy06/24 has new surface. Strip on N side of original centre line. Gliding and parachuting daily throughout the year.
Noise: Avoid over flying villages and habitation in vicinity of AD.

Operating Hrs	SS	**Operator**	Mr R B Harrison
Circuits	Variable		Walltree House Farm
	No over head or cross wind joins		Steane, Brackley, Northants
Landing Fee	Donations welcome		**Tel:** 01295 811235 (PPR)
Maintenance	Holdcroft Aviation		**Tel:** 01295 812300 (Hinton Skydiving)
	Tel: 01295 810287		**Tel:** 01295 811056 (Gliding club)
	Fax: 01295 812247		**Tel:** 01295 812775
Fuel	AVGAS 100LL		(Flight Training Tom Eagles)
Disabled Facilities	Nil		**Fax:** 01295 811147 (Owner)
Restaurants	Light refreshments in club house		**Fax:** 01295 812400 (Hinton Skydiving)
Taxis			
PJ Cars	**Tel:** 01280 704330		
Car Hire	Nil		
Weather Info	AirCen MOEx		

H

50ft 1mb	1nm S of Withernsea N5342.63 E00002.22	PPR	Alternative AD	Humberside Beverley

Hollym	ATIS Humberside 124.125	LARS Humberside 119.125	A/G 129.825 (Microlight freq) Make blind calls

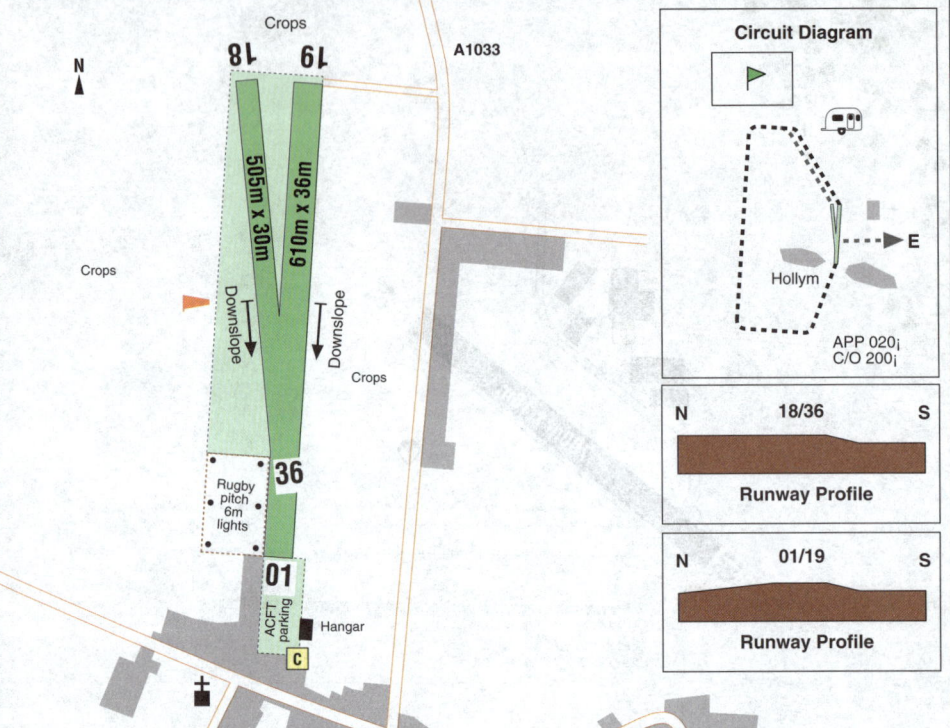

Circuit Diagram

Hollym

APP 020¡
C/O 200¡

N   18/36   S

Runway Profile

N   01/19   S

Runway Profile

RWY	SURFACE	TORA	LDA	LIGHTING
01	Grass	730x36	U/L	Nil
19	Grass	610x36	U/L	Nil
18/36	Grass	505x30	U/L	Nil

Rwy01/19 has grass paddock at S end 120m included in TORA

Remarks

PPR by telephone. ACFT welcome with PPR and at pilots own risk. A slight down slope for 20m portion of both Rwy. Strip is kept close mown and is in excellent condition. Rwy lighting installation is planned for 01/19. Rwy01/19 dimensions are planned to be altered to 690x36m (TORA 690 LDA 690) for both Rwy. Confirm with operator on obtaining PPR.
NB: An additional rugby pitch is established during the season (Winter). Rwy18/36 is closed on match days.

Warnings

Rugby pitch with floodlight stancions 6m high at S end of AD on W side. Large model ACFT use AD. There is an annual fly-in for ACFT & models, some models are up to half size and may be jet powered! Be aware of gulls which congregate on land around AD.
Noise: See circuit diagram showing avoidance areas. ACFT Dept Rwy19 or 18 with sufficient performance may turn E to avoid Hollym village.

Operating Hrs	0900-SS (L)	**Bicycles**	Operator plans to have two loan bikes
Circuits	W 1000ft QFE See circuit diagram	**Weather Info**	AirN MWC www.hollym.org.uk
Landing Fee	Nil but donations towards grass cutting welcome	**Operator**	Ken Wootton KWS Aviation Green Linnet, Northside Rd, Hollym East Yorkshire, HU19 2RS **Tel:** 01964 615622 **Tel:** 07941 698088 steve@hollymairfield.co.uk www.hollymairfield.co.uk
Maintenance	Microlight maintenance available from KWS aviation		
Fuel	Nil		
Disabled Facilities	Nil		
Restaurants	Small cafe in village		
Taxis/Car Hire	Nil		

100ft 3mb	5nm SE of Newark N5300.35 W00041.35	PPR	Alternative AD	Humberside Retford

Hougham	LARS Waddington 127.350	APP Cranwell 119.375	A/G 129.825 (Microlight freq)

N

Crops

East Coast Mainline
4 track with overhead
cables on embankment

18

60 120m x 20m **27**

Crops

Crops

402m x 20m

Crops

Mobile homes
close to strip edge

Crops

Farm track

Crops

Farm buildings

36 Crops

RWY	SURFACE	TORA	LDA	LIGHTING
18/36	Grass	402x20	U/L	Nil
09/27	Grass	120x20	U/L	Nil

Remarks
PPR by telephone. Visiting ACFT & Microlights welcome at pilots own risk.

Warnings
AD is situated close to the boundaries of Cranwell & Barkston Heath CMATZ. Cranwell APP is the controlling authority. Both AD are not normally active at weekends. Care should be taken as E coast mainline with 25kv overhead lines runs on embankment 400m N of Rwy18 Thr. Domestic power cables cross Rwy36 APP 400m S of Thr. Drainage ditch crosses Rwy18/09 Thr. Farm track crosses Rwy36 Thr – pedestrians and farm vehicles. 5ft hedge crosses Rwy27 Thr. Mobile homes are parked along Rwy18/36 E edge.
Noise: Avoid over flying farms & houses in the vicinity.

Operating Hrs	SR-SS	**Operator**	Mike Barnatt-Millns
Circuits	18, 36 E, 09, 27 N, 800ft QFE		The Old Coach House
Landing Fee	Donation appreciated		Coach Road
Maintenance	Nil		Hougham, Grantham
Fuel	Nil		Lincs, NG32 2JF
Disabled Facilities			**Tel:** 01400 250293
			mike.hougham@virgin.net
Restaurants	Nil		
Taxi/Car Hire	Nil		
Weather Info	AirCen MWC		

H

281ft	5nm NNW of Nottingham	PPR	Alternative AD	**Nottingham East Midlands** Nottingham
9mb	N5300.87 W00113.10			

Hucknall	A/G **130.800**

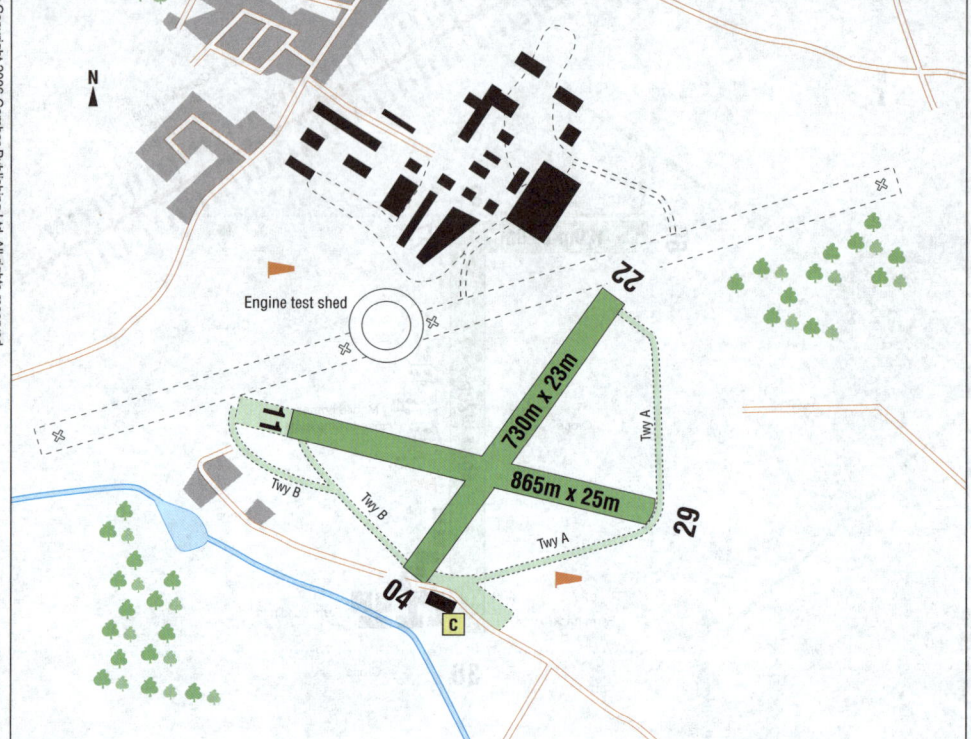

Engine test shed

730m x 23m

865m x 25m

22

11

29

04

Twy A

Twy B

Twy B

Twy A

C

N

RWY	SURFACE	TORA	LDA	LIGHTING
04/22	Grass	730	730	Nil
11	Grass	865	776	Nil
29	Grass	776	776	Nil

Starter extension Rwy11 89m

Remarks
PPR by telephone. Open weekends only to visiting ACFT. AD available Sat-Sun only. AD is not available for public transport passenger flights required to use a licensed AD.

Warnings
Hard Rwy08/26 is disused. Mast 530ft amsl.280°/1.4nm. Mast 530ft amsl 275°/1.9nm. Rwy29 Thr low fence.

Operating Hrs	Mon-Fri closed to visiting ACFT Sat-Sun 1000-1800 or SS (Winter) Sat-Sun 0900-1700 or SS (Summer)	**Operator**	Merlin Flying Club Rolls Royce Ltd Aero Division Hucknall Nottingham, NG15 6EU **Tel:** 0115 975 5153 **Tel:** 0115 964 2269
Circuits	Nil		
Landing Fee	£3		
Maintenance	Nil		
Fuel	AVGAS 100LL Available by prior arr only		
Disabled Facilities	Nil		
Restaurants	Tea & coffee available		
Taxis Streamline	**Tel:** 0115 947 3031		
Car Hire National	**Tel:** 0115 950 3385		
Weather Info	AirCen MWC		

H

825ft 28mb	1.5nm of Huddersfield N5337.28 W00149.72	PPR	Alternative AD	Leeds Bradford Sherburn in Elmet

Huddersfield	APP Leeds 123.750	APP Manchester 135.000	A/G 128.375

RWY	SURFACE	TORA	LDA	LIGHTING
07/25	Asph/Grass	800x22	U/L	Nil

Rwy 550m asphalt 250m grass

Remarks
PPR by telephone. Use restricted to ACFT <2730kg AUW. Whenever possible land and take-off of Rwy25. When Rwy25 is in use pilots are advised to land well beyond the Thr. Fuel available to club ACFT only.

Warnings
Emley Moor TV mast (concrete) 1924ft amsl 6nm to E. Holme Moss TV mast 2490ft amsl 5nm to S. Radio masts 1614ft amsl 2.5nm to NW. Rwy gradient 2.6% down on Rwy07 from start of asphalt. Possible down drafts over head quarry very close to Thr 25.
Noise: Avoid low flying over houses and hospital 0.5m from Thr of Rwy25.

Operating Hrs	SR-SS		Operator	J Whitham
Circuits	LH 1000ft QFE			Huddersfield Aviation Ltd
Landing Fee	Single £5, Twin £10			The Airfield, Crossland Moor
Maintenance	Nil			Huddersfield, HD47AG
Fuel	Limited			**Tel:** 01484 645784/654473
Disabled Facilities	Nil			**Tel:** 07767 483373
Restaurants	Light refreshments available			
Taxis GT	**Tel:** 01484 534565			
Car Hire National	**Tel:** 01484 455050			
Eurocar	**Tel:** 01484 513353			
Weather Info	AirCen MWC			

H

121ft 3mb	10nm W of Grimsby N5334.47 W00021.05	PPR	Alternative AD	Leeds Bradford Sandtoft
Humberside		**ATIS** **124.125**		**APP** **119.125**
RAD **119.125 129.250**		**TWR** **124.900**		**FIRE** **121.600**

RWY	SURFACE	TORA	LDA	LIGHTING
03	Asph/Conc	2070	2070	Ap Thr Rwy PAPI 3.5° LHS
21	Asph/Conc	2196	1950	Ap Thr Rwy PAPI 3° LHS
09	Asphalt	985	985	Nil
27	Asphalt	1025	865	Nil

Remarks

PPR only. Non-radio ACFT NOT accepted. Hi-vis. Training flights subject to ATC approval. Helicopters to land as instructed by ATC. Helicopters operating to and from main apron must avoid over-flying buildings on S edge of apron. Twy to light ACFT parking area and maintenance area is routed behind apron area and marked with a single yellow centre line, exercise caution in this area due to movement of vehicles and personnel. Non handled visiting ACFT are to report to vehicle control post adjacent to the apron. Handling by Servisair.

Warnings

Avoid rifle range 340°/1350m from the ARP below 500ft agl. D306 is located at DME range 15.5nm on the extended centre line of Rwy21. ACFT must not establish on the ILS Rwy21 until DME range is 12nm unless ATC advise that D306 is not active. Light ACFT pilots should be aware of the possible effect of rotor down wash generated by large helicopters operating through the main apron area.

Noise: Avoid over flying Barnetby, Brocklesby and Kirmington villages

Operating Hrs	0530-1925 (Summer) +1Hr (Winter)
Landing Fee	On application
Maintenance	
Eastern Airways	**Tel:** 01652 681059
Hangar 9	**Tel:** 01652 688062
Fuel	AVGAS JET A1 100LL
	Tel: 01652 682044
Hangarage	Hangar 9 **Tel:** 01652 688062

Disabled Facilities

Handling	Hangar 9 **Tel:** 01652 688062
Restaurant	Licensed buffet in Terminal
Taxis	Available at Terminal
Car Hire	
Avis	**Tel:** 01652 680325
Europcar	**Tel:** 01652 680338

Weather Info   M T9 Fax 296 A MWC VN
                   ATIS **Tel:** 01652 682020

Visual Reference Points (VRP)

Immingham Docks	N5337.70 W00011.60
N Tower Humber Bridge	N5342.85 W00027.03
Caistor	N5329.77 W00019.10
Brigg	N5333.20 W00029.20
Laceby Crossroads	N5332.12 W00010.82
Elsham Wolds	N5336.52 W00025.68

Operator   Humberside International Airport Ltd
Kirmington, Ulcerby
North Humberside, DN39 6YH
Tel: 01652 688456 (Admin)
Tel: 01652 682022 (ATC)
Fax: 01652 680244 (ATC)
Fax: 01652 680524 (Admin)
admin@humberside-airport.co.uk

254ft 8mb	2nm NW of Harlow N5148.58 E00004.18	PPR	Alternative AD	Southend Stapleford

Hunsdon Microlight traffic	ATIS Stansted 127.175	APP Essex 120.625	A/G 129.825 (microlight freq)

RWY	SURFACE	TORA	LDA	LIGHTING
08/26	Grass	450x19	U/L	Nil
03/21	Grass	420x20	U/L	Nil
13/31	Grass	350x30	U/L	Nil

Remarks

PPR by telephone essential. Microlight ACFT only accepted. Visitors welcome at own risk. AD situated within Stansted CTR. Flying activities can only be carried out when Essex RAD have been notified AD active daily, it is not a blanket approval. PPR essential for briefing on APP & Dept procedures, routes and noise sensitive areas. Unless requesting transit Stansted CTR do not call Essex RAD but monitor frequency. AD mainly used for microlight training.

Warnings

When entering circuit do not enter Stansted CTR more than 0.5nm to W and S. Stansted CTA base 1400ft QNH.
Noise: Do not over fly Hunsdon & Hunsdonbury. Route clear of all local habitation, and avoid glide descents whenever possible. All APP to AD from the S.

Operating Hrs	Mon-Sat 0800-1900 Sun 0900-1900 (L)	**Operator**	Jay Airsports
Circuits	To N or E 800ft QFE		116 Mount Pleasant New Barnet
Landing Fee	Weekdays £2 Weekends £4		Herts, EN4 9HQ
Maintenance	Nil		**Tel:** 07956 434958
Fuel	Nil		**Tel:** 07904 244035
Disabled Facilities	Nil		**Tel:** 07967 091908
Restaurants	Nil		
Taxis/carhire	Nil		
Weather Info	AirCen		

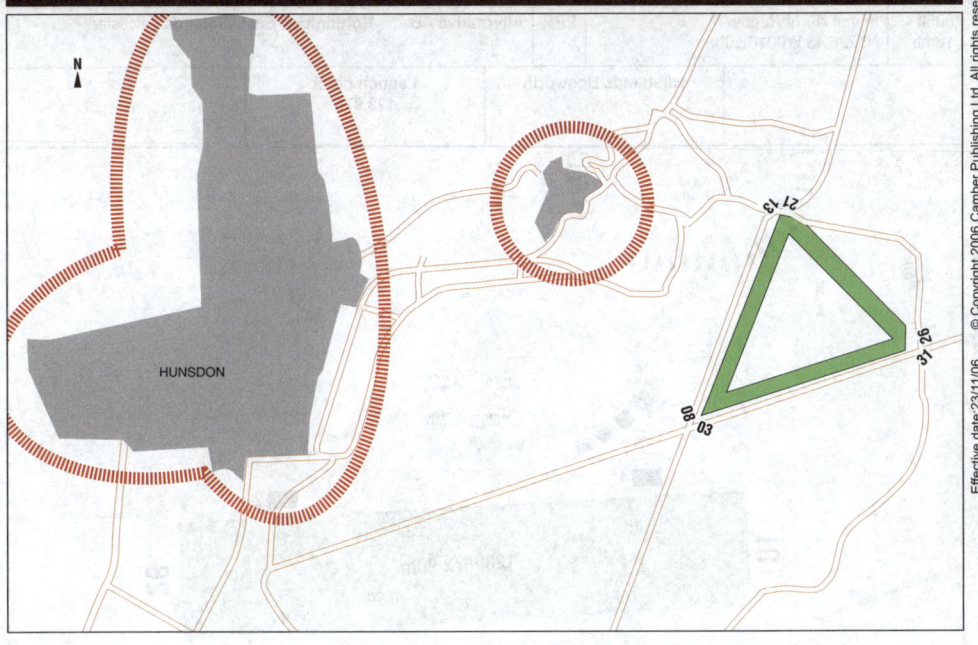

H

HUSBANDS BOSWORTH

505ft 16mb	8.5nm NE of Rugby N5226.43 W00102.63	PPR	Alternative AD	Nottingham East Midlands Leicester

	Husbands Bosworth	Launch point 129.975	

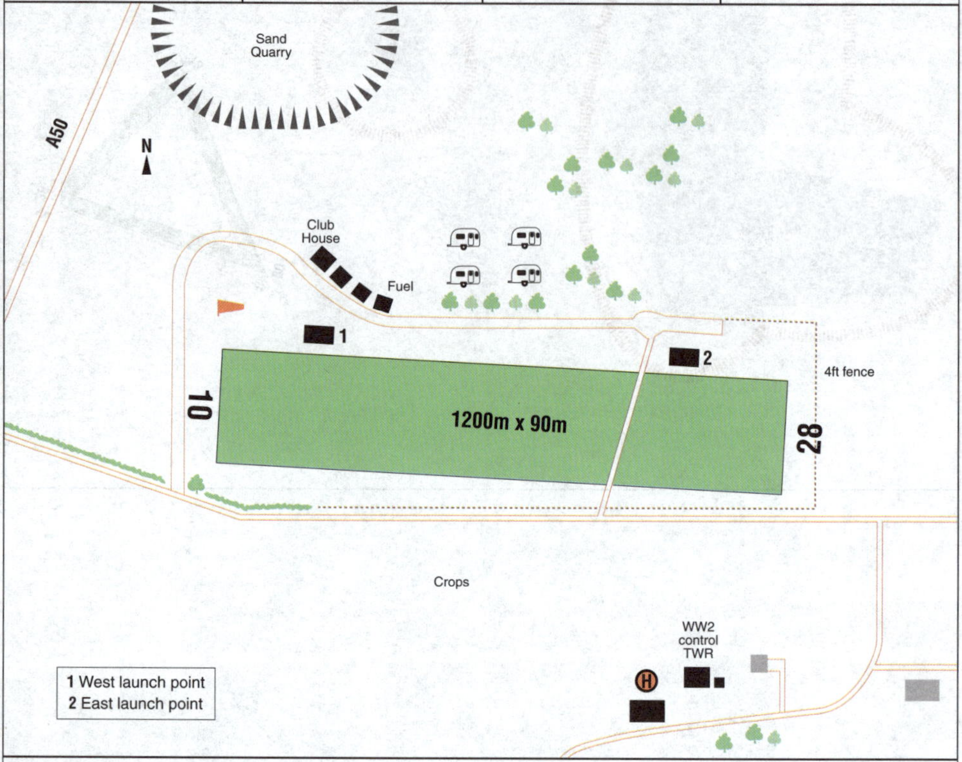

Sand Quarry

A50

N

Club House

Fuel

1

10

1200m x 90m

28

4ft fence

2

Crops

WW2 control TWR

H

1 West launch point
2 East launch point

RWY	SURFACE	TORA	LDA	LIGHTING
10/28	Grass	1200x90	U/L	Nil

Remarks
PPR by telephone. Primarily gliding site with winch & aerotow launching. Cables up to 3000ft agl.

Warnings
Use extreme vigilance – intensive gliding. Although launch point may not acknowledge, please make circuit calls, give preference to aerotow ACFT. Concrete track crosses AD. Police helicopter may lift from helipad on old S portion of AD without warning.
Noise: Dept Rwy28 turn left towards lake & climb to lake before turning on course. Dept Rwy10 turn on course before Sibbertoft village but do not overfly farmhouses E of AD.

Operating Hrs	SR-SS	**Taxis**	
Circuits	28 LH, 10 RH 1000ft QFE	A&B Murphy's	**Tel:** 01858 410210/410776/434935
Landing Fee	£5	ACE Cabs	**Tel:** 01858 462233
Maintenance		**Car Hire**	Nil
Storey ACFT Servs	**Tel:** 01858 880807	**Weather Info**	AirCen MWC
Fuel	AVGAS 100LL by arr only	**Operator**	The Soaring Centre
Disabled Facilities			Husbands Bosworth Airfield Lutterworth, Leics

Tel: 01858 880429 (AD)
Tel: 01858 880521 (Office)
office@soaringcentre.co.uk

Restaurants Refreshments & comprehensive Accomodation list available at AD Local B+B's in Sibbertoft village (2 miles)

Mary Hart **Tel:** 01858 880886
Archway Fmhouse **Tel:** 01858 525623 (Mrs Boulton)

H

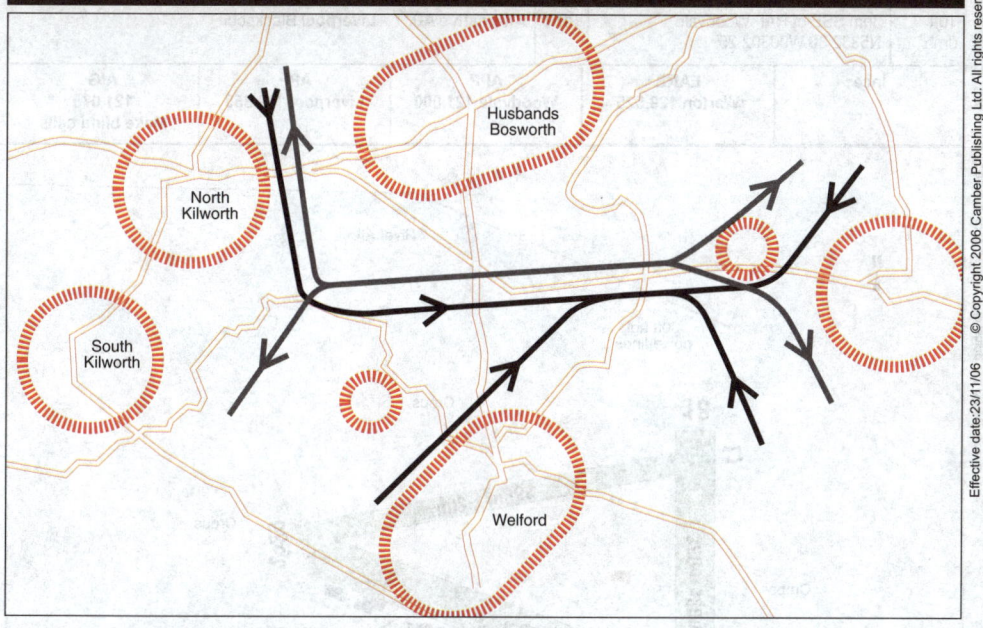

Please avoid over flying any of the areas highlighted on the map.

Towing ACFT will generally fly low level circuits to S of AD.

Dept Rwy27 to W: Hold Rwy heading until reaching the canal, dept to N turn R keeping the canal on your left until passing abeam North Kilworth, then turn on track.

Dept Rwy09 to E: ASAP after take off but not before passing AD boundary, turn L or R to avoid over flying The Wrongs Farm, then after passing abeam the village turn on track.

Arr ACFT from NE: Keep a good look out as you will be passing very close to AD circuit on N side of AD., please use SE arrival preference to help prevent conflicts.

10ft 0mb	3nm SSE of RAF Woodvale N5332.30 W00302.25	PPR	Alternative AD	Liverpool Blackpool

Ince	LARS Warton 129.525	APP Woodvale 121.000	APP Liverpool 119.850	A/G 121.075 Make blind calls

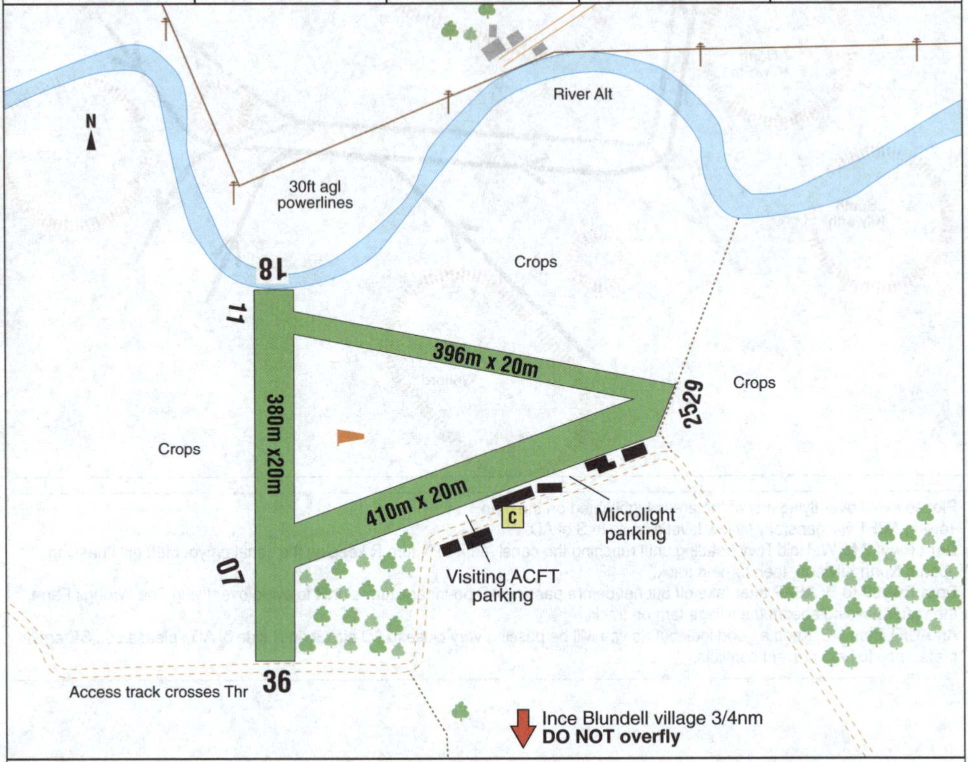

N

River Alt

30ft agl powerlines

Crops

18

11

396m x 20m

25
29

Crops

380m x20m

Crops

410m x 20m

07

C

Microlight parking

Visiting ACFT parking

36

Access track crosses Thr

Ince Blundell village 3/4nm
DO NOT overfly

RWY	SURFACE	TORA	LDA	LIGHTING
07/25	Grass	410x20	U/L	Nil
11/29	Grass	396x20	U/L	Nil
18/36	Grass	380x20	U/L	Nil

I-J

Remarks
PPR by telephone. Primarily a Microlight AD but suitable visiting ACFT are welcome at pilots own risk. Be considerate of ab-initio trainees.

Warnings
Power cables cross Rwy18 APP on short final. An access track crosses the Rwy36 Thr. AD is close to RAF Woodvale ATZ boundary which is 1nm NNW and the Liverpool CTR is 3.5nm to S. University Air Squadron light ACFT carry out general handling exercises in the vicinity.
Noise: Please pay careful attention to the Circuit diagram.

Operating Hrs	SR-SS	**Taxis/Car Hire**	Nil
Circuits	29, 07, 18 RH, 11, 25, 36 LH	**Weather Info**	AirCen MWC

Circuits
Please obtain details with PPR and have circuit diagram to hand. Usual requirement is an overhead join with descent on the deadside to 500ft QFE. (Usual Microlight circuit height)

Operator
Mr John North
West Lancashire Microlight School
Ince Blundell, Formby
Merseyside, L38 6JJ
Tel: 0151 9293319
Tel: 07850 882309
Tel: 07970 234933
www.wlms.co.uk

Landing Fee £2

Maintenance Nil
Fuel MOGAS available by arr from garage 2miles

Disabled Facilities

Restaurants The Weld Ince Blundell
The Red Squirrel Blundell

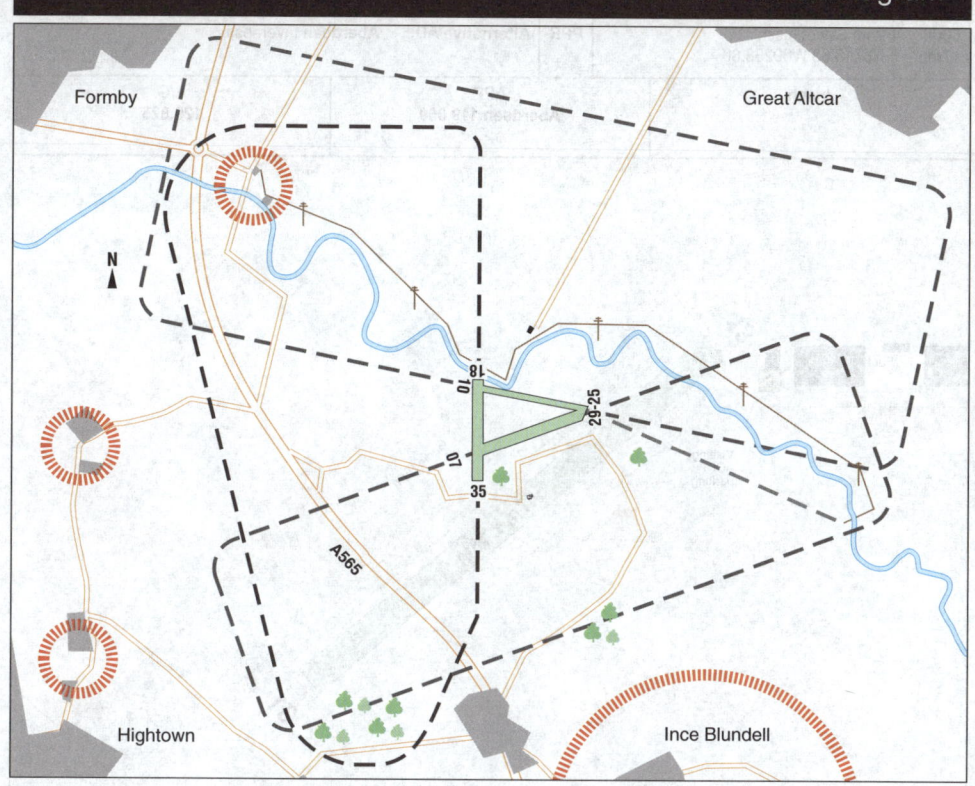

500ft 17mb	2nm SW of Insch N5718.68 W00238.80	PPR	Alternative AD	Aberdeen Inverness

Insch	APP Aberdeen 119.050	A/G 129.825

Fuel

C

Visiting
ACFT
parking

13

31

547m x 18m

Gadie Burn

RWY	SURFACE	TORA	LDA	LIGHTING
13/31	Grass	547x18	U/L	Nil

I-J

Remarks
Strict PPR by telephone. High GND around circuit may cause localised wind effects.

Warnings
Military ACFT avoiding the Aberdeen CTZ tend to over fly. Pilots are advised to keep a good lookout and call Aberdeen for traffic information. DO NOT continue if cars are crossing Rwy31 wait until clear. Power cables 10ft aal 174m before Rwy31 Thr.
Caution: Microlights on AD.
Noise: Avoid over flying Auchleven village 0.5nm E of AD or Leslie village 0.5nm W of AD.

Operating Hrs	By arr	**Operator**	Ken Wood
Circuits	1000ft AGL variable direction for noise abatement		Insch Aerodrome Auchleven, Insch Aberdeenshire, AB5 6PL
Landing Fee	Donation by pilot		**Tel:** 01464 820422 (Home)
Maintenance	Nil		**Tel:** 01464 820003 (AD)
Fuel	Nil		**Tel:** 0771 4531777
Disabled Facilities	Nil		
Restaurants	Local pub		
Taxis/Car Hire	Available via AD		
Weather Info	AirSc GWC		

308

31ft 1mb	7nm NE of Inverness N5732.55 W00402.85	PPR	Alternative AD Diversion AD	Aberdeen

Inverness	ATIS 109.200 (INS VOR)	LARS Lossiemouth 118.900
APP 122.600	**TWR** 122.600	**FIRE** 121.600

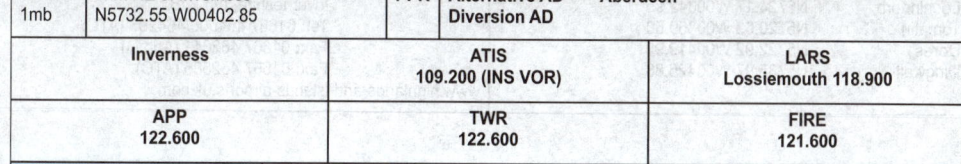

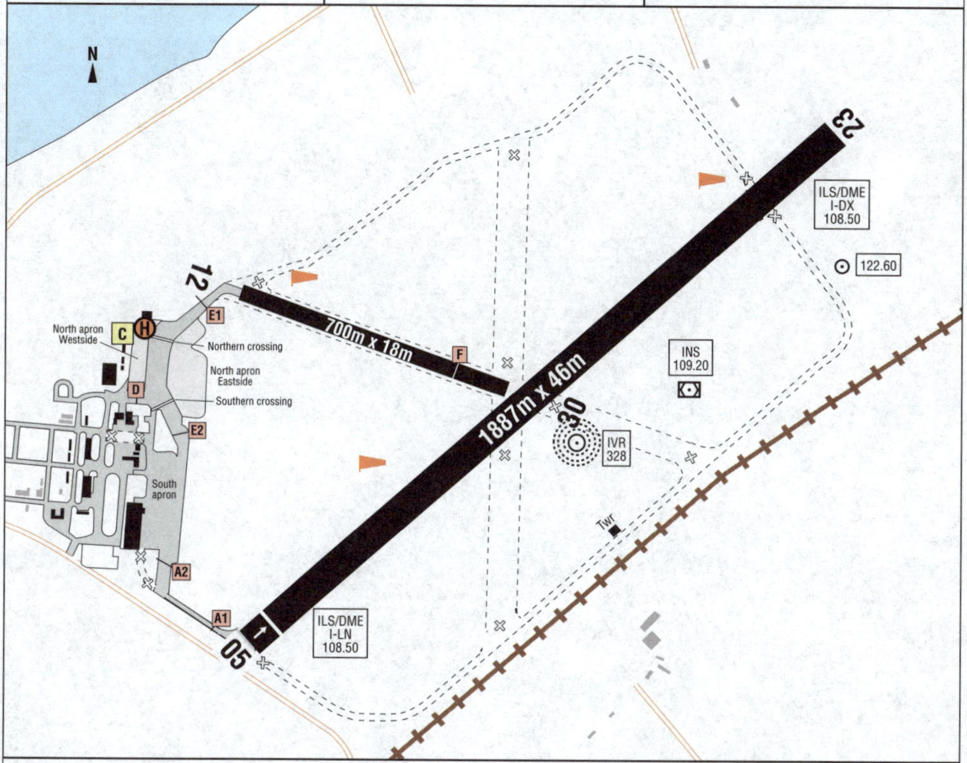

RWY	SURFACE	TORA	LDA	LIGHTING
05	Asphalt	1887	1827	Ap Thr Rwy PAPI 3° LHS
23	Asphalt	1820	1820	Ap Thr Rwy PAPI 3° LHS
12/30	Asphalt	700	700	Nil

I-J

Remarks

No GND signals except light signals. Lossiemouth provides a RAD service for Inverness traffic. All ACFT >2730kg (and any for Customs/Immigration) require handling.

Warnings

Agricultural work takes place on grass areas throughout year. Exercise caution taxiing to hangars No.1 & 2 due close proximity of adjacent security fence. Twy between N end of S apron & Thr12 available for use only by ACFT with wingspan <36m. Grass apron for parking of single piston engined ACFT <1500kg MAUW. Entry to apron E2. AD has constant deer hazard, particularly around dawn/dusk. Patrols mounted whenever the presence of deer is known or anticipated, pilots requested to report to ATC the location of any animals on AD. Birds are constant hazard especially during migration. No hover taxing permitted W of Hold D. All GND movement W of Hold D is at pilots discretion. TV Masts 1074ft amsl 5.6nm to N & 1495ft amsl 8nm WNW. High GND to S 1500ft amsl.

		Disabled Facilities
Operating Hrs	Mon-Sun 0545-2100 (Summer) Mon-Fri 0645-2200 Sat 0645-1915 Sun 0815-2200 (Winter) & by arr	
Circuits	Nil	**Restaurants** Refreshments & Bar
Landing Fee	£11.15 ACFT under 3MT VFR cash/cheque on day if PPR obtained	**Taxis** Available at the terminal **Car Hire**
Maintenance	Nil	AVIS **Tel:** 01667 462787
Fuel	AVGAS 100LL 0730-1800 (L) **Tel:** 01667 462360 JET A1 0600-2000 (L) Fuel available out of Hrs on payment of surcharge	Hertz **Tel:** 01667 462652 **Weather Info** M T9 Fax 298 VSc GWC ATIS **Tel:** 01667 464255

Visual Reference Points (VRP)	
Invergordon	N5741.53 W00410.05
Lochindorb	N5724.17 W00342.95
Tomatin	N5720.03 W00359.50
Dores	N5722.92 W00419.92
Dingwall	N5735.97 W00425.88

Operator	HIAL Inverness
	Inverness Aerodrome
	Inverneshire, IV1 2JB
	Tel: 01667 464000/464293 (ATC)
	Fax: 01667 462041 (Admin)
	Fax: 01667 462586 (ATC)
	www.highlands-and-islands-airports.uk.com

180ft 6mb	8nm NNE of Ipswich N5210.06 E00115.60	PPR	Alternative AD	Norwich Elmsett

Ipswich Radio	APP Wattisham 125.800	A/G 121.000

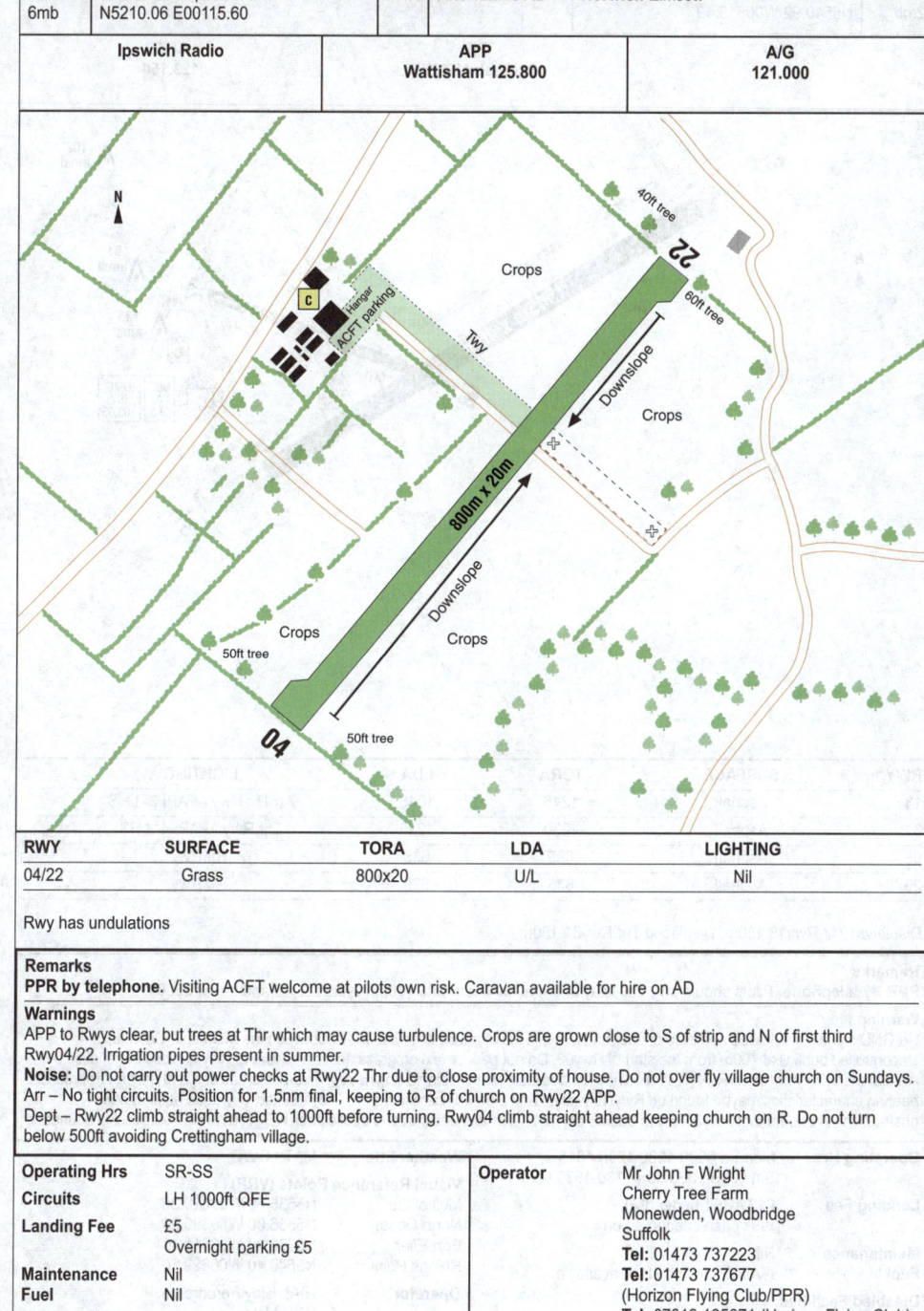

RWY	SURFACE	TORA	LDA	LIGHTING
04/22	Grass	800x20	U/L	Nil

Rwy has undulations

Remarks
PPR by telephone. Visiting ACFT welcome at pilots own risk. Caravan available for hire on AD

Warnings
APP to Rwys clear, but trees at Thr which may cause turbulence. Crops are grown close to S of strip and N of first third Rwy04/22. Irrigation pipes present in summer.
Noise: Do not carry out power checks at Rwy22 Thr due to close proximity of house. Do not over fly village church on Sundays. Arr – No tight circuits. Position for 1.5nm final, keeping to R of church on Rwy22 APP.
Dept – Rwy22 climb straight ahead to 1000ft before turning. Rwy04 climb straight ahead keeping church on R. Do not turn below 500ft avoiding Crettingham village.

Operating Hrs	SR-SS		Operator	Mr John F Wright
Circuits	LH 1000ft QFE			Cherry Tree Farm
Landing Fee	£5			Monewden, Woodbridge
	Overnight parking £5			Suffolk
Maintenance	Nil			**Tel:** 01473 737223
Fuel	Nil			**Tel:** 01473 737677
				(Horizon Flying Club/PPR)
Disabled Facilities	Nil			**Tel:** 07813 105071 (Horizon Flying Club)
Restaurant	Nil			
Taxis	**Tel:** 01728 685883			
	Tel: 07836 676656			
Car Hire	**Tel:** 01728 685883			
	Tel: 07836 676656			
Weather Info	AirS MOEx			

I-J

56ft 2mb	4.5nm NNW of Port Ellen N5540.92 W00615.40	PPR	Alternative AD	Prestwick Campbeltown

Islay	FIS Scottish 127.275	AFIS 123.150

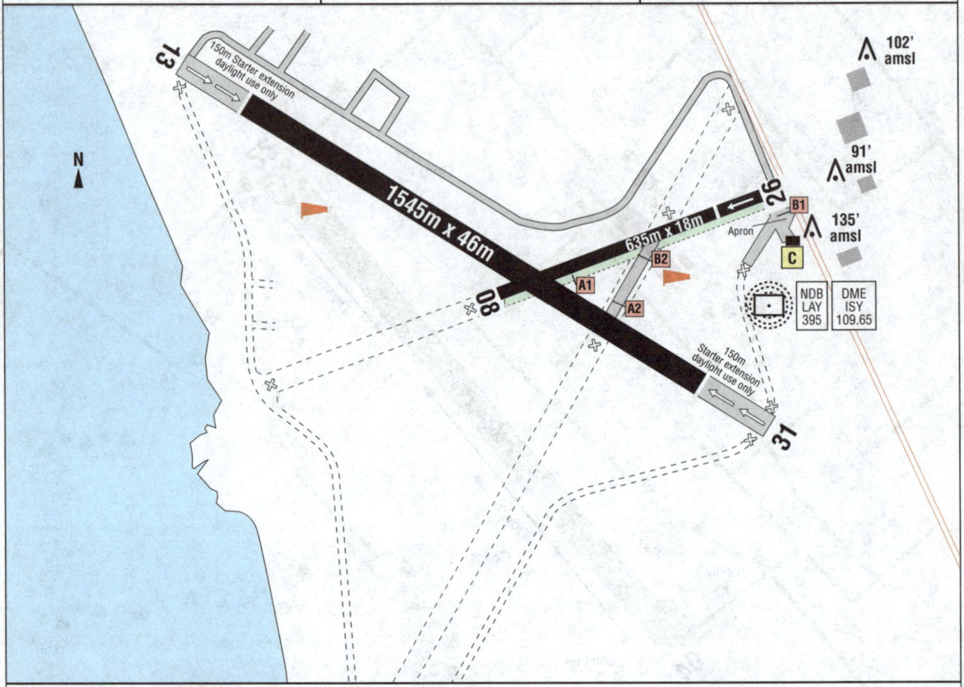

(Aerodrome chart showing runways 13/31 (1545m x 46m), 08/26 (635m x 18m), with 150m Starter extension daylight use only, taxiways A1, A2, B1, B2, C, Apron, NDB LAY 395, DME ISY 109.65, obstructions 102' amsl, 91' amsl, 135' amsl, N arrow)

RWY	SURFACE	TORA	LDA	LIGHTING
13	Asphalt	1245	1245	Ap Thr Rwy APAPI 3° LHS
31	Asphalt	1230	1230	Thr Rwy APAPI 4° LHS
08	Asphalt	635	635	Thr Rwy
26	Asphalt	635	575	Thr Rwy

Displaced Thr Rwy13 150m, Displaced Thr Rwy31 150m

Remarks
PPR by telephone. Pilots should only call Islay Information when within 10nm radius of AD and below 3000ft.

Warnings
No GND signals. Increased numbers of deer and large flocks of geese possible on AD between the months of Oct-Mar. Uncontrolled public Rd 700m from the start of Rwy08. Do not park or taxi on grass areas adjacent to Rwys unless marshalled by AD staff. Link Twy between Rwy13/31 & Rwy08/26 available for light single engine ACFT. Grass areas soft and unsafe. Poor load bearing characteristics maybe found on Rwy/Twy strips and area adjacent to apron. Only marked Twy to be used. Mobile obstructions in undershoot Rwy31. Farm track E of Rwy31 Thr and uncontrolled public track NE of Rwy13/31 outside AD boundary.

Operating Hrs	Mon-Fri 0900-1230 1230-1815 Sat 0900-1000 Sun 1730-1830 (L)	**Weather Info**	M* T9 GWC
Landing Fee	£13 ACFT under 3MT VFR cash/cheque on day	**Visual Reference Points (VRP)** Mull of Oa	N5535.50 W00620.30
		North Coast	N5556.00 W00609.90
Maintenance	Nil	Port Ellen	N5538.00 W00611.40
Fuel	AVGAS Limited stock available	Rhinns Point	N5540.40 W00629.10
Disabled Facilities		**Operator**	HIAL Islay Aerodrome Isle of Islay Argyll, PA42 7AS Tel: 01496 302361 **Fax:** 01496 302096 islayapm@hial.co.uk www.highlands-and-islands.airports.uk.com

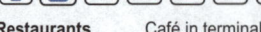

Restaurants	Café in terminal
Taxis	**Tel:** 01496 302155 **Tel:** 07899 756159
Car Hire	**Tel:** 01496 302300
Bike Hire	**Tel:** 01496 810366

I-J

EGNS

52ft 2mb	6nm SW of Douglas N5405.00 W00437.43	PPR	Alternative AD	Belfast City Newtownards

Ronaldsway	ATIS 123.875	APP 120.850	RAD 120.850

TWR 118.900	FIRE 121.600	FIS Scottish 119.875	

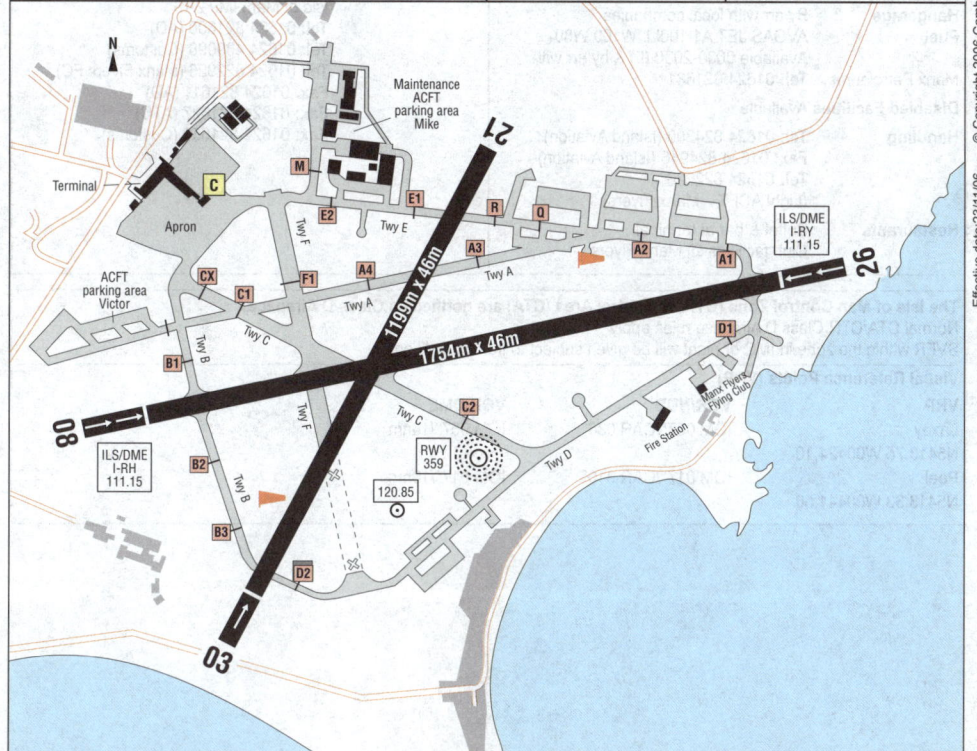

Effective date:23/11/06

RWY	SURFACE	TORA	LDA	LIGHTING
03	Asphalt	1199	1104	Thr Rwy PAPI 3° LHS
21	Asphalt	1104	1104	Ap Thr Rwy PAPI 3.5° RHS
08	Asph/Conc	1631	1463	Ap Thr Rwy PAPI 3° LHS
26	Asph/Conc	1736	1613	Ap Thr Rwy PAPI 3° LHS

I-J

Remarks
PPR for non-radio ACFT. Use governed by regulations applicable to the Isle of Man CTR/CTA. Instrument training is subject to prior permission from ATC. Pilots and passengers of private and charter ACFT Arr from or Dept to GB, the Republic of Ireland or the Channel Islands must report immediately on Arr and immediately before Dept to a Police Examining Officer in the designated security area. Extensions to AD Hrs are frequent, pilots intending to transit Isle of Man CTR outside published AD Hrs must contact Ronaldsway APP. Pilots of helicopters should APP & land in accordance with ATC instructions. Radio communications N of IOM control zone are restricted at low level (<3000ft amsl) due to screening by high GND. Pilots take note of limitations when planing any flight. Ensuring they do not enter IOM controlled airspace without ATC clearance. FIS is available from Scottish Info. Light ACFT are to land and take off on the Rwy, no other landing area is available. When APP Rwy08, ACFT should intercept centre line 1.5nm minimum, should not descend below PAPI indicated APP of 3°. On Dept all prop driven ACFT must climb straight ahead to at least 500ft and must have passed the AD boundary before commencing any turn. In very strong winds into wind parking may be requested with assistance of a marshal. Marshaller available on request. Simulated engine failure Dept Rwy26 not permitted. Handling is compulsory for ACFT needing access to the restricted zone (main apron). Self briefing FBU available

Warnings
No GND signals except light signals. Wind shear exists on short final Rwy08 in SE winds. There is a possibility of turbulence on all Rwys during strong wind conditions. Rwy21due to high GND to the left of the APP for Rwy21, pilots must establish on the Rwy centre line before descending on the PAPI glide path. Due to the presence of an uncontrolled public road Rwy03 APP, Rwy not permitted for use when PAPI's are out of service. The apron flood lighting to the W of the apron area is 7m from the edge of the useable paved apron area. If self parking in this area exercise extreme caution in respect of wing tip clearance. Bird scaring takes place using pyrotechnics.
Noise: Pilots must ensure that ACFT are operated in a manner calculated to cause the least disturbance practicable in areas surrounding the AD, particularly near Castletown and Ballasalla.

Operating Hrs	Mon-Sat 0515-1945		Taxis	Available at terminal
	Sun 0600-1945 (Summer)		**Car Hire**	
	+1Hr (Winter) & by arr		Athol Car Hire	**Tel:** 01624 822481
Circuits	By arr with ATC		Mylchreests	**Tel:** 01624 823533
Landing Fee	£14.52 <1999kgs		**Weather Info**	M T9 Fax 322 VN IOM
	£29.05 2000-3000kgs		**Operator**	The Isle of Man
	> 3000kgs on application			Dept of Transport-Airports Division
	(cash on day)			Isle of Man Airport
Maintenance	Woodgate Aviation			Ballasalla
Hangerage	By arr with local companies			Isle of Man, IM9 2AS
Fuel	AVGAS JET A1 100LL W100 W80			**Tel:** 01624 821600 (AD)
	Available 0630-2030 (L) & by arr with			**Tel:** 01624 439098 (Customs)
Manx Petroleums	**Tel:** 01624 821681			**Tel:** 01624 822926 (Manx Flyers FC)
Disabled Facilities	Available			**Fax:** 01624 821611 (AD)
Handling	**Tel:** 01624 824300 (Island Aviation)			**Fax:** 01624 821627 (ATC)
	Fax: 01624 824946 (Island Aviation)			**Fax:** 01624 821650 (Customs)
	Tel: 01624 822926			
	(Light ACFT – Manx Flyers)			
Restaurants	Buffet & bar at terminal			
	Club facilities @ Manx Flyers			

The Isle of Man Control Zone (CTR) & Control Area (CTA) are notified as Class D Airspace
Normal CTA/CTR Class D Airspace rules apply
SVFR within the zone in IMC or night will be given subject to traffic conditions.

Visual Reference Points (VRP)

VRP	VOR/NDB	VOR/DME
Laxey	IOM 057°/CAR 036°	IOM 057°/16nm
N5413.75 W00424.10		
Peel	IOM 017°/CAR 310°	IOM 017°/10nm
N5413.33 W00441.50		

I-J

34ft 1mb	On the Isle of Skye N5715.19 W00549.68		PPR	Alternative AD	Benbecula Barra

Non-radio	FIS Scottish 127.275	Heli Ops 130.650

N

25

771m x 23m

07

RWY	SURFACE	TORA	LDA	LIGHTING
07/25	Asphalt	771x23	U/L	Emergency Only

I-J

Remarks
PPR 24Hrs notice required.

Warnings
Helicopter operations take place at AD and local areas up to 2000ft within a radius of 25nm. High GND up to 2405ft to E & W of AD.

Operating Hrs	SR-SS	**Operator**	Highland Regional Council
Circuit	Nil		TEC Services
Landing Fee	On application		Glenurquhart Road
Maintenance	Nil		Inverness, IV3 5NX
Fuel	Nil		**Tel:** 01478 612727 (R&T Portree)
			Tel: 01463 702604 (HQ Inverness)
Disabled Facilities	Nil		**Fax:** 01478 612255 (R&T Portree)

Restaurants
Broadford Hotel   **Tel:** 01471 822204 (Bar meals)   **Fax:** 01463 702606 (HQ Inverness)
Claymore Restaurant   **Tel:** 01471 882333 (Broadford)

Taxis
Waterloo   **Tel:** 01471 822630 (Broadford)
Car Hire
Sutherland's Garage   **Tel:** 01471 822225 (self drive)

Weather Info   AirSc GWC

315

55ft 2mb	5nm SE of Newport N5039.18 W00110.92	**PPR**	**Alternative AD**	**Southampton** Bembridge
	Sandown		**A/G** 119.275	

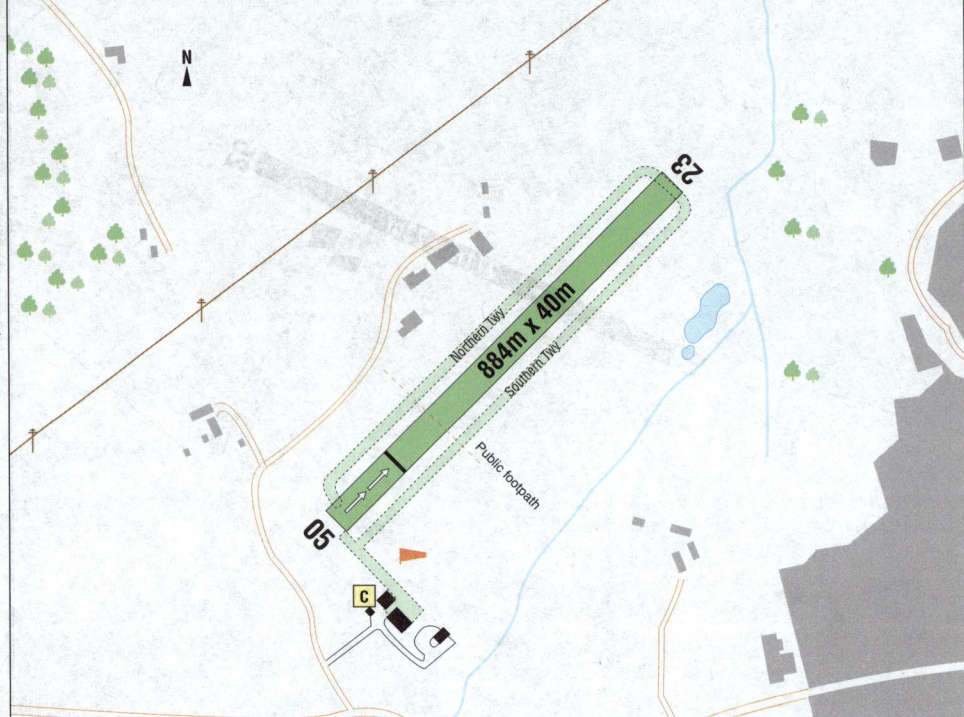

RWY	SURFACE	TORA	LDA	LIGHTING
05	Grass	884	775	Nil
23	Grass	884	884	Nil

Remarks
PPR by telephone.

Warnings
Either Rwy or Twy maybe withdrawn or dimensions changed at short notice. Black & white wing bars mark the landing Thr. Rwy05 QDM markers located before start of Rwy. Taxi with care at all times due to undulating GND in some parts of Twy, active public foot path crosses Rwy 200m upwind of Rwy05 Thr. ATZ over laps Bembridge ATZ, it may be necessary to contact Bembridge after Dept/Arr for transit clearance. Maintain Rwy heading 1nm before turn en-route.
Caution: High sided vehicles cross Rwy05 APP.
Noise: Avoid over flying local towns & villages below 1500ft QNH

Operating Hrs	0800-1700 (Summer) 0900-1700 or SS whichever is earlier (Winter) & by arr	**Weather Info**	AirS MOEx
		Operator	Isle of Wight Airport Ltd
Circuit	05 LH, 23 RH, 1000ft QFE		Isle of Wight Airport
Landing Fee	Single £10 Twin £15		Sandown, Isle of Wight, PO36 0JP
Maintenance	Vectis Aviation Services **Tel:** 01983 405520		**Tel:** 01983 405125 **Tel:** 01983 404838
Fuel	AVGAS 100LL		**Fax:** 01983 406117
Disabled Facilities Nil			tower@isleofwightairport.co.uk
Restaurant	Aviator bar adjacent to TWR		
Taxis Lake	**Tel:** 01983 402641		
Car Hire Wilton Car Hire SW Rentals	**Tel:** 01983 864414 **Tel:** 01983 864263		

JACKRELLS FARM

250ft 8mb	2.5nm SSW of Horsham N5101.90 W00019.88	PPR	Alternative AD	Shoreham Goodwood

Non-Radio	ATIS Gatwick 136.525	APP Gatwick Director 126.825	Safetycom 135.475

45ft trees
Gap in 30ft trees
21
Pasture
550m x 12m
Downslope
Pasture
Hangars amongst 40ft trees
35ft mast
03
6ft hedge
Caravan site

RWY	SURFACE	TORA	LDA	LIGHTING
03/21	Grass	550x12	U/L	Nil

Remarks
PPR Strictly by email to obtain APP map and detailed info to avoid other strips close by. Visiting ACFT welcome at pilots own risk. Visitors are requested to complete movement book by hangars.

Warnings
Downslope on Rwy21. Recommended land Rwy03. Depart Rwy21. Obstacles at Rwy21 Thr. No windsock displayed. Stay on cut surfaces of Rwy and Twy all other surfaces are grass crop.
Caution: There are six other strips in close proximity. One prominent with its own windsock 350m SW of Jackrells Farm close by the Southwater bypass. Airfield is beneath the Gatwick CTA and close to CTR.
Noise: Avoid over flying local houses, particularly to N of AD.

Operating Hrs	SR-SS		**Operator**	Mike & Eileen Hallam
Circuits	To E 1000ft QFE			Birches
Landing Fee	Nil			Ashmore's Lane
Maintenance	Nil			Rusper
Fuel	Nil			Horsham
Disabled Facilities	Nil			West Sussex
Restaurant	Nil			RH12 4PS
Taxi/Car Hire	Nil			mikehallam@btinternet.com
Weather Info	AirSE MOEx			

I-J

274ft 9mb	4nm WNW of St Helier N4912.48 W00211.73			Alternative AD Diversion AD	Guernsey Alderney	
Jersey		**ATIS** 129.725		**ZONE** 125.200		**APP** 120.300
RAD 118.550		**TWR** 119.450		**GND** 121.900 (when notified)		**FIRE** 121.600

I-J

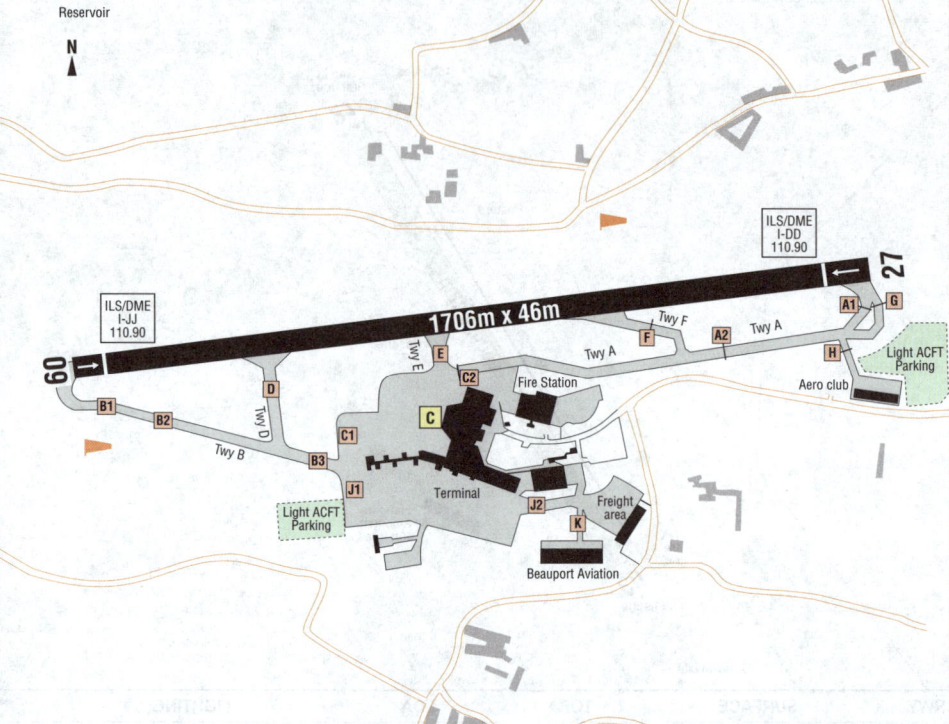

RWY	SURFACE	TORA	LDA	LIGHTING
09	Asphalt	1706	1645	Ap Thr Rwy PAPI 3° LHS
27	Asphalt	1645	1554	Ap Thr Rwy PAPI 3° RHS

Remarks

PPR essential for permit ACFT and microlights. Use governed by regulations applicable to Channel Islands CTR. Proof of insurance should be available for inspection. GND signals other than light signals and letter C not displayed. Light ACFT parking available W of stand 24. Only use designated Twy to access Jersey Aero Club. Access from H to light ACFT park does not meet Twy standards. The centre line is for assistance only, it does not provide the usual clearances. Helicopters are to use the main Twy for all Arr/Dept as no specific helicopter landing area exists. Visiting ACFT under 3 metric tonne will be parked as directed by ATC and will be handled by Jersey Aero Club. ACFT over 3 metric tonnes will be parked as directed by ATC and handled by Aviation Beauport. If passengers need to be conveyed to the main terminal building for customs/immigration, the handling agents will provide transport. For propeller-driven ACFT: Rwy27: Take-off; Climb to at least 500ft aal before turning on to a heading and avoid over-flying land below 1000ft aal. Landing; Maintain at least 1000ft aal until intercepting the ILS glide path or PAPI indication and thereafter descend on the facility. If under 5700kg and making a visual APP, land must not be over flown below 500ft agl until on final APP. Rwy09: Take-off; Climb straight ahead to a minimum of 500ft aal before turning and climb as rapidly as safe to not less than 1000ft aal. Landing. Maintain at least 1000ft aal until intercepting the ILS glide path or PAPI indication and there after descend on the facility. If under 5700kg and making a visual APP land must not be over flown below 500ft agl until on final APP.
Aids to Navigation: NDB JW 329.00

Warnings

All surface movement of ACFT subject to ATC authority, including start-up, push-back and taxi clearance. Turbulence and variable wind conditions may be caused by nearby cliffs on final APP and landing Rwy09. Blasting takes place infrequently on any weekday at quarries adjacent to AD bearing 042° 1.36nm from the VRP. Turning on Rwy for back-tracking only allowed from the Rwy ends with ATC permission.
Caution: Manoeuvring on grass parking areas due to wet and uneven surfaces.

Operating Hrs	0600-2030 (Summer) 0700-2100 (Winter) & by arr	**Restaurant**	Restaurant & buffet in terminal & Aero club
Circuits	When ever cloud base permits maintain at least 1000ft QFE and make the majority of the circuit over the sea.	**Taxis/Car Hire**	Available at terminal
		Weather Info	M T9 Fax 324 A VS JER **Tel:** 0907 155 7777
Landing Fee	On application	**Operator**	States of Jersey
Maintenance	Jersey Aircraft Maintenance **Tel:** 01534 745124 Channel Islands Aero Services **Tel:** 01534 742373		States of Jersey Airport Jersey Channel Islands, JE1 1BY **Tel:** 01534 492000
Fuel	AVGAS 100LL AVTUR JET A1 Refuelling not available after 1930 (L) for AVGAS100LL or after 2000 (L) for JET A1 except by special arrangement through AD switchboard		**Tel:** 01534 747415 (When ATC is not manned) **Tel:** 01534 492226 (ATC) **Fax:** 01534 492131 (Admin) **Fax:** 01534 492430 (ATC)
Handling	**Tel:** 01534 499970 (Jersey Aero Club) **Tel:** 01534 496496 (Beauport Aviation) **Fax:** 01534 496497 (Beauport Aviation)		**Fax:** 01534 492194 (FBU) jacustomerservices@jerseyairport.com www.jerseyairport.com

Disabled Facilities

Channel Islands Control Zone (Class A) & Jersey Control Zone (Class D)
Normal CTA/CTR Class D Air space rules apply
In the event of RAD failure whilst within the Jersey Zone, the ACFT should proceed to overhead Jersey AD at 2000ft and then leave the Zone tracking 225°T.
Carriage of SSR transponders is mandatory within the Channel Islands Control Zone. Mode 'A' for SVFR, Mode 'A+C' for IFR flights.

Channel Island Visual Reference Points (VRP)

VRP	VOR/DME	VOR/DME	VOR/DME
Carteret Lighthouse N4922.00 W00148.00	JSY 051°/13nm	GUR 101°/32nm	
Casquets Lighthouse N4943.00 W00222.00	JSY 340°/32nm	GUR 032°/19nm	
Corbiere Lighthouse N4911.00 W00215.00	JSY 257°/8nm	GUR 141°/21nm	DIN 353°/36nm
Heauville N4934.60 W00148.06	JSY 026°/24nm	GUR 078°/33nm	
NE Point of Guernsey N4930.42 W00230.52	JSY 317°/25nm	GUR 045°/6nm	
NW corner of Jersey N4915.30 W00214.50	JSY 289°/8nm	GUR 131°/18nm	
Point de Rozel N4928.60 W00150.60	JSY 029°/18nm	GUR 088°/30nm	
St. Germain N4914.00 W00138.00	JSY 091°/16nm	GUR 111°/40nm	DIN 028°/43nm
SE Corner of Jersey N4910.00 W00202.00	JSY 176°/3nm	GUR 130°/28nm	DIN 007°/35nm
W of Cap de la Hague N4943.00 W00200.00	JSY 008°/30nm	GUR 058°/29nm	

I-J

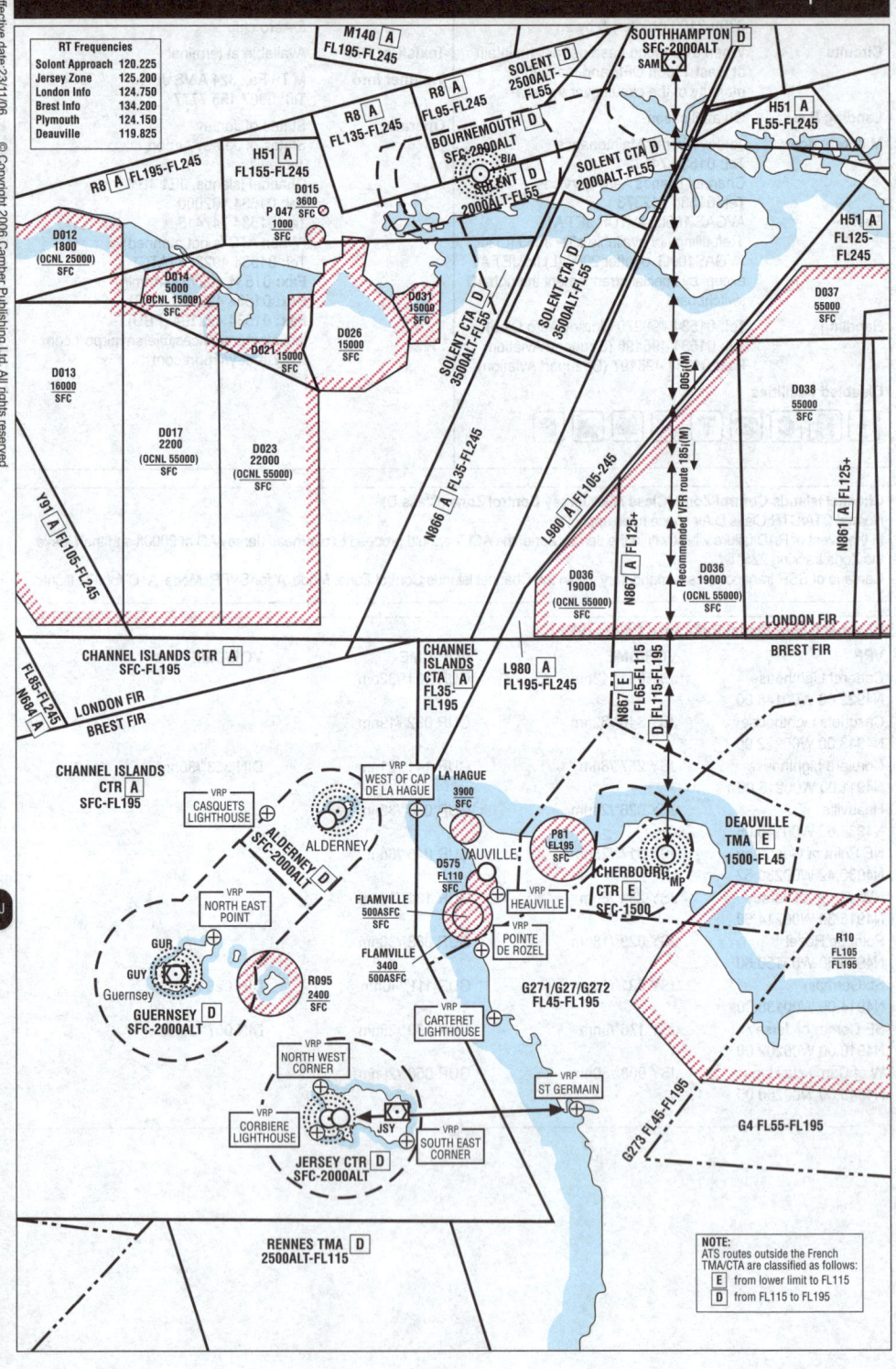

RT Frequencies

Solent Approach	120.225
Jersey Zone	125.200
London Info	124.750
Brest Info	134.200
Plymouth	124.150
Deauville	119.825

M140 A
FL195-FL245

SOUTHHAMPTON
SFC-2000ALT D
SAM

R8 A
FL95-FL245

SOLENT D
2500ALT-
FL55

R8 A
FL135-FL245

H51 A
FL55-FL245

R8 A
FL95-FL245

BOURNEMOUTH D
SFA-2000ALT
BIA

SOLENT CTA D
2000ALT-FL55

H51 A
FL155-FL245

SOLENT D
2000ALT-FL55

H51 A
FL125-
FL245

R8 A FL195-FL245

D015
3600
SFC

SOLENT CTA D
3500ALT-FL55

SOLENT CTA D
3500ALT-FL55

D012
1800
(OCNL 25000)
SFC

P 047
1000
SFC

D037
55000
SFC

D014
5000
(OCNL 15000)
SFC

D031
15000
SFC

D038
55000
SFC

D021 15000
SFC

D026
15000
SFC

D013
16000
SFC

005(M)

N861 A FL125+

D017
2200
(OCNL 55000)
SFC

D023
22000
(OCNL 55000)
SFC

N866 A FL35-FL245

L980 A FL105-245

Recommended VFR route 185(M)

Y91 A FL105-FL245

N867 A FL125+

D036
19000
(OCNL 55000)
SFC

D036
19000
(OCNL 55000)
SFC

LONDON FIR

BREST FIR

FL85-FL245
N684 A

CHANNEL ISLANDS CTR A
SFC-FL195

LONDON FIR
BREST FIR

CHANNEL
ISLANDS
CTA
FL35-
FL195

L980 A
FL195-FL245

N867 E
FL65-FL115

D FL115-FL195

CHANNEL ISLANDS
CTR A
SFC-FL195

CHANNEL ISLANDS
CTA A
FL35-FL195

VRP
WEST OF CAP
DE LA HAGUE

LA HAGUE
3900
SFC

DEAUVILLE
TMA E
1500-FL45

VRP
CASQUETS
LIGHTHOUSE

VAUVILLE

P81
FL195
SFC

ALDERNEY D
SFC-2000ALT

ALDERNEY

D575
FL110
SFC

CHERBOURG
MP

VRP
NORTH EAST
POINT

FLAMVILLE
500ASFC
SFC

VRP
HEAUVILLE

CHERBOURG
CTR E
SFC-1500

R10
FL105
FL195

GUR

FLAMVILLE
3400
500ASFC

VRP
POINTE
DE ROZEL

GUY
Guernsey

R095
2400
SFC

G271/G27/G272
FL45-FL195

GUERNSEY D
SFC-2000ALT

VRP
CARTERET
LIGHTHOUSE

VRP
NORTH WEST
CORNER

VRP
ST GERMAIN

VRP
CORBIERE
LIGHTHOUSE

JSY

VRP
SOUTH EAST
CORNER

G273 FL45-FL195

G4 FL55-FL195

JERSEY CTR D
SFC-2000ALT

RENNES TMA D
2500ALT-FL115

NOTE:
ATS routes outside the French
TMA/CTA are classified as follows:
E from lower limit to FL115
D from FL115 to FL195

I-J

433ft 14mb	5nm SW of Cirencester N5140.08 W00203.42		**Alternative AD** **Diversion AD**	**Gloucestershire** Oxford

Kemble	LARS **Brize 124.270**	Zone **Lyneham 123.400**	AFIS **118.900**

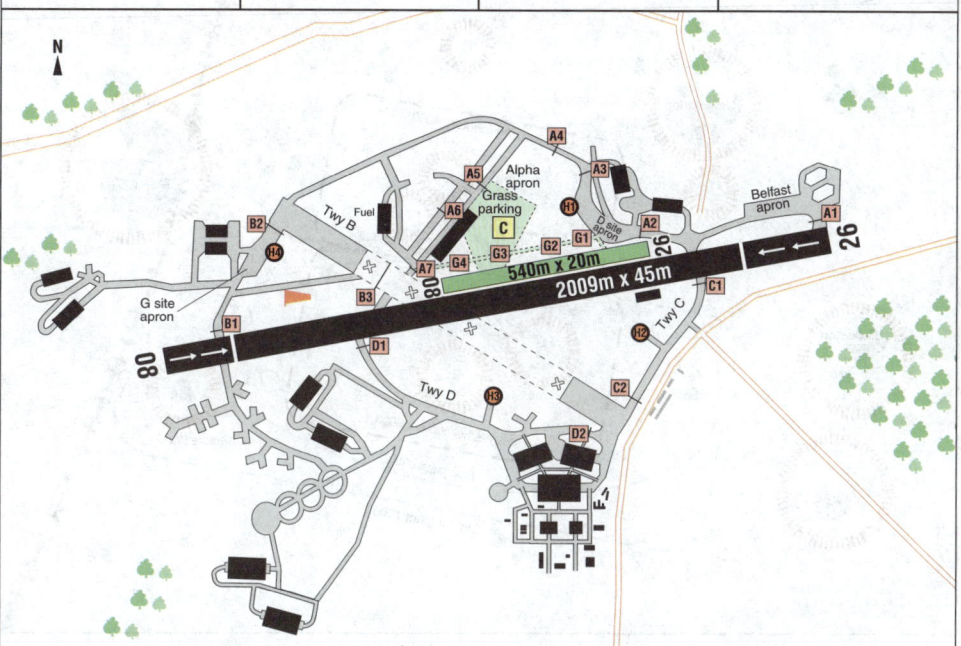

RWY	SURFACE	TORA	LDA	LIGHTING
08	Asphalt	1759	1778	Ap Thr Rwy PAPI 3°LHS
26	Asphalt	1803	1594	Ap Thr Rwy PAPI 3°LHS
08/26	Grass	540x20	U/L	Nil

Rwy08/26 lighting available on request

Remarks

Non Radio ACFT not accepted. Hi-Vis. AD is multi-use including non-aviation use. Look out for microlights & model ACFT. All visitors welcome. Please book-in and pay landing fees in the pilot shop. Fees not settled before Dept will incur an admin charge. All fuel uploads must be paid for on the day. The ACFT commander or person nominated by the ACFT commander is responsible for passenger safety whilst airside.

Warnings

Pilots should avoid Aston Down 3.5nm NW, active cable launch glider site to 3000ft, often mistaken for Kemble. Oaksey Park AD 2.5nm to SE, South Cerney (parachuting) 5nm to ENE, keep good lookout for traffic. AD may close for special events, telephone for information. Turbulence likely on APP Rwy26 with N or S wind.

Noise: Do not over fly any of the local villages. Kemble AD welcomes careful, noise conscious pilots. APP Rwy26 offset to S of Kemble village. APP to Rwy08 offset to N.

Operating Hrs	0800-1700 (Summer) 0900-1700 or SS (Winter) & by arr
Circuits	LH all Rwys unless advised ACFT 1000ft QFE Microlights 600ft QFE Helicopters 700ft QFE Paramotors 300ft QFE
Landing Fee	See website for latest prices
Maintenance Delta Jets	**Tel:** 01285 771494
Fuel	AVGAS 100LL JET A1 0900-1700 (L) by prior arr **Tel:** 01285 771177

Disabled Facilities

Restaurant	AV8
Taxis/Car Hire	Info available **Tel:** 01285 771177
Weather Info	AirSW MOEx
Operator	Kemble Air Services Ltd The Control Tower, Kemble Airfield Cirencester, Glos, GL7 6BA **Tel:** 01285 771177 (Switchboard) **Fax:** 01285 771414 (TWR) atc@kemble.com www.kemble.com

K

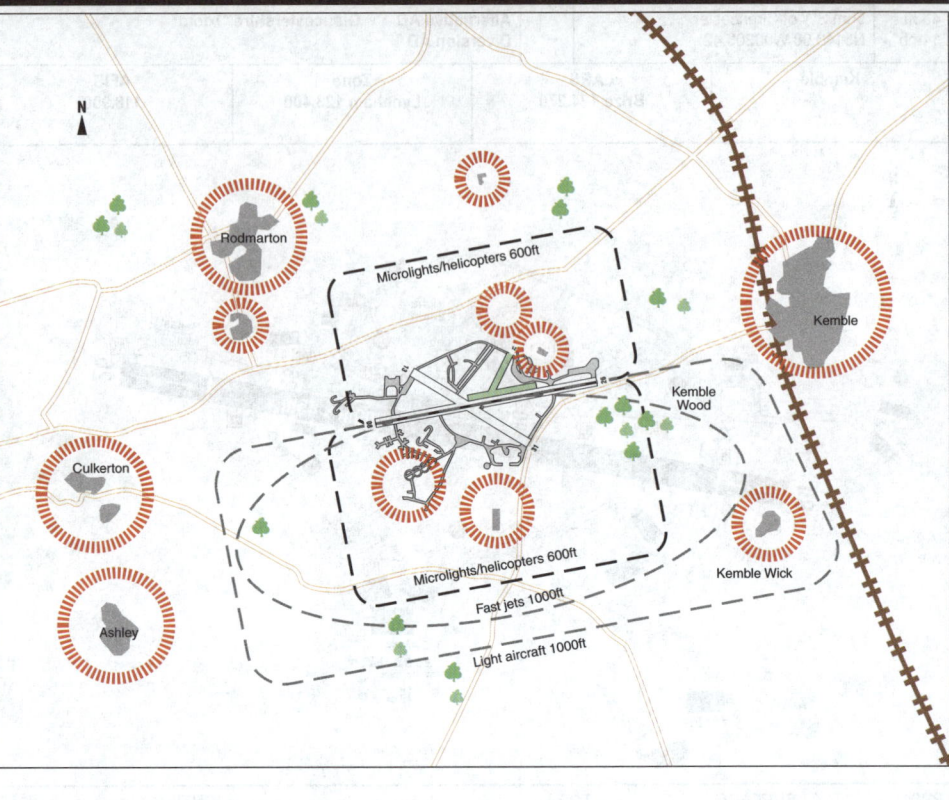

KINGSMUIR

387ft 12mb	3.5nm SE of St Andrews N5616.15 W00245.05	PPR	Alternative AD Diversion AD	Dundee Fife

Kingsmuir	LARS Leuchars 126.500	A/G 129.900 (Weekends)

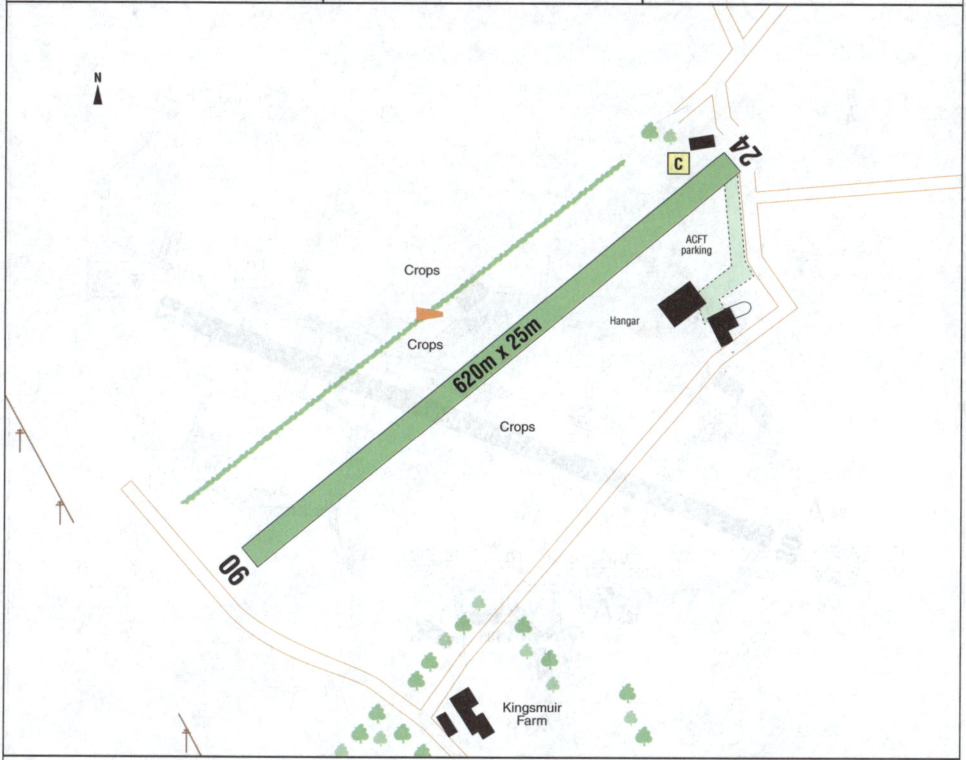

Crops

Crops

620m x 25m

Crops

24

C

ACFT parking

Hangar

06

Kingsmuir Farm

RWY	SURFACE	TORA	LDA	LIGHTING
06/24	Grass	620x25	U/L	Nil

Rwy06 has transverse slope from right to left first 25%

Remarks
Visiting ACFT welcome subject to PPR. Overnight parking is available at owners own risk. Free fall parachuting takes place at the AD. AD close to SE boundary of Leuchars MATZ.
Visual aid to location: Rwy has white flush edge markings but no Thr designators

Warning
Access road crosses Rwy24 Thr. Beware flocks of crows congregate on cut portion of strip. Occasional model ACFT activity on Rwy06 Thr.

Operating Hrs	Available on request	Operator	David & Violet Smith **Tel:** 01333 310619
Circuits	06 RH, 24 LH		
Landing Fee	Nil Donations to up keep gratefully accepted		
Maintenance	Nil		
Fuel	Mogas available in emergency		

Disabled Facilities

  C  T P

Restaurants	Open weekends
Taxis/Car Hire	Nil
Weather Info	AirSC GWC

K

323

| 22ft
0 mb | 2.5nm NE of Forres
N5738.96 W00333.64 | PPR
MIL | Alternative AD
Diversion AD | Inverness Wick | |

| Kinloss | APP
Lossie 118.900 | PAR
Lossie 123.300 118.350 | TWR
122.100 |

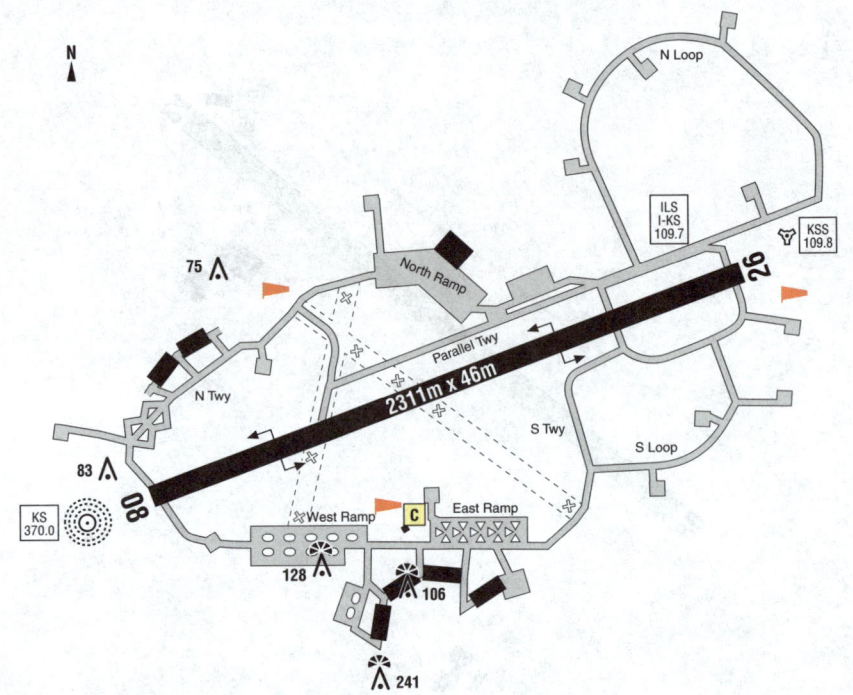

RWY	SURFACE	TORA	LDA	LIGHTING
08/26	Asph/Conc	2311	2311	Ap Thr Rwy PAPI 3° LH

Arrester gear normal ops: APP cable down overun cable up
Arrester gear Rwy26 704m from landing Thr
Arrester gear Rwy08 498m from landing Thr

Remarks
PPR by telephone essential. RAF AD used by heavy ACFT situated in combined MATZ with Lossiemouth. Lossie also provide LARS service within the local area of Intense aerial activity. Civil ACFT not accepted on weather diversion.

Warnings
Inbound ACFT must contact Lossie APP at 50nm if APP at medium/high level and at 20nm when APP from low level.
Caution: Bird hazard, Geese activity may be encountered within 10nm of the AD from Sept-Apr. Glider flying activity on AD Sat-Sun & PH.
Noise: Langcot House (N side Rwy08 Thr) and Binsness House (270°/2.5nm) not to be over flown. Over flight of Forres and Findhorn prohibited. Rwy26 all Dept maintain Rwy heading to 1000ft QFE before turning.

Operating Hrs	H24	Operator	RAF Kinloss
Circuits	Normally LH		Forres
Landing Fees	Charges in accordance with MOD policy Contact Station Ops for details		Tel: 01309 672161 Ex 7608
Maintenance	Not normally available to civil visitors		
Fuel	AVGAS JET A1 100LL by prior arr		

Disabled Facilities

   T

Taxi/Car Hire	Nil
Weather Info	M T Fax326 GWC

38ft 1mb	9.5nm W of Carlisle N5452.94 W00312.32	PPR	Alternative AD	Newcastle Carlisle

Kirkbride	APP Carlisle 123.600	A/G 124.400 (call at 10nm)

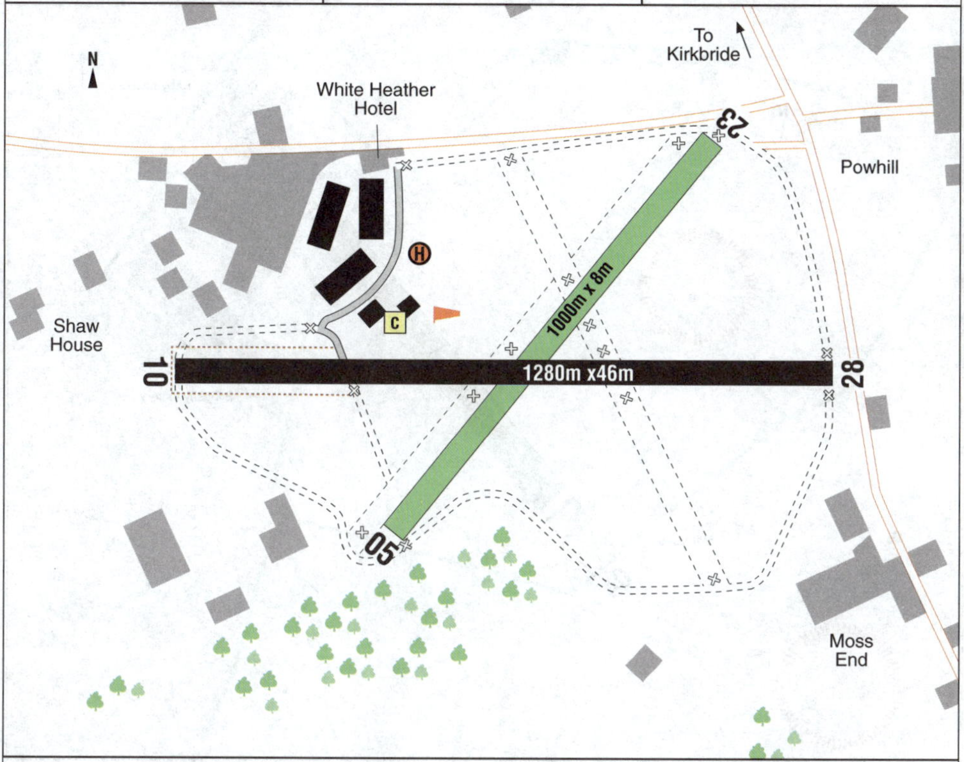

[Aerodrome chart showing runways 05/23 (grass, 1000m x 8m) and 10/28 (asphalt, 1280m x46m). Features include White Heather Hotel, Shaw House, Powhill, Moss End, To Kirkbride, helipad marker (H), control tower (C), compass rose pointing N.]

RWY	SURFACE	TORA	LDA	LIGHTING
05/23	Grass	1000x8	U/L	Nil
10/28	Asphalt	1280x46	U/L	Nil

Remarks
PPR by telephone. Visiting ACFT welcome at own risk. Microlight and autogyro activity at all times. Book in at white control tower. Parking on grass outside hangars.

Warnings
Considerable military low flying activity weekdays. HGV's may use AD manoeuvring area to access storage facilities on AD. Masts: TV 3nm SE of AD 1985ft amsl, 1034ft agl. 3.5nm S 1753ft amsl, 561ft agl & Anthorn Disused AD 2.5nm NW 778ft amsl, 561ft agl. Only one Twy useable. A wire fence 4ft high runs across Thr Rwy10 on both sides of Rwy up to first Twy intersection.
Noise: Do not over fly Kirkbride village.

Operating Hrs	AD manned at weekends but available during week	**Car Hire**	Nil
Circuits	All circuits to S 1000ft QFE	**Weather Info**	AirN MWC
Landing Fee	Nil	**Operator**	Solway Light Aviation Ltd Kirkbride, Cumbria **Tel:** 07710 672089 **Tel;** 07836 272033 photography@rogersavage.co.uk
Maintenance	Nil Hangarage available upon request		
Fuel	AVGAS expected 2007		
Disabled Facilities			

Restaurants	White Heather Hotel on AD Tea & Coffee available in TWR
Taxis	**Tel:** 01697 343148

135ft 4mb	1nm S of Kirkbymoorside N5415.00 W00057.00	PPR	Alternative AD	Durham Tees Valley Full Sutton

Slingsby	LARS Linton 118.550	A/G 129.900

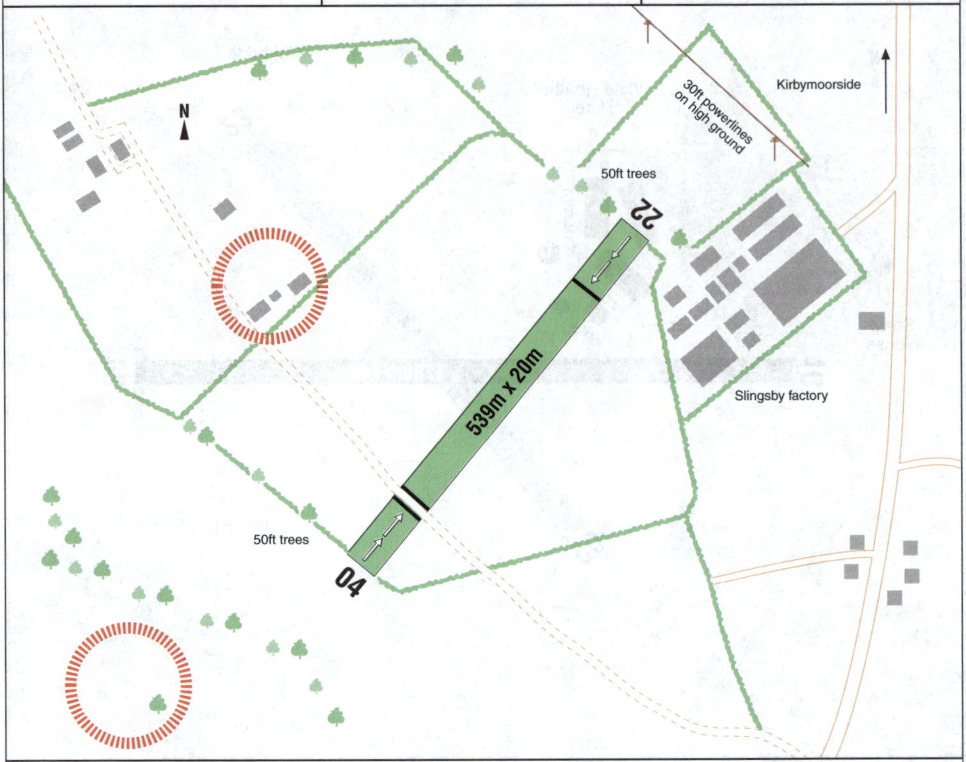

N

30ft powerlines on high ground

Kirbymoorside

50ft trees

22

539m x 20m

Slingsby factory

50ft trees

04

K

RWY	SURFACE	TORA	LDA	LIGHTING
04	Grass	539x20	U/L	Nil
22	Grass	539x20	U/L	Nil

Remarks
PPR by telephone. Use of AD is restricted to visitors to Slingsby Aviation and company flight tests or by prior arr. Operations at pilots own risk.

Warnings
Domestic power lines on high GND on short final Rwy22. Trees close to APP may cause turbulence. After heavy/prolonged precipitation AD may be boggy. Considerable military low-level activity in the area. Wombleton AD is 1.5nm to SW.
Noise: Avoid over flight of local habitation.

Operating Hrs	PPR	
Circuits	04 RH, 22 LH	
Landing fee	Advised with PPR	
Maintenance	Slingsby Aviation	
Fuel	AVGAS 100LL by arr only	
Disabled Facilities		

Taxi	**Tel:** 01751 431670
Car Hire	**Tel:** 01751 431214
Weather Info	AirN MWC
Operator	Slingsby Advanced CompositesLtd Kirkbymoorside Yorkshire, YO62 6EZ **Tel:** 01751 432474 **Fax:** 01751 431173 sal5@slingsby.co.uk

Restaurant/Accomodation
George & Dragon **Tel:** 01751 433334 (Hotel)
Kings Head **Tel:** 01751 431340 (Hotel)
Fox & Hounds **Tel:** 01751 731577 (Hotel, Sinnington approx 3nm from factory)

| 58ft
2mb | 2.5nm SE of Kirkwall
N5857.47 W00254.30 | PPR | Alternative AD
Diversion AD | Wick Sunday | |

Kirkwall	APP 118.300	TWR 118.300	ATIS 108.600	FIRE 121.600

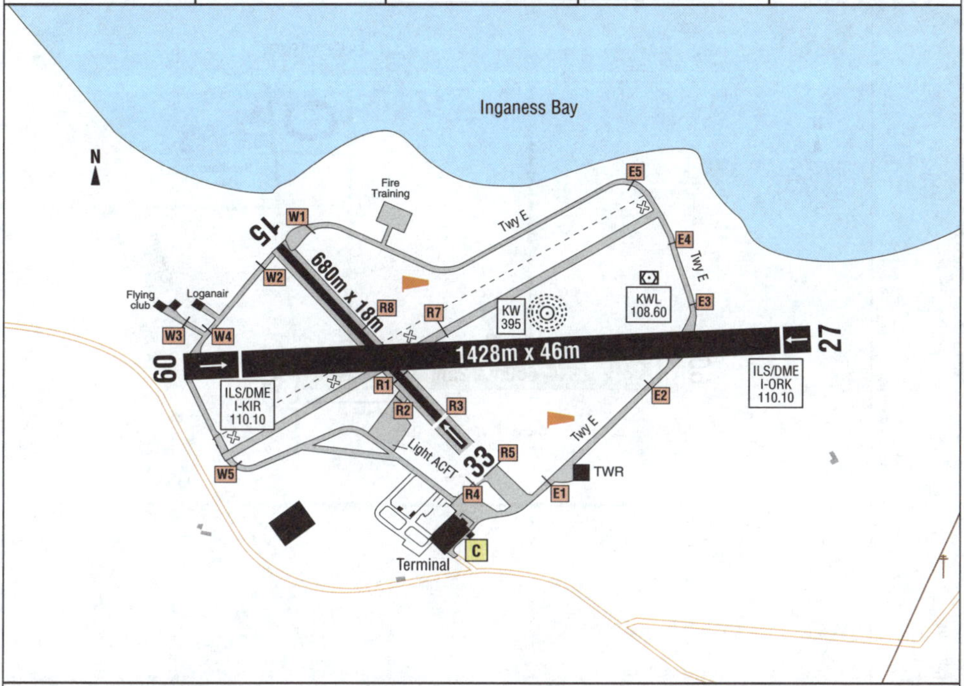

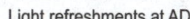

RWY	SURFACE	TORA	LDA	LIGHTING
09	Asphalt	1428	1268	Thr Rwy PAPI 3.5°
27	Asphalt	1368	1326	Ap Thr Rwy PAPI 3.25°
15	Asphalt	560	560	Nil
33	Asphalt	680	560	Nil

Displaced Thr Rwy33 208m

Remarks
Strict PPR. E Twy is only portion of Twy available for use by ACFT requiring licensed AD. Grass areas soft and unsafe only marked Twy to be used. Perimeter Twy is not available to ACFT requiring a licensed AD.

Warnings
Grass areas outside strip are unfit for transit of ACFT because of open drains. Uncontrolled road is located 91m from Rwy09Thr. A section of 549m in length on Rwy15/33 commencing at the SE end of the Rwy, has a down gradient of 1 in 50. AD is subject to water logging. Rwy27 severe turbulence may been countered on short final during periods of strong SW to NW winds. Security post 3m high at edge of apron adjacent to passenger gate.

Operating Hrs	Mon-Fri 0630-1845 Sat 0630-1745 Sun 0800-1845 (Summer) +1Hr (Winter) & by arr	**Car Hire** W R Tullock	**Tel:** 01856 875500
Circuits	Nil	**Weather Info**	M T9 Fax 328 GWC
Landing Fee	ACFT up to 3MT £11.79. Payable on Arr		ATIS **Tel:** 01856 878476
Maintenance	Ltd engineering facilities	**Visual Reference Points (VRP)**	
	available from Loganair on request	Foot	N5901.72 W00248.38
Fuel	AVGAS JET A1 100LL Oil	Lamb Holm Island	N5853.23 W00253.60
	Tel: 01856 872415	Stromberry	N5901.82 W00256.02
Disabled Facilities		**Operator**	HIAL Kirkwall Airport
			Kirkwall
			Orkney, KW15 1TH
			Tel: 01856 872421
			Tel: 01856 886205 (ATC)
			Fax: 01856 875051
Restaurants	Light refreshments at AD		www.highlands-and-islands-airports.co.uk
Taxis	Available at taxi rank outside terminal		

290ft 9mb	4.5nm SE of Oswestry N5248.27 W00259.45		PPR	Alternative AD	Hawarden Sleap

Non-radio	**LARS** Shawbury 120.775	**Safetycom** 135.475

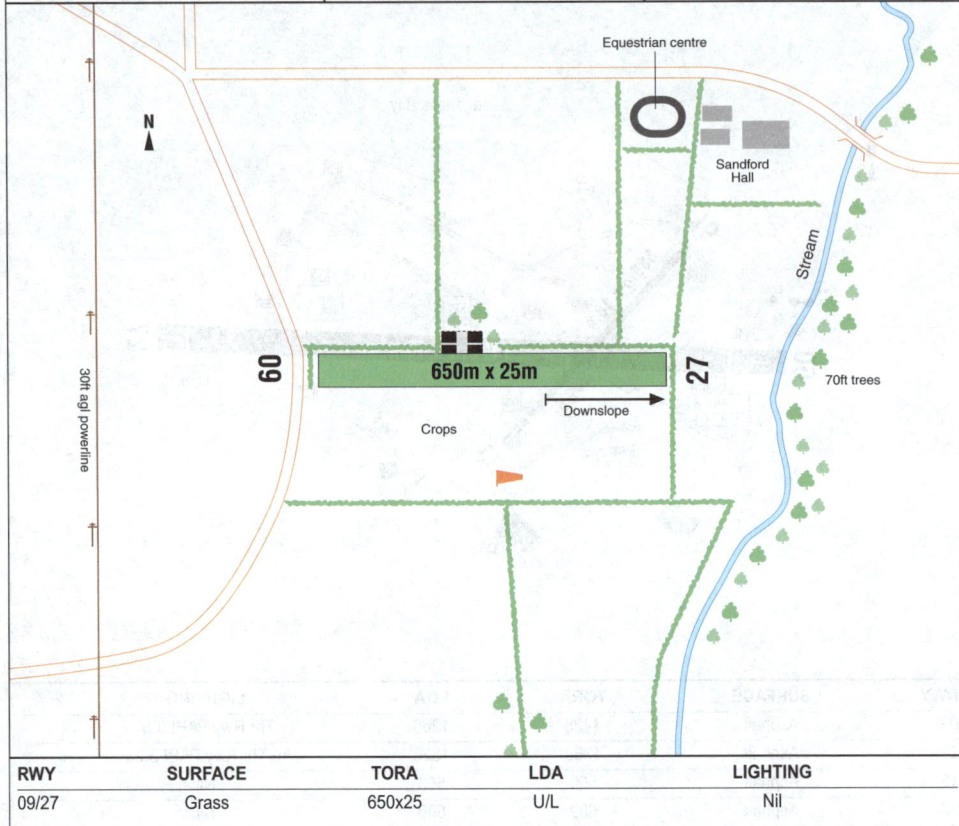

RWY	SURFACE	TORA	LDA	LIGHTING
09/27	Grass	650x25	U/L	Nil

Remarks
PPR by telephone. Well prepared grass strip. Light ACFT visitors welcome at own risk.

Warnings
6ft hedgerow runs along N edge of strip & crosses both Thr. Conifer tree on N edge of strip adjacent to hangars. Down slope in final 1/3rd Rwy09. A copse of mature trees bordering a stream crosses Rwy27 APP 250m from Thr. Power cables 30ft cross Rwy27 APP 400m from Thr. RAF Shawbury helicopter activity in vicinity.

			Operator	Mr T R Jones
Operating Hrs	SR-SS			Sandford Hall, West Felton
Circuits	As you wish, avoid local habitation			Oswestry, SK11 4EX
Landing Fee	Nil			**Tel:** 01691 610889
Maintenance	Nil			(PPR during office Hrs)
Fuel	Nil			**Tel:** 01691 610206 (PPR evenings)
Disabled Facilities	Nil			**Fax:** 01691 690699
Restaurants	Nil			
Taxis	**Tel:** 01691 650651			
Car Hire	Nil			
Weather Info	AirN MWC			

K

LADDINGFORD

Effective date:23/11/06

50ft 1mb	5nm E of Tonbridge N5111.60 E00024.80	PPR	Alternative AD	Manston Rochester

Non-Radio	LARS Southend 130.775	Safetycom 135.475

[Airfield chart showing runways 11/29 (750m x 15m) and 03/21 (450m x 18m), with building labelled C, compass rose pointing N]

RWY	SURFACE	TORA	LDA	LIGHTING
11/29	Grass	750x15	U/L	Nil
03/21	Grass	450x18	U/L	Nil

Remarks
PPR. Visiting ACFT welcome at pilots own risk.

Warnings
ACFT must keep to well-prepared mown strip and manoeuvring areas. Heavy wet land may prevail during the winter months making AD unusable.
Noise: Avoid over flying the villages of Laddingford and Paddock Wood.

Operating Hrs	SR-SS	**Car Hire**	Nil
Circuits	11, 21 LH, 29, 03 RH 1000ft QFE	**Weather Info**	AirSE MOEx
Landing Fee	£5	**Operator**	Laddingford Aero Club
Maintenance	Nil		T/A Laddingford Farm Ltd
Fuel	Nil		c/o Badger Cottage
Disabled Facilities			Sham Farm Road
			Eridge Green
			Tunbridge Wells
Restaurants	Good Pubs in Laddingford village, 1 mile N		TN3 9JD
			Tel: 07712 502030
Taxis	**Tel:** 01892 837799		**Tel:** 07801 721128
	Tel: 01892 835050		2pk@peterkember.co.uk
	Tel: 01892 838383		

L

32ft 1mb	2.5nm SW of Brandon N5224.56 E00033.66	PPR MIL	Alternative AD Diversion AD	Cambridge Old Buckenham

Lakenheath	APP 128.900 (Civil)	APP 136.500 (Military)	TWR 122.100	DEPT 137.250

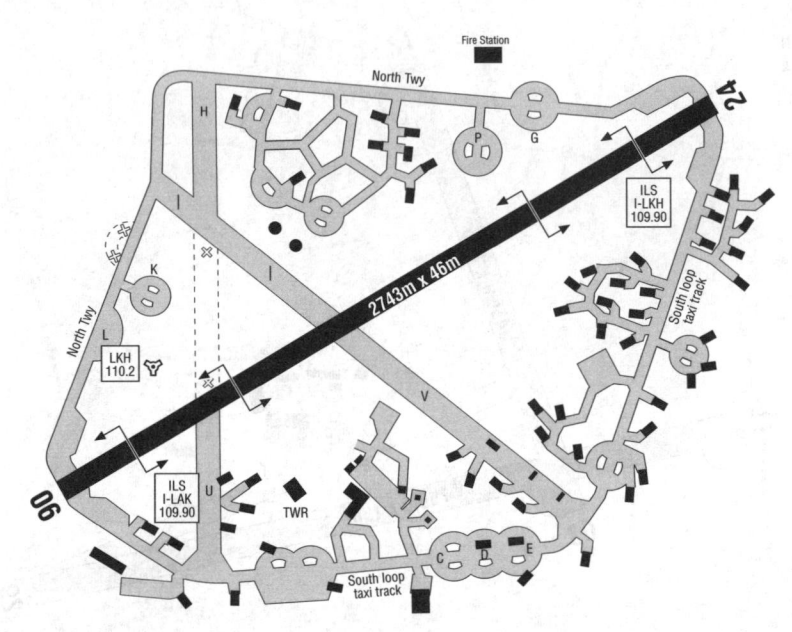

RWY	SURFACE	TORA	LDA	LIGHTING
06/24	Asph/Conc	2743	2743	Ap Thr Rwy PAPI 3° LH

Lighting strobe lead in
Arrestor gear Rwy06 762m from Thr
Arrestor gear Rwy24 365m from Thr

Remarks
24Hr PPR by telephone essential. AD operated by USAF. High performance jet operations. All Arr & Dept must file IFR flight plan.

Warnings
Rwy equipped with arrestor gear. Visiting Piston engined pilots are advised to obtain information on advisability of trampling this equipment with PPR request. All inbound ACFT should contact APP in good time to ascertain state of EGD203, situated 7-12nm finals for Rwy24.
Noise: Jet ACFT should avoid over flying all local towns

Operating Hrs	Mon-Thu 0600-2200 Fri 0600-1800 (Summer) +1Hr (Winter) Sat-Sun & US PH AD closed unless PPR obtained ATZ 24Hrs	Operator	RAF Lakenheath Brandon, Newmarket Suffolk Tel: 01638 524186/2439 (Base Ops)
Circuits	To N		
Landing Fee	Charges in accordance with MOD policy Contact Station Ops for details		
Maintenance	Nil		
Fuel	JET A1 strictly by prior arr		
Disabled Facilities	Nil		
Restaurants	Nil		
Taxis/Car Hire	Nil		
Weather Info	AirS MOEx		

LAMB HOLM

65ft 2mb	4nm S of Kirkwall Airport N5853.18 W00253.60	PPR	Alternative AD Diversion AD	Kirkwall Wick

Lamb Holm	APP Kirkwall 118.300	A/G 129.825 Microlight Ops

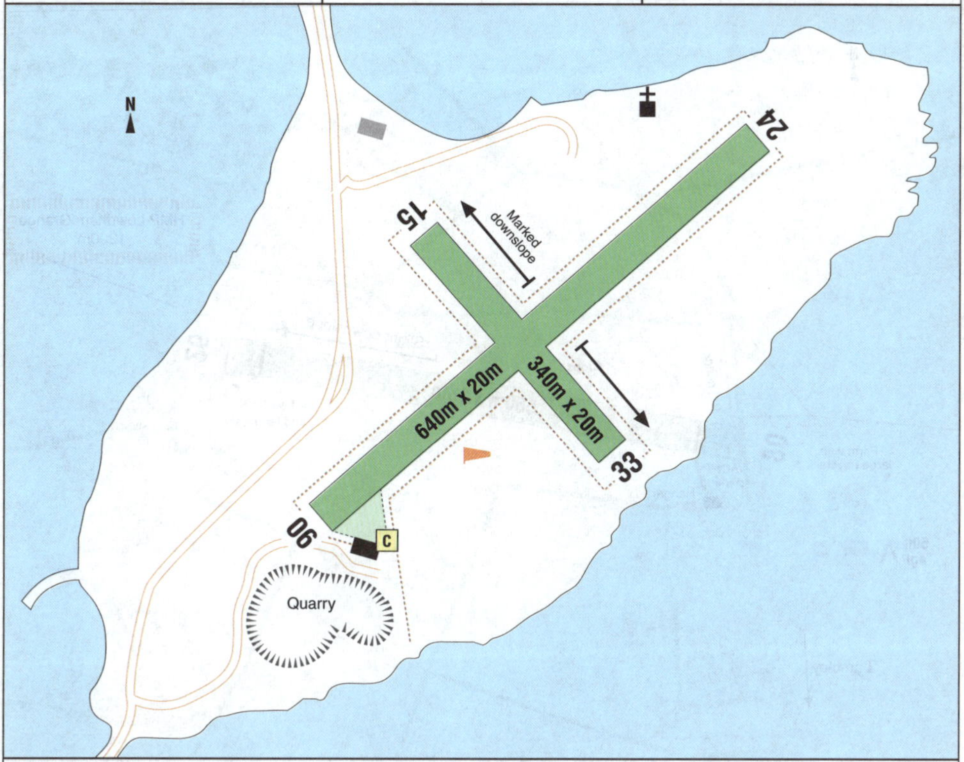

Map of airfield showing runways 06/24 (640m x 20m), 15/33 (340m x 20m), with "Marked downslope" on Rwy 15, Quarry, and Italian chapel (†). Parking marked "C".

RWY	SURFACE	TORA	LDA	LIGHTING
06/24	Grass	640x20	U/L	Nil
15/33	Grass	340x20	U/L	Nil

Rwy06/24 fence to fence distance 658m
Rwy15/33 severe hump-back only use when strong winds preclude

Remarks
PPR by telephone. Visiting ACFT welcome own risk. AD close to S boundary Kirkwall ATZ, keep good look out for commercial traffic operating low level VFR in the area. Inbound make initial call to Kirkwall. Kirkwall town centre approx 7 miles by road. Italian chapel (hand painted to resemble a basilica by Italian prisoners of War) is short walk.

Warning
Width of strip between fencing is 40m, 20m Rwy & 10m each side rough grass. 20ft electricity pole (no wires) 120m from Rwy15 Thr. 4ft boundary fence, wooden poles & barbed wire surrounds AD.
Caution: Turbulence near the quarry.
Noise: Avoid over flying St. Mary's village 1nm NW of AD.

Operating Hrs	SR-SS	**Taxis**	Tel: 01856 876543
Circuits	06, 15 RH, 24, 33 LH	**Car Hire** National	Tel: 01856 872866
Landing Fee	Nil		Tel: 01856 875500
	Donation accepted		Fax: 01856 874458
Maintenance	Nil	**Weather Info**	M T9 Fax 328 GWC
Fuel	Mogas by arr	**Operator**	Tom Sinclair
Disabled Facilities			Tighsith, Holm
			Orkney Islands, KW17 2RX
			Tel: 0780 3088938 (Days)
			Tel/Fax: 01856 781310 (Home/Evenings)

Restaurants 15min walk across causeway food & accomodation
Commodore Motel **Tel:** 01856 781319

300ft 10mb	4nm NE of Nottingham N5300.55 W00103.48	PPR	Alternative AD	Nottingham East Midlands Syerston

Lambley Radio	APP East Mids 134.175	A/G Hucknall 130.800	A/G 123.050 Only occasionally manned

[Aerodrome diagram: North arrow. Runway 08/26 grass strip 550m x 18m with "Slight downslope" toward Rwy26 end. 10ft hedge near Rwy08 Thr. ACFT parking and Hangar near Rwy08. Farm with large haystack, 50ft agl obstacle, Lambley to SW. Crops either side of runway. Low fence and farm track at Rwy26 Thr. HMP Lowdham Grange 1200m to NE.]

RWY	SURFACE	TORA	LDA	LIGHTING
08	Grass	550x18	U/L	Nil
26	Grass	500x18	U/L	Nil

Rwy26 has slight upslope in first third

Remarks
PPR essential. Visiting ACFT welcome at pilots own risk. Windsock may be displayed close to hangar.
Visual aid to location: Rwy has white side markers.

Warnings
Rwy surface may become boggy after prolonged rainfall. Low fence and farm track at the Rwy26 Thr. Public Rd and 10ft hedge at Rwy08 Thr. AD is situated close to a number of AD in busy airspace. Hucknall ATZ (active only at weekends), is close to W. RAF Syerston ATZ to E military gliding school operates daily. A good lookout is strongly recommended. During the summer months straw stacks are present on AD.
Caution: Farm traffic may use strip during the year.
Noise: Avoid local habitation and the villages of Lambley & Woodborough.
DO NOT OVERFLY HMP LOWDHAM GRANGE approx 1200m to N of Rwy26 APP.

Operating Hrs	SR-SS	Weather Info	AirCen MWC
Circuits	LH 800ft QFE	Operator	Mr John Hardy
Landing Fee	Available on request		Jericho Farm
Maintenance	Nil		Green Lane
Fuel	AVGAS in emergency		Lambley, Notts, NG4 4QE
Disabled Facilities			**Tel:** 0115 9313530 (Home/Office)

Tel: 0115 9313639 (Hangar)
Tel: 07768 726279
JW.Hardy@farmline.com

Restaurant	Pub 800yds in village
Taxis/Car Hire	Nil

332

401ft 13mb	5nm W of Penzance N5006.17 W00540.23	**PPR**	**Alternative AD** **Diversion AD**	**St Mawgan** Perranporth

Lands End	LARS **Culdrose 134.050**	TWR **120.250** **(Mon-Sat)**	A/G **120.250** **(Sun)**

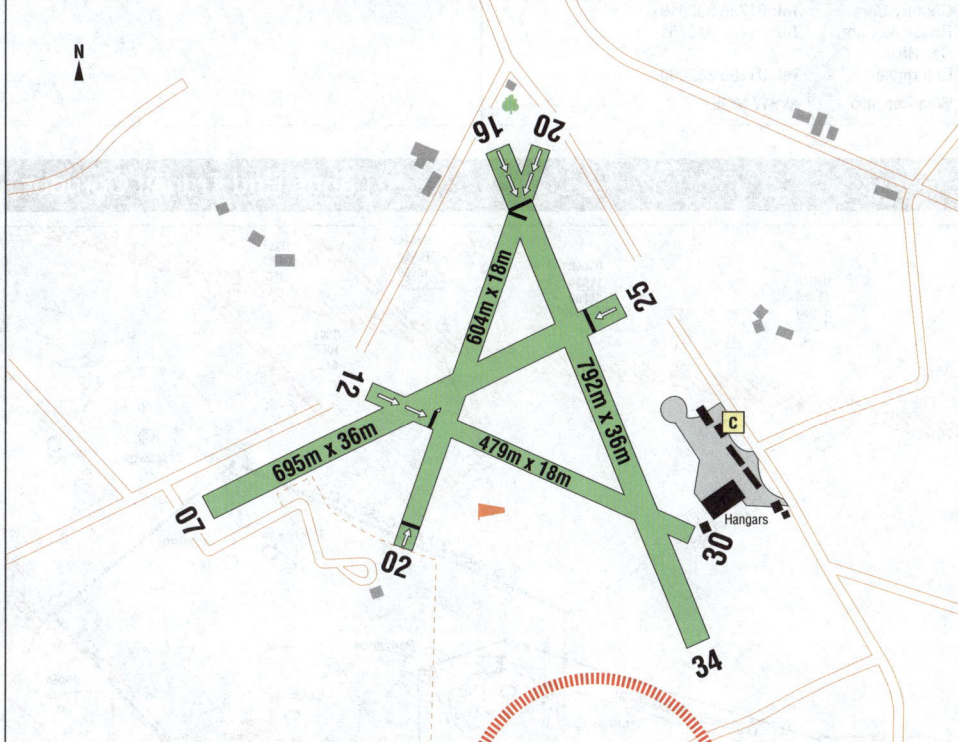

RWY	SURFACE	TORA	LDA	LIGHTING
07	Grass	677	677	Nil
25	Grass	695	630	Nil
16	Grass	792	707	Nil
34	Grass	778	778	APAPI 4° (LHS)
12	Grass	479	417	Nil
30	Grass	506	–	Nil
02	Grass	574	544	Nil
20	Grass	574	436	Nil

Rwy30 not available for ACFT requiring a licensed Rwy for landing
Starter extension Rwy30 27m

Remarks
Strict PPR by telephone. Non radio ACFT not accepted. Hi-vis. Entire grass area is maintained and useable. Rwy17/35 & 07/25 are sufficiently wide to allow differential use of each side of Rwy to conserve grass surfaces. Pilots may be asked to use Rwy (left or right) in order to achieve this. Passengers are not permitted on the refuelling area. Schedule flights to the Scillies operate using transit lane SFC-2000ft QNH.
Aids to Navigation: VOR/DME LND 114.20

Warning
Parts of the manoeuvring area are undulating. Public footpath crosses the AD from NW to SE, entering near Rwy12 Thr, crossing Rwy07/25 and leaving near Rwy03 Thr. Turning circle used extensively by helicopters lifting loads.
Noise: Avoid over flying St Just village N of AD and houses S of AD.

Operating Hrs	Mon-Sat 0800-1700 Sun 0800-1600 (Summer) Mon-Sun 0900-1700 or SS (Winter) & by arr	**Circuits** **Landing Fee**	LH & RH 1000ft QFE Single £10 Twin £15

Maintenance		Operator	Westward Airways Ltd
Westward	**Tel:** 01736 788771		Land's End Aerodrome
Fuel	AVGAS Oil 80 W80 W100		St Just, Cornwall, TR19 7RL
Disabled Facilties	Nil		**Tel:** 01736 788771 (Operator)
Restaurant	Restaurant, club facilities & garden viewing area available		**Tel:** 01736 788944 (ATC)
			Fax: 01736 788366
Taxis			**Fax:** 01736 786450 (ATC)
Country Cars	**Tel:** 01736 333919		
Rosevale Cars	**Tel:** 01736 810751		
Car Hire			
Enterprise	**Tel:** 01736 332000		
Weather Info	AirSW MOEx		

Lands End Transit Corridor

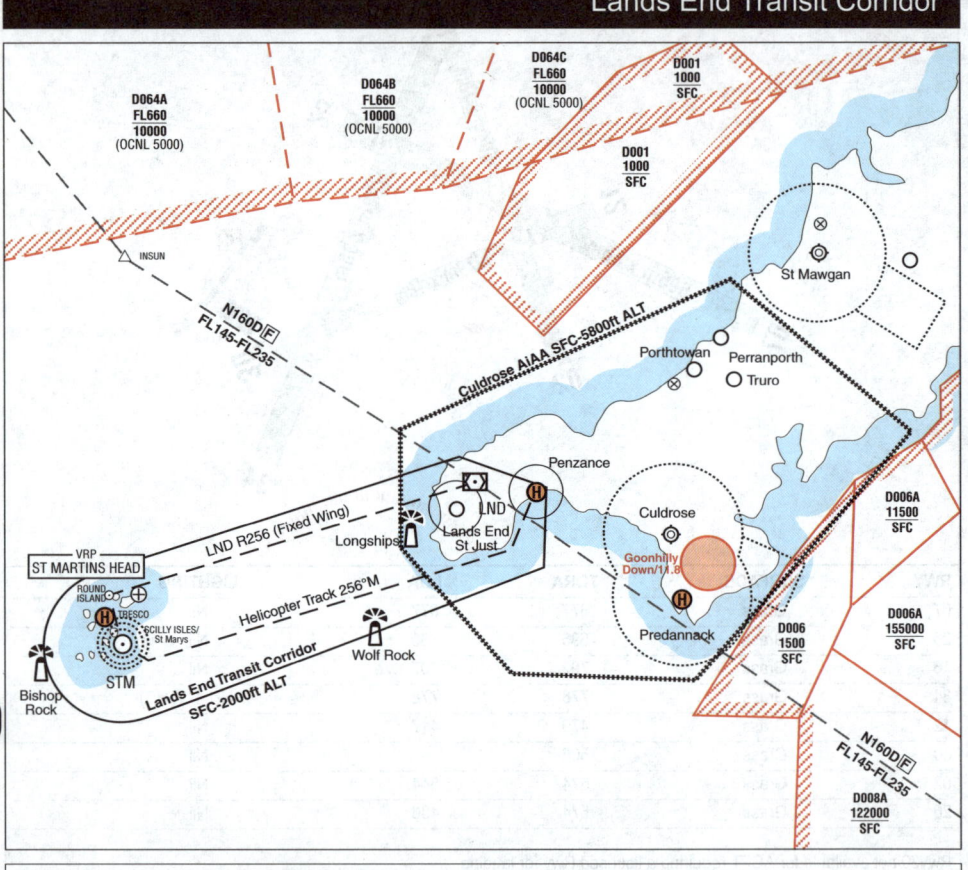

Reporting Points – all nm to run to St Mary's Airport (Scillies)

25	3.5nm to run
Midpoint	11nm to run
Charlie	18nm to run

109ft 4mb	10nm ESE of Nottingham N5253.63 W00054.27	PPR	Alternative AD Diversion AD	Nottingham East Midlands Nottingham
Langar		**LARS** Cottesmore 130.200		**Para Base** 129.900

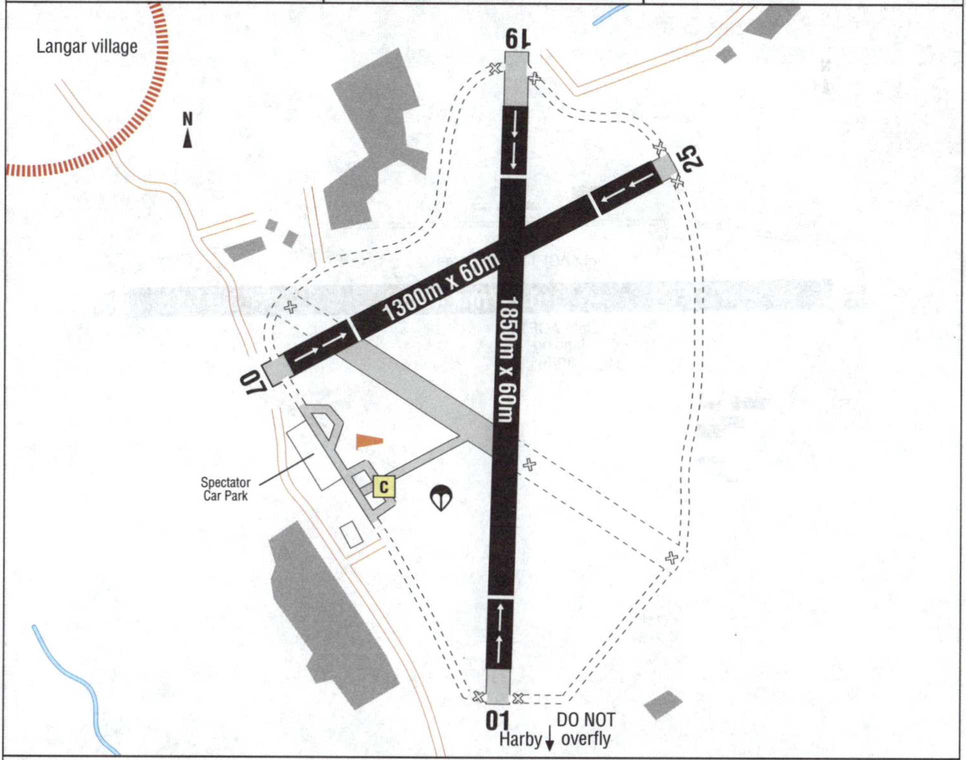

Langar village

N

19

25

1300m x 60m

1850m x 60m

07

Spectator Car Park

C

01
DO NOT
Harby ↓ overfly

RWY	SURFACE	TORA	LDA	LIGHTING
01/19	Asphalt	1850x60	U/L	Nil
07/25	Asphalt	1300x60	U/L	Nil

Remarks
PPR vital in order to obtain briefing on parachuting operation for the day Visiting ACFT welcome. Contact Langar at least 8nm from AD for joining information – normally a straight-in APP or base leg join. Disused Rwy13/31 is available as Twy.

Warnings
Do not over fly AD – intensive para-dropping up to FL150 daily.
Noise: Do not over fly Langar and Harby village 1nm NW and 1nm S of AD.

Operating Hrs	Mon-Sat 0900-2000 Sun 1000-2000 (Summer) Mon-Sat 0900-SS Sun 1000-SS (Winter)	**Operator** British Parachute Schools **Tel/Fax:** 01949 860878
Circuits	See joining procedures	**Langar Joining Proceedures**
Landing Fee	Single £2 Twin £5 No charge if on BPS business	**ACFT MUST NOT over fly AD.** Arr ACFT should call Langar Para Base at least 5-8nm from AD. Straight APP or base leg join will be given
Maintenance	Nil	**Holding Patterns**
Fuel	Jet A1 only	If joining from N: LH orbit on GAM 182°/20nm 1500ft QNH (3.5nm N of Langar)
Disabled Facilities		If joining from S:

LH orbit inbound to TNT 328°/33nm (116°R) 2000ft QNH (3.5nm SE of Langar)

Restaurants	Cafe open weekends
Taxis Bingham	**Tel:** 01949 839000
Car Hire	Nil
Weather Info	AirCen MWC

L

| 618ft | 5nm SE of Basingstoke | PPR | Alternative AD | Farnborough Blackbushe |
| 21mb | N5111.17 W00101.83 | | Diversion AD | |

Lasham	LARS Farnborough 125.250	A/G 131.025

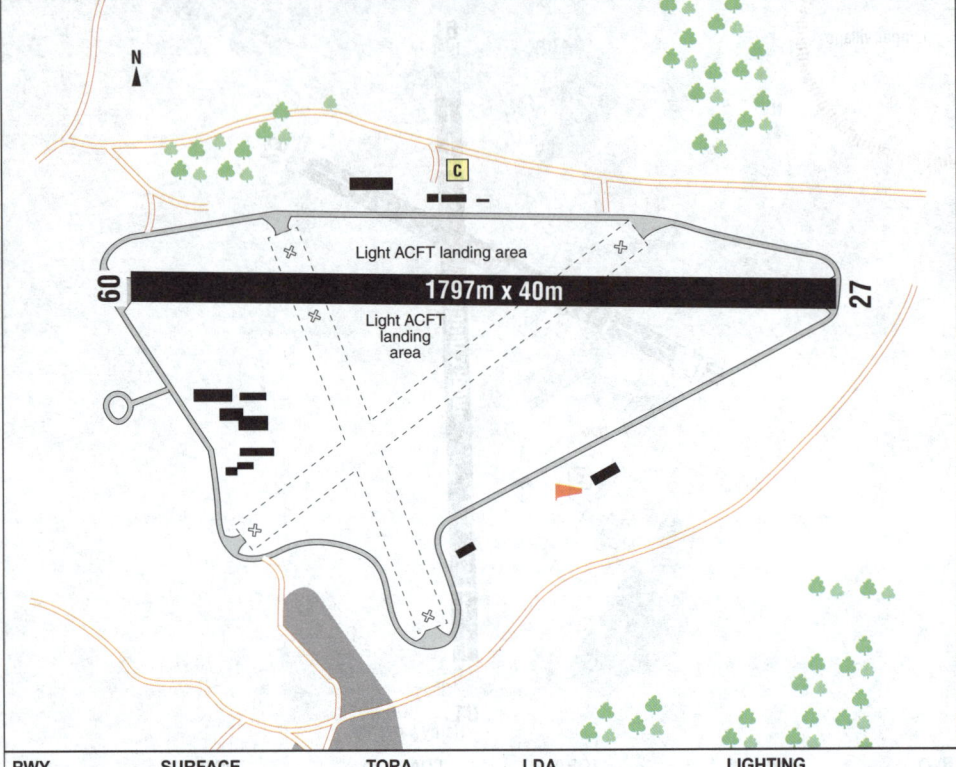

Light ACFT landing area

1797m x 40m

Light ACFT landing area

60

27

C

RWY	SURFACE	TORA	LDA	LIGHTING
09/27	Asphalt	1797x40	U/L	Nil

Rwy not normally available
Landing on grass only

Remarks
PPR strictly by telephone. AD is only available to persons having business with Lasham Gliding Society. Light ACFT must use grass area N of main Rwy or centre triangle dependent on Rwy in use. Visiting pilots & passengers are required to become temporary members, indemnifying the society of all liability. Certain customs facilities are available.

Warnings
Extreme caution due to cables winch launching to 3000ft agl. Parts of AD surfaces are unsuitable for the movement of ACFT. Intense gliding activity takes place on AD. Occasionally AD used by heavy ACFT for maintenance. Contact Farnborough LARS for clearance in Odiham MATZ.

Operating Hrs	Strictly PPR	Operator	Lasham Gliding Society Ltd
Circuits	Nil		Lasham Aerodrome
Landing Fee	Single £10 Others £20 per tonne		Lasham, Alton
Maintenance	Nil		Hants, GU34 5SS
Fuel	Nil		**Tel: 01256 384900**
Disabled Facilities	Nil		
Restaurant	Clubhouse facilities available at AD		

Taxis
Alton **Tel:** 01420 84455
Ames **Tel:** 01420 83309

Car Hire
National **Tel:** 01256 477777

Weather Info AirSE MOEx

72ft 2mb	8nm S of Maidstone N5109.42 E00038.50	PPR	Alternative AD Diversion AD	Manston Rochester

	Lashenden		A/G 122.000

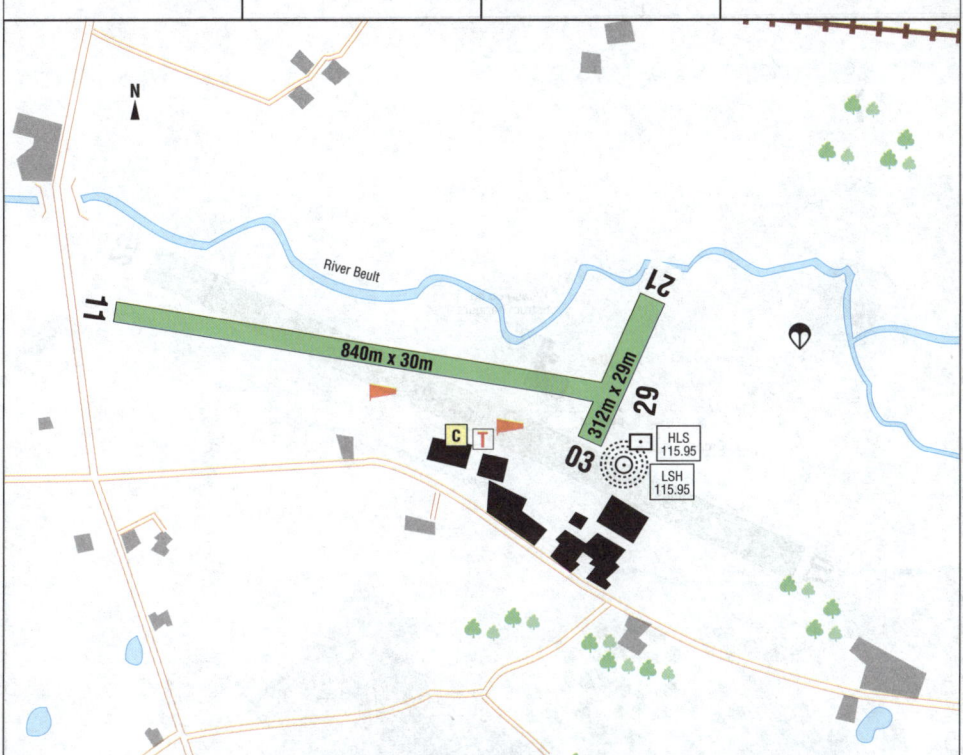

RWY	SURFACE	TORA	LDA	LIGHTING
11/29	Grass	840	840	Nil
03/21	Grass	312x29	U/L	Nil

Rwy03/21 Tiger Moth training

Remarks
PPR. Not available for use at night by flights required to use a licensed AD. Rwy03/21 not available to ACFT flying for public transport or flying instruction.

Warnings
Helicopters must obtain clearance before engaging rotors. Free-fall parachuting takes place up to FL150. Helicopters may not operate & no overhead joins when parachuting in progress. No marked Twys. Taxi to S of Rwy, due to poor condition & undulating surface of AD.
Noise: Avoid over flying local villages

Operating Hrs	0900-SS (L) & by arr	**Taxis**	
Circuits	Fixed Wing LH 1000ft QFE	MTC	**Tel:** 01622 890003
	Rotary 11 LH 700ft QFE,	**Car Hire**	
	29 RH 1000ft QFE	Nathan	**Tel:** 01622 684844
Landing Fee	Single £7 Twin £15	**Weather Info**	AirSE MOEx
	Free with 40lts of fuel or lamb from farm	**Operator**	Shenley Farms (Engineering) Ltd
Maintenance	Available		Headcorn Aerodrome
Fuel	AVGAS Jet A1		Ashford, Kent, TN27 9HX
	Oil 80 W80 100 W100 W100+15W 50		**Tel:** 01622 890226
Disabled Facilties	Nil		**Tel:** 01622 890236 (Out of Hrs)
			Fax: 01622 890876
Restaurant			**Telex:** 966127
Cafe at AD	**Tel:** 01622 890671		
Chequers	**Tel:** 01233 770217		

250ft 8mb	3nm SW of Ledbury N5200.17 W00228.50		**Alternative AD**	**Gloucestershire** Shobdon
Non-radio		**LARS** **Brize 124.275**		**Safetycom** **135.475**

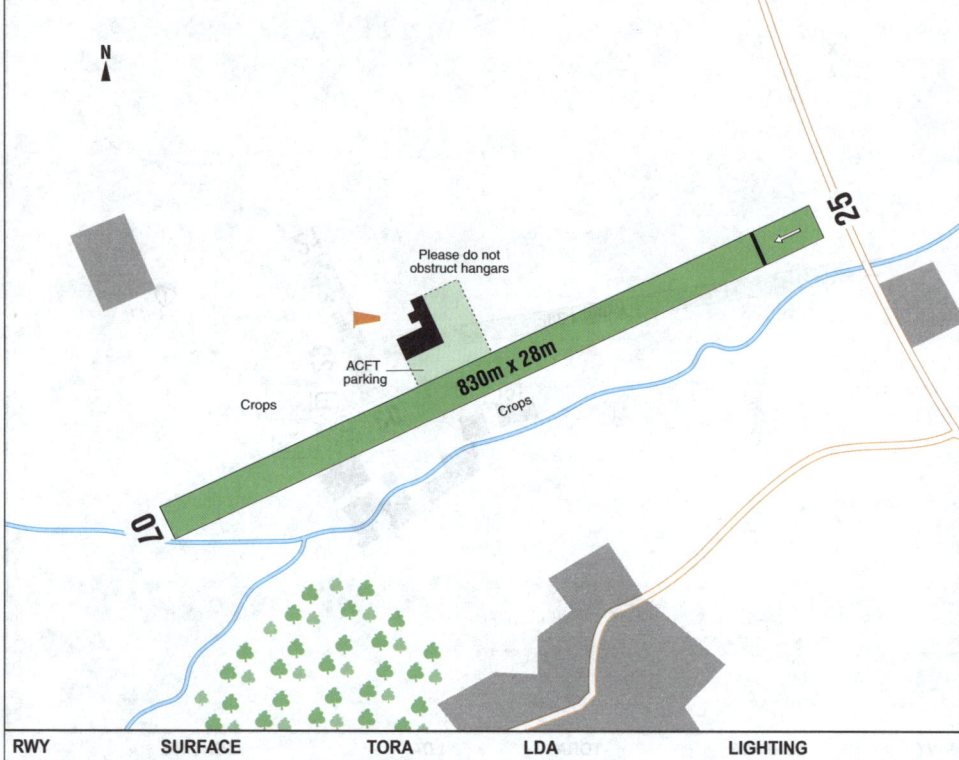

N

Please do not obstruct hangars

ACFT parking

830m x 28m

Crops

Crops

25

07

RWY	SURFACE	TORA	LDA	LIGHTING
07/25	Grass	830x28	U/L	Nil

Rwy25 Thr displaced to avoid high sided vehicles on main road

Remarks
PPR by telephone. AD unmanned. Visitors welcome at own risk. Smooth surface on regularly cut Rwy.

Warnings
Crops grow to edge of strip. Sheep graze AD.30ft power lines cross Rwy25 APP 300m from Thr. Trees SW of Rwy07 can cause turbulence on final in SE wind. TV mast 1210amsl, (540agl) 2nm W AD. Hangar close to mid point of strips N edge. Please do not block access to the hangar.

Operating Hrs	SR-SS		**Operator**	The Bromesberrow Estate
Circuits	LH 1000ft QFE			c/o Robert Killen Chartered Surveyors
Landing Fee	£10 (payable on site)			Littlemead, Tortworth Wotton-under-Edge
Maintenance	Nil			Glos, GL12 8HB
Fuel	Nil			**Tel/Fax:** 01454 261764
Disabled Facilities	Nil			**Tel:** 0778 895803
Restaurant	Nil			
Taxis				
Wyvern (Ledbury)	**Tel:** 01531 633001			
Ames	**Tel:** 01420 83309			
Car Hire	Nil			
Weather Info	AirSW MOEx			

681ft 23mb	6nm NW of Leeds N5351.95 W00139.63	PPR	Alternative AD	Durham Tees Valley Sherburn in Elmet

Leeds	ATIS 118.025	APP 123.750
RAD 121.050	**TWR** 120.300	**FIRE** 121.600

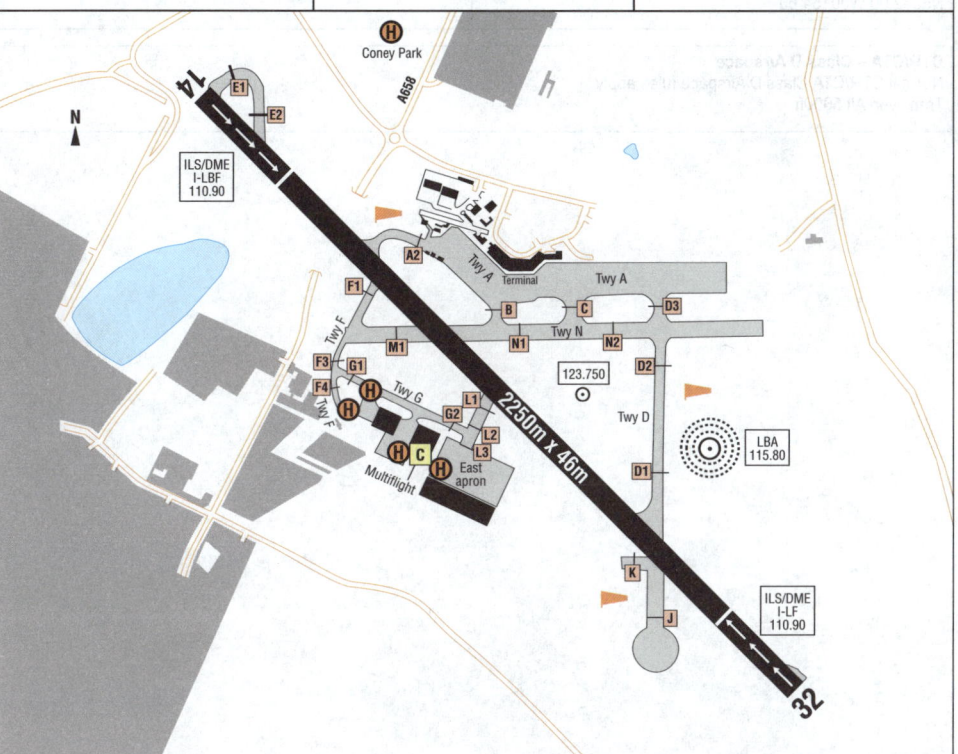

RWY	SURFACE	TORA	LDA	LIGHTING
14	Concrete	2113	1802	Ap Thr Rwy PAPI 3.5° RHS
32	Concrete	2190	1916	Ap Thr Rwy PAPI 3° LHS

Remarks

PPR to all GA ACFT. Microlights NOT accepted. All public transport ACFT must designate a handling agent in advance if operating from the main N side apron. Helicopters to land as instructed by ATC. Rebated fees for training flights subject to prior written approval from the AD Authority. A booking slot system is in operation for ACFT using the AD for training. Pilots transiting the Vale of York AIAA, use LARS offered by Linton or Leeming. Helicopter training is permitted dual only, no circuits. All GA and non-based ACFT must co-ordinate parking with Multiflight.

Handling agents: Northside – Servisair & Aviance. Southside – Multiflight. Customs during AD Ops Hrs.

Warnings

Bird activity noted at this AD – large flocks of Lapwings. ACFT may be delayed while flocks are cleared. The S Twy is restricted to use by ACFT with a wingspan <17m. Windshear my be experienced on APP 190-240° >24kts.

Operating Hrs	H24 PPR 2200-0600 (Summer) +1Hr (Winter)	**Restaurant**	Restaurant buffet & bar available at Terminal
Circuits	Variable	**Taxis**	Available at Terminal
Landing Fee	On application	Telecabs	**Tel:** 0113 2792222
Maintenance	Multiflight **Tel:** 0113 2387100	**Car Hire**	
Fuel	AVGAS JET A1 100LL	Avis	**Tel:** 0113 2503880
		Europcar	**Tel:** 0113 2509066
Fuel available by prior arr AVGAS only available 0800-1800 or by prior arr. AVGAS not available to ACFT with wingspan >17m		Hertz	**Tel:** 0113 2504811
		Weather Info	M T9 Fax 334 A VN MWC
Disabled Facilities Available			
Handling	**Tel:** 0113 2503251 (Servisair) **Tel:** 0113 3913382 (Aviance) **Tel:** 0113 2501410 (Multiflight)		

Visual Reference Points (VRP)		Operator	Leeds Bradford Int Airport Ltd
VRP	**VOR/DME**		Yeadon, Leeds
Dewsbury	POL 105°/17nm		Yorkshire, LS19 7TU
N5341.50 W00138.10			**Tel:** 0113 2509696 (Admin)
Eccup Reservoir	POL 073°/21nm		**Tel:** 0113 3913282 (ATC)
N5352.27 W00132.60			**Tel:** 0113 3913231 (AD Ops)
Harrogate	POL 058°/25nm		**Fax:** 0113 2505426 (Admin)
N5359.50 W00131.60			www.lbia.co.uk
Keighley	POL 047°/10nm		
N5352.00 W00154.60			

CTR/CTA – Class D Airspace
Normal CTR/CTA Class D Airspace rules apply
Transition Alt 5000ft

L

132ft	7nm SW of Northallerton	PPR	Alternative AD	**Durham Tees Valley** Full Sutton
5mb	N5417.54 W00132.11	MIL	Diversion AD	

Leeming	LARS 127.750	APP 123.300	TWR 120.500 122.100

Effective date:23/11/06

[Aerodrome chart: Runway 16/34, 2292m x 46m, Asphalt. ILS LI 110.30. LEE 112.60. Northern Twy. Helicopter positions marked H. Spot heights: 177, 201, 187, 215. PAPI and threshold markings shown.]

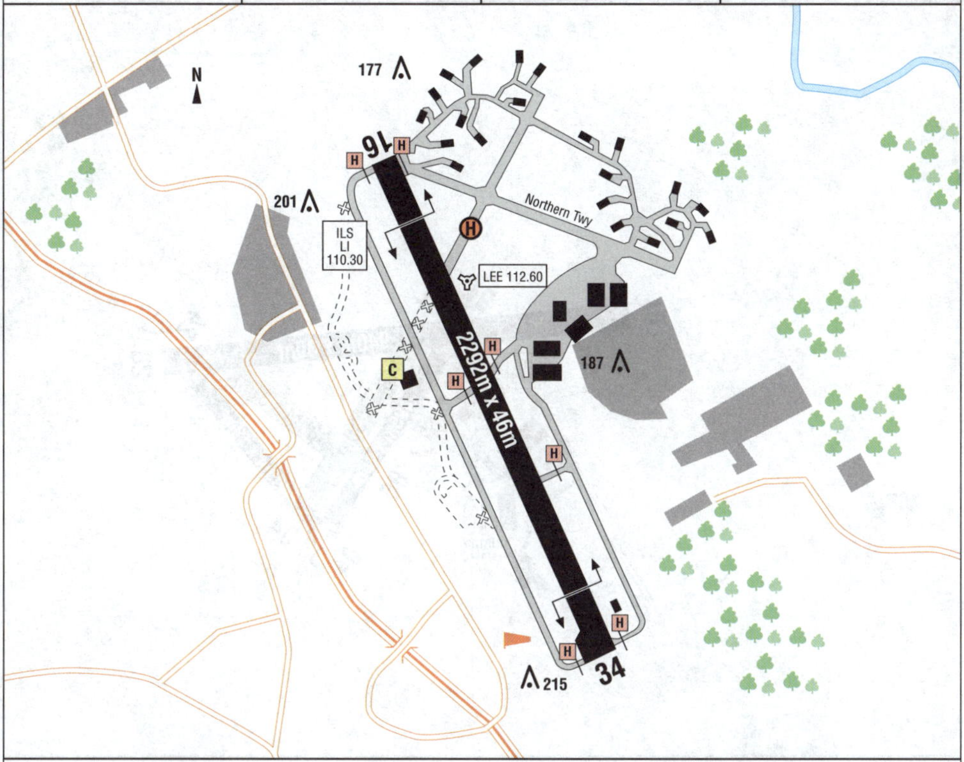

RWY	SURFACE	TORA	LDA	LIGHTING
16/34	Asphalt	2292	2292	Ap Thr Rwy PAPI 2.5°

Arrester gear 390m from Thr

Remarks
PPR 24Hrs required. Resident jet ACFT have priority for take-off, visiting ACFT may have to break-off APP to permit Dept. Limited parking and handling facilities. AD often active at weekends, ATZ active H24. Station based light ACFT operate outside normal Hrs. **Visual aid to location:** IBn LI Red.

Warnings
Strong possibility of wind shear on Rwy16 APP when wind is more than 10 knots in sector 210°-250°. Glider flying at Catterick and Dishforth outside normal Hrs.
Noise: All ACFT are to avoid over flying towns and villages within MATZ unless weather or flight conditions dictate otherwise.

Operating Hrs	Mon-Thu 0800-2359 Fri 0800-1800 Sat-Sun & PH when station based light ACFT operate	**Weather Info**	M T Fax 336 MWC ATIS **Tel:** 01677 423041 Ex 7770
Circuits	Large ACFT 1000ft QFE Small ACFT 800ft QFE	**Operator**	RAF Leeming **Tel:** 01677 423041 Ex 2058/2059 (PPR)
Landing Fee	Charges in accordance with MOD policy Contact Station Ops for details		

Leeming Noise Procedures
All helicopters and light ACFT are not to fly below 500ft QFE within the MATZ, unless weather or operational reasons dictate. Fixed wing ACFT other than light ACFT are not to fly below 1000ft QFE within the MATZ, unless joining the visual circuit. All ACFT must avoid over flying towns and villages within the MATZ – see map for details.
Avoid over flying the local areas of Bedale, Northallerton, Leeming Bar, Leeming village, Laidonderry, Gatenby, Scruton, Scorton Hospital, Breckenborough, Theakeston Hall, Sion Hall. Medium/heavy helicopters msut also avoid, Cross Lanes farm, Grewelmarpe village and Kirkby Mabeard.

Maintenance	Nil
Fuel	AVGAS Jet A1 100LL

Disabled Facilities

Restaurants	In Northallerton
Taxis/Car Hire	Nil

L

EGBG

LEICESTER

469ft	4nm ESE of Leicester	PPR	Alternative AD	Nottingham East Midlands Northampton
16mb	N5236.47 W00101.92		Diversion AD	

	Leicester	A/G	
		122.125	

[Aerodrome chart showing runways: 10/28 (940m x 30m), 15/33, 16/34 (418m x 30m), 06/24 (335m x 30m), 04/22 (490m x 18m), 495m x 18m, 490m x 18m. Labels include ACFT parking, LE 383.5, Fuel pumps, C]

RWY	SURFACE	TORA	LDA	LIGHTING
10/28	Asphalt	940	940	Thr Rwy APAPI 3.25° LHS
06/24	Grass	335	335	Nil
16/34	Grass	418	418	Nil
04/22	Asphalt	490	490	Nil
15/33	Asphalt	495	495	Nil

Remarks
PPR. When using Rwy28, provided the glide clear, requirement of the ANO is maintained at all times, all ACFT to climb straight ahead maintaining Rwy centre line to 1000ft QFE before turning.
Visual aids to location: Ibn, Green, LE.

Warnings
Rwy15/33 used for parking when not active. Helicopters to join circuit not above 500ft. Grass Rwys and Twy are subject to water logging, especially in winter.

Operating Hrs	0800-1600 (Summer) +1Hr (Winter) & by arr	**Taxis** ABC	**Tel:** 01162 555111
Circuits	LH	**Car Hire** National	**Tel:** 01162 510455
Landing Fee	Single £10 Twin £20 Weekends free with 50l of fuel	Europcar	**Tel:** 01162 538531
		Weather Info	AirCen MCW
Maintenance R N Aviation	**Tel:** 01162 593629	**Operator**	Leicestershire Aero Club Ltd Leicester Airport Gartree Road, Leicester, LE2 2FG **Tel:** 01162 592360 **Fax:** 01162 592712
Fuel	AVGAS JET A1 100LL		

Disabled Facilities

Restaurant
Club facilities & bar meals available at AD

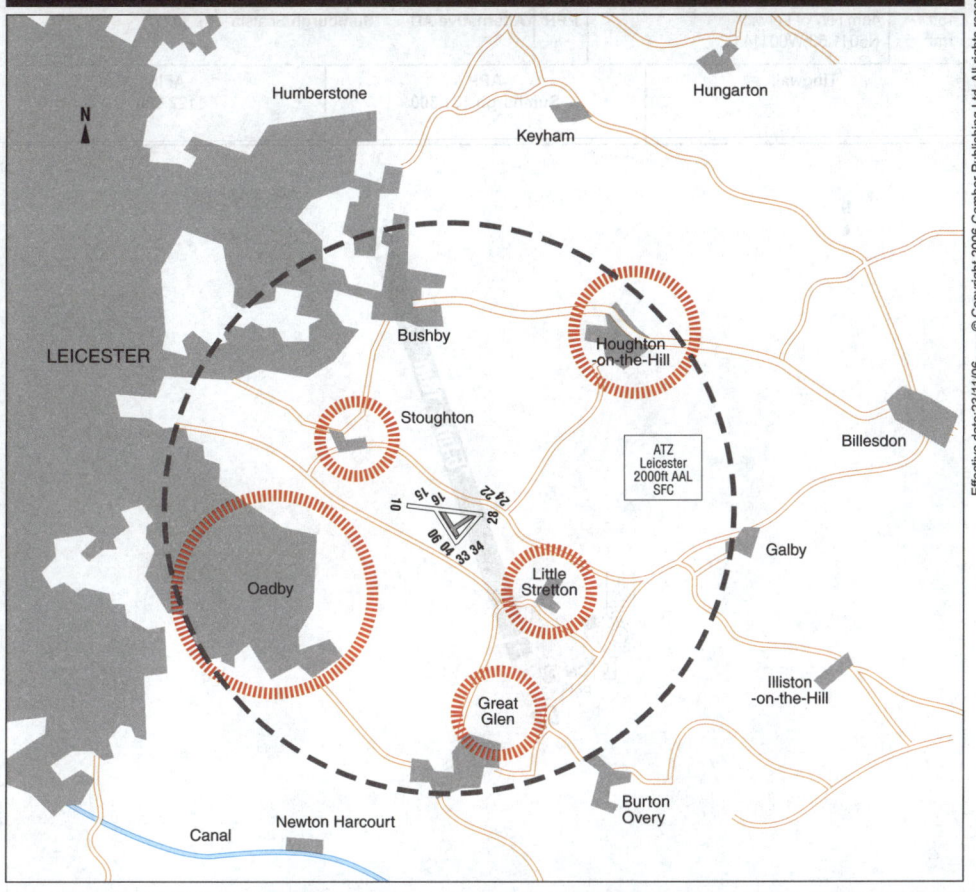

Noise: On Dept please avoid over flying Houghton-on-the-Hill, Little Stretton, Stoughton and Oadby where possible.

EGET

LERWICK

45ft 1mb	4nm NW of Lerwick N6011.53 W00114.62	PPR	Alternative AD	Sumburgh Scatsta

Tingwall	APP Sumburgh 131.300	AFIS 122.600

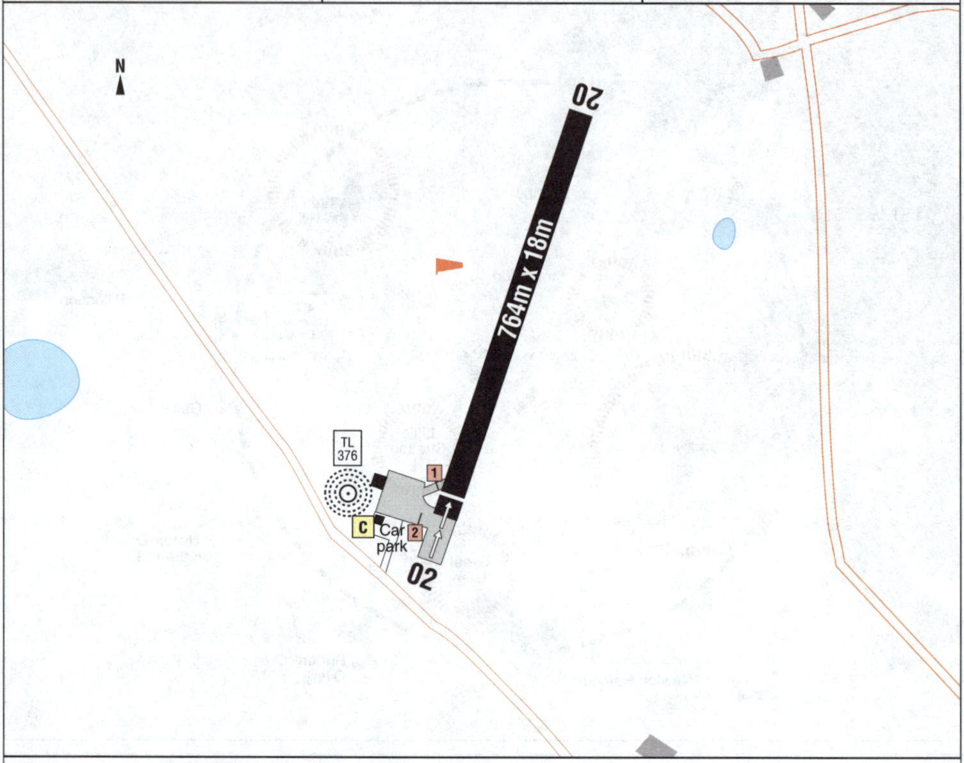

N ↑

TL
376

C Car park

1

2

764m x 18m

20

02

RWY	SURFACE	TORA	LDA	LIGHTING
02	Asphalt	764	744	Ap Thr Rwy APAPI 4° LHS
20	Asphalt	764	764	Thr Rwy APAPI 4° LHS

Displaced Thr Rwy02

Remarks
PPR

Warnings
High GND 449ft aal 1.25nm to NW. High GND 274ft aal 1nm to NE. High GND 407ft aal 1nm to ESE. High GND from S through to W up to 420ft aal within 1.5nm od AD. 5 wind turbines 246ft aal situated on high GND S of AD.

Operating Hrs	Mon-Fri 0830-1700 (Summer) 0830-1700 (Winter)	**Taxis** L Sinclair R Greenwald	**Tel:** 01595 694617 **Tel:** 01595 692080
Circuits	Nil	**Car Hire** J Leask & Son	**Tel:** 01595 693162
Landing Fee	£15 per tonne Parking fees: £2.50 per tonne or part there of for each 24Hrs or part thereof	Bolts Car Hire	**Tel:** 01595 692855
		Weather Info	AirSc GWC
Maintenance	Nil	**Operator**	Shetland Islands Council
Fuel	AVGAS 100LL		Grantfield, Lerwick Shetland, ZE1 0NT **Tel:** 01595 840306 (AD) **Fax:** 01595 744869
Disabled Facilities			

Restaurants Bar meals available at Herrislea House within walking distance

38ft	3.5nm NW ofSt Andrews	PPR	Alternative AD	Edinburgh Fife
1mb	N5622.37 W00252.11	MIL	Diversion AD	

Leuchars	LARS 126.500	APP 123.300	RAD 126.500	TWR/GND 122.100

RWY	SURFACE	TORA	LDA	LIGHTING
09	Asphalt/Conc	2588	2317	Ap Thr Rwy PAPI 3°
27	Asphalt/Conc	2588	2588	Ap Thr Rwy PAPI 2.5°
04	Asphalt	1464	1464	Thr Rwy PAPI 3°
22	Asphalt	1464	1464	Ap Thr Rwy PAPI 3°

Remarks
PPR. All ACFT inbound to Leuchars to call APP before 40nm, unless prior permission has been obtained. All ACFT to avoid St Andrews by 2000ft/2nm. Light ACFT circuits up to 800ft QFE. Airways traffic request start on 122.10. Tutor hold 800ft live side N of N Twy and inside Rwy09/27 Thrs. Helicopters not to hover or taxi in the vicinity of the Watchman RAD TWR 66ft agl W Rwy22 Thr.

Warnings
Arrester gear is fitted 396m from Rwy09/27/22 Thr. There is a possible radiation hazard W Rwy22 Thr. Increased bird hazard on Rwy27 APP, 30 mins either side of sunset (Sep-Mar).
Caution: Windshear on finals Rwy27 when wing 210-240 >15kts.
Noise: Avoid flying over local villages when ever possible.

Operating Hrs	Movements normally only accepted Mon-Fri 0800-1700 (L)	**Operator**	RAF Leuchars Fife, KY16 0JX
Circuits	09 04 LH, 22 27 RH		**Tel:** 01334 839471 Ex 2055
Landing Fee	Charges in accordance with MOD policy Contact Station Ops for details		**Fax:** 01334 838849
Maintenance	Nil		
Fuel	AVGAS JET A1 100LL		
Disabled Facilities	Nil		
Restaurants	Nil		
Taxis/Car Hire	Local taxi by private arr		
Weather Info	M T Fax 338 GWC		

53ft 2mb	9nm NW of York N5402.95 W00115.17	PPR MIL	Alternative AD Diversion AD	Leeds Bradford Full Sutton

Linton	LARS 118.550	APP 118.550

RAD 118.550	TWR 122.100	A/G 118.550 (Weekends & evenings)

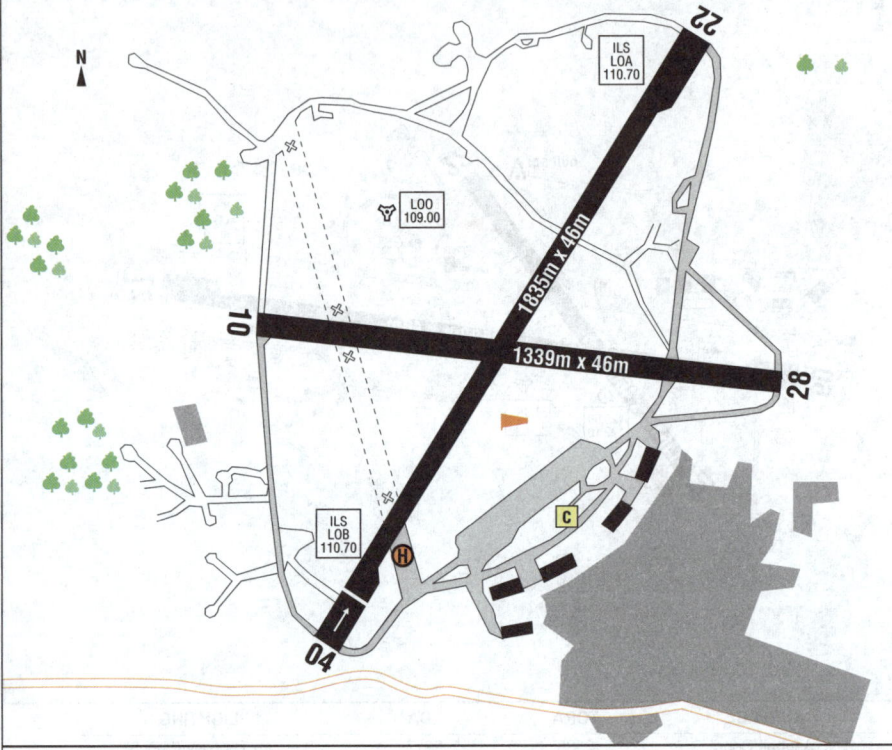

RWY	SURFACE	TORA	LDA	LIGHTING
04	Asphalt	1835	1681	Ap Thr Rwy PAPI 3°
22	Asphalt	1835	1833	Ap Thr Rwy PAPI 3°
10/28	Asphalt	1339	1339	Thr Rwy PAPI 3°

Rwy10 only available for landing in an emergency

Remarks
First 152m of Rwy04 is sterile. A third Rwy17/35 is closed. Circuit directions and heights are variable.
Visual aid to Location: Ibn LO Red.

Warnings
Linton is a high intensity flying training school. 2 Rwys may be in use at the same time. Glider launching at AD takes place in the evenings and weekends.
Caution: Rwy28 trees 110ft 130m from Thr 88m left of centre line. Rwy10 only available for landing in an emergency – High trees within APP area.

Operating Hrs	Mon-Thu 0630-1615 Fri 0630-1600 (Summer) +1Hr (Winter)	**Taxis/Car Hire**	Nil
		Weather Info	AirN MWC ATIS **Tel:** 01347 847467
Circuits	04, 22, 28 RH, 10 LH		
Landing Fee	Charges in accordance with MOD policy Contact Station Ops for details	**Operator**	OC Ops Wing RAF Linton on Ouse York, YO30 2AJ
Maintenance	Nil		**Tel:** 01347 847511 (ATC)
Fuel	Ltd quantities PNR AVGAS JET A1 100LL		**Tel:** 01347 847491/2 (Ops/PPR)
Disabled Facilities	Nil		
Restaurants	Nil		

346

250ft 8mb	5nm SE of St Neots N5210.00 W00009.23	PPR	**Alternative AD Diversion AD**	**Cambridge** Bourn

	Little Gransden	A/G 130.850	

RWY	SURFACE	TORA	LDA	LIGHTING
12/30	Grass	650x28	U/L	Nil
10/28	Grass	570x18	U/L	Nil
03/21	Grass	430x23	U/L	Nil

Starter extension Rwy28 240m

Remarks
PPR by telephone essential. Non-radio ACFT not accepted. In the absence of A/G facility, make normal calls. No dead side, all ACFT join downwind to the S or W of AD. Pilots equipped with constant speed propellers should at safest opportunity set power and propellers to cruise climb configuration.

Warnings
Gransden Lodge Gliding AD is located 2500m to the NE. Rwy03/21 is only for use by experienced pilots, marked power lines cross Thr of Rwys03 & 28.Bridle-path crosses Rwy10/28. Rwy03/21 is unmarked and also used as Twys. Rwy designators positioned in front of Thr.
Noise: Avoid over flying The Gransdens, Gamlingay, Hatley Estate and Waresley.

Operating Hrs	Mon-Sat 0700-1900 Sun 0700-1900 (L)	**Taxis**	
Circuit	03, 28, 30 LH, 10, 12, 21 RH 800ft QFE	Dereks	**Tel:** 01767 260430
Landing Fee	Single £5 Free with 50ltr fuel	Sandy Cars	**Tel:** 01767 682634
Maintenance	YAK UK Ltd	Andys	**Tel:** 01767 260288
	Tel: 01767 651156	**Car Hire**	
	Fax: 01767 651157	Budget	**Tel:** 01223 323838
Fuel	AVGAS 100LL	**Weather Info**	AirCen MOEx
Disabled Facilities	Nil	**Operator**	Skyline School of Flying
Restaurants	Tea & coffee available at AD		Fullers Hill, Little Gransden
			Sandy, Beds, SG19 3BP
			Tel: 01767 651950
			Fax: 01767 651575

196ft 7mb	3nm NE of Fakenham N5251.65 E00054.57	**PPR**	**Alternative AD**	**Norwich** Old Buckenham

Little Snoring	**LARS** Marham 124.150	**A/G** 118.125

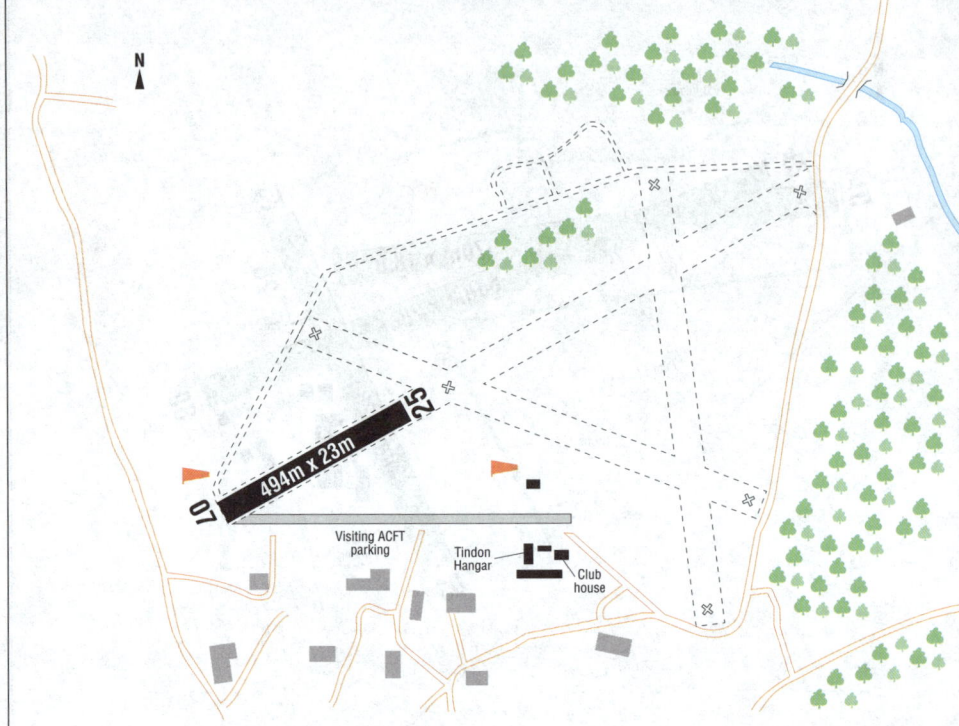

RWY	SURFACE	TORA	LDA	LIGHTING
07/25	Asphalt	494x23	U/L	Nil

Remarks
Strict PPR. Visiting ACFT welcome at owners risk. All fly-ins do not require PPR.

Warnings
Uncontrolled vehicles often on AD.
Noise: Avoid over flying villages and habitation in vicinity of AD.

Operating Hrs	SR-SS	**Operator**	McAully Flying Group Little Snoring Aerodrome Little Snoring Fakenham Norfolk, NR21 0JR **Tel:** 01328 878470 (Mr T Cushing)
Circuits	LH 800ft QFE		
Landing Fee	Donations please box at visiting ACFT parking		
Maintenance	Nil		
Fuel	AVGAS available when Flying Group memebrs present		
Disabled Facilities	Nil		
Restaurants	Good place for a picnic		
Taxis Courtesy Cabs	**Tel:** 01328 855500		
Car Hire Candy	**Tel:** 01328 855348		
Weather Info	AirS MOEx		

348

225ft 7mb	10nm NE of Bedford N5214.57 W00021.85		PPR	Alternative AD	Cranfield Little Gransden
	Little Staughton			A/G 123.925 Make blind calls	

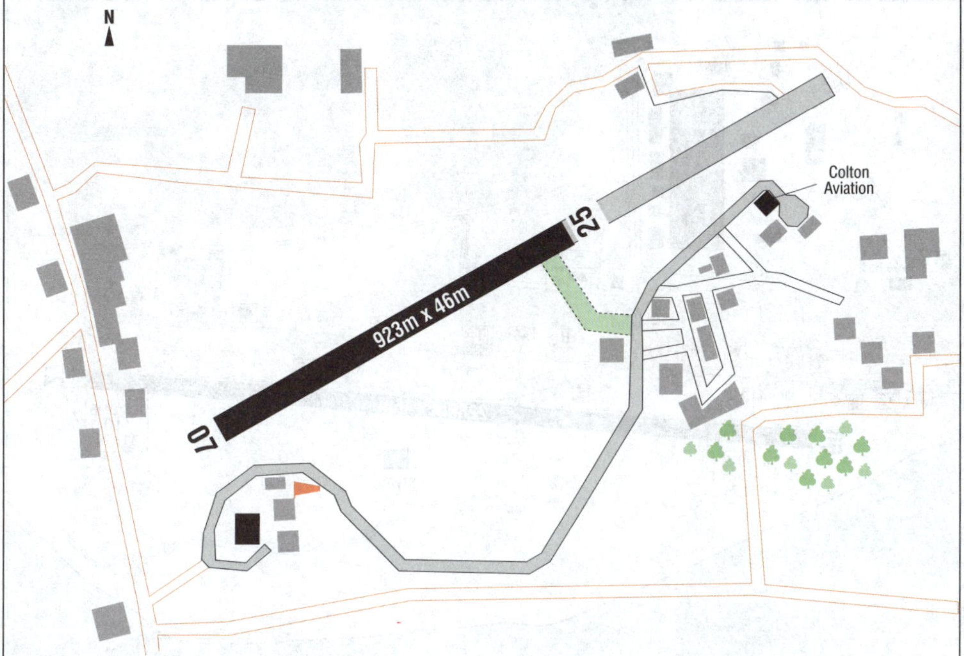

N ↑

Colton Aviation

25

923m x 46m

07

RWY	SURFACE	TORA	LDA	LIGHTING
07/25	Asphalt	923x46	U/L	Nil

Starter extension Rwy25 500m

Remarks
Strictly PPR. Visiting ACFT should proceed to Colton Aviation.

Warnings
Twy leads to perimeter road which acts as an access track. Mast 171ft agl 331ft amsl, 1500m from Rwy25 Thr.
Caution: Vehicles on perimeter road. Gliders may be operating at weekends from Sackville Farm strip 3nm WNW, and from Thurleigh AD.
Noise: Avoid over flight of local villages.

Operating Hrs	0900-2000 (Summer) 0900-SS (Winter)	**Weather Info**	AirCen MOEx
Circuits	07 RH, 25 LH	**Operator**	Colton Aviation Ltd
Landing Fee	Single £5 Twin £10 No charge if in for maintenance		**Tel:** 01234 376775/376705 **Fax:** 01234 376544
Maintenance	Colton Aviation (M3)		
Fuel	AVGAS 100LL		

Disabled Facilities

Restaurants   Local pub in village 20mins walk

Taxis
A1 (Bedford)   **Tel:** 01234 364444
Steve (St Neots)   **Tel:** 01480 471111
CarHire
National   **Tel:** 01234 269565

80ft 3mb	6.5nm SE of Liverpool N5320.02 W00251.00	PPR	Alternative AD Diversion AD	Hawarden Manchester Barton

Liverpool	ATIS 124.325	APP 119.850	RAD 118.450 (as directed by ATC)
TWR 126.350	**GND** 121.950 (as directed by ATC)	**FIRE** 121.600	**Handling** 131.750 (LAS)

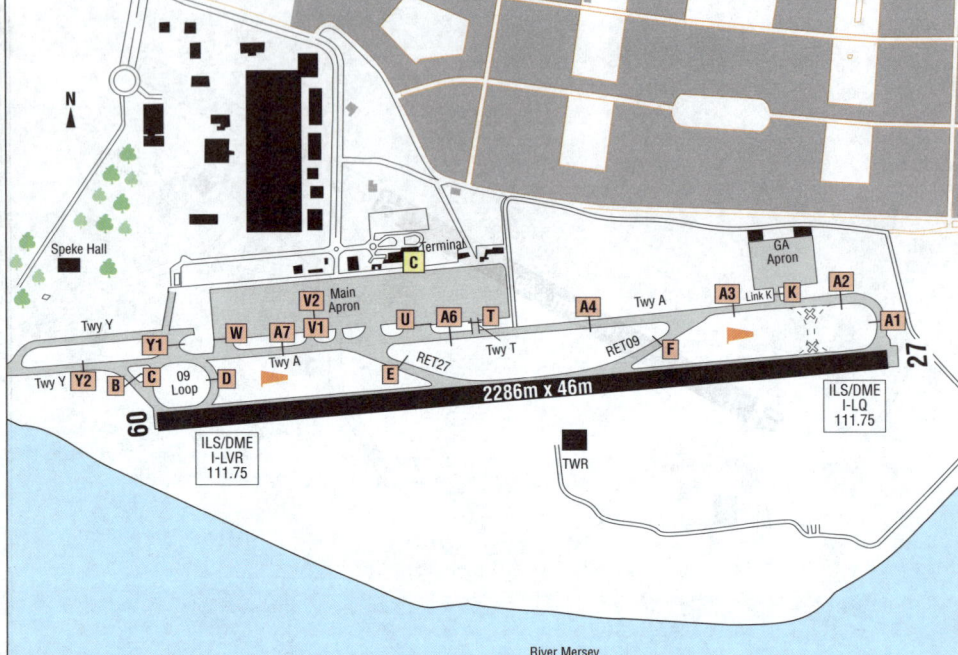

RWY	SURFACE	TORA	LDA	LIGHTING
09	Asphalt	2286	2225	Ap Thr Rwy PAPI 3° LHS
27	Asphalt	2286	2286	Ap Thr Rwy PAPI 3° LHS

Remarks

PPR non-radio ACFT & non-based ACFT via Handling Agent. Mandatory handling for all visiting ACFT. Await signals from marshaller before proceeding on to main apron. Failure to make a booking may result in the ACFT being refused use of the facilities. Payment of landing fees does not constitute booking out. Landing and taxiing on grass area not permitted. All ACFT to enter main apron via Twy V, unless directed by ATC. Hold B only available to ACFT <5700kgs. Twy A abeam holding point C and Twy Y only available for use by Code B ACFT or smaller. Not available at night or in LVP's. Twy G is permanently closed. Circuit training for non-Liverpool based operators is only available by prior arr with ATC and is subject to local circuit traffic. ACFT without PPR could be refused landing permission except in an emergency. For training flights, a booking system is now in operation by ATC. ACFT repositioning on the apron require marshaller guidance. Visiting aircrew not to walk across apron without escort. Inform TWR of any special requests on APP to AD. GA parking area is limited to ACFT <5700kgs.
Aids to Navigation: NDB LPL 349.50

Warnings

Positively identify Rwy27/09 before committing to landing. Be aware of Restricted Area R311, 5nm to the SW. Take care when leaving the main apron not to enter the rapid exit turn off for Rwy09/27. Bird activity on Rwy09/27 APP. Radio controlled ACFT <75 kgs in weight operate 11nm WNW (Arrowe Park) up to 400ft agl (daylight only). Twy A from A3 to Rwy27 Thr is restricted to ACFT with wingspan less than 52m. Overhead join of the CCT is not available. Pilots join as directed by ATC.

Operating Hrs	H24
Circuits	Variable at the discretion of ATC
Landing Fee	Single £26 Twin on application

Maintenance
LAS
Fuel
AVGAS JET A1 100LL
Tel: 0151 486 6161
Tel: 0151 486 7084 (Depot)
Fax: 0151 486 7720
Payment by cash cheque Esso Exxon carnet 3rd Party cards by prior arr or credit card

L

Disabled Facilities	Available
Handling	**Tel:** 0151 486 6161 (LAS)
	Fax: 0151 486 5151 (LAS)
	ops@liverpoolhandling.co.uk
	www.liverpoolhandling.co.uk
Restaurants	Restaurant refreshments in terminal
Taxis	Taxi Rank outside Terminal
Car Hire	
Eurocar	**Tel:** 0151 448 1652
Hertz	**Tel:** 0151 486 7111
Weather Info	M T9 T18 Fax 342 VN MWC

Operator	Liverpool Airport PLC
	Liverpool Airport
	Liverpool L24 1YD
	Tel: 0870 750 8484 (AD)
	Tel: 0151 907 1541 (ATC)
	Tel: 0151 907 1501 (Admin)
	Tel: 0151 907 1551 (AD Ops & PPR)
	Tel: 0151 907 1531 (Flt Plans)
	Fax: 0151 907 1520 (ATC)
	Fax: 0151 907 1500 (Admin)
	Fax: 0151 907 1550 (AD Ops & PPR)
	Fax: 0151 907 1540 (Flt Plans)

CTR – Class D Airspace
Normal CTR/CTA Class D Airspace rules apply
Transition Alt 5000ft
SVFR clearance will not be given to fixed-wing ACFT if the weather conditions are below 1800m visibility or a cloud base below 600ft.
Flights up to 1500ft altitude W of the low level corridor may take place in VMC without compliance with IFR. However, pilots will have to comply (when flying in this area) with Liverpool's Rules which are as follows:
1 Call Liverpool ATC on the appropriate freq giving details of ACFT position, level and proposed track.
2 Obtain permission for the flight.
3 Maintain a listening watch.
4 Obey any instructions given by Liverpool ATC.
A number of standard routes have been established along which VFR/SVFR clearances will be given.

NOISE ABATEMENT PROCEDURES
ACFT must be operated in a manner calculated to cause the least disturbance practicable in areas surrounding the AD. Inbound ACFT, other than light ACFT flying under VFR or SVFR, shall maintain a height of at least 2000ft aal until cleared to descend for landing. ACFT requiring to hold S of AD to minimise flight over Stanlow Oil Refinery (4nm S). ACFT APP without assistance from ILS or RAD must not fly lower than the ILS glide path. Between 2300-0700 (Winter) 2200-0600 (Summer), Rwy09 will only be available for take off when over-riding operational considerations necessitate its use. Avoid over flying Speke Hall.

LIVERPOOL STANDARD ENTRY/EXIT ROUTES:
Rwy27 Outbound
To N – Route via River Mersey, leave CTR via Seaforth, not above 1500ft
To S – Cross River Mersey, follow M53, leave via Chester, remaining E of Capenhurst, not above 1500ft
Rwy27 Inbound
From N – Enter via Kirkby, route E of M57, as directed by ATC, not above 1500ft
From S – Enter via Oulton Park, route W of Helsby, as directed by ATC, not above 1500ft
Rwy09 Outbound
To N – Route E of M57, leave via Kirkby, not above 1500ft
To S – Cross River Mersey, leave CTR via Oulton Park, not above 1500ft
Rwy09 Inbound
From N – Enter via Seaforth, route via River Mersey, as directed by ATC, not above 1500ft
From S – Enter via Chester, follow M53 to Outlet Village, as directed by ATC, not above 1500ft

L

SOUTHPORT
Birkdale Sands
AIRWAY L70
A FL185-FL245
Martin Mere/2
2452 (1015)
MANCHEST
A 3500-

WOODVALE ATZ
MANCHESTR TMA
A 3500-FL245
WOODVALE
Bolton
M61

AIRWAY N864
A FL155-FL245
Wigan
M6

M INCE
M58
MANCHESTR CTA
D 2500-3500ftALT
MANCHESTR
D 2500-3500

AIRWAY L10
A 3500-FL245
E/E MERSEY LANE
VRP KIRBY
St Helens
LOW LEVEL ROUTE
D MAX ALT 1250ft
MANCHESTER QNH
BARTON ATZ

LIVERPOOL CTA
A 2000-3500ftALT
VRP SEAFORTH
VRP AINTREE RACECOURSE
M57
MANCHESTR TMA
A 3500-FL245
M62

GVS/3.1

LIVERPOOL CTA
A 1500-3500ftALT
WAL 114.1
Pier Head
VRP BURTONWOOD
Warrington
VRP THELWALL VIADUCT
Lymm D
Lymm M56

LIVERPOOL LFA
Max Alt 1500ft
Liverpool QNH
Mnm Vis 3km
Clearance by
Liverpool ATC
LIVERPOOL LFA
Jaguar Mushroom
475
678
VRP STRETTON AD
STREETON

M53
LIVERPOOL
LIVERPOOL CTA
2500-3500'ALT
LPL 349.5
MANCHESTR CTR
D SFC-3500ftALT

AIRWAY L975
A 3500-FL245
E/E NESTON LANE
VRP NESTON
663

R311/3.2
Outlet village
(Cheshire Oaks)
Helsby
378
Northwich

994
SEALAND
MANCHESTR CTA
D 2500-3500ftALT
LOW LEVEL ROUTE
D MAX ALT 1250ft
MANCHESTER QNH

AIRWAY N864
A 3500-FL245
HAWARDEN ATZ
VRP CHESTER
576
WHI 368.5
Winsford

HAWARDEN
HAW 340
M WAVERTON
VRP OULTON PARK
ASHCROFT
Middle

POULTON
MANCHESTR CTA
D 2500-3500ftALT
Sandb

1339
MANCHESTR TMA
A 3500-FL245

1083
Crewe

Visual Reference Points (VRP)				
VRP	VOR/VOR	VOR/NDB	VOR/DME	VOR/DME
Aintree Racecourse N5328.60 W00256.58	WAL 057°/MCT 290°	MCT 290°/WHI 331°	WAL 057°/9nm	
Burtonwood Services N5325.00 W00238.28	WAL 089°/POL 227°	WAL 089°/WHI 001°	WAL 089°/18nm	MCT 288°/14nm
Chester N5311.70 W00250.63	WAL 142°/MCT 249°	WAL 142°/WHI 278°	WAL 142°/15nm	MCT 249°/23nm
Kirby N5328.80 W00252.90	WAL 063°/MCT 292°	MCT 293°/WHI 336°	WAL 063°/11nm	MCT 292°/23nm
Neston N5317.50 W00303.60	WAL 160°/MCT 266°	WAL 160°/WHI 296°	WAL 160°/7nm	MCT 266°/29nm
Oulton Park N5310.57 W00236.80	WAL 128°/MCT 233°	MCT 233°/LPL 161°	MCT 233°/17nm	WAL 128°/23nm
Seaforth N5327.68 W00302.08	WAL 044°/MCT 286°	MCT 286°/WHI 322°	WAL 044°/6nm	
Stretton (Disused AD) N5320.77 W00231.58	WAL 101°/POL 215°	MCT 270°/WHI 023°	WAL 101°/22nm	MCT 270°/10nm

19ft 1mb	6nm E of City of London N5130.32 E00003.32	PPR	Alternative AD	Biggin Hill Stapleford

London City	ATIS 136.350	APP Thames RAD 132.700 (0630-2230 L)	APP Heathrow Director 119.725 (2230-0630 L)
TWR 118.075	GND 121.825	RAD Thames 132.700	FIRE 121.600

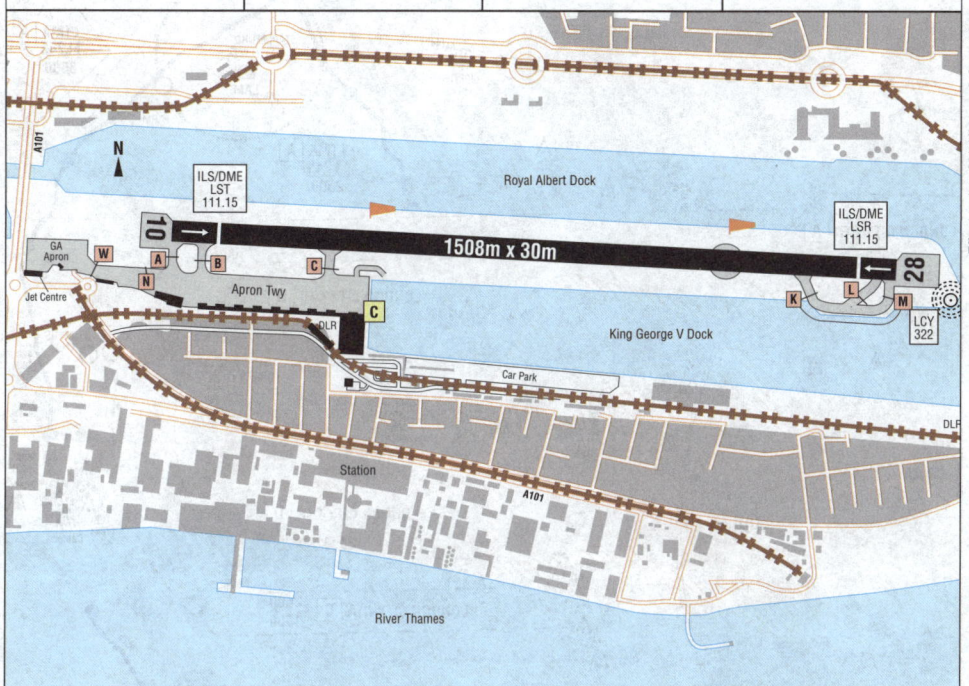

Royal Albert Dock

ILS/DME LST 111.15

ILS/DME LSR 111.15

GA Apron

Jet Centre

Apron Twy

1508m x 30m

King George V Dock

Car Park

LCY 322

Station

A101

River Thames

DLR

RWY	SURFACE	TORA	LDA	LIGHTING
10	Concrete	1508	1319	Ap Thr Tdz Rwy PAPI 5.5° LHS
28	Concrete	1508	1319	Ap Thr Tdz Rwy PAPI 5.5° LHS

Starter extension Rwy10 75m.
Starter extension Rwy28 186m

Remarks
PPR non-radio ACFT not accepted. AD is licensed only for ACFT that have in their Flight Manual data and procedures for APP path angles of 5.5°. The use of AD is subject to prior permission of the AD Director. Operators to provide Noise Certificate details on request. AD not available for use by helicopters, single engined ACFT or for recreational flights. Only training necessary for the operation of ACFT at the AD will be permitted. All training is subject to approval. ACFT landing Rwy28 are not permitted to exit via A unless instructed by ATC. No ACFT to self park without marshaller guidance.

Warnings
Possibility of building induced turbulence and/or wind shear when landing in strong wind conditions.

Operating Hrs	Mon-Fri 0530-2005 Sat 0530-1135 Sun 1130-2000 (Summer) +1Hr (Winter)	**Weather Info**	M T9 Fax 344 MOEx ATIS **Tel:** 0207 6460224
Circuits	Nil	**Operator**	London City Airport Ltd Royal Dock Silvertown London, E16 2PX **Tel:** 0207 6460000 (Admin) **Tel:** 0207 6460205 (ATC) **Fax:** 0207 5111040 (Admin) www.londoncityairport.com
Landing Fee	Available on request		
Maintenance	Scot Airways & BA		
Fuel	AVTUR JET A1		
Disabled Facilities	Available		
Handling	**Tel:** 0207 6460400 (The Jet Centre)		
Restaurants	Restaurant buffet bar	**CTR – Class D Airspace**	
Taxis/Car Hire	Available at Terminal	Normal CTR/CTA Class D Airspace rules apply Transition Alt 6000ft	

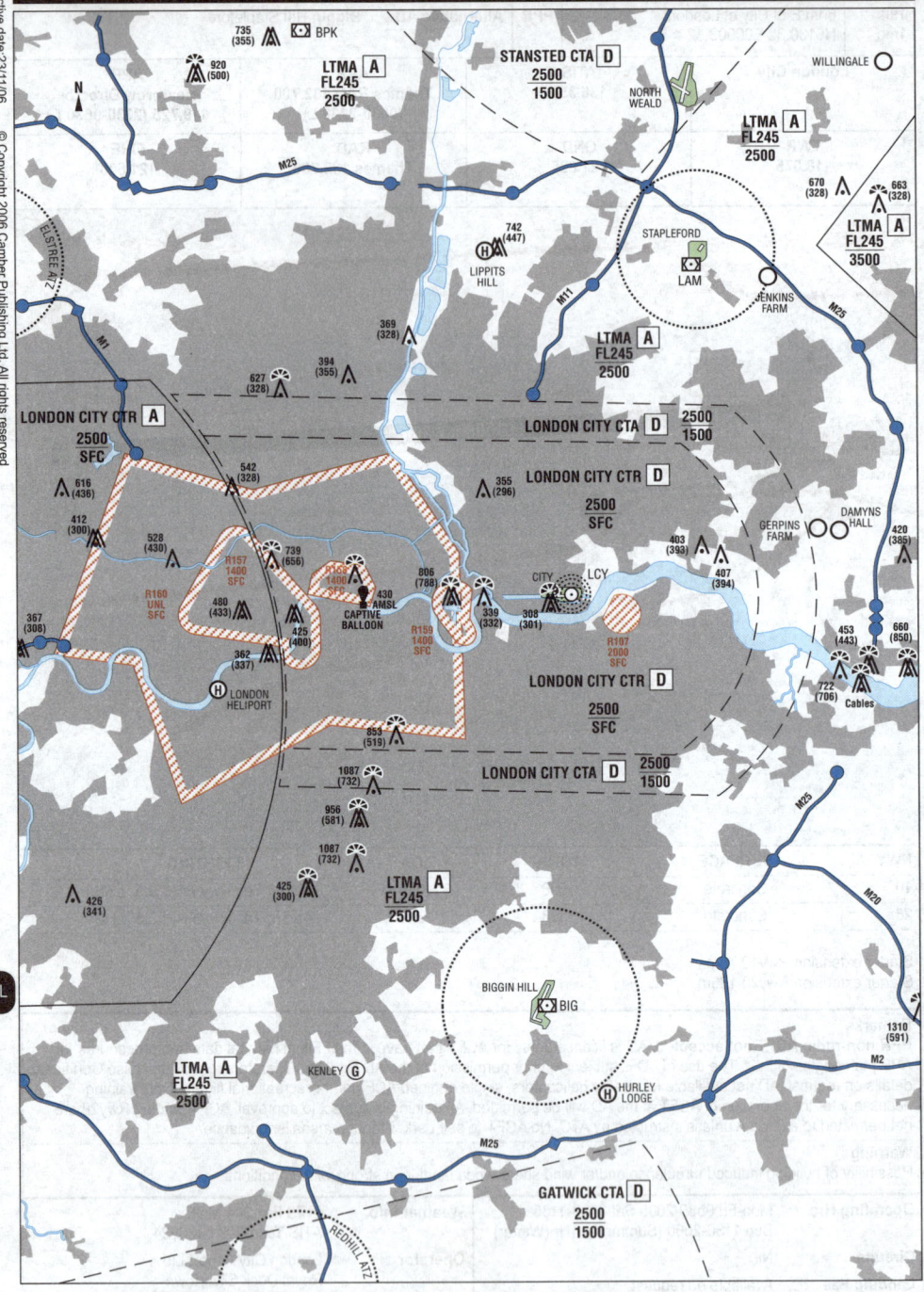

Noise abatement procedures for ACFT Dept London City and joining Controlled Airspace are included in the appropriate Standard Instrument Dept (SID) instructions. ACFT Dept London City CTR into the FIR or Dept on training flights within the London City CTR are to climb straight ahead to a minimum of 1000ft aal before turning on track unless otherwise instructed by ATC. ACFT making APP to London City without assistance from the ILS shall follow a descent path not lower than the ILS glide path. Pilots of ACFT carrying out visual APP to either Rwy or carrying out training circuits visually shall fly at a height of not less than 1500ft QFE until established on the final APP. To reduce noise impact on the local community, ACFT should use the full length of the Rwy for take-offs. ACFT manoeuvring visually (circling) to one Rwy after making ILS APP to the other Rwy shall do so at as high Alt as possible, compatible with the cloud base, retaining visual contact and appropriate published visual manoeuvring (circling) height minima.

196ft 6mb	2.7nm N of Crawley N5108.88 W00011.42	PPR	Alternative AD	Farnborough Redhill

Gatwick	ATIS 136.525		APP 126.825	TWR 124.225
GND 121.800	DEL 121.950		FIRE 121.600	

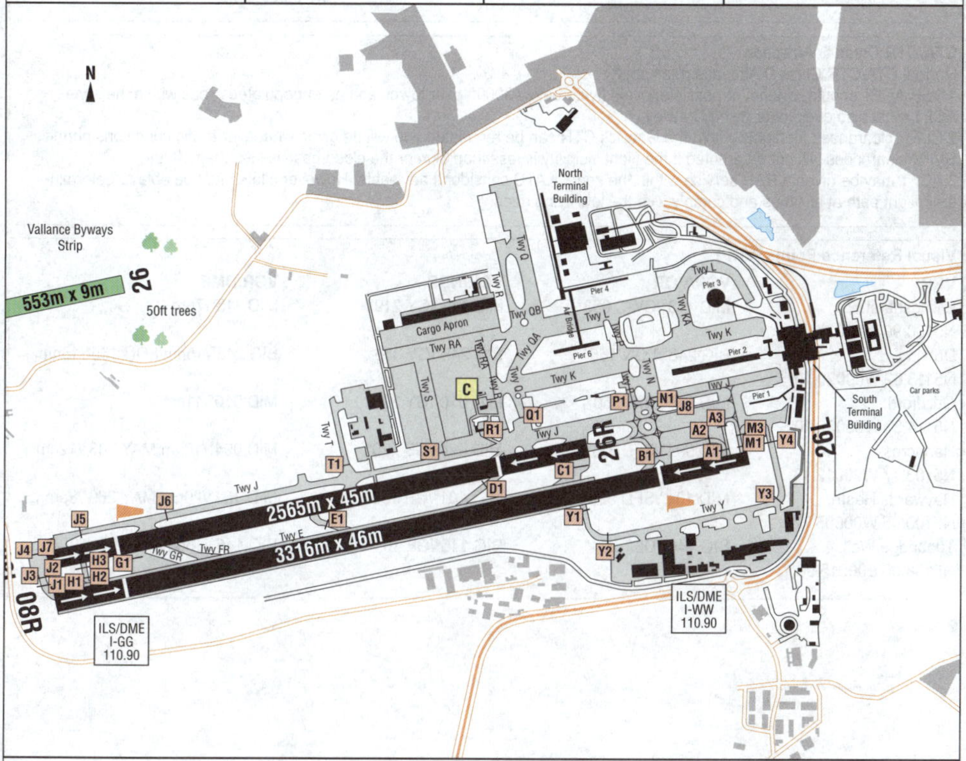

(Airport diagram — London Gatwick. Runways 08R/26L (3316m × 46m, 3159m TORA), 08L/26R (2565m × 45m), Vallance Byways Strip 26/08R (553m × 9m). North Terminal Building, South Terminal Building, Cargo Apron, taxiways. ILS/DME I-GG 110.90, ILS/DME I-WW 110.90.)

RWY	SURFACE	TORA	LDA	LIGHTING
08R	Asph/Conc	3159	2766	Ap Thr Rwy PAPI 3° RH
26L	Asph/Conc	3255	2831	Ap Thr Rwy PAPI 3° LH
08L	Asph/Conc	2565	2243	Ap Thr Rwy PAPI 3° LH
26R	Asph/Conc	2565	2148	Ap Thr Rwy PAPI 3° LH

Remarks

PPR mandatory not more than 10 days, not less than 24Hrs. Non-radio ACFT not accepted. Use governed by regulations applicable to Gatwick CTR. AD may be used by executive and private ACFT GA subject to the following conditions. GA operators must notify details of each flight in advance to their nominated handling agent who will obtain permission from apron control. Operators are advised that before selecting Gatwick as an alternate, prior arr for GND handling should have been agreed with one of the nominated handling agents. The use of this AD for training is prohibited. Helicopter operations: There are no helicopter alighting areas at AD, all helicopters use Rwys. Handling agents to obtain slots. Helicopters may not carry out direct APP to or from apron areas or Twys. After landing helicopters will GND/air taxi to parking slot. Extreme caution to be used due to wing tip clearance whilst helicopters are taxiing. Operator to provide Noise Certificate details on request. All telephones to ATC may be recorded.
Aids to Navigation: NDB GY 365.00. NDB GE 338.00

Warnings

In low visibility at night the apron and car park flood lighting may be seen before APP lights on Rwy26L and Rwy26R APP. Except for light signals, GND signals are not displayed. When landing on Rwy26L/R in strong S/SW winds, there is the possibility of building induced turbulence and windshear.

Operating Hrs	H24
Circuits	Nil
Landing Fee	Available on request
Maintenance	Available by arr with local operators
Fuel	AVTUR JET A1

Disabled Facilities

Handling   GA handling
Tel: 01293 503201 (Interflight)

L

Restaurants		Operator	Gatwick Airport Ltd
Restaurants buffets & bars in N & S terminals			London Gatwick Airport
			West Sussex, RH6 0NP
Taxis	Available at N & S Terminals		**Tel:** 07800 002468 (GAL)
Car Hire			**Tel:** 01293 503089 (Apron Control)
Avis	**Tel:** 01293 529751		**Tel:** 01293 601040 (NATS/FBU)
Hertz	**Tel:** 01293 530555		**Fax:** 01293 601033 (NATS)
			Fax: 01293 505093 (GAL)
Weather Info	M T9 T18 Fax 346 A VM VN MOEx		**Fax:** 01293 505149 (Apron Control)
			www.baa.com

CTA/CTR Class D Airspace

Normal CTA/CTR Class D Airspace rules apply

1 VFR ACFT should, whenever possible, avoid flying below 3000ft over towns and other populated areas within the zone. ACFT must also avoid over-flying Crawley.

2 SVFR clearances for flights within the Gatwick CTR can be requested and will be given whenever traffic conditions permit. SVFR clearances will not be granted if the flight visibility is less than 3km or the cloud base is less than 1000ft.

3 ACFT may be given a RAD service within the zone, if ATC consider it advisable. However pilots must be able to determine their flight path at all times and comply with the low flying rules.

Visual Reference Points (VRP)

VRP	VOR/VOR	VOR/NDB	VOR/DME
Billingshurst N5100.90 W00027.00	MID 113°/GWC 053°	MID 113°/GY 219°	MID 113°/7nm
Dorking N5113.62 W00020.10	BIG 248°/LON 165°	BIG 248°/GY 356°	BIG 248°/15nm/LON 165°/16nm
Guildford N5114.37 W00035.10	MID 010°/BIG 260°	MID 010°/GY 305°	MID 010°/11nm
Handcross N5103.17 W00012.13	MID 094°/SFD 327°	MID 094°/GE 220°	MID 094°/16nm/MAY 283°/12nm
Haywards Heath N5100.45 W00005.77	MID 101°/SFD 333°	MID 101°/GE 189°	MID 101°/20nm/MAY 269°/8nm
Tunbridge Wells N5108.00 E00015.90	BIG 146°/DET 234°	BIG 146°/GE 101°	BIG 146°/15nm/MAY 042°/9nm

L

EGLL   LONDON HEATHROW

83ft 3mb	12nm W of London N5128.65 W00027.68	PPR	Alternative AD	Farnborough Denham

Heathrow	ATIS 121.850 (ARR)	ATIS 128.075 (DEPT)	APP 119.725	RAD 125.625 (SVFR & Heli in CTR)
TWR 118.500 118.700	**GND** 121.900 121.700	**DEL** 121.975	**FIRE** 121.600	

Effective date:23/11/06

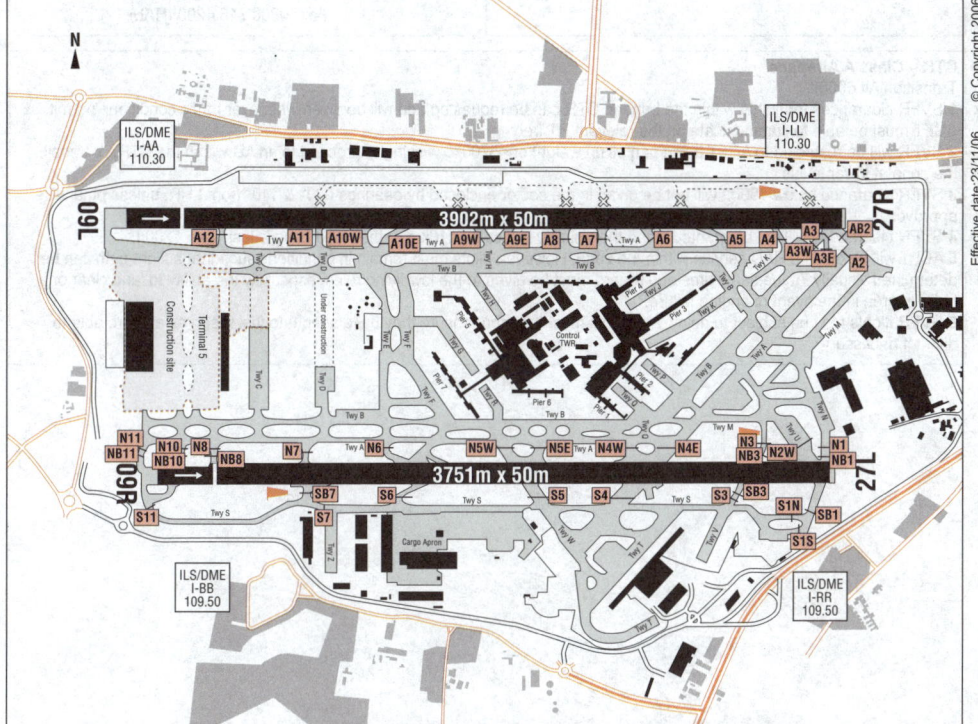

RWY	SURFACE	TORA	LDA	LIGHTING
09L	Conc/Asph	3902	3595	Ap Thr Rwy PAPI 3°
27R	Conc/Asph	3884	3884	Ap Thr Rwy PAPI 3°
09R	Asphalt	3660	3353	Ap Thr Rwy PAPI 3°
27L	Asphalt	3660	3660	Ap Thr Rwy PAPI 3°

L

Remarks
PPR mandatory not more than 10 days not less than 24Hrs. Use governed by regulations applicable to London CTR. IFR procedures apply in all weather conditions. Light single and twin engined ACFT may not use the AD. General and business aviation movements permitted subject to the following conditions. GA operators must notify details of each flight in advance to the Manager Operations Centre. Before selecting Heathrow as an alternate, prior arr for GND handling should have been agreed with one of the nominated handling agents. The use of this AD for training is prohibited. The Arr ATIS is broadcast on the Bovingdon, Biggin, Ockham and Lambourne VOR's.

Helicopter operations
Helicopter aiming point is located at NE end of Block97. Helicopters alighting at the aiming point will GND or air taxi to parking areas as directed by ATC. The following conditions and procedures apply to single-engined and light twin-engined ACFT not fully equipped with radio apparatus (including ILS receiver) as specified in the RAC Section but carrying at least the VHF RT frequencies to allow communication with London Heathrow AD APP/Director, TWR and GND Movement Control: The flight must be made on Special VFR clearance under the weather conditions and along the routes specified in the RAC Section. Operator to provide Noise Certificate details on request. All flights (inc Helicopters) are at all times subject to PPR.

Warnings
When landing on Rwy27R in strong S/SW winds, beware of the possibility of building induced turbulence and large wind shear effects.

Operating Hrs	H24	**Maintenance**	Available by arr
Circuits	Nil	**Fuel**	AVTUR JET A1
Landing Fee	BAA Plc Airports Rates	**Disabled Facilities**	Available

Restaurants	Restaurants buffets & bars in Terminals	Operator	London Heathrow Airport
Taxis	Available at Terminals		Heathrow Point
Car Hire			Middlesex, UB3 5AP
Avis	**Tel:** 0208 897 9321		**Tel:** 0870 000 0123 (HAL)
Hertz	**Tel:** 0208 679 1799		**Tel:** 0208 745 3326 (NATS)
Alamo	**Tel:** 0208 897 0536		**Tel:** 0208 759 4871
			(Manager Ops Centre)
Weather Info	M T9 T18 Fax 348 A VM VSc MOEx		**Tel:** 0208 745 3228
			(Heli route ATC NATS)
			Fax: 0208 745 3491 (NATS)
			Fax: 0208 745 3492 (FBU)
			Fax: 0208 745 4290 (HAL)

CTR – Class A Airspace
Transition Alt 6000ft

1 SVFR clearances for flights within the London CTR can be requested and will be given whenever traffic conditions permit. ACFT must be able to communicate on the relevant RT freq

2 SVFR will be restricted to ACFT having an all up weight of <5700kg wishing to proceed to an AD within the CTR, or transit the zone at lower levels.

3 SVFR clearance below 1500ft will not be given in the sector enclosed by bearings 020° & 140° from LHR, unless otherwise approved.

4 SVFR clearances will not be granted when the visibility is less than10km or the cloud base is less than 1200ft.

5 ACFT will be given a RAD service within the zone. However, pilots must remain in conditions such that a flight path can be determined visually. At the same time due regard must be given to the low flying rules, especially the ability to land clear of a built-up area in the event of engine failure.

6 SVFR flights may be subject to delay, and pilots must therefore ensure they have adequate fuel reserves and are able to divert if necessary.

L

L

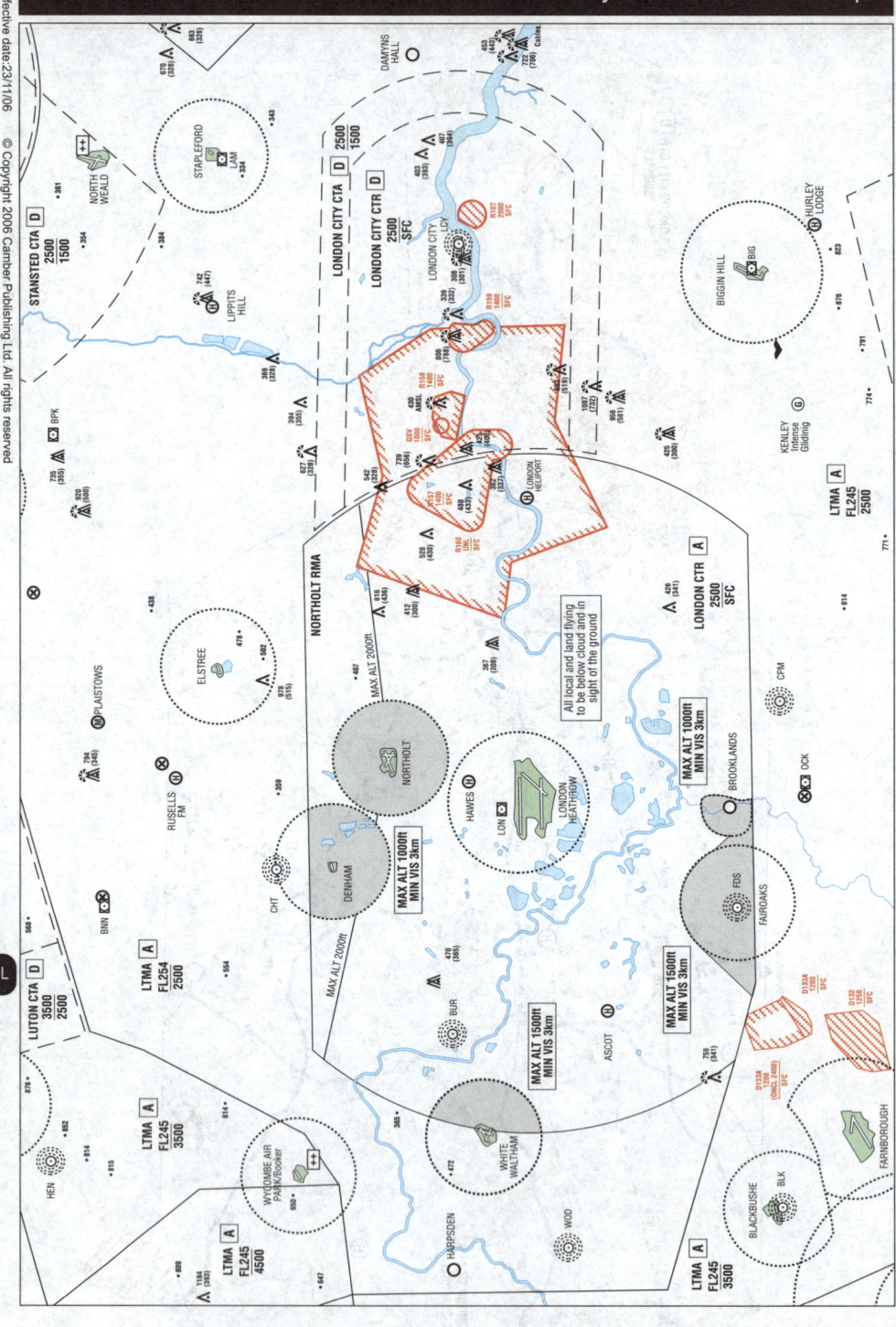

526ft 18mb	1.5nm E of Luton N5152.48 W00022.10	PPR	Alternative AD	Cranfield Panshanger

Luton	ATIS 120.575	APP 129.550
TWR 132.550	GND 121.750	FIRE 121.600

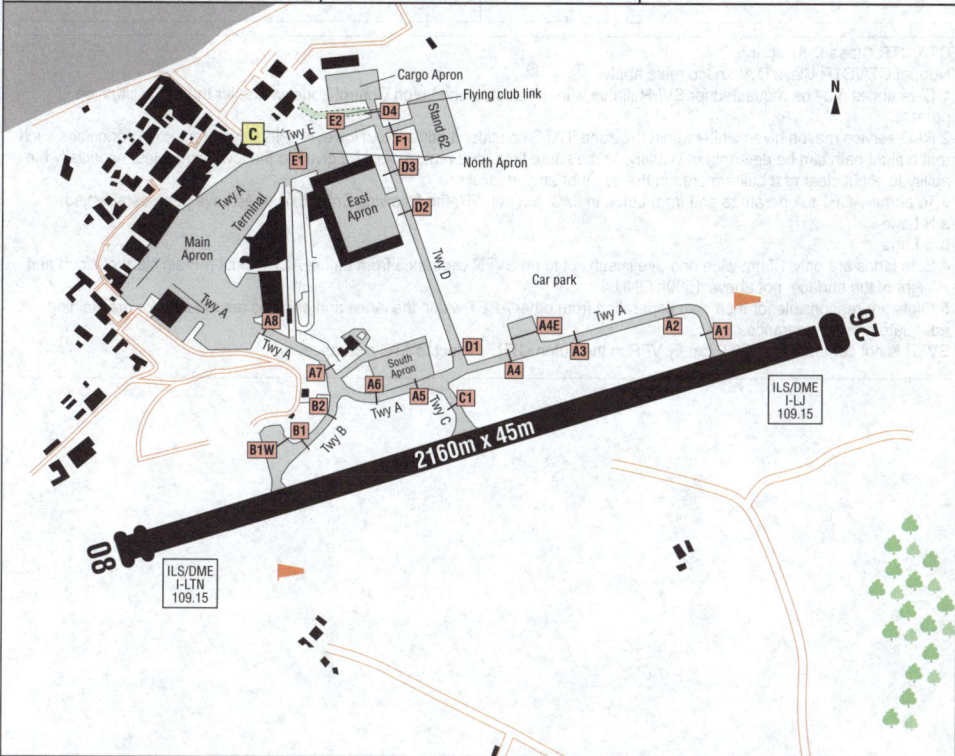

RWY	SURFACE	TORA	LDA	LIGHTING
08	Asphalt	2160	2160	Ap Thr Rwy PAPI 3°
26	Asphalt	2160	2075	Ap Thr Rwy PAPI 3°

Displaced Thr Rwy26 85m

Remarks

Use governed by regulations applicable to Luton CTR. Non-scheduled commercial executive and private ACFT are subject to PPR. All flight training PPR. When taking off from Rwy26 if able to turn cross wind by the end of the Rwy confine circuit to E of London/Luton railway line. To assist parking Arr, details of each flight must be notified in advance to the ATC Watch Manager. All GA flights using the main apron must use a handling agent. AD is available only to qualified pilots. Minimum circuit height for ACFT whose MTWA <5700kg (12500lbs) is 1000ft QFE in the vicinity of AD. Pilots of visiting ACFT to contact apron control before Dept and/or after Arr.

Aids to Navigation: NDB LUT 345.00

Warnings

Grass cutting takes place as required during the summer months. The flying club link is not part of the manoeuvring area, uncontrolled vehicles operate on and close to link. Use is at pilots discretion.

Operating Hrs	H24
Circuits	See Remarks
Landing Fee	On application, mandatory handling
Maintenance	**Tel:** 01582 724182 (Signature Flight Support)
Fuel	AVGAS 100LL (0600-2359 Other times by arr with surcharge) AVTUR JET A1 Out of Hrs contact
Shell UK Ltd	**Tel:** 01582 417659

Disabled Facilities Available

Handling
Tel: 01582 488410 (Air Foyle)
Tel: 01582 402040 (Allied Signal)
Tel: 01582 724182 (Signature)
Tel: 01582 700900 (Aviance)
Tel: 01582 618603 (Servisair)
Tel: 01582 589317 (Harrods Business Aviation)

Restaurant	Restaurant refreshments & Club facilities available at AD	Operator	London Luton Airport Ltd Navigation House Airport Way Luton, Bedfordshire, LU2 9LY
Taxis	Available at Terminal		**Tel:** 01582 405100 (Switchboard)
Car Hire			**Tel:** 01582 395299 (ATC)
Alamo	**Tel:** 01582 468414		**Tel:** 01582 395525 (PPR)
National	**Tel:** 01582 417723		**Tel:** 01582 395029 (NATS)
Europcar	**Tel:** 01582 413438		**Fax:** 01582 395141 (ATC)
Weather Info	M T9 T18 Fax 358 A VS MOEx ATIS **Tel:** 0906 4744474		**Fax:** 01582 395399 (NATS)

CTA/CTR Class D Airspace
Normal CTA/CTR Class D Airspace rules apply.
1 Clearances may be requested for SVFR flights within Stansted and Luton Control Zone whenever the traffic situation permits.
2 RAD service maybe given whilst within the zone if ATC consider it advisable. However, pilots must remain in conditions such that a flight path can be determined visually. At the same time, due regard must be given to the low flying rules, especially the ability to alight clear of a built-up area in the event of engine failure.
3 To permit ACFT to operate to and from Luton in IMC, but not IFR, the following Entry/Exit lanes have been established:
a N Lane
b S Lane
4 Both lanes are only 1.5nm wide and use is subject to an SVFR clearance from Luton. ACFT must remain clear of cloud and in sight of the surface, not above 1500ft QNH.
5 Pilots are responsible for their own separation from other ACFT within the lanes and are also responsible for maintaining adequate ground clearance.
SVFR is not compulsory. ACFT can fly VFR in the Luton CTR, subject to ATC clearance.

L

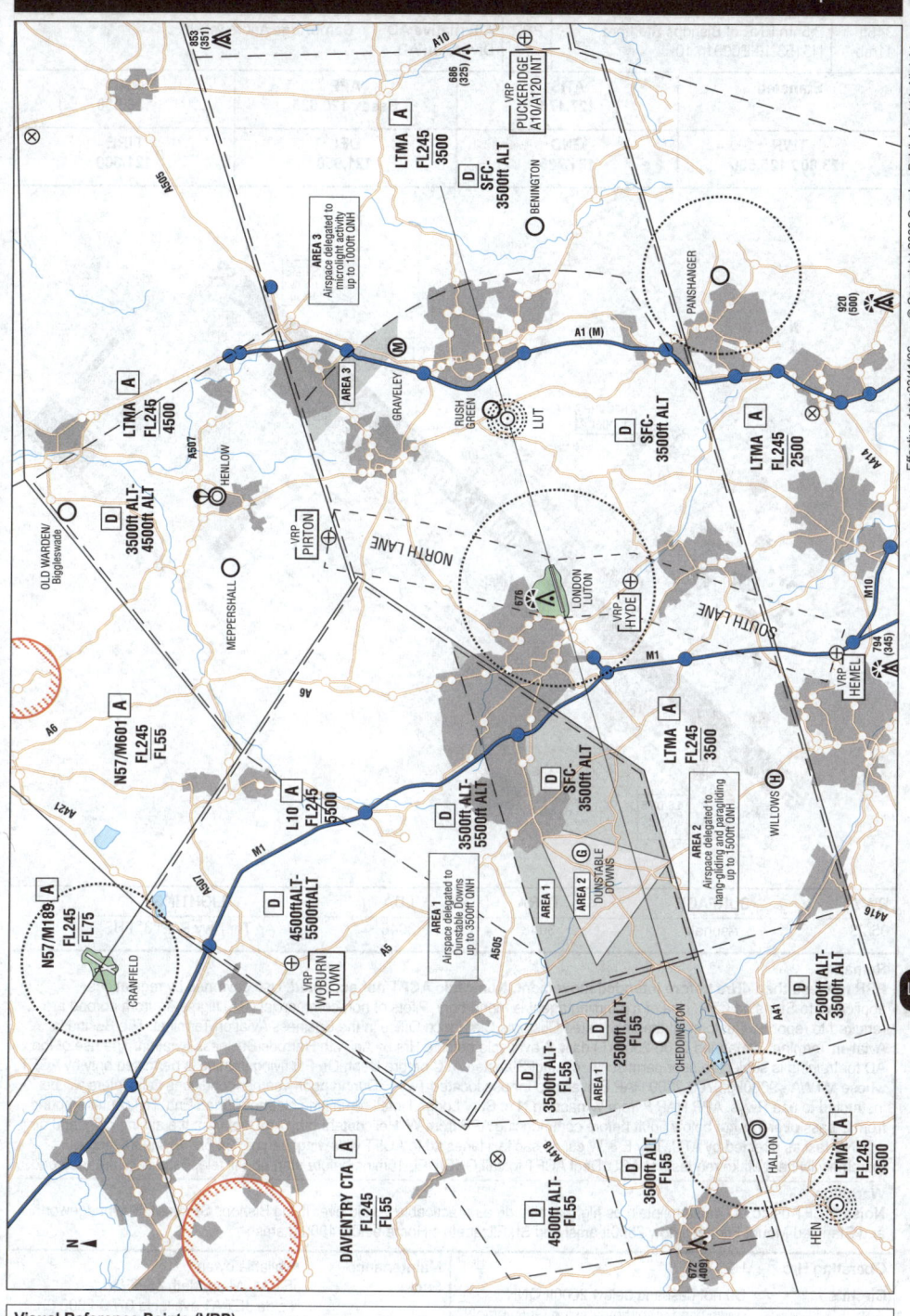

Visual Reference Points (VRP)

VRP	VOR/DME	VOR/DME	NDB
Hemel	BPK 274°/12nm	BNN 073°/5nm	LUT 219°
N5145.37 W00024.97			
Hyde	BPK 303°/11nm	BNN 046°/10nm	LUT 237°
N5150.65 W00021.97			
Pirton	BPK 330°/16nm	BNN 031°/17nm	LUT 331°
N5158.30 W00019.90			

EGSS

LONDON STANSTED

348ft 11mb	2.5nm ENE of Bishops Stortford N5153.10 E00014.10	PPR	Alternative AD Diversion AD	Cambridge Andrewsfield

Stansted	ATIS 127.175	APP Essex 120.625	RAD 126.950

TWR 123.800 125.500	GND 121.725	DEL 121.950	FIRE 121.600

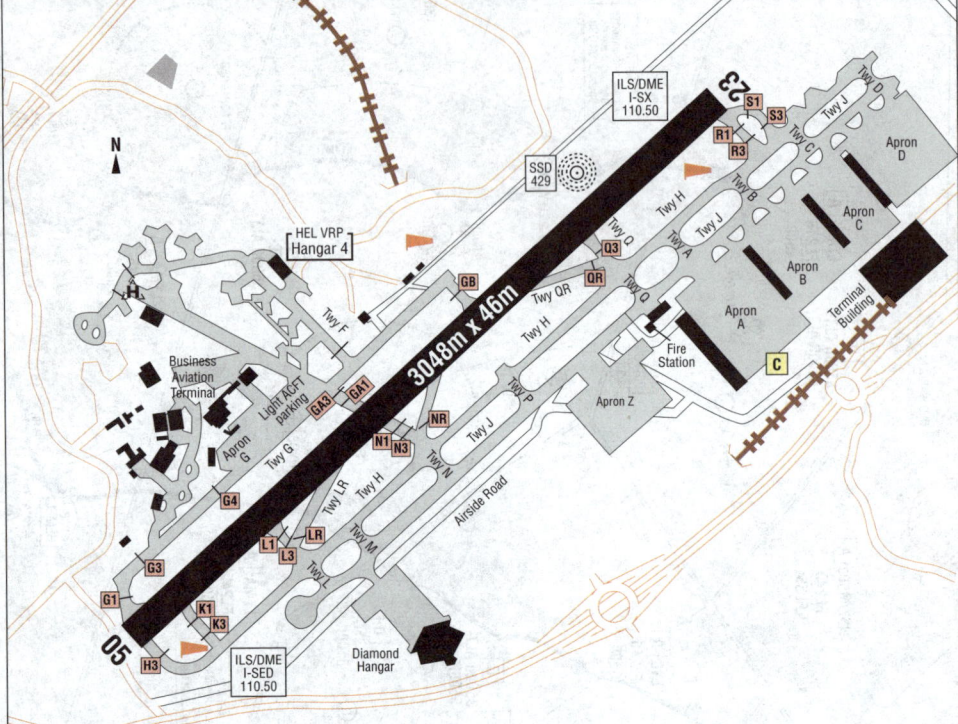

RWY	SURFACE	TORA	LDA	LIGHTING
05/23	Asphalt	3048	3048	Ap Thr Rwy PAPI 3° LHS

L

Remarks

PPR not less than 4Hrs before intended movement. Non-radio ACFT not accepted. Use governed by regulations applicable to Stansted CTR. Use of a handling agent is mandatory. Pilots of non-commercial (GA) flights Arr from abroad are required to report to Customs at the designated Customs Clearance Office in the Business Aviation Terminal. The Business Aviation Terminal is manned 0700-2300 (L) daily & available outside Hrs by Arr with Harrods Business Aviation. The use of the AD for training is subject to prior permission, contact Stansted ATC before Dept. On PH flying training is permitted only by ACFT whose MTWA <9000kg.0700-2300 HAP F available for use located Twy F. During poor weather conditions helicopters will be instructed to use Rwys. APP HAP F from W passing N of Bury Lodge Hotel, remaining clear of Burton End. Helicopter inbound from E pass over Thr not below 500ft before commencing APP from W. Helicopters may Arr/Dept from the aiming point and air or GND taxi as directed by ATC. Twy E & W cul de sac taxi lanes ltd to ACFT with wingspan of <34.5m. Flying training is extremely limited. Make requests to ACL. Dept ACFT to call GND/DEL 10mins before start up. All telephone calls are recorded

Warnings

Noise: ACFT using AD must maintain as high an altitude as practicable. Avoid over flying Bishops Stortford, Sawbridgeworth and Stansted Mount Fitchet below 2500ft amsl and St. Elizabeth's Home below 4000 ft amsl.

Operating Hrs	H24	**Maintenance**	Available by arr
Circuits	Do not descend below 2000ft QNH down wind. Avoid over flying Gt Dunmow & Takeley	**Fuel**	JET A1 Water/Meth 45/55/30 N side JET A1 available 0700-2300 (L). At other times a call out charge of £100.00 will be levied unless fuel is required for medical flight or priorarr has been made
Landing Fee	BAA Plc Airport Rates	**Esso**	**Tel:** 01279 663178/9
		Disabled Facilities	Available

Handling	**Tel:** 01279 665312	Operator	Stansted Airport Ltd
	(Harrods Aviation)		Stansted Essex CM24 1QW
	Tel: 01279 831000 (Inflite Ltd)		**Tel:** 08700 000303 (AD)
	Tel: 01279 680349		**Tel:** 01279 669328 (NATS)
	(Universal Aviation UK)		**Fax:** 01279 662066 (AD)
	Fax: 01279 681367 (Harrods Aviation)		**Fax:** 01279 669336 (NATS/FBU)
	Fax: 01279 837900 (Inflite Ltd)		www.baa.com/stansted
	Fax: 01279 680372 (Universal)		
	(Universal Aviation UK)		
Restaurants	Buffets & bars in Terminal		
Taxis/Car Hire	Available at Terminal		
Weather Info	M T9 T18 Fax 352 A VM MOEx		
	ATIS **Tel:** 01279 669325		

CTA/CFR Class D Airspace

Transition Alt 6000ft

Normal CTA/CTR Class D Airspace rules apply

1 Clearances may be requested for SVFR flights within the Stansted and Luton Control Zone and will be given when ever the traffic situation permits.

2 RAD service may be given whilst within the zone if ATC consider it advisable. However, pilots must remain in conditions such that a flight path can be determined visually. At the same time due regard must be given to the low flying rules, especially in the event of engine failure.

3 Stansted VFR and SVFR Arr/Dept are cleared normally not above 1500ft QNH by the following routes:

a Audley End Railway Station via M11

b Gt Dunmow via A120

c Puckeridge via A120 avoiding Bishops Stortford

d Nuthampstead VRP

4 VFR traffic wishing to transit the Stansted zone can expect a clearance via the routes detailed in 3 a-d Gt Dunmow and either Puckeridge or Nuthampstead routing via the Stansted overhead not above 2000ft QNH. NB Beware of ACFT in the Nuthampstead circuit up to 1500ftQNH.

5 The following areas are notified for the purposes of the low flying rule (Rule5):

a Within 1nm of the A10 and the river Lea from the Ware (VRP) to the intersection with the M25.

b Within 1nm of the M25 from its intersection with the A10 clockwise to its intersection with the M11

c Within 1nm of the track between Ware and Epping (VRP) where the route lies beneath the CTR/CTA.

6 a For clearance contact Essex RAD giving at least 5min notice. Do not enter controlled airspace without clearance.

b Clearance may be subject to delay or re-routing.

c Pilots are reminded of the close proximity of busy minor AD adjacent to CTA/CTR periphery.

Visual Reference Points (VRP)

VRP	VOR/VOR	VOR/DME
Audley End Stn	BKY 083°/LAM 008°	BKY 083°/5nm
N5200.25 E00012.42		
Braintree	BKY 113°/LAM 049°	LAM 049°/20nm
N5152.70 E00033.23		
Chelmsford	BKY 138°/LAM 069°	LAM 069°/13nm
N5144.00 E00028.40		
Epping	BKY 177°/BNN 096°	BNN 096°/25nm
N5142.00 E00006.67		
Gt Dunmow	BKY 125°/LAM 032°	BKY 125°/13nm
N5152.30 E00021.75		
Haverhill	BKY 070°/LAM 024°	LAM 024°/28nm
N5204.95 E00026.07		
Nuthampsted (Disused AD)	BKY VOR site	LAM 353°/21nm
N5159.40 E00003.72		
Puckeridge (A10/A120)	BKY 201°/LAM 342°	BKY 201°/7nm
N5153.10 E00000.27		
Ware	BKY 200°/LAM 329°	LAM 329°/12nm
N5148.70 W00001.60		

Effective date:23/11/06

L

5500+ A

4500+ A

A134

768 (541)

WORMINGFORD G

A120

A12

cables

EARLS COLNE

STOWE MARIES

cables

WAITS FARM

RIDGEWELL G

cables

3500+ A

A131

BOONES Fm

VRP BRAINTREE

RAYNE

A131

3500+ A

A414

A130

FL75+ A

568 (305)

BOREHAM H

2500+ A

VRP CHELMSFORD

506 (365)

WETHERSFIELD G

cables

ANDREWSFIELD

3500+ A D

2500-3500

GVS/3-2

HAVERHILL VRP

VRP GT DUNMOW

SVFR/VFR

HIGH EASTER

659 (325)

3500+ A D

1500-3500

AUDLEY END

SSD

LONDON STANSTED

SVFR/VFR

3500+ A D

SFC-3500

2500+ A

3500+ A

LITTLE SHELFORD

GVS/3-2

DUXFORD

FOWLMERE

J9

AUDLEY END RWY STATION VRP

NUTHAMPSTEAD VRP

BKY

NUTHAMPSTEAD 3500+ A D

2500-3500

SVFR/VFR

M11

NORTH WEALD

EPPING VRP

cables INTENSE GLIDING ACTIVITY

J27

HUMSDON M

3500+ A D

1500-3500

5500+ A

851 (351)

A10

685 (325)

PUCKERIDGE A10/A120 INT VRP

A602

WARE VRP

J26

4500+ A

Royston

3500+ A D

2500-3500

BENNINGTON

739 (656)

J25

BPK

2500+ A

TOP FARM

4500+ A D

3500-4500

972 (790)

A1

GRAVELEY M

920 (500)

728 (328)

PANSHANGER

L

22ft 1mb	7nm ENE of Londonderry N5502.57 W00709.67		Alternative AD Diversion AD	Belfast Aldergrove Bellarena
Londonderry	**APP** 123.625		**TWR** 134.150	**FIRE** 121.600

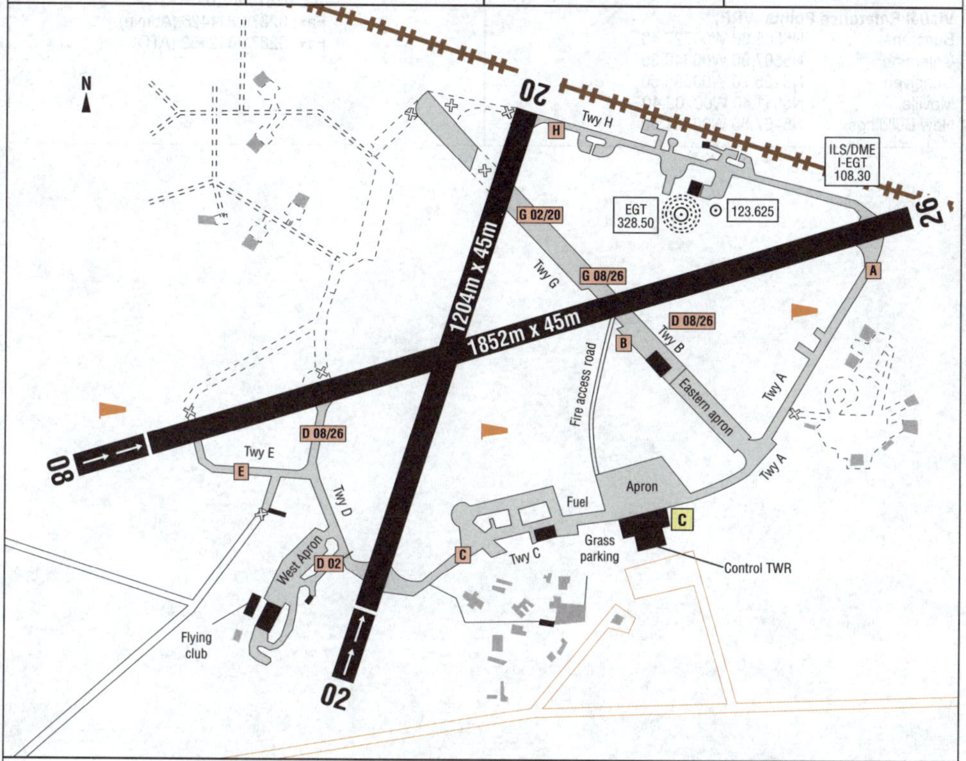

RWY	SURFACE	TORA	LDA	LIGHTING
08	Asphalt	1812	1690	Thr Rwy PAPI 3° LHS
26	Asphalt	1817	1817	Ap Thr Rwy PAPI 3° LHS
02	Asphalt	1204	1086	Thr Rwy PAPI 4° LHS
20	Asphalt	1204	1204	Thr Rwy APAPI 4° LHS

Remarks

PPR. Hi-Vis. Rwy26 –sequenced strobe APP lighting. Rwy through undershoot Rwy26. No ACFT movements Rwy08 Dept/Rwy26 Arr 5 mins prior train. Delays possible. No-radio ACFT subject to ATC approval. Single engine ACFT avoid overflying chemical plant 2-3nm W of AD below 1500ft. Training – book with ATC. Rwy02/20 no training after 2200 (L), Rwy08/26 no training after 2359 (L). ACFT must not execute in-flight turns within AD boundary unless instructed by ATC. Use of AD subject published terms & conditions, (on request). ACFT to/from destinations outside N Ireland use main terminal building customs, Special Branch & Immigration. ACFT minimise noise disturbance. ACFT must not fly below visual glide path indicated by PAPIS Rwy02 & 08. EFATO manoeuvres not permitted Rwy20.
Visual aid to location: Abn, white flashing.

Warnings

Large congregations of sea-birds in APP area Rwy26. Close proximity R503 & Ballykelly 5nm ENE AD, close to the final APP centre line to Rwy26 &, Rwy lighting may be displayed there. Standing water possible Rwy02/20. Pilots should positively identify Eglinton before committing to land.

Operating Hrs	See NOTAMS for latest opening Hrs	Disabled Facilities
Circuits	02, 20 RH 1200ft, 08 1000ft LH 26 LH 1200ft & 1000ft RH. Night 1500ft	
Landing Fee	Single club & private £10.58 Multi club & private £21.15	**Restaurant** Snack bar in main Terminal
Maintenance	Available	
Fuel	AVGAS JET A1 100LL	

367

Taxis	Available at Terminal

Car Hire

Avis	**Tel:** 02871 811708
Hertz	**Tel:** 02871 811994
Eurocar	**Tel:** 02871 812773
Ford Rent a Car	**Tel:** 02871 367137

Weather Info   M T9 Fax 354 BEL

Visual Reference Points (VRP)

Buncrana	N5508.00 W00727.40
Coleraine	N5507.90 W00640.30
Dungiven	N5455.70 W00655.50
Moville	N5511.40 W00702.40
New Buildings	N5457.50 W00721.50

Operator   Derry City Council
City of Derry Airport
Airport Road, Eglinton
Londonderry, BT47 3GY
Tel: 02871 812152
Tel: 02871 811246
Tel: 02871 810784 Ex 208 (Ops)
Tel: 02871 811099 (ATC)
Fax: 02871 811426 (Admin)
Fax: 02871 812152 (ATC)

80ft 2mb	By A1 close to W of Sandy N5207.44 W00018.35	PPR	Alternative AD	Cranfield Little Gransden

Sandy	A/G 129.825	(Microlight freq) make blind calls

RWY	SURFACE	TORA	LDA	LIGHTING
17/35	Grass	365x18	U/L	Nil
09/27	Grass	550x18	U/L	Nil

Rwy27 upslope final third

Remarks
PPR by telephone. Briefing essential. Microlight AD with Ab-initio training but suitable STOL ACFT welcome at pilots own risk.

Warnings
Considerable road traffic crosses Rwy35 short final using A603. 25ft trees adjacent to lake on short final Rwy27. 4ft hedge close to Rwy09 Thr. Sandy TV mast 972ft amsl (790ft agl) 2.5nm E of AD. Shuttleworth AD 2.5nm SSW of AD has regular air displays during the summer period, particularly at weekends.
Noise: Do not over fly Sandy E of AD.

Operating Hrs	SR-SS	Operator	Snowy Barton Long Acres Farm Mogerhanger Road Sandy, Beds, SG19 1ND **Tel:** 01767 691616
Circuits	35 LH, 27, 17, 09 RH No dead side		
Landing Fee	Nil		
Maintenance	Microlight maintenance available		
Fuel	MOGAS available from nearby garage		
Disabled Facilities	Nil		
Restaurants	Tea & Coffee available at AD Little Chef within walking distance adjacent to A1		
Taxis Sandy Taxis	**Tel:** 01767 683333		
Car Hire	Nil		
Weather Info	AirCen MOEx		

369

154ft 5mb	3.5nm SW of Stratford-on-Avon N5208.44 W00145.18	PPR	Alternative AD	Birmingham Wellesbourne Mountford

Long Marston	A/G 129.825 (Microlight freq)

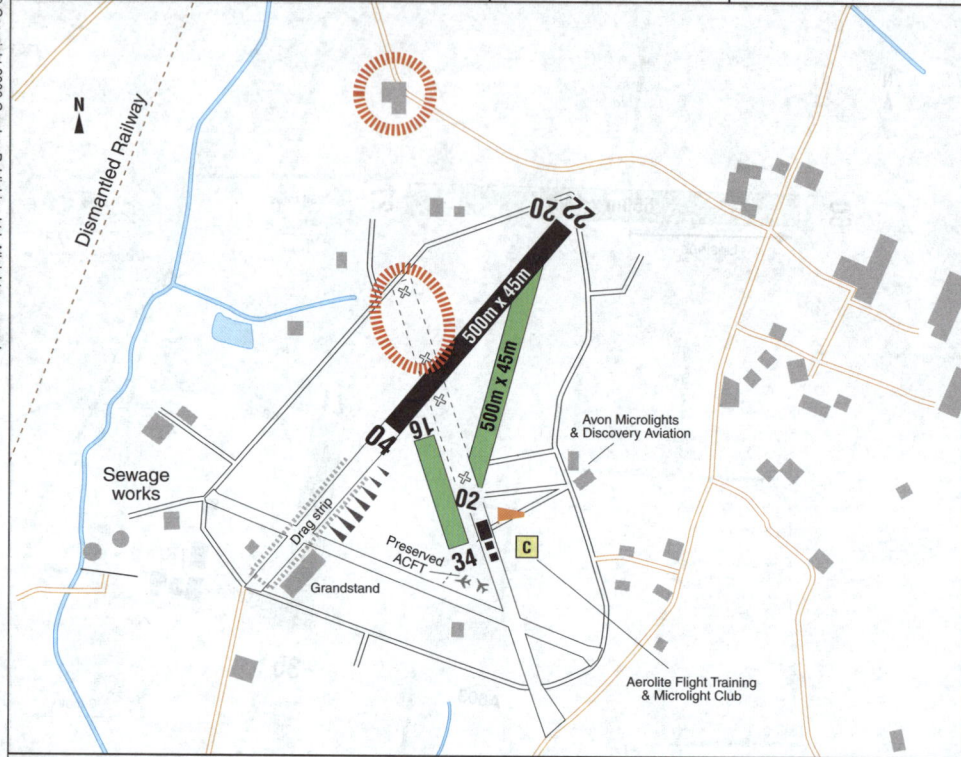

RWY	SURFACE	TORA	LDA	LIGHTING
02/20	Grass	500x45	U/L	Nil
04/22	Asphalt	500x45	U/L	Nil
16/34	Grass	300x45	U/L	Nil

Remarks
PPR by telephone. Visiting ACFT welcome. AD used for microlighting and occasional motor sport.

Warnings
Wellesbourne Mountford ATZ 3nm NE.
Noise: Avoid over flying HMP Long Lartin, 8nm WSW of AD, Long Marston village to W & farm

Operating Hrs	0900-SS (L)	**Operator**	H G Hodges & Son Ltd
Circuits	02, 22 RH, 04, 20 LH 600ft QFE 04, 22 500ft QFE		Long Marston Airfield Stratford on Avon
Landing Fee	Nil £25 without PPR		Warwickshire CV37 8LL **Tel:** 01789 414119
Maintenance	Microlight available		**Tel:** 07768 525567
Fuel	Nil		**Fax:** 01789 262030
Disabled Facilities	Nil		
Restaurant	Tea & coffee making facilities		
Taxis/Car Hire	Can be arr locally		
Weather Info	AirCen MOEx		

370

L

172ft 5mb	11.5nm SW of Norwich AD N5229.30 E00113.00	**PPR**	**Alternative AD**	**Norwich** Seething
	Cheqair Ops		**A/G** **122.950**	

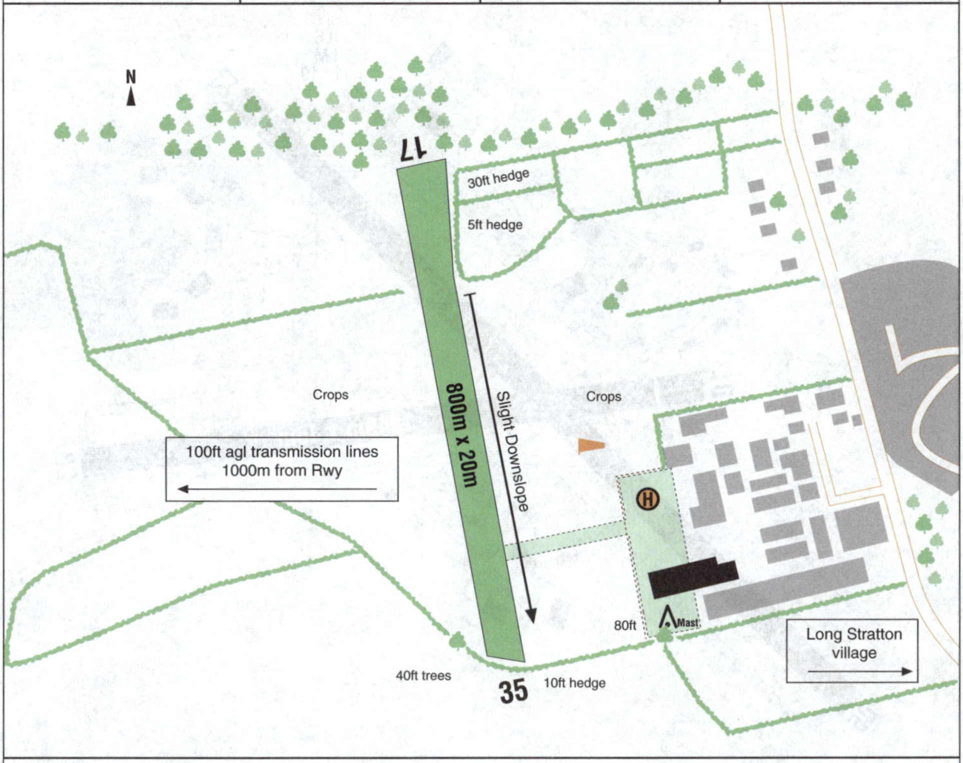

Map of Long Stratton aerodrome. Key features labelled:

- N (north arrow)
- Runway 17/35, 800m x 20m, Grass
- 30ft hedge
- 5ft hedge
- Crops
- Slight Downslope
- 100ft agl transmission lines 1000m from Rwy
- H (helicopter landing area)
- 80ft Mast
- Long Stratton village →
- 40ft trees
- 10ft hedge

RWY	SURFACE	TORA	LDA	LIGHTING
17/35	Grass	800x20	U/L	Nil

Remarks

PPR strictly by telephone and at pilots own risk. Visitors must have business with Cheqair (Ops), SMC Aviation Services or Stratton Motor Co, (Aston Martin Dealership).

Warnings

Pilots must receive briefing from Chief Pilot or Ops. Helicopters are to join via reporting points to N & S of AD. Details provided with PPR. National Grid power line runs 100m W of Rwy 100ft agl.

Noise: Do not over fly the villages of Long Stratton (E) and Wacton (SW).

Operating Hrs	Mon-Fri 0800-1730 Sat 0800-1200 (L) Closed Sun	**Weather Info**	AirS MOEx
Circuits	Fixed wing 35 LH, 17 RH Rotary via entry/exit points	**Operator**	Cheqair Ltd Tharston Ind Site Chequers Lane, Long Stratton Norwich, NR15 2PE **Tel:** 01508 531144 (PPR) **Fax:** 01508 531670 ops@cheqair.com www.cheqair.com
Landing Fee	£15		
Maintenance	Nil		
Fuel	JET A1		
Hangarage	Subject to availability		

Disabled Facilities

Restaurant	Nil
Taxis/Car Hire	Available from Operator by arr

42ft 2mb	4nm N of Elgin N5742.31 W00320.35	PPR MIL	Alternative AD Diversion AD	Inverness Wick

Lossiemouth	LARS 119.350	APP 123.300	TWR 118.200	GND 118.200

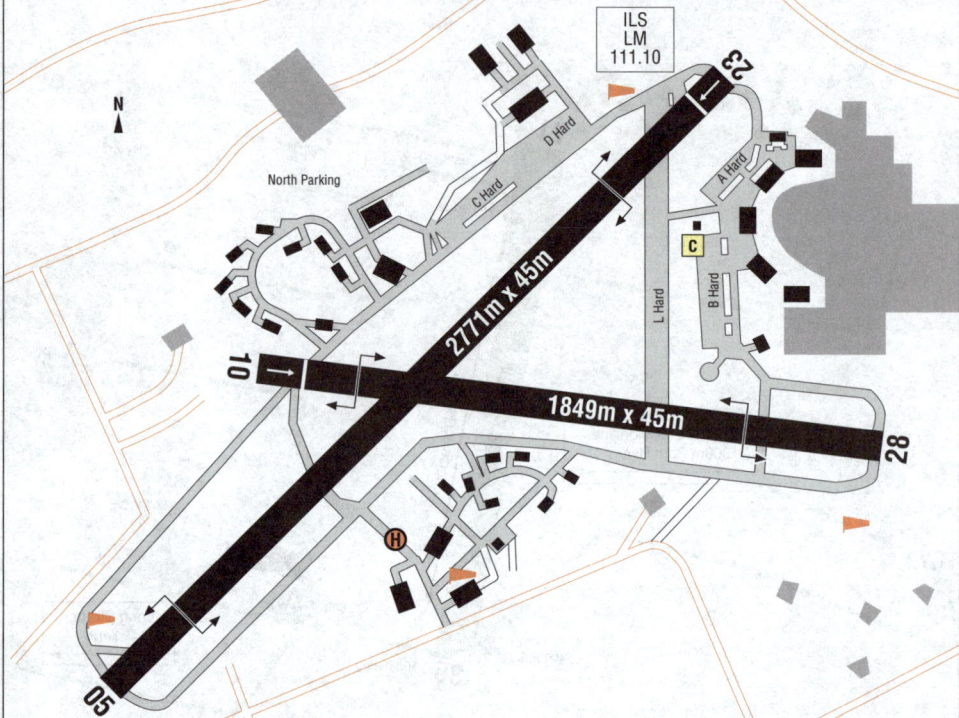

RWY	SURFACE	TORA	LDA	LIGHTING
23	Asphalt	2771	2678	Ap Thr Rwy PAPI 2.5°
05	Asphalt	2771	2771	Ap Thr Rwy PAPI 2.5°
10	Asphalt	1849	1751	Ap Thr Rwy PAPI 3°
28	Asphalt	1849	1849	Ap Thr Rwy PAPI 2.5

Arrester Gear Rwy23/28 426m from Thr
Arrester Gear Rwy05 396m from Thr
Arrester Gear Rwy10 61m from Thr

Remarks
PPR required 24Hrs. ATZ active H24. Aerial farm at Mill town Disused AD 4nm SE of AD.
Visual aid to location: IBn LM Red

Warnings
Noise: Avoid over flying Elgin, Lossiemouth & Gordonstoun school.

Operating Hrs	Mon-Thu 0800-1800 Fri 0800-1700 (L)	**Weather Info**	M T Fax 356 GWC ATIS **Tel:** 01343 817666
Circuits	Join not below 1000ft QFE All circuits LH	**Operator**	RAF Lossiemouth Moray IV31 6SD **Tel:** 01343 817426 (ATC) **Tel:** 01343 816872 (OPS)
Landing Fee	Charges in accordance with MOD policy Contact Station Ops for details		
Maintenance	Nil		
Fuel	Jet A1		
Disabled Facilities	Nil		
Restaurants	Nil		
Taxis/Car Hire	Nil		

60ft 2mb	1.5nm SE of Louth N5321.50 E00002.00		PPR	Alternative AD	Humberside Wickenby

Non Radio	LARS Waddington 127.350	LARS Coningsby 120.800	Safetycom 135.475

N

8ft hedge at Thr

24

Disused railway

Trees up to 40ft

675m x 12-60m

Small trees up to 30ft

Manby disused airfield 1200m SE

To Louth

Hangar

06

15ft hedge

3 silver silos on farm

RWY	SURFACE	TORA	LDA	LIGHTING
06/24	Grass	675x12-60	U/L	Nil

Rwy06 grass run off 100m

Remarks
PPR by telephone. AD of variable width between the Louth to Stewton road and the disused, (and removed), Louth to Mablethorpe railway. The witness marks of the old railway track are clearly visible. Visiting pilots are welcome at pilots own risk. AD is unusual in its location and great care should be taken.

Warnings
AD is bordered by mature hedges and trees which may cause turbulence. AD has undulations in the centre. Identification of the Thr is particularly important. Rwy24 Thr the adjoining field is used for paddocks and a hedge across it. Rwy is to the W of the hedge.

Operating Hrs	SR-SS	Operator	Douglas Electronic Industries Ltd 55 Eastfield Road Louth, Lincs, LN11 7AL **Tel:** 01507 603643
Circuits	As you wish Avoid local habitation 1000ft QFE		
Landing Fee	Nil		
Maintenance	Nil		
Fuel	Nil		
Disabled Facilities	Nil		
Restaurant	Nil		
Taxi/Car Hire	Operator can provide help/assistance		
Weather Info	AirN MWC		

Effective date:23/11/06

4ft 0mb	4nm SE of Louth N5319.50 E00004.40	PPR	Alternative AD	Humberside Wickenby

Non-Radio	LARS Coningsby 120.800	Safetycom 135.475

Track to North Reston

A157

N

White hangar

24

505m x 30m

Slight downslope   Crops

06

Stream

Dismantled railway

Gillwoods Grange

Strip profile

| 06 | mod | slight | flat | 24 |

RWY	SURFACE	TORA	LDA	LIGHTING
06/24	Grass	505x30	U/L	Nil

Remarks

PPR essential by telephone. Visiting ACFT welcome. AD well prepared but has no facilities. Rwy flat at Rwy24 Thr, has a slight down slope in second third, final 60m has increased down slope.
Visual aid to location: Disused railway from Louth to Boston passes close to W of AD.

Warnings

Drainage ditches cross the Thr of both landing directions and run along N side of the strip. APP are clear. Gliding activity at Manby & Strubby (mainly weekends). Crops are grown up to S edge of AD.
Noise: Avoid over flight North Reston to N of AD.

Operating Hrs	SR-SS		Operator	Mr John Read
Circuits	1000ft QFE			Hall Farm
Landing Fee	Nil			North Reston
Maintenance	Nil			Louth, LN11 8JD
Fuel	Nil			**Tel:** 01507 450238
Disabled Facilities	Nil			
Restaurant Royal Oak	**Tel:** 01507 600750 (Cawthorpe)			
Taxis Dixon's	**Tel:** 01507 603864			
Car Hire	Nil			
Weather Info	AirN MWC			

374

LUDHAM

50ft 1mb	11nm ENE of Norwich City Centre N5243.10 E00133.07	PPR	Alternative AD Diversion AD	Norwich Seething

Non radio	LARS Norwich 119.350	Safetycom 135.475

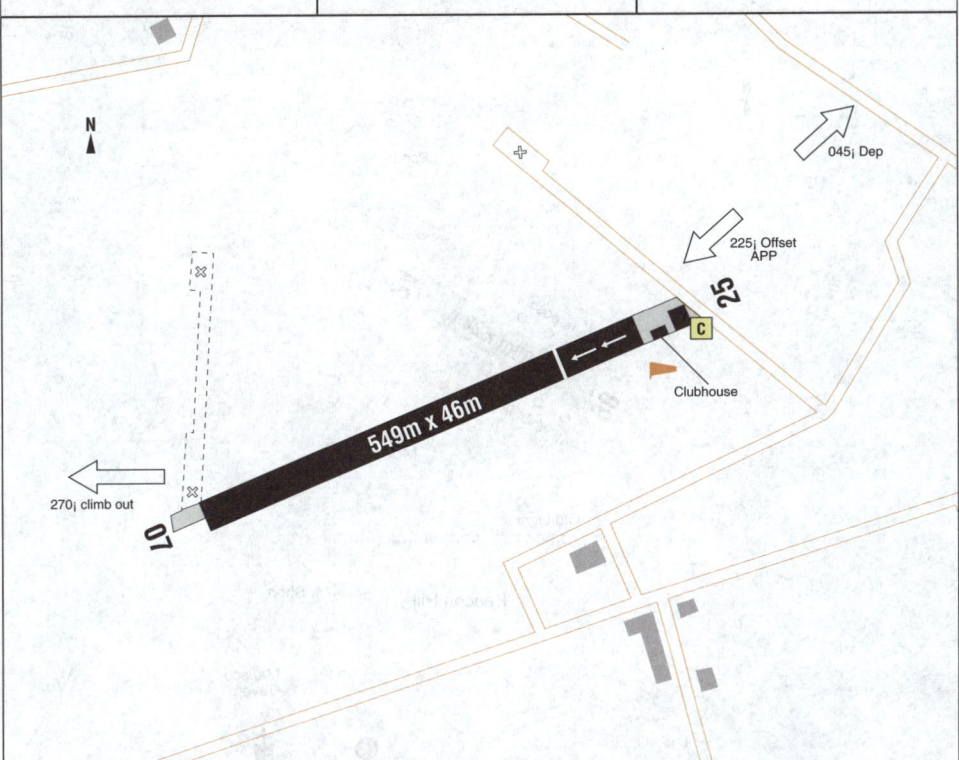

N

045¡ Dep

225¡ Offset APP

25

C

Clubhouse

549m x 46m

270¡ climb out

07

RWY	SURFACE	TORA	LDA	LIGHTING
07	Concrete	420x46	U/L	Nil
25	Concrete	549x46	U/L	Nil

Remarks
PPR essential. No microlights. Situated close to the E boundary of the Coltishall MATZ. Visiting ACFT and vehicle parking on S side of Rwy to W of clubhouse.

Warnings
Hangar at E end of Rwy necessitates an off-set APP Rwy25. Loose stones on Rwy. Large commercial helicopters operate at low altitudes to the E of AD following defined helicopter routes.
Noise: AD situated in the heart of Broadland, please fly with consideration.

Operating Hrs	Available on request	**Operator**	Paul Mahon (Airfield Owner)
Circuits	Nil		Alder Cottage
Landing Fee	£6 Single, Light commercial £20 (Jockeys pls note)		Cess Road
			Martham
			Great Yarmouth
Maintenance	Nil		NR29 4RF
Fuel	Nil		Operated by Ludham Airfield Ltd
Disabled Facilities	Nil		**Tel:** 07787 554389 (Tony Walsh)
Restaurant	Nil		**Tel:** 01493 369969 (Tony Walsh)
Taxis/Car Hire	Nil		**Tel:** 07899 915103 (Mark Tingle)
Weather Info	AirS MOEx		www.ludhamairfield.org

455ft 15mb	11nm NW of Hartland Point N5110.20 W00440.23	PPR	Alternative AD	Swansea Pembrey

Non-radio	FIS London 124.750	Safetycom 135.475

N

Ponds

24

4ft white posts

400m x 28m

06

4ft white posts

Acklands Moor

Old Light

Beacon Hill

Shop

Marisco Tavern

RWY	SURFACE	TORA	LDA	LIGHTING
06/24	Grass	400x28	U/L	Nil

Remarks

PPR by telephone. Light ACFT welcome at pilots own risk. Rwy has no designators but is marked by 4ft white posts at its edges on SW part only. The island has many interesting buildings and much wildlife. The Old Lighthouse is close to SW of strip.

Warnings

This is a difficult strip and for the experienced pilot only! The Rwy is convex in configuration. PPR is essential so that livestock may be moved. Advise land Rwy06 if wind conditions allow, the strip is bumpy and undulating and is only suitable for landing in good weather conditions.

Noise: Please do not low fly in the vicinity of the island to avoid disturbance to bird colonies and possibility of bird strike. However a fly by is advised to examine strip prior to landing.

Operating Hrs	Available on request	**Weather Info**	AirSW MOEx
Circuits	1000ft QFE	**Operator**	The Lundy Island Company
Landing Fee	Administered by the National Trust Landing fee is £10 + £3.50 National Trust admission per person (waived on production of NT membership card)		The Lundy Shore Office The Quay Bideford Devon, EX39 2LY **Tel:** 01237 470074 **Fax:** 01237 477779 admin@lundyisland.co.uk www.lundyisland.co.uk
Maintenance	Nil		
Fuel	Nil		
Disabled Facilities			
Restaurants	Marisco Tavern (within easy walking distance of the strip) B&B sometimes available contact the operator for more info		
Taxis/Car Hire	Nil		

L

EGMD   LYDD

13ft 0mb	1.2nm E of Lydd N5057.37 E00056.35		**PPR**	**Alternative AD** **Diversion AD**	**Manston** Lashenden

Lydd		**APP** **120.700**	**TWR** **120.700**

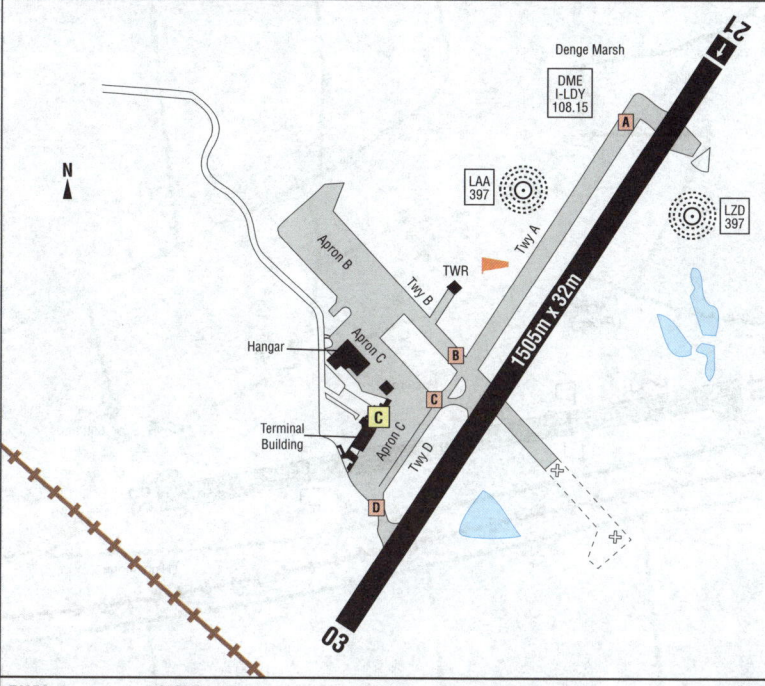

RWY	SURFACE	TORA	LDA	LIGHTING
03	Asphalt	1470	1470	Ap Thr Rwy PAPI 3° LHS
21	Asphalt	1505	1470	Ap Thr Rwy PAPI 3.5° LHS

Remarks

PPR microlights. Hi-vis. Non radio ACFT not accepted. NE. Dept Rwy21, power checks hold C, then as instructed. Handling madatory for ACFT >6000kg. ATC Op Hrs – 0800-1800 (Summer) +1Hr (Winter)
Aids to Navigation: VOR/DME LYD 114.05. NDB LYX 397.00
Visual aid to location: Flashing white strobe.

Warnings

Caution: Do NOT over flying Dungeness Nuclear Power Station 2.5nm SE of the AD below 2000ft. Extensive firing activity on Lydd ranges (EGD-044) DAAIS available on Lydd info during Ops Hrs, outside Hrs from London Info. Twy 6m wide with uneven edges.
Noise: Dept Rwy03: Climb straight ahead to 1000ft, or crossing the coast, whichever is sooner, before turning right or left. **Rwy21:** Climb straight ahead to 800ft before turning left or right. Training Dept involving engine failure practice Not allowed Rwy03. VFR Arr position overhead 1500ft QNH downwind at 1000ft QFE.

Operating Hrs	0900-1900 (L) & by arr	**Restaurant**	
Circuits	03 RH, 21 LH	Biggles	**Tel:** 01797 322440 (bar & restaurant)
Landing Fee	0-1500kg £10	**Taxis**	Arranged at front desk
	1500-2750 £20	**Car Hire**	
	2750-6000kg £59	Sussex Rd Garage	**Tel:** 01797 362404
		Romney Car Hire	**Tel:** 01797 363189
Maintenance			**Fax:** 01797 364505
Skysure	**Tel:** 01797 322430	**Weather Info**	AirSe MOEx
Fuel	AVGAS JET A1 100LL Water/Meth		www.lydd-airport.co.uk
Disabled Facilities		**Operator**	London Ashford Airport Ltd
			Lydd Airport, Lydd

Handling   **Tel:** 01797 322480 (FAL)
                Fax: 01797 322481 (FAL)
                info@falaviation.com
                www.falaviation.com

Romney Marsh, Kent, TN29 9QL
Tel: 01797 320881(ATC)
Tel: 01797 322400 (Switchboard)
Fax: 01797 321964 (ATC)
Fax: 01797 322408 (Switchboard)
frontdesk@lydd-airport.co.uk
www.lydd-airport.co.uk

L

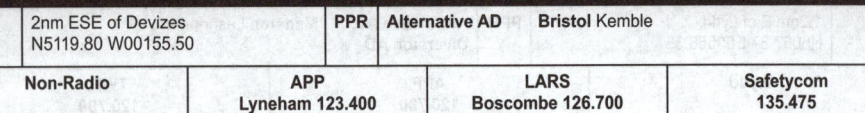

LYDEWAY FIELD

350ft 11mb	2nm ESE of Devizes N5119.80 W00155.50	**PPR**	**Alternative AD**	**Bristol** Kemble

Non-Radio	**APP** Lyneham 123.400	**LARS** Boscombe 126.700	**Safetycom** 135.475

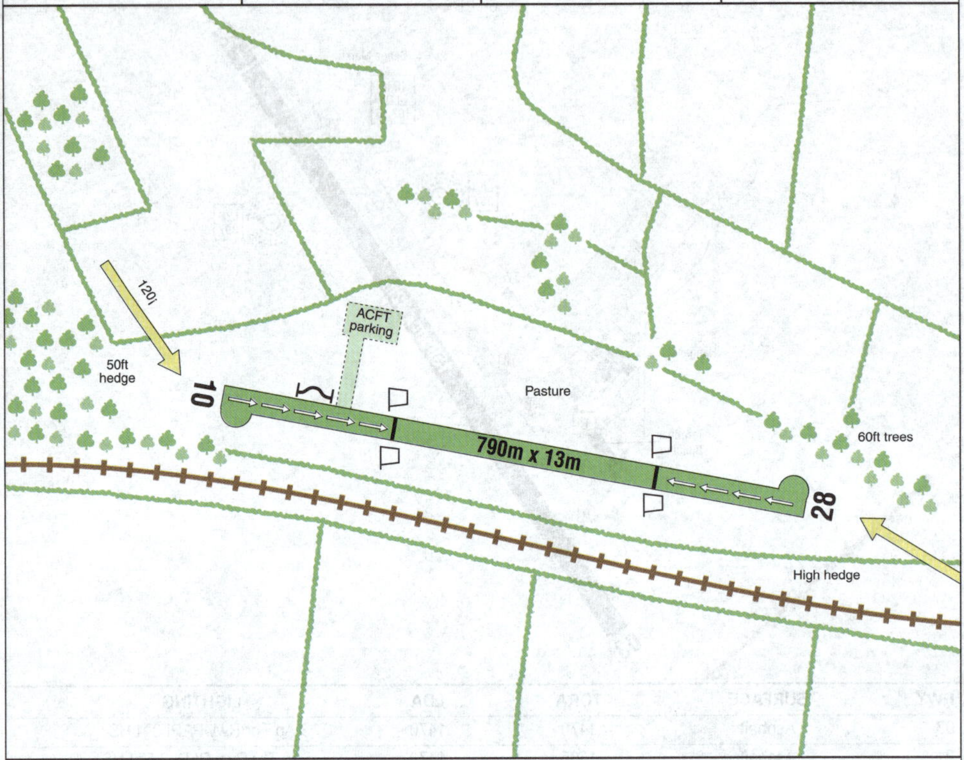

(airfield diagram showing Runway 10/28, 790m x 13m grass strip, 50ft hedge, 60ft trees, High hedge, ACFT parking, Pasture, wind direction arrows labelled 120° and displaced thresholds)

RWY	SURFACE	TORA	LDA	LIGHTING
10/28	Grass	790x13	U/L	Nil

Displaced thr marked with yellow and black chevron wind direction indicators

Remarks
PPR by telephone. Level strip that may become soft after prolonged rain. Figures provided by operator Rwy 10/28 TORA 790 LDA 520.

Warnings
AD is close to Lyneham zone. Keevil gliding site, (7nm SW). Danger areas D123,124,125, (to S). Also Etchilhampton hill 627ft amsl, (1nm NW).
Noise: See arrival and departure instructions

Operating Hrs	SR-SS	**Operator**	Nigel Charles
Circuits	See instructions overleaf		Badgers Cottage
Landing Fee	Nil		Etchilhampton
Maintenance	Nil		Devizes
Fuel	Nil		Wiltshire
Disabled Facilities			SN10 3JL
			Tel: 01380 860620
			Tel: 07764 579860
Taxi/Car Hire	Nil		nwcmc@tiscali.co.uk
Weather Info	AirSW MOEx		

Etchilhampton

Wabi Farm

Hatfield Farm

120°

10

28

295°

ARRIVAL INSTRUCTIONS

Contact with Lyneham APP is recommended for traffic information (or zone transit). Their surface wind and QNH is useful if Lydeway is unmanned.

Call LYDEWAY TRAFFIC using Safetycom to make circuit reports.

This is a noise sensitive area so please avoid over flying villages during approach. The circuit pattern optimises flight path for both noise abatement and obstruction avoidance.

A slow flypast ensures the strip is clear of deer and walkers.

Strong S winds generate from turbulence from hedges along the S AD boundary.

Rwy 10 Beware rising ground on base leg. Turn final over Rwy.

Rwy28 15° offset final APP allows better view and offset from high trees on short final. Due to low crossing altitude of railway line discontinue approach if a train is coming. Full Rwy length is available with care but displaced Thr is marked.

DEPARTURE INSTRUCTIONS

Caution: Trees on both APP may obscure ACFT on final check well before committing to backtrack.

Rwy10 Caution slight hump before Twy which can ski-jump ACFT prematurely into the air. Climb out N of the railway until above 500ft QFE.

Rwy28 As soon as altitude permits TURN RIGHT and fly just W of Wabi Farm. The farmer here likes ACFT and this will avoid noise sensitive areas.

L

LYMM DAM

2150ft 5mb	1nm S of Lymm N5322.00 W00228.00		**Alternative AD**	**Liverpool** Manchester Barton

Non-Radio	**ATIS** Manchester 128.175 (ARR)	**APP** Manchester 135.00	**Safetycom** 135.475

RWY	SURFACE	TORA	LDA	LIGHTING
09/27	Grass	500x10m	U/L	Nil

Remarks

PPR by telephone. Visiting PFA type ACFT welcome at pilots own risk. AD within Manchester CTR, prior notice of flights must be given to Manchester TWR Supervisor. Permission should also be obtained with Manchester APP. Arr ACFT should route along low level route until W of AD then route directly to field. Dept ACFT should route directly into low level route not above 1250ft Manchester QNH.

Warnings

Rwy is flat. There is a small pond to S of Rwy. 5ft hedge and unclassified road cross adjacent Rwy27 Thr. Single telegraph pole is in hedge on right of short final. Wires run away from AD in E direction. Crops grown close to Rwy edges. 4ft wire fence crosses the Rwy09 Thr.

Operating Hrs	SR-SS	**Weather Info**	Air Cen MWC
Circuits	LH 1000ft QFE	**Operator**	Mr Robin Moore
Landing Fee	Nil		5 Orchard Gardens
Maintenance	Nil		Tarporley
Fuel	Nil		Cheshire
			CW6 9GR
Disabled Facilities			**Tel:** 01829 732334
			Tel: 0161 499 5336 (Manchester TWR)
Restaurants	Nil		
Taxis			
Jolly's	**Tel:** 01925 755631		
Car Hire	Nil		

L

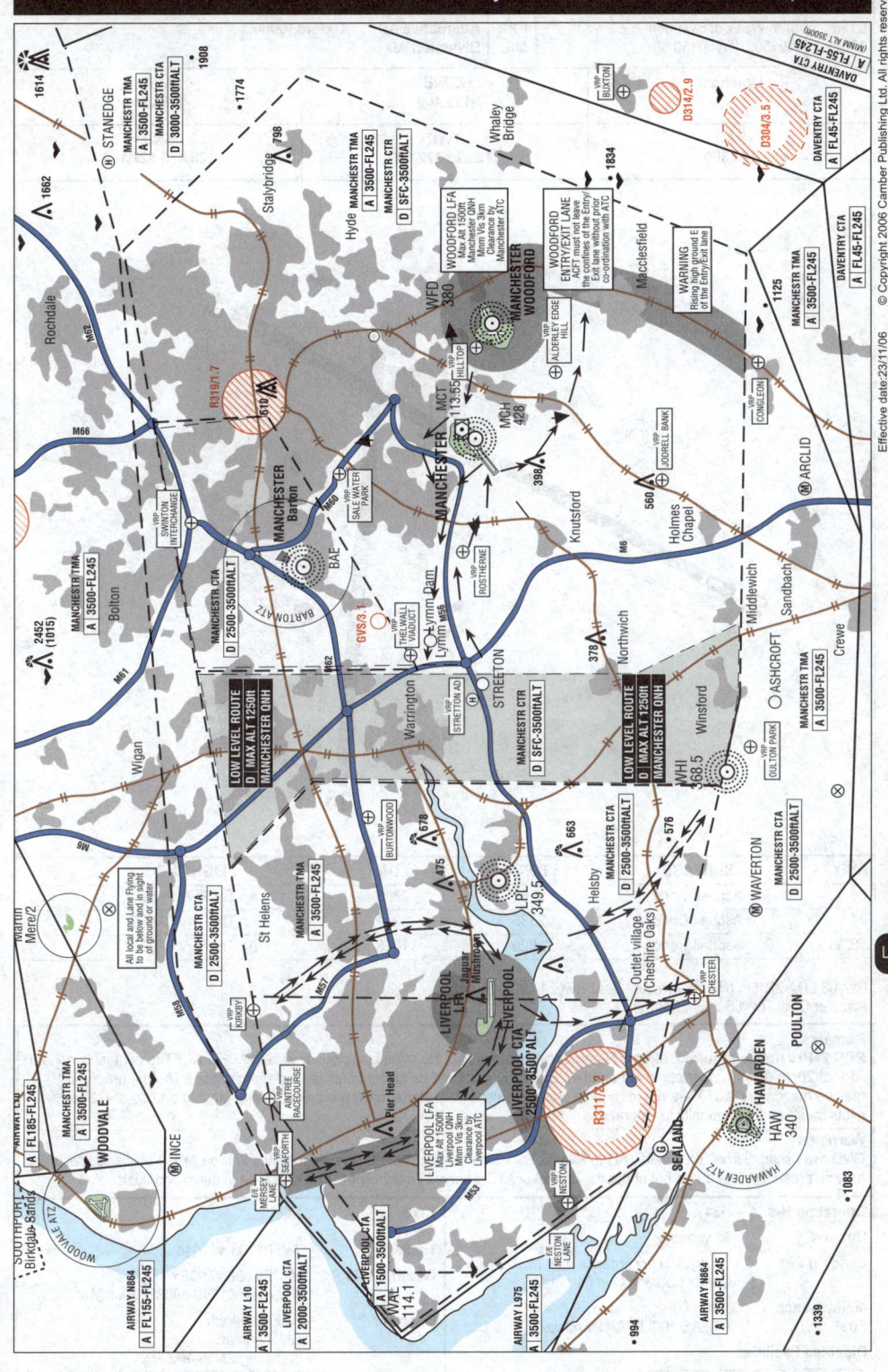

Effective date:23/11/06

513ft 17mb	8nm WSW of Swindon N5130.31 W00159.60	PPR MIL	Alternative AD Diversion AD	Oxford Kemble

Lyneham	ZONE 123.400	APP 118.425
RAD 123.300	**TWR** 119.225 122.100	**GND** 129.475 122.100

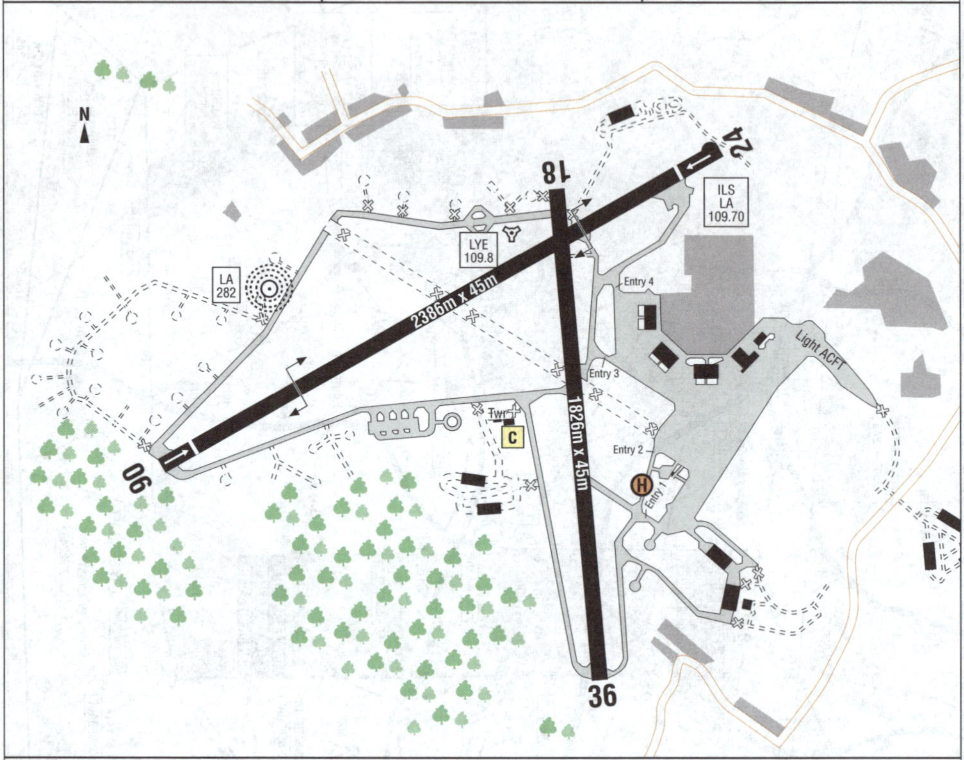

RWY	SURFACE	TORA	LDA	LIGHTING
06	Asphalt/Conc	2386	2386	Ap Thr Rwy PAPI 3°
24	Asphalt/Conc	2386	2204	Ap Thr Rwy PAPI 3°
18/36	Asphalt/Conc	1826	1826	Ap Thr Rwy PAPI 3°

Rwy06 LDA 2235m (Night). Arrester Gear Rwy24 480m from Thr
Arrester Gear Rwy06 510m from Thr

Remarks
PPR 24Hrs notice required. Military Emergency Diversion AD. No night stopping for visiting ACFT. ACFT to contact Lyneham APP at 20nm unless under control of another agency who should be asked to advise Lyneham of the ETA. Instrument APP may be mandatory. ACFT are not to request start-up unless RAF starter crew are present. After landing and before take-off pilots must report personally to Operations.

Warnings
GND rises sharply from 300ft below AD to Rwy06 Thr which may cause turbulence and windshear on APP. Vehicles/pedestrians may be present on the apron not under the control of ATC. Heavy bird concentration in the area at dawn and dusk.

		Taxis	Nil
Operating Hrs	H24	**Car Hire**	
Circuits	06 variable	Thrifty	**Tel:** 01793 422644
Landing Fee	Charges in accordance with MOD policy Contact Station Ops for details	**Weather Info**	M T Fax 364 MOEx ATIS **Tel:** 01249 890381 Ex 6214/7308
Maintenance	Nil	**Operator**	RAF Lyneham
Fuel	AVGAS 100LL (72Hrs notice)		Chippenham Wiltshire, SN15 4PZ
Disabled Facilities			**Tel:** 01249 890381 (AD Switchboard)
			Tel: 01249 890381 Ex 6516 (ATC)

Restaurant Nil

Class D Airspace
Normal CTA/CTR Class D Airspace rules apply
Transition Alt 3000ft
1 To assist Lyneham RAD in ensuring access to its airspace pilots should make an R/T call when 20nm or 5 minutes flying time from the zone boundary, whichever is the earlier.

Visual Reference Points(VRP)

VRP	VOR/VOR	VOR/NDB	VOR/DME
Avebury N5125.68 W00151.28	CPT 264°/SAM 329°	CPT 264°/LA 134°	CPT 264°/24nm
Blakehill Farm N5137.00 W00153.10	CPT 290°/SAM 336°	CPT 290°/LA 038°	CPT 290°/26nm
Calne N5126.20 W00200.30	CPT 267°/SAM 322°	CPT 267°/LA 183°	CPT 267°/30nm
Chippenham N5127.60 W00207.40	CPT 270°/SAM 319°	CPT 270°/LA 240°	CPT 270°/34nm
Clyffe Pypard N5129.40 W00153.70	CPT 273°/SAM 330°	CPT 273°/LA 108°	CPT 273°/25nm
Devizes N5120.80 W00159.30	CPT 257°/SAM 317°	CPT 257°/LA 179°	CPT 257°/30nm
M4 J15 N5131.60 W00143.48	CPT 280°/SAM 340°	CPT 280°/LA 087°	CPT 280°/19nm
M4 J16 N5132.70 W00151.25	CPT 281°/SAM 334°	CPT 281°/LA 072°	CPT 281°/24nm
M4 J17 N5130.88 W00207.30	CPT 276°/SAM 322°	CPT 276°/LA 279°	CPT 276°/34nm
Malmesbury N5135.10 W00206.20	CPT 284°/SAM 326°	CPT 284°/LA 325°	CPT 284°/33nm
Marlborough N5125.20 W00143.70	CPT 261°/SAM 335°	CPT 261°/LA 120°	CPT 261°/19nm
Melksham N5122.50 W00208.30	CPT 262°/SAM 313°	SAM 314°/LA 215°	CPT 262°/35nm
S Marston N5135.40 W00144.10	CPT 291°/SAM 342°	CPT 291°/LA 067°	CPT 291°/20nm
Wroughton N5130.55 W00147.98	CPT 276°/SAM 335°	SAM 336°/LA 093°	CPT 276°/22nm

L

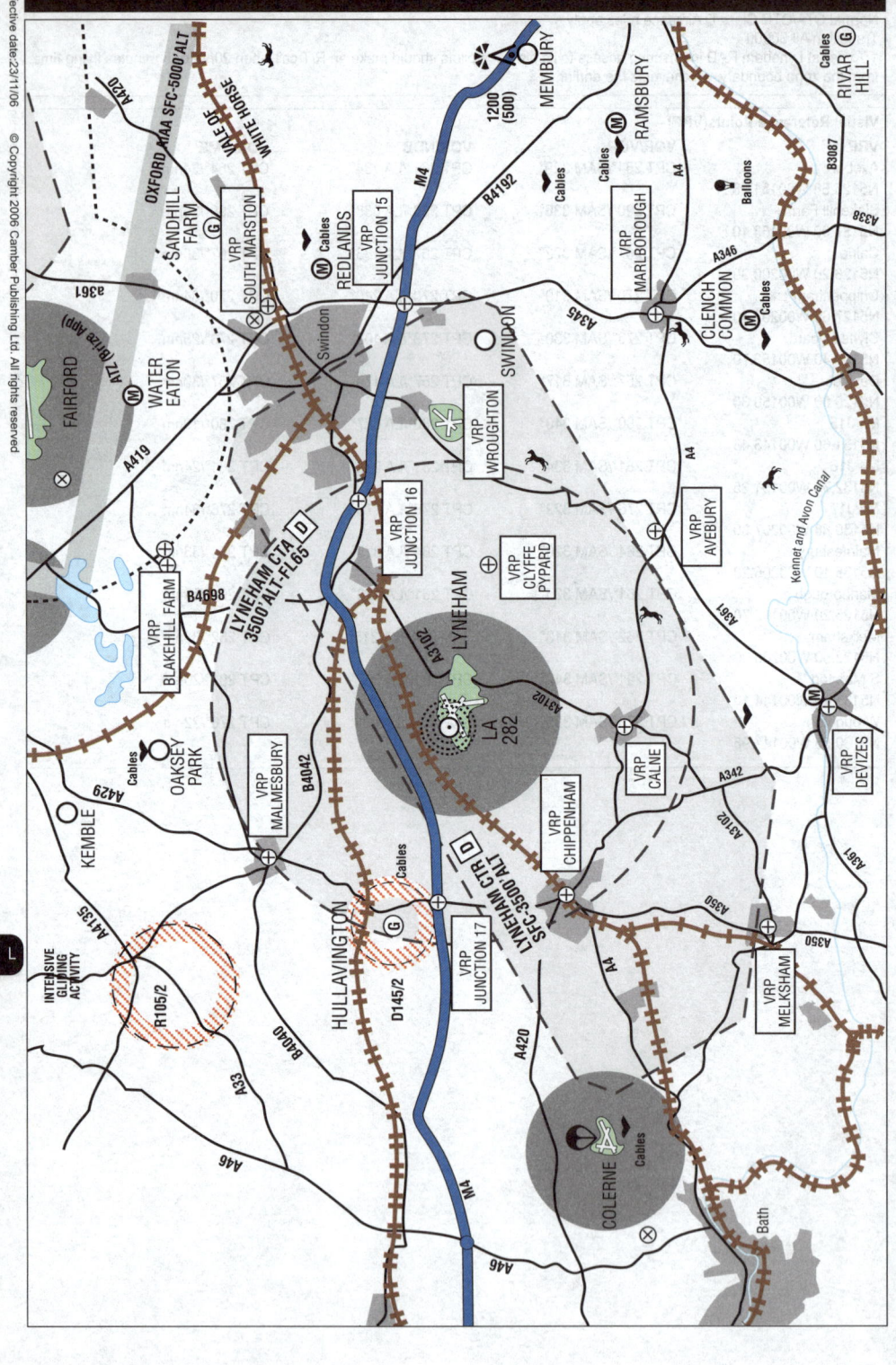

MEMBURY

1200 (500)

RIVAR HILL Ⓖ

Cables

RAMSBURY

Cables

M4

B4192

A4

Balloons

VRP MARLBOROUGH

A346

CLENCH COMMON Ⓜ Cables

B3087

A338

OXFORD MAA SFC-5000' ALT

A420

VALE OF WHITE HORSE

SANDHILL FARM Ⓖ

VRP SOUTH MARSTON

Cables

Ⓜ REDLANDS

VRP JUNCTION 15

A361

a361

ATZ (Brize App) Ⓜ

FAIRFORD

WATER EATON

A419

Swindon

SWINDON

VRP WROUGHTON

VRP JUNCTION 16

VRP CLYFFE PYPARD

A345

A4

VRP AVEBURY

Kennet and Avon Canal

A361

B4698

VRP BLAKEHILL FARM

LYNEHAM CTA Ⓓ 3500' ALT-FL165

A3102

LYNEHAM

LA 282

A3102

Ⓜ

VRP DEVIZES

Cables

OAKSEY PARK

A429

A4042

VRP MALMESBURY

VRP CALNE

A342

A3102

KEMBLE

A4135

Cables Ⓖ

HULLAVINGTON

VRP JUNCTION 17

D145/2

LYNEHAM CTR Ⓓ SFC-3500 ALT

VRP CHIPPENHAM

A350

VRP MELKSHAM

A4

A350

A361

L

INTENSIVE GLIDING ACTIVITY

R105/2

A33

B4040

A46

A420

M4

COLERNE

Cables

Bath

A46

257ft 9mb	7.5nm SW of Manchester N5321.22 W00216.50	PPR	Alternative AD	Liverpool Manchester Barton

Manchester	ATIS 128.175 (Arr) 121.975 (Dept)	APP 135.000	RAD 135.000 118.575	TWR 118.625 (24R/06L) 119.400 (24L/06R)
DEL 121.700	DIR 121.350	GND 121.850	FIRE 121.600	Handling 130.650 (NEA)

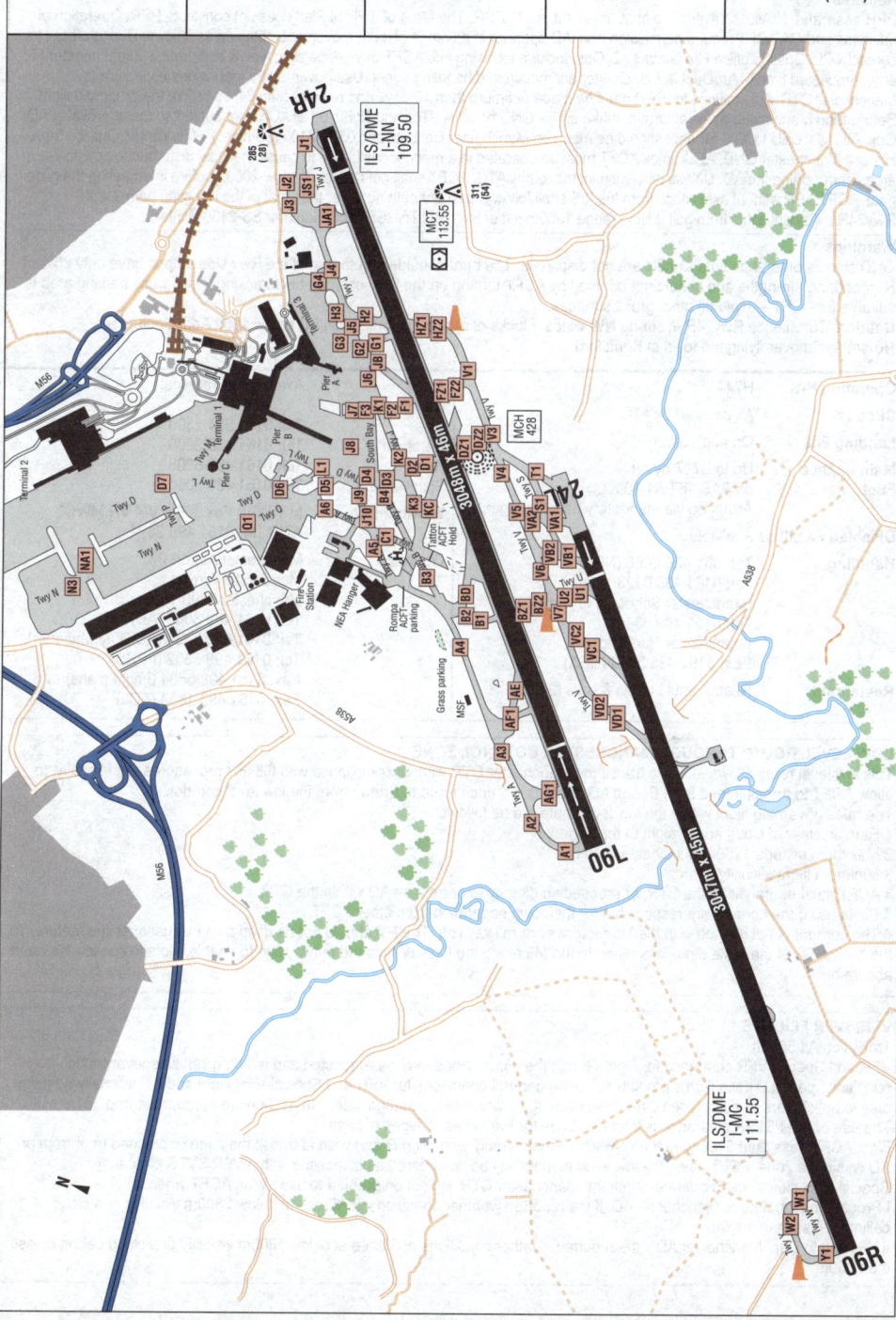

RWY	SURFACE	TORA	LDA	LIGHTING
06L	Conc/Asph	3048	2621	Ap Thr Rwy PAPI 3° RHS
24R	Conc/Asph	3048	2865	Ap Thr Rwy PAPI 3° LHS
06R	Conc/Asph	3047	2864	Ap Thr Rwy PAPI 3° LHS
24L	Conc/Asph	3047	2864	Ap Thr Rwy PAPI 3° LHS

Starter extension Rwy24L 150x30m

Remarks
PPR essential. Hi-Vis. All flights are at all times subject to PPR. The filling of a Flight Plan does not constitute PPR. Operation of business and GA ACFT require permission from AD operator in advance of each movement, obtained as follows: During office Hrs contact ACL. Outside office Hrs contact AD Ops. Include following info ACFT owner/operator, type & registration. Flight number (if any), requested time of Arr/Dept at Manchester and nominated handling agent. Use governed by regulations applicable to Manchester CTR. Applications for PPR must be made not more than 10 days and not less than 24Hrs before the proposed flight Before filing Manchester as an alternate, make arr for GND handling. Training flights by all ACFT are subject to the approval of AD Ops. All initial calls to ATC for dept should be made on Manchester Del between 0530-2100 (Summer) +1Hr Winter. Outside these Hrs call Manchester GND. At all times ACFT must be operated in a manner calculated to cause the least disturbance practicable in areas surrounding the AD. Unless otherwise instructed by ATC, ACFT shall not descend below 2000ft before intercepting the glide path. ACFT APP without assistance from the ILS shall follow a descent path no lower than that of the ILS glide path. Dept Rwy24R/L 4 bright lights from golf driving range 1500m left of Rwy24R Thr (SS-2030 Summer SS-2130 Winter).

Warnings
GND signals other than light signals are not displayed. The hard shoulders outboard of the Rwy side stripes have only 25% of Rwy bearing strengths and should not be used by ACFT turning on the Rwy or when backtracking. Only grass parking area is suitable for ACFT – avoid all other grass surfaces.
Caution: Turbulence Rwy24R in strong NW winds. Flocks of racing pigeons cross AD below 100ft April-September.
Noise: Avoid over flying the town of Knutsford.

Operating Hrs	H24	**Taxis**	Available at Terminal
Circuits	As directed by ATC	**Car Hire**	
Landing Fee	On application	Avis	**Tel:** 0161 934 2300
Maintenance	Up to B747 by arr	Europcar	**Tel:** 0161 436 2200
Fuel	AVGAS JET A1 100LL	Hertz	**Tel:** 0161 437 8208
	Arranged via mandatory handling agent	Sixt Kenning	**Tel:** 0161 489 2666
Disabled Facilities	Available	**Weather Info**	M T9 T18 Fax 368 A VM VN MWC
Handling	**Tel:** 061 436 6666 (NEA)		ATIS **Tel:** 0161 499 2324
	Tel: 0161 436 0123	**Operator**	Manchester Airport Plc
	(Manchester School of Flying)		Manchester Airport
	Tel: 0161 489 6345		Manchester, M90 1QX
	(Manchester Handling)		**Tel:** 0161 489 3000 (AD)
	Fax: 0161 436 3450 (NEA)		**Tel:** 0161 489 3331 (AD Duty Manager)
Restaurants	Restaurants buffets & bars (24Hr)		**Tel:** 0161 499 5502 (FPRS)
			Fax: 0161 499 5504 (Flight plans)
			Fax: 0161 493 1853 (ACL)

LOW LEVEL ROUTE THROUGH MANCHESTER CONTROL ZONE
This low level route allows ACFT to transit the Manchester CTR without compliance with full IFR procedures. Additionally, to allow ACFT to transit to and from Barton AD, there is a branch route to Barton from the low level corridor.
The rules governing flight within the low level route are as follows:
1 Remain clear of cloud and in sight of the surface.
2 Maximum altitude 1250ft (Manchester QNH).
3 Minimum flight visibility4km.
4 ACFT must be transiting the CTR, or proceeding directly to or from an AD within the CTR.
5 Pilots using the corridor are responsible for their own separation from other ACFT.
6 The corridor is not aligned with the M6 motorway or railway line. The M6 should not be used as a navigational line feature. To the NW or SE of the route stubs are alined to the M6 along the Crewe/Winsford railway line to enable pilots to access the route accurately.

VFR/SVFR FLIGHTS
Transition Alt 5000ft
VFR and Special VFR clearance for flights within the control zone may be requested and will be given whenever traffic conditions permit. These flights are subject to the general conditions for VFR and Special VFR flight and will normally be given only to helicopters or aeroplanes other than microlights which can communicate with ATC on the appropriate freq.
The use of VFR/SVFR clearance is intended to be for the following types of flight:
Light ACFT (less than 5700kg MTOW) which cannot comply with full IFR and wish to transit the zone or proceed to or from an AD within the zone. ACFT using the low level corridor will be considered as complying with a VFR/SVFR clearance.
Special VFR clearance to operate within the Manchester CTR will not be granted to fixed-wing ACFT when:
i Proceeding inbound to Manchester AD, if the reported weather conditions at AD are at below 2800m visibility or a cloud ceiling of less than 1000ft.
ii Wishing to Dept Manchester AD if the reported weather conditions at AD are at below 1800m visibility or a cloud ceiling of less than 600ft.

M

Visual Reference Points (VRP)			
VRP	**VOR/VOR**	**VOR/NDB**	**VOR/DME**
Alderley Edge Hill N5317.72 W00212.73	MCT 157°/WAL 103°	MCT 157°/WHI 331°	MCT 157°/4nm
Barton AD N5328.27 W00223.42	MCT 330°/POL 215°	MCT 330°/WHI 029°	MCT 330°/8nm
Buxton N5315.35 W00154.77	MCT 119°/POL 170°	MCT 119°/WHI 084°	MCT 119°/14nm
Congleton N5309.90 W00210.85	MCT 169°/TNT 293°	MCT 169°/WHI 198°	MCT 169°/12nm TNT 293°/20nm
Hilltop N5320.50 W00210.45	MCT 110°/TNT 317°	MCT 110°/WHI 063°	MCT 110°/3nm TNT 317°/25nm
Jodrell Bank N5314.18 W00218.55	MCT 196°/WAL 111°	MCT 196°/WHI 078°	MCT 196°/7nm
Rostherne N5321.23 W00223.12	MCT 271°/POL 206°	MCT 271°/WHI 044°	MCT 271°/4nm
Sale Water Park N5326.00 W00218.17	MCT 346°/POL 204°	MCT 346°/WHI 041°	MCT 346°/5nm
Stretton (Disused AD) N5320.77 W00231.58	POL 215°/WAL 101°	MCT 270°/WHI 023°	MCT 270°/10nm WAL 101°/22nm
Swinton Interchange N5331.40 W00221.60	MCT 344°/POL 218°	MCT 344°/WHI 028°	MCT 344°/11nm
Thelwall (M6 Viaduct) N5323.43 W00230.35	MCT 286°/POL 218°	MCT 286°/WHI 022°	MCT 286°/9nm

Manchester Visual Routes

Standard Inbound Visual Routes

Entry point	Rwy	Max Alt (QNH)	Route
Stretton	06L/06R	1250ft	From Stretton AD VRP route via M56 keep motorway on left join left base Rwy06L
		Remarks:	1 Out bound traffic operates N of M56 2 ACFT may be held at Stretton VRP or Rostherne VRP
Congleton	24R	2500ft	From CTR Boundary E of Congleton VRP, route via the Woodford Entry/Exit Lane (Notes 1 & 4) (keep railway line on left) to Woodford AD. Join left base for Rwy24R
		Remarks:	1 Maximum altitudes 2500ft between CTR Boundary & N edge of Macclesfield 1500ft N of Macclesfield to Woodford ATZ S Boundary 2 ACFT may be held at Hilltop VRP. Pilots must hold by visual reference to ensure that the holding pattern does not deviate to the N, which would come in to conflict with Rwy24R final instrument APP, particularly in a S wind. 3 The Entry/Exit Lane may be under Woodford Control. Pilots should contact Woodford APP initially then, if no contact Manchester APP. 4 **Warning:** High GND to the E of the Entry/Exit Lane. 5 ACFT must not leave confines of Entry/Exit Lane without prior ATC co-ordination 6 ACFT with radio failure inbound to Manchester in Woodford Entry/Exit Lane, or holding at Hilltop, carry out RAD Communication Failure procedure.

Standard Outbound Visual Routes

Entry point	Rwy	Max Alt (QNH)	Route Designator Route
Thelwall	06L	1250ft	**Thelwall 1 Vis.** Cross M56. Route N of M56 to Thelwall Viaduct VRP thence via the low level route.
		Remarks:	1 Avoid over flying Lymm. 2 Inbound traffic operates S of M56 for Rwy06L. 3 **Warning:** Traffic in Low Level Route is unknown to ATC.
Congleton	24R/24L	2500ft	**Congleton 3 Vis.** Left turn towards Alderley Edge VRP. Route W then S of Alderley Edge Hill and join the Woodford entry/exit lane at Prestbury station. Keep railway line on left and leave CTR via Congleton VRP.
		Remarks:	1 Max alt 1500ft between Manchester & N edge of Macclesfield, 2500ft S of N edge to CTR Boundary. 2 **Warning:** High GND to the E of Entry/Exit Lane. 3 Entry/Exit Lane may under Woodford or Manchester control. 4 ACFT may be routed direct from Manchester to Prestbury Station, or via Woodford. 5 ACFT must not leave the Entry/Exit Lane without ATC prior co-ordination. 6 **Caution:** Alderley Edge 650ft amsl.

M

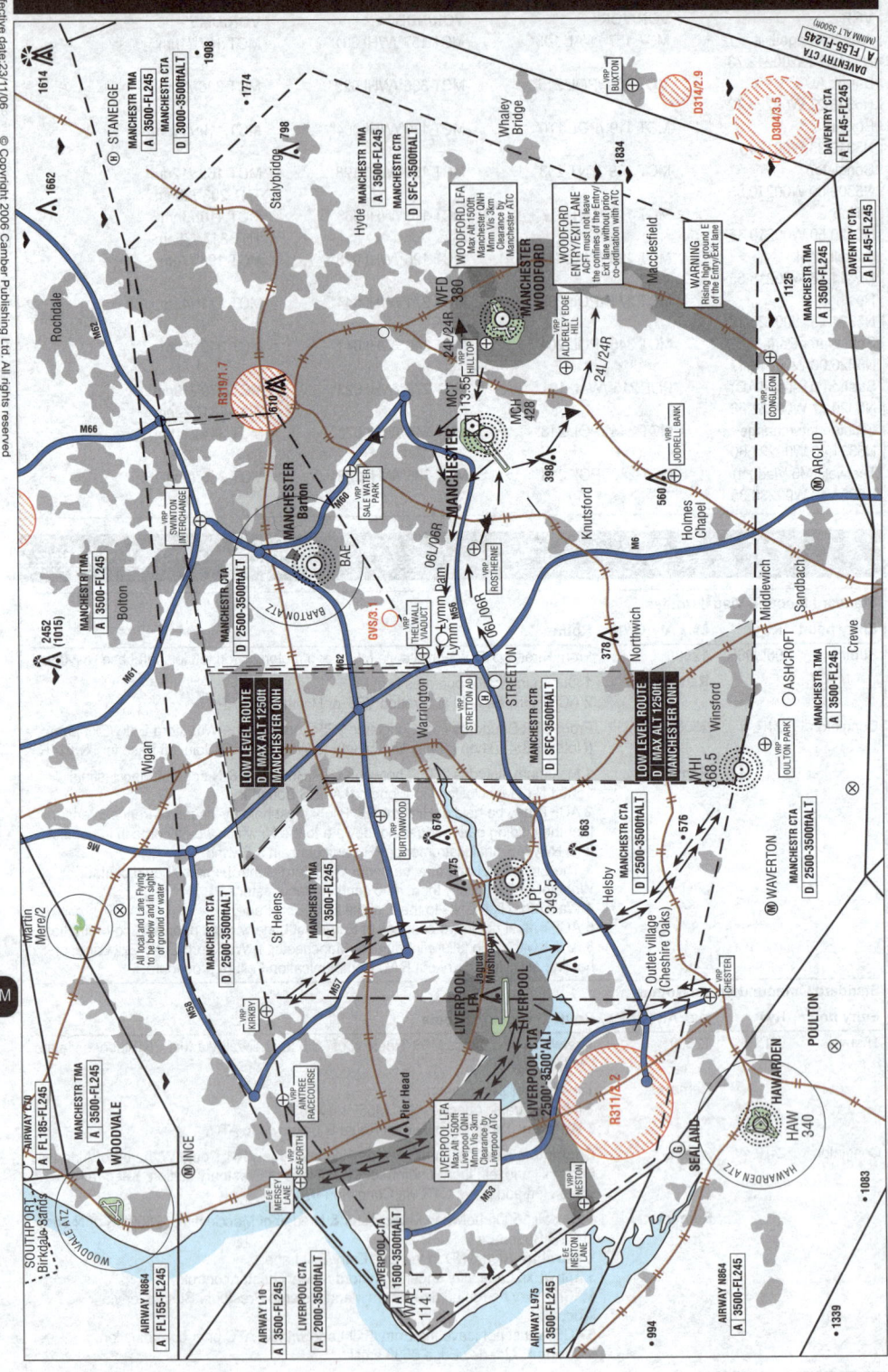

73ft 2mb	5nm W of Manchester N5328.30 W00223.38		**PPR**	**Alternative AD Diversion AD**	**Liverpool** Blackpool

Barton	**AFIS** 120.250	**APP** **Manchester 135.000**

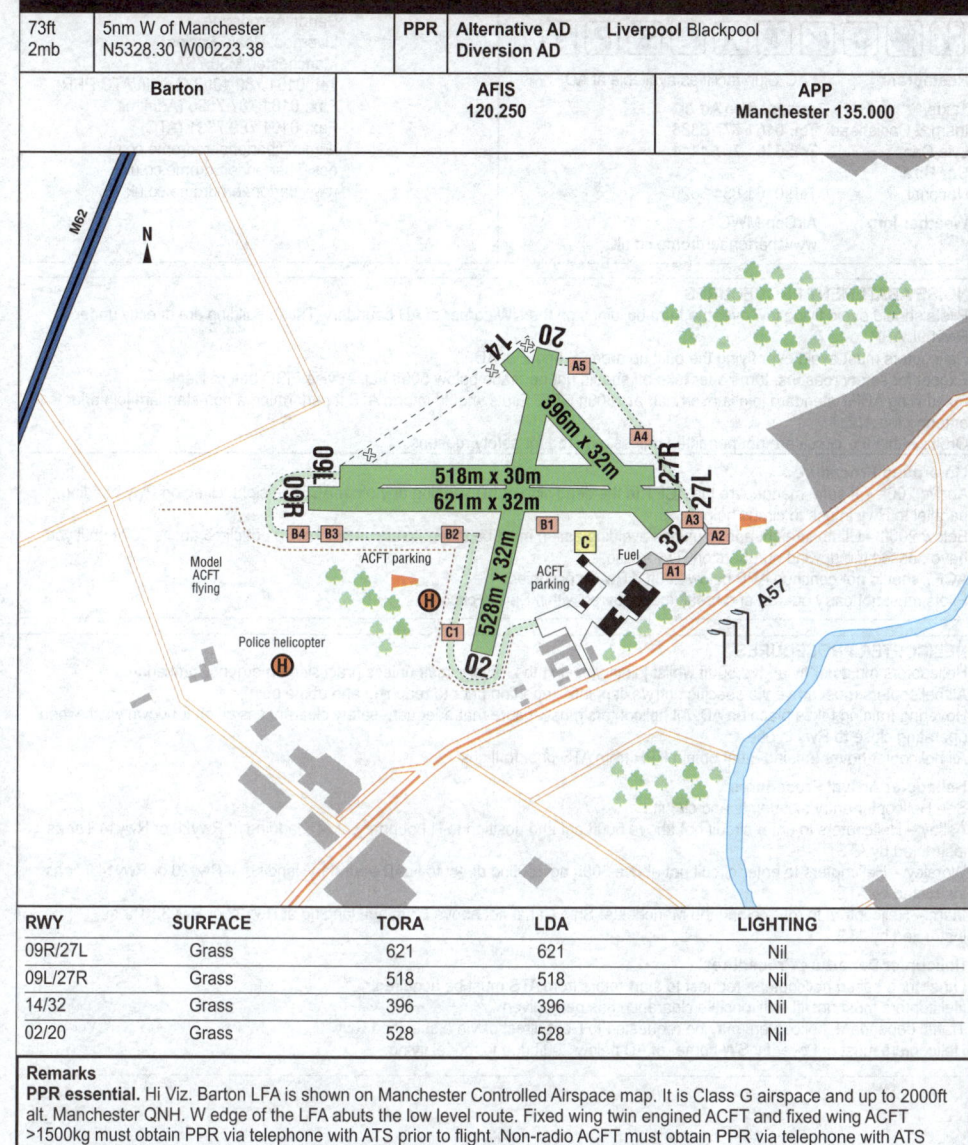

RWY	SURFACE	TORA	LDA	LIGHTING
09R/27L	Grass	621	621	Nil
09L/27R	Grass	518	518	Nil
14/32	Grass	396	396	Nil
02/20	Grass	528	528	Nil

Remarks

PPR essential. Hi Viz. Barton LFA is shown on Manchester Controlled Airspace map. It is Class G airspace and up to 2000ft alt. Manchester QNH. W edge of the LFA abuts the low level route. Fixed wing twin engined ACFT and fixed wing ACFT >1500kg must obtain PPR via telephone with ATS prior to flight. Non-radio ACFT must obtain PPR via telephone with ATS prior to flight. During adverse weather conditions the AD and associated services may be withdrawn. A computer ATIS display is provided for Dept ACFT. A full copy of the Aerodrome Rules and Procedures (Pilot Handbook) is available on request or can be downloaded from the website. Aerobatics may take place overhead the AD with prior approval. Whilst aerobatic detail is in progress overhead joins are not permitted. ATS may request a downwind, base leg or final join for inbound ACFT. Operating Hrs extensions available on request 0700-2300 (L)

Warnings

35ft high lights on the A57 SE and SW of AD. Clay pigeon and game shooting takes place NW of AD within ATZ, helicopters must avoid this area below 500ft agl. Red/white marker boards or non standard markings (cones) may be used to indicate areas of soft GND. Pilots must exercise extreme caution as not all soft areas may be indicated. Surface undulating in places and soft after heavy rain. Rwy14/32 closed at times for ACFT parking. Rwy09/27 pilots must ensure that they have identified the correct Rwy in use. Bird hazard – Herons regularly fly across the aerodrome at 100-500ft. Gulls and pigeon activity increases during period of wet weather and grass seeding. All bird strikes must be reported.

Operating Hrs	0800-SS (Summer) +1Hr (Winter)	**Maintenance**	Light Planes (Lancashire) Ltd **Tel:** 0161 707 8644
Circuits	Fixed Wing 14, 20, 27L, 27R RH, 02, 09L, 09R, 32 LH, 1000ft QFE Overhead joins at 1800ft QFE Helicopter circuits flown in fixed wing circuit at 500ft	**Fuel**	AVGAS JET A1 100LL Fuel not available before 0900 and 15mins prior to last landing
Landing Fee	See website for details		

M

| Disabled Facilities | | Operator | Barton Aerodrome Operations Ltd |

Disabled Facilities		Operator	Barton Aerodrome Operations Ltd
Restaurant	LAC Club facilities available at AD		Barton Aerodrome
Taxis	Arranged on Arr or		Liverpool Road, Eccles
Irlam & Cadishead	**Tel:** 0161 777 8888		Manchester, M30 7SA
Lyle Cars	**Tel:** 0161 707 4444		**Tel:** 0161 789 1362 (Admin/ATC/PPR)
Car Hire			**Fax:** 0161 787 7695 (Admin)
National	**Tel:** 0161 834 3020		**Fax:** 0161 789 7731 (ATC)
Weather Info	AirCen MWC		admin@bartonaerodrome.co.uk
	www.bartonaerdrome.co.uk		ops@bartonaerodrome.co.uk
			www.bartonaerodrome.co.uk

NOISE ABATEMENT PROCEDURES

Pilots should avoid flying low over the farm buildings on the NW corner of AD boundary. These building are directly under Rwy09L APP.

Helicopters must avoid over flying the built up areas S and E of AD.

Except for safety reasons, turns after take off should not be made below 500ft agl. Advise FISO before Dept.

Fixed wing ACFT standard join is overhead at 1800ft QFE. Pilots should inform ATS if performing a non-standard join prior to entering the ATZ.

Orbits within the circuit are not permitted unless required for safety reasons.

Go-around Procedure

Above 200ft – If safe, manoeuvre the ACFT to the dead side of AD keeping any other ACFT in sight, climb on Rwy heading, parallel to Rwy in use to circuit height.

Below 200ft – Climb straight ahead unless avoiding action must be taken, to circuit height. Do not climb above 500ft until you have passed the upwind numbers on Rwy in use.

ACFT should not continue APP below 200ft if Rwy is occupied.

Pilots must not carry out run and break manoeuvres within Barton circuit.

HELICOPTER PROCEDURES

Helicopters must nor fly above 500ft whilst joining/leaving the AD or circuit unless practising emergency procedures.

All helicopters must arrive via specific entry/exit points, reporting prior to reaching and at the point.

Hovering training takes place on AD. All helicopters must ensure that adequate safety clearance is given for down wash when operating close to Rwy in use.

All helicopter hover training must obtain PPR from ATS prior to flight.

Helicopter Arrival Procedures

See Helicopter entry/exit points and circuits

Astley – Helicopters to enter circuit not above 500ft agl and position to N boundary of AD, landing at Rwy20 or Rwy14 Thr as instructed by ATS.

Worsley – Helicopters to enter circuit not above 500ft agl routing direct to N AD boundary, landing at Rwy20 or Rwy14 Thr as instructed by ATS.

Irlam – Helicopters to route along the Manchester Ship Canal not above 500ft agl, landing at Rwy02 or Rwy32 Thr as instructed by ATS.

Helicopter Departure Procedures

Other than based helicopters, request to start rotors from ATS must be acquired.

Helicopters must not lift until positve clearance has been given.

Traffic dependant, helicopters may be requested to Dept direct or via a specified Rwy.

Helicopters must not over fly SW corner of AD below 200ft due to model flying.

M

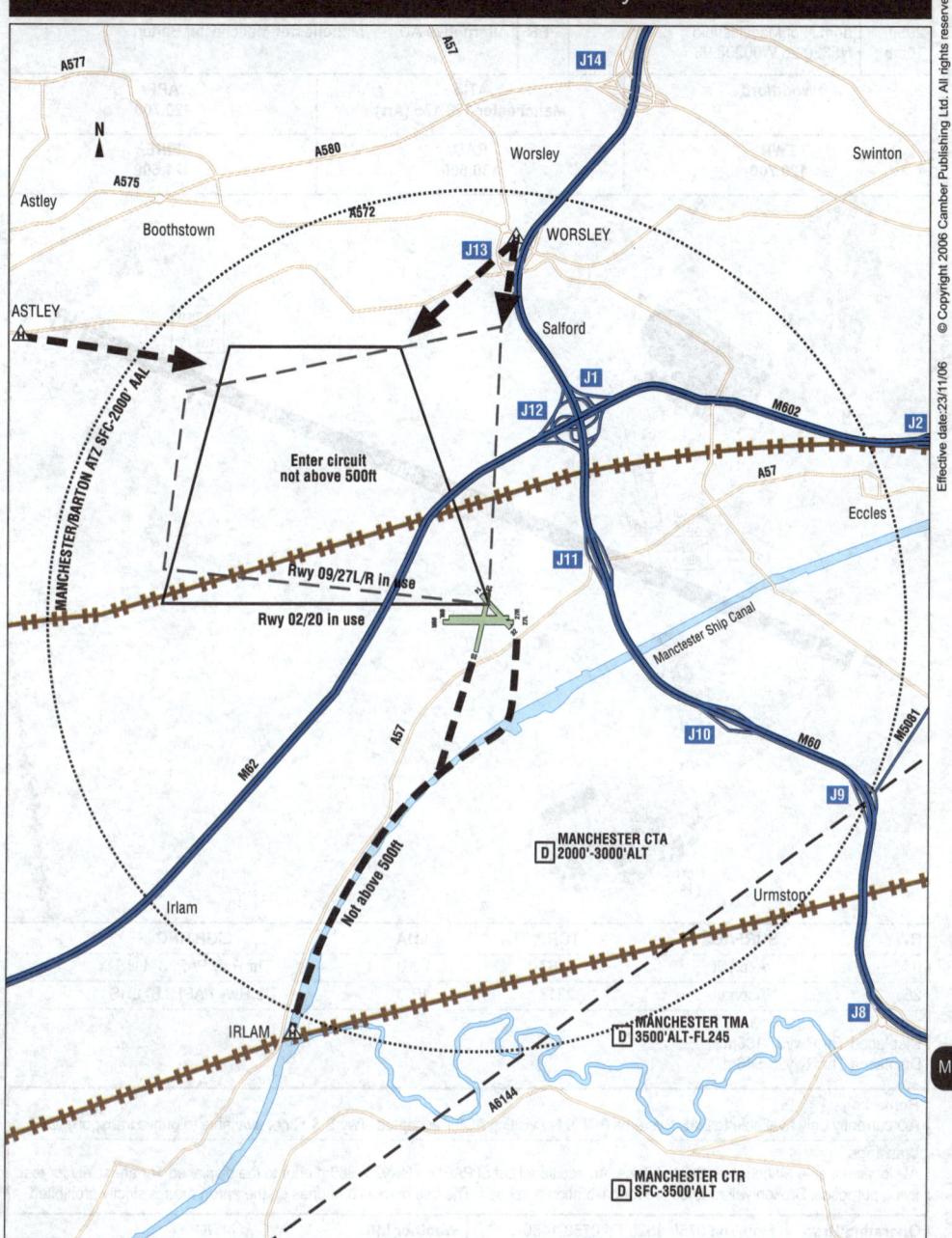

M

295ft 10mb	6nm N of Macclesfield N5320.26 W00208.93	PPR	Alternative AD	**Manchester** Manchester Barton

Woodford	**ATIS** Manchester 128.175 (Arr)	**APP** 120.700
TWR 120.700	**RAD** 130.500	**FIRE** 121.600

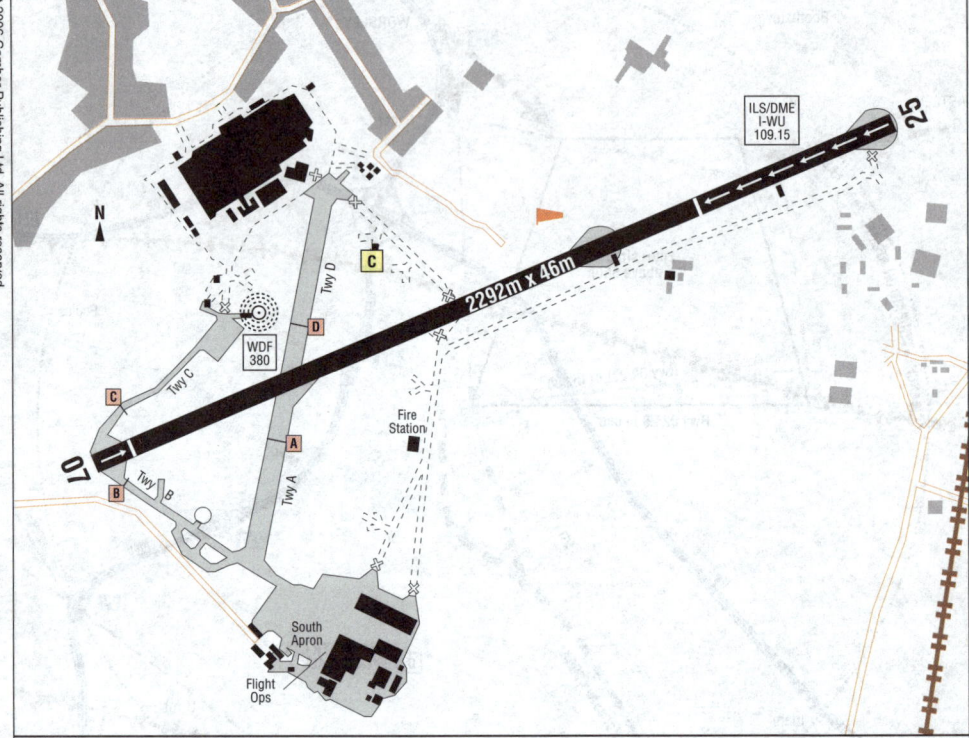

RWY	SURFACE	TORA	LDA	LIGHTING
07	Asphalt	2167	2061	Thr Rwy PAPI 3° LHS
25	Asphalt	2217	1671	Thr Rwy PAPI 3.6° LHS

Displaced Thr Rwy07 106m
Displaced Thr Rwy25 546m

Remarks
AD currently only available to BAE Systems ACFT. No visiting ACFT accepted. Twy B & C not available to public transport ACFT.

Warnings
AD located inside Manchester Control Zone. An additional set of PAPI on Rwy25, 360m prior to the displaced Thr are solely for test flying purposes. Broken yellow lines are for calibration purposes. The use of mobile phones on the apron area is strictly prohibited.

Operating Hrs	Mon-Thu 0750-1525 Fri 0750-1430 (Summer) +1Hr (Winter)	Weather Info	M* AirCen MWC
Circuits	07 RH, 25 LH	Operator	BAe Systems Manchester Woodford Aerodrome Chester Road, Bramhall Cheshire, SK7 1QR **Tel:** 0161 439 5050 Ex 3294 (PPR) **Tel:** 0161 439 3383 (ATC) **Fax:** 0161 955 3316
Landing Fee	N/A		
Maintenance	Nil		
Fuel	JET A1		
Disabled Facilities	Nil		
Restaurants	Nil		
Taxis	**Tel:** 0161 456-7099 **Tel:** 0161 440-9769 **Tel:** 0161 439-9056		
Car Hire	Bramhall Self Drive Hire **Tel:** 0161 439 5826		

M

LOCAL FLYING AREA

Within a local flying area of 1.5nm radius, centred on the AD VFR/SVFR flights may take place subject to ATC clearance from Manchester/Woodford ATC.

ENTRY-EXIT LANE

An Entry-Exit lane is established 1nm wide aligned on the Congleton-Macclesfield railway from the boundary of the LFA to the S boundary of Manchester CTR. VFR/SVFR flights may take place subject to ATC clearance & compliance with the following conditions.

1 ACFT using the lane must remain clear of cloud and in sight of the GND & in a flight visibility of **at least 3km.**

2 ACFT using the lane **must comply with the left hand rule** when following the railway line unless otherwise instructed by ATC for separation purposes.

3 Pilots are responsible for maintaining adequate clearance from the GND and other obstacles, & are warned of **high GND to the E** of the lane.

4 ACFT **must not** leave the confines of the lane unless authorised by ATC.

5 Inbound ACFT should make their first call to Woodford APP to ascertain the controlling agency at the time they wish to join.

It is essential that inbound ACFT follow the flight profile detailed below

Fly not above 2500ft QNH from Congleton to Macclesfield

Fly not above 1500ft QNH from N of Macclesfield to LFA

WOODFORD STANDARD VFR DEPT

To assist in reducing RTF Workload, Woodford ATC will use the following abreviated phraseology to issue the following Dept clearances.

Congleton One VFR Dept Rwy25

A left turn out towards Macclesfield to intercept the Macclesfield-Congleton railway then remain within the confines of the Entry-Exit lane unless other wise instructed by ATC.

Flight Profile ACFT MUST

Fly not above1500ft QNH to the N edge of Macclesfield

Fly not above 2500ft QNH to the Congleton VRP

Congleton Two VFR Dept Rwy07

A right turnout towards Macclesfield & then as the procedure above.

The Woodford Entry-Exit lane is notified for the purpose of Rule 5 (2)(a). That is it is NOT obligatory to comply with the '1500ft rule' but essential that the ACFT be flown at such a height that would enable the ACFT to alight clear of the congested area in the event of failure of a power unit.

Visual Reference Points (VRP)

VRP	VOR/VOR	VOR/NDB	VOR/DME
Congleton	MCT 169°/TNT 293°	MCT 169°/WHI 099°	MCT 169°/12nm
N5309.90 W00210.85			TNT 293°/20nm

Effective date:23/11/06

M

MANOR FARM

Effective date:23/11/06

643ft 21mb	9nm S of Marlborough N5118.30 W00140.00	PPR	Alternative AD	Southampton Thruxton

Non Radio	LARS Boscombe 126.700	DACS Salisbury Ops 122.750	Safetycom 135.475

RWY	SURFACE	TORA	LDA	LIGHTING
10/28	Grass	600x18	U/L	Nil

Remarks

Strictly PPR by telephone, preferably with 24hrs notice as stock may need to be moved . Usually only available to guests staying at Manor Farm B&B. AD well prepared and well drained on top of chalk escarpment. Windsock displayed with PPR. Operator will meet visiting ACFT to help with ground handling to ensure a safe operation. Due to close proximity of D128, visiting pilots are advised to contact Salisbury Plain Ops.

Warnings

Be aware of close proximity of Salisbury Plain Danger area complex to the S & W. C130 para dropping acft regularly operate in close proximity to the AD. Public footpath and solid cross-country horse jumps on the southern edge of the strip. Watch out for people and horses on the strip! Farm machinery may be parked close to the strip.
Noise: App Rwy28. Curved noise abatement approach and departure required between Aughton Farm and Aughton, (Operator can provide information). Please fly with consideration for our neighbours.

Operating Hrs	By arrangement		Operator	James Macbeth
Circuits	To N at 1000ft QFE Join downwind			Manor Farm Collingbourne Kingston Wiltshire SN8 3SD
Landing Fee	Nil			**Tel/Fax:** 01264 850859
Maintenance	Nil			**Tel:** 01980 674710 (Salisbury Ops)
Fuel	Nil			**Tel:** 01980 674730 (Salisbury Ops)
Disabled Facilities	Nil			stay@manorfm.com
Accomodation	4 star B & B Manor Farmhouse www.manorfm.com **Tel:** 01264 850859			www.manorfm.com
Taxi/Car Hire	Operator can assist			
Weather Info	AirSW MOEx			

M

| 178ft | 2.5nm W of Ramsgate | | PPR | Alternative AD | Southend Rochester |
| 6mb | N5120.53 E00120.77 | | | Diversion AD | |

Manston		ATIS 133.675		LARS 126.350		APP 126.350
	RAD 129.450		TWR 119.925		FIRE 121.600	

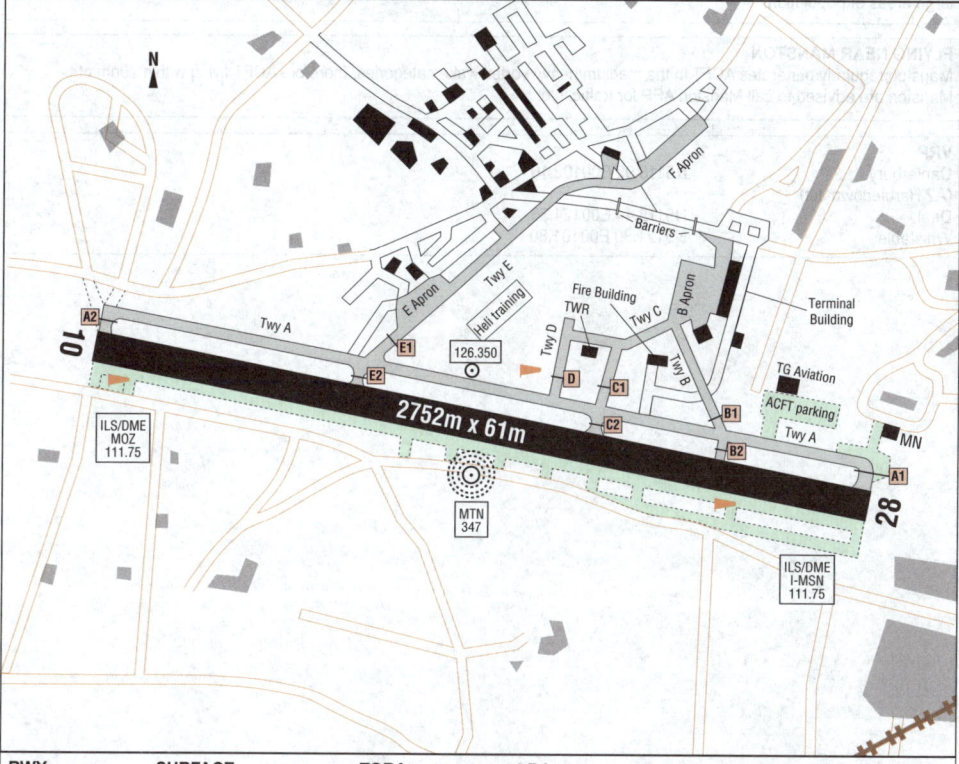

N

Twy A

A2

10

Twy E

E Apron

Heli training

E1

E2

126.350

ILS/DME MOZ 111.75

2752m x 61m

Twy D

Fire Building

TWR

D

C1

C2

Twy C

Twy B

B Apron

B1

B2

Terminal Building

TG Aviation

ACFT parking

Twy A

MN

A1

28

MTN 347

F Apron

Barriers

ILS/DME I-MSN 111.75

RWY	SURFACE	TORA	LDA	LIGHTING
10/28	Asph/Conc	2752	2752	Ap Thr Rwy PAPI 3° LHS

Remarks

Strict PPR inc training. Hi-vis. All ACFT must be handled by agent – ACFT <4 tonnes TG Aviation, ACFT >4 Tonnes AD Ops. Captains of visiting ACFT are responsible for the escort and safety of their passengers whilst airside. LARS available (0900-1700 L Daily). Helicopter training on grass area N Twy A between Apron E & Twy D.
Visual aid to location: Ibn MN Green.

Warnings

Twy B 23m wide, all other 15m wide with sharp turns. Short Twy links Twy A with TG Aviation. Pilots entering Apron B must do so with caution under marshallers instructions. The Y shaped pans off Twy C & D are also used.
Caution: Rwy28 short finals turbulence may be encountered with NW or S winds. Bird concentrations may be present on Rwy APP.

Operating Hrs	0900-1800 (L)		Restaurants	Refreshments available
Circuits	Jets & ACFT 5700kg 1800ft QFE		**Taxis**	
	All other ACFT 1000ft QFE		Minicabs	**Tel:** 01843 581581
	Circuits may be varied		**Car Hire**	
Landing Fee	On application		Budget	**Tel:** 01843 860310
Maintenance			**Weather Info**	M T15 Fax 372 MOEx
TG Aviation	**Tel:** 01843 823656		**Operator**	Infratil Ltd
Fuel	AVGAS 100LL (TG Aviation)			Kent International Airport Manston
	JET A1 (AD Ops)			Manston
Disabled Facilities	Nil			Ramsgate, Kent, CT12 5BP
Handling	**Tel:** 01843 823600/825063 (AD Ops)			**Tel:** 01843 823600 (Switchboard)
	Tel: 01843 823656 (TG Aviation)			**Fax:** 01843 821386 (AD)
	Fax: 01843 821386 (AD Ops)			
	Fax: 01843 822024 (TG Aviation)			

M

MANSTON NOISE PROCEDURES

Unless other wise instructed by ATC or unless deviations are required in the interests of safety, all jet ACFT and all ACFT >5700kgs MTWA dept AD are subject to the following noise preferential routings:

Rwy10 – Climb straight ahead until 3000ft QNH, then as directed by ATC.

Rwy28 – Climb straight ahead to 1.5nm DME I-MSN, then track 310° until 3000ft QNH and passing 5nm DME I-MSN, then as directed by ATC.

Rwy28 – Dept joining airways at DVR VOR: Initially as above, but subject to traffic, after passing 5nm DME I-MSN, R turn on track DVR VOR and arrange flight to pass 4000ft QNH by 15nm DME VOR.

VFR ACFT subject to noise preferential routings will not jeopardise their VFR status, and will be asked where possible to avoid large areas of population.

FLYING NEAR MANSTON

Manston regularly generates ACFT in the medium/heavy vortex wake categories, therefore ACFT flying within 20nm of Manston are advised to call Manston APP for traffic info.

VRP

Canterbury	N5116.92 E00102.10
(A2 Harbledown Jct)	
Deal	N5113.44 E00124.30
Whistable	N5121.80 E00101.60

M

75ft 2mb	9nm ENE of Downham Market N5238.90 E00033.04	PPR MIL	Alternative AD Diversion AD	Norwich Old Buckenham	

Marham	LARS 124.150	APP 124.150	PAR Talkdown 123.300	TWR 122.100

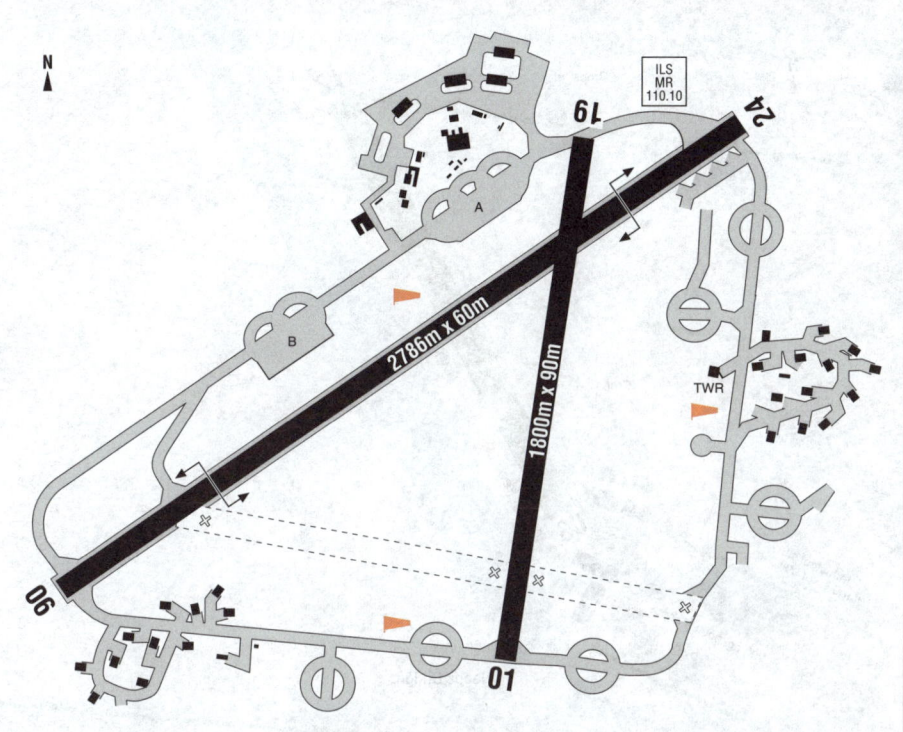

RWY	SURFACE	TORA	LDA	LIGHTING
06/24	Asph/Conc	2786	2786	Ap Thr Rwy PAPI 2.5°
01/19	Concrete	1800	1800	Rwy PAPI 3°

Arrester gear Rwy06 640m from Thr
Arrester gear Rwy24 487m from Thr
Rwy06/24 widths displaced By 50m
Normal ops: app cable down over run cable up

Remarks
PPR strictly by telephone, 24Hrs notice required. Active RAF AD. Intensive fast Jet operations. Civil visitors may be subject to refusal or individual Arr conditions. Inbound ACFT call Marham APP at least 20nm from AD.
Visual aid to Location: I Bn MR red.

Warnings
Considerable bird activity in vicinity of AD. Glider flying takes place outside normal operating Hrs. Under normal operations the APP arrester gear is down trampling of the wires by light ACFT constitutes a hazard.

Operating Hrs	0800-2359 Mon-Thu 0800-1800 Fri (L) ATZ active 24Hrs	**Weather Info**	M T Fax374 AirS MOEx ATIS **Tel:** 01760 337261 Ex 7888
Circuits	24, 01 LH, 06, 19 RH, 1000ft QFE	**Operator**	RAF Marham
Landing Fee	Charges in accordance with MOD policy Contact Station Ops for details		Kings Lynn, Norfolk **Tel:** 01760 337261 Ex 2044/2058 (PPR) **Tel:** 01760 337261 Ex 7282/7412 (ATC)
Maintenance	Not available to Civil visitors		
Fuel	JET A1 by prior arr		
Disabled Facilities	Nil		
Restaurants	Nil		
Taxis/Car Hire	Nil		

-6ft 0mb	5nm ESE of Wisbech N5239.50 E00018.00	PPR	Alternative AD	Cambridge Fenland

Herbert Operations	LARS Marham 124.150	A/G 130.375 Not normally manned

RWY	SURFACE	TORA	LDA	LIGHTING
03/21	Grass	850x20	U/L	Rwy

Remarks
PPR by telephone. Visiting ACFT welcome at pilots own risk. AD is suitable for light twin ACFT with a good level surface.
Visual aid to location: Close proximity to main drain and industrial site with large silver roofed building.

Warnings
AD may be soft after prolonged rain or snow. Rwy03 APP is over group of buildings and trees. Crops are grown up to Rwy on W side. 82m test mast 800m NNW Rwy21 Thr.

Operating Hrs	SR-SS	**Operator**	R J Herbert
Circuits	LH		Harps Hall
Landing Fee	Nil		Walton Highway
Maintenance	Nil		Wisbech, Cambs
Fuel	AVGAS 100LL by arr		**Tel:** 01945 430365 (Evenings)
Disabled Facilities			**Tel:** 01945430666 (Daytime/weekend)
			Fax: 01945 430487
			sales@rjherbert.co.uk

✈ ⛽ C ☎ ✕ T ☕ P

Restaurant	Nil
Taxis/Car Hire	Available on request
Weather Info	AirS MOEx

M

110ft 3mb	3nm NE of Canterbury N5120.31 E00109.34	PPR	Alternative AD	Manston Lashenden

Maypole	LARS Manston 126.350	A/G Maypole 119.400 make blind calls

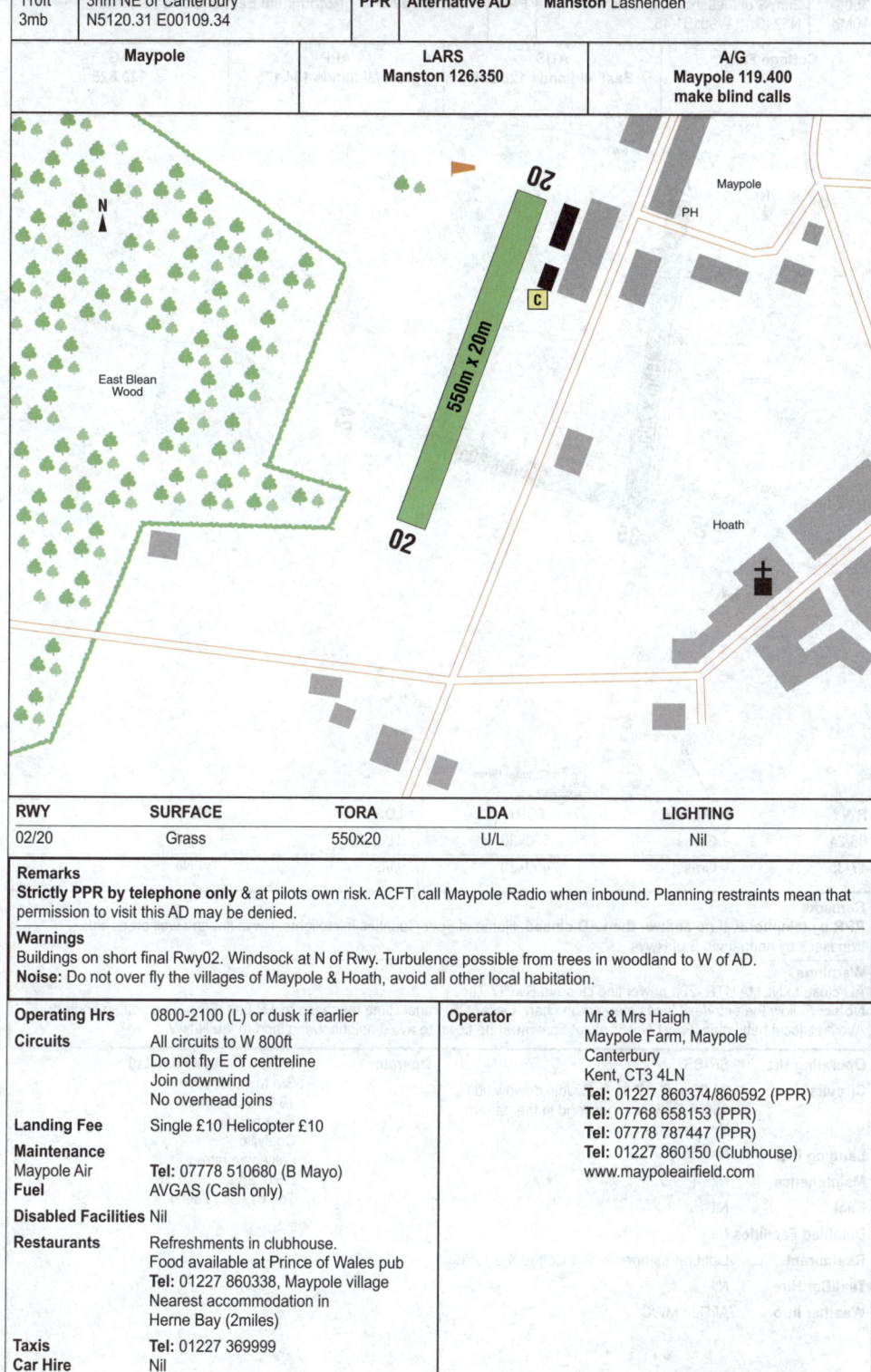

East Blean Wood

Maypole

PH

Hoath

550m x 20m

Effective date:23/11/06

RWY	SURFACE	TORA	LDA	LIGHTING
02/20	Grass	550x20	U/L	Nil

Remarks
Strictly PPR by telephone only & at pilots own risk. ACFT call Maypole Radio when inbound. Planning restraints mean that permission to visit this AD may be denied.

Warnings
Buildings on short final Rwy02. Windsock at N of Rwy. Turbulence possible from trees in woodland to W of AD.
Noise: Do not over fly the villages of Maypole & Hoath, avoid all other local habitation.

Operating Hrs	0800-2100 (L) or dusk if earlier	
Circuits	All circuits to W 800ft Do not fly E of centreline Join downwind No overhead joins	
Landing Fee	Single £10 Helicopter £10	
Maintenance		
Maypole Air	**Tel:** 07778 510680 (B Mayo)	
Fuel	AVGAS (Cash only)	
Disabled Facilities Nil		
Restaurants	Refreshments in clubhouse. Food available at Prince of Wales pub **Tel:** 01227 860338, Maypole village Nearest accommodation in Herne Bay (2miles)	
Taxis	**Tel:** 01227 369999	
Car Hire	Nil	
Weather Info	AirSE MOEx	

Operator

Mr & Mrs Haigh
Maypole Farm, Maypole
Canterbury
Kent, CT3 4LN
Tel: 01227 860374/860592 (PPR)
Tel: 07768 658153 (PPR)
Tel: 07778 787447 (PPR)
Tel: 01227 860150 (Clubhouse)
www.maypoleairfield.com

M

399

350ft 10Mb	2nm S of Measham Leicestershire N5240.12 W00131.46	PPR	Alternative AD	Nottingham East Midland Leicester

Cottage Farm	ATIS East Midlands 128.225	APP East Midlands 134.175	AG 129.825

RWY	SURFACE	TORA	LDA	LIGHTING
06/24	Grass	500x20	U/L	Nil
17/35	Grass	400x20	U/L	Nil

Remarks
PPR by telephone, if no answer then AD closed. Home of Four Counties microlights. Rwys flat and well prepared. Windsock by hangars to S of Rwys.

Warnings
AD close to NEMA CTR. 20ft power line close to Rwy17 Thr .
Noise: Follow the entry/exit lanes marked on chart. Dept ACFT must climb overhead to 1500ft QFE before setting course. Avoid all local habitation. Rwy17– 45° offset final **must** be flown to avoid neighbouring land to the N/NW.

Operating Hrs	SR-SS	**Operator**	William Corbett Farm Ltd
Circuits	24 06 to S, 17 35 to E. Join downwind 1500ft QNH and descend in the pattern No deadside		C/o Mick Moulton 18 Church Lane Ravenstone Coalville
Landing Fee	Nil		Leicestershire
Maintenance	Nil		LE67 2A E
Fuel	Nil		**Tel:** 07712 773601
Disabled Facilities	Nil		
Restaurant	Light refreshments, Tea,Coffee & Snacks		
Taxi/Car Hire	Nil		
Weather Info	AirCen MWC		

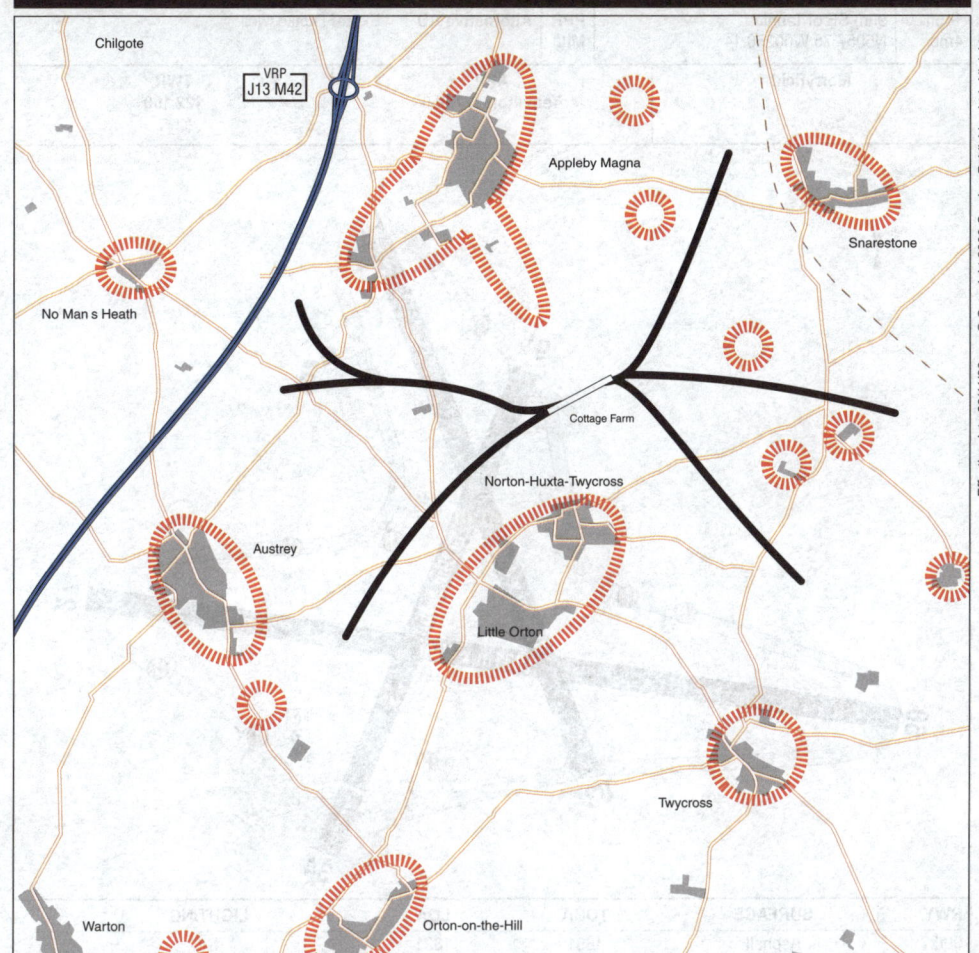

| 146ft 4mb | 9nm SE of Taunton N5057.75 W00256.14 | PPR MIL | Alternative AD | Exeter Dunkeswell |

| Merryfield | APP Yeovilton 127.350 | TWR 122.100 |

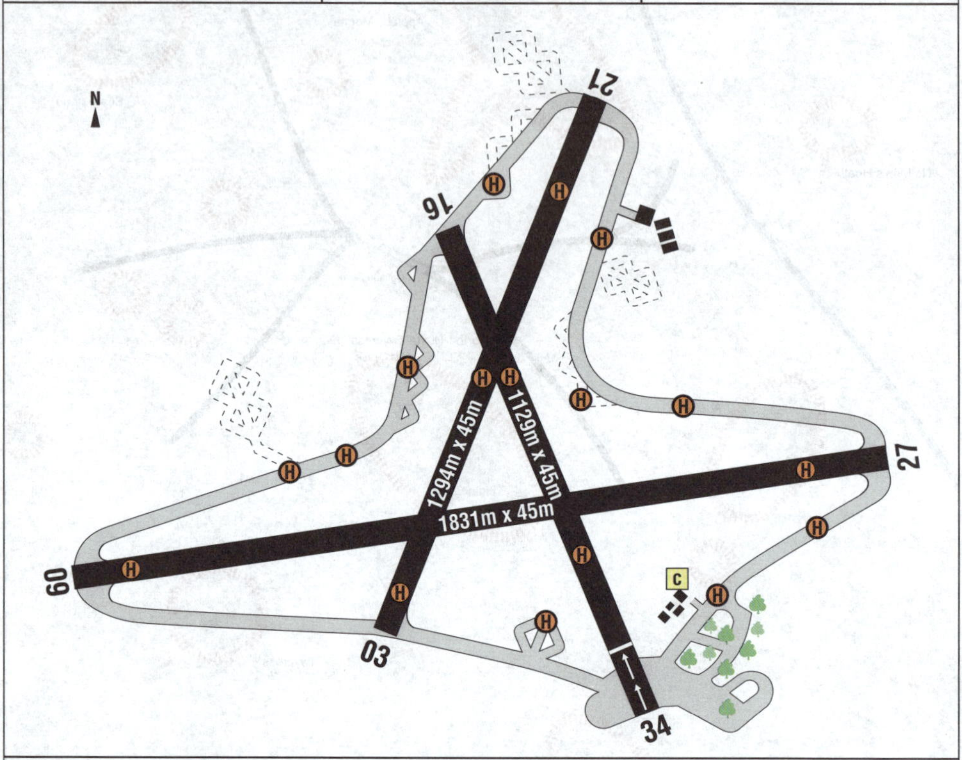

RWY	SURFACE	TORA	LDA	LIGHTING
09/27	Asphalt	1831	1831	Nil
03/21	Asphalt	1294	1294	Nil
16/34	Asphalt	1129	1129	Nil

Remarks
Strictly PPR by telephone. Operated by Royal Navy as a satellite landing area for Yeovilton

Warnings
Helicopter operations normally Mon-Fri as required by Yeovilton. ATZ active H24. Glider flying outside Op Hrs. Rwys have non-standard markings associated with helicopter training. Intensive military helicopter activity within 3nm of AD.

Operating Hrs	As required by Yeovilton	**Operator**	RNAS Yeovilton
Circuits	Helicopters may fly variable circuits No deadside		Yeovilton Somerset
Landing Fee	Charges in accordance with MOD policy Contact Station Ops for details		**Tel:** 01953 455498/7 (PPR) **Tel:** 01460 52018 (AD)
Maintenance	Nil		
Fuel	Nil		

Disabled Facilities

Restaurant	Nil
Taxis/Car Hire	Nil
Weather Info	MT Fax 456 MOEx Tel: 01935 455456

402

297ft 10mb	5nm SW of Andover N5108.57 W00134.05	PPR MIL	Alternative AD	Southampton Thruxton

Wallop	LARS Boscombe 126.700	TWR 118.275

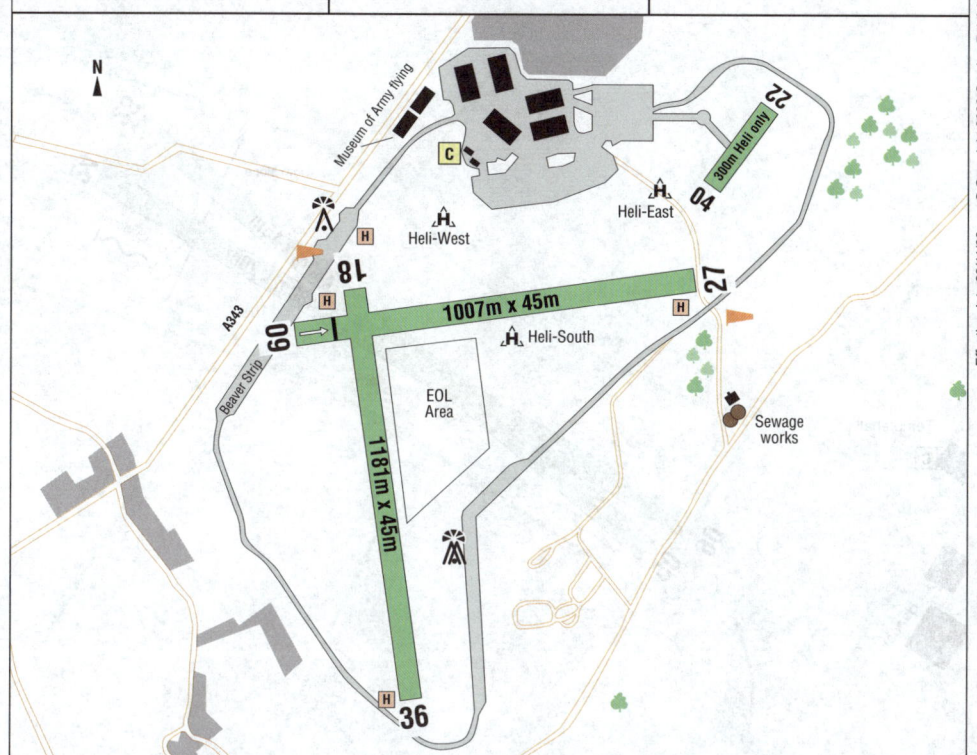

RWY	SURFACE	TORA	LDA	LIGHTING
09	Grass	900	1007	Nil
27	Grass	850	1007	Nil
18/36	Grass	1181	1181	Nil
04/22	Grass	300		Helicopters Only

Remarks

PPR by telephone essential 24Hrs notice required. Visitors will be allowed only if the planned military use is low due to the complicated circuit procedures. Intensive helicopter & fixed wing activity, special procedures apply. Flying may take place at W/E, parascending W/E & PH. Frequent night flying. ATZ active H24. Helicopters Arr/Dept to heli W, E, S while fixed wing circuit is active. Helicopters Arr/Dept Rwy09/27 will pass beneath the fixed wing circuit. Helicopter engine off landing (EOL) circuit will be opposite direction to fixed wing. Visiting ACFT will be held to enable military training to be completed. It is imperative that all visitors are briefed at ATC. DAIS available during working Hrs.
Visual aid to location: IBn MW Red.

Warnings

Operating Hrs	Mon-Thu 0800-0200 Fri 0800-1700 (L) Weekends AD active	**Weather Info**	AirSW MOEx ATIS **Tel:** 01264 784142
Circuits	Helicopters 500ft QFE Fixed Wing 1000ft QFE	**Operator**	Army Air Corps Middle Wallop **Tel:** 01264 784380 (ATC Civil) **Tel:** 01264 784727 (PPR)
Landing Fee	Charges in accordance with MOD policy Contact Station Ops for details		
Maintenance	Not available to civil ACFT		
Fuel	AVGAS Jet A1 100LL		
Disabled Facilities	Nil		
Restaurants	In Museum of Army Flying		
Taxis/Car Hire	Nil		

M

600ft 20mb	5nm SE of Galashiels N5532.00 W00244.00	PPR	Alternative AD	Edinburgh Carlisle

Non-Radio	FIR Scottish 119.875	Safetycom 135.475

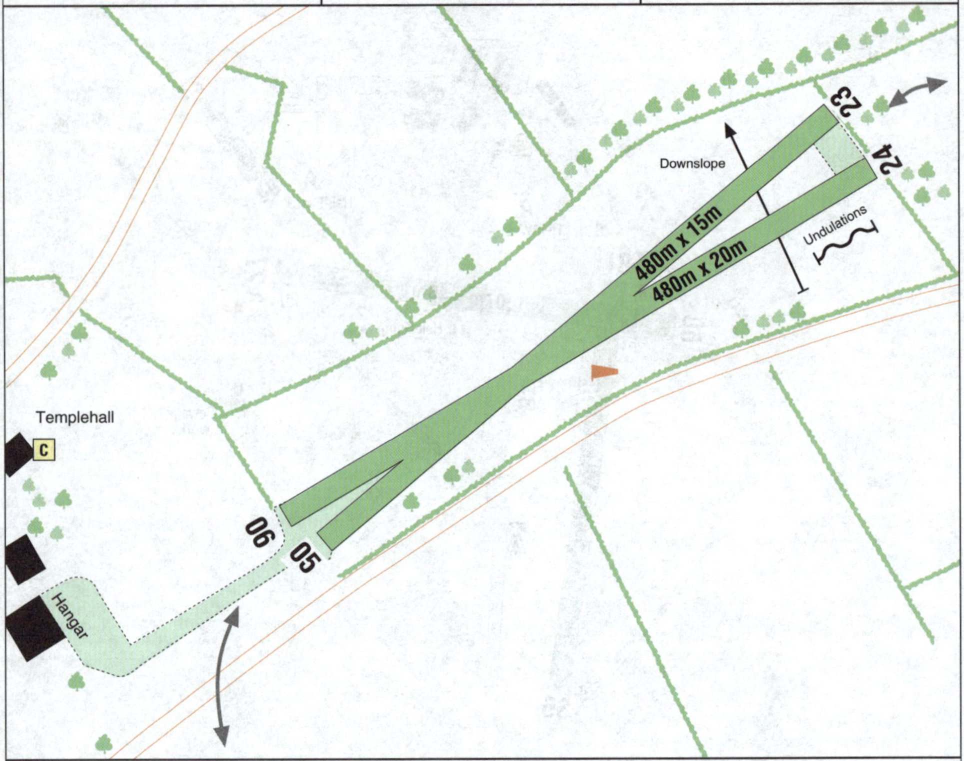

Templehall

C

Downslope

480m x 15m

480m x 20m

23

24

Undulations

06

05

Hangar

RWY	SURFACE	TORA	LDA	LIGHTING
24	Grass	366x20	U/L	Nil
06	Grass	480x20	U/L	Nil
23	Grass	480x15	U/L	Nil
05	Grass	480x15	U/L	Nil

Remarks

PPR by telephone, briefing provided. Visiting pilots welcome at own risk. Windsock S of Rwy intersection.
LDA provided by operator: Rwy24-500m, Rwy06-426m, Rwy23-480m, Rwy05-480m.

Warnings

Rwys have a lateral slope down to N. Rwy24 Thr undulations.
Caution: Power lines 5nm W of AD. Clay pigeon range N of village.
Noise: Avoid over flying local habitation, particularly Midlem village which is on short final for Rwys23/24. Please make curved approaches and climb outs for all Rwys.

Operating Hrs	SR-SS		Taxis/Car Hire	
Circuits	To S 1000ft QFE		Hunters Cabs	**Tel:** 0800 0749613
Landing Fee	Donations please		DJ Taxis	**Tel:** 01750 720354
Maintenance	Nil		Burgh Cabs	**Tel:** 01750 21340
Fuel	MOGAS by arr		Weather Info	AirSC GWC
Disabled Facilities			Operator	Mr R M Johnson
				Templehall Midlem Selkirk TD7 4QB **Tel/Fax:** 01835 870361 robinJ100@aol.com
Restaurants	Nil			

M

33ft 1mb	12nm NW of Bury St Edmunds N5221.72 E00029.18	PPR MIL	Alternative AD Diversion AD	Cambridge Bourn

Mildenhall	LARS Lakenheath 128.900	APP 128.900	TWR 122.550

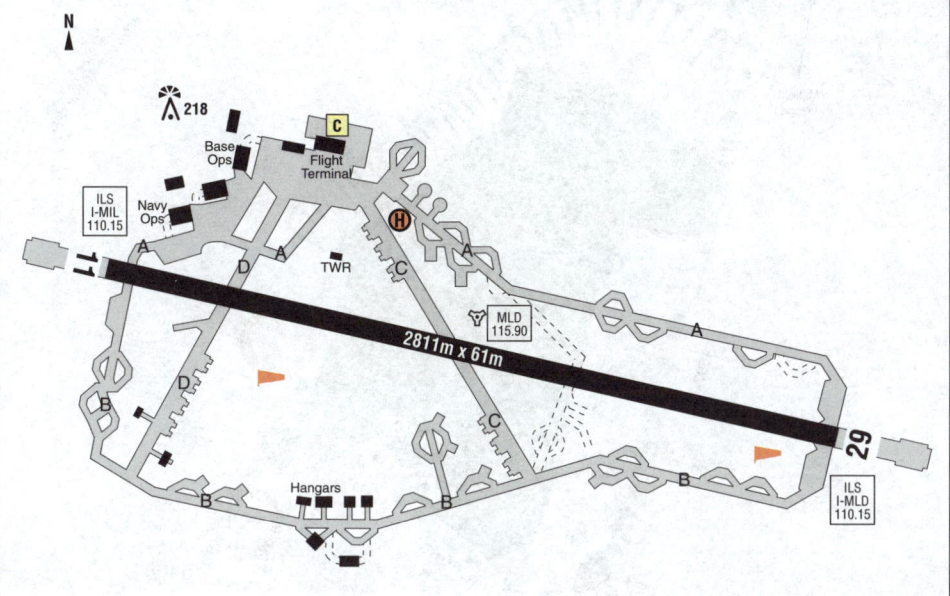

RWY	SURFACE	TORA	LDA	LIGHTING
11/29	Asph/Conc	2811	2811	Ap Thr Rwy PAPI 3° LHS

Remarks

PPR 24Hrs in advance. Military AD operated by USAF. Heavy jet movements may be encountered at any time. ILS for both Rwy29 & 11 uses DME element of TACAN MLD to provide distance from touchdown info.

Warnings

All movements under IFR. Ltd parking for visiting ACFT. Engine start for Dept must be requested from TWR. Rwy11 Dept are to commence turn on course at 1.8 DME MLD or 1nm from the AD boundary.

Operating Hrs	Mon-Thu 0600-2300 Fri-Sun 0600-1800 (Summer) +1Hr (Winter) & by arr ATZ H24	**Operator**	RAF Mildenhall Suffolk **Tel:** 01638 542251/53 (PPR through Base Ops) **Tel:** 01638 542121 (PPR outside office Hrs via 100 ARW/CC)
Circuits	As instructed by ATC		
Landing Fee	Charges in accordance with MOD policy Contact Station Ops for details		
Maintenance	Nil for visiting civil ACFT		
Fuel	JET A1 only by arr to visiting civil ACFT		
Disabled Facilities	Nil		
Restaurants	Nil		
Taxis/Car Hire	Nil		
Weather Info	AirS MOEx		

M

160ft 5mb	4nm NW of Wooler N5535.35 W00205.10	PPR	Alternative AD	Newcastle Charterhall

Milfield	A/G 130.100	Manned during operating Hrs only

Milfield village

N

A697

Quarry

C

Quarry

Crushed stone heaps

Gas venting station
Do NOT overfly below 3100ft

Power lines 180ft agl
600m from AD boundary

RWY	SURFACE	TORA	LDA	LIGHTING

Maximun length 900m on Rwy31/13
All grass surface is useable

Remarks
PPR essential. No visiting ACFT accepted unless directly involved in Gliding Operations or in emergency. All landings at owners risk after radio contact with A/G.

Warnings
Do not over fly GVS on SSW corner of AD under any circumstances. AD is WW2 RAF Milfield, it is now a reclaimed gravel quarry and is 20ft below the surrounding terrain. This, and the slopes into AD at NW & NE boundary, may give an incorrect aspect of surface on APP. Surface is undulating but fairly smooth with well maintained grass surfaces. Wind gradient is severe in a strong S to SW wind with the possibility of MTW rotor down to the surface giving severe turbulence in the circuit and APP. **Noise:** Do not over fly Milfield village or any other settlement on the airfield boundary whilst landing or taking off.

Operating Hrs	Fri-Sun SR-SS & by arr	**Operator**	The Borders (Milfield) Gliding Club Ltd Milfield Airfield Wooler Northumberland, NE71 6HD **Tel:** 01668 216284 www.bordersgliding.co.uk
Circuits	Advised by radio on Arr Join overhead 1500ft QFE		
Landing Fee	Private ACFT £10		
Maintenance	Nil		
Fuel	Nil except in emergency (AVGAS 100LL)		
Restaurants	Tea Coffee and light snacks when gliding in progress. Local Cafes Restaurants and Pubs		
Taxis	By arr		
Car Hire	Nil		
Weather Info	AirN MWC		

M

500ft 16mb	3nm WSW of Cleobury Mortimer N5221.69 W00232.74	PPR	Alternative AD	Birmingham Wolverhampton

Non-radio	ATIS Birmingham 126.275	APP Birmingham 118.050	LARS Shawbury 120.775	Safetycom 135.475

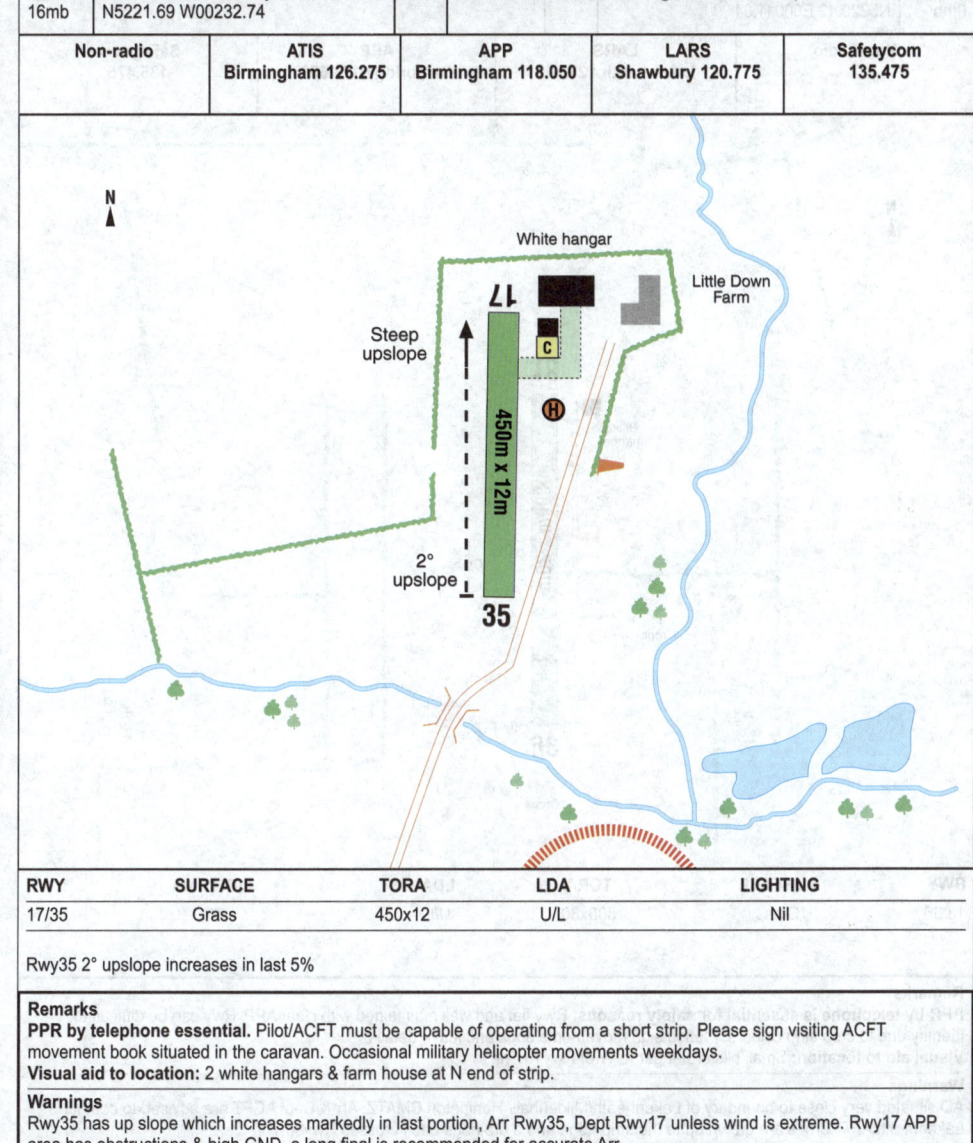

RWY	SURFACE	TORA	LDA	LIGHTING
17/35	Grass	450x12	U/L	Nil

Rwy35 2° upslope increases in last 5%

Remarks

PPR by telephone essential. Pilot/ACFT must be capable of operating from a short strip. Please sign visiting ACFT movement book situated in the caravan. Occasional military helicopter movements weekdays.
Visual aid to location: 2 white hangars & farm house at N end of strip.

Warnings

Rwy35 has up slope which increases markedly in last portion, Arr Rwy35, Dept Rwy17 unless wind is extreme. Rwy17 APP area has obstructions & high GND, a long final is recommended for accurate Arr.
Caution: Clee Hill 1750ft amsl 2nm NW. Cross winds & terrain induced turbulence are often a problem. Model rocket launching Sundays pm.
Noise: Avoid over flying white house SE of AD.

Operating Hrs	10 flights a day is max permissible under planning consent. Arr only (no Dept) 1400-1700 (L) on Sun (April-Sept)	**Operator**	Chris Jones Little Down Farm Milson, Kidderminster Worcs, DY14 OBD **Tel:** 01584 890486 (AD PPR) **Tel:** 0777 5582023 www.milsonairstrip.co.uk	
Circuits	35 LH, 17 RH			
Landing Fee	£2			
Maintenance	Nil			
Fuel	Ltd AVGAS/MOGAS by arr			
Disabled Facilities	Nil			
Restaurants	Nil Toilet facilities available			
Taxis/Car Hire	Nil			
Weather Info	AirN MCW			

M

10ft 0mb	8nm N of Cambridge Airport N5220.42 E00011.04	PPR	Alternative AD	Cambridge Bourn

Non-Radio	LARS Lakenheath 128.900	APP Cambridge 123.600	Safetycom 135.475

N ▲

18

Crops

Blister hangar

800m x 30m

Crops

Crops

36

Crops

RWY	SURFACE	TORA	LDA	LIGHTING
18/36	Grass	800x30	U/L	Nil

Remarks

PPR by telephone is essential for safety reasons. Rwy flat and well maintained with clear APP. Rwy can be difficult to identify due to crop strip colours. Please sign movements book and leave details.
Visual aid to location: Small blister hangar to W of Rwy18 Thr.

Warnings

AD situated very close to boundary of Lakenheath/Mildenhall/ Honington CMATZ. Arr & Dept ACFT are advised to contact Lakenheath APP. Crops are grown up to the strip edge and a drainage ditch crosses Rwy36 Thr.
Noise: Avoid over flight of local habitation, particularly the village of Wilburton to N of AD

Operating Hrs	SR-SS	Operator	Mr A Furness
Circuits	LH 800ft QFE		Mitchells Farm, Millfield Lane Wilburton, Cambs, CB6 3SD
Landing Fee	Nil		**Tel:** 01353 740361
Maintenance	Nil		**Tel:** 07831 148084
Fuel	AVGAS 100LL by arr		

Disabled Facilities

✈ ☎ ✗ 🅿

Restaurants
Kings Head   Tel: 01353 741029

Taxis/Car Hire	Nil
Weather Info	AirCen MOEx

M

408

202ft	2nm W of Llangefni Anglesey	PPR	Alternative AD	Liverpool Caernarfon
7mb	N5315.52 W00422.40	MIL	Diversion AD	

Mona	LARS Valley 125.225	APP 125.225	A/G 118.950 (Flying Club)	TWR 119.175

(Aerodrome chart: Runway 04/22, 1666m x 46m, Asphalt. TWR with C symbol. A5 road. Arrester gear markings shown.)

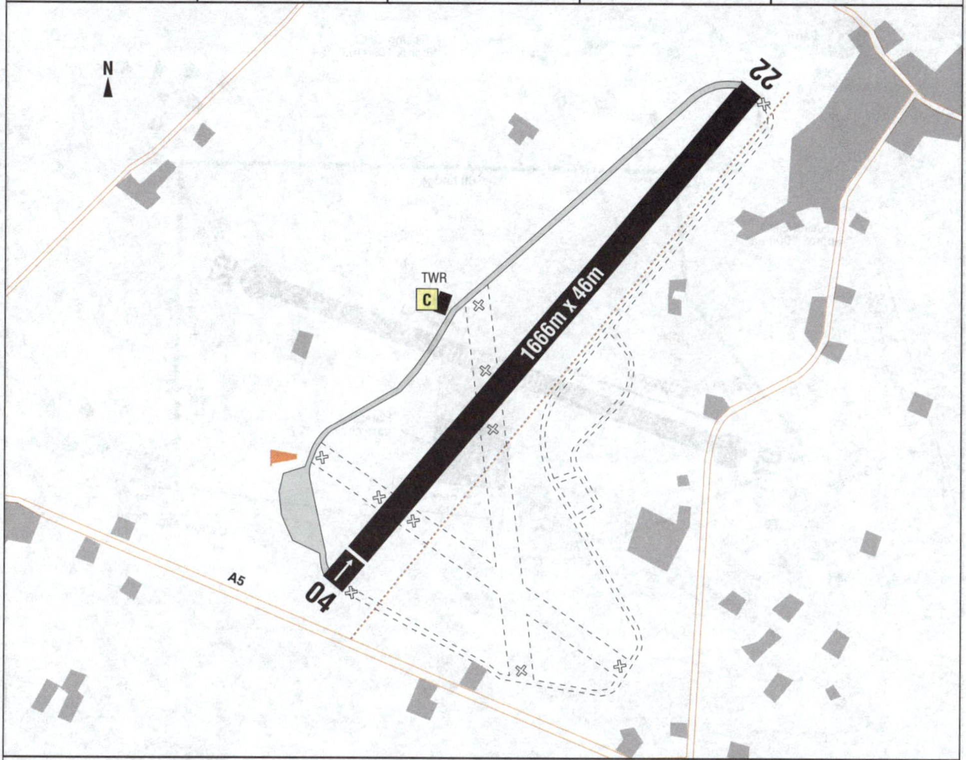

RWY	SURFACE	TORA	LDA	LIGHTING
04	Asphalt	1579	1524	Ap Thr Rwy PAPI 3°
22	Asphalt	1579	1579	Ap Thr Rwy PAPI 3°

Arrester gear Rwy04 Thr & Rwy22 Thr

Remarks
PPR during RAF operating Hrs through Valley Ops. Relief AD to RAF Valley. PPR obtained through Mona Flying Club evenings & W/E during BST. PPL/IMC/Night rating training available through flying club. Visiting pilots report to flying club near hangar.

Warnings
Visiting ACFT contact Valley before entering MATZ. Valley will transfer to Mona. If Valley does not answer contact Mona direct. DO NOT enter Valley MATZ or attempt to land if Valley or Mona cannot be contacted.
Noise: Avoid over flying Bodffordd, particularly downwind & base leg Rwy22.

Operating Hrs	Mon-Thu 0800-1800 Fri 0800-1730 (L)	**Disabled Facilities**	
Mona Flying Club:	Mon-Fri 1800-SS Sat-Sun 0900-1800 (Summer) Sat-Sun 0900-SS (Winter)		
Circuits	04 RH, 22 LH, 800ft QFE Join dead side not below 2000ft QFE On APP Rwy04 cross A5 not below 200ft QFE	**Restaurants**	Nil
		Taxis/Car Hire	Info in clubhouse
		Weather Info	AirN MWC
Landing Fee	Members: free Visitors: Charges in accordance with MOD policy. Contact Station Ops for details	**Operator**	RAF Valley Mona Flying Club RAF Valley Holyhead Gwynedd LL65 3NY **Tel:** 01407 762241 Ex 7450 (PPR RAF Ops Hrs) **Tel:** 01407 720581 (PPR Mona Flying Club Hrs) www.flymona.com
Maintenance	Nil but hangarage available		
Fuel	Nil		

M

180ft 6mb	4nm NW of Kilrea Northern Ireland N5459.25 W00638.81	PPR	Alternative AD	Londonderry

	Movenis Drop Zone		A/G 129.900	

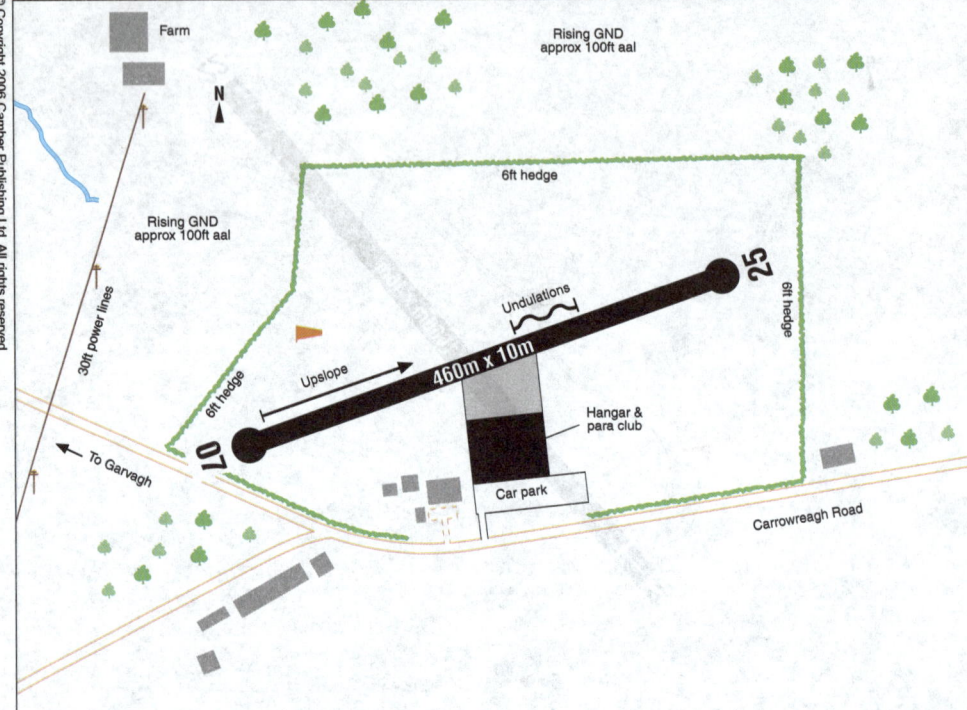

RWY	SURFACE	TORA	LDA	LIGHTING
07/25	Asphalt	460x10	U/L	Nil

Remarks

PPR by telephone. Primarily a parachute centre but light ACFT & microlights welcome. Rwy has undulating surface. No Rwy designators. The AD is situated in a very scenic rural area, Although this AD is not notified as a point of entry/exit under the terms of the Prevention of Terrorism Act permission will normally be granted after contact with The Police Service of Northern Ireland.

Warnings

Inbound ACFT should call Movenis to ascertain parachuting status; free fall parachuting takes place up to FL120. Parachutists use the nearby drop zone at Garvagh. Visiting pilots are requested to avoid transiting this area. AD is surrounded by a hedge and rolling hills.

Operating Hrs	SR-SS	**Operator**	Wild Geese Skydiving Centre
Circuits	Standard overhead join LH both Rwys		Movenis Airfield Garvagh Coleraine Co Londonderry BT51 5LQ
Landing Fee	Nil		**Tel:** 02829 558609 (PPR)
Maintenance	Nil		**Tel:** 02890 650222 (PSNI)
Fuel	Nil		**Fax:** 02829 557050
Disabled Facilities	Nil		jump@skydivewildgeese.com
Restaurants/Accomodation			www.skydivewildgeese.com
	Tea & Coffee at AD. Restaurants & hotel at Garvagh. Accommodation can be provided in the parachute clubhouse for £5 per night. Other neighbouring hotels & B&B's can be recommended		
Taxis/Car Hire	Nil		
Weather Info	AirN BEL		

M

180ft 6mb	5nm NW of Colchester N5158.29 E00051.03	**PPR**	**Alternative AD**	**Southend** Earls Colne

Non-radio	**LARS** Southend 130.775	**APP** Wattisham 125.800	**Safetycom** 135.475

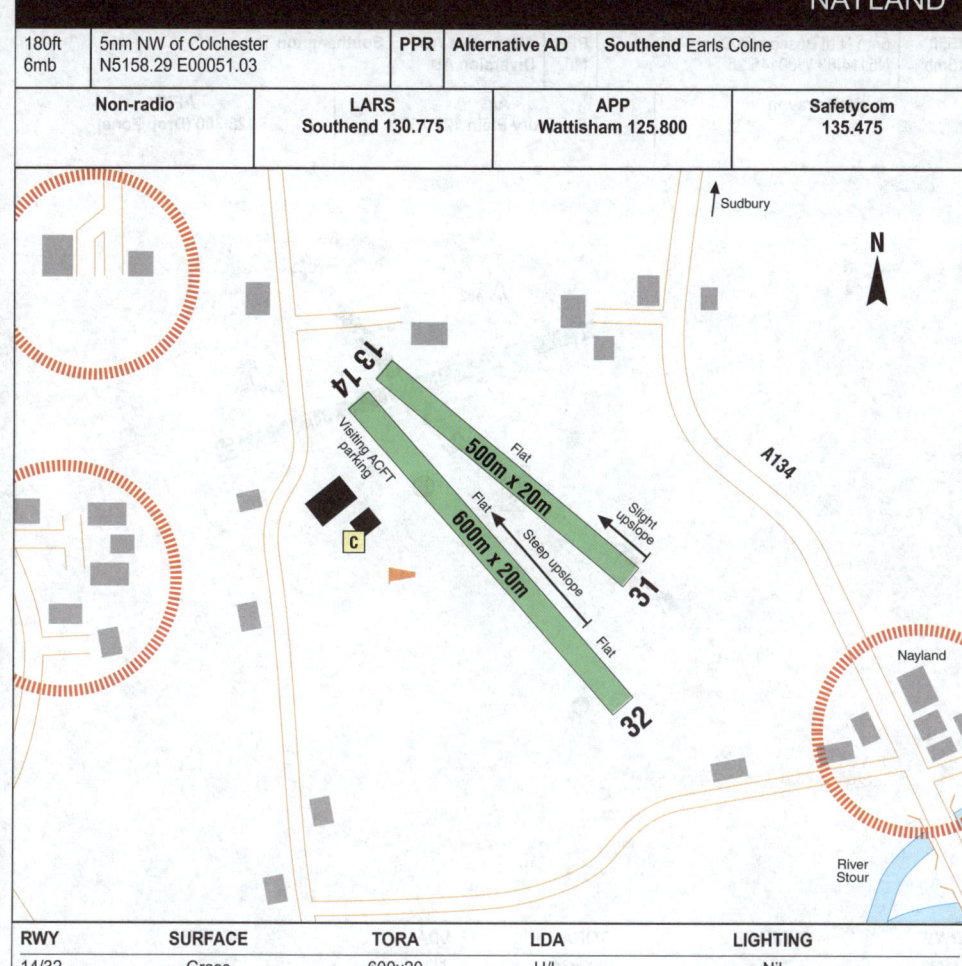

RWY	SURFACE	TORA	LDA	LIGHTING
14/32	Grass	600x20	U/L	Nil
13/31	Grass	500x20	U/L	Nil

Remarks
PPR by telephone for briefing essential. Visitors welcome at own risk. Rwy is delineated with white edge markers. Steep up slope Rwy32. Unless in extreme conditions land Rwy32 Dept Rwy14

Warnings
Noise: Avoid over flying Nayland to SE, hospital to W and large house to NW.

Operating Hrs	SR-SS	**Operator**	Mr R Harris
Circuits	LH 800ft QFE		Nayland Flying Group
Landing Fee	£2		Hill Farm, Wiston
Maintenance	**Tel:** 01206 263178 (Clubroom)		Nayland, CO6 4NL
	Tel: 01206 230333		**Tel:** 01206 262298
Fuel	AVGAS 100LL Cash only		**Tel:** 07887 594355
Disabled Facilities Nil			
Restaurants	Light refreshments available at weekends		
Taxis	**Tel:** 01206 262049		
Car Hire	**Tel:** 07979 640040		
Weather Info	AirS MOEx		

N

411

455ft 15mb	5nm N of Boscombe Down N5114.83 W00145.25	PPR MIL	Alternative AD Diversion AD	Southampton Thruxton

Netheravon	A/G Salisbury Plain 122.750	AFIS 128.300 (Drop Zone)

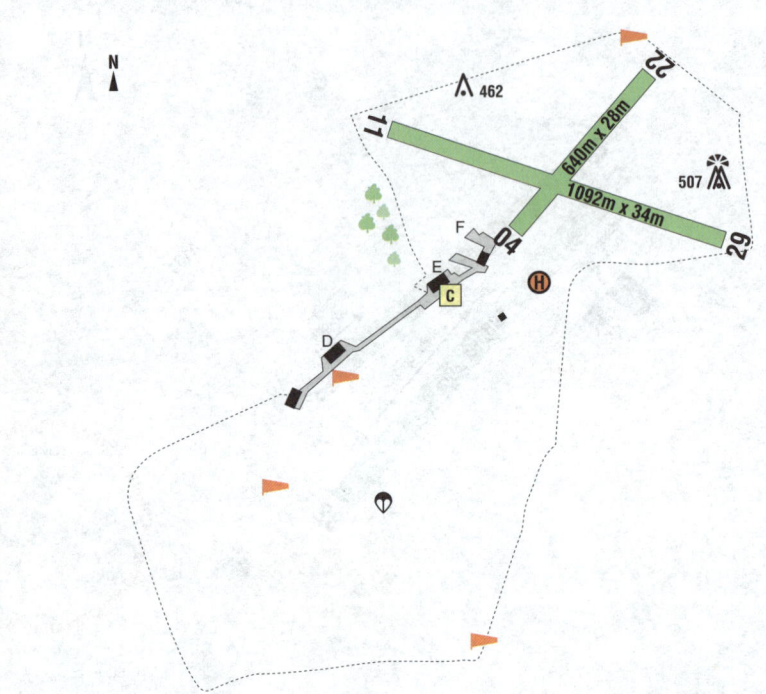

RWY	SURFACE	TORA	LDA	LIGHTING
11/29	Grass	1092x34	U/L	Thr Rwy
04/22	Grass	640x28	U/L	Rwy

Remarks
PPR essential due to special procedures associated with D128. Military AD. Inbound pilots to contact Salisbury Plain to ascertain range status at least 10nm from the Danger Area boundary before contacting Netheravon.

Warnings
AD used for parachuting up to FL150. Outside ATC Ops Hrs parachute Drop zone will operate using call sign Drop Zone. All ACFT must call for start up clearance.

Operating Hrs	Mon-Fri 0800-1700 (L) Military useage may be outside these times	**Operator**	MOD (Army) Netheravon Airfield Salisbury Plain, Wiltshire **Tel:** 01980 678289
Circuits	11, 22 LH, 29, 04 RH, 1000ft QFE remaining outside Boscombe MATZ		
Landing Fee	Charges in accordance with MOD policy Contact Station Ops for details		
Maintenance	Nil		
Fuel	JET A1		
Disabled Facilities	Nil		
Restaurants	Nil		
Taxis/Car Hire	Nil		
Weather Info	AirSW MOEx		

254ft 8mb	2.5nm WNW of Worksop N5319.02 W00111.78	PPR	Alternative AD Diversion AD	Doncaster Sheffield Retford

Netherthorpe	APP Doncaster 126.225	A/G 123.275

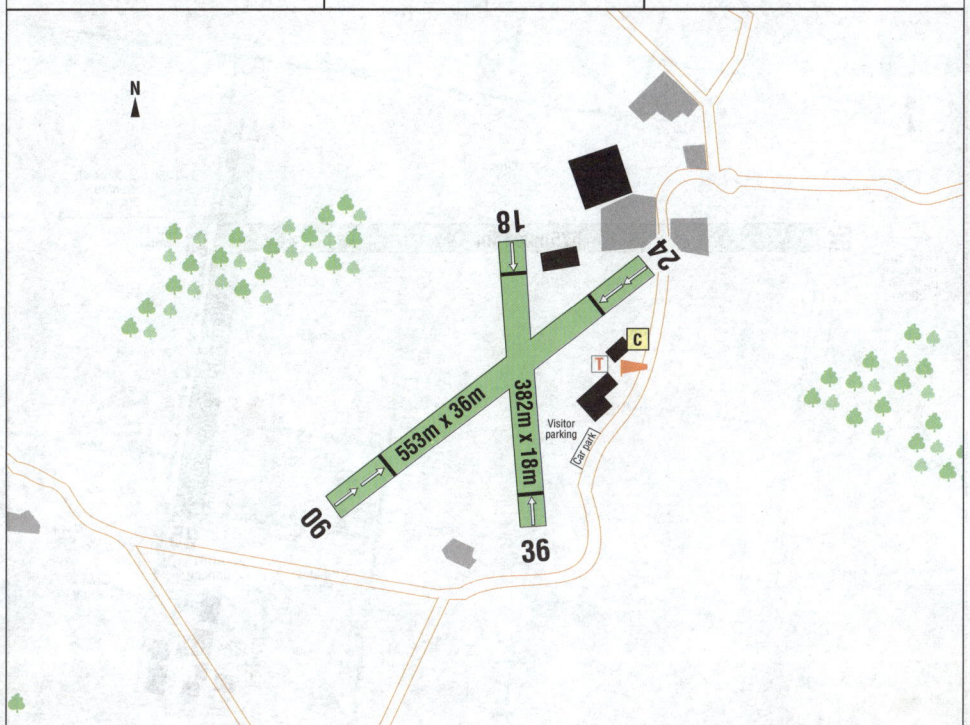

RWY	SURFACE	TORA	LDA	LIGHTING
06	Grass	476	407	Nil
24	Grass	490	370	Nil
18	Grass	382	357	Nil
36	Grass	382	309	Nil

Starter extension Rwy06 38m 1.9% down, Displaced Thr Rwy06 92m, Displaced Thr Rwy24 120m
Displaced Thr Rwy18 25m, Displaced Thr Rwy36 73m

Remarks
Strict PPR by telephone. Inexperienced pilots and/or unsuitable ACFT may be refused due to short Rwy lengths. ACFT Arr/Dept from N or E contact Doncaster APP.

Warnings
When Rwy06/24 in use, ACFT may be parked at S end of Rwy18/36. Pilots whose APP would result in being below 20ft crossing the road must initiate an immediate missed APP.
Noise: Avoid over flying the villages of Shireoaks, Thorpe Salvin and Whitwell.

Operating Hrs	0930-2000 or SS (Summer) 0900-1700 or SS (Winter) & by arr	**Car Hire** Hertz National	**Tel:** 01142 796644 **Tel:** 01142 754111
Circuits	06 36 RH, 18 24 LH, 800ft QFE	**Weather Info**	AirCen MWC
Landing Fee	Single £7.93, Helicopters £16.36 PFA members free. Free with 20L fuel uplift	**Operator**	Sheffield Aero Club Ltd Netherthorpe Aerodrome Thorpe Salvin, Worksop, Notts
Maintenance Dukeries Aviation **Fuel**	Tel: 01909 481802 AVGAS 100LL by arr		**Tel:** 01909 475233 (Ops) **Tel:** 01909 473428 (Clubhouse) **Fax:** 01909 532413 sac@sheffieldaeroclub.force9.co.uk
Disabled Facilities Nil			
Restaurant	Restaurant facilities available at AD		
Taxis Nunns	**Tel:** 01909 500005		

9ft 0mb	1.5nm S of RAF Coningsby N5304.03 W00009.16	PPR	Alternative AD	Nottingham East Midlands Fenland

Non-Radio	LARS Waddington 127.350	APP Coningsby 120.800	Safetycom 135.475

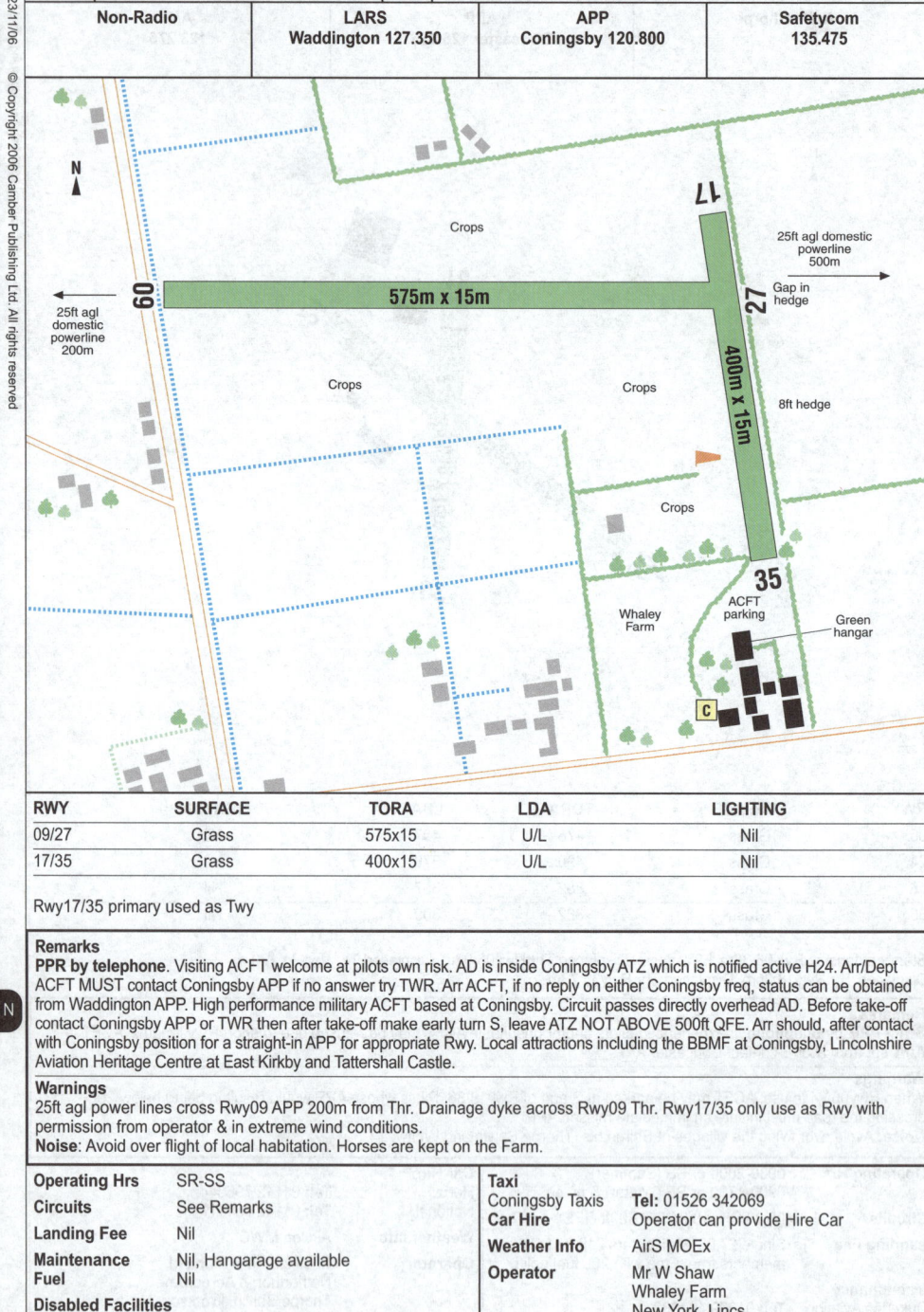

RWY	SURFACE	TORA	LDA	LIGHTING
09/27	Grass	575x15	U/L	Nil
17/35	Grass	400x15	U/L	Nil

Rwy17/35 primary used as Twy

Remarks
PPR by telephone. Visiting ACFT welcome at pilots own risk. AD is inside Coningsby ATZ which is notified active H24. Arr/Dept ACFT MUST contact Coningsby APP if no answer try TWR. Arr ACFT, if no reply on either Coningsby freq, status can be obtained from Waddington APP. High performance military ACFT based at Coningsby. Circuit passes directly overhead AD. Before take-off contact Coningsby APP or TWR then after take-off make early turn S, leave ATZ NOT ABOVE 500ft QFE. Arr should, after contact with Coningsby position for a straight-in APP for appropriate Rwy. Local attractions including the BBMF at Coningsby, Lincolnshire Aviation Heritage Centre at East Kirkby and Tattershall Castle.

Warnings
25ft agl power lines cross Rwy09 APP 200m from Thr. Drainage dyke across Rwy09 Thr. Rwy17/35 only use as Rwy with permission from operator & in extreme wind conditions.
Noise: Avoid over flight of local habitation. Horses are kept on the Farm.

Operating Hrs	SR-SS	**Taxi**	
Circuits	See Remarks	Coningsby Taxis	**Tel:** 01526 342069
		Car Hire	Operator can provide Hire Car
Landing Fee	Nil	**Weather Info**	AirS MOEx
Maintenance	Nil, Hangarage available	**Operator**	Mr W Shaw
Fuel	Nil		Whaley Farm
Disabled Facilities			New York, Lincs
			Tel: 01205 280329
			Tel: 01526 347447 (Coningsby ATC)
			Tel: 07860 386340
			Waltershaw2@aol.com

Restaurants/Accommodation
Tea & Coffee available for visiting pilots. Self Catering accommodation available on AD

414

250ft 8mb	0.5nm E of Newbury N5123.65 W00118.87	PPR	Alternative AD	Oxford Thruxton

Non-radio	LARS Brize 124.270	LARS Farnborough 125.250	Safetycom 135.475

RWY	SURFACE	TORA	LDA	LIGHTING
11/29	Grass	830x30	U/L	Nil

Rwy29 Arrivals, Rwy11 Depts
Rwy has white corner & edge markers

Remarks
PPR by telephone. Visiting ACFT and helicopters welcome at pilots own risk. AD is strictly ONLY available to those involved or attending race meetings. Open race days only. **Pilots should book in & out at the race course office**. Comprehensive briefing notes are essential before Arr and Dept. The strip may be closed from time to time, please check with PPR.

Warnings
Situated in the middle of golf course but play is suspended race days. **ACFT movements are not allowed** 30min before the first race until 30min after the final race or **when horses are on the track**. Copse of mature trees 200m W of Rwy11 Thr. When white X is in place on W end, do not land and all engines are to be shut down. This is changed to a white T when landing appropriate. **AD is periodically closed to fixed wing ACFT.** Helicopters may land when Rwy closed. **Noise:** Avoid built-up areas to W, N & S.

Operating Hrs	Race days only PPR 1st race 2 Hrs until SS	**Taxis** Baileys of Newbury **Car Hire**	**Tel:** 01635 40661 Nil
Circuits	N 1000ft QFE Orbit N for best views of racecourse	**Weather Info** **Operator**	AirSW MOEx Newbury Racecourse PLC
Landing Fee	Nil Groundsman fund donations gratefully appreciated (box in racecourse office)		Newbury, Berks, RG14 7NZ **Tel:** 01635 40015 (PPR/Racecourse Office)
Maintenance **Fuel**	Nil Nil		**Fax:** 01635 528354 info@newbury-racecourse.co.uk
Disabled Facilities	Nil		
Restaurant	Extensive facilities in racecourse stands		

266ft 9mb	5nm NW of Newcastle-upon-Tyne N5502.25 W00141.50	PPR	Alternative AD Diversion AD	Durham Tees Valley Eshott

Newcastle	ATIS 118.375	LARS 124.375	APP 124.375	RAD 118.500
GND 121.725	TWR 119.700	FIRE 121.600	Handling 130.650	

RWY	SURFACE	TORA	LDA	LIGHTING
07	Asphalt	2329	2209	Ap Thr Rwy PAPI 3° RHS
25	Asphalt	2262	2125	Ap Thr Rwy PAPI 3° LHS

Remarks

PPR to non-radio ACFT. Hi-Vis. ACFT towing banners may not operate to or from AD. The grass verges along the sides of the Rwy and Twys are soft in many places. Hangar entrances should remain unobstructed. In association with the Fire Station and Rwy link road located mid-way along the parallel Twy, 2 Twy holding points D6 and D7 are introduced to hold ACFT for AFS deployment. Booking out details should be passed by telephone. (including those inbound from or returning to the EU) are required to nominate a handling agent. For GA flights Samson Aviation operates a full GA Terminal and will arrange any necessary clearances Helicopter Ops 1). As directed by ATC 2) Helicopters must use the Rwy for take-off & landing 3) Helicopters parking on the S apron at positions Papa W or Papa E are restricted to Jet Ranger size and below 4) Limited helicopter training area available, contact ATC. Handling is provided by Swissport UK NE & Servisair.

Aids to Navigation: NDB NT 352.00

Warnings

Gliding may take place at Currock Hill gliding site, 8nm SW of Newcastle AD from dawn to dusk. ATC will advise when active. ACFT using the ILS in IMC or VMC shall not descend on APP to Rwy25 below 1500ft QFE and on Rwy07 below 2300ft QFE before intercepting the glide path and shall not thereafter fly below it. ACFT APP without assistance from RAD or ILS shall follow a descent path not lower than the ILS glide path. ACFT must not join the final APP track to either Rwy at a height of less than 1500ft QFE (1800ft QNH) unless they are a propeller driven ACFT whose MTWA <5700kg when the minimum height shall be 1000ft QFE (1300ft QNH). The portion of Twy E to the W of the Belman hangar has a wing span clearance <17m. When Rwy25 is in use and wind direction is from 160-190° expect turbulence and possible negative gradient. Model ACFT flying takes place at Gosforth Racecourse 2.5nm Se of AD. Bird activity from nature reserve N of NT beacon 1.2nm from Rwy25.

Operating Hrs	H24	**Restaurant**	Restaurant & Club facilities available at AD
Circuits	Variable as advised by ATC	**Taxis**	Available at Main & GA Terminals
Landing Fee	ACFT <2 tonnes £29.38		Metro link to Newcastle
Maintenance			GA Terminal has courtesy coach
M3 GA Terminal	**Tel: 0191 286 4156**	**Car Hire**	
Fuel	Check availability with fuelling companies	Hertz	**Tel: 0870 1221488 Ex 4281**
	AVGAS 100LL	Budget	**Tel: 0870 1221488 Ex 4393**
Samson Av	**Tel: 0191 286 4156**	Europcar	**Tel: 0870 1221488 Ex 4382**
	JET A1	Avis	**Tel: 0191 286 0815**
Swissport Ltd	**Tel: 0191 214 4562**	**Weather Info**	M T9 T18 Fax 376 A VN MWC
Disabled Facilities			ATIS **Tel: 0191 214 3400/3401**

		Operator	Newcastle Int Airport Ltd
Handling	Samson Aviation		Newcastle Airport, Woolsington
	Tel: 0191 286 4156		Newcastle-upon-Tyne, NE13 8BZ
	Tel: 0191 214 5916 (Out of Hrs)		**Tel: 0870 122 1488 (Switchboard)**
	Fax: 0191 286 5347		**Tel: 0870 122 1488 Ex 3244 (ATC)**
			Fax: 0191 214 3254 (ATC)
			www.newcastleinternational.co.uk

© Copyright 2006 Camber Publishing Ltd. All rights reserved

Effective date:23/11/06

CTR-Class D Airspace
Normal CTA/CTR Class D Airspace rules apply
Transition Alt 6000ft
These rules do not apply by day to non-radio ACFT provided they have obtained permission and maintain 5km visibility, 1500m horizontally and 1000ft vertically away from cloud, or for gliders provided they maintain 8km visibility, 1500m horizontally and 1000ft vertically away from cloud.

Visual Reference Points (VRP)

VRP	VOR/DME
Blaydon N5458.10 W00141.62	NEW 181°/4nm
Blyth Wind Farm N5507.40 W00129.62	NEW 057°/9nm
Bolam lake N5507.88 W00152.47	NEW 316°/8nm
Derwent Reservoir N5420.00 W00158.47	NEW 226°/16nm
Durham N5446.43 W00134.60	NEW 168°/16nm
Hexham N5458.25 W00206.17	NEW 257°/15nm
Morpeth Rly Station N5509.75 W00140.97	NEW 007°/7nm
Ouston (Disused AD) N5501.50 W00152.52	NEW 266°/6nm
Stagshaw Masts N5502.00 W00201.42	NEW 272°/11nm
Sunderland Harbour N5455.06 W00121.30	NEW 124°/14nm
Tyne Bridges N5458.05 W00136.42	NEW 146°/5nm

N

D512
18000
(ONCL 2500)
SFC

D512A
22000
SFC

D508
4100
SFC

ESHOTT

CAUSEY PARK

N

L602 A
FL245
FL205

VRP
MORPETH
RWY STA

VRP
BOLAM LAKE

P18 D
FL245
FL155

GVS
1000
SFC

400
(394)

485
(650)

WINDFARM

BLYTH
VRP
BLYTH
WIND FARM

3000 D
FL105

1500 D
FL105

Colt Crag
Reservoir

WINDFARM

Halington
Reservoir
1210
(485)

SFC D
FL105

NEWCASTLE

NT

P18 D
FL125
FL75

1500 D
FL105

HELWOOD

VRP
STAGSHAW
MASTS

VRP
OUSTON

GVS
1000
SFC

FORMER PENNINE RADAR AREA

VRP
HEXAM

465
(327)

VRP
TYNE
BRIDGES

605

cables

418

FL245
FL155

VRP
BLAYDON

302
(295)

CITY HELI

VRP
SUNDERLAND
HARBOUR

1015

CURROCK
HILL

456
(386)

3000 D
FL105

VRP
DERWENT
RESERVOIR

P18 D
FL125
FL55

P18 A
FL245
FL125

1506
(489)

WINDFARM

1552
(765)

WINDFARM

R432
2200
SFC

3000
FL55

VRP
DURHAM

WINDFARM

4500
FL55

CTA D
6000
1000

CTR E
1000
SFC

VRP
HARTLEPOOL

P18 D
FL125
FL55

P18 A
FL245
FL125

CTA D
6000
3000

351
(325)

P18 D
FL125
FL75

P18 A
FL245
FL125

6000
FL75

GSV
3000
SFC

730
(304)

FISHBURN

S'FIELD R'CSE D

R446
2000
SFC

418
(400)

425
(402)

421
(400)

434
(385)

cables

335
(323)

TD

P18 D
FL125
FL75

P18 A
FL245
FL125

DURHAM TEES VALLEY CTR D
6000
SFC

P18 D
FL125
FL105

P18 A
FL245
FL125

TILNI

DURHAM TEES
VALLEY

R408
2500
(ONCL 5600)
SFC

VRP
M'WAY JUNC

VRP
STOKESLEY

N

| 100ft 3mb | 1.5nm W of Newmarket N5214.50 E00022.33 | PPR | Alternative AD | Cambridge Duxford |

| Non-radio | APP Cambridge 123.600 | APP Lakenheath 128.900 | Safetycom 135.475 |

Rowley Mile

Devils Ditch

Rowley Mile Stands

July Landing Strip

National Stud Farm

RWY	SURFACE	TORA	LDA	LIGHTING
18/36	Grass	792x20	U/L	Nil
10/28	Grass	762x20	U/L	Nil
14/32	Grass	914x70	July U/L	Nil

Remarks

PPR open race days only. Visits at pilots own risk. Two separate strips on race course. No flights 30mins before first race until 30mins after last race, unless extreme circumstances, via racecourse manager if horses are within parade ring. Non race days July strip is only available, strictly PPR through Jockey Club Estates.
Rowley mile landing area: Available when racing Rowley mile course 1200-1800 (L) PPR.
July Strip: Restricted use both race & non-race days. PPR, briefing sheet MUST be obtained prior to Arr. Rwy14 arrivals, Rwy32 depts.
All landing & take-offs banned when yellow or white cross is displayed at S end of strip.

Warnings

Noise: Stud farms & training facilities in local area. Correct adherence to local restrictions essential. ACFT are prohibited to fly over the crowd/grandstands on race days.

Operating Hrs	Available on request	**Operator**	Jockey Club Estates
Circuits	Nil		Jockey Club Offices, 101 High Street
Landing Fee	Nil Race days, £23.50 non-race days		Newmarket, Suffolk, CB8 8JL
Maintenance	Nil		**Tel:** 01638 664151 (Non Race Day)
Fuel	Nil		**Tel:** 01638 662762 (Race Day)
			Tel: 01638 663482
Disabled Facilities	Nil		(PPR Non Race Day)
Restaurants	Racecourse facilities		**Tel:** 01638 662758 (PPR Race Day)
Taxis			**Tel:** 01638 663482 (Racecourse Office)
Chilcots	**Tel:** 01638 663282		**Tel:** 01638 664151 (Jockey Club Office)
Car Hire			newmarket@rht.net
Godfrey Davis	**Tel:** 01223 48198		www.newmarketracecourses.co.uk
Weather Info	AirS MOEx		

419

200ft 6mb	2.5nm N of Baldock N5201.42 W00009.45	PPR	Alternative AD	Cambridge Little Gransden

Non-Radio	APP Luton 129.550	Safetycom 135.475

N

30ft trees

Crops

60

750m x 15m

27

Slight upslope

Slight downslope

ACFT parking

15ft hedge

Crops

RWY	SURFACE	TORA	LDA	LIGHTING
09/27	Grass	750x15	U/L	Nil

Rwy27 first 75% slight down slope

Remarks
PPR by telephone. Visiting ACFT and Microlights welcome at pilots own risk. Operator is a BMAA approved inspector and check pilot (Flex-wing & 3 Axis) and welcomes fly-in inspections.

Warnings
Hedge & hangars in undershoot Rwy27. Crops are grown close to strip S edge.
Caution: Farm vehicles may use tracks which run along N of AD and across Rwy09 Thr.
Noise: Avoid over flying Newnham village 1nm to WSW.

N

			Operator	Kevin Woods
Operating Hrs	SR-SS			12 Ennerdale Close
Circuits	N 800ft QFE			Stukeley Meadows
Landing Fee	Nil			Huntingdon, PE29 6UU
Maintenance	Nil			**Tel:** 01480 434439
Fuel	MOGAS by prior arr			**Tel:** 07941 325992
	Lift can be provided to local garage			kevinwoods1@bulldoghome.com

Disabled Facilities

Restaurants	Nil
Taxis/Car Hire	Nil
Weather Info	AirS MOEx

120ft 4mb	4nm SE of Blandford Forum N5047.38 W00206.03	PPR	Alternative AD	Bournemouth Compton Abbas

Non-Radio	ATIS Bournemouth 121.950	LARS Bournemouth 119.475	Safetycom 135.475

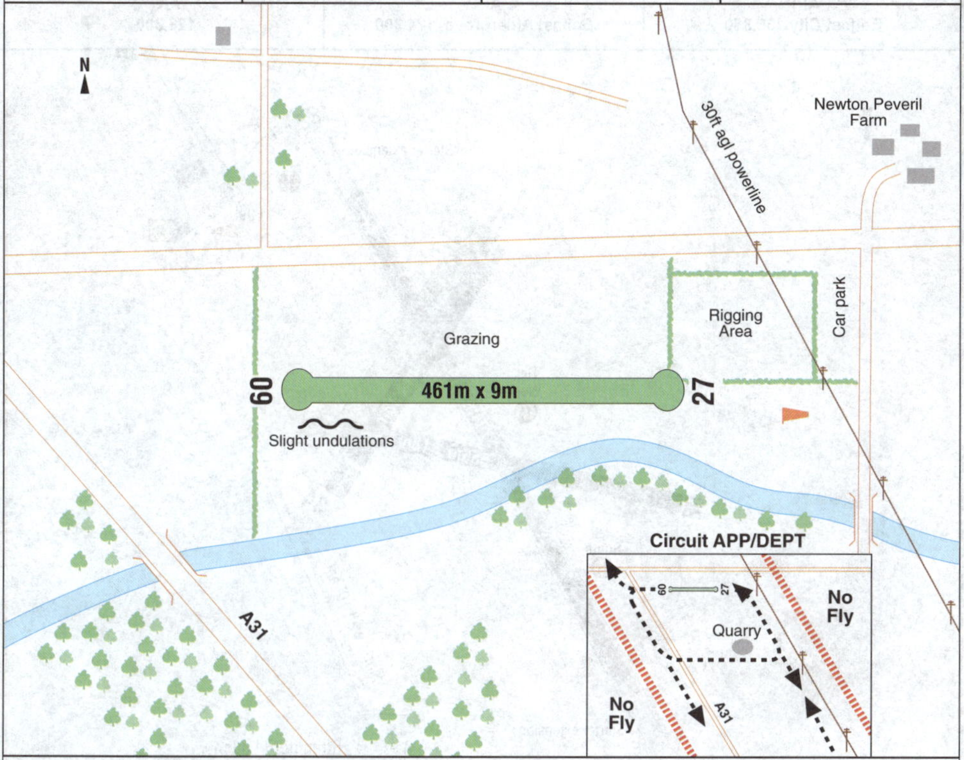

Map showing runway 09/27, 461m x 9m grass runway, Newton Peveril Farm, 30ft agl powerline, Car park, Rigging Area, Grazing, Slight undulations, A31, Circuit APP/DEPT inset with Quarry, No Fly zones

Circuit APP/DEPT

No Fly
No Fly
Quarry
A31

RWY	SURFACE	TORA	LDA	LIGHTING
09/27	Grass	461x9	U/L	Nil

Rwy09 Thr undulations

Remarks
PPR by telephone. Visiting ACFT & Microlights very welcome at pilot's own risk. AD situated under the W end of the Solent CTA, base 2000ft QNH.

Warnings
33,000 volt power cables (on H poles) 30ft agl cross Rwy27 APP on short final. Stream bounded by trees S of Rwy may cause turbulence when wind SW-SE. Cattle maybe grazing.
Noise: Essential that visitors follow the noise abatement circuit pattern shown on the inset to the AD diagram. Landing Rwy27: APP from S along power lines keeping them close to your right. Keep final tight and DO NOT over fly the habitation E or Sturminster Marshall. Landing Rwy09: APP from S along power lines turn LH downwind at the disused quarry. Base leg at the A31. Do not over fly Charborough Park.

Operating Hrs	SR-SS	Operator	Tim Trenchard

Circuits	09 RH, 27 LH, 500ft QFE
Landing Fee	Nil donations to mowing fund welcome
Maintenance	Nil
Fuel	MOGAS. Garage 3.5 miles owner can help if you are desparate

Operator: Tim Trenchard
Newton Peveril Farm
Sturminster Marshall
Wimborne, Dorset, BH21 4AN
Tel: 01258 857205

Disabled Facilities

Restaurants	Black Horse Pub 0.25 mile
Taxis/Car Hire	**Tel:** 01202 604422
Weather Info	AirS MOEx

9ft 0mb	8.5nm E of Belfast N5434.87 W00541.52	PPR	Alternative AD Diversion AD	Belfast Aldergrove Belfast City

Newtownards	ATIS Belfast City 136.620	ATIS Belfast Aldergrove 128.200
APP Belfast City 130.850	APP Belfast Aldergrove 124.900	A/G 128.300

RWY	SURFACE	TORA	LDA	LIGHTING
04	Asphalt	794	794	Thr Rwy APAPI 4.5°
22	Asphalt	794	720	Thr Rwy APAPI 4.5°
16	Asphalt	566	533	Nil
34	Asphalt	559	566	Nil
08	Asphalt	566	N/A	Nil
26	Asphalt	N/A	566	Nil
16/34	Grass	310x25	U/L	Nil

Starter extension Rwy04 150x12m, Starter extension Rwy22 80x12m
Displaced Thr Rwy26 60m, Displaced Thr Rwy22 74m
Displaced Thr Rwy16 85m, Displaced Thr Rwy34 75m
Rwy08 Dept only, Rwy26 landing only
Rwy26 not available to solo students

Remarks

PPR. Visiting ACFT welcome, not a designated AD under the Prevention of Terrorism Act. ACFT operating under restrictions of the act must contact The Police Service of Northern Ireland. AD U/L for ACFT >2730kgs.

Warnings

Situated on the shore of Strangford Lough with high GND & obstructions to W & N. Belfast City CTZ boundary close to N & W. **Obstructions:** Monument (lit) 591ft amsl 267°/0.9nm. HT cables on high GND 232ft aal within 0.5nm Rwy22 APP. Hill 705ft amsl 314°/2.8nm. High GND infringing Rwy26 climb out. Lamp stands on road may affect ACFT making a late decision to go-around on Rwy26. Turbulence may be experienced on a missed APP Rwy26. Pilots APP Rwy26 should satifsy themselves at or above 300ft that they will be able to land and stop. If any doubt exists pilots are advised to carry out a missed APP and early left turn to avoid high GND. ACFT landing Rwy26 without wheels firmly on the GND by Rwy22 intersection are advised to carry out a missed APP. Rwy34 possible pedestrian/vehicle traffic on sea wall, carry out missed APP if necessary. **Noise:** Avoid over flying bird sanctuary at Castle Espie.

Operating Hrs	0800-1600 (Summer) +1Hr (Winter) Late flying Tues & Thur 2000 (L) & by arr	**Operator**
Circuits	04 RH, 22/16/34 LH, 1000ft QFE Microlights 700ft QFE No circuits 26	
Landing Fee	Single £10, Light Twin £25	
Maintenance	Nil	
Fuel	AVGAS 100LL JET A1 by arr	
Disabled Facilities	Nil	
Restaurants	Nil	
Taxis Ards Cabs **Car Hire**	**Tel:** 02891 81111 Lindsay Car Rental **Tel:** 02891 474700	
Weather Info	AirN BEL ATIS **Tel:** 02890 734847 (Belfast City)	

Operator

Ulster Flying Club (1961) Ltd
Newtownards Aerodrome
Portaferry Road, Newtownards
County Down, BT23 8SG
Tel: 02891 813327
Fax: 02891 814575

Effective date:23/11/06

N

10ft 0mb	6nm SE of Grimsby N5330.25 E00003.73	PPR	Alternative AD	Humberside Wickenby

North Coates	DAIS Donna Nook Range 122.750	LARS Humberside 119.125	LARS Waddington 127.350	A/G 120.150

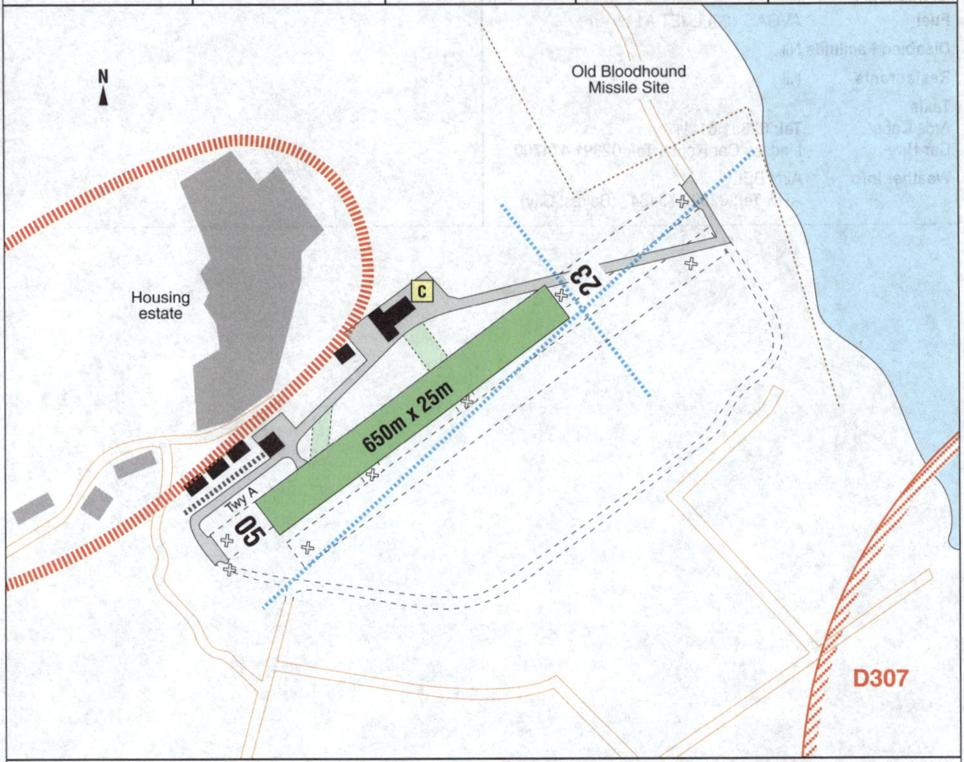

Old Bloodhound Missile Site

Housing estate

C

650m x 25m

23

Twy A

05

D307

RWY	SURFACE	TORA	LDA	LIGHTING
05/23	Grass	650x25	U/L	Nil

Remarks

PPR by telephone. Visiting ACFT welcome at pilots own risk. Inbound ACFT must call Donna Nook range 122.75 at least 5mins or 15nm from North Coates to determine range activity condition. APP AD from the W or SW and, if notified that Donna Nook (D307), N pattern is active, descend to fly at 500ft on Donna Nook QFE when within 2nm of North Coates. Advise Donna Nook when landing complete. D307 is not active at weekends. Please call Microlight School for AD information if no response from the club telephone. AD has a past stretching from WWI to the 80's when it was a bloodhound missile base.

Warnings

Sea breezes can cause localised wind effects.
Noise: Rwy23 Dept, turn left 10° to avoid North Coates village.

Operating Hrs	PPR 7 days	Operator	North Coates Flying Club
Circuits	05 RH, 23 LH or as directed by Donna Nook 500ft aal		Hangar 4 North Coates Airfield North Coates, Lincs, DN36 5XU
Landing Fee	Donations please		**Tel**: 01472 388850 (AD)
Maintenance	Ltd facilities Hangarage available		**Tel**: 01507 358716 Ex 130
Fuel	AVGAS weekends or by arr		(Donna Nook Range)
Disabled Facilities			steve.charters@virgin.net www.northcoatesflyingclub.co.uk **Tel**: 01472 388833 (Robert McKellar Aviation Microlight Flying School) **Tel**: 07881 828514 (Robert McKellar Aviation Microlight Flying School) info@robertmckellaravitaion.co.uk www.robertmckellaraviation.co.uk

Restaurants	Accommodation in village. Snack bar only with light refreshments on AD
Taxis/Car Hire	By arr
Weather Info	AirN MWC

NORTH MOOR

22ft 0mb	3.5nm SSW of Scunthorpe N5332.09 W00040.85	PPR	**Alternative AD** **Diversion AD**	**Humberside** Sandtoft

North Moor	**LARS** **Humberside 119.125**	**LARS** **Waddington 127.350**	**A/G** **119.275**

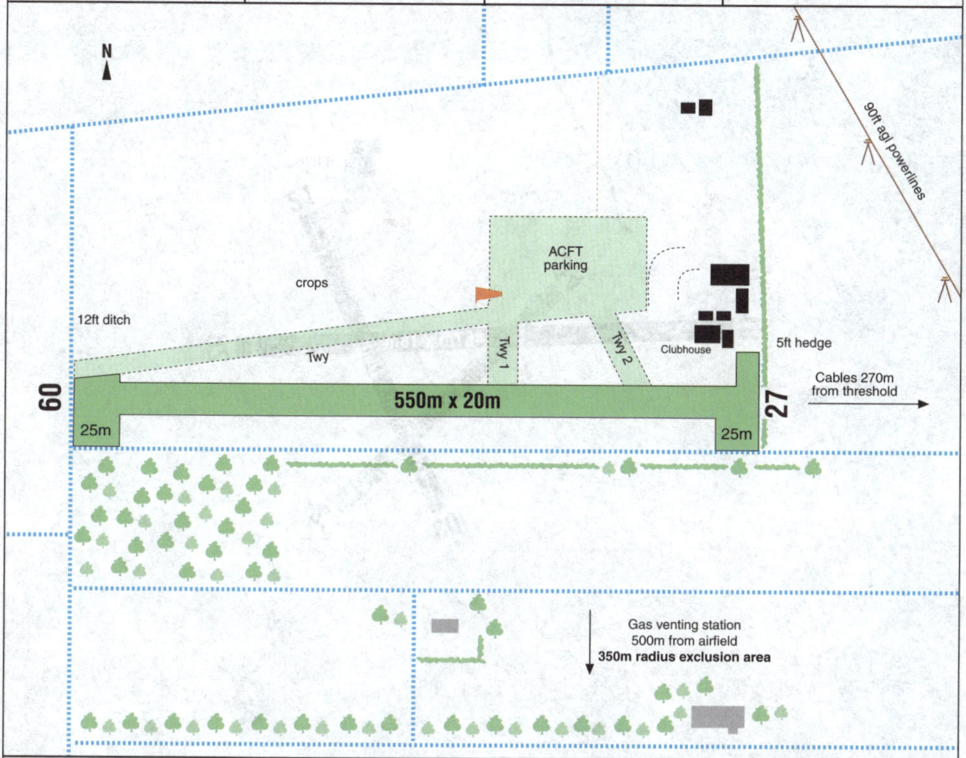

N
90ft agl powerlines
ACFT parking
crops
12ft ditch
Twy
Twy 1
Twy 2
Clubhouse
5ft hedge
09
550m x 20m
27
Cables 270m from threshold
25m
25m
Gas venting station
500m from airfield
350m radius exclusion area

RWY	SURFACE	TORA	LDA	LIGHTING
09/27	Grass	550x20	U/L	Nil

Rwy27 25m run-off area at each end

Remarks

PPR by telephone. Visiting ACFT welcome at pilots own risk. Due to planning restrictions Helicopters and ACFT >2300kgs MAUW cannot be accepted. Distance to go markers adjacent to Rwy show 200 & 400m points. Tie downs are available for visitors.

Warnings

90ft agl transmission lines cross Rwy27 APP 270m from Thr. 5m deep irrigation ditch runs along S AD boundary and crosses W boundary marked by orange & white boards. Gas compressor station 500m S of AD which has an exclusion zone 350m radius up to 3100ft QNH. **THIS MUST NOT BE OVERFLOWN.**

Noise: Avoid over fly Messingham village 1nm E of AD.

Operating Hrs	0730-1930 or SS (L)
Circuits	Variable 1000ft QFE Wide circuits must be flown
Landing Fee	Donations please
Maintenance	Nil
Fuel	Nil
Disabled Facilities	
Restaurants	B & B, Pub lunches & Bar meals available in Messingham 1nm E of AD
Taxis	Can be arr by operator **Tel:** 01724 841000
Car Hire	Nil

Weather Info	AirN MWC
Operator	E W & A Chapman North Moor Aero Club Ltd Low Hill Farm West Common North Road off North Moor Road Messingham, Scunthorpe Lincs, DN17 3PS **Tel/Fax:** 01724 851244 **Tel:** 07724 203764 www.northmoor.flyer.co.uk

Effective date:23/11/06

EGEN

NORTH RONALDSAY

| 40ft | 28nm NE by N of Kirkwall Airport | PPR | Alternative AD | Kirkwall Sanday |
| 1mb | N5922.05 W00226.07 | | Diversion AD | |

| **Non-Radio** | **APP**
Kirkwall 118.300 | **Safetycom**
135.475 |

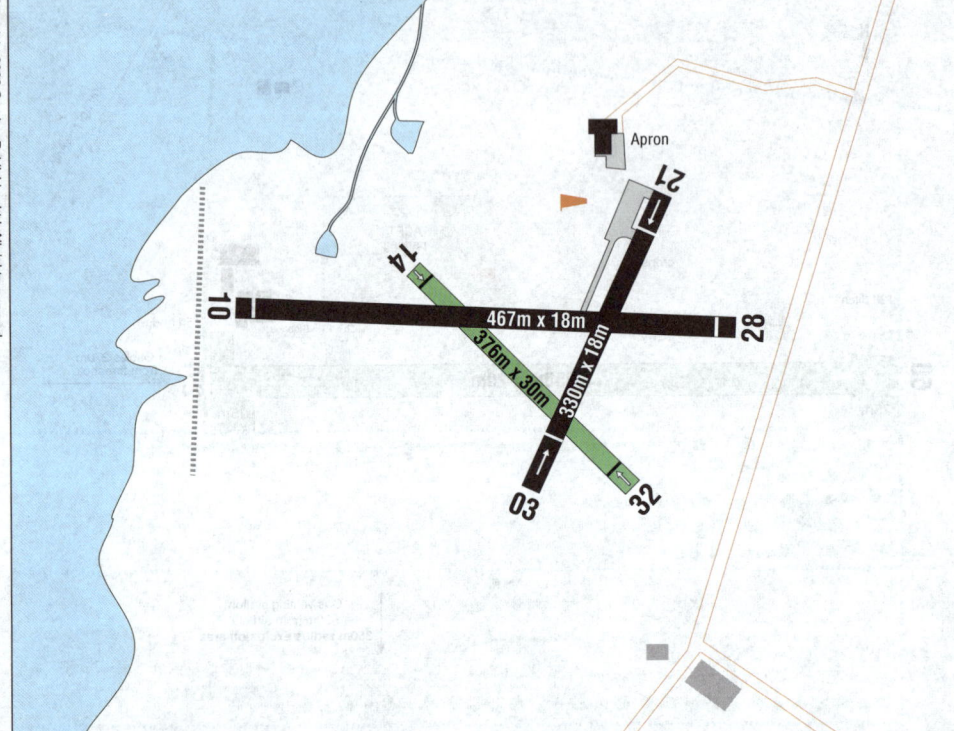

RWY	SURFACE	TORA	LDA	LIGHTING
10/28	Graded Hardcore	467	467	Rwy
14	Grass	336	356	Rwy
32	Grass	326	346	Nil
03	Graded Hardcore	310	276	Rwy
21	Graded Hardcore	314	314	Rwy

Starter extensions 15m available on all Rwys

Remarks
AD is used at pilot's own risk. Licensed AD (day use only).

Warnings
Lighthouse 100ft aal/140ft amsl 2.0nm 051° from APP.

Operating Hrs	SR-SS
Circuits	Nil
Landing Fee	Nil
	Fire cover £20.26 if required
Maintenance	Nil
Fuel	MOGAS (AD Goods & Services) **Tel:** 01857 633220
Disabled Facilities	Nil
Restaurants	Meals & accomodation at North Ronaldsay Bird Sanctuary **Tel:** 01857 633200 alison@nrbo.prestel.co.uk

Taxis/Car Hire	
Garso	**Tel:** 01857 633244
AD Goods & Svcs	**Tel:** 01857 633220
Weather Info	AirN GWC
Operator	Orkney Islands Council Offices Kirkwall, Orkney **Tel:** 01856 873535 **Fax:** 01856 876094

EGSX

NORTH WEALD

321ft 11mb	3.5nm SE of Harlow N5143.30 E00009.25	PPR	Alternative AD Diversion AD	Cambridge Stapleford

North Weald	APP Essex RAD 120.625	A/G 123.525

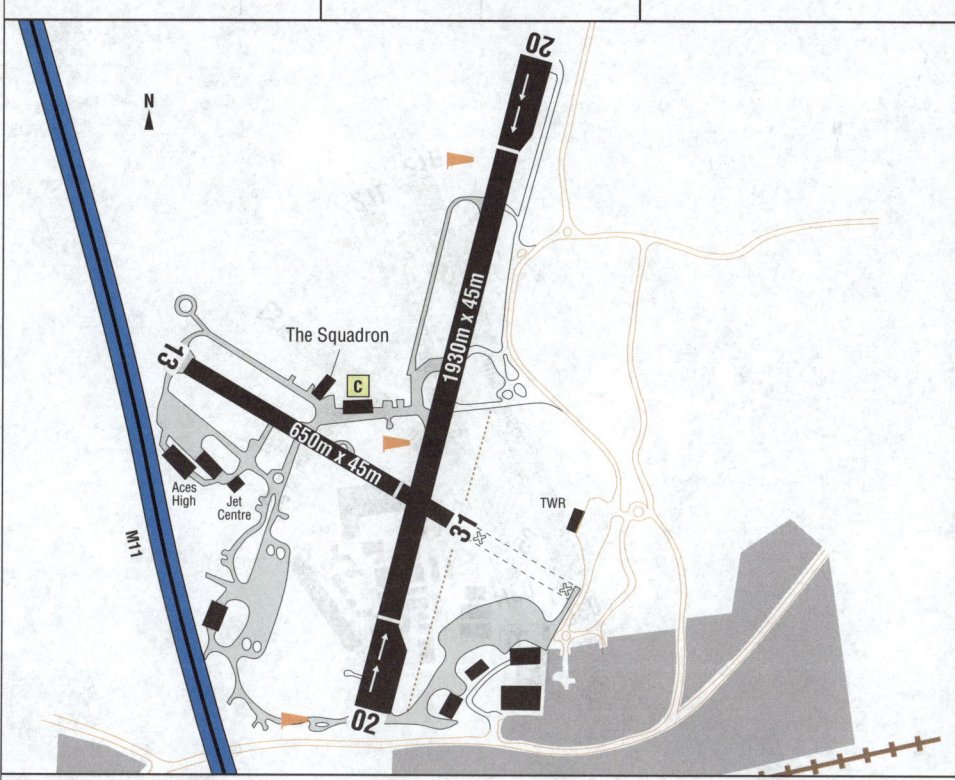

RWY	SURFACE	TORA	LDA	LIGHTING
02/20	Asphalt	1930x45	U/L	Nil
13/31	Asphalt	650x45	U/L	Nil

Remarks
PPR by telephone. Non-radio ACFT not accepted. AD is situated below the Stansted CTA base 1500ft. Contact Essex RAD prior to entering Controlled Airspace at 1500ft. Rwy13/31 is to be used only when strong winds preclude the use of Rwy02/20. During Special Event days contact with Essex RAD is not required except for permission to enter controlled airspace or in an emergency. ACFT Dept AD must continue ahead until 500ft agl, until outside AD boundary.

Warnings
Gliding and model ACFT flying take place on AD. Masts up to 304ft agl/625ft amsl 1nm E of AD. Rwy02/20 PCN varies from 5 at 02 Thr 9 at 20 Thr. High performance ACFT may be encountered in the area and circuit, pilots to keep good look out, contact A/G for info.
Noise: Avoid over flying local villages and houses within the vicinity of AD, obtain briefing.

Operating Hrs	0900-1900 or SS if earlier than 1900 (L)	Operator	Epping Forest District Council

Circuits 02 LH, 20 RH
Gliders operate on opposite circuit

Landing Fee Nil

Maintenance North Weald Flying Services
Tel: 01992 524510

Fuel AVGAS JET A1 100LL

Disabled Facilities Nil

Restaurants The Squadron on AD bar & restaurant

Taxis Can be arranged via The Squadron or
Lawlor Car Services **Tel:** 01992 57888/576094

Car Hire Can be arranged via The Squadron or
Hertz **Tel:** 01279 433316

Weather Info AirSE MOEx

Operator Epping Forest District Council
25 Hemnall Street, Epping
Essex, CM16 4LX
Tel: 01992 524740 (ATC)
Tel: 01992 524510 (The Squadron)
Fax: 01992 522238 (The Squadron)
Fax: 01992 524047 (ATC)

N

Effective date:23/11/06

EGBK

NORTHAMPTON

419ft 15mb	5nm NE of Northampton N5218.32 W00047.58	PPR	Alternative AD Diversion AD	Cranfield Leicester
	Sywell		AFIS 122.700	

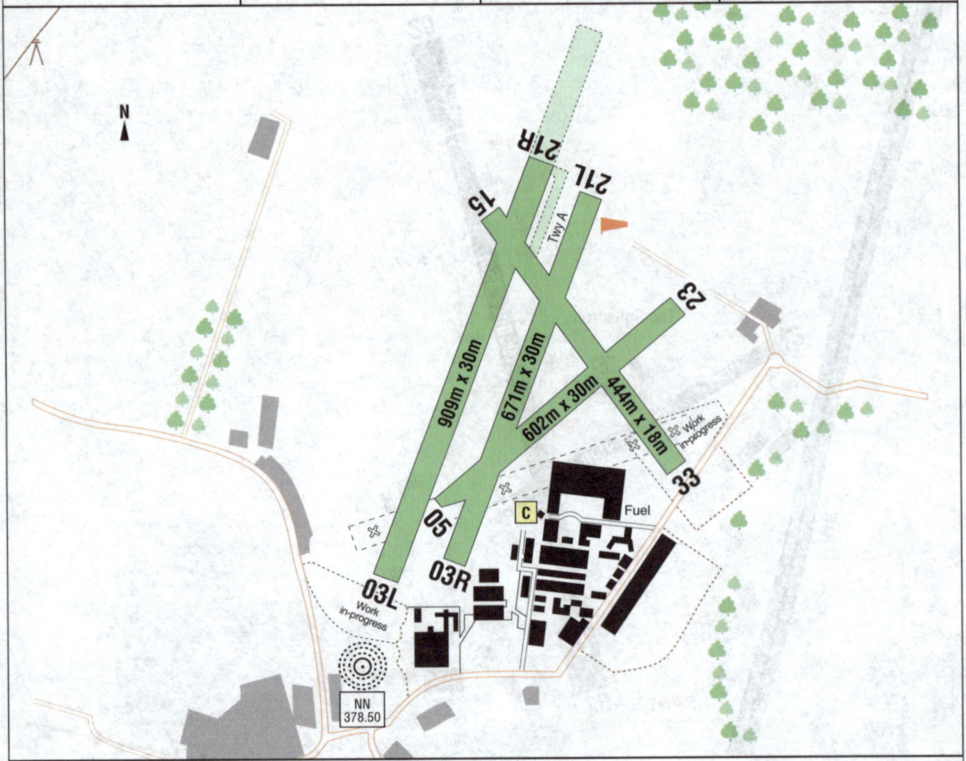

RWY	SURFACE	TORA	LDA	LIGHTING
03L/21R	Grass	909	909	Portable
03R/21L	Grass	671	671	Nil
15/33	Grass	444	444	Nil
05/23	Grass	602	602	Nil

Remarks
PPR by telephone. Non-radio ACFT permitted after obtaining briefing. PPR can be obtained via radio. Only Rwy03L/21R is licensed for night use. Helicopter training circuits are opposite to fixed wing circuits and are flown up to 700ft agl on the dead side of the active Rwy. Resident aerobatic team regular practice and corporate displays upto 5000ft 3nm radius.
Visual aid to location: Ibn NN Green.

Warnings
Public road runs along the SE, S and SW boundaries. S edge of Rwy03/21 and N edge of Rwy15/33 are marked by a number of 2m square white GND markers for helicopter operations; fixed wing pilots should disregard. All Rwys have non-standard white centreline markings.

Operating Hrs	0900-1800 (Summer) 0900-1700 or SS (Winter)	**Restaurants** Aviator Hotel	Restaurants & refreshments available **Tel:** 01604 642111
Circuits	Fixed Wing 05, 21, 33 RH, 03, 15, 23 LH 1000ft Helicopters see Remarks	**Taxis** Northampton Wellingborough	**Tel:** 01604 754444 **Tel:** 01933 441666
Landing Fee	Single/Heli £12, Twin £20, Microlight £10 Special rates at certain times	**Car Hire** National	**Tel:** 01604 259101
Maintenance	Brooklands Engineering	**Weather Info**	AirCen MOEx
Fuel	AVGAS 100LL JET A1 MOGAS	www.skylink-pro.com/airfields/sywell/index.php	
Rotors running refuel avail published Hrs from: Sywell Aerodrome **Tel:** 01604 644917 (credit cards accepted). **Fax:** 01604 499210		**Operator**	Sywell Aerodrome Ltd Sywell Aerodrome Northampton, NN6 0BT **Tel:** 01604 644917 (ATC) **Tel:** 01604 491112 (Admin) **Fax:** 01604 499210 (ATC)

Disabled Facilities

428

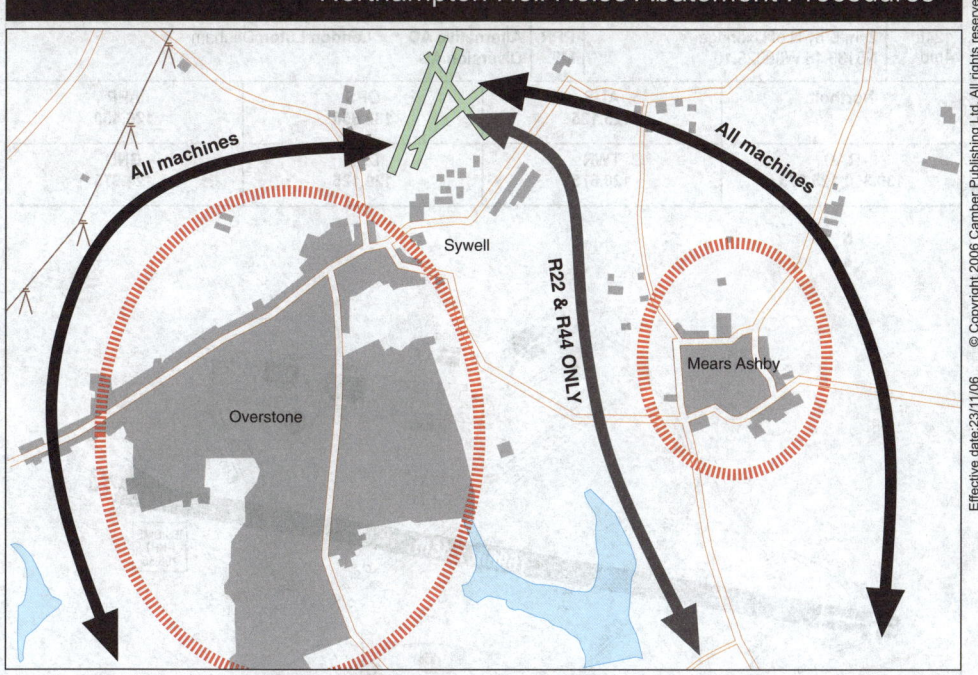

NORTHAMPTON HELICOPTER NOISE ABATEMENT PROCEDURES

All pilots and ACFT operators must comply to the following to reduce the impact of ACFT noise.
1 Avoid over flight of properties and villages close to SE, S and SW AD boundaries, and must not fly on Rwy03 & 33 APP.
2 Multi-engine helicopters arr from S sector, join via overhead at 2000ft QNH, descend dead side, before hover taxi to alight.
3 Helicopters may arr and dept in any direction other than the S.

HELICOPTER ROUTES

SW – Dept to W before turning onto S heading taking a track over Overstone golf course (the same track as downwind for Rwy33L or Rwy15R circuits. Continue to follow the edge of Northampton before taking your track to SW. Avoid over flying villages.
SE – Depart from SE corner of AD and track via Sywell reservoir, continue on route. Avoid over flying villages.
NB: When using either Rwy21L or Rwy03R circuit, it is permissible to enter the large hatched area to use the normal circuit pattern. Do not over fly Mears Ashby village. A109 & B206 ACFT are asked to Arr & Dept via the overhead whenever possible.
Dept to W, NW, N, NE & E remain unaffected. Avoid over flying villages

N

124ft 4mb	2nm E by N of Uxbridge N5133.18.W00025.10	PPR MIL	Alternative AD Diversion AD	London Luton Denham

Northolt	ATIS 125.125	OPS 132.650	APP 126.450
RAD 130.350 125.875	TWR 120.675	DEP 129.125	GND 124.975

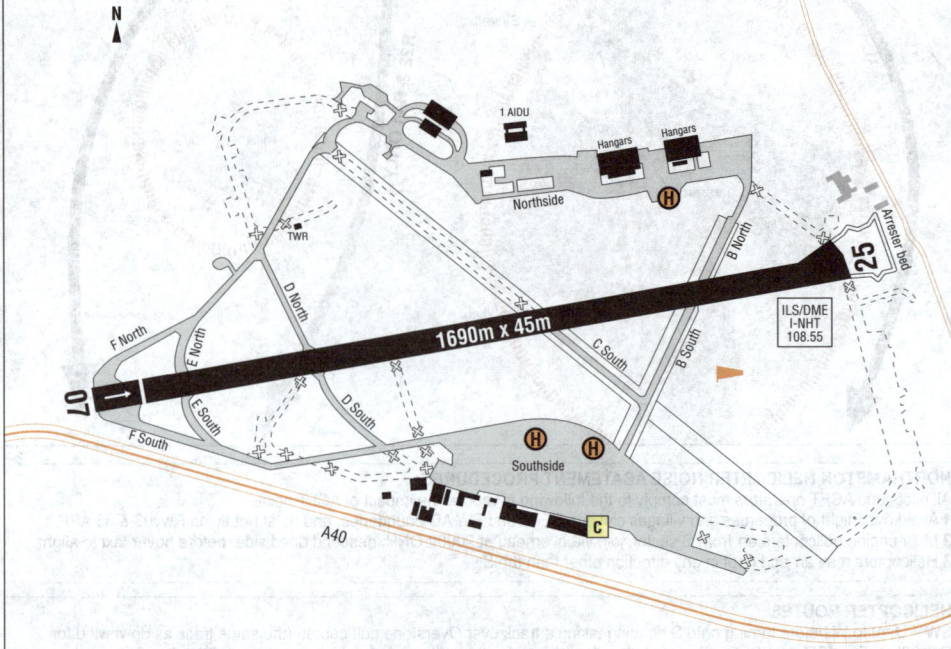

RWY	SURFACE	TORA	LDA	LIGHTING
07	Asphalt	1684	1592	Ap Thr Rwy PAPI 3°
25	Asphalt	1684	1684	Ap Thr Rwy PAPI 3°

Remarks

PPR (before 1300 (Summer) +1 Hr (Winter) for all private, executive and charter flights 24Hrs notice required for all flights. Hi-vis. Between 0800-2000 Sat Sun civil ACFT will only be accepted when AD is planned to be open for military movements. Flight plans showing previously arranged alternatives are to be filed for each flight. Civilian movements at Northolt are limited to 28 per day. Single-engined ACFT are not permitted to land at Northolt. Located within the London CTR. Non Awy inbound to Northolt should work from NW: London RAD from NE: Essex RAD. Pilots are to exercise caution on Echo S at night or during low visability as the Twy is unlit. Exercise caution on the parking areas as wing tip clearance is not assured. Pilots are to make initial call on TWR for start and ATC clearance. No tight turns on Rwy07/25 friction course. Visiting Helicopters to use intersection of disused Rwy for land and takeoff. The full crew of civil flights arr at AD must report to Ramp Control with photo ID. Passports required for flights from outside UK. **Visual aid to location:** Ibn NO Red.

Warnings

Rwy usage dictated by Heathrow. In certain circumstances pilots may have to accept a tailwind. Moderate wind turbulence/wind shear on APP Rwy25 in strong NW wind. Heavy bird activity Oct-Mar adjacent to Rwy25 Thr. **Noise:** Pilots must be familiar with the Northolt procedures.

Operating Hrs	0700-1900 (Summer) +1Hr (Winter) PPR by 1400 previous day	**Handling**	**Tel:** 0208 845 2797 **Fax:** 0208 845 6803
Circuits	25 RH, 07 LH, 1000ft QNH	**Restaurants**	Light refreshments at cafeteria in terminal
Landing Fee	Charges in accordance with MOD policy Contact Station Ops for details	**Taxis/Car Hire**	Nil
		Weather Info	AirSE MOEx **Tel:** 0208 845 2300 Ex 8937
Maintenance	Nil		
Fuel Foster Aviation	JET A1 AirBP via: **Tel/Fax:** 0208 842 1611 **Tel:** 07850 118359 (H24) gary.forster@bp.com	**Operator**	RAF Northolt West End Road Ruislip, Middx, HA4 6NG **Tel:** 0208 845 2300 Ex 4231/4233 **Fax:** 0208 841 9307

Disabled Facilities

117ft 4mb	2.8nm N of Norwich N5240.55 E00116.97	PPR	Alternative AD	Cambridge Seething

Norwich	ATIS 128.625	LARS 119.350
RAD 119.350	TWR 124.250	FIRE 121.600

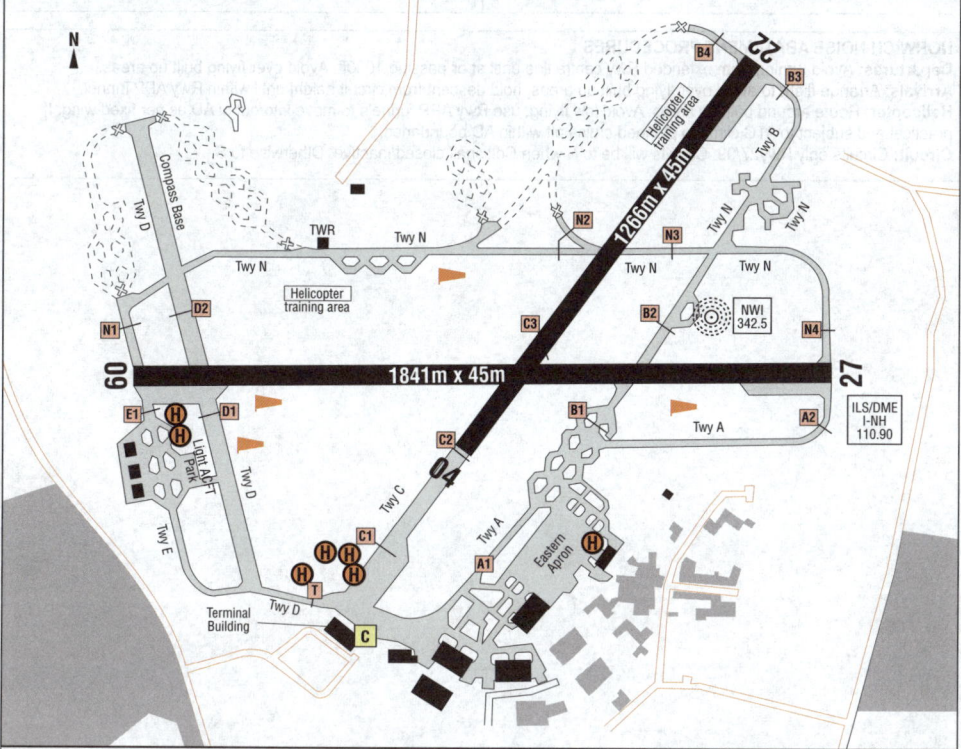

RWY	SURFACE	TORA	LDA	LIGHTING
09	Asph/Conc	1841	1841	Ap Thr Rwy PAPI 3° LHS
27	Asph/Conc	1841	1841	Ap Thr Rwy PAPI 3° LHS
04	Asphalt	1266	1266	Thr Rwy PAPI 4° LHS
22	Asphalt	1266	1266	Thr Rwy PAPI 3.75° LHS

Starter extension Rwy04 305m

Remarks

PPR to non-radio ACFT. Hi-vis. ACFT must contact Norwich APP at least **10 mins before ETA**. Helicopters land as ATC instruct. Light ACFT & microlight activity at Felthorpe AD occasionally with increased activity during summer. All training is subject to ATC approval. ACFT operating for hire or reward must be handled by Norwich Airport Ltd. Proof of insurance must be available for inspection. ACFT book out by telephone.
Visual aids to location: Ibn NH Green

Warnings

Both ends Rwy09/27 width is twice that of associated edge lights due to extra pavement on one side. Rwy centre line lighting is installed, pilots should ensure they are correctly lined up, especially at night. Use Rwy04/22 only when Rwy09/27 unavailable/dangerous due to wind turbulence.

Operating Hrs	Sun-Fri 0530-2115 Sat 0530-2100 (Summer) +1Hr (Winter) & by arr	Restaurants	Restaurant/bar & cafeteria services available in terminal
Circuits	As instructed by ATC Rwy27/09 only	Taxis	Available during AD opening Hrs
Landing Fee	On application	Car Hire	
Maintenance	Available	Avis	**Tel:** 01603 416719
Fuel	AVGAS JET A1 100LL	Europcar	**Tel:** 01603 400280
Disabled Facilities	Nil	Hertz	**Tel:** 01603 404010

N

| **Weather Info** | M T9 Fax 378 VS MOEx
ATIS **Tel:** 01603 420640 | **Operator** | Norwich Airport Ltd
Amsterdam Way
Norwich, NR6 6JA
Tel: 01603 411923 (Admin)
Tel: 01603 420641 (ATC)
Tel: 01603 420642 (Ops)
Tel: 01603 420645 (Duty Manager)
Fax: 01603 487523 (Admin)
dam@norwichinternational.com
www.norwichinternational.com |

NORWICH NOISE ABATEMENT PROCEDURES

Departures: Avoid turning from extended Rwy centre line until at or passing 1000ft. Avoid over flying built up areas.

Arrivals: Arrange flight to avoid over flying built up areas, hold descent from circuit height until within Rwy APP funnel.

Helicopter: Route around built up areas. Avoid low flying, use Rwy APP funnels to move into/out of AD as per fixed wing. If practical and subject to ATC climb to planned cruise alt within AD boundaries.

Circuit: Circuits only Rwy27/09. Circuits will be to N when Coltishall closed/inactive. Otherwise to S.

EGBN					NOTTINGHAM

138ft 5mb	3nm SE of Nottingham N5255.20 W00104.75	**PPR**	**Alternative AD Diversion AD**	**Nottingham East Midlands** Leicester

Nottingham	**APP** East Mids 134.175	**A/G** 134.875

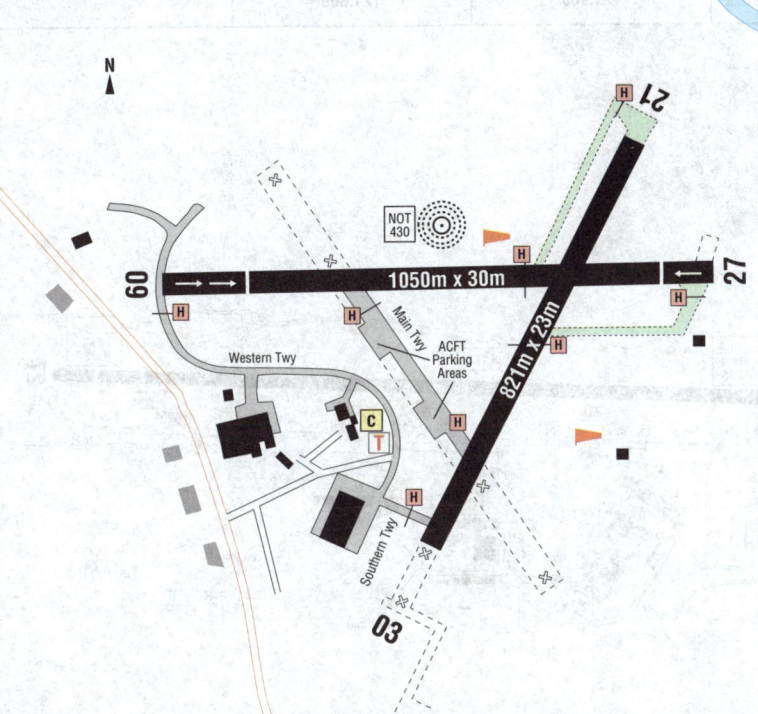

RWY	SURFACE	TORA	LDA	LIGHTING
03/21	Asphalt	821	821	Nil
09	Asph/Conc	989(Day)	837(Day)	Nil
09	Asph/Conc	837(Night)	837(Night)	Thr Rwy LITAS 3.5°
27	Asph/Conc	970(Day)	929(Day)	Nil
27	Asph/Conc	837(Night)	837(Night)	Thr Rwy LITAS 3.75°

Remarks

PPR to non-radio ACFT. AD is situated close to the East Midlands CTR and under the East Midlands CTA (base 2500ft AMSL). Contact East Midlands APP for transit.
Visual aids to location: Ibn NT Green.

Warnings

Chimney 205ft aal/343 ft amsl 1.4nm 285° from the APP. Rwy end lights for Rwy27 are located at the end of the declared TORA. In an emergency pilots should be aware that there is a further 150m of usable Rwy beyond the lighting.

Operating Hrs	Mon-Fri 0800-1700 Sat 0800-1800 Sun 0900-1800 (Summer) Mon-Sat 0900-1700 Sun 1000-1700 Thu 1700-2000 (Winter) & by arr with 24Hrs notice	**Taxis**	Arranged locally
		Car Hire	
		National	**Tel:** 0115 9503385
		Weather Info	AirCen MWC
Circuits	800ft QFE	**Operator**	Truman Aviation Ltd Nottingham Airport Tollerton, Nottingham, NG12 4GA **Tel:** 0115 9811327 (ATC) **Tel:** 0115 9815050 (AD) **Fax:** 0115 9811444
Landing Fee	Single £10 Twin £14 50% discount weekends		
Maintenance			
Trueman	**Tel:** 0115 982 6090		
Fuel	AVGAS JET A1 100LL		
Disabled Facilities Nil			
Restaurant	Club facilities at AD		

433

306ft 10mb	7nm SE of Derby N5249.87 W00119.68	PPR	Alternative AD	Birmingham Leicester

East Midlands		ATIS 128.225		APP 134.175		RAD 120.125
TWR 124.000		GND 121.900		FIRE 121.600		

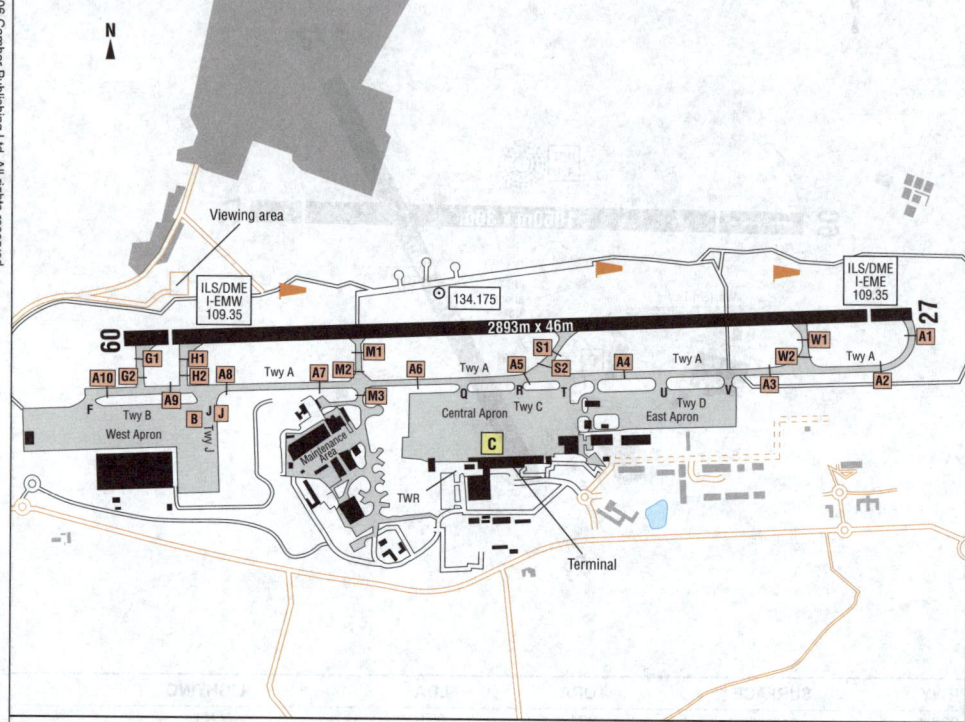

RWY	SURFACE	TORA	LDA	LIGHTING
09	Asphalt	2893	2713	Ap Thr Rwy PAPI 3° LHS
27	Asphalt	2893	2763	Ap Thr Rwy PAPI 3° LHS

7m shoulders either side of Rwy

Remarks
PPR to non-radio ACFT. Hi-Vis. Over night parking on the central apron is limited and requirements should be notified early to handling agents. Training flights are subject to approval and acceptance by ATC, but permission will not be given for any such flights by any type of ACFT 2200-0800 (weekdays). Training flights on Sun & PH only permitted for ACFT <17000kgs MTOW. Operators wishing to take advantage of rebated fees and charges for training must make an application for training rebates in advance to the Airport Authority. Use of a handling agent is mandatory when using all 3 aprons. Handling services available from: British Midland, Donington Aviation, Servisair and Execair.
Aids to Navigation: NDB EME 353.50. NDB EMW 393.00

Warnings
Interference to magnetic compasses may be experienced by ACFT taxiing on Rwy N of final 100m of Twy A S of the Thr of Rwy27 in the areas of W2/W1. Carry out any pre take-off check of Heading Indicator against magnetic compass elsewhere. April-September when grass cutting is taking place in the areas immediately adjacent to the Rwy, circuit flying by light ACFT may be restricted at certain times. In Spring and Autumn bird concentrations maybe present on all areas under agricultural use on the APP to Rwy09/27. A pyrotechnic factory is situated approximately 3nm N of the AD. Rockets, carrying flares of up to 150,000 candela deployed on parachutes, may be tested up to a height on 1000 ft agl by day and night. A flare stack for is situated at Chellaston. The stack is 36ft agl and the flare is 20 ft in length. ACFT must not descend below ILS GP on final APP. When landing Rwy09 in strong S winds, turbulence and windshear possible.
Noise: Pilots must ensure that as far as practicable ACFT are operated in a manner calculated to cause the least disturbance in areas surrounding the AD. Avoid making final turn on APP Rwy27 over Kegworth village.

Operating Hrs	H24	Landing Fee	On application
Circuits	Variable at the discretion of ATC		Reduced rates for light ACFT handled by Execair

Maintenance	Donington Aviation
	East Midlands Flying School
Fuel	AVGAS AVTUR W80 W100 available
	from Donington Aviation & Simon Aviation

Car Hire	
Avis	**Tel:** 01332 811403
National	**Tel:** 01332 853551
Hertz	**Tel:** 01332 811726

Disabled Facilities Available

| **Weather Info** | MT9 T18 Fax247 A VM VN MOEx |
| | **Tel:** 0891 517567 |

Handling	**Tel:** 01332 852204 (British Midland)
	Tel: 01332 812278 (Servisair)
	Tel: 01332 811004 (Donington Aviation)
	Tel: 01332 811179 (Signature)
	Fax: 01332 853584 (Servisair)
	Fax: 01332 811139 (Signature)
	Fax: 01332 852316 (British Midland)
	Fax: 01332 812726 (Donington Avistion)

Operator	East Midlands Int Airport Ltd
	Nottingham East Midlands Airport
	Castle Donington
	Derby, DE74 2SA
	Tel: 01332 852852
	Tel: 01332 850383
	(East Midlands Flying School)
	Tel: 01332 810444 (Donair Flying Club)
	Fax: 01332 852823 (ATC)
	atsm@eastmidlandsairport.com

Restaurants	Refreshments available in AD
	Restaurants at Donington Thistle Hotel
Taxis	Available at terminal
Airport	**Tel:** 01332 814225
Donnington	**Tel:** 01332 810146

HELICOPTER ARRIVAL VFR

Helicopters must APP from N or S, remaining clear of the APP and climb-out of Rwy09/27, not below 500ft QFE or at height/altitude assigned by ATC. Do not over fly Castle Donington to N or Diseworth to S.

Arr from N must obtain specific clearance to cross Rwy09/27 prior to crossing AD boundary, and on crossing boundary are to descend towards the allocated apron stand without over flying equipment or occupied stands

Arr from S must join close base leg, (RB09, LB27) or as directed by ATC. Descend along Rwy or safe path parallel S of Rwy or as directed by ATC. GND or air taxi to parking areas as instructed, following Twys.

Helicopter Dept VFR

Dept as cleared by ATC. Dept must obtain specific clearance to cross Rwy09/27, which must be made at right angle to Rwy. Dept to S must GND or air taxi to Rwy, then on ATC clearance, climb above Rwy to 500ft initially, turning S only when clear of all airport buildings. On reaching AD boundary comply with ATC instructions regarding heading/route & height/altitude.

CTA/CTR Class D Airspace

Normal CTA/CTR Class D Airspace rules apply

Transition Alt 4000ft

Entry/Exit lanes are established to permit ACFT to operate to and from East Midlands Airport in IMC, but not under IFR.

1 Long Eaton Lane

2 Shepshed Lane

(Both are 3nm wide centered on the M1)

Use of the lanes is subject to SVFR clearance. ACFT must remain clear of cloud and in sight of the surface not above 2000ft (QNH). Also recommended for VFR arr and dept.

N

Visual Reference Points (VRP)

VRP	VOR/VOR	VOR/NDB	VOR/DME
Bottesford	TNT 102°/HON 044°	TNT 102°/EME 065°	TNT 102°/33nm
N5257.88 W00046.90	DTY 017°		GAM 166°/20nm
Church Broughton	TNT 189°/HON 001°	TNT 189°/EME 283°	TNT 189°/10nm
N5253.17 W00141.90	DTY 336°	EMW 294°	
Markfield (M1 J22)	TNT 151°/HON 036°	DTY 351°/EME 206°	HON 036°/24nm
N5241.73 W00117.55	DTY 351°		DTY 352°/32nm
Measham (M42 J11)	TNT 172°/HON 015°	HON 015°/EME 239°	HON 015°/20nm
N5241.33 W00132.88	DTY 335°		DTY 336°/34nm
Melton Mowbray	TNT 127°/HON 053°	HON 053°/ DTY 016°	HON 053°/36nm
N5244.37 W00053.57	DTY 016°		DTY 017°/35nm
Trowell (M1 Services)	TNT 114°/HON 024°	TNT 114°/EME 344°	TNT 114°/16nm
N5257.70 W00116.50	DTY 356°		GAM 215°/22nm

460ft 15mb	4nm SE of Royston N5159.40 E00004.07	PPR	Alternative AD	Cambridge Duxford

Non-Radio	APP Essex RAD 120.625	APP Luton 129.550	Safetycom 135.475

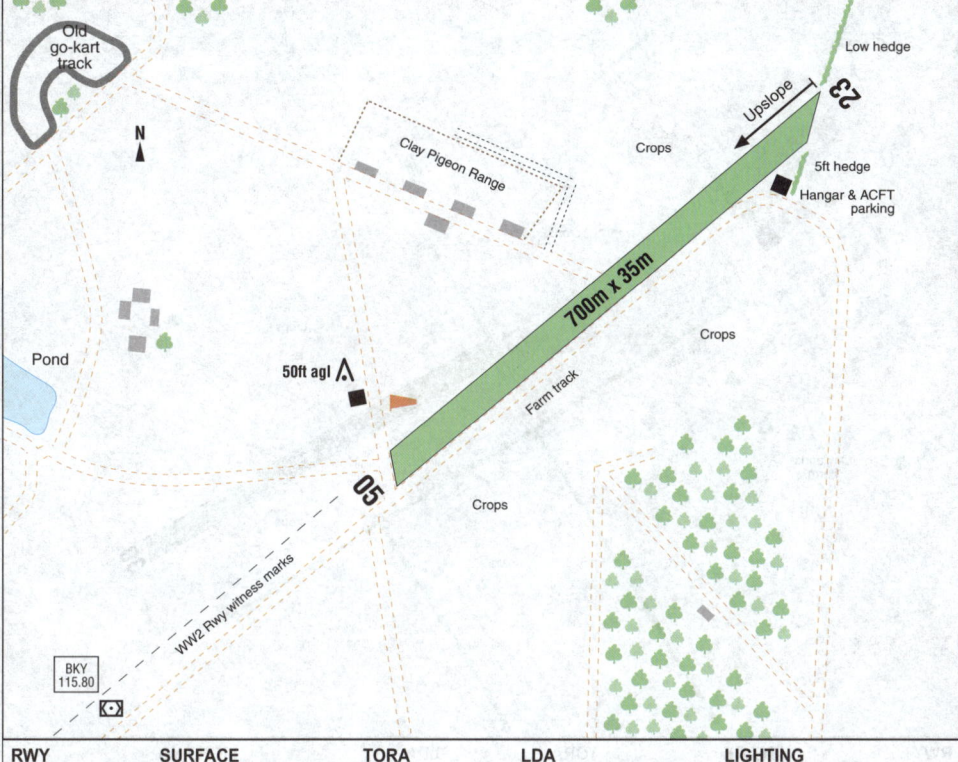

RWY	SURFACE	TORA	LDA	LIGHTING
05/23	Grass	700x35	U/L	Nil

Rwy23 upslope first 100m

Remarks

PPR by telephone. Visiting ACFT welcome with PPR & at pilot's own risk. Situated on WW2 AD, Rwy established on site of wartime hard Rwy with BKY VOR/DME on extended centre line.

Warnings

AD situated beneath the Stansted CTA, base 2500ftQNH. ATZ's of Fowlmere & Duxford are close to N. Vehicles & Pedestrians may use the 6m wide concrete tracks that parallel the Rwy and actually cross it at the mid point. ACFT must operate within the strip markers, as the rest of AD is not consolidated for aviation use. There is a low mast 50ft agl 150m N Rwy05 Thr and a 120ft agl mast approx 1000m 270° from the Rwy05 Thr.

Operating Hrs	SR-SS	**Operator**	Nuthampstead Airfield Associates Ltd
Circuits	05 RH, 23 LH 800ft QFE		Keffords Barley, Royston
Landing Fee	Nil		Herts, SG8 8LB
Maintenance	Nil		**Tel:** 01763 848287
Fuel	Nil		**Fax:** 01763 849616
Disabled Facilities	Nil		
Restaurants	Woodman Pub in Northampstead village		
Taxis			
Drayton's	**Tel:** 01763 848233		
Car Hire	Nil		
Weather Info	AirS MOEx		

370ft 12mbs	3nm WNW of Kidlington N5150.51 W00126.44	**PPR**	**Alternative AD**	**Oxford** Enstone

Non Radio	**ATIS** Oxford 136.225	**LARS** Brize 124.275	**Safetycom** 135.475

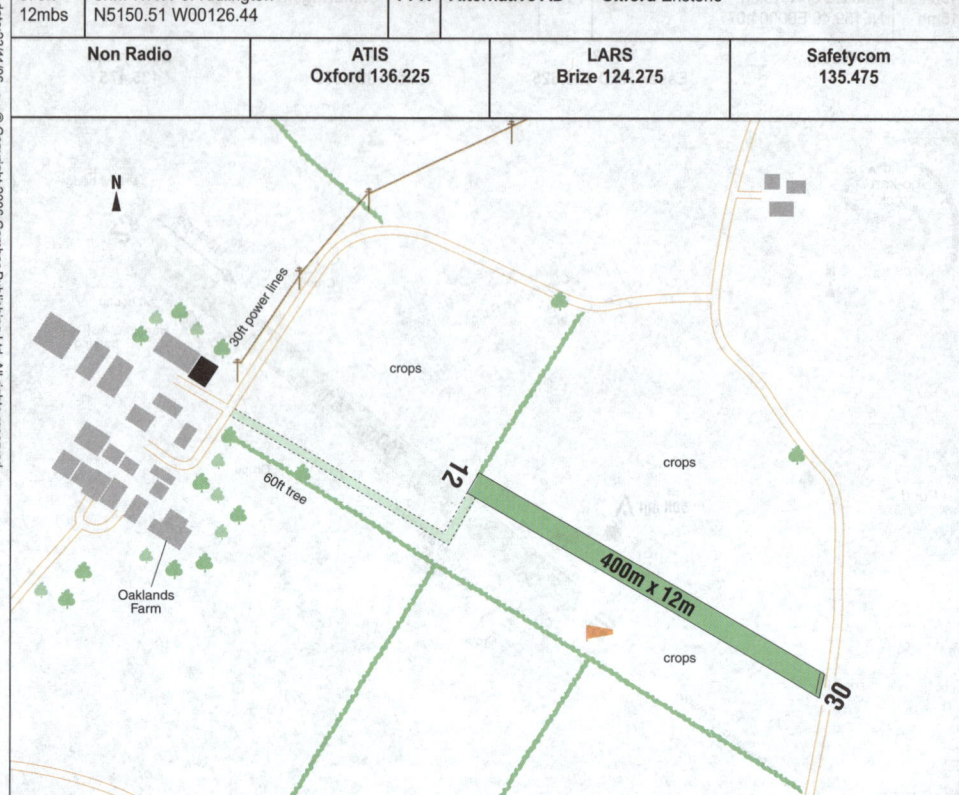

RWY	SURFACE	TORA	LDA	LIGHTING
12/30	Grass	400x12	U/L	Nil

Remarks
PPR by telephone. Visiting ACFT welcome at own risk. Level but narrow strip. Twy to hangar is very restricted in width.

Warnings
Tall crop growth may make the strip unusable for low wing ACFT during certain periods of the farming year. Pole laid across Rwy30 Thr stop vehicle access to strip from the public road which crosses end of Rwy.
Noise: Avoid over flying of local villages and farms.

Operating Hrs	SR-SS
Circuits	To S 600ft QFE
Landing Fee	Nil
Maintenance	Nil
Fuel	Nil
Disabled Facilities	Nil
Restaurant	Nil
Taxi/Car Hire	Nil
Weather Info	AirCen MOEx

Operator	Robert J Stobo Oaklands Farm Stonesfield Oxford OX29 8DW **Tel:** 01993 891226 robstobo@stonesfield.f9.co.uk

438

250ft 8mb	5nm SSE Cirencester N5137.95 W00200.92	PPR	Alternative AD Diversion AD	Bristol Filton Kemble

Oaksey Park	Zone Lyneham 123.400	A/G 122.775

RWY	SURFACE	TORA	LDA	LIGHTING
17/35	Grass	785x20	U/L	Nil
22/04	Grass	975x30	U/L	Nil

Rwy17/35 emergency use only

Remarks

Visitors welcome at own risk. ACFT must be kept to the mown strips and manoeuvring areas. Heavy wet land may prevail during some winter months making AD unusable. No low flying or beat-ups.

Warnings

200Kv national grid power line 1.75km E of AD on Rwy22 APP. " white markers barrels on Rwy22. Land between to avoid bump.
Noise: Visiting pilots must avoid noise sensitive areas of local villages and avoid over flying local farms and houses. Standard circuit joining and Dept must be obeyed at all times.

Operating Hrs	0700-2100 or SR-SS	**Operator**	Mr B & Mrs E Austen
Circuits	04 RH, 22 LH, 1000ft QNH		Oaksey Park Airfield
Landing Fee	Single £12 Twin/Heli £23		The Green
Maintenance	**Tel:** 01666 575111		Oaksey
Fuel	AVGAS JET A1 100LL		Wiltshire
			SN16 9SD
			Tel: 01666 577130 (Manager)
			Tel: 01666 577152 (Clubhouse)

Disabled Facilities

Restaurants	Good pubs in Oaksey village
Taxis	**Tel:** 01285 650850
Car Hire	Nil
Weather Info	AirSW MOEx

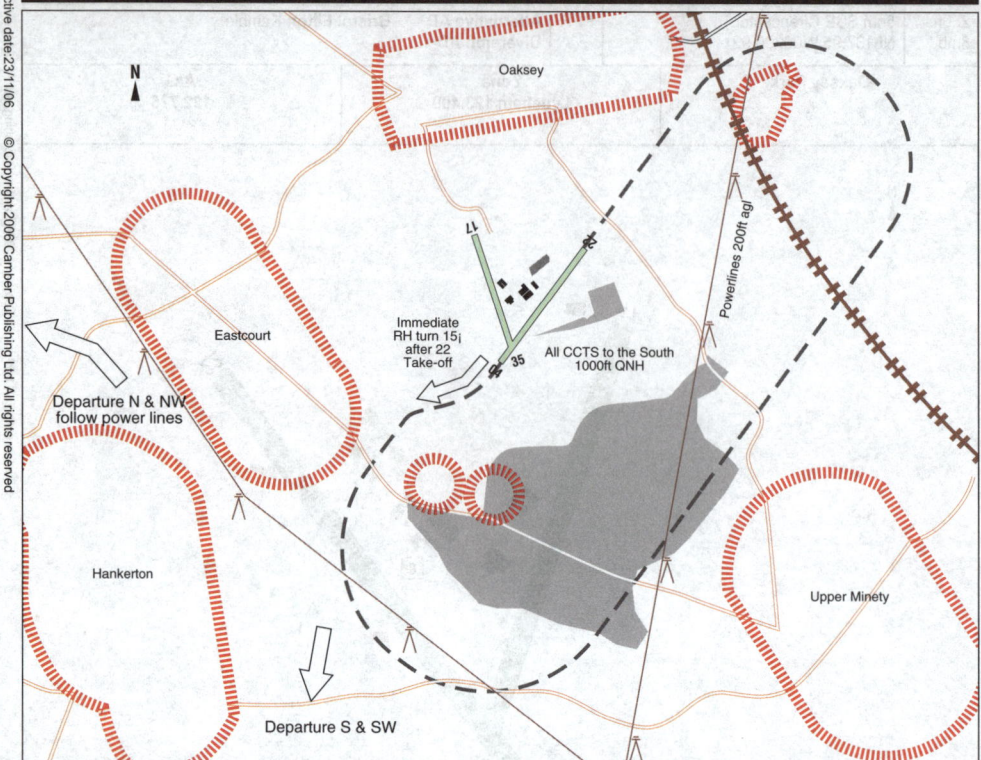

N

Oaksey

Powerlines 200ft agl

Eastcourt

Immediate
RH turn 15¡
after 22
Take-off

35
17

All CCTS to the South
1000ft QNH

Departure N & NW
follow power lines

Hankerton

Upper Minety

Departure S & SW

20ft 1mb	5nm NE of Oban N5627.83 W00523.99	PPR	Alternative AD Diversion AD	Glasgow Glenforsa

Oban Radio	FIS Scottish 127.275	A/G 118.050

RWY	SURFACE	TORA	LDA	LIGHTING
01/19	Asphalt	1240x30	U/L	Nil
03/21	Asphalt	900x30	U/L	Nil

Remarks
AD is increasingly active with light ACFT & light/heavy helicopters.

Warnings
Glider launching and microlight flying takes place at AD. High GND 990ft aal/1010ft amsl 1nm to N and NNE of AD respectively. Gliders are operating when a double cross is displayed N of disused Rwy04/22.

Operating Hrs	0900-1800 & by arr	Taxis	Tel: 01631 710100
Circuits	Powered ACFT to W Gliders to E		Tel: 01631 562834
Landing Fee	Single £10 Twin £15		Tel: 01631 563784
	Public transport £5.75 per 500kgs AUW	Car Hire	Tel: 01631 566553
			Tel: 01631 566476
Maintenance	Nil	Weather Info	AirSc GWC
Fuel	AVGAS 100LL JET A1 H24 7 days		Also observed actuals from AD
	Tel: 01631 710384 (AD)		Tel: 01631 710384/710888
	Tel: 01631 710888	Operator	Total Logistics Concepts
	Tel: 07770 620988		Oban Airport
	Tel: 07796 473670		Oban, Argyll
Disabled Facilities	Nil		Scotland, PA37 1SX
Restaurants	Light refreshments at AD		Tel/Fax: 01631 710384 (PPR)
Lochnell Arms	Tel: 01631 710408		Tel/Fax: 01631 710888
Falls of Lora	Tel: 01631 710483		Tel: 07770 620988
The Ferryman	Tel: 01631 710666		Tel: 07796 473670
			tlc@obanairport.co.uk

405ft 14mb	6nm ESE of Basingstoke N5114.05 W00056.57	PPR MIL	Alternative AD Diversion AD	Farnborough Blackbushe	

Odiham	LARS Farnborough 125.250	APP 131.300	TWR 122.100	AFIS 131.300

Airport diagram showing Runway 10/28, 1835m x 45m, with North Dispersal LIMA, North Dispersal CHARLIE, Eastern Dispersal, Eastern 1, Eastern 2, Southern Dispersal, Compass Base, Southern Specs, Tactical load park, Helicopters / HELILAND area, TWR, ODH 109.60, ILS/DME I-ODH 108.95

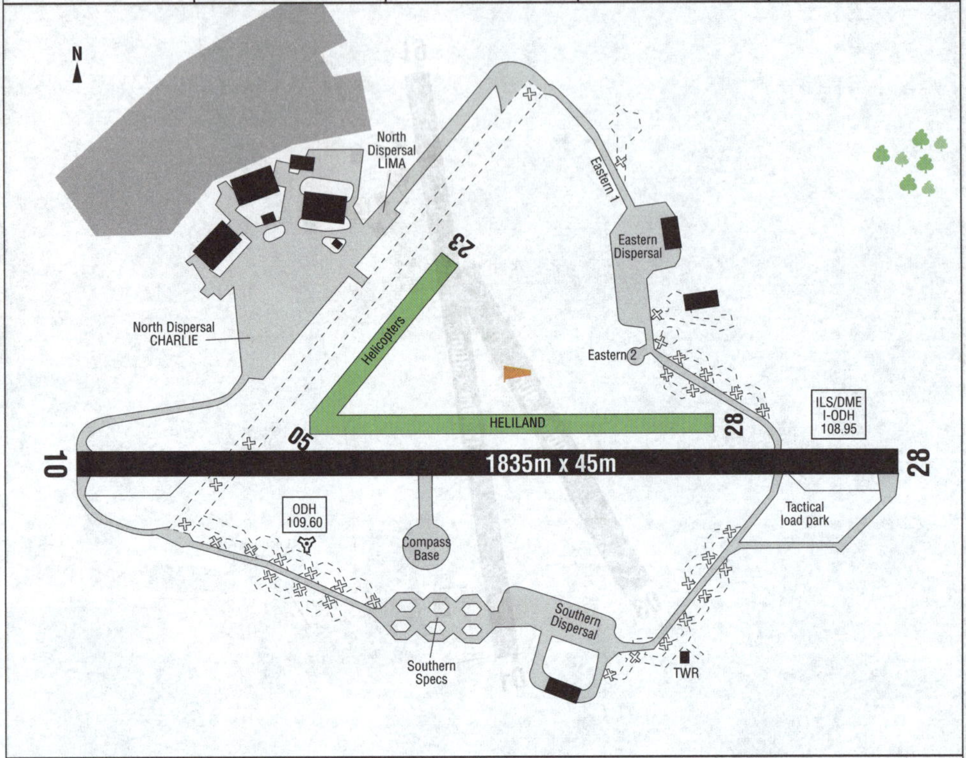

RWY	SURFACE	TORA	LDA	LIGHTING
10	Asphalt	1835	1832	Ap Thr Rwy PAPI 3°
28	Asphalt	1835	1835	Ap Thr Rwy PAPI 3°

Remarks

PPR 24Hrs notice required. Intensive helicopter activity, special procedures apply. Inbound helicopters if flying below 2000ft VFR London/Farnborough QNH, call Odiham APP when inbound before 10nm with details of which cardinal sector they wish to recover from. Variable helicopter circuits, no dead side. All fixed wing visual circuits to S of Rwy. ATZ active H24.
Visual aid to location: IBn OI Red.

Warnings

Glider flying weekends, PH & summer 1700 till dusk. Full bird control measures at not implemented on AD. ACFT to remain outside the MATZ boundary until given clearance and height to fly to join the visual circuit.

		Operator	RAF Odiham
Operating Hrs	HO PPR ATZ H24		Tel: 01256 702134 Ex 7295 (ATC) Tel: 01256 702134 Ex 7254 (OPS)
Circuits	Variable for heli fixed wing to S		
Landing Fee	Charges in accordance with MOD policy Contact Station Ops for details		
Maintenance	Nil		
Fuel	AVTUR Jet A1 by arr		

Disabled Facilities

Restaurants	Nil
Taxis/Car Hire	Nil
Weather Info	M T 382 MOEx

194ft 6mb	12nm SW of Norwich N5229.85 E00103.12	PPR	Alternative AD	Norwich Seething

Old Buckenham	Civil Transit Lakenheath 128.900 (Mon-Fri)	A/G 124.400

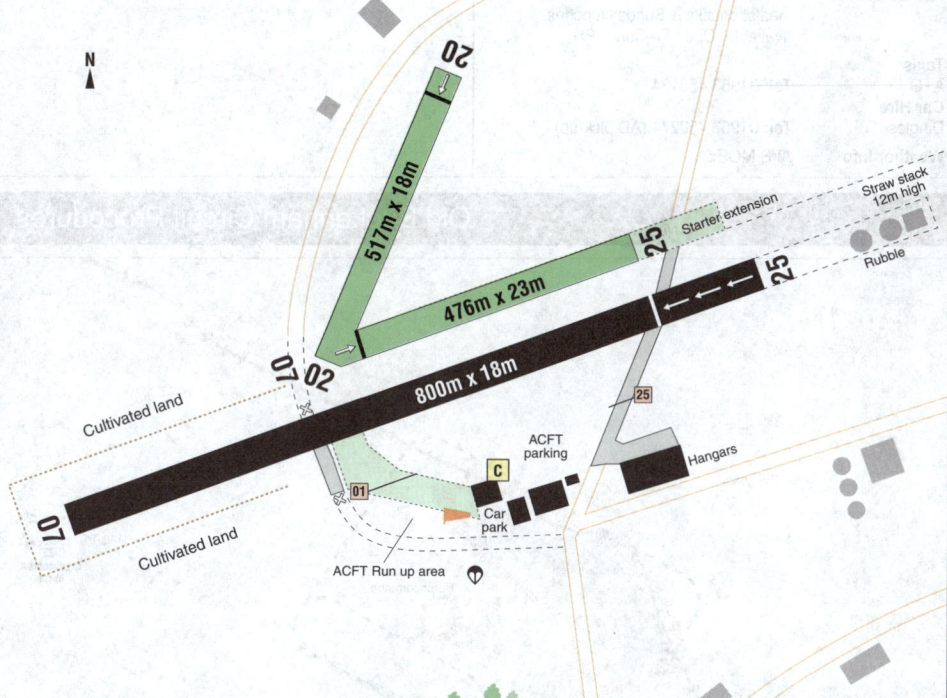

RWY	SURFACE	TORA	LDA	LIGHTING
07	Tarmac	640	640	Thr Rwy
25	Tarmac	800	640	Thr Rwy
07	Grass	430	440	Nil
25	Grass	465	405	Nil
02	Grass	430	517	Nil
20	Grass	517	430	Nil

Starter extension Rwy25 (Tarmac) 160m Concrete

Remarks
PPR by telephone. Helicopters and Microlights not accepted. AD U/L Mon-Thur 0900-SS. Tarmac Rwy constructed on WWII Rwy & partly beyond old perimeter track. Flying training, ACFT hire & sales avail. No mobile phones air side. Passengers are the pilots responsibility airside.

Warnings
No ACFT movements 2000-0700 (L) on any day. Tacolneston TV mast (735ft amsl) 3nm ENE. Considerable gliding activity at Tibenham 4nm SE & Watton 5nm NNW. Disused section short of Rwy25 starter extension, rubble piles & up to 12m high straw stacks. Free-fall parachuting SR-SS Sun-Mon & PH up to FL150. Strictly no ACFT movements within ATZ or running engines on AD when parachuting in progress. All Dept pilots must contact Buckenham Radio for start clearance during para operations.
Noise: Rwy07 LH Arr – Either via downwind N Attleborough or straight in from Snetterton Race track. Dept – Climb straight ahead 1500ft or Tacolneston Mast. Rwy25 RH Arr – Either via downwind N Attleborough or straight in from Tacolneston Mast. Dept – After take-off track 270 to the railway line. In any event avoid over flying Old Buckenham & Attleborough. **No overhead or dead side joins.** No ATZ entry without positive RT contact (non-radio ACFT PPR required). Permission must be obtained from Buckenham A/G to enter the ATZ. If not possible, ACFT must remain clear of ATZ and wait permission to enter zone. During dark all ACFT to access Rwy via Rwy25 Thr hold. Twy centre line delineated by green reflective studs.

Operating Hrs	Fri-Sun 0800-1900 (Summer) Fri-Sun 0900-SS (Winter) & by arr AD licensed Fri-Sun	Circuits	07 LH, 25 RH, 1000ft QFE

Landing Fee	Single £10 Twins £15.00 Members Free
Maintenance	Scanrho Aviation **Tel:** 01953 861351
Fuel	AVGAS JET A1 100LL

Disabled Facilities

Restaurants	Restaurant & bar in clubhouse. Hot meals, snacks & Sunday lunches available. Open Fri-Sun & PH

Taxis
A+G   **Tel:** 01953 453134
Car Hire
Dingles   **Tel:** 01953 452274 (AD pick-up)
Weather Info   AirS MOEx

Operator	Flying School Old Buckenham Aero Club Old Buckenham Airfield, Abbey Road Old Buckenham, Norfolk, NR171PU **Tel:** 01953 860806 **Fax:** 01953 860606 flying@oldbuckaeroclub.co.uk www.oldbuckaeroclub.co.uk

Old Buckenham Circuit Procedures

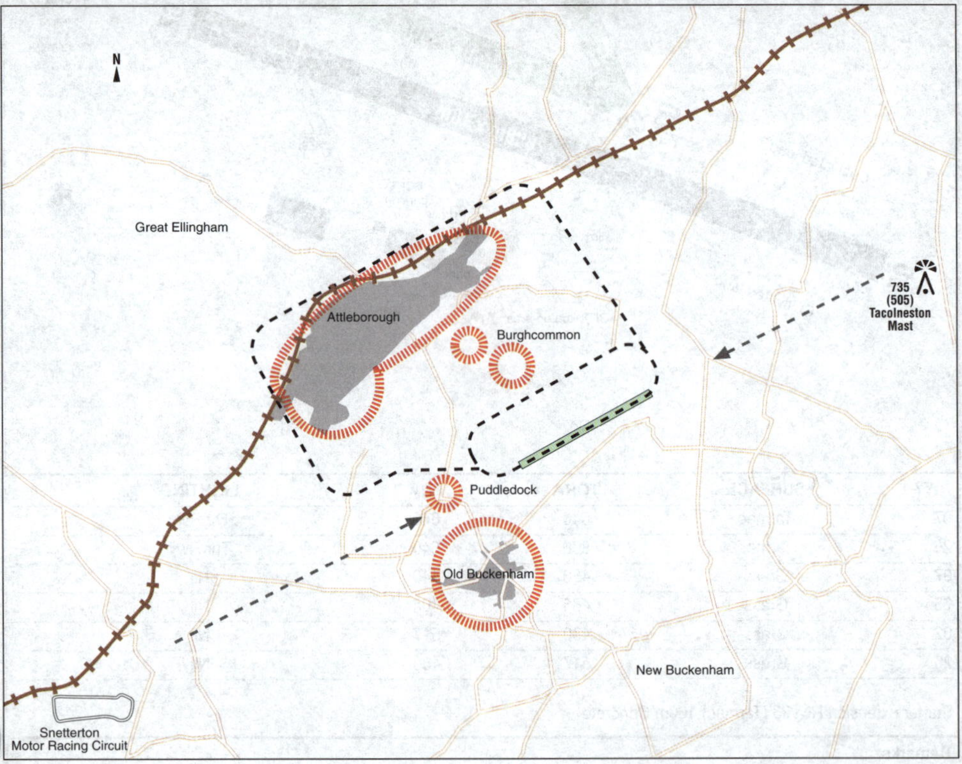

N

Great Ellingham

Attleborough

Burghcommon

Puddledock

Old Buckenham

New Buckenham

735
(505)
Tacolneston
Mast

Snetterton
Motor Racing Circuit

285ft 9mb	2nm NNE of Salisbury N5105.93 W00147.05	PPR	Alternative AD Diversion AD	Southampton Thruxton

Old Sarum	LARS Boscombe 126.700	A/G 123.200

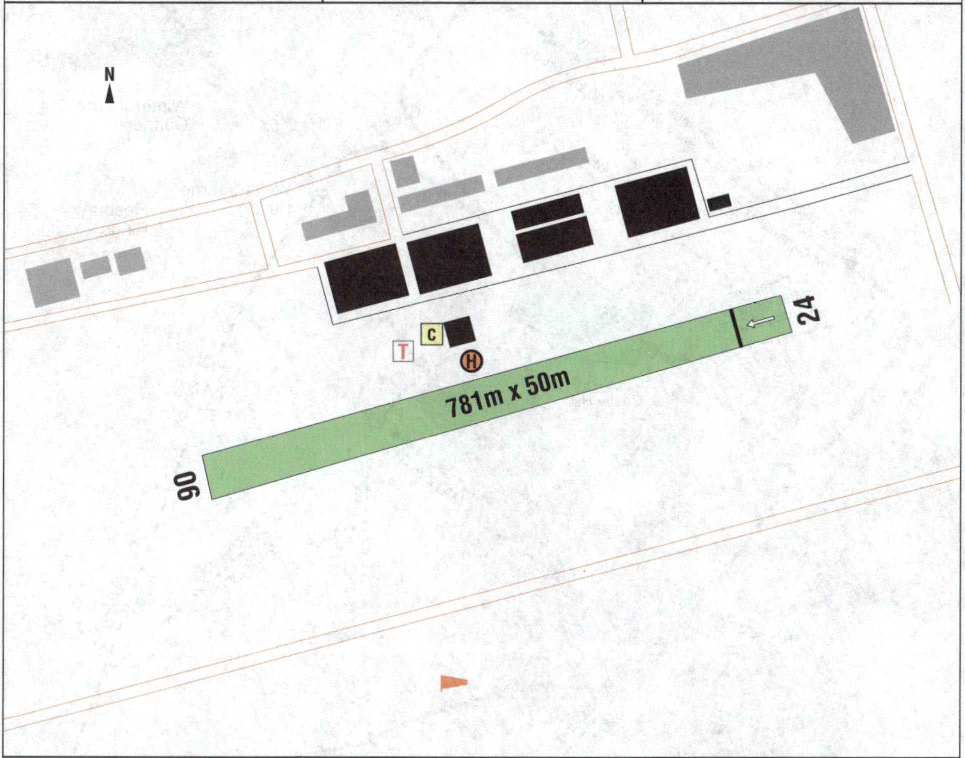

N

781m x 50m

06

24

RWY	SURFACE	TORA	LDA	LIGHTING
06	Grass	781	781	Nil
24	Grass	781	731	Nil

Remarks
PPR to non-radio ACFT. AD is not available at night or by ACFT required to use a licensed AD or for public transport passenger flights.

Warnings
AD is located within the Boscombe Down MATZ, ATZ H24. Danger Area D127 is located 2nm to the E of the AD. Due to a hump on the Rwy, pilots of ACFT with low eye level should exercise caution. Helicopters may operate to the S of the Rwy.

Operating Hrs	Mon-Sun 0830-1830 or SS (L) AD U/L after 2000 Tue-Sun	**Taxis** Assisi Cabs	On request or **Tel:** 01722 415181
Circuits	Variable dependent on Boscombe Zone 800ft QFE	Salisbury Taxis **Car Hire**	**Tel:** 01722 423000 On request or
Landing Fee	Free to members Single £10 Twin £20 Microlights £5	Budget **Weather Info**	**Tel:** 01722 3364444 AirSE MOEx
Maintenance	Old Sarum Engineering **Tel:** 01722 410711	**Operator**	Old Sarum Flying Club, Hangar 3 Old Sarum Airfield
Fuel	AVGAS 100LL		Old Sarum, Salisbury Wilts, SP4 6DZ

Disabled Facilities

Tel: 01722 322525 (Flying club)
Fax: 01722 323702
info@oldsarumflyingclub.co.uk
www.oldsarumflyingclub.co.uk

Restaurants Old Sarum Restaurant on AD. Various others in Salisbury within 2 miles

445

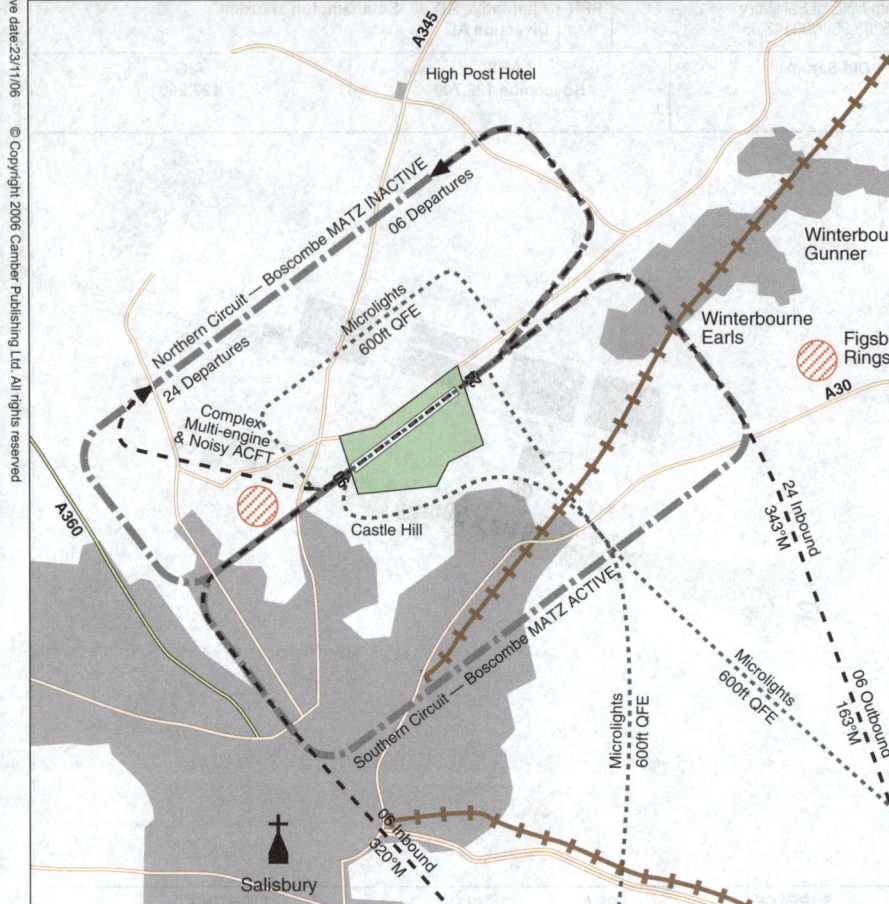

Visual Reference Points (VRP)

Alderbury   N5102.90 W00143.90

Arr pilots must establish contact with Boscombe Down before entering the MATZ at VRP Alderbury 155° 4nm from AD.
When Boscombe Zone is closed standard overhead join at Old Sarum.
Circuit direction when Boscombe Zone is open Rwy06 RH, Rwy24 LH.
Circuit direction when Boscombe Zone is closed Rwy06 LH, Rwy24 RH.
Noise: Avoid flying low level over Salisbury & local villages. Please avoid over flying local habitation
Microlight ACFT operate at 600ft, avoiding all built up areas.

550ft 18mb	1.5nm SSE of Nailsworth N5140.10 W00211.90	PPR	Alternate	Gloucestershire Kemble

Non Radio	LARS Filton 122.725	LARS Brize 124.275	Safetycom 135.475

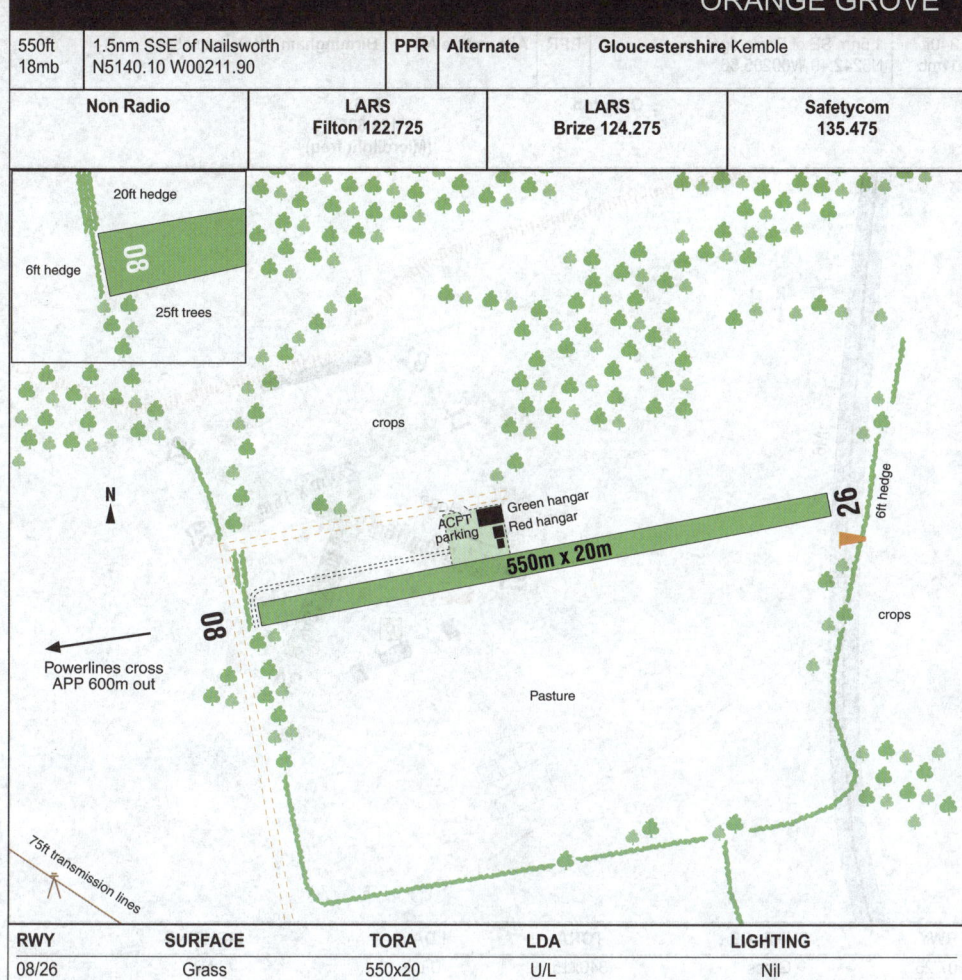

RWY	SURFACE	TORA	LDA	LIGHTING
08/26	Grass	550x20	U/L	Nil

Remarks

PPR by telephone mandatory. Experienced pilots accepted. PFA or Flying Farmers very welcome at own risk. Rwy delineated by small white markers but cut strip clearly visible, particularly during summer months.

Warnings

AD close to Highgrove House, visiting pilots requested to check royal Flight activity. Powerlines cross Rwy08 APP 600m from Thr. High hedges/trees on Rwy08 APP. See inset diagram. ACFT lined up Rwy08 may not be visible to ACFT on APP. Kemble ATZ 2nm to E.

Noise: Avoid all local habitation. Do not fly below 1000ft QFE within the local area except for take-off and landing.

Operating Hrs	SR-SS		Operator	Martin Stoner & George Lowsley-Williams
Circuits	08 RH 26 LH Join overhead 1000ft QFE			Courtyard Cottage 52A Long Street Tetbury
Landing Fee	Nil			Glos GL8 8AQ
Maintenance	Nil			**Tel:** 01666 504884
Fuel	Nil			**Tel:** 01453 833206
Disabled Facilities	Nil			
Taxi/Car Hire	Nil			
Weather Info	AirSW MOEx			

O

447

340ft 11mb	1.5nm SE of Penkridge N5242.49 W00205.56	PPR	Alternative AD	Birmingham Wolverhampton

	Otherton	A/G 129.825 (Microlight freq)	

RWY	SURFACE	TORA	LDA	LIGHTING
07/25	Grass	340x15	U/L	Nil
11/29	Grass	220x15	U/L	Nil
16/34	Grass	340x15	U/L	Nil

Remarks

PPR by telephone small light ACFT ONLY Training school operated by Gordon Faulkner Pilot Training. Training Tue-Sun. A/G only occasionally manned mainly W/E. Visitors should keep a good look out for non-radio ACFT in circuit.

Warnings

Noise: All Arr into overhead at 1000ft QFE from at least 2nm out from E or W. All circuits S only at 500ft QFE. Direction; Rwy07/11 16 RH Rwy25/29/34 LH. Keep circuits tight. Dept: Climb in overhead to min 1200ft QFE then Dept to E or W maintaining heading until at least 2nm from AD before turning on course. Do not over fly Penkridge town, the village, farm buildings to N of AD, or Gailey lake wildlife reserve and farm to S. Rwy25 2% down slope over final 80m.

		Operator	Staffordshire Microlight Centre
Operating Hrs	Mon-Sat 0800-2000 Sun 0900-1700 (L)		**Tel:** 07831 811783 (AD)
Circuits	See Warnings		**Tel/Fax:** 01543 673075 (Evenings)
Landing Fee	Nil donations appreciated		www.sac-gb.com
Maintenance	Nil		
Fuel	MOGAS by arr with the operator (Not Mondays)		
Disabled Facilities	Nil		
Restaurant	Self-service hot drinks available in the clubhouse most days		
Taxi Penkridge Cabs	**Tel:** 01785 712589		
Car Hire	Nil		
Weather Info	AirCen MWC		

448

20ft 0mb	Nr Bruary Out Skerries Shetland N6025.54 W00044.80	PPR	Alternative AD	Sumburgh Scatsta

Skerries	APP Sumburgh 131.300	A/G 130.650

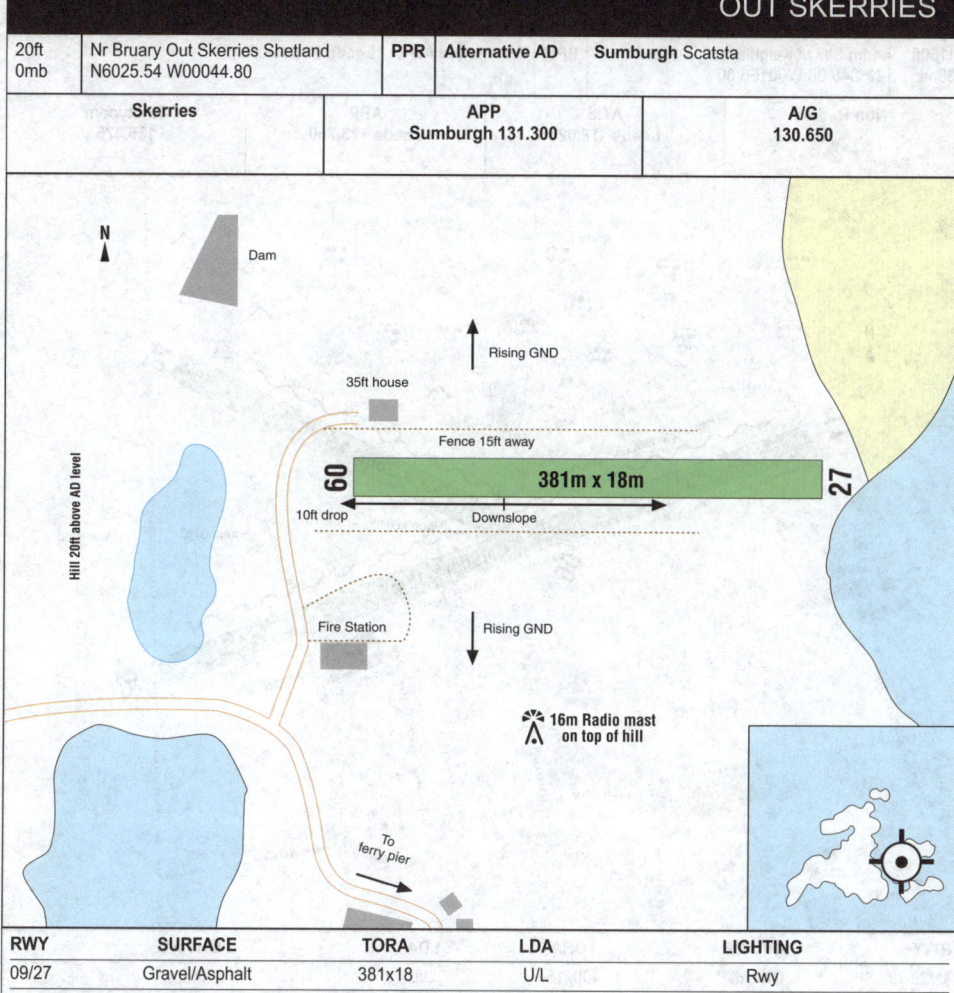

RWY	SURFACE	TORA	LDA	LIGHTING
09/27	Gravel/Asphalt	381x18	U/L	Rwy

Lighting available for emergency night landings

Remarks
PPR by telephone essential. Visiting ACFT accepted. Visitors to contact Loganair to ascertain when their service operates. There is no off-Rwy parking visiting ACFT will constitute an obstruction to vital local services.

Warnings
Rwy surface is poor & uneven fenced on both sides. Due to uneven surface there is danger of prop-strike to nose wheel ACFT with little prop clearance. Rwy profile is hump-backed. The hamlet of Bruray is close to SW of AD. Moss may affect braking action.
Important: ACFT parked on strip restrict scheduled & ambulance services –consult with Loganair.

Operating Hrs	SR-SS	**Operator**	**Tel:** 01806 515253 (Alice Arthur PPR) **Tel:** 01595 840246 (Loganair)
Circuits	1000ft QFE		
Landing Fee	£6.50		
Maintenance	Nil		
Fuel	Nil		
Disabled Facilities	Nil		
Restaurants Accomodation	Alice Arthur can provide B&B		
Taxis/Car Hire	Nil		
Weather Info	AirSc GWC		

449

Effective date:23/11/06

1150ft 38mb	4nm SW of Keighley N5348.00 W00155.00	PPR	Alternative AD	Leeds Huddersfield

Non Radio	ATIS Leeds 118.025	APP Leeds 123.750	Safetycom 135.475

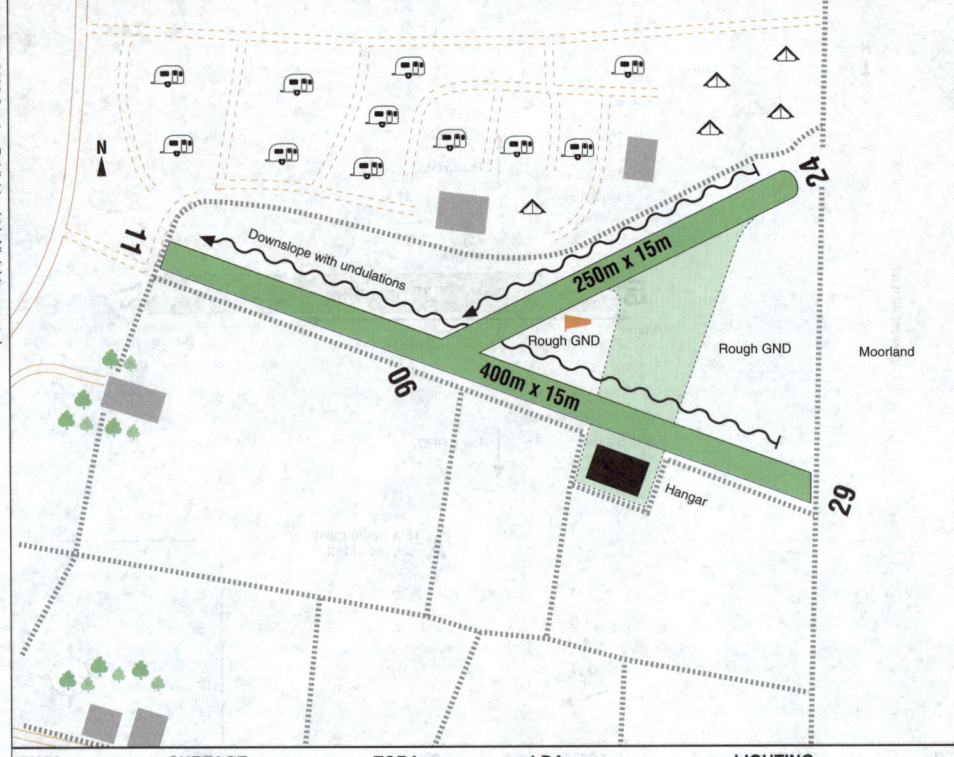

RWY	SURFACE	TORA	LDA	LIGHTING
11/29	Grass	400x15	U/L	Nil
06/24	Grass	250x15	U/L	Nil

Rwys undulate
Rwy29 downslope

Remarks
PPR by telephone. Helicopters not accepted. AD situated on high GND. Worth Valley steam railway is located W of AD and is a short taxi ride away.

Warning
AD situated beneath Leeds CTA, (base 3000ft QNH). Rwys can become waterlogged during winter months. Stone walls at all Thrs.
Noise: Avoid over flying local houses and farms, particularly the caravan site to N of AD.

Operating Hrs	SR-SS
Circuits	LH 600ft QFE
Landing Fee	Donation please
Maintenance	Nil
Fuel	Nil
Disabled Facilities	
Taxi/Car Hire	Nil
Weather Info	AirCen MWC

Operator	Mr J R Heaton Hawksbridge Farm Oxenhope Keighley West Yorkshire BD22 9QU **Tel:** 01535 644863 rodney.heaton@btinternet.com

270ft 9mb	6nm NW by N of Oxford N5150.22 W00119.20	PPR	Alternative AD Diversion AD	Gloucestershire Turweston

Oxford	ATIS 136.225 (Arr)	LARS Brize 124.270
APP 125.325	**TWR** 133.425	**GND** 121.950

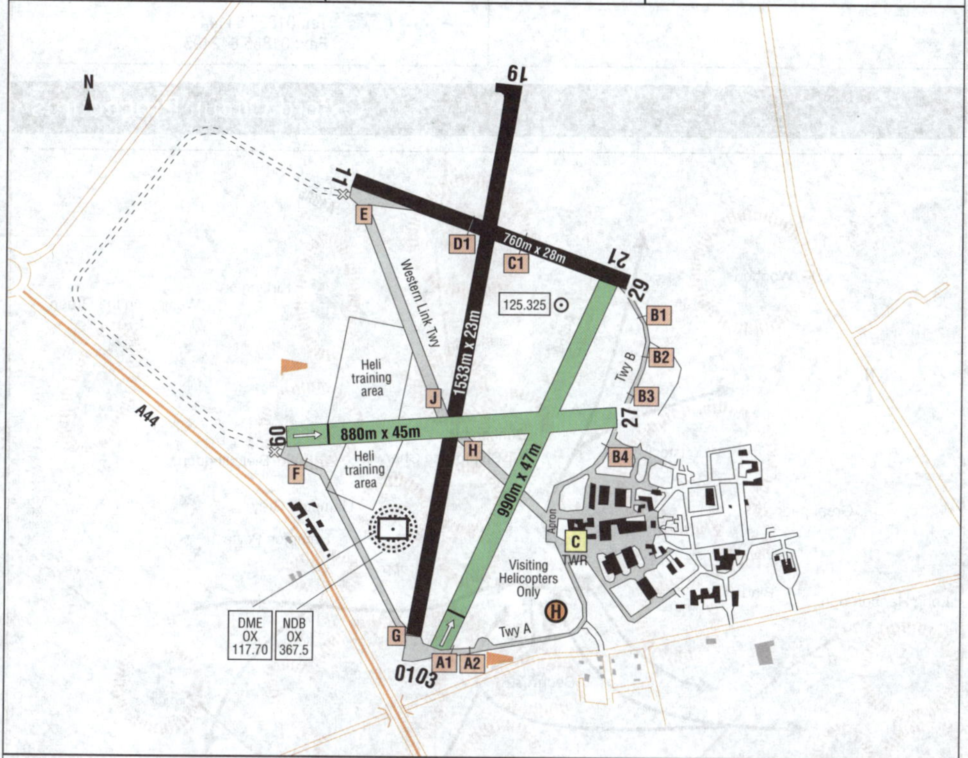

(Aerodrome diagram showing runways 01/19, 03/21, 09/27, 11/29, taxiways, Heli training areas, DME OX 117.70, NDB OX 367.5, frequency 125.325)

RWY	SURFACE	TORA	LDA	LIGHTING
01	Asphalt	1319	1319	Thr Rwy PAPI 3.5° LHS
19	Asphalt	1319	1319	Thr Rwy PAPI 3.1° LHS
03/21	Grass	880	880	Nil
09	Grass	880	880	Nil
27	Grass	880	880	Thr Rwy APAPI 3° LHS
11/29	Asphalt	760	760	Nil

Rwy19 down slope 2.25% over last 200m SW end

Remarks
PPR via Ops. Hi-Vis. Customs parking area N of TWR is for short term use only.
Visual aid to location: Ibn KD Green.

Warnings
Twys Rwy01 Thr to Rwy09Thr disused. Helicopter training takes place in designated areas on AD. Jet fuel installation N of tower, infringes W Twy B, ACFT wingspan >15m; exercise caution. D129 is 4.5nm NE of AD. Work taking place Rwy01/19 & 09/27 during 2007.

Operating Hrs	Mon-Fri 0630-1900 Sat 0730-1700 Sun & PH 0800-1600 (Summer) +1Hr (Winter) & by arr
Circuits	Variable fixed-wing ACFT 1200ft QFE
Landing Fee	Single £12.00, Twin on application
Maintenance CSE	
Fuel	**Tel:** 01865 844200 AVGAS JET A1 100LL

Disabled Facilities

Restaurants Restaurant/refreshments available at AD

Taxis			Operator	Oxford Aviation Services
James Cars	**Tel:** 01865 375742			Oxford Airport
Car Hire				Kidlington
Godfrey Davis	**Tel:** 01865 246373			Oxford, OX5 1RA
Hertz	**Tel:** 01865 319972			**Tel:** 01865 844272 (ATC)
Weather Info	M* A AirCen MOEx			**Tel:** 01865 844267 (PPR/Ops)
				Fax: 01865 841807
				www.oxfordairport.co.uk

≡AFE **Tel:** 01865 841441
Fax: 01865 842495

Oxford Circuit Procedures

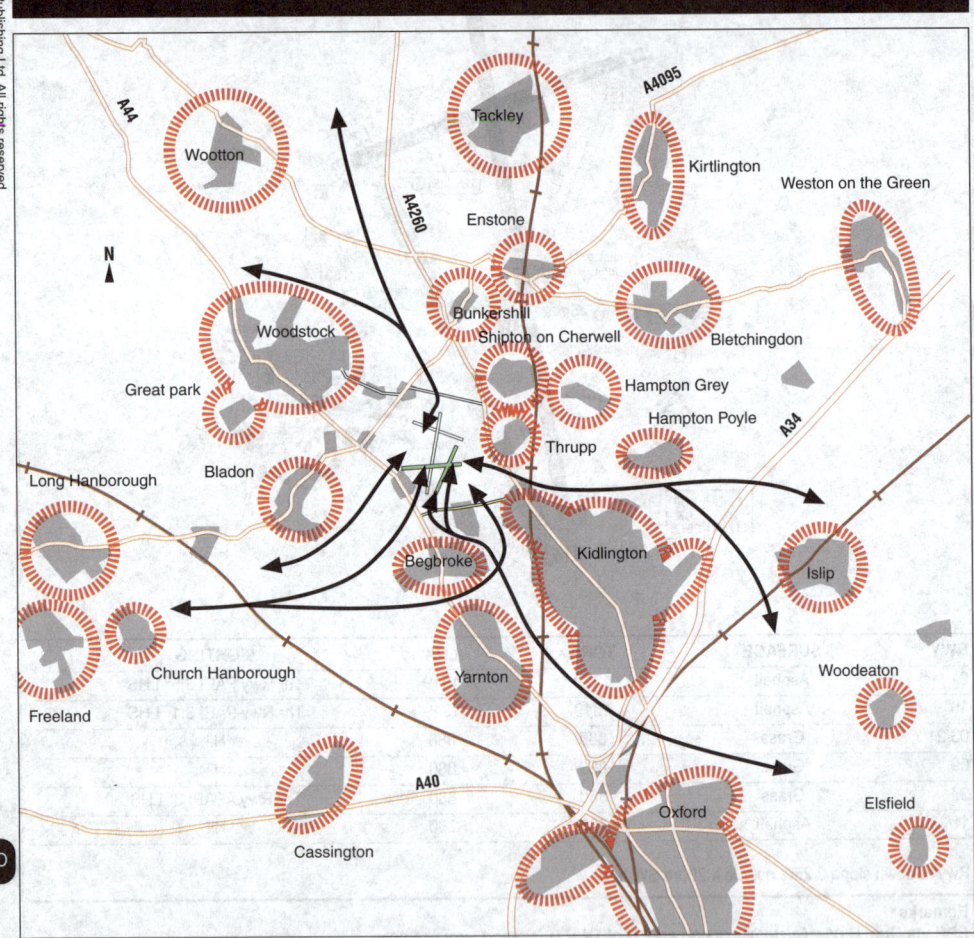

NOISE ABATEMENT PROCEDURES

All Dept fixed-wing ACFT climb straight ahead to 1000ft QNH before turning crosswind, endeavour to complete this before the Mercury satellite station. Rwy19 visual Dept turning left should climb ahead until clear to S of Yarnton village, remaining clear of the Brize CTR. Subject to Rwy & circuit direction pilots should avoid noise sensitive areas as shown on map.
ACFT joining the circuit will join over head unless they request a non-standard join, which will be approved subject to traffic.
ACFT joining will give way to ACFT in the circuit.
Helicopters must avoid built up areas as shown on map or should follow marked track

250ft 8mb	2.5nm W of Hertford N5148.15 W00009.48	PPR	Alternative AD	London Luton Elstree

Panshanger	APP Luton 129.550	A/G 120.250

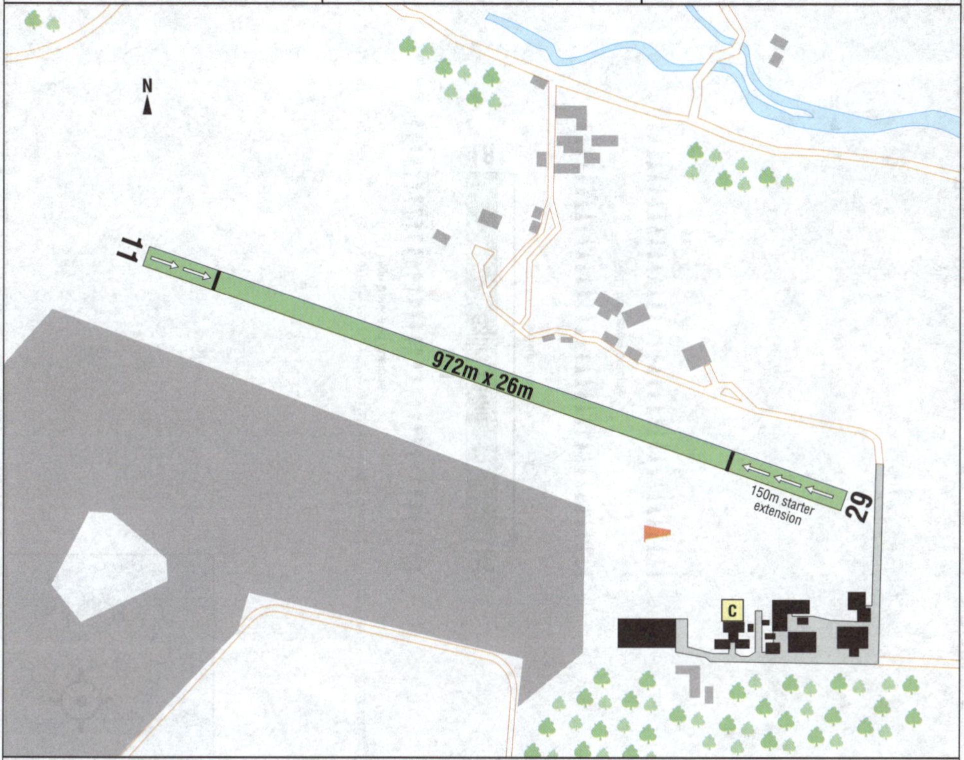

RWY	SURFACE	TORA	LDA	LIGHTING
11	Grass	857	888	Nil
29	Grass	948	788	Nil

Displaced Thr Rwy11 84m
Displaced Thr Rwy29 175m

Remarks
AD strictly PPR. No visitors at weekends.

Warnings
Luton CTR is 1nm to N and ATZ passes into Luton CTR.
Noise: Pilots are to obtain a Dept briefing to avoid noise sensitive areas. Rwy29 After take-off turn right over fly golf clubhouse, turn to Rwy QDM until passing prominent white building (school). Turn right, fly to square wood approx 0.5nm, turn downwind between Tewin and Tewin Wood.

Operating Hrs	0900-1900 (Summer) 0900-SS (Winter)	**Taxis**	
Circuits	11 LH, 29 RH, 800ft QFE	Castle	**Tel:** 01992 501002
	Heli 1000ft QFE standard overhead joins	County	**Tel:** 01992 504111
Landing Fee	Singles/Heli £10 Twins £10	**Car Hire**	
	Commercial £25	Europcar	**Tel:** 01438 715888
		Hertz	**Tel:** 01707 331433
Maintenance	P F Maintenance (M3 & FAA)	**Weather Info**	AirSE MOEx
Fuel	AVGAS 100LL	**Operator**	East Herts Flying School

Taxis **Tel:** 01707 333333

Disabled Facilities

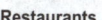

Restaurants Blue Yonder

Panshanger Airfield, Cole Green
Hertford, Herts, SG142NH
Tel: 01707 391791
Fax: 01707 392792
eastherts.flyingschool@virgin.net

82ft 2mb	Isle of Papa Stour Shetland Isles N6120.13 W00145.18	PPR	Alternative AD	Sumburgh Scatsta

Papa Stour	APP Sumburgh 131.300	APP Scatsta 123.600	A/G 130.650 (monitored when flights expected)

RWY	SURFACE	TORA	LDA	LIGHTING
18/36	Grass/Stones	538x18	U/L	Thr

Remarks
PPR by telephone. Visiting ACFT accepted. We recommend visitors seek up to date AD condition advice from A S Glover.

Warnings
Rwy surface is rough & could cause prop-strike to nose wheel ACFT with little prop clearance. Rwy profile has a slight up gradient from Rwy18 to Rwy36 Thr. Rwy is constructed on the side of a hill with an up slope to E & down slope to W. Expect severe turbulence on short finalRwy18 as you cross the cliffs. AD is common land & sheep may stray across the strip at any time.
Important: ACFT parked on strip restrict scheduled & ambulance services – consult Operator.

Operating Hrs	SR-SS	Operator	Papa Stour Airstrip Committee
Circuits	1000ft QFE		**Tel:** 01595 873236 (A S Glover)
Landing Fee	Nil		airstrip@papastour.shetland.co.uk
Maintenance	Nil		www.papastour.shetland.co.uk/airstrip.html
Fuel	Nil		
Disabled Facilities	Nil		
Restaurants	Nil		
Accomodation	Hurdiback **Tel:** 01595 873229		
Taxis/Car Hire	Nil		
Weather Info	AirSc GWC		

91ft 3mb	22nm N of Kirkwall Airport N5921.10 W00254.02	PPR	Alternative AD Diversion AD	Kirkwall Sanday

Non-radio	APP Kirkwall 118.300	Safetycom 135.475

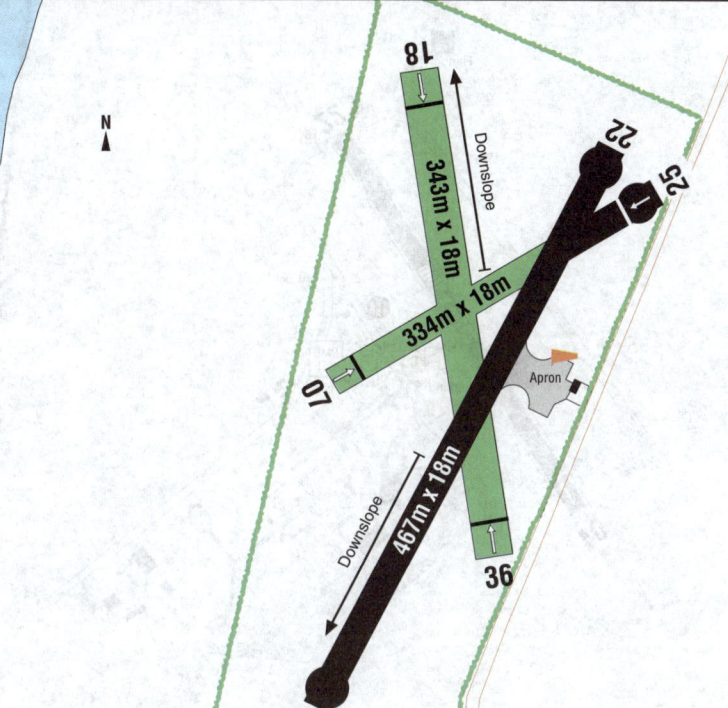

RWY	SURFACE	TORA	LDA	LIGHTING
04/22	Graded Hardcore	467	467	Nil
18	Grass	383	323	Nil
36	Grass	386	323	Nil
07/25	Grass/Graded Hardcore	292	250	Nil

Starter extension Rwy18 40m
starter extension Rwy36 43m

Remarks
PPR from OIC. AD available at pilot's own risk. Rwy conditions contact AD Manager.

Warnings

Operating Hrs	SR-SS	**Operator**	Orkney Islands Council Offices
Circuits	Nil		Kirkwall
Landing Fee	Nil		Orkney, KW15 1NY
	Fire cover £18.90 if req		**Tel:** 01856 873535
Maintenance	Nil		**Tel:** 018567 644225 (AD Manager)
Fuel	Nil		**Fax:** 01856 876094
Disabled Facilities	Nil		
Restaurants			
Beltane House	**Tel:** 01857 644267 (Hotel)		
Taxis	Free guest transport to & from		
Beltane House	**Tel:** 01857 644267 (Hotel)		
Car Hire	**Tel:** 01857 644202		
Weather Info	AirSc GWC		

EGFP

PEMBREY

15ft 0mb	6nm WNW of Llanelli N5142.48 W00418.44	PPR	Alternative AD	Swansea Haverfordwest

Pembrey	DAAIS Pembrey Range 122.750	AFIS 124.400	A/G 124.400

RWY	SURFACE	TORA	LDA	LIGHTING
04	Concrete	797	731	Nil
22	Concrete	731	767	Nil

Displaced Thr Rwy04 66m

Remarks
PPR by telephone weekdays only. 24Hrs notice required. Non-radio ACFT not accepted. Located within D118. Special procedures apply. Active portion is the NE corner of ex-RAF AD. Visitors welcome. Many local attractions of natural & historical significance. Cefn Sidan Beach (Blue flag 20min walk) & Ashburnham Golf Club 2 miles.

Warnings
Access to Pembrey penetrates D118 active Mon-Thu 0830-1700 Fri 0830-1400. All ACFT must call RAF range 24Hrs in advance for permission and slot allocation. All movements during these times must be to E of Rwy centreline. Inbounds must call Pembrey Range 10nm before DA boundary. In-bounds may be instructed to hold if the range is active. Vehicles cross at mid-point.

{P

Operating Hrs	Sat-Sun 0800-1730 (L) & by arr	**Taxis**	**Tel:** 01269 861936
Circuits	22 LH, 04 RH	**Car Hire**	**Tel:** 01554 753040
Landing Fee	On application	**Weather Info**	AirS MOEx
Maintenance	Available also hangarage	**Operator**	Cpt Winston Thomas
Fuel	AVGAS JET A1 100LL		Pembrey Airport
	Cash or cheque only		Pembrey, Carms, SA16 0HZ
Disabled Facilities Nil			**Tel:** 01554 891534
Restaurants	Available on AD at weekend snacks		**Tel:** 01554 890420 (Pembrey Range)
	during the week		**Fax:** 01554 891388

Hotel accommodation

Gwenllian Court	**Tel:** 01554890217
Ashburnham Hotel	**Tel:** 01554 834455
Diplomat Hotel	**Tel:** 01554 756156
Stady Park Hotel	**Tel:** 01554 758171

www.pembreyairport.com

222ft 7mb	5nm S of Market Drayton N5248.36 W00229.52	PPR	Alternative AD	Hawarden Sleap

Non-Radio	LARS Shawbury 120.775	Safetycom 135.475

Crops

21

Crops

Farm track

Farm track

N

Witness marks of Old Wartime Runway

Crops

Rifle Range

800m x 15m

Pig shelters

Red hangar

03

ACFT parking

40ft tree

Crops

Black hangar (not for ACFT use)

40ft trees

24

Crops

600m x 15m

Crops

06

RWY	SURFACE	TORA	LDA	LIGHTING
03/21	Asph/Grass	800x15	U/L	Nil
06/24	Asphalt	600x15	U/L	Nil

Rwy21 has small portion of grass/asphalt at Thr

Remarks
PPR by telephone. Visiting ACFT welcome at pilots own risk. AD established using E side perimeter tracks of WW2 AD. All other parts of AD are not available for ACFT use.

Warnings
Farm vehicles use Rwy, pilots should keep good lookout and beware of debris. Crops grown up to Rwy edges. AD is within Shawbury/Ternhill CMATZ, controlling authority is Shawbury APP. Visiting ACFT call Shawbury when inbound and ASAP after take-off. Weekdays there is considerable military helicopter training at low level.
Noise: Avoid over flight of local habitation.

Operating Hrs	SR-SS	**Weather Info**	AirCen MWC
Circuits	03, 21 RH, 06, 24 LH, 1000ft QFE	**Operator**	Mr D R Williams
Landing Fee	Nil		Standford Service Station
Maintenance	Nil		Standford Bridge, Newport
Fuel	Nil		Shropshire, TF10 8BA
Disabled Facilities			**Tel:** 01952 550261

Restaurants	
Four Alls	**Tel:** 01630 652995
Taxis/Car Hire	
Newport Cars	**Tel:** 01952 8204077

P

457

330ft 11mb	1.5nm SW of Perranporth N5019.90 W00510.65	PPR	Alternative AD Diversion AD	St Mawgan Lands End

Perranporth	LARS Culdrose 134.050	LARS St Mawgan 128.725	A/G 119.750	A/G Glider Ops 130.100

RWY	SURFACE	TORA	LDA	LIGHTING
05	Asphalt	940	940	Nil
23	Asphalt	940	940	Nil
09	Asphalt	750	750	Nil
27	Asphalt	750	750	Nil
01/19	Asphalt	650x27	U/L	Nil

Starter extension Rwy05 204m
Starter extension Rwy09 129m

Remarks
Strictly PPR. ACFT under the control of Culdrose are by agreement permitted to fly in the ATZ at 2000ft QFE & above during Culdrose ATC Hrs of watch. Accordingly ACFT should not fly within the Perranporth ATZ above 1000ft without clearance from either Culdrose ATC orvia relay from Perranporth. Some parts of the manoeuvring area prone to loose gravel. It is also used for taxiing by ACFT using other Rwys

Warnings
Gliding takes place at AD. When gliding is taking place fixed wing ACFT should make wide circuits. AD is located within the Culdrose AIAA. Rwy 01/19 is available for ACFT not required to use a licensed AD. Only the hard Twys from the apron to the Rwy05 hold and Rwy27 hold are useable. Beware of windshear and severe turbulence on Rwy27 in strong NW winds.
Noise: Land Rwy19 and take-off Rwy01 – beware of windshear in NW wind. Pilots should avoid flying directly over St Agnes, Perranporth & villages S of AD. Areas are particularly noise sensitive. After take-off, when practicable, reduce to climb power and turn to track out over the sea to at least 1500ft QNH before proceeding on course. Pilots Arr from E should make contact with St Mawgan.

Operating Hrs	0900-1700 or SS Daily	**Taxis**	
Circuits	N of AD No deadside join	Atlantic **Car Hire**	Tel: 01872 572126 Available on request
Landing Fee	Minimum £6 there after £0.009p/kg gross weight +VAT	**Weather Info** **Operator**	AirSW MOEx Perranporth Airfield Ltd The Airfield, Higher Trevellas
Maintenance **Fuel**	By arr AVGAS 100LL		St Agnes, Cornwall, TR5 0XS **Tel:** 01872 552266 (AD)
Disabled Facilities	Nil		**Fax:** 01872 552261 (AD)
Restaurants	Hotels in Perranporth		www.perranporthairfield.co.uk

P

397ft 13mb	3nm NE of Perth N5626.35 W00322.33	PPR	Alternative AD	Dundee Fife

	Perth	A/G 119.800	

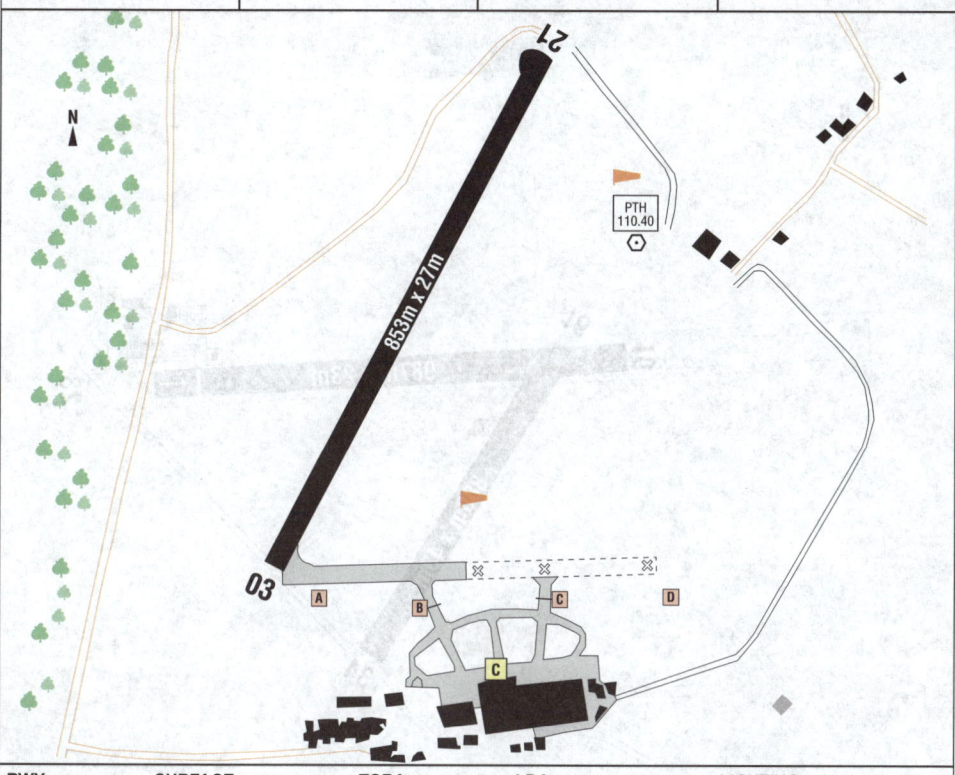

RWY	SURFACE	TORA	LDA	LIGHTING
03/21	Asphalt	853	853	Thr Rwy PAPI 3°

Remarks
PPR Non-radio ACFT not accepted.

Warnings
When landing Rwy03 with the wind from NW, turbulence can be expected from the tree line during the final APP.

Operating Hrs	0800-1600 (Summer) 0900-1700 (Winter) & by arr	**Operator**	Perth Airport (2000) Ltd Unit 3 Perth Airport Scone, PH2 6NP **Tel:** 01738 551631 **Fax:** 01738 553542
Circuits	03 LH, 21 RH		
Landing Fee	Single <1000kg £9 Twin <2000kg £19.86 Others available on request		
Maintenance Tayflite	**Tel:** 01738 554820		
Fuel	AVGAS JET A1 100LL		
Disabled Facilities	Nil		
Restaurants	Restaurant & Club facilities available		
Taxis A & B Taxis	**Tel:** 01738 634567		
Car Hire Thrifty	**Tel:** 01738 633677		
Weather Info	AirSC GWC		

26ft 1mb	7nm S of Peterborough N5228.08 W00015.05	**PPR**	**Alternative AD**	**Cambridge** Fenland

	Coningon		**A/G** 129.725	

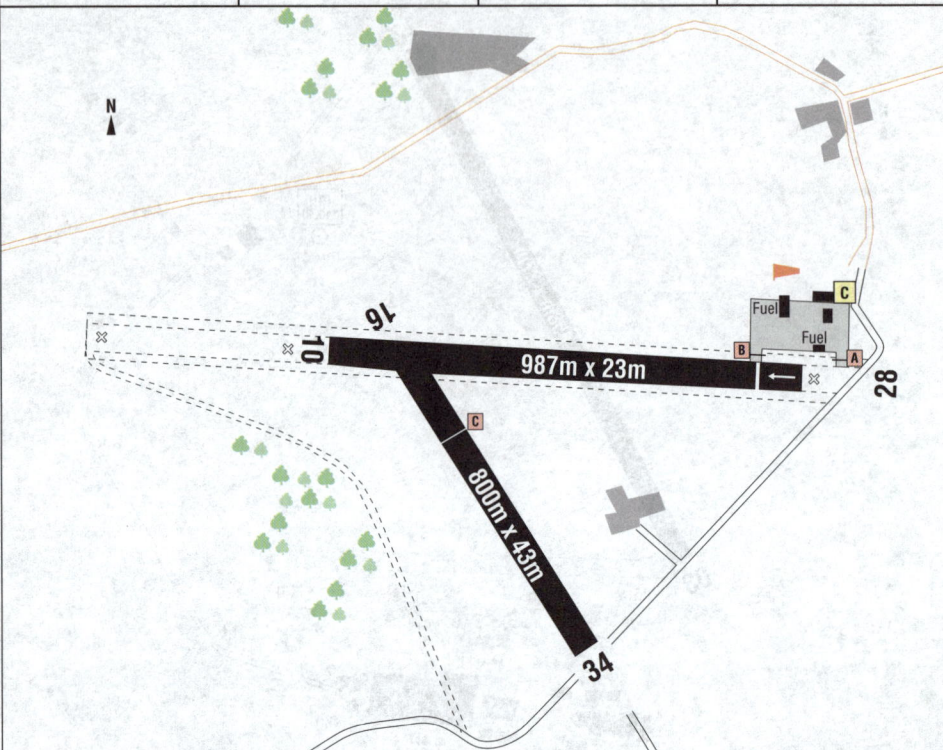

RWY	SURFACE	TORA	LDA	LIGHTING
10	Asphalt	957	957	Thr Rwy LITAS 3.25°
28	Asphalt	987	876	Thr Rwy LITAS 3.25°
16	Asphalt	800x43	U/L	Nil
34	Asphalt	800x43	U/L	Nil

Displaced Thr Rwy28 111m

Remarks
PPR. Non-radio ACFT not accepted. AD is 1nm E of A1M.
Visual aid to location: Ibn PB Green.

Warnings
Avoid Sibson AD (7nm NW). For Pilots of ACFT with wingspan >15m – clearance from obstacles through Hold A is reduced due to AVGAS tank and possible parked ACFT. Rwy lights are at 35m spacing, Rwy is 23m wide.
Noise: All pilots must avoid over flying all local villages.

Operating Hrs	Mon-Fri 0830-1800 Sat-Sun & PH 0900-1800 (Summer). Mon-Fri 0830-1700 Sat-Sun & PH 0900-1700 (Winter)	**Restaurants**	Club facilities with members bar. Snacks & hot meals available 7 days a week 1100-1500
Circuits	1000ft QFE. Direction may be varied to suit local requirements at any time	**Taxis**	**Tel:** 01733 244400 **Tel:** 07971 189242
Landing Fee	Single & R22 £10 Light Twins £15. Free Landings with 40ltr AVGAS per engine or 120ltrs AVTUR. Prices for large twins available on request	**Car Hire**	On request
		Weather Info	AirCen MOEx
		Operator	Aerolease Ltd Peterborough Business Airfield Holme, Peterborough, PE7 3PX **Tel:** 01487 834161 **Fax:** 01487 834246 info@flying-club-conington.co.uk www.flying-club-conington.co.uk
Maintenance Aerolease	CAA M3 Approved **Tel:** 01487 834161		
Fuel	AVGAS JET A1 100LL Oil W80, W100, S80, S100, 15W50		
Disabled Facilities Nil			

{P

130ft 3mb	6nm W of Peterborough N5233.35 W00023.18	PPR	Alternative AD Diversion AD	Cambridge Peterborough Conington

Sibson	LARS Cottesmore 130.200	A/G 122.300

RWY	SURFACE	TORA	LDA	LIGHTING
15	Grass	551	551	Thr Rwy APAPI 4° LHS
33	Grass	551	424	Thr Rwy APAPI 4° LHS
06	Grass	676	468	Nil
24	Grass	468	676	Nil

Displaced Thr Rwy33 127m
Displaced Thr Rwy24 259m
Displaced Thr Rwy06 467m

Remarks
PPR by telephone Non-radio ACFT not accepted. Not available to public transport passenger flights required to use a licensed AD. Inbound ACFT to call Cottesmore MATZ/LARS when no less than 15nm from Wittering. If no R/T contact is made during opening Hrs for Wittering, ACFT must avoid the Wittering MATZ except for that part which lies S of Sibson, and must descend to the Sibson circuit height before entering. Transiting fixed & rotary wing ACFT may not penetrate the ATZ whilst parachuting is in progress. Helicopters may not operate in the ATZ whilst parachuting is in progress.

Warnings
Free-fall parachuting up to FL130. Visiting pilots to contact A/G station to ascertain the latest situation. Do not over fly the AD. Power lines on ARR Rwy25. Surface can become boggy in winter.
Noise: Avoid over flying Eton village downwind Rwy06/24 and Stubbington village left base Rwy15 and climbout Rwy33.

Operating Hrs	0800-2000 (Summer) 0800-SS (Winter) & by arr	**Restaurants** **Taxis**	Nil
Circuits	15, 24 LH, 06, 33 RH, 1000ft QFE No over head joins No dead side		Tel: 01733 566661 Tel: 01733 775555
		Car Hire	
		Avis	Tel: 01733 349489
Landing Fee	Single £10, Twin £20, Microlights £5	Hertz	Tel: 01733 273543
Maintenance	Available (CAA-approved)	**Weather Info**	AirCen MOEx
Fuel	AVGAS 100LL Oils W80 80 W100/100	**Operator**	NSF Sibson
Disabled Facilities			Sibson Aerodrome Wansford Peterborough PE8 6NE Tel: 01832 280289 Fax: 01832 280675

461

450ft 15mb	1.5nm W of Peterlee Co Durham N5446.10 W00123.00	PPR	Alternative AD	Newcastle Durham Tees Valley

Peterlee Drop Zone	APP Newcastle 124.375	APP Durham 118.850	A/G 129.900

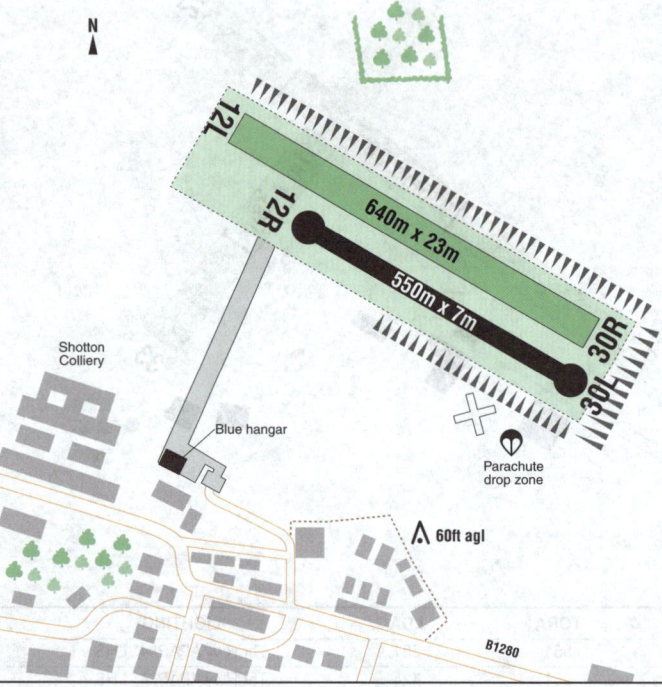

Shotton Colliery

Blue hangar

Parachute drop zone

60ft agl

Industrial Estate

B1280

RWY	SURFACE	TORA	LDA	LIGHTING
12L/30R	Grass	640x23	U/L	Nil
12R/30L	Tarmac	550x7	U/L	Nil

Remarks

PPR by telephone. AD operated primarily as parachute centre with free-fall operations up to FL150. Visiting ACFT welcome with PPR & at own risk. AD constructed on a disused colliery site with slight down slopes E side of Rwy & S end. Rwy has white edge markers & Rwy designators.

Warnings

AD situated on reclaimed land may be water logged after heavy rain. Circuits to N only. AD situated close to N edge of Teeside CTZ, Teeside APP.

Noise: Avoid over flying Peterlee & the village of Shotton Colliery.

Operating Hrs	0830-2030 (L) daylight Hrs only	Operator	Peterlee Parachute Centre The Airfield, Shotton Colliery Co Durham, DH6 2NH **Tel: 0191 5171234**
Circuits	12 LH, 30 RH, 1000ft N of AD only		
Landing Fee	Nil with fuel uplift min 10 litres		
Maintenance	Nil		
Fuel	AVGAS JET A1 100LL Mon-Fri 0930-1600 (phone to book Tue) weekends & PH 0830-2030/SS (L)		
Disabled Facilities	Nil		
Restaurants	Canteen Fri-Sun & PH		
Taxis	Tel: 0191 517 2222		
Car Hire	Nil		
Weather Info	AirN MWC		

PITSFORD

330ft 11mb	South Shore of Pitsford Water N5219.00 W00053.50	**Alternative AD**	**Cranfield** Northampton

Non Radio	**AFIS** Northampton 122.700	**Safetycom** 135.475

RWY	SURFACE	TORA	LDA	LIGHTING
11/29	Grass	450x23	U/L	Nil

Remarks
PPR not required. Visiting ACFT welcome at own risk. AD situated on S bank of Pitsford Water which has adjacent public walks and picnic spots. Please log in using book in red dustbin by parking area.

Warnings
Northampton Sywell ATZ to E of AD and may be contacted if required. AD is well cut and there are undulations for the first two thirds Rwy27.
Noise: Turn N after take-off or climb straight ahead. Avoid over flight of local habitation.

Operating Hrs	SR-SS	**Operator**	Richard Stanley
Circuits	To N 1000ft QFE		Moulton Grange Farm
Landing Fee	Donations to local Air Ambulance fund		Grange Lane
Maintenance	Nil		Pitsford
Fuel	Nil		Northamptonshire
Disabled Facilities	Nil		NN6 9AN
Restaurant	Nil		**Tel:** 01604 645656
Taxi/Car Hire	Nil		inbox@moultongrangefarm.org.uk
Weather Info	AirCen MOEx		

395ft 13mb	2nm SE of Hemel VRP N5143.70 W00022.71		**Alternative AD**	**London Luton** Elstree	
Plaistows	**ATIS** Luton 120.575	**APP** Luton 129.550	**A/G** Elstree 122.400	**A/G** 129.825 (Microlight freq)	

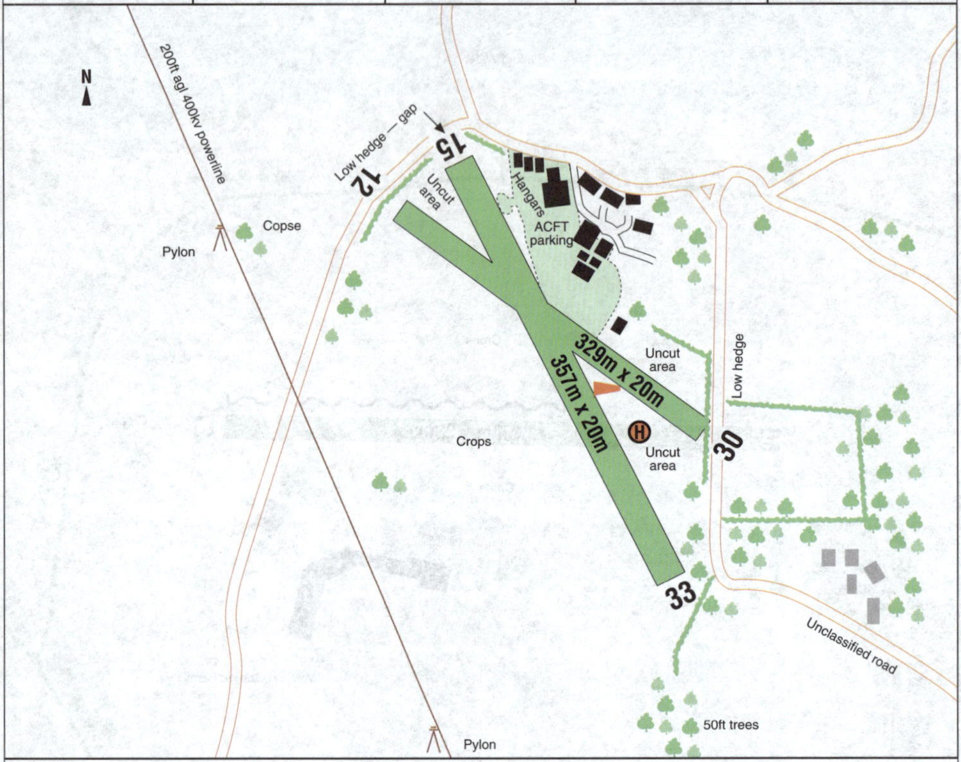

RWY	SURFACE	TORA	LDA	LIGHTING
15/33	Grass	357x20	U/L	Nil
12/30	Grass	329x20	U/L	Nil

Remarks

PPR is not required. Primarily a Microlight AD but suitable STOL ACFT welcome and at pilot's own risk. Rwy always well cut. Please call downwind and on finals.

Warnings

Small copse of trees 50ft high on very short final Rwy33 may cause turbulence in W to NW wind. Power lines 200ftagl run approx 200m W of AD and cross Rwy12 APP. Rwy30 climb out approx 300m from Rwy12 Thr. AD close to S boundary of Luton CTR (Class D) and 2.5nm N of the N boundary of the Elstree ATZ.

Noise: Please avoid over flight of local habitation.

Operating Hrs	SR-SS Dept restricted to between Mon-Sat 0800-1900 Sun 0900-1900	**Operator**	Mr Derrick Brunt Plaistows Farm Chiswell Green Lane St Albans, Herts, AL2 3NT **Tel:** 01727 851642
Circuits	30, 33 LH, 12, 15 RH		
Landing Fee	Donations to Royal Marsden Hospital gratefully received		
Maintenance	Nil		
Fuel	MOGAS		
Disabled Facilities			
Restaurants	The Three Hammers Chiswell Green 1nm E of AD		
Taxis/Car Hire	Nil		
Weather Info	AirSE MOEx		

P

PLOCKTON

Effective date:23/11/06

80ft 3mb	3.5nm NE of Kyle of Lochalsh N5720.12 W00540.32	PPR	Alternative AD	Inverness Isle of Skye

	Plockton	A/G 130.650 make blind calls	

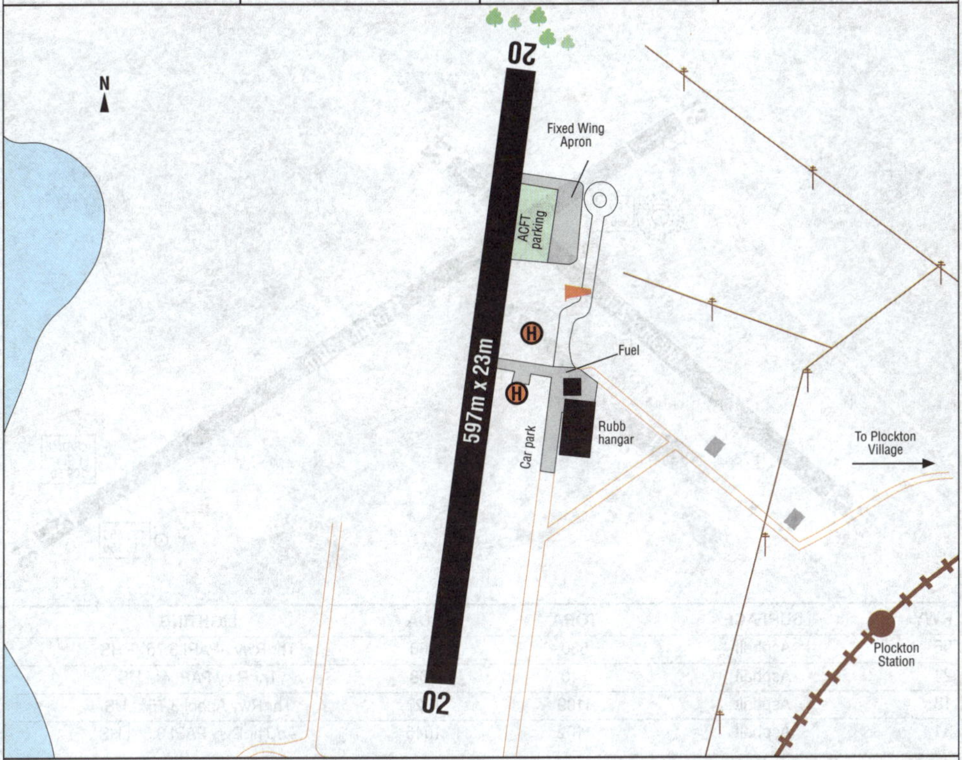

N

20

Fixed Wing Apron

ACFT parking

597m x 23m

H

Fuel

H

Rubb hangar

Car park

02

To Plockton Village

Plockton Station

RWY	SURFACE	TORA	LDA	LIGHTING
02/20	Asphalt	597x23	U/L	Nil

Remarks
Strictly PPR. Visitors welcome at pilots own risk. Fixed wing ACFT parking near windsock or on the short grass between the apron and Rwy. Use Twy to get to both locations.

Warnings
Ridge of high GND up to 140ft amsl 500m to E and up to 400ft amsl 500m to SE. High trees Rwy20 APP. Helicopter operations (Air Ambulance & Coast Guard) take place at AD and local areas up to 2000ft within a radius of 25nm.
Noise: Fly all circuits to W of AD, over the sea, to avoid flying over Plockton village and Plockton High School.

Operating Hrs	24 Hrs	
Circuits	02 LH, 20 RH No dead side	
Landing Fee	TBN	
Maintenance	Nil	
Fuel	AVTUR JET A1 self service Check availability	
Hangarage	Limited	

Disabled Facilities

Restaurants/ Accomodation
Off The Rails — Tel: 01599 544423 www.off-the-rails.co.uk
The Haven — Tel: 01599 544223 www.havenhotelplockton.co.uk

Plockton Hotel — Tel: 01599 544274 www.plocktonhotel.co.uk
Plockton Inn — Tel: 01599 544222 www.plocktoninn.f9.co.uk

Taxis
Kyle Taxi — Tel: 01599 534323
Plockton Taxis — Tel: 01599 544389
Boat Trip — Tel: 01599 544306 www.calums-sealtrips.com

Weather Info — AirSc GWC

Operator — PDG Helicopters (Kyle) BUTEC, Kyle of Lochalsh, Ross-shire IV40 8AJ
Tel/Fax: 01599 534926 (Pete Rawling)
Tel: 07899 936455 (Pete Rawling)
Tel: 07748 656553 (Hugh Vowles)
pdgkyle@btconnect.com
www.pdg-helicopters.co.uk

P

EGHD

PLYMOUTH CITY

| 476ft
16mb | 3.5nm NNE of Plymouth
N5025.22 W00406.21 | | PPR | Alternative AD
Diversion AD | Exeter Bodmin | |

Plymouth	APP 133.550	TWR 118.150	FIRE 121.600

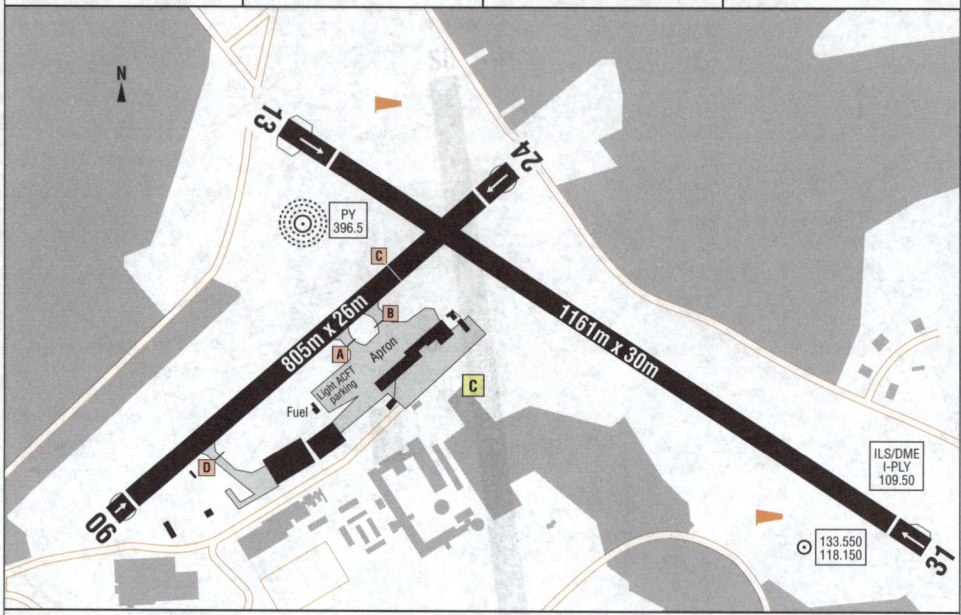

RWY	SURFACE	TORA	LDA	LIGHTING
06	Asphalt	680	680	Thr Rwy APAPI 3.75° RHS
24	Asphalt	740	708	Thr Rwy PAPI 4° LHS
13	Asphalt	1109	1027	Thr Rwy Apapi 3.75° LHS
31	Asphalt	1102	1045	Ap Thr Rwy PAPI 3.5° LHS

Remarks

Strict PPR at all times. Non-radio ACFT not accepted. Rescue & Police heli flights may take place any time outside Hrs. Rwy31 preferential Rwy in zero wind conditions. Helicopter training prohibited. No circuit training flights. Light ACFT parking normally W end main apron subject ATC requirements. Light ACFT & helicopters may be directed park adjacent grass areas. Start up clearance must be requested from ATC. ACFT must cause least disturbance in areas surrounding AD. Aerobatic manoeuvres & low fly pasts prohibited unless ACFT participating organised flying display. Turbo-jet ACFT use subject approval of AD Director/representative. ACFT parking tarmac light ACFT area or stand 5 use & return chocks provided, due sloping GND. Use caution taxiing, wing tip clearance not assured. Grass parking area telephone provided, contact ATC for permission to use pedestrian route across Rwy06/24. Route marked by green lines. Helicopter parking circles on grass between apron & Rwy06/24. **Visual aid to location:** White Strobe.

Warnings

Rwy06 signals visible at night N of extended centre line where normal obstacle clearance is not guaranteed. No APP slope guidance until ACFT is aligned with Rwy. Surface gradients in excess of 2.4% in S W corner of AD. Strong wind windshear & turbulence may be experienced on APP and climb out all Rwys. Downdraughts & sudden changes in W/V possible in light winds. Small flocks wood pigeons up to 2000ft in vicinity Rwy31 TDZ.

Operating Hrs	0530-2130 (Summer) +1Hr (Winter) See remarks for PPR periods	**Taxis** **Car Hire**	Available at terminal
Circuits	06,13 LH, 24,31RH 1000ft QFE or as directed by ATC	Hertz **Weather Info**	**Tel:** 01752 207206 M T9 Fax 386 MOEx
Landing Fee	Available on request from ATC. Out of Hrs surcharges after 1900 (Summer) 2000 (Winter)	**Visual Reference Points (VRP)** Avon Estuary	N5017.00 W00353.00
Maintenance	Nil	Ivy Bridge Saltash	N5023.08 W00355.10 N5025.13 W00414.08
Fuel	AVGAS JET A1 100LL	Yelverton	N5029.52 W00405.22
Disabled Facilities		**Operator**	Plymouth City Airport Ltd North QuayHouse Sutton Harbour, Plymouth Devon, PL4 0RA **Tel:** 01752 515341 (ATC/PPR)
Restaurants	Available in terminal		

{P

87ft 3mb	10nm ESE of York N5355.50 W00047.77	PPR	Alternative AD	Humberside Full Sutton

Pocklington	LARS Linton 118.550	A/G Glider Ops 130.100	GND to GND 129.900

RWY	SURFACE	TORA	LDA	LIGHTING
13/31	Asphalt	1072x50	U/L	Nil
13/31	Grass	1072x25	U/L	Nil
18/36	Asphalt	1167x50	U/L	Nil
18/36	Grass	1167x25	U/L	Nil

Asphalt Rwys in poor condition but safe for landing & take-off

Remarks
Operated by the Wolds Gliding Club Ltd. Primary used for gliding operations. Situated within Vale of York AIAA, pilots are advised to use the LARS of Linton APP. Joining Instructions: During gliding activity plan circuit on Rwy in use by gliders regardless of wind direction. Orbit AD at about 1000ft aal, keeping well outside the traffic pattern, to indicate intention to land. When the Rwy & APP are clear of gliders, land on asphalt or grass Rwy & backtrack to glider launch point. With no glider activity, check windsock, select Rwy and land on either Rwy. Taxi to hangar area.

Warnings
Look out for gliders. DO NOT join overhead below 2000ft agl when gliding is in progress due to cables.
Noise: Avoid over flying the villages of Barmby Moor NW of AD & Pocklington.

Operating Hrs	SR-SS	**Taxis**	
Circuits	Variable no overhead joins	Hessels	Tel: 01759 303176
Landing Fee	Private £5 Commercial £10	**Car Hire** National	Tel: 01904 612141
Maintenance	Nil	**Weather Info**	AirN MWC
Fuel	AVGAS 100LL	**Operator**	Wolds Gliding Club Ltd
Disabled Facilities	Nil		The Airfield, Pocklington
Restaurant			East Yorkshire, YO4 2NR
The Feathers	Tel: 01759 303155		**Tel:** 01759 303579
			Office Hrs Wed, Sat & Sun 1000-1600
			Answer phone at other times

EGHP

POPHAM

550ft 18mb	8.5nm NNE of Winchester N5111.66 W00114.17	PPR	Alternative AD Diversion AD	Farnborough Thruxton
Popham		**LARS** Farnborough 125.250		**A/G** 129.800

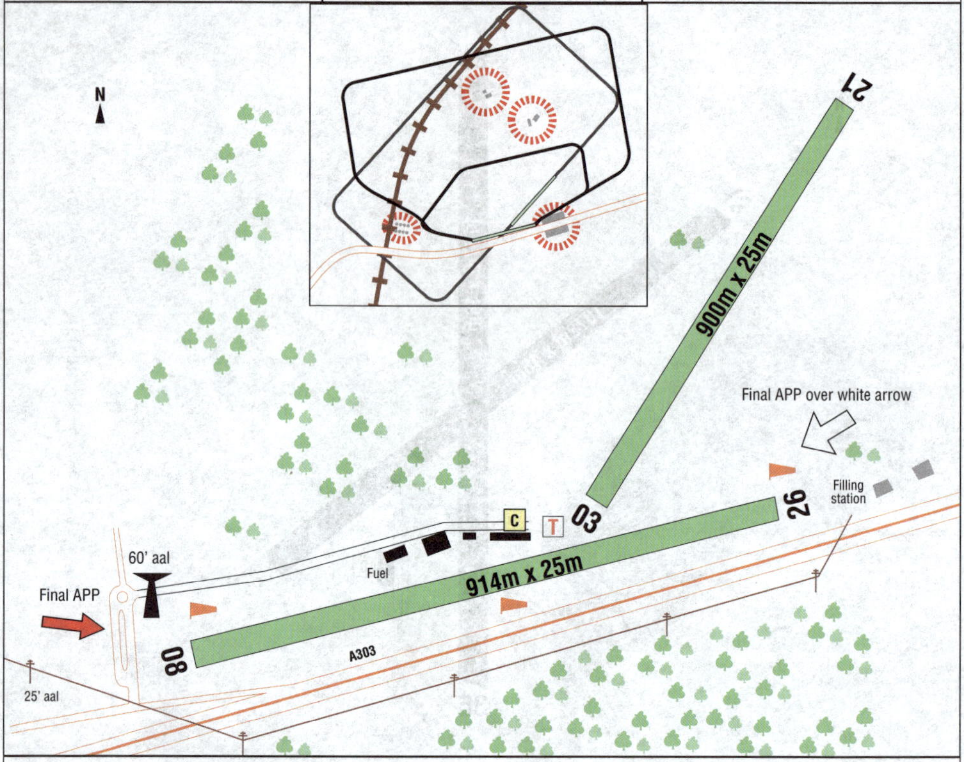

900m x 25m

Final APP over white arrow

21

03

26

Filling station

914m x 25m

60' aal

Final APP

Fuel

C T

08

A303

25' aal

N

RWY	SURFACE	TORA	LDA	LIGHTING
08/26	Grass	914x25	U/L	Nil
03/21	Grass	900x25	U/L	Nil

Rwy03/21 use restricted to certain dates check in advance, Rwy08 thr down slopes 1%, Rwy26 thr down slopes 3.3%

Remarks
PPR to non-radio ACFT. ACFT within 4500lbs MAUW welcome at pilots own risk

Warnings
Caution: Water tower 60ft aal close N of Rwy08 Thr. Microlight activity at AD. During week extensive military flying in local area, mainly helicopters & C130 ACFT often low level & very close to the AD.
Noise: Rwy08/26 APP offset, Rwy26 over white arrow avoiding bungalow & filling station, Rwy08 over silver grain silos avoiding houses W of AD.

Operating Hrs	0800-1700 (L)	
Circuits	N 800ft QFE	
Landing Fee	£5 non-members Free to Members	
Maintenance	Wiltshire ACFT Maintenance **Tel:** 01256 398372	
Fuel	AVGAS 100LL Aeroshell Oils (cash/cheque only)	

Taxis
Grassbys Taxis **Tel:** 01256 464212
Car Hire
Contract Self Drive **Tel:** 01256 322400

Weather Info AirSE MOEx
Operator Charles Church (Spitfires) Ltd
Popham Airfield, Winchester
Hants, SO21 3BD
Tel: 01256 397733
Fax: 01256 397114
pophamairfield@aol.com
www.popham-airfield.co.uk

Disabled Facilities

Restaurants Hot & cold refreshments available 10am-5pm daily

P

360ft 12mb	5nm NW of Kidderminster N5224.01 W00220.30	PPR	Alternative AD	Birmingham Wolverhampton

Non-Radio	ATIS Birmingham 126.275	APP Birmingham 118.050	LARS Shawbury 120.775	Safetycom 135.475

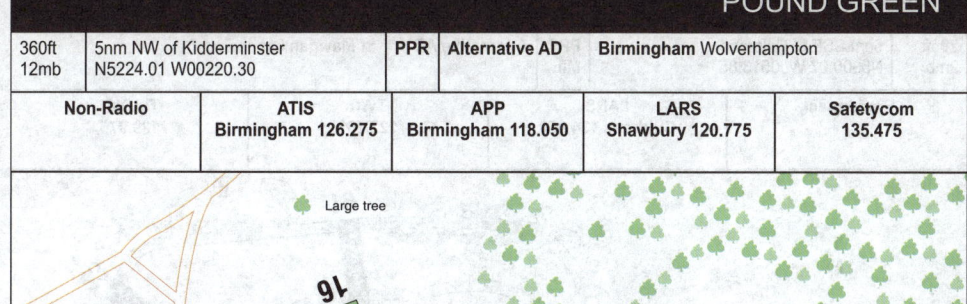

Large tree

16

13

450m x 20m

520m x 20m

Grey farm buildings

Woodhouse Farm

Low hedge

70ft trees

31

34

Timperley Reservoir

13 16

34 31

RWY	SURFACE	TORA	LDA	LIGHTING
15/31	Grass	450x20	U/L	Nil
16/34	Grass	520x20	U/L	Nil

Remarks

PPR by telephone essential. Microlight ACFT only. Briefing given with PPR. AD located between Trimpley Reservoir and River Severn.

Warning

Sheep may be grazing. Power cables before Rwy16 Thr.

Noise: Avoid over flying local houses and keep circuit within farm boundary whenever possible. When APP Rwy16 fly straight in from 3km out. This is a narrow corridor, pilots must avoid white houses to E of APP. Inbound ACFT should follow E bank of River Severn to Trimpley Reservoir. Then fly directly to the field 1km to WSW. Plan circuit using Woodhouse Farm as a guide, (grey sheds are good guide). Keep circuit within farm boundary which is marked by triangle made by roads to S & W. Do not cross these roads.

Operating Hrs	Mon-Sat 0900-2030 Sun 0930-2030 (L)	Operator	Mr E Gatehouse Pinewood Lodge Pound Green, Arley Bewdley, DY12 3LE **Tel/Fax:** 01299 401447
Circuits	LH 500ft QFE		
Landing Fee	Nil		
Maintenance	Nil		
Fuel	Petrol available on request		

Disabled Facilities

Restaurants	Nil
Taxi/Car Hire	Nil
Weather Info	AirCen MWC

P

EGDO   PREDANNACK

295ft 9mb	5nm SSE of Culdrose N5000.07 W00513.85	PPR MIL	Alternative AD	St Mawgan Lands End

Predannack	LARS Culdrose 134.050	TWR 122.100	RADIO 129.975

N

19   23   13   10   05   01   31   28

1814m x 46m
1405m x 46m
916m x 46m
1309m x 46m

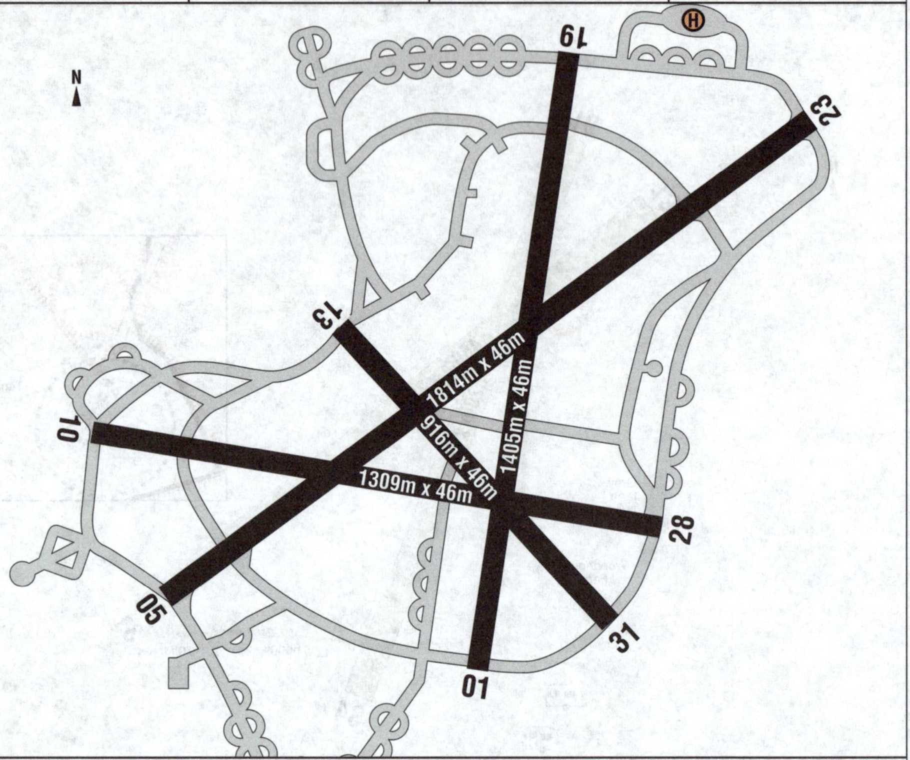

RWY	SURFACE	TORA	LDA	LIGHTING
05/23	Asphalt	1814	1814	Nil
01/19	Asphalt	1405	1405	Nil
10/28	Asphalt	1309	1309	Nil
13/31	Asphalt	916	916	Nil

Rwy01/19 10/28, 13/31 not maintained to normal standard useable by light ACFT only

Remarks
Strictly PPR only. Satellite airfield for RNAS Culdrose. ATZ H24. AD ops are only as required by Culdrose. Landings not authorised.

Warnings
Intensive military helicopter ops at AD and vicinity. Goonhilly Down HIRTA to NE of AD, intrudes into ATZ. Glider and Model ACFT activity outside normal op hrs as required by RNAS Culdrose. Rwys have non-standard markings associated with helicopter training.
Noise: Avoid over flying local habitation.

Operating Hrs	Mon-Fri as required by RNAS Culdrose	Taxi/Car Hire	Nil
Circuits	As instructed	Weather Info	M T Fax 272 MOEx
Landing Fee	Charges in accordance with MOD policy Contact Station Ops for details	Operator	RNAS Culdrose Helston Cornwall, TR12 7RH **Tel:** 01326 574121 Ex 2417 (Culdrose/PPR) **Tel:** 01326 574121 Ex 2319 (AD)
Maintenance Fuel	Nil Nil		
Disabled Facilities			

Restaurants   Nil

EGPK
PRESTWICK

65ft 2mb	1nm NE of Prestwick N5530.47 W00435.20	PPR	Alternative AD Diversion AD	Glasgow Cumbernauld

Prestwick	ATIS 121.125	APP 120.550	Handling 120.500 (Greer Aviation) 129.700 (PIK Handling)
TWR 118.150	RAD 120.550	FIRE 121.600	

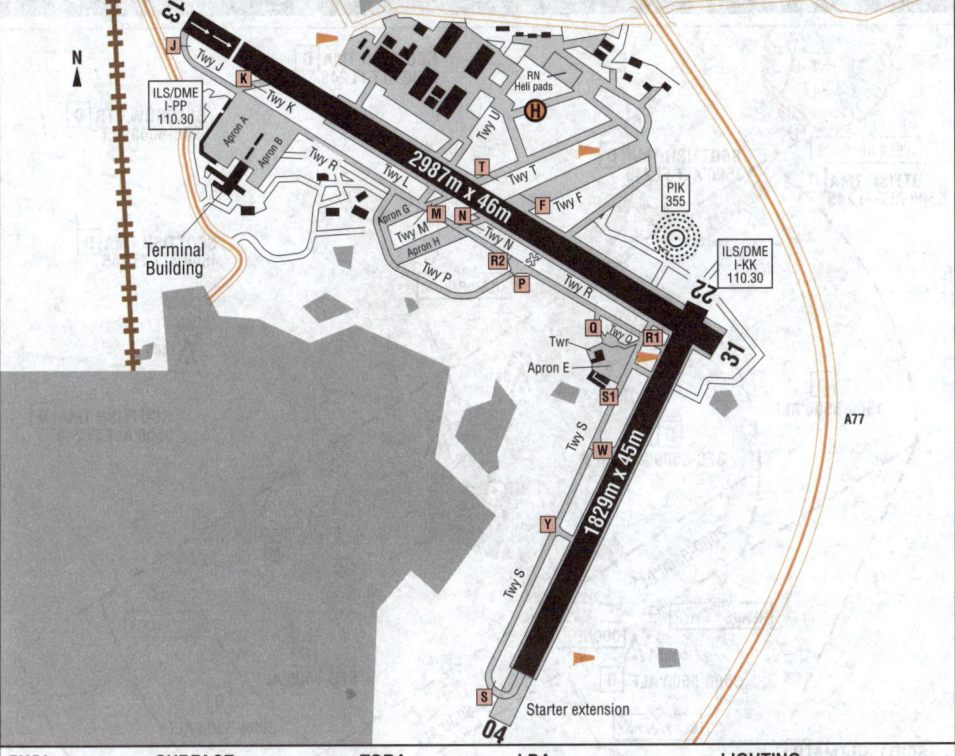

RWY	SURFACE	TORA	LDA	LIGHTING
13	Conc/Asph	2987	2743	Ap Thr Rwy PAPI 3° LHS
31	Conc/Asph	2987	2987	Ap Thr Rwy PAPI 3.5° LHS
04	Asphalt	1829	1829	Thr Rwy PAPI 3° LHS
22	Asphalt	1829	1829	Ap Thr Rwy PAPI 3.5° LHS

Starter extension Rwy04 160m

Remarks
PPR via ATC. Handling mandatory. Training flights PPR from ATC. In VMC or when following a non-standard instrument Dept avoid flying over Troon. ACFT shall maintain as high an altitude as practicable. If APP without assistance from ILS or RAD fly not lower than the ILS glide path. Only marked Twys to be used. Helicopter operations: Civil helicopters normally allocated apron stand. Helicopters to route to apron by APP Rwy13/31 or Rwy04/22 as instructed. Helicopters may air/GND taxi between this area and military parking circles. Apron C only marked designated Twy routes to be used.
Aids to Navigation: NDB PW 426.00.

Warnings
If carrying out circuits on Rwy04/22 be warned of rising GND to the NE. Bird hazard assessed as 'moderate' and severe during migratory periods Oct/Nov and Mar/Apr. Except for light signals, GND signals are not displayed. Traffic flow management of inbound, outbound & local ACFT may be applied without notice. Twys N not to be used at night or in low vis.

Operating Hrs	H24
Circuits	See Warnings
Landing Fee	Light ACFT £35 min charge
Maintenance	Available
Fuel	AVGAS JET A1 100LL
Disabled Facilities	Available

Handling
Tel: 01292 678252 (Greer Aviation)
Fax: 01292 678222 (Greer Aviation)
ops@greeraviation.com
Tel: 01292 478961 (Ocean Sky)
Fax: 01292 479616 (Ocean Sky)
pikops@oceansky.com
Tel: 01292 511260 (PIK Handling)
Fax: 01292 511259 (PIK Handling)
prestwick_handling@glasgowprestwick.com

Effective date:23/11/06

P

Restaurants	Restaurant buffet & bar in terminal	Operator	Glasgow Prestwick Airport Ltd
Taxis	Available at terminal or on request		Aviation House, Prestwick
Car Hire			Scotland, KA92PL
Avis	Tel: 01292 77218		Tel: 01292 511000 (Switchboard)
Hertz	Tel: 01292 79822 Ex 3080		Tel: 01292 511107 (ATC)
			Fax: 01292 475464 (ATC)
Weather Info	M T9 T18 Fax 388 A VSc GWC		www.glasgowprestwick.com

Prestwick Controlled Airspace

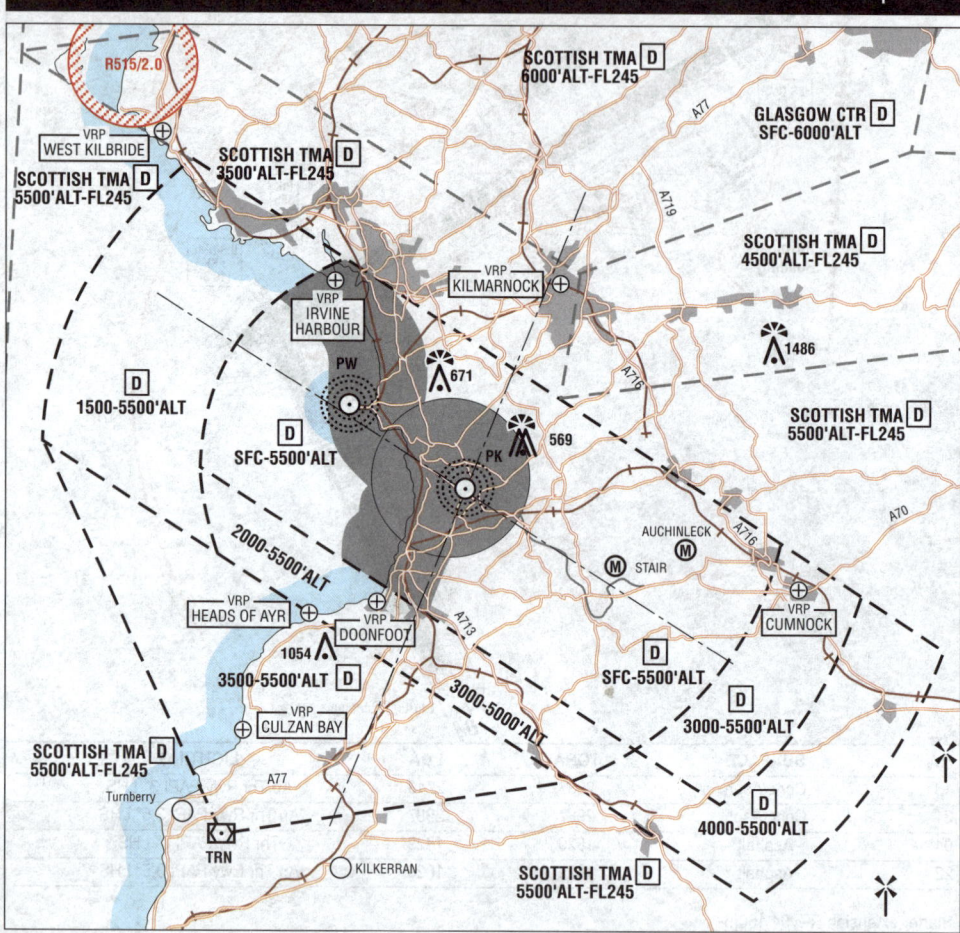

Prestwick CTZ and CTA Class D Airspace. Pilots must flight plan in/out by contacting ATC with brief details of flight.

Visual Reference Points (VRP)

Culzean Bay/Castle	N5522.17 W00446.08
Cumnock	N5527.33 W00415.45
Doonfoot	N5526.42 W00439.05
Heads of Ayr	N5525.97 W00442.78
Irvine Harbour	N5536.65 W00441.92
Kilmarnock	N5536.75 W00429.90
Pladda	N5525.58 W00507.07
West Kilbride	N5541.13 W00452.08

P

210ft 7mb	1.3nm W of Braintree N5153.23 E00031.42	PPR	Alternative AD	Southend Andrewsfield

Rayne	ATIS Stansted 127.175	APP Essex RAD 120.625	A/G 125.050

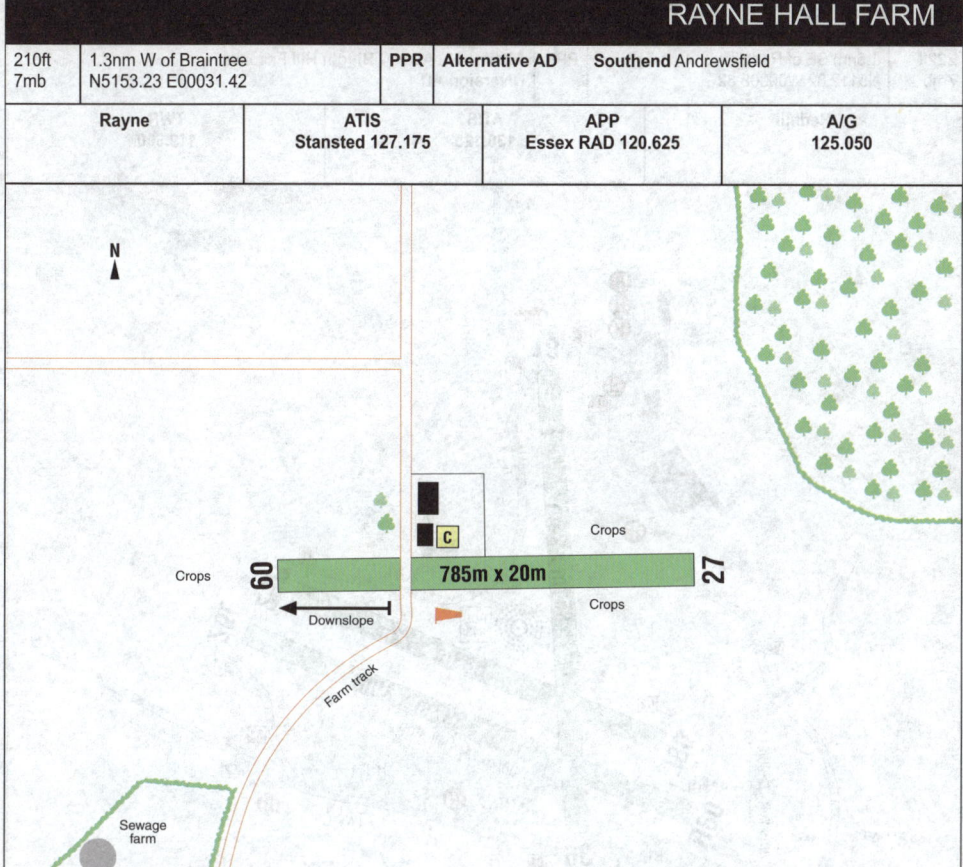

RWY	SURFACE	TORA	LDA	LIGHTING
09/27	Grass	785x20	U/L	Nil

Rwy27 down slope after road crossing

Remarks
PPR by telephone. Visitors welcome at pilots own risk. Microlights operate from AD. Clubhouse at weekends. Picnic table adjacent parking area. Situated under Stansted CTA (base 2000ft QNH). Weather Info can be obtained from Stansted ATIS.

Warnings
Andrewsfield ATZ boundary close to E of AD.
Caution: Crops grow up to edge of strip. Farm road crosses Rwy midpoint loose stones may be encountered when crossing the road.
Noise: Avoid over flying local habitation.

		Operator	Mr D S McGregor
Operating Hrs	Available on request		Rayne Hall Farm, Braintree
Circuits	N 1000ft QFE		Essex, CM7 5BT
Landing Fee	£4		**Tel/Fax:** 01376 321899 (Operator)
Maintenance	Nil		**Tel:** 07850 921961
Fuel	Nil		megregordavidmac@tiscali.co.uk
Disabled Facilities	Nil		
Restaurants	Nil		
Taxis			
T&M Taxis	**Tel:** 01376 347888		
Car Hire	Nil		
Weather Info	AirCen MOEx		

222ft 7mb	1.5nm SE of Redhill N5112.82 W00008.32	PPR	Alternative AD Diversion AD	Biggin Hill Fairoaks

Redhill	ATIS 136.125	TWR 119.600

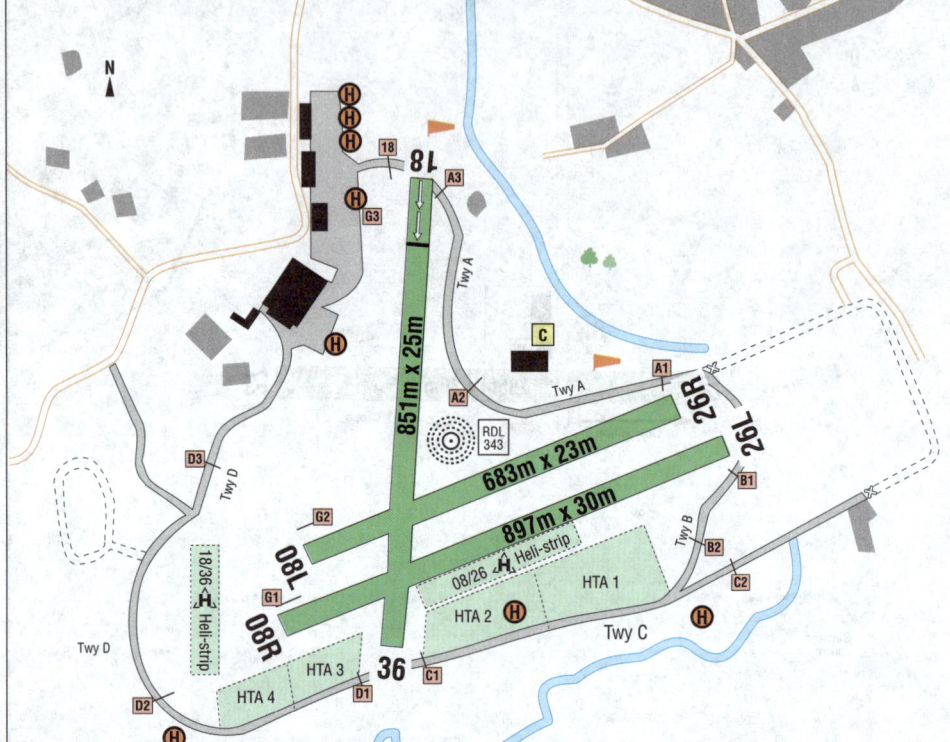

RWY	SURFACE	TORA	LDA	LIGHTING
36	Grass	851	851	Nil
18	Grass	851	699	Nil
08R	Grass	897	897	Thr Rwy APAPI 4.25° LHS
26L	Grass	897	897	Thr Rwy APAPI 3.5° LHS
08L/26R	Grass	683	683	Nil

Displaced Thr Rwy18 151m

Remarks
PPR by telephone. AD based Microlights only. Rwy08R/26L licensed for night use by all ACFT. Fixed wing ACFT ops restricted to marked Rwys and Twys N of Rwy08R/26L. Unmarked Twys not to be used without ATC permission. Training restricted to base Ops and approved helicopter ops. AD has a fixed lighted helipad.
Visual aid to location: Abn white flashing.

Warnings
AD subject to water logging. Surface slopes up 10ft from centre to W boundary. Intensive helicopter ops. Helicopters may not comply with standard R/T procedures. Care must be taken on APP and Dept not to drift into helicopter circuit area. Do not vacate any Rwy until instructed by ATC. Caution down wash from taxiing helicopters. When Rwy36/18 is in use it is not possible to provide separation between helicopters and fixed wing ACFT therefore significant delays will occur.

Operating Hrs	0800-1800 (Summer) 0700-0800 & 1800-1900 24 Hr PNR	Maintenance	Redhill Engineering **Tel:** 01737 822959
Circuits	Variable Fixed wing/Heli 1000ft QFE. See helicopter & fixed wing joining procedures. Helicopters will fly cct pattern opposite to fixed wing ACFT	**Fuel**	AVGAS JET A1 100LL
		Disabled Facilities Nil	
		Restaurant	Cafe in Redhill Aviation
Landing Fee	Single £12 Twin <1500kg £16 <2000kg £22 <2500kg £30		

Taxis		Operator	Redhill Aerodrome Ltd
Bellfry Cars	**Tel:** 01737 766111		Terminal Building, Redhill Aerodrome
Roadrunners	**Tel:** 01737 760076		Surrey, RH1 5YP
Car Hire	See companies listed for London Gatwick		**Tel:** 01737 821801 (Admin)
			Tel: 01737 821805 (Fuel)
Weather Info	AirSE MOEx		**Tel:** 01737 821802 (ATC)
ATIS **Tel:** 01737 832947			atc@redhillaerodrome.com
			www.redhillaerodrome.com

Visual Reporting Points (VRP)

Junction	N5115.83 W00007.68
(Jct M23/M25)	
Godstone	N5114.83 W00004.02
(Jct A25/B2236)	
Reigate Rlwy Station	N5114.52 W00012.25
Godstone Rlwy Station	N5113.08 W00003.07

REDHILL CIRCUIT DIAGRAM

Although the Redhill ATZ is within Gatwick CTR a local flying area has been established which permits ops within this area without reference to Gatwick ATC. Such flights may ONLY be made during the Hrs of watch of REDHILL ATC.

Area A

1 Clear of cloud & in sight of surface in minimum flight visibility (fixed wing ACFT) of 3km.

2 Fly not above 1500ftQNH.

Flight in circuit must not proceed beyond

W: A23 Redhill Horley road

E: Outwood Bletchingley road

S: Picketts & Brownslade farms

Area B

Fly NOT ABOVE 1500ft QNH

All ACFT must obtain clearance from Redhill ATC at least 5min before ETA. (This includes ACFT which have initially contacted Gatwick ATC)

Arr & Dept ACFT must do so N of Gatwick CTR.

Ensure you are familiar with joining/Dept procedures detailed in this section.

JOINING PROCEDURES

ATC will require all VFR ACFT to enter and leave the ATZ via a VRP.

Fixed wing ACFT join at 1300ft QFE. If required to join overhead – enter the ATZ on Rwy QDM remaining within the fixed wing circuit area (N Rwy08/26 or E Rwy36/18). When instructed descend to circuit height and join the visual circuit pattern. Dept at 1500ft QNH.

Helicopters join at 1000ft QFE. When Rwy36/18 is in use helicopters joining from E may be instructed to route from Godstone Station to E AD boundary at500ft QFE. Dept at 1200ft QNH.

NOISE:

Always use best rate of climb. Avoid over flying South Nutfield & East Surrey Hospital. Fixed wing – after Dept Rwy36/08/26 climb straight ahead to 1000ft QNH below turning. After Dept Rwy19 commence left turn at 500ft QNH. Avoid all built up areas within ATZ

R

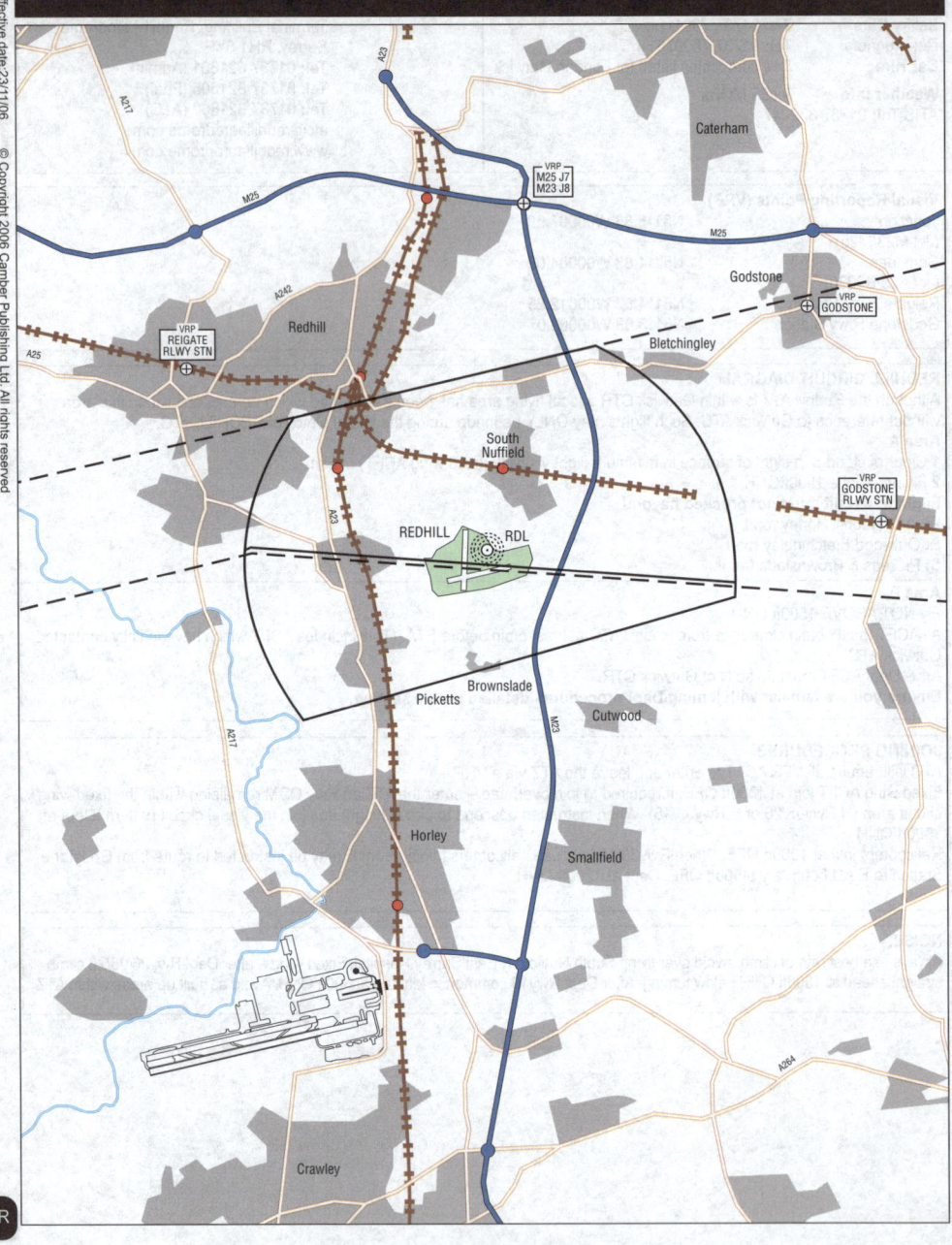

R

322ft 10mb	1nm E of Swindon N5133.65 W00142.27	PPR	Alternative AD	Oxford Kemble

Redlands	Zone Lyneham 123.400	A/G 129.825

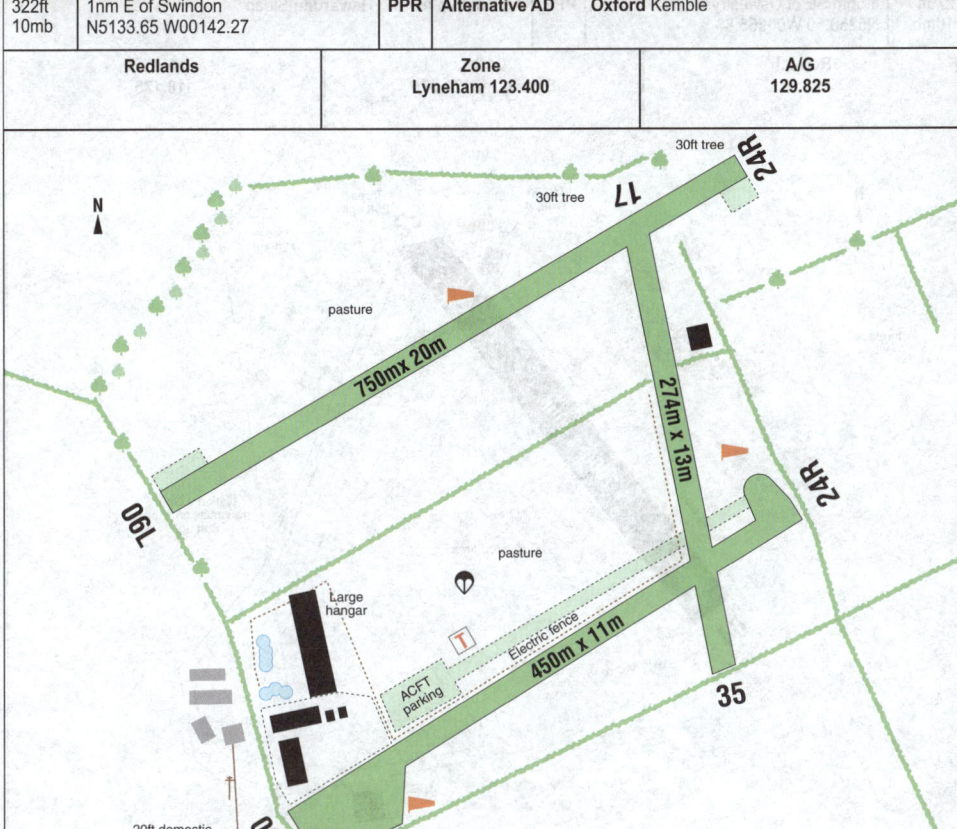

RWY	SURFACE	TORA	LDA	LIGHTING
06L/24R	Grass	450x11	U/L	Nil
17/35	Grass	274x13	U/L	Nil
06L/24R	Grass	750x20	U/L	Nil

Remarks

PPR by telephone essential. GA use only. Microlight ACFT only accepted due to planning constraints. Visitors welcome at own risk. Beware parachute activity weekends & some weekdays. Redlands Radio give details of parachuting activity. Observe signals square. Overnight camping available with toilets on site.
Visual aid to location: New 300ft hangar.

Warnings

AD is close to Lyneham CTR.
Noise: Arr/Dept via N corridor between the twin barns over AD and railway line. Inbound ACFT: 1500ft QFE, join overhead avoiding over flying local habitation and Wanborough. Outbound ACFT: climb out over the barns to railway before setting course.

Operating Hrs	Mon-Sat SR-SS Sun 1000-2000 or SS (L)	Operator	Joe & Sarah Smith
Circuits	06, 35 LH, 24, 17 RH, 500ft aal		Redlands Airfield
Landing Fee	£3.50		Redlands Farm Wanborough, Swindon
Maintenance	Nil		Wilts, SN4 0AA
Fuel	Available by prior arrangement		**Tel:** 01793 791014
Disabled Facilities	Nil		**Tel:** 07703 182756
Restaurants	Help yourself Tea, Coffee & Biscuits Full catering facilities with Hot/cold snacks & lunches during weekends		sarah@redlandsairfield.co.uk www.redlandsairfield.co.uk
Taxis/Car Hire	Can be arranged by operators		
Weather Info	AirSW MOEx		

477

REDNAL

275ft 10mb	4.5nm SE of Oswestry N5250.50 W00255.83	PPR	Alternative AD	Hawarden Sleap

Rednal	LARS Shawbury 120.775	A/G 118.175

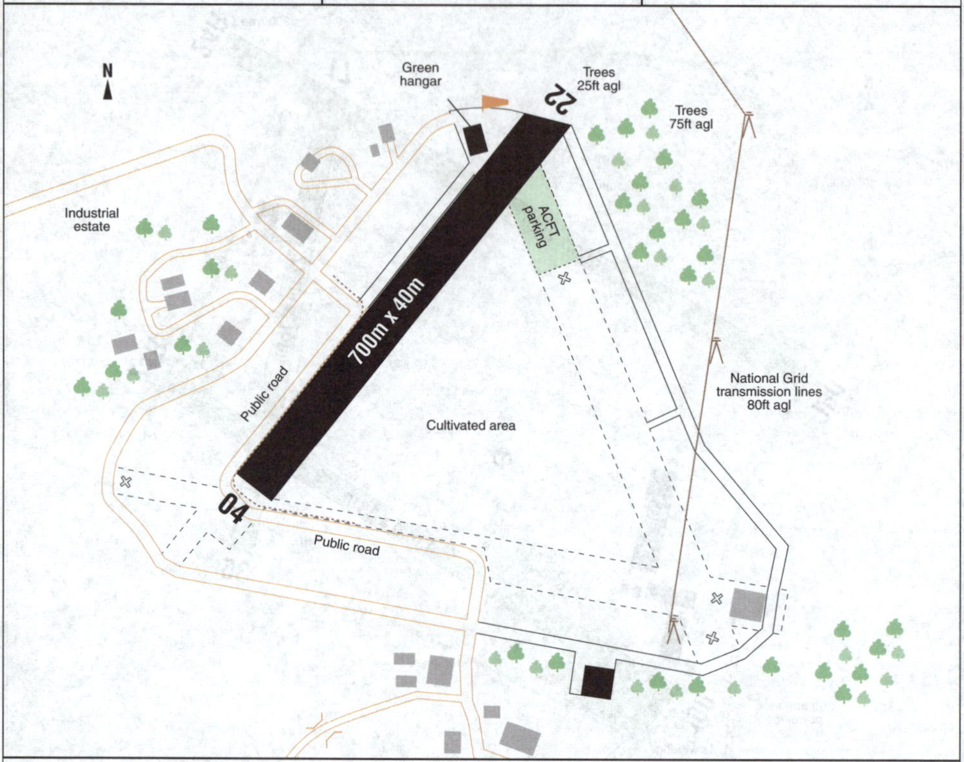

N

Green hangar

Trees 25ft agl

Trees 75ft agl

22

ACFT parking

Industrial estate

700m x 40m

Public road

National Grid transmission lines 80ft agl

Cultivated area

04

Public road

RWY	SURFACE	TORA	LDA	LIGHTING
04/22	Asphalt	700x40	U/L	Nil

Remarks
PPR by telephone, fax or email. Established on W portion of WWII AD. All other Rwys are unavailable.

Warnings
National grid power lines & pylons cross APP Rwy22 80ft aal approx 0.5nm out. Public road crosses Rwy04 Thr & runs along W side for half Rwy length. 4ft wire fence divides the road from the active Rwy. A copse of mature trees, 25ft aal, encroach on the E side of Rwy22 final APP. Rwy surface gritty.
Noise: Avoid over flying all local habitation. No flying to W of AD.

Operating Hrs	SR-SS	**Operator**	Roger Reeves
Circuits	Join overhead 1500ft QFE Circuits E 800ft QFE		Jupiter House Tattenhall Chester, CH3 9PX **Tel:** 07747 618131 (AD) **Tel:** 01829 771440 (Office) **Fax:** 01829 771487 roger.reeves@aviacapital.com
Landing Fee	Nil		
Maintenance	Nil		
Fuel	Nil		

Disabled Facilities

Restaurants/Accomodation
Travelodge **Tel:** 01691 658178 (Oswestry 4m)
Queens Head1m good food (no accom)

Taxis
Berwin Cars **Tel:** 01691 652000
Car Hire Nil
Weather Info AirN MWC

R

87ft 3mb	2nm S of Retford N5316.83 W00057.08	**PPR**	**Alternative AD** **Diversion AD**	**Humberside** Sandtoft

	Gamston		**A/G** **130.475**	

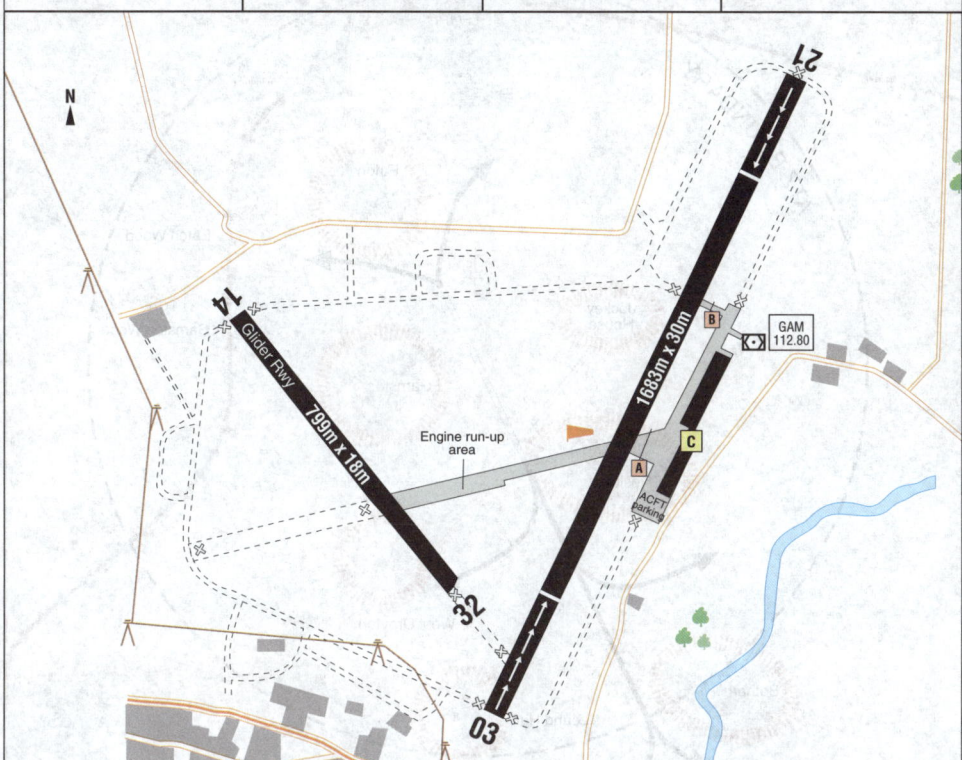

RWY	SURFACE	TORA	LDA	LIGHTING
03	Asphalt	1203	1203	Thr Rwy APAPI 3.5° LHS
21	Asphalt	1203	1203	Thr Rwy APAPI 3° LHS
14/32	Asphalt	799x18	U/L	Nil

Starter extension Rwy03/21 240m
Starter extension Rwy14/32 50m

Remarks

PPR by R/T acceptable. Pilots are to contact A/G 10 mins before ETA. Visiting ACFT asked to park on numbered stands marked by yellow boards on the Twy edges.

Warnings

Pilots taxiing for take-off on Rwy21 at night should not back track further than the red Rwy end lights. Rwy edge lights are positioned at edge of hard surface at a width of 46m. Rwy03/21 is side striped at 30m. Rwy14/32 available on request to powered ACFT. Access to and from Rwy03/21 is via points A and B only.

Operating Hrs	Mon-Fri 0800-1800 Sat-Sun & PH 0900-1800 (L)	Taxis	
		DJ Taxi	**Tel:** 01777 701066
Circuits	1000ft QFE	Hinchcliffe	**Tel:** 01777 702049
Landing Fee	Single £10	**Car Hire**	On request
	Heli £9.40 per half tonne	**Weather Info**	AirCen MWC
	Twin £8.23 per half tonne	**Operator**	Gamston Aviation Ltd
			Retford/Gamston Airport
Maintenance			Retford, Nottingham, DN22 0QL
Diamond Aircraft	**Tel:** 01777 839200		**Tel:** 01777 838593 (Ops/ATC)
Fuel	AVGAS JET A1 100LL		**Tel:** 01777 838521 (Outside Ops Hrs)
Disabled Facilities Available			**Fax:** 01777 838035
Restaurants	Refreshments available at AD Local pubs within 1.5 miles		ops@gamstonairport.co.uk www.gamstonairport.co.uk

R

RETFORD NOISE & CIRCUIT PROCEDURES
1 Do not over fly Bothamsall, Eaton, Elkesley, Gamston, Lound Hall or West Drayton.
2 Whenever possible, backtrack to use all available Rwy for take-off.
3 After take off from Rwy03, turn left or right as appropriate before reaching the end of the Rwy.
4 After take off Rwy21 turn onto the crosswind leg to avoid over flying Elkesley or West Drayton.
5 Reduce power slowly.
6 Keep circuit flying to a minimum, especially at weekends.
7 Low approaches to land should be avoided.

R

650ft 21mb	3nm SE of Prestatyn N5316.58 W00322.07	PPR	Alternative AD	Hawarden Caernarfon

Rhedyn Coch	A/G 129.825 (Microlight freq)	A/G Bryngwyn 118.325 Make blind calls

RWY	SURFACE	TORA	LDA	LIGHTING
18/36	Grass	402x9	U/L	Nil
11/29	Grass	302x9	U/L	Nil

Rwy have no markings
ID by witness marks on large field

Remarks
PPR by telephone. Visiting STOL ACFT and microlights welcome at pilots own risk. Rwys are large part of field which allows run off to either side.

Warnings
Difficult AD to locate, particularly during the winter when there is little aviation use. High GND up to 998ft amsl 0.25nm W of AD. Wood plantations close to AD, particularly on Rwy18 APP which may cause turbulence. There are up slopes on Rwy29 & 18.
Noise: Do not over fly local habitation.

Operating Hrs	SR-SS	**Operator**	Mr Richard Emlyn Jones Rhedyn Coch Rhault, St Asaph, Denbigshire **Tel:** 01745 584051 (Home) **Tel:** 07880 733274
Circuits	Join overhead 1500ft QFE Descend quietly to 600ft QFE 36, 18, 11 LH, 29 RH		
Landing Fee	Nil		
Maintenance	Nil		
Fuel	MOGAS available in cans on request		
Disabled Facilities	Nil		
Restaurant	Tea & coffee available		
Taxi/Car Hire	Nil		
Weather Info	AirCen MWC		

R

436ft 15mb	1.5nm S of Rochester N5121.12 E00030.20	PPR	Alternative AD Diversion AD	Southend Lashenden

	Rochester	AFIS 122.250	

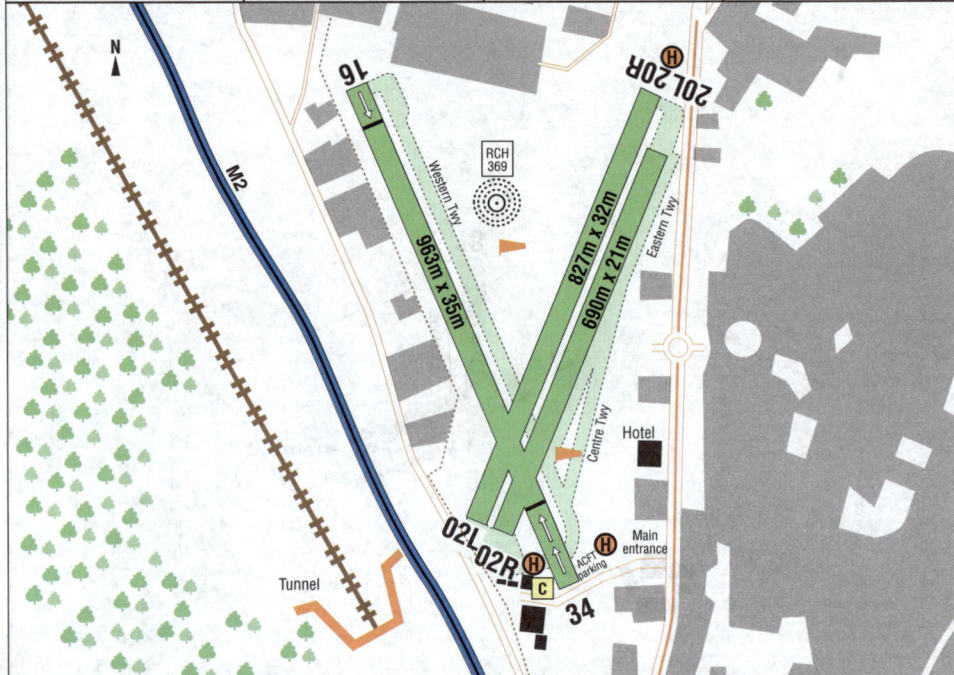

RWY	SURFACE	TORA	LDA	LIGHTING
02L	Grass	827	827	Thr Rwy APAPI 4° LHS
20R	Grass	827	827	Ap Thr Rwy APAPI 3.5° LHS
02R/20L	Grass	690	690	Nil
16	Grass	773	808	Nil
34	Grass	963	773	Nil

Rwy02R/20L additional 35m available

Remarks

PPR by telephone Sat-Sun & PH. Relief Rwy02R/20L has been established parallel to Rwy02/20 used when main Rwy under maintenance. Rwys & Twys may be restricted/withdrawn short notice due surface conditions. Pilots obtain latest info before Arr. Taxi prepared & marked areas only. AD based ACFT may use AD after Hrs in daylight. Police and Air Ambulance helicopters H24 operations.
Visual aid to location: Abn White flashing. AD name displayed.

Warnings

Road used by vehicular traffic runs E/W immediately S of take-off Rwy34 Thr. Rwy16 has non-standard markings. Designator located before landing Thr. Visual glide slope signals for Rwy20R are visible to E of extended Rwy centre line where normal obstacle clearance is not guaranteed. They should not be used until the ACFT is aligned with the extended Rwy centre line.
Noise: Circuits variable to avoid flying over built up areas.

Operating Hrs	0800-1800 (L) ATZ may be active at other times		Taxis	
			Medway	**Tel:** 01634 848848
Circuits	Fixed wing 1000 QFE Heli 800ft QFE. 16, 20 RH, 02, 34 LH		Volkes	**Tel:** 01634 222222/843601
			Car Hire	
Landing Fee	Single £9, Twin £14		Kenning	**Tel:** 01634 845145
Maintenance	RAS Ltd **Tel:** 01634 200008		**Weather Info**	AirSE MOEx
Fuel	AVGAS JET A1 100LL		Operator	Rochester Airport Plc Rochester Airport, Chatham Kent, ME5 9SD **Tel:** 01634 861378 (ATC) **Tel:** 01634 869969 (Admin) **Fax:** 01634 861682 (ATC) **Fax:** 01634 869968 (Admin)
Disabled Facilities	Nil			
Restaurants	Holiday Inn Hotel/Restaurant Several pubs nearby			

171ft 6mb	3nm NE of Lichfield N5242.80 W00144.63	PPR	Alternative AD	Birmingham Tatenhill

Roddige	APP Birmingham 118.050	APP East Mids 134.175	A/G 129.825

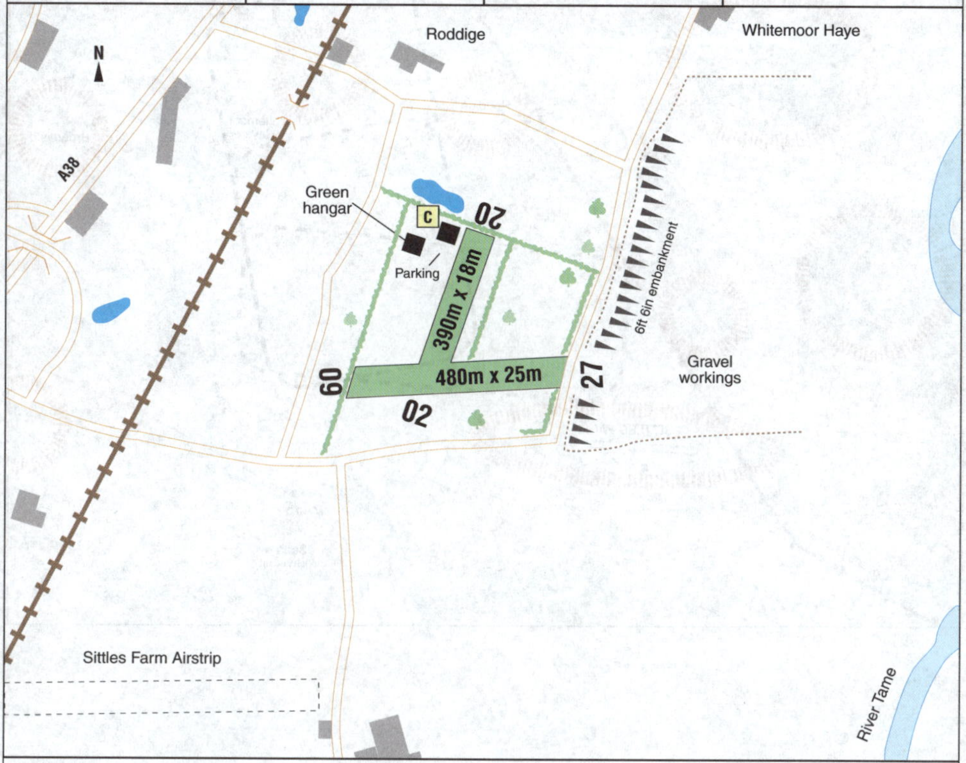

Roddige

Whitemoor Haye

Green hangar

Parking

390m x 18m

480m x 25m

6ft 6in embankment

Gravel workings

Sittles Farm Airstrip

River Tame

RWY	SURFACE	TORA	LDA	LIGHTING
02/20	Grass	390x18	U/L	Nil
09/27	Grass	480x25	U/L	Nil

Remarks
PPR by telephone. Primarily a microlight training AD but light ACFT and pilots with STOL capability welcome at own risk.

Warnings
4ft hedge crosses Rwy27 Thr & 6.5ft embankment screening gravel workings on the opposite side of road from Thr.
Caution: Do not confuse Roddige with Sittles farm strip to S on opposite side of hedge.
Noise: Avoid over flying all local habitation.

Operating Hrs	0900-dusk (L)	**Operator**	Mr Shea
Circuits	27 20 LH, 09 02 RH 500ft QFE Join overhead 1500ft QFE		The Microlight School Roddige Lane, Fradley Lichfield, WS13 8QS
Landing Fee	Nil		**Tel:** 01283 792193
Maintenance	Ltd microlight		**Tel:** 07767 474847
Fuel	MOGAS		www.microlightschool.org.uk
Hangarage	Ltd microlight		

Disabled Facilities

Restaurants	Tea & coffee available
Taxis	**Tel:** 01543 254999
Car Hire	**Tel:** 01543 254825
Weather Info	AirCen MWC

R

483

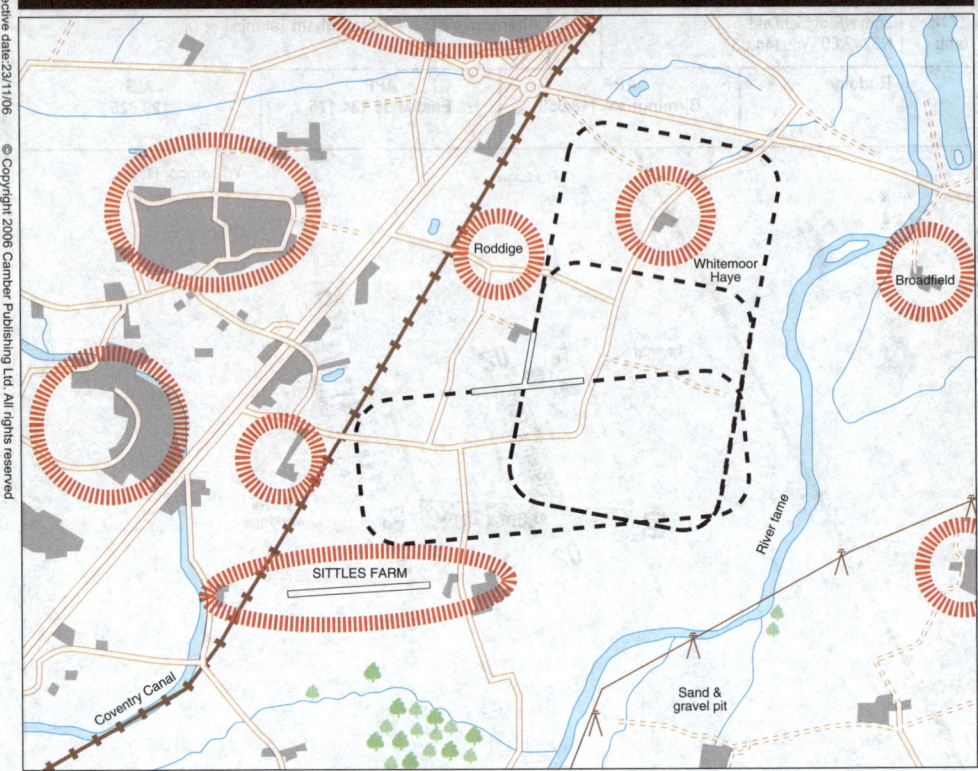

ROSERROW

| 130ft
4mb | 1nm SE of Polzeath
N5033.72 W00454.02 | PPR | Alternative AD | St Mawgan Lands End |

| Non-Radio | LARS
St Mawgan 128.725 | Safetycom
135.475 |

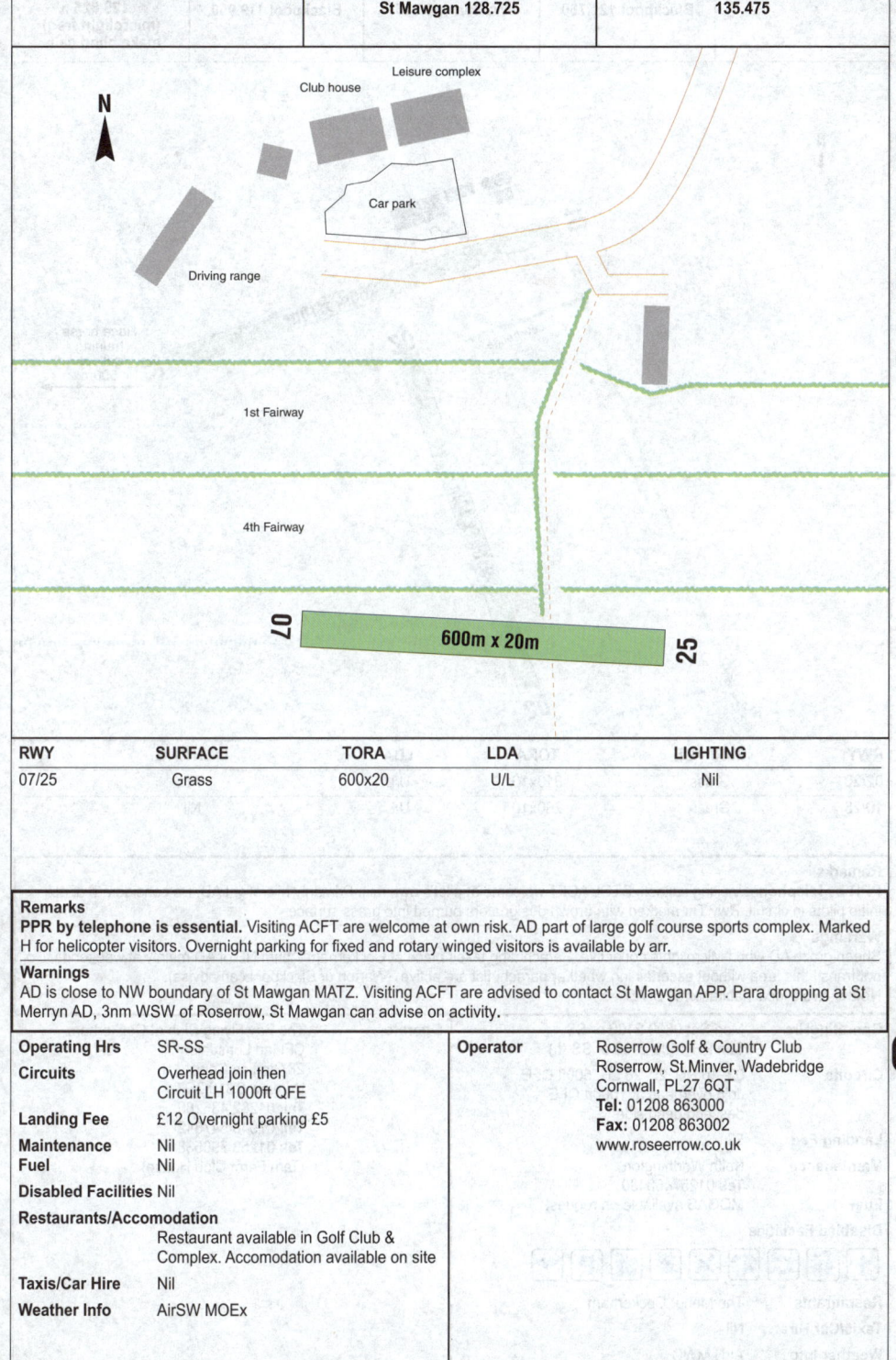

RWY	SURFACE	TORA	LDA	LIGHTING
07/25	Grass	600x20	U/L	Nil

Remarks

PPR by telephone is essential. Visiting ACFT are welcome at own risk. AD part of large golf course sports complex. Marked H for helicopter visitors. Overnight parking for fixed and rotary winged visitors is available by arr.

Warnings

AD is close to NW boundary of St Mawgan MATZ. Visiting ACFT are advised to contact St Mawgan APP. Para dropping at St Merryn AD, 3nm WSW of Roserrow, St Mawgan can advise on activity.

Operating Hrs	SR-SS	**Operator**	Roserrow Golf & Country Club
Roserrow, St.Minver, Wadebridge
Cornwall, PL27 6QT
Tel: 01208 863000
Fax: 01208 863002
www.roserrow.co.uk
Circuits	Overhead join then
Circuit LH 1000ft QFE		
Landing Fee	£12 Overnight parking £5		
Maintenance	Nil		
Fuel	Nil		
Disabled Facilities	Nil		
Restaurants/Accomodation			
	Restaurant available in Golf Club &
Complex. Accomodation available on site		
Taxis/Car Hire	Nil		
Weather Info	AirSW MOEx		

R

485

15ft 0mb	7nm SSW of Lancaster N5356.30 W00250.50	PPR	Alternative AD	Blackpool Manchester Barton

Rossall	ATIS Blackpool 121.750	LARS Warton 129.525	APP Blackpool 119.950	A/G 129.825 (microlight freq) make blind calls

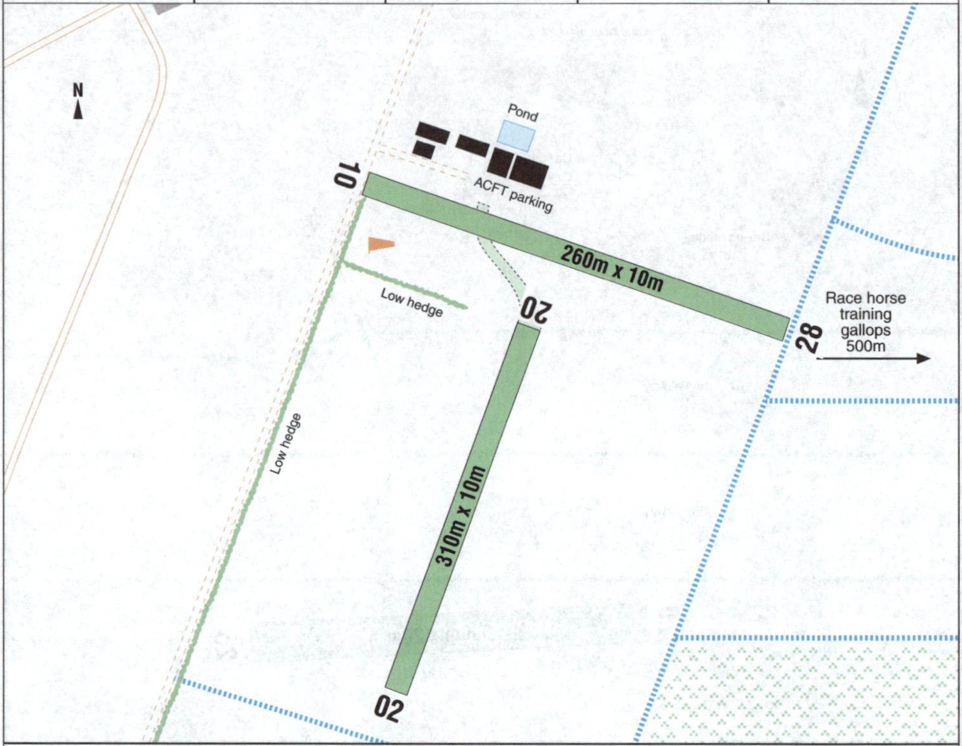

N

Pond

ACFT parking

10

260m x 10m

20

Low hedge

Low hedge

310m x 10m

02

28

Race horse training gallops 500m

RWY	SURFACE	TORA	LDA	LIGHTING
02/20	Grass	310x10	U/L	Nil
10/28	Grass	260x10	U/L	Nil

Remarks
PPR by telephone. Visiting suitable STOL ACFT welcome at pilot's own risk. Primarily Microlight AD. Be considerate of ab-initio pilots in circuit. Rwy Thr marked with brown designators burned into grass surface.

Warnings
Sheep graze AD when Microlights not active. Parachuting takes place at Cockerham 1.5nm NE of AD mainly at weekends. Do not transit this area without ascertaining whether parachutist are active. (Warton or Blackpool can advise).
Noise: Avoid local habitation W of AD

OperatingHrs	Mon-Sat 0800-2100 or SS Sun/PH 1000-2100 or SS (L)	Operator	The Bay Flying Club at Cockerham CFI Ian Lonsdale 28 Sterling Court Burnley, BB10 3QT **Tel:** 01282 436280 **Tel:** 07946 547342 **Tel:** 01253 790538 (Tarn Farm Club House)
Circuits	02, 10 RH, 20, 28 LH, 500ft QFE Join overhead at 1000ft QFE descend dead side		
Landing Fee	£3		
Maintenance	Keith Worthington **Tel:** 01257453430		
Fuel	MOGAS available on request		
Disabled Facilities			

Restaurants	The Manor Cockerham
Taxis/Car Hire	Nil
Weather Info	AirN MWC

400ft 13mb	2nm W of Kettering N5224.70 W00047.40	**PPR**	**Alternative AD**	**Cranfield** Northampton	

Rothwell	**LARS** Cottesmore 130.200	**A/G** 129.900 (Glider freq) make blind calls

Rothwell Services

25ft central reservation lamps

Rothwell Lodge Farm

C

20

Spoil heap

Downslope 500m x 14m

crops

crops

02 Gap in 4ft hedge

Thorpe Malsor Reservoir

N

RWY	SURFACE	TORA	LDA	LIGHTING
02/20	Grass	500x14	U/L	Nil

Rwy20 down slope

Remarks
PPR by telephone. Gliding activity normally weekends & PH with winch launching up to 2000ft agl.
Visual aid to location: AD situated close to A14 and NW of Thorpe Malsor reservoir.

Warnings
25ft lamp standards on central reservation of A14 on short final Rwy20. Farm vehicles use Rwy for access to neighbouring fields. Low flying military ACFT may be encountered during weekdays. Crops are grown close to both Rwy edges. When gliders are operating exercise extreme caution and NO over head joins.
Noise: Avoid over flying Rothwell (NW) & Loddington (SW) villages.

Operating Hrs	SR-SS	**Operator**	Mr G A Pentelow Orton Lodge, Orton Lane Loddington, Kettering Northants, NN14 1LQ **Tel:** 01536 711750
Circuits	LH 1000ft QFE		
Landing Fee	Nil		
Maintenance	Nil		
Fuel	Nil		
Disabled Facilities	Nil		
Restaurants	Nil		
Taxis/Car Hire	Nil		
Weather Info	AirCen MOEx		

R

487

200ft 6mb	2nm E of Bury St.Edmunds N5214.79 E00046.23	PPR	Alternative AD	Cambridge Elmsett

Rougham	APP Lakenheath 136.500	A/G 118.900

Avoid farm 1km from AD

25ft powerline

RWY	SURFACE	TORA	LDA	LIGHTING
09	Grass	780	910	Nil
27	Grass	930	760	Nil
03/21	Grass	400x18	U/L	Nil

Remarks
Strictly PPR by telephone. Visiting pilots welcome at own risk. Non-radio ACFT not accepted on event days. Grass Rwys located on part of old WW2 AD. Join through the overhead at 1500ft, to join circuit at 1000ft QNH. After landing clear Rwy by first exit. Taxi with caution as GND is uneven, (on event days) look out for marshal who will indicate parking spot. All Arr pilots must report to the 'C'. AD holds seasonal licence Jun-Nov.

Warnings
AD not manned on non-event days, pre-landing Rwy inspection essential. Rougham situated on S edge of Honington MATZ which is activated by NOTAM. Lakenheath APP are controlling authority. See joining instructions in Remarks.
Noise: Avoid over flying farm 1km NE Rwy27 Thr. Downwind leg to S of A14 to avoid over flying industrial estate. Avoid over flying houses on base leg/final APP Rwy09.

Operating Hrs	0900-1800 (L) event days Other times by arrangement	Operator	Rougham Estate Office Rougham Bury St Edmunds Suffolk IP30 9LZ Tel: 07840 837952 (PPR Event days) Tel: 01359 270238 (PPR Non event days) Fax: 01359 271555 info@roughamairfield.org www.roughamairfield.org
Circuits	S 1000ft QNH		
Landing Fee	Event days: Pilots & passengers to pay daily show fee Non-event days: All ACFT £5		
Maintenance	Nil		
Fuel	AVGAS by prior arr		
Disabled Facilities	Nil		
Restaurants	Tea & coffee at events		
Taxis/Car Hire	Tel: 01284 766777		
Weather Info	AirS MOEx		

350ft 11mb	3nm S of Hitchin N5154.18 E00014.85	PPR	Alternative AD	London Luton Henlow

Rush Green	ATIS Luton 120.575	APP Luton 129.550	A/G 122.350 by request only

RWY	SURFACE	TORA	LDA	LIGHTING
16/34	Grass	550x10	U/L	Nil
13/31	Grass	550x10	U/L	Nil

Rwy13 has slight downslope

Remarks
PPR by telephone. Light ACFT welcome at pilots own risk. Visitors requested to book in at caravan by hangar.
Visual aid to location: Large scrapyard to S of AD.

Warning
AD situated within Luton CTR, clearance to enter zone must be obtained from Luton . Hay is grown up to Rwy edges. Area of rough GND to E of Rwy16 Thr. AD may be boggy after heavy rain. 40ft trees close to Rwy13 Thr on very short final.

Operating Hours	SR-SS	**Operator**	Mr Maurice Parker
Circuits	To E 500ft QFE		Rush Green Aviation Ltd
Landing Fee	£5 for recreational visitors Commercial landing fee on application		Four Winds Industrial Park Bedford Road Haynes
Maintenance	Outside parking Servicing & repairs available		Bedford, MK45 3QT **Tel:** 07747 864216
Fuel	Nil		
Disabled Facilities	Nil		
Restaurants Royal Oak	**Tel:** 01438 820436		
Taxis	**Tel:** 01438 353562 **Tel:** 07785 347348		
Car Hire	Nil		
Weather Info	AirSE MOEx		

EGDX   ST ATHAN

163ft 6mb	3nm NW of Cardiff Airport N5124.29 W00326.15	PPR MIL	Alternative AD	Cardiff Swansea

St Athan	ATIS Cardiff 128.825	LARS St Mawgan 128.725	APP Cardiff 125.850	TWR 118.125

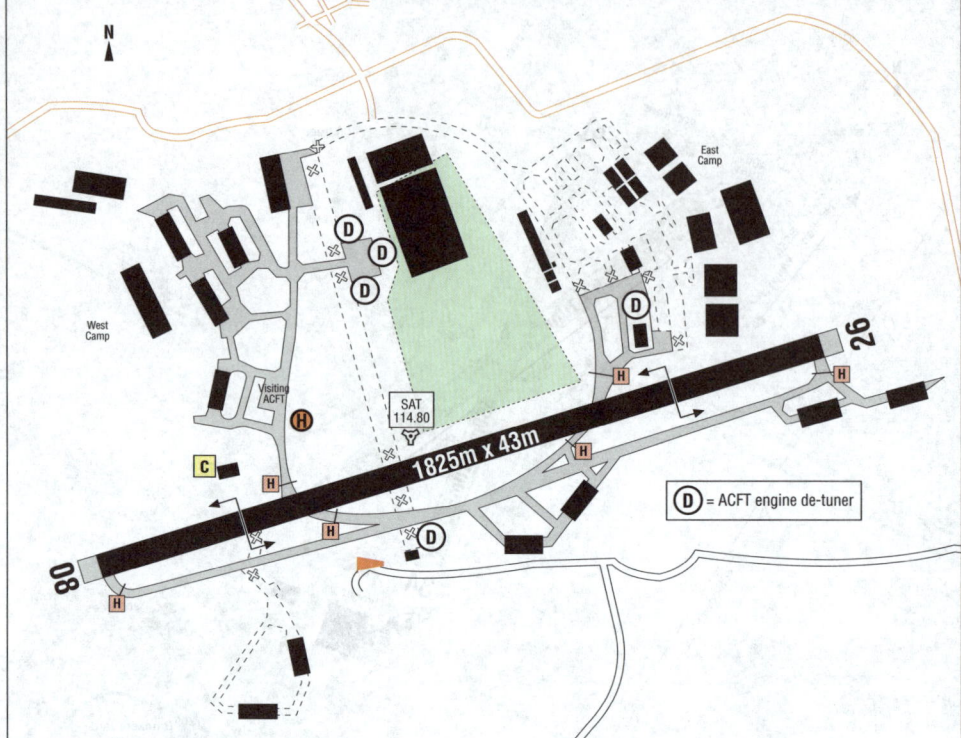

1825m x 43m

D = ACFT engine de-tuner

RWY	SURFACE	TORA	LDA	LIGHTING
08	Asphalt	1825	1825	Thr Rwy PAPI 2.5°
26	Asphalt	1825	1825	Ap Thr Rwy PAPI 2.5°

Arrester gear Rwy08/26 390m from Thr

Remarks
PPR 24Hrs noticed required. AD within Cardiff CTR. Light ACFT & glider flying evening & weekends. ATZ active H24.

Warnings
Beware mis-identifying AD, Cardiff AD (Rwy12/30 & 03/21) 3nm E of AD. Wind shear hazard Rwy26 in strong NW winds. No Twy lighting N of Rwy. Visiting ACFT are to carry out RAD to straight in or RAD to PAR to land only. Visual circuits are not permitted except in an emergency. Railway (282m from Thr) and road (300m from Thr) cross Rwy08 APP.
Noise: Avoid over flying St Athan village.

Operating Hrs	Mon-Thu 0730-1600 Fri 0730-1500 (Summer) +1Hr (Winter)	**Operator**	RAF St Athan Barry Vale of Glamorgan CF62 4WA **Tel:** 01446 755696 (OPS) **Tel:** 01446 798889 (ATC) **Fax:** 01446 798257
Circuits	Nil		
Landing Fee	Charges in accordance with MOD policy Contact Station Ops for details		
Maintenance	Nil		
Fuel	AVGAS JET A1 100LL		
Disabled Facilities	Nil		
Restaurants	Nil		
Taxis Major Cars Car Hire	**Tel:** 01446 794545 Nil		
Weather Info	AirS MOEx		

EGDG					ST MAWGAN

390ft 13mb	3.5nm ENE of Newquay N5026.43 W00459.72	PPR MIL	Alternative AD	Plymouth Perranporth

St Mawgan	LARS 128.725	APP 128.725	DIR 125.550	TWR 123.400

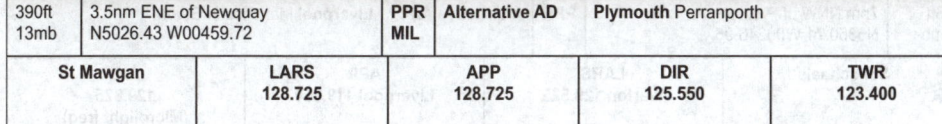

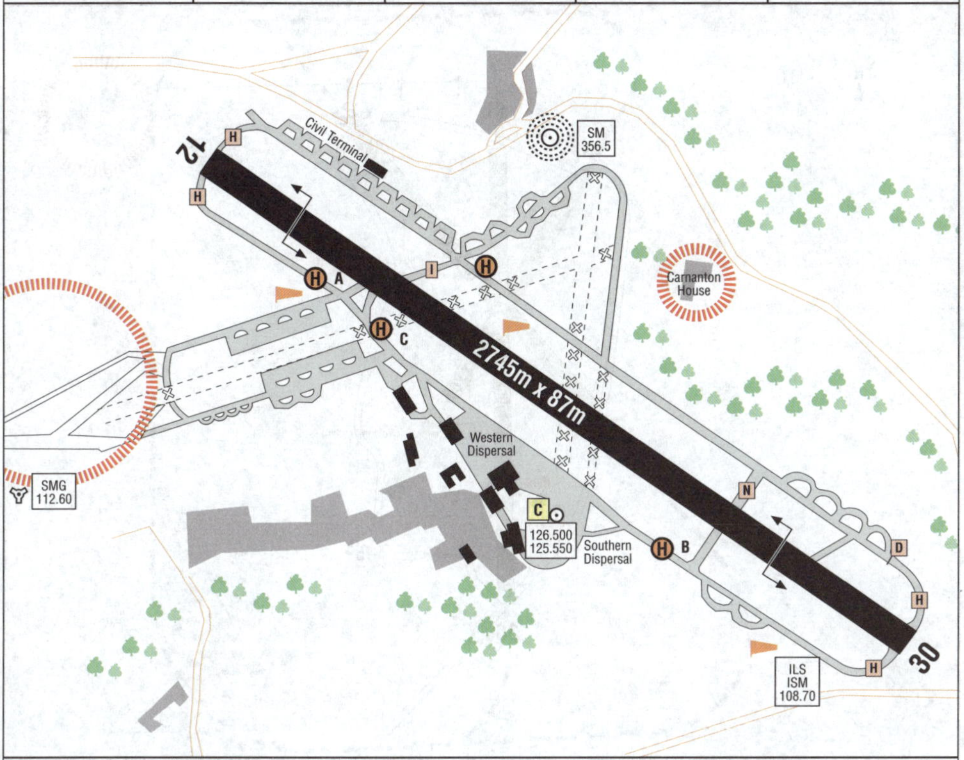

RWY	SURFACE	TORA	LDA	LIGHTING
12/30	Asph/Conc	2745	2745	Ap Thr Rwy PAPI 3°
Reduced dimensions for ACFT unable to trample arrester gear				
12	Asph/Conc	2230	2230	
30	Asph/Conc	2325	2325	

Remarks
PPR 24Hrs civil ACFT wishing to operate at weekends must request PPR not later than 1700hrs Friday. Civil Flight Plans must be sent to Ops for processing EGDGYXYW. All inbound ACFT to contact St Mawgan APP at 20nm. RADAR APP may be mandatory.
Visual aid to location: Ibn SM Red.

Warnings
Risk of bird strikes. Pilots unfamiliar with the area should note that St Eval Disused AD lies 3nm N of St Mawgan. Standard arrester gear configuration is both cables down. There is no dead side when helicopters operate within the visual circuit N Rwy13/31. Fixed wing ACFT do not use dead side without ATC approval. Helis use points N and S Twys and may operate to within 100m of edge of Rwy.
Noise: Avoid over flying Carnanton House 400m NE of AD

Operating Hrs	0700-2200 (L)	**Handling**	**Tel:** 01637 860551(Mid West Aviation)
Circuits	No dead side Fixed wing S, Heli N, 1000ft QFE		**Fax:** 01637 860788 (Mid West Aviation) nqy@midwestexec.com www.midwestexec.com
Landing Fee	Contact Midwest Exec **Tel:** 01637 860551	**Restaurants**	In terminal
		Taxis/Car Hire	Available in terminal
Maintenance	Nil	**Weather Info**	M T Fax 392 MOEx
Fuel	AVGAS JET A1	**Operator**	RAF St Mawgan Newquay, Cornwall TR8 4HP **Tel:** 01637 860551 **Fax:** 01637 857556 www.newquay-airport.co.uk
Disabled Facilities			

S

491

16ft 0mb	7nm NNW of Preston N5350.71 W00246.96	PPR	Alternative AD	Liverpool Manchester Barton

St Michaels	LARS Warton 129.525	APP Liverpool 119.850	A/G 129.825 (Microlight freq)

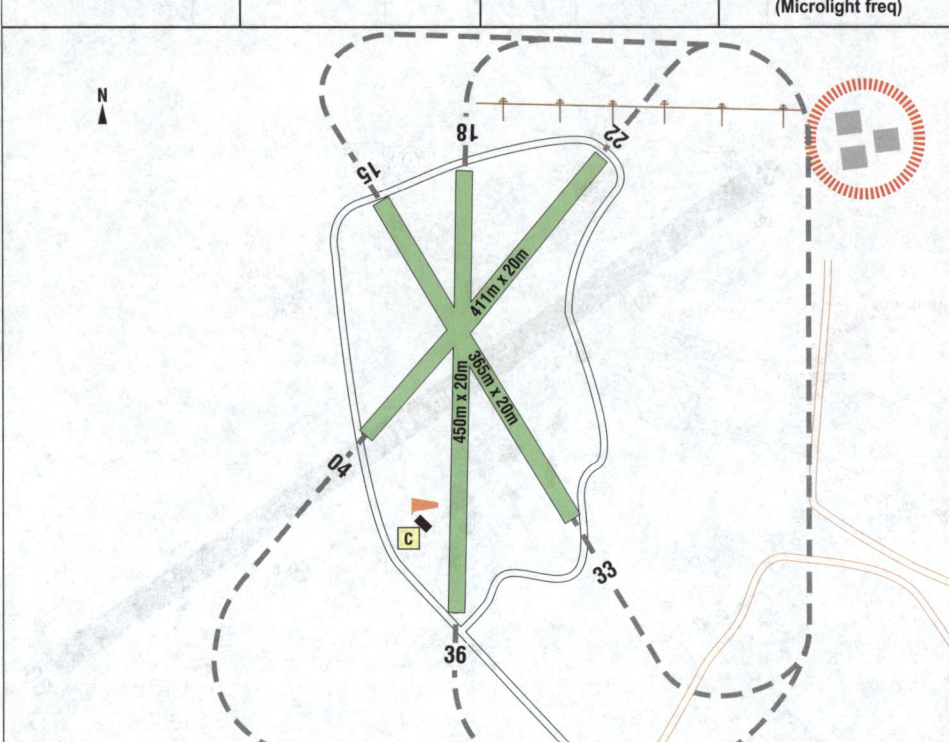

RWY	SURFACE	TORA	LDA	LIGHTING
04/22	Grass	411x20	U/L	Nil
18/36	Grass	450x20	U/L	Nil
15/33	Grass	365x20	U/L	Nil

Remarks

PPR by telephone. Microlight school is particularly active at weekends. Please be considerate of ab-initio students. Although Rwys are marked by cut grass strips, all the field is useable. Take-offs are restricted to Rwys. Student pilots are encouraged to land into wind and not stick blindly to cut Rwys.

Warnings

Occassionaly waterlogged after heavy winter rain/snow. Grass may be long at sides of cut Rwys in summer.
Caution: Telephone poles and lines along N boundary of AD. Dyke 10ft W of AD.
Noise: Avoid over flight of local habitation, Do not over fly the large houses in the trees to NE of AD 1nm.

Operating Hrs	SR-SS	**Operator**	Graham Hobson
Circuits	Join overhead 1500ft QFE Circuits E 500ft QFE		Northern Microlight School 2 Ashlea Cottage Bilsborrow
Landing Fee	£3.50 for as many landings as required in any 1 day		Preston PR3 0RT
Maintenance	Nil Overnight parking available at owners risk		**Tel:** 01995 641058 (Office)
Fuel	MOGAS available by arr		
Disabled Facilities	Nil		
Restaurant	Self brew tea & coffee available		
Taxis/Car Hire	Available by mobile phone		
Weather Info	AirN MWC		

SACKVILLE FARM

Effective date:23/11/06

250ft 8mb	2nm N of Bedford Thurleigh Disused AD N5215.87.W00029.08	PPR	Alternative AD	Cranfield Northampton

Sackville	APP Cranfield 122.850	A/G 119.200

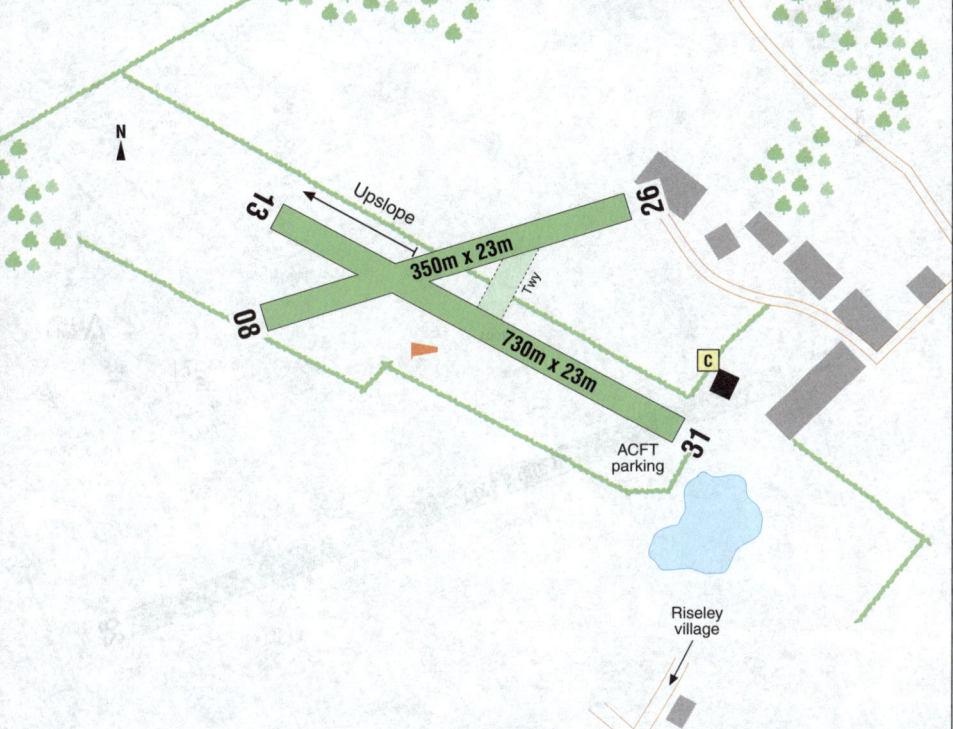

RWY	SURFACE	TORA	LDA	LIGHTING
13/31	Grass	730x23	U/L	Nil
08/26	Grass	350x23	U/L	Nil

Rwy31 upslope in final third

Remarks
PPR by telephone. All ACFT inc microlights welcome at own risk. Glider launching is carried out most weekends by winch & aerotow. Visitors are invited to try gliding.

Warnings
PPR is essential for briefing & removal of livestock from strip.
Noise: Do not over fly Riseley village S of strip.

Operating Hrs	SR-SS	**Operator**	Mr T Wilkinson
Circuits	Nil		Sackville Lodge Farm
Landing Fee	Nil		Riseley, Beds
Maintenance	Nil		**Tel:** 01234 708877 (AD PPR)
Fuel	Nil		**Tel:** 07774 291283
Hangarage	Available		**Tel:** 01933 311895 (Microlight School)
Disabled Facilities	Nil		**Fax:** 01234708862
Restaurants	Tea coffee & snacks weekends		www.sackvilleflyingclub.co.uk
	Fox & Hounds in Riseley village		
	approx 10mins walk		
Taxis	**Tel:** 01234 750005		
Car Hire			
National	**Tel:** 01234 269565 (Bedford)		
Weather Info	AirCen MOEx		

S

420ft 14mb	1nm E of Salcombe N5013.65 W00348.50	PPR	Alternative AD	Plymouth Exeter

Non-Radio	LARS Plymouth Military 121.250	LARS Exeter 128.975	Safetycom 135.475

N

crops

crops

150ft Aerial

C

ACFT parking

11

620m x 18m

Crops (30m wide)

29

RWY	SURFACE	TORA	LDA	LIGHTING
11/29	Grass	620x10	U/L	Nil

Remarks
PPR by telephone essential. Visiting pilots welcome at own risk. Rwy is well prepared. WW II AD. Campsite available at farm. **Visual aid to location**: Large concrete bunker with 150agl aerial on roof.

Warnings
AD can become boggy in winter, generally in good condition. Due to the proximity of sea and nearby cliffs coastal weather effects can be expected including sea mist and downdrafts Rwy29 APP. 4ft hedge Rwy11 Thr. 6ft fence along S side of Rwy. 4ft hedge Rwy29 Thr. **Noise:** All Arr and Dept must avoid over flying all local properties. No over flying of Salcombe and Malborough.

Operating Hrs	SR-SS	**Weather Info**	AirSW MOEx
Circuits	To seaward side 1000ft QFE	**Operator**	Squire Brothers
Landing Fee	£10		Higher Rew Farm
Maintenance	Nil		Malborough
Fuel	Nil		South Devon, TQ7 3BW
Disabled Facilities			**Tel:** 01548 842681

Tel: 07970 654662
www.higherrew.co.uk
Tel: 01548 843927 (Tourist Board)
www.salcombeinformation.co.uk

Restaurant/ Accomodation
Soar Mill Cove Hotel, 1nm from AD
Tides Reach Hotel, South Sands.
(Ferry service from South Sands to Salcombe Mar-Nov)

Taxis
Clarke Cars **Tel:** 01548 842914
Moonraker Taxis **Tel:** 01548 560231
Car Hire Nil

S

480ft 16mb	7nm NE of Melton Mowbray N5249.77 W00042.65	PPR	Alternative AD	Nottingham East Midlands Leicester

Saltby Base	LARS Cottesmore 130.200	A/G 129.975 Not always manned	If no answer make normal circuit calls

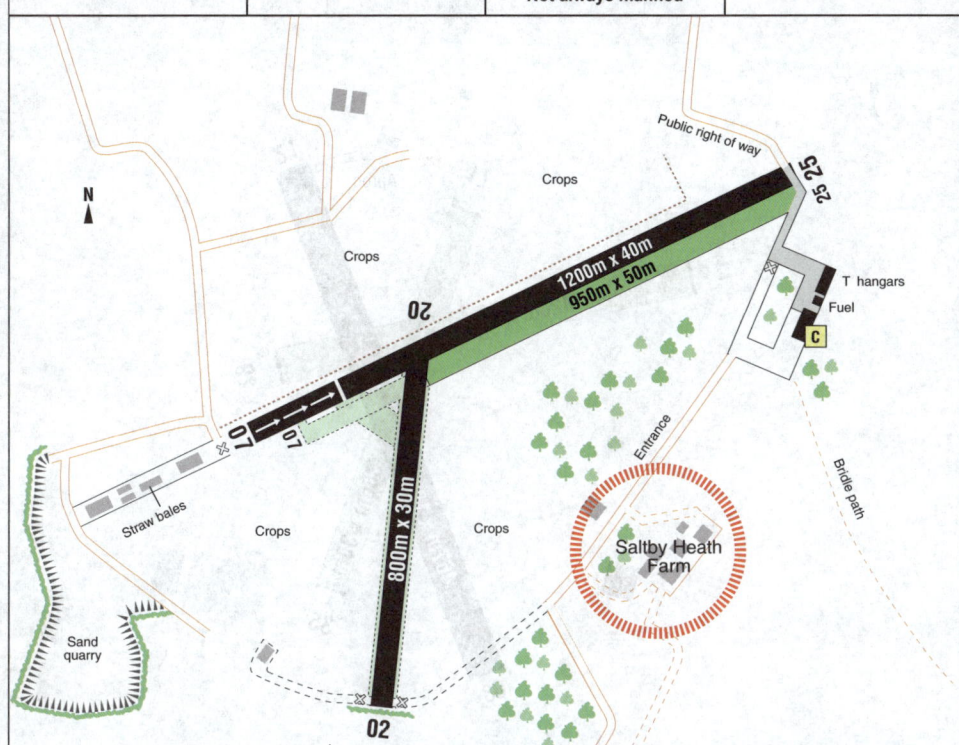

RWY	SURFACE	TORA	LDA	LIGHTING
07/25	Conc/Asph	1200x45	U/L	Nil
07/25	Grass	950x50	U/L	Nil
02/20	Concrete	800x30	U/L	Nil

Rwy20 surface rough

Remarks
PPR by telephone. Primarily a gliding site but light ACFT welcome at own risk. Operated by Buckminster Gliding Club on lease from Buckminster Estates. Due to rural nature/gliding tasks PPR may be denied. Gliders launch by aerotow & winch. Priority should be given to gliding activity. Keep a good lookout at all times. Considering Rwy07/25 surface dates to 1945 it is in excellent condition. A public right of way crosses Rwy25 Thr

Warnings
Wire fence along N side of hard Rwy07/25. Crops grow up to S edge of grass Rwy07/25. Waltham on the Wold TV mast (1487ft amsl, 1050ftagl) 3.5nm Rwy07 APP. Cottesmore MATZ 1.5nm SSE. Inbound/outbound ACFT call Cottesmore. Due to cables NO overhead joins (Mon-Fri 2000ft Weekends 3000ft).
Noise: Avoid over flying local villages.

Operating Hrs	SR-SS	**Weather Info**	AirCen MWC
Circuits	07, 02, 25 LH, 07 RH, 1000ft QFE No overhead joins. Join downwind. Glider circuits variable	**Operator**	Buckminster Gliding Club Saltby Airfield Sproxton Road, Skillington Grantham, Lincs, NG33 5HL **Tel:** 01476 860385 **Tel:** 01476 860947 **Tel:** 07769 955791 **Fax:** 01476 860947 office@buckminstergc.co.uk www.buckminstergc.co.uk
Landing Fee	Contributions gratefully received		
Maintenance	Nil		
Fuel	AVGAS 100LL by prior arr		
Disabled Facilities	Nil		
Restaurants	Snacks tea & coffee at GC		
Taxis/Car Hire	Nil		

S

495

66ft 2mb	20nm NNE of Kirkwall Airport N5915.02 W00234.60	PPR	Alternative AD Diversion AD	Kirkwall Eday

Non-Radio	APP Kirkwall 118.300	Safetycom 135.475

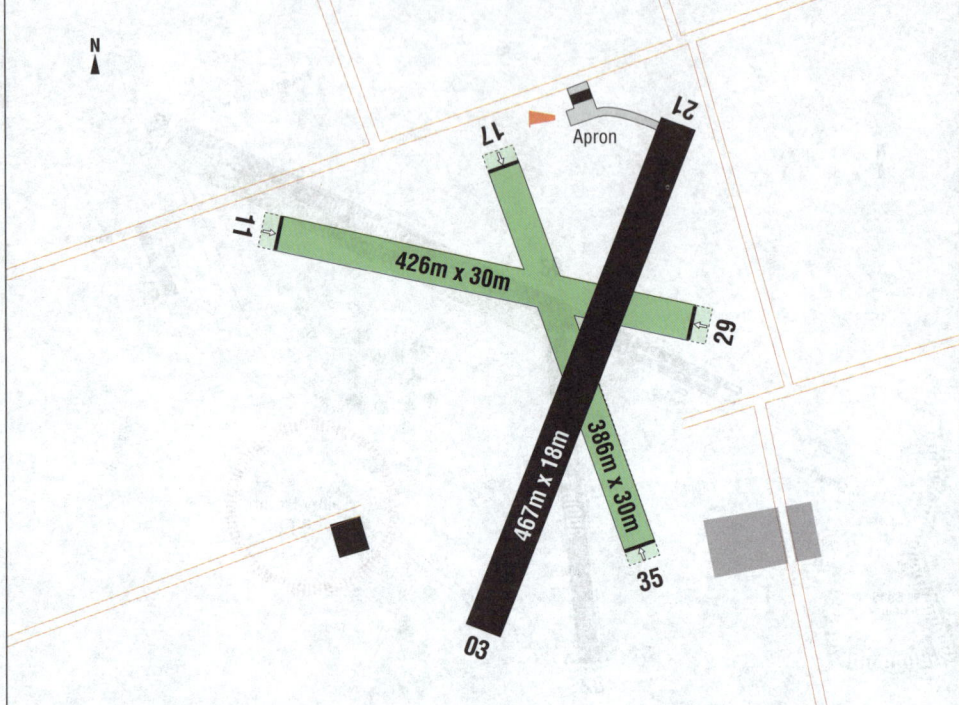

RWY	SURFACE	TORA	LDA	LIGHTING
03/21	Graded Hardcore	467	467	Nil
11/29	Grass	426	396	Nil
17/35	Grass	378	366	Nil

Starter extension 15m on all Rwys

Remarks
Visiting ACFT accepted at pilot's own risk. Scheduled Air Service daily Mon-Sat.

Warnings

Operating Hrs	SR-SS	**Operator**	Orkney Islands Council Offices
Circuits	Nil		Sanday Aerodrome, Kirkwall
Landing Fee	Nil		Orkney, KW15 1NY
Maintenance	Nil		**Tel:** 01856 873535 (PPR)
Fuel	Nil		**Fax:** 01856 876094
Disabled Facilities	Nil		
Restaurants			
Belsair Hotel	**Tel:** 01857 600206		
	Fax: 01857 600453		
Ketteltoft Hotel	**Tel:** 01857 600217		
Taxis/Car Hire			
Ketteltoft Garage	**Tel:** 01857 600321		
B Fleet	**Tel:** 01857 600284		
Weather Info	AirSc GWC		

S

496

350ft 11mb	4nm NE of Swindon N5136.14 W00140.30	PPR	Alternative AD	Oxford Kemble

Non-Radio	Zone Lyneham 123.400	LARS Brize 124.275	Safetycom 135.475

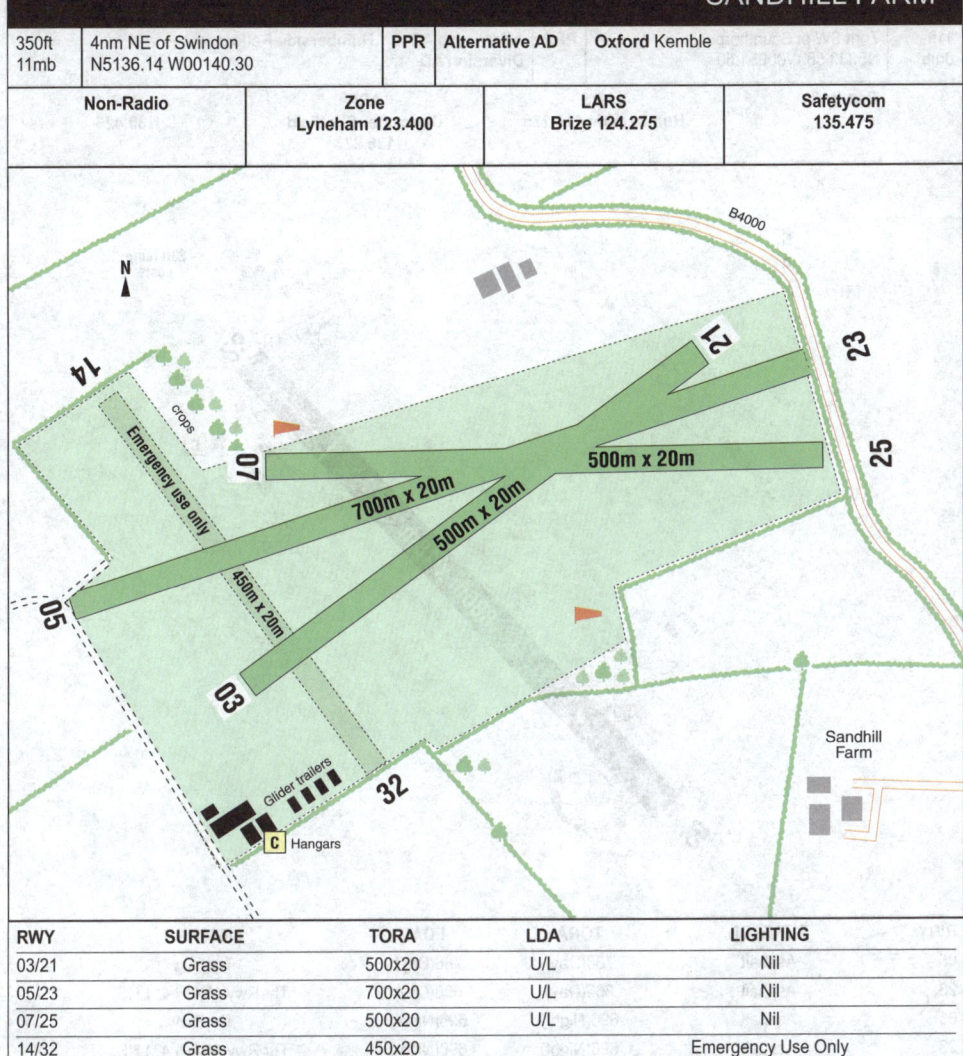

RWY	SURFACE	TORA	LDA	LIGHTING
03/21	Grass	500x20	U/L	Nil
05/23	Grass	700x20	U/L	Nil
07/25	Grass	500x20	U/L	Nil
14/32	Grass	450x20		Emergency Use Only

Rwy03 up slope at narrowest point. Rwy21 down slope after narrowest point. Rwy05 up slope & undulations at narrowest point
Rwy23 down slope after narrowest point. Rwy07 up slope at narrowest point. Rwy25 down slope after narrowest point
Rw14/32 emergency use only, bumpy NW of Rwy05/23 intersection

Remarks
Strict PPR. AD is primarily a gliding site with winch and aerotow launches, beware cables. Powered ACFT circuits to the N of AD, glider circuits either side of AD. Rwys approx 20m wide, but most of year the whole AD can be used. In spring the 'off Rwy' grass may be too long.

Warnings
AD may become waterlogged in winter. Rwy23 or 25 in use gliders will be parked close to hedge adjacent to B4000. Rwy03 or 05 in use gliders will be parked close to boundary fence and adjacent to public footpath. Farm vehicles or pedestrians use farm track Rwy03 & 06 Thr.
Noise: Avoid over flying local villages, particularly two farms either side of B4000 0.5nm N of AD. Do not over fly less than 1000ft agl.

Operating Hrs	SR-SS Weekends only		Restaurants	Tea & Coffee available when gliding in progress
Circuits	03, 05, 07 LH 21, 23, 25 RH 1000ft QFE No over head or dead side joins		Taxi Car Hire	**Tel:** 01793 766666 Nil
			Weather Info	AirSW MOEx
Landing Fee	£6		Operator	Vale of White Horse Gliding Centre Sandhill Farm Shrivenham, Wilts
Maintenance Fuel	Nil Nil			**Tel:** 01793 783685 (AD)
Disabled Facilities	Nil			**Tel:** 01235 224308 (Secretary)

S

11ft 0mb	7nm SW of Scunthorpe N5333.58 W00051.50	PPR	Alternative AD Diversion AD	Humberside Retford

Sandtoft	LARS Humberside 119.125	APP Doncaster Sheffield 126.225	A/G 130.425

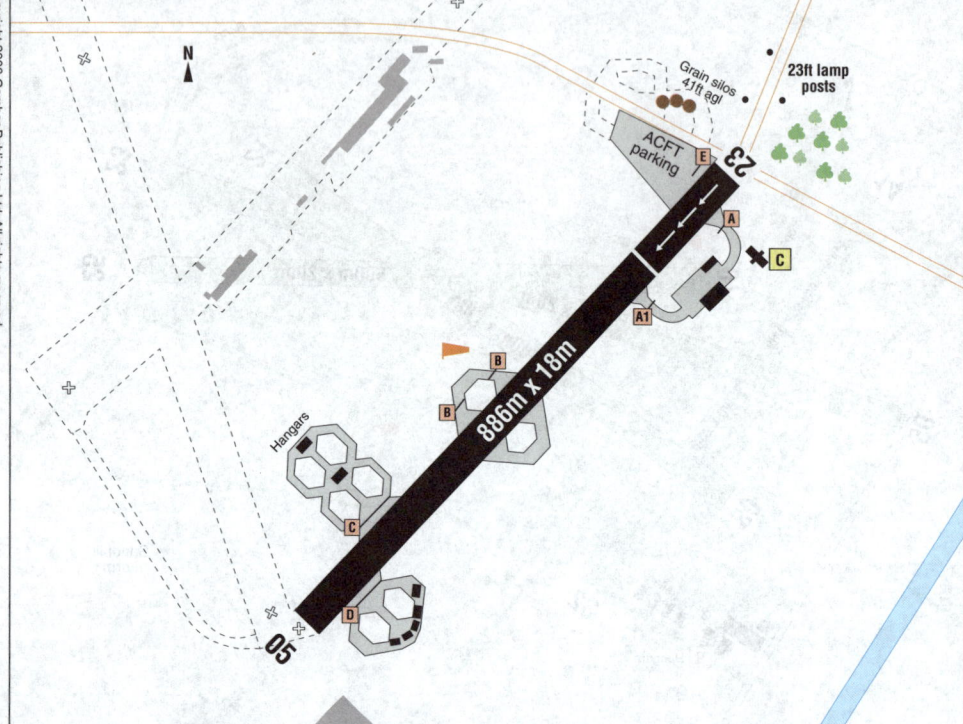

RWY	SURFACE	TORA	LDA	LIGHTING
05	Asphalt	786(Day)	786(Day)	Thr Rwy
23	Asphalt	866(Day)	696(Day)	Thr Rwy APAPI 4° LHS
05	Asphalt	696(Night)	696(Night)	Thr Rwy
23	Asphalt	696(Night)	696(Night)	Thr Rwy APAPI 4° LHS

Remarks
PPR non-radio ACFT not accepted. Rwy05 is not licensed for night use.

Warnings
Street lights on road at Rwy23 Thr. 12.5m agl silos Rwy23 APP
Noise: Avoid over flying the village of Belton to E. Local flying area NE of AD, clear of built-up areas

Operating Hrs	0800-1700 (Summer) 0900-SS (Winter)	**Operator**	New Sandtoft Aviation Ltd
Circuits	05 LH, 23 RH, 1000ft QFE Microlights 700ft QFE		Sandtoft Aerodrome Belton, Doncaster South Yorkshire, DN9 1PN
Landing Fee	Single £5, Twin £10 Heli £10, Microlight £2.50		**Tel:** 01427 873676 (AD) **Fax:** 01427 874656
Maintenance	Nil		
Fuel	AVGAS JET A1 100LL		
Disabled Facilities	Nil		
Restaurant	Restaurant & bar available at AD 0900-1900 (L)		
Taxis Alan Epworth Taxi	**Tel:** 01427 875675 **Tel:** 01427 874569		
Car Hire Europcar	**Tel:** 01724 840655/843239		
Weather Info	AirN MCW		

S

202ft 6mb	5nm N of Lincoln N5318.47 W00033.05		**PPR**	**Alternative AD** **Diversion AD**	**Humberside** Wickenby

	Scampton	**LARS** **Waddington 127.350**	

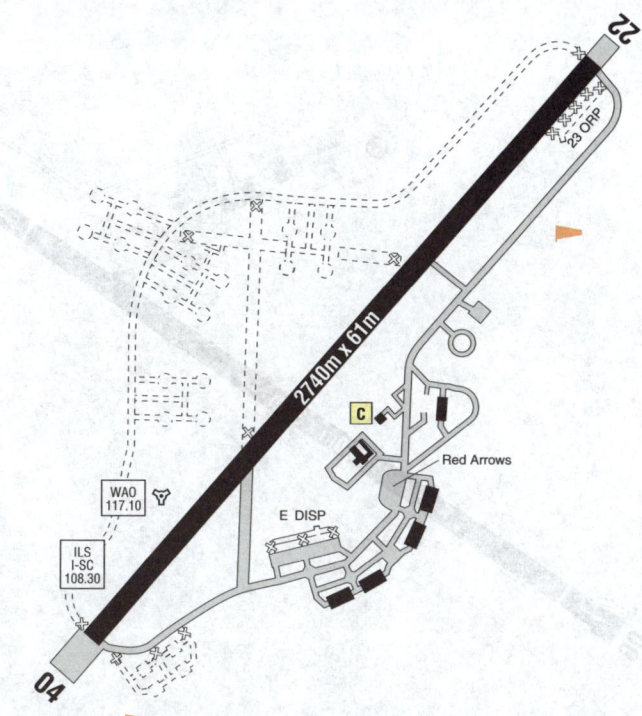

RWY	SURFACE	TORA	LDA	LIGHTING
04/22	Asphalt	2740	2740	Rwy App Thr PAPI 3° LHS

Remarks
Strict PPR by telephone. RAF AD home of Red Arrows, also relief landing GND for RAF Cranwell. AD situated within R313/9.5 which is active when aerobatic practice in progress. Activity status obtained by RTF from Waddington APP, UK AIP ENR 5-1-2-2, or Waddington ATC.

Warnings
ACFT are advised to taxi on all Twy centrelines to ensure clearance from drainage covers, the integrity of which cannot be guaranteed.
Caution: Stadium lights up to 30m agl to W, S & E of Echo dispersal.

Operating Hrs	As required for based/Cranwell Ops	**Operator**	RAF Scampton
Circuits	04 LH, 22 RH, 1000ft QFE		Lincoln
Landing Fee	Charges in accordance with MOD policy Contact Scampton ATC for details		Lincolnshire LN1 2ST **Tel**: 01522 733051 (ATC)
Maintenance	Not available to visiting ACFT		**Tel**: 01522 727451/2
Fuel	Nil		(Waddington ATC)
Disabled Facilities			

Restaurants	Nil		
Taxis/Car Hire	Nil		
Weather Info	Waddington M T Fax 446 MWC **Tel**: 01400 261201 Ex 7262 (Cranwell) **Tel**: 01522 733051 (Scampton ATC)		

S

81ft 2mb	17nm N of Lerwick N6025.97 W00117.77	PPR	Alternative AD	Sumburgh Lerwick	
Scatsta	**APP** **123.600**	**TWR** **123.600**		**RAD** **122.400**	**FIRE** **121.600**

N

1360m x 31m

191 (110)

06

24

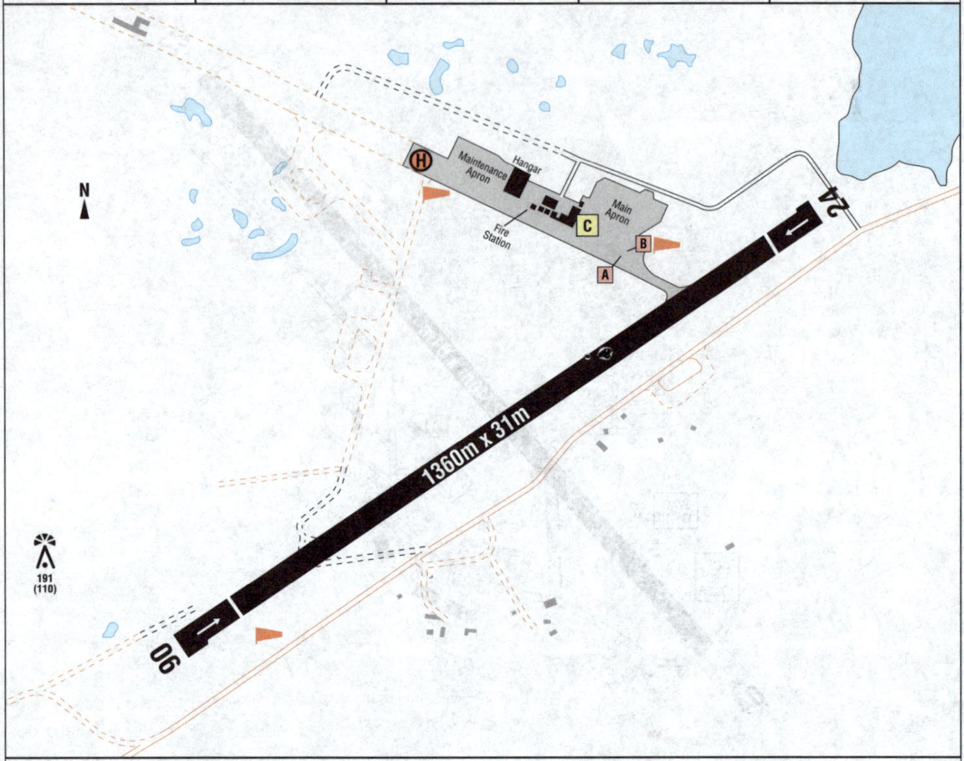

RWY	SURFACE	TORA	LDA	LIGHTING
06	Asphalt	1253	1138	Ap Thr Rwy PAPI 4° LHS
24	Asphalt	1262	1168	Ap Thr Rwy PAPI 3.25° LHS

Remarks
Strict PPR 24Hrs notice required. Non-radio ACFT not accepted. No training flights.
Aids to Navigation: NDB SS 315.50
Visual aid to location: Strobe alignment beacons for Rwy06 APP.

Warnings
Area of poor GND in strip near Rwy06 Thr on S side suitably marked with 'bad GND' markers. Unpaved surfaces are liable to be soft, particularly after periods of heavy rain. High GND in vicinity of AD. Twy S side of main apron has semi-width of only 6.6m. Rwy lights 15in above agl.
Noise: Avoid over flying oil terminal area

Operating Hrs	Mon-Fri 0630-1830 Sat 0700-1300 (Summer) +1Hr (Winter) & by arr	**Car Hire** Bolts Car Hire	**Tel:** 01595 692855
Circuits	Nil	**Weather Info**	M T9 Fax 394 GWC
Landing Fee	On application	**Visual Reference Points (VRP)**	
Maintenance	Nil	Brae	N6023.82 W00121.23
Fuel	AVTUR JET A1 (2Hrs PNR)	Fugla	N6026.95 W00119.43
Disabled Facilities		Hillswick	N6028.55 W00129.32
		Linga Island	N6021.40 W00121.58
		Voe	N6021.00 W00115.97

Restaurants	Nil	
Taxis		**Operator**
W Hurson	**Tel:** 01806 522550	Serco Ltd on behalf of BP Scatsta Aerodrome, Brae Shetland, ZE2 9QP **Tel:** 01806 242791 **Fax:** 01806 242110
G Johnson	**Tel:** 01806 522443	

S

116ft	1nm E of Hugh Town	PPR	Alternative AD	St Mawgan Lands End
4mb	N4954.80 W00617.50		Diversion AD	

Scillies	APP 123.825	TWR 123.825	FIRE 121.600

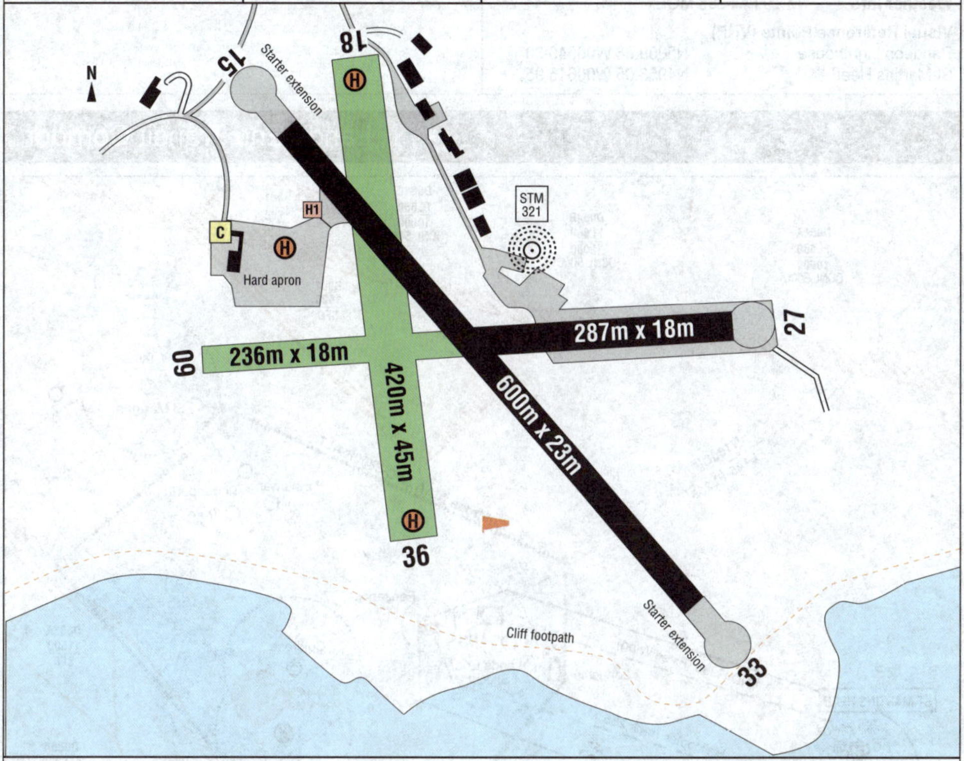

RWY	SURFACE	TORA	LDA	LIGHTING
09	Grass/Asph	523	523	Thr Rwy
27	Asph/Grass	523	523	App Thr Rwy
15	Tarmac	600	600	Thr Rwy PAPI 3.5° LHS
33	Tarmac	600	600	Thr Rwy PAPI 3.5° LHS
18/36	Grass	400	400	Helicopter Rwy

Starter extension Rwy15 13m
starter extension Rwy33 38m

Remarks
Strict PPR by telephone. Non-radio ACFT not accepted. Asphalt strips marked by white centre lines, grass strips have grass edge markings. AD is closed to all other ACFT Sundays. DO NOT attempt to land. Dept by arr 1500-1600 (L). Flight plans should be filed for all flights to and from Scilly Isles/St Mary's – SEE LANDS END TRANSIT CORRIDOR MAP.
Visual aid to location: Ibn Green SC.

Warnings
Caution: Landing/take-off AD is markedly hump-backed. Turbulence may be experienced at lower levels on all APP. The gradients increase to 1 in 13 at Rwy ends. Pilots – different braking characteristics of the grass/asphalt sections Rwy09/27. Perimeter road runs around N part of AD & vehicular traffic crosses Rwy15 APP. Coastal footpath crosses Rwy33 APP. Pilots exercise great care when using Rwy33 turning circle due reduced clearance SSE – granite outcrop present. SAR & local ACFT activity may take place outside published Hrs.

Operating Hrs	Mon-Sat 0730-1900 (L, Mon-Fri 0830-1230 1330-1700 Sat 0830-1230 (Nov-Feb), 1400-1700 (14 Feb-21 Mar) (Winter)	Maintenance	Nil
		Fuel	Nil
Circuits	As directed by ATC	Disabled Facilities	
Landing Fee	Single £18.10, Twin £26.38		
Parking Fee	Single £8.13 after 2Hrs		
	Twin £10.67 after 2Hrs	Restaurants	Buffet & bar available at AD

Taxis		Operator	Council of the Isles of Scilly
Marks Taxi	**Tel:** 01720 423424		St. Mary's Airport
Scilly Cabs	**Tel:** 01720 422901		St Mary's
	Tel: 0836 253063		Isles of Scilly, TR21 0NG
St Mary's Taxis	**Tel:** 01720 422555		**Tel:** 01720 422677 (ATC)
Island Taxis	**Tel:** 01720 422635		**Tel:** 01720 424338 (AM)
Car Hire	Nil		**Fax:** 01720 424337 (ATC)
Weather Info	M T9 Fax 396 MOEx		

Visual Reference Points (VRP)

Pendeen Lighthouse	N5009.88 W00540.30
St Martins Head	N4958.05 W00615.95

Lands End Transit Corridor

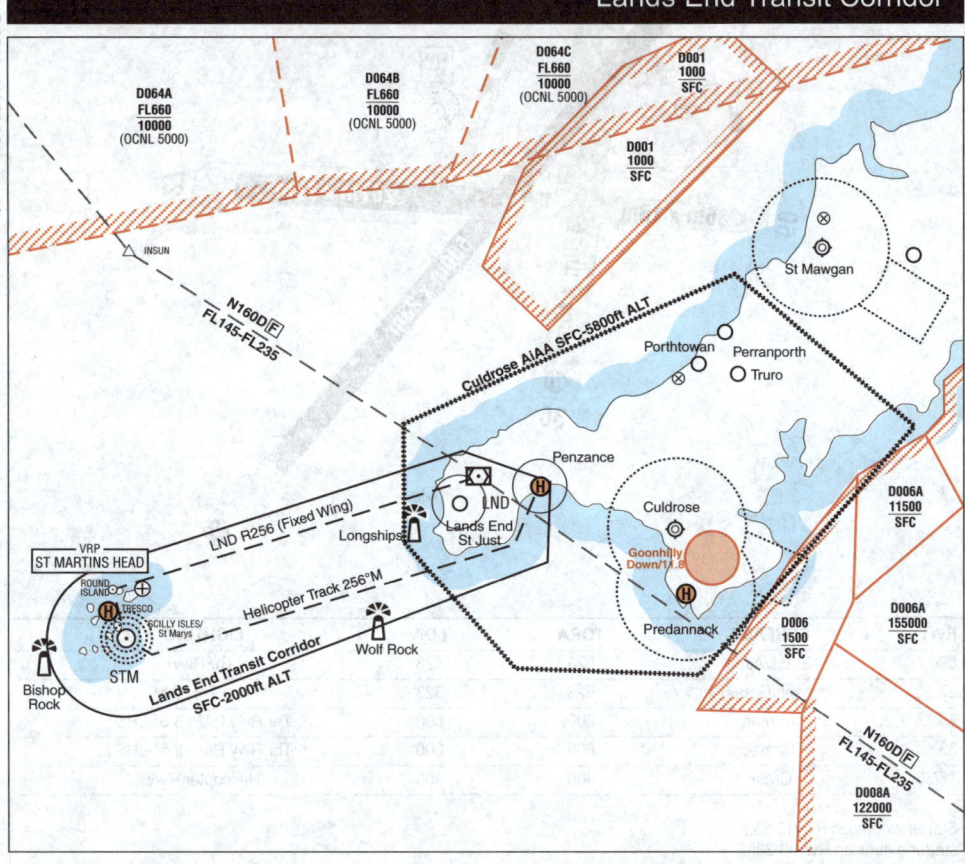

130ft 4mb	9nm SSE of Norwich N5230.67 E00125.03		**Alternative AD** **Diversion AD**	**Norwich** Beccles

Seething	**LARS** **Norwich** 119.350	**A/G** **122.600**

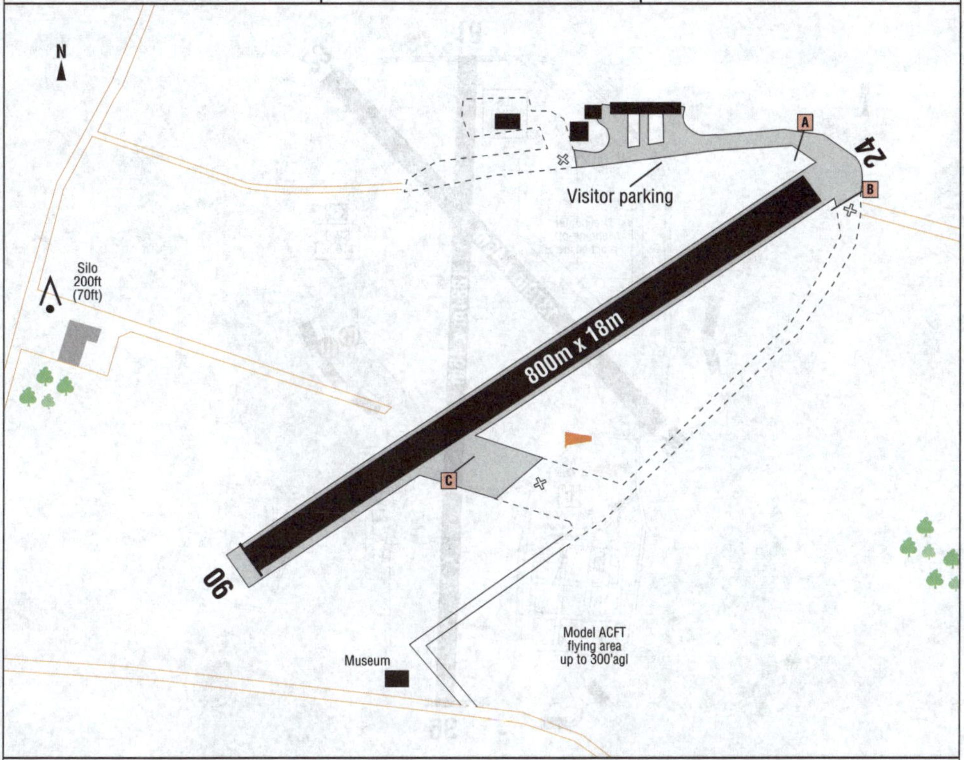

N

Silo 200ft (70ft)

A

B

Visitor parking

24

800m × 18m

06

C

Museum

Model ACFT flying area up to 300'agl

RWY	SURFACE	TORA	LDA	LIGHTING
06/24	Asphalt	800	800	Nil

Remarks
Flying activity may take place outside published Ops Hrs.

Warnings
Agricultural vehicles and equipment may cross close to Rwy24 Thr. Silo 70ft aal/200ft amsl 0.13nm 277° from APP. Windshear may be experienced on Rwy24 APP with S winds. Model ACFT flying takes place on AD.
Noise: Avoid over flying surrounding villages below 1000ft. Pilots taking-off to leave the circuit from Rwy24 should climb straight ahead to 500ft before turning. Dept Rwy06, turn right 30°, climb to 1000ft before turning. ACFT must fly away from the village SE of AD. Also avoid small hamlet 1.24nm from Rwy.

Operating Hrs	0800-SS (Summer) 0900-SS (Winter)	**Weather Info**	AirS MOEx
Circuits	06 RH, 24 LH, 1000ft	**Operator**	Wingtask 1995 Ltd
Landing Fee	Business Flights: Single £6 Twin £12 GA ACFT: no landing fees but a donation to the group to assist in Rwy maintenance would be appreciated		Seething Aerodrome Brooke Norwich, NR15 1EL **Tel:** 01508 550453 (AD)
Maintenance	Ltd		**Tel:** 07778 592150 (PPR out of Hrs)
Fuel	AVGAS 100LL (Ltd)		**Fax:** 01508 558653
Disabled Facilities			www.seething-airfield.co.uk

  X P

Restaurants Snacks available at AD

Taxis
Bungay **Tel:** 01502 712625
Car Hire
Godfrey Davis **Tel:** 01603 45798

S

249ft 8mb	6nm NNE of Shrewsbury N5247.89 W00240.08	PPR MIL	Alternative AD Diversion AD	Hawarden Sleap	

Shawbury	LARS 120.775	APP 120.775	RAD 123.300	TWR 122.100

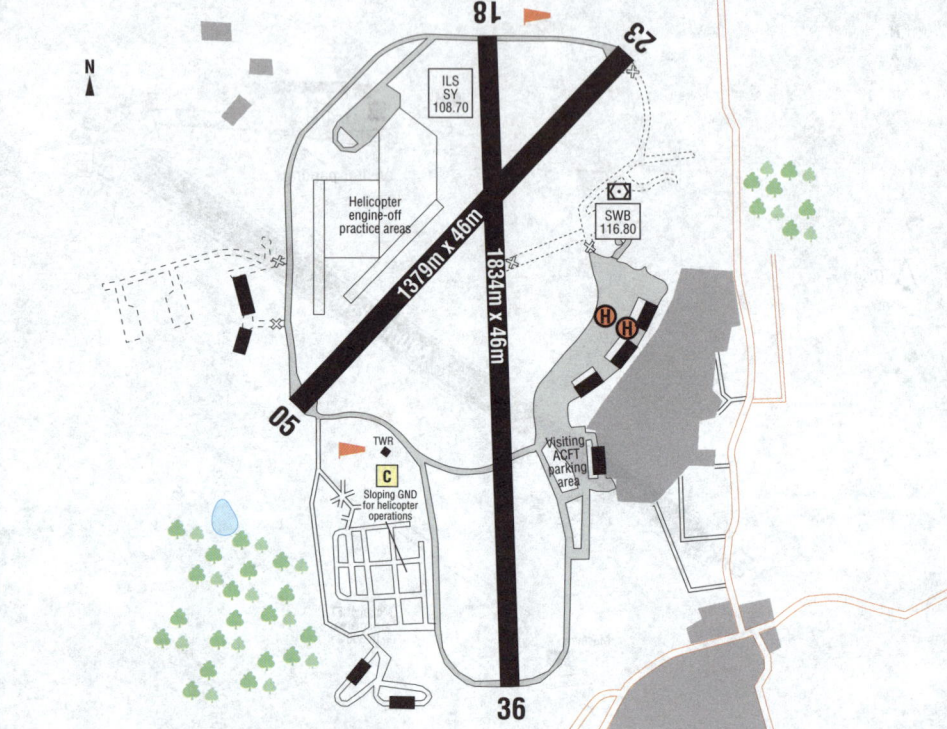

RWY	SURFACE	TORA	LDA	LIGHTING
18/36	Asph/Conc	1834	1834	Ap Thr Rwy PAPI 3°
05/23	Asph/Conc	1379	1379	Thr Rwy PAPI 3°

Remarks
Visiting pilots wishing to operate out of Shawbury are to contact Shawbury Ops.
Visual aid to location: Ibn SY Red

Warnings
Helicopters operate within 50m of either side of the active Rwy below1500ft. Go-arounds to be made down the full length of Rwy. There is no dead side in AD. PAPI Rwy18 coincides with ILS touchdown only. PAR APP will result in incorrect PAPI indications. Visitors contact LARS at 20nm for instrument or RAD visual APP. All fixed wing ACFT to carry out instrument APP, subject to traffic and weather. A RAD vectored visual straight into land may be permitted, providing ACFT is visual and in line with Rwy at 2nm.

Operating Hrs	Mon-Thu 0830-1730 Fri 0830-1700 (L) ATZ H24	**Operator**	RAF Shawbury Shrewsbury Shropshire, SY4 4DZ **Tel:** 01939 250351 Ex 7232/7233
Circuits	05, 36 RH, 18, 23 LH, 1500ft QFE No dead side		
Landing Fee	Charges in accordance with MOD policy Contact Station Ops for details		
Maintenance	Nil		
Fuel	AVTUR JET A1		
Disabled Facilities	Nil		
Restaurants	Nil		
Taxis/Car Hire	Nil		
Weather Info	M T Fax 398 MWC ATIS **Tel:** 01939 250351 Ex 7574		

S

310ft 10mb	15nm E of Bude N5050.10 W00409.50	PPR	Alternate AD	Exeter Eaglescott

Non Radio	LARS Exeter 128.975	Safetycom 135.475

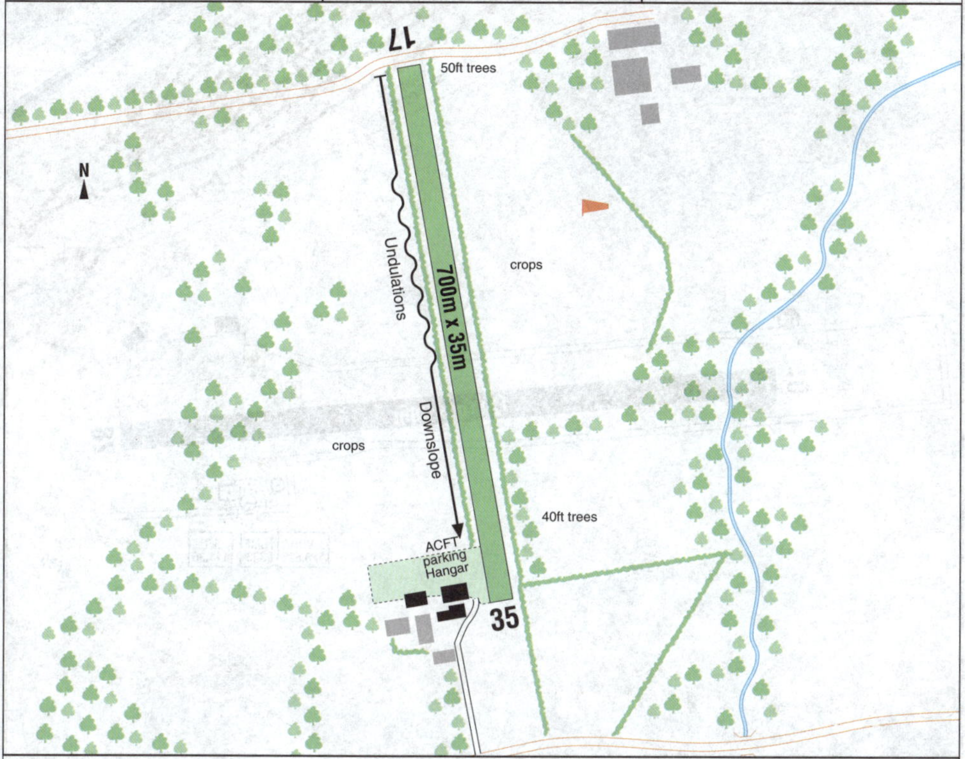

17

N

50ft trees

Undulations

700m x 35m

Downslope

crops

crops

40ft trees

ACFT parking Hangar

35

RWY	SURFACE	TORA	LDA	LIGHTING
17/35	Grass	700x35	U/L	Nil

Rwy17 downslope with undulations on mid section

Remarks
PPR by telephone. Experienced pilots welcome at own risk.

Warnings
Rwy slope and undulations mean ALL landings must be on Rwy35. Take-off on Rwy17 only. Windshear and roll-over may be experienced. Large trees border AD. High tensile stock fences surround AD. Public footpath on E bounday of AD. Do not land if footpath in use.
Noise: Avoid all local villages.

Operating Hrs	SR-SS	Operator	Roger Appleton Westover Sheepwash Devon EX21 5HQ **Tel:** 01409 231619 roger@westover-sheepwash.co.uk www.westover-sheepwash.co.uk
Circuits	Overhead join LH 1000ft QFE Rwy35		
Landing Fee	Donation to upkeep appreciated		
Maintenance	Nil		
Fuel	Nil		

Disabled Facilities

Taxi/Car Hire	Nil
Weather Info	AIRSW MOEx

S

EGSY | SHEFFIELD CITY

231ft 7mb	3nm ENE of Sheffield City Centre N5323.65 W00123.32	PPR	Alternative AD Diversion AD	Leeds Bradford Retford Gamston

Sheffield	LARS Waddington 127.350	A/G 128.525	FIRE 121.600

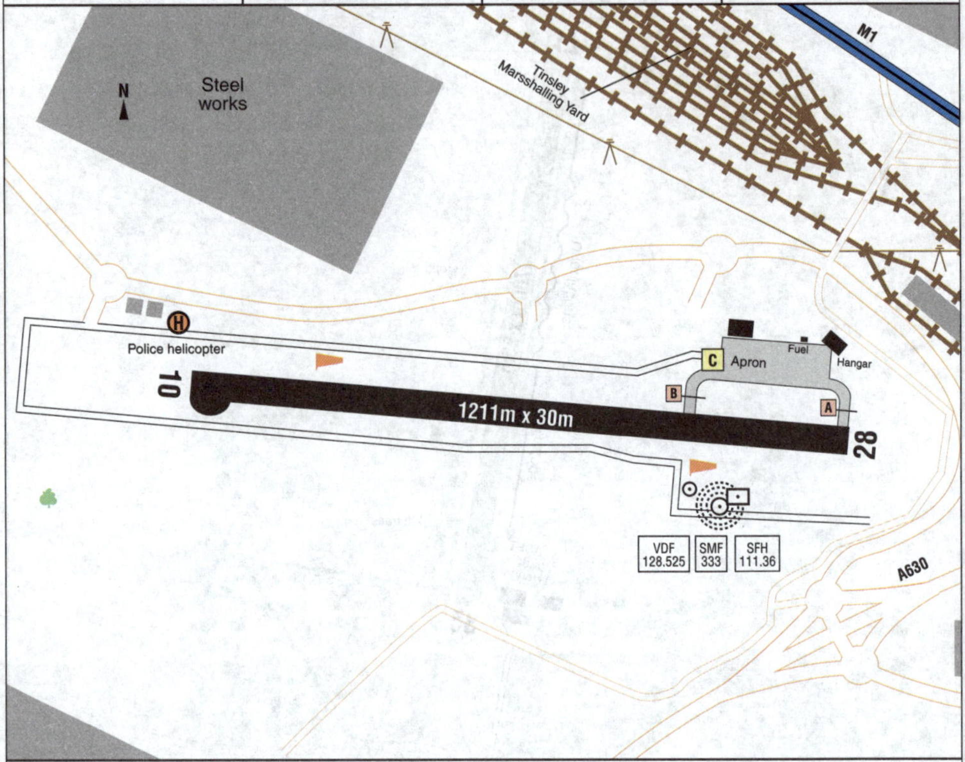

(Airport diagram)

- Steel works
- Tinsley Marsshalling Yard
- M1
- N
- (H) Police helicopter
- 10
- 1211m x 30m
- 28
- C Apron
- Fuel
- Hangar
- B
- A
- VDF 128.525 | SMF 333 | SFH 111.36
- A630

RWY	SURFACE	TORA	LDA	LIGHTING
10/28	Asphalt	1199	1199	Ap Thr Rwy PAPI 3° LHS

Remarks
PPR by fax. Hi-vis. Non-radio ACFT not accepted. Pilots must be in receipt of Guide to single engine aeroplane pilots using Sheffield City Airport. AD available to single engine ACFT, but not available for use by solo student pilots flying single engined fixed wing ACFT.

Warnings
Turbulence strong SW wind effects APP & climb-out Rwy28. AD in highly populated & industrial area. Major obstacles: Chimney 405ft amsl259/2.33nm. Mast 559ft amsl 044°/1.92nm. Steel works 332ft amsl (lit) 0.24nm N of Rwy. High GND 372ft amsl (lit) S of Rwy. Yellow Rwy edge lights for final 400m of LDA Rwy10/28.

Operating Hrs	Mon-Sun 0830-2000 (L)	**Visual Reference Points (VRP)**	
Circuits	Nil	Barnsley Railway Station	N5333.27 W00128.65
Landing Fee	See website or Tel: 0114 201998 Free with >50L AVGAS (singles only)	Old Coates	N5323.52 W00107.12
		Chesterfield Railway Station	N5314.25 W00125.22
Maintenance	Nil	M1/M18 JCT 32	
Fuel	AVGAS JET A1 100LL Mon-Sun 0830-1930 (L)	Redmires Reservoir	N5321.92 W00136.42
Disabled Facilities		**Operator**	Sheffield City Airport Ltd Europa Link, Sheffield, S9 1XZ Tel: 0114 2011998 (PPR) Fax: 0114 2011888 enquiry@sheffieldcityairport.com www.sheffieldcityairport.com

Restaurants	Cafe in terminal Free meal for twin engined ACFT crew
Taxis/Car Hire	Available on request in terminal
Weather Info	AirCen MCW Tel: 0114 2015545

S

SHEFFIELD CITY JOINING INSTRUCTIONS

Arrivals:

All APP and dept routes must be followed:

All APP by single engine ACFT are to be via VRP (M1/M18 Jct 32)

All joining single engine ACFT must be over head AD at 2000ft QFE via the VFR. Keep a good lookout at all times for other joining ACFT.

All ACFT must NOT over fly the City of Sheffield.

All ACFT landing Rwy23/28 use turning circle

Pilots making visual APP Rwy28 should avoid flying over village of Laughten en le Morthen situated 6nm on extended centre line easily identified by tall church spire.

Depts:

All Dept ACFT must use the full length Rwy

ACFT Rwy10 climb out, turn right 500ft QFE

ACFT Rwy28 climb out, turn left 500ft QFE

Helicopters:

Helis MUST Arr/Dept via

North – Tinsley Power Station

East – Steel works

South – Tinsley Park Golf Course

S

642ft 21mb	5nm NW of Banbury N5205.10 W00128.38	**PPR**	**Alternative AD**	**Oxford** Wellesbourne Mountford

	Shennington		**A/G** **130.100** **make blind circuit calls**	

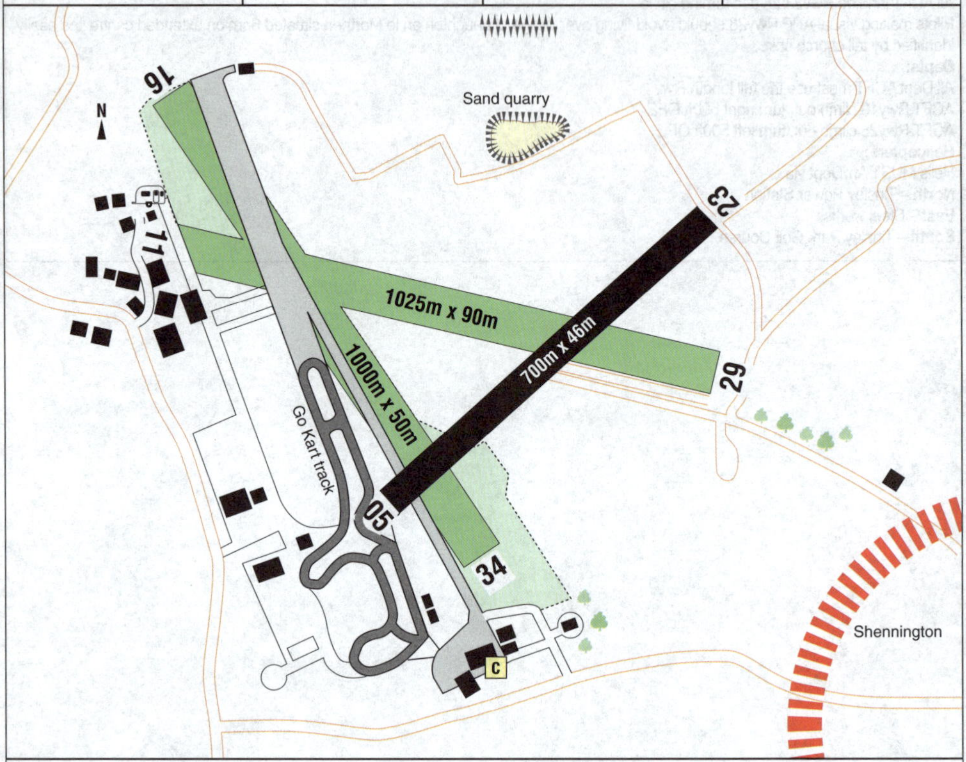

RWY	SURFACE	TORA	LDA	LIGHTING
16/34	Conc/Grass	1000x50	U/L	Nil
05/23	Concrete	700x46	U/L	Nil
11/29	Grass	1025x90	U/L	Nil

Remarks

PPR by telephone. Primarily a Gliding site. Visiting powered ACFT are welcome at pilots own risk. Telephone PPR is required to receive info on the days gliding operations or competitions.

Warnings

Winch launching takes place on AD. No overhead joins. Take care not to trample winch cable. Keep a good lookout for gliders in the circuit, which may not be monitoring A/G freq. Beware of tractors and pedestrians associated with Glider retrieval. There is a Go-Kart track at Rwy05 Thr.

Noise: Avoid local habitation particularly Shenington village SE of AD.

Operating Hrs	SR-SS daily	**Operator**	Oxfordshire Shenington Gliding Club
Circuits	Available on request with PPR		Shenington Airfield
Landing Fee	Nil		Shenington, Oxon
Maintenance	Nil		**Tel:** 01295 688121
Fuel	Nil		

Disabled Facilities

Restaurants	Refreshments available on AD
Taxis/Car Hire	Nil
Weather Info	AirCen MOEx

| 26ft | 5.5nm W of Selby | **PPR** | **Alternative AD** | **Leeds Bradford** Full Sutton |
| 1mb | N5347.07 W00113.03 | | **Diversion AD** | |

| **Sherburn** | **APP** Fenton 126.500 | **LARS** Linton 118.550 | **A/G** 122.600 |

RWY	SURFACE	TORA	LDA	LIGHTING
01	Grass	553	553	Nil
19	Grass	553	521	Nil
11/29	Grass	616	616	Nil
06	Grass	723	676	Nil
24	Grass	696	703	Nil
11	Tarmac	616	830	Nil
29	Tarmac	830	616	Nil

Displaced Thr Rwy01 32m, Displaced Thr Rwy19 32m
Displaced Thr Rwy06 87m, Displaced Thr Rwy24 60m
Displaced Thr Rwy29 214m

Remarks
PPR. AD situated within Church Fenton MATZ. AD not available for use by public transport passenger flights required to use licensed AD. Inbound ACFT contact Fenton MATZ when at 15nm or 5mins flying time from MATZ boundary and are to enter MATZ at 1500ft on Sherburn QFE. If unable to make contact with Fenton APP, pilots to contact Sherburn Radio or Linton MATZ and advise inability to contact Fenton. Dept ACFT are to contact Fenton MATZ before leaving Sherburn circuit and are to leave MATZ below 1500ft QFE. Refuelling: Follow yellow line on Twy onto apron, then follow arrows anti-clockwise around the pump. DO NOT park nose to the pump.

Warnings
Paved Rwy N of grass Rwys is closed to ACFT. It is used as a vehicle test track.
Noise: ACFT must not over fly the villages of Sherburn-in-Elmet, South Milford, Monk Fryston or Hambleton.

| **Operating Hrs** | 0830-SS (Summer) 0900-SS (Winter) Fri closed 1700 | **Landing Fee** | Single £10 Twin £20 Commercial rate available No charge with fuel uplift >40l AVGAS, >80l JET A1 |
| **Circuits** | 01, 19 variable 1000ft QFE 24, 29 LH, 06, 11 RH 1000ft QFE | | |

Maintenance	Sherburn Engineering **Tel:** 01977 685296	Operator	Sherburn Aero Club Ltd Sherburn-in-Elmet Aerodrome Lennerton Lane, Sherburn-in-Elmet West Yorkshire, LB25 6JE **Tel:** 01977 682674 **Fax:** 01977 683699

Fuel AVGAS JET A1 100LL
Sherburn Aero Club **Tel:** 01977 682674

Disabled Facilities

Restaurants Bar & Cafe

Taxis
A1 Private Hire **Tel:** 01977 681100
South Milford **Tel:** 01937 689200
Private Hire
Car Hire
National **Tel:** 0113 277 7957
Weather Info AirN MWC

Sherburn-in-Elmsett Circuit Procedures

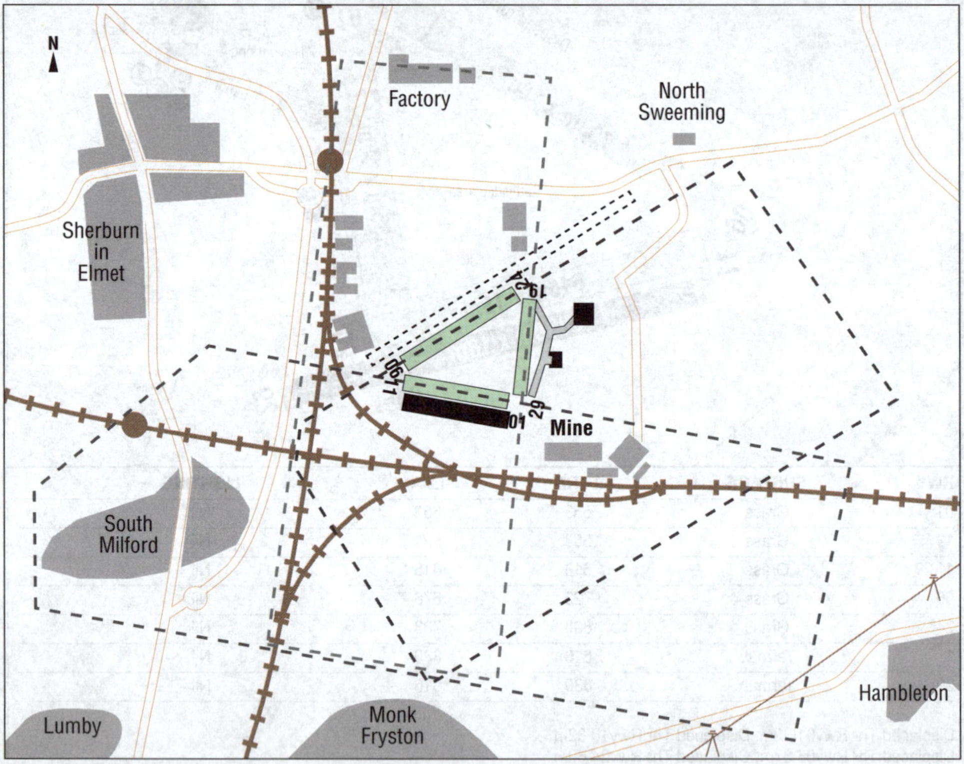

Rwy06 RH: Taxi out along Rwy29.After Dept turn right, not above 500ft QFE. Turn base leg before Monk Fryston. Turn final no further W than Sherburn by-pass. DO NOT over fly South Milford.

Rwy24 LH: Turn left onto 190°, when height & speed permit turn crosswind before South Milford. Turn downwind before Monk Fryston. DONOT extend downwind due to Church Fenton circuit. DO NOT over fly farmhouse at North Sweeming. After landing exit along grass.

Rwy11 RH: Taxi out along Rwy24. Turn crosswind before Hambleton. Turn downwind N of Monk Fryston. Turn base leg W of South Milford, DO NOT over fly built up areas on APP. Complete final turn not below 400ft QFE. DO NOT over fly South Milford or Lumby

Rwy29 LH: After Dept climb out between Sherburn & South Milford. DO NOT over fly South Milford or Lumby. Turn base leg before Hambleton. After landing exit along grass.

Rwy01 LH: After Dept turn left crosswind at 400ft or abeam factory (whichever is first). Continue to 700ft QFE max until downwind. DO NOT over fly Sherburn or South Milford downwind leg. Turn base leg before Monk Fryston.

Rwy19 RH: Turn crosswind before Monk Fryston. DO NOT over fly South Milford or Sherburn on downwind leg. Turn base leg no further N than abeam factory.

510

SHERLOWE

210ft 7mb	4.5nm SE of RAF Shawbury N5244.13 W00236.09	PPR	Alternative AD	Hawarden Sleap

Sherlowe	LARS Shawbury 120.775	A/G 119.300 Not always manned

RWY	SURFACE	TORA	LDA	LIGHTING
15/33	Grass	680x25	U/L	Nil

Rwy33 2° upslope first 430m

Remarks
Strict PPR by telephone. Visiting ACFT welcome at own risk. AD located 1.5nm to SW of High Ercall disused AD. AD within Shawbury MATZ. Arr/Dept ACFT to contact Shawbury.

Warnings
Ditch at Rwy33 Thr. Farm track crosses Rwy keep a good lookout for farm traffic particularly on landing.
Noise: Pilots join at own discretion to avoid over flying local habitation. Avoid over flying High Ercall village 1nm N AD. Noise reduction routes on clubhouse notice board.

		Operator	Mr R F Pooler
Operating Hrs	0800-2000 or SS (L)		Lower Grounds Farm
Circuits	Nil		Sherlowe, High Ercall
Landing Fee	Donations appreciated		Shropshire, TF6 6LT
Maintenance	Nil		**Tel:** 01952 770189
Fuel	Nil		**Fax:** 01952 770762
Disabled Facilities	Nil		**Tel:** 07768 333030
			pooler@aol.com
Restaurants	Tea Coffee & Snacks available in clubhouse "Terminal 1"		
Taxis	Operator can advise		
Car Hire	Nil		
Weather Info	AirCen MWC		

210ft 7mb	3.5nm S of East Dereham N5237.77 E00055.68	PPR	Alternative AD Diversion AD	**Norwich** Old Buckenham

Shipdham	**LARS** Marham 124.150	**A/G** **132.250** make blind calls

RWY	SURFACE	TORA	LDA	LIGHTING
02/20	Asphalt	862x18	U/L	Nil

Remarks
PPR by telephone. Visiting ACFT welcome at own risk.

Warnings
All movement on AD is confined to the paved surfaces.
Noise: Avoid over flying Shipdham village 0.5nm W of AD

Operating Hrs	Sat-Sun 0900-1700 (L) Weekdays by arr	**Operator**	Shipdham Aero Club Shipdham Aerodrome Thetford, Norfolk, IP25 7SB **Tel:** 01362 820709 www.shipdhamaeroclub.co.uk
Circuit	1000ft QFE Powered ACFT to E of Rwy Gliders to W of Rwy		
Landing Fee	Single £5		
Maintenance	Nil		
Fuel	AVGAS 100LL weekends only		
Disabled Facilities	Nil		
Restaurant	Cafe on AD at weekends		
Taxis Anglia	**Tel:** 01362 690050		
Car Hire Hertz	**Tel:** 01842 761362		
Weather Info	AirS BNMC		

S

512

EGBS

SHOBDON

317ft 11mb	6nm W of Leominster N5214.50 W00252.88	PPR	Alternative AD Diversion AD	Gloucestershire Wolverhampton

Shobdon	AFIS 123.500	A/G 123.500

© Copyright 2006 Camber Publishing Ltd. All rights reserved

Effective date:23/11/06

N

Car Park

C C SH 426

Twy B

T

Grass Twy A A

B

Grass glider strip 900m x 25m

60

836m x 18m

27

280m x 20m Microlight Rwy

Crops

Gravel pit

RWY	SURFACE	TORA	LDA	LIGHTING
09	Asphalt	799	836	Thr Rwy
27	Asphalt	799	836	Thr Rwy APAPI 3.5° LHS

Remarks
PPR. Rwy09 not licensed for night use.

Warnings
Parallel asphalt Twy and W access Twy are suitable only for ACFT with a wing span <8m and wheel span <4.5m. Deviation from marked movement area can be hazardous. When Rwy27 is in use, gliders land on grass strip to N of Rwy. Grass microlight strip 280m S of main Rwy09/27. Fence 4.5ft high, 97m W of Rwy09Thr. During heavy rain the Rwy is liable to have patches of standing water. Pilots should use the centre of the Rwy at night as the outer sections are rough.

Operating Hrs	Nov-Mar Fri-Wed 0900-1630 Thu 0900-2100 Apr 0800-1700 May-Aug 0800-1830 Sep-Oct 0800-1700 daily	**Restaurants**	Café & bar on AD 0900-2100 (L) **Tel:** 01568 708783 Camping and caravan site on AD
Circuits	Powered ACFT wide 09 RH, 27 LH, 1000ft QFE. Microlight/Heli using microlight strip tight 800ft QFE (Heli) 500ft QFE (Micro). Overhead joins 1500ft QFE min dead side. Descend to circuit height S of Rwy, see noise chart.	**Taxis** Markham's **Car Hire** Watson's Leominster Hereford Vehicle Rent. **Weather Info** **Operator**	**Tel:** 01568 708208 **Tel:** 01568 612060 **Tel:** 01432 277887 AirN MWC Herefordshire Aero Club Ltd Shobdon Aerodrome Leominster, Hereford, HR6 9NR **Tel:** 01568 708369 **Fax:** 01568 708935 hac@aeroclub.co.uk www.aeroclub.co.uk
Landing Fee	Single £8 Twin £16 Microlight £3		
Maintenance	Herefordshire Aero Club Maintenance **Tel:** 01568 709170		
Fuel	AVGAS JET A1 100LL		
Disabled Facilities	Nil		

S

7ft 0mb	1nm W of Shoreham by Sea N5050.13.W00017.83	PPR	Alternative AD Diversion AD	Farnborough Chichester

Shoreham	ATIS 125.300	APP 123.150	TWR 123.150 125.400	A/G 123.150

RWY	SURFACE	TORA	LDA	LIGHTING
02	Asphalt	960	871	Thr Rwy PAPI 3.5° LHS
20	Asphalt	916	865	Thr Rwy PAPI 4.5° RHS
02/20	Grass	700x18	U/L	Nil
07	Grass	877	877	Nil
25	Grass	877	794	Nil
13/31	Grass	400	400	Nil

Starter extension Rwy31 130m

Remarks

PPR for non-radio ACFT, Microlights, IR Training and qualifying cross-countries. Unless otherwise instructed, join circuit by over-flying AD at 2000ft aal, when instructed descend to circuit height on dead side of Rwy in use and join circuit by crossing upwind end. More than 1 Rwy may be in use at any one time.Rwy02/20 will always be preferred subject to operational limitations. ACFT Dept Rwy20 should avoid over-flying as much of built-up area to S as practical. Noise abatement techniques should be practised at all times, area to E & W being particularly sensitive. Training: Touch and go training is not permitted on Sundays or before 1000 and after 1800 local Mon-Sat. Rwy13/31 is not available for 'touch and go' landing. Only Rwy02/31 may be used for practice engine failures after take-off. Use of NDB or VDF for training by arr with ATC and subject to IFR and scheduled movements.
Parking for Customs: ACFT for Customs clearance should park as instructed by ATC. After heavy rain, standing water may persist on grass areas.
Helicopter Operations: Extensive helicopter training takes place in area W of **Rwy02/20 ('W')** alongside E perimeter fence **('E')** and N of VDF aerial **('X')**. Helicopter circuits will vary in direction. Helicopter Arr & Dept should follow ATC instructions closely and will be subject to specific ATC authorisation to cross Rwys, more than one of which may be in use at any one time. Helicopters should avoid over-flying built up areas that are adjacent to the Arr/Dept routes.
Radio failure procedures: In the event of an ACFT experiencing radio failure during daytime, join over head AD, fit into the traffic pattern, over fly Rwy in use at 500ft before positioning for landing. Standard light signals should be followed.
Visual aid to location: Ibn SH Green.

Warnings

Caution soft GND either side of Twy K. Enter/exit using marked points only. Caution on Twy A, ensure adequate wing tip separation from ACFT holding at Hold C. Mobile obstructions (up to 50ft) on adjacent roads and railways. ACFT APP Rwy02 (hard) are reminded of the displaced Thr due to the elevated railway line. Kite flying/Surfing between Shoreham beech up to 132ft daily during daylight Hrs. Model ACFT flying up to 100ft, approx 1nm from Rwy20 Thr.

Operating Hrs	Mon-Sat 0700-1900 or SS Sun 0730-1930 or SS (Summer) Mon 0800-1800 Tue-Sat 0800-1900 Sun 0830-1800 (Winter), & by arr	**Taxis**	At terminal **Tel:** 01273 414141
		Car Hire	
Circuits	Variable ACFT 1100ft QFE Heli 600ft QFE	Europcar Avis Hertz	**Tel:** 01273 329332 **Tel:** 01273 673738 **Tel:** 01273 738227
Landing Fee	500kgs-1.5MT £16.50 1.5MT-2.5MT £33	**Weather Info**	M T9 Fax 422 A MOEx ATIS **Tel:** 01273 296900 Ex 3

Maintenance

AS Engineering	**Tel:** 01273 464791
MCA	**Tel:** 01273 464222
KB Air	**Tel:** 01273 453333
Apollo Aviation	**Tel:** 01273 440737
Fuel	AVGAS JET A1 100LL

Operator

Brighton Hove & Worthing
Joint Municipal Airport Committee
Shoreham Airport
Shoreham-by-Sea
West Sussex BN43 5FF
Tel: 01273 296900/296888(ATC)
Fax: 01273 296899
admin@shorehamairport.co.uk
www.shorehamairport.co.uk

Disabled Facilities

Restaurants Restaurant refreshments
& Club facilities available
Tel: 01273 296900

Shoreham Arrival & Departures

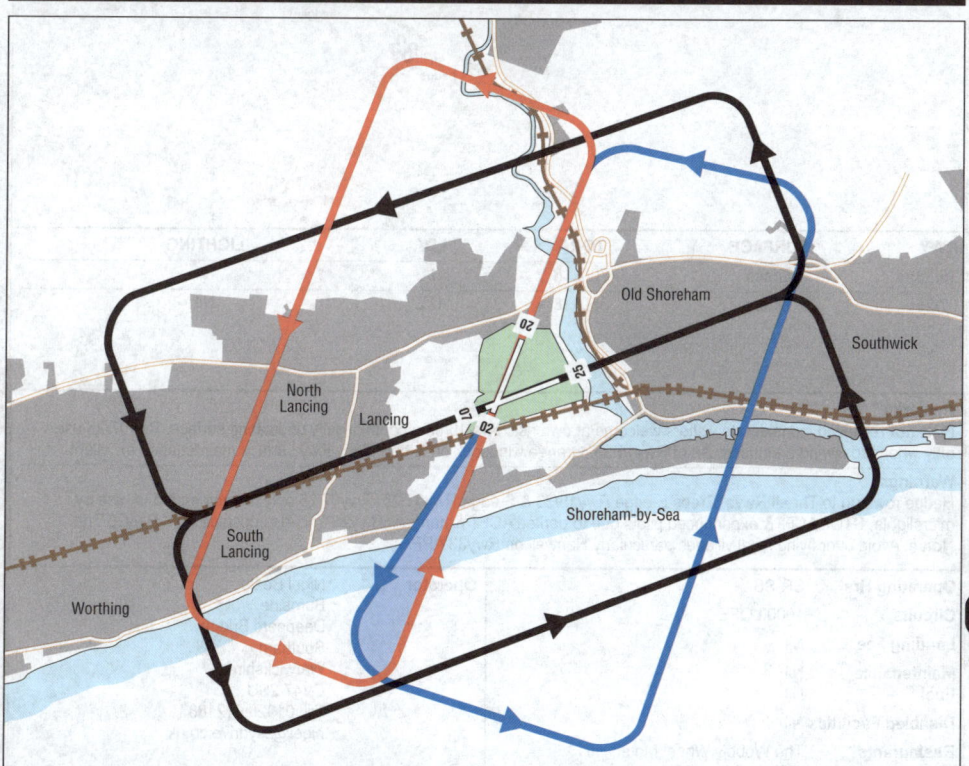

Visual Reference Points (VRP)

Brighton Marina	N5048.65 W00006.05
Lewes Intersection	N5051.87 W00001.45
Littlehampton	N5048.77 W00032.78
Washington Intersection	N5054.57 W00024.47

SHOTTESWELL

530ft 17mb	3nm N of Banbury N5206.25 W00122.80		**Alternative AD**	**Cranfield** Wellesbourne Mountford

Non-radio	**APP** Birmingham 118.050	**Safetycom** 135.475

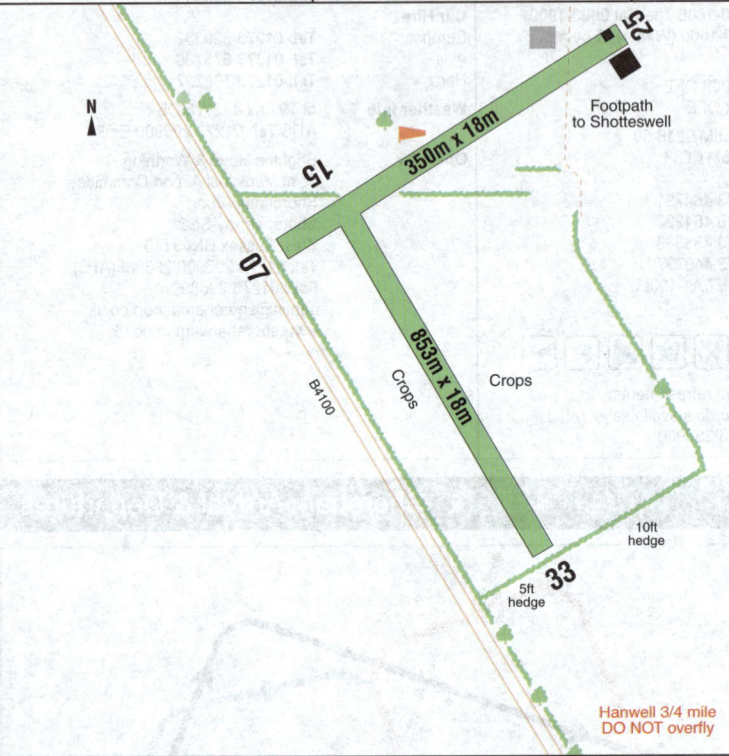

RWY	SURFACE	TORA	LDA	LIGHTING
15/33	Grass	700x18	U/L	Nil
07/25	Grass	350x18	U/L	Nil

Remarks
PPR not required, considerate visitors welcome at own risk. Rwy15/33 smooth slightly undulating surface. Rwy07/25 use only when crosswind precludes use of Rwy15/33. Orange windsock on N boundary. Rwy surface maintenance excellent.

Warnings
Hedge rows up to Thr all Rwys. Crops E edge Rwy15/33 & S edge Rwy07/25. Rwy07/25 only recommended for use by microlights, STOL ACFT& experienced pilots due to parked ACFT & hangars Rwy25 Thr. Also upslope from Rwy25 Thr. **Noise**: Avoid over flying local villages particularly Hanwell on Rwy33 APP.

Operating Hrs	SR-SS	**Operator**	Nigel Beale Burnside Deeppers Bridge Southam Warwickshire CV47 2SU Tel: 01926 612188 nigel@skydrive.co.uk
Circuits	1000ft QFE		
Landing Fee	Nil		
Maintenance	Nil		
Fuel	Nil		
Disabled Facilities	Nil		
Restaurants	The Wobbly Wheel Motel 0.75 mile from AD		
Shotteswell Hse	**Tel: 01295 738227 (B&B)**		
Taxis	**Tel: 01295 270011** **Tel: 01295 264774**		
Car Hire	Nil		
Weather Info	AirCen MOEx		

516

EGTH — SHUTTLEWORTH

110ft 4mb	6nm ESE of Bedford N5205.33 W00019.09	PPR	Alternative AD Diversion AD	Cranfield Little Gransden

Shuttleworth	A/G 130.700	AFIS 130.700 Display days & occasional events only

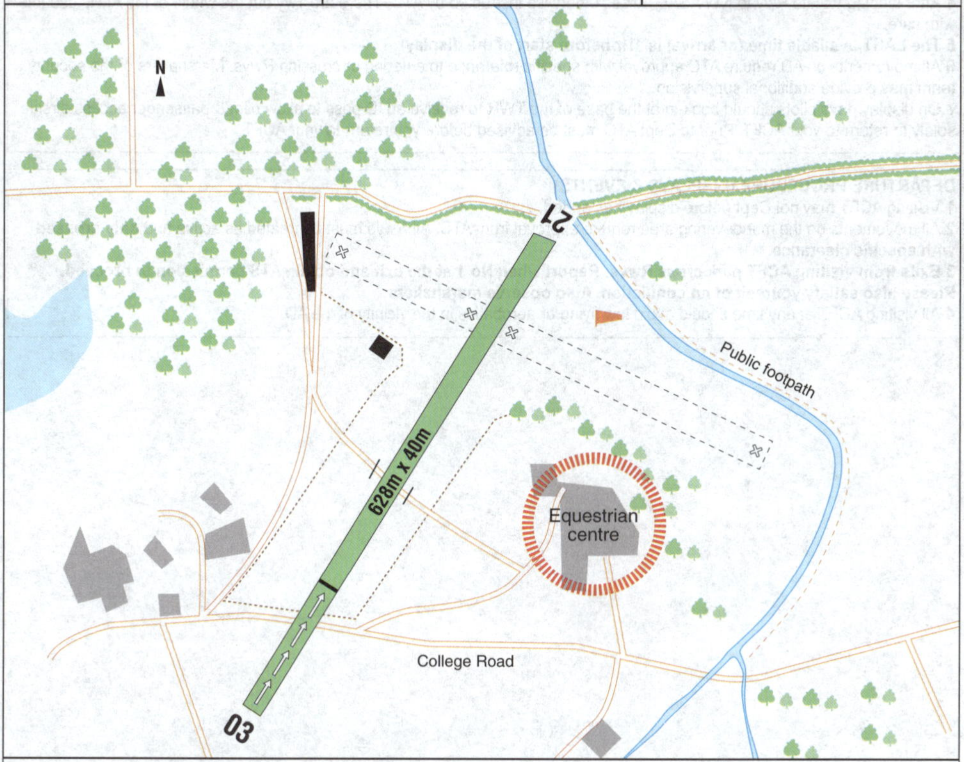

N

628m x 40m

21

03

Public footpath

Equestrian centre

College Road

RWY	SURFACE	TORA	LDA	LIGHTING
03/21	Grass	628x40	U/L	Nil

Rwy03 has marked down slope
Section of rwy s of college rd not available to visiting ACFT

Remarks

PPR by telephone essential. AD closed some days for public events, consult NOTAMs. On non-event days please book in at Shuttleworth shop. High sided vehicles use College Rd keep good lookout! On flying days & for events parking is limited PPR should be obtained well in advance A slot time will be issued. Special admission charges apply. During Winter sheep may be grazing. Aero-modellers may be present, normal circuit should be flown to enable them to clear Rwy. Non-radio ACFT from the collection may be conducting flight trials or practice displays.

Warnings

Operating Hrs	0900-1700	**Taxis**	
Circuits	Join overhead 21 LH, 03 RH, 800ft QFE	Maurice	**Tel:** 01767 316438 **Tel:** 01234 262222
Landing Fee	See website	**Car Hire** Biggleswade Mtr Co	On request or **Tel:** 01767 313788
Maintenance	Available in emergency only	**Weather Info**	AirCen MOEx
Fuel	AVGAS 100LL Flying days only must be requested immediately on Arr, cash payment only	**Operator**	The Shuttleworth Trust Old Warden/Biggleswade Aerodrome Northill, Biggleswade Beds, SG189EP **Tel:** 01767 627927 **Fax:** 01767 627949 collection@shuttleworth.org www.shuttleworth.org

Disabled Facilities

Restaurants
Full facilities avail until 1700 (1600 Nov-Mar)

517

ARRIVAL PROCEDURE (DISPLAYS & EVENTS)

1 On first contact state Booking ref & ACFT details. If unable to meet your slot time please advise early as others are keen to visit. Pilots should be aware that a practice display may be in progress using conflicting Rwy. ATC will advise and may request a delay.

2 Non-radio ACFT are required to Arr within +/-10 mins of slot time. Pilots should be aware that a practice display may be in progress using conflicting Rwy. LOOK OUT FOR LIGHT SIGNALS.

3 All ACFT to make a standard overhead join and visual circuit. Keep a good lookout for non-radio ACFT

4 After landing vacate Rwy to NW ASAP unless otherwise instructed by ATC. There are Twy but the whole of the AD is useable with care.

5 The LAST available time for arrival is 1Hr before start of the display

6 All movements on AD require ATC approval with specific reference to entering or crossing Rwys. Marshallers or the security team may provide additional supervision.

7 On display days pilots should book-in at the base of the TWR to receive an ID pass to allow pilot & passenger access airside solely to return to your ACFT. Prior to Dept ATC must be advised before you return to your ACFT

DEPARTURE PROCEDURE (DISPLAYS & EVENTS)

1 Visiting ACFT may not Dept before display has ended.

2 All movements on the manoevering area require approval from ATS. All Rwys must be treated as active and **only crossed with specific clearance.**

3 Exits from visiting ACFT park cross Rwys. Report when No 1 at the exit and obtain ATS permission to proceed. **Please also satisfy yourself of no confliction. Also observe marshallers.**

4 All visiting ACFT at any time should avoid low flying or aerobatics in the vicinity of the AD.

SITTLES FARM

190ft 6mb	3nm E of Lichfield N5242.30 W00144.50	**PPR**	**Alternative AD**	**Birmingham** Tatenhill

Non Radio	**APP** **Birmingham 118.050**	**A/G** **Roddige 129.825**	**Safetycom** **135.475**

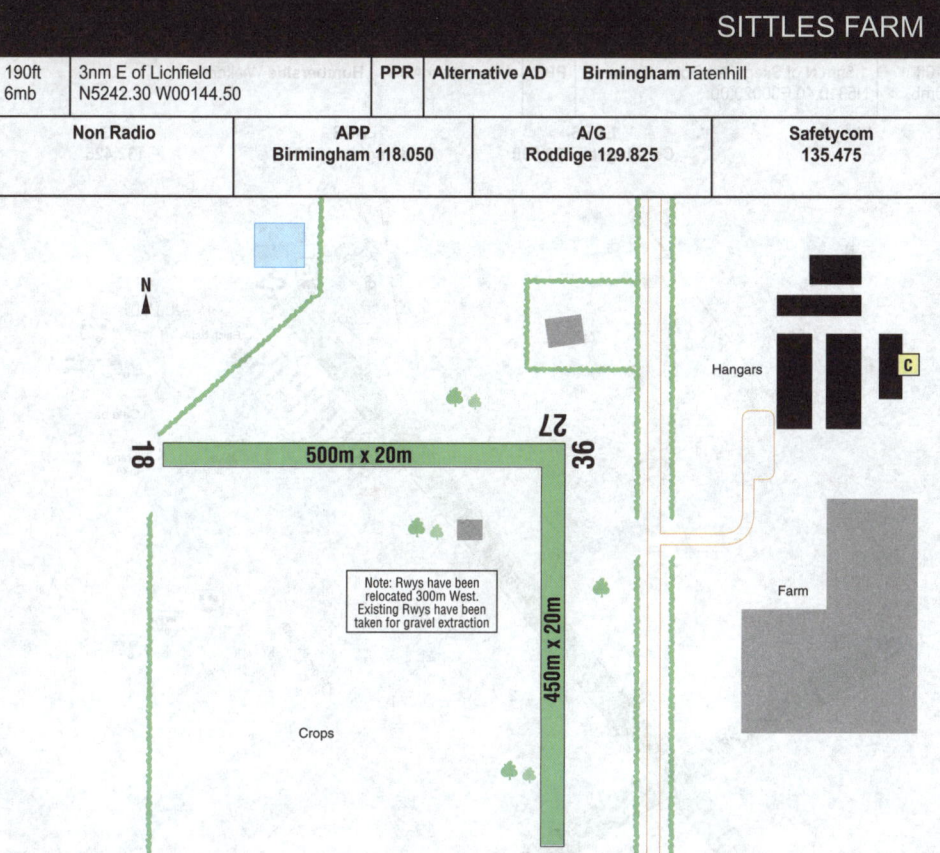

Note: Rwys have been relocated 300m West. Existing Rwys have been taken for gravel extraction

Hangars

Farm

Crops

500m x 20m

450m x 20m

18   27   36   09

N

C

RWY	SURFACE	TORA	LDA	LIGHTING
09/27	Grass	500x20	U/L	Nil
18/36	Grass	450x20	U/L	Nil

Remarks
PPR by telephone. Visiting ACFT welcome at own risk. Rwy well maintained.

Warnings
Roddige AD is close to N AD boundary with daily Microlight activity. Crops grown up to edge of strip.
Noise: Avoid over flying all local villages. See circuit details.

Operating Hrs	SR-SS	**Operator**	Mr John Boulton
Circuits	27, 36 LH, 09, 18 RH 800ft QFE Join overhead		20 Yewtree Avenue Lichfield
Landing Fee	Nil		Staffs WS14 9UA
Maintenance	Nil		**Tel:** 01543 418555
Fuel	MOGAS available from garage 0.5nm		**Tel:** 07860 436003
Disabled Facilities	Nil		john.boulton@virgin.net
Restaurant	Tea & Coffee available Farm can provide group catering on open days for 200-300 people		
Taxi/Car Hire	Nil		
Weather Info	AirCen MWC		

S

10ft 0mb	1.5nm N of Skegness (Town Ctr 4nm) N5310.40.E00020.00	PPR	**Alternative AD**	**Humberside** Wickenby

Skegness	**LARS** Conningsby 120.800	**LARS** Waddington 127.350	**A/G** 132.425

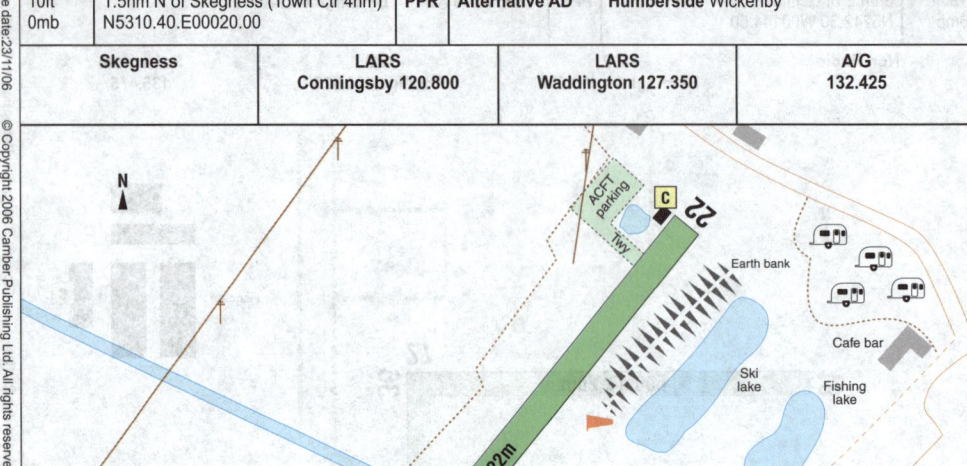

RWY	SURFACE	TORA	LDA	LIGHTING
11/29	Grass	540x22	U/L	Nil
04/22	Grass	755x22	U/L	Nil

Starter extension Rwy11 192m
Starter extension Rwy29 45m

Remarks
AD situated within Water Leisure Park complex 0.5nm from Butlins Fun Coast World (day tickets available).

Warnings
AD close to N boundary of the Wash AIAA. ACFT Arr from S must contact Conningsby during their Ops Hrs, other times Waddington. Rwy11 displaced Thr due to over head power lines on AD boundary.
Noise: Rwy22 make crosswind turn keep church on left. Do not turn downwind until over coast. Rwy04 ensure base leg turn is made before built up area of Skegness

Operating Hrs	Request only	**Operator**	Mr F Ellis
Circuits	LH 800ft QFE		Skegness Water Leisure Park
Landing Fee	£6 pay at hangar or site reception		Walls Lane, Skegness
Maintenance			**Tel:** 07957 595835
M3	**Tel:** 01754 611127		**Tel:** 01754 611127
Fuel	Nil		**Fax:** 01754 611127
Disabled Facilities Nil			www.skegnessairfield.co.uk
Restaurants	Available in Water Leisure Park during summer season		
Taxis			
Rainbow	**Tel:** 01754 612222		
Car Hire	Available by arr		
Weather Info	AirCen MWC		

275ft 9mb	10nm N of Shrewsbury N5250.03 W00246.30	PPR	Alternative AD Diversion AD	Hawarden Wolverhampton

Sleap	LARS Shawbury 120.775	A/G 122.450

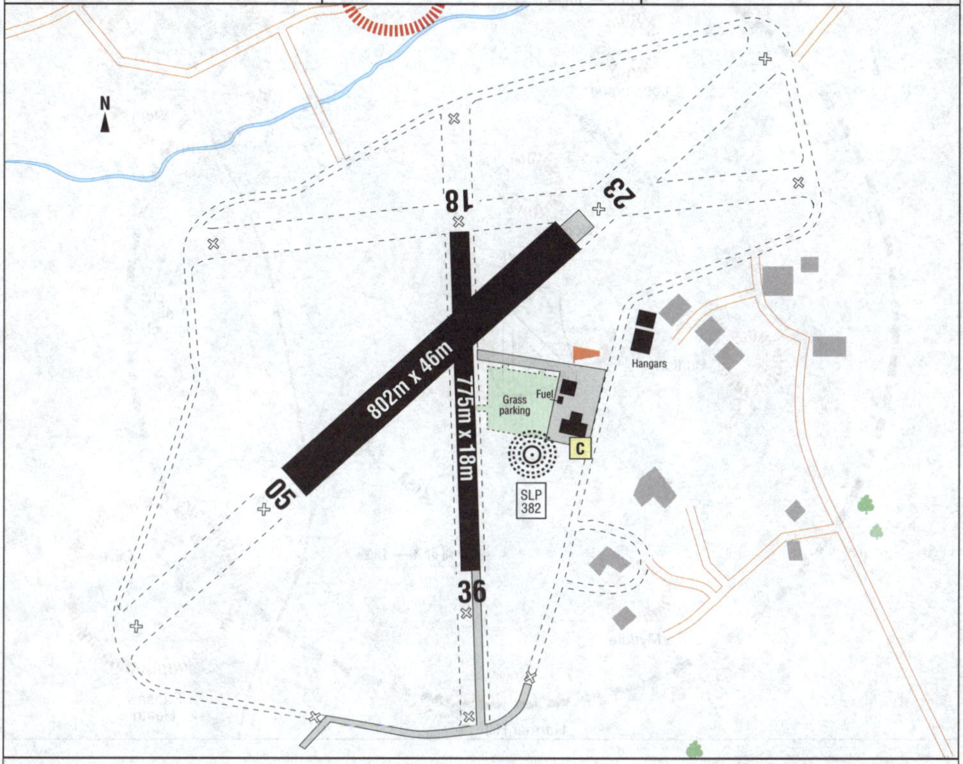

(Aerodrome chart: Runway 05/23 802m x 46m, Runway 18/36 775m x 18m, N arrow, Grass parking, Fuel, Hangars, SLP 382, C)

RWY	SURFACE	TORA	LDA	LIGHTING
05/23	Asphalt	802	802	Thr Rwy LITAS 3.5°
18/36	Asphalt	775	775	Nil

Starter extension Rwy23 50m (day only)

Remarks
Strict PPR by telephone. AD not available for public transport passenger flights and civil helicopter training flights or jet ACFT. Inbound ACFT are to contact Shawbury. ACFT not to be parked on grass parallel to Twy or opposite to fuel pumps. Used for helicopter training Mon-Fri visiting ACFT must obtain a telephone briefing.
Visual aid to location: Ibn Green SP

Warnings
Glider launching takes place on AD. Pilots are warned that deviation from the marked movement area can be hazardous. Circuits to W of AD are active with intense military rotary activity when RAF Shawbury are active.

Operating Hrs	Fri-Wed 0830-1600 Thu 0830-2015 (Summer) +1Hr (Winter)	**Taxis** Wem Taxis Shawbury Taxis	**Tel:** 01939 233673 **Tel:** 01939 250777
Circuits	Variable – See circuit procedures	**Car Hire**	Nil
Landing Fee	Single £10, Twin £20	**Weather Info**	AirCen MWC
Maintenance	Shropshire Light Aviation **Tel:** 01939 290861	**Operator**	Shropshire Aero Club Ltd Sleap Aerodrome Myddle Shropshire, SY4 3HE **Tel:** 01939 232882 **Fax:** 01939 235058 info@shropshireaeroclub.com www.shropshireaeroclub.com
Fuel	AVGAS Jet A1 100LL		
Disabled Facilities			
Restaurants	Hot & cold food/drinks available		

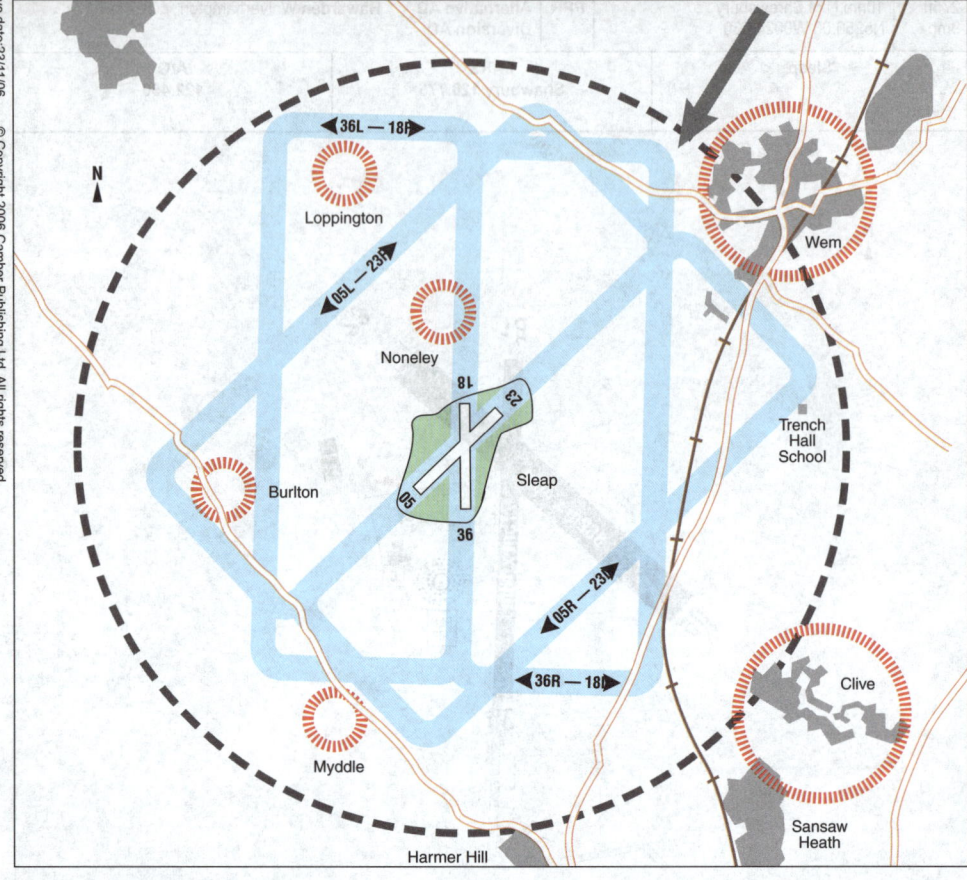

Joining procedures: Weekend standard joins 2000ft QFE. Weekdays ACFT should carry out non-standard centre line join 2000ft QFE. Call for briefing.
Circuit Height 1000ft QFE
Circuits generally LH except when RAF Shawbury is active, when circuits will be E of AD.
Circuits should be contained within ATZ(large broken circle).
Circuit patterns shown are required maxima.
Avoid over flying Wem, Clive, Myddle, Loppington, Noneley & Burlton.
Arr ACFT should carry out standard 2000ft overhead joining procedure except when RAF Shawbury are active when ACFT should carry out a centre line join at 2000ft QFE. A full briefing on this procedure must be obtained by contacting the operator before dept.
ACFT APP Rwy23 on a straight-in or long final should keep to W of Wem (220°).
ACFT especially high-powered singles or twins Dept Rwy36 should make a10° right turn after take-off to avoid Noneley village.

460ft 15mb	8nm WNW of Hull N5346.30 W00034.62	PPR	Alternative AD	Humberside Beverley

Non-radio	LARS Humberside 119.125	Safetycom 135.475

RWY	SURFACE	TORA	LDA	LIGHTING
07/25	Grass	732x20	U/L	Nil

Rwy25 2.3° down gradient

Remarks
PPR. Visitors welcome at pilots own risk. Pilots of visiting ACFT must obtain a briefing on landing and take-off procedures. Available by telephone from AD operator at weekends.

Warnings
Caution: Steeply rising GND and trees on W boundary produce roll-over which should be anticipated at any time, particularly with strong winds. Public footpath crosses undershoot of Rwy07 95m short of Thr. Radio masts 208ft agl close to N of Rwy25 APP 1300m from Thr. Low flying high speed military ACFT may be encountered in the vicinity of AD.
Noise: Avoid over flying village of South Cave W of AD.

Operating Hrs	No takeoff before 0800 or after 2000 (L) Landings are permitted	**Operator**	N & L May Mount Airy Farm South Cave Brough, East Yorkshire, HU15 2BD **Tel:** 01430 422395/422973 (Operator) **Fax:** 01430 422395
Circuits	07 RH, 25 LH 1000ft QFE		
Landing Fee	Singles £3 Twins £5 Business use £5		
Maintenance	Can be arr on a call out basis		
Fuel	Nil		
Disabled Facilities	Nil		
Restaurants	Food available in South Cave (1.25nm)		
Taxis/Car Hire	Courtesy Car usually available or taxi arr		
Weather Info	AirN MWC		

S

523

EGHI

SOUTHAMPTON

44ft 2mb	3.5nm NNE of Southampton N5057.02 W00121.40	PPR	Alternative AD Diversion AD	Bournemouth Thruxton

Southampton	ATIS 113.350 (SAM VOR)	ZONE Solent APP 120.225	APP 128.850

	RAD 128.850	TWR 118.200	FIRE 121.600	

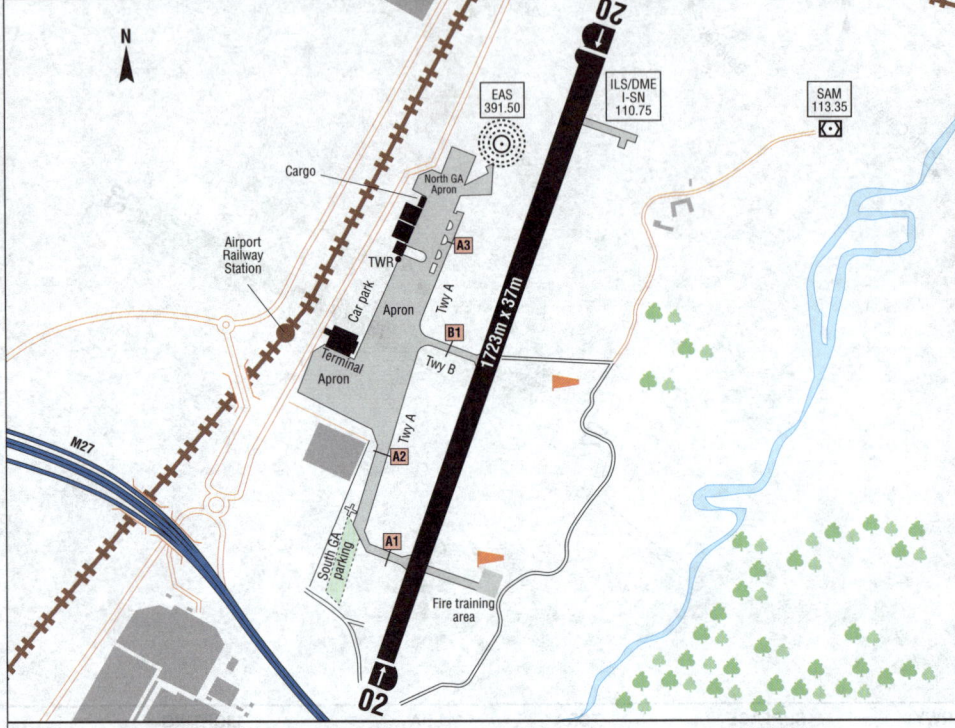

RWY	SURFACE	TORA	LDA	LIGHTING
02	Asphalt	1723	1650	Ap Thr Rwy PAPI 3°
20	Asphalt	1650	1605	Ap Thr Rwy PAPI 3.1°

Displaced Thr Rwy02 73m, Displaced Thr Rwy20 45m

Remarks
PPR for visiting GA ACFT. Non-radio ACFT not accepted. Landing/taxiing grass areas prohibited. Use of AD by training flights subject approval from AD operator. Requests for approval to ATC briefing unit.

Warnings
GA ACFT parking stands 9-11, S/N GA aprons required to use AD GND transport. ACFT commanders responsible for safety of themselves, passengers/crew when airside. When GND transport not provided all passengers/crew to be escorted by ACFT commander, Circuit training by helis not permitted.

Noise Preferential Routes & Procedures: After take-off Rwy20 ACFT not below 500ft agl, turn right make good track of 218°M maintain track to 2000ft (Southampton AD QNH) or Southampton Water (compatible with ATC requirements), individual cases may be varied by ATC.

Operating Hrs	Mon-Thu 0545-2030 Fri 0545-2115 Sat 0630-1915 Sun 0830-2000 (Summer) Mon-Fri 0625-2100 Sat 0615-2000 Sun 0900-2100 (Winter)	**Taxis** Airport Cars	**Tel:** 02380 627100
		Car Hire Avis/Hertz/	**Tel:** 02380 629600
Circuits	Day 1000ft QNH, Night 1500ft QNH	**Weather Info**	M T9 A Fax 424 VS MOEx ATIS **Tel:** 02380 627103
Landing Fee	Available with PPR	**Operator**	BAA Southampton, Southampton Airport, Southampton, SO18 2NL **Tel:** 02380 629600 (AD Switchboard) **Tel:** 02380 627113 (AD Duty Manager) **Tel:** 02380 627102 (AD Ops) **Tel:** 02380 627243 (ATC) **Fax:** 02380 629300 **Fax:** 02380 627104 (Duty Ops Mgr)
Maintenance Signature Aviation **Tel:** 02380 620727			
Fuel	AVGAS JET A1 100LL		
Disabled Facilities Nil			
Handling	**Tel:** 02380 616600 (Signature) **Fax:** 02380 629648 (Signature)		
Restaurants	Cafe bar at AD		

S

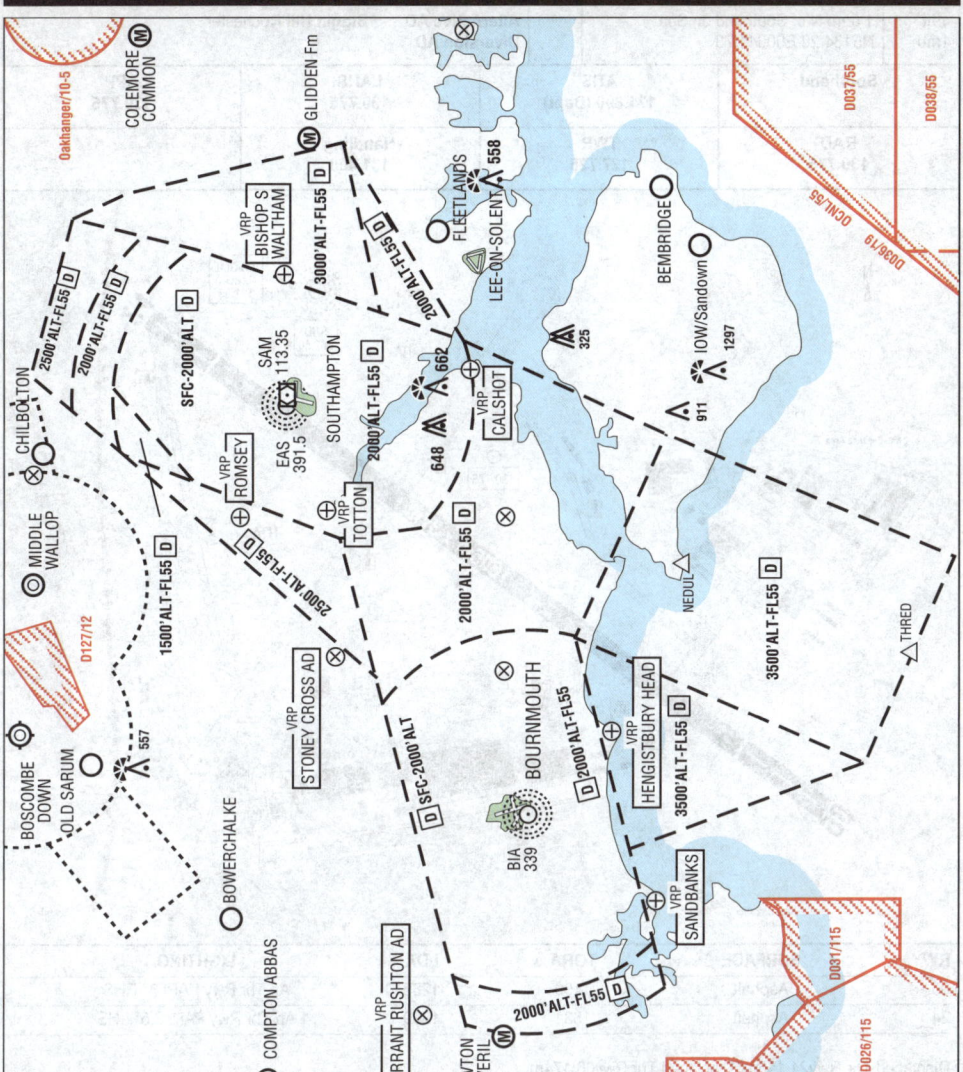

CTA/CTR Class D Airspace

Normal CTA/CTR Class D Airspace rules apply.
Transition Alt 4000ft.
These rules do not apply to non-radio ACFT by day provided they have obtained permission and maintain 5km visibility, 1500m horizontally and1000ft vertically away from cloud, or for gliders provided they maintain 8km visibility, 1500m horizontally and 1000ft vertically away from cloud.

VFR Transit Traffic

VFR traffic wishing to transit the Southampton CTR from the E or W should plan to route via ROMSEY-SAM Bishops Waltham or vice versa.

Visual Reference Points (VRP)

VRP	VOR/NDB	VOR/DME
Bishops Waltham	SAM 093°/EAS 093°	SAM 093°/5nm
N5057.28 W00112.58		
Calshot	SAM 178°/BIA 086°	SAM 178°/8nm
N5049.07 W00119.75		
Romsey	SAM 293°/EAS 295°	SAM 293°/6nm
N5059.45 W00129.75		
Totton	SAM 251°/EAS 250°	SAM 250°/6nm
N5055.20 W00129.33		

49ft 1mb	1.5nm N of Southend on Sea N5134.28 E00041.73		Alternative AD Diversion AD	Biggin Hill Rochester

Southend	ATIS 121.800 (Dept)	LARS 130.775	APP 130.775
RAD 130.775	TWR 127.725	Handling 131.400	

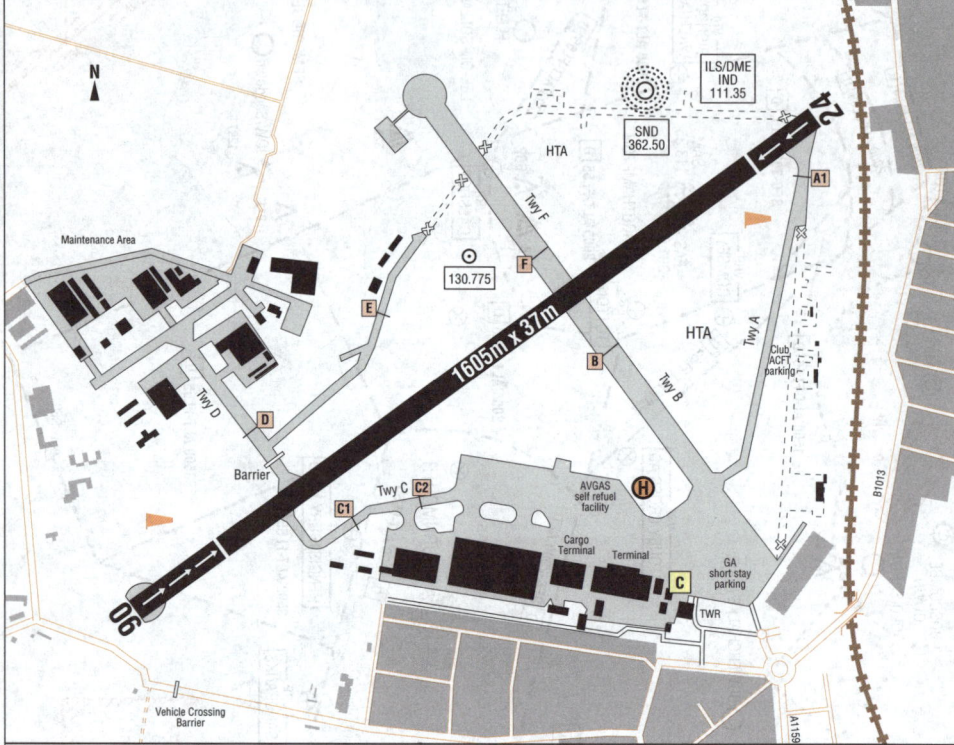

RWY	SURFACE	TORA	LDA	LIGHTING
06	Asphalt	1459	1285	Ap Thr Rwy PAPI 3° RHS
24	Asphalt	1531	1399	Ap Thr Rwy PAPI 3.5° LHS

Displaced Thr Rwy24 146m, Displaced Thr Rwy06 174m

Remarks
PPR Instrument training, QXC's, examination flights & non-radio ACFT. Hi-Vis. Dept all propeller driven ACFT must climb straight ahead at least 600ft aal before turning. Dept Rwy24 propeller driven ACFT requiring a left turn shall, pass 600ft aal, maintain track 190° to N bank River Thames, or until Detling DME 13nm or less, before setting course. Busy public road crosses extended Rwy centreline at SW end Rwy06/24. APP Rwy06/24 in VMC intercept Rwy extended centreline min range 2nm from touchdown not below PAPI APP slope 3° Rwy06 or 3.5° Rwy24. Heli training S of Rwy between Twy A & B and N of Rwy. Heli circuits normally parallel fixed wing Rwy in use at 500ft/1000ft as advised by ATC. Twy barriers installed across Twy D S of Hold D max height 3ft agl. Barriers controlled by ATC and lit. AVGAS self-fuelling facility for Southend account card holders/Air BP holders only. GA park by TWR ACFT <PA31 self parking. ACFT nose wheel must be left on, but perpendicular to broken line. Pilots operating into AD must read and accept the terms and conditions of use. Slots required for instrument APP and circuit training, advise ATC of cancellations or delays of >10mins.
Visual aid to location: Abn White flashing.

Warnings
Not all Twy are available for use, ATC will advise. Deviation from marked movement area hazardous. Twy D is un-lit, use at pilots own discretion. Extensive instrument flying takes place 0800-2000.

Operating Hrs	H24	Parking Fee	<2.5 tonnes <2Hrs Free, 2-4 Hrs £6.46, 4-8 Hrs £12.04, 8-24 Hrs £14.69 Night surcharge £58.75 2300-0600 (L)
Circuits	Variable at the discretion of ATC		
Landing Fee	£19.98 per 1000kg Discount for circuits & go-arounds	Maintenance Fuel	Available (major) AVGAS JET A1 100LL

Disabled Facilities							Operator	Regional Airports Ltd

Operator

Regional Airports Ltd
London Southend Airport
Southend-on-Sea
Essex, SS2 6YF
Tel: 01702 608125 (FBO)
Tel: 01702 608120 (ATC)
Fax: 01702 608128(ATC)
fbo@southendairport.net
www.southendairport.net

Handling   **Tel:** 01702 608150
                  handling@southendairport.net

Restaurant   Restaurant in Terminal
                  (Mon-Fri 0800-1530 Sat-Sun 1000-1500)
                  Tel: 01702 608138
                  McDonalds 300m SE Terminal

Taxis
At terminal   **Tel:** 01702 334455
Car Hire
Budget   **Tel:** 01268 772774
Hertz   **Tel:** 01702 546666

Weather Info M T9 A Fax 426 VS MOEx

Effective date:23/11/06

Visual Reference Points (VRP)

Billericay	N5138.00 E00025.00
Maldon	N5143.70 E00041.00
Sheerness	N5126.50 E00044.90
St Marys Marsh	N5128.50 E00036.00
South Woodham Ferrers	N5139.00 E00037.00

Pilots are requested to contact APP prior to reaching abeam any of the VRP's when inbound or over flying the area.

ARRIVALS & DEPARTURES

VFR flights and over flight must establish communications with ATC at least 5 minutes before ETA overhead Southend and prior to reaching abeam any of the VRP's. Instructions may be issued with a restriction, this does not absolve pilots from any requirement they may have to remain in VMC at all times, pilots must advise ATC if they are unable to comply.

Arr or over flying VFR flights must avoid the instrument APP let down areas and dept climb outs at all times, unless ATC have indicated no traffic. ATC may specify a specific route or track requirement to assist pilots. Pilots wishing to make a standard overhead join are to request this on initial contact.

VFR DEPARTURES

Depts may be issued with a level and/or routing restrictions by ATC to assist in deconflicting traffic and is circuit integration. Pilots are advised that IAP's may be flown that do not conform to the Rwy in use.

335ft 11mb	6nm SW of RAF Wittering N5233.95 W00036.34	PPR	Alternative AD	Nottingham East Midlands Peterborough Conington

Non-Radio	LARS Cottesmore 130.200	Safetycom 135.475

640m x 13m

60

27

crops

crops

3m concrete strip

20ft trees

ACFT parking

C

Windmill Aviation

N

RWY	SURFACE	TORA	LDA	LIGHTING
09/27	Conc/Grass	640x13	U/L	Rwy

Rwy27 grass touchdown zone with narrow concrete strip lighting on request only

Remarks
Strictly PPR by telephone. Home of Windmill Aviation (M3). AD situated on S. perimeter track of WW2 AD, all other areas unsuitable for aviation use.

Warnings
AD situated beneath the SW MATZ stub of RAF Wittering, (controlling authority Cottesmore). Arr/Dept ACFT may be requested to contact Wittering TWR. Inbound ACFT contact Cottesmore and prior to Dept. Caution: Vehicles occasionally use Rwy.
Noise: Avoid over flight of local villages.

Operating Hrs	Mon-Sat 0800-1900 (L) by arr Closed Sunday	**Taxis** Corby Cabs	**Tel:** 01536 260033
Circuits	Variable 1000ft QFE	**Car Hire**	Nil
Landing Fee	Advised with PPR	**Weather Info**	AirCen MOEx
Maintenance	Windmill Aviation **Tel:** 01780 450205 Hangarage available for visiting ACFT by arr	**Operator**	Windmill Aviation Spanhoe Airfield
Fuel	AVGAS 100LL		Laxton, Corby
Disabled Facilities Nil			Northants, NN17 3AT
Restaurants/Accomodation			**Tel/Fax**: 01780 450205
Spanhoe Lodge	**Tel:** 01780 450328		
Guest House	**Tel:** 01780 450328		
White Swan	**Tel:** 01572 747543 (Harringworth)		

S

185ft 6mb	4.5nm N of Romford N5139.15 E00009.35	PPR	Alternative AD Diversion AD	Southend Elstree

Stapleford	APP Thames RAD 132.700	APP Stansted 120.625	A/G 122.800

RWY	SURFACE	TORA	LDA	LIGHTING
04R Day	Grass/Asph	1127	1077	Ap Thr Rwy APAPI 4.5° RHS
04R Night	Grass/Asph	900	900	Ap Thr Rwy APAPI 4.5° RHS
22L Day	Asph/Grass	1100	900	Ap Thr Rwy APAPI 4.25° LHS
22L Night	Asph/Grass	900	900	Ap Thr Rwy APAPI 4.25° LHS
10	Grass	698	698	Nil
28	Grass	715	500	Nil
04L	Grass	900	900	Nil
22R	Grass	900	900	Nil

Rwy22L 600mx18m asphalt insert starts 17m after beginning of TORA
Starter extension Rwy04 50x44m
Starter extension Rwy22L 23x48m
Displaced Thr Rwy28 215m
Displaced Thr Rwy22L 177m

Remarks
PPR 2Hrs outside published Hrs of operation. Licensed relief Rwy has been established to W, parallel to and adjoining Rwy04/22. Rwy is marked with white corners and white painted edge markers. Pilots may be asked to use this Rwy at certain times.
Aids to Navigation: VOR/DME LAM 115.60

Warnings
Radio mast 295ft aal SW of AD and 1.2nm from Rwy04 Thr in line withRwy04/22. Do not land short of displaced Rwy22L/22R Thr. Power cables 210ftagl running NW/SE 1nm NE of Rwy22 Thr. Not all Twys available for use during winter months, deviation from marked manoeuvring area can be hazardous. E Twy closed, clear right after landing Rwy22L.
Noise: Avoid over flying villages of Abridge and Lambourne below 1000ft agl. Rwy28 Dept ACFT should maintain Rwy heading until passing 1000ft agl. Rwy22Dept: No right turn below 1000ft agl.

Operating Hrs	0830-SS (L) & by arr	Circuits	LH 1200ft QNH

Landing Fee	Single £10 Twin/Heli £20
	£3 per night parking
	Out of Hrs by arr
Maintenance	Stapleford Maintenance
	Tel: 01708 688449
Fuel	AVGAS JET A1 100LL
	with PPR

Disabled Facilities

Restaurants	Cafe & bar at AD
Taxis	
Theydon Bois	**Tel:** 01992 814335
Car Hire	
Hertz	**Tel:** 01708 721882
Weather Info	AirSE MOEx

Operator	The Herts and Essex Aero Club Ltd
	Stapleford Aerodrome
	Stapleford, Romford
	Essex, RM41SJ
	Tel: 01708 688380
	Fax: 01708 688421
	www.flysfc.com

10ft 0mb	4nm W of Sheerness N5126.64 E00037.96	Alternative AD	Southend Rochester

Stoke	LARS Southend 130.775	A/G 118.925

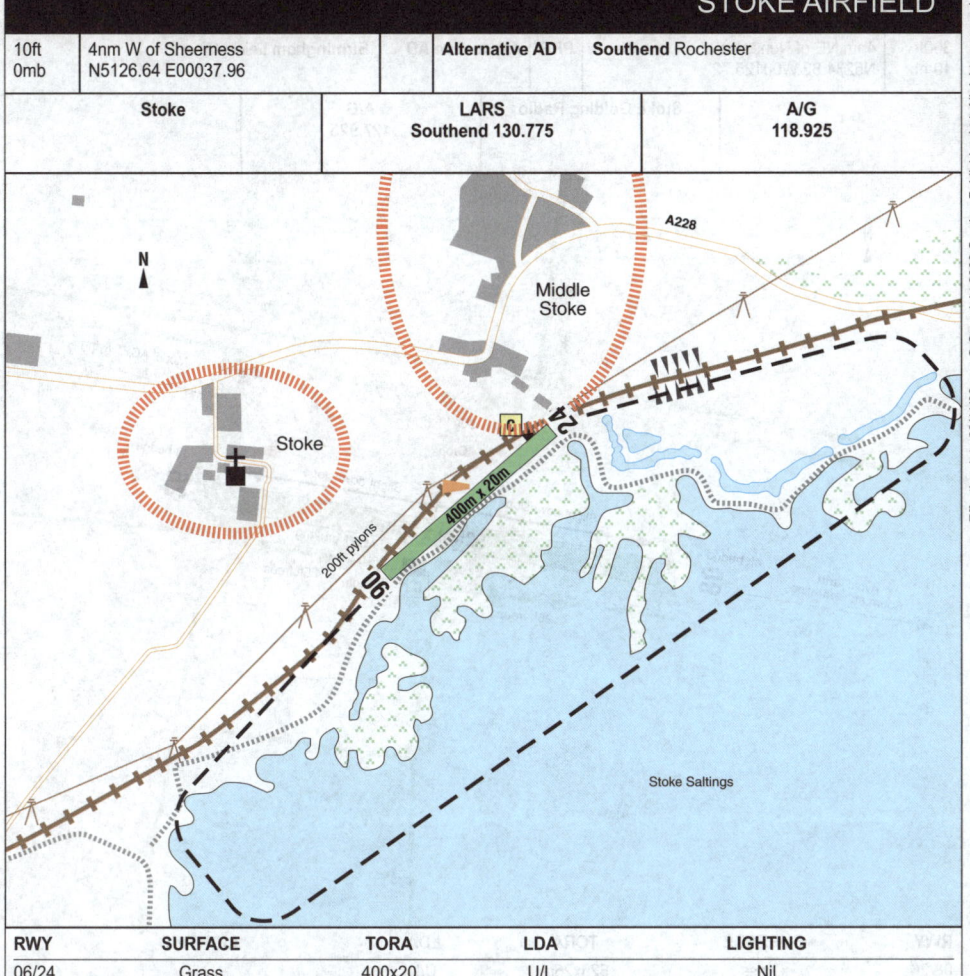

RWY	SURFACE	TORA	LDA	LIGHTING
06/24	Grass	400x20	U/L	Nil

Remarks

PPR not required visiting ACFT & microlights welcome. Intense microlight training site please keep a good lookout & make blind calls if no reply. Strip has a very slight curve over its entire length. Taxi on the sea wall side of Rwy & park with propeller close to bushes, first 4 spaces used by school ACFT only. Visitors book in at club hut.

Warnings

National grid transmission lines 200ft high parallel to Rwy and final APP on land ward side. Railway passes along this side of AD between Rwy & pylons. The seaward marsh is SSSI do not over fly below 500ft QFE.
Noise: Do not over fly Stoke village or St Mary's Marsh to N of AD.

Operating Hrs	SR-SS Last permitted take-off 2000 (L)	**Taxis**	
Circuits	06 RH, 24 LH 800ft QFE Join overhead 1500ft QFE (Slightly offset final APP to avoid transmission lines)	Hoo Cabs **Car Hire** **Weather Info** **Operator**	Tel: 01634 251234 Nil AirSE MOEx Medway Microlights
Landing Fee	Mon-Fri £2 Sat-Sun & PH £4		Stoke Airfield Stoke, Rochester
Maintenance	Medway Microlight Factory 200 yds from AD Mon-Fri 0900-1700 sales service & maintenace		Kent, ME3 9RN **Tel:** 01634 270236 (AD) **Tel:** 01634 270780 (Factory)
Fuel	MOGAS at local village 0800-2000 (L) 7-days (transport avail with notice)		
Hangarage	Available for de-rigged microlights & 3 axis		
Disabled Facilities Nil			
Restaurants/Accomodation			
	Hot & cold drinks Mon-Fri Food available weekends Accomodation can be arr		

S

300ft 10mb	4nm NE of Nuneaton N5234.82 W00125.72	PPR	Alternative AD	Birmingham Leicester

	Stoke Golding Radio	A/G 127.925	

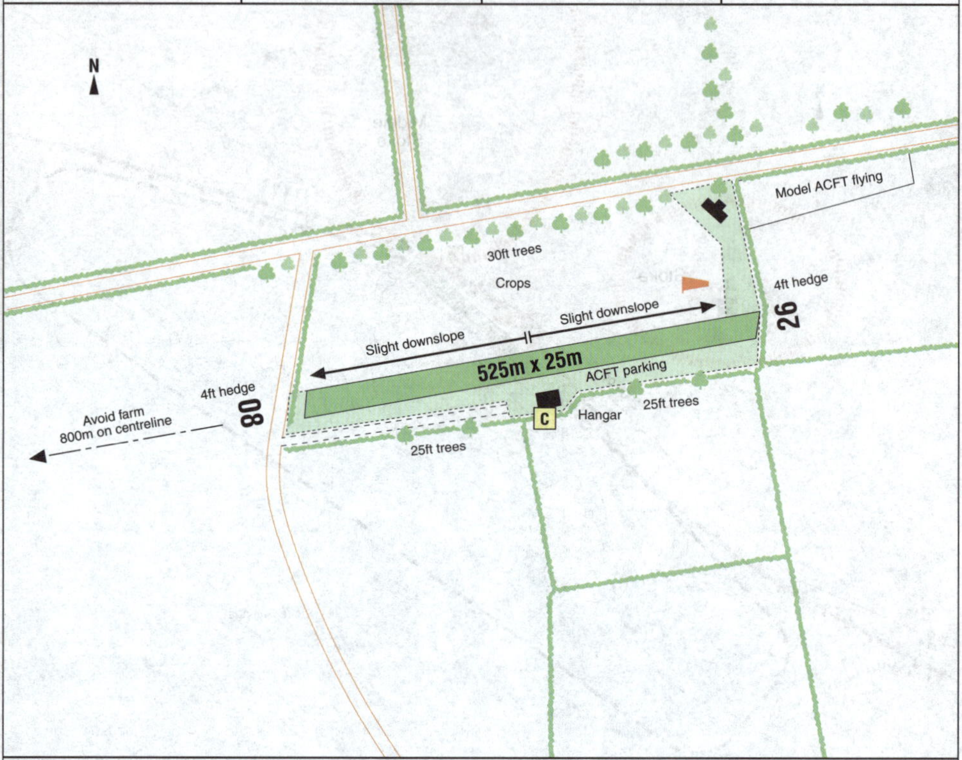

Model ACFT flying

30ft trees

Crops

Slight downslope

Slight downslope

Slight downslope

525m x 25m

4ft hedge

26

ACFT parking

C

Hangar

25ft trees

4ft hedge

80

Avoid farm 800m on centreline

25ft trees

N

RWY	SURFACE	TORA	LDA	LIGHTING
08/26	Grass	525x25m	U/L	Nil

Remarks

PPR by telephone or Website. Very friendly strip, visiting ACFT and microlights welcome at pilots own risk. Battle of Bosworth site and Shackerstone steam railway short distance from AD.

Warnings

Large model ACFT may operate at W/E, PH & some evenings. Modellers will land on observing ACFT making overhead join to circuit. **Noise:** Avoid over flying Stoke Golding village, particularly farm 800m from Rwy08 Thr. Rwy26 depts make early turn to avoid farm.

Operating Hrs	SR-SS
Circuits	26 RH, 08 LH 1000ft QFE
Landing Fee	Donation to grass-cutting welcomed
Maintenance	Nil
Fuel	AVGAS available by prior arr

Disabled Facilities

Restaurant	Refreshments normally available at W/E Dog & Hedgehog restaurant Dadlington village **Tel:** 01455 212629
Taxi/Car Hire	Operator can assist
Weather Info	AirCen MWC

Operator	Tim Jinks Sminks Aviation 95 Main Road Baxterley Warwickshire, CV9 2LE **Tel:** 01827 712706 **Tel:** 07771 701498 e-mail via website www.stokegoldingairfield.co.uk

S

26ft 1mb	2nm E of Stornoway N5812.93 W00619.87		Alternative AD **Benbecula**	
			Diversion AD	
Stornoway		**ATIS** 115.100 (on STN VOR)		**APP** 123.500
TWR 123.500		**AFIS** 123.500		**FIRE** 121.600

RWY	SURFACE	TORA	LDA	LIGHTING
18/36	Asphalt	2080	2080	Ap Thr Rwy PAPI 3°
07	Asphalt	1000	1000	Thr Rwy APAPI 4° LHS
25	Asphalt	1000	1000	Thr Rwy APAPI 3.5° LHS

Starter extension Rwy18 not available

Remarks
Rwy36 APP lights terminate 150m short Thr. Rwy07/25 no night landings. Flight clearance, Weather info and Customs (General Declaration) all available from ATC.
Aids to Navigation: VOR/DME STN 115.10

Warnings
Grass areas soft & unsafe. No GND signals except light signals. N & S Twys on E side of AD 15m wide. Use only marked Twys. Rwy36 Thr displaced a public road crosses APP. Use minimum APP angles of 3° as indicated by PAPI. 120m asphalt Rwy extending beyond Rwy36 Thr not avail for ACFT manoeuvring or starter extension. Western apron surface uneven, mashalling instructions must be complied with. SK61 Coast Guard helicopter operates priority over other traffic for SAR duties.

Operating Hrs	Mon-Fri 0645-1730 Sat 0645-1600 (Summer) +1Hr (Winter) & by arr	**Restaurants**	Refreshments & bar Pubs & restaurants in Stornoway
Circuits	18, 25 LH, 07, 36 RH	**Taxis** Central	**Tel:** 01851 706900
Landing Fee	£12 ACFT up to 3MT VFR cash, cheque or credit card on day	**Car Hire** Stornoway Car Hire	**Tel:** 01851 702658
Maintenance	Nil	**Weather Info**	M T9 T18 Fax 428 VSc GWC
Fuel	AVGAS JET A1 100LL **Tel:** 01851 703026 Available outside published Hrs by arr with ATC		ATIS **Tel:** 01851 707444
		Operator	HIAL Stornoway Aerodrome Isle of Lewis, HS2 0BN
Disabled Facilities	Nil		**Tel:** 01851 707415 (ATC)
Handling	**Tel:** 01851 701282 (Highland Airways) **Tel:** 01851 703673 (British Airways)		**Tel:** 01851 707400 (Admin) **Fax:** 01851 707402 (ATC) **Fax**: 01851 707401 (Admin) stornatc@hial.co.uk www.hial.co.uk

S

534

STRATHALLAN

Effective date:23/11/06

120ft 4mb	4nm SE of Crieff N5619.50 W00344.91	PPR	Alternative AD	Dundee Perth

	Strathallan	A/G 129.900	

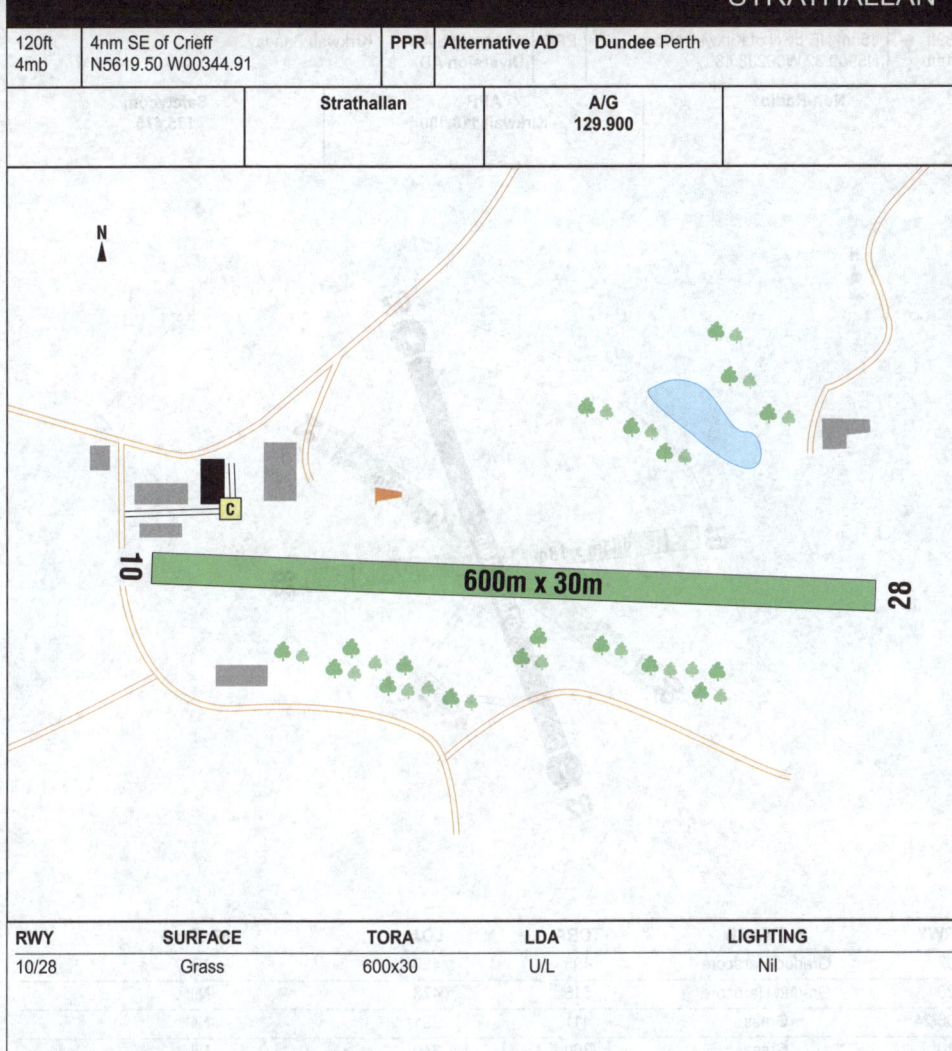

600m x 30m

10 — 28

N

C

RWY	SURFACE	TORA	LDA	LIGHTING
10/28	Grass	600x30	U/L	Nil

Remarks
PPR by telephone. Non-radio ACFT not accepted. Call Strathallan, if no response, assume no parachuting. Para-dropping ACFT will advise. Before starting engines, obtain permission.

Warnings
Intensive free-fall parachuting takes place up to FL120. High GND 1225ft aal (1345ft amsl) 4nm SE of AD. Sheep may graze on AD.
Noise: ACFT must not over fly AD.

Operating Hrs	Fri-Sun & PH 0900-2100 or SS (L)	**Operator**	Scottish Parachute Club
Circuits	10 RH, 28 LH, 1000ft QFE No over head joins		Strathallan Aerodrome Auchterarder Tayside Region, PH3 1LA
Landing Fee	Nil		**Tel:** 01764 662572 (Weekends)
Maintenance	Nil		**Tel:** 01698 832462
Fuel	Nil		(Kieran Brady Weekdays)
Disabled Facilites	Nil		
Restaurants	Cafe at weekends 0900-2100 (L)		
Taxis/Car Hire	Available on request		
Weather Info	AirSc GWC		

S

39ft 1mb	15nm NE by N of Kirkwall Airport N5909.32 W00238.48	**PPR**	**Alternative AD** **Diversion AD**	**Kirkwall** Sanday

Non-Radio	**APP** **Kirkwall 118.300**	**Safetycom** **135.475**

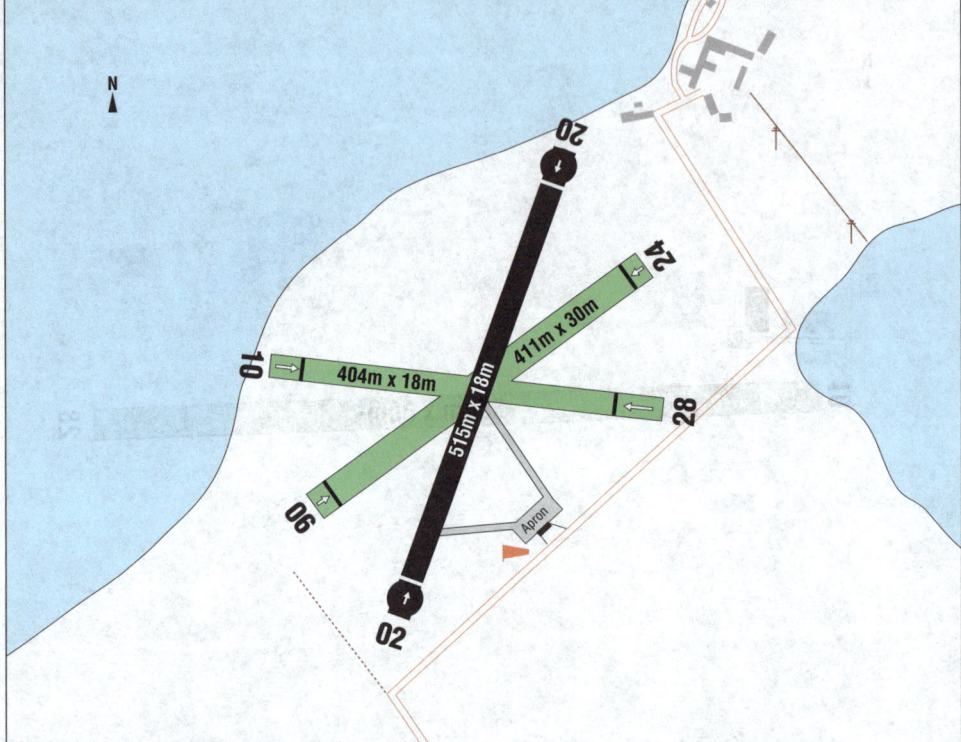

RWY	SURFACE	TORA	LDA	LIGHTING
02	Graded Hardcore	495	480	Nil
20	Graded Hardcore	515	478	Nil
06/24	Grass	411	391	Nil
10	Grass	360	340	Nil
28	Grass	384	340	Nil

Remarks
Licensed AD (day use only). Visiting ACFT accepted at pilot's own risk. Scheduled Air Services daily Mon-Sat.

Warnings

Operating Hrs	SR-SS	**Operator**	Orkney Islands Council
Circuits	Nil		Stronsay Aerodrome, Kirkwall
Landing Fee	Nil		Orkney, KW15 1N
Maintenance	Nil		**Tel:** 01856 873535
Fuel	Nil		**Fax:** 01856 876094
Disabled Facilities	Nil		
Restaurants (Wed & Sat-Sun)	Woodlea Restaurant & Takeaway **Tel:** 01857 616337		
Taxis Peace Williamson	**Tel:** 01857 616335 **Tel:** 01857 616255		
Car Hire Peace	**Tel:** 01857 616335		
Weather Info	AirSc GWC		

47ft 1mb	4nm SW of Mablethorpe N5318.28 E00010.20	PPR	Alternative AD	Humberside Wickenby

Strubby Base	DAIS Donna Nook 122.750	A/G 118.750	Gliders 130.100

N ↑

Strubby (old heliport)
750m x 15m
80 **26**
450m x 25m
Hangar
ACFT parking
Crops

Crops
Glider strip no powered ACFT
850m x 46m
80 **26**
ACFT parking
Crops
Crops

B1373

Crops

Garden centre

Old WWII tower

C

STRUBBY GLIDING

RWY	SURFACE	TORA	LDA	LIGHTING
08/26	Asph/Conc	850x46	U/L	Nil

Rwy surface rough. Grass section not suitable for powered ACFT

STRUBBY OLD HELIPORT

RWY	SURFACE	TORA	LDA	LIGHTING
08	Asphalt	650x15	U/L	Nil
26	Asphalt	750x15	U/L	Nil
08/26	Grass	450x25	U/L	Nil

Displaced Thr Rwy26

Remarks
PPR. Both strips established on WW2 AD. Visiting ACFT are welcome at pilots own risk.
Strubby Gliding: Gliders operate mainly at WE & PH using Winch and Aerotow.
Strubby Old Heliport: Due to planning constraints is only available to ACFT <5700kgs MAUW.

Warnings
Strubby Gliding: Keep good lookout for Gliders and Winch cables. No overhead joins. Radio rarely manned but make blind circuit calls. Small manouvering area marked, all other hard surfaces not available for ACFT use.
Noise: Do not over fly villages of Strubby Maltby le Marsh or Withern.
Strubby Old Heliport: No circuit training, touch and goes, or intentional go arounds. Fence runs up to N side Rwy26 Thr and along N side of Twy to hangar and parking area. Visitors must transmit their intentions to Strubby Base, usually there will be no reply, in which case make blind calls and keep a good lookout because Gliders may launch from Rwy close to S by winch or aero tow. Gliders can and do operate over the Old Heliport. Most of the gliders do not carry radios, so although base may be able to inform you where they are, and will attempt to inform Dept pilots. Gliders already airborne will not normally be aware of you.
Noise: Do not over fly villages of Strubby, Maltby le Marsh or Withern.

S

Operating Hrs		**Taxi/Car Hire**	Nil
Strubby Gliding	SR-SS	**Weather Info**	AirN MWC
Old Heliport	0830-2000 or SS whichever is earlier (L)	**Operators**	
Circuits		**Strubby Gliding**	Lincolnshire Gliding Club Ltd
Strubby Gliding	Advised with PPR		Strubby Airfield
Old Heliport	N 1000ft QFE		Alford, Lincs, LN13 1AA
Landing Fee			**Tel:** 01507 463726
Strubby Gliding	£5	**Strubby Old Heliport**	
Old Heliport	ACFT £5 Microlights £2.50		Strubby Aviation Club
Maintenance	Nil		C/o Mr Ron Larder
Fuel	Nil		Orme Lane
			Louth, Lincs
Disabled Facilities	Nil		**Tel:** 01507 600588 (Work)
			Tel: 01507 450498 (Home)
Restaurants	Café at nearby Garden Centre is a short walk from Gliding field but some distance from Old Heliport		

S

58ft 2mb	4nm SE of Gainsborough N5322.87 W00041.12	PPR	Alternative AD Diversion AD	Humberside Retford

Sturgate	LARS Waddington 127.350	A/G 130.300

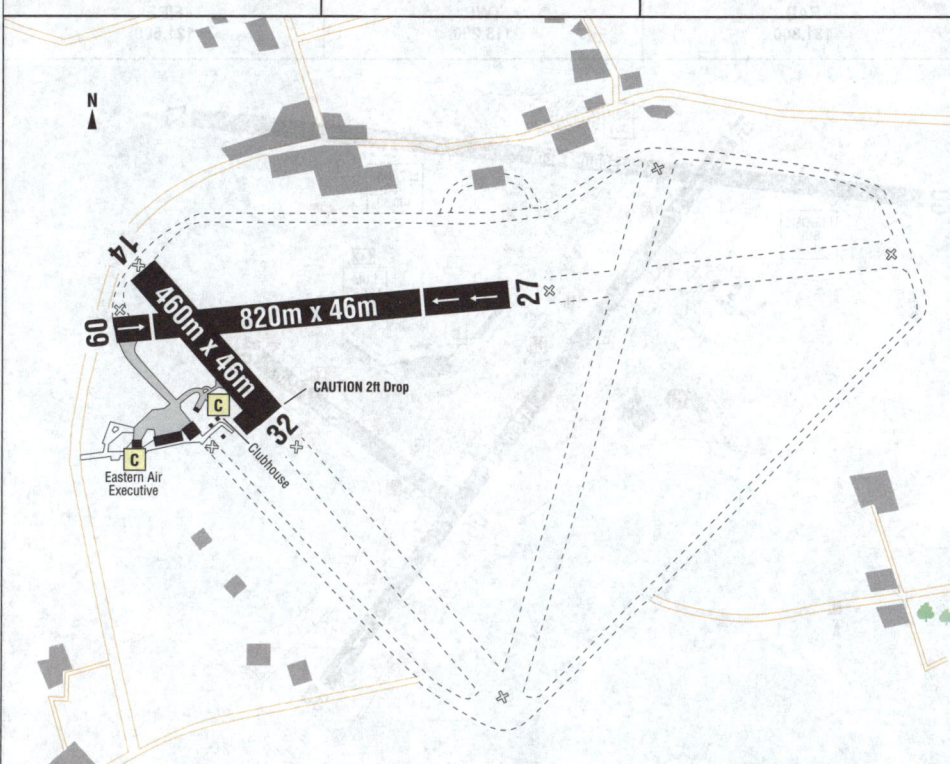

RWY	SURFACE	TORA	LDA	LIGHTING
09	Asphalt	805x46	U/L	Thr Rwy PAPI 3° RHS
27	Asphalt	790x46	U/L	Thr Rwy AVASIS 3°
14/32	Asphalt	460x46	U/L	Nil

Starter extension Rwy27 30m (day only)

Remarks
Microlights not accepted. AD is NOT available for public transport passenger flights required to use a licensed AD. Non-radio ACFT should remain well clear of the MATZ. Flights to Sturgate AD is limited to 1500ft aal unless prior arr has been made with Waddington. When within 10nm of Sturgate, pilots should use the MATZ altimeter setting.
Visual aid to location: Ibn SG Green.

Warnings
SE end Rwy14/32 ends abruptly in a 2ft drop indicated by a white line and a row of crosses. A road crosses the APP short of Rwy09 Thr. EG R313 Scampton abuts the S of ATZ. Home of the Red Arrows.

Operating Hrs	Mon-Fri 0800-1600 (Summer) Mon-Fri 0900-1600 (Winter) & by arr	Operator	Eastern Air Executive Ltd Sturgate Aerodrome, Gainsborough Lincs, DN21 5PA **Tel:** 01427 838280 (Mon-Fri) **Tel:** 01427 838305 (Sat-Sun) **Fax:** 01427 838416
Circuits	Variable		
Landing Fee	Single £5 Twin £20		
Maintenance Eastern Air	**Tel:** 01427 838280		
Fuel	AVGAS 100LL		
Disabled Facilities	Available		
Restaurants	Nil		
Taxis/Car Hire	Arr can be made via Eastern Executive Ops		
Weather Info	AirN MWC		

S

20ft 1mb	17nm S of Lerwick N5952.73 W00117.73		**Alternative AD Diversion AD**	**Scatsta** Lerwick	
Sumburgh			**ATIS 125.850**		**APP 131.300**
RAD 131.300			**TWR 118.250**		**FIRE 121.600**

RWY	SURFACE	TORA	LDA	LIGHTING
09	Asphalt	1319	1245	Ap Thr Rwy PAPI 3° LHS
27	Asphalt	1319	1260	Ap Thr Rwy PAPI 3° LHS
15	Asphalt	1426	1239	Ap Thr Rwy APAPI 4° LHS
33	Asphalt	1426	1239	Thr Rwy
06	Asphalt Heli Rwy	550x45	U/L	Thr Rwy
24	Asphalt Heli Rwy	550x45	U/L	Ap Thr Rwy

Remarks

SAR, Bristow Helicopters (HMCG) & Coast guard SK61 and Bond Offshore Helicopters AS3B operates from Sumburgh & will be given priority over all other traffic when operating on SAR duties. These operations may take place 24Hrs using the call sign "RESCUE GBDOC". Use of Rwys: Except helicopters, night landings are not permitted on Rwy15/33 except in an emergency. Night take-offs from Rwy15/33 are restricted to operators with procedures accepted by the CAA. The helicopter Rwy06/24 is not to be used by fixed wing ACFT. Pilots not using a resident handling agent must ensure that all relevant AD documentation is completed upon initial Arr. Such documentation may be obtained from the AD security staff in the Wilsness terminal. Start-up must be requested on TWR freq. Grass areas soft and unsafe only marked Twys to be used.

Warnings

During strong wind conditions turbulence may be expected on APP to or climb out from any Rwy. Bird colonies are active throughout the year. No GND signals except light signals. Pilots using the N Twy are reminded to adhere to the marked centreline. A separate vehicle route is marked on the N part of this Twy. Thr Rwy09/27 are positioned 98m and 90m respectively from concrete sea defences and the open sea.

Operating Hrs	Mon-Fri 0630-1915 Sat 0800-1630 Sun 0930-1700 (Summer) +1Hr (Winter) & by arr	**Landing Fee**	£13 ACFT under 3MT VFR cash/cheque on day
		Maintenance	Nil
Circuits	Nil	**Fuel** AirBP	AVGAS JET A1 100LL **Tel:** 01950 460367 **Fax:** 01950460182

Disabled Facilities

Restaurant	Terminal ground floor buffet
Taxis	Available at Terminal
Car Hire	Europcar & Avis agents
Bolts Car Hire	**Tel:** 01950 460777
Star Rentacar	**Tel:** 01950 460444
Weather Info	M T9 Fax 432 A VSc GWC
	Tel: 01950 461037

Visual Reference Points (VRP)

VRP	VOR/DME
Bodam	SUM 018°/2.4nm
N5955.10 W00116.10	
Mousa	SUM 033°/8.2nm
N6000.00 W00109.60	

Operator

HIAL, Sumburgh Airport,
Virkie, Shetland, ZE3 9JP
Tel: 01950 460654 (HIAL)
Tel: 01950 460173 (ATC)
Tel: 01244 727199 (Sumburgh APP)
Fax: 01950 460218 (HIAL)
Fax: 01950 460718 (ATC)

Effective date:23/11/06

CTA/CTR-Class D Airspace
Normal CTA/CTR Class D Airspace rules apply.
Helicopter operating VFR, or at night SVFR, may be routed via a VRP.

HELICOPTER OPERATIONS
Helicopter operations in support of N Sea oil rigs may take place outside the published Hrs of AD availability. Helicopters are treated as fixed wing traffic and should normally GND taxi, unless skid equipped, between the Rwys and parking areas. In adverse weather conditions and during snow-clearing operations, hover taxiing of wheeled helicopters may be permitted by ATC. 'Rotors running' refuelling of helicopters with passengers onboard is only permitted during exceptionally severe wind conditions and with the permission of ATC. Helicopter parking spots 1-9 are designated quick turn round spots and should not be occupied for more than 15 minutes. Long term parking spots 10-19.

FIXED WING PARKING
Stands 20-22 for schedule services
Stands 23-26 for all other fixed wing ACFT

8ft 0mb	5nm W of Ely N5223.12 E00003.84		**PPR**	**Alternative AD**	**Cambridge** Bourn

	Sutton Meadows	**A/G** 129.825 (Microlight Freq)

Tubbs Farm

480m x 15m
470m x 15m
490m x 15m

24 19
10 06
28
01

C

20ft powerlines

RWY	SURFACE	TORA	LDA	LIGHTING
10/28	Grass	490x15	U/L	Nil
06/24	Grass	480x15	U/L	Nil
01/19	Grass	470x15	U/L	Nil

Remarks
PPR by telephone. Visiting ACFT welcome at pilots own risk. Well maintained level grass strip. AD is primarily a microlight training field but is not challenging for fixed wing ACFT/pilots with reasonable short field performance. Signal square near clubhouse, gliding symbol near square when hang gliders active. Cambridgeshire Aerotow Club now on AD. Hang gliders and tug can be at any height, have the right of way both air and GND, may not be using the designated Rwy. All hang gliders circuits usually inside normal circuit.

Warnings
Power lines 20ft agl S & E of AD.
Noise: Do not over fly Tubbs Farm. Be considerate of local habitation.

Operating Hrs	SR-SS		**Taxis/Car Hire**	Nil
Circuits	Join overhead 1000ft QFE 06, 10, 19 LH, 01, 24, 28 RH, 500ft QFE		**Weather Info**	AirCen MOEx
			Operator	Peter Robinson
Landing Fee	PPR £2 otherwise £5 free with reciprocal arr			Argents Farm House 114 High Street
Maintenance	Nil			Sutton, Ely, Cambs
Fuel	MOGAS Ltd quantities by arr			**Tel:** 01353 778446 (Operator) **Tel:** 01487 842360
Disabled Facilites				(Pegasus Flight Training)
				www.cambsmicrolightclub.fsnet.co.uk/index.htm
Restaurants	Clubhouse open for light refreshments when microlight flying is in progress			

S

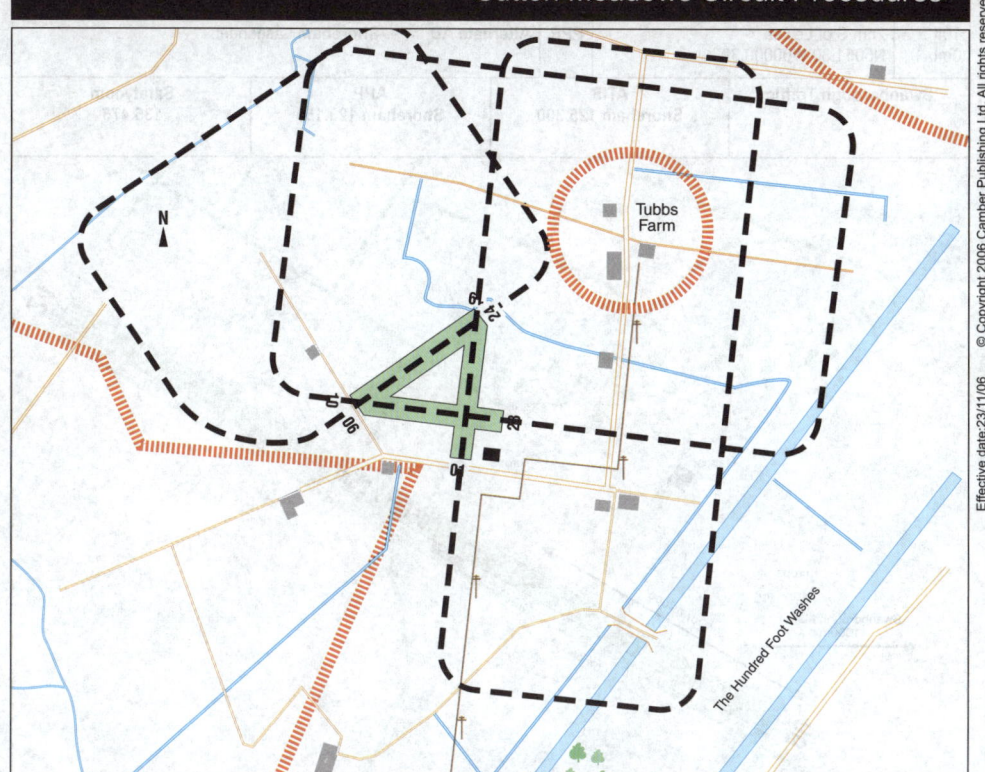

10ft 0mb	2nm S of Lewes N5051.30 W00000.30	PPR	Alternate AD	Shoreham Lashenden

Swanborough Traffic	ATIS Shoreham 125.300	APP Shoreham 123.150	Safetycom 135.475

RWY	SURFACE	TORA	LDA	LIGHTING
24/06	Grass	650x25	U/L	Nil

Rwy06 downslope to midpoint

Remarks
PPR by telephone. Visiting ACFT welcome at pilots own risk. AD not suitable for inexperienced pilots. Windsock may be displayed at Rwy midpoint on S side. Day tickets available for angling lakes to N of AD (owned by operator).

Warnings
Low hedge and ditch Rwy24 Thr. Rwy may be waterlogged after heavy rain.
Noise: Avoid over flying all local habitation.

Operating Hrs	SR-SS	Operator	Mr Will Greenwood
Circuits	S 1100ft QNH		Swanborough Farm
Landing Fee	Nil		Lewes
Maintenance	Nil		East Sussex
Fuel	Nil		BN7 3PF
Disabled Facilities	Nil		**Tel:** 01273 477388
Taxi/Car Hire	Nil		**Tel:** 07850 811704
Weather Info	AIRSE Moex		will.greenwood@btconnect.com

299ft 10mb	5nm WSW of Swansea N5136.32 W00404.07		Alternative AD Diversion AD	**Cardiff** Pembrey
	Swansea		A/G **119.700**	

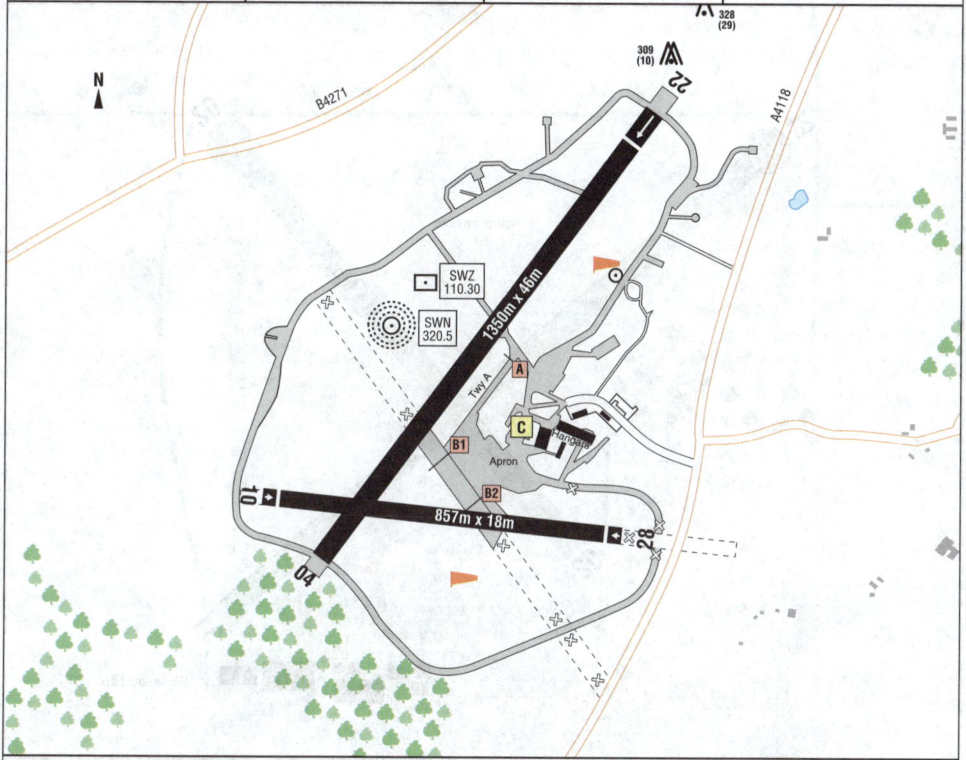

SWZ 110.30

SWN 320.5

Twy A

A

B1

C Hangar

Apron

B2

1350m x 46m

857m x 18m

10

04

28

328 (29)

309 (10)

22

B4271

A4118

N

RWY	SURFACE	TORA	LDA	LIGHTING
04	Concrete	1260	1200	Ap Thr Rwy PAPI 3° LHS
22	Concrete	1290	1260	Ap Thr Rwy PAPI 3.25° LHS
10	Asphalt	857	824	Nil
28	Asphalt	824	794	Nil

Remarks

Strict PPR. Non-radio ACFT not accepted. Hi-Vis. Light ACFT experiencing radio failure in VMC are to carry out the standard overhead join for Rwy in use as notified by either previous dept or joining information passed by A/G. Gliding operations by Air Training Corps at weekends. Operations by emergency service helicopters occur outside normal operating hrs.

Warnings

Unusable parts of Rwys short of Rwy10/28 and Rwy04/22 Thr are marked by white crosses. Not all Twy are usable. Road crosses near Rwy28 Thr and is marked by orange triangular markers outside the AD and orange/white circular markers on the AD side. Deviation from marked manoeuvring area can be hazardous.

Operating Hrs	0900-1730 (L) & by arr Hrs available with PPR	**Taxis** Exec Travel Servcs	**Tel:** 01792 203080
Circuits	04, 28 LH, 10, 22 RH Helicopters must conform with standard circuits	**Car Hire** Europcar Hertz	**Tel:** 01792 650526 **Tel:** 01792 587391
Landing Fee	Private singles £11.00	**Weather Info**	M T9 Fax 434 MOEx
Maintenance	Nil	**Operator**	Swansea Airport Ltd
Fuel	AVGAS JET A1 100LL		Swansea Airport Fairwood Common Swansea, SA2 7JU **Tel:** 01792 204063 (Reception) **Fax:** 01792 207550 (ATC)

Disabled Facilities

Restaurants   Restaurant on AD 0900-1730 (L)

S

492ft 16mb	5nm NE of Rugby N5225.60 W00109.65	PPR	Alternative AD	Nottingham East Midlands Leicester

	Swinford		A/G 129.825 (microlight freq)	

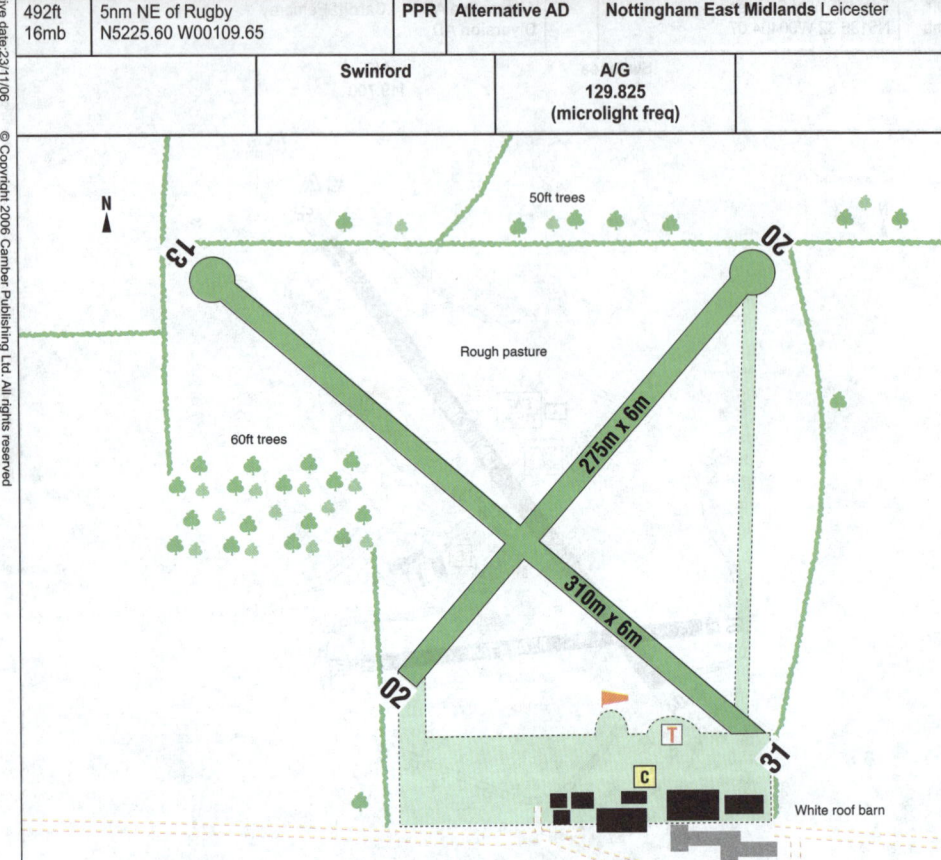

RWY	SURFACE	TORA	LDA	LIGHTING
13/31	Grass	310x6	U/L	Nil
02/20	Grass	275x6	U/L	Nil

Remarks
PPR by telephone. Microlights only. Windsock and signals square displayed when AD is active. AD slopes slightly down to the S.

Warnings
Turbulence may be encountered in W winds. Keep a good lookout for hang gliders. AD may be water logged in winter.
Noise: Avoid over flying three farms N of AD and Swinford village to S.

Operating Hrs	SR-SS	**Operator**	Barry Underwood
Circuits	02, 13 RH, 20, 31 LH 500ft QFE.		3 Jackson Close
Landing Fee	Nil		Hampton Magna
Maintenance	Nil		Warwickshire
Fuel	MOGAS avail from local garage		CV35 8SZ
Disabled Facilities	Nil		**Tel:** 01455 558791 (AD)
Restaurants	Tea & Coffee avail in club caravan		**Tel:** 01926 494906 (Club)
Taxis/Car Hire	Nil		barry@lmac.org.uk
Weather Info	AirCen MWC		www.lmac.org.uk

S

546

228ft 7mb	4nm SW of Newark N5301.06 W00054.60	PPR MIL	Alternative AD	Nottingham East Midlands Nottingham

Syerston	LARS Waddington 127.350	A/G 125.425

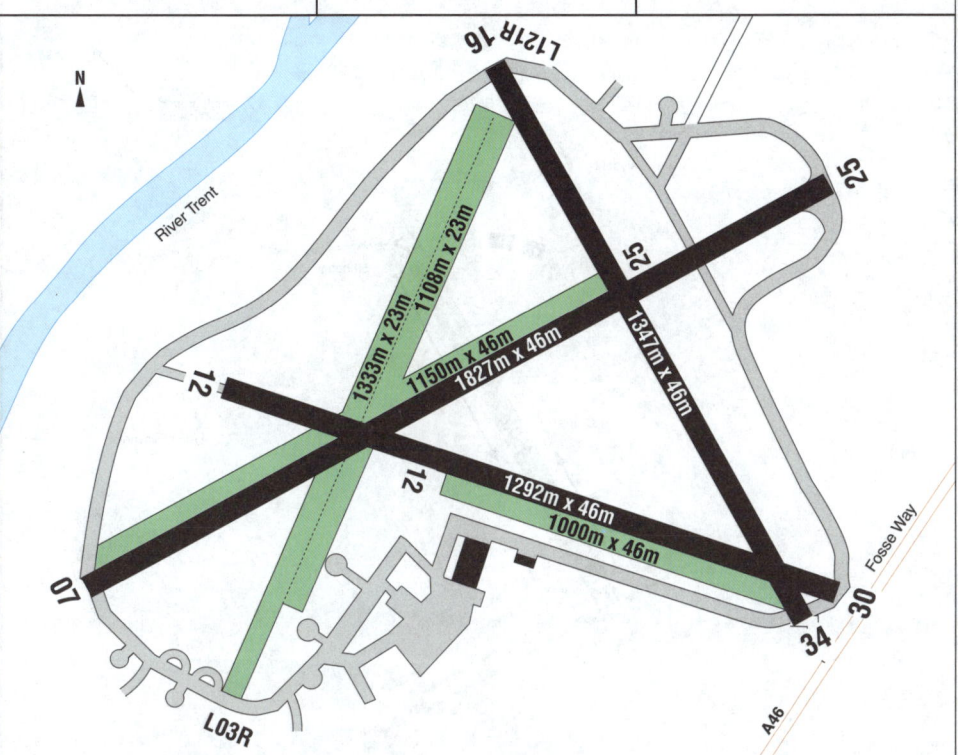

RWY	SURFACE	TORA	LDA	LIGHTING
07/25	Asphalt	1827	1727	Nil
07/25	Grass	1100	1150	Nil
16/34	Asphalt	1347	1247	Nil
16/34	Grass	1200	1100	Nil
12/30	Asphalt	1292	1192	Nil
12/30	Grass	1000	900	Nil
03l/21R	Grass	1400	1300	Nil
03r/21L	Grass	1400	1300	Nil

2 dayglo markers at Thr may mark grass Rwy in use. Rwy30 surface poor, Rwy03R/21L used by motor gliders if wind allows

Remarks
Strict 48Hrs PPR required by telephone. RAF glider operations have priority at all times. WW2 AD with aged Asphalt surfaces, loose stones may be present.

Warnings
Intense cable launched and motor glider activity during operational hours up to 5000ft agl. Full obstacle clearance criteria not met on APP to all Rwys. No fire cover available for visiting civil ACFT. Rwy markings becoming indistinct.

Operating Hrs	0830-SS (L) Gliders Mon-Fri 0830-1700 or SS Sat-Sun 0630-SS (L)	**Taxi/Car Hire**	Nil
		Weather Info	AirCen MWC
Circuits	Full briefing must be obtained with PPR	**Operator**	RAF Syerston
Landing Fee	Charges in accordance with MOD policy Contact Station Ops for details		Fosse Road, Syerston Newark, Nottinghamshire NG23 5NG
Maintenance	Nil		**Tel:** 01636 525467 Ex 4525
Fuel	Nil		(General Office)
Disabled Facilities	Nil		**Tel:** 01636 525467 Ex 4523
Restaurants	Nil		(Officer Commanding)

S

40ft 1mb	1nm NE of Tywyn N5236.70 W00404.50	PPR	Alternative AD	Pembrey Caernarfon

Talybont Micro Base	LARS Valley 125.225	A/G 129.825

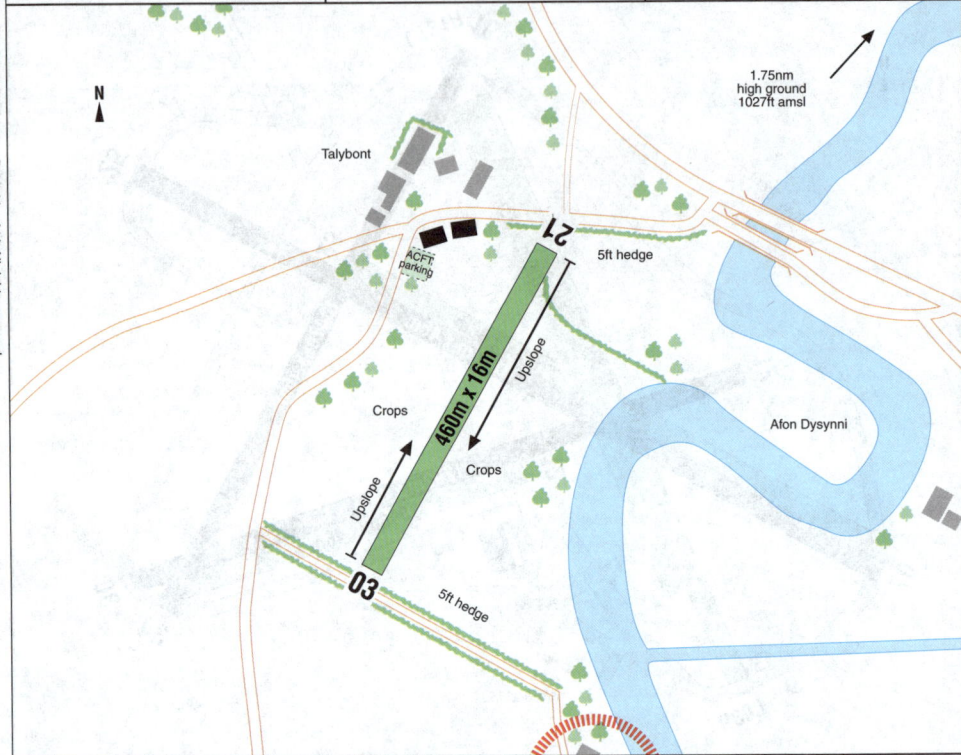

RWY	SURFACE	TORA	LDA	LIGHTING
03/21	Grass	460x16	U/L	Nil

Rwy03 rises 10ft in first 200m then has down slope
Rwy21 rises 20ft in first 300m then has down slope

Remarks
Strictly PPR by telephone. Gyros not accepted. Grass strip high GND close proximity must be treated with respect. Experienced pilots with STOL ACFT welcome at pilot's own risk. Sheep live on AD.

Warnings
Operator publishes AD bulletin identified by information code as ATIS broadcast. Visitors must obtain this by E-mail, phone, Fax, or post quote code letter on Arr overhead or no landing! Sheep graze AD will be kept off the field for 1Hr after notified ETA. AD suffers rotor in N & NW winds, particularly Rwy21. Pilots should also be aware of coastal wind effects. Grass can be very slippery when wet so please do not land long as Rwy gradient will not assist. Operator advises you be lightly loaded on first visit. Valley to NE rises 3000ft in 7nm should be treated with respect! Fast flying ACFT advised avoid slow-flying cormorants!
Noise: Avoid over flying local habitation and do not 'Buzz' AD as noise sensitive neighbours will report offenders.

Operating Hrs	SR-SS	**Taxis/Car Hire**	**Tel:** 01654 711788
Circuits	21 LH, 03 RH, 1200ft QNH Join overhead 1200ft QNH	**Weather Info**	AirN MWC
		Operator	Mr William Williams-Wynne
Landing Fee	Nil with PPR £500 without PPR		Peniarth, Tywyn Gwynedd, LL36 9UD **Tel:** 01654 710101 (Day)
Maintenance	Nil		**Tel:** 01654 710102 (Evening)
Fuel	MOGAS Ltd avail check with PPR Microlight pilots must bring their own Oil		**Tel:** 07831 131000 **Fax:** 01654 710103
Disabled Facilities	Nil		www@wynne.co.uk
Restaurants Peniarth Arms Penhelig Arms	B&B/Bar snacks at **Tel:** 01654 711505 (0.5m) **Tel:** 01654 767215 Aberdovey (6m)		

T

548

EGBM

Effective date:23/11/06

450ft 15mb	4nm W of Burton on Trent N5248.88 W00145.67	PPR	Alternative AD Diversion AD	Nottingham East Midlands Wolverhampton

Tatenhill	APP East Mids 134.175	APP Birmingham 118.050	A/G 124.075

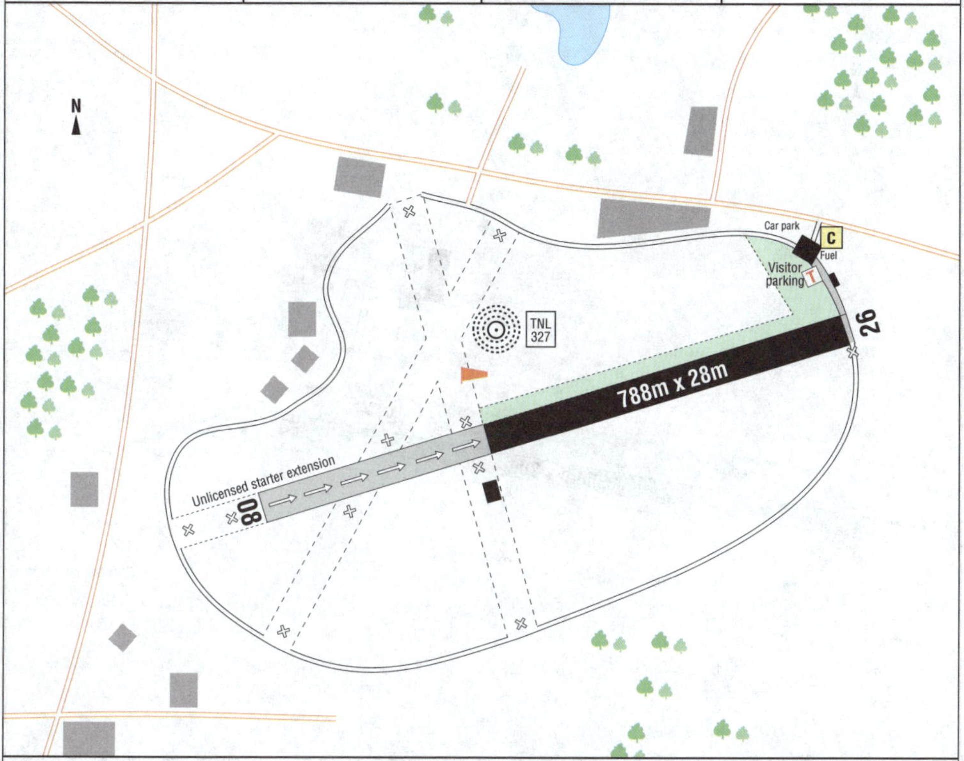

[Aerodrome chart: Runway 08/26, 788m x 28m, TNL 327, Car park, Fuel, Visitor parking. "Unlicensed starter extension".]

RWY	SURFACE	TORA	LDA	LIGHTING
08/26	Asphalt	700	700	by arr

Starter Extension Rwy08 500m U/L

Remarks
PPR non-radio ACFT not accepted. **AD not available to weight shift microlights.** Pilots should note proximity of Birmingham & East Midlands CTA and are advised to call Birmingham or East Midlands for traffic info before calling Tatenhill. Night flying by arr.

Warnings
Rwy08/26 used as Twy, contact AD for permission to use as Rwy. Pilots are advised to keep a good lookout for military traffic. Gliding may take place at Cross Hayes (N5247.40 W00149.14).

Operating Hrs	0800-1600 (Summer) +1Hr (Winter)	**Operator**	Tatenhill Aviation Ltd
Circuits	08, 22, 26 LH, 04 RH, 1000ft QFE Join overhead		Tatenhill Airfield Newborough Road, Needwood Burton on Trent, Staffs, DE13 9PD
Landing Fee	Single £10 Twin £20		**Tel:** 01283 575283
Maintenance	Tatenhill Aviation Ltd **Tel:** 01283 575283		**Fax:** 01283 575650 www.tatenhill.com
Fuel	AVGAS 100LL JET A1 (by arr)		

Disabled Facilities

Restaurants	Tea, coffee & sandwiches available Catering at weekends only
Taxis/Car Hire	By arr
Weather Info	AirCen MWC

240ft 8mb	8Nm S of Lincoln N5304.60 W00030.70	PPR	Alternative AD	Doncaster Sheffield Retford/Gamston

Non Radio	APP Cranwell 119.375	LARS Waddington 127.350	Safetycom 135.475

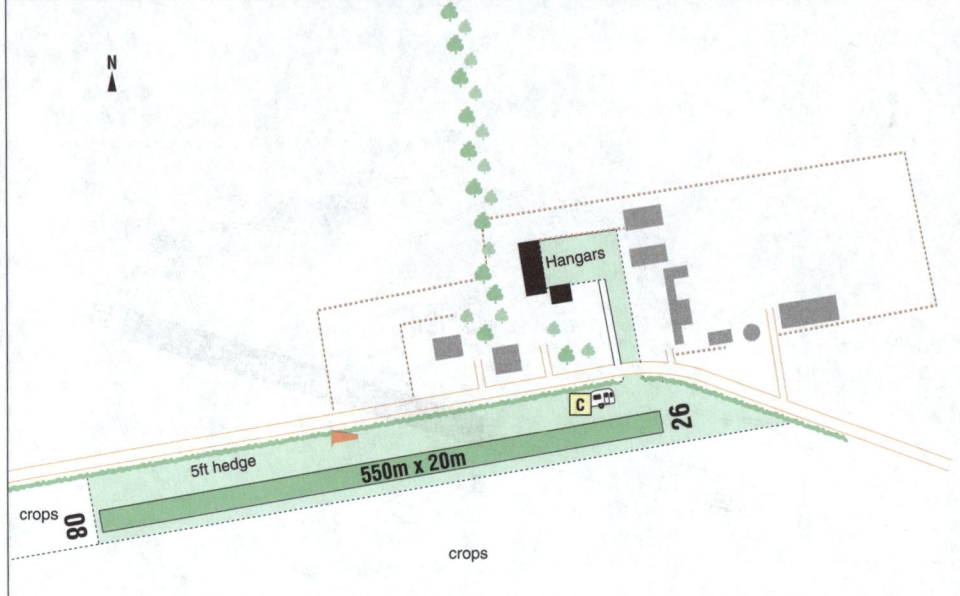

N

Hangars

5ft hedge
550m x 20m
crops

08
26

C

crops

RWY	SURFACE	TORA	LDA	LIGHTING
08/26	Grass	550x20	U/L	Nil

Remarks
PPR strictly by telephone. Briefing will be given. Planning limitations restrict visits to 5 per day, permission for visiting ACFT may be refused. Level strip with crops grown close to the S side.

Warnings
AD situated within Cranwell MATZ. Contact Waddington when Cranwell closed. Gliding takes place from Cranwell North, (2nm S of AD).

Operating Hrs	0800-SS	**Operator**	Mr D A Porter
Circuits	LH 500ft QFE		The Old Granary
Landing Fee	Single £5 Twin & Helicopter £10		Holly Lane
Maintenance	Nil		Temple Bruer
Fuel	Nil		Lincoln
Disabled Facilities	Nil		LN5 0DF
Restaurant	Nil		**Tel/Fax:** 01522 810840
Taxi/Car Hire	Nil		
Weather Info	AirN MWC		

T

272ft 9mb	2nm SW of Market Drayton N5252.27 W00232.01	PPR MIL	Alternative AD	Hawarden Sleap

Ternhill	LARS Shawbury 120.775	TWR 122.100

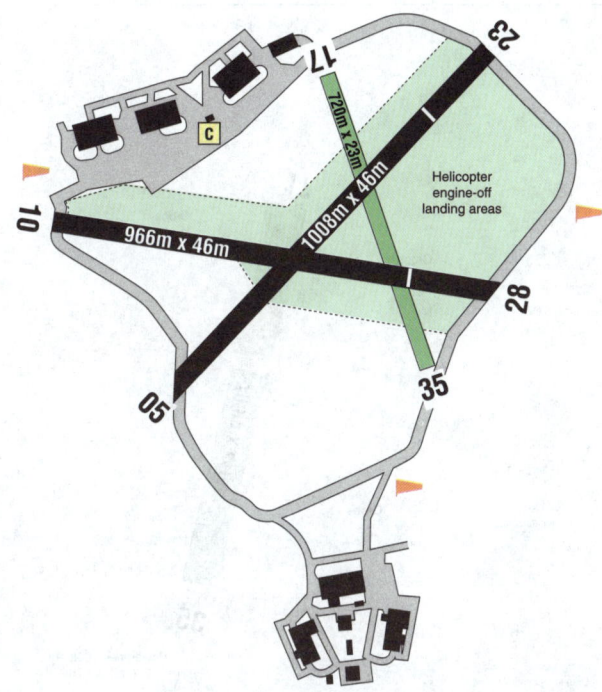

Helicopter engine-off landing areas

720m x 23m
1008m x 46m
966m x 46m

RWY	SURFACE	TORA	LDA	LIGHTING
05	Asphalt	980	980	Nil
23	Asphalt	980	791	Nil
10	Asphalt	948	948	Nil
28	Asphalt	948	756	Nil
17/35	Grass	720	720	Nil

Remarks
Strict PPR by telephone. No fixed wing movements accepted. RAF relief landing ground for Military helicopter training and ATC Glider/Motor glider activity. Master AD is RAF Shawbury.

Warnings
Intensive military training weekdays. Glider flying outside normal Hrs and weekends up to 3000ft. ACFT not to cross Rd adjacent to Rwy23/28 Thr below 50ft. Thr have non standard markings.

		Operator	RAF Shawbury
Operating Hrs	ATZ 24 Hrs AD active as required by RAF Shawbury		Shrewsbury Shropshire, SY4 4DZ **Tel:** 01939 250351 Ex 7227 (Shawbury Ops)
Circuits	Variable in direction & height		
Landing Fee	Charges in accordance with MOD policy Contact Station Ops for details		
Maintenance	Nil		
Fuel	Nil		
Disabled Facilities	Nil		
Restaurants	Nil		
Taxis/Car Hire	Nil		
Weather Info	M T Fax 398 MWC		

10ft 0mb	1nm E of Thorne Town N5337.20 W00055.41	PPR	Alternative AD	Humberside Sandtoft

Non Radio	ATIS Doncaster 134.95	LARS Waddington 127.350 Humberside 119.125

APP Doncaster 126.225	Safetycom 135.475	

RWY	SURFACE	TORA	LDA	LIGHTING
17/35	Grass	700x24	U/L	Nil

Remarks
PPR by telephone. No microlights. Business use prefered. Good flat strip. Give way to farm vehicles on track.

Warnings
AD subject to water logging in winter months. National Grid power lines to S. Keep good lookout for low flying military ACFT in local area.
Caution: AD under final APP for Rwy20 at Doncaster Sheffield AD.
Noise: Circuits flown to E to avoid over flight of local habitation.

		Operator	
Operating Hrs	SR-SS		Paul Burtwistle
Circuits	Standard overhead join Circuits E 1000ft QFE		Dairy Farm, Coulman Road, Thorne Doncaster, South Yorkshire
Landing Fee	Advised with PPR		**Tel:** 01405 812260
Maintenance	Nil		**Tel:** 07836 693943
Fuel	Nil		**Fax:** 01405 740084
Disabled Facilities	Nil		p.h.burtwistle@talk21.com
Restaurant	Nil		
Taxi/Car Hire	Available via operator		
Weather Info	AirN MCW		

319ft 11mb	4.5nm W of Andover N5112.63 W00136.00	PPR	Alternative AD Diversion AD	Southampton Old Sarum

Thruxton	LARS Boscombe 126.700	A/G 130.450

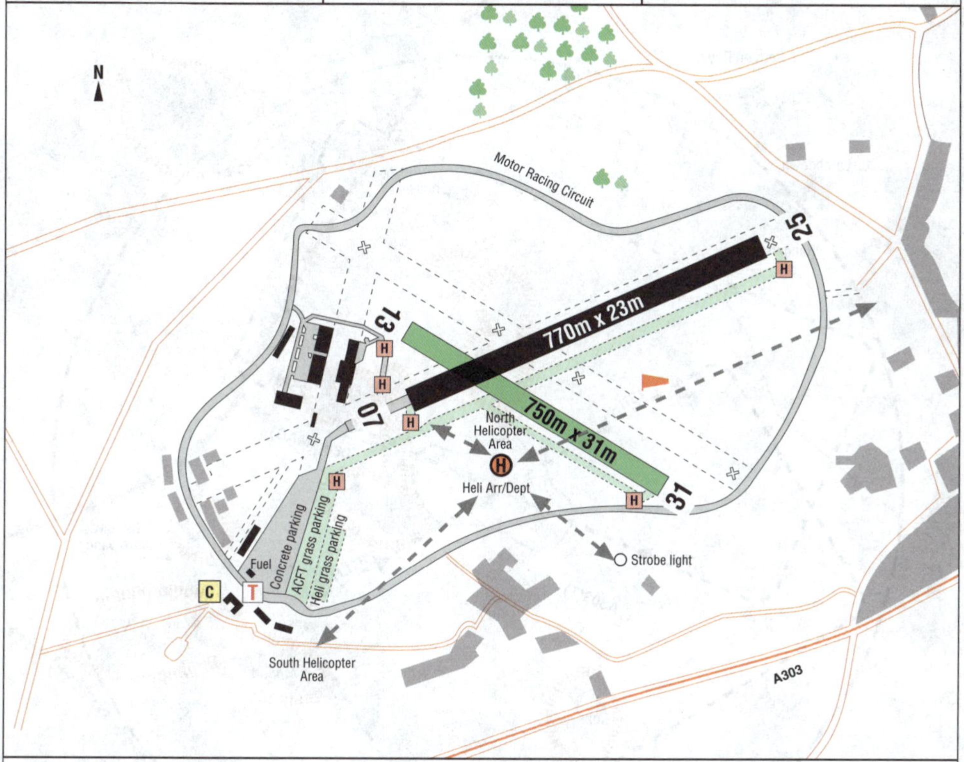

[Airport diagram: Thruxton aerodrome with Motor Racing Circuit, runways 07/25, 13/31, North Helicopter Area, Heli Arr/Dept, South Helicopter Area, Concrete parking, ACFT grass parking, Heli grass parking, Fuel, Strobe light, A303. Runway markings: 770m x 23m, 750m x 31m]

RWY	SURFACE	TORA	LDA	LIGHTING
07	Asphalt	770	760	Thr Rwy APAPI 4° LHS
25	Asphalt	770	770	Thr Rwy APAPI 4° LHS
13/31	Grass	750	750	Nil

Starter extension Rwy07 220m U/L

Remarks
Certain Microlights not accepted. HI-Vis. Non radio ACFT PNR. Race days helicopters by arrangement only. No dead side Rwy07/25 due variable circuit directions Circuit joining height 1200ft QFE or 1500ft QFE when CMATZ not in operation. ACFT vacating Rwy13/31 must vacate to W. ACFT commanders responsible for passengers and crew members.

Warnings
APP Thruxton avoid Danger Areas D123, D125, D125A, D126 & D127. Middle Wallop AD 4nm S of Thruxton intensive rotary flying training. Instrument APP service operates 070°-080° up to 8nm from Middle Wallop & may be used for practice VMC conditions. Perimeter track permanently obstructed not available for ACFT. Power cables cross final APP Rwy25 200m from Thr.

Operating Hrs	0800-1600 (Summer) +1Hr (Winter) & by arr	**Restaurants** Jackaroo	**Tel:** 01264 882217 (0900-1700 (L)
Circuits	Fixed Wing 07/31 LH, 25/13 RH, 800ft QFE. Helicopter (via heli north) HA 07, 31 LH HA 25, 13 RH. HA 07/25 1000ft HA31/13 800ft. Circuit height 1000ft QFE when Boscombe MATZ is closed	**Taxis** **Car Hire** Eurodollar **Weather Info**	**Tel:** 01264 359000 **Tel:** 01264 338181 AirSW MOEx
Landing Fee	Single £10 Twin £20. Free for qual cross countries. Consessions on fuel uplift	**Operator**	Western Air (Thruxton) Ltd Thruxton Aerodrome Andover, Hampshire, SP11 8PW
Maintenance Jade Air Aeromaritime **Fuel**	 **Tel:** 01264 773362 (Fixed wing) **Tel:** 01264 771700 (Rotary) AVGAS JET A1 100LL		**Tel:** 01264 772352 (TWR) **Tel:** 01264 772171 (Admin) **Fax:** 01264 773913 www.westernairthruxton.co.uk

Disabled Facilities

T

N

Ludgershall

Perham Down

Lambdown

Rangers

house

Kimpton

Appleshaw

Fyfield

25RH

080i (MAG)

13RH

Thruxton

07LH

The Hawk
Consevancy

A303(T)

31LH

Monxton

Amport

Quarley

Quarley Hill

Grately

Arrivals:
When Boscombe MATZ is active, ACFT should call Boscombe Down for MATZ penetration. ACFT being provided ATS from Boscombe are not to enter the Thruxton ATZ unless contact has been established with Thruxton A/G and relevant information obtained.

Departures:
All ACFT should dept to E or NE.
Climb to 1200ft QNH or 900ft QFE or remain VMC before free calling Boscombe APP, or climb when clear from the CMATZ.
W bound depts should call Boscombe APP prior to take off.

Noise: Avoid over flying the following villages– Kimpton, Fyfield, Thruxton, Quarley & Thruxton Down, also avoid Hawk Conservancy 1.5m SE of AD
Dept Rwy07 – Fixed wing ACFT should turn R onto 080° on passing the AD boundary or when safe to do so.

T

25ft 0mb	5nm SW of Basildon N5132.17 E00022.00	PPR	Alternative AD	Southend Stapleford

Non-Radio	APP Thames RAD 132.700	LARS Southend 130.775	Safetycom 135.475

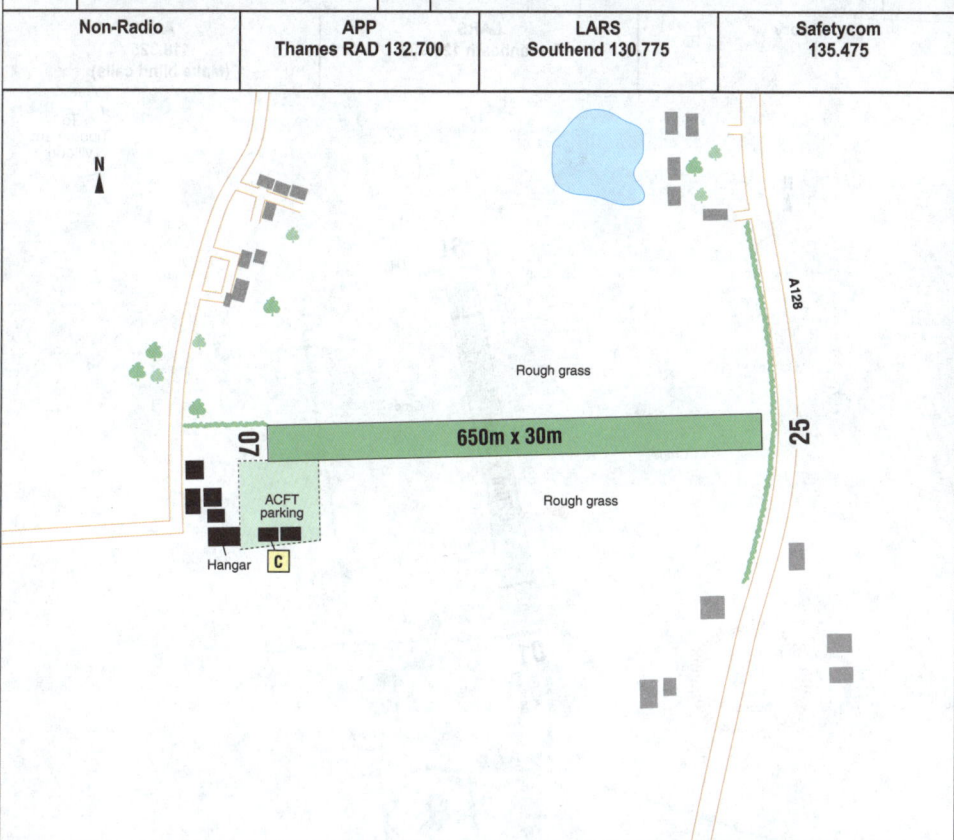

RWY	SURFACE	TORA	LDA	LIGHTING
07/25	Grass	650x30	U/L	Nil

Rwy is part of large field which allows run-off to S & N of strip

Remarks
PPR by telephone. Visitors welcome at pilots own risk. NO TRAINING.
Visual aid to location: Light ACFT parked on AD.

Warnings
High sided vehicles on A128 crosses Rwy25 Thr. 6ft hedge between road and Thr. Trees and hedge adjacent Rwy09 Thr.
Noise: Avoid over flight of local habitation.

Operating Hrs	SR-SS	**Operator**	Thurrock Leisure Ltd Thurrock Airfield Tilbury Road, Orsett, Essex **Tel:** 01375 891165
Circuits	25 LH, 07 RH, 1000ft QFE		
Landing Fee	Yes available with PPR		
Maintenance	Hangarage & parking by arr		
Fuel	AVGAS 100LL		
Disabled Facilities	Nil		
Restaurant	Nil		
Taxis Abbey Cars	**Tel:** 01277 812812		
Car Hire	Nil		
Weather Info	AirSE MOEx		

T

TIBENHAM

186ft 6mb	1nm W of Tibenham AD N5227.00 E00107.00	PPR	Alternative AD	Norwich Old Buckenham

Priory	LARS Lakenheath 128.900	A/G 118.325 (Make blind calls)

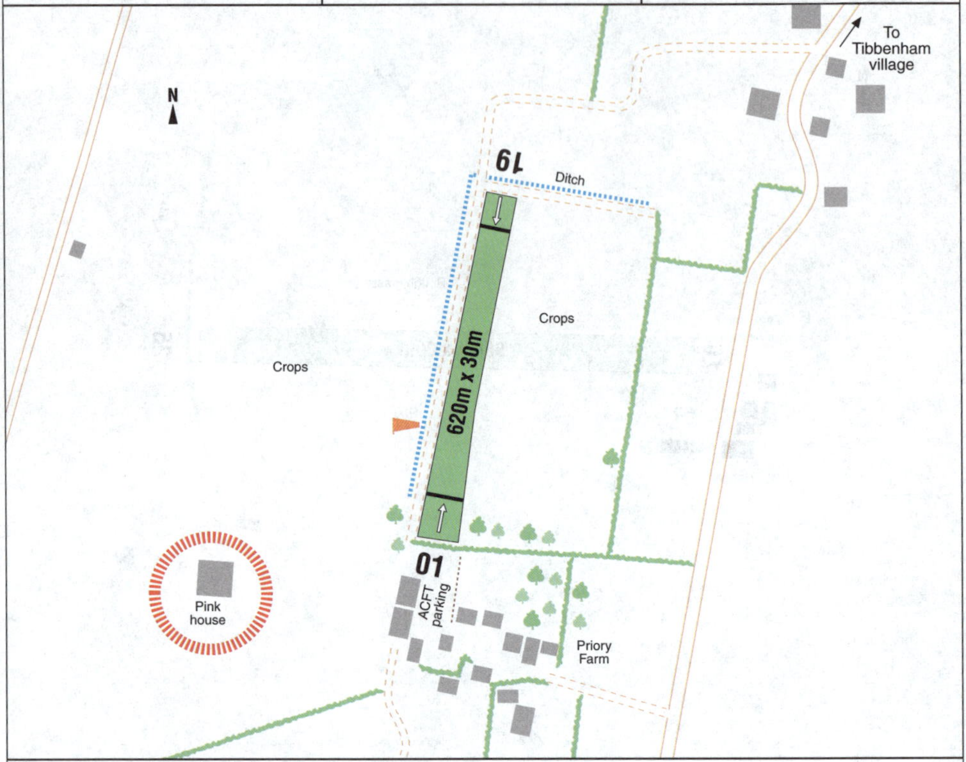

N

To Tibenham village

19

Ditch

Crops

620m x 30m

Crops

01

ACFT parking

Pink house

Priory Farm

RWY	SURFACE	TORA	LDA	LIGHTING
01/19	Grass	620x30	U/L	Nil

Remarks
PPR by telephone. Visiting ACFT welcome at own risk. Annual fly-in, check aviation press for details.

Warnings
Keep good lookout for glider activity from Tibenham AD 1nm to E. APP Rwy01 over farm buildings with group of trees to left of Thr. Low hedge extends across Rwy01 Thr from right. Use Rwy19 for landing when conditions permit. A ditch runs along full length of Rwy19 Thr. Crops grow up to edge of strip on E side.
Noise: Do not over fly the Pink House and Tibenham village NNE of AD.

		Operator	Bob Sage
Operating Hrs	1000-2000 (L)		Priory Farm, Tibenham
Circuits	Overhead joins 01 LH, 19 RH, 500ft QFE		Norwich, NR1 6NY **Tel/Fax:** 01379 677334
Landing Fee	Donation please		bobs.airstrip@btinternet.com www.bobs.airstrip@btinternet.com
Maintenance	Nil		
Fuel	AVGAS 100LL by arr		
Hangarage	Available by prior arr		

Disabled Facilities

Restaurants	By arr
Taxis Diss	**Tel:** 01362 696161
Car Hire	Nil
Weather Info	AirS MOEx

T

301ft 10mb	2nm SE of Whitchurch N5255.93 W00238.83	**PPR** **Alternative AD** Hawarden Sleap

Tilstock	LARS Shawbury 120.775	TWR Shawbury 122.100	A/G 118.100

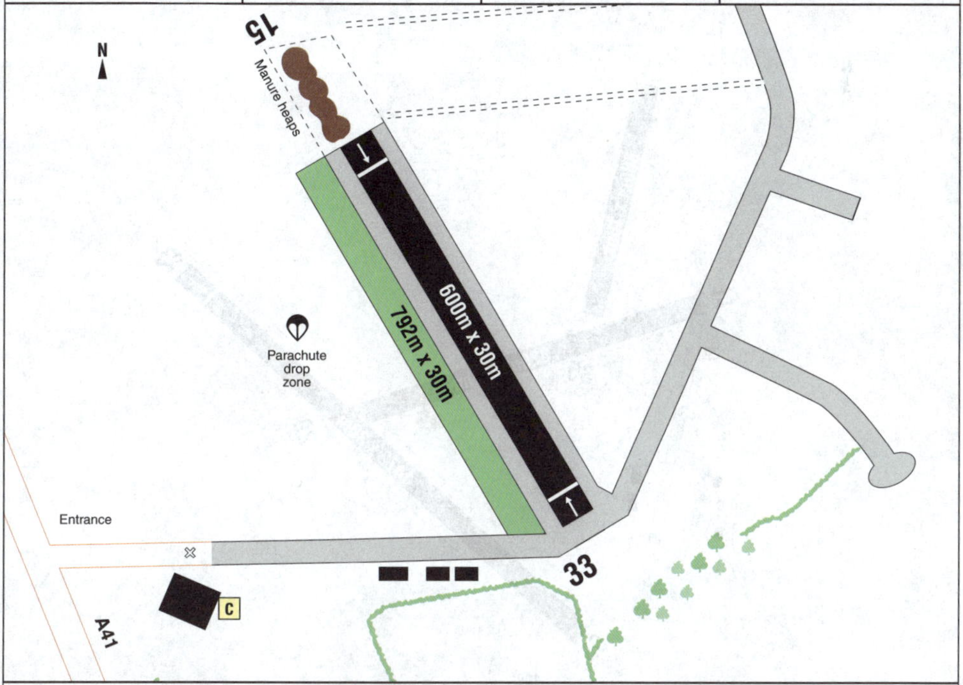

(Aerodrome diagram showing Runway 15/33, manure heaps at N end, parachute drop zone, parking area, entrance off A41, taxiways)

RWY	SURFACE	TORA	LDA	LIGHTING
15/33	Tarmac	600x30	U/L	Nil
15/33	Grass	792x30	U/L	Nil

Remarks
PPR by telephone closed Sunday. Visiting light ACFT welcome at owner's risk. Intensive parachute activity up to FL150. AD is situated under N portion of Shawbury MATZ.

Warnings
No overhead joins or circuits. Narrow Twy between parking area & Rwy with no passing places. AD frequently closed for other activities. Manure piles up to 15ft high are often present on N end of Rwy.

Operating Hrs	Available on request
Circuits	Join downwind 1000ft QFE
Landing Fee	£10 cash
Maintenance	Nil
Fuel	AVGAS 100LL available by prior arr

Disabled Facilities

Restaurants	Snacks tea & coffee available at AD
Taxis Halls	**Tel: 01948 662222**
Car Hire	Nil
Weather Info	AirCen MWC
Operator	The Parachute Centre Tilstock Aerodrome Whitchurch Shropshire, SY13 2HA **Tel: 01948 841111** (Parachute Centre) **Tel: 01948 663239** (Landowner/PPR Mr Matson) **Tel: 01939 250351 Ex 7232** (Shawbury ATC)

Tilstock Arrival & Departure Procedures
Arrival
contact Shawbury when 20nm from Tilstock. Contact Tilstock when 5nm from Tilstock if no reply from Shawbury.

Departure
Telephone Shawbury ATC at least 10 mins before Dept stating "Tilstock Dept" with flight details. Then:

1 Maintain VMC & climb not above 1000ft Tilstock QFE until in contact Shawbury or well clear extended centreline Shawbury Rwy18/36.

2 After initial (or if no) contact turn heading 050°, remain VMC continue climb. After Shawbury contact turn onto agreed track, otherwise turn onto desired track after passing AUDLEM 050°/6.5nmTilstock.

3 W/E PH & evenings when Shawbury limited activity/LARS unavailable, call Shawbury TWR when airborne for info on Shawbury & Ternhill activity.

38ft	2.5nm NNE of Balemartin	PPR	Alternative AD	Islay Barra
1mb	N5629.93 W00652.15		Diversion AD	

Tiree	FIS Scottish 127.275	AFIS 122.700

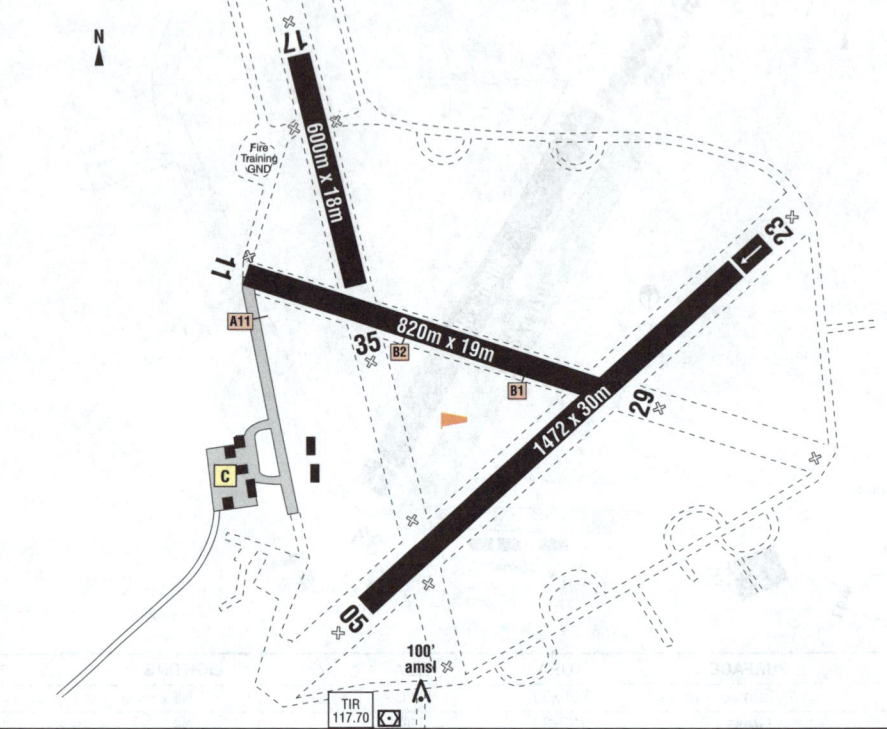

RWY	SURFACE	TORA	LDA	LIGHTING
05	Asphalt	1402	1402	Thr Rwy APAPI 3° LHS
23	Asphalt	1402	1350	Thr Rwy APAPI 3° LHS
11/29	Asphalt	820	820	Nil
17/35	Asphalt	600	600	Nil

Displaced Thr Rwy23 122m

Remarks
Grass areas soft and unsafe. Use marked Twys only.
Visual aid to location: Abn White flashing.

Warnings
All Twys are closed except between the control TWR & Rwy11 Thr. Unserviceable sections of Rwy are fenced off and marked with crosses. No GND signals except light signals. The useable portion of Rwy17/35 is marked with white sidelines. Windsurfing and kite surfing takes place on beaches near AD. Large flocks of geese in vicinity of AD Oct-Mar.

Operating Hrs	Mon-Fri 1000-1500 Sat 0830-1000 (L)
Circuits	Nil
Landing Fee	£12 under 3MT VFR cash/cheque
Maintenance	Nil
Fuel	Nil
Disabled Facilities	Nil

Restaurants

Mart Café	200m from AD
Scarinish Hotel	**Tel:** 01879 220308
Lodge Hotel	**Tel:** 01879 220368 (Bar lunches)

Taxis

A J Mackechnie	**Tel:** 01879 220419

Car Hire

Tiree Motor Co	**Tel:** 01879 220469
A MacLennan Mtrs	**Tel:** 01879 220555

Weather Info	M T9 Fax 438 GWC
Operator	HIAL, Tiree Aerodrome Isle of Tiree, Argyll, PA77 6UW **Tel:** 01879 220456 **Fax:** 01879 220714 tireeapm@hial.co.uk

TOP FARM

200ft 6mb	7nm NW of Royston N5207.45 W00007.20	PPR	Alternative AD Diversion AD	Cambridge Little Gransden

Non-radio	A/G Little Gransden 130.850	Safetycom 135.475

RWY	SURFACE	TORA	LDA	LIGHTING
06/24	Grass	440x24	U/L	Nil
15/33	Grass	380x15	U/L	Nil

Rwy06/24 over runs 230m at either end
Rwy15/33 only for use in strong winds
Rwy15 has marked upslope

Remarks
PPR by telephone. Visitors welcome at own risk. Well prepared strip. Rwy06/24 level and smooth. No take-offs after 1400 (L) on Sundays.

Warnings
Intense gliding activity at Gransden Lodge 2.5nm to N. Little Gransden ATZ boundary is 1nm to N and NW of Top Farm. Sandy TV mast (972ft amsl) is 3nm WNW.
Noise: Avoid over flying local habitation. Do not over fly house on 1nm final for Rwy06

Operating Hrs	Available on request No take-offs after 1400Hrs Sundays	**Taxis** Mayalls	**Tel:** 01763 243225
Circuits	06 RH, 24 LH, 1100ft QFE	**Car Hire**	Nil
Landing Fee	£5	**Weather Info**	AirCen MOEx
Maintenance Barmoor Aviation	**Tel:** 01767 631377	**Operator**	David Morris Barmoor House Top Farm, Croydon, Royston Herts, SG8 0EQ **Tel:** 01767 631377 **Tel:** 07711 197738
Fuel	AVGAS 100LL		
Disabled Facilities Nil			
Restaurants Randall's Queen Adelaide	**Tel:** 01223 207229 (B&B) **Tel:** 01223 208278		

559

| 92ft | 2.5nm SW of Thirsk | PPR | Alternative AD | **Durham Tees Valley** Full Sutton |
| 3mb | N5412.33 W00122.93 | MIL | Diversion AD | |

Topcliffe	**LARS** **Leeming 127.750**	**APP** **125.000**
TWR **122.100**	**A/G** **129.900**	**A/G** **125.000 (Glider freq)**

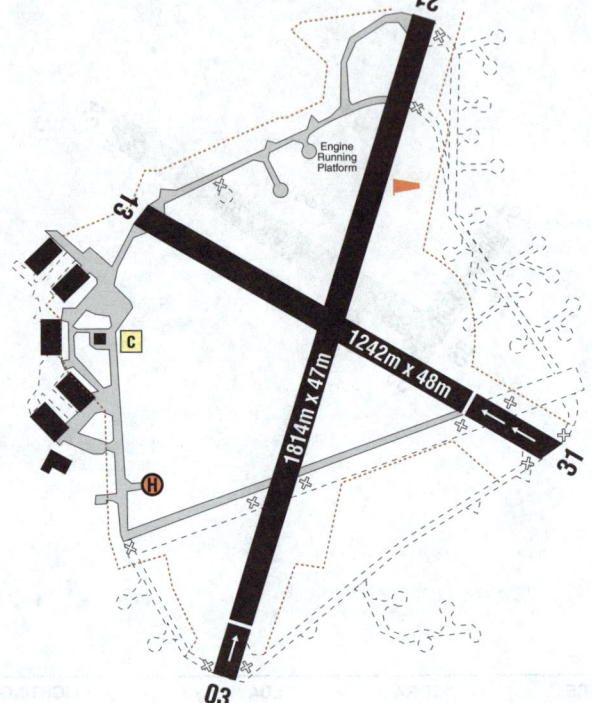

RWY	SURFACE	TORA	LDA	LIGHTING
03	Asphalt	1814	1434	Thr Rwy PAPI 3°
21	Asphalt	1814	1814	Ap Thr Rwy PAPI 3°
13	Asphalt	1242	1242	Thr Rwy PAPI 3°
31	Asphalt	1242	946	Thr Rwy PAPI 3°

Remarks
PPR 24 Hrs notice required via Linton Ops. Satellite to Linton-on-Ouse

Warnings
Glider flying Mon-Fri evenings, Sat-Sun all day.

Operating Hrs	Mon-Fri 0900-1615 & as required by Linton-on-Ouse	Operator	RAF Topcliffe Topcliffe
Circuits	13, 21 RH, 03, 31 LH		Thirsk North Yorkshire
Landing Fee	Charges in accordance with MOD policy Contact Station Ops for details		YO7 3QE **Tel:** 01845 595340 (ATC)
Maintenance	Nil		**Tel:** 01347 848261 Ex 7491 (PPR)
Fuel	Jet A1		**Tel:** 01347 848261 Ex 7486
Disabled Facilities	Nil		**Tel:** 01347 848261 Ex 7491 (Linton Ops)
Restaurants	Topcliffe village 2 miles S		**Fax:** 01845 595227 (ATC)
Taxis/Car Hire	Nil		**Fax:** 01845 595367 (Ops)
Weather Info	AirN MWC		

T

400ft 13mb	3nm WNW of Truro N5016.72 W00508.55	PPR	Alternative AD Diversion AD	St Mawgan Perranporth

Truro	APP Culdrose 134.050	APP St Mawgan 128.725	A/G 129.800

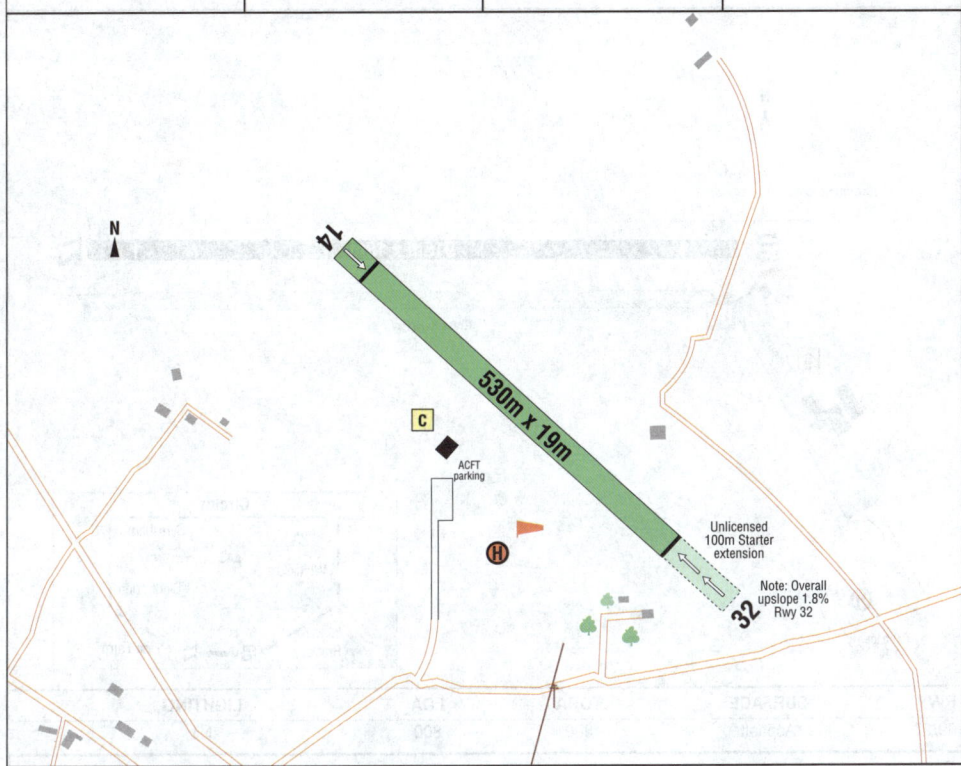

530m x 19m

Unlicensed 100m Starter extension

Note: Overall upslope 1.8% Rwy 32

ACFT parking

RWY	SURFACE	TORA	LDA	LIGHTING
14	Grass	530	491	Nil
32	Grass	500	500	Nil

Starter extension Rwy32 100m
Displaced Thr Rwy14 39m
Rwy32 Upslope 5.5%

Remarks
PPR by telephone. Inbound & outbound ACFT to and from NE are requested to call St Mawgan. AD situated below Culdrose AAIA for info contact Culdrose. AD available to ACFT requiring a licensed AD Sat-Sun only.

Warnings
AD is located under RNAS Culdrose AIAA.
Noise: Climb straight ahead for 0.75nm after take-off before turning on-route.

Operating Hrs	0800-1900 or SS whichever earliest (Summer) +1Hr (Winter) Licensed Sat-Sun & Wed 0800-1800 (L)	**Car Hire** Hertz Car Rental	**Tel:** 01872 223638 **Tel:** 01872 676797
Circuits	To N 800ft QFE	**Weather Info**	AirSW MOEx
Landing Fee	Single £8.81, Twin & Heli £11.75	**Operator**	Graham Barall Truro Aerodrome Truro, Cornwall TR4 9EX **Tel:** 01872 560488
Maintenance	Nil		
Fuel	To be advised		
Disabled Facilities	Nil		
Restaurants	AD owner will advise		
Taxis City Taxis	**Tel:** 01872 273053 **Tel:** 0800 318708		
Avcab	**Tel:** 01872 241214		

T

448ft 15mb	2nm E of Brackley N5202.45 W00105.73	PPR	Alternative AD Diversion AD	Oxford Wellesbourne Mountford

	Turweston	A/G 122.175

915m x 18m

60 09 27 27

(Driving School)

N

Grass Rwy/Twy

C Apron

PFA

H

Cabbage patch

Circuit

Syresham

Whitfield

A43

Biddlesdon

Brackley

60 27

Farm

RWY	SURFACE	TORA	LDA	LIGHTING
09/27	Asphalt	800	800	Nil

Remarks

PPR by telephone or website form to all users, not all ACFT types accepted. Essential due to restrictions in number and type of movements. AD not available for use at night by flights required to use licensed AD. Connecting service available to Silverstone Circuit. AD U/L on Sundays, no dept after 1600.

Warnings

Radio Masts 232° aal/680ft amsl 220°/3.5nm. Power cables run NW/SE 1nm W of AD. Not all Twys are available for use. Deviation from the marked manoeuvring area can be hazardous. Tail wheel ACFT may with prior permission land & take-off on the grass Twy. Rwy09 APP fly offset 20° to N of centre line.
Caution: EG D129 Weston on the Green Active H24.
Noise: Dept Rwy27: after take-off turn right 20° to climb between Brackley and Whitfield. **Dept Rwy09:** after take-off turn left 20° to avoid over-flying farmhouse on extended centreline. Avoid over-flying local habitation and maintain circuit position on downwind legs to the N ofA43.
Rwy27: FLY OFFSET final track 250° to Thr.

Operating Hrs	Mon-Fri 0900-1800 0800-2000 on request Sat 0900-1800 Sun 1000-1800 (L)	**Taxis** R&R	**Tel:** 01280 814239/823636
Circuits	09 LH, 27 RH, 1300ft QFE	**Car Hire**	Budget will pick up at AD contact ATC for details
Landing Fee	Single £10 (Free with up lift of fuel 60ltr) Twin £15 (Free with up lift of fuel 80ltr)	**Weather Info**	AirCen MOEx
Maintenance	Akki Enterprises (JAR145) **Tel:** 01280 706616 (Day) **Tel:** 01933 355127 (Evening)	**Operator**	Turweston Flight Centre Ltd Turweston Aerodrome Brackley, Northants, NN13 5YD **Tel:** 01280 705400 (TWR/Admin)
Resprays	**Tel:** 01280 840661 (Mick Allen) **Fax:** 01280 840662		**Tel:** 01280 701167 (Turweston Flying School)
Fuel	AVGAS 100LL		**Tel:** 01280 846786 (PFA)
Disabled Facilities Nil			**Fax:** 01280 704647
Restaurants/ Accomodation			**Fax:** 01280 840465 (Turweston Flying School)
Wellington's Café	**Tel:** 07968 966241		info@turwestonflight.com
Mrs Owen	**Tel:** 01280 704843		www.turweston.co.uk www.turweston.flight.com www.turwestonflyingschool.co.uk

T

62ft 2mb	On the Isle of Unst (Shetland Islands) N6044.83 W00051.23	**PPR**	**Alternative AD**	**Scatsta** Lerwick

Unst	**APP** Sumburgh 131.300	**A/G** 130.350

RWY	SURFACE	TORA	LDA	LIGHTING
12	Asphalt	640x28	U/L	Thr Rwy PAPI 4.5° LHS
30	Asphalt	610x28	U/L	Ap Thr Rwy PAPI 4.5° LHS

Displaced Thr Rwy12

Remarks
ACFT operators are reminded to check with ATC availability of services before nominating this AD as a Diversion AD.
Visual aid to location: IbnGreen UT.

Warnings
Rising GND exists in take-off path Rwy30. Frequent helicopter activity outside AD Hrs. No GND signals except light signals.

		Operator	Shetland Islands Council
Operating Hrs	Emergency use or ambulance flights UFN		Unst Aerodrome
Circuits	30 RH, 12 LH, 1000ft QFE		Baltasound, Shetland, ZE2 9DT
Landing Fee	On application		**Tel:** 01957 711877 (AD)
Maintenance	Nil		**Tel/Fax:** 01957 711541
Fuel	Nil		
Disabled Facilities	Nil		
Restaurants	Nil		
Taxis PT Coaches	**Tel:** 01957 711666		
Car Hire	Nil		
Weather Info	M T9 Fax 442 GWC		

575ft 19mb	8nm NNW of Boscombe Down N5117.17 W00146.92	PPR MIL	Alternative AD	Farnborough Thruxton

Upavon	LARS Boscombe 126.700	OPS Salisbury 122.750

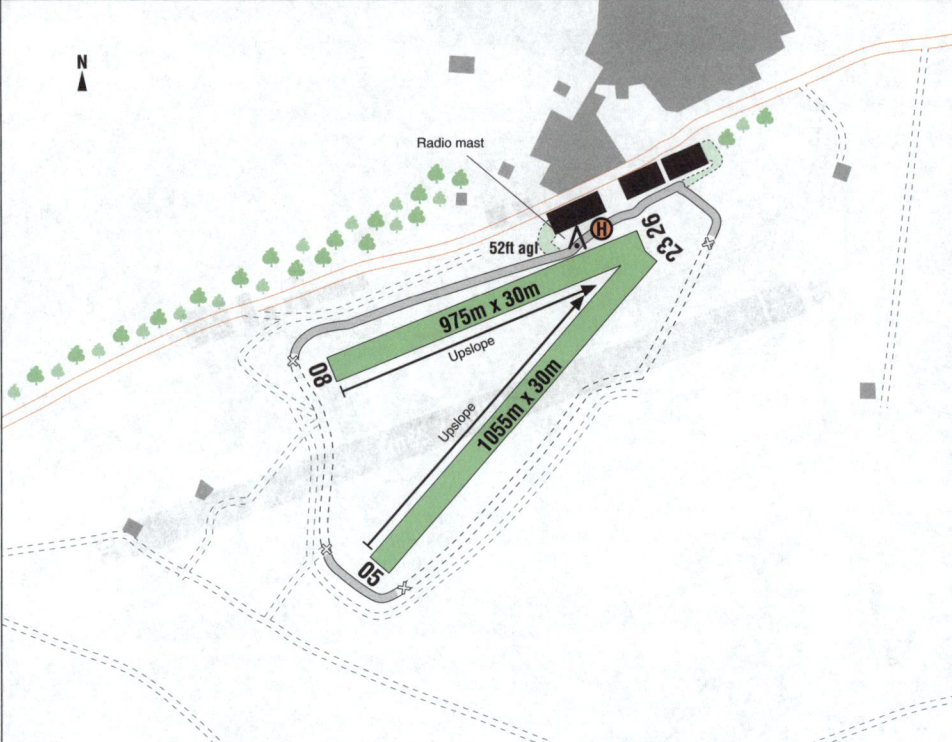

Radio mast

52ft agl

23 26

975m x 30m
Upslope

1055m x 30m
Upslope

08

05

N

RWY	SURFACE	TORA	LDA	LIGHTING
05/23	Grass	1055	1055	Nil
08/26	Grass	975	975	Nil

Rwy26 surface suitable for ACFT equipped with low pressure tyres
Rwys upslope W-E 1.77%

Remarks
Strict PPR by telephone, 24Hrs notice. Army AD. ATC manned for certain pre-notified operations. Non-ATC qualified personnel give advisory information on UHF freq. During daylight hours call Salisbury Ops, 5 minutes before ETA passing ACFT type, ETA & intentions.

Warnings
AD situated within EG D126/128 range information available from 'Salisbury Ops'. S Twy closed to Helicopter and fixed wing operations. Glider flying takes place during daylight hrs.
Caution: Radio mast 52ft agl just to W of TWR. Netheravon AD is 2.5nm S, Larkhill Range 3nm W. Everleigh drop zone 3.5nm to the SE.
Noise: Arr/Dept will be at pilots own discretion. All APP to be from N sector (290-040°).

Operating Hrs	SR-SS	Operator	MOD (Army)
Circuits	Info available with PPR		Upavon Airfield
Landing Fee	Charges in accordance with MOD policy Contact Station Ops for details		Salisbury Plain, Wilts **Tel:** 01980 615238 (PPR)
Maintenance	Nil		**Tel:** 01980 615066
Fuel	Nil		**Tel:** 01980 674710/674730
Disabled Facilities	Nil		(Salisbury Ops)
Restaurant	Nil		
Taxi/Car Hire	Nil		
Weather Info	AirSW MOEx		

U-V

UPFIELD

10ft 0mb	4nm SE of Newport N5133.50 W00253.00	PPR	Alternative AD	Bristol Filton Bristol

Upfield	LARS Filton 122.725	LARS Cardiff 126.625	A/G 130.400 (Manned with PPR)

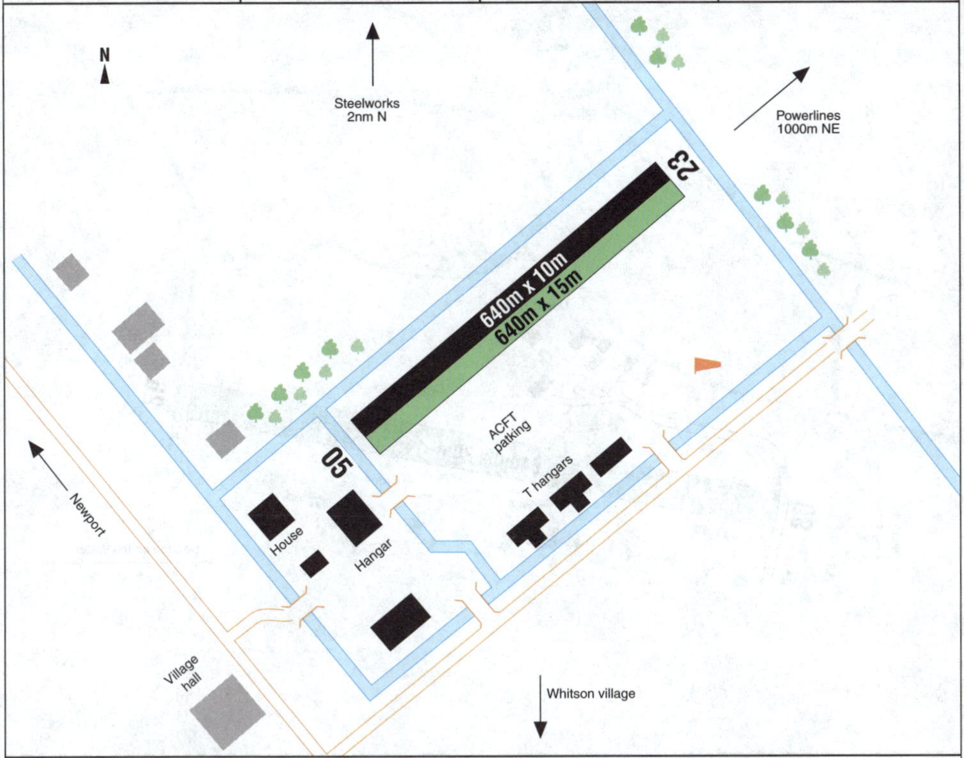

(Aerodrome diagram)

- N
- Steelworks 2nm N
- Powerlines 1000m NE
- 23
- 640m x 10m
- 640m x 15m
- 05
- ACFT parking
- T hangars
- Newport
- House
- Hangar
- Village hall
- Whitson village

RWY	SURFACE	TORA	LDA	LIGHTING
05/23	Concrete	640x10	U/L	Nil
05/23	Grass	640x15	U/L	Nil

Concrete Rwy raised 4ins agl, flood avoidance
Grass Rwy very bumpy

Remarks
PPR. Visiting ACFT welcome at own risk. AD situated 1nm N of N edge of Severn Estuary and 2nm S of Newport Steelworks.

Warnings
All ACFT movements must be confined to Rwy only. Other areas are very soft all year round. Rwy may become boggy after heavy rain. Grass is bumpy and visiting pilots are advised to touchdown 1/3 down Rwy from either end. Maintain height between two houses on Rwy05 APP. Use full length of Rwy for take-off. Sheep may be grazing. Low flying military ACFT may be encountered in vicinity, particularly during the week.
Noise: Operate considerately. Avoid over flying Redwick village to NE and houses on Whiston Road to SE. Ensure downwind leg is over the coast. Climb out on Rwy centre line to 1000ft before turning onto course.

Operating Hrs	SR-SS	**Taxis**	Operator can advise
Circuits	To S 1000ft QFE	**Car Hire**	Nil
Landing Fee	Single £5, Twin £10, Microlight £3	**Weather Info**	AirS MOEx
Maintenance	Emergency repairs, PFA inspector on site Long term parking available	**Operator**	K M Bowen Upfield Farm Whitson, Newport Gwent, NP18 2PG **Tel:** 01633 279222 **Fax:** 01633 279922
Fuel	MOGAS available on request		
Disabled Facilities			

   P

Restaurants	Local Pub B & B Celtic Manor (Ryder Cup Venue) 6 miles from AD

U-V

750ft 25mb	2.5nm W of Bourton on the Water N5153.32 W00149.28	PPR	Alternative AD	Gloucestershire Kemble

Non-Radio	LARS Brize 124.275	Safetycom 135.475

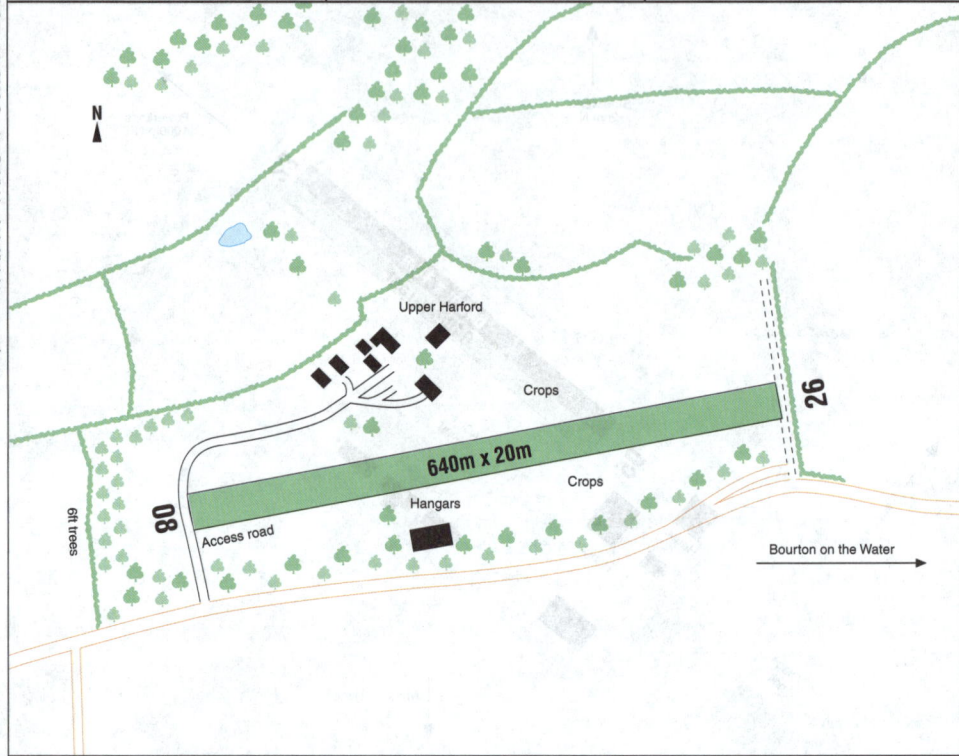

RWY	SURFACE	TORA	LDA	LIGHTING
08/26	Grass	640x20	U/L	Nil

Remarks

Strictly PPR by telephone. AD operated by flying community, which has strict planning constraints on visiting ACFT. PPR for visitors will normally only be granted for pilots visiting residents or local villages. Casual visitors will not be accepted. Strip is well maintained and is located between a disused railway line and Bourton on the Water.

Warnings

Hedge at Rwy08 Thr and disused electrical supply poles, (no wires), adjacent to Rwy26 APP.
Noise: Avoid over flight of all local habitation.

Operating Hrs	SR-SS daily	**Operator**	Mr M Jones
Circuits	N 1000ft QFE		Upper Harford House
Landing Fee	Nil		Upper Harford
Maintenance	Nil		Bourton on the Water, GL54 3BY
Fuel	Nil		**Tel/Fax**: 01451 821455
Disabled Facilities	Nil		
Restaurants	Nil		
Taxis/Car Hire	Nil		
Weather Info	AirCen MOEx		

U-V

| 37ft | 5nm SE of Holyhead | PPR | Alternative AD | Hawarden Caernarfon |
| 1mb | N5314.89 W00432.12 | MIL | Diversion AD | |

Valley	ATIS 120.725	LARS 125.225	APP 123.300

RAD 125.225	TWR 122.100	GND 122.100	

RWY	SURFACE	TORA	LDA	LIGHTING
14/32	Asphalt	2290	2290	Ap Thr Rwy PAPI 3°
01	Asphalt	1572	1572	Thr Rwy PAPI 3°
19	Asphalt	1571	1571	Ap Thr Rwy PAPI 3°
08	Asphalt	1280	1066	Nil
26	Asphalt	1280	1158	Nil

Remarks

PPR to all ACFT other than emergency. Inbound civil ACFT make contact with ATC at min range 30nm. Flying training takes place 0800-1800, helicopter training H24. Valley can only accept 1 visiting ACFT movement during any 30 min period. Ltd RAD service at a range exceeding 12nm in sector SE of AD.
Visual aid to location: Ibn VY Red.

Warnings

Intensive visual circuit flying at Mona (094°/6nm). Arrester gear 390m from Rwy14/32 Thr.
Noise: Avoid over flying Rhosneigr (SSE of AD) below 1000ft agl.

Operating Hrs	Mon-Thu 0800-1800 Fri 0800-1700 (L)	**Restaurants**	Nil
Circuits	32, 19 RH	**Taxis/Car Hire**	Nil
	2 Rwys may be in use at once	**Weather Info**	M T Fax 444 MWC
Landing Fee	Charges in accordance with MOD policy	**Operator**	RAF Valley
	Contact Station Ops for details		Holyhead, Ynys Mon
Maintenance	Nil		Gwynedd, LL65 3NY
Fuel	JET A1		**Tel:** 01407 762241 Ex 7582 (Ops)
Disabled Facilities			**Fax:** 01407 767335

Effective date:23/11/06

U-V

			PPR MIL	Alternative AD Diversion AD	Nottingham East Midlands Wickenby
231ft 8mb	3.5nm S of Lincoln N5309.97 W00031.43				

Waddington	LARS 127.350	APP 127.350	RAD 123.300	TWR 122.100

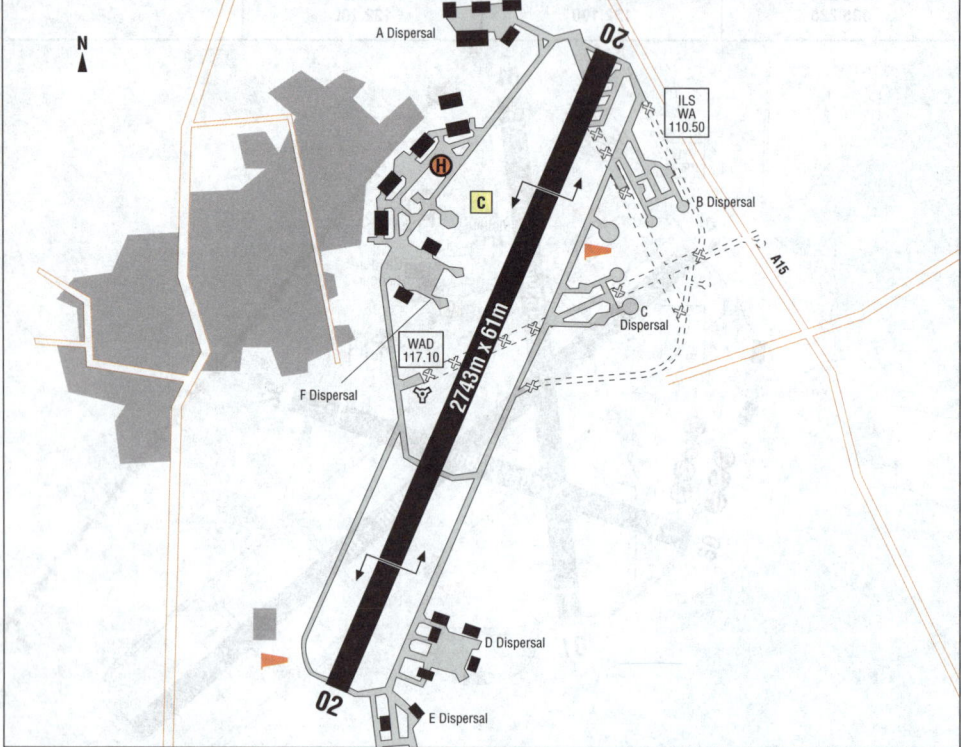

RWY	SURFACE	TORA	LDA	LIGHTING
02/20	Asphalt	2743	2743	Ap Thr Rwy PAPI 3°

Arrester gear Rwy02/20 610m from Thr

Remarks

PPR 24Hrs notice required. ATZ active H24. Inbound ACFT contact Waddington Zone 20nm before MATZ boundary. For Scampton MATZ crossings, contact Waddington Zone. Air Ambulance and flying club operate outside normal Hrs.

Warnings

Public Rd cross final APP Rwy20. Due to high usage slot times must be adhered to. Dept into sector 130-220 will not normally be approved due to Cranwell Ops, plan to avoid this sector. Strong W Winds can produce marked turbulence on final for Rwy20.
Noise: Pilots joining or flying in visual circuit are to avoid over flight below 1000ft QFE of Harmston & Waddington villages, do not over fly Boothby Graffoe, Bracebridge Heath, Branston, Washingborough, Heighington, Coleby & Navenby villages below 500ft QFE.

Operating Hrs	PPR from Ops Ex 7301	**Operator**	RAF Waddington
Circuits	02 RH, 20 LH, 1000ft QFE		**Tel:** 01522 727451 (ATC)
Landing Fee	Charges in accordance with MOD policy Contact Station Ops for details		**Tel:** 01522 727301 (Ops)
Maintenance	Nil		
Fuel	AVTUR		
Disabled Facilities	Nil		
Restaurants	Nil		
Taxis/Car Hire	Nil		
Weather Info Waddington Met Office	M T Fax 446 MWC **Tel:** 01522 726522 **Fax**: 01522 726525 **Tel:** 01522 727305		

W

0ft 0mb	1nm NNE of Whittlesey N5234.70 W00007.15	**PPR**	**Alternative AD**	**Cambridge** Peterborough Sibson

Non-Radio	**LARS** **Cottesmore 130.200**	**Safetycom** **135.475**

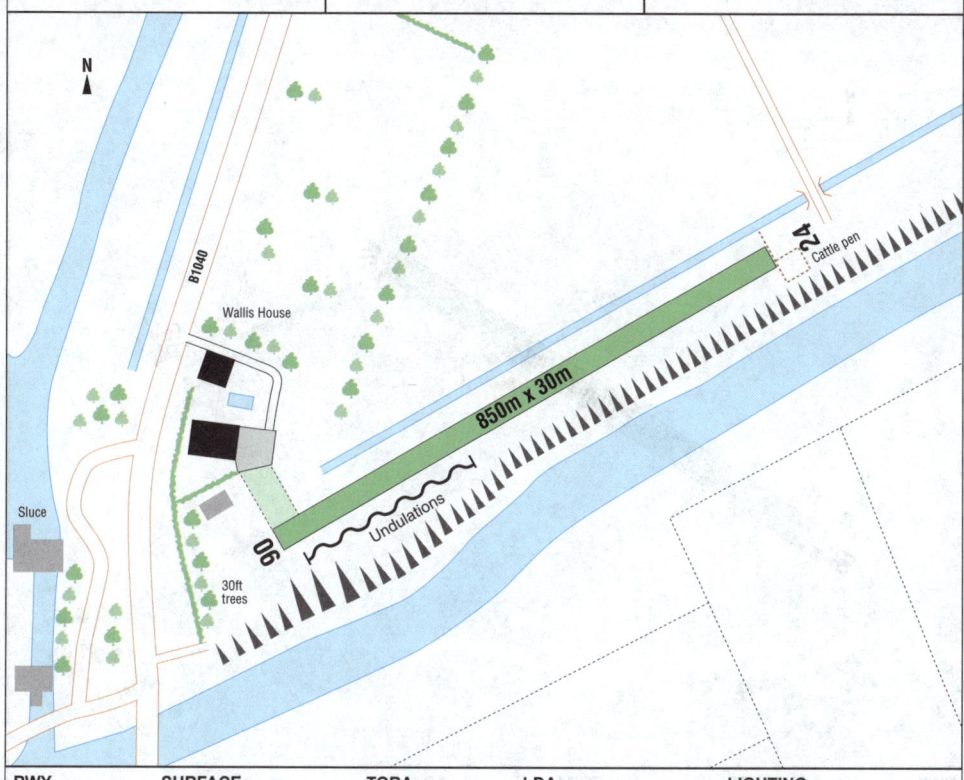

RWY	SURFACE	TORA	LDA	LIGHTING
06/24	Grass	850x30	U/L	Nil

Remarks

PPR by telephone. Visiting ACFT welcome at pilots own risk. AD situated close to River Nene, midway between Thorney & Whittlesey. Strip is mainly flat but there are undulations for first third of Rwy06.

Warnings

30ft trees on short final Rwy06. Wire fence 4ft high and cattle pen Rwy24 Thr.
Noise: Avoid over flight of local houses.

Operating Hrs	SR-SS	**Operator**	Tony Wallis Wallis House Thorney Peterborough Cambridgeshire PE6 0RL **Tel:** 01733 202070 **Tel:** 07958 224545 jrfisher.farming@virgin.net
Circuits	LH 1000ft QFE		
Landing Fee	Nil		
Maintenance	Nil		
Fuel	Nil		
Disabled Facilities	Nil		
Restaurant	Pub adjacent strip (5 min walk)		
Taxi/Car Hire	Nil		
Weather Info	MOEx		

W

| 180ft
6mb | 4.5nm S of Pontefract
N5337.77 W00115.55 | PPR | Alternative AD
Diversion AD | **Leeds Bradford** Sherburn in Elmet |

| | **Walton Wood** | **A/G**
123.625 |

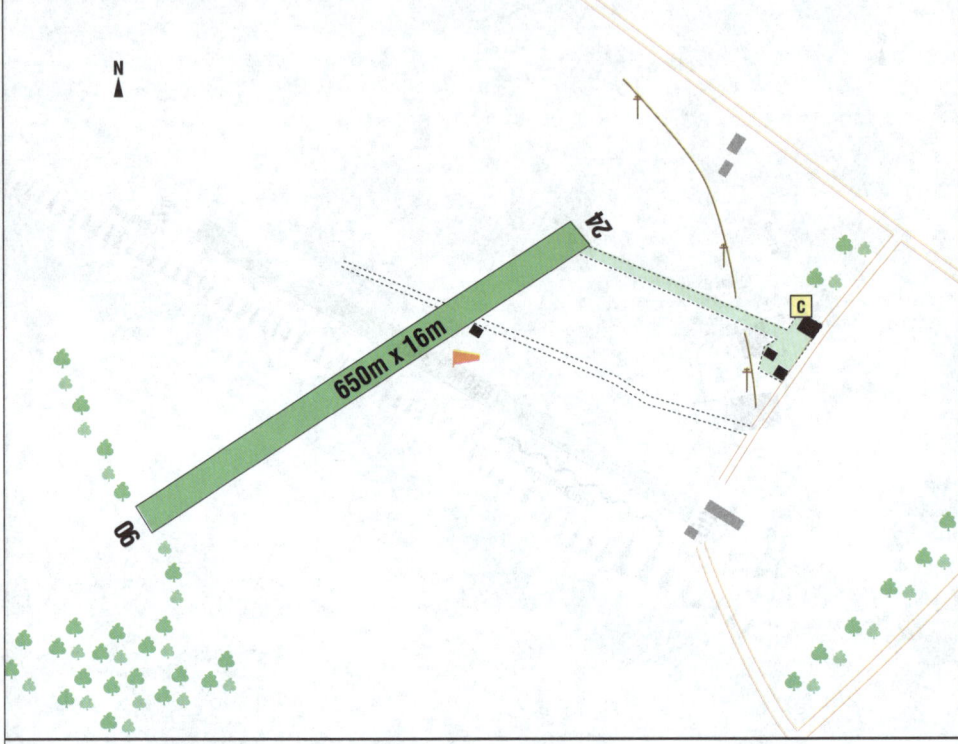

RWY	SURFACE	TORA	LDA	LIGHTING
06/24	Grass	650x16	U/L	Nil

Remarks
PPR by telephone. Visiting ACFT welcome at own risk. Rwy can become water logged in winter.

Warnings
Power lines cross Rwy24 APP 10m from Thr. Public footpath & bridle way cross Rwy.
Noise: Avoid over flying all local villages.

Operating Hrs	Available on request	**Operator**	Heliscott Ltd
Circuits	24 LH, 06 RH 1000ft		Walton Wood Airfield
Landing Fee	Single £10 Twin £20		Thorpe Audlin
			Pontefract, Yorkshire, WF83HQ
Maintenance	Helicopter JAR 145		**Tel:** 01977 621378
Fuel	AVGAS Jet A1 100LL		**Tel:** 01977 620631
			Fax: 01977 620868
Disabled Facilities	Nil		info@heliscott.com
Restaurants	Nil		www.heliscott.com
Taxis/Car Hire	Nil		
Weather Info	AirCen MWC		

W

55ft 2mb	6nm W of Preston Docks N5344.70 W00252.98	PPR	Alternative AD Diversion AD	Blackpool Manchester Barton

Warton	ATIS 121.725	LARS 129.525
APP 129.525	TWR 130.800	FIRE 121.600

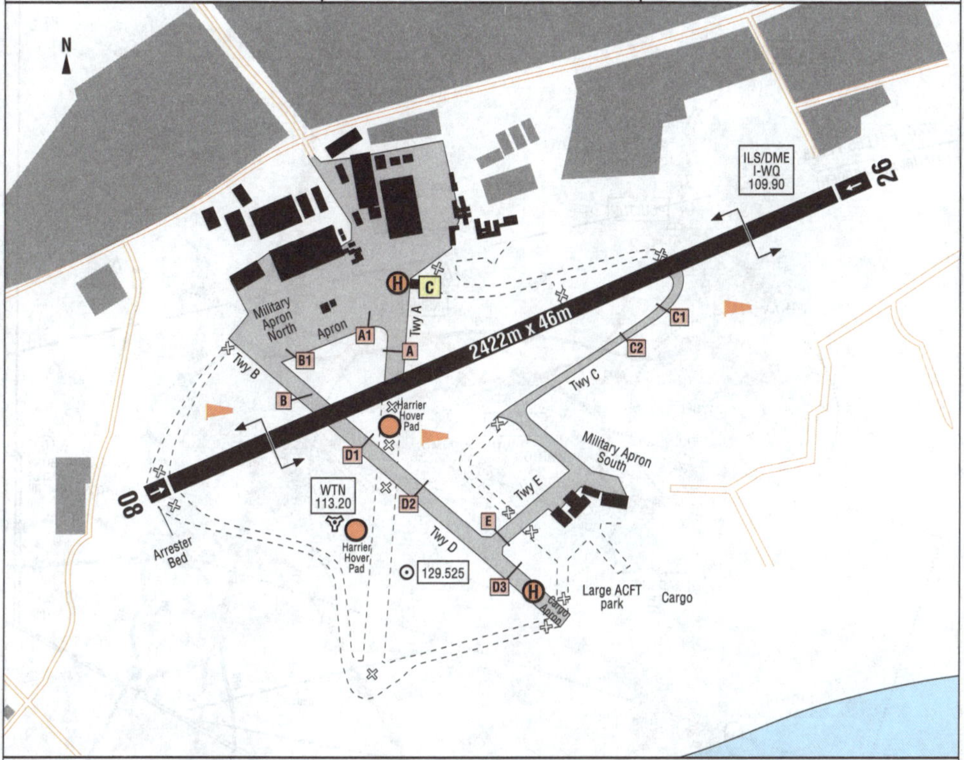

(Aerodrome chart: Runway 08/26, 2422m x 46m, Asphalt. Taxiways A, B, C, D, E. Military Apron North, Apron, Military Apron South, Harrier Hover Pad, Arrester Bed, Large ACFT park, Cargo. ILS/DME I-WQ 109.90, WTN 113.20, 129.525. Taxiway markers A1, A, B1, B, C, C1, C2, D1, D2, D3, E.)

RWY	SURFACE	TORA	LDA	LIGHTING
08	Asphalt	2422	2358	Ap Thr Rwy PAPI 3°
26	Asphalt	2341	2341	Ap Thr Rwy PAPI 3°

Remarks

PPR non-radio ACFT not accepted. Hi-vis. Visiting ACFT on business with BAE only. Red & white marker boards positioned 35m S Rwy08/26 for its full length, 1000m apart. A marshaller must be present for engine starts. Model ACFT flying on AD when closed. Lancashire Police Helicopter operates H24.
Aids to Navigation: NDB WTN 337.00

Warnings

Arrester gear on Rwy08/26. Arrester cable housing located 395m after the start of the full width pavement flush with Rwy. Pilots of light ACFT advised to touchdown after cable housing. Beware close proximity of Springfields Restricted Area and Blackpool AD.
Noise: Avoid over flying factory buildings.

Operating Hrs	0630-1730 (Summer) +1Hr (Winter) & by arr	**Restaurants** Birley Arms	Pub & Motel nr AD **Tel:** 01772 632201
Circuits	All circuits S	**Taxis/Car Hire**	Can be arr on site
Landing Fee	On application	**Weather Info**	M* AirCen MWC ATIS **Tel:** 01772 856060
Maintenance	Ltd	**Operator**	BAE Systems
Fuel	JET A1		Warton Aerodrome, Preston

Disabled Facilities

Handling **Tel:** 01772 852303

Lancashire, PR4 1AX
Tel: 01772 633333 (AD)
Tel: 01772 852303 (Civil Ops)
Tel: 01772 852374 (ATC)
Fax: 01772 634706

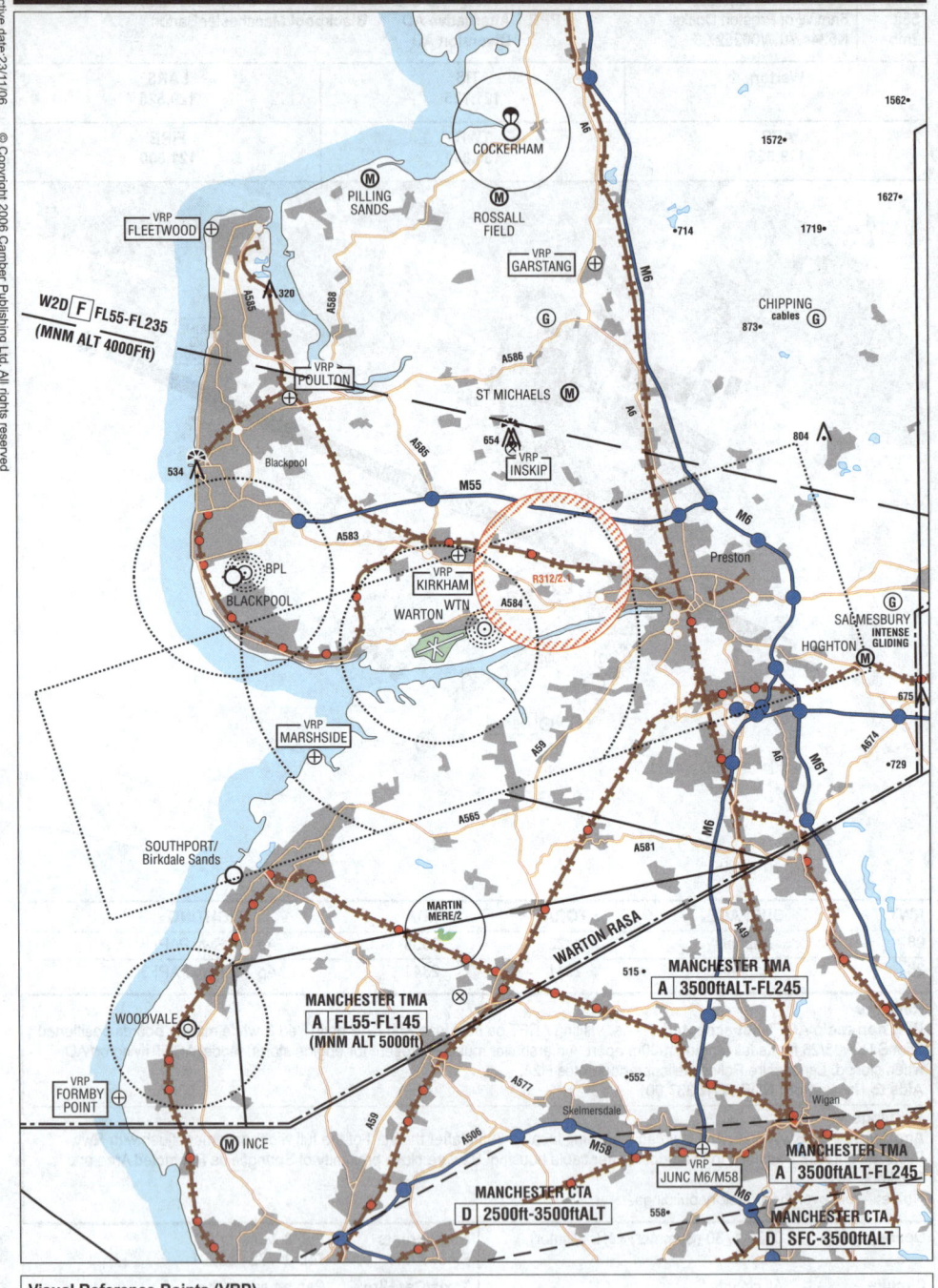

Visual Reference Points (VRP)

Blackburn	N5344.85	W00228.78
Formby Point	N5333.12	W00306.32
Garstang	N5354.38	W00246.55
M6/M58 Junction	N5332.07	W00241.87

W

284ft 9mb	8.5nm NW of Ipswich N5207.64 E00057.64	PPR MIL	Alternative AD	Southend Elmsett

Wattisham	APP 125.800	RAD 123.300	TWR 122.100	A/G 125.800

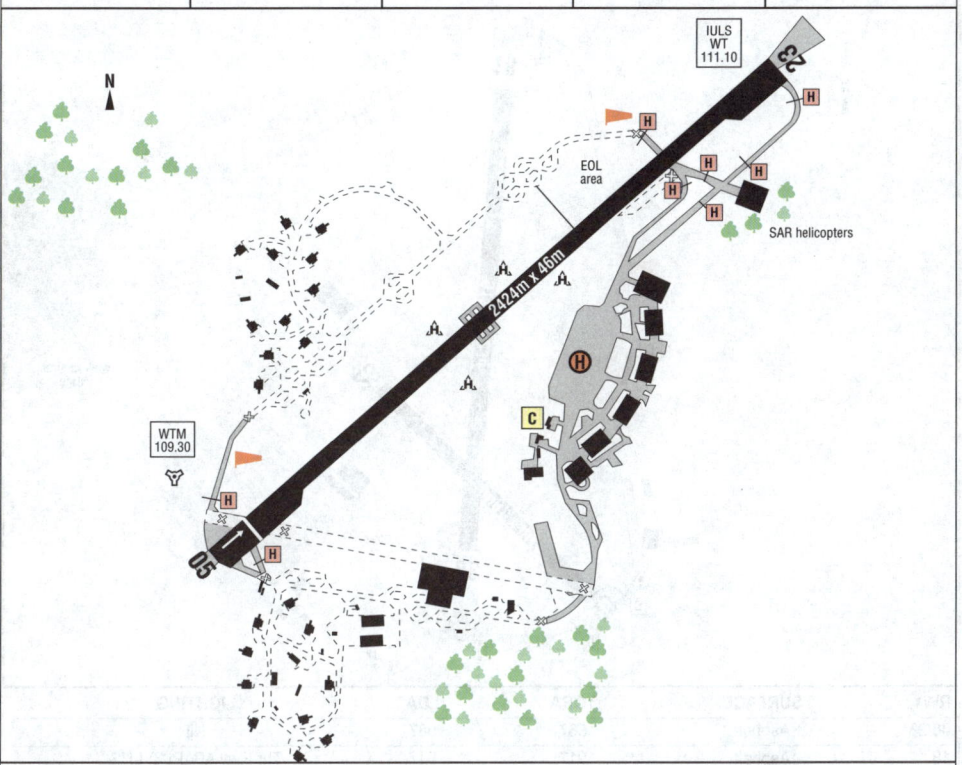

RWY	SURFACE	TORA	LDA	LIGHTING
05	Asphalt	2424	2284	Ap Thr Rwy PAPI 3°
23	Asphalt	2424	2422	Ap Thr Rwy PAPI 3°

Remarks
Strict PPR. Flight plans must be addressed to EGUWZGZX and EGUWYWYO.
Visual aid to location: Ibn WT Red.

Warnings
Intense helicopter flying at all times. Possible laser hazards on apron when Apache helicopters running. Avoid 10m from nose area. Glider flying daily SR-SS. Aeromodel flying takes place on AD on Friday evenings, W/E & PH. Outside normal Ops Hrs if no answer on APP/TWR freq call A/G freq and request gliders to cease launching prior to Arr & Dept. Full time bird control unit in operation on AD. Elmsett AD 2nm S.
Caution: SAR & Police Helicopters operate H24. Deer on AD. 3m fence Rwy23 undershoot. TV mast 933ft aal/1217ft amsl 9nm NE of AD.

Operating Hrs	Mon-Fri 0800-1800 (L)	**Operator**	Army **Tel:** 01449 728234/35 **Tel:** 01449 728234 Ex 8241
Circuits	Variable up to 1000ft QFE No dead side		
Landing Fee	Charges in accordance with MOD policy Contact Station Ops for details		
Maintenance	Nil		
Fuel	AVTUR FS 11		
Disabled Facilities	Nil		
Restaurants	Nil		
Taxis/Car Hire	Nil		
Weather Info	M T Fax 448 MWC		

W

159ft 5mb	3.3nm E of Stratford upon Avon N5211.53 W00136.87	PPR	Alternative AD Diversion AD	Birmingham Turweston

Wellesbourne	APP Birmingham 118.050	AFIS 124.025

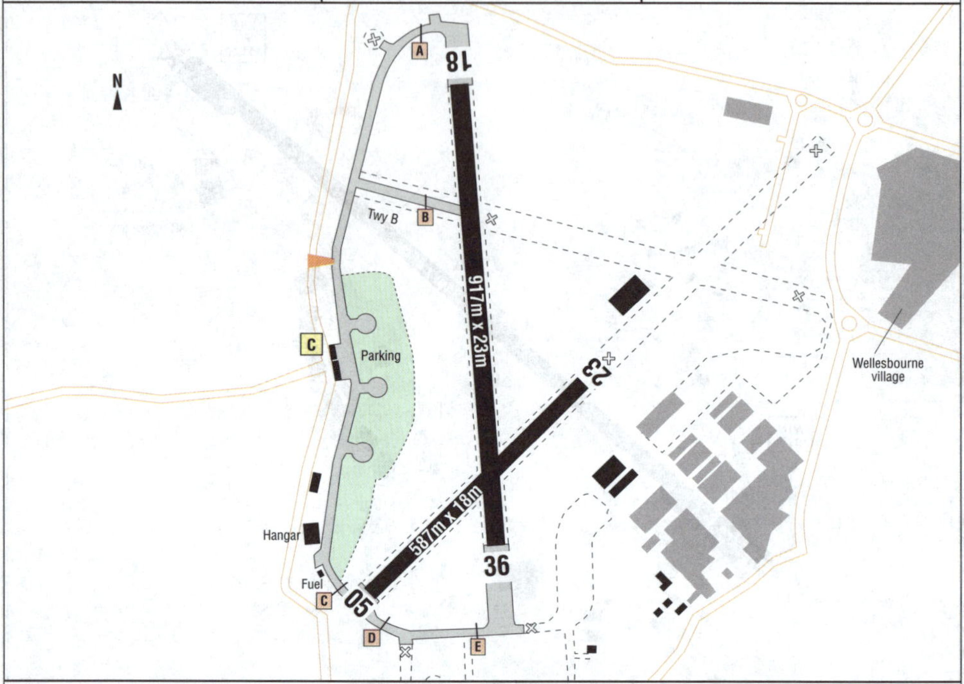

RWY	SURFACE	TORA	LDA	LIGHTING
05/23	Asphalt	587	587	Nil
18	Asphalt	917	917	Thr Rwy APAPI 3° LHS
36	Asphalt	917	917	Thr Rwy APAPI 4.25° LHS

Rwy23 not available Sat & PH due to market

Remarks

PPR non-radio ACFT not accepted. Pilots requested to contact Wellesbourne at least 10 mins before ETA Wellesbourne. Certain customs facilities available.
Visual aid to location: Abn white flashing

Warnings

AD situated 3nm S boundary of Birmingham CTA (base 1500ft) & below CTA base 3500 ft. Deviation from marked manoeuvring area hazardous. Industrial buildings E of AD may cause turbulence and/or wind shear.
Noise: Avoid over flying villages of Loxley, Charlecote, Hampton Lucy, Wellesbourne. Whilst in the circuit avoid over flying Wellesbourne village & built up areas. Rwy36 Dept immediate turn track 030° climb 1000ft QFE before turning

Operating Hrs	0800-1630 (Summer) 0900-1730 or SS +30mins whichever earlier (Winter) & by arr	**Taxis** Local Stratford	Tel: 07900 616673 Tel: 01789 414514
Circuits	Fixed wing variable 1000ft QFE Heli variable 600ft QFE	**Car Hire**	Nil
Landing Fee	Fixed wing Single £10, Twin £15 Heli Single £5, Twin £10	**Weather Info**	AirCen MOEx www.wellesbourneairfield.com
Parking	Single £5.00, Twin £10, over night	**Operator**	Radarmoor Ltd Wellesbourne Mountford Aerodrome Wellesbourne Warks, CV35 9EU Tel: 01789 842007 Tel: 01789 842000 (TWR) Tel: 01789 470112 (Office) Fax: 01789 470465 tower@wellesbourneairfield.com www.wellesbourneairfield.com
Maintenance	Nil		
Fuel	AVGAS JET A1 100LL 0900-1715 or SS (L) (Winter) 0800-1715 (L) (Summer)		

Disabled Facilities

Restaurants
Touchdown Inn   Tel: 01789 470575

233ft 8mb	2nm S of Welshpool N5237.72 W00309.20		PPR	Alternative AD Diversion AD	Hawarden Sleap
	Welshpool			A/G 128.000	

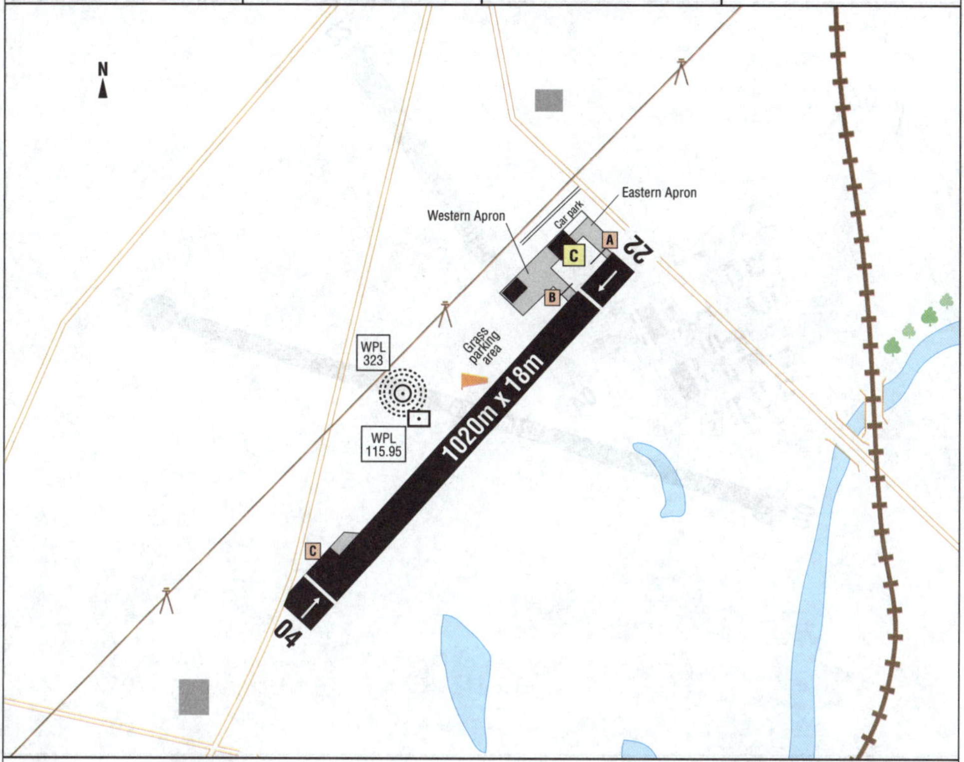

Western Apron   Eastern Apron   Car park
22
A
C
B
C
WPL 323
WPL 115.95
Grass parking area
1020m x 18m
C
1
04
N

RWY	SURFACE	TORA	LDA	LIGHTING
04	Asphalt	880	902	APAPI 3° LHS
22	Asphalt	880	879	APAPI 3° LHS

Lighting available to based operators
Displaced Thr Rwy04 100m
Displaced Thr Rwy22 123m

Remarks
PPR non-radio ACFT not accepted.

Warnings
AD situated in the Severn Valley with high GND on both sides. Pilots should not descend below safety height until the Rwy has been positively identified. The fins of parked ACFT on the W apron may infringe AD transitional area. Trees infringe the transitional surface by 2nm ESE AD.

Operating Hrs	0900-1700 (L)	**Taxis**	
Circuits	LH 1500ft QFE	Amber Cabs	**Tel:** 01938 556611
Landing Fee	Single £10, Twin £20	Yellow Cabs	**Tel:** 01938 555533
Maintenance	Nil	**Car Hire**	Nil
Fuel	AVGAS JET A1 100LL	**Weather Info**	AirN MWC
	Hrs as AD	**Operator**	Mid Wales Airport Ltd
Disabled Facilities			Welshpool Aerodrome
			Welshpool, Powys, SY21 8SG
			Tel: 01938 555560
			Fax: 01938 555062
Restaurants	Cafe at AD		www.welshpoolairport.co.uk

W

428ft 15mb	4nm E of Cardigan N5206.92 W00433.42	PPR	Alternative AD	Pembrey Haverfordwest

West Wales	A/G 122.150	AFIS 122.150	Range Control 119.650

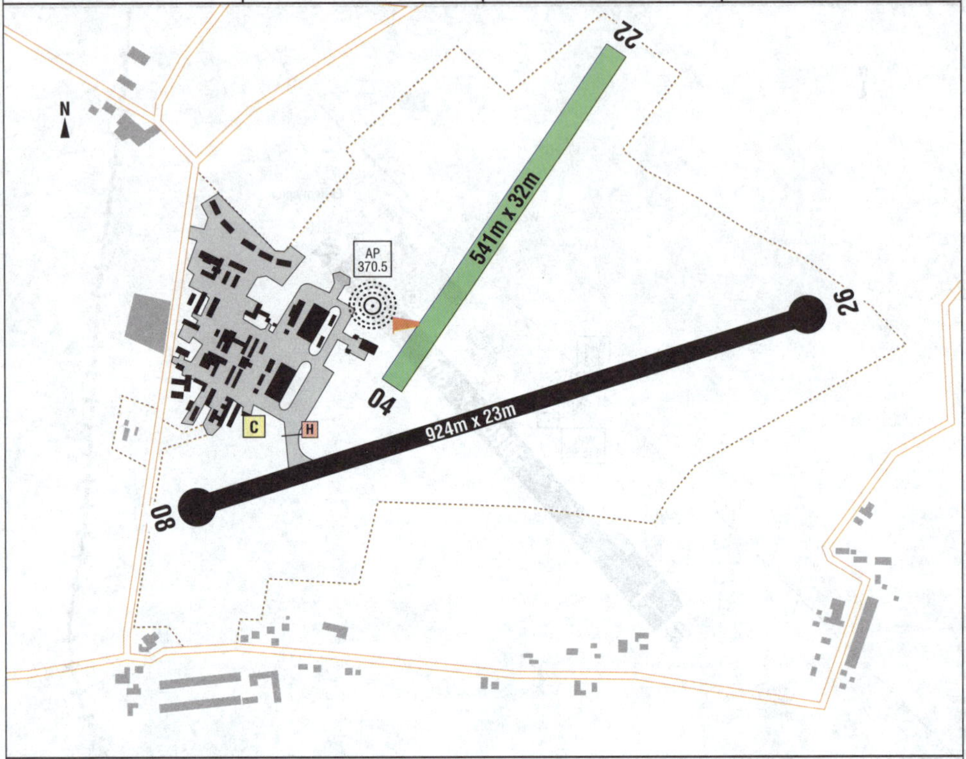

RWY	SURFACE	TORA	LDA	LIGHTING
08	Asphalt	883	845	Nil
26	Asphalt	886	845	Nil
04/22	Grass	541x32	U/L	Nil

Remarks

Strict PPR by telephone. Non-Radio ACFT not accepted. Hi vis. AD U/L weekends & PH, licensed operations by arr. While airside pilots are responsible for safety of passengers and other crew members. Carriage of dangerous goods as specified in ANO is prohibited without written approval of AD manager.

Warnings

Part of ATZ located within Danger Area EGD201. ACFT must NOT penetrate range without permission during notified hours of range ops. PPR & Radio contact with West Wales Radio is sufficient for ACFT Arr/Dept AD. Subject to Rwy in use circuit entry must be made via downwind or base leg aircraft are to specify where the circuit will be joined. Helicopters must fly fixed wing circuit procedures unless otherwise approved. All wheel equipped Helicopters must use the Rwy. Road close to Rwy08 APP. Road traffic is controlled by traffic lights. A/G station will advise if any vehicles are observed not complying with signals.
Caution: Turbulence Rwy08 Try with strong N winds
Noise: ACFT should operate in such a manner as to create minimum noise impact.

Operating Hrs	0800-1600 (Summer) 0900-SS (Winter) & by arr	**Taxis**	Information available with PPR
		Car Hire	Hourly bus service passes AD
Circuits	26 LH, 08 RH, 1000ft QFE. No O/H joins	**Weather Info**	AirS MOEx
Landing Fee	Single £10 Twin £15, Other £7.50/tonne	**Operator**	West Wales Airport Ltd
Maintenance	Nil		Blaenanarch
Fuel	AVGAS Jet A1 100LL		Ceredigion
			SA43 2DW
			Tel: 01239 811100
			Fax: 01239 811555

Disabled Facilities

Restaurants   Light refreshments available

30ft 1mb	4nm SE of Bridgewater N5106.60 W00255.58	PPR	Alternative AD	Exeter Dunkeswell

Zoyland Microbase	LARS Yeovilton 127.350	A/G 129.825

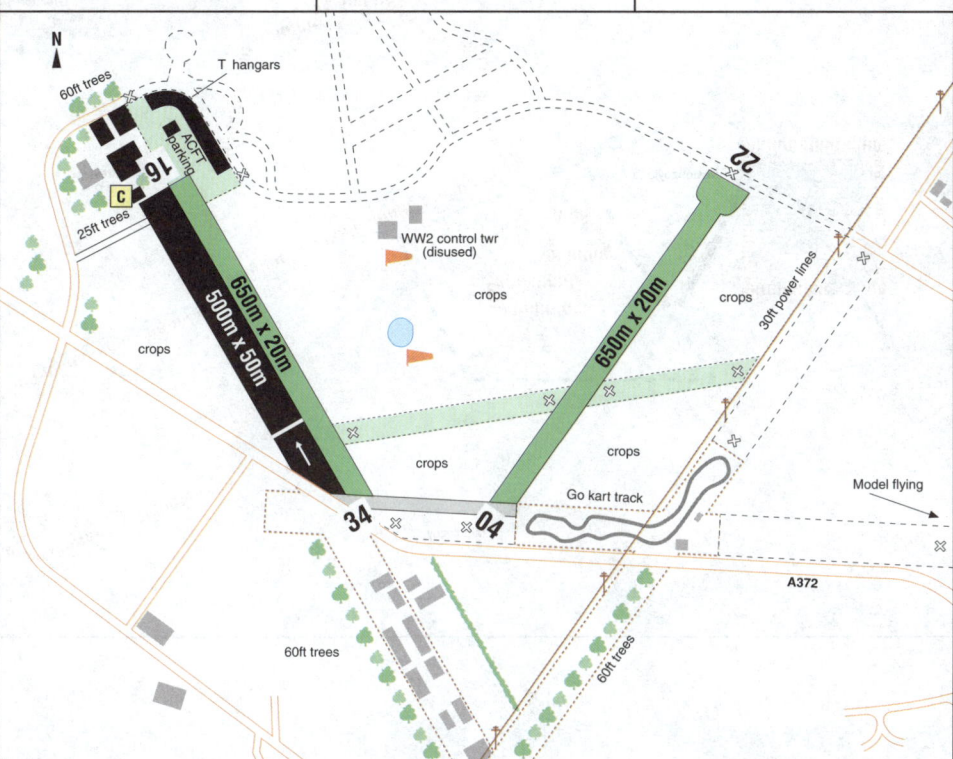

RWY	SURFACE	TORA	LDA	LIGHTING
16/34	Asphalt	500x50	U/L	Nil
16/34	Grass	650x20	U/L	Nil
04/22	Grass	650x20	U/L	Nil

Remarks
PPR by telephone. Visiting ACFT welcome at pilots own risk. Ab Initio Microlight training takes place. AD uses part of WW2 site, marked areas are useable. AD has other uses. On Sunday preferential Rwy04/22. New Twy between Rwy16/34 and Rwy04/22 opening during 2007

Warnings
Rwy16/34 Asphalt in good condition there are substantial trees final APP Rwy16 which may cause turbulence/windshear. Garden Centre on Rwy34 final.
Noise: ACFT to join overhead the windsock on control TWR at 1500ft, descending to deadside, remaining clear of Westonzoyland village. Resident ACFT join circuit downwind 800ft. See circuit diagram.

Operating Hrs	SR-SS	Operator	Westonzoyland Microlight School
Circuits	See Circuit diagram 800ft QFE		13 Taunton Road
Landing Fee	£3 for non members		Bridgwater
			Somerset
Maintenance	Nil		**Tel:** 07816 597063 (Club Mobile)
Fuel	Nil		**Tel:** 07970 710453 (Roger Whittall)
Disabled Facilities	Nil		info@westonzoylandflyingclub.co.uk
Restaurant	Nil		whittallmax@aol.com
Taxi/Car Hire	Nil		www.westonzoylandflyingclub.co.uk
Weather Info	MOEx		

W

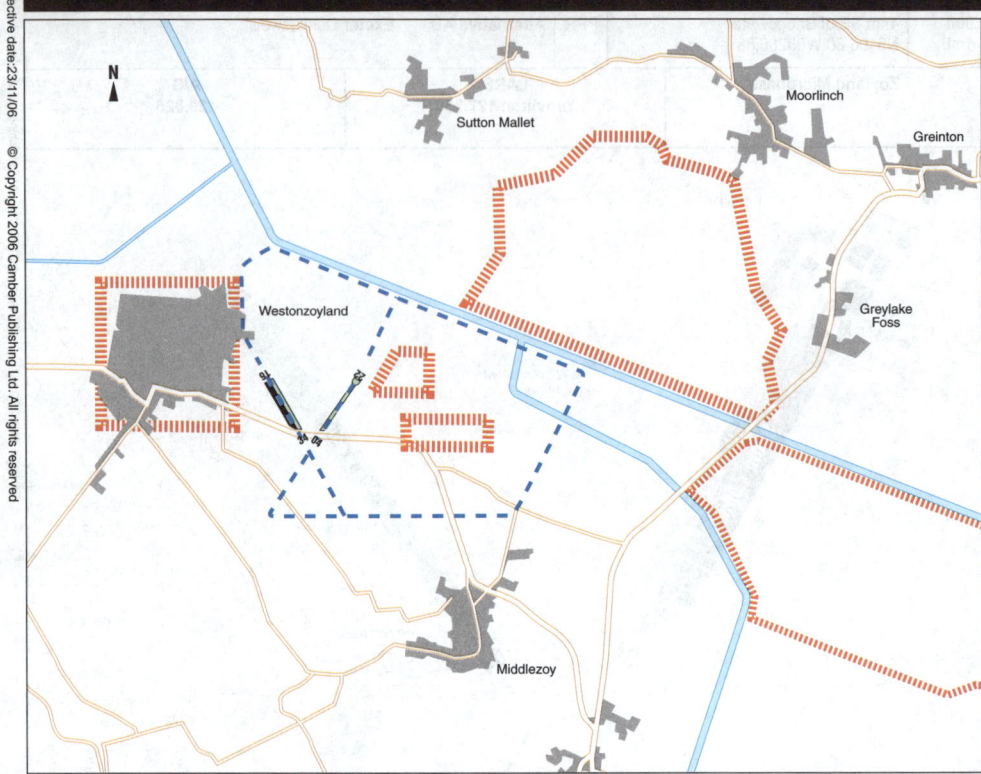

29ft 1mb	22nm N of Kirkwall Airport N5921.02 W00257.00	PPR	Alternative AD Diversion AD	Kirkwall Sanday

Non-radio	APP Kirkwall 118.300	Safetycom 135.475

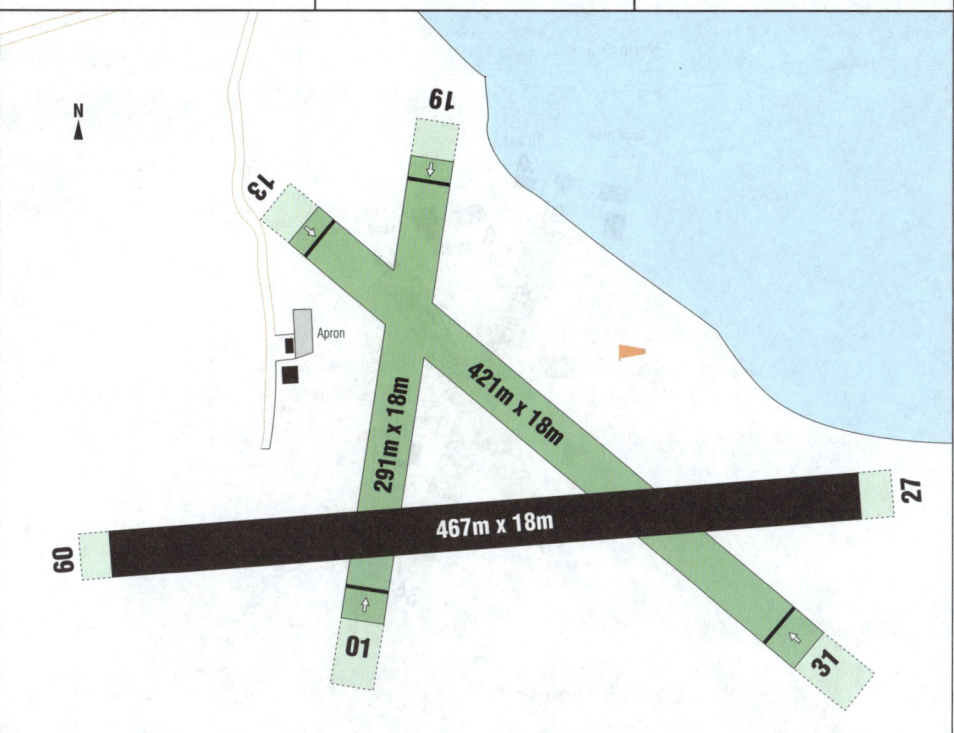

RWY	SURFACE	TORA	LDA	LIGHTING
09	Hard Core	467	467	Nil
27	Hard Core	467	467	Nil
13	Grass	394	359	Nil
31	Grass	421	359	Nil
01	Grass	261	235	Nil
19	Grass	291	218	Nil

Remarks
Scheduled service operates Mon-Sat. Contact AD Manager before landing.

Warnings
Rwys flooded after heavy rain.

Operating Hrs	SR-SS
Circuits	Nil
Landing Fee	Nil
Maintenance	Nil
Fuel	Nil
Disabled Facilities	Nil

Restaurants
Cleaton House   **Tel:** 01857 677508
cleaton@orkney.com

Taxis/Car Hire
Logies   **Tel:** 01857 677220
Harcus   **Tel:** 01857 677450
Mrs Groat   **Tel:** 01857 677374 (Sand O'Gill)

Bike Hire
Mrs Bain   **Tel:** 01857 677319 (Rapness)
Mrs Groat   **Tel:** 01857 677374 (Sand O'Gill)

Weather Info   AirSc GWC

Operator   Orkney Islands Council
Kirkwall, Orkney
Tel: 01856 873535
Fax: 01856 876094
Tel: 01857 677226 (AD Manager)
stephenhagan@onetel.net.uk

W

| 30ft 1mb | 3nm W of Sheringham N5256.81 E00107.32 | PPR | Alternative AD | Norwich Old Buckenham |

| Non-radio | LARS Norwich 119.350 | Safetycom 135.475 |

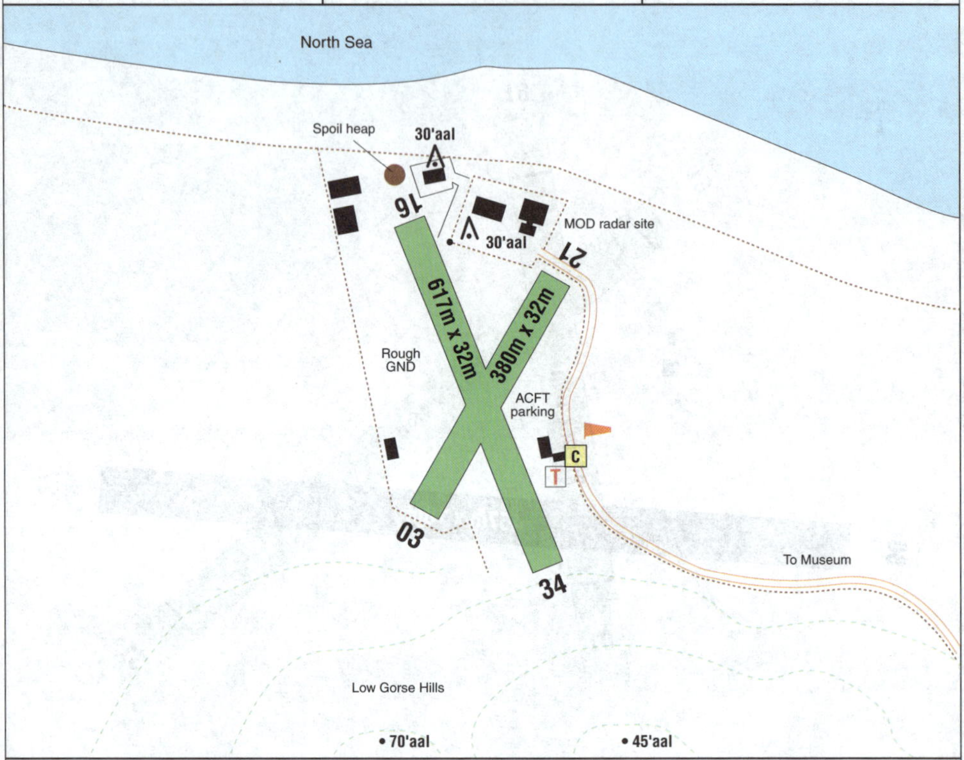

North Sea

Spoil heap

30'aal

30'aal

MOD radar site

16

617m x 32m

380m x 32m

21

Rough GND

ACFT parking

C

T

03

34

To Museum

Low Gorse Hills

• 70'aal   • 45'aal

RWY	SURFACE	TORA	LDA	LIGHTING
16/34	Grass	617x32	U/L	Nil
03/21	Grass	380x32	U/L	Nil

Rwy21 slight upslope
Rwy16 slight upslope first half

Remarks
Smallest WW2 RAF AD. Housing Muckleburgh collection of military vehicles (open Feb-Nov). Strips very well prepared & cut. PPR not required but third party insurance essential. Book-in at caravan key at side. Museum is short walk. Fly-ins welcome, special facilities can be arr (ie tank demonstrations). For personal tours or party arr at restaurant contact Collection manager.

Warnings
Rwy suface may suffer from rabbit scrapes, please exercise caution. Low gorse hills S of strip. White post at corner of MOD perimeter fence, encroaches edge Rwy16 Thr. Model ACFT may operate, one circuit before landing will GND aero-modellers.
Noise: Avoid over flying Weybourne & Kelling villages & MOD RAD site close Rwy21Thr. RAD site also has a number of other antennae (see AD chart).

Operating Hrs	SR-SS	Car Hire	Nil
Circuits	1000ft QFE	Weather Info	AirS MOEx
Landing Fee	£5 (Donation if not going to museum) £5.50 (Museum admission)	Operator	Muckleburgh Estates Weybourne Norfolk, NR25 7EG **Tel:** 01263 588210/588608 (Museum Office) **Fax:** 01263 588425
Maintenance	Nil		
Fuel	Nil		

Disabled Facilities

| Restaurants | Restaurant in museum complex |
| Taxis | **Tel:** 01263 822228 |

100ft 3mb	Shetland Islands N6022.62 W00055.33	**PPR**	**Alternative AD**	**Scatsta** Lerwick

Non-radio	**APP** Sumburgh 131.300	**Safetycom** 135.475

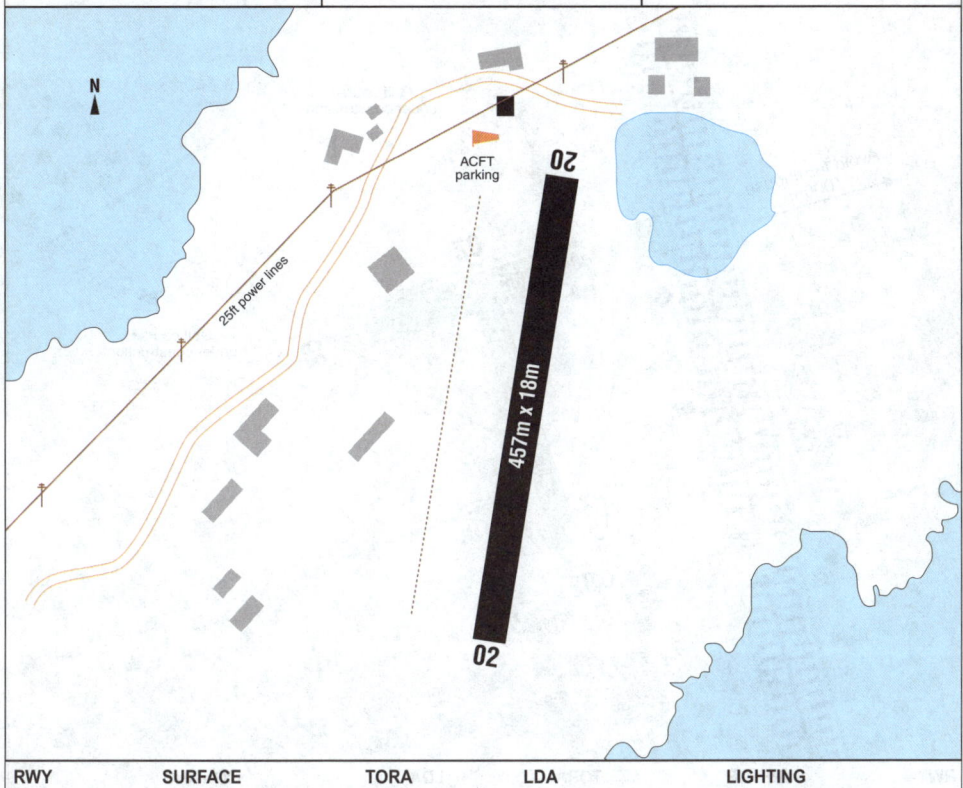

RWY	SURFACE	TORA	LDA	LIGHTING
02/20	Asphalt	457x18	U/L	Nil

Heavily weathered surface with many loose stones

Remarks
PPR by telephone. Main function is Air Ambulance Ops.

Warnings
Rwy surface poor with loose stones. Hill 390ft amsl 222° 3.4nm. AD used during daylight Hrs only. Sheep may be present on Rwy. Fence W of Rwy has been known to blow across the strip after high winds.

Operating Hrs	SR-SS	**Operator**	Whalsay Development Committee
Circuits	Suggest standard overhead join LH 1000ft QFE		Whalsay Aerodrome, Skaw Whalsay, Shetland Islands **Tel:** 01806 566449 (PPR via agent Mr Williamson)
Landing Fee	£4		
Maintenance	Nil		
Fuel	Nil		
Disabled Facilities	Nil		
Restaurants	Nil		
Taxis Angus Irvine	Transport can be provided by **Tel:** 01806 566208		
Car Hire	Nil		
Weather Info	AirSc GWC		

295ft 9mb	0.25nm W of Market Bosworth N5237.40 W00124.59	PPR	Alternative AD	Nottingham East Midlands Leicester

Non Radio	ATIS East Mids 128.225	APP East Mids 134.175	Safetycom 135.475

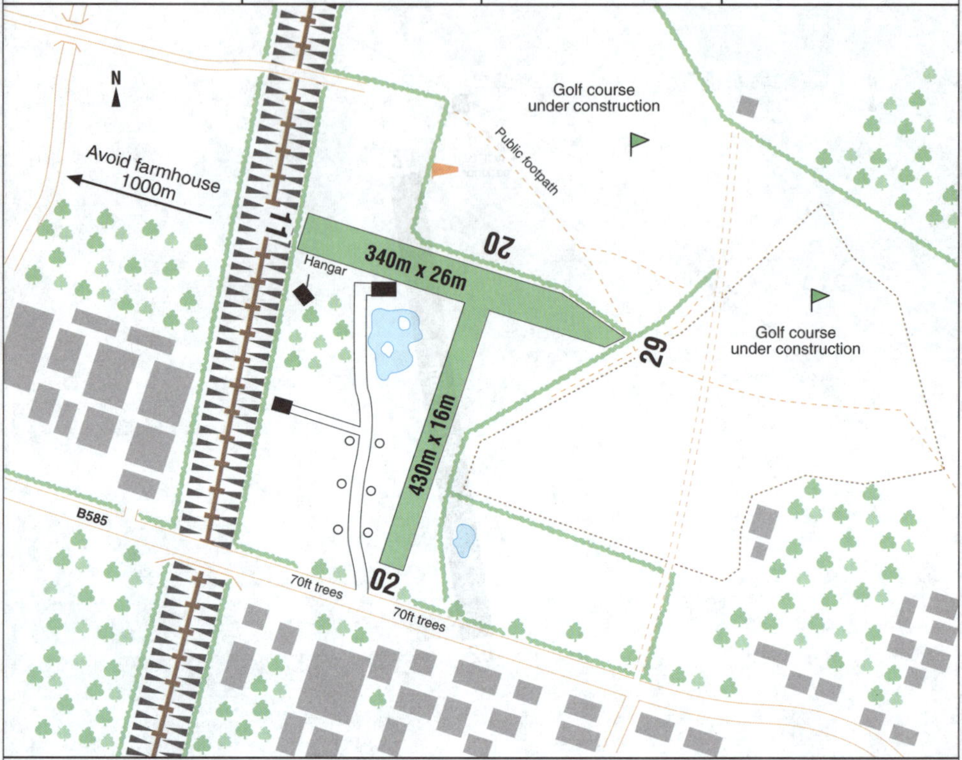

(Aerodrome diagram)

- N
- Avoid farmhouse 1000m
- 11
- 20
- 29
- 02
- Golf course under construction
- Public footpath
- 340m x 26m
- 430m x 16m
- Hangar
- B585
- 70ft trees
- 70ft trees
- Golf course under construction

RWY	SURFACE	TORA	LDA	LIGHTING
02/20	Grass	430x16	U/L	Nil
11/29	Grass	340x26	U/L	Nil

Remarks
PPR by telephone. Suitable STOL ACFT welcome at pilots own risk.

Warnings
Mature trees either side of short final Rwy02. Industrial buildings on opposite side of B585 from Rwy. Public footpath crosses short final Rwy29.Railway cutting crosses short final Rwy11, operated by Battlefield line preserved steam railway, operates at weekends only.
Caution: Position of low hedges adjacent to Rwy Thr. Electric fences at the side of Rwy. Construction traffic Crosses Rwy29 Thr,
Noise: Avoid over flying Market Bosworth E of AD and farmhouse 1000m out on Rwy29 climb out.

Operating Hrs	SR-SS	**Operator**	Mr L James
Circuits	02, 20 W, 11, 29 N, 800ft QFE		Wharf Farm
Landing Fee	Nil		Station Road, Market Bosworth
Maintenance	Nil		Leicestershire, CV13 0PG
Fuel	Nil		**Tel:** 01455 290258
Disabled Facilities			wharf.farm@tiscali.co.uk
Restaurants	Nil		
Taxis/Car Hire	Nil		
Weather Info	AirCen MWC		

360ft 12mb	7nm N of Aberdeen Airport N5719.40 W00214.30	**PPR**	**Alternative AD**	**Aberdeen** Insch

Non-Radio	**APP** Aberdeen 119.050	**Safetycom** 135.475

RWY	SURFACE	TORA	LDA	LIGHTING
10/28	Grass	595x46	U/L	Nil
18/36	Grass	700x18	U/L	Nil

Starter extension Rwy10 275m, Rwy10 downslope over first 300m, Rwy36 upslope on initial portion

Remarks

PPR by telephone essential. AD situated within Aberdeen CTR Class D Airspace. Hangarage available by arr. Pilots must read & comply with booking out procedure posted on hanger door.

Warnings

Exercise caution taxiing to hangar due to close proximity of parked ACFT at Rwy edge. Agricultural work takes place on grass up to Rwy edges.

Caution: 30ft trees Rwy28 Thr and along S egde of Rwy for first 150m. Grass cutting may be in progress periodically. Hills 678ft amsl 1.5nm SE. Windmill generator 0.8nm S. TV masts (Meldrum VRP) 1245ft amsl 5.5nm WNW. There are specific restrictions applied to Inbound and Dept ACFT by Aberdeen ATC please see specific VFR/SVFR routings.

Operating Hrs	Mon-Fri 0630-SS Sat-Sun 0730-SS	**Restaurant**	Nil
Circuits	Circuit patterns must be strictly followed to avoid conflict with Aberdeen APP traffic. Circuits should be kept within 1nm laterally from AD & maximum of 1.5nm final. 10 LH 28 RH 800ft but not above 600ft on base leg 36 LH 18 RH 800ft. All altitudes QNH	**Taxi** Swift Taxi **Car Hire**	Tel: 01651 862862 Nil
		Weather Info	AirSc GWC
		Operator	Arthur Simmers 1 Lochrew Place Bridge of Don AB23 8QG **Tel:** 07786 395961 paul@rhodes908.fslife.co.uk john@gadiehse.demon.co.uk bgfdl@btinternet.com
Landing Fee	£5		
Maintenance	Nil		
Fuel	Nil		
Disabled Facilities	☒		

W

583

WHITERASHES INBOUND & OUTBOUND ROUTES

Mandatory Actions

PPR essential and contact with Aberdeen ATC for flights to/from AD.

Pre-Take Off Actions:

Contact Aberdeen APP by Telephone to book out Tel: 01224 727159

A dept slot must be adheres to ± 5mins, or re-negotiated.

Attempt to establish contact with Aberdeen APP on GND, or at very latest 500ft, if unsuccessful, you **must** return to field and phone Aberdeen ATC.

Approach & Departure Routes:

Standard APP – from the N at less than 1000ft QNH. APP Old Meldrum Mast from N, (golf course with country house is entry point). Track 138°M to AD. DO NOT CONTINUE FURTHER S INTO THE ZONE IF AD NOT IN SIGHT.

Standard Dept – Track 312°M from AD to Old Meldrum Mast.

Alternative arr may be made with ATC, but remember you are in Controlled Airspace, close to ILS APP Rwy16.

133ft 5mb	2nm SW of Maidenhead N5130.05 W00046.47		Alternative AD Diversion AD	Farnborough Wycombe
	Waltham		**A/G 122.600**	

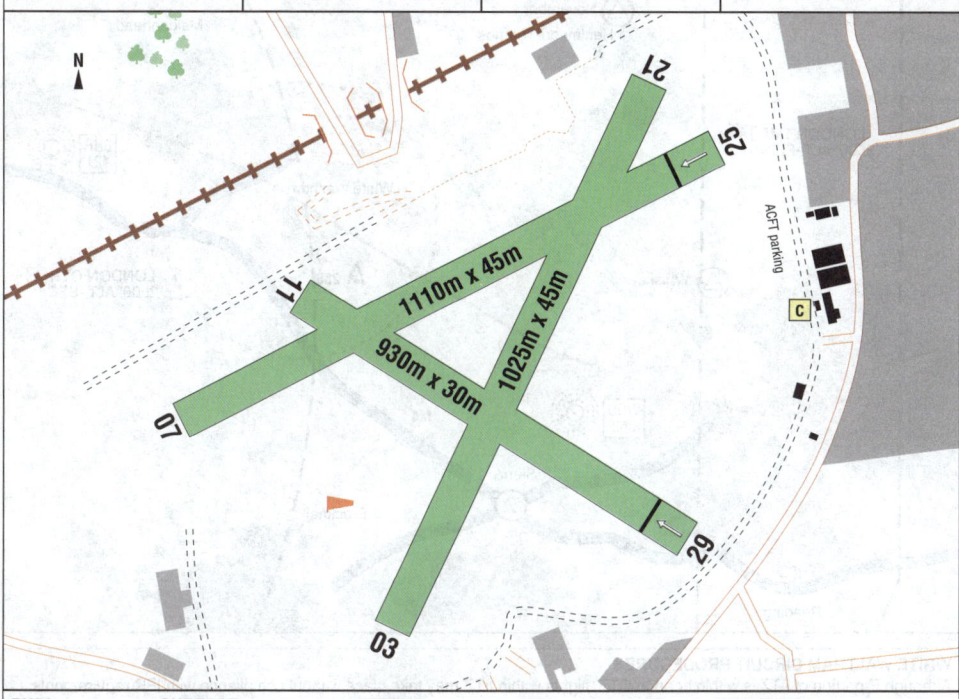

RWY	SURFACE	TORA	LDA	LIGHTING
03/21	Grass	1025	1025	Nil
07	Grass	1110	1110	Nil
25	Grass	1110	1045	Nil
11	Grass	930	930	Nil
29	Grass	930	867	Nil

Displaced Thr Rwy25 65m, Displaced Thr Rwy29 63m

Remarks
Aerobatic practice takes place on AD. No night operations on AD. No overhead depts. Run and break manoeuvres prohibited.

Warnings
Vehicular traffic not under control of AD uses the perimeter track which bounds the manoeuvring area to N & E of AD Pilots are to exercise extreme vigilance when taxiing.
Noise: Pilots of Dept ACFT are requested to conform with local noise abatement procedures. Available in the briefing room.

Operating Hrs	0700-SS +30mins or 1900 if earlier (Summer) 0800-SS +30mins (Winter) & by arr	**Taxis** Airport U-want	**Tel:** 01628 836726 **Tel:** 01628 822110
Circuits	07, 29 RH, 03, 11, 21, 25 LH, 800ft QFE Join overhead 1300ft QFE	**Car Hire** National	**Tel:** 0118 9352088
Landing Fee	Single £10, Twin £15. Free with fuel uplift, single 50ltr, twin 100ltr	**Weather Info** **Operator**	AirSE MOEx West London Aero Club
Maintenance WLAC **Fuel**	**Tel:** 01628 823276 AVGAS JET A1 100LL 0800-SS or 1900 if earlier (Summer) 0800-30 mins before SS (Winter)		White Waltham Aerodrome, Maidenhead, Berks, SL6 3NJ **Tel:** 01628 823272 **Fax:** 01628 826070 www.wlac.co.uk
Disabled Facilities Nil			
Restaurant	Licensed restaurant & club facilities available		

W

LONDON TMA [A]
2500' ALT–FL245

November
Henley-on-Thames

Maidenhead

LONDON TMA [A]
3500' ALT–FL245

BUR
421

White Waltham

Whiskey

⋀ 280

LONDON CTR [A]
2500' ALT–SFC

WOD
352

M4

Sierra

Bracknell

Reading

WHITE WALTHAM CIRCUIT PRODEDURES
Although E portion of ATZ is within London CTZ, flights within ATZ may take place without compliance with IFR requirements provided that:
1 ACFT must remain clear of cloud & in sight of surface.
2 ACFT must fly **not above 1500ft QNH** provided that ACFT can remain at least **500ft below cloud otherwise 1000ft QNH.**
3 Minimum flight visibility **3km.**
Pilots operating in local flying area are responsible for their own separation from other air traffic.
Dept Rwy07RH turn at end of Rwy onto 100°M

W

WHITE WALTHAM JOINING PROCEDURES
Fixed Wing – join overhead at 1300ft QFE.
Helicopters – Arr and Dept low level avoiding fixed wing circuit traffic and noise sensitive areas.

Visual Reporting Point (VRP)

From N:	**November**	Bend in the Thames N of Henley-on-Thames
From W:	**Whiskey**	N of gravel pits by Reading gasometers
From S:	**Sierra**	M4/A329M Jct N of Wokingham (M4 Jct 10)

EGPC   WICK

126ft 4mb	1nm N of Wick N5827.53 W00305.58	**PPR**	**Alternative AD Diversion AD**	**Kirkwall** Sanday

Wick	**ATIS** 113.600	**APP** 119.700	**AFIS** 119.700

TWR 119.700	**FIRE** 121.600	**Handling** Farnor 130.375	

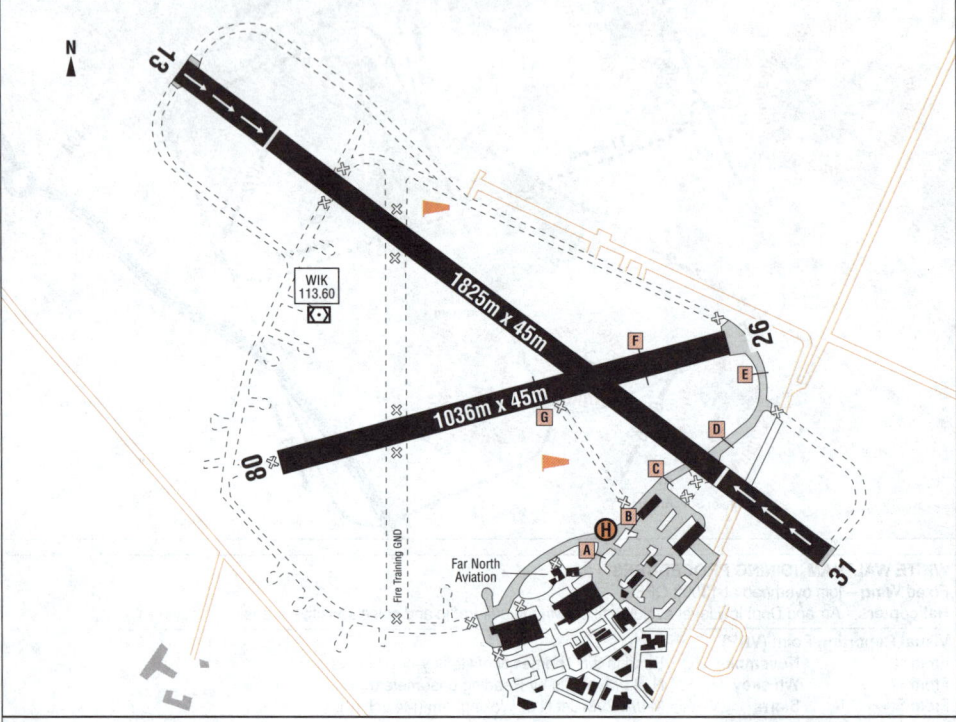

RWY	SURFACE	TORA	LDA	LIGHTING
08/26	Asphalt	1036	1036	Thr Rwy APAPI 4° LHS
13	Asphalt	1740	1400	Ap Thr Rwy PAPI 3° LHS
31	Asphalt	1708	1398	Ap Thr Rwy PAPI 3° LHS

Remarks
Grass areas soft sand unsafe, only marked Twys to be used. GA handling available from Far North Aviation free service with fuel uplift. Far North can provide accommodation & other useful advice.
Aids to Navigation: NDB WCK 344.00

Warnings
No GND signals except light signals. AD has deer hazard, particularly during dawn/dusk. Pilots are requested to report any animals on AD to ATC. Loop Twy (N of disused Control TWR, linking apron with Hangar 2) is available for ACFT with outer main gear span <6m.

Operating Hrs	Mon-Fri 0600-1730 1800-1945 Sat 0800-0924 1000-1345 (Summer) + 1Hr (Winter) & by arr	Handling	**Tel:** 01955 602201 (Far North Aviation) **Fax:** 01955 602203 (Far North Aviation) www.farnorthaviation.co.uk
Circuits	Nil	Restaurant	Buffet facilities available at AD
Landing Fee	£12 ACFT under 3MT VFR cash/cheque on day	Taxis Car Hire Practical Car Hire	Via Far North Via Far North or **Tel:** 01955 604125
Maintenance Fuel	By arr with Far North Aviation AVGAS JET A1 100LL Refuelling Hrs during AD Hrs with Far North outside AD Hrs by arr **Tel:** 01955 602201 (H24)	Weather Info	M T9 Fax 452 GWC ATIS **Tel:** 01955 607596
Disabled Facilities	Nil		

Visual Reference Points (VRP)	
Castletown	N5835.12 W00321.02
Duncansby Head Lighthouse	N5838.60 W00301.50
Keiss Village	N5832.00 W00307.40
Loch Watten	N5829.00 W00320.10
Lybster	N5818.00 W00317.10
Thrumster Masts	N5823.58 W00307.43

Operator	
	HIAL, Wick Aerodrome
	Wick, Caithness, KW1 4QP
	Tel: 01955 602215 (HIAL)
	Fax: 01955 604750 (ATC)
	wicksatco@hial.co.uk
	www.hial.co.uk/wick-airport.html

W

EGNW

WICKENBY

84ft 3mb	8nm NE of Lincoln N5319.02 W00020.93	PPR	Alternative AD	Humberside Retford Gamston

Wickenby	LARS Waddington 127.350	A/G 122.450

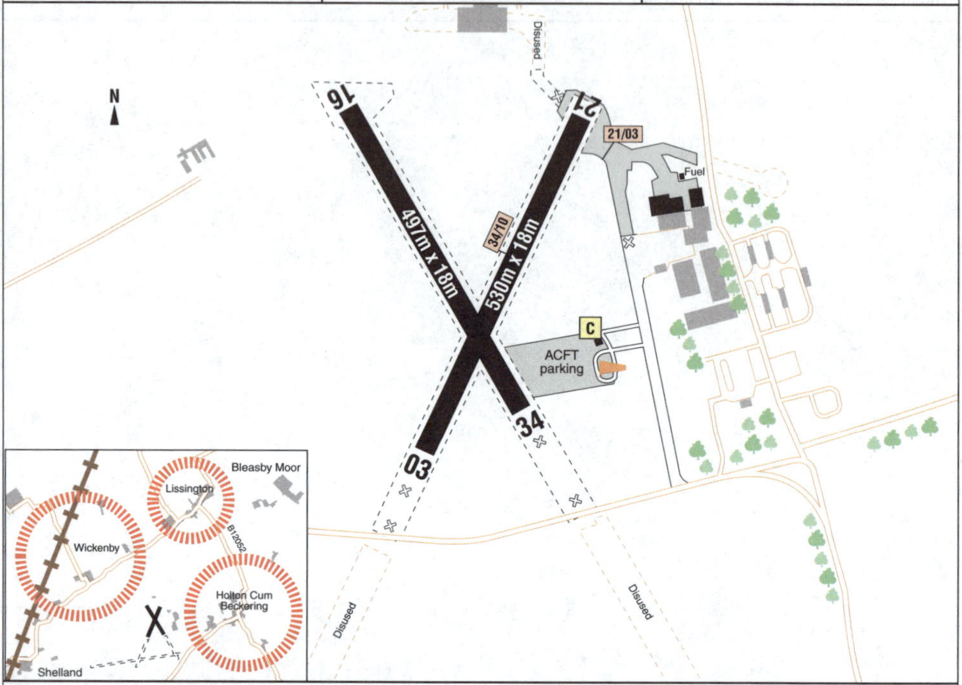

N

21/03

Fuel

497m x 18m

530m x 18m

34/10

C

ACFT parking

16

21

34

03

Disused

Bleasby Moor

Lissington

Wickenby

Holten Cum Beckering

Shelland

Disused

Disused

RWY	SURFACE	TORA	LDA	LIGHTING
03	Concrete	530	530	Nil
21	Concrete	530	530	Nil
16	Concrete	497	497	Nil
34	Concrete	497	497	Nil

Displaced Thr Rwy03 128m, Displaced Thr Rwy21 15m, Displaced Thr Rwy16 30m, Displaced Thr Rwy34 164m

Remarks
PPR by telephone. AD U/L on Monday. Inbound ACFT requested to contact RAF Waddington.
Visual aid to location: Ibn WN Green.

Warnings
Aerobatic training takes place SE corner of ATZ 800-3000ft, times notified by radio. No overhead join sduring active periods.
AD is divided by public road and only Rwys N of road can be used. A third Rwy09/27 is closed. HGVs cross Rwy21 Thr. All
ACFT flying in ATZ must contact Waddington before climbing above 1500ft QFE.
Noise: Avoid over flying the villages of Wickenby, Holton Cum Becking and Lissington.

Operating Hrs	0900-1800 (Summer) 0900-SS (Winter)	
Circuits	LH Light ACFT 1000ft QFE LH Microlights & Helicopters 700ft QFE	
Landing Fee	Single £7, Twin £14, Microlights £3.50	
Maintenance	JAR 145, FAA & PFA **Tel:** 01673 885966	
Fuel	AVGAS 100LL	

Taxis/Car Hire
Marriot Taxis   **Tel:** 01673 858541
   Tel: 07813 932282
County Cars   **Tel:** 01522 567878
Weather Info   AirN MWC
Operator   Wickeny Aerodrome LLP
The Old Control Tower
Wickenby Aerodrome
Langworth, Lincoln, LN3 5AX
Tel/Fax: 01673 885000
cas.projects@talk21.com
Tel: 01673 885111
(Fly365 Ltd Microlight School)
info@fly365.co.uk
www.fly365.co.uk

W

Disabled Facilities

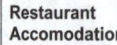

Restaurant Club facilities & restaurant
Accomodation
Redhurst B&B   **Tel:** 01673 857927

WING FARM

420ft 14mb	2nm SSW of Warminster N5109.80 W00212.51	PPR	Alternative AD	Bristol Compton Abbas

Non-Radio	LARS Boscombe 126.700	LARS Yeovilton 127.350	Safetycom 135.475

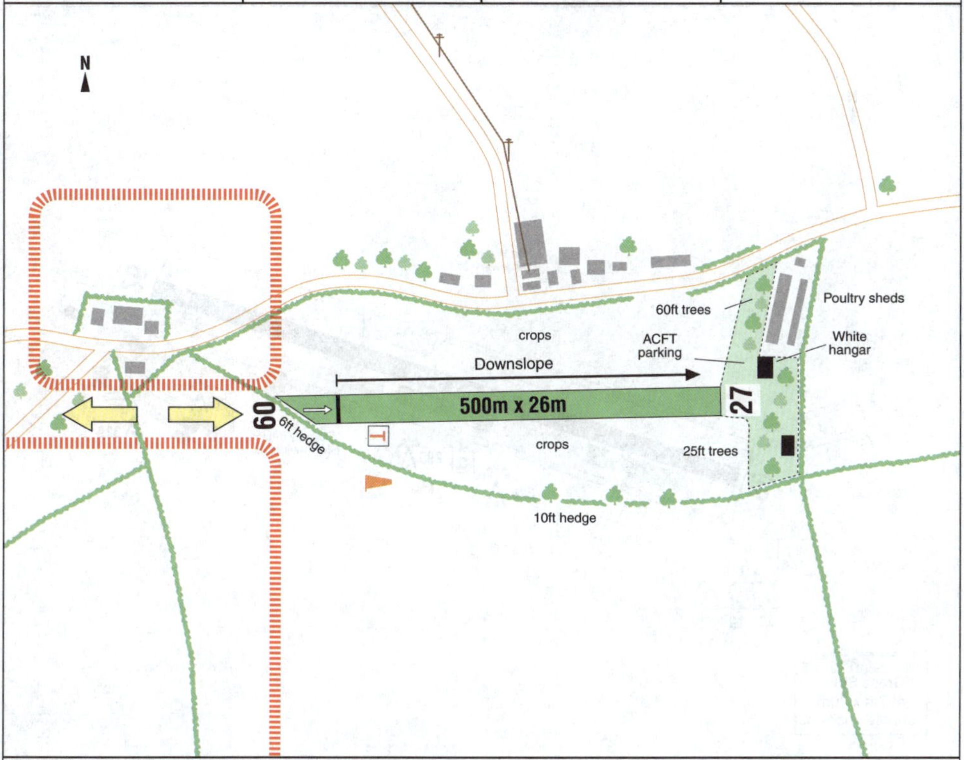

N

Poultry sheds

60ft trees

ACFT parking

White hangar

crops

Downslope

500m x 26m

60

6ft hedge

27

crops

25ft trees

10ft hedge

RWY	SURFACE	TORA	LDA	LIGHTING
09/27	Grass	350x26	U/L	Nil

Rwy09 2.2% downslope

Remarks
PPR. Visiting ACFT welcome at pilot's own risk. Pilots MUST be capable of STOL operations. Take off run ltd to 350m, leaving 150m stopping distance. Rwy is well prepared cut strip. White 'T' markers mark Rwy & Thrs. Long-term parking available.

Warnings
Surface may be soft especially Jan-Apr. Movements confined to strip and parking area. Electric power cables 500m out on Rwy09 APP. Glider site, 'The Park' 3nm SSW of AD. Beware cables up to 3000ft agl. D123 3nm NNE of AD activity info available from Boscombe APP.
Noise: Avoid low flying over the local habitation, particularly the houses marked either side of Rwy09 APP. Make straight in APP/climb-out until well clear of the houses.

Operating Hrs	SR-SS	**Taxis**	
Circuits	500ft QFE	DJ's Taxis	**Tel:** 01985 215151
Landing Fee	Private ACFT £5, Microlights £3	**Car Hire**	
	Have correct money, no change available	**Weather Info**	AirSW MOEx
	Overnight parking: Private ACFT £3, Microlights £2	**Operator**	Mr Earl W B Trollope
Maintenance	Airbourne Composites		Wing Farm
	Tel: 01985 840981		Longbridge Deverill
Fuel	Nil, Petrol station 0.75 of mile		Warminster
Disabled Facilities			Wilts BA12 7DD
			Tel/Fax: 01985 840401

Restaurants/Accommodation
The George Inn   **Tel:** 01985 840396 Longbridge Deverill

W

273ft	3nm S of Stamford	PPR	Alternative AD	Nottingham East Midlands
9mb	N5236.75 W00028.60	MIL	Diversion AD	Peterborough Conington

Wittering	LARS Cottesmore 130.200	DIR Cottesmore 123.300	TWR 125.525

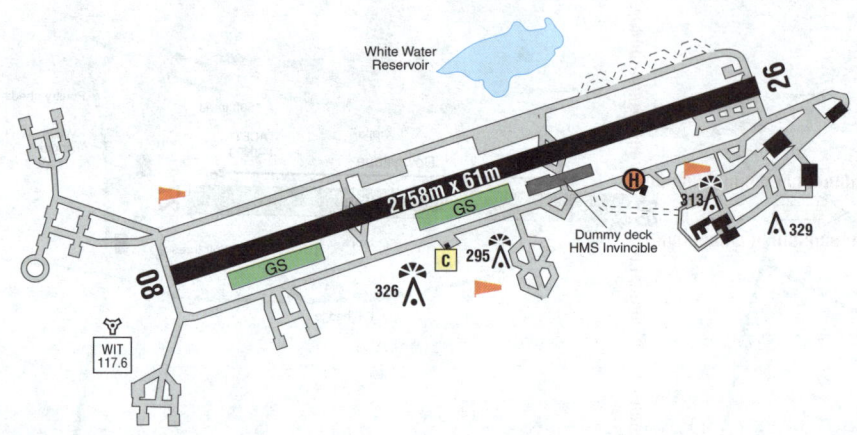

RWY	SURFACE	TORA	LDA	LIGHTING
08	Asphalt	2759	2744	Ap Thr Rwy PAPI 3° LHS
26	Asphalt	2759	2759	Ap Thr Rwy PAPI 3° LHS

Remarks

PPR by telephone essential. RAF AD with based high performance ACFT. AD Situated within CMATZ with Cottesmore who are the controlling authority.
Visual aid to location: Ibn Red

Warnings

AD has various areas of Twy & dispersals carrying non-standard markings associated with Harrier STOL strips. Also numerous cut grass strips within AD boundary. These areas are for use of based AD ONLY. Hovering and variable ciruits in operation at all times. Gliding winch launch to 3000ft Mon-Fri 0800-1515 Sat 0900-1030 1600-SS Sun 1200-1300 1600-SS (Summer) + 1Hr (Winter) & by arr
Noise: Over flight of domestic site to SE and fenced compounds to SW is forbidden to fixed wing ACFT below 1000ft QFE.

		Operator	RAF Wittering
Operational Hrs	0800-1730 (Summer) 0800-1700 (Winter)		Stamford, Lincs
Circuits	Light ACFT 26 LH, 08 RH, 800ft QFE Jet ACFT 1200ft No deadside		**Tel:** 01780 783838 Ex 7052
Landing Fee	Charges in accordance with MOD policy Contact Station Ops for details		
Maintenance	Not available to visiting ACFT		
Fuel	JET A1 strictly by prior arr only		
Disabled Facilities	Nil		
Taxi/Car Hire	Nil		
Weather Info	M T Fax454 MOEx		

283ft 10mb	5nm E by S of Bridgnorth N5231.05 W00215.57	**PPR**	**Alternative AD**	**Birmingham** Tatenhill

	Wolverhampton	**AFIS** 123.000

RWY	SURFACE	TORA	LDA	LIGHTING
04	Asphalt	635	605	Nil
22	Asphalt	635	545	Nil
10/28	Asphalt	880	880	Thr Rwy APAPI 4° LHS
16	Asphalt	1079	872	Nil
34	Asphalt	1096	909	Nil
10/28	Grass	350x18	U/L	Nil

Starter extension Rwy10 49m
Starter extension Rwy28 45m
Displaced Thr Rwy04 30m
Displaced Thr Rwy22 90m
Displaced Thr Rwy10 158m
Displaced Thr Rwy28 140m
Displaced Thr Rwy16 219m
Displaced Thr Rwy34 187m

Remarks
PPR. Hi Vis only. Rwy10/28 licensed for night use. Pilots are responsible for their passengers whilst airside. Helicopters not to be flown within 50m of DME mast NE of apron.
Visual aid to location: IBn flashing green WBA.

Warnings
Rwy10/28 lighting outside Hrs for police ops only. Police helicopters may operate outside normal Hrs.
Noise: Dept Rwy16 to maintain track for 600m before turning, avoid Highgate Farm Completely. No fan stop Rwy34 until beyond 1000m past Thr.

Operating Hrs	Mon-Fri 0700-1900 Sat-Sun & PH 0900-1900 (L)	**Circuits**	Helicopters RH 800ft QFE. Joining ACFT keep >1300ft QFE dead side

Landing Fee	Singles £10, Twin <3Tonne £20.00, Twin >3 Tonne £35 + £15 per tonne, Microlights £7.50	**Operator**	Wolverhampton Airport Ltd

Landing Fee — Singles £10, Twin <3Tonne £20.00, Twin >3 Tonne £35 + £15 per tonne, Microlights £7.50

Maintenance

MAM — **Tel:** 01384 221302

Fuel — AVGAS JET A1 100LL
Oil W80 W100.80 100 by arr

Disabled Facilities

Restaurants — Café OK open daily

Taxis — **Tel:** 01384 404040
Tel: 01384 296362

Car Hire — **Tel:** 01384 424666

Weather Info — AirCen MWC

Operator

Wolverhampton Airport Ltd
Wolverhampton Airport
Stourbridge
West Midlands, DY7 5DY
Tel: 01384 221350 (Admin)
Tel: 01384 221378 (ATC)
Tel: 0808 1003362
Fax: 01384 221514 (ATC)
info@wolverhamptonairport.co.uk
atc@wolverhamptonairport.co.uk
www.wolverhamptonairport.co.uk

594

W

120ft 4mb	8nm W of Pickering N5414.02 W00058.13	PPR	Alternative AD Diversion AD	Humberside Sherburn in Elmet

Non-radio	LARS Leeming 127.750	Safetycom 135.475

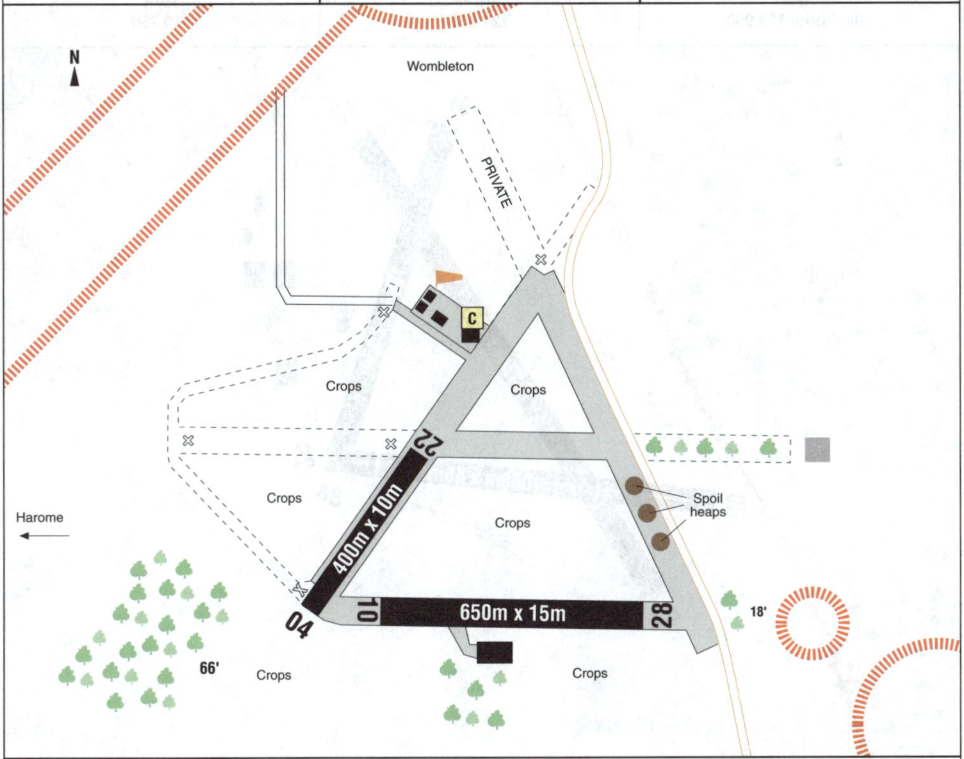

Map of Wombleton airfield showing N arrow, villages of Wombleton and Harome, PRIVATE area, runways, Crops areas, Spoil heaps, trees (66', 18'), and runway layout labelled 22, 04, 10, 28, 400m x 10m, 650m x 15m, with C marker.

RWY	SURFACE	TORA	LDA	LIGHTING
10/28	Concrete	650x15	U/L	Nil
04/22	Asphalt	400x10	U/L	Nil

Rwy10/28 prefered

Remarks
PPR by telephone. Visitors welcome at own risk. Park ACFT near old TWR & enter flight details in AD log. Microlight activity. Former Twy and Rwy to W of Rwy04/22 are unusable by ACFT.

Warnings
Farm vehicles, pedestrians, animals & model ACFT may be encountered on AD, please be alert to Rwy incursion at any time. AD surfaces rough with loose stones & grass growth at joints. 70ft trees 200m Rwy10 Thr. Public road bounded by25ft trees 150m Rwy28 Thr. 2 private strips in N portion of AD not to be used by visitors. Kirkbymoorside AD 1.5nm NE of Wombleton.
Noise: Do not over fly the villages of Wombleton & Harome to W & N of AD. Please modify APP to avoid local houses & obstructions.

Operating Hrs	Available on request	**Weather Info**	AirN MWC
Circuits	Light ACFT 04, 10 RH, 22, 28 LH, 1000ft QFE. Microlights 04, 28 RH, 10, 22 LH, 500ft QFE	**Operator**	Windsports Centre Ltd Wombleton Airfield North Yorkshire **Tel/Fax:** 01751 432356
Landing Fee	Private Nil Commercial may be charged a small fee		
Maintenance	Nil		
Fuel	Nil		
Disabled Facilities			

  P

Restaurant	Tea & coffee available
Taxis/Car Hire	Can be arr on Arr

EGOW

WOODVALE

37ft 1mb	4.5nm SSW of Southport N5334.89 W00303.33	PPR MIL	Alternative AD Diversion AD	Liverpool Blackpool

Woodvale	LARS Warton 125.925	APP Liverpool 119.850

APP Blackpool 119.950	APP 121.000	TWR 119.750

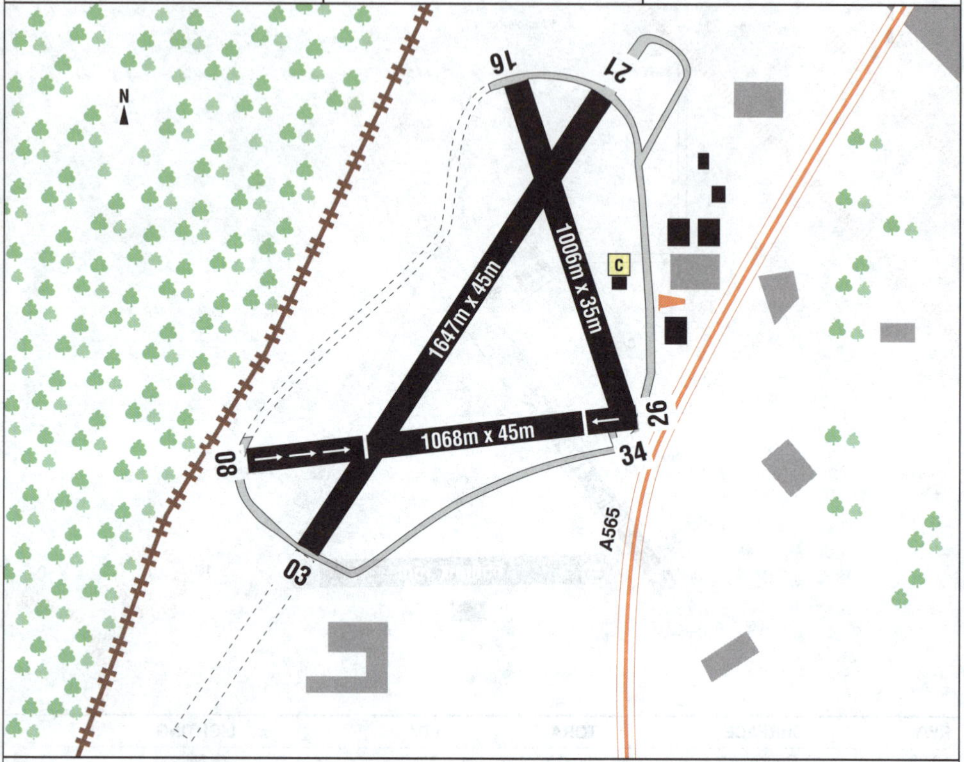

Airport diagram showing runways 16/34, 03/21, 08/26 with dimensions 1647m x 45m, 1006m x 35m, 1068m x 45m. Taxiway marked C. Road A565 to the east.

RWY	SURFACE	TORA	LDA	LIGHTING
03/21	Asphalt	1649	1644	Nil
08	Asphalt	1056	710	Nil
26	Asphalt	1056	918	Nil
16	Asphalt	1006	610	Nil
34	Asphalt	1006	869	Nil

Remarks
PPR to private and charter ACFT. Light ACFT activity SR-SS +30min outside AD Hrs. Circuit can be very busy with University Air Squadron ACFT. Police helicopter activity H24.

Warnings
Full obstacle clearance criteria not met on APP to all Rwys. Considerable risk of bird strike. Taxi routes as per ATC.

Operating Hrs	Tue-Sun 0700-1700 or SS if earlier (Summer) +1Hr (Winter) Available in summer any 6 days out of 7 Sometimes 7 days a week notified by NOTAM	**Restaurants**	Numerous in Southport
		Taxis	
		White	**Tel:** 01704 527777
		Yellow	**Tel:** 01704 531000
		Car Hire	
Circuits	03 08 LH, 21 26 RH 800ft QFE	Dewerdens	**Tel:** 01704 533066
Landing Fee	Charges in accordance with MOD policy Contact Station Ops for details	**Weather Info**	AirCen MWC
		Operator	RAF Woodvale
Maintenance	Nil		Formby, Liverpool, L37 7AD
Fuel	AVGAS 100LL (Ltd) Military Account holders only		**Tel:** 01704 872287 Ex 7243 **Fax:** 01704 834805 (Flight Plans)

Disabled Facilities

520ft 19mb	2.4nm SW of High Wycombe N5136.70 W00048.50	PPR	Alternative AD Diversion AD	Oxford White Waltham

Wycombe	TWR 126.550	GND 121.775

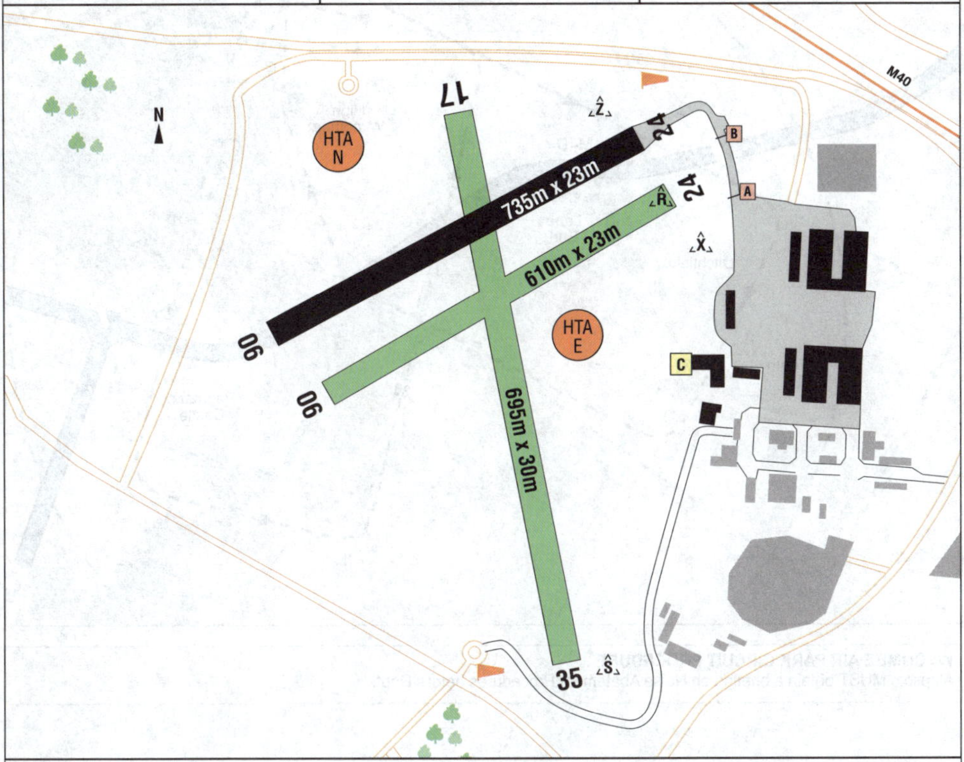

[Aerodrome chart: runway diagram showing Rwy 17/35, Rwy 06/24 Asphalt 735m x 23m, Rwy 06/24 Grass 610m x 23m, Rwy 17/35 Grass 695m x 30m, with HTA N and HTA E helicopter areas, taxiways A, B, C, and M40 motorway. North arrow shown.]

RWY	SURFACE	TORA	LDA	LIGHTING
06/24	Asphalt	735	735	Thr Rwy APAPI 4°
06/24	Grass	610	610	Nil
17/35	Grass	695	695	Nil

Remarks

PPR. When Rwy17/35 in use, Rwy06/24 is PPR Mon-Fri Sat-Sun 2Hrs. Gliders fly a circuit opposite direction to powered ACFT. Joining ACFT must position to over fly AD at 1200ft QFE on Rwy QDM. When overhead the midpoint of Rwy turn left or right (depending on circuit direction) to level at circuit height 1000ft QFE on cross wind leg prior to turning downwind. Helicopter circuit height 750ft QFE.
Visual aid to location: Ibn WP Green.

Warnings

AD is situated below London Terminal Control Area. AD is liable to water logging. Intense gliding takes place on & around AD. Helicopters operate inside fixed-wing circuits. Helicopters must remain well clear of housing area E of Rwy17/35.
Noise: Procedures are enforced – pilots must obtain a briefing before dept Visiting ACFT will not be accepted without PPR including a briefing

Operating Hrs	0800-1630 (Summer) 0900-1600 (Winter) & by arr	**Car Hire** National	Tel: 01494 527853
Circuits	Variable 1000ft QFE	**Weather Info**	AirSE MOEx
Landing Fee	£13 up to 1.5MT	**Operator**	Airways Aero Associations Ltd Wycombe Air Park, Booker, Marlow Buckinghamshire, SL7 3DP **Tel:** 01494 529261 (Admin/ATC) **Tel:** 01494 529262 (BA Flying Club) **Fax:** 01494 438657 (ATC) **Fax:** 01494 461237 (Admin) www.bafc.co.uk
Maintenance	Available		
Fuel	AVGAS JET A1 100LL		

Disabled Facilities

Restaurants   Restaurant & refreshments available

Taxis
Neales   **Tel:** 01494 463399

WYCOMBE AIR PARK CIRCUIT PROCEDURE
All pilots MUST obtain a briefing on Noise Abatement Procedures before Dept.

135ft 4mb	3nm NE of Huntingdon N5221.43 W00006.47	PPR MIL	Alternative AD Diversion AD	Cambridge Peterborough Conington

Wyton	APP 134.050	GND 122.100	TWR 119.975	A/G 134.050

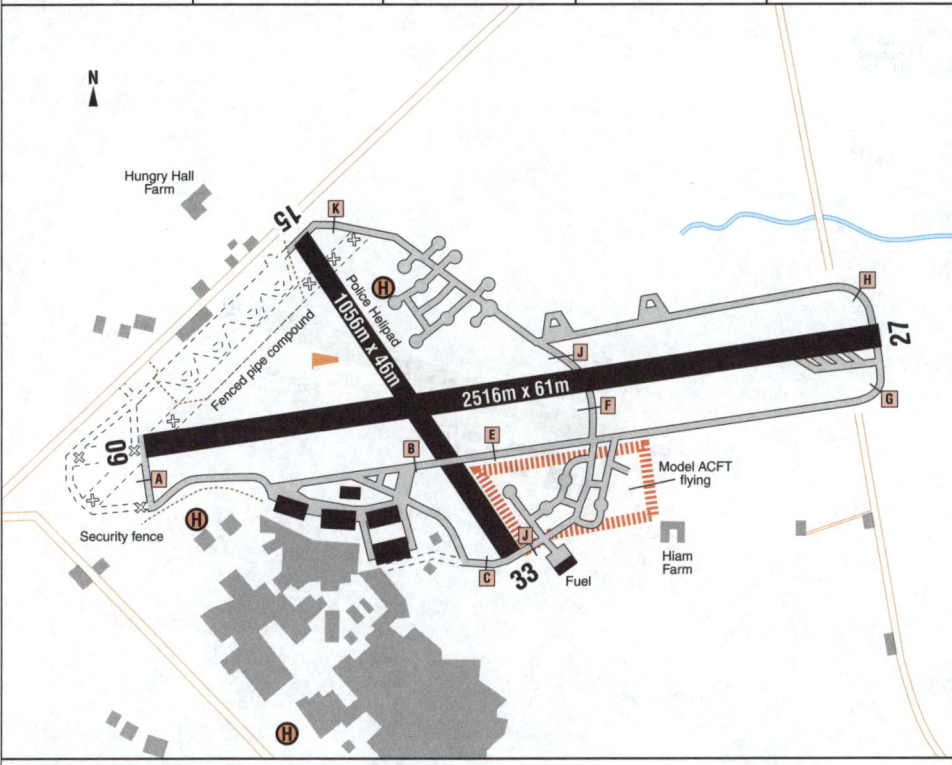

RWY	SURFACE	TORA	LDA	LIGHTING
09/27	Asph/Conc	2516	2516	Nil
15	Asph/Conc	1056	770	Nil
33	Asph/Conc	1056	1056	Nil

Remarks
PPR. Strictly by telephone. RAF AD, intensive ab-initio flying training by UAS ACFT.

Warnings
Turbulence may be encountered over Rwy when wind from S and greater than 15kts. Twy clearance reduced to 17.5 m from centreline to fence S of Rwy09 holding point, Twy available to light ACFT only. Locally based ACFT and Microlights operate outside normal AD Hrs. Model ACFT operate outside AD Hrs within designated area. Rwy27 non standard markings.
Noise: Avoid Huntingdon town, the village of Woodhurst 1.5nm N of Rwy27 Thr and Raptor foundation 2.75nm Rwy27 final APP.

Operating Hrs	0830-1700 & by arr	**Operator**	VT Aerospace
Circuits	09 LH, 27 RH, 800ft QFE		RAF Wyton
Landing Fee	Charges in accordance with MOD policy Contact Station Ops for details		Huntingdon, Cambs **Tel:** 01480 52451 Ex 6412 **Fax:** 01480 446783 (ATC)
Maintenance	Nil		
Fuel	AVGAS 100LL by prior arr		
Disabled Facilities	Nil		
Restaurant	Nil		
Taxi/Car Hire	Nil		
Weather Info	AirCen MOEx		

W

30ft 1mb	2nm S of Redcar N5435.01 W00103.93	PPR	Alternative AD	Durham Tees Valley Fishburn

Non-radio	LARS Durham 118.850	Safetycom 135.475

ICI industrial complex

A174

N

Crops

635m x 12m

25

07

Low hedge

Farm track

C

Pond

125ft power lines

B1269

Yearby village

RWY	SURFACE	TORA	LDA	LIGHTING
07/25	Grass	635x12	U/L	Nil

Remarks
PPR by telephone essential. Windsock displayed with PPR. AD situated close to boundary of Durham Tees Valley CTR/CTA. Contact Durham APP on Arr/Dept. Full airstrip details on website.

Warnings
Power lines 125ft agl cross Rwy25 final APP approx 600m from Thr with a pylon on the centreline.
Noise: Avoid over flying village of Yearby, ICI chemical plant NW & Redcar.

Operating Hrs	SR-SS	**Taxis**	**Tel:** 01642 474849
Circuits	Any convenient height Over head joins essential	**Car Hire**	Nil
		Weather Info	AirN MWC
Landing Fee	Private Nil Commercial rates with PPR	**Operator**	Yearby Airstrip Trust Turners Arms Farm
Maintenance	Nil		Yearby
Fuel	Nil		Redcar
Disabled Facilities			North Yorkshire
			TS11 8HH

Tel: 01642 470322 (Barry Smith)
acro@btinternet.com
www.acro.co.uk

Restaurants Nil

EGHG

YEOVIL

202ft 7mb	1nm W by S of Yeovil N5056.40 W00239.52	PPR	Alternative AD Diversion AD	Bristol Compton Abbas

Westland	LARS Yeovilton 127.350	APP Yeovil 130.800	TWR Yeovil 125.400	A/G 125.400

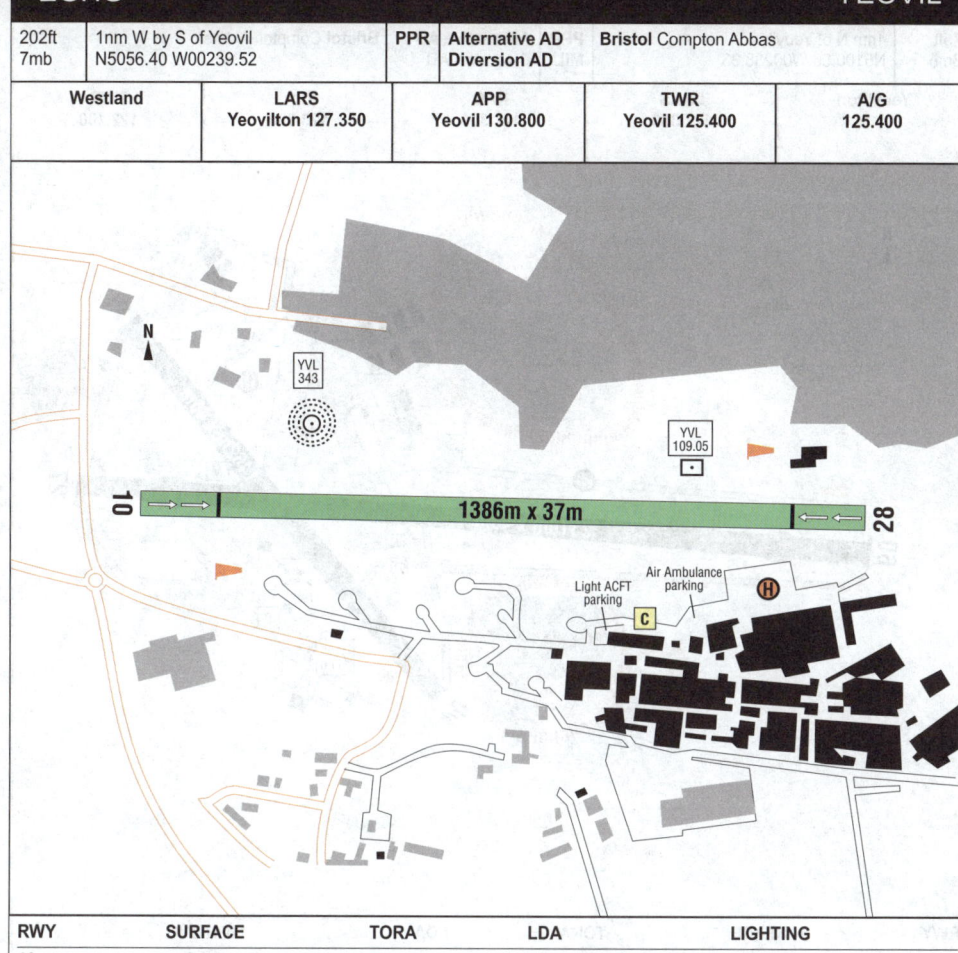

RWY	SURFACE	TORA	LDA	LIGHTING
10	Grass	1319	1224	Nil
28	Grass	1319	1124	Nil

Remarks
PPR 24Hrs Licensed for night Ops by helicopters only. Circuits S of Rwy due to proximity of Yeovilton. Visiting ACFT may be delayed due to helicopter test flying.

Warnings
Windshear on Rwy28 APP. Displaced landing Thr. AD surface is convex with a pronounced gradient to S at Rwy10 Thr. Caution required after heavy rain. Model ACFT, light ACFT & helicopter flying takes place outside normal Hrs. High GND rising to 442ft amsl 2.5nm to SW with radio mast 528ft amsl. Trees on high GND rising to 400ft amsl 1nm to E. Aerial mast 471ft amsl 0.8nm NW. Beware of bird concentrations.
Noise: Avoid over flying houses adjacent to NW, N & E boundaries.

Operating Hrs	Mon-Thu 0800-1530 Fri 0800-1430 except PH (Summer) +1Hr (Winter)	**Operator**	Westland Helicopters Ltd Yeovil Aerodrome, Yeovil Somerset, BA20 2YB **Tel:** 01935 475222 ask for ATC **Fax:** 01935 703055
Circuits	S 1000ft See Remarks		
Landing Fee	Available with PPR		
Maintenance	Nil		
Fuel	JET A1 by arr with PPR		
Disabled Facilities	Nil		
Restaurant	Light refreshments available		
Taxis/Car Hire	On request to ATC before or after landing (Booked via ATC to comply with security restrictions)		
Weather Info	M* T9 MOEx		

75ft 3mb	4nm N of Yeovil N5100.56 W00238.33	PPR MIL	Alternative AD Diversion AD	Bristol Compton Abbas

Yeovilton	LARS 127.350	RAD 127.350	DIR 123.300	TWR 122.100

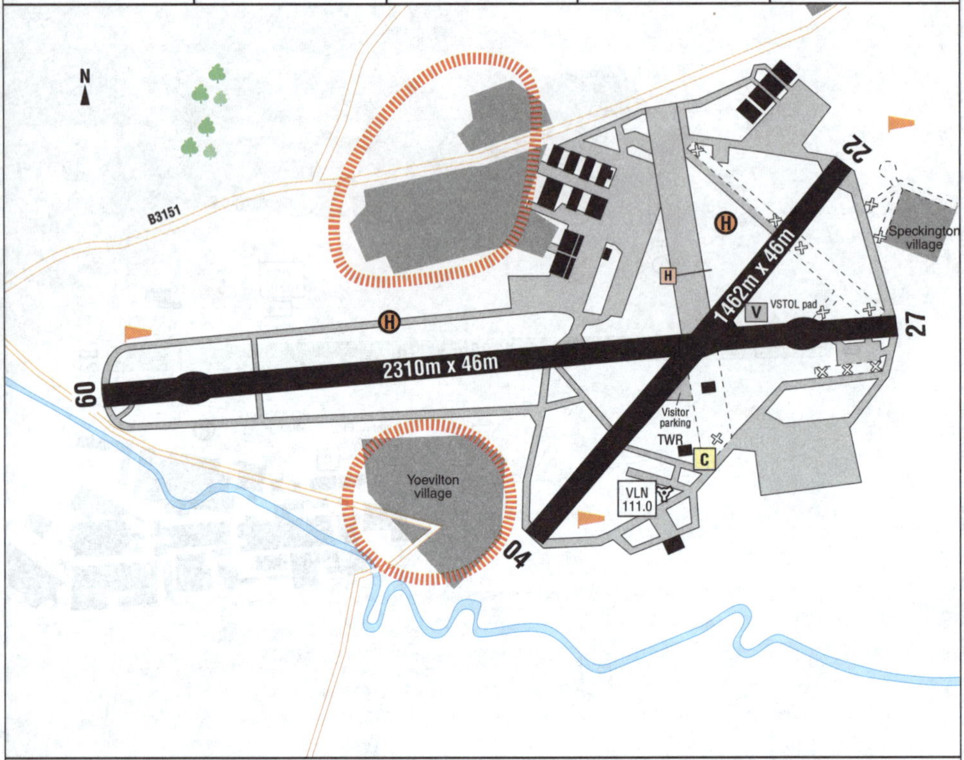

RWY	SURFACE	TORA	LDA	LIGHTING
09	Concrete	2310	2310	Ap Thr Rwy PAPI 3°
27	Concrete	2310	2287	Ap Thr Rwy PAPI 3°
04	Concrete	1462	1462	Ap Thr Rwy PAPI 3°
22	Concrete	1462	1462	Ap Thr Rwy PAPI 3.25°

Remarks
Visiting ACFT call APP at 20nm range. Outside published Ops Hrs AD is not available to civil ACFT.

Warnings
Glider flying takes place outside normal Ops Hrs. High intensity mixed jet and helicopter activity. 2 Rwys may be in use at the same time. Special rules for helicopters. Constant helicopter transit traffic between Yeovilton and Merryfield 7nm WSW. Turbulence and windshear may be experienced on short final Rwy27.

		Operator	RNAS Yeovilton
Operating Hrs	Mon-Thur 0830-1700 Fri 0800-1400 (L)		Yeovilton, Somerset, BA22 8HT
Circuits	04, 09 RH, 22, 27 LH, 1000ft QFE		**Tel:** 01935 455497 (PPR)
Landing Fee	Charges in accordance with MOD policy Contact Station Ops for details		**Tel:** 01935 455262 (ATC)
Maintenance	Nil		
Fuel	AVGAS JET A1 100LL		

Disabled Facilities

Restaurants	Nil
Taxis/Car Hire	Nil
Weather Info	M T Fax 456 MOEx **Tel:** 01935 455426

65ft 2mb	3nm W of York N5356.83 W00110.24		**PPR**	**Alternative AD Diversion AD**	**Leeds Bradford** Sherburn in Elmet

Rufforth	**LARS** Linton 118.550	**LARS** Fenton 126.500	**A/G** 129.975

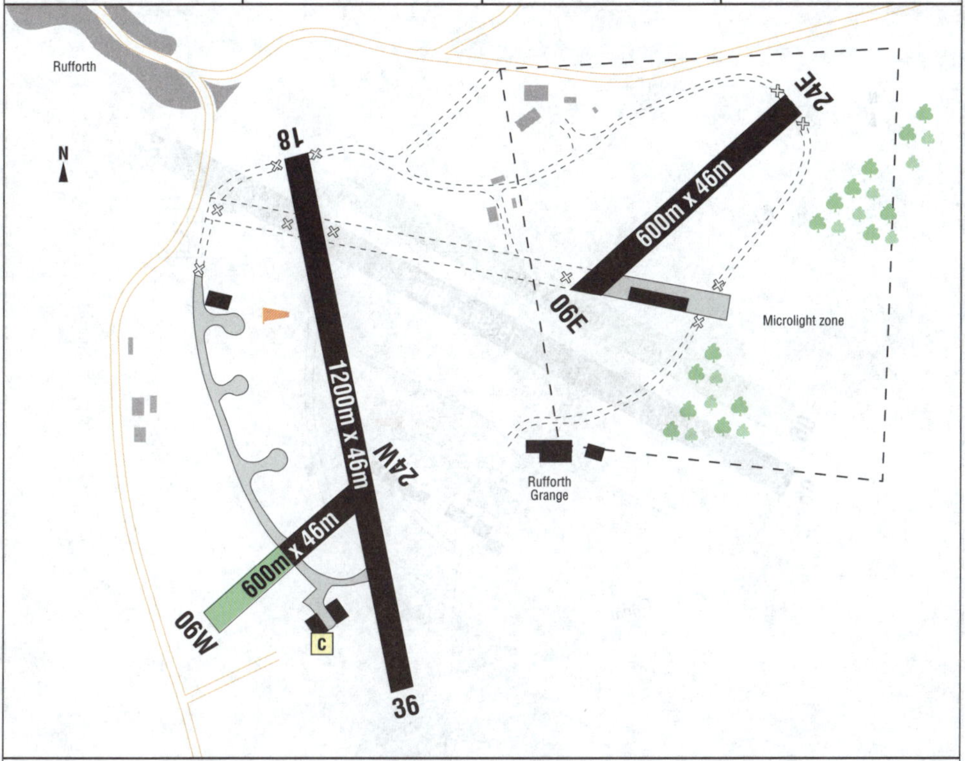

Rufforth

N

Microlight zone

18

24E

600m x 46m

06E

1200m x 46m

24W

600m x 46m

06W

36

Rufforth Grange

C

RWY	SURFACE	TORA	LDA	LIGHTING
18/36	Asphalt	1200x46	U/L	Nil
06/24W	Asph/Grass	600x46	U/L	Nil
06/24E	Asphalt	600x46	U/L	Nil

Rwy36 ignore Displaced Thr markings, Rwy24W 300m grass & 300m tarmac, Rwy24E microlight acft only

Remarks
ACFT landing Rwy24W avoid microlight circuits on Rwy24E/06E. Beware gliders and powered ACFT on same circuit. Tug ACFT operate variable circuits.

Warnings
AD located on part of disused AD. Disused parts of AD are obstructed by farm buildings & equipment. AD is between Church Fenton and Linton-on-Ouse MATZs. Intense gliding activity. Rwys18/36 have displaced Thr marks which should be ignored. Microlights operating from disused Rwy at NE side of AD which is now re-activated as Rwy06E/24E. No overhead joins due to cables up to 2000ft agl. No dead side, join downwind.
Noise: Avoid over flying local farms and villages

Operating Hrs	SR-SS		
Circuits	18 RH, 36 LH 24W RH, 06W LH, 800ft QFE Microlights 24E LH, 06E RH, 500ft QFE	**Restaurants**	Vending machine in clubhouse Pub lunches The Tankard Rufforth 1m
		Taxis	**Tel:** 01423 359000
		Car Hire	
Landing Fee	Rufforth E Nil Rufforth W £6-£50 depending on size	National	**Tel:** 01904 612141
		Weather Info	AirN MWC
Maintenance	Nil	**Operator**	York Gliding Centre
Fuel	AVGAS 100LL (Rufforth W)		Rufforth Aerodrome York, YO23 3NA **Tel:** 01904 738694 (W) **Fax:** 01904 738109 (W) **Tel:** 01904 738877(Microlights E)

Disabled Facilities

Y

LFAC

CALAIS-DUNKERQUE

11ft 0mb	3.5nm ENE of Calais N5057.65 E00157.80	PPR	Alternative AD	Le Touquet

Calais	ATIS Lille 119.320	ATIS Calis 135.450	APP Lille 120.275	TWR 128.920

RWY	SURFACE	TORA	LDA	LIGHTING
06	Asphalt	1535	1535	Thr Rwy
24	Asphalt	1535	1535	Ap Thr Rwy
06/24	Grass	1050	1050	Nil

Remarks

PPR for Ops at certain times see Ops Hrs. Situated within Calais TMA (Class E airspace). SVFR flights requested to contact Lille APP if above 2000ft QNH, if operating below this alt, call Calais direct. Non-radio ACFT MUST use grass Rwy. DZ is to NW Rwy06/24 grass. Customs available 0800-1900 (L).
Aids to Navigation: NDB MK 418.00

Warnings

AD surface unusable outside marked or asphalt areas. Danger area 1.5nm NNW AD 0.5nm radius, up to 1650ft agl/ Coastal location gives high risk of sea fog. Heli & parachute activity on AD.

Operating Hrs	0800-1900 (1900-2300 PPR for IFR or training flights only). PPR requests must be made before 1700 same day. PPR for flights wishing to operate 0600-0800 must be obtained previous day	**Weather Info**	MT **Fax:** 552
		Operator	**Tel:** 00 33 321 00 1100 (ATC) **Tel:** 00 33 32182 7066 (AD) **Tel:** 321 97 90 66 (Customs) **Fax:** 00 33 328 613 327 (AD)
Circuits	Asphalt 06 RH, 24 LH, 1000ft QFE Grass 06 LH, 24 RH, 1000ft QFE		
Landing Fee	On application		
Maintenance	Nil		
Fuel	AVGAS Jet A1 100LL		
Hangarage	by arr		
Disabled Facilities	Nil		
Restaurants	On AD		
Taxis/Car Hire	Arranged locally		

219ft 7mb	3nm S of Dinard N4835.26 W00204.80	PPR	Alternative AD	Avranches Dinard

Dinard	ATIS 124.575	FIS Brest 122.800
APP Rennes 124.900	TWR 120.150	Lighting 120.150

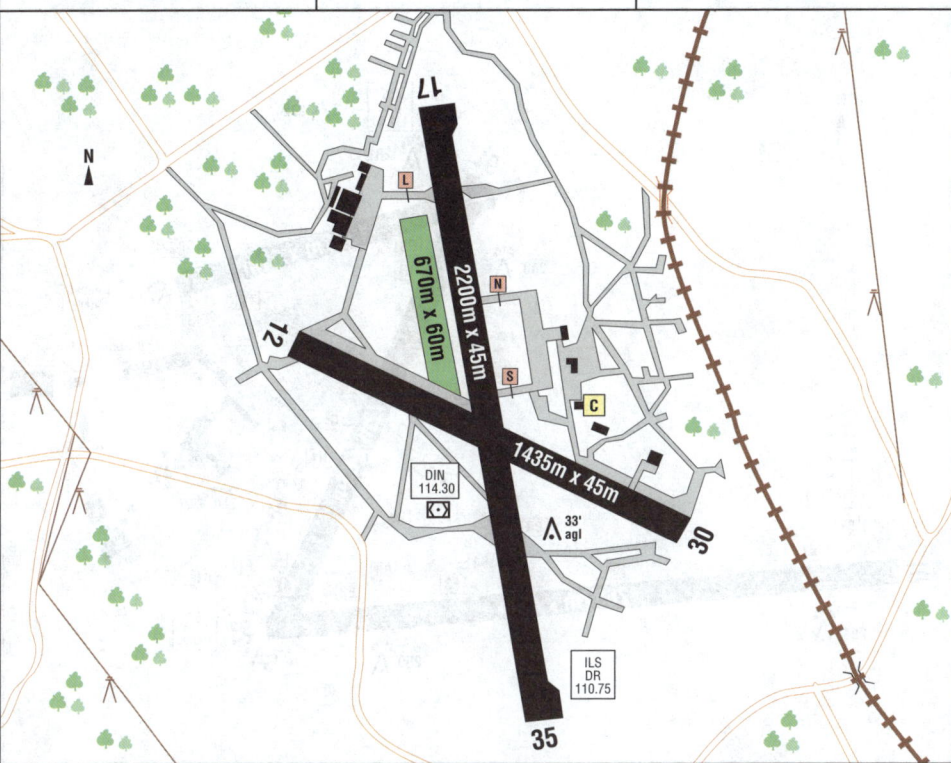

RWY	SURFACE	TORA	LDA	LIGHTING
35	Asphalt	2200	2200	Ap Thr Rwy PAPI 3° LH
17	Asphalt	2200	2200	Thr Rwy PAPI 3.9° LH
30/12	Asphalt	1500	1500	Nil
35/17	Grass	670	670	Nil

Rwy17 local club ACFT use only

Remarks
PPR non-radio and SVFR. SVFR weather minima 5000m/1000ft ceiling. Rwy35/17 grass usually available only to locally based ACFT. SVFR flight PPR by telephone. Customs normally available 0730-2030 (L)

Warnings
Mandatory SVFR routing, please check with SVFR request. Rwy unuseable outside ATC Hrs.

Operating Hrs	Mon-Fri 0515-1845, Sat 0615-2015, Sun 0615-1845 (L)	**Weather Info**	M T Fax 544 A ATIS **Tel:** 00 33 299 163 158	
Circuits	Asphalt 30 RH, 12, 17, 35 LH, 1000ft QFE Grass 17 RH, 35 LH, 1000ft QFE	**Visual Reference Points (VRP)**		
		Echo/Pont du Port St Hubert	DIN 131°/5nm	
		November/Ile de Cezembre	DIN 010°/5nm	
Landing Fee	On application	November Bravo/Barrage de la Rance	DIN 054°/3nm	
Maintenance	Available	November Echo/Pointe du Grouin	DIN 057°/12nm	
Fuel	AVGAS Jet A1 100LL	November Whisky/Cap Frehel	DIN 307°/11nm	
		Sierra Whisky/Ploancoet	DIN 241°/7nm	
Disabled Facilities	Nil	Whisky Juliet/LeGuildo	DIN 264°/5nm	
Restaurants	In the terminal	**Operator**	**Tel:** 00 33 299 16 3803 (AD)	
Taxis	At the terminal		**Tel:** 00 33 299 16 3805 (Operator)	
Car Hire	Available in Dinard			

For

242ft 8mb	5nm N of Dublin City N5325.52 W00615.12	PPR	Alternative AD	Belfast City Trim

Dublin	ATIS 124.525	APP 121.100 119.550 119.925	DEL 121.875
GND 121.800	FIS 118.500	RAD 129.175	TWR 118.600

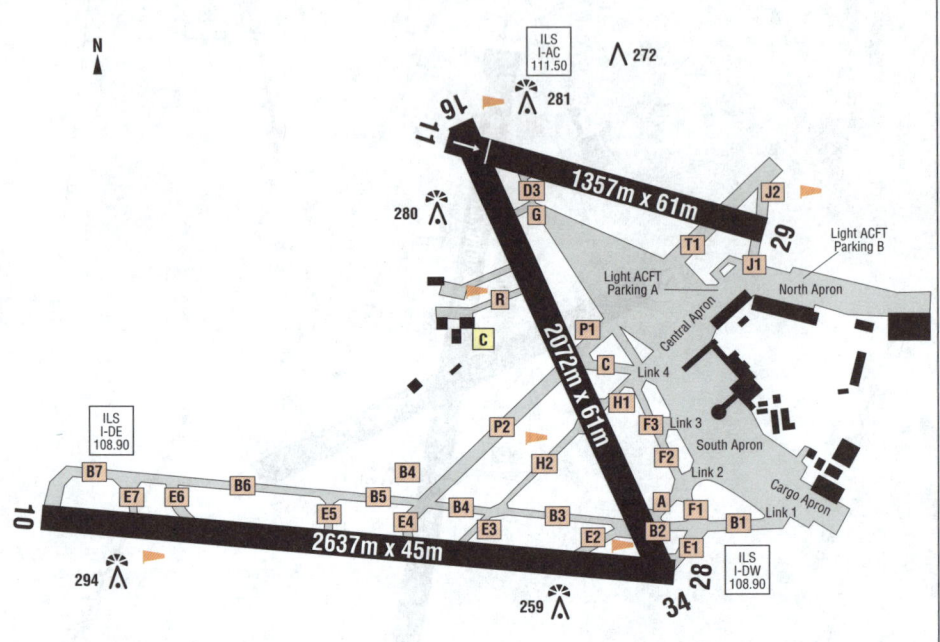

RWY	SURFACE	TORA	LDA	LIGHTING
10/28	Concrete	2637	2637	Ap Thr Rwy PAPI 3°
16/34	Asphalt	2072	2072	Ap Thr Rwy PAPI 3°
11	Asph/Conc	1339	1254	Ap Thr Rwy PAPI 3.5°
29	Asph/Conc	1339	1339	Ap Thr Rwy PAPI 3°

Remarks

PPR. Flight plans are mandatory for all ACFT wishing to use Dublin AD and CTA. Contact DEL at least 15 minutes prior to start up. ACFT prohibited from entering stands without marshalling guidance. ACFT are prohibited to hold on Twy B2. Twy E4 for daylight use only, ACFT with wingspan <30m taxiing from Rwy28. Twy E5 for use by ACFT with wingspan <36m. Twy T1 for daylight use only. Mandatory GND handling for all ACFT. AD closed on Christmas day.
Visual aid to location: Abn White Green

Warnings

Obstacle 700ft amsl 5nm SE of Rwy34 Thr.
Noise: ACFT operators must ensure at all times that the ACFT is operated in a manner that will cause the least disturbance practicable to areas surrounding the AD. Dept ACFT from all Rwys must maintain heading straight after take-off to 5nm before commencing turn unless otherwise instructed by ATC.

Operating Hrs	H24	**Restaurants**	Available inside terminal
Circuits	Not available on Rwy10/28 & Rwy16/34 11 LH 29 RH 800ft aal	**Taxi/Car Hire**	Available outside terminal
		Weather Info	**Tel:** 00 353 570 123123 **Fax:** 00 353 570 131838
Landing Fee	Available with PPR	**Operator**	Aer Rianta Cpt
Maintenance Fuel	Available AVGAS 100LL (0700-2230 (L) AVTUR JET A1 (H24)		Dublin airport Co Dublin **Tel:** 00 353 18141111 **Fax:** 00 353 18144643 www.dublin-airport.com
Disabled Facilities	Available		
Handling	Tel: 00 353 18145232 (Signature)		

DUBLIN CIRCUIT PROCEDURES

Rwy10/28 & Rwy16/34 are not available for circuit traning.

Rwy11
LH 800ft

After take-off/passing end of Rwy turn onto 100°M. Turn onto crosswind leg before crossing N1 main road.
Downwind leg - to be flown to S of Rathingle House and Rivervalley Estate.
Base leg – turn to be E of Rivermeade Estate.
Finals – ACFT must not position S of Rwy centreline.

Rwy29
RH 800ft

Dept on Rwy heading, climb to 500ft by 0.75nm upwind. Climb and turn through crosswind at 800ft aal remaining E of Rivermeade (Toberburr) Estate.
Downwind – Must be S of rathingle House and Rivervalley Estate.
Base leg – to be over the N! road.
Finals – ACFT must not position So of Rwy29 extended centreline.

DUBLIN VISUAL APPROACH CHART

Flight plans are mandatory for flights within Dublin CTR/CTA. When the flight destination is not an AD licensed for public use the address, telephone number and name of property owner of the place of intended landing must be included in field 18.
Special VFR is available within Dublin CTR.
Flight information Service is H24. 118.50 is allocated for ACFT in class G airspace.
Landing lights should be shown at all times during flights within Dublin CTR.
Take-off without 2 way communications with Dublin ATC either by RTF or telephone is not permitted.

DUBLIN CTA/CTR CLEARANCE PROCEDURES

Prior to penetration of Dublin CTA/CTR contact must be made at least 10 minutes before ETA at airspace boundary to the relevant ATSU as follows:
Dublin TWR 118.60 for entry into Dublin CTR
Dublin ACC North Sector 129.17 for entry to Dublin CTA North Sector
Dublin ACC South Sector 124.65 for entry to Dublin CTA South Sector
Dublin ACC North Sector is divided from Dublin ACC South Sector by:
Rwy10/28 active – boundary line along extended centreline of Rwy10/28
Rwy16/34 active – boundary line along extended APP line of Rwry16/34

DUBLIN VFR ARRIVAL & DEPARTURE ROUTES

Flights arr/dept at Dublin AD are cleared as follows:
N arr/dept: via Skerries VFR route
W arr/dept: via Skerries VFR route or Dunshaughlin VFR route
S arr/dept: as instructed by TWR.
SW arr: fixed wing via Dunboyne or Dunshaughlin. Helis via Redcow Roundabout or The Square, Tallaght.
S dept: as instructed by ATC or flights intending to transit EIR15 are cleared to either Palmerston Roundabout Hold or Marley Park to await onwards clearance from Baldonnel TWR.

Flights with arr/dept destinations other than Dunlin AD are normally cleared as follows:
N arr/dept: As instructed by Dublin TWR or Skerries VFR route
W arr/dept: As instructed by Dublin TWR or Dunshaughlin VFR route
SW arr: as Instructed by Dublin TWR or Heli – via Red Cow roundabout or The square, Tallaght. Fixed wing – via Dunboyne or Dunshaughlin
S arr: as instructed by Dublin TWR
S dept: as instructed by Dublin TWR or flights intending to transit EIR15 route either the Palmerstown Roundabout Hold or the Marley Park Hold to await onwards clearance from Baldonnel TWR.

DUBLIN HOLDING PATTERNS

Broad Meadows Bridge
N532756.45 W00611.25

LH pattern based on the M1 motorway bridge, which crosses Broad Meadow estuary. Outbound leg is 1 minute at 90 kts on track 190°M. Minimum holding alt 100ft QNH.
Arr overhead, turn L onto outbound leg before southern shore of the Broad Meadow estuary.
Turn L onto inbound leg E of N1 road, remaining E of N1 road at all times.

Finglas Church Spire
N5323.17 W00618.41

LH pattern based on the W Finglas Church Spire. Outbound leg is 1minute at 90 kts on track 010°M. Minimum holding alt 1700ft QNH.
Arr overhead, turn onto outbound leg before M50 motorway remaining S of the motorway at all times.
Turn L onto inbound leg remaining W of N2 road at all times.

Palmerston Roundabout
N5321.25 W00623.00

LH pattern based on Palmerston roundabout which intersects the M50 motorway and N4 road.
Outbound leg is 1 minute at 90 kts on track 281°M.
Minimum alt is 1700ft QNH.

Marley Park House
N5316.36 W00616.00

RH pattern based on Marley Park House (large manor house in Marley Public Park)
Outbound leg is 1 minutes at 90 kts on track 291°M.
Minimum Alt is 1700ft QNH.

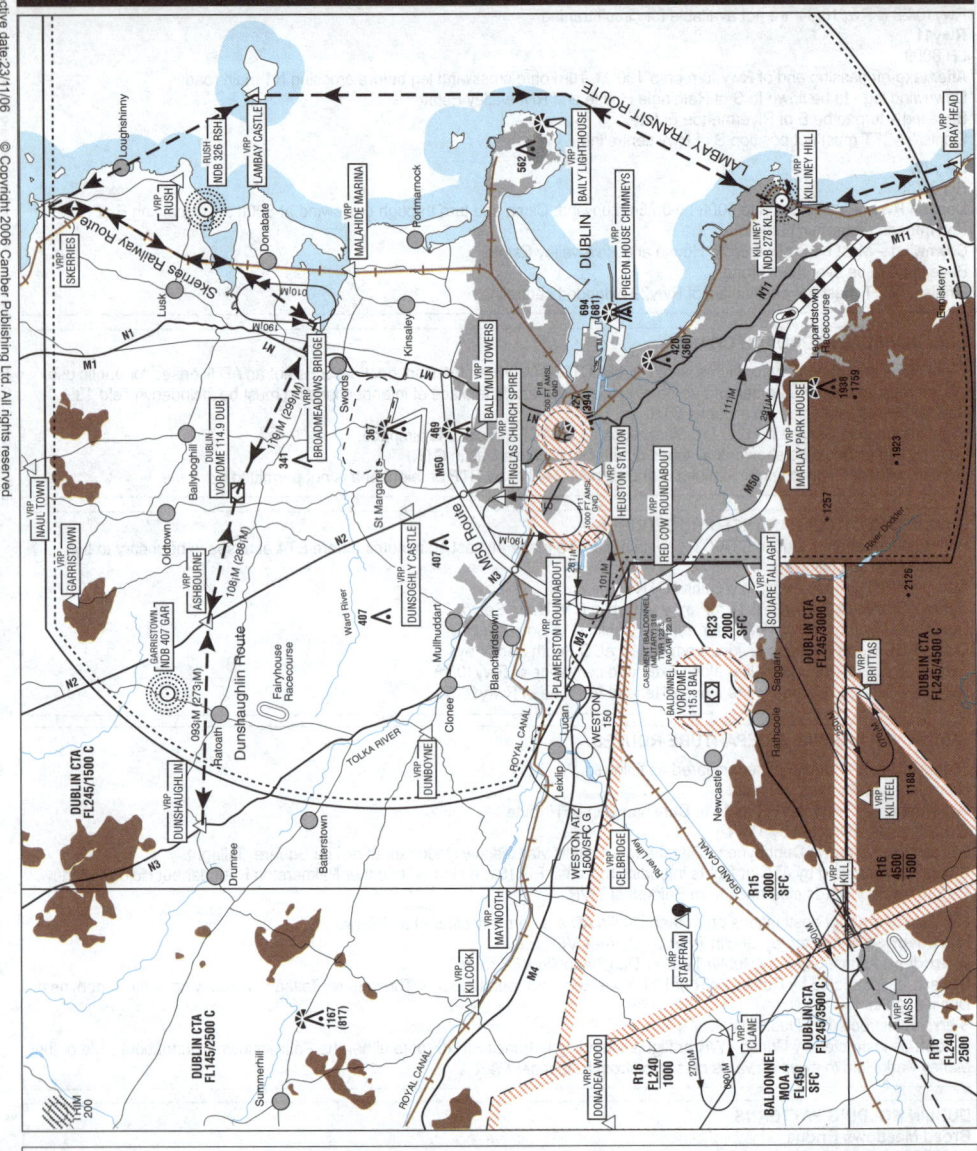

VRP		VRP	
Ashbourne	N5330.70 W00623.90	Kill	N5314.80 W00635.50
Baily Lighthouse	N5321.80 W00603.30	Killiney Hill	N5315.80 W00606.90
Ballymun Towers	N5323.80 W00615.80	Kilteel	N5314.10 W00631.30
Bray Head	N5311.70 W00604.80	Lambay Castle	N5329.40 W00601.80
Brittas	N5314.20 W00627.20	Malahide Marina	N5327.10 W00609.10
Broadmeadows Bridge	N5327.90 W00611.40	Marley Park House	N5316.60 W00616.00
Cellbridge	N5320.30 W00632.20	Maynooth	N5322.90 W00635.40
Clane	N5317.60 W00641.20	Naas	N5313.50 W00639.20
Donadea Wood	N5320.60 W00645.00	Naul Town	N5335.20 W00617.30
Dunboyne	N5325.10 W00628.50	Palmerston Roundabout	N5321.40 W00623.00
Dunshaughlin	N5330.80 W00632.50	Pigeon House Chimneys	N5320.40 W00611.40
Dunsoghly Castle	N5325.60 W00619.30	Red Crow Roundabout	N5319.10 W00622.10
Finglas church Spire	N5323.30 W00618.70	Rush	N5331.40 W00605.40
Garristown	N5334.00 W00623.00	Skerries	N5334.70 W00606.50
Heuston Station	N5320.80 W00617.70	Square Tallaght	N5317.20 W00622.30
Kilcock	N5324.00 W00640.00	Straffan	N5318.70 W00636.40

74ft 3mb	1.4nm NW of La Rochelle N4610.75 W00111.71		Alternative AD	Le Thou

La Rochelle	ATIS 126.870	FIS Bordeaux Info 125.300	APP 124.400	TWR 118.000

RWY	SURFACE	TORA	LDA	LIGHTING
28	Asphalt	2140	1605	Thr Rwy PAPI 3.1° LHS
10	Asphalt	2140	1940	Thr Rwy PAPI 3° LHS
28/10	Grass	690	–	Nil
22/04	Grass	550	–	Nil

Rwy28/10 available only to local ACFT

Remarks
Microlights not accepted. SVFR minima 1500m, ceiling 700ft. Rwy28 preferred in winds of less than 4 kts.
Aids to Navigation: NDB RL 322.00

Warnings
Only Rwys and marked Twys available for the movement of ACFT.
Noise: In the visual circuit avoid over flying built-up areas.

Operating Hrs	Mon-Fri 0400-2100 Sat/Sun & PH 0600-2000 (Summer) Mon-Fri 0500-2200 Sat/Sun & PH 0800-1800 (Winter) & by arr	**Visual Reporting Points (VRP)** Charron Usseau Nieul-s-Mer & St Vivien	
Circuits	28, 22 RH, 700ft QFE	**Operator**	CCI LaRochelle 14 Rue du Palais, 17000 La Rochelle
Landing Fee	On application		**Tel:** 00 33 46 42 3026 (AD)
Maintenance	Available plus hangerage		**Fax:** 00 33 46 43 1254 (AD)
Fuel	AVTUR JET A1 100LL		
Disabled Facilities	Nil		
Restaurants	In the terminal		
Taxis/Car Hire	Available in the terminal		
Weather Info	M T		

Effective date:23/11/06

LFAT

LE TOUQUET

36ft	1nm E of Le Touquet		PPR	Alternative AD	Calais
1mb	N5030.90 88137.65				

Le Touquet	ATIS 129.125	FIS Paris N 125.700	APP 125.30 118.450
APP Lille 120.275	**TWR** 118.450	**GND** 125.300	

RWY	SURFACE	TORA	LDA	LIGHTING
14	Asphalt	1850	1554	Ap Thr Rwy
32	Asphalt	1850	1700	Thr Rwy PAPI 3° LHS

Remarks

PPR non-radio ACFT. Call TWR before starting engine for Dept. SVFR weather minima 3000m/820ft ceiling (Arr); 1500m / 660ft ceiling (Dept) fixed wing. In winds of less than 4kts use of Rwy14 is preferred.

Aids to Navigation: NDB LT 358.00

Warnings

Due to AD location is it susceptible to sea fog which can arrive without warning, have an in-land diversion planned. Mandatory SVFR routing, please check with SVFR request.

Operating Hrs	Mon-Fri 0800-1700 (Summer) Mon-Sat 0900-1700 (Winter)
Circuits	32 RH, 14 LH, 1000ft QFE
Landing Fee	On application
Maintenance	Available
Fuel	AVGAS Jet A1 100LL
Disabled Facilities	Nil
Restaurants	In the terminal
Taxis	At the terminal
Car Hire	Available in Le Touquet
Weather Info	M T Fax 552 A ATIS Tel: 00 33 2105 5126

Visual ReferencePoints (VRP)

Echo/Neuville	N5028 50 E00146.70
November/Hardelot Plage	N5038 00 E00168.00
November Echo/Samer	N5038 10 E00144.80
November Mike/Wimereux	N5045 90 E00138.00
Sierra/Rang duFliers	N5025.00 E00138.60

Operator	Tel: 00 33 321 05 0066 (ATC)
	Tel: 00 33 321 050 399 (AD)
	Fax: 00 33 321 055 934 (AD)

Effective date:23/11/06

13ft 1mb	3nm S of Ostend N5111.93 E00251.73	PPR	Alternative AD	Kokjoide

Ostend	FIS Brussels 126.900	APP 120.600	TWR 118.175	GND 121.900

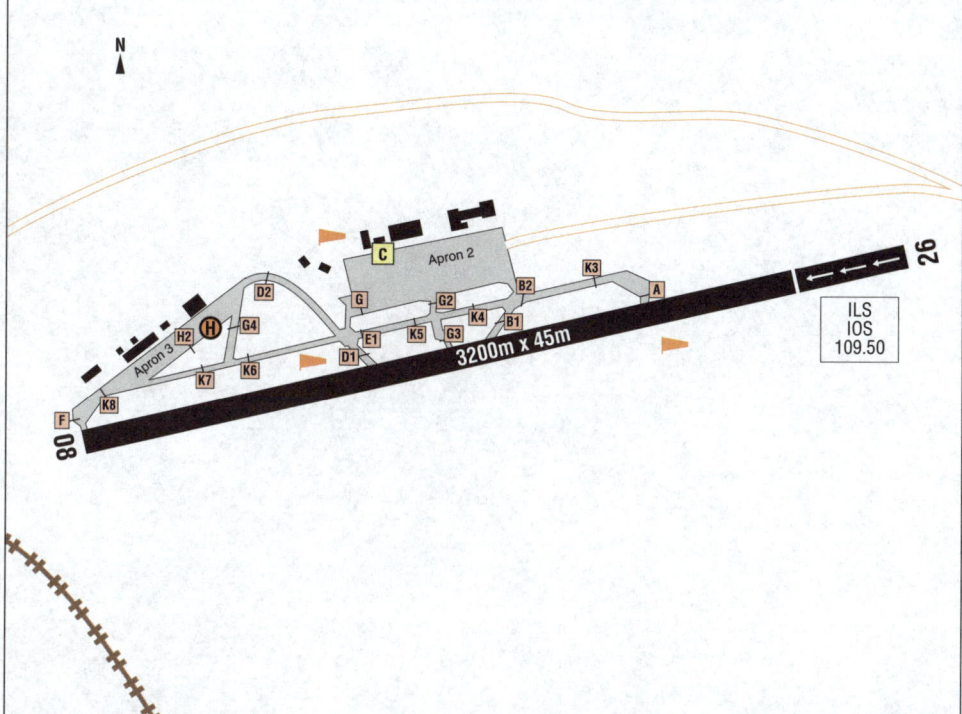

RWY	SURFACE	TORA	LDA	LIGHTING
26	Asphalt	3200	2785	Ap Thr Rwy PAPI 3° LH
08	Asphalt	2400	2900	Ap Thr Rwy PAPI 3° LH

Remarks
PPR non-radio ACFT (may be subject to prohibition). AD situated within Class C Airspace.
Aids to Navigation: NDB ONO 399.50. NDB DD 352.50. NDB OO 375.262.

Warnings
ACFT APP visually should not descend below 1500ftamsl before intercepting the PAPI glide slope, or fly below this slope once established.

Operating Hrs	H24	**Operator**	**Tel:** 00 32 59 551411 (AD)
Circuits	Nil		**Tel:** 00 32 59 551464 (Self briefing)
Landing Fee	On application		**Tel:** 00 32 59 551452 (Met)
Maintenance	Available		**Fax:** 00 32 59 512951 (AD)
Fuel	AVGAS Jet A1 100LL		
Disabled Facilities	Nil		
Restaurants	In the terminal		
Taxis/Car Hire	At the terminal		
Weather Info	M T **Fax:** 562 A **Tel:** 00 32 59 551452		

Visual Referenc Points (VRP)
Aalter	N5105.12 E00327.00
Breskens	N5125.00 E00333.00
Dunkerque	N5102.00 E00222.30
Torhout	N5104.10 E00306.11

UK VFR Flight Guide
Private Airfields

Private Airfields
DELETED this year

The AD below has been deleted from this guide for various reasons. Often because of inconsiderate visitor use that has caused annoyance to neighbours and put the strip at risk. The owners therefore have requested that we no longer publish details. The fact that an AD is listed below **does not necessarily mean that the AD no longer exists.**

Kirkcudbright

Seighford

Thorpe Le Soken

Private Airfields
ADDED for 2007

The ADs below have agreed to let us publish details for the first time this year. **Please remember that should you use them – and they are all strictly PPR – consideration and good airman ship will ensure they are still available in future years.**

Binstead

Craysmarsh Farm

Grassthorpe Grange

Lower Botrea

ABOYNE
N5704.52 W00250.08, 1.1nm W of Aboyne (N of River Dee), 460ft amsl

Rwy09L/27R Tarmac 520x5.5m Rwy09R/27L Tarmac 540x7m. **Remarks:** Gliding or maintenance related ACFT only. Gliders launch by Aerotow, keep good look out at all times. Field grazed by cattle at times. Windsock N of Rwy. **Circuits:** Nil. **Fuel:** Nil. **Maintenance:** Light ACFT & Glider available Alan Middleton, Aboyne ACFT Maintenance **Tel:** 01339 885236. **Landing Fee:** Gliding Club business or Maintenance £6. Non Gliding Club business £17 Motor Gliders £4 Light ACFT £7.50. **Operator:** Deeside Gliding Club, Waterside, Dinnet. **Tel:** 01339 885339 (Club Office) deeside@glidingclub.co.uk www.deeside.glidingclub.co.uk **Disabled Facilities:**

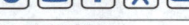

ALLENSMORE
N5200.02 W00250.07, 4nm SW of Hereford, 300ft amsl

N/S Grass 550x50m. **Remarks:** Animals grazing. Large letter A on white back ground on hangar roof at N end of strip. **Landing Fee:** Subscription to Mission Aviation Fellowship. **Circuits:** Nil. **Maintenace/Fuel:** Nil. **Operator:** Mr Powell, Locks Garage, Allensmore, Hereford HR2 9HS. **Tel:** 07879 883406

BINSTEAD
N5043.00 W00112.00, 2nm W of Ryde, 150ft amsl

Rwy18/36 Grass 400x16m. **Remarks:** PPR. Microlights not accepted. Well maintained strip. Power lines APP Thr Rwy36 but go underground APP. **Visual Aid to Location:** 0.5nm S of Abbey on N coast of Isle of Wight. Southampton CTR close by. **Noise:** Do not over fly the abbey and villages. **Operating Hrs:** SR-SS. **Circuits:** Please fly straight in APP. **Fuel:** Nil. **Operator:** John Cleaver, Newnham Farm, Binstead, Isle of Wight, PO33 4ED. **Tel:** 01983 882423

BREIDDEN
N5242.30 W00305.00, 4nm NNE Welshpool, 200ft amsl

Rwy01/19 Grass 500x10m. **Remarks:** PPR by telephone essential to check availability and conditions of AD. Windsock displayed E of Rwy. Orange markers placed either end of Rwys. **Warnings:** Public footpath crossed Rwy01 APP. Sheep and cattle graze strip. Welshpool AD to SW, call stating intentions. **Operating Hrs:** SR-SS. **Circuits:** All to E. **Landing Fee:** Nil. **Maintenance/Fuel:** Nil. **Operator:** Trevor Pugh, 1 Melverley View, Crew Green, Shropshire. **Tel:** 01743 884450

BROADMEADOW
N5202.00 W00246.00. 3nm SW Hereford. 325ft amsl

Rwy09/27 Grass 400x18m. **Remarks:** PPR by telephone. Microlight ACFT only. Windsock at both ends of Rwy. Good clear APP to both Rwy. **Warnings:** Slight Rwy upslope. Madley AD close to S of strip. **Noise:** Avoid over flying all local houses and villages, especially to E of AD. Over fly the field to identify not below 1500ft agl. Decend to circuit height over open farmland 1nm W of AD for ling final Rwy10R and tight circuit for Rwy28L. **Radio:** 129.825. **Operating Hrs:** 0900-2000. **Circuits:** All to N. 500ft agl **Landing Fee:** Nil. **Maintenance/Fuel:** MOGAS by arrangement. **Operator:** Mr Powell, Broadmeadow Farm, Haywood, Hereford, HR2 9RU. **Tel:** 01432 278421 **Tel:** 07749 702699 (PPR) **Tel:** 07787 564170 (PPR)

BROMSGROVE (Stoney Lane)
N5220 W00159, 2nm NW of Redditch. 425ft amsl

Rwy075/255 Grass 375x15m. **Remarks:** PPR is essential. Strip is only suitable for experienced STOL pilots due to windshear and turbulence. Rwy slope to SW. A windsock may be shown in S of AD. Join overhead at 1500ft QFE. **Noise:** Avoid over flying Blakenhurst Prison 0.5m to S and all local habitation. **Circuits:** SE at 800ft QFE. **Landing Fee:** £5 for business use, £2.50 for recreational flyers. **Fuel:** Available (MOGAS) 3nm away 24 Hrs. **Accommodation:** Immediately to S of AD. **Operator:** P Whittaker, 'Longlands', Stoney Lane, Bromsgrove, Worcs, B60 1LZ. **Tel:** 01527 875228 **Tel:** 07966 275154 (Mobile)

CAMPHILL
N5318.28 W0143.80, 12nm WSW of Sheffield. 1300ft amsl

Rwy02/20 Grass 1400x50m. **Remarks:** Gliding Site, Strictly PPR. No powered ACFT except motor gliders permitted. Surface is undulating, APP can be hazardous in poor weather. Area of intense gliding activity with winch launches up to 2000ft agl (3300ft asml). **Noise:** Avoid over flying adjacent villages. **Fuel:** Nil. **Accommodation:** Available in club house inc food. **Operator:** Derbyshire & Lancashire Gliding Club, Camphill, Great Hucklow, Tideswell, Buxton, SK17 8RQ. **Tel:** 01298 871270/871207 dlgc@gliding.u-net. com www.dlgc.org.uk

CAUNTON

N5307.05 W00053.50, 4.5NM NW of Newark, 160ft amsl

Rwy03/21 Grass 400m, Rwy11/29 Grass 400m. **Radio:** Caunton Radio 129.825. **Remarks:** PPR essential. Microlights only enter and leave AD from E or W. Arrive 1000ftagl, desend in circuit. High performance 3-axis microlights may use alternative circuit pattern – call for briefing if flying said machine. **Warnings:** Rwy21 has displaced Thr– keep finals short and land 1/3 along Rwy. Rwy03/11 down slope. High power cables to E. Keep a good look out for hang gliders on aerotow and foot launched powered hang gliders. **Circuits:** 03/11 RH, 21/29 LH 500ft agl. No deadside **Landing Fee:** Nil. **Hangarage:** Ltd available. **Fuel:** Available on request. **Accommodation:** B & B available on site. **Operator:** Andy Buchan, Pebbles, Southwell Road, Farnsfield, Notts, NG22 8EB. **Tel:** 01623 883802 **Tel:** 07850 942096 (Mobile) andy@lightflight.co.uk. **Disabled Facilities:**

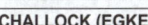

CHALLOCK (EGKE)

N5112.50 E00049.75, 4nm NNW of Ashford, 600ft amsl

NE/SW Grass 800m, N/S Grass 800m. **Remarks:** PPR by telephone essential. Glider towing by winch and aerotow takes place here. **Warnings:** There are unmarked electric lines along NE side of AD. All APP are over tall trees. Rwy surface is undulating and SW corner is not useable. **Noise:** Do not join over head. **Operating Hrs:** By arrangement. **Fuel:** Nil. **Landing Fee:** Nil. **Operator:** Kent Gliding Club, Challock Aerodrome, Squids Gate, Challock, Ashford, Kent, TN25 4DR. **Tel:** 01233 740274 **Tel:** 01233 740307 **Fax:** 01233 740811. **Disabled Facilities:**

COLL (Ballard)

N5635.92 W00637.17, Island of Coll, Inner Hebrides, 41ft amsl

Rwy11/29 Grass 434x18m. **Remarks:** ACFT Arr or Dept Coll are to call Tiree as Tiree APP procedure passes close to Coll circuit. Field N of Rwy is subject to flooding, manoeuvring is restricted to marked Rwy and area adjacent to hut S of Rwy. The owner has no objection to the strip being used but takes no responsibility for its operation. **Operator:** Mr A C Brodie, Coll/Ballard Aerodrome, Inner Hebrides, Argyll & Bute Region, Scotland. **Tel:** 01879 230323

CRAYSMARSH FARM

N5121.80 W00205.30, 4nm N of Keevil AD, 250ft amsl

Rwy18/36 Grass 500x15m. **Remarks:** PPR. Rwy waterlogged during winter months. **Warnings:** Power cables 800m from Rwy18 APP. **Noise:** Avoid over flying all local villages. **Operating Hrs:** SR-SS. **Landing Fee:** Available with PPR. **Circuits:** Operator will advise with PPR. **Fuel:** MOGAS available with PPR. **Operator:** Mr Cottle, Craysmarsh Farm, Melksham, Wiltshire, SN12 6RG. **Tel:** 01380 828258

DONEMANA

N5453.42 W00717.55, 10nm S of Londonderry, 340ft amsl

Rwy06/24 paved hardcore 300x30m. **Remarks:** PPR. STOL visitors welcome at pilots own risk. Due to the difficult nature of this strip a telephone briefing for first time visitors is mandatory. AD is not notified as a designated point of entry/exit for Northern Ireland under the terms of the prevention of terrorism act but this can be arranged via PSNI. **Warnings:** TV mast 1931ft amsl, (1031ft agl), 3nm SSW of the AD. **Landing Fee:** Nil. **Fuel:** MOGAS, Ltd supplies available by prior arr. **Operator:** Mr Alfie Danton, Raspberry Hill Farm, 29 Bond's Glen Road, Londonderry, BT47 3ST **Tel/Fax:** 02871 397860. alfie@raspberryhill.freeserve.co.uk **Disabled Facilities:**

DOWLAND

N5053.00 W00402.00, 3.5nm W Winkleigh Disused AD. 450ft amsl

Rwy09/27 Grass 461x8m. **Remarks:** Strict PPR. Rwy in excellent condition. Windsock displayed at W end of Rwy. **Warnings:** Slight upslope Rwy09. Trees on APP Rwy27. High GND to NE of AD. Eaglescott ATZ close to NNE. **Noise:** Avoid over flying Dowland village. **Operating Hrs:** SR-SS. **Circuits:** LH at 800ft QFE. **Landing Fee:** Nil. **Maintenance/Fuel:** Nil. **Operator:** Mr W.G. Dunn, Croft, Dowland, Winkleigh, Devon, EX19 8PD. **Tel:** 01805 804627 wgdunn100@tiscali.co.uk. **Disabled Facilities:**

DUNSTABLE DOWNS

N5151.98 W00032.90, 1nm SW of Dunstable, 500ft amsl

Rwy04/22 Grass 900x50m, Rwy15/33 Grass 750x50m, Rwy18/36 Grass 500x50m. **Radio:** A/G 119.900. **Remarks:** PPR essential. Permission for use normally restricted to pilots with at least a Silver Gliding Badge and on gliding business. Inbound ACFT contact Luton APP. AD located within the Luton CTR. ACFT to taxi behind glider launch points. Intensive gliding activity including winch launching takes place. There are no AD markings. The Downs up to 817ft amsl are located to E & S of AD. Rwys have undulating surfaces. For landing information please telephone. Intensive hang gliding takes place along the ridge. **Operating Hrs:** by arr. **Circuits:** variable to NW of Downs, powered ACFT circuit is outside glider circuit. **Fuel:** AVGAS 100LL available by arr. **Maintenance:** London light ACFT **Tel:** 01582 663419. **Operator:** London Gliding Club, Dunstable Downs, Dunstable, Bedfordshire, **Tel:** 01582 663419 (PPR) **Fax:** 01582 665744 andy@londonglidingclub.com www.londonglidingclub.com.

EAST LOCHLANE FARM

N5622.00 W00352.30, 1.5nm W of Crieff, 800ft amsl

Rwy06/24 Grass 440x15m. **Remarks:** PPR essential for brief on AD conditions. Animals graze on field. Windsock displayed N Rwy06 Thr. **Warnings:** Upslope Rwy24 Thr. Trees border S edge of strip, may cause turbulence. **Noise:** Avoid over flying all houses and farms, especially the stud farm next door. **Operating Hrs:** SR-SS. **Circuits:** Nil. **Landing Fee:** Nil. **Maintenance/Fuel:** Nil. **Operator:** Gordon Halley, East Lochlane Farm, Crieff, **Tel:** 01764 653702 **Fax:** 01764 753042 gordon@lochlane.co.uk

EAST WINCH

N5243.33 E00031.90, 4nm SE of Kings Lynn, 49ft amsl

Rwy10/28 Grass 850x16m. **Remarks:** Situated on edge of Marham MATZ. Pilots Arr & Dept should contact Marham APP Visiting ACFT not normally accepted unless a customer of Scanrho Aviation. Crop spraying ACFT operate from AD. **Noise:** Avoid over-flying East Winch village **Circuits:** 10 LH, 28 RH, 800ft QFE. **Maintenance:** Scanrho Aviation. **Operator:** Three Ways, East Winch, Kings Lynn, Norfolk. **Tel:** 01553 840396 **Tel:** 01553 840262 (Mr Burman) **Fax:** 01485 600413

ERROL

N5624.30 W00310.92, 6nm SW of Dundee Airport, 31ft amsl

Rwy05/23 Asphalt 630x46m (E of disused AD). **Radio:** A/G 123.45 **Remarks:** Contact Leuchars APP & Dundee APP. Before entering circuit call DZ Control Errol. Free-fall parachuting up to FL150. Visiting pilots should report to Fife Parachuting Centre, Muirhouses Farm or Harbour Sawmills Ltd (on disused Rwy11). **Noise:** On APP/climb-out maintain Rwy heading for at least 1nm to avoid houses. **Operating Hrs:** SR-SS closed Mon & Thur. **Landing Fee:** Single £5, Twin £10. **Operator:** Mr L Doe, Muirhouses Farm, Errol. **Tel:** 01821 642555 (Operator-work) **Tel:** 01821 642333 (Operator-home) **Tel:** 01821 642355 (Harbour Sawmills AD) **Tel:** 01821 642454 (Parachute Club) **Fax:** 01821 642825 (Mr Doe)

FANNERS FARM

N5147.00 E00026.00, 4nm N Chelmsford. 210ft amsl

Rwy06/24 Grass 415x14m. **Remarks:** Strict PPR by telephone. **Warnings:** 8ft hedges at both Thrs. Rwy 06 APP is between two large poplars. Also electricity poles on Rwy24 APP. AD is on SE edge of Stansted CTA, (base 2000ft). **Noise:** Avoid over flying Great Waltham and Chignall Smealy villages. **Operating Hrs:** SR-SS. **Circuits:** 800ft QFE to NW. **Landing Fee:** Nil. **Maintenance/Fuel:** Nil. **Operator:** Peter Lee, Fanners Farm, Great Waltham, Essex, CH3 1EA. **Tel:** 01245 360470

FEARN

N5745.48 W00356.58, 1nm S of Fearn, 25ft amsl

Rwy11/29 Asphalt 1097x46m (other Rwys are obstructed by fences). Rwy surface – Asphalt over concrete, W 2/3rds very broken, Loose surface on all Rwy. **Remarks:** AD situated in D703. An entry/exit sector is established from GND level to1000ft agl in the segment S of a line joining N5745.00 W00400.42 & N5745.00 W00353.25. Maximum height S of this line is 1000ft agl. DAAIS Tain Range 122.750. Wind monitoring mast adjacent Rwy11/29 to N side on west cross Rwy. **Operator:** Mrs D Sutherland, Tullich Farm, Fearn, Ross-Shire, Highland Region, IV18 0PE **Tel:** 01862 832278

FELIXKIRK

N5415.11 W00117.93, 2nm NE of Thirsk, 226ft amsl

Rwy01/19 Grass 500x40m. **Remarks:** Strict PPR. Rwy can be soft after prolonged precipitation. National Grid transmission pylons 120ft agl run N-S close to W of AD. AD is the home of Sport Air UK and is situated within Topcliffe MATZ (controlling authority Leeming APP, ACFT may be transferred to Topcliffe APP. ACFT Dept Felixkirk are advised to call Topcliffe APP initially, it may be possible to get two-way communication on the GND). **Noise:** Please avoid local habitation and particularly Felixkirk village close to SE of AD **Operating Hrs:** Mon-Fri 0830-1700 (L) Closed Weekends. **Circuits:** LH. **Landing Fee:** Nil. **Fuel:** Nil. **Maintenance:** Sport Air UK, Rans ACFT specialists. **Restaurants:** Carpenters Arms, Felixkirk. **Operator:** Mr G McDill, Sport Air UK Ltd, The Airfield, Felixkirk, Thirsk, Yorkshire, YO7 2DR. **Tel:** 01845 537465 **Fax:** 01845 537791

FLOTTA

N5849.58 W00308.53, 9.5nm SE of Stromness, Orkney, 70ft amsl

Rwy16/34 Asphalt 759x18m. **Remarks:** Heliport operated by Talisman Energy (UK) Ltd. Fixed wing ACFT accepted when operating Ambulance flights or in emergency only. There is a significant longitudinal slope on Rwy. No facilities. **Visual aid to Location:** A flare stack 1.4nm from AD. **Operator: Tel:** 01856 884359. **Disabled Facilities:**

FOLKESTONE (Lyminge)

N5109 E00104, 7nm S of Canterbury, 600ft amsl

Rwy06/24 Grass 440x10m. **Remarks:** Strip is surrounded to W, E and N by Lyminge Forest – a large wooded area. **Caution:** trees to 50ft are a hazard at N end of strip. PPR is essential as there may be farm machinery or people working in soft fruit fields in close proximity. **Noise:** Visiting ACFT are requested to avoid all houses. **Circuits:** 24 LH, 06 RH, 800ft QFE. **Operator:** Mr G G Boot **Tel:** 01624 801027 geoffreyboot@supanet.com

GRASSTHORPE GRANGE

N5311.70 W00048.40, 5nm N of Newark AD, 35ft amsl

Rwy08/26 Grass 575x25m **Remarks:** PPR by telephone essential. Well maintained strip. Windsock displayed near buildings. Powelines approach strip from S but go underground to cross Rwy. **Warnings:** AD close to Scampton/Waddington MATZ. **Nosie:** Avoid over flying all villages in surround area. **Operating Hrs:** SR-SS. **Circuits:** To N at 800ft QFE. **Landing Fee:** Nil. **Fuel:** Nil. **Operator:** Bob Beard, Grange Farm, Grassthorpe, Newark, Notts, NG23 6QX. **Tel:** 01636 822140 **Tel:** 07708 248571. bobatgrangefarm@hotmail.co.uk

GREEN FARM

N5209.00 W00133.30, 3nm SE of Wellesbourne Mountford AD, 375ft amsl

Rwy04/22 Grass 613x30. **Remarks:** Displaced Thr Rwy04 marked by red cones to avoid hedge close to Rwy04 Thr and rough GND which reduces take off run on Rwy04 also. Rough area is suitable as over run Rwy22. Call Wellsbourne Radio due to close proximity of ATZ. Ettington strip is 1.5nm to WSW. Strip is regularly over flown by low level fast jets. Windsocks displayed. AD regularly crossed by horse riders. **Warnings:** Rwy04 undershoot slopes steeply upwards, suitable for Rwy22 over run. **Noise:** Do not over fly Kineton and Butlers Marston village E of AD. **Circuits:** 22 LH, 04 RH. **Landing Fee:** Nil. **Operator:** Terry Cooper, Green Farm, Combrook, Warwickshire. CV35 9HP. **Tel:** 01926 640162. **Disabled Facilities:**

GUNTON PARK (Hanworth)

N5250.30 E000119.16, 2nm N of Suffield and 3nm W of Antingham, 100ft amsl

N/S Grass 800x30m. **Remarks:** PPR imperative due to location of Rwy in middle of a deer park. Rwy has 2m deer fence at each end, some high trees on S APP, also undulating with mown dry grass. Electric power line goes under GND in centre of Rwy. There is a line of trees S of Rwy and also trees at N end. Windsock is displayed on E side. **Noise:** Visiting ACFT are requested not to over fly Observatory TWR 1nm N and Hall 1nm W of AD. **Operator:** Sally Martin, Gunton Park, Hanworth, Norwich, Norfolk NR11 7HJ. **Tel:** 01263 761202 **Tel:** 01263 768667 (Office) **Fax:** 01263 768642

HALWELL

N5021.55 W00342.35, 5nm WNW of Dartmouth, 625ft amsl

Rwy09/27 Grass 480x12m. **Remarks:** PPR. Rwy09 has up slope. Well prepared/mowed Rwy. Mainly used by Microlights but light ACFT are welcome at pilots own risk. **Noise:** All ACFT APP AD from NW. Do not over fly houses to the W of the AD. **Operating Hrs:** SR-SS. **Circuits:** should be to N and kept very tight. **Landing Fee:** Nil. **Fuel:** MOGAS available by prior arr. Restaurant/Accomodation: The Old Inn, Halwell (shortwalk from AD) **Tel:** 01803 712329. **Operator:** Keith Wingate, South Hams Flying Group, Chakdina, 16 Buckwell Road, Kingsbridge, South Devon, TQ7 1NQ. **Tel:** 01548 857513 **Fax:** 01548 853556 **Tel:** 07971 480078 keithwinga@aol.com www.btinernet.com/~south.hams/shfc/index.html

HATTON

N5724.45 W00154.93, 1nm S of Hatton, 265ft amsl

Rwy08/26 Grass 650x24m. **Remarks:** Visiting ACFT welcome with PPR at owners own risk. 2% up slope on Rwy08. 30ft agl domestic power line crosses Rwy26 APP on short final. Strip may be waterlogged during winter months. Strip is close to boundary of Aberdeen CTA/CTR Aberdeen APP, and is beneath HMR Whiskey, a published helicopter route for off shore traffic. Heavy commercial helicopters can be expected entering/leaving Aberdeen zone. Useful weather information can be obtained from Aberdeen ATIS. **Noise:** Avoid over flight of local habitation. **Landing Fee:** Donations to upkeep welcomed. **Circuits:** 26 LH, 08 RH, 800ft QFE. **Operator:** James Anderson, Ardiffery Mains, Hatton, Peterhead, Aberdeenshire AB42 0SD. **Tel:** 01779 841207. **Disabled Facilities:**

HOME FARM

N5206.50 W00143.00, 5nm S Stratford upon Avon, 250ft amsl

Rwy02/20 Grass 650x20m. **Remarks:** Strict PPR. **Warnings:** Rwy has up slope at S end. Power lines cross APP Rwy20. Large oak tree 2/3 along Rwy on W side. Low flying military ACFT operate in AD vicinity. **Caution:** Microlight activity from Long Marston 2nm NW. **Noise:** Avoid over flying local villages to NW and NE. **Operating Hrs:** SR-SS. **Circuits:** To W 500ft QFE. **Fuel/Maintenance:** Nil. **Operator:** Paul Collicutt, Lower Farm, Admington, Shipton on Stour, Warks, CV36 4JW. **Tel:** 01789 450329 **Tel:** 07801 466990 paul@ebonystar.demon.co.uk

HOOK

N5116.50 W00056.53, 5nm E of Basingstoke, 225ft amsl

Rwy08/26 Grass 609x20m. **Remarks:** Slight up slope on Rwy08, grass can become water logged in winter. Power lines and trees on both APP. Preferred landing Rwy26, take off Rwy08. Windsock by Rwy08 Thr. **Noise:** Do not over fly Hook village. **Operator:** Chris Hill, Scotland Farm, Holt Lane, Hook, Hampshire, RG27 9ES **Tel:** 01256 762423. **Disabled Facilities:**

JUBILEE FARM (Wisbech)

N5238.00 E00003.89, 4.5nm SW of Wisbech, 5ft amsl

Rwy01/19 Grass 565x20m **Remarks:** PPR essential. Flat strip with farm buildings very close to Rwy19 Thr. These not only constitute a hazard but may generate turbulence. Telegraph poles close to Rwy01 Thr on either side of APP but wires run under ground as they cross the APP. R212, (up to 2000ft) is 4nm S of strip but this is applicable to helicopters only. Keep a good lookout for low flying military ACFT in the vicinity, particularly during the week. **Noise:** Avoid over flight of local habitation, particularly to E of AD. **Circuits:** 01 LH, 19 RH, 1000ft QFE **Landing Fee:** Nil. **Fuel:** Nil. **Operator:** Frank Ball, Jubilee Farm, Tholomas Drove, Wisbech St. Mary, Cambs, PE13 4SP **Tel:** 01945 410261

KIMBOLTON (Stow Longa)

N5218.98 W00022.75, 8nm W of Huntingdon. 1nm W of Grafham Water (reservoir), 246ft amsl

Rwy10/28 Grass 600x12m, Rwy13/31 Grass500x18m, **Remarks:** PPR by telephone essential. Rwy13/31 is not available on kart racing days (2nd Sat & Sun of month). Light ACFT welcome at pilot's own risk. Windsock displayed. Gas Booster Station and tall mast on Rwy31 APP. **Landing Fee:** Nil. **Operator:** R C Convine, Yendis, Stow Longa, Hunts **Tel:** 01480 860300. **Disabled Facilities:**

KINGFISHER BRIDGE

N5219.50 E00016.50. 5nm S of Ely. 16ft asml

Rwy09/27 Grass 570x38m. **Remarks:** PPR by telephone. Rwy in excellent condition. Windsock displayed N of Rwy. **Visual aid to location:** Cement works to N of AD. River cam to W of AD. **Warnings:** Power lines 400m W of Rwy27 Thr. AD situated within Lakenheath/Mildenhall MATZ, call for info. **Operating Hrs:** SR-SS. **Circuits:** LH 1000ft QFE. **Landing Fee:** Nil. **Maintenance:** Nil. **Fuel:** Nil. **Operator:** Andrew Green, Kingfishers Bridge, High Fen Farm, Wicken, Ely, Cambs, CB7 5XJ. **Tel:** 01353 72112. agreen@plr.net

KING'S LYNN (Tilney St. Lawrence)

N5243 E00019. 4.5nm SW of Kings Lynn,2nm W of River Great Ouse, 10ft amsl

Rwy16/34 Grass 400x32m. **Remarks:** Operated for private use, Strict PPR, visiting ACFT welcome at pilot's own risk. Pylons 200ft high 0.5nm to N. Orange Windsock displayed. **Landing Fee:** Nil. **Operator:** J. Goodley & Sons, Hirdling House, Tilney St. Lawrence **Tel:** 01945 880237. **Disabled Facilities:**

KNOCKBAIN FARM

N5735.75 W00428.00, 1nm SW Dingwall, 600ft amsl

Rwy08/26 Grass 650x15m. **Remarks:** PPR. AD well marked, located on top of hill between Dingwall and Loch Ussie, may not suitable for use during winter months. PFA types welcome. 2 windsocks displayed on AD. Power lines present E of AD. Beware low flying jets. Rwys slope up to centre, Rwy08 6%, Rwy26 4%. **Noise:** Dept: Rwy26 turn right as soon as practicable possible. **Operating Hrs:** SR-SS. **Circuits:** To N at 800ft. Make standard calls on 135.475. **Landing Fee:** Nil. **Maintenance:** Nil. **Fuel:** Nil. **Operator:** David Lockett, Knockbain Farm, Dingwall, Ross-shire, IV15 9TJ. **Tel:** 01349 862476 davidlockett@avnet.co.uk. **Disabled Facilities:**

LAINDON

N5135.67 E00026.76, 1.25nm NNW of Basildon, 90ft amsl

Rwy08/26 Grass 475x18m. **Remarks:** Up slope on Rwy26. Crops may be grown right up to strip edge. There is a public road at Rwy26 Thr, keep a good lookout for vehicles and pedestrians. Power lines 80ft agl parallel the strip to S. AD located within Southend LARS. Preferred landing Rwy in light winds Rwy26. **Noise:** Do not over fly built up area to S of AD. **Circuits:** 1000ft to N. **Operator:** George French, High View, 16 Wash Road, Basildon, Essex, SS15 4ER. **Tel:** 01268 411464 **Tel:** 07802 887338

LANE FARM

N5207 W00312, 4nm NW of Hay-on-Wye, 830ft amsl

Rwy06/24 Grass 730x50m (strip width narrows to min of 30m). **Remarks:** Strip situated in a valley with high GND all around up to 1671ft amsl to W and 1361ft amsl to SW. 50ft trees on N side of AD and close to both Thrs. Cables run close down NW side of AD and cross Rwy06 APP on very short final (30ft agl). Windsock displayed when AD active. Lane farm is on the NW side of AD. This strip is ONLY available to pilots visiting the locality or using Lane farm for B&B or their holiday properties. No casual visitors or strip training. Farmed deer graze AD. **Noise/Circuits:** To be flown to avoid local villages, the area is very rural. **Landing Fee:** £5. **Operator:** John Bally, Lane Farm, Paincastle, Hay-on-Wye, Radnorshire LD2 3JS. **Tel:** 01497 851605

LANGHAM

N5256.30 E00057.38,9nm W of Sheringham, 120ft amsl

Rwy10/28 Concrete 700x15m (former Twy), Rwy02/20 Grass 550x18m. (SW end of disused AD). **Remarks:** Mast 98ft aal, 250m N of Rwy25 Thr. Trees and huts on Rwy28 APP. Due to obstructions exercise extreme caution. **Circuits:** Nil. **Landing Fee:** £20. **Maintenance:** M3 available. **Fuel:** AVGAS 100LL by arr. **Operator:** H Labouchere Esq **Tel:** 01328 830003 **Fax:** 01328 830232

LARK ENGINE FARMHOUSE

N5224.96 E00022.18, 4.5nm ENE of Ely, 0ft amsl

Rwy06/24 Grass 600xm. **Remarks:** Flat strip situated within the Mildenhall/Lakenheath CMATZ. Call Lakenheath APP 128.900. Trees very close to Rwy24 APP on very short final which, as well as constituting an obstruction may also generate rotor in S winds. Farm equipment may be parked close to Rwy edge. Windsock displayed. **Noise:** Do not over fly the village of Prickwillow 1nm NW of AD. **Operating Hrs:** SR-SS. **Circuits:** Join directly downwind LH for both Rwys 1000ft QFE. **Landing Fee:** Nil. **Fuel:** Nil. **Operator:** Mr Clinton Judd, Lark Engine Farmhouse, Lark Bank, Prickwillow, Ely, Cambs. CB7 4SW, **Tel/Fax:** 01353 688428

LITTLE CHASE FARM

N5221.00 W00137.00, 1.5nm WNE of Kenilworth, 325ft amsl

Rwy08/26 Grass 500x30m. **Remarks:** PPR essential. Experienced STOL pilots welcome at own risk. Rwy in good condition. **Warnings:** Live stock graze AD, removed with PPR. AD within Birmingham CTR. **Caution:** High level power lines cross Rwy26 Thr and electric fence half way along Rwy. **Noise:** Avoid over flying local houses and farms. **Operating Hrs:** SR-SS. **Circuits:** To S of AD, avoiding Birmingham CTR. **Landing Fee:** Nil. **Maintenance/Fuel:** Nil. **Operator:** David Sansome, Little Chase Farm, Chase Lane, Kenilworth, Warks, CV8 1PR. **Tel:** 01926 853029

LOWER BOTREA

N5007.00 W00538.00, 1.5nm SE of St Just, 400ft amsl

Rwy07/25 Grass 600x50m. Rwy17/35 Grass 500x50m. **Remarks:** PPR essential. Strip may be water logged and unusable during winter months. Windsock displayed at Rwy intersection. Trees surround AD. **Noise:** Avoid over flying all local habitation. **Operating Hrs:** SR-SS. **Circuits:** Any direction - See noise. **Fuel:** Nil. **Operator:** Mr Hunt, Lower Botrea Farm, Newbridge, Penzance, Cornwall. **Tel:** 01736 787768

MELBOURNE (Melrose Farm)

N5352.03 W00050.27, 6nm SSW of Pocklington, 25ft amsl

Rwy06/24 Tarmac 1000x46m. **Remarks:** Only active Rwy on disused AD. Power line 120ft, crosses Rwy06 APP, farm tractors maybe on AD. Drag racers, microlights and autogyros all operate here. Windsock displayed to N of Rwy24 Thr. **Noise:** Avoid over flying local habitation. **Operator:** J Rowbottom, Melrose Farm, Melbourne, York, YO42 4SS, **Tel:** 01759318392 **Fax:** 01759 318948

NETHER HUNTLYWOOD

N5540.60 W00236.42, 8nm NW of Kelso, 550ft amsl

Rwy07/25 Grass 400x25m. **Remarks:** PPR essential. Sheep graze AD. Always fly low past Rwy to check status. Windsock displayed N edge of AD. Rwy has small undulations. **Warnings:** Power lines 1nm W of AD. **Operating Hrs:** SR-SS. **Circuits:** To S of Rwy. **Landing Fee:** Nil. **Maintenance:** Nil. **Fuel:** MOGAS by arrangement. **Restaurants:** Toilets on site. **Operator:** Richard Lawrence, Nether Huntlywood, Earlston, Berwickshire, TD4 6BB. **Tel:** 01573 410502 **Tel:** 07968 862518

NEWARK (Beeches Farm)

N5309 W00044. 2nm W of Swinderby AD and 5nm NE of Newark. 50ft amsl

Rwy10/28 Grass 517x18m. **Remarks:** Visiting ACFT welcome PPR. Rwy is level with good surface. Windsock displayed on hangar roof. Newark – Lincoln railway runs at 90° close to Rwy28 Thr. N side of AD there is a ditch running from hangar to railway. Contact Waddington MATZ when in the area. **Noise:** Avoid over flying local villages. **Circuits:** 800ft aal. **Operator:** P L Clements, Beeches Farm, South Scarle, Newark, Notts NG23 7JH. **Tel:** 01636 892273 **Fax:** 01636 893556

NYMPSFIELD (Stroud)

N5142.51 W00217.01, 4nm SW of Stroud,700ft amsl

E/W Grass 1120m. **Remarks:** PPR by telephone essential for gliding business only. Visiting ACFT welcome at pilots own risk. Field is undulating, areas N & S side of AD very boggy. Gliding site, caution cables!. Trees close to AD boundary and hilly situation of site generates turbulence and wind gradients in cross winds. NW wind is to be avoided. **Landing Fee:** £5.00. **Maintenance:** Roger Targett Sailplanes **Tel:** 01453 860861. **Operator:** Bristol & Gloucestershire Gliding Club **Tel:** 01453 860342/860060. office@bggc.co.uk. **Disabled Facilities:**

OLD HAY

N5110.00 E00026.30, 2nm W of Paddock Wood, 55ft amsl

Rwy09/27 Grass 750x50m, Rwy02/20 Grass 500x50m. **Radio:** A/G 119.500 (not always manned, transmit blind). **Remarks:** Strict PPR by telephone, AD not normally manned. Strip in excellent condition, with very good APP Rwy09/27. Rwy02/20 emergency use only. Windsock displayed N Rwy09/27. Laddingford AD (with similar layout) to NW of AD. **Warnings:** High tension wires on APP Rwy02/20, use only in emergencies. **Noise:** Avoid over flying Paddock Wood Village. **Operating Hrs:** SR-SS. **Circuits:** S of railway line. **Landing Fee:** Donation required. **Maintenance/Fuel:** Nil. **Operator:** Old Hay Farms Ltd, PO Box 39, Rye, East Sussex, TN31 6ZT. **Tel:** 01892 832216 (PPR)

PAYDEN STREET

N5115.12 E00044.50, 7nm NE of Ashford. 630ft amsl

Rwy02/20 Grass 1000x12m. **Remarks:** Strict PPR by telephone. Rwy in good condition. Windsock displayed to W of Rwy midpoint. **Visual aid to location:** 2 Dutch barns on Rwy02 APP. AD located in the middle of arable land. **Noise:** Avoid over flying all local houses especially house adjacent Rwy02 Thr. **Operating Hrs:** SR-SS. **Circuits:** Join over head, descend on dead side. **Landing Fee:** £20. **Maintenance:** Nil. **Fuel:** Nil. **Operator:** John Boyd, Court Lodge Farm, Lenham, Maidstone, Kent, ME17 2QD. **Tel:** 01622 858403 **Tel:** 07791 040578 **Fax:** 01622 850624 jarthurboyd@aol.com

PENT FARM

N5106.32 E00104.30, 2.5nm NNW Hythe, 240ft amsl

Rwy06/24 Grass 670x10m. **Remarks:** Strict PPR by telephone. AD not suitable for inexperience pilots due to proximity of hills. Windsock displayed on N side approx mid point. Model ACFT active at weekends. **Warnings:** Rwy06 slight up slope. Hills rising to 550ft amsl at NE end of AD. Masts 221ft agl 1nm NE of AD. **Noise:** Avoid over flying the villages of Stanford and Postling. **Operating Hrs:** SR-SS. **Circuits:** N at 1000ft. **Landing Fee:** £5. **Maintenance:** M3 & M5 available **Fuel:** Nil. **Operator:** Mr C R Reynolds, Pent Farm, Postling, Hythe, Kent, CT21 4EY. **Tel:** 01303 862436. **Tel:** 07850 628981

PORTMOAK (Kinross)

N5611.21 W00319.45, 0.5nm E of Loch Leven, 4nm ESE of Kinross, 360ft amsl

Rwy09/27 Grass 700x15m, Rwy10/28 Grass 900x15m. **Remarks:** Powered ACFT only to use Rwy10/28 (N field). Strict PPR light ACFT accepted at pilot's own risk. Caution Winch cables. Pilots of nose wheel ACFT should exercise extreme caution. Beware of large flocks of birds around the area at all times of the year. Winch and aerotow launching seven days a week. Pilots intending to land at Portmoak should contact Leuchars APP and advise inbound to Portmoak. When within 5nm of Portmoak make all calls blind on 129.975. Do not expect a reply. Keep a good lookout for gliders which regularly fly between ground level and 20000ft. Windsock displayed. **Noise:** Do not over fly the site or the nearby villages of Scotlandwell, Kinnesswood or the Vane RSPB Centre on S side of Loch Leven. **Landing Fee:** £7. **Fuel:** Nil. **Operator:** Scottish Gliding Centre **Tel:** 01592 840543 (Office) **Tel:** 01592 840243 (Club)

RHIGOS

N5144.34 W00335.05, 8nm W of Merthyr Tydfil, 780ft amsl

Rwy09/27 Grass 550m. **Remarks:** Hill top site, primarily for gliding. Surface is rough. Field slopes down from E to W. After rain due to soft surface. Not suitable for light ACFT in strong S & N winds. Beware of launch cables. **Noise:** Avoid over flying Rhigos village. **Circuits:** 09 RH, 27 LH. **Operator:** Vale of Neath Gliding Club, Rhigos Airfield, Aberdare, Glamorgan, South Wales. **Tel:** 01685 811023

ROSEMARKET

N5144.32 W00458.59, 4nm S of Haverford W, 160ft amsl

Rwy08/26 Grass 600x15m. **Remarks:** Up slope on Rwy08. Can be unusable after heavy rain. Public road close to Rwy08 Thr, look out for vehicles and pedestrians. Car park close to Rwy08 Thr. Windsock displayed at E end of strip. Strip is part of a leisure complex and is situated within a 9 hole Golf course. Because of the Rwy site prior telephone contact would be appreciated. Golfers are particularly welcomed. **Noise:** Avoid over flying riding school on N edge of woods to NE of strip **Circuits:** 800ft QFE. **Fuel:** MOGAS at Haverfordwest. **Operator:** Bill & Bridie Young, Dawn till Dusk Golf course, Rosemarket, Milford Haven, Pembrokeshire SA73 1JY **Tel:** 01437 890281 www.dawntilldusk.co.uk. **Disabled Facilities:**

SHACKLEWELL

N5239.00 W00034.00, 3nm W Stamford, 535ft amsl

Rwy06/24 Grass 600x15m. **Remarks:** PPR by telephone. Well prepared strip, with clear APP. Windsock displayed at E end. Contact Cottesmore MATZ inbound and before Dept. **Noise:** Avoid over flying Empingham village 1nm S of AD. **Operating Hrs:** SR-SS. **Circuits:** Nil. **Landing Fee:** Nil. **Maintenance/Fuel:** Nil. **Operator:** Richard Watt, Shacklewell Lodge, Empingham, Oakham, Rutland, LE15 8QQ. **Tel:** 01780 460646 **Tel:** 07801 585480 **Fax:** 01780 460306 wattrichard@hotmail.com

SOLLAS

N5739.51 W00719.33, Beach 1nm NE of Sollas Village, North Unst. SL

Rwy04/22 no markings sand approx 1 mile in length parallel to shoreline. **Remarks:** Firm Sand public beach strip. No facilities. The useable portion is situated below the High water mark. Pilots should exercise caution during flare and hold-off as height judgement may be difficult over the feature less surface. Preferred landing technique is to use power down to touchdown. S end of strip is sometimes subject to ridgeing and standing water which will be clearly seen by carrying out an inspection over flight. To calculate tide timesuse times and heights published for Lochmaddy. A public telephone is situated on the main road 0.5 miles from the end of the landing area. Annual Fly-in held during September. **NB:** A general rule for beach operations. Carry out engine run-up on a suitable area of firm sand around the high-water mark. If ACFT stops on the beach before commencing take-off run for run-up there is a danger of the wheels settling into the sand. This particularly applies to nose wheel ACFT. Beach is used for agricultural vehicles as a route to adjacent farm lane. Pilots must ensure that vehicles have cleared and keep a good look out for people walking. Information can be obtained from Mr J A Macleod (who is a local PPL based in Stornoway), 17 Balallen, Isle of Lewis, H52 9PN **Tel:** 01851 830366 **Tel:** 07778 673513. jaml.bal@tiscali.co.uk

STOODLEIGH BARTON

N5057.50 W00332.00, 4nm NW of Tiverton, 830ft amsl

Rwy09/27 Grass 800x75m. **Remarks:** Rwy27 has up slope and lateral slope down to S. A building on short final Rwy09 and power lines approx 30ft agl running along E side of road to Stoodleigh village. **Noise:** Avoid Stoodleigh village. **Operating Hrs:** SR-SS. **Circuits:** S 1000ft QFE. **Landing Fee:** donation to the RNLI would be most welcome. **Fuel:** MOGAS available by prior arr. **Restaurant:** Red Lion, Oakford **Tel:** 01398 351219. **Operator:** Mr W Knowles, Stoodleigh Barton, Tiverton, Devon **Tel:** 01398 351568 **Tel:** 07850 384000

STRATHAVEN

N5540.80 W00406.25, 1.3nm W of Strathaven, 847ft amsl

Rwy08/26 Grass 730x90m (marked by white flush slabs). **Radio:** A/G 130.100. (Glider Ops). **Remarks:** Parts of the grass strip are very bumpy. PPR. ACFT welcome at pilot's own risk. Glider flying at W/E & Wed evenings during summer. **Caution:** Cables, also intensive Microlight activity. "Strathaven" in white letters is displayed on red hangar roof. Livestock grazing when no gliding in progress. HT wires and trees 35ft high approx 90m obliquely from E boundary fence. Trees on RH side – do not touchdown before end of trees. Windsock displayed. Microlights use 129.825. **Landing Fee:** £3. **Operator:** Strathclyde Gliding Club **Tel:** 01357 520235 (AD)

STRETTON

N5320.70 W00231.50, 3nm SE of Warrington, 270ft amsl

Rwy09/27 parallel Concrete/Grass 400x20m. **Remarks:** Rwy N of disused Rwy09/27 Rwy on Stretton disused AD. 6ft high hedge and public road close to Rwy27Thr. APP from S directly to base leg. When landing Rwy09 make offset APP to avoid M56. This will also provide clearance from a cellular telephone mast 130ft agl, 700m out and to N Rwy09 APP. Located within the Manchester Low Level Route – intensive light ACFT traffic up to 1250ft amsl, also VRP for Liverpool/Manchester VFR traffic. PFA or Vintage type ACFT only accepted. **Noise:** Do not over fly house E of AD. **Operator:** J Sykes, Invergordon Nurseries, Swineyard Lane, High Leigh, Knutsford, Cheshire **Tel:** 01925 754027

SUTTON BANK (Thirsk)

N5413.62 W00112.72, 5nm E of Thirsk,18nm N of York, 920ft amsl

E/W Grass 549m NE/SW Grass 732m. **Radio:** A/G 129.975. **Remarks:** PPR Surface may be soft in places. There are trees to N & E. Do not APP over steep S & W cliffs with insufficient speed to overcome local down draughts. Windsock displayed. **Landing Fee:** Nil. **Operator:** Yorkshire Gliding Club (PTY) Ltd, Sutton Bank, Thirsk, North Yorkshire YO7 2EY. **Tel:** 01845 597237. enquiry@ygc.co.uk. www.ygc.co.uk. **Disabled Facilities:**

THORNBOROUGH GROUNDS

N5201.00 W00058.30, 2nm ENE of Buckingham, 260ft amsl

Rwy06/24 Grass 500m. **Remarks:** Visiting ACFT welcome with PPR and at pilots own risk. Field wet in winter. **Warnings:** Pylons and power lines on both Rwy APP. **Noise:** Avoid over flying local farm houses, village and stud farm N of Rwy. **Landing Fee:** Voluntary. **Fuel/Maintenance:** Nil. **Operator:** C M Moore, Thornborough Grounds, Buckingham MK18 2AB. **Tel:** 01280 814675 cmm@morecorporation.com. **Disabled Facilities:**

TIBENHAM

N5227.40 E00109.25, 12nm SW of Norwich, 186ft amsl

Rwy08/26 Tarmac 700x46m, Rwy03/21 Tarmac 914x46m, Rwy15/33 Tarmac 1600x46m. **Radio:** Tibenham 129.975 **Remarks:** Gliding Site. PPR. ACFT welcome at pilots own risk. Exercise caution due to rope dragging circuits by tug ACFT, winch launching and aerotows up to 3000ft. Club facilities available. (powered ACFT). **Operating Hrs:** Mon-Sun (Summer) Wed-Thur & W/E (Winter). **Fuel:** Avgas 100LL. **Landing Fee:** Nil, donation to upkeep of Rwy appreciated. **Operator:** Norfolk Gliding Club, Tibenham Airfield, Norfolk **Tel:** 01379 677207 secretary@ngcglide.co.uk. **Disabled Facilities:**

TOWER FARM

N5215.44 W00039.55, 2nm SSE of Wellingborough, 370ft amsl

Rwy10/28 Grass 640x24m. **Remarks:** Briefing essential for first time visitors. Rwy28 has up slope which increases in severity at midpoint then becomes less severe from midpoint on. This aids landing but could constitute a significant hazard on Dept. Owner recommends that visitors call or listen out with Sywell A/G for local traffic information. Beware microlights operating from field to w of AD. AD is situated 2nm NW of Podington disused AD, (Santa Pod Raceway) where large numbers of spectators congregate for drag racing events spring to autumn mainly PH & weekends. **Visual aid to location:** White concrete water TWR at W end of strip. **Noise:** Avoid Wollaston, to W of AD. **Operating Hrs:** SR-SS **Circuits:** To N. **Fuel:** Nil. **Landing Fee:** Nil. **Operator:** Mrs S Sumner and Chris Sumner, Tower Farm, Wollaston, Wellingborough, Northants, NN29 7PJ **Tel:** 01933 664225 **Tel:** 07803 715736. pgs@clara.co.uk

TRULEIGH FARM

N5053.85 W00015.30, 3nm SSE of Henfield VRP (Shoreham), 132ft amsl

Rwy10/28 Grass 500x15m. **Remarks:** Sheep may be grazing so PPR essential. Strip slopes upward from E until midpoint. Rwy is situated between two groups of trees which may cause rotor/windshear. AD can be very wet after prolonged precipitation. Power lines to E of AD crossing the Rwy28 APP 900m from Thr. Radio masts on hill 1nm S of AD. There are numerous Hang gliding and Paracending sites in the area around AD. Shoreham ATZ is close to S. Arr/Dept ACFT are advised to contact Shoreham APP. Useful weather information can be obtained from Shoreham ATIS. Windsock displayed to NW of Rwy. **Noise:** Avoid all local habitation, especially the houses 0.5nm NE of AD. **Operating Hrs:** SR-SS. **Circuits:** LH 1000ft QFE. **Landing Fee:** Nil. **Fuel:** Nil. **Operator:** Robin Windus, Truleigh Manor, Edburton, Henfield, Sussex. BN5 9LL **Tel:** 01903 813186. **Disabled Facilities:**

VALLANCE BY-WAYS GATWICK

N5109.17 W00011.40, Adjacent to NW corner of Gatwick AD, 202ft amsl

Rwy08/26 Grass 553x9m. **Remarks:** PPR strictly required. Helicopter welcome handled by Interflight **Tel:** 01293 509000 **Fax:** 01293 567010. Permission from Gatwick must be obtained. 60ft trees Rwy26 APP and deer may encroach the strip. Windsock displayed. **Circuits:** To N away from Gatwick but avoiding Charlwood NW of AD. **Landing Fee:** Donation to Gatwick Aviation Museum on AD. **Fuel:** Nil. **Operator:** P G Vallance Ltd, Lowfield, Heath Road, Charlwood, Surrey. RH6 0BT **Tel:** 01293 862915 or **Tel:** 07836 666817 gpvgat@aol.com www.gatwick-aviation-museum.co.uk. **Disabled Facilities:**

WADSWICK STRIP

N5124 W00212, 2.2nm SE of Colerne AD, 400ft amsl

Rwy10/28 Grass 700x25m. **Caution:** Access road crosses the strip at W end. Traffic is controlled by traffic lights, which are activated on Freq 123.100. Ensure you use this facility before landing and take off. Wires at E end of strip are buried. The pole is still in position close to Thrs on S side of Rwy. Windsock displayed. AD within Lynham CTR always contact APP. **Noise:** Avoid over flying he village to N of strip on initial APP particularly avoiding Hazelbury Manor which is close to W of strip. **Circuits:** to S. **Operator:** Tim Barton, Manor Farm, Wadswick, Corsham, Wiltshire. SN13 8JB. **Tel:** 01225 810706 **Fax:** 01225 810307. tim@wadswick.co.uk

WEST HORNDON

N5133.72 E00021.30, 3nm S of Brentwood. 80ft amsl

Rwy06/24 Grass 500x20m. **Remarks:** PPR by telephone. Rwy in good condition. Windsock displayed S of Rwy24. Lunches available Thursday Apr-Jul £4 donation to National Garden Scheme. **Warnings:** Power lines run close ro N AD boundary parallel with Rwy. **Caution:** Farm machinery on AD. **Noise:** Avoid over flying all local houses and farms. **Operating Hrs:** SR-SS. **Circuits:** To S 1000ft QFE. **Landing Fee:** Nil. **Maintenance/Fuel:** Nil. **Restaurants:** Nil. **Operator:** Bernard Holmes, Barnards Farm, Brentwood Road, West Hordon, Essex, CM13 3LX. **Tel:** 01277 811262 www.barnardsfarm.org. **Disabled Facilities:**

WESTON-ON-THE-GREEN (Oxford)

N5152.80 W00113.10, 7nm N of Oxford, 4nm NE of Oxford AD, 282ft amsl

Rwy01/19 Grass 690m, Rwy06/24 Grass 830m, Rwy10/28 Grass 910m. **Radio:** A/G RAF Weston-on-the-Green 133.650. **Remarks:** D129 radius 2nm centred on AD is RAF parachute drop zone up to FL120, including free-fall parachuting. Military ACFT may fly pre-set range patterns. DAAIS is available via Brize RAD. The area should be avoided at all times unless PPR has to been obtained. **Landing Fee:** Nil Cafe at weekends. Owned by MOD & leased by Oxford Gliding Club and RAFSPA (Sport Parachute Association) **Tel:** 01869 343246 (AD) **Tel:** 01869 343265 (Gliding Club) **Tel:** 01869 773210 (Launch Point) **Tel:** 01993 842551 Ex 7555/7551 (Brize Norton)

WHITBY (Egton)

N5427.00 W00045.00 4nm W of Whitby, 3nm NE of Grosmont, 650ft amsl

E/W Grass 450x100m. **Remarks:** Level, but surface may be bumpy and strip is surrounded by trees. During summer sheep graze on Rwy. Situated beside the main Whitby to Guisborough road. Windsock S side at midpoint. **Operator:** P A Jackson, Fimble Bottoms, Great Freyup, Whitby, North Yorkshire. **Tel:** 01947 897367 (Home)

WIGTOWN

N5450.93 W00426.95, 1nm S of Wigtown, 20ft amsl

Rwy06/24 Concrete 446x18m, (30m starter extensions available at both ends of Rwy). **Remarks:** Rwy surface rough. Baldoon Hill – 129ft amsl/109ft aal – located 300m NW Rwy06 Thr, care should be taken when APP/Dept from this direction. **Operating Hrs:** PPR by arr. **Circuits:** 06/24 LH 800ft. **Landing Fee:** Nil. **Operator:** Mr A H Sproat **Tel:** 01988 402215

WOODLANDS (Roche)

N5025.31 W00448.80, 5nm SW of Bodmin, 531ft amsl

Rwy16/34 Grass 320x15, Rwy01/19 Grass 320x15m, Rwy13/31 Grass 320x15m, Rwy07/25 175x15m. **Remarks:** Strict PPR. AD situated very close to St Mawgan MATZ. No facilities on AD. Rwy34/31 APP trees and power lines present. Rwy07 APP large hedge on short finals. Windsock displayed 200m on E side Rwy31. **Noise:** Avoid over flying all local habitation, especially the farm to S of AD and N of main Rd. **Operating Hrs:** SR-SS. **Circuits:** No local circuits. **Fuel:** Nil **Operator:** Woodlands Flying Group, Woodlands Aerodrome, Camelford, Cornwall, PL32 9YF. **Tel:** 01872 560771 (Mr Hanley) **Tel:** 01872 510495 (Mr Gibbs)

WOONTON

N5209.72 W0256.74, 5nm SSW of Shobdon AD, 400ft amsl

Rwy16/34 Grass 500x15m. **Remarks:** Rwy34 has a marked up slope. Land Rwy34, Dept Rwy16 only. Surface can be soft after prolonged precipitation. Sheep graze the strip so PPR essential. Public footpath crosses Rwy34 touchdown point. Windsock displayed. Low flying military ACFT transit area during weekdays. Operator can sometimes provide transport if arranged in advance. **Noise:** Avoid local habitation, particularly the village of Woonton to N of AD. **Operating Hrs:** SR-SS. **Landing Fee:** Nil. **Fuel:** Available by arr. **Operator:** Mike Hayes, Chapel Stile Cottage, Woonton Almeley, Herefordshire. HR3 6QN. **Tel:** 01432 377371 (Office Hrs) **Tel:** 01544 340635 (Evenings) **Fax:** 01432 355988 mike.hayes@denco.co.uk

BALLYKELLY (EGQB)

N5503.69 W00700.89, 2nm W of Limavady, 18ft amsl

Rwy08/26 Tarmac 1676x46m, Rwy02/20 Tarmac 1835x46m. **Remarks:** Active army AD. Beware of mast 305ft amsl between Rwy20 & 26 Thrs. Note that Londonderry 5nm W has same Rwy directions. ACFT carrying out instrument APP Rwy26 at Londonderry pass through the overhead at 1200ft. TACAN BKL 109.1 on AD. Call Londonderry APP. **Tel:** 02877 763221

FAIRFORD (EGVA)

N5141.01 W00147.41, 7nm N of Swindon, 286ft amsl

Rwy09/27 Asphalt 3047m. Military AD activated by NOTAM. MATZ actvated by NOTAM. Rwy27 is preferred Rwy, pilots may be required to accept a tail wind. TWR approval is needed for start up clearance. Initial inbound call to Brize RAD , Brize APP. Fairford TWR. TACAN (on AD) FFA 113.40. ILS/DME Rwy27 IFFA 111.1, Rwy09 I-FFD 111.1. **Noise:** Avoid over flying local villages and built-up areas in the circuit.VFR traffic pattern involves an overhead join at 2000ft QNH then circuit at 700ft QFE. This may be varied by ATC. **Fuel:** JET A1 available strictly by arrangement only. **Tel:** 01285 714805. Advice via Mildenhall. **Tel:** 01638 542125/2627 **Fax:** 01638 543389 (PPR through local Duty Officer. Please state who, where from and why)

NESSCLIFFE CAMP

N5245.83 W00256.92, 7nm NW of Shrewsbury, 253ft amsl

Rwy11/29 Grass 381m. **Remarks:** PPR. Strip established for Army use only. NO civil visitors. Strip established within Shawbury AIAA. There are deep ruts in undershoot Rwy29. Rwy marked with white concrete side and corner markers. Airstrip is used for grazing. **Radio:** Non radio APP/LARS Shawbury. **Operating Hrs:** PPR. **Tel:** 01743 262376. **Fuel:** Nil

SENNYBRIDGE

N5201.22 W00339.68, Within EGD203, 1130ft amsl

NNE/SSW Grass 305m. **Remarks:** Strip established for Army use only, NO civil visitors. Operational whenever required for Army operations. **Tel:** 01874 636361